ENCYCLOPEDIA OF AMERICAN RELIGION AND POLITICS

Paul A. Djupe
Laura R. Olson

Facts On File, Inc.

Encyclopedia of American Religion and Politics

Facts On File, Inc.
132 West 31st Street
New York NY 10001

Library of Congress Cataloging-in-Publication Data

Djupe, Paul A.
Encyclopedia of American religion and politics / Paul A. Djupe and Laura R. Olson.
p. cm.
Includes bibliographical references and index.
ISBN 0-8160-4582-8
1. Religion and politics—United States—Encyclopedias. 2. United States—
Religion—Encyclopedias. 3. United States—Politics and government—Encyclopedias.
I. Olson, Laura R., 1967– II. Title.
BL2525 .D58 2003
322'.1'097303—dc21   2002033921

Facts On File books are available at special discounts when purchased in bulk
quantities for businesses, associations, institutions, or sales promotions. Please call
our Special Sales Department in New York at (212) 967-8800 or (800) 322-8755.

You can find Facts On File on the World Wide Web at http://www.factsonfile.com

Text design by Joan M. Toro
Cover design by Cathy Rincon

Printed in the United States of America

VB Hermitage 10 9 8 7 6 5 4 3 2 1

This book is printed on acid-free paper.

Contents

List of Entries

★ ─────────────────────────────────

Introduction

An understanding of religion and politics is essential to an understanding of American politics. Throughout American history, religious views have pervaded and infused American politics, whether through challenges to the status quo—as exemplified by the movements to end slavery, abortion, and the sale of alcohol—or in the worldviews of politicians and voters. Religious views play important roles in informing and structuring the specific policy objectives political actors pursue. Such political actors strategically use religious rhetoric as a campaign tool, targeting specific groups of voters on the basis of their faith traditions. And mass-level religious groups are among the most potent petitioners of government on behalf of a wealth of causes that span the ideological spectrum.

By design, government's effect on religion is less obvious, although government has shaped the destiny of many, often small, religious groups throughout American history. The Latter-day Saints (Mormons), for example, have had profound conflicts with the U.S. government but have in recent years emerged as some of the most ardent advocates of American patriotism. Other religious minority groups, such as the Jehovah's Witnesses, have sought refuge in the courts from local oppression and have on balance received some measure of protection.

Historically, the United States has maintained a wall of separation between church and state, though this wall has often appeared quite porous. Only since the World War II era has the Supreme Court begun to plug some of the wall's holes by extending federal constitutional protections to cover the states. At the same time, several prominent religious movements with political goals have arisen in response to the Court's challenge to their belief systems and communities, including numerous conservative Christian movement organizations that have sprung up since the 1980s. They have advanced policy proposals for government to return prayer to public schools and to offer vouchers to families who wish to send their children to religious schools. Meanwhile, increasing numbers of candidates for public office make their faith commitments explicit. All of these recent developments suggest the sensitive nerve that was struck during the rapid social change of the 20th century and show a desire to "return God" to a prominent place in the public square.

We composed this volume intending it to have comprehensive coverage of the most significant connections between religion and politics in the United States from both contemporary and historical perspectives. Our goal is to bring together in one place "the facts" about the people, groups, jurisprudence, forces, and phenomena that together tell the story of the interaction between religion and politics in America. The entries in this encyclopedia were written by a team of 135 established scholars of religion and politics in the United States and abroad. It is our hope that it will be the key reference source for people searching for basic and detailed information about religion and politics in America. It is also a gateway to further information, because contributors provide lists of books, articles, and websites for further reading. We also include a comprehensive general bibliography for those who wish to delve deeper into the study of religion and politics in America.

We focused on several organizing themes in determining what to include in the encyclopedia. Here is a list of those themes, in addition to some related entries:

- We emphasize the roles played by religious organizations and beliefs during the colonial and founding periods (e.g., ANNE HUTCHINSON, MARYLAND, PENNSYLVANIA, RELIGIOUS ESTABLISHMENT IN THE COLONIES, VIRGINIA, and JOHN WINTHROP).
- We place substantial attention upon religion and the U.S. Constitution, including scores of path-breaking First Amendment cases from the 19th century to the present day, including almost all cases that have reached the Supreme Court (e.g., ESTABLISHMENT CLAUSE, FREE EXERCISE CLAUSE, and cases such as *ENGEL V. VITALE*).
- Also included are entries that address the intersections between theology, political theory, and political practice (e.g., ECO-THEOLOGY, ECUMENISM, FUNDAMENTALISM, and TOLERATION).
- The encyclopedia includes numerous entries on the burgeoning world of religious interest groups, associations, and social movements (e.g., BREAD FOR THE WORLD, FOCUS ON THE FAMILY, INTERFAITH ALLIANCE, and PROMISE KEEPERS).
- We further emphasize the relationships among religious groups, elections, and political parties, with specific entries on key recent and historical elections (e.g., CATHOLICS AND THE DEMOCRATIC PARTY, CHRISTIAN RIGHT AND THE REPUBLICAN PARTY, and RELIGION IN THE 1980 ELECTION). On a related note, we include entries that explore the role of religious organizations and beliefs in citizens' political behavior (e.g., CIVIC SKILLS and POLITICAL PARTICIPATION).
- The complicated relationships between public policy and religion constitute another key theme (e.g., ABORTION, AID TO POOR NATIONS, CENSORSHIP, EUTHANASIA, and HEALTH CARE).
- Also included are entries that address specific American religious traditions and their distinctive takes on the appropriate relationship between religion and politics (e.g., AFRICAN METHODIST EPISCOPAL CHURCH, EPISCOPAL CHURCH, ROMAN CATHOLIC CHURCH, and SOUTHERN BAPTIST CONVENTION).
- A few distinctive historical events merited inclusion (e.g., CIVIL RIGHTS MOVEMENT, FIRST GREAT AWAKENING, and VIETNAM WAR).
- Finally, we include biographies of leading individuals who have shaped the relationship between religion and politics in the United States most profoundly (e.g., JERRY FALWELL, ABRAHAM JOSHUA HESCHEL, THOMAS JEFFERSON, JOHN CARDINAL O'CONNOR, and WILLIAM PENN).

Literally hundreds of people contributed to the writing of this encyclopedia. We would like to thank Owen Lancer at Facts On File for proposing this project and for his excellent advice and assistance throughout the project. We also offer many thanks to our outstanding contributors for their excellent work. They made this project possible and we appreciate them enormously for their valuable intellectual contributions and for complying with our deadlines with good humor. We are particularly grateful to the Religion and Politics organized section of the American Political Science Association, the Society for the Scientific Study of Religion, and the University of Chicago Divinity School for their assistance in recruiting contributors. Finally, we thank our families and friends for their love and support throughout the course of this project.

Contributors

★

Susan Gleason Anderson, University of Chicago
Jacquelyn A. Anthony, Emory University
David T. Ball, Ohio Legal Assistance Foundation
Ryan Barilleaux, Miami University
Staci L. Beavers, California State University–San Marcos
Sara C. Benesh, University of Wisconsin–Milwaukee
Robert Benne, Roanoke College
Claudia Bergmann, University of Chicago
R. Lorraine Bernotsky, West Chester University
Whitney L. Bevill, Clemson University
Kraig Beyerlein, University of North Carolina–Chapel Hill
John Blakeman, Baylor University
Stephanie Clintonia Boddie, Washington University in St. Louis
Louis Bolce, Baruch College–City University of New York
Florence Caffrey Bourg, College of Mount St. Joseph
Leah Boyd, Azusa Pacific University
David G. Bromley, Virginia Commonwealth University
Aaron L. Broomall, Denison University
Ron Brown, Wayne State University
Kurt Buhring, University of Chicago
Wendy Cadge, Princeton University
Allison Calhoun-Brown, Georgia State University
Zachary R. Calo, University of Virginia
David E. Campbell, University of Notre Dame
Damon M. Cann, State University of New York–Stony Brook
Tony Carnes, Columbia University
Brett M. Clifton, Brown University
Ram A. Cnaan, University of Pennsylvania
Clarke E. Cochran, Texas Tech University
Scott Comparato, Southern Illinois University
Kimberly Conger, Ohio State University

Michael Coulter, Grove City College
Kendra Cover, Virginia Commonwealth University
Alison L. Davis, Denison University
Derek H. Davis, Baylor University
Matthew DeBell, Georgetown University
Melissa M. Deckman, Washington College
Gerald DeMaio, Baruch College–City University of New York
Kevin R. den Dulk, Grand Valley State University
Robert E. Dewhirst, Northwest Missouri State University
Veronica Donahue DiConti, American University
David B. Djupe, Glenview, Illinois
Paul A. Djupe, Denison University
Carrie B. Dohe, University of Chicago
Marc Dollinger, San Francisco State University
Matthew L. Eanet, Georgetown University
Eldon J. Eisenach, University of Tulsa
Maurice M. Eisenstein, Purdue University–Calumet
Bette Novit Evans, Creighton University
Paul Fabrizio, McMurry University
Jonathan Fidani, Azusa Pacific University
Jeffrey C. Fox, Fort Lewis College
Beverly Gaddy, Georgia Southwestern State University
Brian J. Glenn, Harvard University
Philip Goff, Indiana University–Purdue University Indianapolis
Sarah Gossman, Howard Payne University
TeResa C. Green, Eastern Michigan University
Susan E. Grogan, St. Mary's College of Maryland
Sara A. Grove, Shippensburg University
David E. Guinn, De Paul University
James L. Guth, Furman University
Hans J. Hacker, Wheeling Jesuit University
Perry T. Hamalis, University of Chicago
Ron E. Hassner, Stanford University

Jeanne M. Heffernan, Pepperdine University

Thomas Heilke, University of Kansas

Ryan P. Hite, Denison University

J. David Holcomb, University of Mary Hardin-Baylor

Dennis R. Hoover, Trinity College

Donald L. Huber, Trinity Lutheran Seminary

Steven D. Jamar, Howard University School of Law

Ted G. Jelen, University of Nevada–Las Vegas

Matthew V. Johnson Sr., Greensboro, North Carolina

Timothy R. Johnson, University of Minnesota

Esther V. Kay, Center for Public Justice

James Keating, Pontifical College Josephinum

Stephen M. King, Stephen King Ministries

Joseph M. Knippenberg, Oglethorpe University

Drew Noble Lanier, University of Central Florida

Thomas Lansford, University of Southern Mississippi

John R. LaRaia, Denison University

William Lasser, Clemson University

William Lester, Howard Payne University

Steven C. Leidinger, Denison University

Geoffrey Brahm Levey, University of New South Wales

Roland Marden, University of Sussex

Allen McDuffee, The Center for Policy Analysis on Palestine

Susan McKee, Indianapolis, Indiana

Krista McQueeney, University of North Carolina–Chapel Hill

Jean L. McSween, University of Virginia

Emmet V. Mittlebeeler, American University

Robert L. Montgomery, Ridgewood, New Jersey

Andrea E. Moore, University of Wisconsin–Madison

Hubert Morken, Regent University

Susanna Morrill, University of Chicago

StanLey M. Morris, Attorney at Law, Cortez, Colorado

Vincent Phillip Muñoz, North Carolina State University

Andrew R. Murphy, Valparaiso University

Elisabeth Newberry, Seneca, South Carolina

Franklyn C. Niles, John Brown University

Caroline M. Nordlund, Brown University

Jim Ohlson, Center for Public Justice

James Paul Old, Valparaiso University

Laura R. Olson, Clemson University

Erik Owens, University of Chicago

Keith Pavlischek, Center for Public Justice

James M. Penning, Calvin College

Santiago O. Piñon Jr., University of Chicago

Anthony J. Pogorelc, Catholic University of America

Stephen R. Prescott, Southeastern College at Wake Forest of Southeastern Baptist Theological Seminary

Jane Gurganus Rainey, Eastern Kentucky University

Malia Reddick, American Judicature Society

Boris E. Ricks, University of Southern California

Matthew M. C. Roberts, University of Minnesota

Alonford James Robinson Jr., Harvard University

Mark J. Rozell, Catholic University of America

Jillian Savage, University of Canberra

Deborah Schildkraut, Oberlin College

Jason A. Scorza, Fairleigh Dickinson University

Mary C. Segers, Rutgers University–Newark

Said Sewell, State University of West Georgia

Stephen K. Shaw, Northwest Nazarene University

Caroline R. Sherman, Princeton University

Mara S. Sidney, Rutgers University–Newark

David J. Siemers, University of Wisconsin–Oshkosh

Adam L. Silverman, University of Florida

Martin W. Slann, Pennsylvania State University Wilkes–Barre

Julie Smith, Howard Payne University

Mark Caleb Smith, Calvin College

Robert W. Smith, Clemson University

Anand E. Sokhey, Denison University

Ryan S. Solomon, Clemson University

Lora L. Stone, University of New Mexico

Daniel D. Stratton, University of Arizona

Gregory W. Streich, Central Missouri State University

Stephen Sussman, Economic Council of Palm Beach County, Florida

Joanne Tetlow, Catholic University of America

Eric L. Thomas, Hartwick College

Carolyn R. Wah, Watch Tower Bible and Tract Society of Pennsylvania

Andrew D. Walsh, Culver–Stockton College

Beth Ann Waltz, National Woman's Christian Temperance Union

Jeffrey Walz, Concordia University Wisconsin

Hillary Warren, Otterbein College

Keith Warren, Ohio State University

Chaim I. Waxman, Rutgers University

David L. Weeks, Azusa Pacific University

Charles F. Williams, American Bar Association

Kelli R. Williams, Clemson University

J. Matthew Wilson, Southern Methodist University

Robert Wilson-Black, University of St. Francis

J. David Woodard, Clemson University

David O. Woodyard, Denison University

ENTRIES
A TO Z

Abernathy, Ralph (1926–) *civil rights leader*

Born in Linden, Alabama, in 1926, Ralph Abernathy became an ordained Baptist minister in 1948, received a B.S. in mathematics from Alabama State College in 1950 and an M.A. in sociology from Atlanta University in 1951, and became pastor of the First Baptist Church in Montgomery, Alabama. In Montgomery, Abernathy, together with E. D. Nixon, Jo Ann Robinson, and MARTIN LUTHER KING JR. founded the Montgomery Improvement Association (MIA) in 1955 to organize a BUS BOYCOTT after Rosa Parks was arrested for refusing to give up her bus seat to a white man. The MIA successfully organized the Montgomery bus boycott, filing a lawsuit in federal court seeking an injunction against Montgomery's segregated seating practices. The Supreme Court upheld this injunction in 1956.

The success of the bus boycott and of the MIA as a community-based organization signaled the beginning of a sustained effort to attack segregation through nonviolent protest. In 1957, civil rights organizers such as Ella Baker and BAYARD RUSTIN, together with ministers such as Abernathy, King, Joseph Lowery, and Fred Shuttlesworth, formed the SOUTHERN CHRISTIAN LEADERSHIP CONFERENCE (SCLC) as an umbrella organization of southern black churches that helped coordinate the nonviolent direct action as a political strategy to end segregation. King was president of the SCLC, Abernathy served as the "bagman," and activists such as Ella Baker did much of the behind-the-scenes organizing. With the SCLC, Abernathy assisted in organizing economic boycotts of merchants, sit-ins, and marches to win civil and voting rights.

In 1961, Abernathy became pastor of the West Hunter Street Baptist Church in Atlanta, Georgia. Abernathy was one of King's closest associates and felt overshadowed by King's reputation. Upon King's assassination in 1968, Abernathy became president of the SCLC and went on to lead a march in April in support of the black striking sanitation workers in Memphis, Tennessee, the city in which King was assassinated. In May 1968, Abernathy led the Poor People's Campaign march and encampment in Washington, D.C., an event the SCLC had planned prior to King's death, in an effort to bring together a multiracial protest movement to draw attention to issues of ongoing poverty that President Lyndon Johnson's Great Society programs had not addressed.

Following King's assassination, the SCLC lost influence and support. Abernathy credited this decline to the success of the SCLC in helping eliminate "virtually all of the statutory barriers to our own advancement and equality"; the attempt to take the Civil Rights movement to Northern cities such as Chicago; the loss of faith in nonviolent protest by newer black leaders emerging in black power organizations like the Black Panther Party; the difficulty of linking civil rights to issues of economic inequality; and the fact that activists were weary of the struggle after fighting for over a decade. Additionally, Abernathy knew that King's leadership was irreplaceable.

In 1976, SCLC leaders requested Abernathy's resignation as president. To avoid embarrassment, Abernathy timed his retirement in 1977 with an announcement that he would run for the seat in the U.S. House of Representatives that opened up when Andrew Young was appointed the U.S. ambassador to the United Nations by President JIMMY CARTER. Abernathy viewed his campaign as a vindication of all that he and the SCLC had worked for since its inception. With little organizational and financial support, Abernathy finished third in the primary, behind Wyche Fowler and the eventual winner, John Lewis, a former member of the STUDENT NONVIOLENT COORDINATING COMMITTEE.

Abernathy published his autobiography in 1989, one year before his death, which is as much King's story as his own. Abernathy states, "No one knew Martin better than I did. . . . When he went to jail, I went with him. . . . And when he was gunned down in Memphis, I was the one who rode with him in the ambulance; and after the doctors had given up on him, it was I who cradled him in my arms until he died." Because Abernathy wanted to tell the personal struggle behind the civil rights struggle, he wrote about King as a person the reader would "love to have as a friend" but also felt compelled to write of King's "personal weaknesses." Because he discussed King's alleged extramarital affairs, many in the civil rights community criticized him for airing information that would damage the image of the martyred King. Abernathy argued that discussing the personal side of King would not damage him but would humanize him and make King's story all the more remarkable.

Further reading: Abernathy, Ralph David. *And the Walls Came Tumbling Down: An Autobiography.* New York: Harper-Perennial, 1989.

—Gregory W. Streich

Abington Township, School District of v. Schempp 374 U.S. 203 (1963)

In *Schempp,* the Supreme Court ruled a violation of the ESTABLISHMENT CLAUSE of the First Amendment Pennsylvania's requirement that "At least ten verses from the Holy Bible shall be read, without comment, at the opening of each public school on each school day." Another case, MURRAY V. CURTLETT, was also decided concurrently with *Schempp;* its distinguishing feature was the appellant, Madalyn Murray O'Hair, later known for her leadership of atheist organizations.

After their seminal decision in ENGEL V. VITALE voiding the New York Regent's prayer, public reaction was swift and strongly opposed. Less than one-fifth of the public supported the decision according to polls, church leaders condemned it, and over 150 proposals were considered by Congress to overturn it, none of which garnered the two-thirds vote of both chambers to send it to the states for ratification. Separationist groups continued their campaign to remove religious practices from public schools by challenging Bible readings, a more common practice in school than prayer.

The state of Pennsylvania required Bible reading, although it allowed, "Any child shall be excused from such Bible reading, or attending such Bible reading, upon written request of his parent or guardian." The Schempps, members of a Unitarian church, did not want their children to be exposed to Bible reading in school, nor did they want to exempt them from the practice because of the probable pressure and recriminations that would ensue. Edward Schempp, the father, feared his children would be labeled "oddballs" or "atheists," that they would miss important announcements, or that other students would think the Schempp children had been punished after seeing them standing in the halls.

Writing for the 8-1 majority, Justice Tom Clark built upon previous establishment clause case law, addressing several themes: the importance of coercion in establishment cases; whether schools establish SECULAR HUMANISM when religious practices are removed; and a new standard for establishment clause jurisprudence.

The majority denied the necessity of coercion being present in order to strike down the exercise of religious practices in public schools: "The distinction between the two clauses is apparent—a violation of the FREE EXERCISE CLAUSE is predicated on coercion while the Establishment Clause violation need not be so attended." Belying the content of a test emerg-

ing, Clark argued that if a practice is indeed a religious one and appears in school as part of the curriculum under supervision of school employees, it constitutes an establishment of religion. Clark sides with JAMES MADISON in his *Memorial and Remonstrance:* "It is proper to take alarm at the first experiment on our liberties."

The lone dissenter in 1963, Justice Potter Stewart, whose views would later become majoritarian on the Court, argued that coercion was a necessary component for striking down a statute. If no one was compelled to engage in the practice, the practice should be allowed to stand. The practical import of Stewart's argument is that a provision to allow students to be exempted from the religious practice, as the Pennsylvania statute contained, would likely provide sufficient grounds to uphold it.

The majority also denied that removing Bible reading from the public schools would establish a religion of secular humanism, which the Court also would oppose. Instead, schools are allowed to use the Bible "when presented objectively as part of a secular program of education," which might include a comparative, historical, or literary study. Nothing in the Pennsylvania program, though, suggested to the majority that the Bible reading was an academic exercise.

A long line of dissent to separationist jurisprudence tried to insert a free exercise argument to prevent striking down religious practices in schools. The majority argument would later fall (ROSENBERG V. UNIVERSITY OF VIRGINIA and GOOD NEWS V. MILFORD CENTRAL SCHOOL), Justice Clark argued, "While the Free Exercise Clause clearly prohibits the use of state action to deny the rights of free exercise to anyone, it has never meant that a majority could use the machinery of the State to practice its beliefs."

The test articulated in the landmark *Schempp* decision consisted of two prongs, to which the Court in LEMON V. KURTZMAN would add the third concerning entanglement: "What are the purpose and primary effect of the enactment?" Any state action must have a secular legislative purpose and neither advance nor inhibit religion. The Pennsylvania statute violated both prongs of this test, according to the majority.

This definitive statement by the Court did little to quell public displeasure with *Engel.* Public sentiment remained opposed, and though it has inched upward ever since, noncompliance has remained high, especially in the South, and attempts have continued to add an amendment permitting prayer and other religious practices in public schools, such as the RELIGIOUS FREEDOM AMENDMENT, offered in Congress by Representative Ernest J. Istook Jr. (R-Okla.).

See also ATHEISM; UNITARIAN UNIVERSALIST.

Further reading: Birkby, Robert. "The Supreme Court in the Bible Belt: Tennessee Reaction to the *Schempp* Decision." *American Journal of Political Science* 10, no. 3 (1966): 304–319; Epstein, Lee, and Thomas Walker. *Constitutional Law for a Changing America.* Washington, D.C.: CQ Press, 1995.

—Paul A. Djupe

abolitionist movement

The abolitionist movement was an effort spanning three centuries characterized by a network of people, organizations, and publications all promoting the immediate, unconditional end to the institution of slavery.

The abolitionist movement in America represents one of the most compelling examples of the interaction between religion and politics, asking: Should American Christians participate in the international slave trade? Was it immoral to own a slave? Was the institution of slavery itself sinful? These were among the issues at the core of the American debate over slavery. That debate featured the voices of some of America's most influential ministers and politicians.

Antislavery and *abolition* are terms often used interchangeably, but before the mid-1830s, the tactics and objectives of the two movements were very different. Antislavery was a much broader movement that endorsed a gradual, conditional end to slavery. Antislavery activists were usually white moderates who often disagreed on when and how to begin dismantling slavery. Some limited their demands to prohibition of the slave trade, others to restrictions on the type of slave trade. Some argued that slavery should be excluded from all new territories in America, others that slavery could exist everywhere as long as it was humane.

In contrast, within the larger antislavery movement, abolitionists were considered to be radicals. Many of the earliest white abolitionists were ministers, typically QUAKERS or Presbyterians, and they tended to live in the Northern colonies of PENNSYLVANIA, New York, and MASSACHUSETTS. Early black abolitionists were most often former slaves who had managed to escape to the North. Working separately and occasionally together, white and black abolitionists represented a small but vocal community in the earliest years of the movement. What united all abolitionists irrespective of color, gender, or class was support for the immediate and unconditional end to all forms of slavery.

Among the first known antislavery petitions in America was one printed in 1688 by a small group of Quakers in Germantown, Pennsylvania. Their petition represented a politicization of an issue that threatened to divide the religious group in a bitter debate that did not end until the latter half of the 18th century. Although they were slaveholders themselves, many Quakers challenged the notion that Christianity condoned slavery.

Abolitionist Quakers initially encouraged other Quakers to treat their slaves with kindness. But by 1750, Quakers in Pennsylvania and New Jersey had freed their slaves and were demanding that other Quakers do the same. Ten years later, the Quakers passed an official resolution that punished those choosing to break the strict laws against owning slaves or participating in the slave trade. In 1775, led by Anthony Benezet and John Woolman, the Quakers in Philadelphia founded the first antislavery organization in America—The Pennsylvania Society for the Abolition of Slavery. Fifteen years later the Quakers remained at the forefront of the movement when

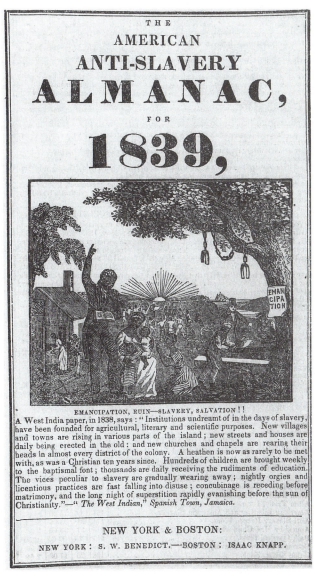

Shown here is *The Anti-Slavery Almanac,* published yearly by the American Anti-Slavery Society. *(Library of Congress)*

they submitted the first antislavery petition to the U.S. Congress.

Although the Quakers were the first and most active, Presbyterians, Methodists, Baptists, and Congregationalists also participated in the movement to abolish slavery. The activities of these denominations led to the formation, in 1774, of the American Convention for Promoting the Abolition of Slavery and Improving the Condition of the African Race. Founded in Philadelphia, the convention was attended by delegates from New York, New Jersey, Pennsylvania, Delaware, and Maryland. Although influential, the American Convention never succeeded in lifting the issue of abolition to prominence outside of these states. In fact, throughout the 18th century, abolition was primarily restricted to the North, and almost exclusively to the cities of Philadelphia, New York, and Boston.

The tremendous political power that slavery's proponents enjoyed in the U.S. Congress initially hindered the growth of the abolitionist movement. It forced the movement to emerge in waves. The first wave, culminating in 1807, pushed for an end to the international slave trade. During the second wave, abolitionists demanded that Congress prevent the introduction of slavery in all newly formed states in the nation. By 1833, the abolition and antislavery forces had converged, and both demanded an immediate eradication of all forms of slavery in the United States.

After 1833 and the formation of the American Antislavery Society, the movement to end slavery began to win public support. It was a long and dangerous crusade that claimed the lives of hundreds, perhaps thousands, of abolitionists. Black abolitionists often suffered tremendously. Many faced certain death if caught by the white lynch mobs that roamed the borders between Northern and Southern states. But the movement overcame these obstacles and celebrated on January 1, 1863, when President ABRAHAM LINCOLN signed the Emancipation Proclamation.

See also BROWN, JOHN; SECTIONAL DIVIDE OF THE CHURCHES OVER SLAVERY.

—Alonford James Robinson Jr.

abortion

Abortion, in contemporary parlance, refers to the intentional termination of pregnancy. Abortion became one of the most divisive issues of the last quarter of the 20th century and remains an important question in contemporary political discourse in the United States.

Throughout most of American history, abortion had been legal prior to "quickening," or the perception of fetal movement on the part of the woman. Most state legislatures did not pass laws proscribing the practice until the late 19th century.

The idea of liberalizing abortion laws became culturally salient during the late 1960s, and several state legislatures passed relatively permissive abortion laws during this period. The trend toward gradual liberalization was interrupted by the Supreme Court's landmark 1973 decision ROE V. WADE, which held virtually all state abortion laws to be unconstitutional. Although public opinion generally moved in a more pro-choice direction following Roe, the decision mobilized opposition from several, often religious, sources. Many cultural and religious conservatives opposed legal abortion because legal abortion was thought to encourage sexual promiscuity by reducing the risks of sexual activity outside of marriage. Another early source of opposition to legal abortion came from the African-American community. Several African-American leaders denounced legal abortion as "genocide" and suggested that easy access to abortion would ultimately be used by whites to limit societal responsibility to care for children born into poverty.

The most visible opposition to Roe came from ROMAN CATHOLIC CHURCH and Evangelical Protestant leaders, who regarded abortion as the taking of human life. Indeed, since the Roe decision, opponents of legal abortion have been characterized by themselves and opponents as "pro-life." Catholics opposed legal abortion on the ground that intentional termination of pregnancy constituted a violation of natural law. Since the early 1950s, the fetus was regarded as "ensouled" (and, therefore, fully human) from the moment of conception. Evangelical Protestants came to oppose abortion on the basis of biblical passages in Exodus, Leviticus, and Proverbs.

Conversely, support for legal abortion has come primarily from people who regard a woman's right to control her own fertility as fundamental. Abortion, to some activists, has come to be regarded as an issue of women's rights, and proponents of legal abortion have generally been characterized as "pro-choice."

At the activist level, the abortion issue has been regarded as one in which compromise is difficult or impossible, as suggested by constitutional law scholar Laurence Tribe's book on abortion politics entitled *Abortion: The Clash of Absolutes* (1989). Because both pro-life and pro-choice advocates cast their arguments in terms of (nonnegotiable) rights and abortion politics in the United States has largely been conducted in the courts may have contributed to the apparent intractability of the issue. However, mass opinion on the abortion issue reflects a strong ambivalence, in that most Americans value both the potential life of the fetus and the privacy rights of women who may wish to terminate pregnancies. A plurality of Americans might be characterized as "situationalists," in that they regard abortion as appropriate in some circumstances but not others. Interestingly, religiosity appears to increase the incidence of pro-life sentiment in virtually all religious denominations, despite the fact that many denominations take nuanced or explicitly pro-choice positions.

An intriguing aspect of abortion politics is the changing nature of pro-life rhetoric since the Roe decision. Initially following Roe, antiabortion arguments were generally couched in religious language, in which considerations of morality, natural law, or Scripture were paramount. Gradually, however, the focus of attention has shifted from religious to scientific arguments for opposition to legal abortion. Pro-life leaders are increasingly likely to argue that a fetus is a genetically unique entity that develops identifiable human characteristics very early in the gestation period. While much opposition to legal abortion still has religious sources, the arguments posed have become increasingly secularized, and correspondingly less likely to evoke concepts from a specific theological tradition.

In the period following Roe v. Wade, the Supreme Court generally struck down attempts by state governments to regulate the practice of abortion. This trend came to an end in the 1989 case of WEBSTER V. REPRODUCTIVE HEALTH SERVICES, which upheld several state restrictions on abortion. Webster was regarded by abortion activists on both sides of the issue as a victory for pro-life forces. But despite the willingness of the

Supreme Court in the post-*Webster* era to uphold state regulations on access to abortion services, the Court has stopped short of overturning the precedent set in *Roe*. In *Planned Parenthood v. Casey*, the Court explicitly upheld the core ruling in *Roe* while simultaneously upholding a number of regulations intended to make abortions more difficult to obtain.

One possible consequence of these changes in abortion jurisprudence is that, since the early 1990s, abortion has become a highly partisan issue. Among both party leaders and members of the mass public, the abortion issue has become more polarized along party lines, with the Democratic Party taking a generally consistent pro-choice position and the Republicans becoming more uniformly pro-life. Abortion has become a very important issue in many elections in the United States.

In response to the continued legality of abortion, many pro-life activists have resorted to "direct action," which has included sidewalk counseling near abortion clinics, obstructing access to such facilities, vandalism of abortion clinics, and occasional violence against abortion providers. Many of these activists are motivated by religious zeal, although their actions are generally condemned by most religious leaders.

Abortion activists on both sides of the issue have been challenged by a number of developments in the evolution of the issue. Contemporary abortion debate now centers around the morality and legality of so-called partial birth abortions, which are late-term abortions performed for medical reasons. Other controversies surround the use of the drug RU-486, which provides an alternative to surgical abortions in the early stages of pregnancy, and the appropriateness of research on fetal tissue. Fetal tissue research has appeared to be a promising avenue of inquiry for curing such maladies as Alzheimer's disease and juvenile diabetes, but the morality of such research has been challenged by pro-life advocates.

See also CATHOLIC ALLIANCE; CATHOLIC BISHOPS' 1975 PASTORAL LETTER ON ABORTION; CATHOLICS FOR FREE CHOICE; CONSISTENT ETHIC OF LIFE; *CULTURE WARS;* MORAL MAJORITY; RELIGIOUS COALITION FOR REPRODUCTIVE CHOICE; and *STENBERG V. CARHART.*

Further reading: Blanchard, Dallas A. *The Anti-Abortion Movement and the Rise of the Religious Right.* New York: Twayne, 1994; Cook, Elizabeth Adell, Ted G. Jelen, and Clyde Wilcox. *Between Two Absolutes: Public Opinion and the Poli-*

Thousands of antiabortion protesters gather outside the White House before the start of the rally in Washington, D.C., on the anniversary of *Roe v. Wade. (Jamal Wilson/Getty)*

tics of Abortion. Boulder, Colo.: Westview, 1992; Luker, Kristin. *Abortion and the Politics of Motherhood*. Berkeley: University of California Press, 1984; Mohr, James C. *Abortion in America: The Origins and Evolution of National Policy, 1800–1900*. New York: Oxford University Press, 1978; Tribe, Laurence H. *Abortion: The Clash of Absolutes*. New York: Norton, 1989.

—Ted G. Jelen

Adams, Henry Carter (1851–1921) *scholar*

After attending Iowa (later Grinnell) College and Andover Theological School, Adams received the first Ph.D. degree awarded by Johns Hopkins University, then spent a year of study in Germany at Heidelberg and Berlin. The son of Ephraim Adams, an early antislavery activist, cofounder of Iowa College, and member of the "Iowa Band" of New England evangelicals dedicated to erecting a Christian commonwealth in the Midwest, in 1885 Henry became a founding member, with Richard Ely, of the American Economics Association (AEA), a group dedicated to the substitution of English laissez-faire political economy for one that made the state an active agent in economic and moral progress. For Adams and the AEA, the discipline of political economy was part of a larger evangelical project of Social Christianity, later called the SOCIAL GOSPEL.

As professor of political economy at the University of Michigan from 1886 until his death in 1921, Adams was instrumental in defining the emerging profession of economics in America. Two of his articles, "The Relation of the State to Industrial Action" (1887) and "Economics and Jurisprudence" (1896), became the benchmarks of professional identity, asserting that the new industrial order, if properly shaped and understood, would usher in a "true republic" whose moral code is no longer expressed in the language of individual rights against society, but in the language of social duty and mutual obligation. Because the new social relationships created by this interdependent industrial order are the major source of wealth creation, all participants in these relationships, especially wage earners, should possess "industrial property" and thus share in its benefits. Through collective bargaining, arbitration boards, and subsidiary laws of industrial agency that define the duties of corporations, trusts, and unions to the public at large, the new industrial order would embody a higher morality than earlier small-producer capitalism. For this to happen, however, citizens must see the state as the source and the articulator of these higher standards of justice, and not merely as the guarantor of private property rights or as a standing threat to personal liberty.

Adams's textbook, *The Science of Finance: An Investigation of Public Expenditure and Public Revenues* (1898), encoded these new ideals of civic responsibility and was continuously revised and used for more than a quarter of a century. Many of the ideas foundational to the new academic discipline of political economy were foreshadowed in his early essay, "Democracy," which appeared in the *New Englander* in 1881. In it, Adams maintained that a cooperative commonwealth could be achieved not through state socialism but through the abandonment of the wages system in favor of shared industrial ownership. The early essays on democracy by JOHN DEWEY, a University of Michigan colleague of Adams's, reflect many of these same ideas. Another colleague at Michigan, Charles H. Cooley, shaped the new field of social psychology and shared many of the same "kingdom" ideals for American society. Together, these three came to be presidents of four academic professional societies: the American Economics Association (Adams, 1896); the American Sociological Society (Cooley, 1905); the American Psychological Association (Dewey, 1899); and the American Philosophical Association (1904).

See also ECONOMIC DEVELOPMENT; LIBERALISM.

Further reading: Dombrowski, James. *The Early Days of Christian Socialism in America*. New York: Octagon, 1966.

—Eldon J. Eisenach

Adams, John (1735–1826) *U.S. president*

Perhaps more than any other American president, John Adams sought to discover the proper relationships among religion, politics, and the social order. Born and reared in Braintree, Massachusetts, in a nonrevivalist congregation during the FIRST GREAT AWAKENING, he thought from early on about issues related to one's private faith, the role of reason, and how these relate to politics and society.

Adams was deeply affected by Old Light preaching as a child, as its emphasis on reason and human ability to choose good dominated his thought and behavior throughout his life. Hearing Jonathan Mayhew, Boston's Lockean liberal minister and early Unitarian, on a number of occasions, Adams virtually memorized the preacher's famous *Discourse Concerning Unlimited Submission and Non-Resistance to the Higher Powers* in 1750. Adams wrote THOMAS JEFFERSON nearly 70 years later that, as a 14-year-old, he read that sermon repeatedly "till the Substance of it was incorporated into my Nature and indelibly engraved on my Memory."

Mayhew's Enlightened understanding of the complementary natures of religion, politics, and society were further engraved on Adams's thinking by his training at Harvard in the early 1750s. Each of his mentors emphasized a "moderate Enlightenment" understanding of the world in which balance and symmetry marked every aspect of life: science, theology, government, and the social order. By applying the early Enlightenment methods of reason to each of these arenas, students formulated a reasoned, balanced understanding of the relation of all things.

This ran Adams into trouble, for he had planned to enter the ministry, just as the firstborn males of the Adams clan had done for generations. But on the heels of the divisive Great Awakening, his emphasis on Enlightenment reason could prove especially troublesome to parishes looking to hire a minister. Doubting everything from the Trinity to biblical accounts of miracles, Adams instead chose to study law while he served as schoolmaster in Worchester. Finding other like-minded individuals, he spent his twenties working out his ideas on reasonable religion and balanced government by constantly arguing and fine-tuning his thoughts with friends. His views on tyranny of the conscience—both spiritual through "priestcraft" and political through social cruelties—were largely shaped during this early period.

He had the opportunity to put those ideas into print when the Stamp Act crisis arose in 1765. Published throughout the colonies and in England as "A Dissertation on the Canon and Feudal Law," this four-part series argued that ignorance historically had enabled religious and secular tyrants to rule over people in a "wicked conspiracy." This cabal remained in power until the Protestant Reformation, when Martin Luther led the charge for increased knowledge and liberty of conscience. The PURITANS, who through religion and "a love of universal Liberty" settled America, furthered that spirit. New England's heritage, Adams argued, was to see liberty "at all hazards." "We have a right to it," he explained, since it was derived from God and won by the blood of their forebears.

Adams often used religious imagery in his pseudonymous writings to describe the political and social struggles leading up to the violence that broke out in the mid-1770s. As "Clarendon," he tied America's struggle to principles based on the moral law, the law of God, the British constitution, and the welfare of English citizens. As "Humphrey Ploughjogger," he linked the governor's behavior to the evil spirits who animated people since humanity's fall in the Garden of Eden. As old Plymouth's "Governor Bradford," he deplored human nature's ambition and the cruel oppressions that spring from it. Overall, these writings exhibited his private understanding of true religion, the danger of ambitious leaders, and America's providential position in history.

His private commitment to a faith that balanced the biblical God of the Puritans with the Enlightenment deity of the "Age of Reason" was but one aspect of a mentality that consistently sought to understand the world as an equilibrium. Thus some early patriots mistrusted Adams's commitment to the cause when he decried the destruction of private property in defense of "American rights" and even defended the British soldiers charged in the Boston Massacre. Tyranny, he believed, could take many forms, including a tyranny of the masses as they attacked the cruelties of the monarchy or aristocracy.

Not surprisingly, then, Adams formulated a political theory by the time of the war's outbreak that balanced government along the lines of the social order, which he considered a perfect equilibrium among interests. By arguing in *Thoughts On Government* in 1776 for "mixed government" in each colony, wherein democracy (lower house), aristocracy (upper house), and monarchy (governorship) jointly held power, he believed he offered the best chance for stability. The body politic should reflect the human mind, which was made by God to hold at once different passions and interests, constantly balancing various needs against one another. Seven of the 13 colonies adopted precisely the form of government Adams suggested after reading the document.

Adams took those concerns with him to Europe when Congress sent him as an envoy to the Netherlands, then to France to negotiate peace, and then to England as the first American minister after the war. His writings during this period show a constant critique of European and American societies, judging them according to religious tolerance and balanced government. When he returned to the United States nearly a decade later, he joined the new government as the nation's first vice president under a Constitution that he largely approved, finding it in accord with his own ideas on mixed government.

But while Adams had remained very consistent in his thought, America itself had changed significantly in his absence. That fact was made clear during his presidency (1797–1801), when he tried to override party politics with his brand of balanced government. Utilizing the New England tradition of Fast Day each spring, he twice called for National Days of Prayer during the XYZ affair, as the country flirted with war with France. In 1798, when faced with internal challenges from the Republicans, his message was the need for national unity. Thousands took to the streets in Philadelphia to march on the president's mansion for misusing his authority and breaching the SEPARATION OF CHURCH AND STATE. The following year, however, defending himself from charges by both the more democratic Republicans led by Thomas Jefferson and the aristocratic Arch-Federalists led by ALEXANDER HAMILTON, Adams called for a National Day of Prayer by pointedly attacking both sides, insisting on a balanced policy that played into neither party's hand.

Having eschewed what he considered the tyranny of the masses (Republicans) and the tyranny of aristocracy (Federalists), Adams sat alone politically. Although the leaders of neither party supported him, he nearly won reelection in 1800, losing instead to Jefferson in a close contest. Adams retired to his home in Massachusetts, not suspecting that he had more than a quarter of a century left to live, during which he would read widely and write volumes of letters and newspaper articles.

And write he did—thousands of letters covering everything from politics to theology, from agriculture to literature, poured from his quill. To this day they remain a testament to his broad mind and constant self-education. Still, he considered himself an expert in only two areas: In 1816 he wrote his son, John Quincy Adams, "For fifty years I have neglected all Sciences but Government and Religion."

In retrospect, Adams's public behavior, previously viewed as erratic by his contemporaries and later scholars, was in fact very consistent, based as it was on certain underlying principles. First, his view of human nature and its effects on society were evident in such actions as the defense of the British soldiers in 1772, his derision of both the Republicans and the

High Federalists in the 1790s, and his concern for slavery's consequences. Borrowing from Puritan notions of human nature, he understood people as constitutionally ambitious and selfish. Only a mixed government that pitted competing interests against one another could offer social stability. Second, the independent streak he developed early in life that took him to the heights of power resulted from his personal quest for freedom of conscience, both in the spiritual and political realms. Dissuaded from the ministry because he feared reprisals for his religious ideas, he exalted his own struggle for independence to a national level. Finally, both his views on human nature and his notions of personal and national independence found fruit in his presidency. His Fast Day Proclamations employed religious rhetoric to expose political and social movements that threatened to undo the balanced government Americans enjoyed.

See also LOCKE, JOHN; WASHINGTON, GEORGE; UNITARIAN UNIVERSALIST.

Further reading: Ellis, Joseph. *Passionate Sage: The Character and Legacy of John Adams.* New York: Norton, 1993; Goff, Philip. *The Soul of John Adams.* Chapel Hill: University of North Carolina Press, 2003; McCullough, David. *John Adams.* New York: Knopf, 2001.

—Philip Goff

Addams, Jane (1860–1935) *activist*

Born in Illinois, the daughter of a prominent Republican state senator who had led a military company during the Civil War, Jane Addams attended college in Illinois, then traveled and studied in Europe in the mid-1880s. In England, she visited Toynbee Hall, an experimental "settlement house" in an industrial district of London. An early activist in women's political and labor movements, her lasting achievement was the founding of Hull-House, on the west side of Chicago in 1889. Given her strong ties to the emerging academic disciplines of sociology and social work, Hull-House functioned at once as a neighborhood community center, as a center and clearinghouse for a host of reform organizations and movements, and as a working laboratory linking reform activism and the academic social sciences.

Although not associated with any particular religious body, Addams's many reform causes overlapped considerably with those of the SOCIAL GOSPEL movement, whether the cause was rights for black Americans, SOCIAL JUSTICE for the immigrant, adult education, woman suffrage, tenement house legislation, mother's pensions, or factory inspection and worker's compensation. Although her local constituency comprised urban immigrants, her primary national audience was morally earnest middle-class women whom she prodded out of the increasing comforts of the home and into lives of public and social service through the new medium of national women's magazines, such as *Ladies' Home Journal* and *Woman's Home Companion*, monthlies such as *Atlantic*

Jane Addams *(Library of Congress)*

Monthly, and professional journals such as the *American Journal of Sociology*. These ideas were systemized in her book *Democracy and Social Ethics* (1902), where she shows that personal ethics ("righteousness"), impelled by the newer conception of democracy, was manifested in social obligations and standards of conduct informed by ideals of social justice.

In time, she became something of a secular saint and even the focus of public adulation. In a 1906 contest to discover "Who is the best woman in Chicago," Addams not only won hands down, but the next three winners were her fellow settlement-house workers. A poem dedicated to Addams combined the images of biological and social motherhood and Christian missionary, beginning, "Mother of races fusing into one, / and keeping open house with presence sweet / In that loud city where the nations meet" and concluding, "When I behold the wild tribes thou hast won / And see thee wooing from the witching street / By thy own saintly face the erring feet / I know Love still has power beneath the sun."

Her influence was also manifested in institutions of substantial national and international reach. She was a founding member of the American Sociological Society in 1905 and the first woman president of the National Council of Social Work in 1910. At the Progressive Party convention in 1912, she seconded the nomination of THEODORE ROOSEVELT for president. In 1915, she chaired the International Congress of Women, meeting at The Hague, which culminated in the founding of the Women's International League for Peace and Freedom, which she also headed. In 1931, she received the Nobel Peace Prize.

See also ADAMS, HENRY CARTER; ECONOMIC DEVELOPMENT; LIBERALISM.

Further reading: Eisenach, Eldon. *The Lost Promise of Progressivism.* Lawrence: University Press of Kansas, 1994; Elshtain, Jean Bethke, *Jane Addams and the Dream of American Democracy.* New York: Basic Books, 2001.

—Eldon J. Eisenach

African Americans and faith-based initiatives

By almost any measure, Congress's Personal Responsibility and Work Opportunity Reconciliation Act (PRWORA) was a radical piece of legislation. It abruptly dismantled a social safety net that had been in place since the New Deal of President FRANKLIN DELANO ROOSEVELT. It replaced a "tried and true" safety net with an untested welfare-to-work program that requires welfare recipients to find jobs, sets time limits for their job searches, and ultimately withdraws welfare assistance from individuals whose long-term searches for employment prove to be futile. August 22, 1996, marked the end of "the welfare state" as we formally knew it. WILLIAM JEFFERSON CLINTON signed PRWORA into law and said that it should "be remembered not for what it ended, but for what it began: a new day that offers hope, honors responsibility, rewards work, and changes the terms of the debate."

PRWORA established the Temporary Assistance for Needy Families (TANF) Program as the cash assistance program for needy families with children. A major focus of the TANF program is to move clients from cash assistance into employment. The CHARITABLE CHOICE provision was also part of the welfare reform legislation. "Charitable Choice" specifically encourages the public sector to contract directly with faith-based organizations for welfare-related programs such as childcare and job training, as well as relaxing some of the traditional barriers that have inhibited provision of public funding to the religious community. This provision allows states to contract with faith-based organizations to provide federally funded welfare services to poor families and needy communities.

The legislation created an instant fault line in the African-American community, dividing minister from minister and activist from activist. CIVIL RIGHTS MOVEMENT leaders within the black community voiced their fears that the black church would lose its autonomy by accepting government money, whereas conservatives were concerned that the black church would become too dependent on federal dollars. While black churches have been setting up nonprofit organizations and community development corporations for years, the faith-based initiative offers something new in that tax credits and federal dollars may go directly to a church-based organization. This is of particular interest for the black church, which traditionally has been the source of many social services for the black community. In inner-city and low-income areas throughout the country, black churches operate homeless shelters, distribute food and clothing to the needy, run drug and alcohol treatment programs, in addition to meeting diverse spiritual needs.

African-American clergy, faith-based organizations, and the black community are all partners in the efforts to pull people out of poverty, as a result of the new welfare reform law. Some churches and other religious groups are responding to what they see as a crisis facing people who have severely suffered from welfare cutbacks, but others say the law offers an unprecedented opportunity to make a difference in the lives of the nation's needy. This concept is no different in the African-American community. The black church has been at the forefront of nearly every major social, moral, and political movement in the black community. With the Charitable Choice provisions in the federal welfare reform legislation, federal policy makers opened the door for the black religious community to play a larger role in providing services to welfare recipients.

Given this unprecedented situation, however, black churches certainly need to address a series of issues in the attempt to build new partnerships with government. First, black churches must develop a system of partnerships that transcends "government mistrust" and historic notions of paternalism and take advantage of the resources each has to offer. Second, black churches must cultivate the idea of public-private partnerships (within their congregations) to bring together principals with a shared interest in the social and economic development of their community. Third, churches must start to focus their attention on education issues (education is the engine that can drive African Americans out of poverty) in minority communities, especially because clergy are often not involved in the discussions concerning the public schools' obligation to provide quality education to all its students. Fourth, black churches and community-based organizations must work more collaboratively to ameliorate the conditions of poverty. As opposed to competing for government funds, public trust, and media sympathy, black churches and community-based organizations simply need to work together.

U.S. Attorney General and former U.S. senator John Ashcroft, the architect of Charitable Choice, has repeatedly asserted that welfare reform legislation was specifically designed to invite faith-based organizations back into the social safety-net roles that had been taken from them during the New Deal era. The law's authors take for granted that faith-based organizations possess the capacity and the will to reclaim these roles, that religious leaders perceive these roles to be compatible with the fundamental missions of their organizations, and that both the public sector and religious leaders are comfortable with the kind of church-state relations that welfare reform creates.

See also ECONOMIC DEVELOPMENT; SEPARATION OF CHURCH AND STATE; WELFARE REFORM; WHITE HOUSE OFFICE OF FAITH-BASED INITIATIVES.

Further reading: Carson-Thies, Stanley W. "Introduction." In *A Guide to Charitable Choice: The Rules of Section 104 of the 1996 Federal Welfare Governing State Cooperation with Faith-Based-Social-Service Providers.* Washington, D.C.: Center for Public Justice, 1997.

—Boris E. Ricks

African-American voting behavior since the Civil Rights movement

The passage of the 1965 Voting Rights Act represented the end of legal racial discrimination in the electoral system of the United States. It represented the beginning of an opportunity for full POLITICAL PARTICIPATION by African Americans in this country. Today African Americans vote at rates similar to whites. The religiosity of African Americans is one of the major reasons for this parity. African Americans display high levels of religiosity attending church, participating in church activities, praying, and reading the Bible more than whites. Such activities do not just produce spiritual benefits; they have significant political effects. Research indicates that religiously inclined blacks are more likely to engage in electoral activities. Although blacks as a group possess lower levels of education, income, and other variables associated with political participation, religion helps to make up the difference by serving as an important group-based psychological and institutional resource for political mobilization among blacks. Models of African-American political participation emphasize such group-based political resources in explaining why African Americans vote despite a lack of traditional motivational factors.

Both private and public expressions of religiosity promote the development of the group-based resources associated with individual political action. Chief among these resources in the African-American community is the development of a racial consciousness. Racial consciousness involves identification with a racial group and a perception that the group is unfairly discriminated against or disadvantaged on the basis of race. This consciousness has led African Americans to engage in collective behaviors like voting more than those who do not have a similar collective orientation. Among African Americans, private religious expressions of devotionalism like praying, reading religious books, or watching religious programming all contribute to the development of racial consciousness. Public expressions such as attending politically active African-American churches also contribute significantly to racial consciousness.

It is not surprising that African-American religiosity contributes to a racial identification and consciousness. From the earliest slave experiences, African-American religion was one of the few societal sources mediating messages of inferiority and subordination. Because churches were the most segregated institutions in American society and because under systems of segregation so many other avenues for political, social, and civic expression were closed, many African-American churches became centers for political socialization and organization around racial issues. They helped to provide definition to the African-American community as well as information on what it meant to be a part of it.

The more people pray and read their Bibles, the more likely they are to feel personally and politically empowered and conclude that their participation can truly make a difference. The collective orientation of the church environment can also contribute to feelings of empowerment. Churches can also be rich contexts for the dissemination of political information and can effectively communicate messages of civic awareness and participation to those who attend them. African-American churches vary greatly in the extent to which they actually present racial or political messages, but collectively they remain a major influence on political socialization and political learning among blacks, and there is a lot of support in the black community for the involvement of churches in political matters.

Politically, churches also have a considerable impact on African-American voting behavior. Organizationally, churches are significant institutional resources and can offer facilities, finances, communication networks, leadership, and an audience to political causes and candidates. The power of black churches organizationally was most clearly demonstrated during the CIVIL RIGHTS MOVEMENT. However, even today political parties and candidates seeking to mobilize the African-American community commonly work through churches to do so. The most successful national examples of the organizational capacity of African-American churches in electoral politics are the 1984 and 1988 presidential campaigns of the Rev. JESSE JACKSON. Jackson's candidacies were based on the legitimacy of African-American ministers as political leaders and on the ability of African-American churches to turn out voters. Not only did Jackson go to churches to legitimize his candidacy; he relied on them and their resources to reach and mobilize the people and to provide core organization in the states. The strategy was effective because the organizational strength of churches individually and denominations collectively has been considerable. For instance, when the Rev. T. J. JEMISON, president of the NATIONAL BAPTIST CONVENTION USA Inc., endorsed Jackson, 40,000 churches and nearly 7 million congregants were put at Jackson's disposal. While the Jackson case is sensational, church-based support for politicians occurs as dramatically, but on a smaller scale, at the state and local level every time an electoral contest is held. Many elected officials owe their political lives to the ability of churches to access and to activate African-American voters.

Because African Americans are overwhelmingly Democratic in partisan identification, the political activities of black churches often benefit Democratic more than Republican candidates. Despite the fact that most black churches and churchgoers are evangelical in theological orientation, among blacks EVANGELICALISM is not associated with conservative political behavior. Organizations of the Christian Right have had little success bringing blacks into their coalitions by appealing to their conservative religious beliefs. Black attitudes toward many moral-cultural issues like ABORTION and homosexuality are even more conservative than whites. However, their liberal positions on the appropriate role of government in society as well as on many economic issues are more congruent with Democratic political positions and, for blacks, more salient to vote choice.

Further reading: Allen, Richard, Michael Dawson, and Ron Brown. "A Schema Based Approach to Modeling an African American Racial Belief System." *American Political Science Review* 83 (1989): 421–444; Brown, Ron, and Monica Wolford. "Religious Resources and African American Political Action." *National Political Science Review* 4 (1994): 30–48; Calhoun-Brown, Allison. "African American Churches and Political Mobilization: The Psychological Impact of Organizational Resources." *Journal of Politics* 58 (1996): 935–953; Harris, Fredrick. *Something Within: Religion in African American Political Activism.* New York: Oxford Books, 1999; Lincoln, C. Eric, and Lawrence Mamiya. *The Black Church in the African American Experience.* Durham, N.C.: Duke University Press, 1990; Morris, Aldon. *The Origins of the Civil Rights Movement: Black Communities Organizing for Change.* New York: Free Press, 1984; Smith, Robert, and Richard Seltzer. *Race, Class and Culture: A Study in Afro-American Mass Opinion.* Albany: State University of New York Press, 1992; Tate, Katherine. *From Protest to Politics: The New Black Voters in American Elections.* Cambridge, Mass.: Harvard University Press, 1994.

—Allison Calhoun-Brown

African Methodist Episcopal (A.M.E.) Church
The African Methodist Episcopal Church (A.M.E) has approximately 2.5 million members, 5,000 churches, and 19 Episcopal districts located in North America, the Caribbean islands, and Africa. Its history may be traced back to the beginnings of U.S. history. In 1786, blacks represented 10 percent of the Methodist Episcopal Church. If one act in particular led to the beginning of a free Methodist African Church movement, it occurred in 1787 in St. George's Methodist Episcopal Church in Philadelphia. According to Richard Allen, founder and first elected bishop of the A.M.E. Church, on a November Sunday in 1787, at the first Sabbath service after the church's renovations, a sexton ushered Allen, Absalom Jones, and William White (a prominent black church member) to seats in the new gallery that was situated above the old part of the church. The

trio instead took seats near where they had formerly sat before the renovation. This led to a confrontation because the section was now reserved for white members only. White trustees attempted to pull Jones and Williams from their knees, all to no avail. Allen recalls, "By the time the prayer was over, and we all went out of the church in a body, and they were no more plagued by us in the church."

In late 1790, Allen joined with other black leaders in Philadelphia to raise money for an independent African church, which would formally be known as Mother Bethel. Members of Bethel drew up what Allen called the African Supplement, which gave trustees the right to nominate and appoint one or more persons of African extraction to exhort and preach in Bethel Church or any other church. Independence from white Methodism would become official only in 1816. Black Methodists called a general conference in April 1816 that led to the formal establishment of the A.M.E. Church and the election of Richard Allen as its first bishop.

Under Allen's leadership, the A.M.E. Church would engage in both spiritual and sociopolitical matters. Allen felt that moral persuasion, black economic independence, and protest activism would eventually lead to full citizenship. Hence, long before Dr. MARTIN LUTHER KING JR.'s notion of

Richard Allen, the first bishop of the African Methodist Episcopal Church *(Library of Congress)*

the beloved community, Allen's faith led him to believe, much like John Wesley, that the message of Christ could change the hearts of slave owners, thereby eventually causing racial enslavement to end. Moreover, black economic freedom, which meant ownership of church property and small businesses, would make blacks less dependent on whites, thereby showing whites that blacks were willing to work hard to obtain economic wealth. Hence, the A.M.E. Church is a forerunner of black economic determinism that would exhibit itself in the 20th century in the Garvey Movement, the NATION OF ISLAM, and Operation Breadbasket–PUSH. Allen's political involvement would include co-founding the Free African Society, a group that fostered self-help and economic self-determinism. He also established day and night schools and operated a station on the Underground Railroad.

The twin notions of ECONOMIC DEVELOPMENT and political agitation would take on different forms for the A.M.E. Church in the remainder of the 19th century. The failed reconstruction would lead Bishop Henry Neil Turner, an ousted Georgian state senator, to promote pan-Africanism. In 1893, Turner founded a journal, *Voice of Missions,* that provided a platform for his views on missionary and commercial development in Africa and plans for resettlement there. Turner wrote and preached that the only way blacks could gain respect and power in the United States was to establish independent A.M.E. missions in Africa. These missions would provide black Americans and Africans with a common basis for creating a black Christian nation that would be independent of white power. Of equal importance in Turner's thought was his radical suggestion (which looked forward to Marcus Garvey as well as to formulations by MALCOLM X and the Nation of Islam) that blacks would forever be degraded in their faith as long as they worshipped a white God. Finally, Turner was instrumental in forming an alliance between the A.M.E. Church and the Ethiopian Church of South Africa in 1896. The South African government viewed this alliance as a political threat because it might provide blacks with the basis of a nationalist movement. The political role of the A.M.E. Church in South Africa would undergo numerous changes, largely because of government repression and fear among American bishops that too much overt political activism would retard the development of the missionary work of the church. In the end, the A.M.E.–South African connection failed to produce the pan-African political movement that Turner envisioned. The church dialogue was a cultural one, with black Americans and Africans learning a great deal about the similarities and differences in their struggles for human dignity.

During the CIVIL RIGHTS MOVEMENT and black power era in the United States, local churches would provide the spark for political activism. For example, both the building and the members of Brown Chapel A.M.E. Church played pivotal roles in the Selma, Alabama, marches that helped lead to the passage of the 1965 Voting Rights Act. The starting point of the Selma-to-Montgomery marches, Brown Chapel, also hosted meetings of the SOUTHERN CHRISTIAN LEADERSHIP CONFERENCE (SCLC) for the first three months of 1965. It was also at Brown Chapel that the Rev. JESSE JACKSON first talked to King about the possibility of establishing Operation Breadbasket in Chicago, an idea that would come into being just six months later when Jackson was named to King's staff.

The A.M.E. Church seeks to continue its legacy of activism, and to confront and meet new challenges. The church made history on July 11, 2000, by electing Vashti McKenzie as the first female bishop in church history. A recent Internet survey conducted by the Rev. William P. DeVeaux, president of the Council of Bishops, 2000–2001, of lay members reveals that the church is confronting a number of challenges that will shape its future direction. Lay members are calling for more AIDS/HIV community outreach efforts, increased efforts to appoint women to visible positions within the church, and, finally, the appointment of indigenous African and Caribbean leaders to top leadership positions.

See also AFRICAN METHODIST EPISCOPAL (A.M.E.) ZION CHURCH; CHRISTIAN METHODIST EPISCOPAL CHURCH; RACISM.

Further reading: Campbell, James. *Songs of Zion: The African Methodist Episcopal Church in the United States and South Africa.* New York: Oxford University Press, 1995; Lincoln, C. Eric. *The Doctrine and Discipline of the African Methodist Episcopal Church, 1996–2000.* Nashville: African Methodist Episcopal Church A.M.E.C. Sunday School Union, 1996; Lincoln, C. Eric, and Lawrence H. Mamiya. *The Black Church in the African American Experience.* Durham, N.C.: Duke University Press, 1990.

—Ron Brown

African Methodist Episcopal (A.M.E.) Zion Church

The African Methodist Episcopal (A.M.E.) Zion Church encompasses 3,000 churches and has an active membership of 1.5 million. Much like the AFRICAN METHODIST EPISCOPAL (A.M.E.) CHURCH, the A.M.E. Zion Church came into existence because of the expressed desire among some blacks in New York City to create an independent black church. A number of black people, most of whom were members of the John Street Methodist Episcopal Church in New York City, took the first step toward independence in 1796. They had not been disturbed in their worship to the extent experienced by the founders of the A.M.E. Church in Philadelphia, but they had a "desire for the privilege of holding meetings of their own, where they might have an opportunity to exercise their spiritual gifts among themselves, and thereby be more useful to one another."

Peter Williams, a former slave employed at John Street Church, and some black members of the church organized an African chapel in a cabinetmaker's shop owned by another of the members, William Miller. Worship there continued until 1800, when they erected a building. The following year, members named the chapel the African Methodist Episcopal Zion Church. The year 1820 is commonly accepted as the date of the official incorporation of the African Methodist Episcopal Zion denomination. It was then that the denomination sought to make clear its distinction from those affiliated with A.M.E. Church founder Richard Allen. The new denomination also made clear its desire to break away from the predominantly white Methodists in 1824. In 1848, the word *Zion* was officially added to the African Methodist Episcopal to clearly distinguish between this denomination and the A.M.E. Church that originated in Philadelphia.

The A.M.E. Zion Church, much like its sister denomination, the A.M.E. Church, places a significant degree of emphasis on political activism. For example, St. James A.M.E. Zion Church of Ithaca, New York, built in 1836, was an Underground Railroad station. The congregation officially expressed its antislavery sentiments through the writings and preaching of pastors such as Thomas James, who was known to have assisted fugitive slaves. HARRIET TUBMAN, an antislavery advocate, played an active role in A.M.E. Zion Church affairs, as well as did Frederick Douglass, who was ordained as an A.M.E. Zion preacher. St. James Zion Church continued to play a critical role in the political and social lives of African Americans in the 20th century. In 1906, in the basement of St. James, seven African-American Cornell University students, frustrated by discriminatory all-white fraternities, formed Alpha Phi Alpha, the nation's oldest official black fraternity.

The CIVIL RIGHTS MOVEMENT and black power era would again find some black local A.M.E. Zion churches involved in the struggle. Butler Chapel in Tuskegee, Alabama, was the focal point of a multiyear grassroots project that united and empowered African Americans to fight for the right to vote. In a 1957 effort to minimize the number of black voters in Tuskegee, Alabama's municipal elections, the state legislature simply redrew the town's political districts, placing Tuskegee Institute and all but a small fraction of black residents outside the city limits. To protest this action, Tuskegee's middle-class black community and Macon County's poor black citizens joined forces in a seven-year "Crusade for Citizenship." On June 25, 1957, 3,000 area black residents showed up at Butler Chapel for the first of many weekly mass meetings. Only 500 attendees could fit into the church's small sanctuary; the rest listened outside. Charles Gomillion, a professor at Tuskegee Institute and the driving force of the black Tuskegee Civic Association, urged the crowd to join a "Trade with Friends" boycott of local white merchants. "We are going to buy goods and services from those who help us, from those who make no effort to hinder us, from those who recognize us as first-class citizens," he promised.

See also AFRICAN METHODIST EPISCOPAL (A.M.E.) CHURCH; CHRISTIAN METHODIST EPISCOPAL CHURCH; RACISM.

Further reading: Lincoln, C. Eric, and Lawrence H. Mamiya. *The Black Church in the African American Experience.* Durham, N.C.: Duke University Press, 1990.

—Ron Brown

agnosticism

Agnosticism is the belief that knowledge of God's existence has not yet been achieved or is not achievable. The word was created in the 19th century as a result of the successes of modern science in solving problems previously left to religion to solve. The term "agnosticism" was coined by the British professor Thomas H. Huxley in the 1840s, to mean the method of free and rational inquiry, unhindered by tradition and religious assumptions. Huxley's meaning of the term is different from the most common meaning of the word in the 21st century. Today, agnosticism is often applied to the question of God, claiming that the existence of God is not known, or not knowable.

Robert G. Ingersoll is the most famous American agnostic. A staunch Republican, lawyer, abolitionist, colonel in the Union Army in the Civil War, and magnificent orator, Ingersoll was a freethinker who championed reason and science over religious traditions. Following the general trend of the Enlightenment regarding ethics and justice, he criticized the idea that God would go against the moral standards equally applicable to humans: a true God would not kill innocent people (as depicted in the story of Noah's flood, for instance). In the late 19th century, various groups of agnostics formed, often meeting weekly to provide support and fellowship. In 1876, Felix Adler founded what became the American Ethical Union, an organization centered on a rationally ethical approach to social issues.

Today, proponents of agnosticism often find fellow like-minded thinkers in organizations dedicated to religious and/or SECULAR HUMANISM. The AMERICAN HUMANIST ASSOCIATION and the Council for Secular Humanism are two main groups in the United States. These groups are prominent in legal debates on church-and-state separation, the right to privacy, creationism versus evolutionism, and the freedom of, and from, religion.

See also ATHEISM.

—Eric L. Thomas

Agostini v. Felton No. 96-552 (1997)

In a 5-4 decision, the conservative majority on the Supreme Court continued their assault on the *LEMON V. KURTZMAN ESTABLISHMENT CLAUSE* regime, dealing *Lemon* a near fatal blow. The case readdressed a claim by appellants in *AGUILAR V. FELTON*, a 1987 decision that struck down a New York use of Title I federal education monies to fund private school teachers. In *Aguilar*, Justice WILLIAM BRENNAN found that the administration of the program constituted excessive entanglement between church and state. By 1997, though, Brennan had retired and the balance on the Court had shifted by one seat, which was enough to shift the prevailing sentiment. The losing side in *Aguilar* wanted the Court to revisit the issue in light of their recent Establishment Clause rulings.

Title I of the Elementary and Secondary Education Act of 1965 was meant to ensure the adequate education of economically less-fortunate children. Title I funds are channeled through local educational agencies for remedial education, guidance, and job counseling. Title I funds come with more restrictions when used in a private school: they cannot be used to replace services already offered and instead must only supplement them; they cannot be used for schoolwide services; they must provide the services through individuals not affiliated with the private school; the state must retain ownership of materials provided with Title I funds; and they must be used in a manner that is "secular, neutral, and nonideological."

Applying the three prongs of the *Lemon* test to the facts in *Aguilar*, Brennan found that the New York application of Title I funds to provide public school teachers for remedial purposes in private schools was secular in intent and did not advance religion (though see Powell's concurring opinion), but did encourage an entangling relationship between the religious school and the state. Brennan found that ensuring that Title I funds were being used in a secular manner required "comprehensive, discriminating, and continuing state surveillance." Such surveillance would inhibit free exercise of the religion practiced at the school (see FREE EXERCISE CLAUSE).

Justice Sandra Day O'Connor delivered the opinion of the Court in *Agostini*, joined by Chief Justice William Rehnquist and Justices ANTONIN SCALIA, Anthony Kennedy, and Clarence Thomas. In that opinion, O'Connor established the opinion, considered mere *dicta* in the KIRYAS JOEL VILLAGE SCHOOL DISTRICT V. GRUMENT decision, that *Aguilar* should be overruled. The majority placed heavy emphasis on their ruling in ZOBREST V. CATALINA FOOTHILLS SCHOOL DISTRICT, in which the Court allowed a program whereby the state paid for an interpreter for a deaf student attending a sectarian institution. The 5-4 majority in *Zobrest* found that the interpreter was in no way advancing religion simply by translating for the student and that the state aid program certainly was not motivated by religion. Justice Harry Blackmun sharply criticized the *Zobrest* majority: "Until now, the Court never has authorized a public employee to participate directly in religious indoctrination. Yet that is the consequence of today's decision."

Zobrest was aimed at the heart of *Aguilar*—nullifying the entanglement prong of the *Lemon* test—and *Zobrest* was taken to the logical next step in *Agostini*. The majority in *Agostini* argued that if the translator in *Zobrest* did not constitute an advancement of religion nor generate an entangling relationship, then hiring a public school teacher to teach secular subjects was even less of a threat to establishing a religion. The majority claimed that the legislative commandment to use the money for secular ends, along with unannounced monthly visits by the state, provided enough insurance against promoting religion that further state surveillance was not necessary.

The dissenting opinions held to the conclusion that "The result is to repudiate the very reasonable line drawn in *Aguilar* and *Ball*, and to authorize direct state aid to religious institutions on an unparalleled scale, in violation of the Establishment Clause's central prohibition against religious subsidies by the government." The dissenting justices, some of whom constituted the majority in *Aguilar*, argued that a public school teacher in a private location would advance religion in three ways: via inadvertent sympathy with the sectarian institution, through a symbolic union of church and state, and by providing, and hence subsidizing, services the school would otherwise have to provide. They distinguished *Aguilar* and *Agostini* from *Zobrest*, claiming this last distinction—*Zobrest* does not address the *Agostini* facts since in *Zobrest* the state provided a service private schools were not required to provide (the interpreter—"indirect and incidental aid"), though private schools do have to provide basic educational instruction as provided for in *Agostini*. Thus, the *Agostini* majority opinion seems to allow "direct and substantial" aid to private schools for required instruction, even though it serves to free up resources that may be spent elsewhere, including on religious instruction.

—Paul A. Djupe

Agudat Israel

Almost from the beginning of the Zionist enterprise that was born at the end of the 19th century, some of its most vociferous opponents were Jews. While much of the Jewish opposition to ZIONISM came from secularized communities in western Europe and North America, a significant proportion was also from a segment of the Orthodox Jewish constituency. Agudat Israel was the foremost anti-Zionist expression to emanate from ORTHODOX JUDAISM. These Jews believed that political Zionism was a heretical travesty. They believed that ISRAEL could only be reestablished by the intervention of the Messiah. In the view of Agudat Israel, the state of Israel is different from other countries. It is a sacred polity that cannot be dominated by the same sort of political process that has been applied everywhere else. Agudat Israel also has an affiliated American arm, Agudath Israel of America.

Agudat Israel horrified the overwhelming proportion of Jews living in Palestine during the 1920s. They were particularly put off by Agudat Israel's hostility to Zionism, which was then so intense that it included collaboration with opponents of Zionism in both the Palestinian population and the British mandate authority. Agudat Israel agents even lobbied the League of Nations to blunt the implementation of the Balfour Declaration, a British government document published in 1917 that called for the creation of a Jewish homeland. Anti-Jewish riots at the Western Wall in 1929 persuaded Agudat Israel to moderate its stance. The rioters did not distinguish between pro- and anti-Zionist Jews. By 1931, Agudat Israel had ceased its opposition to the Zionist movement and gradually established cordial relations with it.

During the life of the Israeli state since 1948, Agudat Israel has been politically active. It is one of several religiously orthodox parties that have inconsistently cooperated with conservative or labor governments. Ironically, while Agudat Israel continued to adhere to an anti-Zionist posture, it became very opposed to any Israeli withdrawal from the West Bank. It has also attempted to work with other religious parties to bring greater spirituality to Jewish life in Israel. Agudat Israel has been in the forefront of activities to pressure the government to enforce dietary laws and ban the sale of pork products; apply censorship to literature and films it thinks are pornographic; and, above all, to determine "who is a Jew." The latter issue has been particularly vexing since many Israeli citizens have mixed parentage, particularly within the Russian immigrant community. Like most religious authorities, Agudat Israel holds that no child can be safely Jewish unless its mother is Jewish.

Agudat Israel's religious motivations have not been discouraging to certain segments of nonreligious voters. Israeli Jews on the lower socioeconomic rungs recently have voted for Agudat Israel in significant numbers. Like other religious parties in Israel, Agudat Israel has become a vehicle for voters who feel they have been neglected by the political mainstream.
—Martin W. Slann

Aguilar et al. v. Felton et al. 473 U.S. 402 (1985)

In this case, decided on July 1, 1985, the Supreme Court considered the constitutionality of programs in New York City funded under Title I of the Elementary and Secondary Education Act of 1965. Under these programs, federal funds were used since 1966 to pay the salaries of public school employees who provided some instruction to "educationally deprived children from low-income families" on the premises of the parochial schools they attended. Writing for a five-justice majority, Justice William Brennan applied the three-prong test first articulated in LEMON V. KURTZMAN (1971) and found that the administration of the program involved "excessive entanglement" of church and state.

Brennan's argument relied on the analogy between New York's Title I program and those found unconstitutional in Lemon and MEEK V. PITTENGER (1975). In all three instances, assuring that publicly funded teachers did not engage in impermissible advancement of religion required a "comprehensive, discriminating, and continuing state surveillance." This state surveillance inhibited the religious freedom of the parochial school authorities. Furthermore, matters such as assigning and scheduling classrooms required a continuing cooperation between public and parochial teachers and administrators that amounted to another kind of entanglement. While publicly funded teachers could continue to instruct students enrolled in parochial schools, they could do so only away from those schools.

In his concurring opinion, Justice Louis Powell highlighted another dimension of excessive entanglement, "a considerable risk of continuing political strife over the propriety of direct aid to religious schools and the proper allocation of limited governmental resources." He further suggested that the program might violate the "effects" prong of the Lemon test, since it "amounts to a state subsidy of the parochial schools by relieving [them] of the duty to provide the remedial and supplemental education their children require."

Each of the four justices in the minority wrote a dissent. Chief Justice Warren Burger emphasized the substantive evil that the ESTABLISHMENT CLAUSE of the First Amendment meant to avoid (the establishment of a state religion) and observed that "[f]ederal programs designed to prevent a generation of children from growing up without being able to read effectively are not remotely steps in that direction." Justice William Rehnquist's brief dissent dwelled on the paradoxical character of the "excessive entanglement" test, through which steps taken to avoid establishment or promotion of religion led to the invalidation of the program. Justice Byron White's dissent, which applied both to Aguilar and to GRAND RAPIDS, SCHOOL DISTRICT OF THE CITY OF V. BALL, a companion case, recalled his long-standing opposition to the framework articulated in Lemon.

Only Justice Sandra Day O'Connor, whose dissent was joined in part by Rehnquist, was willing to apply part of the Lemon test. While she agreed that a program whose purpose or effect was to promote religion is constitutionally infirm, she denied that the record developed through New York's administration of Title I programs supported such a conclusion. As she observed, the professionalism of publicly funded teachers was not likely to vary, and has evidently not varied, from setting to setting. Because such teachers needed and received no more supervision in Title I programs than they did in the ordinary course of teaching, it was hard to see how this supervision amounts to excessive entanglement. Furthermore, citing LYNCH V. DONNELLY (1984), which dealt with a publicly owned nativity scene, O'Connor wondered about the worries of some members of the majority concerning the divisiveness of this sort of program, especially when the only evidence for it was the lawsuit that raises that concern. To the extent that the Court took such evidence seriously, one need only file a lawsuit in effect to win it. Finally, O'Connor indicated that she shared the concerns of others in the minority regarding the paradoxical character of the "excessive entanglement" prong of the Lemon test.

While the majority in this case continued to support and apply the Lemon test, the minority did not waver in their doubts, finding an additional ally, Justice O'Connor, in their objections to the "excessive entanglement" prong. Nevertheless, as applied in this case, the Lemon test led to the requirement that publicly funded teachers do their work outside the parochial schools whose students they are supposed to serve.
—Joseph M. Knippenberg

aid to poor nations

The U.S. Agency for International Development (USAID), an independent federal agency under the direction of the secretary of state and operating with less than half of 1 percent of the federal budget, provides assistance to various countries, identified as poor and developing, located in sub-Saharan Africa, Asia and the Near East, Latin America and the Caribbean, and Europe and Eurasia that are undergoing both natural and human-made disasters. USAID's purpose in assisting these regions is to further "America's foreign policy interests in expanding democracy and free markets," and "improve the lives of the citizens of the developing world." Unfortunately, the State Department has used USAID disaster assistance to advance foreign policy goals through a variety of means, including "punishing enemies by its denial of relief." However, most nations make humanitarian decisions based on how their political interests will be furthered.

In addition to USAID, the U.S. Department of Agriculture also provides food aid to poor nations consisting of wheat, rice, soybean products, and milk powder. According to the Bureau for Humanitarian Response, a U.S. Agency for International Development with its headquarters in Washington, D.C., reports that 70 percent of the funds spent on U.S. food assistance activities is spent in the United States. Nonetheless, funds that the U.S. government provides are significant. For example, in response to a drought in Central America, which has affected Honduras, Nicaragua, El Salvador, and Guatemala, America will provide $84.5 million in food aid.

When aiding poor nations, the U.S. government distributes its aid through nongovernment organizations such as the United Nations. Additionally, various faith-based domestic organizations distribute aid provided by the United States. For example, U.S. Catholic bishops founded the Catholic Relief Services (CRS), based in Baltimore, Md., in 1943 to help the poor and disadvantaged outside the country. Church World Service (CWS), headquartered in New York, is another organization that responds to disasters. Founded in 1946, CWS is composed of 36 Protestant, Orthodox, and Anglican denominations. The American Jewish Joint Distribution Committee, Inc., based in New York, founded the Non-Sectarian International Development Program (IDP), which aids victims of natural and human-made disasters. Funding for IDP is obtained from the U.S. government, international agencies, and private foundations and donors. The Lutheran World Relief is another faith-based organization that assists the disadvantaged in poor nations. Initially, the Lutheran World Relief, like the American Jewish Joint Distribution Committee, Inc., was sectarian, but worldwide disasters prompted the Lutheran World Relief to provide emergency relief on a nonsectarian basis.

The influence of faith-based communities is evidenced by the fact that they are numbered among the nongovernment agencies that raised nearly $4.5 billion in private and public assistance. Furthermore, political influence of religious communities is demonstrated by organizations such as BREAD FOR THE WORLD. Bread for the World, founded in 1972 and based in Washington, D.C., consists of both Roman Catholics and Protestants. Although it provides neither direct relief nor development assistance, Bread for the World has been able to successfully lobby, in 2001, for the Africa: Hunger to Harvest resolution, which provides $400 million in debt relief and poverty-focused aid to Africa.

Historically, faith-based communities have refused to accept and not applied for government funds because of questionable foreign policy implementation. However, these communities unknowingly support foreign policy in several ways.

In 1996, the World Food Summit, held in Rome, Italy, urged heads of state and international leaders to resist using food as an instrument for political and economic pressure. Local governments receiving aid from the U.S. government will distribute food to the middle classes and elite populations to elude political pressure. The result is that poverty-stricken populations, including women, often fail to receive the food and aid that was meant to improve their lot. Often, these injustices took place in the presence of nongovernment organizations unable to exercise any political influence because they refused to accept federal aid.

See also HEIFER INTERNATIONAL; HUNGER AND HUMANITARIAN AID.

Further reading: Belgrad, Eric. "The Politics of Humanitarian Aid." In *The Politics of International Humanitarian Aid Operation*. Edited by Eric Belgrad and Nitza Nachmias. Westport, Conn.: Praeger, 1997; Natsios, Andrew S. *U.S. Foreign Policy and the Four Horsemen of the Apocalypse*. Westport, Conn.: Praeger, 1997; Pottier, Johan. *Anthropology of Food: The Social Dynamics of Food Security*. Malden, Mass.: Blackwell, 1999.

—Santiago O. Piñon Jr.

aid to religious schools

When it comes to education, strict SEPARATION OF CHURCH AND STATE does not exist in the United States. Federal and state governments have long provided some degree of aid to sectarian schools, although its nature and extent varies. Such provision raises constitutional questions related to the ESTABLISHMENT CLAUSE and the Fourteenth Amendment's Equal Protection Clause. On the one hand, advocates, elected officials, and judges have debated whether aid to religious schools represents excessive government intervention in religious organizations. On the other hand, they have contested whether limits on public aid discriminate against individuals on the basis of their religion. Often, perspectives for or against aid to religious schools stem from how one defines the primary beneficiary—parents and children, or religious schools. Increasingly, the Supreme Court has ruled that public aid is constitutional if its primary purpose is to benefit children, and seems less concerned about the commingling of government and religion. Vouchers and school choice has now become the central issue raising controversy about aid to religious schools—particularly with regard to voucher programs that enable parents to send their children to parochial schools with state funds. Although religious organizations have reservations about accepting government aid, most of their political activity has sought to secure it, rather than to oppose it.

Legislatures design the programs that provide public aid to religious schools, but these programs often generate legal challenges. Thus, the Supreme Court has set the boundaries of permissible public aid to religious schools. Cases dealing with aid to religious schools date from 1930. Jurisprudence tended toward a separationist approach through the mid-1980s, with the Court striking down programs providing various forms of direct aid. In at least one instance, the Court did permit public aid to parochial schools where it found the goal was to protect the safety and welfare of children rather than to advance religion (EVERSON V. BOARD OF EDUCATION). With its 1971 ruling in LEMON V. KURTZMAN, the Court developed a test to determine constitutionality of public aid to religious schools. Aid had to have a secular purpose, could neither advance nor impede religion, and could not result in excessive entanglement with religion. Using this test, the Court struck down several state and local programs. But since 1992, the Court has criticized or ignored the *Lemon* test and reversed several of its earlier rulings.

Public aid to religious schools comes in both direct and indirect forms. Direct aid consists of funds, supplies, or personnel provided at state expense to religious schools. Today, children attending religious schools may receive publicly funded transportation to school, academic testing, and student diagnostic services. Public school districts may loan religious schools computers, textbooks, and other materials paid for with federal funds. Disabled students may receive state-funded interpreters and aides. Parochial schools may use the services of federally funded remedial teachers. Religious organizations currently operate charter schools in some states, receiving public funds based on pupil enrollment. Indirect forms of aid to religious schools consist of subsidies to parents who select private schools for their children. When parents choose a religious school, the school benefits from the subsidy. For example, the Supreme Court has upheld tuition tax credit programs, as long as they apply to all private schools. In the few cities where school voucher programs exist, religious schools receive government money for tuition when parents select their school. Opponents claim these programs violate the First Amendment. Supporters argue that vouchers are neutral relative to religion because parents have freedom of choice when selecting a school. They argue that no public money flows directly to parochial schools, and that the bulk of state spending on education remains for public, secular schools. In February 2002, the Supreme Court heard oral arguments in ZELMAN V. SIMMONS-HARRIS, a case involving a voucher program in Cleveland, Ohio, where nearly every participating student uses vouchers to attend parochial schools.

Generally, religious groups have sought public aid for their schools, and usually place such efforts in the context of general support for increasing equity in education. This is especially true for the ROMAN CATHOLIC CHURCH. The UNITED STATES CATHOLIC CONFERENCE supports school choice programs and the inclusion of religious schools in them. In some cases, Catholic advocates and clergy see aid as critical to their survival; for example, Chicago's Catholic schools are declining in number as costs rise, especially in the inner city. Others argue for equal treatment of public and parochial

school systems; that is, families choosing religious-based education should not suffer for the choice. Advocates portray their schools as providing a public service by producing educated citizens. Historically, Protestants opposed government aid to Catholic schools, but recently they too support forms of aid such as tax credits or scholarships for students in their schools. Some religious groups oppose government aid because they fear losing control over their schools. But others engage in the political process to limit conditions that may come with aid. They thus resist regulations on religious schools' curriculum, hiring, and student selection, and may oppose "opt-out" provisions that enable students to choose not to attend religious services and instruction.

Further reading: McCarthy, Martha. "Religion and Education: Whither the Establishment Clause?" *Indiana Law Journal* 75 (2000): 123–166; Morken, Hubert, and Jo Renee Formicola. *The Politics of School Choice.* Lanham, Md.: Rowman and Littlefield, 1999.

—Mara S. Sidney

Allegheny, County of v. ACLU Greater Pittsburgh Chapter 492 U.S. 573 (1989)

This case concerns the constitutionality of two recurring holiday displays located on public property in downtown Pittsburgh. The first is a crèche placed on the grand staircase of the Allegheny County Courthouse. The second is a Chanukah menorah placed just outside the City-County Building beside a Christmas tree and a sign saluting liberty. The Court of Appeals for the Third Circuit ruled that each display violates the ESTABLISHMENT CLAUSE of the First Amendment because each has the effect of endorsing religion. The Supreme Court agreed that the crèche display is unconstitutional but reversed the Court of Appeals' judgment regarding the menorah display. Justice Harry Blackmun announced the judgment of the Court and delivered its opinion. Justices John Paul Stevens and Sandra Day O'Connor joined in part.

Since 1981, the county had permitted the Holy Name Society, a Roman Catholic Church group, to display a crèche in the county courthouse during the Christmas holiday season. A banner by the display read "Gloria in Excelsis Deo." On November 17, 1986, city employees erected and decorated a 45-foot Christmas tree near the entrance to the City-County Building. A sign displayed the mayor's name and the phrase "A Salute to Liberty: during this holiday season, the city of Pittsburgh salutes liberty. Let these festive lights remind us that we are the keepers of the flame of liberty and our legacy of freedom." On December 22 of the same holiday season, the city placed an 18-foot Chanukah menorah beside the Christmas tree. Although a Jewish group owned it, the menorah was stored, erected, and removed by the city.

The U.S. Supreme Court examined the constitutionality of these two separate holiday displays on public property. The Court affirmed in part and reversed in part, ruling that while the crèche was unconstitutional, the menorah and Christmas tree display were not. In his opinion, Blackmun reasoned that the Supreme Court found that the display of a Christmas tree and menorah did not violate the Establishment Clause since they were merely symbolic recognitions of a holiday season that has attained secular status in American society and, as such, is not explicitly religious by nature. The Court relied strongly on the fact that a reasonable observer would not view the Christmas tree or the menorah as either endorsements or disapprovals of individual religious views. The Court said that displays of Christmas trees and menorahs are temporary in nature and represent symbolic recognition of the winter holiday season. As such, they do not violate the Establishment Clause of the First Amendment. However, the crèche display was not used in conjunction with seasonal decorations. Not only did it stand alone, but it also held a prominent position on the courthouse grounds, signifying government endorsement and violating the Establishment Clause.

Justice Anthony Kennedy concurred in part and dissented in part. He reasoned that the crèche should be permissible because it did not have the effect of advancing or inhibiting religion. Furthermore, the statute allowing the crèche does not violate the Establishment Clause because the clause does not mandate that there be no contact between government and religion. As a result, he thought that both displays were permissible.

Justice WILLIAM BRENNAN concurred in part and dissented in part. In his dissenting opinion he argued that the display of an object that "retains a specifically Christian religious meaning" is contrary to the SEPARATION OF CHURCH AND STATE. As a result, he thought that both displays violated the Establishment Clause.

—Stephen Sussman

America-Israel Public Affairs Committee (AIPAC)

The American Israel Public Affairs Committee (AIPAC) is considered by virtually all scholars, commentators, and analysts as the preeminent Jewish lobbying organization. AIPAC, originally called the American ZIONIST Committee for Public Affairs (AZCPA), was established in 1954 as an official, permanent American Jewish pro-ISRAEL lobby, chartered with the task of "coordinating and directing public actions on behalf of the American Zionist movement . . . with a view to maintaining and improving friendship and good will between the United States and Israel." In the latter half of the 20th century, AIPAC has worked to exert its influence on virtually every American political decision affecting Israel.

AIPAC serves several functions via several different means. In one sense, AIPAC is very much a "traditional" lobbying organization. Through both its political and its financial clout in Washington, it deals with the congressional and executive branches of the federal government to promote financial and military aid to Israel. AIPAC's action on Capitol Hill is often carefully coordinated with the Israeli government to maximize the effectiveness of its lobbying efforts. AIPAC's political efforts also involve grassroots political mobilization, exercised through direct mailings, the Internet, and "action alerts." Finally, AIPAC serves as a source of information, through the regular publication of the *Near East Reporter,* as well as other scholarly books, pamphlets, and studies regarding Israel, the Middle East, and U.S. foreign policy.

It is difficult to clearly articulate the success of AIPAC's lobbying efforts. Israel has generally enjoyed a uniquely favored place in America's foreign policy. But a number of other factors readily figure into this calculus: Israel's military status as a "strategic asset" in the region, often leading it to be characterized as the sole "democratic foothold" in the Middle East, overall American sympathy for the plight of world Jewry in the aftermath of the HOLOCAUST, and the messianic significance of the state of Israel for many Evangelical Christians. Nonetheless, AIPAC has had a hand in some of the most important U.S. foreign policy decisions affecting Israel. This success has inspired animosity toward the group among some politicians and observers, leading to former congressman Paul Findley's publication of *They Dare Speak Out,* a scathing indictment of AIPAC's political influence.

Nor has AIPAC won all of its political battles. In the wake of the cold war, it became unclear how active a role AIPAC and the rest of the Israel lobby would have in shaping U.S. foreign policy. Perhaps the first major test of this new dynamic revolved around the PERSIAN GULF WAR, Israeli settlements, and $10 billion in U.S. loan guarantees. President George H.W. Bush, in an effort to promote the linkage of humanitarian aid to Israel with a moratorium on building Jewish settlements in the Occupied Territories, sought to postpone congressional debate on the loan guarantees for 120 days—after the 1991 Madrid Peace Congress. In response, AIPAC mounted a massive lobbying campaign to convince Congress to consider the guarantees immediately. Not only did AIPAC fail in its efforts, but President Bush successfully linked the humanitarian assistance to the cessation of building in the Occupied Territories.

Even in the wake of the cold war, an era in which Israel is often viewed more as a "strategic liability" to the United States than an asset, AIPAC has survived as an effective lobbying group. In May 2001, *Forbe's* magazine ranked AIPAC the fourth most powerful political lobby in the United States. Moreover, it was the number-one foreign policy lobby and the only Jewish group to make the list of the "Power 25."

See also AMERICAN JEWISH COMMITTEE; AMERICAN JEWISH CONGRESS; ANTI-DEFAMATION LEAGUE; B'NAI B'RITH INTERNATIONAL.

Further reading: Ben Zvi, Abraham. *The United States and Israel: The Limits of the Special Relationship.* New York: Columbia University Press, 1993; Findley, Paul. *They Dare to Speak Out: People and Institutions Confront Israel's Lobby.* Westport, Conn.: Lawrence Hill, 1985; Goldberg, David Howard. *Foreign Policy and Ethnic Interest Groups: American* *and Canadian Jews Lobby for Israel.* New York: Greenwood, 1990; Lipson, Charles. "American Support for Israel: History, Sources, Limits." *U.S.-Israeli Relations at the Crossroads,* ed. Gabriel Sheffer. London: Frank Cass, 1997; Mansour Camille. *Beyond Alliance: Israel in U.S. Foreign Policy.* Trans. James Cohen. New York: Columbia University Press, 1994.

—Matthew L. Eanet

American Baptist Churches in the U.S.A.
(ABC-USA)

Claiming 1.5 million members in more than 5,800 congregations, ABC-USA is a progressive mainline Protestant denomination known for its racial diversity and Ecumenical cooperation (see ECUMENISM). Formerly called the American Baptist Convention (1950–72) and the Northern Baptist Convention (1907–50), the denomination traces its history back to 1907, when a group of Baptists met in Washington, D.C., to form the Northern Baptist Convention and elected as its first president the governor of New York and future Chief Justice of the Supreme Court, Charles Evans Hughes. Consistent with the historic identity of the larger Baptist tradition, the ABC-USA has been an advocate of religious liberty and SEPARATION OF CHURCH AND STATE. Although the denomination is politically and theologically diverse, its adopted policies and resolutions have reflected a more liberal political orientation.

Over the years the denomination has called for protecting human rights and advancing SOCIAL JUSTICE in both the international and domestic arenas. A charter member of the Federal Council of Churches of Christ (later NATIONAL COUNCIL OF CHURCHES), the ABC-USA has historically been a leader in ecumenical cooperation. While Baptist ecclesiology is rooted in the autonomy of the local church, the national denomination has regularly adopted policy statements and resolutions reflecting the "peace and justice" emphases of other mainline Protestant denominations and the National Council of Churches. Past statements have called for the elimination of the death penalty, support for affirmative action, reduction of nuclear arms, liberalization of immigration laws and support for the SANCTUARY MOVEMENT, freedom of choice regarding ABORTION, support of the EQUAL RIGHTS AMENDMENT, advancing human rights in Haiti, El Salvador, and Nicaragua, opposition to Soviet intervention in Afghanistan, struggle against APARTHEID IN SOUTH AFRICA, advocacy of a national health insurance program, and tax reform that would be more equitable and just for the poor. At the 2001 biennial meeting of the denomination, a "statement of concern" calling for implementation of "restorative justice" as an alternative to traditional criminal justice was adopted. An additional proposal listing concerns regarding President GEORGE W. BUSH's proposal to provide federal funds for faith-based social service programs won a majority of votes, but was not formally passed because of the lack of a quorum.

American Baptists frequently assert their commitment to religious freedom and separation of church and state as a key distinguishing mark of the Baptist heritage. Consequently, denominational policy statements have called for opposition to organized PRAYER IN PUBLIC SCHOOLS, the appointment of an ambassador to the Vatican, and federal AID TO RELIGIOUS SCHOOLS. At the same time, the ABC-USA has defended CONSCIENTIOUS OBJECTION to military service, religious freedom for Native Americans and other religious minorities and fought religious discrimination in the workplace. Through its office of Governmental Relations and in cooperation with the BAPTIST JOINT COMMITTEE on Public Affairs, the ABC-USA has filed briefs in a variety of First Amendment cases in the federal courts. In FREE EXERCISE disputes, the denomination filed friend-of-the-court briefs that defended both the fundamentalist Bob Jones University and the Unification Church leader Sun Myun Moon against government interference in their internal affairs. Critical of the U.S. Supreme Court's decision in *EMPLOYMENT DIVISION OF OREGON V. SMITH* (1990), the ABC-USA has argued for the reinstatement of the compelling state interest test. ABC-USA briefs have also asserted a broad reading of the ESTABLISHMENT CLAUSE calling for a high wall of separation between church and state. These briefs regularly challenge VOUCHERS and other forms of government aid to religious schools. In the 1992 *LEE V. WEISMAN* graduation prayer case, an amicus curiae brief was filed by the ABC-USA that not only challenged the constitutionality of clergy-led prayers at public school graduation exercises, but also criticized calls for the Court to abandon the traditional "neutrality" test in favor of a less stringent "coercion" test.

In addition to Charles Evans Hughes, several other prominent politicians have been active members of ABC-USA churches, including Oregon U.S. senator Mark Hatfield and fellow Republican senator Harold Stassen of Minnesota. Historically, a larger percentage of American Baptists (as with other mainline Protestants) have identified with the Republican Party than with the Democratic Party, although current research shows that this affiliation is in decline.

See also AFRICAN AMERICANS AND FAITH-BASED INITIATIVES; MAINLINE PROTESTANTS AND THE REPUBLICAN PARTY; WHITE HOUSE OFFICE OF FAITH-BASED AND COMMUNITY INITIATIVES.

Further reading: American Baptist Quarterly. "American Baptist Policy Statements and Resolutions." *American Baptist Quarterly* 50 (1986): 92–324; Byrd, Kenny. "American Baptists Elect 33-year-old President." *Associated Baptist Press News,* July 11, 2001; Fowler, Robert Booth, Alan D. Hertzke, and Laura R. Olson. *Religion and Politics in America.* Boulder, Colo.: Westview Press, 1999; Torbet, Robert G. *A History of the Baptists.* Valley Forge, Pa.: Judson Press, 1973.

—J. David Holcomb

American Center for Law and Justice (ACLJ)

In 1990, PAT ROBERTSON founded the American Center for Law and Justice (ACLJ) as a conservative evangelical counterpart to the AMERICAN CIVIL LIBERTIES UNION. Jay Alan Sekulow, a constitutional lawyer, serves as chief counsel of the organization. The ACLJ, which focuses primarily on high-profile litigation over church-state relations and "family values," is currently the largest evangelical public-interest law firm, both in terms of budget and staff.

Most ACLJ cases address religious speech in public schools, equal access of religious groups to public resources, and ABORTION protest. With Sekulow as the lead attorney, the group litigated a string of controversial cases addressing the First Amendment rights of abortion protesters in the 1990s (*Bray v. Alexandria Health Clinic* 1993; *NOW v. Scheidler* 1994; *Schenck v. ProChoice Network* 1997; *Hill v. Colorado* 2000). Sekulow and the ACLJ also took part in important First Amendment cases such as *LAMB'S CHAPEL V. CENTER MORICHES UNION FREE SCHOOL DISTRICT* (1993), which granted a church access to public school property, and *SANTA FE INDEPENDENT SCHOOL DISTRICT V. DOE* (2000), which banned certain prayers at high school sporting events. In fact, since 1990, Sekulow and his team have participated as lead counsel or amicus curiae in nearly every church-state and abortion-related case to reach the Supreme Court, as well as in hundreds of other disputes litigated in lower courts or settled out of court.

The ACLJ has also taken a keen interest in implementation of court rulings. In this regard, its participation in *LEE V. WEISMAN* (1992) was perhaps most controversial. In response to the Supreme Court's ruling that invited clergy may not pray at public school commencements, Sekulow directed the ACLJ to send thousands of letters to school districts around the country suggesting that *student*-initiated prayers would pass constitutional muster. Critics dismissed his interpretation as an attempt to confuse implementation of the Court's decision, but the campaign is widely credited with motivating changes in some state laws to accommodate student-initiated graduation prayers. The ACLJ's action also brought public exposure that Sekulow and his associates have managed to maintain throughout the 1990s.

As evident in the *Lee v. Weisman* example, Sekulow has a well-deserved reputation as an aggressive and confrontational chief counsel. He has also been quite successful. Even before joining ACLJ, Sekulow had begun to make a name for himself as a litigator before the Supreme Court. A Jewish-born Christian, he successfully defended the free-speech rights of an evangelistic Jewish group in *Board of Airport Commissioners of Los Angeles v. Jews for Jesus* (1987). He also won a unanimous ruling in *WESTSIDE COMMUNITY BOARD OF EDUCATION V. MERGENS* (1990) that upheld the access of student religious groups to public school facilities. Pat Robertson hired Sekulow as ACLJ's chief counsel shortly after the *Mergens* victory.

The ACLJ operates on a yearly budget of roughly $10 million, which is well short of its chief rival, the ACLU. Yet the ACLJ's tight focus has allowed it to develop a strong track record on a relatively narrow range of issues. Furthermore, though today it is an independent organization, Robertson provided the start-up money and the ACLJ remains closely connected to his other groups. Indeed, Robertson, a Yale law school graduate, envisioned the ACLJ as the legal complement to his media (CHRISTIAN BROADCASTING NETWORK), political (CHRISTIAN COALITION), and educational organizations (Regent University, including Regent's College of Law). These groups not only provide a steady source of conservative leaders for the ACLJ—Robertson; Herbert Titus, former dean of the Regent law school; and RALPH REED, former executive director of the Christian Coalition, have all served on ACLJ's board of directors—but they also generate publicity, fundraising, and expertise. Sekulow has considerable visibility as a frequent guest on Robertson's popular CBN television program, *700 Club*, and Regent's law school houses the ACLJ's headquarters and provides student interns. The ACLJ has even received legal business from Robertson's other groups, including the Christian Coalition in its dispute with the IRS over its TAX-EXEMPT STATUS.

The ACLJ has had an uneasy relationship with other organizations sympathetic to its goals. Some Christian legal groups have expressed concern that the ACLJ has been blinded by the desire for publicity, causing it to sue too much or appeal cases too quickly. Nevertheless, the ACLJ has emerged as a leader among rights-advocacy groups that identify with conservative evangelicalism.

See also AMERICAN FAMILY ASSOCIATION; CHRISTIAN LEGAL SOCIETY; CONSERVATIVE CHRISTIAN LITIGATORS; HERITAGE FOUNDATION; RUTHERFORD INSTITUTE.

Further reading: Den Dulk, Kevin R. "Prophets in Caesar's Court." Ph.D. diss., University of Wisconsin-Madison, 2001; Ivers, Gregg. "Please God, Save This Honorable Court: The Emergence of the Conservative Religious Bar." In *The Interest Group Connection: Electioneering, Lobbying, and Policymaking in Washington.* Edited by Paul Herrnson, Ronald G. Shaiko, and Clyde Wilcox. Chatham, N.J.: Chatham House, 1998.
—Kevin R. den Dulk

American Civil Liberties Union (ACLU)

The ACLU was founded on January 19, 1920, largely owing to the efforts of Roger Baldwin and Crystal Eastman, two social workers committed to a principled defense of the BILL OF RIGHTS. The ACLU evolved from two earlier national organizations: the American Union Against Militarism (AUAM), formed in 1914, and the National Civil Liberties Bureau (NCLB), created in 1917. Headquartered in New York, with state chapters or affiliates throughout the country, the ACLU has been at the forefront of protecting civil liberties in the United States.

Founded at a time when the promises of the Bill of Rights were largely devoid of any real legal content, the ACLU has played an essential (and often controversial) role in the establishment and development of a substantive body of law in the United States regarding civil liberties, including SEPARATION

OF CHURCH AND STATE and the free exercise of religion. With respect to issues surrounding the meaning of the ESTABLISHMENT CLAUSE and the FREE EXERCISE CLAUSE of the First Amendment, the ACLU's historic and continued opposition to state-imposed religious dogma has been the keystone of the organization's lobbying and litigation strategies.

Initially the ACLU dedicated itself to defending CONSCIENTIOUS OBJECTION during World War I and to advancing the doctrine of PACIFISM. With its involvement in the 1925 SCOPES MONKEY TRIAL, however, the ACLU began to confront the de facto establishment of Protestantism in the United States, such that over the course of several decades in the 20th century, the greatest impact of the ACLU has been its role in aiding the courts, especially the U.S. Supreme Court, in constitutionalizing numerous public controversies concerning the role of religion in American public life. The net effect has been the disestablishment of Protestantism as the nation's unofficial religion. In the 1930s and 1940s, for instance, the ACLU sponsored, litigated and filed AMICUS CURIAE BRIEFS in numerous cases involving JEHOVAH'S WITNESSES. These cases, such as *CANTWELL V. CONNECTICUT* in 1940 and *WEST VIRGINIA BOARD OF EDUCATION V. BARNETTE* in 1943, involved the religion clauses from the First Amendment and signaled a crucial shift in the Court's jurisprudence concerning a constitutional safe haven for religious dissenters.

The ACLU sponsored the watershed case of *EVERSON V. BOARD OF EDUCATION of Ewing Township, New Jersey* in 1947, in which the Supreme Court constitutionalized THOMAS JEFFERSON's "wall of separation" metaphor concerning the proper relationship between church and state in the United States. The *Everson* ruling, still controversial in many quarters today, committed the High Court to a separationist stance with respect to the Establishment Clause, although the immediate consequence of the decision was to sanction permissible financial aid to parochial education.

Throughout almost the rest of the 20th century, the vast amount of the litigation of the ACLU before the Supreme Court dealt with the meaning of the Establishment Clause, primarily with respect to state-sponsored or state-endorsed religious activities in public schools. In 1962, the ACLU was directly involved in the school prayer case of *ENGEL V. VITALE*, and in 1963 it focused on overturning state-mandated Bible readings in public schools, a position adopted by the Court in *ABINGTON TOWNSHIP V. SCHEMPP*. These victories on the part of the ACLU produced a national backlash against it and the Court, as 75 members of Congress "introduced 147 separate bills to allow prayer in school by statute or constitutional amendment." In turn, the ACLU organized and conducted aggressive and ultimately successful public education and political lobbying campaigns to defeat such proposals.

In the latter half of the 20th century, the ACLU worked not only to maintain the "wall of separation" regarding the Establishment Clause, as in cases involving school aid, nativity scenes, and religious practices in public schools; the organization also labored to give teeth to the Free Exercise Clause, as in cases concerning military dress regulations and non-mainstream religious actions, such as peyote use and animal sacrifice. Over the course of the 20th century and continuing into the 21st, a vital relationship between the ACLU and the judiciary emerged, in which the organization litigated various issues and as the Supreme Court accepted and decided numerous cases (often in the ACLU's favor). The ACLU in turn was encouraged by its successes to be more energetic. As a result, primarily through its state affiliates, the ACLU brought new and often successful challenges to traditional practices such as graduation prayers in public schools in rural areas throughout the country.

The principal characteristic of the ACLU in its 80-plus years of existence is its nonpartisan, public defense of civil liberties, including and perhaps especially religious liberty as guaranteed by the Establishment and Free Exercise Clauses of the First Amendment. The ACLU regards the First Amendment as the fountainhead of democracy, and its commitment to civil liberties has fueled its efforts in rewriting U.S. constitutional law and social policy.

Further reading: Walker, Samuel. *In Defense of American Liberties: A History of American Civil Liberties Union.* 2nd ed. Carbondale: Southern Illinois University Press, 1999.

—Stephen K. Shaw

American Council of Christian Churches

The American Council of Christian Churches (ACCC) was founded on September 17, 1941, in New York City at a meeting of the Bible Protestant Church and the Bible Presbyterian Church. The organizing impetus behind the ACCC was the protection of Protestant orthodoxy against the encroaching theological modernism represented by the Federal Council of Churches (FCC)—now known as the NATIONAL COUNCIL OF CHURCHES (NCC). The Rev. Carl McIntire, a staunch separatist and militant defender of orthodoxy, was the first president of the ACCC (1941–70). The ACCC is currently a member-based, multidenominational organization composed of churches and individuals based in the fundamentalist Christian tradition.

During his tenure as president, McIntire argued that the FCC, in advocating ECUMENISM, had compromised the truth of the gospel in its attempt to build a "one world church." McIntire was unable to convince other evangelicals to join the ACCC, which led to a division between the ACCC and the more moderate NATIONAL ASSOCIATION OF EVANGELICALS (NAE). The ACCC, however, did achieve two early political victories: it was granted free radio time from the FAA and was allocated a quota of chaplains in the U.S. armed forces.

The ACCC claims over 1 million members, 49 state branches, and a budget of $125,000. Denominations affiliated with the ACCC include the General Association of Regular Baptist Churches, Evangelical Methodist Churches, the Fellowship of Fundamental Bible Churches, FREE PRESBYTERIAN

Churches of North America, and hundreds of independent churches. In 1987, the ACCC formed the World Council of Biblical Churches as its international counterpart. The ACCC maintains ten commissions, which include Chaplaincy, Education, Laymen, Literature, Missions, Radio, Audio/Visual, Relief, and Youth. Additionally, the ACCC publishes *Fundamental News Service*, a bimonthly newsletter, and maintains a research library available to fundamentalist pastors.

The purpose of the ACCC is to "*provide* information, encouragement, and assistance to Bible-believing churches, fellowships, and individuals; to *preserve* our Christian heritage through exposure of, opposition to, and separation from doctrinal impurity and compromise in current religious trends; to *protect* churches from political restrictions . . . that would hinder their ministries for Christ; and to *promote* [biblical obedience]."

Theologically, the ACCC holds to "biblical inerrancy, the deity of Jesus Christ, His virgin birth, His literal bodily resurrection and His Second Coming." Not surprisingly, the ACCC places great emphasis on maintaining doctrinal purity and is thus committed to exposing "LIBERALISM, New EVANGELICALISM, the Charismatic movement, and compromise in all areas of life and ministry." According to the ACCC constitution, members must remain separate from all liberal, modernist, and apostate influences. As such, to be a member of the ACCC, one cannot be associated with the WORLD COUNCIL OF CHURCHES, the NCC, the World Evangelical Fellowship (WEF), the NAE, the modern charismatic movement, or the ecumenical movement.

Beyond championing religious causes, the ACCC has been an issue-based organization that exists, among other things, "to expose and oppose . . . socialism, and near-communism threatening the very life of our nation." During the 1950s, McIntire and the ACCC, in collaboration with the Church League of America and Billy James Hargis of the Christian Crusade, led the anticommunist crusade among religious conservatives. Additionally, McIntire focused attacks on the NCC and WCC, believing they were "apostate, un-American, pro-Communist, and treasonous ecclesiastical organizations." McIntire and other fundamentalists held "McCarthy-style" exposés of prominent NCC and WCC leaders and assembled lists of suspected communists among clergy that were passed on to Senator Joseph McCarthy. With the demise of communism, the ACCC has shifted its political efforts and is now intent on combating and exposing liberals and "humanists" in government, society, and the news media.

Membership in the ACCC made no gains in the 1960s, and while its membership is significantly greater in 2002 than in the 1960s—there were only an estimated 265,000 members in 1965—the independent influence, both religiously and politically, of the ACCC (and other fundamentalist groups) has diminished greatly over the past four decades. While the ACCC was politically influential during the 1950s, its long-term influence fell short of expectations. In part, this was due to fundamentalists as a group being absorbed into mainstream evangelicalism during the 1960s, and divisions arising from a dispute over funds and tactics in 1968 within the ACCC. Still, given the continuing existence of the ACCC and its uncanny ability to shift its agenda to address new issues, the ACCC will no doubt be an active voice for fundamentalist concerns into the foreseeable future.

See also ANTICOMMUNISM.

Further reading: American Council of Christian Churches. website. URL: http://www.amcouncilcc.org/constitu.htm. Hunter, James Davison. *Evangelicalism: The Coming Generation.* Chicago: University of Chicago Press, 1987; ———. *American Evangelicalism: Conservative Religion and the Quandary of Modernity.* New Brunswick, N.J.: Rutgers University Press, 1983; Jorstad, Erling. *The Politics of Doomsday: Fundamentalists of the Far Right.* Nashville, Tenn.: Abingdon Press, 1970; Speer, James A. "The New Christian Right and Its Parent Company." In David Bromley and Anson Shupe, eds., *New Christian Politics.* Macon, Ga.: Mercer University Press, 1984.

—Franklyn C. Niles

American Family Association (AFA)

Based in Tupelo, Mississippi, the American Family Association is one of the premier conservative Christian organizations committed to representing the moral positions of grassroots supporters. Founded in 1978 by Methodist minister Rev. Donald Wildmon, the AFA boasts over 2 million members and more than 500 local chapters nationwide. Originally named the National Federation for Decency, the organization was run out of Wildmon's home, and he used it to launch campaigns against PORNOGRAPHY, offending student textbook adoptions, GAY RIGHTS, and the programming choices of major TV networks. He defines the mission of the AFA as protecting Christians from "an erosion of the civil and Constitutional rights of people of faith, particularly Christian groups." Further, he seek to force corporations to abandon practices to which the AFA objects on moral grounds.

After years of campaigning through mass boycotting against the policies of American Airlines, K-Mart (owners of Walden Books), and Disney, Wildmon changed the name of the organization in 1987 and started what has become a nationwide network of over 160 radio affiliates. These stations provide an array of programming including contemporary religious music, preaching, Bible and life lessons, and communications to members about AFA-sponsored boycotts. The AFA also maintains a network of "Faithful and True" support groups that function as "AA for the pornographically addicted."

Relying on its nationwide network, the AFA steers new members to local chapters when they contact the national office. These local chapters mount their own campaigns against local business and support the national office in its broader efforts. Examples of locally led boycotts include campaigns against CBS affiliates that aired ads for condoms during the Howard Stern Show, and against Pepsi, which started a nationwide advertising campaign involving pop artist

Madonna. National campaigns include lobbying Congress over funding for the National Endowment for the Arts. The AFA has won some impressive victories, including a halt to the Madonna ad campaign and an agreement with the 7-11 Corporation not to sell pornographic magazines. In 1998, the AFA scored its greatest victory, convincing the Texas State Board of Education to divest its $44 million worth of Disney stock.

During the 1980s, opponents of the AFA sought to limit its boycott activities by bringing suit against it in federal court. As a result, in 1988 Wildmon formed an in-house legal arm, called the AFA-Center for Law and Policy (AFA-CLP), after the AFA was threatened with legal action for a boycott directed at *Penthouse* magazine, the Playboy Corporation, and the American Booksellers Association. These organizations alleged that the federal Racketeering Influenced and Corrupt Organizations (RICO) Act prohibited the AFA from encouraging its members to boycott stores that sold pornography. The AFA-CLP gained an impressive victory in its first case, securing the dismissal of the lawsuit "without prejudice." In effect, the ruling insulates the AFA from any further RICO lawsuits.

From this high-profile beginning, the AFA-CLP has become the leading trial-oriented public-interest law firm representing conservative Christians in the United States. Its purpose is to serve as a "grassroots law firm" capable of defending rank-and-file Christians during the initial stages of litigation. According to former chief counsel, Bruce Green, the AFA-CLP's goal is to "defend the existing constitutional rights of believers when those rights are infringed, or where we perceive an erosion of those rights." Thus, the AFA-CLP emphasizes the provision of legal services to AFA members and other Christians who are involved in conflicts over religion and religious expression in their communities. As a grassroots law firm, the AFA-CLP maintains strong ties to street preachers, ABORTION protesters, and local churches serving blue-collar and lower-income neighborhoods.

The AFA-CLP has an organizational structure traditional for conservative Christian law firms. It functions under the auspices of a powerful, nonlegal parent organization that defines its mission and provides it with all necessary resources. But while AFA-CLP attorneys and staff do not expend energy raising funds, the mission of the parent organization restricts the possible range of goals the AFA-CLP can pursue. For example, unlike some conservative Christian litigating firms, it does not attempt to galvanize grassroots support or seek the attention of the media. Its parent organization exists for those purposes.

While it is a leading conservative Christian litigation firm, the AFA-CLP is also one of the best funded. Estimates suggest that the activities of the firm account for approximately 15 percent of the AFA's annual budget, or more than $1 million. Throughout its history, the firm has undergone extensive changes in structure and personnel while scoring victories in court. Currently it is composed of six attorneys, including its general counsel and a litigation specialist.

The AFA-CLP combines litigation strategies pioneered by liberal organizations with an agenda comprised of issues commonly associated with religious conservatives. In pursuing these goals, the AFA-CLP employs a multiple strategy. First, it sponsors cases that offer the courts an opportunity to clarify old rulings and occasionally to rule on new issues. It adapts case sponsorship to its particular goal of defending Christians at the trial level—the AFA-CLP rarely litigates at the appellate level and has never taken a case to the Supreme Court (although it has on occasion petitioned the Court for review). Furthermore, the AFA-CLP primarily litigates cases in areas where interpretations of law are settled and long-standing. Thus, it influences precedent by extending its implementation to trial-level conflicts involving Christians.

Second, it uses a punishing and aggressive approach to trial-level litigation. The firm has consistently moved to challenge social policies that do not square with conservative Christian beliefs. On its agenda are core issues that resonate with its membership, including defending abortion protesters, challenging public school book selections in state educational systems, opposing gay-rights legislation, defending zoning ordinances aimed at stopping pornography, and litigating conflicts over religious expression in public schools and places, such as crèche displays in town squares. The firm has filed one of only two constitutional challenges to the Freedom of Access to Clinic Entrances (FACE) Act (*Cook v. Reno*, 859 F. Supp. 1008). It won a major victory in a FREE EXERCISE case (*Brown v. Woodland Independent School District*, 27 F.3d 1373) and successfully defended abortion counselors accused of violating the FACE act from prosecution by the U.S. Department of Justice (*United State v. Vasquez*, 145 F.3d 74). The firm is also responsible for crafting several anti–partial-birth abortion initiatives that have appeared on state ballots.

See also AMERICAN CENTER FOR LAW AND JUSTICE; AMERICAN CIVIL LIBERTIES UNION; CHRISTIAN LEGAL SOCIETY; CONSERVATIVE CHRISTIAN LITIGATORS; HERITAGE FOUNDATION; RUTHERFORD INSTITUTE.

—Hans J. Hacker

American Friends Service Committee

In 1917 in Philadelphia, the Religious Society of Friends (QUAKERS) founded the American Friends Service Committee (AFSC) to give CONSCIENTIOUS OBJECTORS a way to aid civilian victims during World War I. AFSC was started by Quaker representatives from the Philadelphia Yearly Meeting, the Friends General Conference, and the Five Years Meeting. Rufus Jones was the first chair. From the start, the committee aimed to bring Quakers together, to reaffirm the peace witness, to provide conscientious objectors with an alternative to fighting, to give Friends in the United States a method of witnessing their faith in wartime, and to accomplish social reconstruction abroad. The work of AFSC is based on the Quaker belief in the worth of every person and faith in the power of love peacefully to overcome violence and injustice. Today the committee has programs in the United States, Africa, Asia, Latin America, and the Middle East focused on issues related to economic justice, peace building, demilitarization, SOCIAL JUSTICE, and youth. Throughout its development, Quaker support of the peace testimony has unified groups within AFSC.

After World War I, AFSC did relief work throughout Europe, especially in Germany, Poland, Austria, Serbia, and Russia. AFSC worked closely with British Quakers, the American Red Cross, the U.S. government, and European governments. After the war, AFSC began to develop programs in the United States, particularly around peace work. They were also involved in relief work in Appalachia in the 1920s, which continued into the 1930s at the request of Herbert Hoover. Young volunteers began Home Service, a precursor to Work Camps in the 1930s. Volunteers in Home Service and Work Camps served at social service organizations, summer camps, and special schools across the United States. AFSC worked with British Quakers, Mennonites, and Church of the Brethren representatives in Spain during the Spanish Civil War.

During World War II, AFSC assisted refugees abroad and worked with other peace churches in the United States to establish the Civilian Public Service Program, which worked with conscientious objectors. AFSC also worked with people of Japanese ancestry incarcerated in the United States during the war. When the war ended, AFSC became involved again with relief work in European countries. The American Friends Service Committee and the British Friends Service Council received the Nobel Peace Prize in 1947 for humanitarian service and work for reconciliation.

In the second half of the 20th century, AFSC was active in the United States and abroad. In the 1950s, the AFSC began new programs in the United States focused on factory conditions, mental hospitals and correctional facilities, and nuclear weapons. Programs developed in the 1960s focused on equal opportunities for minorities in schooling, employment, and housing. In addition to its international work in postwar Europe, AFSC was present internationally in Japan and China in the 1940s; Kenya, the Congo, and the Middle East in the 1950s; Vietnam, Latin America, and South Africa in the 1960s and 1970s; and Zimbabwe, Cambodia, Honduras, Nicaragua, and the Middle East in the 1980s.

In addition to its direct service work, AFSC was involved in supporting the League of Nations, the International Court, and the United Nations. Since 1948, the Society of Friends has had an office at the United Nations aimed at helping the U.N. decision-making process function more effectively and monitoring U.N. negotiations. This office works closely with a similar office in Geneva, Switzerland, supported by British Quaker Peace and Service. The committee also operates a national office in Washington, D.C., designed to bring AFSC insights and advocacy to bear on policy makers, opinion leaders, and diplomats. The office has existed in its current form since 1982.

At present, AFSC's work is divided among community relations, international programs, and peace-building programs. AFSC is headquartered in Philadelphia, and programs are run through regional offices in the United States Funds

that support the committee have come primarily from non-Quakers from the start, and Quakers currently make up a minority of AFSC employees.

See also MENNONITE TRADITION; VIETNAM WAR.

Further reading: American Friends Service Committee website. URL: http://www.afsc.org; Barbour, Hugh, and J. William Frost. *The Quakers.* New York: Greenwood Press, 1988.

—Wendy Cadge

American Humanist Association

The American Humanist Association (AHA), a national organization based in Washington, D.C., and founded in 1941 to promote SECULAR HUMANISM in the United States, represents both secular and religious naturalistic humanism interests. It is the oldest and largest humanist organization in the United States. Organized into local humanist chapters in numerous American cities, it also coordinates with other national and international societies whose liberal political and religious agenda are similar (see UNITARIAN-UNIVERSALIST; AMERICAN CIVIL LIBERTIES UNION). Its membership size is disputed but definitely fewer than 50,000; however, its members participate in similarly aligned political groups, making it a liberal parachurch organization. Political activism among AHA members and chapters has included the protection of the rights of those considered to be in danger of religious or political intolerance and presenting AMICUS CURIAE BRIEFS to the U.S. Supreme Court and lower courts on similar issues. AHA and its members advocate the extension of participatory democracy and the expansion of an open society, supporting human rights and SOCIAL JUSTICE. Among its many publications are its journal, *The Humanist Magazine,* its past presidents including scientist and author Isaac Asimov, and signers of the 1933 and 1973 Humanist Manifestos.

AHA's central doctrine is: "Free of supernaturalism, it recognizes human beings as a part of nature and holds that values—be they religious, ethical, social, or political—have their source in human experience and culture. Humanism thus derives the goals of life from human need and interest rather than from theological or ideological abstractions, and asserts that humanity must take responsibility for its own destiny." AHA attempts to provide a quasi-religious alternative to Christian, Jewish, and other organized religious rituals, beliefs, and communities. AHA provides chaplains, advocates, speakers, and advisers to help individuals and organizations that need nonsectarian assistance from a naturalistic philosophical viewpoint.

Humanism, though variously defined through the centuries, is in the North American context an early-20th-century philosophical reaction against religious particularism, most notably Fundamentalist Protestant Christianity. This modern humanism's basic principles include an affirmation that every individual should be allowed to actualize his or her highest aspirations and successfully achieve a happy and fulfilling life without any acknowledgment or need for a higher power or divine reality. Humanists generally assert that individuals should take responsibility for their own morals and their own lives, and for the lives of their communities and the world in which we live, instead of leaving these to God, the church, or implementation of biblical interpretation. Members of AHA emphasize reason and scientific inquiry, individual freedom and responsibility, human values and compassion, and the need for TOLERANCE and cooperation. Humanists reject supernatural, authoritarian, and antidemocratic beliefs and doctrines. AHA holds sacred a strict separationist interpretation of the constitutional principle of SEPARATION OF CHURCH AND STATE and has been active in local and national political initiatives to ensure that an alternative to the "religious Right" is provided.

Further reading: Schulz, William. "Making the Manifesto: A History of Early Religious Humanism." Ph.D. diss., Meadville Lombard Theological School, 1975. Available on-line. URL: http://www.americanhumanist.org.

—Robert Wilson-Black

American Indian Religious Freedom Act (AIRFA)
(1978)

The American Indian Religious Freedom Act of 1978 states, in part: "On and after August 11, 1978, it shall be the policy of the United States to protect and preserve for American Indians their inherent right of freedom to believe, express, and exercise the traditional religions of the American Indian, Eskimo, Aleut, and Native Hawaiians, including but not limited to access to sites, use and possession of sacred objects, and the freedom to worship through ceremonials and traditional rites" (42 U.S.C. 1996). At one time, the policy of the federal government was to assimilate Native Americans into the mainstream of American society, and the suppression of native religions played a central role in achieving this goal. Tribes were systematically assigned to specific mainstream religions to aid in this process, thereby supplanting the traditional native religions. By the 1930s, federal policy changed substantially and the practice of actively suppressing native religions ended.

Despite the government's shift in policy, it was not until 1978 that AIRFA was passed. And even with AIRFA to support them, the ability of Native Americans to exercise these rights has been uneven. The act provides for federal review of any and all policies that deprive or impede access to traditional NATIVE AMERICAN SACRED GROUNDS. However, this has not led directly to greater levels of protection for native religious practices. Agencies are only required to review their policies for potential conflicts, but the act does not require any substantive changes in policy if conflicts are found. The problem is even greater at the state level, where state governments are free to deny tribes access to religious areas, the right of state prisoners to engage in traditional ceremonies, and children the

opportunity to obtain excused absences from school to attend religious ceremonies.

In response, a number of tribes took to the courts to press their rights under AIRFA. In 1988, the Supreme Court ruled that the United States Forest Service had the right to construct a road on Forest Service land, even though it would significantly disturb a Native American cemetery and, hence, the ability of the tribe to practice its religion in LYNG V. NORTHWEST INDIAN CEMETERY PROTECTIVE ASSOCIATION (1988). There were also challenges to laws limiting the ability of Native Americans to engage in traditional religious practices. In EMPLOYMENT DIVISION, DEPARTMENT OF HUMAN RESOURCES V. SMITH (1990), the Supreme Court was asked to decide whether or not the state of Oregon could deny unemployment benefits to members of the Native American church for using peyote, a hallucinogen outlawed in the state. Two members of the church who were denied benefits challenged the state action, relying on previous Supreme Court cases that, they argued, protected their right to engage in activity mandated by their religion. Justice Antonin Scalia, writing for the majority, argued that none of the Court's previous decisions would support the contention that personal religious beliefs provide an excuse for noncompliance with an otherwise valid law prohibiting certain forms of behavior that a state is free to regulate. It has been argued that the decision in *Smith* is one of the most regressive treatments of religious freedom that the Court has ever offered, curtailing the rights of those who practice minority religions, while maintaining protections for more widely practiced faiths.

In response to the Court's decision in *Smith,* and the resulting public outcry, Congress passed the RELIGIOUS FREEDOM RESTORATION ACT (RFRA) in 1993. Binding on both state and federal governments, RFRA protected the FREE EXERCISE of religion even more explicitly than did AIRFA. The act prevented the government from restricting religious practices, even if the restriction is made applicable to the general public, unless the government could show that the restriction is in furtherance of a compelling government interest and is the least restrictive means in furthering that interest.

Despite the efforts of Congress to expand the rights of Native Americans, the courts have not been as accommodating, ruling that Congress has overstepped its constitutionally defined powers. In response to these court decisions, a number of groups have attempted to revive RFRA in another form, but it appears that these groups are having more success at the state than the federal level. The Religious Liberty Protection Act was proposed in Congress during the 2000 term but stalled in the Senate. However, by the year 2000, more than 10 states had passed religious freedom laws designed to offer similar protections as those outlined in RFRA and earlier in AIRFA.

Further reading: Marquard, Robert. "High Court's Colorful Man in Black." *Christian Science Monitor,* March 3, 1998; O'Brien, Sharon. "Federal Indian Policies and the International

Protection of Human Rights." In *American Indian Policy in the Twentieth Century*. Edited by Vine Deloria Jr. Norman: University of Oklahoma Press, 1992; Petoskey, John. "Indians and the First Amendment." In *American Indian Policy in the Twentieth Century*. Edited by Vine Deloria Jr. Norman: University of Oklahoma Press, 1992.

—Scott Comparato

American Jewish Committee (AJC)

Organized in 1906 after Russian authorities instituted a series of pogroms (government-sponsored acts of anti-Semitism), the American Jewish Committee (AJC) sought "to prevent the infraction of the civil and religious rights of the Jews, in any part of the world." A small group of 20 men including Jacob Schiff, Louis Marshall, Oscar Strauss, and Cyrus Adler decided all policy while its expanded "corporate members" numbered only 327 by 1941. AJC leaders descended from German Jews forced out of Europe by the political upheaval of the 1840s. As members of REFORM JUDAISM, German-American Jews resisted the use of Hebrew in worship, replaced the bar mitzvah with confirmation, and did not support ZIONISM when it first emerged. Among national Jewish organizations, the AJC became the most important in the first half of the 20th century.

Owing in part to the German-American Jewish community's tremendous successes in business and social life, the AJC embraced an accommodationist approach to American life, favoring quiet negotiations and dialogue over confrontational tactics. In one famous experiment, the Galveston Project, the well-known German-American Jewish banker Jacob Schiff offered to pay the transatlantic boat fare for any eastern European Jew willing to settle in Texas. By dispersing Jews in the West, Schiff hoped to hasten Jewish integration into the American mainstream. For Schiff and many others in the AJC, America represented the new Zion.

AJC leaders enjoyed a friendly relationship with government leaders who appreciated their approach to American life. In one of its earliest political efforts, in 1913 the AJC successfully abrogated an 1832 U.S.-Russian trade treaty on the grounds that the anti-Jewish policies of the czarist regime violated basic human rights standards. The committee also took action, though ultimately failed, to prevent Congress from limiting Jewish immigration to the United States. After World War I, the AJC and its sister organization, the Joint Distribution Committee, provided relief needs for European Jewish refugees.

In the 1920s, the AJC established itself as a leading organization for interfaith dialogue and understanding. When Henry Ford published the anti-Semitic *Protocols of the Elders of Zion* in his Dearborn, Michigan, newspaper, AJC head Louis Marshall secured a public apology from the automaker. As Adolf Hitler rose to power in Europe, the AJC began domestic programs designed to celebrate cultural diversity and American democratic pluralism. Always fearful of dual loyalty conflicts, the AJC refused to participate in many American Zionist activities during the 1930s and offered only limited political and strategic support for the Jewish state during the war years. Even after Israel's creation in 1948, the AJC maintained strict allegiance to the United States and rebuffed any Jewish communal embrace of nationalist ideals.

In the postwar period, the AJC reinvented itself as a more democratic organization, opening its membership to individuals for the first time. Through its preference for face-to-face dialogue and legal appeal, the AJC worked with civil rights organizations, filed AMICUS CURIAE BRIEFS on many church-state separation issues, opened lines of communication with a variety of non-Jewish religious groups, and sponsored many social-scientific studies of human relations. Always committed to education as the keystone of social progress, the AJC sponsored dozens of conferences and helped educational institutions develop programming geared toward better intergroup understanding. Its allied publication, *Commentary*, emerged in the 1960s under the editorial stewardship of Norman Podhoretz as a leading voice of Jewish neo-CONSERVATISM in the United States.

In the 1970s, the AJC took a leading role in defining the emerging white ethnic movement. Seeking to capitalize on the nation's newfound respect for diversity, the AJC's Irving Levine spearheaded a Jewish-focused reinterpretation of multicultural America. By the 1990s, the AJC, suffering from budget constraints, eliminated many programs and refocused its organizational thrust on fighting anti-Semitism, promoting interfaith dialogue, and supporting the state of ISRAEL.

See also AMERICAN JEWISH CONGRESS.

Further reading: Adler, Cyrus. *I Have Considered the Days.* Philadelphia: Jewish Publication Society, 1945; Cohen, Naomi. *Not Free to Desist: The American Jewish Committee, 1906–1966.* Philadelphia: Jewish Publication Society, 1972; Svonkin, Stuart. *Jews Against Prejudice: American Jews and the Fight for Civil Liberties.* New York: Columbia University Press, 1997.

—Marc Dollinger

American Jewish Congress (AJC)

The American Jewish Congress, organized in 1918 "to create in the United States an all-inclusive representative Jewish body for the defense of Jewish rights," provided a powerful alternative to the German-American dominated AMERICAN JEWISH COMMITTEE (AJC). Under the leadership of Rabbi Stephen S. Wise and Supreme Court Justice Louis D. Brandeis, the American Jewish Congress enjoyed early support from newly arrived eastern European Jews dissatisfied with the assimilationist and elitist stance of the AJC. Representing 30 different national Jewish organizations, the first American Jewish Congress met in Philadelphia on December 15, 1918. Throughout its history, the American Jewish Congress called for a more vocal defense of European Jews, supported Jewish claims to Palestine, and sought to define American democracy in a way that accented their belief in religious pluralism, intergroup understanding, and TOLERANCE. It adopted a democratic approach to Jewish communal life and claimed to be the Jewish community's most representative body. Although the American Jewish Committee initially supported the notion of a national American Jewish Congress, it eventually left the body and over the years inspired fierce debate on a number of political issues.

In its first political act, the American Jewish Congress sought representation at the Versailles peace conference following World War I. Congress leaders drafted statements aimed at protecting Jews and other minorities from persecution and celebrated when they learned that the Paris peacemakers had adopted some of their proposals. The American Jewish Congress raised its political profile during the 1930s when it backed a controversial boycott of German-made goods. Created in 1933 by the Jewish Labor Committee, the anti-German boycott followed Adolf Hitler's call for an anti-Jewish boycott in Germany. Eventually, most of the organized Jewish community joined in the action, propelling the American Jewish Congress and its leader, Stephen Wise, into the forefront of American Jewish politics. During the 1930s, the American Jewish Congress also led the movement to revitalize American ZIONISM. Constantly at odds with the non-Zionist American Jewish Committee, the congress emerged by the late 1930s as the voice of most American Jews on the question of Jewish statehood. During World War II, the American Jewish Congress proved instrumental in forging an American Jewish Conference, established to offer a unified American-Jewish voice on issues of anti-Semitism, European Jewish refugees, and creation of a Jewish state.

In the postwar period, the American Jewish Congress reorganized itself as a powerful voice for social change in the secular world. The congress fought for passage of antiquota laws, Fair Employment Practices legislation, and antilynching laws. It established the Commission on Law and Social Action, engaged the services of leading attorneys, and launched legal battles on behalf of Americans of all faiths. In the CIVIL RIGHTS MOVEMENT, the American Jewish Congress established a close association with the NAACP. The American Jewish Congress head, Rabbi Joachim Prinz, joined MARTIN LUTHER KING JR. as the Jewish community's official representative to the 1963 MARCH ON WASHINGTON.

By 1964, much of the American Jewish Congress's civil rights work ended with passage of the Civil Rights Act. The rise of militant black nationalism, the Black Power movement, and the purge of whites from leading civil rights groups hastened a rapid retreat by the American Jewish Congress from the Civil Rights movement. While the congress initially supported affirmative action programs, it flinched when government officials adopted strict race-based quotas in their hiring practices. When many American Jews pulled their children from public schools in the wake of court-ordered busing, the American Jewish Congress sent experts into the field to find

new, more creative solutions to achieve racial integration. Despite the congress's ambivalence on some of the new group-based liberal programs, it remained the Jewish community's most progressive national political organization.

Further reading: Frommer, Morris. "The American Jewish Congress: A History 1914–1950." Ph.D. diss., Ohio State University, 1978; Svonkin, Stuart. *Jews Against Prejudice: American Jews and the Fight for Civil Liberties.* New York: Columbia University Press, 1997; Urofsky, Melvin. *A Voice That Spoke for Justice: The Life and Times of Stephen S. Wise.* Albany: State University of New York Press, 1982.

—Marc Dollinger

American Muslim Council

Founded in 1990 by Abdurahman Alamoudi, the American Muslim Council (AMC) is the largest membership American Muslim nonprofit organization. With headquarters in Washington, D.C., and more than two dozen chapters throughout the United States, its membership comprises Muslims from all ethnic backgrounds. An educational and lobbying organization, the AMC's primary goal has been to increase the political participation of the American Muslim population in mainstream political and policy arenas. In both domestic and foreign policy agendas, AMC "aims to promote ethical values that enhance the quality of life for all Americans" by reconciling Muslim values and American interests and ideals.

AMC encourages the U.S. government to take a stronger role in promoting peace and stability in the Middle East, with primary focus on the Palestinian-Israeli conflict. It supports an independent Palestinian state with East Jerusalem as its capital, the right of return for Palestinian refugees to ISRAEL and the future state of Palestine, and employment of U.N. Resolutions 242 and 338 as the basis for peace negotiations. AMC advises the United States to develop a new policy on Iraq, which would meet U.S. security concerns in eradicating weapons of mass destruction, without the devastating repercussions for the Iraqi people. It also advocates democratization and civil society development as a U.S. foreign policy objective throughout the Middle East. Among other AMC foreign policy concerns are U.S. assistance with debt relief and the AIDS epidemic in Africa, a heightened U.S. role in the Indian-Pakistani-Kashmiri conflict, developing an international standard of women's rights, and the ratification of the 1997 International Mine Ban Treaty.

Although primarily known for its work on foreign policy, AMC's domestic agenda covers a broad range of issues, including secret evidence, education, HEALTH CARE, tax policy, legislative and campaign finance reform, and immigration policy reform. AMC has been one of the primary organizations at the forefront of the secret evidence debate by endorsing the Secret Evidence Repeal Act of 1999, sponsored in the House of Representatives by Tom Campbell (R-Calif.) and David Bonior (D-Mich.); Senators Edward Kennedy (D-Mass.) and

Spencer Abraham (R-Mich.) introduced a concurrent resolution in the Senate. This legislation would revoke the ability of law-enforcement agencies to utilize secret evidence in the form of classified information currently protected by the 1996 Antiterrorism and Effective Death Penalty Act, which established a new court charged only with hearing cases in which the government seeks to deport aliens accused of engaging in terrorist activity. The 1996 Illegal Immigration Reform and Immigrant Responsibility Act expanded the secret evidence court so that secret evidence could be more easily used to deport even lawful permanent residents. It also included provisions allowing the government to use secret evidence to deny bond to all detained noncitizens and to deny various discretionary immigration benefits such as asylum to all noncitizens, including those not accused of being terrorists.

AMC encourages Congress to enact education legislation that promotes greater resource accessibility, increased school funding, equal opportunity, and higher standards of academic excellence for teachers and students. In support of the public education system, AMC discourages the reallocation of public school funds to a VOUCHER system and supports affirmative action initiatives to provide equal opportunities to the disadvantaged. AMC strongly advocates high-quality health care availability to all Americans through sustaining Medicare and Medicaid programs, the Patient's Bill of Rights, health maintenance organization accountability, and diversity of healthcare plans to accommodate patients of various religious and ethnic backgrounds. To ensure the economic welfare of families throughout the 1990s and the beginning of the 21st century, AMC argues that there is a need for tax relief. It favors tax cuts in general and specifically a repeal of the Marriage Penalty Tax, estate tax reform, Adoption Tax Credit, and it strongly supports the Earned Income Tax Credit.

At the grassroots level, AMC organizes regular voter registration drives to encourage American Muslim participation in local, state, and national elections. It conducts other activities such as polling American Muslims on a variety of issues, developing a VOTER GUIDE on candidates for elections, and hosting hospitality suites at Republican and Democratic Party conventions. Additionally, AMC was among the first Muslim organizations to publicly condemn the attacks of SEPTEMBER 11, 2001, while simultaneously serving as advocates for victims of HATE CRIMES following the attacks on the World Trade Center and the Pentagon.

See also ISLAM; NATION OF ISLAM.

—Allen McDuffee

Americans United for the Separation of Church and State

In 1947 a group of religious, political, and educational leaders formed what is today called Americans United for the Separation of Church and State. While the organization has Protestant roots, Americans United now claims more than 50,000 members of all faiths and representation in nearly 4,000

churches, synagogues, and other places of worship. Barry Lynn, an ordained minister in the United Church of Christ and former attorney for the AMERICAN CIVIL LIBERTIES UNION, is its current executive director. The group's chief focus has been political and legal advocacy for the principle of strict SEPARATION OF CHURCH AND STATE in educational settings, though it has applied the principle in many other arenas as well.

Americans United was created out of mainline Protestant fears that the ROMAN CATHOLIC CHURCH was beginning to mount a successful campaign for public funding of parochial schools. Its original name—Protestants and Other Americans United—suggests the primary place of Protestant churches in the formation of the group. In its early years, the group's zealous opposition to public aid for Catholic schools often crossed a line into vitriolic attacks on the Catholic Church itself. For example, Paul Blanshard, a longtime leader and spokesperson for Americans United, published *American Freedom and Catholic Power* in 1949, which charges that Catholic and American values were incompatible and that the American Catholic hierarchy was under the control of a foreign power. The group's uncompromising approach to the separation of church and state also contributed to its uneasy relationship with other religious and civil liberties organizations. Despite their shared commitment to church-state separation, the AMERICAN JEWISH COMMITTEE, AMERICAN JEWISH CONGRESS, and the BAPTIST JOINT COMMITTEE ON PUBLIC AFFAIRS were wary of building coalitions with Americans United.

Beginning in the 1960s, Americans United refashioned its role in the politics of church and state. The organization dropped the "Protestants and Other" from its name in 1964, signaling its desire to broaden its membership and cast off its public reputation as the leading Protestant critic of the Catholic Church. By the late 1980s, it had turned much of its attention toward the activities of conservative evangelical Christians. Americans United, which today describes one of its roles as a "watchdog of the religious Right," has been particularly critical of evangelical efforts to introduce PRAYER IN SCHOOL, educational VOUCHERS, public funds for religious nonprofit groups, and the teaching of creationism in public schools.

Americans United views its primary task as educational. Its major publication, *Church and State*, is a monthly magazine that, through news reporting and editorializing, advocates strict church-state separation. The group generates a steady stream of legislative alerts, press releases, and informational papers on a wide variety of concerns, including frequent reports on the "religious Right." The group's leaders also take a very public role in spreading the separationist message. Lynn has shown remarkable media savvy and is frequently called on to provide public commentary on church-state issues.

In addition to these efforts at public education, Americans United has participated heavily in the legal battles over church and state. The group was formed in the wake of the landmark decision in *EVERSON V. BOARD OF EDUCATION* (1947), in which the Supreme Court upheld state transportation reimbursements to parents of parochial school children. Leaders in the group were concerned that *Everson* marked the beginning of greater judicial accommodation of Catholic claims to public funds. Since *Everson*, Americans United has participated as case sponsor, or amicus curiae, in dozens of legal disputes. For example, it opposed the state aid programs for church-affiliated schools at issue in *LEMON V. KURTZMAN* (1971), an important case that laid out legal doctrine still used by some members of the Supreme Court to guide their church-state decisions. Americans United also participated in *Flast v. Cohen* (1968), which established procedural rules for taxpayers wishing to dispute the use of federal funds for religious purposes.

Americans United has complemented its educational and legal activities with legislative lobbying. One of its first actions as an organization was to urge U.S. representatives to pass a constitutional amendment banning government aid to religious schools, and it continues to have a role in most legislation relating to church and state. The group uses a range of tactics, from hearings testimony to mass letter-writing campaigns.

Further reading: Sorauf, Frank J. *The Wall of Separation: The Constitutional Politics of Church and State.* Princeton, N.J.: Princeton University Press, 1976.

—Kevin R. den Dulk

amicus curiae briefs

An amicus curiae (friend of the court) brief is a legal brief filed by either an individual or a group that is not a party to the case. Perhaps it is more accurate to refer to these briefs, which are pervasive in First Amendment ESTABLISHMENT CLAUSE and FREE EXERCISE CLAUSE cases, as "friend of the *cause*" briefs, for those who file them are particularly interested in rulings favorable to the viewpoint they represent. From the mid-20th century on, these briefs were transformed from literally an impartial voice aiding the work of the judiciary into a voice of advocacy concerning the meaning of either the Establishment Clause or the Free Exercise Clause.

Individuals, private organizations, or governmental entities may file amicus curiae briefs. However, with respect to First Amendment religion clause cases, religious bodies, religious associations, and civil liberties organizations normally file such briefs. These briefs normally are filed after a case has been accepted for review, although some briefs are submitted in connection with the filing of a petition of certiorari. Amicus curiae briefs seek to clarify the issues involved in the case and to aid in the development of legal doctrine with respect to either the Establishment Clause or the Free Exercise Clause. The briefs also help to set the agenda, legally and politically, concerning religion clause issues, such as public schools and religious activities or the degree to which an individual is exempted from the regulatory state because of his or her religious beliefs. Amicus curiae briefs are a form of "politics by other means," for they seek not only to influence the development of constitutional and legal doctrine but also to influence social policy and inform public debate about such policy. Thus, amicus curiae briefs in essence are forms of "lobbying by litigation" and reflect the growth of public interest law in the last 100 years in the United States.

It is difficult to measure precisely the influence on judges and justices of amicus curiae briefs, or to gauge the particular use the Supreme Court, for instance, makes of these briefs when deliberating and deciding cases and issuing written opinions. But the number of amicus curiae briefs in any one case invariably attests to the importance of that case and its legal and political ramifications. Cases regarding either the Establishment Clause or the Free Exercise Clause are no exception. For example, throughout the 20th century and into the 21st century, the American Civil Liberties Union has filed amicus curiae briefs in almost all the major Establishment Clause and Free Exercise Clause cases, such as *WEST VIRGINIA BOARD OF EDUCATION V. BARNETTE, MCCOLLUM V. BOARD OF EDUCATION, EPPERSON V. ARKANSAS, WALLACE V. JAFFREE,* and *EMPLOYMENT DIVISION V. SMITH.*

In recent years the number of amicus curiae briefs submitted in Establishment Clause and Free Exercise Clauses cases has mushroomed, given the controversial nature of many of the issues involved and the overall increase in public-interest litigation. For instance, in 1997 the Supreme Court heard the case of *CITY OF BOERNE V. FLORES.* At issue was the constitutionality of the 1993 RELIGIOUS FREEDOM RESTORATION ACT (RFRA), which Congress has passed with only three dissenting votes and which was signed into law by President WILLIAM JEFFERSON CLINTON. A federal district court, in a case involving RFRA and the denial of a building permit to enlarge St. Peter Catholic Church in a small town outside of San Antonio, Texas, struck down RFRA, but it was reversed by a federal appellate court. The Supreme Court accepted the case and, in 1997, ruled that RFRA was indeed unconstitutional under the Court's understanding of the doctrine of separation of powers. The amicus curiae briefs filed in the case reveal an interesting (and somewhat unusual) coalition of organizations that collectively were asking the Court to uphold RFRA: the AMERICAN CENTER FOR LAW AND JUSTICE, the AMERICAN CIVIL LIBERTIES UNION (ACLU), the AMERICAN JEWISH CONGRESS, the BAPTIST JOINT COMMITTEE ON PUBLIC AFFAIRS, the CHRISTIAN LEGAL SOCIETY, the NATIONAL COUNCIL OF CHURCHES, the Union of Orthodox Jewish Congregations of America, PEOPLE FOR THE AMERICAN WAY, AMERICANS UNITED FOR SEPARATION OF CHURCH AND STATE, the COALITION FOR THE FREE EXERCISE OF RELIGION, and the EVANGELICAL LUTHERAN CHURCH IN AMERICA, among others.

Earlier in the 20th century, organizations such as the NAACP and the ACLU pioneered the use of amicus curiae briefs in their attempt to influence the development of constitutional law and social policy in the United States. Today, such briefs are commonplace, and with respect to the nexus of religion and law, especially in the context of the two religion clauses of the First Amendment, by all accounts will continue to be a standard feature for some time to come.

Further reading: Krislov, Samuel. "The Amicus Curiae Brief: From Friendship to Advocacy." *Yale Law Journal* 72 (1963); Noonan, John T., Jr., and Edward M. Gaffney Jr. *Religious Freedom: History, Cases, and Other Materials on the Interaction of Religion and Government.* New York: Foundation Press, 2001.

—Stephen K. Shaw

Amish

The Amish (who also refer to themselves as "The Plain People") are a conservative Christian group residing mostly in Pennsylvania, Ohio, Indiana, Illinois, Iowa, Nebraska, Kansas, and Ontario, Canada. They trace their roots back to the Mennonite elder Jakob Amman, who in 17th-century Switzerland caused a schism between his followers and the existing Mennonite communities by refusing to worship in state-run churches. They began emigrating to Pennsylvania in the early 1700s and are now found only in North America.

The Amish are best known for their use of horse and buggies, refusal to operate many modern-day machines and appliances, and their distinctive dress. Clothing is worn with hooks, not buttons. Married men adopt beards without mustaches, and women wear plain dresses with bonnets and aprons. The distinctive attire and refusal to farm with tractors is not merely a subgroup clinging to antiquated tradition. The Amish are very much a modern society in the sense that they are aware of and actively strive to control their own destiny. They use clothing, social structures, rules, and financial dealings to protect and preserve their culture.

As a social system, the Amish are noteworthy for their rich and pervasive system of mutual assistance, which is predicated on biblical interpretations of separation from the outside world and care for one another. The Plain People point to II Corinthians 6:14–17, which instructs the follower, "Be ye not unequally yoked together with unbelievers: for what fellowship hath righteousness with unrighteousness? . . . Wherefore come out from among them, and be ye separate." The simple dress, German dialect, and use of horse and buggy all distinguish the Amish from outsiders. While they avoid commercial insurance policies that link them to the outside world, formal and informal mutual welfare practices are part of the very fiber of Amish society. Following Galatians 6:2, "Bear ye one another's burdens, and so fulfill the law of Christ," the Amish strive to ensure that none of their brethren fall into dire need. The large barn raisings and quilting parties are perhaps the best-known examples of this, but just as important are the day-to-day practices such as helping out with household and farmwork during times of illness and when there is a death in a family.

In 1955, the Eisenhower administration announced that the Old-Age, Survivors, and Disability Insurance program, commonly known as Social Security, was being extended to self-employed farmers—including the Amish. The Plain People saw this both as linking them to the outside world and also as an undesired method of mitigating their obligation to bear each other's burdens. Most refused to pay the Social Security tax, often closing their bank accounts so that the Internal Revenue Service (IRS) could not seize their assets. In 1961, Amish farmer Valentine Byler was in the field using his horses to pull his plow for spring planting when IRS agents pulled up with a trailer and carted away his horses. Politicians were outraged, and in 1965 members of Amish communities were given permission to opt out of the Social Security system, which they universally now do.

Although they themselves do not litigate, the Amish still try to protect their interests both politically and in the courts, benefiting from the help of friendly politicians and attorneys who act on their behalf. Slow-moving vehicle laws affect using horse and buggies on public roads, draft laws demand negotiations on finding alternative ways for the Amish (who are CONSCIENTIOUS OBJECTORS) to serve, while regulations affect how they store their milk and how they dispose of animal waste. The most famous court case involving the Amish is undoubtedly *WISCONSIN V. YODER* (1972), in which the Supreme Court unanimously ruled that the Old Order Amish were not required to send their children to high school or to keep their children in school until the age of 16, as most state laws required. Chief Justice Warren Burger explained that "almost 300 years of consistent practice, and strong evidence of a sustained faith pervading and regulating respondents' entire mode of life support the claim that enforcement of the State's requirement of compulsory formal education after the eighth grade would gravely endanger if not destroy the free exercise of respondents' religious beliefs."

Thus the Amish are both traditional in lifestyle but modern in social practice, refusing to engage in law and rarely in politics, but still benefiting from others who will act for them to protect their interests.

See also FREE EXERCISE CLAUSE; MENNONITE TRADITION.

Further reading: Hostetler, John A. *Amish Society.* 4th ed. Baltimore: Johns Hopkins University Press, 1993; Kidder, Robert L., and John A. Hostetler. "Managing Ideologies: Harmony as Ideology in Amish and Japanese Societies." *Law & Society Review* 24, no. 4 (1990): 895–922; Kraybill, Donald B., ed. *The Amish and the State.* Baltimore: Johns Hopkins University Press, 1993; Kraybill, Donald B., and Marc Olshan. *The Amish Struggle with Modernity.* Hanover, N.H.: University Press of New England, 1994; Loomis, Charles. "The Old Order Amish as a Social System." In *Social Systems: Essays on Their Persistence and Change.* Edited by Charles Loomis. New York: D. Van Nostrand, 1960.

—Brian J. Glenn

Anabaptists

Transliterated from the Greek word for "re-baptizer," Anabaptist refers to members of what has sometimes been called the

"Radical Reformation" or the "left wing of the Protestant Reformation." The appellation was a serious matter; under a law from the Justinian code (529 C.E.) used by the religious and political authorities of the day, "re-baptism" was a capital crime. Anabaptists themselves did not use this name, preferring versions of "Brethren," or, in the Netherlands, *Doopsgezind* (baptism-minded).

The first recorded "rebaptism" occurred near Zurich, Switzerland, on January 21, 1525, although Anabaptist ideas were in evidence in southern German territories one or two years earlier. Anabaptist origins reside in multiple locations and sources, some of which date back several more centuries. Christian groups that stem from the Anabaptist movements of the 16th century include various permutations of Mennonites (see MENNONITE TRADITION) and AMISH, along with Swiss Brethren, Dunkards, Brethren in Christ, Hutterites, and others. It is difficult to identify precisely what was and was not "Anabaptist" in the 16th century, because the movement as a whole was highly diverse (as are its modern American relatives), and it did not originate in a single place or under a single recognized leader, as did the primary churches of the Magisterial (Calvinist, Lutheran, and Zwinglian) Reformation.

Identifying characteristics of early Anabaptist teachings include anticlericalism, PACIFISM, adult baptism for church membership, local congregational autonomy, strict SEPARATION OF CHURCH AND STATE, emphasis on moral purity and good works, and rigorous biblicism. Few of these markers, however, would pertain absolutely to all groups or individuals labeled Anabaptist. An early confession of faith, the so-called Schleitheim Confession (1527), provides important points of common reference but is neither definitive nor exhaustive. No Anabaptist church was officially sponsored or supported by government authorities, as were the ROMAN CATHOLIC CHURCH, various EASTERN ORTHODOX CHURCHES, and Magisterial Reformation churches.

Important early Anabaptist leaders include Georg Blaurock (ca. 1492–1528), Hans Denck (ca. 1500–27), Conrad Grebel (ca. 1498–1526), Balthasar Hubmaier (ca. 1480–1528), Melchior Hofmann (ca. 1495–1543), Hans Hut (ca. 1490–1527), Jakob Hutter (d. 1535), Felix Manz (ca. 1498–1527), Pilgram Marpeck (ca. 1495–1556), Wilhelm Reublin (ca. 1480–1560), Melchior Rinck (ca. 1492–ca. 1560), and Michael Sattler (ca. 1490–1527).

Protestants and Catholics alike reviled Anabaptists. Most Magisterial Reformation leaders, including Johannes Bader, Heinrich Bullinger, John Calvin, Martin Luther, Philip Melanchthon, Justus Menius, Johannes Oecolampadus, Urbanus Rhegius, and Ulrich Zwingli, wrote substantial, often vitriolic tracts against them, as did a number of Catholic theologians. As their dates show, many of the early Anabaptist leaders perished in persecutions by 1530, and others who lived longer languished in prison. Thieleman Von Braght's 1,290-page *Martyrs' Mirror* (1660) gives a lengthy account of Anabaptist sufferings.

Menno Simons (1496–1561), a Catholic priest who joined the Anabaptists in 1536 after a gradual conversion, was a major leader in the next generation. Together with Dirk Philips (1504–68), Simons is generally credited with consolidating the Anabaptists in Holland and the north German territories into a coherent body of believers from which stem the several Mennonite groups that now bear his name.

While persecution of Anabaptists was widespread and sometimes intense, it was not uniform. In the mid-16th century, Archduke Ferdinand of Austria, for example, made strenuous efforts to eradicate Anabaptists from his kingdom root and branch, while individual noblemen elsewhere gave refuge to Anabaptist groups, inviting them to farm fallow or unworked land or to establish cottage industries. Thus, Hutterite Anabaptists settled in Moravia, and Mennonite Anabaptists settled and flourished for periods of time in eastern German territories and later in Russia, eventually beginning a migration to the United States in the later 1800s. By the 17th century, Mennonites became officially tolerated in the Netherlands, where they participated in the flowering of Dutch art and commerce. Anabaptists in the Swiss and southern French territories succeeded in agriculture, one of the few occupations from which they were not legally excluded there.

Anabaptist groups immigrated to North America as early as the 1680s. Successive waves throughout the 18th, 19th, and early 20th centuries populated areas in Pennsylvania and Midwestern and Plains states. Communities of Mennonites also settled in California and Manitoba (Canada), while Hutterites established colonies in South Dakota, Montana, Alberta, and Manitoba. The North American churches descended from the Anabaptists have generally retained an emphasis on pacifism, benevolence, community service, and moral integrity, and they currently span the entire theological spectrum.

See also CALVINISM.

—Thomas Heilke

Anthony, Susan B. (1820–1906) *activist*

Born February 5, 1820, in Adams, Massachusetts, Susan B. Anthony would become the most famous American champion of women's rights. An ardent social reformer, Anthony was devoted to a variety of causes, working for temperance, campaigning against slavery, and, most notably, crusading for the political and social advancement of women for over 50 years. Though by the time of her death on March 13, 1906, Anthony's main political goal—national voting rights for women—went unfulfilled, yet her extraordinary efforts would be rewarded in 1920 with the passage of the Nineteenth Amendment for women's suffrage.

Raised in an unconventional home, Susan B. Anthony's family life powerfully shaped her character and achievements. Her father, Daniel, had a fiercely independent mind and a passionate dedication to progressive causes, especially temperance and abolition. He supported women's rights, too, insisting that his daughters as well as his sons receive a formal education and cultivate self-reliance. In a more public vein, in 1848 Daniel Anthony and his wife, Lucy Read Anthony, signed the

Susan B. Anthony *(Library of Congress)*

feminist Declaration of Sentiments, drafted at the Seneca Falls Convention that same year. These commitments to social reform sprang from strong QUAKER convictions concerning egalitarianism and moral rectitude, beliefs that permeated the Anthony home.

Susan B. Anthony absorbed this Quaker spirit of equality and moral seriousness and brought these convictions to her work as an educator and temperance activist, two fields in which she early encountered gender inequities. As a young teacher in the 1840s, Anthony learned firsthand of the gross disparity in pay between male and female teachers. Similarly, in the temperance movement, she encountered stubborn male resistance to the equal participation of women. In protest against a particularly stinging rebuff she received at an 1852 Sons of Temperance meeting, Susan and her new acquaintance, ELIZABETH CADY STANTON, founded the Woman's State Temperance Society. Though the organization was short-lived, the friendship forged in it between Anthony and Stanton became a lifelong, legendary partnership in social activism.

By the 1850s, convinced that beyond temperance laws women's advancement required comprehensive political and legal gains, including the suffrage, property rights, and divorce reform, Anthony shifted her focus. Refining her skills as a grassroots organizer, she worked diligently for feminist changes in New York state law, circulating petitions, giving speeches, and hosting women's rights conventions (see FEMINISM). Her efforts were rewarded with the 1860 passage of the Married Woman's Property Act, which gave New York women the novel right to own property, transact business, and share custody of their children.

Anthony perceived a basic similarity between women's oppression and slavery, and struggled against both. Her exceptional energy and aptitude for social activism earned her a

prominent role in the abolition movement, whose leading figures, including Frederick Douglass and William Lloyd Garrison, were frequent visitors at her family home. In addition to cofounding an emancipation organization with Stanton, Anthony assumed a leading position in 1865 as the chief New York agent of Garrison's American Anti-Slavery Society. After the Civil War, she and Stanton campaigned vigorously to render the Fourteenth and Fifteenth Amendments gender-inclusive—a position that alienated several longtime abolitionist allies, who were fearful that the conjunction of black and woman suffrage would be deemed too radical.

In other groundbreaking initiatives, Anthony began in 1868 to publish a feminist weekly, *The Revolution*, and in 1869 she cofounded with Stanton the National Woman Suffrage Association, dedicated to securing a constitutional amendment enfranchising women. Starting in the early 1870s, an indefatigable Anthony canvased the country for over a decade speaking on behalf of this goal. In 1872, in a bold attempt to challenge electoral law using Fourteenth Amendment protections, Anthony cast a vote for president in Rochester, New York. Promptly arrested and fined for civil disobedience, she was released on bail but refused on principle to pay the fine.

In the late 1870s Anthony contributed to women's advancement in yet another way by initiating a history of women's political activism, a project that would eventually yield a multiauthored six-volume series on *The History of Woman Suffrage*. More an activist than a scholar, however, Anthony remained tirelessly engaged in political action, founding the International Council of Women in 1888, presiding over the National American Woman Suffrage Association from 1892 to 1900, and speaking on behalf of women's rights up to the very month of her death in 1906.

See also MOTT, LUCRETIA; WILLARD, FRANCES.

—Jeanne M. Heffernan

anticommunism

The major debate over anticommunism in American religion and politics has not been about whether to be anticommunist, but rather about what is the most realistic and effective anticommunist stance. The bipolar nature of American politics, in which public policy is forged in the competition and cooperation of two major political parties, has meant that each party often portrayed the other as dangerous in its approach to communism. Those on the Left, usually Democratic, were labeled as "weak on communism," allowing communists to take over various nations, as well as infiltrate the U.S. government. Those on the Right, usually Republican, were labeled as "right-wing extremists," who supported oppression and who would lead the nation to war. Parallel to and in interaction with the political realm, religious groups and their leaders were linked to these terms and to the public policies formed in the debate between perspectives identified as liberal and conservative.

Soon after the Bolshevik triumph in Russia in 1917, a Red Scare arose in the United States, primarily in Attorney General A. Mitchell Palmer's rounding up and imprisonment of suspected Communists in 1919. This approach was soon discredited as extremist. The boom times of the 1920s reduced the fear of communism, and, in the 1930s, the dangers of fascism and militarism diverted attention from communism. In the 1930s the U.S. Communist Party adopted a new policy of seeking allies through "united front" organizations. The fight against fascism in World War II brought a period of strategic alliance with the Soviet Union, which also minimized pressure against the U.S. Communist Party. At the same time, the developments of the 1930s and 1940s increased the opportunities for American Communists to spy on and exert influence in government.

After World War II, a new Red Scare appeared with the cold war. A high point in the scare came in 1954 with the investigations into internal subversion by the House Un-American Activities Committee (HUAC), led by Senator Joseph R. McCarthy (R-Wisc.) (1908–57). The paradox of the extreme anticommunism associated with Senator McCarthy and others is that although there was a reaction against the anticommunist hysteria of McCarthy and others (just as there had been against Palmer), examination of Soviet archives since the breakup of the Soviet Union has shown that the U.S. Communist Party was used from its earliest days for spying on and infiltrating the U.S. government.

In 1960, a U.S. Air Force manual contained the famous and subsequently discredited statement regarding communist influence in the churches. In spite of the charges by those on the Right that communists had infiltrated the mainline Protestant churches and the NATIONAL COUNCIL OF CHURCHES, Ralph Roy makes clear in his study that very few ministers ever had membership in the Communist Party. Even when the Communist Party adopted the policy of forming "united fronts," relatively few ministers lent their names to organizations formed by Communists to recruit allies. In these cases, ministers joined front groups because of the causes of peace, democracy, or labor unionization that were being promoted. Basically, the large majority of religious leaders in America identified communism as misguided and harmful. Conservatives tended to emphasize the evils of communism, particularly its antireligious beliefs and policies and its repression of freedoms. Liberals viewed the conservatives as lacking in understanding and compassion for the poor and as direct or indirect supporters of cruel and corrupt dictatorships simply because they were anticommunist. Basically, however, no CHRISTIAN ANTI-COMMUNIST CRUSADE or movement with a large following could be developed in America.

Since the 1960s, the Religious Right has generally muted its anticommunist rhetoric. The Rev. BILLY GRAHAM, who had been strongly anticommunist, is a major example of moderation among evangelicals. In spite of criticism from some on the extreme right, he made a series of visits to Communist countries and was generally well received. The ROMAN CATHOLIC CHURCH, although strongly anticommunist, was clearly divided in its support of Senator McCarthy and of Father

CHARLES COUGHLIN earlier, and, in the end, saw McCarthyism as a political, not a religious, question, which meant that many Catholics supported the political repudiation of extreme anticommunism.

Americans in general have remained anticommunist, without forming an anti-Communist movement, over the whole period from the Russian Revolution of 1917 to the end of the century, when communism appeared to be on the decline. The strange combination in communism of idealism and cruel oppression tended to produce contrasting reactions among the most liberal and most conservative in the American public. In the meantime, American politics continued to be dominated by practical rather than ideological goals, producing the policies of both containment and détente toward communist countries. Americans continue to prefer to believe that most people in communist countries are not driven by a communist ideology.

Further reading: Haynes, John E. *Red Scare or Red Menace?* Chicago: Ivan R. Dee, 1996; Martin, William. *With God on Our Side.* New York: Broadway Books, 1996; Roy, Ralph Lord. *Communism and the Churches.* New York: Harcourt, Brace and Company, 1960.

—Robert L. Montgomery

anticult movement

A variety of groups historically have taken as their mandate identifying problematic or illegitimate religious organizations. With respect to contemporary religious movements, these oppositional organizations have been of two kinds, religious and secular. The focus here is on secular organizations, which have been the primary source of opposition to groups they regard as "cults." Anticult groups began with a movement opposing the Children of God (now The FAMILY), and gradually evolved into national organizations, most notably the Cult Awareness Network (CAN) and the American Family Foundation (AFF). Ultimately, CAN was connected to an illicit deprogramming event and was forced into bankruptcy in an ensuing civil suit. Opponents of CAN purchased its name and files, and reopened the organization with a staff and perspective more favorable to the religious movements CAN had condemned.

The religious anticult organizations formed long before the 1970s cult controversy erupted. They typically challenged sectarian Christian and non-Christian churches, such as the JEHOVAH'S WITNESSES, SEVENTH-DAY ADVENTISTS, LATTER-DAY SAINTS, and Christian Scientists. With the advent of the cult controversy, these organizations simply added the contemporary cohort of new religions to their lists of target cults. Religious anticult organizations, drawing their membership largely from the ranks of conservative denominational groups, conceive of themselves as engaged in spiritual warfare. Cults are defined principally in theological terms as groups that propagate doctrinal heresy. Secular anticult organizations began as family-based groups concerned with the conversions of relatives to new religious movements. The battle in which secular anticultists are engaged, therefore, is for adherents' hearts and minds rather than for their souls. Secular antic-ultists are more politically active than their religious counter-parts, attempting to ally with mental health professionals and government agencies to gain access to sanctioning power.

In its initial form, secular anticult ideology depicted cults as rapidly growing, unprecedented in their organization, tactics, and destructiveness, capable of dramatically altering individual beliefs and behaviors, and of creating long-term emotional damage to anyone subjected to them. The linchpin concepts in ACM ideology are "brainwashing" (alternatively, mind control, coercive persuasion, thought reform) and "cults." There are numerous, diverse models for both cults and brainwashing. However, brainwashing typically refers to a deliberate, potent program of indoctrination and control that reduces individual autonomy, voluntarism, and self-directed-ness. Cult typically refers to groups in which there is a domi-nant, authoritarian leader who claims total personal allegiance and a totalistic control structure that encapsulates members. Early versions of anticult ideology focused on the destructive-ness of cults to family ties; later versions emphasize damage to individual selfhood, which has created a role for therapeu-tic treatment.

The first organized anticult group, FREECOG (Parents Committee to Free Our Sons and Daughters from the Chil-dren of God), was formed in 1972 in response to the recruit-ment of young adults to the Children of God. A number of other local groups subsequently were formed to oppose other new religious groups that also drew members from the youth counterculture. Within a short time there was an initiative to create a national coordinating group to create a more eco-nomically viable, politically effective organization. The most important of these organizations were the Citizens Freedom Foundation, which became the Cult Awareness Network (CAN) in 1984, and a new organization, the American Family Foundation (AFF). The former became the public rela-tions/education wing of the anticult movement and the latter the intellectual wing, supporting and reporting research on "destructive cultism." With the development of anticult orga-nizations came an increased demand from families of con-verts for information and means for extricating members from cults. The latter service was termed "deprogramming," a pro-cess that putatively reverses the effects of cultic programming. Entrepreneurs rapidly entered this market, and the number of forcible deprogrammings soared. Opposition to deprogram-ming soon developed as it frequently involved the forcible abduction and restraint of adults who insisted their conver-sions were voluntary. In the face of this mounting opposition and the legal liabilities it posed, AFF/CAN officially withdrew support for coercive deprogramming, but CAN continued links and referrals to deprogrammers. The anticult movement then pursued alternative strategies. One was to obtain conser-vatorship orders from courts that granted parents legal cus-

tody of their offspring for purposes of deprogramming. Legal support for this practice quickly waned. The second was to ini-tiate civil suits against groups for infliction of mental distress as a product of brainwashing. This alternative ultimately foundered when courts began to reject brainwashing testi-mony as lacking scientific standing.

CAN's demise traces to its continued involvement in deprogrammings. The pivotal case was one in which a mem-ber of the United Pentecostal Church International, Jason Scott, was deprogrammed by Rick Ross, a deprogrammer hired by Scott's mother. The deprogramming was unsuccessful and led to a civil suit against Ross and CAN. In 1996, the court issued a judgment against CAN that included a multimillion dollar penalty, and the organization was forced into bankruptcy. A coalition of groups purchased the corporate name, phone number, and files, which were auctioned to pay the settlement. The "New CAN" was then established to dispense what the organization regards as more accurate, objective, and balanced information about new religious movements.

Further reading: Bromley, David G. "Deprogramming as a Mode of Exit from New Religious Movements: The Case of the Unification Church." In *Falling from the Faith*. Edited by David G. Bromley. Beverly Hills, Calif.: Sage, 1988; Freedom Magazine. "Exposing the Criminal Clique Called 'CAN': Dis-closure of Criminality and Perversions Rock Anti-Religious Hate Group." *Freedom Magazine* (October 1991): 28–32; Coates, Priscilla. "The History of the Cult Awareness Net-work." In *Anti-cult Movements in Cross-Cultural Perspective*. Edited by Anson Shupe and David Bromley. New York: Gar-land, 1994; Melton, J. Gordon. "Anti-cultists in the United States: An Historical Perspective." In *New Religious Move-ments: Challenge and Response*. Edited by Bryan Wilson and Jamie Cresswell. London: Routledge, 1999; Shupe, Anson, and David G. Bromley. *The New Vigilantes*. Beverly Hills, Calif.: Sage, 1980.

—David G. Bromley

Anti-Defamation League (ADL)

Founded in 1913, the Anti-Defamation League (also known as the Anti-Defamation League of B'NAI B'RITH) is dedicated to fighting anti-Semitism and other forms of bigotry and hatred in the United States and around the world. The activities of the league include collecting and disseminating information on organized hate groups, terrorists, and extremists in the United States and abroad; combating hate crimes; building support for ISRAEL among U.S. policy makers, opinion leaders, and the general public; and promoting the SEPARATION OF CHURCH AND STATE in the United States.

The creation of the ADL was prompted by the infamous case of Leo Frank, who was wrongly convicted of murder in the death of a teenage girl employed at an Atlanta pencil fac-tory. The trial was only the most infamous example of anti-Semitism in America; discrimination was widely practiced and widely accepted, and negative stereotypes of Jews were commonplace. Frank himself was killed in 1915 by a lynch mob out for what they called "justice" against the "Yankee Jew."

The ADL's founder, Sigmund Livingston, began operations in Chicago in the wake of the Frank case, with support from the Independent Order of B'nai B'rith. The aims of the organization, as Livingston put them, were "to stop, by appeals to reason and conscience, and if necessary, by appeals to law, the defamation of the Jewish people . . . to secure justice and fair treatment to all citizens alike . . . [and to] put an end forever to unjust and unfair discrimination against and ridicule of any sect or body of citizens." Throughout its history, the ADL has consistently linked its fight against anti-Semitism with the broader struggle for civil rights for all minority groups.

The ADL's major focus in its early years was to combat negative Jewish stereotypes in newspapers and magazines (the very name "Anti-Defamation League" suggests this primary purpose). The leaders of the organization eschewed legal action to force an end to discrimination against Jews; they believed that social progress would come about only with changes in public opinion. Fittingly, a leading member of the ADL's executive committee was Adolph Ochs, the publisher of the *New York Times.*

The ADL was remarkably successful in its early efforts to combat negative stereotypes of Jews. Ochs himself wrote a letter to newspaper editors urging the elimination of "objectionable and vulgar" references to Jews. The organization was especially active in protesting the negative depiction of Jews in the media during the period of World War I and the Russian Revolution.

The rise of the KU KLUX KLAN in the 1920s prompted the ADL to turn its attention to monitoring and exposing the activities of hate groups, an activity it continues to pursue to this day. The ADL currently keeps its eye on a wide range of extremist groups, including those that promote various forms of RACISM, engage in or support terrorism, and deny the reality of the HOLOCAUST. Most recently, the ADL has actively monitored hate groups on the Internet.

Over the years, the ADL has become increasingly aggressive in pursuit of its agenda, adding to its arsenal not only appeals to public opinion but also efforts to promote change through Congress, the courts, and state legislatures. The Holocaust marked a key turning point, convincing the ADL (along with other Jewish advocacy groups) of the need, as one ADL activist put it, for "the Jew to consider himself as a natural partner in a government of the people and by the people."

Thus the ADL became part of a broad coalition fighting in the courts and in the legislatures to promote a strict separation of church and state—early on, with efforts to ban release time for public school children to pursue religious education, and more recently, by opposing VOUCHER programs that would benefit religious schools. The ADL has been a consistent opponent of organized PRAYER IN PUBLIC SCHOOLS, and has actively lobbied to convince Congress and the state legislatures to pass laws banning, or increasing the punishments

for, HATE CRIMES, and in the legal efforts to defend the constitutionality of such laws. In recent years, the ADL has become increasingly outspoken in defense of Israel and in opposition to those whom it sees as opposing Israel's interests.

Further reading: Ivers, Gregg. *To Build a Wall: American Jews and the Separation of Church and State.* Charlottesville: University Press of Virginia, 1995.

—William Lasser

Anti-Masonic Party

The Anti-Masonic Party was established in 1828 after a drowning in Lake Ontario in upstate New York, to combat perceived conspiracies and secret deals made among Masons. Anti-Masonic sentiment was based on the belief that Masons were wealthy men who conspired to promote their mutual economic, political, and social self-interest at the expense of everyone else. The first third party in American history, the Anti-Masons tapped growing anti-Masonic feelings that had been building for decades, particularly among residents of rural upstate New York, but also in the New England states and PENNSYLVANIA.

The party's primary founder was Thurlow Weed, a journalist and political activist who gathered like-minded anti-Masons together in September 1826, in response to a much-publicized disappearance and rumored murder of a Mason, William Morgan, just before the promised release of his book exposing the rituals and activities of FREEMASONRY. Masons reportedly kidnapped Morgan and carried him through several counties in upstate New York. Although Morgan's body was never found, Weed's messages of a conspiracy to silence Morgan, coupled with widespread anti-Masonic fears, fueled the quick growth of the party.

The party reportedly gained the support of many evangelical Protestants who scorned what they saw as selfish, elite-promoting, and underlying anti-Christian principles of Freemasonry. The Masons were a secret fraternal organization imported the previous century from England. Many non-Masons thought their members were guided by the use of reason over religious faith. Its known membership was filled with stalwarts found in every community, such as judges, major business and civic leaders, and public officials at all levels of government. Critics viewed the Masons as an aristocratic organization of men seemingly operating above the law, seeking to govern society for themselves alone, and were attacked for allegedly having stolen the government from the rest of society. In addition, the secret rituals were thought to be somehow related to those associated with the ROMAN CATHOLIC CHURCH, another major religious institution feared and distrusted at that time by many American Protestants supporting the Anti-Masons.

In contrast, the Anti-Masons saw themselves as guided by God as they struggled to return the nation to its constitutional and Christian roots by preserving the basic governing, social, and economic institutions of America. The Anti-Masons claimed to have completely egalitarian goals and to speak on behalf of the average person. They saw themselves as wholesome and guided by true religious principles struggling against the essentially sectarian, selfish, and urban Masons.

Politically, the Anti-Masonic Party recorded several successes in its brief history. The party's populist message complemented perfectly a major contemporary governing development—the rapid expansion of the franchise. Their antielite message was well suited to appeal to many of the newly enfranchised voters rapidly swelling the ranks throughout much of the 1820s and 1830s. In 1828, the party won four senate and 17 assembly seats in the New York legislature. Later they won the governorships of Pennsylvania and Vermont. In 1831, the party won 150 of 490 seats in the MASSACHUSETTS general assembly.

In 1832, the Anti-Masons became the first American political party to hold a national convention to nominate a candidate for president. However, their nominee, William Wirt of MARYLAND, carried only Vermont and its seven electoral votes, which likely siphoned votes from the Whig Party's nominee, Henry Clay, and helped assure reelection for the Democratic-Republicans' Andrew Jackson. Undoubtedly, the intensity of the Anti-Masonic Party's effort was fueled by the widespread knowledge that both Clay and Jackson were Masons. An early policy goal of the party was to end Sunday postal service, initiated in 1825, which Anti-Masons saw as a desecration of the Sabbath made into law by the Masons through their control of the Democratic Party in Congress. Another Anti-Masonic goal was to make illegal extrajudicial oaths in government.

The party's political strength essentially died in the early 1830s. By the 1836 presidential election, most of its members had drifted toward the Whig Party, which by then was the major rallying point for those opposed to the Democratic Party, which Anti-Masons viewed as the political home of Masons and Roman Catholics alike.

See also KNOW-NOTHING PARTY.

Further reading: Formisano, Ronald, and Kathleen S. Kutolowski. "Anti-Masonry and Masonry: The Genesis of Protest, 1826–1827." *American Quarterly* 29, no. 2 (1997): 139–165; Goodman, Paul. *Towards a Christian Republic: Anti-Masonry and the Great Transition in New England, 1826–1836.* New York: Oxford University Press, 1988; Hofstadter, Richard. *The Paranoid Style in American Politics and Other Essays.* New York: Knopf, 1966.

—Robert E. Dewhirst

apartheid in South Africa

In South Africa, the struggle against apartheid—the Afrikaner National Party policy of racial separation and oppression—started in 1948. Antiapartheid resistance was taken up by several organizations and individuals, and manifested in various ways. Antiapartheid organizations and movements included the African National Congress (ANC), the Pan Africanist Congress (PAC), the Black Consciousness Movement (BCM), and the United Democratic Front (UDF), as well as other student, labor, and church resistance.

The earliest major organization to oppose apartheid was the African National Congress (ANC), formed in 1910, whose aims were national freedom, political independence, and self-determination: The goal of the ANC's 1952 Defiance Campaign was to undermine the practicality of the apartheid policy through strikes, boycotts, stay-at-homes, CIVIL DISOBEDIENCE, and noncooperation. By the end of 1952, ANC membership had grown to 100,000 members. The 1955 Freedom Charter, written in part by the ANC, called for the formation of a nonracial society characterized by legal equality for all citizens and a sharing of the land and wealth of the nation. In 1956 some 150 ANC leaders, including Nelson Mandela, were arrested on treason charges, though were later acquitted. In 1960, in Sharpeville, a demonstration against "pass laws" erupted in violence when police opened fire and killed almost 70 protesters. As a result of the massacre, martial law was declared, and, in 1964, both the ANC and the PAC leaders were banned.

The Black Consciousness Movement (BCM) refers to the philosophy of the antiapartheid resistance efforts of the South African Students Organization (SASO) and the Black People's Convention (BPC). SASO was formed in December 1968 with Steve Biko as its first president. It stressed black consciousness and black economic and cultural self-reliance. The BCM struggled not only for sociopolitical liberation but also, perhaps more important, for psychological liberation from white domination. In distinction from previous antiapartheid movements, the BCM believed that black self-understanding and formation were necessary preconditions for direct confrontation with the white South African government. Though not a direct manifestation of the BCM, which advocated nonviolence, the student uprisings in Soweto in June 1976 that resulted in police violence and rioting were a by-product of the BCM. Biko, the popular BCM leader, died in 1977 in police detention.

Throughout the late 1970s and into the 1980s, antiapartheid resistance continued, led by students, labor organizations, and churches. Formed in 1979, the Azanian People's Organization (AZAPO) interpreted apartheid as an economic issue rather than as an exclusively racial one. The United Democratic Front (UDF), growing out of AZAPO in 1983, was highly influenced by South African black LIBERATION THEOLOGY, especially the writings and activities of Archbishop Desmond Tutu and Allan Boesak, who understood apartheid to be heresy. The UDF advocated unity of all opponents of apartheid, including whites, and favored mass action that would potentially lead to direct confrontation with the government.

In addition to resistance movements internal to South Africa, international pressure mounted to force business pullouts, economic sanctions, and a cultural boycott during the 1980s. Religious and theological solidarity with South African resistance to apartheid was evident in the writings of African-

American theologians such as JAMES CONE and GAYRAUD WILMORE. These African-American theologians of liberation argued that the demand for political and cultural liberation united BLACK THEOLOGY in America and South Africa. They asserted the Christian scriptures proclaimed that God had liberated the oppressed of society and profoundly identified with those who are powerless and outcast in the incarnation of Jesus Christ. They maintained that the meaning of Christ's resurrection was that God identified with and liberated the oppressed of all times. Since God was where the oppressed were, they concluded, God is active among black freedom movements, both in the United States and in South Africa.

American theologians both influenced and were influenced by South African theologians such as Tutu, Boesak, Manas Buthelezi, Bonganjalo Goba, Takatso Mofokeng, and Itumeleng Mosala. As a result of resistance and liberation movements in South Africa and elsewhere, black American theologians of liberation developed a more nuanced understanding of oppression and liberation. They came to see that liberation theology must include social and class analysis in addition to race analysis in order to struggle better against forms of oppression, such as apartheid.

The movement in the United States against South African apartheid found resonance largely in mainline Protestant churches, liberal Jewish movements, and among some Catholics, not to mention higher education institutions. Their SOCIAL JUSTICE orientation and large pension and endowment funds made the institutions targets for the antiapartheid movement, often leading to decisions over whether institutional funds should be divested from companies doing business in South Africa.

In 1990, South African president F. W. de Klerk removed bans on antiapartheid organizations and released Nelson Mandela after 27 years in prison. After negotiations, a transitional government was formed, and in 1994 South Africa's first free elections made Mandela president and the ANC the new ruling party.

Further reading: Byrnes, Rita M., ed. *South Africa: A Country Study.* 3d ed. Washington, D.C.: Library of Congress, 1997; Hopkins, Dwight N. *Black Theology USA and South Africa: Politics, Culture, and Liberation.* Maryknoll, N.Y.: Orbis Books, 1989; Mandela, Nelson. *Long Walk to Freedom: The Autobiography of Nelson Mandela.* Boston: Little, Brown, 1994; Motlhabi, Mokgethi. *Challenge to Apartheid: Toward a Moral National Resistance.* Grand Rapids, Mich.: Eerdmans, 1988; Motlhabi, Mokgethi. *The Theory and Practice of Black Resistance to Apartheid: A Socio-Ethical Analysis.* Johannesburg, South Africa: Skotaville Publishers, 1984.

—Kurt Buhring

Aryan Nations

Aryan Nations is the name of Pastor Richard Girnt Butler's movement and compound in Coeur d'Alene, Idaho. Aryan Nations comprises one of the largest CHRISTIAN IDENTITY communities, along with Butler's Church of Jesus Christ Christian. Aryan Nations has given rise to some of the most violently racist literature, ideology, and behavior in the United States. In September 2000, Pastor Butler and his followers lost a civil suit (*Keenan v. Aryan Nations*) that forced them to surrender their compound to pay for the judgment against them.

Richard Girnt Butler, an engineer at Lockheed Martin and follower of Christian Identity leader Wesley Swift, founded the Church of Jesus Christ Christian in Coeur d'Alene in 1973. Aryan Nations grew out of Butler's church and became the political wing of Butler's movement. Butler held annual Aryan Nations World Congresses at his compound for a number of years. These meetings, attended by a variety of racialists and white supremacists, came close to approximating an umbrella organization. Many of the most violent white supremacists have ties to Butler's Aryan Nations.

In the early 1980s, The Order, led by an Aryan Nations follower named Robert Mathews, was involved in several major violent incidents. Mathews, galvanized into action by the shoot-out death of Gordon Kahl, a tax dissenter, took an oath to God as an Aryan warrior to deliver his people from "the Jew." After several high-profile armored car heists, the assassination of Jewish talk-show host Alan Berg in Denver, and several lesser bias-motivated crimes, Mathews died in a standoff with federal agents in Smugglers Cove, Washington.

More recently, in August 1992, federal law enforcement engaged in a violent standoff with the Weaver family in Ruby Ridge, Idaho. The Weavers had ties to Pastor Butler's Aryan Nations and his Church of Jesus Christ Christian in Coeur d'Alene. Randy and Vicki Weaver, their children, and family friend Kevin Harris held U.S. marshals and the Federal Bureau of Investigation at bay for several weeks. The confrontation began when Deputy Marshal William Degan and another marshal attempted to serve a warrant and apprehend Randy Weaver on weapons violations. Degan shot the family dog, shot and killed Sammy Weaver, and was shot and killed in return.

The nearly two-week standoff ended after FBI sharpshooter Lon Horiuchi shot and killed Vicki Weaver. Horiuchi was following rules of engagement that had been modified on site by Deputy Director Larry Potts. Randy Weaver and Kevin Harris were subsequently acquitted of murder and conspiracy charges. Involuntary manslaughter charges against Agent Horiuchi were dropped, Deputy Director Potts and others were disciplined, the federal government made a multimillion-dollar settlement with the Weaver family, and both the House of Representatives and the Senate held numerous investigations into the incident.

In the summer of 1999, two separate Christian Identity–related incidents occurred. On July 4, Benjamin Smith, a follower of Matthew Hale (head of the World Church of the Creator), went on a shooting spree. Upset over the Illinois Bar's refusal to grant Hale permission to practice law on the grounds that he was morally unfit, Smith committed suicide after shooting 11 Asian Americans, African Americans, and Jews, killing two (including former Northwestern University basketball coach Ricky Byrdsong). On August 10, Buford Furrow, a follower of Pastor Butler and the second husband of Vicki Mathews (Robert Mathews's wife), violently entered a Los Angeles Jewish Community Center and wounded five, including several children, then killed a U.S. postman of Filipino descent while attempting to flee.

Pastor Butler and the Aryan Nations lost their Coeur d'Alene compound as the result of a civil suit in September 2000. Morris Dees and the Southern Poverty Law Center brought the lawsuit against Aryan Nations on behalf of Victoria and Jason Keenan. The Keenan's vehicle was pursued and forced from the road by Aryan Nations security after it backfired while they traveled near the Aryan Nations compound. After they were pulled from the vehicle, Aryan Nations security guards beat them. It remains to be seen whether or not Pastor Butler's Aryan Nations can survive the $6.3 million judgment rendered against it.

See also ANTI-SEMITISM; KU KLUX KLAN.

Further reading: Barkun, Michael. *Religion and the Racist Rights.* Chapel Hill: University of North Carolina Press, 1994; Hellwege, Jean. "Hate in the Crosshairs: Lawyers, Legislators Battle Hate Crime." *Trial* 37, no. 1 (January 1, 2001): 14–19; Wessinger, Catherine. *How the Millennium Comes Violently: From Jonestown to Heaven's Gate.* New York: Seven Bridges, 2000.

—Adam L. Silverman

asceticism

Asceticism is derived from the Greek verb *aske,* meaning both "to form by art" and "to practice, exercise, or train." The term was traditionally used in reference to the preparatory activities of athletes. But, at least since Plato, *asksis* took on an ethical meaning, referring to training in the virtuous life. Its meaning has since expanded further to refer generally to the disciplines of moral and religious traditions that seek to "form" or "re-form" human behavior to make possible the attainment of higher ethical or spiritual modes of existence.

Like ritual, asceticism constitutes a part of almost every religious tradition. Ascetic forms like (1) seclusion or "withdrawal from the world," (2) fasting, (3) voluntary poverty, (4) continence (especially in matters of sexuality), (5) voluntary suffering (both physical and nonphysical), and (6) meditation or silent prayer can be found in each major world religion, although the meaning of these forms and the details of their appropriation vary significantly.

In monotheistic traditions like Judaism, Christianity, and ISLAM, asceticism is often regarded as the necessary path to union with God. Put differently, mysticism tends to presuppose asceticism; the Divine cannot be experienced directly without proper preparation or purification through ascetic practices. Christian monasticism, for example, has historically incorporated such ascetic forms as seclusion, celibacy, fasting, poverty, and silent prayer, not as ends in themselves but, rather, as means toward intimacy with the Divine. Nonmonotheistic traditions like Advaita Vedanta HINDUISM, BUDDHISM, and Jainism similarly incorporate ascetic practices (frequently drawn from Yoga doctrine) as integral means toward the highest spiritual states. The Theravada Buddhist monk, for example, embraces material simplicity, practices sexual continence, and engages in extended meditation to approach the ideal state of *nirvana.*

A kind of dualism (i.e., spirit v. flesh, afterlife v. present life, or nonmaterial v. material) frequently characterizes asceticism and has lead to the claim made famous by Friedrich Nietzsche (1844–1900) in *The Genealogy of Morals* that ascetics are "world-rejecting" or "body-rejecting." Some form of "world-rejection" and somatic discipline has undoubtedly defined EASTERN ORTHODOX and ROMAN CATHOLIC monasticism. However, defenders of such practices contend that monasticism is essentially an affirmation, not a rejection—a positive, not a negative, way of life—because its ascetic aim is, finally, the deeper love of God and neighbor.

Protestant Christians, since the time of Luther, have been generally critical of traditional forms of asceticism like celibacy and fasting. Luther, himself a former Roman Catholic monk, renounced such ascetic practices as being efforts to gain righteousness through works instead of solely through God's grace. With the exception of such groups as the AMISH, North American Protestants have generally relegated traditional ascetic forms to a minimal role in the Christian life. One of the most controversial claims about Protestant asceticism, however, has carried direct and important consequences for thinking about American political, social, and economic life. Shortly after the turn of the 20th century, the German economist and sociologist Max Weber (1864–1920) proposed the thesis that modern capitalism developed and flourished in part because of "Protestant asceticism." Weber argued that Protestantism, and especially CALVINISM, endorsed and cultivated "inner-worldly asceticism (*inner-weltliche Askese*)," a form of asceticism that taught that the sole way of being certain of one's salvation was through the loyal and disciplined fulfillment of one's vocation *within* the institutional framework of the world. Within such a "Protestant ethic," according to Weber, the accumulation of wealth that capitalism's development demanded was not regarded as being morally suspect, as it had been by many religious traditions; rather, when coupled with a frugal lifestyle, wealth was regarded as a sign of God's favor and of one's membership among the predestined elect.

Forms of asceticism continue as part of contemporary American life. Not only are there traditional monasteries and religious communities that seek to continue ancient ascetic practices; novel forms of asceticism have also grown, for example, out of the 1960s counterculture. Even America's popular culture evinces a kind of asceticism with its emphasis on fitness, diets, and vacation "retreats." In contemporary religious and philosophical ethics, asceticism's importance has again surfaced through renewed interest in religious formation and spiritual exercises.

Further reading: Creel, Austin B., and Vasudha Narayanan, eds. *Monastic Life in the Christian and Hindu Traditions.* Lewiston, N.Y.: Edwin Mellen, 1990; Harpham, Geoffrey. *The Ascetic Imperative in Culture and Criticism.* Chicago: University of Chicago Press, 1987; McGinn, Bernard. *The Foundations of Mysticism.* New York: Crossroad, 1991; Weber, Max. *The Protestant Ethic and the Spirit of Capitalism.* Trans. T. Parsons. New York: Scribner, 1958; Wimbush, Vincent L., and Richard Valantasis, eds. *Asceticism.* New York: Oxford University Press, 1995.

—Perry T. Hamalis

Assemblies of God

In April 1914, the General Council of the Assemblies of God was formed out of a meeting with more than 300 people in Hot Springs, Arkansas. Over the course of the next several decades, the Assemblies of God grew from a loosely organized collection of local congregations to one of the largest PENTECOSTAL denominations in the United States, with over 2.5 million adherents (1.5 million members) in 2001. With the politicization of evangelicals in the 1980s, the Assemblies of God came to be considered a core constituency of the Christian Right.

For the initial meeting in 1914, Eudorus N. Bell served as the temporary chairman with J. Roswell Flower as secretary. Both men became influential in the Assemblies of God through their work on the *Word and Witness,* edited by Bell, and the weekly paper *Christian Evangel,* edited by Flower. The first meeting sought to establish a loosely connected collection of local congregations, hoping to avoid becoming too highly structured, which, they claimed, was a flaw in the mainline denominations.

But, the Assemblies of God soon found it necessary to move toward a more organized structure as disputes arose among its members. For instance, the Oneness advocates claimed that one could be baptized in the name of the Lord, Jesus, and Christ as an appropriate counterpart to the old Trinitarian formula of Father, Son, and Holy Ghost. In 1916, the Fourth General Council of the Assemblies of God adopted the Statement of Fundamental Truths to refute the Oneness movement and state their beliefs. The following year the General Council agreed to require credentialed ministers to accept the statement.

Women's roles in the Assemblies of God became another matter needing resolution. At the initial meeting in 1914, women were not permitted a vote. Although a few women, such as AIMEE SEMPLE MCPHERSON and Edith Mae Pennington, were affiliated with the Assemblies of God as ministers, the denomination reaffirmed its opinion that women could not be ordained as ministers. In 1935, the General Council voted to accept women as elders, though, in most cases, women act as co-pastors with their husbands, not as sole pastors.

In the late 1940s, tensions emerged within the Assemblies of God as critics challenged its organizational structure. The "latter rain" movement claimed that the organized Pentecostal movement had died because of its acquiescence to worldly concerns and its loss of spontaneity and spiritual gifts. A more substantial challenge to the Assemblies of God came from the popular healing revivalism. This movement forced the denomination to reexamine and affirm its commitment to the spiritual gift of healing, thereby helping ministers, such as Oral Roberts, to gain notoriety.

In the 1960s, the Assemblies of God was drawn into regular conflicts with American culture. They attacked the World and NATIONAL COUNCIL OF CHURCHES for their work on ecumenism, which they viewed as a rejection of Christianity. Their opposition to ecumenism included distrust of the ROMAN CATHOLIC CHURCH and opposition to the election of the nation's first Catholic president, JOHN F. KENNEDY. In the 1970s, the Assemblies of God renewed their belief that homosexuality is a sin. However, they did accept remarriage in the 1973 "Statement on Divorce and Remarriage." The conflict between culture and the church was also present in the denomination's initial support for and later rejection of the TELEVANGELISM of Jim Bakker and JIMMY SWAGGART after they became involved in sex scandals.

In the 1980s, the Assemblies of God became part of the Religious Right's entrance into politics. The unsuccessful candidacy of Marion "PAT" ROBERTSON for the Republican presidential nomination drew support from Assemblies of God members. In one study, 89 percent of Assemblies of God ministers identified with the Republican Party, and 98 percent voted for George H. W. Bush for president in the 1988 election. Assemblies support for Republicans stems from its conservative religious and political views on social issues, particularly on ABORTION, though at one time Pentecostals had a more natural fit in the Democratic Party in the South because of a lower socioeconomic status, which is now less evident. To confirm this shift pivoting around social issues, the General Council of the Assemblies of God passed a resolution in 1989 supporting CIVIL DISOBEDIENCE in the fight to end abortion.

See also RELIGION IN THE 1988 PRESIDENTIAL ELECTION; SOUTHERN REPUBLICAN REALIGNMENT.

Further reading: Blumhofer, Edith Waldvogel. *Restoring the Faith: The Assemblies of God, Pentecostalism, and American Culture.* Urbana: University of Illinois Press, 1993; Guth, James L., John C. Green, Corwin E. Smidt, Lyman A. Kellstedt, and Margaret M. Poloma. *The Bully Pulpit: The Politics of Protestant Clergy.* Lawrence: University Press of Kansas, 1997; Poloma, Margaret M. *The Assemblies of God at the Crossroads: Charisma and Institutional Dilemmas.* Knoxville: University of Tennessee Press, 1989.

—Jean L. McSween

Association of Catholic Conscientious Objectors

A ROMAN CATHOLIC CHURCH organization that supported Catholic CONSCIENTIOUS OBJECTORS during World War II, the Association of Catholic Conscientious Objectors (ACCO) was founded in 1940 and headquartered at DOROTHY DAY's Catholic Worker organization building on Mott Street in New York City. By April 1941, the ACCO had received over 400 claims for conscientious objection. The ACCO affiliated with the National Service Board for Religious Objectors (NSBRO) to support Catholic conscientious objectors (COs) who chose Civilian Public Service (CPS) camps as an alternative to military service. The ACCO published a quarterly newspaper, the *Catholic CO,* from January 1944 until June 1948. Although the number of Catholic COs was never large, the ACCO was the only Catholic organization to provide them assistance.

During World War II, PAX, a pacifist branch of the CATHOLIC WORKER MOVEMENT, endeavored to form a permanent group of Catholic COs that would offer mutual assistance and promote a Catholic pacifist tradition. In its monthly column in the *Catholic Worker,* PAX included the 1938 pastoral letter of the only U.S. bishop to urge Catholic conscientious objection, Archbishop John T. McNicholas of Cincinnati ("A Mighty League of COs"). After Dorothy Day was reprimanded by local church officials for the inclusion of a PAX notice in the *Catholic Worker* urging noncompliance with the draft, PAX changed its name to ACCO, and William Callahan and Arthur Sheehan assumed leadership.

With the NSBRO, the ACCO ran a CPS camp for Catholic COs in Stoddard, New Hampshire, beginning in August 1941. When the facility was outgrown in the autumn of 1942, a second, larger camp, in Warner, New Hampshire, was opened and operated until March 17, 1943. But, unlike COs from the Protestant Peace Churches, Catholic COs did not receive financial support from their church. Instead, Catholic COs supported themselves with some assistance from the ACCO. The conditions for Catholic COs in these camps were severe. After the Warner, New Hampshire, CPS camp closed, Catholic COs were permitted to accept alternative service in hospitals, asylums, and training schools. In 1945 the ACCO withdrew from the NSBRO and repudiated their participation in the CPS camps as cooperation with the military establishment and a form of slave labor and imprisonment. The NSBRO also repudiated the CPS camp model on similar grounds.

The ACCO, through the efforts of Arthur Sheehan, also provided support services to Catholic COs in prison. The NSBRO counted 61 Catholics imprisoned for noncompliance with the draft; the largest number, 18, were imprisoned at Danbury Federal Prison in Connecticut.

The ACCO's quarterly publication, the *Catholic CO,* was edited by William Strube, Richard Lion, Gordon Zahn, Ray Pierchalski, and Robert Ludlow, all of whom were COs. Funds raised supported the newspaper and Catholic COs in CPS camps. During its existence, the *Catholic CO* took over the peace writings and news of the *Catholic Worker.* With the end of publication in 1948 and the close of the CPS camps, the ACCO ceased to exist.

The U.S. Roman Catholic Church hierarchy has never denied the right of individual conscientious objection to war.

However, neither has there been much support for such a position. Among other reasons, the U.S. Catholic Church has historically been careful to show the patriotism of a largely immigrant church. Catholic COs have never been significant in number. Fewer than five were counted as COs during World War I; up to 200 were counted during World War II. But at VATICAN II, conscientious objection was upheld as a right and duty of individual conscience, and Catholic COs to the VIETNAM WAR numbered nearly 2,500.

The Catholic Worker, PAX, and ACCO were the first organizations associated with the U.S. Catholic Church to develop a judgment against war without using the just-war tradition. Writing for the *Catholic Worker* in 1935, the Rev. Paul Hanley Furfey, a priest and educator from the Catholic University of America, used the gospel counsel of perfection and the precedents of the Christian's duty to God's kingdom over the state as the basis for an antiwar stance. Among the contributions of the ACCO and the Catholic Worker was the introduction of this Christian pacifist stance to Catholic thought that has largely defined the American Catholic peace movement since.

See also JUST WAR; NATIONAL CATHOLIC WAR COUNCIL/NATIONAL CATHOLIC WELFARE CONFERENCE; PACIFISM.

Further reading: McNeal, Patricia. *Harder than War: Catholic Peacemaking in Twentieth-Century America.* New Brunswick, N.J.: Rutgers University Press, 1992; Piehl, Mel. *Breaking Bread: The Catholic Worker and the Origin of Catholic Radicalism in America.* Philadelphia: Temple University Press, 1982.

—Susan Gleason Anderson

atheism

The word *atheism* is a transliteration of the Greek word *atheos* (without god). In the strictest sense, atheism is a disbelief in the existence of God or any other deity. There are two kinds of atheists, however, each type a reflection of the reasons for rejecting theism. An individual who believes that "God does not exist" is referred to as a positive atheist, or in popular usage, just atheist. A person who believes there is no reason to accept as true the existence of God or gods is a negative atheist (often called an agnostic).

Atheists justify their rejection of theism in different ways. For example, contemporary American philosopher Theodore Drange (b. 1934) bases his rejection of the existence of God on the "Argument of Non-Belief," which asserts that because there is a large amount of non-belief in the world, the existence of God is improbable.

Other atheists reject the existence of God because of the "problem of evil." Positive atheists argue that theism does not provide convincing arguments for why suffering affects innocent beings, such as children and animals. Charles Darwin (1809–82) illustrates this argument well when he rejects God on grounds that nature is inherently cruel. According to these atheists, a better explanation for evil is that God does not exist.

From a sociological perspective, Ludwig Feuerbach (1800–34) argued that ideas about God are simply projections of human ideas about humanity onto an imaginary supernatural being. Similarly, Émile Durkheim (1858–1917) suggested that religion is a product of human society and is instrumental in providing meaning to group members and reinforcing moral codes.

More recently, George Smith (b. 1949) argues that since "the concept of god is unknowable," belief in a supernatural god is irrational. Similarly, Michael Martin (b. 1932) says that negative atheism is justified, since "religious language is unverifiable and hence factually meaningless."

Atheism is not a comprehensive worldview or philosophy but, rather, simply a negation of theism. Indeed, atheists are a diverse group in terms of philosophical beliefs. For example, atheism has often been associated with MARXISM, which argues that religion encumbers human progress; materialism, which asserts that only what can be seen truly exists; and rationalism, which claims that logical reasoning, as opposed to other sources of information, is the primary way that knowledge is acquired. There are no necessary connections, however, between atheism and these philosophies. For instance, René Descartes (1596–1650), a rationalist, believed in God, whereas, Jean-Paul Sartre, (1905–80), an existentialist, was an atheist. Even within a philosophical school, adherents often maintain opposing views concerning atheism: British analytic philosopher A.J. Ayer (1910–89) and Danish philosopher Søoren Kierkegaard (1813–55) were both existentialists. Yet, the former was an atheist, while the latter believed in God.

One of the most visible and politically active atheists of the 20th century was Madalyne Murray O'Hair (1919–95), whose efforts influenced the 1963 Supreme Court decision (*MURRAY V. CURTLETT*), which declared mandatory prayer and Bible reading in school classrooms unconstitutional. Bolstered by her success in removing religious practices from schools, Murray O'Hair founded American Atheists Inc., which currently claims 45,000 members, is affiliated with American Atheist Women (AAW) and United World Atheists (UWA), and publishes *American Atheist Newsletter.* The expressed goals of American Atheists Inc. are to secure freedom from religion, advance SEPARATION OF CHURCH AND STATE, and protect the civil liberties of atheists in America.

Estimates of the number of atheists in America are unreliable at best. A massive survey by the City University of New York estimates that 902,000 (0.4 percent) Americans identify themselves as atheist, while American Atheists Inc. claims there are 25,000,000 atheists in America. A survey by Angus Reid Group in 1996 finds that 1.0 percent of Americans are atheist, while Andrew Kohut finds that 0.4 percent of Americans claim to be atheist. One consideration when interpreting these data is that many atheists identify themselves as humanists, free thinkers, or persons of no religion. If atheists, agnostics, and other nonreligious individuals are considered as one group, then in 2001 nonreligious persons comprised over 14 percent of the population, an increase of 6 percent from 1990.

Despite the growing number of nonreligious people in America, and the relative success of American Atheists Inc. in championing political causes, organized atheism remains a very small and disorganized movement. Obviously, this limits the political influence of atheists. If atheists desire an increased role in American politics, mobilizing nonreligious individuals must be a priority. Given the ideological and political diversity of atheists, this is admittedly a difficult task. Still, issues dealing with church-state separation and civil rights are possible areas of connection.

Further reading: Martin, Michael. *Atheism.* Philadelphia: Temple University Press, 1990; Smith, George H. *Atheism, The Case Against God.* New York: Prometheus Books, 1989.

—Franklyn C. Niles

B

Ba'al Shem Tov, Israel (1698–1760) *rabbi*

Israel Ba'al Shem Tov (The Master of the Good Name) was born Israel ben Eliezer. His early life is shrouded in uncertain information, including his place of birth. Some accounts place his birth in western Ukraine, while others place it in Galicia in southern Poland or Romania. There is even debate concerning his date of birth, which some contend was 1700 rather than 1698. What is not in doubt is that Rabbi Israel Ba'al Shem Tov is responsible for one of the most important religious and therefore political movements in Jewish history, Hasidism, or HASIDIC JUDAISM. In spite of its decimation during the HOLOCAUST, the movement rejuvenated itself and exerts significant political clout for its interests in both the United States and Israel.

In the 19th century, especially in Ashkenazi eastern Europe, the Hasidic movement resulted in significant sociological and cultural changes in Jewish life. From a sociological perspective, the Hasidic movement resulted in greater religious equality among different classes of Jews. Further, from a theological perspective, Hasidism placed greater emphasis on the emotion or heart as the source of piety than on the mind.

It is generally accepted that Israel Ba'al Shem Tov was born in Okop, a small village in the Ukraine on the Polish border. His parents, Eliezer and Sarah, who had him late in life, died early, leaving him an orphan under community care. During his youth and through his teenage years, he developed a strong emotional relationship with God that, in later years, became the central defining characteristic of Hasidism.

When the community's responsibility for him ended, he was provided a job as a teacher's assistant (*bahlefer*), after which he became the caretaker of the local synagogue. While a caretaker, he had the opportunity to study and attain a remarkable level of knowledge of the complete Jewish works, including the mysteries of the Kabbalah, the book of Jewish mysticism. During this time, he maintained a simple life, and his fellow Jews of the town were unaware of his achievements.

He emerged from obscurity in 1736 when he became well known as a mystical healer and attained the name of Ba'al Shem Tov. The itinerant mystics were known as *baal shem* as

they plied their trade in invoking a holy prescription in the process of healing. Although this is how Israel Ba'al Shem Tov began his career, he did not practice it long, but the name remained. During his lifetime, he produced very little in the way of literary works. Rather, most of his ideas were made available through the writings of his many disciples. Ba'al Shem Tov's foremost disciple, Rabbi Yakov Yosef of Polonoye, was the author of the first Hasidic work ever published, *Toldot Yakov Yosef,* which is now the main source for our knowledge of the ideas of the Ba'al Shem Tov. He returned Jewish mysticism and mystical works, the Kabbalah and the Zohar, to a central place in Jewish theology.

There are three basic doctrines that the Ba'al Shem elucidated that are central to Hasidism. First, the source of piety is the heart, or emotion, rather than the mind. Second, God is everywhere and immediately present. Finally, the goal of piety and the religious experience was to achieve oneness with the almighty. This perspective seeks a unity with God rather than an analytic relationship with him. According to the Ba'al Shem Tov, the only way to approach God is through joyous experience. Music and song thus became a central part of Hasidic prayers.

Hasidism grew significantly in eastern Europe's Jewish community predominantly because it created class equity across the religion. Most of eastern European Jewry lived a subsistence life and were generally uneducated. Therefore, Hasidism, with its emphasis on emotion, presence, and oneness, was equally available to all, irrespective of education or wealth. It reemphasized the equality of the Jew's relationship with God.

Although the followers of Israel Ba'al Shem Tov grew in number slowly during his tenure on earth, by the turn of the century, Hasidism was the most influential force in Jewry in terms of new cultural, literary, and social developments. The movement swept eastern European Jewish communities and included many branches, depending on the particular rebbe, or learned leader, that the group followed. With the Holocaust, though, practically all traces of Hasidism in Europe were destroyed. Since the Holocaust, a renewal of Hasidic communities has occurred in both America and Israel. In both countries the Hasidic rebbes have tremendous political influence in excess of their small overall numbers. Their influence resides in New York State and large metropolitan areas in the United States where they can produce a significant turnout and provide political resources for elections. In Israeli elections, the Hasidic block supports the religious parties that have gained significant representation in the Knesset (parliament).

—Maurice M. Eisenstein

Bakker, Jim (1941–   ) *televangelist* and
Bakker, Tammy Faye (1942–   ) *televangelist*
Jim (born in Muskegon, Michigan) and Tammy Faye Bakker (born in International Falls, Minnesota) were household names in the Christian television world during the early to mid-1980s. After marrying in 1961, they spent the next five years preaching in several cities around the United States. By 1966, they had been introduced to PAT ROBERTSON, who was in the midst of trying to launch the CHRISTIAN BROADCASTING NETWORK (CBN). At Robertson's request, they moved to Portsmouth, Virginia, where Jim and Tammy Faye launched and hosted the new Christian talk show, *The 700 Club*. The show became immensely popular and was the seed that allowed CBN to grow into the most influential Christian network in the world today.

Later, in 1973, the Bakkers cofounded the Trinity Broadcasting Network with Jan and Paul Crouch. One year later, they started the *Praise the Lord* (PTL) show, which debuted on their own separate Christian television network, called Inspirational Network. Soon, with donations from their rock-solid audience, they were able to finance a 2,300-acre Christian theme park, Heritage USA. Located in Fort Hill, South Carolina, this ministry empire required at its zenith approximately a half-million dollars per day in donations to operate. Based on the Bakkers' grasp and implementation of the prosperity message so popularized by other televangelists such as ORAL ROBERTS, JIMMY SWAGGART, and the now-defunct Texas-based preacher Robert Tilton, they were able to persuade millions of donors to contribute to their ministry media empire.

In 1987, however, amid allegations—which later turned out to be true—of a sexual tryst in 1980 between Jim Bakker and Jessica Hahn, his then-21-year-old personal secretary at Heritage USA, and his later confession of having paid $265,000 to Hahn to keep quiet, the Bakkers' rise to spiritual fame was soon to crash.

The ASSEMBLIES OF GOD pulled his ordination as a direct reaction to his sexual encounter with Hahn. And by 1989, after a relatively short (six-week) trial and conviction, he was sentenced to 45 years (although the sentence was reduced to six years) for fraudulently overselling time shares at Heritage USA's hotels and for taking nearly $4 million of the $158 million he bilked from his followers to support the lavish lifestyle he led with Tammy Faye.

In 1992, after a 31-year marriage, Tammy Faye served divorce papers on Jim while he was still in prison. In his recent "tell all" book, *I Was Wrong* (1996), Jim Bakker profusely apologized to those he offended. Even though Bakker believes that the PTL ministry was stolen from him and Tammy Faye, in the end he blames himself for his demise. He notes in his book: "Had I simply stopped long enough to think, to seek God's direction, to surround myself with a group of wise counselors as the Bible instructs, I would not have allowed a group of men, many of whom I barely knew, to take the reins of PTL." He contends he is innocent of fraud, but he does admit to being cocky and foolish concerning his lifestyle and poor business practices.

Tammy Faye married Jim's former business partner, Roe Messner, in 1993. Shortly after their marriage, Messner was convicted and imprisoned of bankruptcy fraud, but he has since been released. They then moved from California to Charlotte, North Carolina. In 1996 Tammy Faye teamed with Jim J. Bullock, the former star of *Too Close for Comfort*, to host a short-lived daily talk show titled *The Jim J. and Tammy Faye Show*. That same year she published an autobiography, *Tammy: Telling It My Way*. Most recently, in 2000, she was the subject of a well-received documentary titled *The Eyes of Tammy Faye*. It chronicles her own rise and her rise with Jim to fame in the televangelism world.

After being released from prison in 1994, Jim Bakker moved to a remote North Carolina farm. In 1996 he published his *I Was Wrong* biography, where he chronicled his rise to fame, then his descent to poverty and imprisonment. While in prison, where he was assigned menial clean-up tasks, he lost his sanity, dignity, and even confidence in his faith. Eventually, of course, he also lost his wife. Asked why he wrote the memoir, he said in a recent interview, "I owed it to my children, my grandchildren, and the people who supported and watched me for twenty-five years. I want them to understand what I learned in prison, that my previous philosophy of life was flawed."

By 1998, after being given permission by his parole board to travel, Bakker began speaking at selected sites around the country, including the Dream Center, a large, former hospital complex associated with the Los Angeles International Church, located in the inner-city neighborhood of Echo Park. He met his future wife, Lori Beth Graham, at Dream Center. They now travel the country preaching and living a message of forgiveness and God's grace. In addition, they have opened a center called Morning House, a refuge where ministers may receive spiritual healing.

See also TELEVANGELISM.

—Stephen M. King

Baptist Joint Committee on Public Affairs

The Baptist Joint Committee on Public Affairs (BJC) is a denominational advocacy agency headquartered in Washington, D.C., that represents and is supported by 14 separate Baptist organizations. The BJC was formed in 1945 as the result of the collective recognition among the AMERICAN BAPTIST CHURCH, the NATIONAL BAPTIST CONVENTION, U.S.A., the National Baptist Convention of America, and the SOUTHERN BAPTIST CONVENTION out of their belief that there was a need for a stronger Baptist voice in American public affairs. However, the BJC's perceived liberal politics caused one of its founding institutions, the more conservative Southern Baptist Convention, to withdraw its support for the agency in 1992.

The BJC is a staunch defender of religious liberty, and it engages in political and legal activities to protect the rights of all persons in the free exercise of their religious beliefs. Its political activities include lobbying members of Congress on legislation involving religious issues and participating in ecumenical coalitions formed for the advocacy of religious liberty, human rights, and other causes. The BJC's legal activities include the filing of AMICUS CURIAE BRIEFS and the provision of other legal services in cases involving questions of religious freedom and often concerning the religion clauses of the FIRST AMENDMENT. A critical phrase from the BJC's mission statement emphasizes its commitment "to defend and extend God-given religious liberty for all, bringing a uniquely Baptist witness to the principle that religion must be freely exercised, neither advanced nor inhibited by government."

The BJC publishes a biweekly newsletter, "Report from the Capital," to apprise constituents of its activities, to alert them to pending legislation and legal cases, and to call particular attention to threats to the American tradition of religious liberty.

See also MAINLINE PROTESTANT WASHINGTON OFFICES.

—Derek H. Davis

Barth, Karl (1886–1968) *theologian*

Karl Barth was born in Basel, Switzerland, on May 10, 1886, and died on December 10, 1968. Until Hitler's rise to power, Barth held appointments successively at universities in Göttingen, Münster, and Bonn. His refusal to take the oath of loyalty to Hitler and employ the Nazi salute in classes led to his dismissal in 1935. He returned to his homeland and became professor of theology at the University of Basel. His career began in the pastorate, however, and the church was always the setting for his reflections. Many, if not most, would agree that Barth was one of the two most influential theologians of the 20th century, along with PAUL TILLICH.

The centerpiece of his theology is the claim that God is God's own witness and alone creates the possibility of knowing the deity. Knowledge of God comes from God and is on God's terms. Nothing in or of this world serves as a preparation for faith or a wedge in support of it. Knowledge of God begins in what he called "the divine ingression." Neither erudition nor intuition is a lever upon the divine reality. Self-disclosure, not human discovering, is the basis of revelation. Barth was determined that secularity not invade the theologian's articulation of the faith. After the publication of the first volume of his monumental *Church Dogmatics*, he detected an unsavory

dependency on an existentialist philosopher. Barth repudiated his own work and created a new volume that was to become the first of 16.

Part of what triggered this stern resolve to protect the purity of the faith was the failure of the liberal theology in which he had been schooled to stand up to the state. In August 1914, 93 German intellectuals came out in support of the war policies of Wilhelm II. Among them were virtually all his esteemed teachers. From that point on, Karl Barth resolved to explain the Christian faith on its own terms and resist the intrusion of secular agendas.

Given the priority of the knowledge of God from God, it is not surprising that every doctrine is conceived through the prism of Christ and is grounded in what God did in that event. Through Christ the universe is created, the reality of God is disclosed, and the purpose and promises of God for humankind are made evident. God declares himself for sinful man and sinful man for Godself through Christ. In a sense, God works both sides of the aisle. We are elected by God in Christ and through Christ our response is generated. For Barth, Christ was with God from the beginning, including the decision to create. And we are turned toward God through the work of God in Christ. We have no capacity for God. At the very least, this is a radical Christology.

Some would argue that Barth's theology is apolitical. While he made a political statement in refusing loyalty to Hitler, his retreat to Switzerland was seen as searching for a safe haven for his scholarly work, far removed from the torturous situation of the German people. But Barth in effect claimed that theological affirmations were political statements. A true statement of faith unmasks the world as world and its sinful ways. Barth was instrumental in creating the Barmen Confession for the church, and critics landed directly on the absence of explicit political references. But Karl Barth believed that an affirmation of the Lordship of Jesus Christ directly intercepted the claim of Hitler. If Jesus is Lord, Hitler is not. Hence, we are thrown into a situation of crisis; the crisis is now the human pretension revealed by divine disclosure. His entire theological project was a critique of totalitarianism.

In all of this, Scripture is central and the Word of God is defining. His career began with *The Epistle to the Romans* (1933), a commentary written while he was in a Swiss parish. It was said to land on the theological scene like a bomb. Its effect was to call the theological and ecclesiastical community back to the text on its own terms. And it taught a generation to listen for the Word God delivers without the apparatuses of the age intruding their ideologies upon it.

Karl Barth may be rejected in times to come, but he will be forgotten at the peril of theological legitimacy.

Further reading: Barth, Karl. *A Shorter Commentary on Romans*. Richmond, Va.: John Knox Press, 1960; ———. *The Humanity of God*. Richmond, Va.: John Knox Press, 1960; ———. *Church Dogmatics—A Selection*. Edinburgh: T. & T.

Clark, 1961; ———. *Evangelical Theology: An Introduction.*
New York: Holt, Rinehart and Winston, 1963.

—David O. Woodyard

Bauer, Gary (1946–) *conservative activist*

Born in Newport, Kentucky, Gary Bauer is best known for
serving as president of the FAMILY RESEARCH COUNCIL, a conservative, pro-family lobbying organization and think tank
based in Washington, D.C. Bauer has been politically active
most of his adult life, serving eight years in the administration
of RONALD REAGAN, and more recently, undertaking a failed
run for the Republican presidential nomination in 2000. Bauer
is a politically conservative Baptist with strong commitments
to preserving the traditional family and the Judeo-Christian
values he believes are the foundation of American society.

Bauer graduated from Georgetown Law School in 1973
and later went on to spend nearly eight years in various posts
under President Reagan. Bauer served as a domestic policy
adviser, eventually becoming the director of the White House's
Office of Policy Development. In 1988, he resigned his position in the Reagan administration to become president of the
Family Research Council. There, he became extremely influential as one of the most outspoken representatives in Washington of conservative Evangelical Protestants. Under Bauer,
the Family Research Council became a powerful fund-raising
force and began its own political action committee, the Campaign for Working Families. This PAC has since raised millions of dollars to support political candidates who share its
commitment to a morally conservative policy agenda. Though
the Family Research Council and the Republican Party were
natural allies, Bauer did not hesitate to criticize the Republican
Party when he believed it was compromising on issues like
PRAYER IN PUBLIC SCHOOLS and ABORTION for the sake of
political success. Bauer preferred a confrontational strategy
toward the party, and on this issue, he and his counterpart at
the Christian Coalition, Executive Director RALPH REED, disagreed. Whereas Reed believed they would be more successful
in promoting Christian values in government and public policy
by cooperating with the Republicans, Bauer felt that the
Republicans needed to be taken to task over what he and many
other evangelicals saw as a failure by the Republicans to remain
loyal to conservative Christian values.

In 1999, Bauer took a leave from his position at the Family Research Council to campaign for the 2000 Republican
presidential nomination. Against the advice of many who
thought his campaign would be a sure failure, he decided to
pursue it anyway. He dropped out of the race early in March
2000, but not before establishing his influence and angering
many of his supporters and friends, particularly those at the
Family Research Council. When Bauer withdrew from the
race, he publicly endorsed Arizona senator John McCain, a
moderate Republican. Most of his fellow Christian conservatives were lending their support to then-governor GEORGE W.
BUSH, whose views were closer to their own and who appeared
to have the best chance of winning the Republican nomination
and the presidency. During the Republican primary campaign,
McCain had made disparaging remarks about JERRY FALWELL
and PAT ROBERTSON, both of whom were quite influential in
conservative Christian circles. Hence, Bauer's endorsement
was seen as both politically unwise and morally offensive.

Even though his endorsement of Senator McCain left
Bauer with far less support than he had enjoyed before entering the presidential race, Bauer has stood by his decision. He
has not returned to the Family Research Council but remains
based in Washington, working on issues that are important to
him, in particular, strengthening the traditional family and
advocating greater restrictions on abortion. Since his departure
from the Family Research Council, he has been a frequent
public speaker and talk-show guest. He also continues to write;
his best-known early work, *Children at Risk: The Battle for the
Hearts and Minds of Our Kids*, was coauthored with his friend
and mentor, JAMES DOBSON of FOCUS ON THE FAMILY.

See also CHRISTIAN RIGHT AND THE REPUBLICAN PARTY.

Further reading: Fowler, Robert Booth, Allen D. Hertzke,
and Laura R. Olson. *Religion and Politics in America: Faith,
Culture, and Strategic Choices.* Boulder, Colo.: Westview
Press, 1999; Hofrenning, Daniel J.B. *In Washington but Not of
It: The Prophetic Politics of Religious Lobbyists.* Philadelphia:
Temple University Press, 1995.

—Andrea E. Moore

Bernardin, Joseph Cardinal (1928–1996) *Roman Catholic cardinal*

Born in Columbia, South Carolina, Joseph Bernardin, the son
of Italian immigrants, was ordained a ROMAN CATHOLIC
CHURCH priest in 1952 and a bishop in 1996. He served as an
auxiliary in Atlanta until 1972, when he was named archbishop
of Cincinnati. In 1982 Bernardin became archbishop of
Chicago, and in 1983 was named a cardinal.

In 1968, Bernardin was recruited by Archbishop John
Dearden to serve as general secretary (or chief operating
officer) for the NATIONAL CONFERENCE OF CATHOLIC BISH-
OPS (NCCB) and its administrative arm, the UNITED STATES
CATHOLIC CONFERENCE (USCC). Dearden was the NCCB's
first president; the organization was successor to the
NATIONAL CATHOLIC WAR COUNCIL. These groups had coordinated Catholic services in response to World Wars I and
II. They were also known for progressive public policy proposals that were paralleled in President FRANKLIN DELANO
ROOSEVELT's New Deal. Nevertheless, they were voluntary
organizations; not all bishops took part. After VATICAN II, the
NCCB was to be the official forum where American bishops cooperated on matters of importance to the entire
nation.

At the NCCB, Bernardin gained experience in the national
church and developed a reputation for promoting cooperation
and reconciliation among diverse people. Organizing the bish-

ops to collaborate was a challenge. Structures had to be developed to facilitate communication and implementation of their goals; at a more basic level, bishops needed to be reeducated to think of themselves as a group that should function collegially, not simply as individuals in their own jurisdictions. One of the first political projects under Bernardin's administration was the Campaign for Human Development, launched in 1970. This collection funded secular and religious groups that redress systemic causes of poverty and empower disadvantaged people to help themselves. Bernardin was elected NCCB/USCC president from 1974 to 1977; he also served as chair of the committee responsible for an important statement on U.S. military policy, *The Challenge of Peace* (1983) and chair of the conference's pro-life committee (1983–89).

In these posts and at the diocesan level, Bernardin cultivated an enriched understanding of the teaching role of bishops. As moral teachers, both individually and collectively, they should be pastorally sensitive and politically well informed. This would enhance credibility within their church and among wider audiences, especially on divisive issues such as nuclear weaponry and ABORTION. To this end, one tool not customary for bishops of a prior generation but that became a hallmark of Bernardin and the NCCB/USCC was the consultation process. For instance, in preparation for *The Challenge of Peace,* testimony was sought from Catholic and non-Catholic experts, ranging from peace activists to military chaplains to current and former U.S. secretaries of defense. Bernardin used speaking engagements with groups such as the American Bar Association and the National Press Club to clarify proper understanding of the First Amendment of the U.S. Constitution. Employing the thought of theologian John Courtney Murray, Bernardin said the amendment creates a nation where church and state are institutionally separate, but where religious individuals or groups are free to share beliefs on political matters. Bernardin agreed with Murray that in a pluralistic culture, religious people must articulate their concerns not only with religious language but also with arguments that could be persuasive to secular audiences. Bernardin modeled this approach in formulating the CONSISTENT ETHIC OF LIFE, which advocates respect for human dignity from conception to natural death. In speeches on the consistent life ethic and in *The Challenge of Peace*, Bernardin articulated an important distinction relevant to bishops' teaching role. The bishops expected agreement at the level of general moral principles and church teaching, but when it came to practical application of these truths, it was recognized that persons of good conscience could disagree on the most prudent strategies. Bernardin thought that in most cases, open consultation could broker consensus among constituencies who considered themselves ideologically and politically divided.

On September 9, 1996, shortly before his death from cancer, Bernardin received the Presidential Medal of Freedom from President WILLIAM JEFFERSON CLINTON. His trip to receive the award was coupled with a Capitol Hill protest of Clinton's veto of legislation restricting partial-birth abortion. In his final days, Bernardin submitted a letter to the Supreme Court, which was soon scheduled to hear cases involving EUTHANASIA. Bernardin distinguished the right to forgo medical treatment from deliberate suicide. He wrote, "Creating a new right to assisted suicide would endanger society and send a false signal that a less than 'perfect' life is not worth living."

See also CATHOLIC BISHOPS IN AMERICAN POLITICS; CATHOLIC BISHOPS' 1975 PASTORAL LETTER ON ABORTION; CATHOLIC BISHOPS' 1986 PASTORAL LETTER ON THE ECONOMY; CATHOLIC BISHOPS' 1983 PASTORAL LETTER ON WAR AND PEACE.

Further reading: Kennedy, Eugene. *Cardinal Bernardin.* Chicago: Bonus, 1989.

—Florence Caffrey Bourg

Bill of Rights

The first 10 amendments to the U.S. Constitution are collectively known as the Bill of Rights. Largely the product of JAMES MADISON, the 10 amendments officially became part of the Constitution in 1791, after being approved by Congress in its initial session in 1789. Initially, 12 amendments were adopted by Congress and sent to the states for ratification or rejection; the first two amendments were not approved, thus leaving the 10 amendments as we know them today. Madison's speech in the U.S. House of Representatives on June 8, 1789, in which he argued persuasively for the insertion of a document to the Constitution that would protect "the great rights of mankind," still stands today as one of the most consequential speeches in the annals of Congress.

Within the Bill of Rights, the critical provisions concerning religion are contained in the first 16 words of the First Amendment: "Congress shall make no law respecting an establishment of religion, or prohibiting the free exercise thereof." These words mandate that the American political system in general and the judiciary more specifically address the nature and extent of the role of religion in American public life. While religion is in no way defined in these two clauses, the ESTABLISHMENT CLAUSE and the FREE EXERCISE CLAUSE, we do know that laws respecting religion's establishment are prohibited, as are laws precluding its free exercise.

The interpretation and application of the First Amendment's religion clauses has been the peculiar province of the judiciary, especially the U.S. Supreme Court, and particularly since roughly the midpoint of the 20th century. Although several cases concerning these clauses transpired in the 19th century, the effective "making sense" of the two clauses began in the 1940s, beginning with the case of CANTWELL V. CONNECTICUT in 1940. In *Cantwell,* the Supreme Court ruled for the first time that the Free Exercise Clause applied to the states as well as to the national government. However, for most of the rest of the 20th century, the primary work of the Court with the religion clauses centered on the Establishment

Clause, beginning with the case of *EVERSON V. BOARD OF EDUCATION OF EWING TOWNSHIP, NEW JERSEY.*

In *Everson* the Supreme Court incorporated or applied the Establishment Clause to the states for the first time. In so doing, the Court, through the majority opinion of Justice Hugo Black, constitutionalized THOMAS JEFFERSON's "wall of separation" metaphor as the animating principle of the Establishment Clause. According to Black, "In the words of Jefferson, the clause against establishment of religion by law was intended to erect a 'wall of separation' between church and state." Black continued in his opinion for a bitterly divided Court: "The First Amendment has erected a wall between church and state. That wall must be kept high and impregnable. We could not approve the slightest breach." However, in *Everson* the Court, in spite of its rhetoric, did permit what it considered "permissible" aid to be given to students attending parochial schools, thus unleashing the debate concerning the difference between permissible and impermissible aid—a debate that continues in American constitutional law and politics, as witnessed in the case of *MITCHELL V. HELMS.*

The bulk of the Court's work with respect to the Establishment Clause has dealt with state-sponsored or state-mandated religious exercises in public schools. For instance, in 1962, in *ENGEL V. VITALE,* the court, again in an opinion by Justice Black, struck down a New York State statute that required the reading of this generic prayer written by state officials: "Almighty God, we acknowledge our dependence upon Thee, and we beg Thy blessings upon us, our parents, our teachers, and our Country." The Court concluded that the Establishment Clause "must at least mean that in this country it is no part of the business of government to compose official prayers for any group of the American people to recite as part of a religious program carried on by government." Moreover, Justice Black wrote, the "first and most immediate purpose [of the Establishment Clause] rested on the belief that a union of government and religion tends to destroy government and degrade religion."

The Court's initial forays into trying to make sense of the Establishment Clause relied more on historical analysis than judicial precedent, such that as the Court's doctrines "matured" in the latter part of the 20th century, debates over the meaning and role of history became more prominent and sharper. The debate within the Court over the degree to which the meaning of the clause could be found in an accurate reading of history reflected as well the debate within the Court over the role of religion in American public life, and the manner in which religion should be kept separate or accommodated to reflect the reality of religious belief and practice in the United States. And with respect to religious belief and practice, in the 1960s and beyond the Court also began to try to make sense of the Free Exercise Clause, as witnessed by its work in cases such as *SHERBERT V. VERNER, WISCONSIN V. YODER, GOLDMAN V. WEINBERGER, EMPLOYMENT DIVISION V. SMITH,* and *LUKUMI BABALU AYE INC., CHURCH OF, V. CITY OF HIALEAH.* The Court's Free Exercise Clause jurisprudence today rests on the precedent of *Smith* from 1990, where Justice ANTONIN SCALIA, writing for the Court, concluded that if an otherwise valid law happens to burden the free exercise of religion, there is no violation of the First Amendment unless the law specifically targets a certain religious group or faith.

See also FOURTEENTH AMENDMENT AND THE INCORPORATION DOCTRINE.

Further reading: Amar, Akhil. *The Bill of Rights.* New Haven, Conn.: Yale University Press, 1998; Witte, John Jr. *Religion and the American Constitutional Experiment: Essential Rights and Liberties.* Boulder, Colo.: Westview Press, 2000.
—Stephen K. Shaw

Black Church in the African American Experience, The (1990) By C. Eric Lincoln and Lawrence H. Mamiya. Durham, N.C.: Duke University Press

This book is a significant contribution to the literature on the black church in America. Lincoln and Mamiya provide a wide-ranging study of the churches and clergy that the seven major historic black denominations comprise: the AFRICAN METHODIST EPISCOPAL (A.M.E.) CHURCH; the AFRICAN METHODIST EPISCOPAL (A.M.E.) ZION CHURCH; the CHRISTIAN METHODIST EPISCOPAL (C.M.E.) CHURCH; the NATIONAL BAPTIST CONVENTION, U.S.A., Incorporated (NBC); the National Baptist Convention of America, Unincorporated (NBCA); the Progressive National Baptist Convention (PNBC); and the CHURCH OF GOD IN CHRIST (COGIC). The authors acknowledge that the black church in America has long been recognized as the most independent, stable, and dominant institution within the black community. They combine historical overview, sociological description, comparative analysis, and cultural understanding as tools for interpreting the black church and the black religious experience.

In their analysis, Lincoln and Mamiya advance with the basic premise that black religion, whatever its distinctive expressions, is significantly part and parcel of the American experience in religion. As the black church became the institutional heart of the black community, cultural heritage, affirmation of faith—and social activism—would have profound implications for the preservation of black culture. The impact of the black church on the spiritual, social, economic, educational, and political interests that structure life in America is examined in this 13-chapter, 10-year study. The authors interviewed more than 1,800 black clergy in both urban and rural settings to examine the contextual structure of the black church and the black religious experience. According to Lincoln and Mamiya, much of black culture is heavily indebted to the black religious tradition, including most forms of black music, drama, literature, storytelling, and even humor.

Lincoln and Mamiya suggest that the potential power of the black church as a social institution has never been fully realized. The authors contend that black churches are the only stable and coherent institutions to emerge from slavery; they were not only dominant in their communities, but they also became the center of black culture. While the social processes of migration, urbanization, and differentiation have diminished aspects of this centrality and dominance, black churches have continued their interactions within the spheres of politics, economics, education, and culture so that only a partial differentiation has occurred.

Of all the book's contributions, the most significant may be its reassessment of Hart Nelsen and Anne Kusener Nelsen's *Black Church in the Sixties* (1975) interpretative schemes based on their work on the black church, which can be summarized as the "dialectical model" of the black church. The Nelsens maintain that black churches are institutions involved in a constant series of dialectical tensions. The dialectic holds polar opposites in tension, constantly shifting between the polarities in historical time. The dialectical model of the black church is helpful in explaining the pluralism and the plurality of views that exist in black churches and black communities.

For example, with regard to politics, the dialectical model of the black church is helpful in understanding the complexity of black churches, some of which are both conservative and radical at the same time. The dialectical model allows for a more objective analysis of black churches as social institutions because it takes into account a broader, more comprehensive perspective. This model moves beyond the simplistic positive or negative assessments of personal observation and places black churches along a dynamic continuum, allowing for the blend of politics, protest, and Christianity. According to Lincoln and Mamiya's reassessment, the task of the social analyst is to examine the social conditions of any particular black church, including the situation of its leadership and membership, to determine their major orientation in relation to any pair of dialectical polarities.

The theoretical assumptions made by the authors contribute to the scholarly dialogue regarding ways of interpreting the black church and the black religious experience. The religious dimension of black churches is found in the black sacred cosmos, a unique Afro-Christian worldview, which was forged among black people from both the African and the Euro-American traditions during the 18th and 19th centuries. The black sacred cosmos permeated all the social institutions and cultural traditions of black people. *The Black Church in the African American Experience* filled a large gap in the literature on the black church in America.

See also BLACK THEOLOGY.

Further reading: Nelsen, Hart, and Anne Kusener Nelsen. *Black Church in the Sixties.* Lexington: University of Kentucky Press, 1975.

—Boris E. Ricks

black theology

Black theology has theological, cultural, and political dimensions. Theologically, the majority of African Americans prac-

tice some form of PROTESTANTISM resulting from the spread of evangelical Christianity among free and enslaved blacks in the SECOND GREAT AWAKENING of the early 1800s. While white Southerners defended slavery as divinely ordained and viewed Christianity as a method of social control for producing obedient and passive slaves, enslaved blacks adopted and refashioned Christianity as a method of spiritual and social resistance in the "invisible institution" of underground slave religion.

This invisible institution of slave religion included Protestant, ROMAN CATHOLIC, ISLAMIC, and African folk practices unconnected to formal churches. The Old Testament appealed most strongly to black Protestants as they identified with the enslaved children of Israel who were to be delivered to freedom by a liberating God, and themes of exodus and deliverance resonated in the secret meetings, ceremonies, and the music of enslaved blacks. While the prayer meetings, shouts, and spirituals of black Protestants were foreign to black Catholics, Catholicism offered enslaved blacks the ritual use of sacred objects and devotion to saints that were modified and fused with African theology and rituals. Though fewer enslaved blacks were practitioners of Islam, the religion did survive the middle passage. Additionally, a rich tradition of folk belief and practice, including conjure, herbalism, and fortune-telling, flourished in the slave quarters.

While 15 to 20 percent of black religious affiliates are Roman Catholic and mainline Protestant, 80 percent of black religious affiliation is found in seven major black denominations representing Methodist, Baptist, and PENTECOSTAL faiths: the AFRICAN METHODIST EPISCOPAL (AME) CHURCH, founded in 1816; the AFRICAN METHODIST EPISCOPAL ZION (AMEZ), founded in 1821; the CHRISTIAN METHODIST EPISCOPAL (CME) CHURCH, founded in 1870; the NATIONAL BAPTIST CONVENTION, U.S.A., Incorporated (NBC), founded in 1895; the National Baptist Convention of America, Unincorporated (NBCA), founded in 1915; the Progressive National Baptist Convention (PNBC), founded in 1961; and the CHURCH OF GOD IN CHRIST (COGIC), founded in 1907. These denominations are organized in a coalition called the Congress of National Black Churches, and together they include roughly 60,000 black churches, 50,000 clergy, and a membership of about 17 million.

Also an important strand of black theology, Islam is the fastest-growing religion in the United States, with blacks making up 30 percent of affiliates and two-thirds of new converts. A uniquely black American version of Islam is the NATION OF ISLAM (NOI), founded by WALI D. FARD in 1931 and led by ELIJAH MUHAMMAD until his death in 1976. Brought to national attention in the 1960s by MALCOLM X, the NOI posits Christianity as a European religion and Islam as the true religion of blacks. After Muhammad's death, his son WARITH DEEN MUHAMMAD, influenced by Malcolm X's 1964 turn to traditional Islam, renamed it the African Muslim Mission (AMM), transformed it into an orthodox Islam organization, and encouraged a multiracial following, but eventually dissolved it in 1985. In

1977, a faction led by LOUIS FARRAKHAN revived the original name and teachings of the NOI. Currently the NOI has an estimated 20,000 members and millions more followers.

Given that "'freedom' has found deep religious resonance in the lives and hopes of African Americans," black theology is also politically important. First, as institutions controlled by black people, black churches allow ministers to acquire a degree of political power that was denied them in mainstream institutions. Many black elected officials from Reconstruction to the present exemplify the "preacher-politician" phenomenon, whereby ministers' status within black communities enables them to enter mainstream political institutions as social reformers.

Second, the combination of biblical prophesy, themes of the unity of humankind and of religious and political freedom, and criticism of American slavery and discrimination has produced the black jeremiad as a powerful source of social criticism and reform in the United States. From Frederick Douglass's abolitionist oratory to MARTIN LUTHER KING JR.'s "I Have a Dream" speech given at the MARCH ON WASHINGTON in 1963, the black jeremiad has long challenged the United States to live up to its self-professed vision of equality under the laws of God and humans.

Third, black churches serve as centers for political organization and mobilization. During slavery, the major revolts in the early 1800s were largely planned at secret meetings in black religious settings, and many black churches were stops on the Underground Railroad. During the CIVIL RIGHTS MOVEMENT of the 1950s and 1960s, black churches created the local movement centers within which blacks planned and organized nonviolent direct action. Many of these churches formed the PNBC in 1961 as a pro–civil rights alternative to the more conservative NBC. Black churches continue to anchor voter registration, fund-raising, and mobilization drives, as religiosity promotes high levels of POLITICAL PARTICIPATION among blacks.

Last, Christian and Islamic theology within black communities embody a self-help ethos, especially in the economic and social development of black communities. Historically, black churches created mutual aid–benefit societies and insurance companies, and established schools and universities. Black churches continue to promote small business creation, provide social services, and finance support for education.

See also ABOLITIONIST MOVEMENT; AFRICAN AMERICANS AND FAITH-BASED INITIATIVES; AFRICAN-AMERICAN VOTING BEHAVIOR SINCE THE CIVIL RIGHTS MOVEMENT; CONE, JAMES; LIBERATION THEOLOGY.

Further reading: Howard-Pitney, David. *The Afro-American Jeremiad*. Philadelphia: Temple University Press, 1990; Lincoln, C. Eric, and Lawrence Mamiya. *The Black Church in the African American Experience*. Durham, N.C.: Duke University Press, 1990; Raboteau, Albert. *Slave Religion*. New York: Oxford University Press, 1978.

—Gregory W. Streich

Bliss, William Dwight Porter (1856–1926) *activist*

Born in Turkey, the son of Congregational missionaries, William Dwight Porter Bliss attended Amherst College and Hartford Theological Seminary but pursed a journalistic vocation of social and political activism rather than the ministry. Founder of the Christian Socialist Society in 1889 and editor of its publication, *Dawn,* he went on to become editor of *American Fabian* and national lecturer for the Christian Social Union. In 1899 Bliss served as president of the National Social Reform Union, an alliance of America's most prominent progressive intellectuals and leaders that included George Herron, RICHARD ELY, JANE ADDAMS, Eugene Debs, Henry Demarest Lloyd, and Graham Taylor. He later was an investigator for the U.S. Department of Labor during THEODORE ROOSEVELT's presidency and then served on the staff of Josiah Strong's Institute of Social Service, a center for SOCIAL GOSPEL research and publication.

Bliss's greatest achievement was the manner in which he established institutional and intellectual linkages between American religion and social reform and between these American projects and those in Europe in his *New Encyclopedia of Social Reform* (1908). Successor to a less ambitious earlier version, this new edition was a compendium of "all social-reform movements and activities, and the economic, industrial, and sociological facts and statistics of all countries and all social subjects." The articles, statistical tables, reform organization listings and, especially, the biographies portray social reform as the common enterprise of the civilized world, flowing inexorably from the lives and thoughts of its most intellectually and morally advanced citizens. Article contributors to the *New Encyclopedia* are overwhelmingly American Progressives, with a sprinkling of British Fabians and Liberal members of Parliament and a few German Social Democrats and academics. American contributors include social workers Edward Devine and Florence Kelley, economists John R. Commons and Arthur Twining Hadley, sociologists Franklin Giddings and Charles Ellwood, labor leaders Samuel Gompers and Morris Hilquit, clergymen-reformers Graham Taylor and J. Cardinal Gibbons, and celebrity reformers and warhorses such as Booker T. Washington and William Lloyd Garrison. Billed also as "contributing," but only because their writings are extensively quoted, are Jane Addams, Richard Ely, Josiah Strong, Sidney Webb, and President Theodore Roosevelt.

Bliss's religious background and convictions permeated his writings, and his writings constituted an important source of the internationalist impulses that permeated Progressive political culture. The topic headings of the *New Encyclopedia,* for example, included "Christ and Social Reform," "Christian Socialism," "Christianity and Social Reform," and "Church and Social Reform" and rivaled in extent and scope such seemingly more central topics as "Child Labor" and "Factory Legislation." Indeed, the *New Encyclopedia* can be read as a handbook for a Social Gospel Internationale; encoded in its pages is a church invisible, headquartered in America but with powerful centers throughout the English-speaking world and in the advanced states in Europe, especially Germany. Its leading lights were academic social scientists and reform leaders whose ideas and spirit radiate throughout the hundreds of reform organizations, thousands of periodicals, books, and pamphlets, and millions of enthusiastic followers. America is the leading national actor, Bliss's *New Encyclopedia* seems to say, and its stage is the whole world.

See also ADAMS, HENRY CARTER; LIBERALISM; SOCIAL JUSTICE.

Further reading: Dombrowski, James. *The Early Days of Christian Socialism in America.* New York: Octagon Books, 1966; Eisenach, Eldon. "Progressive Internationalism." In *Progressivism and the New Democracy.* Edited by Sidney M. Milkis and Jerome M. Mileur. Amherst: University of Massachusetts Press, 1999.

—Eldon J. Eisenach

blue laws

Blue laws, or Sunday closing laws, are state and local laws that compel nonessential businesses to close on Sundays. Called blue laws because of the color of paper on which they were initially printed, these decrees date back to America's Colonial era. The laws originated as governments' express efforts to sanctify the Sabbath through legislation. State and local courts routinely upheld these laws throughout the 19th and early 20th centuries.

The First Amendment's Establishment Clause was first incorporated, or applied to states and localities, in *EVERSON V. BOARD OF EDUCATION* (1947). After *Everson,* the Supreme Court began to delineate the relationship between state laws and the ESTABLISHMENT CLAUSE, particularly in the realm of PRAYER IN PUBLIC SCHOOLS. The school prayer decisions (*ENGEL V. VITALE* [1962]; *ABINGTON TOWNSHIP SCHOOL DISTRICT V. SCHEMPP* and *MURRAY V. CURLETT* [1963]) from this era have garnered much publicity, but during this time the Court also ruled on the constitutionality of blue laws. Though the Court generally ruled that prayer in school was an unconstitutional establishment of religion at the state level, blue laws survived intact.

A pair of 1961 Supreme Court cases directly addressed the constitutionality of blue laws. In *MCGOWAN V. MARYLAND* (1961), Chief Justice Warren, writing for the majority, addressed the claim that blue laws were instituted by the legislature to encourage attendance of Christian worship services, thereby making them an unacceptable establishment of religion. Warren noted that "despite the strongly religious origin of these laws . . . nonreligious arguments for Sunday closing began to be heard more distinctly and the statutes began to lose some of their totally religious flavor." In fact, "proponents of Sunday closing legislation are no longer exclusively representatives of religious interests. Recent New Jersey Sunday legislation was supported by labor groups and trade associations." The Court's ruling in *McGowan* recognizes a secular as well as religious purpose

behind Sunday closing laws. The day of worship for some could be a well-deserved day of rest for others, and the fact that this day of rest coincides with the Sabbath does not necessarily constitute an establishment of religion by the government.

The choice of Sunday as a legally enforced day of rest was convenient for many Americans, but it was a burden on Orthodox Jews (see ORTHODOX JUDAISM) and others for whom Saturday, or another day, was their day of worship. These groups wanted to work on Sundays to make up for the loss of business incurred by closing on their own holy days. In *BRAUNFELD V. BROWN* (1961), Braunfeld was an Orthodox Jew, and his religion forbade business activities from Friday night through Saturday night. Philadelphia laws forced Braunfeld to close on Sundays, so he was doubly burdened, he claimed, by the Sunday closing law. This burden, according to Braunfeld, hampered his free exercise of religion, which is guaranteed in the First Amendment. Chief Justice Warren wrote that Sunday closing laws may impose an indirect burden on Braunfeld, but this alone did not violate the FREE EXERCISE CLAUSE. The legislation did force Braunfeld to make financial sacrifices to practice his religion, but that "is wholly different than when the legislation attempts to make a religious practice unlawful." Had the legislation forced Braunfeld to be open on Saturday, then, it may have violated Braunfeld's civil liberties.

Though still on the books in some places, during the past several decades blue laws have become a historical artifact driven largely by economic pressures. Some localities still ban the sale of alcohol on Sundays, but most businesses are free to engage in commercial activities if they choose to do so.

—Mark Caleb Smith

B'nai B'rith International

B'nai B'rith (Hebrew for "Children of the Covenant") is an international Jewish organization dedicated to human rights and philanthropic, social, and Jewish community causes. It has branches in 58 countries and some 500,000 members. The international headquarters are in Washington, D.C. Its divisions, which cover the programming areas of public policy, Jewish identity, community action, and youth and senior services, include the ANTI-DEFAMATION LEAGUE (a civil rights organization combating anti-Semitism, bigotry, and RACISM); Hillel Foundation (for Jewish college students); B'nai B'rith Youth Organization (a peer-led youth movement for 13 to 18 year olds); and B'nai B'rith Women. Groups are often organized in terms of "Lodges"; however, B'nai B'rith has no connection to FREEMASONRY. The organization is nonsectarian, drawing its membership from across the wings of contemporary Judaism—ORTHODOX, CONSERVATIVE, REFORM (and, outside the United States, the Masorti, Liberal, and Progressive movements)—as well as secular Jews.

B'nai B'rith is the oldest Jewish service organization and the most enduring such organization, Jewish or non-Jewish, in the United States. Founded in 1843 by 12 German-Jewish immigrants in New York City as a mutual aid society, B'nai

B'rith soon became an effective force against discrimination and the persecution of Jews. It spearheaded opposition to General Ulysses Grant's attempt to expel Jews from several states under military rule during the Civil War; President ABRAHAM LINCOLN overturned the order. In 1870, it petitioned another U.S. president to intervene on behalf of Jews in Romania, where sustained anti-Semitic attacks were occurring, a move that inaugurated the organization's advocacy for the welfare of Jews everywhere. In 1913, after a B'nai B'rith member by the name of Leo Frank was framed on a murder charge and subsequently lynched, B'nai B'rith established the Anti-Defamation League (ADL), a body committed to combating all forms of bigotry, and now perhaps its best-known agency. The ADL has proved particularly effective in lobbying governments and leaders to action. Its achievements include extracting commitments from Argentine president Carlos Menem in 1995 and from Croatian president Franjo Tudjman in 1997, to bring Nazi war criminals to justice, commitments that both leaders honored.

In addition to its civil rights activity, B'nai B'rith draws on traditional Jewish values to mandate other areas of community work. For example, appealing to *gemilut chasidim,* loving-kindness to others, B'nai B'rith members offer a range of volunteer services, including feeding the hungry through projects such as the Bagel Brigades, and teaching literacy skills to those in need. Similarly, appealing to the Jewish value of *tikkun olam*—repair of the world—the organization raises money for disaster relief and has helped, for example, survivors of the Oklahoma City bombing, Hurricane Mitch, the war in Kosovo (1999–2000), and the 1999 Turkish earthquake.

B'nai B'rith has also been at the forefront of secular and informal Jewish learning, establishing community centers (including Covenant Hall in New York, the nation's first Jewish community center), libraries, and adult education classes of various kinds. Another well-known arm, the Hillel Foundation, was established in 1923 and has serviced generations of Jewish students at colleges and universities across the United States and in 16 other countries.

B'nai B'rith participated in the 1948 San Francisco Conference that established the United Nations. Through its Center for Public Policy, it is the only Jewish organization with a full-time presence at the United Nations and at the European Union, in Brussels. It also has nongovernmental status at the Organization of American States and MERCOSUR, South America's economic development bloc. The B'nai B'rith World Center in Jerusalem deals with important issues affecting Israel and the Jewish people. A Bureau of International Affairs, recently established in London, serves as a major information clearinghouse and lobbying body on issues of Jewish concern throughout the world.

Further reading: B'nai B'rith USA website. URL: http://bbi.koz.com; Moore, Deborah Dash. *B'nai B'rith and the Challenge of Ethnic Leadership.* Albany: State University of New York Press, 1981.

—Geoffrey Brahm Levey

Board of Education v. Allen 392 U.S. 236 (1968)

In *Board of Education of Central School District No. 1 et al v. Allen, Commissioner of Education of New York, et al.,* a majority of the U.S. Supreme Court affirmed an opinion of the New York Court of Appeals that upheld as constitutional a New York statute that provided for the loan of textbooks to children attending both public and parochial schools. The law had been challenged by members of school boards in two New York counties who sought a declaration that the law was invalid and an order preventing the commissioner of education of New York (Mr. Allen) from removing board members who failed to comply with the contested law. The persons challenging the law relied on both the state and the federal Constitutions, claiming in respect to the federal Constitution that the law violated the ESTABLISHMENT CLAUSE of the First Amendment. Justice White delivered the majority opinion, which was supported by Justices Brennan, Stewart, and Marshall. Justice Harlan delivered a brief concurring opinion, with Justices Black, Douglas and Fortas each delivering separate dissenting judgments.

The case involved a challenge to the constitutionality of §701 of the Education Law of the State of New York, which required public school boards to purchase textbooks and lend them without charge to all children residing in their school district who were enrolled in grades seven through 12 of a public or private school, as long as that school was in compliance with the compulsory Education Law. It was a requirement of the law that textbooks designated for use in a public or private school be approved by the relevant board of education and that only "secular" books could receive such approval.

The majority relied on this requirement of board approval as ensuring that the books purchased and loaned to private school students were books that were not unsuitable for use in public schools because of the religious content. Relying on this assumption, the majority determined that the New York law was able to survive the test of state neutrality toward religion that was established in EVERSON V. BOARD OF EDUCATION. The test derived from *Everson* and applied by the majority in *Allen* required the Court to ascertain the purpose and primary effect of the challenged law. If either the purpose or the effect was the advancement or inhibition of religion, then the enactment would fail to pass constitutional muster.

In applying the *Everson* test to the facts of this case, the majority reached the conclusion that the express purpose of the law was to further educational opportunities available to the young. The majority further found that the person challenging the law had no evidence to suggest that the necessary effect of the statute was contrary to this facially neutral legislative purpose. In *Everson,* the Court upheld a law that provided free bus transport to all students in the state, whether they attended public or private schools. The majority regarded the textbook loan scheme established by §701 of the Education Law as sufficiently analogous to the provision of free buses to school children, or indeed the provision of water or sewerage services to properties owned by religious organizations, to pass the *Everson* test provisions.

The separate dissenting opinions issued by Justices Black, Douglas, and Fortas are all strident in their opposition to the majority view. Justice Black describes the challenged law as a "flat, flagrant, open violation of the First and Fourteenth Amendments." He regards the law as taking "great strides" toward the establishment of a state religion. The recurring theme in the dissenting judgments is the inherent ideological and educational nature of textbooks, in contrast to the provision of buses or sewerage services. The justices found that the constitutional safeguard relied on by the majority to support the challenged law (namely, the requirement that school boards approve only "secular" books) is too fragile a barrier to support the constitutionally mandated separation between church and state. Justice Douglas noted that there is "no reliable standard by which secular and religious textbooks can be distinguished from each other," and that it is to be expected that sectarian schools will request textbooks that are most favorable to their religious persuasion.

Justice Douglas gave numerous examples of the range of perspectives available within "secular" subjects like science or history to illustrate his concern as to the difficulty of distinguishing the secular from the sacred in education. He concluded that the tendency or effect of the system created by the contested law is to cause the insidious infiltration of the secular into the sacred, or vice versa—with either result violating the constitutional safeguards contained in the First and Fourteenth Amendments.

—Jillian Savage

Bob Jones University and Goldsboro Christian School, Inc. v. United States 461 U.S. 574
(1983)

In 1970, the Internal Revenue Service (IRS) ruled that schools with racially discriminatory policies toward students do not qualify for tax-exempt status as charitable organizations. On religious grounds, Bob Jones University refused admission to prospective students who practiced or advocated interracial dating and/or marriage, and as a result the IRS revoked the university's tax-exempt status. The university denied that its policy constituted racial discrimination and claimed that the revocation of tax-exempt status violated its rights under the FREE EXERCISE CLAUSE and ESTABLISHMENT CLAUSE of the First Amendment. The Supreme Court disagreed, upholding both the IRS policy of denying tax-exempt status to racially discriminatory organizations and the finding that Bob Jones University's policy was racially discriminatory. Chief Justice Berger wrote for the 8-1 majority, with Justice Rehnquist dissenting, in an opinion issued May 24, 1983.

Bob Jones University v. U.S. raises a perennial question arising under the Free Exercise Clause of the First Amendment: when do religious beliefs justify an exemption from the normal requirements of law? Conversely, when do otherwise lawful government actions become unlawful in the face of religiously grounded objections? The university claimed that its

religious rationale for racial discrimination (based on its particular interpretation of fundamentalist Christianity) should trump the IRS's ruling that the revenue code prohibits granting tax exemptions to racially discriminatory organizations.

In upholding the IRS decision, the Supreme Court followed the precedents established in SHERBERT V. VERNER (1963), WISCONSIN V. YODER (1972), and THOMAS V. REVIEW BOARD OF INDIANA EMPLOYMENT SECURITY DIVISION (1981). In these cases, the Court followed the principle that the government can infringe on the free exercise of religion only when the infringement is necessary for the fulfillment of a compelling state interest and when the infringement employs the least restrictive means possible. As the Court observed in its *Bob Jones* opinion, "the Government has a fundamental, overriding interest in eradicating racial discrimination in education. . . . That governmental interest substantially outweighs whatever burden denial of tax benefits places on petitioners' exercise of their religious beliefs. The interests asserted by petitioners cannot be accommodated with that compelling governmental interest; . . . and no 'less restrictive means' . . . are available to achieve the governmental interest."

The university also claimed that its ban on intermarriage and interracial dating was not racially discriminatory because the rules applied to all races. The Court rejected this claim, observing that "decisions of this Court firmly establish that discrimination on the basis of racial affiliation and association is a form of racial discrimination."

In his dissent, Justice Rehnquist picked up on a point argued by the university, claiming that the IRS lacked statutory warrant to revoke the tax-exempt status of racially discriminatory organizations. Under Rehnquist's reading of the Internal Revenue Code, Congress's definition of a charitable organization does not give the IRS the authority to rule that a racially discriminatory organization is not charitable, with the result that there is no legal basis to withdraw the university's tax-exempt status.

The Supreme Court undermined the logic of the *Bob Jones* decision seven years later when it adopted a narrower reading of the Free Exercise Clause. See EMPLOYMENT DIVISION, DEPARTMENT OF HUMAN RESOURCES OF OREGON V. SMITH, in which the Court held that the clause prohibits only laws that place an intentional burden on religion rather than an incidental one, thus eliminating the requirement that any burden on religion by justified by a compelling state interest.

—Matthew DeBell

Boerne, City of v. Flores 521 U.S. 507 (1997)

The congregation of St. Peter the Apostle Catholic Church in Boerne, Texas, had grown too large for its sanctuary. Plans to expand the building were halted when the City of Boerne denied construction permits, stating that the church was part of a protected historic district. Archbishop Patrick Flores filed suit against the city, relying in part on the 1993 RELIGIOUS FREEDOM RESTORATION ACT (RFRA), which sought to secure the free exercise of religion against incidental infringement by laws of general applicability. The Supreme Court ultimately ruled against Flores and the church in *City of Boerne, Petitioner v. P. F. Flores, Archbishop of San Antonio, and United States,* decided on June 25, 1997. Writing for a 6-3 majority, Justice Anthony Kennedy ruled that the RFRA was an unconstitutional use of Congress's powers under the FOURTEENTH AMENDMENT.

The RFRA itself was the direct result of the High Court's decision in EMPLOYMENT DIVISION V. SMITH (1990). In *Smith,* the Court explicitly refused to apply the standard established in SHERBERT V. VERNER (1963), instead holding that when the burden to religion was the incidental result of a neutral law of general applicability, no offense was done to the First Amendment. Widely decried by religious critics, the *Smith* precedent prompted Congress to pass the RFRA. The act sought to enshrine the *Sherbert* standard in law, forbidding all levels of government from substantially impairing FREE EXERCISE without a demonstration of compelling interest and least restrictive means.

This history, however, must be set in the context of the Court's wider Fourteenth Amendment jurisprudence. The most controversial part of the RFRA was its blanket application to all state and local actions, statutory or otherwise. Congress defended this expansive power under section five of the Fourteenth Amendment, claiming that the RFRA was remedial legislation aimed at helping to enforce the rest of the amendment's provisions—in particular, the application of the First Amendment to the states. Proponents of the RFRA argued for its similarity to previous congressional actions, such as the Voting Rights Act of 1965.

The Court failed to agree. If the RFRA was intended as a remedial measure, it was a poor one at best. The legislative record made no showing from recent history of generally applicable laws enacted because of religious bigotry. Only a stretch of the imagination could hold that the incidental impact created by generally applicable laws represented religious animus, hostility, or a widespread pattern of religious discrimination. The RFRA also suffered from a startling case of overbreadth. Here comparison is useful. The Voting Rights Act included remedial measures that targeted specific acts of discrimination in specific geographic regions, providing a phaseout period for federal intervention. On the other hand, the RFRA would have applied to state and local governments everywhere without possibility of termination. The act effectively opened every act of state or local government to challenge at any time by any individual who perceived a substantial burden to his or her free exercise. Governments had almost no recourse in the face of such challenges, because the act also required them to meet a compelling interest and least-restrictive means test—one of the most stringent standards that could be established.

If the RFRA could not be considered remedial action, it had to be seen for what it was—an effort to change substantively the content of the Free Exercise clause. The act was offensive in part because of the drastic change it created in the structure of federalism, potentially invalidating hundreds if not thousands of laws. Congress had removed the states' recognized ability to legislate for the health and welfare of their citizens. However, the RFRA also breached the traditional separation of powers. The Fourteenth Amendment, argued the Court, denied Congress the power to interpret and elaborate on its own meaning by conferring self-executing substantive rights against the states. Referring to *Marbury v. Madison* (1803), Justice Kennedy noted the impermissibility of using ordinary legislation to alter the content of constitutional provisions. Within our system, the Supreme Court retains the ultimate power of interpretation. Given the RFRA's unconstitutionality, Kennedy had no choice but to decide the case in line with the Court's own precedent— *Smith.*

Two factors suggest that *Boerne* is only the latest, not the final chapter in the history of free exercise. First, the RFRA had widespread support within Congress and in the public at large; this means that further congressional action might still follow. Second, each of *Boerne's* dissenters left open the possibility of revisiting and possibly overturning the *Smith* standard.

—Matthew M. C. Roberts

Bonhoeffer, Dietrich (1906–1945) *theologian*

Dietrich Bonhoeffer is best known for his neoorthodox theology, his participation in the failed 1943 plot to assassinate Adolf Hitler, and his consequent execution days before the end of World War II. Born in Breslau, the sixth of eight children, he was raised in Berlin amid stimulating intellectual support and encouragement. There his father held a prestigious university chair in psychology.

Bonhoeffer enrolled to study theology at Tübingen at the age of 17. After two semesters there and a semester in Rome, he continued his studies in Berlin with Adolf von Harnack and Reinhold Seeberg, receiving a doctorate in 1927. At age 22, he became assistant pastor of a German-speaking Lutheran congregation for a year in Barcelona, Spain. In September 1930, at age 24, he went to Union Theological Seminary in New York City as a Sloan Fellow. The ethical (rather than theological) emphasis of American Christian thinking, the strongly pacifist outlook of many American churches, and the general ignorance among seminary students of the theology of KARL BARTH, on which Bonhoeffer lectured to them, were both a surprise and a challenge to him. He began to reject the traditional Lutheran separation of the spheres of politics and faith, and he became increasingly attracted to Christian PACIFISM. His summary thought on the American churches was: "Protestantism without Reformation."

After his return to Germany, Bonhoeffer was actively involved in various forms of resistance against the Nazi government, especially in opposing the policies of the "German Christians," the overwhelming majority of Germans who had accepted National Socialist doctrines and policies as authoritative for the church. Despite his many political-ecclesiastical activities in Germany, he accepted a call to become minister to two German-speaking congregations in London, England, in October 1933. His success in persuading the leaders of the international ecumenical movement that the Confessing Church, not the Reich Church, was the true church in Germany gave the Confessing Church a voice in the movement, enabling church leaders internationally to stay accurately informed of events in Germany.

In April 1934, Bonhoeffer returned to Germany to establish a seminary for the Confessing Church at Finkenwalde, which was closed by the Nazis in 1937. Bonhoeffer's high-level connections in the German administration, despite being subject to a ban on speaking and publishing, allowed him to become an official in a counterintelligence agency, which permitted him to travel extensively, by means of which he carried out various assignments for the German resistance movement. British refusal to guarantee that a new government would not be subject to "unconditional surrender" demands (this in 1942, when the Germans were victorious nearly everywhere) led the conspirators to move away from plans for a coup and an alternative government toward plans for assassination. Bonhoeffer was arrested for his part in the conspiracy on April 5, 1943. After 18 months in a Berlin prison and a tighter confinement after the failed July 1944 assassination attempt, Bonhoeffer was hanged at Flossenburg concentration camp on April 8, 1945.

Considered by many to be a leading figure in the so-called neoorthodox school of theology, Bonhoeffer is often remembered for his provocative formulations, which sometimes became slogans, including "costly grace," "religionless Christianity," and "the church for others." Bonhoeffer was at core an ecclesiocentric, Christ-centric thinker who, much like Augustine, saw the church as God's vehicle for providing the means of salvation, and who saw Christ as the central sine qua non of the faith. For Bonhoeffer, "Christianity is community through Jesus Christ. . . . A Christian needs others because of Jesus Christ *and* a Christian comes to others through Jesus Christ." Bonhoeffer recognized the many shortcomings of the institutional church in fulfilling its God-ordained roles, and he worked through ways of addressing these faults. He nevertheless remained faithful to his high view of the church and the promise this vision of the church holds.

Bonhoeffer's work in ecclesiology is paralleled by his work in Christian ethics. His post-liberal, "post-Barthian" ethics, expressed especially in *The Cost of Discipleship* (1934) and the posthumously published *Letters and Papers from Prison* (1962) and *Ethics* (1965), are an effort to articulate the shape of a responsible freedom before God, apart from law, but in the world; practical, but not legalistic. Bonhoeffer looked to "conformation," the shaping of people to the form of Christ in the Incarnation, Crucifixion, and Resurrection, as a way of accomplishing this articulation and realization of the Christian ethical life in the everyday.

—Thomas Heilke

born-again experience

The point of origination for the term "born-again" can be found in John 3:3, which reads, "Jesus answered and said to him, 'Truly, truly, I say to you unless one is born again he cannot see the kingdom of God.'" Nicodemus, a Pharisee, had come to Jesus by night to learn more about Jesus and his teachings. He was confronted with the need to be born again. This required a radical break from Nicodemus's past. Some Protestant Christians, particularly Evangelical Protestants, glean from this encounter a need for a personal life-changing break with the past. Also, the same people who claim to be born again ordinarily hold a very high or literal view of Scripture. According to this literal interpretation, one must be born again. Therefore, the term "born-again" is used to describe an intense, once-in-a-lifetime experience of repenting of sins and giving one's life over to the Lord Jesus. From this point in life, one is said to be born again.

Born-again Christians see the experience as being absolutely essential to becoming a Christian. Often the view that one must be born again is misunderstood by both those who are familiar and unfamiliar with the term. For instance, all ROMAN CATHOLIC, EASTERN ORTHODOX, and Protestant Christians would agree that it is necessary for one to turn one's life over to God. This turning over of one's life to God, however, need not be a once-in-a-lifetime experience, according to those who hold this view. Instead, it can be a process of growth and maturity over the years. So, there are those who insist that a born-again experience is a necessity for entering heaven and those who see the possibility of a slower life process of coming to know God.

Approximately 44 percent of the American public claims to be born again, a sizable portion of the population. It demonstrates how pervasive this idea has become in the American religious culture and in the broader American culture. We now see the term applied in a quite secular way. For example, we now have born-again companies and born-again sports franchises. Without a societal familiarity with the term, it would not be bandied about so much. Many people in America understand that it means to be regenerated or to start over. In many ways, the term is now firmly entrenched in the American lexicon.

A theologically based understanding of being born again requires a broader look at the doctrine of regeneration. From about the second century to the 15th century, regeneration was almost exclusively linked to the rite of baptism. It was understood that the outward act of baptism was accompanied by an inner regeneration. Augustine (Bishop of Hippo, 395–430) offered a view that conversion and baptism were two different things when he wrote, "the sacrament of baptism is one thing, the conversion of the heart is another." This allowed a view of regeneration that, to some degree, approximated a life-changing experience. Still, Augustine's view was far from pronouncing the need for a once-in-a-lifetime climactic experience with God.

Aquinas (1225–74) helped set in place a view that denoted baptism as the means by which regeneration occurred. When these Aquinan ideas were accepted at the Council of Florence (1438–45), it set the stage for the Protestant Reformers in the 16th century. The Reformers returned to a more Augustinian view of baptism and regeneration. However, the term "new birth" began to appear quite often in association with the term "baptism." In the midst of the Reformation, ANABAPTISTS stressed the need for spiritual rebirth, which is accomplished through an internal baptism. The act of baptism thereby becomes an outward picture of an internal event.

Through Lutheran, Calvinist, and Wesleyan thought, an emphasis on individual experience began to move to the forefront. The necessity for a new birth was clearly the focal point of the evangelical revivals of the mid-1700s. An unbroken string connects modern evangelists like BILLY GRAHAM (1918–   ) and their use of the term "born again" with the preaching evangelists of the mid-1700s. The stress on being born again has only sharpened over the years. The largest Protestant denomination in America, the SOUTHERN BAPTIST CONVENTION, and numerous other Baptist groups along with charismatic, PENTECOSTAL, and independent groups have focused theologically on the need for a singular born-again experience. These groups make up a growing portion of the American religious population.

Confusion over the term seems to linger. Still, all major Christian groups stress the importance of turning over one's life to God.

See also EVANGELICALISM; FIRST GREAT AWAKENING; SECOND GREAT AWAKENING; TELEVANGELISM.

Further reading: Augustine. *Confessions.* Edited by E. M. Blaiklock. Nashville: Thomas Nelson, 1983; Catholic Center at Rutgers University website. URL: http://www.catholic-center.rutgers.edu/born.html. Downloaded March 13, 2002; Southern Baptist Convention: Baptist Faith and Message 2000. URL: http://sbc.net/default.asp?url=bfam_2000.html, Downloaded March 13, 2002; Toon, Peter. *Born Again: A Biblical and Theological Study of Regeneration.* Grand Rapids, Mich.: Baker House Books, 1987.

—William Lester

Bowen, Secretary of Health and Human Services, et al., v. Roy et al. 476 U.S. 693 (1986)

This case concerns a religious objection to the government's use of Social Security numbers (SSN). Petitioner Stephen Roy, who was a descendant of the Abenaki Native American tribe, believed that allowing the government to use a SSN for his daughter, Little Bird of the Snow, would "rob her spirit" by infringing on her uniqueness. The Supreme Court rejected the claim that government use of SSNs violates the FREE EXERCISE CLAUSE. Chief Justice Burger wrote for an 8-1 majority in an opinion issued June 11, 1986.

Little Bird of the Snow's parents (the petitioners) applied for Food Stamps and Aid to Families with Dependent Children in Pennsylvania. Federal law required that applicants for such assistance furnish the state with the SSN of everyone residing in their household. The petitioners refused to furnish the number of their child on the ground that doing so would violate their Native American religious beliefs, and they claimed that the federal law requiring them to inform government agencies of the SSN violated the Free Exercise Clause of the First Amendment. In a parallel claim, they argued that the government's use of the child's SSN would also violate the Free Exercise Clause.

By an 8-to-1 majority, the Court rejected Roy's second claim. Chief Justice Burger wrote, "The Free Exercise Clause simply cannot be understood to require the Government to conduct its own internal affairs in ways that comport with the religious beliefs of particular citizens. . . . As a result, Roy may no more prevail on his religious objection to the Government's use of a Social Security number for his daughter than he could on a sincere religious objection to the size or color of the Government's filing cabinets." Rather, the Free Exercise Clause protects the rights of individuals to believe and act in accordance with their faith.

The Court was divided on the claim that the government may not demand the provision of an SSN over religious objections. Burger distinguished the facts of this case from circumstances in which the government has criminalized religious conduct or compelled conduct, despite religiously inspired objections, noting that in this case the requirement that welfare recipients submit a SSN is neutral with respect to all religions and is a condition that religiously scrupulous people may choose to accept or reject. Joined only by Justices Powell and Rehnquist, Burger argued for a new jurisprudential standard. Burger contended that the standard in WISCONSIN V. YODER (that, when infringing the free exercise of religion, the government is justified only when using the least restrictive means to satisfy a compelling state interest) should not apply. Instead, Burger argued that the appropriate requirement is that the law be neutral and uniform in its application and be a reasonable means of promoting a legitimate public interest—a lower burden on the state.

A majority of the Court disagreed with this part of Burger's opinion. Justice O'Connor, joined by Justices Brennan and Marshall, would have upheld the lower court's ruling that the government may not condition the offering of public welfare benefits upon the provision of an SSN in this case. Justice Stevens argued that the issue was moot (that the issue was resolved), because at the time of the Supreme Court's decision, the government already had the SSN it had previously sought. He concurred in the remainder of the injunction. Justice Blackmun, noting the possibility of mootness, agreed with O'Connor that the government may not deny welfare assistance on the ground that an SSN is withheld for religious reasons. Justice White dissented from the opinion.

The use of SSN is also opposed on religious grounds by some fundamentalist Christians who regard the SSN as the "mark of the beast." This belief is based on an interpretation of the New Testament Book of Revelation to indicate (primarily in chapter 13) that one day a number will be required to engage in commerce, will be used as a universal identifier, and that those who accept this number will endure the wrath of God.

See also EMPLOYMENT DIVISION V. SMITH; NATIVE AMERICAN SACRED GROUNDS.

—Matthew DeBell

Bowling Alone: The Collapse and Revival of American Community (2000) By Robert D. Putnam. New York: Simon and Schuster

The thesis of *Bowling Alone* is simply that SOCIAL CAPITAL in America is in decline. As Putnam uses the term, *social capital* refers to "connections among individuals—social networks and the norms of reciprocity and trustworthiness that arise from them." The book uses an array of data to demonstrate that since roughly the mid-1960s, Americans have been increasingly less engaged in a wide variety of activities that contribute to social capital. These include POLITICAL PARTICIPATION, belonging to groups, and socializing with friends. According to Putnam, religious participation is no exception. Both church membership and attendance have declined over the last 40 years.

For Putnam, the decline in religious participation is an especially telling indicator of social capital's decline, because religious institutions arguably constitute the largest reservoir of social capital in America. Relative to most other nations, a high percentage of Americans regularly participate in a faith community. Religious participation, in turn, is strongly correlated with many types of civic activity, including membership in secular organizations, philanthropy, and volunteering.

The phrase *bowling alone* was first popularized by Putnam when he used the term in a 1995 article in the *Journal of Democracy*. It refers to the somewhat whimsical fact that along with a decline in such activities as group memberships and church attendance, fewer and fewer Americans are bowling in leagues (thus, it is not that more Americans are literally bowling alone—that is, as individuals—rather, they are not bowling in leagues). Putnam's article attracted considerable attention, both inside and outside of academia. It struck a chord with many readers, but also attracted numerous critics. Articles in a number of journals and magazines were devoted to debates about Putnam's thesis.

Putnam's alarm about declining rates of civic engagement in the United States was motivated by his research in Italy, as detailed in his 1993 book, *Making Democracy Work: Civic Traditions in Modern Italy*. In that book he first used the term *social capital,* arguing that it was the primary factor affecting the performance of Italy's regional governments. He found that throughout Italian history, high levels of civic engagement in seemingly nonpolitical associations—not bowling leagues perhaps, but soccer leagues and choral societies—have had tangible political consequences, namely, the smooth functioning of various government institutions.

The book *Bowling Alone* can be read as both a response to the criticism leveled at the article "Bowling Alone" and an extension of Putnam's Italian research to the United States. Although the original article reported on only a few indicators of social capital from widely available sources, the book chronicles trends in numerous activities, many with original data. The analysis of social capital's consequences also extends beyond the performance of government institutions. Drawing on a wide body of literature across many academic disciplines, Putnam links social capital to such diverse outcomes as crime rates, economic growth, and life expectancy.

Unlike his earlier work, in *Bowling Alone* Putnam is careful to distinguish between two different forms of social capital, that which "bonds" and that which "bridges." The former consists of homogeneous groups, while the latter connects people across social cleavages. Both can have positive social consequences, although Putnam warns that bonding social capital is rooted in exclusion and thus has a "dark side." This warning is particularly appropriate in the context of religion. In discussing religious trends in postwar America, Putnam notes that the denominations experiencing growth are likely to foster bonding social capital among their members, while those losing members are generally characterized as sources of bridging social capital.

Bowling Alone identifies four contributing factors to the decline in social capital. The first, and smallest, is the decrease in Americans' free time and disposable income, particularly owing to the rise of two-career families. Second is suburbanization. Third is the privatization of leisure time, with television mostly to blame. Fourth, and most important, is generational change. The "long civic generation"—those born between roughly 1910 and 1940—have been replaced in the population be generational cohorts with ever-lower levels of social capital.

Even though its tale of decline seems pessimistic on its face, Putnam pointedly stresses that Americans responded to a similar period of social transformation—at the turn of the 19th century—by engineering new ways to build social capital. He thus concludes with a call for social capitalists at the turn of this century to be as innovative as the Progressive reformers at the turn of the last.

Further reading: Putnam, Robert D. "Bowling Alone: America's Declining Social Capital." *Journal of Democracy* 6, no. 1 (1995): 65–78; ———. *Making Democracy Work: Civic Traditions in Modern Italy*. Princeton, N.J.: Princeton University Press, 1993; ———. *Bowling Alone: The Collapse and Revival of American Community*. New York: Simon and Schuster, 2000.

—David E. Campbell

Boy Scouts of America v. Dale 530 U.S. 640 (2000)

In *Boy Scouts of America v. Dale*, the U.S. Supreme Court held (5-4) that the Boy Scouts of America's (BSA) right to freedom of association trumped the state's interest in preventing discrimination against homosexuals. Specifically, the Court determined that a New Jersey public accommodations law did not prevent the BSA from expelling a homosexual scoutmaster, because such an application of the law would violate the organization's right of "expressive association." Chief Justice William Rehnquist delivered the majority opinion on June 28, 2000, with dissenting opinions filed by Justices John Paul Stevens and David Souter.

Shortly after enrolling at Rutgers University in 1989, James Dale first acknowledged to himself and others that he is gay. A former Eagle Scout, he was at the time an assistant scoutmaster in the Monmouth, New Jersey, Boy Scout Council. After reading a newspaper article about Dale's leadership in the university's Lesbian/Gay Alliance, leaders of the Monmouth BSA Council revoked his membership, stating that the organization "specifically forbids membership to homosexuals." Dale sued the BSA, alleging that it violated a state antidiscrimination statute by revoking his membership solely because of his sexual orientation. New Jersey's Law Against Discrimination prohibits, among other things, discrimination on the basis of sexual orientation in places of public accommodation. The state trial court ruled in favor of the BSA, but the first appellate court reversed the decision; the State Supreme Court affirmed the reversal, prompting the BSA's appeal to the U.S. Supreme Court.

Though the right of "association" is not specifically enumerated in the U.S. Constitution, the Supreme Court has determined, in *NAACP v. Alabama* (1958), that "freedom to engage in association for the advancement of beliefs and ideas is an inseparable aspect of the 'liberty' assured by the Due Process Clause of the Fourteenth Amendment, which embraces freedom of speech." Group membership—and, conversely, the exclusion of certain persons from a group—allows for more effective articulation and advocacy of beliefs and ideas, and therefore is generally protected as an aspect of free speech. Like free speech, however, freedom of association is not absolute; the state can regulate the membership policies of a private association when the state's compelling interest (for example, the promotion of equality by banning discrimination based on gender, race, religion, or sexual orientation) cannot be accomplished with less restrictive measures.

Nevertheless, the Court has limited the state's power in three important ways: (1) the state may not restrict association to suppress ideas or beliefs; (2) discrimination among "intimate associations" (small, private gatherings) is fully protected; and (3) larger organizations created for the purpose of "engaging in those activities protected by the First Amendment" (speech, assembly, petition for redress of grievances, and exercise of religion) may discriminate when admitting members, but only when the discrimination is integral to the "expressive message" of the organization. Thus the KU KLUX KLAN would have the right to exclude African Americans from its membership (since RACISM is central to the group's identity), but a business club cannot exclude women so long as being male was not central to the group's expressive activity.

Demonstrators protest outside the National Capital Area Council for the Boy Scouts of America, August 21, 2000, in Bethesda, Maryland. *(Michael Smith/Getty)*

The issue in *BSA v. Dale*, therefore, was whether the BSA's exclusion of homosexual scoutmasters was consistent with one of these protected types of discrimination.

The BSA sought protection as an expressive association, claiming that the forced inclusion of a gay troop leader would impair its ability to express the views that brought Scouts together, including the opinion that homosexuality was immoral. Although neither the oath, the mission statement, nor the bylaws of the BSA specifically mentions homosexuality, the plaintiffs argued that the oath's pledge to be "morally straight" implied a rejection of homosexuality, and that a 1978 BSA Executive Committee statement made this position clear. Writing for the Court, Chief Justice Rehnquist accepted the plaintiff's assertion that "homosexual conduct is inconsistent with the values [the BSA] seeks to instill," and held that the existence of a gay troop leader would "force the organization to send a message, both to the young members and the world, that the Boy Scouts accepts homosexual conduct as a legitimate form of behavior." Forcing the BSA to admit a gay scoutmaster would thus violate its right of expressive association.

By allowing associations more leeway in defining their expressive message, the *Dale* Court effectively expanded the ability of large associations to discriminate against groups that state laws are designed to protect. Furthermore, in accepting the claim that the mere presence of a gay troop leader impairs the BSA's ability to express its values, the Court also accepted the view that homosexuality is a form of speech (which the plaintiffs ipso facto deemed immoral), not a status or self-identity distinguishable from speech. Ever since the decision was released, several cities have banned the BSA's use of public facilities, and legislation was introduced (and resoundingly defeated) in Congress that would revoke the BSA's federal charter.

See also GAY RIGHTS.

Further reading: Chemerinsky, Erwin, and Catherine Fisk. *"Boy Scouts of America v. Dale:* The Expressive Interest of Associations." *William & Mary Bill of Rights Journal* 9 (April 2001): 595–617; Endejann, N. Nicole. "Coming Out Is a Free Pass Out: *Boy Scouts of America v. Dale." Akron Law Review* 34 (2001): 893–917.

—Erik Owens

Bradfield v. Roberts 175 U.S. 291 (1899)

In *Bradfield v. Roberts*, decided on December 4, 1899, the U.S. Supreme Court was faced with an application for an injunction to prevent the treasurer of the United States from paying any moneys to the directors of Providence Hospital ("the Directors") pursuant to an agreement entered into between those directors and the Commissioners of the District of Columbia ("the Commissioners") for the construction of a hospital. A general appropriation of $30,000 authorized the Commissioners to construct two hospitals in the District of Columbia, with the details of the construction to be at the discretion of the Commissioners. The Commissioners had entered into an agreement with the Directors for the construction of one of the hospitals, and it was payment in respect of this agreement that the defendant sought to have enjoined by the Court.

The basis of the defendant's objection to the payment by the Treasury to the Directors was the "private eleemosynary" nature of the Directors' corporation. The defendant asserted that the Directors' corporation was composed solely of members of a monastic order, or sisterhood of the ROMAN CATHOLIC CHURCH, and that the activities of the corporation were conducted under the auspices of that church. Accordingly, the defendant argued that any payment by the Treasury to the Directors amounted to "an appropriation of the funds of the United States for the use and support of religious societies," contrary to the dictates of the First Amendment ESTABLISHMENT CLAUSE. As such, it is one of the first establishment clause cases considered by the Court.

In an opinion by Justice Peckham, the Court refused to issue the injunction sought by the defendant. The Court looked to the act of Congress that had created the corporation here in issue and determined that there was nothing expressly religious in the limited, authorized purposes of that corporate body. In undertaking this analysis, the Court stated that it was prepared to assume (solely for the purposes of the present exercise) that the religious nature of the corporation might render the contested appropriation unconstitutional. However, given that the defendant had wholly failed to establish that the relevant corporation was of such a religious nature, the issue simply did not arise. As the formal, legal character of the corporation was purely secular (according to the law that created it), the individual beliefs of those employed by the corporation or those who incorporated it were irrelevant. The mere influence of a particular religious sect in the management of a corporation that was established for certain defined secular purposes could not alter the essentially neutral nature of the organization.

In summary, the Court concluded that the act of Congress establishing the corporation showed that there was nothing sectarian about that corporation. Rather, the specific and limited object of the corporation was the opening and keeping of a hospital in the city of Washington for the care of such sick and invalid persons as may place themselves under the care of that corporation. Accordingly, the agreement entered into between the Commissioners and the Directors was a reasonable exercise of the discretion vested in the Directors by Congress, and the consequent appropriation was therefore constitutional.

—Jillian Savage

Branch Davidians

The Branch Davidians are an apocalyptic offshoot of the SEVENTH-DAY ADVENTISTS. They are best known for their involvement in a standoff with agents of the Federal Bureau of Investigation and the Bureau of Alcohol, Tobacco, and Firearms between February and March 1993. After Ellen G. White, the first leader of Seventh Day Adventism, died in 1915, its leaders were unable to choose a clear spiritual successor or establish a strong theological base for continuing the movement. When the Seventh Day Adventists were unable to replace White, replacements came to the fore on their own. Among these was a Hungarian immigrant named Victor Houteff. Houteff led a reform movement within the movement during the late 1920s that failed to gain majority support. The result of his failure led Houteff and his followers to move to Waco, Texas, in 1935, where they established the Davidian community. Among Houteff's additions to Adventist theology were the beliefs that the apocalypse was imminent and that there would be only 144,000 selected to enter the heavenly kingdom, which would soon be established in Palestine. Houteff died in 1955, failing to lead his people into the heavenly kingdom.

Upon his death, Houteff's wife, Florence, took control of the community and announced that the actual date of the Apocalypse would be April 22, 1959. When the Apocalypse did not take place on this date, a split occurred within the Davidian community, and most of Houteff's followers moved under the aegis of another Davidian leader named Ben

Roden. Roden named his community the Branch Davidians, since it was a branch of Houteff's original Davidian movement.

Roden's major addition to Davidian theology was a return to Old Testament praxis. He instituted the celebration of all the ancient Jewish festivals that would have been kept by Jesus. Under Roden's leadership, the Branch Davidian community flourished and grew both in the United States and abroad. When Roden died in 1978, his wife, Lois, took over. In 1977 Lois Roden began to assert that the Holy Spirit was feminine. She claimed to have received this revelation directly from the Holy Spirit Mother. Moreover, she asserted that when the Second Coming occurred, the Messiah would appear in female form. From this point on, Lois Roden's vision of the Davidian mission was one in which the femininity of God was made known to the world.

When Lois Roden died, her estranged son George attempted to take control of the community; however, his attempt was doomed to failure, as Lois Roden had already selected her successor: Vernon Howell (a.k.a. David Koresh). Howell became Lois Roden's spiritual heir and eventually took control of the Branch Davidians after an armed standoff and firefight. The matter ended up in court, and Howell and his followers were awarded possession of the group's complex. At this time, in 1988, Howell firmly cemented his control over the Davidian community. Koresh was considered to be the seventh seal of prophecy, as he was the seventh leader of the Davidian community, a community that viewed itself as the only legitimate successors to Ellen White, the first Adventist seal of prophecy.

Koresh's contribution to Davidian theology was to emphasize a few very select pieces of the Christian tradition. Foremost among these was the belief that Koresh was the avatar of the biblical Cyrus, the ancient Persian king. The biblical passage that contains the prophecy about Cyrus indicates that he was an anointed one, a messiah. Koresh came to believe he was anointed, but not necessarily the messiah that Jesus was. Koresh also believed that he needed to spread his messianic seed and create as many pure offspring as possible. The result of this was Koresh's impregnation of many of the women in the Branch Davidian community—women to whom he was not legally married. He also believed he was the only person who was actually able to open the apocalyptic seals, and that he was the Lamb mentioned in the biblical text, though not Jesus Christ.

See also MESSIANISM; RAID ON WACO.

Further reading: Pitts, William L. "The Davidian Tradition." In *From the Ashes: Making Sense of Waco.* Edited by James R. Lewis. Lanham, Md.: Rowman and Littlefield, 1994; ———. "Davidians and Branch Davidians: 1929–1987." In *Armageddon in Waco: Critical Perspectives on the Branch Davidian Conflict.* Edited by Stuart A. Wright. Chicago: University of Chicago Press, 1995; Reavis, Dick J. *The Ashes of Waco: An Investigation.* New York: Simon and Schuster, 1995; Tabor, James D. "The Waco Tragedy: An Autobiographical Account

of One Attempt to Divert Disaster." In *From the Ashes: Making Sense of Waco.* Edited by James R. Lewis. Lanham, Md.: Rowman and Littlefield, 1994.

—Adam L. Silverman

Brandeis, Louis D. (1856–1941) *U.S. Supreme Court justice*

Louis Dembitz Brandeis, who was born on November 13, 1856, in Louisville, Kentucky, had a heart for the common man. Although his family was prosperous, it strongly supported the idea of individual liberty after emigrating from Prague after the 1848 revolution. During the Civil War, the Brandeis family sided with the abolitionists (see ABOLITIONIST MOVEMENT). Brandeis's moral philosophy supported individual initiative, creativity, and development. Originally named Louis David Brandeis, he changed his middle name to Dembitz, the last name of his highly admired uncle, Lewis Naphtali Dembitz. Brandeis's uncle Dembitz was a lawyer who wrote on jurisprudence and had wide-ranging intellectual interests and strong political convictions. Brandeis in many respects became very similar to the portrait of his uncle. However, Philippa Strum commented: "Dembitz's ORTHODOX JUDAISM was of no interest to the secular Brandeises, but it would affect Louis Brandeis dramatically later in his life."

An 1878 graduate of Harvard Law School, Brandeis had a successful law practice in Boston. "He was a millionaire by 1907, a millionaire twice over when he joined the Supreme Court in 1916, and in spite of substantial charitable contributions, he left an estate worth over [three million dollars] in 1941." Nevertheless, the themes of Brandeis's life as a man, lawyer, and judge are concerns for popular democracy, public service, morality, concrete facts, and ordinary people. Against the exploitation of big business, Brandeis supported labor unions against corporate management and upheld congressional legislation that sought to protect workers' interests.

President Woodrow Wilson appointed Brandeis to the U.S. Supreme Court in 1916. His nomination was very controversial and engendered protracted debate, hearings, and testimony about his suitability as a Supreme Court justice. Critics attacked him as a radical without a proven record of judicial temperament. Despite opposition from the American Bar Association, former president Howard Taft, and various probusiness groups, Brandeis was approved. He became the first Jewish justice on the Supreme Court and served from 1916 to 1939, the years when Progressivism was challenging the conservative Republicanism of years gone by. Brandeis brought to the Supreme Court a philosophy of practical justice, social jurisprudence, and constitutional interpretation that expressed his political Progressivism. He wrote the opinion for the majority in the landmark case *Erie v. Tompkins* (1938), overturning the long-standing principle of federal general common law articulated in *Swift v. Tyson* (1842). Strum sums up Brandeis's jurisprudence: "He went to the Court with a fully developed philosophy of democracy and law. His fear of bigness, his emphasis on facts as the key to knowledge and good law-making, and his belief in experimentation as central to progress came together in his judicial opinions."

Brandeis's jurisprudence was also reflected in his later embrace of ZIONISM. Brandeis had not been raised as an observant Jew, and until age 54, Brandeis showed no interest in his Judaic heritage. Being highly principled and ethically conscientious did not translate into a vibrant faith for Brandeis. "He never became religious, but in the second decade of the twentieth century he threw himself into the Zionist cause." Brandeis's interest in Zionism began in his encounter with working-class eastern European Jews during the New York garment workers' strike in 1910. By that time Brandeis was sympathetic to the Zionist movement, but he believed that the Jewish people should consider themselves Americans first and Jews second. What really changed Brandeis's mind on the issue was learning for the first time that his beloved uncle, Lewis Dembitz, was a Zionist. Brandeis began to immerse himself in Zionist literature and attended an American Zionist meeting after the outbreak of World War I. He soon became a key leader of American Zionism and founded the AMERICAN JEWISH CONGRESS, the Palestine Endowment Fund, and the Palestine Co-operative Company. Applying his political Progressivism, Brandeis saw Jewish settlements in Palestine as an advancement of democracy. In 1919, Brandeis visited Palestine and enthusiastically supported democratic ideals for the Jewish homeland. Despite the emergence of LIBERALISM, Jews worldwide were not being accorded individual rights. The anti-Semitism that arose in Germany was spreading to other lands, and this fact deeply concerned Brandeis. Individuals may have been given universal rights, but groups such as Jews had not. In a 1915 address to the Conference of Eastern Council of Reform Rabbis, Brandeis defined Zionism as the right of Jews collectively to live as a distinct, ethnic nation in Palestine.

Brandeis's ideas about Judaism had clearly changed. Rather than viewing Judaism through the lens of Americanism, Brandeis came to view Americanism through the lens of Judaism. To be a good Jew required one to be a good Zionist. Brandeis argued, "by battling for the Zionist cause, the American ideal of democracy, of social justice and of liberty will be given wider expression." In his 1916 speech as chairman of the Jewish Congress Organization Committee, Brandeis called for all Jews to become Zionists and to act, unify, and organize to further the Zionist cause through the American Jewish Congress.

Until his death in 1941, Brandeis was an active Zionist and advised Presidents Woodrow Wilson and FRANKLIN DELANO ROOSEVELT about developing a Jewish nation-state in Palestine. In essence, Brandeis's Zionism was political rather than religious. His inspiration, motivation, and organization of the Zionist cause came from his political Progressivism, inventive INDIVIDUALISM, and moral philosophy of equal rights.

See also BRENNAN, WILLIAM JOSEPH, JR.

Further reading: Brandeis, Louis D. *Brandeis on Zionism: A Collection of Addresses and Statements by Louis D. Brandeis.* Washington, D.C.: Zionist Organization of America, 1942; Strum, Philippa, ed. *Brandeis on Democracy.* Lawrence: University Press of Kansas, 1995.

—Joanne Tetlow

Braunfeld v. Brown 366 US 599 (1961)

Braunfeld v. Brown was one of four challenges to Sunday closing laws (BLUE LAWS), which the Supreme Court decided concurrently. See also MCGOWAN V. MARYLAND (1961), TWO GUYS FROM HARRISON-ALLENTOWN V. MCGINLEY (1961), GALLAGHER V. CROWN KOSHER SUPERMARKET (1961). In this case, the Supreme Court upheld Pennsylvania's Sunday closing law against a claim that it violated the First Amendment guarantee of free exercise of religion.

Pennsylvania, like many states, prohibited the sale of certain commodities on Sundays, the Christian Sabbath. Although Sunday closing laws were historically adopted for religious reasons, the Court majority reasoned that they now served important secular ends, by providing a common time for leisure and recreation. In *Braunfeld v. Brown*, the Court considered the claim that Sunday closing laws violated the FREE EXERCISE CLAUSE of the First Amendment.

This challenge was brought by an Orthodox Jewish merchant, whose religion required him to close his business between sundown Friday and sundown Saturday (see ORTHODOX JUDAISM). Being additionally prohibited from opening his business on Sunday meant that the most important business days were not open to him, thus impeding his ability to earn a living. The law, therefore, imposed serious economic costs on the exercise of his religion.

Chief Justice Earl Warren, writing for the majority, distinguished between laws that prohibit a religious practice, and those that simply made a religious practice more expensive:

> the statute at bar does not make unlawful any religious practices of appellants; the Sunday law simply regulates a secular activity and, as applied to appellants, operates so as to make the practice of their religious beliefs more expensive. Furthermore, the law's effect does not inconvenience all members of the Orthodox Jewish faith but only those who believe it necessary to work on Sunday.

The Constitution does not forbid states from enacting ordinary secular legislation that inadvertently imposes a burden on someone's religion. Given the wide range of religious practices among the American people, innumerable ordinary statutes unintentionally result in a burden to some religious practice:

> But we are a cosmopolitan nation made up of people of almost every conceivable religious preference. . . . Consequently, it cannot be expected, much less required,

that legislators enact no law regulating conduct that may in some way result in an economic disadvantage to some religious sects and not to others because of the special practices of the various religions.

The majority concluded that the law is not unconstitutional on its face, nor is the state required to grant exemptions for those religiously obligated to close on Saturdays:

> If the purpose or effect of a law is to impede the observance of one or all religions or is to discriminate invidiously between religions, that law is constitutionally invalid, even though the burden may be characterized as only being indirect. But if the State regulates conduct by enacting a general law within its power, the purpose and effect of which is to advance the State's secular goals, the statute is valid despite its indirect burden on religious observance unless the state may accomplish its purpose by means which do not impose such a burden.

Justice WILLIAM BRENNAN, dissenting, would have required the state to show a compelling state interest any time a religious exercise is burdened. And, he argued, the administrative convenience of having a common day for rest and leisure did not rise to the level of such importance. In short, administrative convenience did not justify the economic burdens suffered by the Jewish merchants.

One of the most puzzling aspects of this decision is that it was followed only a term later by the landmark decision in SHERBERT V. VERNER (1963), which took an opposite approach on every major question. In that decision, the Court required a state to accommodate Saturday religious observance. Moreover, the majority rejected the *Braunfeld* distinction between an act overtly penalizing a religion and simply making it more expensive to practice, and required a state to show a compelling state interest when its laws burdened religion. Thus, without being overturned, the *Braunfeld* precedent seemed short-lived. But in light of the decisions in EMPLOYMENT DIVISION OF OREGON V. SMITH (1990) and BOERNE, CITY OF V. FLORES (1997), the Court seems to have returned to *Braunfeld*'s approach to legitimizing secular, religiously neutral laws.

—Bette Novit Evans

Bread for the World

Founded in 1974 by the Reverend Arthur Simon, this Christian citizens' organization has been devoted to hunger issues around the globe since its inception. What began as a small group of Roman Catholics and Protestants grew to more than 45,000 members by the 1990s and continues to maintain a large membership base. This nonpartisan, multidenominational organization is composed of concerned Christians and is devoted primarily to lobbying the government to make real and lasting improvements for the world's poorest people. Bread for the World does not provide direct relief, but instead focuses its grassroots efforts on contacting members of Congress, encouraging them to propose and support hunger-relief legislation and antipoverty measures more generally. Based in Washington, D.C., Bread for the World is considered politically liberal, particularly in relation to some of its fellow Christian lobbying organizations such as the MORAL MAJORITY and its successor, the CHRISTIAN COALITION.

Reverend Simon served as the organization's first president, from 1974 to 1991. The brother of former Illinois senator Paul Simon, he was part of a small group of Christians who began meeting in 1972 to discuss how Christians could be more effective in influencing hunger-related policies in the United States. By 1973, this small group had grown to 500, and it continued that growth for the next two decades. Under Simon's leadership, Bread for the World enjoyed several legislative victories; most notably, it was successful in passing the Hunger and Global Security bill in 1981. This bill dealt primarily with the relationship between the United States and developing nations, and stated that the United States would make combating hunger its top priority in those areas of the world. Bread for the World has continued its influence in Washington under the leadership of the Rev. David Beckmann, a Lutheran clergyman, who became president in 1991 after Simon stepped down. Simon and Beckmann recently collaborated on a book about the issues for which they share a passion entitled *Grace at the Table: Ending Hunger in God's World* (1999).

Today, Bread for the World is one of the largest grassroots organizations devoted to hunger and poverty issues. It has a staff of 45 but relies on its members to call, write, and visit their congressional representatives, urging them to support legislation that will benefit the hungry and the poor. The organization has a monthly newsletter and a website that keeps members and staff connected to each other. Bread for the World also has a partner organization, Bread for the World Institute. The institute conducts research on hunger and poverty issues, analyzing the root causes of those phenomena, then uses those findings to inform their eventual policy recommendations. The primary issue to which the organization and its members are devoted is hunger, but this is part of a larger crusade to eliminate poverty, in all its manifestations, around the globe. Recently, this crusade has included a campaign to urge members of Congress and the presidential administration of GEORGE W. BUSH to increase the minimum wage in the United States. So far, this effort has not been as successful as the organization had hoped, but it remains a prominent part of its agenda. The organization has also lent its voice and influence recently in support of full funding for debt relief to the poorest nations as part of the worldwide International Debt Relief/Jubilee 2000 campaign. Jubilee is a biblical concept that calls for the cancelling of debts at regular intervals to provide people with a new beginning and diminish inequality. Bread for the World, along with other supporters of Jubilee 2000, has been successful in eliminating some debt owed to the United States by developing nations but continues to lobby for the complete cancellation of these debts.

See also CALL TO RENEWAL; HUNGER AND HUMANITAR-IAN AID; SIDER, RON.

Further reading: Sider, Ronald J. *Rich Christians in an Age of Hunger.* Downers Grove, Ill.: InterVarsity Press, 1984.
—Andrea E. Moore

Brennan, William Joseph, Jr. (1906–1997) *U.S. Supreme Court justice*

William Joseph Brennan Jr. was born on April 25, 1906, in Newark, New Jersey. After a prolonged illness, Brennan died on July 24, 1997, in Arlington, Virginia. Brennan served as an associate justice on the U.S. Supreme Court from 1956 until 1990.

Republican president DWIGHT EISENHOWER nominated Brennan, a Democrat, during the middle of the 1956 presidential campaign; Brennan's nomination was politically motivated by Eisenhower's desire to court Democratic voters. Brennan's nomination also restored the Roman Catholic seat on the Court; the seat had been vacant since the death of Justice Frank Murphy in 1949.

Brennan received a recess appointment in October 1956 and his confirmation hearings were delayed until after the presidential election; he was confirmed by a voice vote on March 19, 1957. According to Stephen Wermeil, "the only dissent [was] shouted audibly by [Senator] Joseph McCarthy." In later life, Eisenhower remarked that his selection of Brennan was one of his worst mistakes as president, undoubtedly only

Associate Justice William Joseph Brennan Jr. *(U.S. Supreme Court)*

second to naming Earl Warren as the chief justice of the Court in 1953.

During his 33 years on the Court, Justice Brennan was a prolific writer, authoring 2,988 opinions, many of which reflected his vision that the Supreme Court could serve as an agent for political and social change. While he is recognized more for his decisions in obscenity and racial and gender discrimination cases, Justice Brennan authored the majority opinions in SHERBERT V. VERNER (1963), a landmark decision addressing the FREE EXERCISE CLAUSE, and in EDWARDS V. AGUILLARD (1987), a major ESTABLISHMENT CLAUSE decision.

In *Sherbert*, Justice Brennan established that state laws are subject to strict scrutiny if the laws infringe, even indirectly, on individual religious beliefs. To survive a constitutional challenge, states must show that the law in question is justified by a compelling state interest. South Carolina's denial of unemployment benefits for Adeil Sherbert because of her refusal to accept employment that required her to work on her Sabbath violated the Free Exercise guarantee in the First Amendment. The "compelling interest test" in *Sherbert* guided the Court's decisions in conflicts between neutral laws designed to promote societal objectives and religious freedom until the Court's decision in EMPLOYMENT DIVISION, OREGON DEPARTMENT OF HUMAN RESOURCES V. SMITH (1990), which narrowed the scope of *Sherbert* to unemployment compensation cases.

Aguillard involved Louisiana's statute that mandated the teaching of creation science if the theory of evolution was taught in a public school. In the 7-2 decision, Justice Brennan, writing for the majority, applied the standards outlined in LEMON V. KURTZMAN (1971) for determining whether an establishment of religion has occurred. Justice Brennan rejected the state's contention that the law had a secular purpose. Returning to the language in WALLACE V. JAFFREE (1985), Justice Brennan noted that the "State's articulation of a secular purpose . . . [must] be sincere and not a sham." He reviewed the legislative history of the act and found numerous instances when the sponsor of the legislation, State Senator Bill Keith, stated "his disdain for the theory of evolution." To Justice Brennan, the purpose of the Creationism Act was not to promote academic freedom but to "restructure the science curriculum to conform with a particular religious viewpoint," and therefore was unconstitutional.

Beyond the majority opinions in *Sherbert* and *Aguillard*, Justice Brennan is remembered for his 70-page concurrence in ABINGTON TOWNSHIP, SCHOOL DISTRICT OF V. SCHEMPP and MURRAY V. CURLETT (1963), as well as his passionate dissents in TILTON V. RICHARDSON (1971), MARSH V. CHAMBERS (1983), and LYNCH V. DONNELLY (1984).

Despite being a devout Roman Catholic, Justice Brennan's opinions on issues involving the Free Exercise and Establishment Clauses reflected "his creed that under our Constitution the state must resolutely stay out of the church and the church must resolutely stay out of the state."

Further reading: Abraham, Henry J. *Justices, Presidents, and Senators: A History of U.S. Supreme Court Appointments from Washington to Clinton.* Lanham, Md.: Rowman and Littlefield, 1999; Wermeil, Stephen. "William J. Brennan, Jr." In *The Supreme Court Justices: Illustrated Biographies, 1789–1993.* Ed. Clare Cushman. Washington, D.C.: Congressional Quarterly, 1993.

—Sara A. Grove

Brown, John (1800–1859) *abolitionist*

John Brown was born May 9, 1800, in Torrington, Connecticut, and died December 2, 1859, in Charles Town, Virginia. Brown, a self-described radical abolitionist, led several violent confrontations with proslavery supporters in Kansas and led the 1859 raid on the federal armory at Harpers Ferry, Virginia (now West Virginia).

John Brown's name is synonymous in American history with the violent confrontation over slavery that would plunge the country into civil war. But he is a powerful reminder of the potentially volatile reaction that can be produced when religious beliefs and political convictions collide. In the great American struggle over slavery, the lines between political conviction and religious crusade often blurred, and no one embodies that lesson more clearly than John Brown.

Brown was raised in Hudson, Ohio, a community known for its strong support for antislavery and an active participant in the ABOLITIONIST MOVEMENT. His father, Owen Brown, was a successful businessman, a leader in his community, and was instrumental in the founding of Oberlin College, a leading center for antislavery thought and activity. Owen Brown's children inherited his discipline and deep religious convictions; among the convictions picked up by young John Brown was an intense hatred for slavery.

But slavery did not define John Brown's childhood. Throughout his adolescent years, John was consumed by a quest to mimic his father's tremendous business success. While growing up, John tried his hand at several different occupations, but he proved to be less astute at running and managing a business.

Over the next few years, John struggled financially to meet the needs of his large family (he had a total of 20 children). Then, in November 1837 in nearby Illinois, an abolitionist and newspaper editor, Elijah Lovejoy, was brutally attacked and murdered by a mob of proslavery supporters, sending shockwaves throughout the North.

John was deeply disturbed by the events in Illinois and grew increasingly concerned when he joined some of his sons on their homestead in Kansas. The intense political battle over whether Kansas should be admitted as a slave or free state thrust Brown and his family right into the heart of the struggle over slavery. Events took a volatile turn on March 30, 1855, when proslavery supporters invaded the Kansas territory and routinely harassed antislavery settlers.

In 1856, Brown decided to take action. Emerging from the woods after a brief isolated excursion, Brown reportedly

Issued in the North during the Civil War, this melodramatic portrayal of John Brown meeting a slave mother and her child on his way to execution was symbolic and used for propaganda purposes. *(Library of Congress)*

told his family and friends that he had experienced a spiritual awakening. According to his testimony, God called him to seek retribution for the evil and violence waged on behalf of slavery.

Brown assembled a small band of followers and immediately began to exact what he saw as justice. Brown and his men believed they were doing God's will, and they justified their violence as an "eye for an eye."

Brown's actions soon made him a wanted man. After fleeing Kansas, he made his way through antislavery circles throughout the North, trying to enlist support for what had become a religious crusade. Among those he met with were black abolitionist Frederick Douglass and writers RALPH WALDO EMERSON and HENRY DAVID THOREAU. Most abolitionists did not support Brown's plan to violently overthrow slavery. However, he did manage to secure funding from a wealthy group of Northern abolitionists who called themselves the "Secret Six."

With their financial assistance, Brown (and a few of his sons) marched an army of 22 men into Harpers Ferry, Virginia, and stormed the federal armory. His plan was to seize the weapons and to encourage slaves in the surrounding area to join his army to wage a full-scale war against slavery. Brown did seize the armory, but fewer than 36 hours later, his insurrection was over. Ten of his men were killed, seven fled into the hills, and five were captured, including Brown. He was tried, convicted of treason, and executed on December 2, 1859.

During his trial, Brown was asked if he had any last words. He made the following comments: "Had I interfered in behalf of the rich every man in this court would have deemed it an act worthy of reward. I see a book kissed here, the Bible, that teaches me to 'remember them that are in bonds.' I endeavored to act up to that instruction. I believe that to have interfered in behalf of His despised poor was not wrong, but right. Now, if it is deemed necessary that I should forfeit my life, and mingle my blood further with the blood of my children and with the blood of millions in this slave country, I say let it be done!"

See also SECTIONAL DIVIDE OF THE CHURCHES OVER SLAVERY.

—Alonford James Robinson Jr.

Bryan, William Jennings (1860–1925) *politician*

William Jennings Bryan fused religion and politics into a career of powerful rhetoric, social foresight, and unfailing vigor. Bryan was a member of Congress, secretary of state dur-

William Jennings Bryan *(Library of Congress)*

ing a portion of the Wilson administration (1913–15), and a three-time Democratic Party nominee for the presidency. Bryan's political career was varied and influential, but later in his life he was a noted advocate of fundamentalist Christianity. He died less than a week after his participation in the famous SCOPES "MONKEY" TRIAL, on July 26, 1925.

Born on March 19, 1860, in Salem, Illinois, Willy Bryan was precocious and active. His father, Silas Bryan, was a fence builder, turned one-room schoolhouse teacher, turned politician. Silas Bryan, a Democrat, wrestled an Illinois state senate seat from the Whigs by taking his campaign directly to the people—a style his son would later emulate. The Bryans were also fixtures in Salem's religious community. Silas was a Baptist deacon, while Mariah Jennings Bryan, Willy's mother, led the choir at Salem Methodist Church. By age eight, Willy was a devout Christian and remained one throughout his life.

William Jennings Bryan was the valedictorian when he graduated from Illinois College in 1881. He attended Union College of Law in Chicago, and in 1883 he passed the bar examination and graduated. Bryan married Mamie Baird in 1884. The couple eventually had three children.

The Bryans moved to Lincoln, Nebraska, still the frontier, in 1887 because of increased business and political opportunities there. Bryan was elected to Congress in 1890 and was reelected in 1892. He ran a failed bid for the U.S Senate in 1894. Bryan then edited the *Omaha World-Herald* and continued to speak at Chautauqua meetings and political rallies. Bryan reentered formal politics at the 1896 Democratic Convention in Chicago. The party was divided between hardened advocates of the existing gold standard and proponents of the expanded coinage of silver, which would make money more available for the poor, farmers, and others who relied on credit. Bryan was a dedicated "silverite," and his spirited delivery of the Cross of Gold speech garnered him the presidential nomination and made him a celebrity. In a memorable synthesis of religious imagery and political rhetoric, Bryan told the convention, "You shall not press down upon the brow of labor this crown of thorns, you shall not crucify mankind upon a cross of gold." While the Republican nominee, William McKinley, made his campaign speeches from his front porch, Bryan's revolutionary campaign crisscrossed the nation several times on his whistle-stop train tour. Bryan lost the 1896 election, and though named the Democratic nominee again in 1900 and 1908, he lost those as well.

The Great Commoner remained active in politics, and in 1913 he became Woodrow Wilson's secretary of state. Bryan promoted peace, so he resigned when he thought Wilson was steering the country into World War I. Bryan's later years were consumed with his dedication to conservative religious ideals. Bryan was at the front of the battle between theological liberals (who championed a scientific, or "higher critical," view of the Bible and Darwin's theories of evolution), and fundamentalists (who held to religious orthodoxy and social conservatism). Bryan spoke out against liberalism as it became a force in many Protestant denominations, and he was the impetus behind bills that prohibited public schools from teaching evolution. One such bill became law in Tennessee, from which the famed Scopes "Monkey" Trial, in Dayton, Tennessee, resulted. Bryan was one of the prosecution's attorneys at the trial, which became a clash between religious orthodoxy and modern science. Foolishly, Bryan allowed the shrewd defense attorney, Clarence Darrow, to place him on the stand as a defender of the Christian faith. Bryan, well past his rhetorical prime, performed poorly and became a target of derision for many Americans. Bryan died only a week later, on July 26, 1925.

Bryan's legacy still survives in three ways. First, he argued for many policies well before they became fashionable. Bryan stumped for the direct election of U.S. senators, female suffrage, a national highway system, the protection of bank deposits, a minimum wage, and secret ballot elections. Second, Bryan's political style, which emphasized charisma and personal contact with voters, is now the rule, not the exception, in American politics. Third, Bryan's legacy also includes a nondenominational Christian college named in his honor. William Jennings Bryan College is located in Dayton, Tennessee, the site of the famous Scopes trial.

See also RELIGION IN THE 1896 PRESIDENTIAL ELECTION; ROOSEVELT, THEODORE.

Further reading: Levine, Lawrence W. *Defender of the Faith.* Cambridge, Mass.: Harvard University Press, 1987; Wilson, Charles Morrow. *The Commoner: William Jennings Bryan.* Garden City, N.Y.: Doubleday, 1970.

—Mark Caleb Smith

Buchanan, Patrick J. (1938–   ) *conservative activist*

Patrick "Pat" Buchanan is a conservative activist, author, and media commentator. Buchanan served as an adviser to three Republican presidents and gained national fame as a syndicated columnist and television personality. By the 1990s, Buchanan had established himself as one of the foremost proponents of Christian conservatism and advocated a return to more traditional moral values as a means to renew American culture. However, his rigid adherence to Roman Catholicism also led to accusations of ANTI-SEMITISM and homophobia.

Pat Buchanan was born in Washington, D.C. He was educated at Jesuit schools, where he internalized strict Catholic moral codes. Buchanan went on to graduate with honors from Georgetown University with a degree in English and philosophy. In 1962, he received a master's degree in journalism from Columbia University. At age 23, Buchanan became one of the nation's youngest editorial writers when he began working for the *St. Louis Globe-Democrat.*

In 1966, Buchanan launched his political career just three years later when he joined the staff of RICHARD M. NIXON's presidential campaign. Buchanan served for the next eight years as a White House staffer. He wrote foreign policy speeches for Nixon and accompanied the president on a number of major

Patrick J. Buchanan *(Michael Smith/Getty Images)*

summits, including the 1972 historic journey to open U.S. relations with mainland China. Throughout the Watergate crisis, Buchanan remained loyal to Nixon and was bitterly disappointed when the president resigned. Buchanan also served as an assistant and policy adviser to President Gerald Ford. While working at the White House, Buchanan met and married a fellow staffer, Shelley Ann Scarney. From 1985 to 1987, Buchanan served as the White House director of communications.

After he left the White House in 1987, Buchanan launched a career in broadcasting. He worked on three of the most successful political talk shows in television broadcast history. These included *The McLaughlin Group* on NBC, and *Capital Gang* and *Crossfire,* both on CNN. He also became a noted syndicated columnist and published essays in a variety of newspapers and journals. Buchanan wrote five books, two of which, *Right from the Beginning* and *A Republic Not an Empire,* were best-sellers. He also hosted a radio show, *Buchanan and Company.* Buchanan built his reputation by being outspoken. However, his controversial stance on many issues led to charges of RACISM and anti-Semitism. He strongly opposed affirmative action and the traditional support of the United States for ISRAEL.

In 1991, Buchanan decided to campaign for the presidency. He went on to run for the office three times: in 1992, 1996, and 2000. Buchanan came close to defeating President George H. W. Bush in the New Hampshire Primary in 1992, and beat the eventual Republican nominee, Robert Dole, in New Hampshire in 1996. In 2000, Buchanan left the Republican Party and gained the nomination of the Reform Party. But, while his two previous campaigns had a significant impact on the election, the influence of his 2000 campaign was negligible.

Buchanan's electoral popularity has been limited to conservatives disenchanted with the mainstream candidates. These voters, who called themselves the "Buchanan Brigades," were drawn to Buchanan's populist message. Buchanan's three campaigns were all based on the same central message: that mainstream politicians had become disassociated with the beliefs and values of average Americans. Buchanan asserted that there were "two Americas"—one affluent and prospering and one increasingly under siege, economically and culturally, by special-interest groups. The candidate's version of the morals and values of common Americans was centered on conservative Christianity and traditional nativist sentiments. Buchanan also decried the erosion of the nation's manufacturing base. These messages brought together both conservative Democrats and Republicans.

During his campaigns, Buchanan took a strong stand against ABORTION. He specifically proposed banning the abortion pill RU-486 and advocated the appointment of pro-life judges. Buchanan also opposed homosexuality and equated the GAY RIGHTS movement with the nation's moral and cultural decline. On educational issues, the candidate proposed reintroducing PRAYER IN PUBLIC SCHOOLS and offering VOUCHERS so that children could attend private schools, including religious schools. He also endorsed HOMESCHOOLING. Buchanan's positions on these cultural concerns attracted the support of a number of Christian conservatives.

Further reading: Buchanan, Patrick J. *Right from the Beginning*. Boston: Little, Brown, 1988; Berman, William C. *America's Right Turn: From Nixon to Bush*. Baltimore: Johns Hopkins University Press, 1994; Rozell, Mark J., and James F. Pontuso, eds. *American Conservative Opinion Leaders*. Boulder, Colo.: Westview Press, 1990; Oldfield, Duane Murray. *The Right and the Righteous: The Christian Right Confronts the Republican Party*. Lanham, Md.: Rowman and Littlefield, 1996.

—Thomas Lansford

Buddhism

Buddhism originated on the Indian subcontinent and was founded on the teachings of Siddhartha Gautama, who lived in the sixth century B.C.E. Today, both Asian immigrants and native-born American converts make up Buddhist communities in the United States; one source lists the 1990 American Buddhist population at 0.4 percent of the population.

The first Buddhists in America were Chinese and Japanese immigrants who found work in the West, especially in California and Hawaii. In 1899, Japanese-American Buddhists, with the help of missionary priests from Japan, established the first Buddhist institution in the United States, the Buddhist Churches of America. Immigration restrictions in the late 1800s limited the growth of the East Asian population in the United States, but teachers of Buddhism from Japan began to visit the United States in the early 20th century, including the scholar of Zen, D. T. Suzuki, and the Zen teacher Shunryu Suzuki. A few Buddhist teachers from Japan and Southeast Asia also came to the World's Parliament of Religions in 1893.

With the Immigration and Nationality Act of 1965, Buddhists from other Asian countries were allowed to immigrate to America. Buddhists from Southeast Asia fled war-torn Vietnam and surrounding nations, bringing with them both Mahayana and Theravada Buddhism (two of the three main forms of Buddhism). Tibetan Buddhists (representing the third main form of Buddhism), whose most famous representative is the Dalai Lama, came in the form of both lay Buddhist refugees from occupied Tibet and spiritual teachers, or lamas. The movement to free Tibet from Chinese occupation became a political goal for many Americans in the 1990s.

Zen achieved popularity in the 1960s and 1970s, thanks to American-born teachers such as Robert Aitken and Philip Kapleau. Theravada Buddhism is represented by centers such as the Insight Meditation Society, in Barre, Massachusetts. One Japanese form of lay Buddhism, Soka Gakkai International-USA, has spread quickly in American cities, often appealing to members of African-American and Hispanic communities. The presence of Buddhism in America has led to many innovations, collectively called the "Americanization" of Buddhism: the role of monasticism has lessened, women have entered leadership roles (e.g., becoming abbots of Zen centers), and democratic procedures have been adopted for the governing of Buddhist organizations. What is called "Engaged Buddhism" is in part a continuation the activism of the 1960s as informed by Buddhist thought, as well as by American Protestant traditions of social justice and Buddhist social movements in Asia.

Further reading: Kosmin, Barry A., and Seymour P. Lachman. *One Nation under God*. New York: Crown, 1993.

—Eric L. Thomas

Bully Pulpit, The: The Politics of Protestant Clergy (1997) James L. Guth, John C. Green, Corwin E. Smidt, Lyman A. Kellstedt, and Margaret M. Poloma. Lawrence: University Press of Kansas

The Bully Pulpit is the most comprehensive and useful study of the politics of Protestant clergy in the United States yet written. Building on and extending the pathbreaking work of Hadden (1969) and Quinley (1994), the book embodies the collaborative efforts of five of the U.S. foremost students of religion and politics—James L. Guth, John C. Green, Corwin E. Smidt, Lyman A. Kellstedt, and Margaret M. Poloma. This important book reflects the growing realization among scholars that clergy not only are potentially important political actors in American politics but that the nature of their political roles is complex and changes over time.

The core of the book's analysis "is based on national surveys of more than 5,000 clergy in eight church bodies": the ASSEMBLIES OF GOD (AOG), the SOUTHERN BAPTIST CONVENTION (SBC), the Evangelical Covenant Church, the Christian Reformed Church (CRC), the Reformed Church in America (RCA) (see DUTCH REFORMED TRADITION), the UNITED METHODIST CHURCH, the PRESBYTERIAN CHURCH IN THE UNITED STATES OF AMERICA (PCUSA), and the Christian Church (Disciples of Christ—DOC). In addition to these surveys, conducted in 1989, the authors rely on a variety of other sources, including a 1992 survey of Evangelical Covenant clergy, 1992, and 1996 studies of Southern Baptist clergy, a 1992 survey of Christian Reformed ministers, and the 1990–91 Wheaton Religious Activist Survey.

Guth et al. posit a simple model of pastoral politics: "ministers' theological beliefs, expressed in a social theology and modified by social context, generate political goals and activities. Because ministers' theology, social theology, and social context differ, their goals and activities will vary as well."

The authors begin their analysis with a discussion of the history and theology of their eight denominations. While these denominations by no means constitute a comprehensive roster of all American Protestant denominations, they arguably do constitute a theologically representative sample, including relatively modernist denominations such as the PCUSA and DOC, as well as relatively orthodox denominations such as the AOG and the SBC. Including such denominational diversity is important since the *Bully Pulpit*'s data reveal that the old "two-party" division "between the orthodox and their modernist opponents still characterizes the theological landscape of American Protestantism." The authors find distinct theological differences between clergy from various denominations, with some denominations proving to be far more orthodox than others.

To the authors of *The Bully Pulpit,* theological views are important, in part, because they help to shape ministers' social theology. Guth et al.'s data support common perceptions of orthodox Protestants as holding a more individualist social theology and modernist Protestants as holding a more communication social theology, regardless of denominational affiliation.

When Guth et al. examine the issue positions of Protestant clergy, they find "the historic political agendas of the Evangelical and Mainline Protestant traditions largely intact," with more orthodox, evangelical ministers tending to support a moral reform agenda and more modernist, mainline ministers tending to support a social justice agenda. Furthermore, Guth et al.'s analysis of clergy political ideology demonstrates that there is "an increasingly firm ideological basis for a 'two-party' system in American Protestantism," with evangelical clergy generally representing the political right and mainline clergy representing the political left. While the most powerful influence on issue positions and ideology proved to be theological perspectives, religious tradition and membership in competing religious movements also mattered.

The final chapters of *The Bully Pulpit* examine the partisanship and political activities of Protestant clergy. In this analysis we learn that Protestant clergy "have chosen party affiliations consistent with their theological and ideological perspectives," with orthodox clergy tending to be more Republican than their more modernist peers. We also learn that while modernist ministers tend to be more supportive of political activism than are orthodox ministers, "positive attitudes about political involvement are on the rise among orthodox ministers." Similarly, the data suggest that although modernist, liberals still have a participatory edge among clergy, the "participation gap" has narrowed. The authors conclude that "the critical differences" among clergy are primarily "ideational"; that is, issues of theology, social theology, and political attitudes matter.

Further reading: Djupe, Paul A., and Christopher P. Gilbert. *The Prophetic Pulpit: Clergy, Churches and Communities in American Politics.* Lanham, Md.: Rowman and Littlefield, 2003; Hadden, Jeffrey. *The Gathering Storm in the Churches.* Garden City, N.Y.: Doubleday, 1969; Olson, Laura R. *Filled with Spirit and Power: Protestant Clergy in Politics.* New York: State University of New York Press, 2000; Quinley, Harold. *The Prophetic Clergy.* New York: Wiley, 1974.

—James M. Penning

bus boycotts

Boycotting buses was one of the most effective protest methods used during the early days of the CIVIL RIGHTS MOVEMENT, though the tactic was employed earlier against streetcars. The bus boycotts and the subsequent social and economic ramifications demonstrated the power of nonviolent and direct-action protest tactics. Targeting public transportation was crucial, because these business were owned by whites but utilized primarily by blacks; thus, blacks wielded significant economic power: "Let us touch to the quick of the white man's pocket. Tis there his conscience often lies." The major bus boycotts were organized in three capital cities in the South, Baton Rouge, Louisiana; Tallahassee, Florida; and Montgomery, Alabama, in which the boycotts caused enormous economic and social disruption.

The success of the first bus boycott in Baton Rouge (1953), though short (seven days), greatly influenced two ministers from Montgomery: MARTIN LUTHER KING JR. and RALPH ABERNATHY, who would later become leaders of the Civil Rights movement. The Montgomery bus boycott began in 1955 when Rosa Parks refused to give up her seat to a white man. The boycott lasted more than a year and culminated in a Supreme Court ruling that banned segregated busing. The

Tallahassee bus boycott started five months after the Montgomery boycott and put the bus companies out of business. The larger significance of the Tallahassee boycott was that nonviolent protest methods could be utilized with great success in smaller as well as larger southern cities.

The rear seating of the buses in Baton Rouge was marked "colored section" and the front was marked "white section." In June 1953, the Rev. T. J. JEMISON called on African Americans in Baton Rouge not to ride the buses. Nightly meetings were held at the Mt. Zion Baptist Church, and the boycott mobilized the African-American community. A "free car lift" of private cars was organized to replace the bus system. The Baton Rouge boycott highlighted the black church as an organizing and mobilizing force, and its success sparked the more famous Montgomery bus boycott. The boycott was, in Jemison's words, "100 percent effective."

The Montgomery bus boycott became one of the most storied events in the Civil Rights movement. It began when Rosa Parks would not give her seat to a white man; her subsequent arrest touched off a yearlong bus boycott. The role of the churches and ministers in the organization and implementation of the boycotts is illustrated by the leaders of the boycott: the Reverends King and Abernathy. These leaders called on other ministers and churches throughout Montgomery to build a network that would get people to and from work, as well as help workers who lost their jobs because of the boycotts. The churches produced a new organization created to oversee the boycott, the Montgomery Improvement Association (MIA), of which Reverend King was the first leader. This longest of the bus boycotts resulted in the Supreme Court ruling ending bus segregation in November 1956.

The Tallahassee bus boycott began on the heels of the Montgomery bus boycott in May 1956. During that month, two women students from Florida A&M University refused to give up their seats to whites. Inspired by the successful boycott in Baton Rouge and the positive nature of the Montgomery bus boycott, Tallahassee became the third city to utilize the strategy. Though students were the first to begin mobilizing citizens not to ride the bus, church leaders soon became involved. Reverend Steele, president of the Tallahassee NAACP, and James Hudson, head of the interdenominational organization of black ministers, began calling on congregations around the city to boycott the bus system. Soon after the bus boycott was in full effect, private cars and other transportation were organized. Organizational meetings were held at different churches around the city, and the boycott continued until the Supreme Court ruling. Despite the ruling, African Americans were still forced to sit at the back of the bus. To counter this massive white resistance, the boycotts were kept in place until segregation ended, nearly two years after the protests began.

Further reading: Morris, Aldon D. *The Origins of the Civil Rights Movement: Black Communities Organizing for Change.* New York: Free Press, 1984.

—Caroline M. Nordlund

Bush, George W. (1946–) *U.S. president*

George W. Bush was born on June 2, 1946, in Midland, Texas. After serving as governor of Texas (1995–2000), he was elected the 43rd president of the United States in 2000. Bush attributes his success in politics to how his life turned around after becoming a born-again Christian (see BORN-AGAIN EXPERIENCE). As the oil boom faded by the mid-1980s, Bush was experiencing the grinding fears and tensions of owning an oil business on the rocks. He started drinking heavily but also went through a period of intense introspection. After a conversation with evangelist BILLY GRAHAM percolated in his thinking, Bush renewed his Christian faith. He recalled in his autobiography *A Charge to Keep* (1999), "Most lives have defining moments. Moments that forever change you. Moments that set you on a different course. Renewing my faith, getting married and having children top my list of those memorable moments."

Bush's career took a sharp turnabout by 1989. With the help of his father's wealthy friends, Bush became managing general partner of the Texas Rangers, which also gave him considerable media exposure in the state. In 1994 he defeated the incumbent Democratic governor, Ann Richards, rallying his supporters around the message "Take a stand for Texas values."

Subsequently, the relation of Bush's faith and politics has met at four pivotal events: the birth of his faith-based social service policy; the execution in Texas of Karla Faye Tucker; his decision to run for president; and the terrorist attacks on SEPTEMBER 11, 2001.

During Bush's first term as governor of Texas, Teen Challenge, a pentecostal drug rehabilitation ministry with a branch in San Antonio, opposed the State of Texas's demands that the ministry hire only staff trained according to the state's psychiatric standards. The ministry claimed that its unique blend of biblical counseling, intense fellowship, prayer, and cold-turkey abstinence would be fatally undermined by the state's secular standards. Consequently, in 1995 the Texas Commission on Alcohol and Drug Abuse moved to close down the ministry. Teen Challenge's supporters gathered at the Alamo, where Bush met with them.

The governor came away from the meeting determined to make government user-friendly to faith-based organizations (FBOs). The germs of his "compassionate conservatism," which advocates government FBO partnerships to solve social problems, arose out of the confrontation. Bush sided with Teen Challenge against his own state agency. Then, he passed legislation institutionalizing equal legal treatment for faith-based approaches, issued an executive order establishing the option that the state could use private and religious charities to deliver welfare services (called CHARITABLE CHOICE), and made Texas the first state to permit a ministry to operate a state prison. At least by 1997, Bush started to call his package of government reforms, which included cooperation with FBOs, "compassionate conservatism." Earlier politicians had used the phrase, but Bush made it his own.

Bush's faith-based politics was sharply challenged in 1998, however, with the debate over the death penalty for Karla

Faye Tucker, who was on death row in Texas. A recent convert to Christianity, Tucker appealed for clemency from the death penalty imposed for her pickax murders of two people. Religious broadcaster PAT ROBERTSON and other conservative Christian leaders joined her appeal. In this case, Governor Bush faced two questions: did his Christian faith allow the death penalty, and should his sympathy for a fellow Christian believer override his sense of justice? Bush recalls announcing his decision as "one of the hardest things I have ever done." On February 3, 1998, Bush signed the death warrant for Tucker. "I have sought guidance through prayer," he said at a news conference at the time. "I have concluded judgements about the heart and soul of an individual on death row are best left to a higher authority." Just before the execution of Tucker, Bush "felt like a huge piece of concrete was crushing me as we waited. Those remain the longest 20 minutes of my tenure as governor."

Bush's next pivotal crossing of faith and politics came in his decision to run for president. While listening to a sermon during the festivities for his second inauguration as governor, Bush told friends that he felt the call of God to run for president. During the presidential campaign, Bush relied on Christian conservatives to help him win a crucial primary in South Carolina. But, as the campaign segued north, Bush mainly courted the white ethnic Catholic vote and used appearances with African-American pastors to give him a more liberal image. After the campaign, Bush's manager, Karl Rove identified the Roman Catholic vote as crucial to the Republican strategy. Also, Evangelical Protestants made up 40 percent of Bush's voters.

One of the first acts that Bush did on becoming president was to establish the WHITE HOUSE OFFICE OF FAITH-BASED AND COMMUNITY INITIATIVES. The goals of the office continued similar ones that Bush had pursued while he was governor of Texas. He wanted to make the federal bureaucracy interface more easily with FBOs, and he hoped to pass legislation allocating money to the social services they ran. However, the legislation allocating money to FBOs stalled in the face of concerns about the SEPARATION OF CHURCH AND STATE.

The terrorist attacks of September 11, 2001, also diverted the Bush administration from the parts of its domestic agenda that lacked support. The White House Office of Faith-Based and Community Initiatives was reorganized to focus more on community service in other countries. However, the Septem-

President George W. Bush shakes hands with John DiIulio, director of the White House Office of Faith-Based and Community Initiatives. *(Getty Images)*

ber catastrophes also posed a moment of decision for Bush. The nation wondered if its new president was up to the task. American Muslims wondered if the Christian president would unleash a crusade against them. In response, Bush seemed to find a new resoluteness and maturity. He easily talked of his faith while also warmly embracing U.S. Muslim leaders. The president told a gathering of religious leaders shortly after the attacks, "I think this is part of a spiritual awakening in America." The president told friends that he understood God's call to service with greater clarity. He told the nation in a televised memorial service, "In our grief and anger we have found our mission and our moment."

See also AMERICAN MUSLIM COUNCIL; RELIGION IN THE 2000 PRESIDENTIAL ELECTION.

Further reading: Bush, George W. *A Charge to Keep.* New York: William Morrow, 1999; Carnes, Tony. "A Presidential Hopeful's Progress." *Christianity Today* (October 3, 2000): 62–64; Carnes, Tony. "Bush's Defining Moment." *Christianity Today* (November 12, 2001): 38–42; Olasky, Marvin. *Compassionate Conservatism.* New York: Free Press, 2000.

—Tony Carnes

C

Call to Action

Call to Action was the name of the 1976 justice conference sponsored by the NATIONAL CONFERENCE OF CATHOLIC BISHOPS (NCCB) to observe the U.S. Bicentennial. It is also the name of an independent social movement organization inspired by that conference, which promotes internal church reform and social justice. The name itself is the subtitle of *Octogesima Advenians* (1971), an apostolic letter marking the 80th anniversary of *RERUM NOVARUM* (1891), the papal encyclical that inaugurated modern Catholic social teaching.

Progressive cardinal John Dearden headed the NCCB committee that selected "Liberty and Justice for All" as the theme of the Catholic bicentennial observance. Consistent with the American ethos and ROMAN CATHOLIC CHURCH social teaching, the program sought to stimulate reflection, planning, and action for SOCIAL JUSTICE. The program had three phases:

1. In 1975, consultation was undertaken at the local church level. Six "justice hearings" were held that gathered panels of bishops in various regions of the country to listen to both experts and victims of injustice.
2. Data from these consultations were used as the basis for resolutions to be discussed and voted on at a conference to formulate a national church policy on social justice. The conference was held in Detroit on October 21–23, 1976. Delegates numbered 1,331; of these, 47 percent were laity, 34 percent were clergy, 17 percent were nuns, and 64 percent were church employees. The conference passed 182 resolutions focused on eight areas: Church, Ethnicity and Race, Family, Humankind, Nationhood, Neighborhood, Personhood, and Work.
3. From 1976 to 1981, policies based on conference resolutions were supposed to be implemented, monitored, and evaluated.

Conference delegates affirmed a progressive political agenda rooted in Catholic social teaching. They called for the American Catholic Church to become more multicultural.

The bishops' pastoral letter on RACISM was commissioned. The assembly condemned the production, possession, and proliferation of nuclear arms and supported conscientious objection to military service and the payment of war taxes. The delegates endorsed the EQUAL RIGHTS AMENDMENT to the U.S. Constitution.

Approximately 10 conference resolutions called for changes in church policies, such as ending the bans on the ordination of married persons and women, reconsidering the contraception stance, being more tolerant of gays and lesbians, and democratizing the process of selecting bishops. Delegates interpreted these resolutions as attempts to promote equality and dialogue within the church. NCCB president Archbishop JOSEPH BERNARDIN saw the resolutions as inappropriate and unrepresentative of the views of the majority of American Catholics. Conservative bishops increased their control as the third phase began and made sure the 10 resolutions were rejected. Both bishops and delegates agree that this stifled the momentum of the program.

Liberal Chicago Catholics, already angry about the autocratic rule of John Cardinal Cody, perceived the bishops' action as an abandonment of Call to Action and VATICAN II reforms. In 1978 a group of liberal Chicago Catholic organizations cosponsored an unofficial follow-up to the Call to Action conference. Dan Daley became the coordinator of this movement.

Chicago Catholics had a tradition of progressivism, and the city was a center for Catholic Action, a movement that emphasized an active role for laity in the mission of the church. The "Chicago style" of this movement encouraged laity to work with clergy, but not to be dominated by them. Catholics influenced by this tradition joined forces to form the social movement Chicago Call to Action (CTA). To facilitate communication, a regular newsletter, "Call to Action News," began publication in 1978. Early meetings of the movement centered on the Detroit conference resolutions. The group challenged Cody's authoritarian style and financial secrecy. It also focused on local and national justice issues. Since 1981 the movement has sponsored annual conferences.

After Cody's death in 1982, Joseph Bernardin was appointed as Chicago's archbishop. CTA had a direct and cordial relationship with him. During the 1980s, CTA participated in consultations for the bishops' peace (1983) and economics (1986) pastorals. Its performing arts ministry won a 1987 Vatican Communications Day award for writing and producing a play on the pastorals.

In 1990, Call to Action sponsored an ad in the *New York Times,* signed by 4,500 people, that echoes some controversial themes from the 1976 conference. This inaugurated CTA as a national movement with local chapters. In 1996, CTA gained national attention when the bishop of Lincoln, Nebraska, excommunicated all members of the local chapter.

Today Call to Action is a social movement with 20,000 members. It stresses that the inner life of the church must be evaluated by the same norms used to evaluate society in regard to justice and equality. It continues to promote a progressive politics agenda rooted in Catholic social teaching.

See also CATHOLIC BISHOPS' 1975 PASTORAL LETTER ON ABORTION; CATHOLIC BISHOPS' 1986 PASTORAL LETTER ON THE ECONOMY; CATHOLIC BISHOPS' 1983 PASTORAL LETTER ON WAR AND PEACE; *CATHOLIC BISHOPS IN AMERICAN POLITICS;* CATHOLICS FOR FREE CHOICE.

—Anthony J. Pogorelc

Call to Renewal

Formed in 1995, Call to Renewal (CTR) is a loosely organized, Christian-based movement that initially set a very broad goal—to offer an alternative to both the Christian Right and secular left that mobilizes individuals, churches, and other faith-based organizations to fight poverty, dismantle RACISM, promote healthier families and communities, and reassert the dignity of human life. Later, CTR elevated poverty fighting as its primary raison d'être. CTR's agenda, rhetoric, and strategies largely reflect the influence of its primary convener, *Sojourners* editor JIM WALLIS.

CTR is not a mass-membership organization; in 1999 its mailing list reportedly numbered only about 7,500. It is more like a federation—a network that, according to Wallis, is mobilized on the model of the black CIVIL RIGHTS MOVEMENT (minus the close identification with the Democratic Party). CTR has worked hard and with some success to attract support from black Protestants, mainline Protestants, Mennonites, Roman Catholics, and moderate and conservative Evangelical Protestants. Liberal evangelical groups (e.g., *Sojourners,* EVANGELICALS FOR SOCIAL ACTION) play a leading role, as does the DUTCH REFORMED TRADITION.

CTR grew out of the "Cry for Renewal," a protest/media event held in Washington, D.C., on May 23, 1995. In the wake of the 1994 election, in which the Christian Right helped Republicans gain power in Congress, liberal evangelicals felt a renewed urgency to get out the message that not all evangelicals are right-wing, a message journalists then found novel and newsworthy. *Sojourners* seized the opportunity, taking the lead in drafting a statement that criticized both the religious right and the religious left for being driven by ideology and lust for power via partisan politics. It called for a new "spiritual politics" that is biblical and transcends the ideological left and right.

Nearly a hundred Christian leaders from across the political spectrum signed on as "initiating endorsers." Encouraged by the response, Cry for Renewal sponsors continued to cultivate the network and set up a February 1996 organizing conference for CTR.

CTR's diversity proved to be a blessing and a challenge, as there was early confusion and disagreement over tactics and goals. For instance, although early CTR rhetoric emphasized the need for a politically influential alternative to the Christian Right, distrust of traditional lobbying and electoral tactics ran deep among some CTR constituencies. Thus, on an organizational continuum from social movements to party factions, it became clear that whereas the Christian Right tacked toward the party faction end of the scale, CTR would gravitate to the social movement model—with a focus toward changing society rather than working within a governing coalition.

The idealistic vision of a comprehensively biblical agenda also ran into the hard realities of coalition maintenance. The earliest articulation of CTR planks linked the goals of affirming "life" (signaling openness to moderately conservative views on abortion) with antipoverty and antiviolence efforts, a linkage akin to the CONSISTENT ETHIC OF LIFE advocated by many Catholics and liberal evangelicals. However, some liberal CTR supporters promised to quit the coalition if any policy substance was ever attached to these vaguely pro-life sentiments. CTR delayed action on such issues, focusing instead on poverty, a high biblical priority for all members.

With an eye on achieving a unified religious voice on behalf of the poor, CTR began in 1997 to bring together religious leaders—including some from the Christian Right—for a series of National Roundtables on Churches and Poverty. CTR also began holding annual summit meetings. At the 2000 summit, CTR launched its Covenant and Campaign to Overcome Poverty. The covenant, an eloquently worded pledge to fight poverty, was promoted in a manner similar to a petition with the goal of attracting a million signers. As for policy recommendations, CTR's campaign remained rather broad, pointing in generally left-of-center directions on welfare policies. But CTR did give guarded support for public funding of faith-based social services according to the principles of CHARITABLE CHOICE, a signature issue in GEORGE W. BUSH's "compassionate conservatism." John DiIulio, a Catholic political scientist on CTR's board of directors, was named to head Bush's WHITE HOUSE OFFICE OF FAITH-BASED AND COMMUNITY INITIATIVES.

While CTR did employ stock advocacy techniques such as VOTER GUIDES, church study materials, and local forums, it demonstrated a particular knack for attracting media attention—e.g., during the 2000 national party conventions, CTR helped stage "Shadow conventions" on issues of poverty, campaign finance, and drugs. Such events also underscored CTR's affinity for alternative, "prophetic" politics.

See also CHRISTIAN RIGHT AND THE REPUBLICAN PARTY; RELIGION IN THE CONGRESSIONAL ELECTIONS OF 1994; WELFARE REFORM.

Further reading: Koopman, Douglas L. "The Call to Renewal." Paper presented at the annual meeting of the American Political Science Association, Washington, D.C., 1997; VanDerWerff, Jeffrey A. "Capturing the Countervailing Power of Call to Renewal." Paper presented at the annual meeting of the American Political Science Association, Atlanta, 1999.

—Dennis R. Hoover

Calvinism

The term *Calvinism* refers to the theology and beliefs developed and promoted by the 16th-century theologian John Calvin. These beliefs, as well as the principles of church polity and the social ethics derived from these beliefs, have had a profound influence on Protestantism and continue to influence Western culture in important respects.

Calvin, trained in both theology and law, was born and educated in France but is best known for his work as a scholar, pastor, and politician in southern Germany, Basel, and, especially, Geneva. Calvin's theology is most completely developed in his 1536 magnum opus, *Institutes of the Christian Religion,* one of the most important statements of Protestant belief ever written. Calvin also articulated his thought in a variety of other writings, including a series of biblical commentaries. Although Calvin's theology was firmly rooted in Scripture, he recognized the troublesome nature of hermeneutics and stressed the need for an informed clergy to interpret Scripture to the laity. This, in part, helps to explain his stress on education, as well as on frequent public worship.

At the heart of Calvinism are the concepts of the "sovereignty of God" (God rules over all) and the "total depravity" of humans (sin has fundamentally corrupted all creation, making it impossible for humans to achieve salvation through their own efforts). Much flows from the concept of total depravity, including Calvinism's emphasis on the need for salvation and sanctification, a belief in the necessity of redeeming culture, and a stress on the importance of civil authority (to restrain evil). Other key elements of Calvinism include a belief in the doctrines of predestination (God has foreordained all things), election (God chooses whom he wishes to save), irresistible grace (God's saving grace is all-powerful), limited atonement (Christ died for those whom God gave him to save), and the preservation of the saints (once saved, a person remains saved).

Although John Calvin is sometimes perceived as cold, rigid, and overly intellectual, there is evidence that this perspective is misleading. Calvin did place great emphasis on spirituality, the importance of God's love, and the inability of

humans to fully comprehend the mind of God. After his death, however, some leading Calvinists, including his Geneva lieutenant, Theodore Beza, attempted to systematize Calvinism, producing a kind of latter-day scholasticism that placed greater emphasis on systematic theology than on the gifts of the spirit.

As Calvinism spread throughout northern Europe, England, Scotland, and later, America, different variants of Calvinism developed, making it difficult to speak of a single "Calvinism." Calvin himself had encouraged the spread of Calvinism by inviting scholars and clergy from across Europe to study at Geneva before returning to their home countries. Through this method, as well as through his writings, Calvin had a significant impact on religious groups as diverse as the PURITANS, the Reformed Church in the Netherlands, the Church of Scotland, and Presbyterian, Baptist, and Reformed churches in central Europe and North America. It is hardly surprising that these diverse groups produced a number of Calvinist emphases, including the COVENANT THEOLOGY, embodied in the Westminster Confession, the emphasis of Dutch theologian and politician Abraham Kuyper on transforming all culture in the name of Christ, and the Puritan stress on piety and individual salvation.

Calvinism not only has had a major impact on Protestantism but, in a larger sense, Calvinism has also had a major impact on Western culture. Max Weber, for example, made a well-known effort to link Calvinism's discipline and work ethic to the rise of modern capitalism. Others have attempted to link Calvinistic rationalism to the rise of modern science.

Perhaps most important, historians have argued that Calvinism has had notable political consequences, helping to pave the way for the rise of liberal democracy. Calvin himself rejected monarchy in favor of a form of republican government. And his emphasis on the value of each individual before God may well have had important implications for democratic POLITICAL PARTICIPATION. But Calvin also stressed the importance of subjection to the "higher powers" as "ordained by God," admitting to only a limited right of citizens to challenge government authority or foment revolution. This may help explain why Calvinism, following the lead of Calvin himself, has tended to foster conservative politics and conservative political movements.

See also DUTCH REFORMED TRADITION; FREE PRESBYTERIANS; PRESBYTERIAN CHURCH IN AMERICA; PRESBYTERIAN CHURCH USA; SOUTHERN BAPTIST CONVENTION.

—James M. Penning

Campolo, Anthony (Tony) (1935–) *activist*

Anthony Campolo was born on February 25, 1935, in Philadelphia, Pennsylvania. He did his undergraduate work at Eastern College in St. David's, Pennsylvania, and earned a Ph.D. from Temple University. A uniquely controversial figure in the world of religion and politics, Campolo is a veteran of the religious and academic world. He came to prominence in the mid-1980s for his religious and political activism. Campolo has authored 28 books, many of which have been controversial. As a dedicated believer in ECUMENICISM among evangelicals, he has become recognized for his ministry of reconciliation and revitalization, both within the church and within the community. Campolo is the founder and president of the Evangelical Association for the Promotion of Education, an organization involved in educational, medical, and economic development programs in a number of developing countries, including Haiti and the Dominican Republic. This organization also has done widespread work with at-risk youth in urban America. Campolo is professor emeritus of sociology and director of the Urban Studies Program at Eastern College. Previously, he taught for 10 years on the faculty of the University of Pennsylvania.

In May 1995, saying that they had had enough of politics as usual, Campolo and more than 100 other Christian leaders from "a diversity of traditions" stepped forward to sign a document called "Cry for Renewal." The group, calling itself CALL TO RENEWAL, was formed to respond to the so-called Religious Right. In response to religious opposition, Campolo remains active in defense of his beliefs. He believes that Christians should be much more involved in helping to alleviate suffering in the world. His activism on social issues is a direct outgrowth of this belief. Campolo developed Cornerstone Christian Academy for inner-city children with learning disabilities and founded an organization that helps to set up Christian hospices for AIDS victims. Campolo also serves on the international board of directors for Habitat for Humanity.

Campolo provided regular counsel to President WILLIAM JEFFERSON CLINTON during his terms in office on social policy, including the problems affecting the nation's inner cities and nationalized health care. Additionally, Campolo was widely publicized as providing President Clinton with spiritual counsel following the Monica Lewinsky affair. Some conservative evangelicals were critical of Campolo's support for the president and critical of some of his theological stances. For his part, Campolo has questioned some of the theological and social policy positions of conservative evangelicals. He has been referred to as a "progressive evangelical" because of his many stances on social issues and his drive to see changes made in public policy. He has been featured on JAMES DOBSON's FOCUS ON THE FAMILY radio show and has produced educational materials for David C. Cook, a respected publisher of Christian instructional materials. He has been on the frontline of the debates between the different elements within EVANGELICALISM. The response Campolo elicits covers a wide range of opinions, as evidence above. It is this penchant for "stirring things up" that continues to challenge evangelical thinking on issues and theology.

He is a regular guest on a wide range of television programs including *Nightline, Politically Incorrect,* and CNN's *Crossfire.* He cohosted his own television series, *Hashing It Out,* on the Odyssey Network and currently hosts *From Across the Pond,* a weekly program on the Premier Radio Network in England.

Campolo is an ordained minister and currently serves as an associate pastor of the Mount Carmel Baptist Church in West Philadelphia. He is married and has two grown children and four grandchildren.

See also EVANGELICALS FOR SOCIAL ACTION; SIDER, RON; WALLIS, JIM.

Further reading: Wallis, Jim. "A Network for Renewal." *Sojourners* (July–August 1995): 6.
　　　　　　　　　　　—William Lester and Sarah Gossman

canon law

Tracing its origins back to the Apostles, canon law continues today to govern the ROMAN CATHOLIC CHURCH. Further, this body of law developed within the Catholic Church has exerted considerable influence on legal systems around the globe, including that of the United States.

The church developed its law over time, as bishops and various church councils and local leaders legislated on matters of Christian faith and behavior. Decrees by popes (known as "papal letters" or "decretals") also came to play a key role in the growth of this law. Canon law was inspired by such sources as biblical texts and "the Holy Spirit."

Scattered across geography and over time, these religious decrees varied widely and on occasion conflicted with one another. The scholar Gratian first began the task of compiling these scattered writings into a comprehensive, systematic collection in the 12th century. Gratian's work, widely known as the "decretum," also drew heavily from Roman law; his hybrid of Roman and canon law became known as the *"ius commune,"* or the "common law" of medieval Europe.

From the time of Gratian until the Protestant Reformation in the early 16th century, the church and its laws provided much of the stability and structure that existed in medieval Europe. Throughout the Christian world, the laws of the church heavily influenced the laws of the land. For example, Reid and Witte suggest "until the sixteenth century, the Church's canon law of marriage was the law of the West."

Canon law continues to govern spiritual matters within the Catholic Church, including such sacraments as baptism and marriage, as well as all matters relating to the clergy. For example, the church's requirements for nullities (annulments) and the prohibitions against ABORTION and the ordination of women as priests are enshrined in canon law.

The church's law continues to evolve over time. In signing the Code of Canon Law of 1983, Pope JOHN PAUL II signed into effect a number of revisions. While many of these revisions focused on procedural and administrative matters, this new code was heavily influenced by reforms instituted by Pope John XXIII's Second Vatican Ecumenical Council (popularly known as VATICAN II). The new code places a heavy emphasis on "defining and protecting the rights and obligations of the church members in their relationships with each other and the church." Brennan has argued that the 1983 code also significantly changed the church's conception of marriage, deemphasizing the primacy of procreation as the purpose of marriage in favor "of a fresh theology of married love."

Canon law has also contributed significantly to secular law around the world. For example, it is widely credited with influencing the development of the English common law. With respect to American law, Helmholz has asserted that "such principles as the Fifth Amendment's prohibition against double jeopardy (being tried twice for the same offense) can be traced back to Roman law as incorporated by the Church." Helmholz has made similar claims about the origins of the Fifth Amendment's protection against self-incrimination. In the area of family law, the American legal conception of marriage as a form of contract has drawn heavily from classical canon law.

The effects of canon law also continue to reverberate in spiritual matters even outside the Roman Catholic Church. For example, while the Church of England (Anglican Church) split off from Rome in 1534, the Anglican Communion has drawn heavily from Catholic laws in developing its own canons. In short, the canon law of the Roman Catholic Church remains a powerful force across the globe, for Catholics and non-Catholics alike.

Further reading: Alesandro, John A., Msgr. "A Study of Canon Law: Dismissal from the Clerical State in Cases of Sexual Misconduct." *Catholic Lawyer* 36 (1996): 257–300; Brennan, Patrick McGinley. "Review Essay: Of Marriage and Monks, Community and Dialogue." *Emory Law Journal* 48 (1999): 689–732; Helmholz, R. H. "Origins of the Privilege against Self-Incrimination: The Role of the European *Ius Commune*." *New York University Law Review* 65 (1990): 962–990; ———. *The Spirit of Classical Cannon Law.* Athens: University of Georgia Press, 1996; Reid, Charles J., Jr., and John Witte, Jr. "Review Essay: In the Steps of Gratian: Writing the History of Canon Law in the 1990s." *Emory Law Journal* 48 (1999): 647–688.

—Staci L. Beavers

Cantwell v. Connecticut 310 U.S. 296 (1940)

On May 20, 1940, the Supreme Court handed down its decision in *Cantwell et al. v. Connecticut.* Like many early FREE EXERCISE cases, *Cantwell* involved members of the JEHOVAH'S WITNESSES. Here, a father and his two sons had been arrested while proselytizing in New Haven, Connecticut. Their conviction rested on a state law that prohibited solicitation without prior approval. Appellants argued that the statute was unconstitutional: a deprivation of their rights to free speech and free exercise without the FOURTEENTH AMENDMENT's requirement of due process. Writing for a unanimous court, Justice Owen Roberts overturned the convictions, ruling that the Connecticut law represented an impermissible prior restraint of speech and religious exercise. The Court also set aside one son's separate conviction of inciting a breach of the peace, ruling that he had engaged in no action that could sustain the conviction. To prosecute him for unpopular religious beliefs was to violate his very right to hold them.

Two important constitutional concepts stand at the heart of the *Cantwell* opinion. First, the decision relied on the concept of incorporation. Before its 1937 decision in *Palko v. Connecticut,* the Court lacked a clear statement of how the BILL OF RIGHTS should be applied to the states. In language reminiscent of *Palko,* Justice Roberts held that all aspects of the First Amendment were included in the "fundamental concept of liberty." As such, the Fourteenth Amendment prohibited the states from passing laws that infringe on the free exercise of religion. Were it not for incorporation, the Cantwells could not have claimed that a state law violated their federal rights.

Roberts's opinion also relied on the so-called belief-action dichotomy, traceable to REYNOLDS V. UNITED STATES (1879), a Mormon POLYGAMY case. This view holds that freedom of religion comprises two parts: an inviolable freedom of conscience and a corresponding freedom to act on one's chosen beliefs. This second component, however, is never absolute. In particular, it can be circumscribed when necessary for the protection of society as a whole. Both state laws at issue—the regulation of solicitation and the preservation of the public peace—were permissible uses of state police power. The real question was whether the laws were written to avoid an undue infringement of protected freedoms.

This was where the Connecticut law failed. The establishment of general and nondiscriminatory measures to regulate solicitation—such as by time, place, and manner restrictions—would have presented no constitutional problem. Connecticut, however, chose to require solicitation permits that would be granted only if a public official decided that the cause was sufficiently religious or worthwhile. This official's power to prevent individuals from exercising their First Amendment rights, based solely on his own judgment as to what constituted "true religion," represented an impermissible prior restraint. The Court was unimpressed with the state's claim that abuses of discretion would be remedied through judicial channels. Such oversight may have a role but does nothing to correct the problem of prior restraint.

The Court overturned Jesse Cantwell's separate conviction by first disputing the facts of the case. While Cantwell's religious beliefs might have been offensive to some, nothing in his actual behavior amounted to a breach of the peace or an attempt to incite a breach. The state had offered no evidence of a clear and present danger, as defined by Justice Holmes in *Schenck v. U.S.* (1919). In addition, Cantwell had not engaged in the use of "fighting words," which would later be held as unprotected speech in *Chaplinsky v. New Hampshire* (1942). To deem Cantwell's behavior unlawful, Connecticut would have needed a statute narrowly tailored to his specific actions.

The test outlined in *Cantwell* sought to balance individual rights against the state's interest in neutrally pursuing legitimate interests. Known as the "valid secular policy test," it figured prominently in several subsequent and conflicting cases, including: MINERSVILLE SCHOOL DISTRICT V. GOBITIS (1940), WEST VIRGINIA BOARD OF EDUCATION V. BARNETTE (1943), and

PRINCE V. MASSACHUSETTS (1944)—all of which involved Jehovah's Witnesses. In more recent years, the Court has distinguished *Cantwell* as a hybrid case, encompassing both freedom of speech and religion (*EMPLOYMENT DIVISION V. SMITH*, 1990).

Attention to the details of this case serves as an important reminder about the history of free exercise. Perhaps what angered New Haven most was that the Cantwells were preaching their anti-Catholic views in an area dominated by the ROMAN CATHOLIC CHURCH. More often than not, the contours of free exercise have been established not in the struggle between religion and nonreligion, but between competing religions.

See also JEHOVAH'S WITNESSES.

—Matthew M. C. Roberts

Carroll, John (1735–1815) *Jesuit priest*

John Carroll was born in 1735 to a Catholic family of the Maryland aristocracy. They were prominent patriots, and John's cousin, Charles Carroll, was a signer of the DECLARATION OF INDEPENDENCE. At age 13, John was sent to Europe to study at the Jesuit School of St. Omer in French Flanders. He joined the Jesuits in 1753 and was ordained a priest in 1769. When Pope Clement XIV suppressed the Jesuits, in 1773, Fr. Carroll returned to Maryland. There a group of American former Jesuits selected him to lead them in the reorganization of their mission.

During the Revolutionary War, Carroll lived on his mother's estate and traveled, as a missionary, to serve Roman Catholics in Maryland and Virginia. In April 1776, he became a reluctant diplomat joining Samuel Chase, BENJAMIN FRANKLIN, and his cousin Charles in a diplomatic mission to Canada to seek help for the colonies in their struggle against Britain. Carroll's patriotism showed in his congratulatory message, on behalf of colonial Catholics, to GEORGE WASHINGTON for his 1789 inauguration.

Carroll led in developing structures for the ROMAN CATHOLIC CHURCH in the United States. In 1782, he drafted a plan to organize the lifetyle of priests, financial arrangements, arbitration and conciliation, and the administration of material assets. In 1784, Rome named Carroll superior of the Mission of the Thirteen United States of North America, a post he held for five years. Benjamin Franklin, who was posted as a diplomat in Paris, was consulted by Rome and recommended Carroll.

Carroll believed the religious situation in the United States had "undergone a revolution . . . more extraordinary than our political one." He believed acceptance of the church in the American context required bishops to be elected by the clergy, not appointed by a foreign power. Conveying these sentiments in March 1788, the priests petitioned Rome to create a diocese. Rome granted the request and left the choice of a bishop and see city to the priests. On May 18, 1789, Carroll was elected bishop of Baltimore by a vote of 24-2. He was consecrated in England on August 15, 1790.

Carroll fostered a church with a clear American identity that acknowledged the pope only as its spiritual head. Those wanting ethnic churches rather than one Catholic American church frustrated him. A national clergy was central to his vision. To recruit and educate future priests, he founded in 1791 the Georgetown Academy (later University) and St. Mary's Seminary in Baltimore. In 1800 Bishop Carroll ordained the first American-born priest, but for the most part he remained dependent on immigrant European clergy. Carroll never secured bishop-collaborators to effectively extend his vision.

Tension characterized the mixture of American democratic forms and the European forms of Catholicism. This tension was embodied in Carroll himself. The influence of enlightenment thought is seen in his strong belief in the separation of church and state. He advocated religious freedom and opposed attempts to make PROTESTANTISM the religion of the republic. He articulated a Catholic apologetic based on reason and intelligibility. Carroll promoted the celebration of the sacraments in English, and when an English Catholic translation of the Bible came out, he was its most energetic salesman.

In parishes, democratic orientations were expressed through the parishioners' election of lay trustees. Some parishioners also wanted to have the right to choose and discharge parish priests at their pleasure. Carroll opposed this, saying "trusteeism" would end "the unity and Catholicity of our church." Carroll upheld a bishop's prerogative to rule his diocese and in 1798 won a lawsuit (the Fromm case) that legally established the authority of the bishop over parishes and priests.

As a bishop, Carroll increasingly was swayed by the designs of Rome. This factor moved American Catholicism into a more traditional, conservative posture. The Synod of 1791 adopted laws issued by European synods and lost the innovative spirit that had characterized earlier days in America. The church was growing, and by 1810 there were five separate dioceses in the United States. Initially Carroll consulted the clergy, and together they selected new bishops. But, after 1807, Carroll submitted names to Rome without consulting the priests. He even sought papal advice on the replacement of bishops. He also retracted his position and opposed the English Mass.

In 1808 Baltimore was raised to the status of an archdiocese, and Carroll became the first American archbishop. John Carroll died in 1815. His voluminous writings remain the best available record of the early period of Catholicism in the United States.

Further reading: Dolan, Jay. *The American Catholic Experience: A History from Colonial Times to the Present.* Garden City, N.Y.: Doubleday, 1985; Hennesey, James. *American Catholics.* New York: Oxford University Press, 1981.

—Anthony J. Pogorelc

Carter, James Earl (1924–)   *U.S. president*

The 39th president of the United States (1977–81), James Earl Carter is widely considered to have been the most religious U.S. president of the 20th century. As a "born-again" Christian, church deacon, and member of the SOUTHERN BAPTIST CONVENTION, Carter frequently asserted publicly that his deep faith in God was the central fact of his life, both personally and professionally. A weekly news magazine dubbed Carter the "most unabashed moralist" candidate for the presidency since WILLIAM JENNINGS BRYAN.

His religious background was never far from the surface throughout his public life. As a presidential candidate (and similar to the treatment of JOHN F. KENNEDY as a candidate), Carter frequently was pressed to assure voters that he would be tolerant of those not sharing his viewpoints and would not try to impose his beliefs on the rest of society. In a likely effort to eliminate those fears, Carter agreed to an interview for *Playboy* magazine. In this interview Carter tried to explain his religious views and to assure the nation that he could separate his beliefs from how he would act as president. His statements likely could have been directed at trying to ease the concern of some voters who viewed him as prude and self-righteous. However, his admission of committing sins, such as lust, caused a furor among his critics and religious supporters alike. In general, Carter's presidential candidacy ignited a nationwide discussion of defining a born-again Christian.

Carter was the first president ever to call himself "born again," and his religious beliefs likely affected his presidency in many ways. Those beliefs probably stimulated his promoting worldwide human rights as an anchor of his foreign policy and his strongly promoting civil rights domestically. His religious beliefs also probably contributed to the crucial role he played in helping negotiate an historic peace settlement between Egypt and Israel brokered at Camp David. The heart of his commitment to helping antagonists negotiate was reportedly his devotion to the Christian doctrine of agape,

meaning love. Carter's deeply held religious beliefs continued to be the key part of his public and political persona throughout his presidency.

Carter was an active Christian throughout his formative years, joining his home church as a youth and participating in activities there throughout his life. Intellectually, he read a number of prominent theologians, such as PAUL TILLICH. Yet he frequently admitted to being most influenced by the writings of REINHOLD NIEBUHR. Also, since the age of 18, Carter was a Sunday school teacher and remained one throughout his life. He even taught some Sunday school classes as a midshipman at the U.S. Naval Academy, to crew members aboard a submarine while on active duty, and later at the First Baptist Church of Washington, D.C., during his presidency.

After leaving the White House, Carter continued his active Christian life. Following publication of his political memoirs, *Keeping Faith*, in 1982, Carter went on to publish what he termed his spiritual autobiography (*Living Faith*) in 1996, plus several other books on his beliefs. He established and worked to fund the Carter Center at Emory University in Atlanta, a nonprofit organization devoted to resolving local, regional, or national conflicts throughout the world. Citizen Carter also took an active role in international peacekeeping. He traveled around the world to help resolve disputes and monitored elections in troubled nations. Carter became active in the Habitat for Humanity worldwide project to build homes for the homeless. He helped raise funds, served on its governing board, and worked on projects himself (together with his wife, Rosalynn) at least one week every year.

In 2000, Carter again made religious headlines by severing his ties to the Southern Baptist Convention, an organization to which his family had been affiliated for three generations. Carter explained his action by saying that he viewed convention leaders as becoming increasingly rigid in their views and intolerant of those who differed with them. He reportedly was particularly troubled by the convention's recent call for literal interpretation of Scripture and for women to play a subordinate role to men in church and family life. His announcement did not affect the active role he continues to play in his home Maranatha Baptist Church in Plains, Georgia, which remained affiliated with the convention. In 2002, Carter was awarded the Nobel Peace Prize.

See also BORN AGAIN EXPERIENCE; RELIGION IN THE 1976 PRESIDENTIAL ELECTION; RELIGION IN THE 1980 PRESIDENTIAL ELECTION.

James Earl Carter *(Jimmy Carter Library)*

Further reading: Bourne, Peter G. *Jimmy Carter: A Comprehensive Biography from Plains to Postpresidency.* New York: Scribner, 1997; Carter, Jimmy. *Keeping Faith: Memoirs of a President.* New York: Bantam Books, 1982; ———. *Living Faith.* New York: Random House, 1996; Haas, Garland. *Jimmy Carter and the Politics of Frustration.* Jefferson, N.C.: McFarland, 1999.

—Robert E. Dewhirst

Catholic Alliance

The Catholic Alliance, a grassroots organization of American Catholics, was formed in 1995 as an offshoot of the CHRISTIAN COALITION, to expand the coalition's support beyond the confines of evangelical Protestantism. The alliance has over 125,000 members and has drawn support from prominent Catholic laypeople, including Bowie Kuhn (the former commissioner of Major League Baseball), Tom Monaghan (the former CEO of Domino's Pizza), and Raymond Flynn (former Democratic mayor of Boston and U.S. ambassador to the Vatican), the latter of whom now serves as the alliance's president. The alliance has advanced a generally conservative agenda, and it has drawn fire from some Catholic bishops and liberal Catholic organizations because of its alleged Republican partisanship and its positions on the death penalty, immigration, and other controversial issues. In recent years, the alliance has severed both organizational and financial ties with the Christian Coalition and now advocates a narrower and more conventionally Catholic set of public policy objectives.

The Catholic Alliance generated controversy within the hierarchy of the ROMAN CATHOLIC CHURCH in America from the moment of its founding. The organization burst onto the scene in October 1995, shortly after Pope JOHN PAUL II's visit to the United States. At that time, the Catholic Alliance sent letters to over 1 million American Catholics and distributed flyers at a number of Catholic churches calling on Catholics to join in "a fight with the radical Left for the soul of our great nation," and identifying the primary enemies of Catholicism as "militant homosexuals, radical feminists, and Big Government liberals." Many priests and bishops were angered by the organization's apparent partisan tilt and by its claim to speak for Catholics when it was at best indifferent to the church's teachings on poverty, war, and capital punishment. The extent of liberal Catholic hostility toward the alliance is apparent from an editorial in *National Catholic Reporter,* which dismissed the organization's policy stances as "the narrow, cribbed agenda of those who claim a divine mandate for their fundamentalist politics" and assailed its leaders as "smiling theocrats who know what is best for all of us." At the 1995 General Meeting of the NATIONAL CONFERENCE OF CATHOLIC BISHOPS, Bishop Howard Hubbard of Albany, New York, cautioned his fellow bishops to be suspicious of the Catholic Alliance and to resist its overtures. At the same time, however, other bishops were much more open to the new organization. BERNARD CARDINAL LAW of Boston stressed that the church neither supported nor opposed the alliance but lauded the efforts of Catholic laypeople to band together for political action, while Bishop James McHugh of Camden, New Jersey, welcomed the alliance as a positive step toward ecumenical dialogue between Catholics and Evangelical Protestants.

Partly in response to this debate, the Catholic Alliance, since its organizational and financial separation from the Christian Coalition in 1998, has backed away from some of the more explicitly political and tangentially Christian policy objectives in its original statement of purpose. Although the organization originally endorsed a very diffuse conservative agenda that included a balanced-budget amendment, congressional term limits, welfare cuts, and tort reform, its website (www.catholicvote.org) now advances a more modest set of goals rooted in traditional Catholic teaching, focusing chiefly on opposition to ABORTION and homosexuality and support for the institution of the family. The organization now lists its priorities as fourfold: the dignity of all human life, the primacy of the family, authentic freedom, and solidarity with the poor and needy. With this reformulation of objectives and with the choice of respected Democrat Raymond Flynn as its president, the Catholic Alliance has managed to curb some of the hostility initially directed at it from the American episcopal hierarchy, and has positioned itself to play a less overtly partisan role in American politics.

See also CATHOLIC LEAGUE FOR RELIGIOUS AND CIVIL RIGHTS.

Further reading: "Catholic Alliance Agenda One of Fear, Exclusion," *National Catholic Reporter* 32 (1995): 24; Kantz, Matt. "Raymond Flynn to Lead Catholic Alliance." *National Catholic Reporter* 35 (1999): 8; McManus, James G. "Christian Coalition Takes Aim at Boston." *National Catholic Reporter* 32 (1995): 3; Small, Nancy. "A Strategy of Fear: The Christian Coalition Stalks Catholics." *Sojourners* 25 (1996): 11–12; "Truths and Untruths about the Catholic Alliance." Unsigned editorial. *First Things* 60 (1996): 7–9.

—J. Matthew Wilson

Catholic Bishops in American Politics (1991) *By Timothy A. Byrnes. Princeton, N.J.: Princeton University Press*

Timothy A. Byrnes's *Catholic Bishops in American Politics* is the first book-length study dealing with the political activities of the episcopate of the ROMAN CATHOLIC CHURCH in America. Byrnes's purpose in the book is threefold: "to fill a substantial gap in the literature on the American Catholic hierarchy, suggest a more politics-centered approach to the study of religion and politics in general, and contribute to the discussion of realignment theory and its applicability to contemporary American politics." The book, generally well received by reviewers, was deemed by Marilyn Harran to be "required reading for those who wish to understand how, in spite of the separation of church and state, politics and religion continue to intersect in setting the national agenda."

Byrnes begins by establishing a distinction between the traditional and modern eras of political activity for American bishops. In the traditional era, running from the 1790s through the 1950s, the bishops' political activity was characterized by three main features: a local focus, guided by individual bishops; a parochial emphasis on defending the interests of an immigrant church; and unflagging support for U.S. foreign policy and war efforts, to establish Catholics' patriotic credentials. In the 1960s, however, a variety of forces came together to render this traditional approach obsolete. The focus of American politics was shifting from localities to Washington, Catholics had largely been accepted into the American social mainstream, and VATICAN II called for the formation of national episcopal conferences that would challenge, where appropriate, government policy. Thus, beginning in the late 1960s, the American bishops embarked on a distinctly modern course of political activity, speaking collectively through the NATIONAL CONFERENCE OF CATHOLIC BISHOPS and addressing issues of national scope. As examples of this modern approach, Byrnes cites the bishops' pro-life ABORTION activities and their major statements on nuclear weapons and economic justice in the 1980s.

Byrnes's central point, however, is that these developments did not occur in a political vacuum. Rather, the nationalization of the bishops' political activities coincided with the fragmenting of the Democrats' New Deal coalition and the advent of a competitive era in American politics. As a result, both parties, but especially the Republicans, sought to associate themselves with the bishops in an effort to bring Catholic voters into their electoral coalition. The problem for Republicans, however, was that while they agreed with the bishops on abortion, the bishops' views on nuclear weapons and the economy were more in line with the Democrats. Thus, the Republican appeal to the bishops, and thereby to Catholic voters, focused heavily on abortion and "family issues," while obscuring disagreements on other questions.

The bishops, Byrnes argues, divided into two camps in their response to these political overtures. One group, led by JOHN CARDINAL O'CONNOR of New York, emphasized abortion as the central moral issue in American politics. All other questions, in their view, paled in comparison. These bishops were generally willing to be associated with (if not to endorse) pro-life Republican candidates and to make common cause with conservative political forces. A second group of bishops, led by JOSEPH CARDINAL BERNARDIN of Chicago, took a different view, stressing that abortion was part of a "CONSISTENT ETHIC OF LIFE," or a "seamless garment" of concerns. These bishops, perceiving that their agenda cut across the existing partisan cleavage in American politics, tended to be more wary of political involvement. The clash between these two approaches, while present in every election since 1976, was particularly acute in 1984, when the Democrats nominated Geraldine Ferraro, a pro-choice Catholic, for vice president. It remains, in Byrnes's view, the principal political division in the American episcopate.

In conclusion, Byrnes mentions several major factors that, he believes, will shape the political activity of American bishops in the coming decades. One is the influx of Latino Catholics into the United States, a development that may once again cast the bishops as defenders of an embattled minority. Another is the increasing skepticism, from the Vatican and from some American bishops, about the role and teaching authority of national episcopal conferences. But the final and most critical factor will be the actions of the two

major political parties. The current political activities of American bishops are largely driven by the fact that Republicans agree with them on abortion while Democrats agree with them on poverty issues. Should this alignment change, Byrnes fully expects that the political focus of the bishops will change as well. This prediction underscores the central message of *Catholic Bishops in American Politics:* that the political focus of the American Catholic hierarchy is as much a product of the external partisan environment as it is of the bishops' issue stances themselves.

See also CATHOLIC BISHOPS' 1975 PASTORAL LETTER ON ABORTION; CATHOLIC BISHOPS' 1986 PASTORAL LETTER ON THE ECONOMY; CATHOLIC BISHOPS' 1983 PASTORAL LETTER ON WAR AND PEACE; UNITED STATES CATHOLIC CONFERENCE.

Further reading: Harran, Marilyn J. Review of *Catholic Bishops in American Politics* by Timothy A. Byrnes. *Political Science Quarterly* 108 (1993): 757–758; Wald, Kenneth D. Review of *Catholic Bishops in American Politics* by Timothy A. Byrnes. *American Political Science Review* 86 (1992): 795–796.

—J. Matthew Wilson

Catholic Bishops' 1975 pastoral letter on abortion

The ROMAN CATHOLIC CHURCH had been seeking a constitutional amendment prohibiting ABORTION beginning just before *ROE V. WADE* was handed down in 1974. By 1975, the NATIONAL CONFERENCE OF CATHOLIC BISHOPS had promulgated a "Pastoral Plan for Pro-Life Activities: A Campaign for Life" to express "a precise and vigorous reaffirmation of the value of human life and its inviolability, and at the same time a pressing appeal addressed to each and every person, in the name of God: respect, protect, love and serve life, every human life." It called for passage of a constitutional amendment, passage of federal and state laws, and adoption of administrative policies that would restrict the practice of abortion as much as possible, narrow interpretation of *Roe*, and support legislation that would provide alternatives to abortion.

The plan included four components. The first, public information and communication with the Catholic and wider public, called on the full and considerable organizational diversity of the church to mount a concerted information campaign incorporating the most recent medical research but ultimately grounded in moral and theological terms—"the most intellectually compelling terms." Lay and religious persons, priests, Catholic organizations, parochial school teachers, Catholic social service agencies, other Catholic professionals, and parents were urged to disseminate information to the Catholic community. The pitch to the public was structured as a typical information campaign, directed to "the development of pro-life attitudes and the rejection of abortion and euthanasia." The plan asserted that "[e]ven today, there remains a need for accurate information about these threats to life."

The second facet, pastoral care, includes pregnancy counseling, material and information support for pregnant women, and a campaign to encourage chastity outside of marriage and natural family planning. The third feature was directed at public policy; the plan referenced THOMAS JEFFERSON's words in the DECLARATION OF INDEPENDENCE to build support for the idea that "Protecting and promoting the inviolable rights of persons is the most solemn responsibility of civil authority." The plan called on Catholic civic leaders to back it, laying out a variety of long- and short-term goals of ending abortion and euthanasia through the courts, the passage of a constitutional amendment, the passage of laws, election of pro-life local party officials, monitoring of the abortion position of every elected official and potential candidate, and other grassroots initiatives. The last component of the plan is prayer and worship, encouraging "dioceses and parishes to sponsor programs of prayer and fasting as well as paraliturgical programs and to encourage Catholics to adopt programs of private prayer."

Under the plan, the bishops laid out a "model for organizing and allocating the Church's resources of people, services, institutions, and finances at various levels to help restore and advance protection in law for unborn children's right to life and to foster a true culture of life." Similar to a public lobby with tremendous organizational resources, each state was to create a State Coordinating Committee, functioning under the authority of the State Catholic Conference or its equivalent, to coordinate the Pro-Life Committees that were to be created in each diocese, which in turn were to support the formation of pro-life committees in each parish. Further, in each congressional district, bipartisan, nonsectarian pro-life action groups were to be formed in conjunction with other supporters of the goals of the plan. Under the plan, Roman Catholic priests were asked to set aside the Sunday preceding January 22 annually to mark the decision in *Roe v. Wade,* and a nationwide "Respect for Life" Sunday was recommended each October. In October 1976, "pro-life affirmation cards" were distributed for signature on Respect for Life Sunday.

While the Catholic Church is not the entire pro-life movement, it spearheaded its initial formation, starting the National Committee for a Human Life Amendment, which was the first national lobby against abortion, and provided many of the organizational resources and participants of the movement. Efforts sparked by the plan resulted in some counties banning funding for abortion, grassroots support for the HYDE AMENDMENT banning federal funding of abortions through Medicaid, the Pro-Life Party in New York, and an annual march on the Capitol bringing media attention and hence increased exposure, among other successes. Evangelical Protestants joined the movement in 1978 and shifted its center of gravity, but involvement of the Catholic Church in the movement has remained high. Although the bishops never wavered on their opposition to abortion and euthanasia, a struggle has occurred over the priority of abortion on the agenda, with the late JOSEPH CARDINAL BERNARDIN arguing that abortion was one of many important life issues, and oth-ers, including the late JOHN CARDINAL O'CONNOR, insisting on abortion as the top institutional priority of the church.

See also CATHOLIC BISHOPS IN AMERICAN POLITICS; CATHOLIC BISHOPS' 1983 PASTORAL LETTER ON WAR AND PEACE; CATHOLIC BISHOPS' 1986 PASTORAL LETTER ON THE ECONOMY.

Further reading: Craig, Barbara Hinkson, and David M. O'Brien. *Abortion and American Politics.* Chatham, N.J.: Chatham House, 1993; U.S. Conference of Catholic Bishops. "Pastoral Plan for Pro-Life Action." URL: http://www.nccbuscc.org/prolife/pastoralplan.htm.

—David T. Ball and Paul A. Djupe

Catholic Bishops' 1983 pastoral letter on war and peace

In May 1983, the NATIONAL CONFERENCE OF CATHOLIC BISHOPS (NCCB) issued a pastoral letter on "The Challenge of Peace: God's Promise and Our Response." The letter sparked significant controversy. The period of the early 1980s was one of turmoil in international relations. Beginning in 1981, President RONALD REAGAN embarked on a policy aimed at bringing about the breakup of the Soviet empire in Eastern Europe. This was to be accomplished in part by an aggressive buildup in U.S. defensive forces, which Reagan and his advisers believed the Soviet economy would be unable to match. This buildup was accompanied by more confrontational rhetoric by the president, who had secret intelligence revealing weaknesses in Moscow's political and economic infrastructure. Reagan's policies drew sharp criticism from the Left, including the rise of a movement to freeze the production of all nuclear weapons. The nuclear freeze movement gained strength in Europe and, to a lesser extent, in the United States. It argued that the Reagan administration's policies threatened to stimulate a nuclear crisis, and potentially war, between the superpowers. The president responded that the United States and its allies had to stand up to threats from the Soviet Union and that his policies were strictly defensive.

The ROMAN CATHOLIC CHURCH entered this debate with its bishops' statement on "The Challenge of Peace." Drafted primarily by Father J. Bryan Hehir of the UNITED STATES CATHOLIC CONFERENCE, the statement was long and quite detailed in its prescriptions for nuclear weapons policy. It advanced four major themes: (1) primary emphasis in developing nuclear weapons policy should be on means for promoting security and peace rather than ends; (2) peace is a necessary condition for achieving the fullness of the Kingdom of God; (3) PACIFISM and JUST WAR theory are equally authentic Christian traditions for public affairs; (4) there is almost no situation in which the use of nuclear weapons would be morally acceptable. The document essentially sided with the call for a nuclear freeze and made clear the bishops' criticism of Reagan's policies.

The statement was in the form of a pastoral letter, which means that it was based on each bishop's role as teacher of the faithful. An important ambiguity underlay the letter, however, because it was unclear whether rank-and-file Catholics were bound in conscience to follow the judgments and policy prescriptions of the statement. The teaching authority of the bishops—on faith and morals—was not usually interpreted to include the ability to make such detailed policy prescriptions as were included in the letter. Moreover, rumors abounded that the Vatican had discouraged the NCCB from issuing the letter, in part because its denigration of just-war theory and endorsement of pacifism as public policy (as opposed to individual choice, the traditional interpretation) put the letter on the margins of the Catholic tradition. This question of the authority of the letter was especially pertinent for the many American Catholics who played prominent roles in the Reagan national-security team. Indeed, many Catholics—government officials, commentators, and some theologians—argued that the bishops had overstepped their teaching authority by trying to prescribe policies that only the laity could construct to promote the public interest of the civil community.

In any event, the letter had little effect on public policy or the course of events. President Reagan continued to pressure the Soviet Union with programs such as the "Star Wars" missile-defense project, and by 1989 it was clear that Moscow could no longer maintain its grip on Eastern Europe. By 1991, the Soviet Union itself collapsed. The West had won the cold war. In retrospect many observers credited the policies of the Reagan administration with promoting the downfall of the Soviet empire. Many who were critical of Reagan's policies in the early 1980s changed their views when reports from former Soviet officials revealed that Reagan's pressure on Moscow helped bring down communism in Europe.

From the perspective of the 21st century, the bishops' statement seems almost irrelevant. It drew little attention from most American Catholics, was ignored by those who made policy, and seems to have taken the wrong side at a crucial moment in the events of the 20th century. Furthermore, it stimulated organized resistance by Catholic intellectuals to the bishops' next major pastoral letter—on the U.S. economy—and in subtle ways undermined the authority and respect that American Catholics have for their leaders.

See also CATHOLIC BISHOPS IN AMERICAN POLITICS; CATHOLIC BISHOPS' 1975 PASTORAL LETTER ON ABORTION; CATHOLIC BISHOPS' 1986 PASTORAL LETTER ON THE ECONOMY.

—Ryan Barilleaux

Catholic Bishops' 1986 pastoral letter on the economy

In 1986, the NATIONAL CONFERENCE OF CATHOLIC BISHOPS issued "Economic Justice for All: Pastoral Letter on Catholic Social Teaching and the U.S. Economy," authored principally by the Rev. J. Bryan Hehir. The six-year process of constructing this consensus document is noteworthy. After consulting with over 200 experts in public policy, theology, ethics, labor, and business, the committee submitted pre-

liminary drafts to the conference in 1984 and 1985. Because these preliminary drafts created heated debates among the bishops, the final version of this consensus document, accepted by a vote of 225 to 9, is somewhat less bold than earlier versions.

"Economic Justice for All" was the most celebrated statement of the bishops on economics since the bishops' "Program of Social Reconstruction" of 1919. The hierarchy's practice of issuing statements on national political, social, and economic affairs began following the formation of the NATIONAL CATHOLIC WELFARE CONFERENCE (NCWC) in 1919. The NCWC marked the first attempt of the American Catholic bishops to create a permanent institution that could address the entire American Church and promote Catholic interests and perspectives at the national level. Apart from the bishops' "Program of Social Reconstruction" and "Economic Justice for All," the bishops commented on economics in "The Present Crisis" (April 25, 1933), "Statement on Church and Social Order" (February 4, 1940), and "The Economy: Human Dimensions" (November 20, 1975).

The bishops appear to have created this pastoral letter in response to two related movements. First, the Christian Right had provided a reconstruction of American history that identified Christianity with laissez-faire capitalism and the welfare state with Marxist ATHEISM. This historical reconstruction clearly dismisses the role of the ROMAN CATHOLIC CHURCH in helping to legitimate the welfare state in the first place. Second, the Catholic bishops feared that their emphasis on the single issue of ABORTION during the 1980 presidential election had been interpreted as unequivocal support for the Republican platform. In November 1980, Catholics who had provided over one-third of the total Democratic presidential vote throughout the New Deal era, tilted Republican for the first time, and many embraced Reaganomics, President RONALD REAGAN's version of supply-side economics. Consistent with Catholic social thought as articulated in Pope Leo's RERUM NOVARUM (1891), JOHN RYAN's Program on Social Reconstruction (1919), Pope Pius XI's Quadragesimo Anno (1931), and more recent pronouncements by popes and bishops, the National Conference of Catholic Bishops rejected communism and laissez-faire capitalism. Although claiming to present a balanced critique of individualistic and socialistic ideologies, this document is clearly a reaction against what the Catholic bishops perceived to be an individualistic assault on the institutions that provide a safety net for the poorest and most vulnerable Americans.

"Economic Justice for All" consists of five chapters. Chapter one describes the economic setting of the United States as including failures and hopes. Chapter two outlines a Christian vision of economic life. Chapter three examines specific policy issues such as employment, poverty, and food and agriculture. Chapter four calls for a new American experiment that emphasizes a greater commitment to the common good, community, partnership, and wider economic participation for the poor. Chapter five describes the meaning of Christian vocation in the modern world and outlines how Christians can be moral actors in the contemporary economy.

The letter is not, the bishops emphasize, "a blueprint for the American economy." It instead "turns to Scripture and the social teachings of the Church" to develop basic moral principles of economic practice. Six principles are emphasized: First, economic decisions and institutions must be judged in light of whether they protect or undermine the dignity of the human person. Second, love of neighbor requires not only individual responsibility but also "a broader social commitment to the common good." Third, discrimination in or exclusion from the economic sphere of life is a violation of human rights. Fourth, all members of society have an obligation to assist the poorest and most vulnerable members of society. Fifth, "all people have a right to life, food, clothing, shelter, rest, medical care, education, and employment." Sixth, society as a whole, acting through public and private institutions, has the moral responsibility to enhance human dignity and protect human rights, and "government has an essential responsibility in this area." Instead of retreating from the war on poverty, the Catholic bishops advocated expanding job-training programs, using monetary policies to achieve full employment, strengthening labor unions, increasing the minimum wage and welfare benefits, supporting farm subsidies, and giving development assistance to developing countries.

The pastoral generated a marked response among Catholic and non-Catholic commentators. Nine out of 10 Catholic parishes conducted educational sessions on economic justice following release of the letter. Yet the document was highly controversial. Like the NCCB's 1983 statement on nuclear war, "The Challenge of Peace, Economic Justice for All" received extensive criticism, in large part because of the liberal position the bishops take. However, unlike the CATHOLIC BISHOPS' 1983 PASTORAL LETTER ON WAR AND PEACE, which shifted Catholic attitudes toward nuclear deterrence, inspired other religious communities to issue their own pastoral letters, and, arguably, changed the tone of the policy debate in the United States, the 1986 pastoral letter on the economy had relatively little national impact. Ignored by most Americans, some fiscally conservative Catholics, nonetheless, took it seriously enough to respond critically. Some critics argued the letter stood in tension with the principle of subsidiarity—a prominent aspect of Catholic social theory that teaches problems should first be addressed at the local level. Others questioned what authority the bishops conference had to speak on these matters and what obligation Catholics had to follow the document's guidelines. The Lay Commission on Catholic Social Teaching and the U.S. Economy issued its own letter, entitled "Toward the Future," to suggest that the free market, along with the principle of self-interest, rightly understood, would be more effective at reducing poverty than the expansion of the welfare state advocated by the bishops. Adherents of LIBERATION THEOLOGY, on the other hand, argued that the Catholic bishops were far bolder in articulat-

ing their ethical principles than they were in constructing specific policy recommendations.

Although this pastoral letter was not particularly well received, its construction has played a crucial role in articulating the Catholic bishops' "consistent ethic of life," which refuses to conform to the platform of either political party in the United States, but, nevertheless, demonstrates more sympathy for the Republican Party on issues such as abortion and for the Democratic Party on issues related to political economy. The bishops issued a document on the 10th anniversary of "Economic Justice for All" entitled "A Decade After Economic Justice for All: Continuing Principles, Changing Context, New Challenges," which urged Catholics to renew their efforts to act on behalf of the poor.

See also CATHOLIC BISHOPS' 1975 PASTORAL LETTER ON ABORTION.

Further reading: Byrnes, Timothy A. *Catholic Bishops in American Politics.* Princeton, N.J.: Princeton University Press, 1991; Copeland, Warren R. *Economic Justice: The Social Ethics of U.S. Economic Policy.* Nashville: Abingdon Press, 1988; Gannon, Thomas, ed. *The Catholic Challenge to the American Economy: Reflections on the U.S. Bishops' Pastoral Letter on Catholic Social Teaching and the U.S. Economy.* New York: Macmillan, 1987; Lay Commission on Catholic Social Teaching and the U.S. Economy. *Toward the Future: Catholic Social Thought and the U.S. Economy.* New York: Lay Commission on Catholic Social Teaching, 1984; National Conference of Catholic Bishops. *Economic Justice for All: Pastoral Letter on Catholic Social Teaching and the U.S. Economy.* Washington, D.C.: United States Catholic Conference, 1986; Royal, Robert, ed. *Challenge and Response: Critiques of the Catholic Bishops' Draft Letter on the U.S. Economy.* Washington, D.C.: Ethics and Public Policy Center, 1985; Walsh, Andrew D. *Religion, Economics, and Public Policy: Ironies, Tragedies, and Absurdities of the Contemporary Culture Wars.* Westport, Conn.: Praeger, 2000.

—Zachary R. Calo and Andrew D. Walsh

Catholic Charities

Catholic Charities refers to the ROMAN CATHOLIC CHURCH's efforts to provide social services to people in need and to call their faithful to participate in this effort as a requirement of Christian charity. In the United States through the late 19th century, Catholic efforts at relief for the poor were directed primarily in and through the local parish through volunteer efforts, especially through lay women's charities and the Society of St. Vincent de Paul, as well as through professed religious communities such as the Sisters of Charity. Efforts focused on the care of children, the sick, and the aged and were largely directed toward fellow Catholics with shared nationalities. At the beginning of the 20th century, efforts were begun to organize and coordinate these local efforts through a national organization. In 1910, the National Conference of

Catholic Charities held its first meeting at the Catholic University of America in Washington, D.C., bringing together 400 delegates from around the country. The National Conference of Catholic Charities sought to bring together and support the efforts of a variety of different types of Catholic charitable organizations, including parish relief efforts, communities of religious sisters and brothers, and diocesan agencies.

Among the first tasks of the National Conference of Catholic Charities was to collect and disseminate information regarding the successes and problems of charitable organizations affiliated with the Catholic Church and to develop a literature of Catholic social work. To this end, in 1916 the National Conference of Catholic Charities began to publish the monthly *Catholic Charities Review* (1917–74), which, with the cooperation of the Society of St. Vincent de Paul, replaced the *St. Vincent de Paul Quarterly* (1895–1916) as the source of information regarding the Catholic charities.

The National Conference of Catholic Charities advocated more professional standards among Catholic charitable organizations, including record keeping and public review of the effectiveness of these organizations and activities. The National Conference devoted itself to training volunteers and recommended that Catholic dioceses organize to support Catholic charitable activities. These efforts met with some success but were not without difficulties and critics.

While providing support and direction for direct social service efforts, the National Conference of Catholic Charities also attended to the larger questions of social reform in an effort to address the causes of poverty. The National Conference was influential in the development of Social Security, public housing legislation, and health insurance. The National Conference saw its mission to empower the lay faithful to engage in efforts of social reform. In this regard especially, the National Conference understood itself to be a movement rather than an agency.

In the 1930s, the National Conference expanded its vision beyond the national scene to encompass Latin America and Europe, particularly the problems of refugees. The National Conference was influential in the creation of the International Conference of Catholic Charities, formed in 1951, which gained consultative status in the U.N.'s Economic and Social Council.

The National Conference of Catholic Charities was renamed Catholic Charities USA in 1985. The mission of Catholic Charities USA, in continuity with its history, is to provide service to those in need, to advocate for just social structures, and to call the church and others to do the same. Catholic Charities USA publishes a magazine; *Charities USA* (since 1975) and *Social Thought,* a quarterly professional journal of social work.

The history of the National Conference of Catholic Charities is indicative of the movement of the Catholic Church from an insular, immigrant church to a more confident player on the American political scene. Initially, Catholic Charities were protective of their clientele and efforts. But throughout the 20th century, Catholic charitable efforts have become more open to adopting contemporary standards of social work. In addition, Catholic Charities have come to support government efforts to provide public assistance to those in need, as long as this assistance does not infringe on the rights and responsibilities of individuals. The organized efforts of Catholic charities have been influential in working out the relationship between the private social-service agency and the government.

See also CONSISTENT ETHIC OF LIFE; NATIONAL CONFERENCE OF CATHOLIC BISHOPS; UNITED STATES CATHOLIC CONFERENCE.

Further reading: Froehle, Bryan T., and Mary L. Gautier. *Catholicism USA: A Portrait of the Catholic Church in the United States.* Maryknoll, N.Y.: Orbis, 2000; Gavin, Donald P. *The National Conference of Catholic Charities, 1910–1960.* Milwaukee: Bruce Press, 1962; O'Grady, John. *Catholic Charities in the United States: History and Problems.* Washington, D.C.: National Conference of Catholic Charities, 1930.

—Susan Gleason Anderson

Catholic League for Religious and Civil Rights

The Catholic League for Religious and Civil Rights is an organization of predominantly lay Catholics founded in 1973 by Jesuit priest Virgil Blum to protect Roman Catholics in America from discrimination and bigotry in government and in the culture at large. The organization originally relied primarily on education campaigns and occasional lawsuits to achieve its objectives. In 1993, the small, low-profile group chose William Donohue as its president, and since then it has both increased its membership substantially (to as many as 350,000: Che 1998) and adopted much more aggressive tactics. The league's board of directors is a virtual who's who of American Catholic conservatives, including Linda Chavez, Dinesh D'Souza, Alan Keyes, Michael Novak, and Kate O'Beirne, among others. But the group rejects the label "conservative" and eschews involvement in internal church politics. While some liberal Catholic groups view the league with suspicion, it claims on its website (www.catholicleague.org) to have the support of all American cardinals and many of its bishops. In recent years, the Catholic League has emerged as a prominent voice for traditional Catholics in America's CULTURE WARS.

Most of the Catholic League's high-profile battles have centered on fighting perceived anti-Catholic bigotry in the arts and entertainment industries. "There is something terribly perverse going on in the artistic community," argues league president Donohue. "The need to offend Catholics is so deep and so sick that it can only be described as pathological." Major Catholic League efforts have included protests and boycotts launched against the film *Priest,* the ABC television series *Nothing Sacred,* and the Showtime production of *Sister Mary Explains It All.* The league claims credit for a string of victories, including cancellation of *Nothing Sacred,* relatively favorable coverage of Pope JOHN PAUL II's 1995 visit to the

United States, and a series of media apologies for anti-Catholic bias in various stories. The organization closely monitors the government, the media, and Hollywood, publicizing instances of what it feels to be bigotry, blasphemy, or religious insensitivity on its website and in its membership newsletter, "Catalyst." According to Donohue, the league is most concerned with attacks on Catholic dogma (as opposed to the disciplines of the church), as well as irreverence toward Jesus, Mary, or the church hierarchy.

Under Donohue's leadership, the Catholic League for Religious and Civil Rights has increased its membership more than tenfold and now includes over 140,000 people who contribute to the organization every month. It has come to be regarded by many as the preeminent organization representing the views of American lay Catholics (though the league is careful to point out that it does not speak authoritatively for the church as a whole). At the same time, it has earned increased attention and ire from the Christian Left, at least some of whom, such as John Swomley, consider it "one of the least known and most dangerous of the far-right organizations." The surge in both influence and criticism have resulted from the league's much more aggressive and combative style. "The threat of a lawsuit is the only language that some people understand," argues Donohue. "The specter of public humiliation is another weapon that must be used." This aggressive approach has earned the league much more attention from media elites than it ever enjoyed in the past but has led some to question whether an attempt at dialogue might be more effective than boycotts, condemnations, and legal actions. Yet the increased visibility gained from campaigns against major forces in the entertainment industry has made the Catholic League, in the words of board member George Weigel, "a player" in any battles involving the depiction of things Catholic.

See also CATHOLIC ALLIANCE.

Further reading: Allen, John L., Jr. "League's Dark Vision Divides Catholics: Dispute over TV Show Affords New Visibility." *National Catholic Reporter* 34 (1997): 3–4; Che, Cathay. "Censorship: Offending Catholics—What's the Catholic League Got Against 'Priest,' 'Nothing Sacred,' and Now Terrence McNally's new play 'Corpus Christi'?" *The Advocate* 763 (1998): 49; Swomley, John M. "A League of the Pope's Own." *The Humanist* 58 (1998): 32–34.

—J. Matthew Wilson

Catholics and the Democratic Party

Roman Catholics have long been recognized by students of politics as an important component of the Democratic Party coalition. This was not always the case—prior to the 1830s, for example, Catholics who gained national political prominence were mainly Federalists and Whigs—and since the 1970s, this characterization has become less accurate as the political orientations of Catholics have become less distinguishable from those of other Americans.

The American party system historically has been a vehicle used by ethnic and religious minorities to attain status in the political community and protection from hostile social forces. In broadest terms, Catholics have viewed the Democratic Party as more receptive to their concerns. The historical identification of Catholics with the Democratic Party took form during the 1840s and 1850s. Catholics began voting solidly Democratic in reaction to a virulent nativist backlash spurred by the arrival of record numbers of Catholic immigrants, particularly the Irish, into northeastern cities. Anti-Catholic fervor gave rise to the KNOW-NOTHING (AMERICAN) PARTY and gained a foothold in the Whig Party—leading Bishop John Hughes of New York to order Catholic laity to vote against the Whigs in the 1844 election. With the collapse of the second American political party system in the 1850s, anti-Catholic sentiment coalesced in the new Republican Party, where it remained throughout the remainder of the century, and was reflected in Sabbatarian and temperance laws, defense of Protestant public schools (exemplified by the failed Blaine amendment), and English-only language instruction.

Ethnocultural historians of 19th-century party coalitions have posited three explanations of Catholic identification with the Democratic Party (and the affiliation of Protestants with the Republicans): negative reference group voting, cultural domain conflicts, and clashes among faith traditions. Catholics became politically conscious when their religion and cultural practices became politically salient to pietistic and "morally imperialist" Protestants. It would take the economic upheavals of the 1890s, the capture of the Democratic Party by Populist (and fundamentalist) WILLIAM JENNINGS BRYAN in the 1896 election, and a realignment of the party system to deflect Catholics from their traditional voting patterns and into the Republican column, a partisan home where many remained for a quarter of a century.

The high point of Catholic Democratic identification came during the religiously polarizing election of 1928, with the nomination of New York governor AL SMITH. The first Roman Catholic to appear at the top of a major party ticket and against Prohibition, Smith exacerbated preexisting cleavages stemming from the second rise of the KU KLUX KLAN, prohibition, and a new wave of nativism and restrictive immigration legislation associated with the Republican Party. The 83 percent support that Catholics gave to this Democratic presidential candidate has never been repeated. But, with the election of FRANKLIN DELANO ROOSEVELT in 1932 and the enactment of the New Deal, Catholic fidelity to the Democrats remained solid for a generation, though not immune to the national electoral drift toward the popular World War II hero and Republican candidate, Dwight Eisenhower in the 1950s. Not until the 1960 candidacy of JOHN F. KENNEDY, the second Catholic on a major party ticket and the first to win the presidency, would the Catholic Democratic vote approach the levels it reached in 1928.

The tumultuous 1960s and 1970s shaped American political behavior in ways not seen previously. In response to the rise of new and divisive social issues such as ABORTION, school busing, and alternative lifestyles, Catholics grew more politically independent and emerged as a swing bloc. They cast their ballots in favor of Republican presidential candidates in 1972, 1980, 1984, and 1988, supported JAMES EARL CARTER in 1976, and backed WILLIAM JEFFERSON CLINTON twice. Transformations within the Catholic community (e.g., changes in ethnic composition as a result of immigration, rising social and economic status, assimilation, religious disaffection, and CULTURE WAR conflicts) have led students of religion and politics to argue for the need to differentiate among subsets of Catholics or among "multiple Catholic political cultures" when describing Catholic partisanship and voting behavior.

See also BLUE LAWS; CHRISTIAN RIGHT AND THE REPUBLICAN PARTY; EQUAL RIGHTS AMENDMENT; MAINLINE PROTESTANTS AND THE REPUBLICAN PARTY; PROHIBITION PARTY; *ROE V. WADE.*

Further reading: Appleby, R. Scott. "Catholics and the Christian Right: An Uneasy Alliance." In *Sojourners in the Wilderness: The Christian Right in Comparative Perspective.* Corwin E. Smidt and James M. Penning, eds. Lanham, Md.: Rowan and Littlefield, 1997; Holt, Michael. *The Rise and Fall of the Whig Party.* New York: Oxford University Press, 1999; McCormick, Richard L. "Ethno-Cultural Interpretations of Nineteenth Century American Voting Behavior." *Political Science Quarterly* 89 (1974): 351–377; Prendergast, William. *The Catholic Voter in American Politics: The Passing of the Democratic Monolith.* Washington, D.C.: Georgetown University Press, 1999.

—Louis Bolce

Catholics for a Free Choice

Catholics for a Free Choice (CFFC), founded in 1973, is an independent, not-for-profit organization engaged in research, policy analysis, education, and advocacy on issues of gender equality and reproductive health. CFFC promotes contraceptive rights, including access to ABORTION. CFFC's specific focus is the "intersection of Catholic teaching and public policy" (Catholics for a Free Choice website). Frances Kissling leads the group, headquartered in Washington, D.C., which has had a budget of approximately $2.5 million in recent years. In its early years, CFFC's main focus was defending abortion rights in the United States. In recent years, the organization has sought to promote abortion and contraception throughout the world.

Three members of the National Organization for Women—Joan Harriman, Meta Mulcahy, and Patricia McQuillan Fogarty—founded CFFC and led the organization until 1976, during which time the organization's office was in New York City. Fogarty moved the organization to Washington, D.C., and led the organization until 1979. From 1979 to 1982, Pat McMahon served as president of CFFC.

During the course of its history, CFFC has been very critical of the ROMAN CATHOLIC CHURCH's position that abortion should be illegal and that artificial contraception is illegitimate. They claim to represent American Catholics who disagree with the church's present leaders. Representatives of CFFC regularly criticize pronouncements by the Vatican and the American Catholic hierarchy.

Frances Kissling is CFFC's longtime president. Early in her life, she studied to be a nun but left the order. She then became active in feminist causes. She operated an abortion clinic and was a founder and director of the National Abortion Federation (1976–80). In 1980, she became a member of CFFC's board of directors, and in 1982 she became president. She organized pro-choice hearings with members of Congress presenting testimony that reproductive rights could be compatible with Catholicism. Kissling benefited from a statement from Democratic vice presidential candidate, Geraldine Ferraro, during the 1984 campaign in support of abortion rights. After New York archbishop JOHN CARDINAL O'CONNOR criticized Ferraro, Kissling put together an advertisement in the *New York Times* with over 70 signatories, including several Catholic theologians, supporting Ferraro. This ad generated much attention for CFFC.

CFFC was recognized by the United Nations in 1992 as a nongovernmental organization and has participated in several U.N. conferences. CFFC has led the effort to remove the Vatican's permanent U.N. observer status. This initiative is called the "See Change" campaign.

CFFC has also published several books and many pamphlets dissenting from the Catholic Church's antiabortion position and criticizing the Catholic Right. These include *A History of Abortion* and *A New Rite: Conservative Catholic Organizations and Their Allies,* which criticizes politically conservative Catholic organizations and was funded by the Robert Sterling Clark Foundation and the Albert A. List Foundation. In 1983, CFFC published *Abortion: A Guide to Making Ethical Choices* by Marjorie Reiley Maguire and Daniel C. Maguire, a professor of theology at Marquette University, which argues that abortion can be morally justified. They also published *Reflections of a Catholic Theologian on Visiting an Abortion Clinic* by Daniel Maguire in 1984, wherein Maguire criticized antiabortion leaders and empathized with those seeking an abortion. In addition to books and pamphlets, CFFC publishes *Conscience,* a quarterly that examines issues related to CFFC's mission. CFFC reports that *Conscience* has a readership of approximately 15,000.

CFFC receives funding from individuals and from many significant foundations, such as the Ford Foundation, Buffett Foundation, John D. and Catherine T. MacArthur Foundation, and Rockefeller Foundation. But they have no formal association with any organization that is part of the international Catholic hierarchy. They are associated with liberal Catholic organizations such as Catholic Organizations for Renewal (COR), Women-Church Convergence (WCC), and Catholics for a Changing Church. It is associated with liberal religious groups such as the RELIGIOUS COALITION FOR REPRODUCTIVE CHOICE.

CFFC has been denounced by the NATIONAL CONFER-ENCE OF CATHOLIC BISHOPS: "CFFC is, practically speaking, an arm of the abortion lobby in the United States and throughout the world. It is an advocacy group dedicated to supporting abortion. It is funded by a number of powerful and wealthy private foundations, mostly American, to promote abortion as a method of population control." Bishop Fabian Bruskewitz of Lincoln, Nebraska, said that members of CFFC who live in his diocese would be subject to excommunication.

Further reading: Catholics for a Free Choice. URL: www. cath4choice.org; "The Cardinal of Choice." *Washington Post,* August 24, 1986.

—Michael Coulter

Catholic Worker movement

Founded in 1933 in New York City by Peter Maurin and DOROTHY DAY, the Catholic Worker movement is a lay apostolate serving the poor. Day repeatedly credited Maurin with beginning the movement, although she was the moving force behind much of its success and continues to be the person most associated with its ideals.

The Catholic Worker advocated a radical commitment to SOCIAL JUSTICE at a time when the ROMAN CATHOLIC CHURCH in America was just beginning to involve itself in social-reform movements. In contrast to liberal Catholic social thinkers like JOHN AUGUSTINE RYAN, Day and Maurin did not seek moderate social reform through political means. They instead advocated the creation of what Maurin called "a new society within the shell of the old." Epitomizing the evangelical strand of Christian social action, the Catholic Worker believes Christians are called to perform radical acts of sacrifice and charity in imitation of Christ.

In his famous essay "What the Catholic Worker Believes," Maurin described the movement's principles as "gentle personalism," "the personal obligation of looking after the needs of our brother," "the daily practice of Works of Mercy," and "Houses of Hospitality for the immediate relief of those who are in need." The movement drew its guiding philosophy from a variety of sources. Of particular importance were the personalist philosophies of Jacques Maritain and Emmanuel Mounier, which regarded the freedom and dignity of each person as the basis of ethics, and the distributist thought of Hilaire Belloc and G. K. Chesterton, which advocated small proprietorship and opposed capitalism. The Catholic Worker criticizes both socialism and capitalism as dehumanizing systems of social and economic organization. It advocates a decentralized and simpler society based on COMMUNITARIAN-ISM and the practice of love in action. The movement does not oppose technology per se but does call for its use in ways that foster human dignity and community.

The most effective aspects of the movement remain the *Catholic Worker* newspaper and the Houses of Hospitality. The first issue of the paper was distributed on May 1, 1933, in New York's Union Square at the price of a penny per copy. The paper's editorial stated: "In an attempt to popularize and make known the encyclicals of the Popes in regard to social justice and the program put forth by the Church or the 'reconstruction of the social order,' this news sheet, *The Catholic Worker,* is started."

The first House of Hospitality was also opened in 1933: St. Joseph's, at 36 East First Street in New York City. The house served as a source of food and shelter for the poor and a residence for members of the movement. The movement continues to attract a diverse group of people, ranging from scholars to reformers. Catholic Workers live in voluntary poverty and dedicate themselves to serving the poor and pursuing social justice in conformity with the principles of the movement. The Houses of Hospitality and their worker occupants are supported entirely by donations. The movement receives no financial support from the institutional church or the U.S. government. There are currently over 175 Catholic Worker communities around the world, with 155 in 36 U.S. states.

Maurin also called for the creation of farming communes to be called "agronomic universities." Their purpose was to enable workers and scholars to join in common work on the land and establish an authentically cooperative society. The first farm was formed in 1936 near Easton, PENNSYLVANIA. Other farms have also been founded, but this aspect of the Catholic Worker has not defined the movement nearly to the extent that the newspaper and houses have.

In accord with its commitment to radical gospel ideals, the movement has remained steadfast in its commitment to Christian PACIFISM. Day's pacifism created a split in the movement during World War II when 15 Houses of Hospitality closed and subscriptions to the *Catholic Worker* declined precipitously, but she remained steadfast in holding pacifism as a central tenet of the movement. Her example has inspired left-wing Catholics in America such as Thomas Merton and Daniel and Philip Berrigan.

Further reading: Day, Dorothy. *The Long Loneliness: An Autobiography.* San Francisco: Harper and Row, 1952; Piehl, Mel. *Breaking Bread: The Catholic Worker and the Origin of Catholic Radicalism in America.* Philadelphia: Temple University Press, 1982; Roberts, Nancy L. *Dorothy Day and the Catholic Worker.* Albany: State University of New York Press, 1984.

—Zachary R. Calo

censorship

The First Amendment to the U.S. Constitution states, "Congress shall make no law . . . abridging the freedom of speech, or of the press." Yet in spite of this seemingly absolute statement in favor of free expression in the United States, debates over censorship have plagued the nation from its founding up to the present.

Just as important as the *language* of the First Amendment's protection for freedom of speech and press is its *interpretation* by the courts. For example, though the First Amendment states only that the *Congress* shall not interfere with freedom of speech or press, the Supreme Court has extended the amendment's reach to protect freedom of expression from *all* levels of American government. On the other hand, the Supreme Court has also determined that some forms of expression have so little value that they simply do not merit any First Amendment protection. As Justice Murphy wrote for the Court in *Chaplinsky v. New Hampshire* (1942), in which JEHOVAH'S WITNESS Chaplinsky was distributing literature and became involved in a public disturbance: "such utterances are no essential part of any exposition of ideas, and are of such slight social value as a step to truth that any benefit that may be derived from them is clearly outweighed by the social interest in order and morality."

Materials excepted from First Amendment protection include those legally designated as obscenity, child pornography, libel, and those posing a "clear and present danger" to society. Once a speech or work is placed into one of these legal categories, government can regulate and even ban materials at will.

But many ideas and expressions that are protected by the First Amendment are also threatened with censorship, and religion is often at the center of censorship controversies in the United States. Religious ideology has been claimed as the justification for regulating or banning many controversial ideas and materials; on the other hand, religious ideas and expressions can themselves become targets of censorship. Some even credit TEXTBOOK CONTROVERSIES in public schools with sparking the modern Christian conservative movement.

British author J. K. Rowling's "Harry Potter" books may provide the most prominent contemporary American censorship controversy. Harry Potter is a fictional boy wizard who plays a pivotal role in the fight against the dark arts of magic from his school in Britain while still finding time to study for his exams and learn about girls. Rowling's books are international best-sellers, but they have also become among the most controversial books in America. While Harry is a "good" wizard who fights evil, some Christian conservative critics argue that the books' very attention to witchcraft celebrates evil. According to the American Library Association, the Harry Potter books were the "most challenged" books in American libraries and schools in 1999, 2000, and 2001. Copies of her books have been burned and cut apart in public by demonstrators, and some schools have conceded to public pressure and removed the books from their library shelves. Harry Potter's experience in America clearly demonstrates that neither the First Amendment nor enormous worldwide acclaim can automatically guarantee that a work is easily accessible to the American public.

While the First Amendment requires that government not endorse or establish religion, great care must be taken to ensure that religious viewpoints themselves are not unduly restricted. Finding an acceptable balance is a delicate task. For example, though the First Amendment's ESTABLISHMENT CLAUSE bars prayers in public school classrooms (*ENGEL V. VITALE*, 1962), can religious organizations for students legitimately be denied equal access to the same school facilities that are made available to secular groups without raising claims of unfair treatment? The Supreme Court has determined that such "viewpoint discrimination" does indeed violate the Free Speech clause of the First Amendment, even at the elementary school level (*GOOD NEWS CLUB V. MILFORD CENTRAL SCHOOL*, 2001). Religious organizations must also be accorded free speech considerations under the First Amendment. In short, pains must constantly be taken on all sides to ensure that a free exchange of ideas is possible.

Further reading: American Library Association. "Harry Potter Series Tops List of Most Challenged Books for Third Year in a Row." Available on-line. URL: http://www.ala.org. Downloaded January 21, 2002.

— Staci L. Beavers

Center for Public Justice

The Center for Public Justice is an independent, national civic-education and policy research organization that grounds its work in a comprehensive Christian political perspective. Its mission is to equip citizens, develop leaders, and shape policy. A volunteer board of trustees governs the center. Its president, James Skillen, has served as the center's director since 1981, when the organization established its office in Washington, D.C. The center is now located in Annapolis, Maryland.

The center mines both ROMAN CATHOLIC CHURCH and Protestant pluralist traditions, particularly the reformed Kuyperian and Catholic Social Teaching traditions. It interprets politics as part of the unfolding drama of world history, in which God's rule is being established by the lordship of Jesus Christ. This lordship calls for neither church-governed societies nor Christian-majority-governed societies. The center's "Christian democratic" or "pluralist" politics recognizes that all human beings are upheld by God's grace, receiving the same rain and sunshine and countless other public blessings. The true basis, then, for constitutionally limited government, the protection of civil rights, the equal treatment of all citizens under law, and the right of all citizens to have a public voice in politics through elected representatives is God's providential maintenance and eschatological restoration of creation through Jesus Christ.

The center's philosophy of principled *pluralism* flows directly from its conviction that governments have the high calling to uphold public justice for all people. States are public-legal communities of law and exist for the protection and enhancement of the common good. Different religions, ideologies, and philosophies contend with one another over the shaping of society and not simply over different creeds and modes of worship. Principled pluralism means, among other things, that no philosophy, ideology, or religion should be given a privileged place within society.

The center pursues a multi-issue approach to lawmaking and governance. It views policy issues as interrelated and works for long-term solutions. The center focuses on both constitutional and institutional issues in its policy work. It also researches and writes on such issues as the right to life, a sustainable environment, educational choice, welfare reform, religious freedom, and just-war doctrine.

The center helped to develop the CHARITABLE CHOICE provision of the 1996 federal welfare reform law. Charitable Choice requires government's equal treatment of faith-based organizations and churches in the delivery of public welfare services. Since 1996, the center has been assisting officials and religious leaders throughout the country with the nuts and bolts of welfare reform. The center's former director of social policy studies, Stanley Carlson-Thies, accepted an appointment in February 2001 to the WHITE HOUSE OFFICE OF FAITH-BASED AND COMMUNITY INITIATIVES.

Through its publications, speeches, and programs, the center inspires citizens with a Christian perspective and equips them with tools for civic responsibility. The center produces periodicals, books, and other publications to reach people in churches, service agencies, schools, universities, and government. Its periodicals include the biweekly *Capital Commentary* and its quarterly *Public Justice Report*. Staff members speak at events across the county and abroad. In 1995, the center established the annual Kuyper Lecture, in honor of Abraham Kuyper, the influential Dutch statesman who pursued the implications of faith in education, journalism, and politics. The annual lecture gives leaders the opportunity to address important questions of public life. A recent two-year "Saints and Citizens" project assessed the quality of Christian civic education programs in various churches and nonprofit organizations. It aims to produce publications describing the most effective approaches for encouraging Christians to understand and exercise their civic responsibilities in light of their faith commitment. Moreover, the center organizes domestic and international conferences on a wide range of topics. The center is also one of three participating institutions, including the Brookings Institution and the American Enterprise Institute, in the Civitas Program in Faith and Public Affairs, a program of the Pew Charitable Trusts.

Further reading: Center for Public Justice. URL: http://www.cpjustice.org.

—Esther V. Kay and Jim Ohlson

charitable choice

The relationship between faith-based nonprofit organizations and the federal government changed significantly in 1996 with the passage of the charitable choice provision (Section 104) of the 1996 welfare law (Personal Responsibility and Work Reconciliation Act of 1996, see WELFARE REFORM). This provision

aimed to expand the involvement of community and faith-based organizations in public antipoverty efforts (*A Guide to Charitable Choice*). Before the "charitable choice" provision was passed, faith-based organizations that administered social service programs generally formed separate nonprofit organizations to receive federal funds and were subject to a great deal of ambiguity about how "religious" the social services they provided could be. The 1996 charitable choice provision requires states that contract with social service organizations to deliver services to the poor to allow faith-based organizations also to apply for those contracts. Faith-based organizations that receive contracts are no longer required to form separate nonprofit organizations to receive federal funds, and their work can be more explicitly "religious" than it could in the past. In January 2001, President GEORGE W. BUSH announced a WHITE HOUSE OFFICE OF FAITH-BASED AND COMMUNITY INITIATIVES designed to "coordinate a national effort to expand opportunities for faith-based and other community organizations and to strengthen their capacity to better meet social needs in America's communities."

The 1996 charitable choice legislation lays out specific requirements for faith-based organizations and the government in their new partnerships. First, as a condition of receiving a contract, the state cannot require a religious organization to "alter its form of internal governance" or "remove religious art, icons, scripture, or other symbols" from its buildings. Second, the religious organization retains its independence from federal, state, and local governments including its "control over the definition, development, practice, and expression of its religious beliefs" throughout the duration of the contract. Third, religious organizations awarded a contract to provide social services can be audited, but they may receive the federal funds in a separate account so that only the "financial assistance provided with such funds shall be subject to audit." Fourth, funds received through the charitable choice provision may not be used for "sectarian worship, instruction, or proselytization." Fifth, faith-based organizations are prohibited from discriminating against individuals receiving their services on the "basis of religion, a religious belief, or refusal to actively participate in religious practice." Religious organizations do, however, retain their right (granted through an exemption clause to the 1964 Civil Rights Act) to hire program staff on the basis of their religious beliefs. Finally, the charitable choice legislation stipulates that if a recipient of assistance objects to the religious nature of an organization providing services, the government must find an alternative service provider of the same quality within a reasonable amount of time. While this legislation requires that states allow faith-based organizations to apply for these government contracts, it does not guarantee that faith-based organizations will be awarded contracts (it is not an affirmative action program).

Charitable choice was a hotly debated issue among religious leaders during the 1996 welfare policy debates. Religious liberals generally opposed charitable choice in the early debates, while religious conservatives supported it. Religious liberals worried about the potential negative consequences of more entanglement between church and state. Some expressed concern about the constitutionality of the legislation, and many feared that legal challenges to charitable choice would have to be decided by the Supreme Court. Others argued that churches' critical stance toward government would change if they received government money, as would churches' relations with the poor. And others were concerned that the government would overestimate churches' abilities and significantly cut back on other forms of government social-service support. Government agencies, they argued, are better suited to providing public assistance than are religious organizations. Conservative religious leaders tended to support charitable choice, emphasizing how it would expand their opportunities to provide social services to the poor.

President Bush announced the White House Office of Faith-Based and Community Initiatives by executive order in January 2001 and appointed political scientist John DiIulio as its director. After stating that faith-based and community organizations are central to meeting the needs of the poor throughout the United States, Bush described a plan to "promote public-private partnerships that enable diverse sacred places and grassroots secular programs to achieve civic purposes." The White House office would identify barriers to such partnerships in federal regulations and work with similar centers in other federal agencies to promote such regulations. The response to Bush's order was fervent and swift on all sides, and details of the programs were slow to emerge.

Further reading: Center for Public Justice and the Christian Legal Society. *A Guide to Charitable Choice.* URL: http://www.cpjustice.org/~cpjustice/CGuide/Guide.html. Posted 1997. Executive Order: Establishment of White House Office of Faith-Based and Community Initiatives. January 29, 2001.

—Wendy Cadge

Christian Anti-Communist Crusade

The relationship between Christianity and communism became complicated in the 1930s by a shift in the strategy of the Communist Party. Instead of attacking both conservative and liberal Christianity, as it had done in the 1920s and early 1930s, the Communist Party sought allies through united front organizations. This meant that some liberal Christian leaders, like their political liberal counterparts, would become involved in some of the causes that were promoted by Communists. As early as 1941, the Rev. Carl McIntire formed the right-wing AMERICAN COUNCIL OF CHRISTIAN CHURCHES to "expose Communist infiltration of the Church," such as in the NATIONAL COUNCIL OF CHURCHES (NCC). But this was only part of the larger purpose of the organization to fight "modernism."

The era of U.S. friendship with the Soviet Union during World War II was not conducive to forming an anticommunist

crusade. After World War II and the development of the cold war, however, a New Red Scare emerged. The particular concern of promoters of this scare with ideology and internal subversion was very congenial to the concern of extreme religious conservatives with "right teaching" and in distinguishing orthodoxy from heresy. Thus, some Christians on the right supported the effort of the nation's most conservative ideologues to fight communism. A theme of the Christian anticommunist leaders was that liberal Christians had allowed themselves to become part of the communist apparatus. This paralleled and lent support to the right-wing political attack on liberals in government.

Two names were closely associated with Christian anticommunist crusade organizations. Fred Schwarz, an Australian physician and lay preacher, organized the Christian Anti-Communist Crusade in 1952. His main purpose was to check the spread of communism through the organization of study groups to understand that ideology. His largest following consisted of business and professional people. He extended his study conferences to other countries, such as Thailand, the Philippines, and India, where he sought to educate people on the dangers to freedom of communist domination. His book, *You Can Trust the Communists (to be Communists)*, published in 1960, sold over 1 million copies. A tireless and effective lecturer, Schwarz spoke to numerous groups and by the end of the 1960s had collected almost $3 million. Because of his ability to present an analysis of communism and to debate intellectuals, Schwarz continued to be influential with both religious and political conservatives. He thus contributed to the rise of the Religious Right and its influence in American politics. Schwarz's autobiography, published in 1996, included supportive comments on the cover from RONALD REAGAN and vice-presidential candidate Jack Kemp.

Another approach in Christian anticommunist organization is represented by the Rev. Billy James Hargis. He left his pastorate in 1950 to fight communism and built up a large radio audience from his base in Oklahoma to support his organization, Christian Crusade. The crusade included a Summer Youth Anti-Communist University in Colorado, Anti-Communist Leadership Schools, and numerous publications. Unlike Schwarz, Hargis's audience came primarily from working-class Protestants, likely to be traditional Democrats. His targets included liberal Christians and organizations, especially the National Council of Churches, and intellectuals in general. However, Hargis's approach was less academic, as well as less positive, than that of Schwarz, and, therefore, was less influential with conservative intellectuals. Together, however, Schwarz and Hargis never attracted more than a small fraction of even conservative Christians.

Meanwhile, among Roman Catholics, FRANCIS CARDINAL SPELLMAN of New York became very aggressive in his speaking of the danger of "Communist conquest and annihilation." Also, Bishop Fulton J. Sheen, known for his popular radio broadcasts and books, often attacked communism, as did Father CHARLES COUGHLIN earlier. But, rather than organizing a separate "Anti-Communist Crusade," as among conservative Protestants, the anticommunist movement in Roman Catholicism was expressed through established organizations, such as the Catholic War Veterans and the KNIGHTS OF COLUMBUS, as well as in the speeches of Catholic leaders.

After the 1950s and 1960s, ANTICOMMUNISM became only one of many causes even among the most conservative Christians. Although strongly anticommunist, BILLY GRAHAM, on his trips to communist countries, placed people before ideology. In addition, the overtures of President RICHARD NIXON to China, the opening to China, and, finally, the breakup of the Soviet Union after 1989 all helped to remove the fear of communist domination. The Christian anticommunist crusade basically failed to gain the interest and support of the large majority of Christians, including the most conservative among both Protestants and Roman Catholics. Although they were never drawn into a single focus on anticommunism, conservative Christians have become important supporters of political CONSERVATISM in American politics, which generally includes an anticommunist stance.

See also CHRISTIAN RIGHT AND THE REPUBLICAN PARTY; MARXISM/COMMUNISM; ROMAN CATHOLIC CHURCH.

Further reading: Bennett, David H. *The Party of Fear: From Nativist Movements to the New Right in American History.* Chapel Hill: University of North Carolina Press, 1988; Haynes, John Earl. *Red Scare or Red Menace?* Chicago: Ivan R. Dee, 1996; Schwarz, Fred. *Beating the Unbeatable Foe.* Washington, D.C.: Regnery, 1996.

—Robert L. Montgomery

Christian Broadcasting Network (CBN) and the *700 Club*

In 1960, PAT ROBERTSON founded the Christian Broadcasting Network (CBN). It was the first Christian television network established in the United States. Over 1 million viewers daily watch CBN's signature show, the nationally televised religious program, the *700 Club* (www.cbn.com). It is one of the most popular religious programs on television and is, perhaps, the quintessential "parachurch" organization. Through strategic mass communication, CBN's mission is to "prepare the United States of America, the nations of the Middle East, the Far East, South America and other nations of the world for the coming of Jesus Christ and the establishment of the kingdom of God on earth" (CBN website). At its peak, CBN reached 16 million households each month, and *700 Club* phone-bank volunteers received 4 million calls requesting prayers.

In 1959, Robertson purchased a defunct television studio, WYAH-TV, in Portsmouth, Virginia, for $70 and immediately began preaching on the air. It was from that one television station that Robertson built the nonprofit CBN empire, which includes Regent University, a 24-hour telephone prayer hotline, and various international broadcasting entities and relief agencies. Robertson added satellite capacity in 1977, convert-

ing to a 24-hour cable network in 1981. CBN brought about a revival of television shows deemed morally acceptable by Robertson and his supporters. Robertson intended his television network to act as a means of combating the decay of the American family. Indeed, CBN, later renamed the Family Channel, found an eager market of parents desperate for wholesome programming, such as *Leave It to Beaver, The Waltons,* and *Lassie,* for their children. The Family Channel was so successful and generated such large profits that the Internal Revenue Service demanded its divestiture from the tax-exempt CBN in 1989. Robertson complied with the IRS, selling the Family Channel in 1990 to International Family Entertainment Inc. (IFE), but retained controlling shares in the company. Fox Kids Worldwide, Inc., bought IFE in 1997. Hence, today the *700 Club* appears on the renamed Fox Family Channel and on many local Fox network affiliates around the United States.

The "700 Club" pioneered modern television ministries. Cohosted by Robertson, it has been on the air every day since 1966. In news magazine format, Robertson offers viewers the latest news, practical advice about finances and family relations, prayer and inspirational music, and interviews with leading Christians. Although faith healing and altar calls have been deemphasized, they do remain a part of "700 Club" programming.

The *700 Club* has also provided a valuable forum for political and religious leaders. Although there is no financial relationship between Pat Robertson's CHRISTIAN COALITION and CBN, the "700 Club" has provided the Christian Coalition with an enormous amount of free promotion. It also provides the coalition with an instant base of communication to its supporters. Robertson has used the show to stir up the faithful to contact their elected representatives about issues important to conservative Christians. In 1995, for example, former Indiana Republican representative David McIntosh pushed a bill to curb lobbying by liberal nonprofit groups while appearing on the *700 Club.* The coalition and Robertson heavily supported this bill, so viewers were encouraged to pay attention to McIntosh's explanation of the bill—and then to contact their representatives in Congress. The show has also been used, arguably, for electioneering. Shortly before the 1992 Republican National Convention, for example, President George H. W. Bush appeared on the *700 Club,* hoping to reconnect with a constituency he needed to carry in order to retain the presidency.

Additionally, in September 1986, Robertson used the *700 Club* to promote his potential presidential candidacy, encouraging viewers to sign petitions endorsing his campaign. He announced that he would run for president if he received at least 3 million petition signatures by September 1987. Once he declared his candidacy, Robertson used the network to communicate with and convert an already loyal audience into a formidable political base. CBN provided Robertson with a complex organizational structure and operation that rivaled most contemporary presidential campaign organizations. Not only did CBN maintain a donor list of more than 900,000 individuals, it had the experience and savvy to pry donations from these individuals through the use of direct mail and television. In 1986, for example, the organization raised $230 million, mostly from small individual contributions, exactly the type of donation needed to run a presidential campaign. Although Robertson's presidential campaign failed to resonate with Republican primary voters, CBN and the *700 Club* continue to offer political leaders the ability to make direct appeals to viewers.

See also CHRISTIAN RIGHT AND THE REPUBLICAN PARTY; FALWELL, JERRY; PAX TV; RELIGION IN THE 1988 PRESIDENTIAL ELECTION; RELIGION IN THE 1992 PRESIDENTIAL ELECTION; ROBERTS, ORAL; TELEVANGELISM.

Further reading: Christian Broadcasting Network. URL: http://www.cbn.com; Hertzke, Allen D. *Echoes of Discontent: Jesse Jackson, Pat Robertson, and the Resurgence of Populism.* Washington, D.C.: CQ Press, 1993; Oldfield, Duane M. *The Right and the Righteous: The Christian Right Confronts the Republican Party.* Lanham, Md.: Rowman and Littlefield, 1996; Regan, Mary Beth, and Richard S. Dunham. "Gimme That Old-Time Marketing." *Business Week,* November 6, 1995; Watson, Justin. *The Christian Coalition: Dreams of Restoration, Demands for Recognition.* New York: St. Martin's, 1997.

—Brett M. Clifton

Christian Coalition

In 1989, PAT ROBERTSON founded the Christian Coalition of America. Robertson is a well-known religious broadcaster who made an unsuccessful bid for the Republican presidential nomination in 1988 but emerged from that loss with a substantial following. Those supporters largely comprised evangelical Christians who suddenly felt they had found, in Robertson, a candidate who spoke to their concerns about the perceived erosion of traditional morality in America. From its outset, the coalition was a prominent part of the Christian Right movement in the United States and became virtually synonymous with it in the eyes of the public. With its agenda of strengthening families, making schools effective, and limiting government, the Christian Coalition quickly became the voice of a previously silent sector of the population.

The Christian Coalition is based in Washington, D.C., but focuses much of its effort at the state and local levels, where it has enjoyed moderate success. Its primary objective and stated mission is to promote Christian values in government and public policy. It espouses a socially and economically conservative message, placing the preservation of the traditional family at the center. The Christian Coalition urges its members to engage in grassroots lobbying of public officials. To that end, it circulates a newsletter and maintains a website that advises its supporters about effective ways of contacting their congressional representatives, and offers general suggestions regarding involvement in local politics. Members of the Christian

Coalition have been quite successful in winning seats on local school boards, for example. While it remains fundamentally a grassroots lobbying organization, the Christian Coalition has also worked to elect national candidates who share its vision, and to use the courts when necessary. The AMERICAN CENTER FOR LAW AND JUSTICE, created by Robertson and supported, in part, by the Christian Coalition, frequently accepts cases on behalf of issues dear to the coalition and its members, such as PRAYER IN PUBLIC SCHOOLS and other types of religious expression that they feel are threatened.

From the beginning, the coalition has relied on its members for support, but strong leadership has also played an integral role in its emergence in the political sphere. Until his resignation in 1997 from the coalition, former executive director RALPH REED was a regular presence on a number of political talk shows, promoting and defending the Christian Coalition and its vision against its many critics. Reed was a tireless advocate for the conservative politics whose high point came in the 1994 elections, in which the Republican Party captured a majority of seats in both houses of Congress. This sweeping victory came thanks in part to the electoral mobilization of pro-family conservative voters by the Christian Coalition. The coalition and its members waged a particularly energetic mobilization campaign in the 1994 elections in response to their vehement dislike of President WILLIAM JEFFERSON CLINTON's political agenda. Clinton was not up for reelection that year, but conservative Christians were determined to eliminate the Democratic majorities in Congress, thereby eroding support for Clinton's policies and impeding their implementation. The influence of conservative Christians on the 1994 elections was evidenced by numerous subsequent proposals in Congress for downsizing and decentralizing the federal government in favor of private, nonprofit organizations.

One of the main tools used by the Christian Coalition to get its message to a larger audience are the VOTER GUIDES it publishes and distributes in churches and other religious venues before political elections. The guides list a number of issues of interest to Christian conservatives and offer an issue-by-issue comparison of the candidates. The issues included in the guides vary by election but generally include family-related issues such as ABORTION, taxes, and education. The guides have been effective in expanding support for conservative candidates but have also become the source of an intense controversy. At issue is the coalition's tax-exempt status. The federal tax code prohibits churches from partisan political activity if they want to maintain tax-exempt status. The Christian Coalition maintains that the guides are intended to serve an educational role and do not endorse particular candidates. Critics like AMERICANS UNITED FOR THE SEPARATION OF CHURCH AND STATE, however, argue that these guides are thinly disguised campaign propaganda for Republican office seekers. The Federal Election Commission (FEC) agrees and believes the coalition is a partisan political organization. The IRS subsequently denied the coalition its tax-exempt status.

The coalition countersued, and the issue remains an ongoing controversy with no clear resolution.

More recently, the Christian Coalition has undergone changes in an attempt to recapture its once prominent role. Despite its earlier successes and large membership, the coalition's resources and influence have declined steadily since Reed's departure in 1997. In addition, by the late 1990s, the coalition itself was beginning to be eclipsed in stature by other conservative political organizations like the FAMILY RESEARCH COUNCIL. In 1997, Randy Tate took over as the coalition's executive director. Roberta Combs, the current executive director, later replaced Tate. In an internal restructuring done in preparation for the 2000 elections, Pat Robertson's role in the coalition was expanded to compensate for the loss of Reed, who, by most accounts, was largely responsible for the coalition's early successes. Plagued by dwindling contributions, the coalition's magazine, *Christian American,* ceased publication to save money. The issue of the coalition's tax-exempt status continues to threaten its financial viability, but many of the coalition's strengths remain intact. Its base of support, while smaller than it once was, has remained loyal to the conservative vision. The Christian Coalition, despite recent declines in membership and resources, remains one of the best examples of Christian political mobilization in the United States.

See also CHRISTIAN RIGHT AND THE REPUBLICAN PARTY; CHRISTIAN RIGHT SCHOOL BOARD CANDIDATES; RELIGION IN THE 1988, 1992, 1994, 1996, 2000 PRESIDENTIAL ELECTIONS; TAX-EXEMPT STATUS OF RELIGIOUS ORGANIZATIONS.

Further reading: Hofrenning, Daniel J. B. *In Washington but Not of It: The Prophetic Politics of Religious Lobbyists.* Philadelphia: Temple University Press, 1995; Lienesch, Michael. *Redeeming America: Piety and Politics in the New Christian Right.* Chapel Hill: University of North Carolina Press, 1993; Monsma, Stephen V. *When Sacred and Secular Mix: Religious Nonprofit Organizations and Public Money.* Lanham, Md.: Rowman and Littlefield, 1996.

—Andrea E. Moore

Christian Identity

Christian Identity, the guiding force behind a large portion of the extremist and racist Right in America, is based on a fusion of Anglo/Israelism, the insurrectionist interpretation of the Second Amendment, and a belief in the organic constitution (the Ten Commandments, the Articles of Confederation, and the BILL OF RIGHTS). Anglo/Israelism is in the most general sense the belief that the descendants of the Anglo-Saxons are in fact descendants of the ten lost tribes of ISRAEL. In the years between the end of World War II and the mid-1970s, Anglo/Israelism as presented in successive incarnations of American Christian Identity became infused with a virulently intolerant ideology regarding race and religion. It also came to embrace the beliefs that the federal government is illegitimate and that it is conspiring with Jews and communists to take over

and destroy both whites and the United States itself. Christian Identity also developed the theory that Satan, in the avatar of the serpent in the Garden of Eden, had sexual relations with Eve and that the ensuing offspring, sometimes identified with Cain, became the Jews. The leaders of today's Christian Identity movement include Richard G. Butler of ARYAN NATIONS, Bob Miles, Pete Peters, and others. These leaders dispense religiously inspired hatred from their pulpits.

At the core of Christian Identity theology is the belief that only whites—the descendants of the Anglo-Saxons and other northern Europeans—are truly human. This belief is rooted in the fact that the Hebrew word *Adam,* the first man, literally means "red man." Christian Identity teaches that if you smack a white person's face, blood rushes to it in a blush. Since it is not possible to see nonwhites blush, then they must not be human. If you cannot see blood rush to a person's face, then that person must not be human. This understanding of who is a human and who is not, including Jews, Africans, Asians, Hispanics, indigenous peoples, and people of mixed ethnicity (called "mud people"), provides a theological justification for Christian Identity–based violence. As the theory goes, if nonwhites are not really human, then it is acceptable to kill them.

Since the early 1980s, adherents of Christian Identity have perpetrated several HATE CRIMES and terrorist incidents in the United States. The Order, or Silent Brotherhood, is perhaps the best known of the Christian Identity groups. The Order's leader was Robert Mathews, a follower of Pastor Butler. Mathews, galvanized into action by the shoot-out death of Gordon Kahl, a tax dissenter, took an oath to God as an Aryan warrior to deliver his people from "the Jew." After several high-profile armored car heists, the assassination of Jewish talk-show host Alan Berg in Denver, and several lesser hate crimes, Mathews died in a standoff with federal agents in Smugglers Cove, Washington.

More recently, in August 1992, federal law enforcement engaged in a violent standoff with the Weaver family in Ruby Ridge, Idaho. The Weavers had ties to Butler's Aryan Nations in Coeur d'Alene, Idaho. In the summer of 1999, two separate Christian Identity–related incidents occurred. On July 4, Benjamin Smith, a follower of Matthew Hale (head of the World Church of the Creator), went on a shooting spree. After shooting 11 Asian Americans, African Americans, and Jews (and killing two), Smith committed suicide. On August 10, Buford Furrow, another follower of Butler, violently entered a Los Angeles Jewish Community Center and wounded five, including several children. He then killed a U.S. postman of Filipino descent while attempting to flee.

See also RACISM.

Further reading: Barkun, Michael. *Religion and the Racist Right.* Chapel Hill: University of North Carolina Press, 1994; Kaplan, Jeffrey. *Radical Religion in America: Millenarian Movements from the Far Right to the Children of Noah.* Syracuse, N.Y.: Syracuse University Press, 1997; Ridgeway, James. *Blood in the Face: The Ku Klux Klan, Aryan Nations, Nazi*

Skinheads, and the Rise of a New White Culture. New York: Thunder's Mouth Press, 1991; Wessinger, Catherine. *How the Millennium Comes Violently: From Jonestown to Heaven's Gate.* New York: Seven Bridges, 2000.

—Adam L. Silverman

Christian Legal Society

Founded in 1961, the Christian Legal Society (CLS) is a non-profit, grassroots network of Christian law practitioners, judges, law school students, and laypeople. It is modeled after the Christian Medical and Dental Society and other Christian professional associations. The organization defines its mission broadly as providing a social and professional mechanism for Christian lawyers and preparing students for the practice of law. Furthermore, it identifies "biblical conflict reconciliation, public justice, religious freedom and the sanctity of human life" as centrally important concerns for the organization and its ministry to lawyers and society.

Initially, the CLS existed for the purposes of fellowship, sharing religious and professional concerns, and providing legal services to the poor, the church, and other charitable religious organizations. But in the mid-1970s, the CLS expanded its mission to include law student ministries, conflict mediation, and legal advocacy. The CLS now provides a portfolio of legal aid programs, member benefits, and professional networking opportunities. Specific services include a nationwide legal referral service, professional development conferences, conflict mediation programs, local-level mobilization, and religious freedom litigation services. From modest beginnings as an informal meeting group of Chicago lawyers, the CLS has grown to include 85 local chapters and over 3,500 dues-paying members in all major U.S. cities and 10 foreign countries.

To achieve its broad goals, the CLS has organized into four divisions: Membership Ministries, Law Student Ministries, the Christian Legal Aid/Conciliation Division, and the Center for Law and Religious Freedom. Membership dues fund all services and programs. Additional revenue comes from contributions, gifts, and (to a lesser extent) external grants. The CLS Membership Ministries provides members with publications, free Internet access, and long-term care benefits, and are directed to a local chapter where they can participate in dispute mediation and community service. Members may elect to participate in local legal aid programs or law student chapters.

The Christian Legal Aid/Conciliation Division of the CLS provides two types of community service programs for members. The CLS Legal Aid program is designed to coordinate efforts among membership to provide pro bono legal services. Within the organization, provision of services to the poor and socially downtrodden is perceived as a biblical duty for members. Through local chapters, the CLS provides training to volunteer members in removing "key legal and other impediments" for the poor and homeless. Volunteer attorneys provide legal counsel on a variety of issues, including "wrong-ful denial of jobs, of housing, of food, of medical, and of other benefits." Services are usually offered through partnership with an established community service provider such as the SALVATION ARMY.

CLS founded the Center for Law and Religious Freedom in 1975 as the legal advocacy arm of the organization. Thus, it is the only litigation firm within the Conservative Christian Bar supported by a professional association. The center initially engaged in legislative lobbying and litigation to protect and advance religious liberties within the legal system. In the 1990s this mandate was extended to sanctity-of-life issues. Legally, the center is a separate entity from the CLS. But the CLS controls it, providing a budget of over $500,000 per year, hiring staff and attorneys, and overseeing its caseload. Furthermore, the center does not charge legal fees to its clients but largely relies on contributions from CLS members above and beyond regular dues.

The center is composed of a general counsel, three full-time attorneys, and a network of 4,500 volunteer attorneys. Though the center is involved in dispute mediation, it is primarily known for appellate litigation. It files between 10 and 15 AMICUS CURIAE BRIEFS each year supporting religious interests in court. The center has recently developed plans to pursue its own litigation agenda by sponsoring cases up through the courts. It is currently active on a range of issues, including religion in public schools, First Amendment FREE EXERCISE cases, and stem cell research litigation. Recently, the center experienced brain drain as some of its more prominent attorneys (including two former general counsels) moved into civil service or government positions. But it continues to build a stable and active firm with a defined mission within the courts.

See also AMERICAN CENTER FOR LAW AND JUSTICE; AMERICAN CIVIL LIBERTIES UNION; AMERICAN FAMILY ASSOCIATION; CONSERVATIVE CHRISTIAN LITIGATORS; HERITAGE FOUNDATION; RUTHERFORD INSTITUTE.

—Hans J. Hacker

Christian Methodist Episcopal (C.M.E.) Church

The Christian Methodist Episcopal (C.M.E.) denomination has about 900,000 members, 3,000 churches, 10 Episcopal districts, and missions in Africa. It was established during the Reconstruction era and changed its first name from "Colored" to "Christian" in 1954. In the late 19th century, both black and white Methodists actively recruited recently freed black Americans into their respective denominations. Southern black Methodists, affiliated with the predominantly white Methodist Episcopal Church, South, wanted their own independent religious organization. Forty-one men convened in Jackson, Tennessee, on December 16, 1870. With advice and assistance from the predominantly white Southern Methodist Church, the black religious leaders organized what was then known as the "colored branch" of Methodism. On December 20, they adopted the Methodist South's *Book of Discipline,* and on

December 21, William H. Miles of Kentucky and Richard H. Vanderhorst of Georgia were elected as their bishops.

The harshness of Jim Crow laws, the KU KLUX KLAN, lynching, and the threat of being jailed and sent to penal farms all severely restricted the political mobilization of Southern black Methodists. Nonetheless, working for racial justice was always part of the creed of the C.M.E. Church. This is best illustrated in the opening editorial of the *Gospel Trumpet* of 1879, where Bishop Lucius H. Holsey stated that the denomination's purpose would be to "discuss without hesitation, any phase of the civic, social, economic and political questions that may affect the well-being of the Church and the race." This policy of active participation in the quest for SOCIAL JUSTICE has not been restricted to literary and journalistic endeavors. It can be seen in the individual contributions of some of the leaders of the C.M.E. Church during its history. Bishops such as Locus H. Holsey, Isaac Lane, C. H. Phillips, Randall A. Carter, J. A. Hamlet, J. Abray, J. A. Martin, and Channing H. Tobias were actively involved in the CIVIL RIGHTS MOVEMENT. *The Social Creed* of the church also calls for the church to develop and implement programs and practices that directly address crime, poverty, and racial injustice. More specifically, *The Social Creed* endorses collective bargaining, the United Nations, and the right of individual church members to refuse military service if they have a moral objection to war.

See also AFRICAN METHODIST EPISCOPAL (A.M.E.) CHURCH; AFRICAN METHODIST EPISCOPAL (A.M.E.) ZION CHURCH; CONSCIENTIOUS OBJECTION; RACISM.

Further reading: Lincoln, C. Eric, and Lawrence H. Mamiya. *The Black Church in the African American Experience.* Durham, N.C.: Duke University Press, 1990.

—Ron Brown

Christian Right and the Republican Party

The Christian Right of the 1980s and 1990s has been most active within the Republican Party. The Christian Right's dominant personalities work with the Republicans; RALPH REED, JAMES DOBSON, and JERRY FALWELL are all active in the party's politics, while PAT ROBERTSON, Alan Keyes, and GARY BAUER, all of whom hold sterling Christian Right credentials, made bids for the Republican Party's presidential nomination. Christian Right interest groups (such as CHRISTIAN VOICE, MORAL MAJORITY, CHRISTIAN COALITION, and the FAMILY RESEARCH COUNCIL) have lobbied Republican legislators with varying degrees of success over time, and studies of Christian Right delegates to the Republican National Convention have shown the dramatic differences between Christian Right Republicans and more traditional Republican delegates. However, very little work has explicitly examined the relationship between the Republican Party and the Christian Right. This relationship has been symbiotic on the surface, with both entities gaining from their interaction, but beneath the facade, the union is often strained.

There is scholarly evidence that Evangelical Protestants, who are the dominant component of the Christian Right, have realigned into the GOP, and that Southern evangelicals have become more Republican over time. Clyde Wilcox notes that the Christian Right—as of 1994—was a dominant or substantial influence in 31 state Republican parties. According to a survey conducted by the Pew Research Center, the Religious Right is not, however, a partisan monolith. Though those affiliated with the Religious Right are more Republican than other white Americans (51 percent to 31 percent), nearly half identify as either Independents (27 percent) or Democrats (21 percent).

While not all members of the Christian Right are Republicans, many commentators have assumed that those who are have divided the GOP. Very little research has explored the presence and nature of this schism, but evidence suggests that conservative Christians who claim Republican Party affiliation are significantly different from their fellow Republicans. Though the two camps agree on broad economic matters and on the amount of government involvement in society, members of the Christian Right are more conservative on civil rights and social attitudes—particularly ABORTION.

These attitudinal differences are significant, but their scope is undetermined. All political parties have factions, but unless they are inherently electoral, where general election candidates can rise and fall on the basis of these factions, they may be essentially meaningless. In this case, the factions are meaningful and potentially damaging. Religious Right Republican voters are among the most loyal in the electorate, supporting all GOP general election candidates 85 percent or more of the time, regardless of the candidates' association with the Christian Right. In some cases, rank-and-file Republicans abstain or vote for Democratic candidates when a Christian Right candidate lifts the party's banner in November. This sort of electoral behavior may make it difficult for Christian Right Republicans to elect their own candidates, which can have serious ramifications. The Christian Right may become less enthusiastic about politics if it works to externalize its values through the electoral process. This dampening effect could damage the Republican Party in many states and throughout the South. Electoral friction may also exacerbate conflicts that already exist between the Christian Right and the Republican Party.

Pat Robertson ran for the Republican presidential nomination in 1988. His sound defeat convinced many of the Christian Right's fall from power within the Republican Party. This was followed by the Republican Convention of 1992, where the Christian Right's profile was stark and noticeable. George H. W. Bush's loss further crippled the movement. The Christian Right was widely credited with aiding the Republican takeover of Congress in 1994, giving the Christian Right "a seat at the table" where decisions are made. After the victory, many of those associated with the Christian Right expected immediate policy gains on the pro-family front. The results have been mixed, and some within the movement are thoroughly unsatisfied. James Dobson, arguably the most powerful man in the Christian Right, has threatened to leave the Republican Party and take his multitudes of followers with him, if it does not act on the movement's pro-family agenda. Such a public threat is unusual at the highest levels of American politics, but it may have signaled the beginning of intra-party warfare.

Gary Bauer, a close associate of Dobson's and former head of the Family Research Council, which Dobson founded, ran for the GOP's presidential nomination in 2000. Pat Robertson, Dobson's most visible rival within the Christian Right, favors a more pragmatic political approach that allows for incremental policy gains. He spurned both Bauer and Dobson by endorsing GEORGE W. BUSH. John McCain, Bush's capable but unsuccessful opponent for the GOP nomination, attempted to connect Bush to the Christian Right while distancing himself from the movement. While campaigning in Virginia, which is a Christian Right stronghold, McCain characterized Robertson and Jerry Falwell, who are each based in the state, as prophets of hate. The Republican primaries of 2000 highlighted the current and historical tensions within the Christian Right, for the movement is still in search of unification. The primaries also illustrated the strained ties that bind the Christian Right to the Republican Party.

See also CHRISTIAN RIGHT IN VIRGINIA; CHRISTIAN RIGHT SCHOOL BOARD CANDIDATES; CONTRACT WITH THE AMERICAN FAMILY; *CULTURE WARS;* IMPEACHMENT OF WILLIAM JEFFERSON CLINTON; NEW EVANGELICALS IN CONGRESS; QUAYLE, DAN; REAGAN, RONALD; RELIGION IN THE 1980, 1984, 1988, 1992, 1996, AND 2000 PRESIDENTIAL ELECTIONS [SEE SEPARATE ENTRIES]; SOUTHERN REPUBLICAN REALIGNMENT.

Further reading: Green, John C., Lyman A. Kellstedt, Corwin E. Smidt, and James L. Guth. "The Soul of the South: Religion and the New Electoral Order." In *The New Politics of the Old South: An Introduction to Southern Politics.* Edited by Charles S. Bullock III and Mark J. Rozell, Lanham, Md.: Rowman and Littlefield, 1998, 261–276; Green, John C., and James L. Guth. "The Christian Right in the Republican Party: The Case of Pat Robertson's Supporters." *Journal of Politics* 50 (1988): 150–165; Kellstedt, Lyman A. "Evangelicals and Political Realignment." In *Contemporary Evangelical Political Involvement: An Analysis and Assessment.* Edited by Corwin E. Smidt. Lanham, Md.: University Press of America, 1989, 99–117; Moen, Matthew C. *The Transformation of the Christian Right.* Tuscaloosa: University of Alabama Press, 1992; The Pew Research Center. *The Diminishing Divide: American Churches, American Politics.* Washington, D.C.: Brookings Institution, 2000; Smith, Mark Caleb. "With Friends Like These . . . The Religious Right, the Republican Party, and the Politics of the American South." Ph.D. diss. Athens: University of Georgia Press, 2001; Wilcox, Clyde. *Onward Christian Soldiers? The Religious Right in American Politics.* Boulder, Colo.: Westview Press, 1996.

—Mark Caleb Smith

Christian Right in Virginia

In some respects, Virginia is the birthplace and home of the modern Christian Right movement. In the mid-late 1970s, the Rev. PAT ROBERTSON, the son of a former Democratic U.S. senator from Virginia, was instrumental in mobilizing conservative evangelicals to participate in Democratic Party nomination battles. He recruited an evangelical conservative to run for Norfolk City Council in 1976. After that candidate won the race, Robertson was emboldened to lead an impressive mobilization of evangelicals to participate in the 1978 Democratic U.S. Senate nominating convention. Although Robertson's candidate ultimately was unsuccessful, observers took notice of the impressive number of first-time political activists who had signed up as convention delegates.

The Rev. JERRY FALWELL in 1978 successfully led a largely church-based opposition to a statewide racetrack betting referendum. Falwell called his ability to mobilize various church leaders and activists a "portent of future endeavors together." Out of this victory, Falwell most famously formed the MORAL MAJORITY and launched the most successful national political mobilization of evangelical Christians in modern times. As GOP presidential nominee RONALD REAGAN openly appealed to evangelical voters in the 1980 campaign, and as conservatives became energized to defeat President JAMES EARL CARTER, the Christian Right mobilized in the Republican Party and has been most active there ever since.

As the GOP won impressive victories in presidential campaigns in the 1980s, the Virginia Republican Party lost a string of gubernatorial elections in 1981, 1985, and 1989. In each of those statewide elections, the Christian Right played an important role in GOP nominations. Democrats successfully saddled the Republican Party with the image of being "extremist" on social issues, and some statewide polls showed that Falwell was the most unpopular political figure in the state. Falwell and Robertson had each made campaign appeals on behalf of the GOP gubernatorial candidates in 1981 and 1985, and in each case the nominee experienced a decline in public support. Close to election time in 1985, the GOP gubernatorial nominee promised to make the teaching of creationism mandatory in the public schools. In 1989 the GOP gubernatorial nominee had taken a strong position against abortion, saying he would favor legal restrictions even in the cases of rape and incest. As the Virginia GOP lost the 1980s elections at a time when the party was thriving elsewhere, the Christian Right leadership began to take a careful look at the role of the movement in Republican losses.

A major part of the problem was that the demands movement leaders and activists in the 1980s placed on GOP candidates hindered the party's electoral chances. The Christian Right demanded that these candidates openly express commitments to unpopular social policy positions as a condition for support and thereby made it possible for Democrats to characterize the GOP as too closely linked to party extremists. Democratic campaigns frequently ran ads picturing GOP candidates with Falwell, Robertson, or both.

By the time of the 1993 statewide campaigns, Christian Right leaders had become politically more sophisticated. Movement leaders backed a gubernatorial candidate, George Allen, who said little about abortion and even said he would support abortion rights in the first trimester. Christian Right leaders refrained from pushing Allen to make specific policy commitments as a condition for support, and they advocated that movement activists similarly allow the GOP nominee to say whatever was necessary to win. Interviews with movement leaders for a book on the Virginia Christian Right revealed that there was a conscious strategy to become politically "pragmatic," as some put it. Some even said that they had adopted a strategy of "incrementalism" and that they needed time to "grow up" politically and learn the lesson that politics is not an all-or-nothing game. Consequently, they adopted a strategy of backing mainstream GOP candidates who had a chance to win elections, rather than supporting "purist" candidates who might take more congenial policy positions but could not win.

In the 1990s the Christian Right witnessed the fruits of its strategy of pragmatism. By backing mainstream candidates in elections, the movement was much in favor within the GOP, rather than getting blamed for party defeats. Prominent movement leaders and some activists found themselves appointed to leading positions in the Allen and Jim Gilmore administrations. In the 1990s the movement also experienced some big policy victories in the state, including the enactment of a parental notification requirement for young women seeking abortions. Such legislation had bottled up in the state legislature for nearly two decades and finally became law during the Gilmore administration. The GOP-led legislature also passed a bill allowing a moment of silence at the beginning of public school days. The law specifically mentioned prayer as an option for children to exercise during the moment of silence. Court rulings upheld the law after a number of challenges to its constitutionality.

In 2000, the Christian Right celebrated former governor Allen's defeat of incumbent Democratic senator Charles Robb, a prominent proponent of abortion rights and GAY RIGHTS. With that victory, the once moribund state GOP achieved a complete sweep of the Virginia political landscape. By 2002, the party controlled both houses of the state legislature, all three statewide elected offices (governor, lieutenant governor, attorney general), both U.S. Senate seats, and a majority of the House of Representatives delegation.

Just as the Christian Right was instrumental in the declining fortunes of the state GOP in the 1980s, the movement played a prominent role in the party's march to dominance in the 1990s and the beginning of the 2000s. A movement that was once marginalized politically and largely written off as too extreme had become a major force in the state.

See also CHRISTIAN RIGHT AND THE REPUBLICAN PARTY; PRAYER IN PUBLIC SCHOOLS.

—Mark J. Rozell

Christian Right school board candidates

The Christian Right has been involved in education policy debates throughout the 20th century. Unique to Christian Right activism in the 1990s, though, has been the effort by some Christian Right organizations to encourage, recruit, and train conservative Christian candidates to run for school board seats. For example, Citizens for Excellence in Education—a Christian Right group that has focused extensively on local school board elections—claims to have helped elect more than 25,000 candidates to school boards across the nation in the past decade. Critics often accuse the Christian Right of running "stealth campaigns," in which conservative Christian candidates with ties to Christian Right interest groups are coached to hide or downplay such connections before the general public while campaigning on more moderate education platforms. Meanwhile, critics claim that these stealth candidates quietly organize sympathetic voters in conservative churches. Since school board elections are often marked by low voter turnout, carefully targeted campaigning in local churches can lead to success in such races.

Evidence regarding the frequency and success of such stealth campaigns, however, is mixed. Several cases in Florida, California, Texas, and New Hampshire made national headlines when slates of fundamentalist Christians won school board elections using stealth techniques in 1993 and 1994. Once in office, these newly elected board members voted to make controversial curriculum changes, which led to abstinence-only sex education, PRAYER IN PUBLIC SCHOOLS, and the teaching of creationism in biology classes. However, such drastic changes brought considerable media attention to these school districts, and most of these candidates were either recalled or defeated in subsequent elections.

One national study found few if any significant differences between the campaign techniques of Christian Right and non–Christian Right candidates. Although they significantly campaign on more conservative issues than do their non–Christian Right counterparts (such as increasing discipline or raising academic scores), Christian Right candidates shy away from controversial topics such as sex education in their campaigns. Christian Right candidates are no more likely than non–Christian Right candidates to campaign in churches. Instead, the study found that Christian Right candidates and their non–Christian Right counterparts generally use similar campaign techniques and strategies. The study also found few ties between Christian Right school board candidates and Christian Right groups such as the CHRISTIAN COALITION, despite national media coverage to the contrary. Only 1 percent of Christian Right candidates in the study reported receiving any sort of candidate training from the Christian Coalition or Citizens for Excellence in Education.

One area where Christian Right candidates differ significantly from non–Christian Right candidates, however, is their motivation in running for office. Christian Right candidates are significantly more likely than non–Christian Right candidates to run for religious reasons.

While Christian Right organizations do not have a widespread impact on most school districts, they do have influence in select school districts, particularly those where voters are conservative and tend to share the same values as Christian Right candidates. Further, Christian Right candidates appear to have similar rates of success in their election campaigns: 58 percent of Christian Right candidates in Deckman's study won their elections, compared with 64 percent of non–Christian Right candidates (a difference that is not statistically significant). In addition to candidate training and recruitment, some Christian Right organizations, such as the Christian Coalition and the EAGLE FORUM, assist school board candidates by distributing VOTER GUIDES that contain candidates' responses to hot-button education issues such as VOUCHERS, creation science, and sex education. In addition, the Christian Right has tried to influence the membership of state boards of education. The Christian Right has had initial success electing or getting members appointed to state boards in Virginia, Texas, and, perhaps most notably, in Kansas, which voted in 1999 to pass new science standards that would reduce the likelihood that evolution would be taught in public high schools. Yet, the actions by the Christian Right–led board drew national headlines and subsequently led to the defeat of three candidates who voted to exclude evolution from the Kansas state science test guidelines in their reelection bids in August 2000.

See also AID TO RELIGIOUS SCHOOLS; TEXTBOOK CONTROVERSIES; TUITION TAX CREDITS FOR RELIGIOUS SCHOOLS.

Further reading: Deckman, Melissa M. "Christian Soldiers on Local Battlefields: Campaigning for Control of America's School Boards." Ph.D. diss., American University, 1999; ———. "School Board Elections and the Christian Right: Strategies and Tactics at the Grassroots." *American Review of Politics* 20 (1999): 123–140; People for the American Way. *A Right Wing and a Prayer: The Religious Right and Your Public School.* Washington, D.C.: People for the American Way, 1997; Simonds, Robert. "President's Report—January." Costa Mesa, Calif.: National Association of Christian Educators/Citizens for Excellence in Education, 1998.

—Melissa M. Deckman

Christian Science

MARY BAKER EDDY founded Christian Scientism in 1875 in Lynn, Massachusetts. In 1875, Eddy also published the first edition of *Science and Health,* which, along with the Bible, became the central scripture of the church. In 1879, the group adopted the name Church of Christ (Scientist) and became legally incorporated. After a period of turmoil and controversy within the church in the late 1880s, Eddy lived most of the rest of her life in carefully guarded seclusion. In 1894, under her guidance, the mother church in Boston was completed and became the headquarters of the group. Eddy continued to have tight control over the policies and direction of the church until her death in 1910, but she also established a number of boards, most notably the Board of Directors and the Board of Trustees, that continued the institutional and leadership structure of the church after her death.

The group is best known for Eddy's central discovery that sickness and disease are simply errors of the mortal mind that can be cured with correct understanding and prayer. This seemingly simply assertion, however, rests on an intricate theology that argues that God, or Mind, is the ultimate reality of the world and that humans are simply the reflection of that Mind: "The Scriptures imply that God is All-in-All. From this it follows that nothing possesses reality nor existence except the divine Mind and His ideas." Eddy argued that the material, sensuous world was misperceived by humans to be the most immediate and highest reality, and that to have a correct understanding of God and transcend disease, humans had to undergo an internal transformation and revelation of the true structure of divinity and the universe. To spread this understanding, Eddy created a system of teachers, practitioners, and readers who act in the role of lay ministers, preachers, and healers as they tend to the emotional and physical needs of the church membership.

Historically, the membership of the Christian Scientist Church was largely white, well-educated, and middle class to wealthy. Since the theology of the church preaches that one must come to understand the material and mortal world as a misperception, this membership and the church as an institution usually have not actively and openly engaged with the political arena or taken a stand on political issues, except as these issues impact the beliefs and practices of the church. So, for instance, the church and its membership have advocated for the passage of legislation that protects the rights of parents to deny on the grounds of religious beliefs medical treatment and inoculations for their children. The church has also lobbied for Medicare and Medicaid coverage of care at Christian Scientist sanatoriums and nursing homes. The group has consistently been successful in numerous court challenges in gaining these religious rights. Thus especially as it is enunciated in *Science and Health,* though the theology of Christian Science is rather abstract and urges a kind of internal disconnection from the world, leadership and membership have been motivated by this theology to expertly and proactively advocate for the right to live out and act on this belief system.

The church has also been deeply involved in the political and social realms by way of its well-respected periodical, the *Christian Science Monitor,* founded in 1908 by Eddy, who wanted to introduce a more objective alternative to the often sensational journalism of the day. Later, less successful media ventures into television and radio have also established the church's commitment to observing, reporting, and recording worldwide political and social news.

In terms of numbers and influence, Christian Scientism peaked in the middle decades of the 20th century, with membership reported at more than a quarter of a million. However, owing to rapid advances in medical treatment, as well as continuous internal dissension and litigation, the church has been in gradual but steady decline. In 2000, membership was estimated at well under 100,000. With increasing financial difficulties and the gradual disintegration of local congregations, the church has even less influence on and interest in the political and social discourses of the day.

Further reading: Eddy, Mary Baker. *Science and Health with Key to the Scriptures.* Boston: The Writings of Mary Baker Eddy, 2000.

—Susanna Morrill

Christians in Racial Crisis: A Study of the Little Rock Ministry (1959) By Thomas F. Pettigrew and Ernest Q. Campbell. Washington, D.C.: Public Affairs Press

Pettigrew and Campbell's study provides an account of what clergy and churches did in Little Rock, Arkansas, after the U.S. Supreme Court issued its desegregation order in *Brown v. Board of Education.* More important, the study attempts to explain why clergy acted as they did. In this one of the early social scientific analyses of the political actions of clergy, Pettigrew and Campbell suggest the actions of clergy result from three pressures: personal beliefs, denominational pressures and leadership, and relations with and needs of the church membership.

Their point of departure is the realization of an "enforced" silence in the South of those who may not have agreed with segregationist policies, but whose connections to society impeded their ability and desire to speak out. Clergy were largely in the same boat, although other forces outside of the community also affected them. Because some clergy were willing to take a public stand against segregation, one commentator noted that ministers were "perhaps the greatest threat to the unity sought by organized segregationists."

In their exploration of the forces working on clergy to shape their public behavior, Campbell and Pettigrew settle on the interrelationships among three: the personal, professional, and congregational. They focus on pro-integration clergy because of the tensions involved among these three systems: "As things turned out in 1957 the Little Rock minister who believed in integration was confronted with the impossible pressure between personal integrity and social pressure." Not one of the pro-integration clergy perceived a supportive congregation; in fact, the median perceived opposition to integration was 75 percent of the church (the highest perceived support was 40 percent).

One would be led to believe that if each of these three forces was of equal weight, the cause of integration would have triumphed quickly, in part thanks to the active role of clergy in the conflict. Yet Campbell and Pettigrew argue that internal inconsistencies in the personal and professional systems would nullify their influence in favor of the raw force of congregational opposition. Denominations, while taking a strong stand in favor of integration (the appendix of *Christians*

in Racial Crisis contains the statements of a number of different denominations on desegregation), were not configured to confer rewards or penalties for deviating stances among clergy. Moreover, while a denomination urges clergy to take specific stands in accord with their statements, the primary message to clergy is to maintain and minister to their flocks. One church administrator told two of his ministers, "It's OK to be liberal, boys, just don't stick your neck out." The absence of penalty and the charge to organizational maintenance did not provide a strong impetus for clergy to take action.

The effect of the personal system, too, weakens from inner conflict. While theology and the reinforcement of guilty feelings urged clergy to take a stand, several forces allowed either an escape hatch or wiggle room. Clergy could lessen their guilt if political work was perceived to be a hindrance to their ministerial role or the mission of the church. When they made a public statement, even if ambivalent and veiled, most often it was met by the cries of the opposition. Campbell and Pettigrew argue that hearing segregationists call these clergy "race mixers" would have the effect of suggesting to integrationist clergy that they had indeed satisfied their moral imperative. Inaction was the typical response.

They conclude:

> Seen in this manner, it is not surprising that most Little Rock ministers [of mainline Protestant churches] have been far less active and vocal in the racial crisis than a knowledge of the policies of their national church bodies, their sense of identification with these bodies, and their own value systems would lead one to expect. Rather, what is surprising is that a small number . . . continued . . . to express vigorously the moral imperative as they saw it, in the face of congregational disaffection, threatened reprisal, and the lukewarm support or quiet discouragement of their superiors and peers.

Campbell and Pettigrew launched an understanding of the political behavior of clergy that went unnoticed for 30 years. The dominant strain of research on clergy has focused on the differences among religious traditions in the aggregate, which has consequently meant that attention has been focused on theological differences. *Christians in Racial Crisis* compels us to consider the context in which clergy live and work to understand if, when, and how they confront the political world.

See also BULLY PULPIT, THE; CIVIL RIGHTS MOVEMENT; GATHERING STORM IN THE CHURCHES, THE.

—Paul A. Djupe

Christian social ethics
Christian social ethics describes the ways in which Christians seek to live in the world of politics and culture while striving to be faithful to Christ, according to the Christian tradition to which they belong. Christian *social* ethics may be distinguished

from Christian *personal* ethics, though the line is not sharp. Both vary according to the many Christian traditions. There is no single system, no single account. Yet Christian social ethics are not infinitely plural; many useful categorizations exist. Such categories themselves, however, have multiplied by the 21st century, and this article describes only the major systems.

The distinction between church and sect, developed early in the 20th century by Max Weber and Ernst Troeltsch, remains influential but is inadequate to capture the complexity of Christian social ethics today. Church-type ethical systems compromise with the "world" and accommodate faith to existing structures of political and social power. Sect-type ethical systems protest against accommodation, rejecting worldly power in favor of faith's strict ethical demands. H. Richard Niebuhr refined these categories into five representative types of Christian response to society and politics, which he summarized under the heading of "culture." These include:

1. *Christ against culture,* characteristic of sectarian groups such as Anabaptists and Christian pacifists (Troeltsch's sect-type ethics).
2. *Christ of culture* is the opposite extreme, Troeltsch's church-type, in which the ethical demands of Christianity and the best aspects of one's present culture are indistinguishable.
3. In *Christ above culture,* which Niebuhr identifies with classic Roman Catholic natural law ethics, the demands of the faith accept, but go beyond, the ethics of one's culture.
4. *Christ and culture in paradox* describes classical Lutheran dualism, in which legitimate duties to one's culture coexist in tension with ultimate loyalty to the Gospel's demands.
5. *Christ the transformer of culture* describes prophetic ethical approaches that seek to make Christ's redemptive work real for society as well as for individuals.

Niebuhr's categories are still widely cited, but his terminology is not much used.

Cultural revolutions traceable to the 1960s and 1970s had their impact on theology as well as secular ethical systems. Though the conversation stretches back many decades, the most characteristic feature of Christian social ethics in the last two decades is the intensified dialogue among theological ethics, social movements, and social science. This development is particularly true for mainline PROTESTANTISM and Roman Catholicism (see ROMAN CATHOLIC CHURCH). "Situation ethics," the antiwar, CIVIL RIGHTS, environmental movements, FEMINISM, and the sexual revolution had profound influence on Christian social ethics. They opened both mainline and Catholic theologians to greater respect for PACIFISM (and intensified attention to the tradition of JUST WAR) within Christianity, but also to awareness of the sinfulness of social structures (beyond individual sin) that create oppression of women, racial minorities, immigrants, and homosexual persons.

Latin American LIBERATION THEOLOGY, initially Roman Catholic in origin (Gutierrez 1973), has had a deep effect on Protestant social ethics as well. Liberation theology focuses on liberation of the poor from oppression, particularly within developing nations and on class structures within those nations. It also emphasizes the role of international economics in the promotion of such oppression. More important, God is viewed from the perspective of the Hebrew Bible's Exodus account as a God of hope and liberation. In the United States, BLACK THEOLOGY, gay liberation, and FEMINIST THEOLOGY drew on these themes to fashion liberation ethics within the North American context. Environmental stewardship has also emerged as a principal motif in these approaches to social ethics.

Roman Catholic social ethics was shaped in the 20th century by the revival of natural law philosophy in figures such as Jacques Maritain and the development of the social encyclicals with Pope Leo XIII's *RERUM NOVARUM* (1891) and continuing especially in the papacy of JOHN XXIII (1958–63), VATICAN II (1962–65), and Popes Paul VI and JOHN PAUL II. Catholic social teaching emphasizes themes of common good, preferential option for the poor, social justice, human rights, and peace. These themes are echoed in mainline Protestant social ethics as it developed from the SOCIAL GOSPEL movement early in the 20th century, and there is rich social dialogue within the WORLD COUNCIL OF CHURCHES and between ethicists and activists working in the Catholic, mainline Protestant, and EASTERN ORTHODOX traditions. A strong spirit of global ECUMENISM is pervasive. Christian social ethics in this vein takes an activist approach to government and the possibilities of justice, peace, and social transformation.

Until recent decades, a separationist, "Christ against culture" orientation characterized evangelical social ethics. This changed with the rise of the Christian Right in the 1980s and the continued activity of groups on the political left such as EVANGELICALS FOR SOCIAL ACTION, led by RONALD J. SIDER, and groups in the political middle such as the CENTER FOR PUBLIC JUSTICE, led by James Skillen. The convergence of such groups, combined with political issues having intense moral content (ABORTION, homosexuality, family life), generated a new vibrancy in evangelical social ethics and strong engagement with social and political issues. Despite their differences at the policy level, evangelical social ethicists share a strong commitment to biblical authority as the ultimate norm for ethical thinking and a commitment to Christian moral life as a transformative leaven for social improvement.

More recently, neoconservatives, grouped around Richard John Neuhaus's journal, *First Things,* have emerged from the Catholic, mainline, and evangelical traditions to challenge the dominant LIBERALISM of Catholic and mainline academic and activist social ethics and the biblicism of the most visible evangelical movements.

Finally, a self-consciously "sectarian" Christian social ethics inspired by the late ANABAPTIST theologian John Howard Yoder has won adherents among some Catholics and mainline scholars. Its most prominent figure is ethicist Stanley Hauerwas. This movement of "radical discipleship" insists that

Christian social ethics can be learned and practiced only within the church, which must be a strong and clear alternative to the dominant secular culture. All other Christian social ethics, proponents of this movement insist, have been captured and compromised by the political, cultural, and economic powers of modern Western culture.

No reconciliation of these variant interpretations of Christian social ethics appears on the horizon. However, they increasingly share common concerns (for example, the social consequences of the biotechnical revolution) and attend to each other's interpretations of the Christian tradition. Each movement will continue to produce significant implications for the political activity of Catholic, mainline, and evangelical Christians in the 21st century.

Further reading: Budde, Michael L., and Robert W. Brimlow, eds. *The Church as Counterculture*. Albany: State University of New York Press, 2000; Coleman, John A., S.J. *One Hundred Years of Catholic Social Teaching: Celebration and Challenge*. Maryknoll, N.Y.: Orbis Books, 1991; Gutierrez, Gustavo. *A Theology of Liberation: History, Politics, and Salvation*. Trans. Caridad Inda and John Eagleson, Maryknoll, N.Y.: Orbis Books, 1973; Hollinger, Dennis, and David P. Gushee. "Evangelical Ethics: Profile of a Movement Come of Age." In *The Annual of the Society of Christian Ethics*. Vol. 20. Atlanta: Society of Christian Ethics, 2000; Niebuhr, H. Richard. *Christ and Culture*. New York: Harper, 1951; Wogaman, J. Philip. *Christian Perspectives on Politics*. Louisville, Ky.: Westminster John Knox Press, 2000.

—Clarke E. Cochran

Christian Voice

Christian Voice was among a group of four prominent Christian Right interest groups founded in 1978 and 1979. Christian Voice, MORAL MAJORITY, the RELIGIOUS ROUNDTABLE, and the National Christian Action Coalition all enjoyed times of prominence but were reduced to rubble by the end of the RONALD REAGAN presidency.

Christian Voice, founded by the Reverends Robert Grant and Richard Zone, was formed out of several California antigay and antiPORNOGRAPHY groups. PAT ROBERTSON, who later founded the CHRISTIAN COALITION, furnished some early financial resources for Christian Voice. Christian Voice made its reputation as a lobbying organization, mostly owing to Grant's decision to hire Gary Jarmin, a Washington insider and Republican politico, to run Christian Voice's lobbying efforts on Capitol Hill. Jarmin, in a strategy later mimicked by RALPH REED at the Christian Coalition, urged Jews, fundamentalists, ROMAN CATHOLICS, PENTECOSTALS AND CHARISMATICS, and others to put aside their theological differences to work together for common notions of political change. This stood Christian Voice in contrast to Moral Majority, the Religious Roundtable, and the National Christian Action Coalition, all of which were more narrowly FUNDAMENTALIST in their theol-

ogy, and were initially less willing to build political bridges to other religious communities.

Christian Voice attracted several powerful conservatives to its cause. At one point, Republican U.S. senators Orrin Hatch (Utah), Roger Jespen (Iowa), and James McClure (Idaho) all served on the organization's board of directors. President JAMES EARL CARTER, a Democrat who embraced the label "born-again Christian," disappointed many Christian conservatives by supporting the Panama Canal Treaty and by taking what many Christian conservatives thought was a soft line on communism. This perception caused Christian Voice, and others, to support Ronald Reagan, the Republican nominee, in 1980. Christian Voice organized "Christians for Reagan" as a subdivision within the group, and it also sponsored an advertising campaign that implied Carter approved of homosexual lifestyles. The group gained more notoriety when it issued "moral report cards" to grade the social voting patterns of members of Congress. The bare-knuckle politics angered many Christian Voice supporters, including some of the congressmen on the board of directors.

Christian Voice's primary legislative objective, a constitutional amendment to allow for PRAYER IN PUBLIC SCHOOLS, failed near the end of Ronald Reagan's first term. After Reagan's second term began, Christian Voice shifted its activities away from lobbying and toward the publication of campaign literature, especially the aforementioned "report cards." The group claimed to distribute some 30 million report cards during the 1986 election cycle. Funding and leadership flagged after the 1986 elections, which saw the Republicans lose control of the U.S. Senate, and many of the key members of Christian Voice fled the organization to found the American Freedom Coalition. This reduced Christian Voice to little more than a "letterhead" organization.

Several explanations have been offered for the collective failure of the four early Christian Right interest groups, including Christian Voice. First, the groups—particularly Moral Majority—were the initial efforts to institutionalize the Christian Right of this era. As such, they ignited followers and enemies alike, and they displayed what many saw as a lack of political sophistication. Groups that followed this first wave, like the Christian Coalition and FAMILY RESEARCH COUNCIL, showed an increased level of sophistication, but only time will tell if that sophistication translates into membership and resource stability. Second, all four groups attempted to organize local constituents through national issues via direct-mail campaigns. This strategy worked initially but failed to retain key supporters, who soon grew tired of battles fought in far away Washington. This pointed toward a new direction, and newer organizations, like the Christian Coalition, labored to make themselves grassroots organizations flexible enough to address both local and national issues. Finally, all four organizations, including Christian Voice, struggled to set effective political agendas. Christian Voice and Moral Majority set their agendas so broadly that successes were difficult, if not impossible, to attain and claim, and organizations that cannot achieve stated institutional objectives find it difficult to maintain and recruit members.

See also *GOD'S WARRIORS; VOTER GUIDES.*

Further reading: Moen, Matthew C. *The Transformation of the Christian Right.* Tuscaloosa: University of Alabama Press, 1992; Reed, Ralph. *Active Faith: How Christians Are Changing the Soul of American Politics.* New York: Free Press, 1996; Wilcox, Clyde. *Onward Christian Soldiers? The Religious Right in American Politics.* 2d ed. Boulder, Colo.: Westview Press, 2000.

—Mark Caleb Smith

church burnings

From 1995 to 1996, 27 black churches were destroyed by fire in the southern United States. The unusual number of fires in the three-week period, which began December 1995, sparked national interest in the wave of attacks and rekindled fears of a white supremacist conspiracy. For the black community, the arson of the mid-1990s was a throwback to the 1950s and 1960s. In the years following the Supreme Court's landmark 1954 decision in *Brown v. Board of Education* to end racial segregation in schools, hundreds of attacks and attempted attacks on black-owned churches and buildings blanketed the American South.

The outbreak of church fires spurred the passage of the Church Arson Prevention Act of 1996, making "destructive hate crimes against houses of worship a federal crime." Likewise, PRESIDENT WILLIAM JEFFERSON CLINTON created the National Church Arson Task Force out of a number of federal agencies, "to catch and to prosecute arsonists, to prevent further burnings, and to help communities rebuild." Following the creation of the act and the task force, the number of reported arson incidents began to drop, from a high of 297 in 1996. Although a number of arrests were made linking suspects to white supremacist organizations, a report issued in October 1998 found "no evidence that the fires were connected to a national conspiracy based on race or religion." Rather, the findings of the task force showed RACISM to be but one of several motivators, including "religious hate, satanic rituals [see SATANISM], revenge" and money. In late 1999, a minister and several other individuals were charged with burning a black Texas church in the hopes of collecting a $270,000 insurance policy. Also in 1999, a member of an Indiana satanic church, Jay Scott Ballinger, was arrested and charged with the burning of 29 churches nationwide. A number of the churches had been marked with satanic symbols.

"Many scholars and students of American society have argued that, with the exception of the family, Black churches are incontestably the most important social institutions within the Black community." In the decade following *Brown v. Board of Education,* black churches were chosen as targets because they were the backbone of the CIVIL RIGHTS MOVE-MENT. Today, black churches still serve as stages for political organization and mobilization.

Although recent investigations have indicated that racism was not the motivation for all the church burnings of the mid-1990s, many incidents were nonetheless traceable to the hatred of blacks. The targeting of churches is significant—they are chosen because they are still the heart of close-knit communities. A South Carolina KU KLUX KLAN rally held shortly before a 1996 burning disseminated the message "that black churches were where blacks were taught how to get on the dole." In a strange way, by targeting the black church, white supremacist groups actually acknowledge its importance.

The burning of churches tries to destroy the spirit of empowerment embodied in these structures and weaken black representation in the public sphere. The terrorism of the 1950s and 1960s was a result of white resistance to change in the status quo, and in many ways its revival in the 1990s was an attempt to return to that time. As they have been, black churches continue to be preyed upon by those espousing white supremacy and racial inequality.

See also RELIGIOUS PERSECUTION.

Further reading: Cannon, Angie, and Chitra Ragavan. "Another Look at the Church Fire Epidemic," *U.S. News and World Report* (Accessed 3-4-02); Clayton, Obie, Jr. "The Churches and Social Change: Accommodation, Moderation, or Protest." *Deadalus* 124, no. 1; 101, no. 18 (1995); Clinton, William Jefferson. "Remarks on the Church Arson Prevention Act of 1996." *Weekly Compilation of Presidential Documents* 32, no. 28; 1221, no. 2 (1996); Morris, Aldon D. *The Origins of the Civil Rights Movement: Black Communities Organizing for Change.* New York: Free Press, 1984; "No Sanctuary: Black Politics (African-American church burnings in southern states)." *The Economist* 339, no. 7970; 27, no. 1 (1999).

—Anand E. Sokhey

Churches of Christ

A loosely but recognizably affiliated aggregate of autonomous congregations, the Churches of Christ in the United States number roughly 15,000 congregations with a total membership of about 1.5 million. There are no central denominational offices or officers; affiliated publications and institutions are either under local congregational control or are independent entities. Church of Christ members reject all creedal formulations beyond the one developed early in the movement's history: "Where the Bible speaks, we speak, and where the Bible is silent, we are silent."

In matters concerning the nature of God and of the Trinity, the divine inspiration of the scriptures, and standards of Christian moral conduct, Churches of Christ are recognizably orthodox within the wider Christian tradition. Antipedobaptism, the baptismal practice of adult immersion for the forgiveness of sins and entry into church membership, a weekly celebration of the Lord's Supper, along with belief in a specific, discernible "New Testament pattern" for matters of salvation and church organization are perhaps the most distinctive features of the movement. Like many American Protestant groups in the 19th century, Churches of Christ were predominantly pacifist, but the doctrine was dropped in U.S. churches during World War II. Some Canadian Churches of Christ retain their pacifist teaching. Demographically, the overwhelming majority of Churches of Christ members are located in a few southern states, especially Tennessee and Texas. Growth in other parts of the country, and especially in the rest of the world, has been small relative to other Christian groups.

The historical roots of the Churches of Christ are in the early-19th-century activities of Barton W. Stone (1772–1844), Thomas Campbell (1763–1854), his son, Alexander Campbell (1788–1866), and various associates, including Walter Scott (1796–1861). In the first decade of the 1800s, Stone, an ordained minister in the Presbyterian Church in Kentucky, became discouraged by the denominational particularism that dominated Presbyterian thinking of the time. He began working toward a model that would be more inclusive and unifying. Based on practices of independent churches that Methodist lay preachers James O'Kelly and Rice Haggard had recently established in Virginia, Stone called the new church movement simply "Christian," with the individual, locally autonomous churches often being called "Churches of Christ" as a way of signifying their rejection of denominational particularity and a return to strictly biblical sources for guidance in all matters of church polity and individual moral practice. Similar independent churches were emerging elsewhere on the frontier. The most important of these for future leadership and in the gradual mergers of fellowships were those founded in Pennsylvania out of similar motives by Thomas and Alexander Campbell. The intention of these leaders was to unite all Christian denominations on a model of the church they purported to find in the New Testament. The effort became known as the Restoration Movement.

The experiences of the Campbells led them to develop an approach to scriptural authority that would fulfill the purpose of uniting all Christians around a single model of church order and governance. A hermeneutic based in Lockean rationalism, emphasizing the immediacy of the written word, a careful distinction between essentials and freedom of opinion in nonessentials, and a rejection of the polluting influences of human tradition in determining the meaning of texts, gave the Campbells the tools they hoped would provide unity combined with freedom among Christians.

Current denominations or un-denominations with their roots in the Restoration Movement include the widely disparate but generally theologically conservative Churches of Christ and the theologically more liberal Christian Church (Disciples of Christ), along with the center-of-spectrum Christian Churches/Churches of Christ. Divisions into these three groupings occurred during the later 1800s over issues concerning the use of instrumental music in worship, theistic evolution, theological approaches to biblical texts, and establishment of missionary societies (implying a centralization of church activities). The economically less endowed southern churches, which became identified as the Churches of Christ, tended to reject instrumental music, higher criticism, doctrines of theistic evolution, and any centralization of church programs. The principles of individual scriptural interpretation and an emphasis on specifically correct institutional practice have led to numerous splits within this wider fellowship, with as many as two or more dozen distinct Churches of Christ splinter groups now identified.

Major colleges and universities associated with the Churches of Christ include Harding University Graduate School of Religion, Harding Christian University, Lubbock Christian University, Pepperdine University, Abilene Christian University, Oklahoma Christian University, and Lipscomb University.

—Thomas Heilke

Church of God in Christ (COGIC)

From its beginnings as a small sect, COGIC has matured into the largest black Pentecostal religious organization in the country. COGIC has grown from an estimated membership of 10 congregations in 1907 to the second-largest PENTECOSTAL group in America. The church grew from 3 million in 1973 to an estimated 8 million in 1997 and is the only black Pentecostal group that has been characterized as a denomination as opposed to a sect.

COGIC was one of the several new denominations formed around the beginning of the 20th century as an outgrowth of what came to be known as the Holiness Movement (see HOLINESS CHURCHES). Characterized by an emphasis on the necessity of sanctification, the church sought to cleanse the faith of the corrupting political and social influences that had crept into black middle-class churches.

Charles Harrison Mason was the founder of the Church of God in Christ. He had been a former Baptist minister until he became sanctified in 1893. In 1896, he was excluded from the state Baptist Association because he, along with others, held a revival in Jackson, Mississippi. This resulted in the formation of the Church of God, and the denomination was incorporated in Memphis, Tennessee, as the Church of God in Christ.

COGIC became a Pentecostal denomination after Mason attended a revival in Los Angeles between 1906 and 1908. The revival was lead by a black preacher named William Seymour, who is generally acknowledged as being the founder of the Pentecostal movement. Contrary to the black Methodists and Baptists, black Pentecostals did not emerge from white denominations; instead, the foundation of the white branch of the Pentecostal movement was profoundly affected and influenced by both Mason and Seymour. Further, COGIC was the only incorporated Pentecostal body in existence between 1907 and 1914. In this role, it was the only body of authority that independent white Pentecostal churches could appeal to. As a result, many white ministers were obtained by Mason and formally appointed as COGIC ministers. When the Pentecostal movement began to capitulate to white social and political approval of segregation, the white pastors who had been ordained by Mason organized the largest white Pentecostal denomination, the ASSEMBLIES OF GOD.

COGIC, although independent from white denominations, was formed during the beginning of the 20th century, a period of severe repression for African Americans, which may have a bearing on the often-mentioned apolitical nature of the denomination. In the last three decades COGIC, however, with its theologically conservative tradition, has become more immersed in political and social activism. It is notable that these churches have joined and founded local community organizations dedicated to ECONOMIC DEVELOPMENT in their communities. The extremely visible church participation in the CIVIL RIGHTS MOVEMENT and Black Power movement of the 1960s and 1970s galvanized some members of the latest generation of black Pentecostal clergy to form activist interpretations of their faith. Many of the denomination's ministers were active during this time in community services and antipoverty programs.

COGIC is committed to social transformation and the brotherhood of humanity, with an appeal to all Christians to develop common respect for one another. To defend their activism, pastors use fundamental components of the Pentecostal religion, specifically the significance their teachings place on the tangible workings of the spirit, the pertinence of biblical teachings to everyday life, and the importance of closely knit community life. In many poor, inner-city neighborhoods, black Pentecostal churches are key advocates for political, economic, and social change. Once the domain of poor rural African Americans, COGIC has become more urban, middle class, and upwardly mobile as it has pushed for economic growth. This has empowered the denomination politically and encouraged voter mobilization efforts and other political actions by various congregations. The Church of God in Christ is now surpassing the historic black denominations in both membership and authority in many black communities.

Further reading: Baer, Hans A., and Merrill Singer. *African American Religion in the Twentieth Century: Varieties of Protest and Accommodation.* Knoxville: University of Tennessee Press, 1992; Lincoln, C. Eric, and Lawrence H. Mamiya. *The Black Church in the African American Experience.* Durham, N.C.: Duke University Press, 1990; McRoberts, Omar M. "Understanding the New Black Pentecostal Activism: Lessons from Ecumenical Urban Ministries in Boston." *Sociology of Religion* 60, no. 1 (1999): 47–70; Sawyer, Mary R. *Black Ecumenism: Implementing the Demands of Justice.* Valley Forge, Pa.: Trinity Press International, 1994.

—TeResa C. Green

Church of Scientology

The Church of Scientology is a uniquely American religion that grew out of the popular self-help therapy, Dianetics, in 1950. Both Dianetics and Scientology are the discoveries of the late L. RON HUBBARD (1911–86). He headed the church from its inception in 1954 until 1966, when he resigned his official positions to continue his research and writing. Scientology is one of the most successful of the new religious movements. Over the last 50 years, Scientology has grown rapidly both in North America and around the world. Scientology claimed centers in over 100 nations by the late 1990s and estimates that 8 million individuals have participated in various church-sponsored programs. Estimates of active membership vary widely, from as few as 50,000 to several hundred thousand.

Scientology emerged out of Dianetics when practitioners began reporting experiences from previous lives during therapy. Hubbard postulated the existence of the "thetan," an immortal entity within humans. Thetans created the material universe and then experimented with taking on a corporeal form. They gradually lost knowledge of their higher origins and became trapped in the bodies of humans in the material universe.

Scientology's explanation for how thetans in human form have become trapped in the material world is based on Hubbard's model of the human mind. The mind contains three components—analytic, reactive, and somatic—with the first two being central. The analytic mind is a conscious, completely rational mechanism that is also very delicate and can be disrupted by traumatic events. The reactive mind, by contrast, operates on a stimulus-response basis and protects the analytic mind from traumatic experiences. In times of stress, the analytic mind shuts down and the reactive mind takes over and records every detail of sensory experience. Scientologists refer to the individual memory records of traumatic events stored in the reactive mind as "engrams." Engrams are reactivated whenever any part of an earlier traumatic experience reoccurs. Humans fail to understand their true nature and fail to be able to relate to others appropriately because engrams stored across lifetimes have severely diminished the capacity for self-understanding and adaptive behavior.

The most central ritual practice in Scientology, auditing, is directed toward eliminating engrams. The auditor engages in a command/question–response exchange with the practitioner designed to locate engrams. Diagnosis is assisted through use of the "e-meter," a skin galvanometer that sends a small electrical charge through the body and then registers the electrical flow on its meter. Engrams are thought to possess an actual mass and so offer resistance to the electrical charge. When a stored emotional charge (engram) is identified and is discussed sufficiently (audited), it will no longer produce an emotional response (the charge it contains will be released), and the e-meter needle will register no reaction (it has been "cleared"). Progressive clearing of engrams allows the individual to relate to experiences directly rather than through the distorting filter of the reactive mind. Scientolo-

A snow-covered Hollywood scene behind Santa Claus helps the Church of Scientology seek converts to their religion on Hollywood Boulevard, December 2000, in Hollywood, California. *(David McNew/Newsmakers)*

gists identify several stages of progress in freeing practitioners from the reactive mind, with "Clear" and "Operating Thetan" being the most important.

Scientology practice is organized on several different levels. There are hundreds of missions and churches where introductory-level training is offered. One feature of these missions/churches that is most striking, and controversial, is that they are set up as licensed franchises. These organizations offer practitioners beginning-level auditing for a fee, and they return a stipulated percentage of their revenues to the church. Advanced training is offered through organizations designated as Saint Hill Organizations, the Flag Ship Service, and the Flag Service Organization.

Scientology is one of the most controversial new religions. At the heart of the controversy is whether Scientology is a religion at all, given its mixing of religion, therapy, philosophy, corporate organization, and technology. The church has produced a description of its doctrines and organization. There are also numerous analytic treatments that are critical. Other analyses examine the church more historically and contextually.

Further reading: Bednarowski, Mary. *New Religions and the Theological Imagination in America.* Bloomington: Indiana University Press, 1989; Bromley, David, and Mitchell Bracey. "Religion as Therapy, Therapy as Religion," pp. 141–156. In William Zellner and Marc Petrowsky, eds. *Sects, Cults, and Spiritual Communities.* Westport, Conn.: Praeger, 1998; Church of Scientology. *What Is Scientology?* Los Angeles: Bridge Publications, 1992; Passos, Nikos, and Manuel Castillo. "Scientology and Its 'Clear' Business." *Behavioral Sciences and the Law* 10 (1992): 103–116; Wallis, Roy. *The Road to Total Freedom.* London: Heinemann, 1976.

—David G. Bromley

civic skills

In *VOICE AND EQUALITY,* Sidney Verba, Kay Lehman Schlozman, and Henry Brady (VSB) (1995) make an important contribution to the social scientific study of POLITICAL PARTICIPATION, as they introduce the notion of civic skills—"communications and organizational abilities that allow citizens to use time and money effectively in political life." While these researchers point out that civic skills are obtained throughout the life course, their work concentrates mainly on adult civil skill acquisition, especially the role of nonpolitical organizations in this acquisition. Along with workplaces and other voluntary associations, they found that churches are important settings in which civic skills are learned, sustained, and honed. VSB measured civic skills by asking individuals on the job, in voluntary associations, and in churches whether they had, in the past six months, done the following activities: (1) written a letter, (2) gone to a meeting where they took part in making decisions, (3) planned or chaired a meeting, or (4) given a presentation or speech. Compared with workplaces and other voluntary associations, citizens were least likely to practice all forms of civic skills in churches. Thirty-two percent of church members attended a meeting where decisions were made (versus 69 percent of the employed and 39 percent of those involved in voluntary associations); 17 percent planned or chaired a meeting (versus 35 percent of the employed and 19 percent involved in other voluntary associations); 12 percent wrote a letter (versus 58 percent of the employed and 19 percent of those involved in voluntary associations); and 19 percent gave a speech or presentation (versus 40 percent of the employed and 19 percent of those involved in voluntary associations). Although citizens practice civic skills less often in churches than in workplaces or voluntary associations, churches, as these percentages indicate, are still important institutions for generating civic skills.

When the standard demographic factors of socioeconomic status, gender, and race enter the picture, churches become even more important for developing civic skills. Practicing civic skills is strongly stratified in workplaces and, to a lesser extent, in voluntary associations, as individuals with higher incomes practice civic skills more often in these settings. On the other hand, exercising civic skills in churches is not systematically related to socioeconomic status. With respect to gender and race, the workplace is again the most stratified setting. Women practice fewer civic skills on the job than men, and Latinos practice fewer civil skills than African Americans and, especially, whites. Although somewhat less pronounced, such is the pattern in voluntary associations. In churches, however, there are only slight gender differences in practicing civic skills, and African Americans actually practice more civic skills in churches than do whites, although Latinos practice the least number of civic skills in churches of the three racial groups. Regarding civic skill development, then, churches are the least stratified of these nonpolitical institutions along socioeconomic status, gender, and racial lines. Therefore, one way that churches foster political participation among disadvantaged citizens more than workplaces or other voluntary associations is by providing them with greater amounts of civic skills.

Variations in socioeconomic status, gender, and race do not differentiate, in large part, those who exercise civic skills in churches from those who do not. Religious affiliation—that is, Protestant versus Catholic—does produce such differentiation, however. Protestants are much more likely to practice civic skills in their churches than Roman Catholics. Since Latinos are disproportionately Catholic, they practice fewer civic skills in their churches than African Americans or whites. The Protestant-Catholic difference in practicing civic skills remains after relevant demographic and religious characteristics are controlled. Thus, this Protestant-Catholic difference seems to be the result of differences in church structure between Protestants and Catholics, and not individual differences between Protestants and Catholics. The following three differences in church structure between Protestants and Catholics may explain the civic skill disparity between these two religious traditions. First, Protestant churches are generally smaller than Catholic churches. Second, Protestant laity participate more in the lives of their churches than Catholic laity in the lives of theirs. Finally, authority within most Protestant churches resides in the church itself, whereas authority for most Catholic churches resides in the church hierarchy.

Further reading: Verba, Sidney, Kay Lehman Schlozman, and Henry E. Brady. *Voice and Equality.* Cambridge, Mass.: Harvard University Press, 1995.

—Kraig Beyerlein

civil disobedience

Civil disobedience is usually understood to entail deliberate lawbreaking in response to an intolerable evil for the sake of conscience, conjoined with a willingness to accept the lawful punishment for one's illegal acts. Persons engaging in civil disobedience often appeal to particular religious beliefs as justification for their actions, as did many American conscientious objectors during World War I, World War II, and the VIETNAM WAR. But, civil disobedience is also associated with a secular moral belief advanced by HENRY DAVID THOREAU that a responsibility to resist evil falls upon anyone with the slightest power to resist.

The earliest arguments on behalf of civil disobedience in America come from religious dissenters, such as QUAKERS and MENNONITES, seeking freedom of conscience. For instance, when PENNSYLVANIA decided to arm against Native American attacks during the French and Indian War, John Woolman, a Quaker and antislavery advocate, refused to pay the war tax and encouraged others to do the same. Woolman explains, "To refuse the active payment of a Tax which our Society generally paid, was exceedingly disagreeable; but to do a thing contrary to my Conscience appeared yet more dreadfull."

The tactics of civil disobedience were subsequently adopted by abolitionists, first among the Quakers and then by groups such as the New England Non-Resistance Society, led by William Lloyd Garrison. In 1846, reformer Adin Ballou explained a concept called "Christian non-resistance" to a meeting of the society, contending that it involved not absolute passivity in the face of evil but, rather, active resistance to evil excluding, of course, violent means such as revenge. In the wake of the Fugitive Slave Law of 1850, however, many abolitionists, including Frederick Douglass and Garrison himself, began to doubt the effectiveness of a purely nonviolent strategy.

During the late 1840s, Thoreau too began by advocating noncooperation with the law, refusing first to pay a church tax (arguing that he should not be expected to support an organization of which he was not a member) and later refusing to pay a poll tax (arguing that this tax went to support the institution of slavery and an unjust war with Mexico). Thoreau's famous 1848 lecture, "On the Relation of the Individual to the State," explains the rationale for his refusal to pay these taxes. Later published as "Civil Disobedience," the lecture reveals that Thoreau is under no illusion about the political effectiveness of his conscientious refusal. His mission, it seems, is not to organize the overthrow of the American slave system but, rather, to deny this great injustice even his modest passive support. This, according to Thoreau, is a moral responsibility that falls to all individuals. It is worth noting that although the tactics recommended by Thoreau in "Civil Disobedience" happen to be nonviolent, and his essay on civil disobedience was an important influence on Mohandas Gandhi, Thoreau himself never claimed to adhere to PACIFISM.

Civil disobedience was reborn as a political tactic during the CIVIL RIGHTS MOVEMENT of the late 1950s and 1960s. The spontaneous act of disobedience of Rosa Parks, in Montgomery, Alabama on December 1, 1955, helped to energize the Montgomery Bus Boycott of 1955–58. Parks had refused to give up her seat to a white passenger and move to the back of the bus, where blacks were required by law to sit. Subsequently, organizations such as the SOUTHERN CHRISTIAN LEADERSHIP CONFERENCE (SCLC), the CONGRESS OF RACIAL EQUALITY (CORE), and the STUDENT NONVIOLENT COORDINATING COMMITTEE (SNCC) would organize thousands of students and African Americans in sit-ins and other nonviolent acts of civil disobedience in the cause of integration.

During the 1960s, the practice of civil disobedience was frequently subjected to sharp criticism, including condemnation by religious leaders who favored negotiation over confrontational, direct action. In his 1963 "Letter from Birmingham City Jail," Martin Luther King Jr. responds to such criticism, arguing that nonviolent direct action, including acts of civil disobedience, sometimes are required to force those who have refused to negotiate to confront the relevant issues. King's letter is rich in biblical references and quotations of contemporary theologians, such as Martin Buber and Paul Tillich. It is simultaneously a subtle defense of civil disobedience in the light of the Judeo-Christian tradition and also a spirited nonviolent call to arms on behalf of racial equality.

See also ABOLITIONIST MOVEMENT; CONSCIENTIOUS OBJECTION.

Further reading: Bedau, Hugo Adam, ed. *Civil Disobedience: Theory and Practice.* Indianapolis: Bobbs-Merrill, 1969; King, Martin Luther, Jr. *Why We Can't Wait.* New York: Harper and Row, 1964; Lynd, Staughton. *Nonviolence in Amer-*

ica: A Documentary History. Indianapolis: Bobbs-Merrill, 1966; Thoreau, Henry David. *Walden and Other Writings of Henry David Thoreau.* New York: Random House, 1937.
—Jason A. Scorza

civil religion

The French philosopher Jean-Jacques Rousseau coined the phrase "civil religion." In Book 4, Chapter 8 of his *On the Social Contract* of 1762, a chapter titled "On Civil Religion," Rousseau argues that religion can be "divided into two kinds, namely, the religion of man and the religion of the citizen." He called for "a purely civil profession of faith" through which citizenship would be inculcated properly.

Rousseau's concept was resurrected and given new meaning in the American context by the American sociologist Robert Bellah in a groundbreaking article in 1967. He wrote that "there actually exists alongside and rather clearly differentiated from the churches an elaborate and well-institutionalized civil religion in America." Bellah's thesis, further elaborated in subsequent writings, is that the political realm in the United States entails a certain religious dimension. "This public religious dimension," he argued, "is exercised in a set of beliefs, symbols and rituals" that he called "the American civil religion."

Civil religion, in Bellah's eyes, is not synonymous with Christianity or a blind fealty to the American civil religion. Instead, according to Bellah, "at its best [civil religion] is a genuine apprehension of universal and transcendent religious reality as seen in . . . the experience of the American people." Civil religion, Bellah contends, is "that religious dimension, found I think in the life of every people, through which it interprets its historical experience in the light of transcendent reality." As such, American civil religion has its sacred scriptures (DECLARATION OF INDEPENDENCE, Gettysburg Address, ABRAHAM LINCOLN's Second Inaugural Address), its own icons (GEORGE WASHINGTON and especially Lincoln), and its peculiar liturgy (Thanksgiving Day proclamations and presidential addresses).

Civil religion is protean, transdenominational, and nonsectarian. It provides meaning to the American political experience and is essential to American national political, historical, and cultural narrative. It can be and has been invoked for both noble and pedestrian purposes. According to MARTIN MARTY, American civil religion is both "priestly" and "prophetic," and as such is used to celebrate and admonish the behavior of the governors and governed alike. Sydney Mead argues that American civil religion, which he calls "the religion of the Republic," is essentially prophetic, "which is to say that its ideals and aspirations stand in constant judgment over the passing shenanigans of the people."

American civil religion, poorly conceived or practiced, however, runs the risk of comprising both bad politics and bad religion. Lincoln's "almost chosen people" can also become, in the wrong hands, easily conflated with a "Christian

America," "righteous republic," or "God in the Oval Office" perspective, by which "the universal God of the Bible" is reduced to "the tribal god of America." Ideally, American civil religion recognizes and properly pursues the thesis, as in Lincoln's Second Inaugural Address, which is arguably the central text or most sacred political scripture in the American testament, that the public square does or should entail a common religious ethic or ethos that enables the citizenry to understand, appreciate, and operate on a real sense of national purpose or common mission.

American civil religion clearly reminds us of the salient fact that religion, from the inception of the country; as in an "American Israel" theme of the 17th and 18th centuries, has a unique place in our polity and culture. According to Bellah, civil religion is "a genuine vehicle of national religious self-understanding." It is part of our public philosophy, our political theology, our democratic faith, and our political hopes and even our fears. Ultimately, civil religion "is unique in that it has reference to power within the state, but because it focuses on ultimate conditions, it surpasses and is independent of that power." From the time of its founding, the American republic has been "a proving ground for the relating of religion to politics." And as history so clearly reveals, American civil religion is neither unalloyed nor unimportant, and arguably at its center is the American president as chief priest and prophet. The chief exemplar here is Abraham Lincoln, best represented in that insightful phrase from his Second Inaugural Address, "The Almighty has His own purposes."

Further reading: Bellah, Robert N. "Civil Religion in America," *Daedalus* 90 (Winter 1967); ———. *The Broken Covenant: American Civil Religion in Time of Trial.* 2d ed. Chicago: University of Chicago Press, 1992; Marty, Martin E. *The New Shape of American Religion.* New York: Harper and Row, 1958; Mead, Sydney E. *The Nation with the Soul of a Church.* New York: Harper and Row, 1975; Pierard, Richard V., and Robert D. Linder. *Civil Religion and the Presidency.* Grand Rapids, Mich.: Zondervan, 1988; Thompson, Kenneth W. "The Religious Transformation of Politics." *Review of Politics* 50 (Fall 1988).

—Stephen K. Shaw

Civil Rights movement

The modern Civil Rights movement (1954–68) outlawed legal segregation in public accommodations and gave African Americans voting rights. The movement was a freedom or liberation struggle that heavily emphasized grassroots participation by black people. It was also viewed as a moral crusade in the manner of the abolitionist fight against slavery. The movement sought to end RACISM, racial discrimination, and segregation through mass organization, direct action, lawsuits, and participation in politics and negotiation. The modern Civil Rights movement struggled to break down racial barriers and raised fundamental questions about race and destiny.

The faith experience of American churches provided the context in which the Civil Rights journey took place. In 1955, Montgomery, Alabama's, chapter of the NAACP found in the defiance of a municipal segregation ordinance and arrest of member Rosa Parks a workable legal case for challenging segregation in public transportation. The arrest of Parks sparked the Montgomery BUS BOYCOTT (1955–56). Everywhere in the South, African Americans arranged alternative public transportation during the boycott, as well as nonviolence workshops, and a massive fund-raising effort in one of the most comprehensive illustrations of collective action and self-government of the 20th century. It was the nonviolent character of the Montgomery uprising and MARTIN LUTHER KING JR.'s capability in popularizing a Christian belief in nonviolent direct action that first attracted social activists beyond Montgomery.

Massive black protests and boycotts in Birmingham, Alabama, in the spring of 1963 pressed liberal churches toward more involvement in the Civil Rights movement. King represented a younger generation of black clergy whose direct-action tactics were transforming the civil rights struggle in the South. King's willingness to engage in civil disobedience and to preach forcefully to white churches about the effects of discrimination was tremendously compelling. By 1963, he was the leading black interpreter of the civil rights struggle to white church people all over the country.

After his arrest in 1963 for participating in a march in Birmingham, King wrote his "Letter from the Birmingham City Jail," responding not only to the circumstances of his arrest but to criticism from other clergy. King supported his actions by citing a broad range of doctrines, philosophies, and thinkers that he connected to the experiences of his Christian ministry and the secular ideals of liberty and justice articulated in the DECLARATION OF INDEPENDENCE, the Federalist Papers, and the U.S. Constitution.

The Civil Right movement asked Americans to judge themselves and their institutions according to values and commitments that transcended and informed constitutional choice. From the perspective of African Americans, the injustices of ordinary law and flaws in the federal Constitution compelled not only constitutional tests but also a movement to redirect American constitutionalism toward natural rights, equality, and justice. The movement viewed the political principles of equality and liberty expressed in the Declaration of Independence as religious insights regarding the essential worth of all God's creations.

To those who participated in the movement, segregation was a moral as well as political problem, one of many indications of America's alienation from God. Since the Declaration made no mention of a graded scale of fundamental worth, it followed, according to civil rights activists, that there was no divine right of one race that superseded the divine right of another. The pursuit of justice was not only the will of God but also an essential part of the heritage of the nation. The Declaration of Independence made it clear that American political institutions could be judged by their ability to allow citizens to recognize and address moral imperatives.

The Civil Rights movement presented an opportunity for the nation to realign its political institutions with the fundamental principles of justice. The goal of nonviolence was to correct injustice by evoking universal moral principles. Activists used nonviolent CIVIL DISOBEDIENCE and other forms of direct action to address serious breeches of fundamental civil rights. Many of these demands were accommodated by legislative change. Direct action was used to engage citizens in the task of evaluating ordinary law against constitutional law and both of these against universal moral claims. Additionally, the movement emphasized that it was the citizen's responsibility to take direct action to bring injustice to light, rather than wait for government agencies to act. In his widely cited definition of civil disobedience, King described the moral and political obligations of citizenship.

The Civil Rights movement's demand for equality under the law presupposed that citizens are moral equals, and that basic proposition provided the foundation for general demands of equal opportunity and corrective action to remove obstacles that were built based on mistaken assumptions of moral (e.g., racial) superiority. Church people were interested in the Civil Rights movement from a moral standpoint. Some reasoned that the moral demands placed on Christians meant they had no choice but to support civil rights. Many citizens were especially sensitive to the clear ethical issues posed by the Civil Rights movement. The fact that considerable numbers of Americans were still denied the right to vote and have access to public accommodations because of their race was a moral contradiction that outweighed for a short time other misgivings or prejudices about race that many churchgoers may have felt.

The struggle for the passage of the Civil Rights Act of 1964 marked the dramatic entry into national politics by American churches. The direct commitment of the churches in 1963 and 1964 to the national racial struggle was a return to the activism of the early-20th-century's SOCIAL GOSPEL movement. The results suggest that religious groups had begun to make their political presence felt. Representatives of mainline Protestant churches quickly learned methods of applying political pressure and influencing the legislative process in Washington.

Demonstrating idealism and a sense of moral concern stemming from their religious commitments, the mainline churches spoke out in a sustained and effective way on the primary domestic problem facing the nation. By the end of the 1960s, other emerging social movements splintered the Civil Rights movement, which collapsed under the weight of incompatible demands and agendas.

However, the moral and political force of the early Civil Rights movement mobilized the citizens of the United States to challenge and change political inequality in the nation.

See also ABERNATHY, RALPH; AFRICAN-AMERICAN VOTING BEHAVIOR SINCE THE CIVIL RIGHTS MOVEMENT; BLACK THEOLOGY: *CHRISTIANS IN RACIAL CRISIS;* CHURCH BURNINGS; CONE, JAMES; CONGRESS OF RACIAL EQUALITY; *GATHERING STORM IN THE CHURCHES, THE;* JACKSON, JESSE; KU KLUX KLAN; LIBERATION THEOLOGY; MALCOLM X; PROTESTS AND RALLIES; SOUTHERN CHRISTIAN LEADERSHIP CONFERENCE; STUDENT NONVIOLENT COORDINATING COMMITTEE; YOUNG, ANDREW.

Further reading: Allen, Barbara. "Martin Luther King's Civil Disobedience and the American Covenant Tradition." *Publius* 30, no. 4 (2000): 71–113; Branch, Taylor. *Parting the Waters: America in the King Years 1954–63.* New York: Simon and Schuster, 1989; Dittmer, John, George C. Wright, and W. Marvin Dulaney. *Essays on the American Civil Rights Movement.* Edited by W. Martin Dulaney and Kathleen Underwood. College Station: Texas A&M University Press, 1993; Findlay, James F. "Religion and Politics in the Sixties: The Churches and the Civil Rights Act of 1964." *Journal of American History* 77, no. 1 (1990): 66–92; Morris, Aldon D. *The Origins of the Civil Rights Movement: Black Communities Organizing for Change.* New York: Free Press, 1984.

—TeResa C. Green

Clinton, William Jefferson (Bill) (1946–)
U.S. president

William Jefferson Clinton served as the 42nd president of the United States (1993–2001). During his tenure, Clinton drew on religious themes, leaders, and people to support his "New

William Jefferson Clinton *(Spencer Platt/Getty Images)*

Democratic" policies, but not without evoking strong antipathy from conservative religious groups.

Clinton's early life prepared him well to deal with religious matters. Although his family was not religious, he attended a ROMAN CATHOLIC CHURCH school for two years, had a deeply religious nanny, and began frequenting a SOUTHERN BAPTIST CONVENTION church on his own initiative at the age of eight. Education at Georgetown University deepened his understanding of the Catholic tradition, adding to his already considerable facility with religious language. Marriage to Hillary Rodham, a UNITED METHODIST steeped in the SOCIAL GOSPEL tradition, connected him to the liberal wing of mainline Protestantism.

Although Clinton's religious involvement apparently waned after graduation from Georgetown, his surprising 1980 defeat for reelection as Arkansas governor a decade later elicited a return to his religious roots. He joined Little Rock's Immanuel Baptist Church, sang in the choir, attended revivals and, upon reelection in 1982, appointed new staff with ties to Southern Baptists, PENTECOSTALS, and other religious conservatives. In his 1992 presidential campaign, Clinton tried to downplay the social LIBERALISM of the Democratic Party with rhetorical appeals to "family values" and "personal responsibility," wrapped in a biblical call for a "new covenant" between citizens and government. Although he still endorsed freedom of choice on ABORTION, GAY RIGHTS, and other policies anathema to religious conservatives, these appeals bolstered support among mainstream religious voters.

As president, Clinton tried to sustain a religious profile. Inauguration Day began with ecumenical prayer services attended by an army of religious leaders. Invited by several Baptist pastors to join their Washington flocks, Clinton chose instead Foundry United Methodist Church, Hillary's preference, and was often pictured in the media leaving church, Bible in hand. He did not appoint a staff liaison for religious groups, but often played that role himself, especially in meetings with liberal Protestants from the NATIONAL COUNCIL OF CHURCHES, elated by the end of their 12-year exile from the White House during the presidencies of RONALD REAGAN and GEORGE H. W. BUSH. Clinton's personal ties with Catholic clergy and his familiarity with Catholic social teaching helped propitiate the NATIONAL CONFERENCE OF CATHOLIC BISHOPS, as he stressed common interests in social welfare while minimizing differences over abortion. Finally, the president assiduously cultivated the Jewish and African-American Protestant communities, always vital in Democratic politics.

Clinton had a talent for appealing simultaneously to different religious traditions, framing his appeal in universalistic terms, but leaving his listeners hearing the language of their own faith. He applauded Stephen Carter's contention in *The Culture of Disbelief* that religious values should infuse politics, while Hillary Rodham Clinton lauded the "politics of meaning" propounded by Jewish publicist Michael Lerner. The Clinton's progressive, humanistic religious perspective was attractive to many mainline Protestant, Catholic, and Jewish groups, which frequently endorsed administration policy.

Clinton was much less successful at wooing Evangelical Protestants, who were long skeptical of his religious credentials. Well-publicized prayer sessions with prominent evangelicals, support for the RELIGIOUS FREEDOM RESTORATION ACT of 1993, regular phone conversations with his Baptist pastor in Little Rock, and recruitment of evangelical leaders such as William Hybels and ANTHONY CAMPOLO as "spiritual mentors"—all failed to create much enthusiasm for Clinton among evangelicals. In any event, Clinton's early decisions frustrated his personal diplomacy. Evangelicals were ignored and Catholics underrepresented in administrative and staff appointments. And some hotly contested nominations, such as that of Surgeon General Joycelyn Elders, raised conservative hackles. Nor were Clinton's religious credentials burnished by the First Family's hobnobbing with the Hollywood elite, anathema among traditionalists. And Clinton's early actions to rescind Reagan-Bush–era abortion restrictions and to allow homosexuals to serve in the military only intensified the antagonism.

By 1994 Clinton's growing feud with religious conservatives threatened Democratic prospects in the congressional elections, especially in the South. After considerable indecision among White House strategists over the best approach, Democratic National Congressional Committee chair Vic Fazio precipitated a decision by attacking Christian Right groups directly, and was quickly followed by other Democrats. The sweeping Republican victory, bolstered by Christian conservative votes, clearly called for a course adjustment.

After much political soul-searching, Clinton adopted a strategy of "triangulation," emphasizing moderate or even conservative stances on some social issues but reverting occasionally to liberal stands to mollify vital Democratic constituencies. Clinton was soon making both symbolic and policy appeals to religious traditionalists. The president first renewed public references to his own spirituality, telling a television interviewer about his "deep" and "humble" faith, while musing on devotional readings in the Psalms. Drawing on a Department of Education policy guideline drafted with the help of religious groups, Clinton declared that schools were not required to be religion-free, and even hinted that he might accept a bill about PRAYER IN PUBLIC SCHOOLS. Clinton later signed a drastic WELFARE REFORM law that had the strong endorsement of religious conservatives, talked up the "V-chip" that would permit parents to control children's TV viewing, and even signed the Defense of Marriage Act, pushed through Congress by conservative religious groups fearing legalized homosexual unions.

Clinton refused to budge, however, on other issues with religious overtones. He protected affirmative action, rejected massive reductions in immigration, and opposed media CENSORSHIP. Above all, he refused to sign a congressional ban on "partial-birth" abortion, passed by substantial majorities in both houses, despite a fervent plea from the Catholic bishops and fierce lobbying by a coalition of religious conservatives.

Mainline Protestant and Jewish groups backed Clinton once again, and despite the furor, his veto did not prevent an impressive reelection victory in 1996.

Upon return to office, Clinton tried to follow the same "mixed" strategy on social issues that had proven so successful during the campaign. By this time, however, the lines of religious division had solidified once more, with Clinton drawing support from religious liberals and secularists and strong opposition from religious traditionalists, especially Evangelical Protestants. These alignments achieved special clarity during the battle over Clinton's impeachment in 1998–99.

See also GAY AND LESBIAN MARRIAGE; IMPEACHMENT OF BILL CLINTON; RELIGION IN THE 1992 PRESIDENTIAL ELECTION; RELIGION IN THE CONGRESSIONAL ELECTION OF 1994; RELIGION IN THE 1996 PRESIDENTIAL ELECTION.

Further reading: Guth, James L. "Clinton, Impeachment, and the Culture Wars." In Steven E. Schier, ed. *The Postmodern Presidency: Bill Clinton's Legacy in U.S. Politics.* Pittsburgh: University of Pittsburgh Press, 2000; Maraniss, David. *First in His Class: The Biography of Bill Clinton.* New York: Simon and Schuster, 1995.

—James L. Guth

cloning/genetic engineering

Genetic engineering, the transfer of DNA from one organism to another, and cloning, the induction of asexual reproduction of an organism, are two of the most ethically, legally, and religiously controversial scientific developments of the last century. This technology has the potential for conquering world hunger and curing, or even eliminating, many inherited diseases. But, it also forces society to question the nature of life itself and could have horrifying consequences whether intended or not.

Genetic engineering has applications in agriculture, medicine, and the environment. In agriculture, both animals and crops are being altered to increase production and disease resistance. In medicine, gene therapy, which involves using altered cells or viruses to deliver new genes into an organism's genes, may be used to improve the treatment of patients with genetic diseases and cancer, and perhaps one day cure them, by manipulating those very patients' own genes. Finally, another use of genetic engineering is in environmental crises. Genetically engineered microbes may be used in combating pollutants and poisonous wastes by converting hazardous materials into nontoxic products.

Many scientists and scholars believe that genetic engineering may have negative consequences, some still unforeseeable. Additionally, some critics raise the question of who will control new biotechnologies—scientists, governments, or corporations. Potential negative uses of genetic engineering include genetic screening and discrimination by employers and/or insurance companies. Opponents warn that the new technology will be developed on medical advancements only for profit, such as cures for baldness or wrinkles, at the risk of ignoring less economically though perhaps more ethically valuable uses.

Cloning is a form of induced asexual reproduction in which genetic material may or may not be altered. Though they had previously cloned other animals from fetal cells, in 1997 Ian Wilmut and Keith Cambell of Roslin Institute in Scotland cloned the first mammal, a sheep named Dolly, from an adult body cell. This distinction means that clones may be produced from adult organisms without having to use fetal tissue. This has been a highly controversial ethical and political debate, to say nothing of the technological difficulties involved. The next year the Roslin team cloned Dolly to produce Polly, and, this time, also genetically altered Polly's genetic makeup. This showed that genetic material might be added, deleted, or altered.

After Dolly was cloned, reaction worldwide ranged from wonder to horror because of the potential ramifications the new technology would have for human cloning. President WILLIAM JEFFERSON CLINTON placed a ban on federal funding of human-cloning research in March 1997. From 1998 to 2000, other animals, including mice, calves, goats, and pigs, were cloned. While the international community debated the merits and dangers of human cloning, the first cloned human embryos were created at Advanced Cell Technology's (ACT) lab in Massachusetts in October 2001. The ACT team removed DNA from a human egg, then delivered new genes into that egg. The researchers then tricked the egg into action using electricity, rather than sperm, resulting in stem cells. The stem cells were then induced to specialize and grew into six-cell embryos.

Many say that genetic engineering, and specifically human cloning, is unethical because it is unnatural and therefore immoral. Some of these critics assert that using the technology is akin to playing God and that science has gone too far. Furthermore, the production of embryos for "spare parts" is morally reprehensible to most people, they argue. Proponents of the technology respond that the moral should not be equated with present conceptions of the natural. Others point to resistance to previous technological developments to argue that biotechnology is being rejected simply because it is new. Supporters of genetic engineering and cloning also believe that the use of fetal cells in therapeutic cloning treatments outweighs any ethical concern over the cells used. These people explain that the cells being used are the building blocks of life, really no different from any other cell in the human body, and must be understood as not yet being a person. Finally, they answer that fears that human cloning will be used to mass-produce humans are unfounded since a consensus exists that such actions should and would be illegal. Time will tell whether cloning and genetic engineering are beneficial or harmful to humanity and the world.

See also ABORTION.

Further reading: Fischer, Joannie. "The First Clone." *U.S. News & World Report.* December 3, 2001; Torr, James D., ed. *Genetic Engineering: Opposing Viewpoints.* San Diego: Greenhaven Press, 2001; Wilmut, Ian, Keith Campbell, and Colin Tudge. *The Second Creation: Dolly and the Age of Biological Control.* New York: Farrar, Straus and Giroux, 2000.

—Kurt Buhring

Coalition for the Free Exercise of Religion

The Coalition for the Free Exercise of Religion is an ecumenical advocacy group formed in 1991 for the specific purpose of aiding passage of the RELIGIOUS FREEDOM RESTORATION ACT (RFRA) in the U.S. Congress. The coalition represents at least 70 religious groups and civil liberties organizations as diverse as the AMERICAN CIVIL LIBERTIES UNION, NATIONAL ASSOCIATION OF EVANGELICALS, LATTER-DAY SAINTS, UNITED METHODIST CHURCH, and the TRADITIONAL VALUES COALITION.

The impetus for the formation of the Coalition for the Free Exercise of Religion was the Supreme Court's 1990 decision in the case of *EMPLOYMENT DIVISION OF OREGON V. SMITH.* In the *Smith* case, which involved the denial of state unemployment benefits to two Native Americans for their ritual use of peyote in religious ceremonies, the Court abandoned its traditional principle for assessing the constitutionality of state actions that restrict religious practices. That principle held that for a particular state action (which results in the restriction of religious exercise) to be constitutional, the state must be able to demonstrate a "compelling interest" for taking that action. In *Smith,* the Court also rejected its previously applied "least restrictive means" test, which determined that once a compelling interest for state action has been established, the state must act in such a way as to be least restrictive of the rights of religious groups. Rejection of these constitutional tests for the adjudication of First Amendment cases was seen as a grave threat to religious liberty in the United States and especially threatening to the religious rights of minority groups.

RFRA was designed to restore these two tests for the determination of the constitutionality of state actions that impact religious practice, and the coalition was successful in aiding passage of RFRA in 1993. Three years later in *BOERNE, CITY OF V. FLORES,* however, the Supreme Court ruled that Congress had overstepped its bounds in passing RFRA by engaging in constitutional interpretation, a function reserved exclusively for the judiciary in the American constitutional system. In response to the *Boerne* decision, the coalition set about once again to achieve a legislative remedy to the perceived threat to religious rights by lobbying for passage of the Religious Liberty Protection Act (RLPA). Yet, support for this bill within the coalition and within Congress ultimately fragmented, and the legislation never reached a vote. As of the year 2000, the Coalition for the Free Exercise of Religion was working actively to achieve passage of various "state RFRAs" in state legislatures across the United States.

—Derek H. Davis

Colson, Charles (1931–) *Christian activist*

Charles Wendell "Chuck" Colson was born in Boston, Massachusetts, where he learned about the mainline Protestant establishment firsthand. He was a self-described "Swamp Yankee," a Protestant left behind when the old stock withdrew to the shelter of Beacon Hill and Commonwealth Avenue. He earned a bachelor's degree from Brown University in 1953 and a law degree from George Washington University in 1959. He married after college and divorced in 1964, then married his present wife the same year.

Today, Colson is a popular Christian author, speaker, and radio commentator. He served as a special counsel to President RICHARD NIXON and was a prominent figure in the Watergate scandal of the early 1970s. He left the White House in 1972 because of his association with the conspirators but remained in the headlines. Colson's dramatic conversion to Christianity in August 1973 made news because he had a reputation as a ruthless politico who crushed opponents and demanded complete loyalty from friends.

Colson was socialized into politics in the ethnic enclaves of Boston, where in 1960 he helped engineer a remarkable upset victory for Republican Leverett Saltonstall on the same day that JOHN F. KENNEDY was winning the electoral votes of Massachusetts and also the presidency. Colson practiced law in Boston with a comfortable six-figure salary until he joined the Nixon campaign in 1968.

His work as an "issues man" in the campaign led to an invitation to join the White House staff in 1969, where a journalist later described him as a "white collar bully." Colson was Nixon's "hatchet man," working to identify the president's opposition and establishing a White House "enemies list" of antagonistic journalists, politicians, academics, and entertainers. His devotion to the president was such that he was quoted as saying, "I would walk over my grandmother if necessary to get Nixon re-elected."

Colson brought E. Howard Hunt into the White House. Hunt later became the ringleader of the infamous "plumbers," the group responsible for the 1972 burglary of the Democratic National Committee headquarters in the Watergate complex. The plumbers also burglarized the offices of the psychiatrist for Daniel Ellsburg. Ellsburg was a former federal official who had angered the White House by publicizing documents about the VIETNAM WAR, known as the "Pentagon Papers."

While awaiting trial for his part in Watergate, Colson met an old friend who had recently had a BORN-AGAIN EXPERIENCE. At the same time, Colson read C. S. Lewis's *Mere Christianity.* These influences stirred him to accept Christ, and later to plead guilty to an obstruction of justice charge rather than delay his court proceedings any further. Colson's conversion is detailed in his book *Born Again.* The sincerity of his religious experience was questioned when he had his born-again experience because he was facing other charges for the illegal activities in the Nixon White House, but later even his political enemies were impressed with his commitment.

On March 1, 1974, Colson was indicted, along with six others, on charges of perjury and conspiracy to obstruct justice in connection with the Watergate burglary. After serving a seven-month prison term, he founded an international Christian ministry called PRISON FELLOWSHIP. By the 1990s, this organization had more than 40,000 volunteers in all 50 states, with branches overseas.

Colson has written several books, including *Born Again, Life Sentence, Loving God, Kingdoms in Conflict, The Body,* and *How Now Shall We Live.* Collectively, these books have shaped social and political thinking within the evangelical Christian community and given Colson an international pulpit. He also coauthored a novel with Ellen Vaughn, *Gideon's Torch,* and has a syndicated radio program called *Breakpoint.* The commentary on a variety of social and political issues is a popular feature on both Christian and secular radio stations.

The major sign of the earnestness of Colson's religious convictions is his fervent devotion to Christian ministry during the three decades since Watergate. He has become a leading spokesman for criminal justice reforms, including the "Inner-change" approach used in one Texas prison. The 18-month prerelease program became a model for Texas governor GEORGE W. BUSH to use as a successful example of a "faith-based" policy initiative when he campaigned for the presidency in 2000.

The success of the Prison Fellowship ministry has vindicated Colson in the eyes of the evangelical community. As a result, he has assumed the role of spokesman for many conservative Christian causes. In 1993 he was recognized for his service and awarded the Templeton Prize for Progress in Religion, which is awarded for extraordinary leadership and originality in advancing humanity's understanding of God.

Further reading: Colson, Charles W. *Born Again.* Grand Rapids, Mich.: Fleming H. Revell, 1976; Whalin, W. Terry. *Chuck Colson.* Grand Rapids, Mich.: Zondervan, 1994.

—J. David Woodard

Committee for Public Education and Religious Liberty (CPEARL) et al. v. Nyquist, Commissioner of Education of New York, et al. (413 U.S. 756) (1973)

In this case, decided on June 23, 1973, the Supreme Court considered the constitutionality of a number of forms of public aid to religious schools and the parents of children attending them. At issue in particular were provisions of a New York State law that would subsidize the maintenance and repair costs of certain nonpublic, primarily religious schools, give a partial reimbursement to some parents of children attending all nonpublic schools, and offer a limited tax credit to other parents not eligible for the reimbursement. Justice Lewis Powell, writing for a six-justice majority, utilized the three-pronged test first fully articulated two years earlier in *LEMON V. KURTZMAN,* and found all three programs in violation of the

ESTABLISHMENT CLAUSE of the First Amendment, as applied to the states through the FOURTEENTH AMENDMENT. Three justices argued that the reimbursement and tax credit programs were constitutional, but only one (Justice Byron White) argued on behalf of the constitutionality of the maintenance and repair subsidy.

The three parts of the *Lemon* test require that, to be constitutional, a law "must reflect a clearly secular legislative purpose," "must have a primary effect that neither advances nor inhibits religion," and "must avoid excessive government entanglement with religion." Failure on any one of these counts is sufficient to invalidate the legislation. In the case of the New York programs at issue, the majority found that all three failed the second test.

The maintenance and repair program, aimed at the appropriate secular purpose of securing the health, safety, and welfare of schoolchildren, provided for direct payments to nonpublic schools serving substantial numbers of low-income students. Because "[n]o attempt is made to restrict payments to those expenditures related to the upkeep of facilities used exclusively for secular purposes," this program had the unavoidable effect of advancing religion.

The remaining two programs were distinguished from the first by the fact that grants and tax credits were provided to parents, rather than directly to the nonpublic schools. Although in two previous cases—*EVERSON V. BOARD OF EDU-CATION* and *BOARD OF EDUCATION V. ALLEN*—this sort of aid had passed constitutional muster, the Court distinguished the current programs. In both previous cases, it was possible to separate out secular functions the state could support, whether reimbursements for bus fares (*Everson*) or the provision of secular textbooks (*Allen*). In this case, however, the grants appeared to be "offered as an incentive to parents to send their children to sectarian schools." Similarly, the majority regarded the tax credit as a "form of encouragement and reward" given to parents who send their children to nonpublic schools. As such, both the grant and the tax credit could be said to advance religion, violating the second prong of the *Lemon* test.

There were three dissenting opinions, authored by Chief Justice Warren Burger, Justice William Rehnquist, and Justice White. Burger, joined by Rehnquist and White, took issue with the majority's attempt to distinguish this case from *Everson* and *Allen*. In all three cases, the state law could be said to be aimed at "enhancing a recognized freedom of individuals," which was permissible, even if "many of those individuals may elect to use [the law's] benefits in ways that 'aid' religious instruction or worship." It was merely "simple equity," Chief Justice Burger contended, "to grant partial relief to parents who support the public schools they do not use."

Justice Rehnquist's dissent, joined by Burger and White, took issue with the majority's effort to distinguish the current programs from the tax exemptions for churches upheld three years earlier in *WALZ V. TAX COMMISSION.* The two programs were, he insisted, "indistinguishable in principle"; if the one were upheld, so should be the other. In addition, he argued that the state's "benevolent neutrality" with respect to religion that the Court acknowledged and upheld in *Everson* and *Allen* ought equally to be upheld here. After all, the aid went to parents, not to schools; furthermore, it served to relieve overburdened public schools and to relieve some of the costs absorbed by parents who are "compelled to support public school services unused by them."

Justice White, joined in part by Burger and Rehnquist, would uphold all three programs. In his dissent, he reminded his brethren that the second prong of the *Lemon* test "is one of 'primary' effect not any effect." By this standard, even the maintenance and repair program would pass muster, since the grants given to schools "[do] not and could not, by its terms, approach the actual repair and maintenance cost incurred in connection with the secular education services performed for the State in parochial schools."

See also TAX-EXEMPT STATUS OF RELIGIOUS ORGANIZATIONS; TUITION TAX CREDITS FOR RELIGIOUS SCHOOLS.

—Joseph M. Knippenberg

Committee for Public Education and Religious Liberty (CPEARL) et al. v. Regan, Comptroller of New York, et al. (444 U.S. 646) (1980)

The case of *CPEARL v. Regan*, decided on February 20, 1980, involved a challenge to the constitutionality of a New York law that provided direct reimbursement by the state to private schools for staff time spent in keeping records of student attendance and grading standardized tests. In an opinion authored by Justice Byron White, a majority of the Supreme Court held that the law did not violate the ESTABLISHMENT CLAUSE of the First Amendment (made applicable to the states through the Fourteenth Amendment). In *LEVITT V. CPEARL* (1973) the Supreme Court struck down an earlier version of the same law on the basis that it did violate the Constitution. The Court in the present case was faced with a revised version of the same statute drafted by the legislature with a view of overcoming the constitutional infirmities that had been fatal to their earlier attempt.

The decision to uphold the revised New York law was reached by a 5-4 majority. However, eight of the nine justices were able to agree on the appropriate standard of constitutional review applicable on these facts; it was the application of this standard of review that divided the Court. The legal test approved by all justices (except for Justice Stevens, who applied an inflexible divide between church and state to strike down the law) contained the three prongs of the *Lemon* test. For a law to pass constitutional muster under the Establishment Clause, it must have a secular legislative purpose; its principal or primary effect must neither advance nor inhibit religion; and it must not foster an excessive government entanglement with religion.

Justice White (with whom Chief Justice Burger and Justices Stewart, Powell, and Rehnquist agreed) found that both the testing provisions as well as the record-keeping provisions

of the New York law passed all three prongs of the applicable standard of review. On the topic of the grading of tests, the majority noted that the purpose of standardized testing was clearly secular. Further, the nature of the tests (largely comprising multiple-choice questions) left little room for the exercise of educational discretion that might be influenced by the religious mission of the teachers employed in private schools. The tests were set by the state (not the private school teachers), and thus were incapable of being used as part of the religious curriculum of sectarian schools. Accordingly, the practice of reimbursing the schools for time spent grading the tests did not impermissibly infringe on the First Amendment.

The majority adopted similar reasoning in relation to state reimbursement for attendance record keeping by private schools. They noted that this task was purely ministerial, lacking any ideological content or use. Therefore, it was not possible that the practice could have a religious purpose or effect. On the issue of excessive entanglement, the majority concluded that the discrete and clearly identifiable nature of the services for which the schools were to be reimbursed negated any tendency toward undue entanglement between the secular and the sacred. In recognition of the dissenting justices, the majority acknowledged that "Establishment Clause cases are not easy" and looked forward to the future development of a more unified approach to such cases.

Justice Blackmun wrote a dissenting opinion, joined by Justices Brennan and Marshall. The minority agreed with the standard of review identified by the majority and further agreed that the New York law manifested a "clear secular purpose." But they reached a different conclusion in relation to the last two elements of the test. The fact that the assistance provided by the state to private schools was in the form of direct cash payments was a key element supporting the minority view that the legislation did have the proscribed effect of advancing religion. Justice Blackmun reasoned that as all private schools were required to perform the record-keeping and testing functions anyway (in order to be accredited by the state), the effect of reimbursing the schools for carrying out these functions was to facilitate generally the provision of sectarian education. In effect, the law acted as a direct subsidy of the operating costs of private schools.

Further, given that some parts of the standardized tests involved the teachers having to exercise subjective judgment, the grading process would have to be supervised by the state to ensure that purely secular standards were being applied by private-school teachers. This practice would tend to foster the kind of excessive entanglement between church and state prohibited by the First Amendment. For these reasons, Justice Blackmun concluded the law was unconstitutional.

—Jillian Savage

Commonweal

Commonweal is an independent journal of opinion published biweekly by ROMAN CATHOLIC CHURCH laypeople. Founded in 1924 by Michael Williams as *The Commonweal* (the journal's title was shortened to *Commonweal* in 1965), it has consistently provided intelligent coverage of politics, religion, ethics, and the arts. Its purpose is to engage the principles of Catholic Christianity with contemporary thought, literature, art, and public affairs at a high intellectual level.

Commonweal is independent, without direct church subsidy or control. Headquartered in New York City, it is published by the nonprofit Commonweal Foundation, which was incorporated in 1983. It has a circulation of 21,000 and a readership of 35,000. Fifteen staff members and six columnists produce the biweekly magazine.

Through provocative essays by distinguished writers, *Commonweal* has sought to bring Catholic faith and modern life—especially the experience of American freedom and diversity—into fruitful contact. Among the noted thinkers and writers who have appeared in *Commonweal,* are Michael Harrington, Willa Cather, Graham Greene, Thomas Merton, Evelyn Waugh, Jacques Maritain, Walter Kerr, Wilfrid Sheed, Eugene McCarthy, Abigail McCarthy, Andrew Greeley, Daniel Berrigan, Gordon Zahn, REINHOLD NIEBUHR, Walter Lippmann, Lewis Mumford, Hannah Arendt, DOROTHY DAY, Will Herberg, Harvey Cox, and Robert Coles. Feminist theologians and writers such as Mary Daly, Elizabeth Schussler-Fiorenza, Rosemary Ruether, Elizabeth Johnson, and Karen Sue Smith wrote for *Commonweal.* The magazine has also published poetry of W. H. Auden, Robert Lowell, Padraic Colum, John Updike, Phyllis McGinley, Ned O'Gorman, and Sister M. Madaleva.

Commonweal addresses controversial issues of continuing relevance within both the Catholic Church and American society in general. Throughout the 20th century, its editors and writers have commented vigorously on such issues as the presidential nominations of Al Smith and JOHN F. KENNEDY, the Spanish Civil War, foreign policy debates prior to World War II, Nazism and fascism, the dropping of the atomic bomb, the McCarthy era, the CIVIL RIGHTS MOVEMENT, the sixties, the VIETNAM WAR, the renewals and disappointments of VATICAN II, the Watergate and Iran-Contra scandals, RICHARD NIXON's resignation as president, and the IMPEACHMENT OF WILLIAM JEFFERSON CLINTON, Pope JOHN PAUL II's pontificate, the RONALD REAGAN administration, the collapse of communism in Eastern Europe, the PERSIAN GULF WAR, the boom of the 1990s, and the extraordinary presidential election of 2000. Combining liberal convictions and Catholic tradition, the editors of *Commonweal* bring a moral perspective to bear on complicated policy issues such as the legality of ABORTION, CLONING, stem-cell research, religious pluralism, GAY RIGHTS, economic justice, the environment, church and state, war and peace, race and gender, poverty and WELFARE REFORM. The magazine also features articles on liturgical reform, dissent within the Catholic Church, theological controversy, and Jewish-Christian dialogue.

Like any first-rate journal of opinion, *Commonweal* has a distinctive outlook; ultimately, it is known as a liberal journal.

It has consistently sought to defend a commitment to government activism in regulating the economy and redistributing public goods. It has opposed censorship and the ANTICOMMUNISM of the McCarthy era, defended civil liberties and civil rights, and supported organized labor. True to its Catholic tradition, however, *Commonweal* has sometimes parted ways with secular liberals over issues concerning reproduction and sexuality, bioethics and technology, and the role of religion in politics and society. In short, as one of its former editors wrote, "Independence . . . has been a *Commonweal* hallmark, independence from church structure or subsidy, independence from liberal orthodoxy, independence from the post-sixties factions, whether Catholic or secular." Such independence is not easy to bankroll, and *Commonweal* has relied for financial support on the modest donations of loyal readers and the thrift and sacrifices of its editors and writers. The magazine celebrated its 75th anniversary in 1999 with a public lecture by Alice McDermott and a grand feast at Fordham University's Lincoln Center campus.

Further reading: Commonweal on the Internet. URL: http://www.commonwealmagazine.org; Jordan, Patrick, and Paul Baumann, eds. *Commonweal Confronts the Century: Liberal Convictions, Catholic Tradition.* New York: Simon and Schuster, 1999; Steinfels, Peter. "Introduction." In *Commonweal Confronts the Century: Liberal Convictions, Catholic Tradition.* Edited by Patrick Jordan and Paul Baumann. New York: Simon and Schuster, 1999; Van Allen, Rodger. *The Commonweal and American Catholicism: The Magazine, The Movement, The Meaning.* Philadelphia: Fortress Press, 1974; Van Allen, Rodger. *Being Catholic: Commonweal from the Seventies to the Nineties.* Philadelphia: Fortress Press, 1993.

—Mary C. Segers

communalism

Communalism derives from *commune,* a term first used by newly formed towns in 12th- and 13th-century France to denote their claims to political autonomy and social solidarity, values that communalism still represents. The short-lived revolutionary Paris communes of 1792 and 1871 gave a more radical political edge to communalism, leading to its association with extreme egalitarianism and common property and, therefore, locally based MARXISM/COMMUNISM. In America, communalism is most strongly associated with, and derives its energy and meanings from, the religiously based utopian experiments begun in the late 17th century (Labadists in Maryland, Women in the Wilderness in Pennsylvania) but mostly formed in the early and mid-19th century. The most notable of these later experiments are the many SHAKER communities first formed in New York in 1787, the Amana colonies in New York and Iowa—and, most famously, the Perfectionist community at Oneida, New York, founded by John Humphrey Noyes in 1848, and the LATTER-DAY SAINTS, based on the inspiration and teachings of JOSEPH SMITH, also in upstate New York, in 1830. Running parallel with these religiously based communities were secular experimental communities as well, some influenced by the French socialist Charles Fourier (Brook Farm, in Massachusetts, and Icaria, in Nauvoo, Illinois, after the Mormon exodus) and others founded by the English socialist Robert Owen (New Harmony, Indiana).

New York State figures so prominently in the story of American communalism because many of its ideas and experiments were inspired by the SECOND GREAT AWAKENING, a long period of revival movements especially strong among New England migrants to upstate New York. This same mid–nineteenth-century region of religious enthusiasm—popularly called the "burned-over" district—attracted many other segments of the PURITAN diaspora to the Sunday school movement, campaigns for Sunday BLUE LAWS and asylum reform, ABOLITIONIST MOVEMENT, women's rights, temperance, and the anti-Masonic league, the last a party-political movement against Jacksonian Democrats. After the Civil War, communalism largely ceased to inspire utopian community formation but, in alliance with new variants of earlier northern evangelical Protestant religious, moral, and economic reform movements, influenced a host of organizations and movements that came to be called Christian socialism or social Christianity and, later, the SOCIAL GOSPEL movement. Prominent intellectual and organizational leaders in this period were Edward Bellamy, author of *Looking Backward* (1888), and William Dwight Porter Bliss, cofounder (with Richard Ely) of the Society of Christian Socialists (1889–96) and editor of *Dawn* (1889) and *American Fabian* (1895–96). Other leaders in this period were George Herron, famous revivalist and later supporter of Eugene Debs, Washington Gladden, Richard Ely, cofounder and secretary of the American Economics Association, and Walter Rauschenbusch, whose *Christianity and the Social Crisis* (1907) provided the theological underpinnings for a non-Marxist and cooperative form of socialism. Women were also prominent, especially FRANCES WILLARD, founder-president of the WOMEN'S CHRISTIAN TEMPERANCE UNION, and JANE ADDAMS, the settlement house founder and publicist.

In the 1960s and 1970s, the term "commune" received a new lease on life as the name for urban and rural experiments in collective living and political activism inspired mainly by the New Left counterculture and, to a lesser degree, by Eastern religions. Almost all were as short-lived as their 19th-century predecessors, although some evolved either into small businesses (such as organic foods) or exemplars of energy-conserving environmentalism. Those parts of President Lyndon Johnson's Great Society antipoverty programs stressing "maximum feasible" community participation to build communal-political solidarity outside of established political bodies also echo communitarian aspirations and values. The rise of black nationalism in this period also called forth many communal experiments.

From its first discovery by Europeans through today, America has always been seen as a fertile field for religious bodies to plant their communal aspirations. While Reformed Protestant movements, charismatic leaders, and church organizations have provided the dominant examples and continue to dominate our historical understanding, this should not blind us to the fact that HASIDIC JEWS, BUDDHISTS, Black Muslims, and secular utopians of all stripes have made their communal statements as well. The chief contemporary legacy of communalism in America, however, is in the more wide-ranging and intellectually and religiously diverse movement known as COMMUNITARIANISM.

See also TRANSCENDENTALISM.

Further reading: Cross, Whitney. *The Burned-Over District: The Social and Intellectual History of Enthusiastic Religion in Western New York, 1800–1850.* Ithaca, N.Y.: Cornell University Press, 1950; Nordhoff, Charles. *The Communistic Societies of the United States from Personal Visit and Observation.* New York: Dover Publications, 1966 [1875]; Noyes, John Humphrey. *The History of American Socialisms.* New York: Dover Publications, 1966 [1870].

—Eldon J. Eisenach

communitarianism

The reemergence of communitarianism during the 1980s and 1990s bespoke a growing disenchantment with liberal INDIVIDUALISM in American public and private life. In a sense, this phenomenon was hardly a reemergence at all: the decline of community has been a perennial theme in social theory and criticism, and contemporary communitarians draw on such varied thinkers as Rousseau, Tonnies, and Burke. As we shall see, the relationship between communitarianism and American religion encompasses areas of agreement as well as divergence.

American communitarians lament the increasing predominance of individualistic, rights-oriented rhetoric within the citizenry; the growth of central state power and the corresponding decline of community cohesion, participation in governmental and nongovernmental institutions, and the notion of civic obligation; and the erosion of personal ties, particularly but not exclusively family and traditional ones. Robert Bellah and his collaborators voice their concern that American individualism "may have grown cancerous—that it may be destroying those social integuments that Tocqueville saw as moderating its more destructive potentialities, that it may be threatening the survival of freedom itself."

A deeper problem, according to communitarians, lies in the widespread liberal view of individuals as autonomous, instrumental choosers, rather than as "embedded in the story of those communities from which [they] derive [their] identity," and with liberal governments, which contribute to the erosion of community through their commitment to neutrality in all public actions and their endorsement of market mechanisms over community norms and values. Market individualism, with its "cancerous effects on community life," has created a society in which "selfishness becomes a moral code."

Michael Sandel describes liberal societies as "procedural republics" filled with "unencumbered selves"—governments dedicated to neutrality between citizens' competing conceptions of the good, conceiving of their citizens as autonomous, willing selves independent of their claimed ends. Communitarians call into question the ability of such unencumbered selves to engage in fulfilling relationships, let alone politics, with other people, *and* the ability of a politics of unencumbered selves to address the issues of meaning, value, and identity that bind real people in real communities.

With regard to American religion and history, communitarians argue that the neutralist, individualist understanding of American freedom that dominates contemporary liberal discourse does not accurately represent the theory or practice of American life for much of the nation's past: a collective, often religious, context always undergirded American professions of individualism (as pointed out in, for example, Tocqueville's DEMOCRACY IN AMERICA), and these contexts prevented such individualism from degenerating into atomization and moral anarchy. Communitarians offer a powerful historical narrative depicting the steady erosion of such communal contexts by the forces of commercialism, industrialism, and capitalism, or by the introduction of television and the steadily increasing commuting times of American workers. Over time, communitarians argue, a radical individualism has crowded out more civic, religious, or morally grounded traditions in American thought, and modern liberalism has brought about "a willful abnegation of an ethics of mutual concern."

Clearly, then, contemporary communitarianism shares conceptual and political ground with the perennial communalist impulse in American history, driven as it so often was by religious values of one sort or another. At the same time, the relationship between communitarianism and religion has not always been smooth. The commitment among some contemporary communitarians to community per se has drawn the ire of self-identified religious conservatives, for whom the position resembles a dangerous version of rootless communal relativism. Without a grounding in transcendent truth, they argue—without a clear connection between community values and religious values (such as, on this view, characterized the American Founding and the early national period)—communitarianism merely replicates the liberal relativism it seeks to criticize.

See also BOWLING ALONE; COMMUNALISM; HABITS OF THE HEART; SOCIAL CAPITAL; UTOPIANISM; VOICE AND EQUALITY.

Further reading: Bellah, Robert, et al. *Habits of the Heart: Individualism and Commitment in American Life.* New York: Harper and Row, 1986; Etzioni, Amitai. *The Spirit of Community: Rights, Responsibilities, and the Communitarian Agenda.* New York: Crown, 1993; MacIntyre, Alasdair. *After Virtue: A Study in Moral Theory.* Notre Dame, Ind.: Notre Dame University Press, 1981; Putnam, Robert D. *Bowling Alone: The Collapse and Revival of American Community.* New York: Simon and Schuster, 2000; Sandel, Michael. *Democracy's Discontent: America in Search of a Public Philosophy.* Cambridge, Mass.: Harvard University Press, 1996; Selznick, Philip. "The Communitarian Persuasion." In *Communitarianism and Citizenship,* ed. Emilios A. Christodouldis. Aldershot, U.K.: Ashgate, 1998; Tam, Henry. *Communitarianism: A New Agenda for Politics and Citizenship.* New York: New York University Press, 1998.

—Andrew R. Murphy

community organizing

Regardless of the method or ideology, community organizing mediates the power relationships between the government, businesses, and powerful groups, on the one hand, and citizens on the other. Although other mediating organizations serve similar functions, few are found with such frequency in every neighborhood across the country, with reputations as trusted and stabilizing entities in residential areas, with regular attendance of at least half the adult population, and with an organizational norm to serve its community as are local congregations. The distinct contribution of religious-based organizations is linked to the translation of their religious values and beliefs into acts of advocacy and service that build and sustain local and regional communities.

Religious-based organizations, particularly congregations, are an existing power base, political unit, and social organism driven by values and united with the community to serve in the best interests of its neighbors. Religious-based organizations command resources that include people, space and facilities, materials and equipment, expertise, economic power, relationships, values, and political influence. These entities are vital links as organizational networks and community resources that can effect change in communities and the government. Many social change efforts like the CIVIL RIGHTS MOVEMENT were originated by religious groups. Similarly, a major opposition to the 1996 welfare reform came from religious circles. Several months after the law was signed by President WILLIAM JEFFERSON CLINTON (1993–2001), the religious CALL TO RENEWAL organized some 300 Washington, D.C., homeless people and their advocates on the U.S. Capitol lawn for a soup-and-sandwich meal, press conference, and prayer service.

The most noted examples of community organizing efforts by religious-based organizations are undertaken by congregations in some 133 local areas in 33 states and the District of Columbia (Warren and Wood 2001). These efforts are under the auspices of four national networks: the INDUSTRIAL AREAS FOUNDATION (IAF), the Pacific Institute for Community Organization (PICO), Gamaliel Foundation, and Direct Action & Research Training (DART) Centers. Each local federation is composed of 10–40 congregations or religious groups affiliated with and supported by the national organization. These organizations galvanize large numbers of people to advocate for an initiative, which is a compelling reason for politicians and business owners to listen and attempt to cooperate. According to Warren and Wood, faith-based community organizing represents one of the most vital and expansive efforts that builds democratic power, challenges the status quo, calls for social justice, and enhances public life in the United States.

The IAF is the most prominent national organization committed to serving as a change agent at the local level. IAF, founded by Saul Alinsky in 1940, had its beginnings in Alinsky's "Back of the Yards" organization, a coalition of ROMAN CATHOLIC congregations and Labor/Communist Party organizers that sought to enhance the quality of life in Chicago's neighborhoods through advocacy and lobbying.

One example of an IAF affiliate is Tie Nashville Together (TNT) in Nashville, Tennessee. In the months following the founding convention in 1993, TNT members visited schools, conducted public hearings regarding nursing homes, and held "Accountability Nights" for school board and local political candidates. Leaders also formulated an after-school program for K-8 and a "strategy for labor force development and ECONOMIC DEVELOPMENT," both of which were based on IAF initiatives in other communities. In addition, TNT members convinced the mayor's office to open and fund a Neighborhood Justice Center for mediating disputes without police intervention as a means of fostering a sense of community.

In New York, a coalition of East Brooklyn Churches (EBC) joined with the Industrial Area Foundations (IAF) to redevelop deteriorating neighborhoods that were experiencing financial instability, a growing number of abandoned properties, and out-migration of most working-class families. As first steps, street signs were replaced; food quality and sanitary conditions in local supermarkets were improved; long-abandoned buildings were demolished; smoke shops (place for selling illegal narcotics) were closed; and a voter registration campaign boasted an increase of 10,000 new voters in 1984. EBC later took on the task of building 1,000 new homes in Brooklyn. The coalition garnered the FINANCIAL CAPITAL of many denominational and community groups and pressured the city of New York to donate the land, pay for landfill removal, and provide $10,000 in interest-free loans to new home owners. This is one of the many accomplishments of community organizing by religious organizations.

Further reading: Byrd, M. "Determining the Frames of Reference for Religiously Based Organizations: A Case for Neo-Alinsky Efforts to Mobilize Congregational Resources." *Nonprofit and Voluntary Sector Quarterly* 26 (1997): 122–138; Cnaan, R. A., S. C. Boddie, F. Handy, G. Yancey, and R. Schneider. *The Invisible Caring Hand: American Congregations and the Provision of Welfare.* New York: New York University Press, forthcoming; Cnaan, R. A., R. J. Wineburg, and S. C. Boddie. *The Newer Deal: Social Work and Religion in Partnership.* New York: Columbia University Press, 1999; Warren, M. R., and R. L. Wood. "Faith-Based Community Organizing: The State of the Field." Available on-line. URL: http://comm-org.utoledo.edu/papers2001/faith/faith.htm. Accessed 2001.

—Ram A. Cnaan and Stephanie Clintonia Boddie

Concerned Women for America

Describing itself at the largest U.S. public policy women's organization, Concerned Women for America (CWA) claims 500,000 members nationwide. CWA was founded in 1979 by Beverly LaHaye, wife of MORAL MAJORITY cofounder Tim LaHaye, as a direct reaction to a claim by Betty Friedan (then president of the National Organization for Women) that she spoke for the interests of the women of the United States. Organizational literature states: "Mrs. LaHaye was stirred into action. She knew the feminists' anti-God, anti-family rhetoric didn't represent her interests, and she didn't believe it represented the interests of the vast majority of women." After an initial meeting to discuss opposing the EQUAL RIGHTS AMENDMENT, the number of "concerned" women grew to 1,200. Shortly thereafter, CWA was officially established. In 1985, in light of the tremendous growth of CWA's membership, the organization established a headquarters in Washington, D.C., "in order to have a greater impact preserving, protecting, and promoting traditional Judeo-Christian values."

Although CWA's national headquarters is in Washington, D.C., there are "prayer and action" chapters organized in most of the 50 states. The national office is responsible for setting the overall agenda for the organization, and it provides research and position papers for state and local chapters. Chapter leaders who report to regional directors represent local chapters. Regional directors report to the national office, thereby completing the link between grassroots activists and the organizational national leadership. This structure is an important element of CWA's continued organizational success, as it allows for a small number of activists (seven make up a local chapter) to mobilize around an issue and be linked very easily to a state, regional, and national support structure. For political activity by members, this means that their efforts can be felt at all levels of government, from local to national.

CWA's political activities follow a pattern similar to other Christian Right organizations. Relying originally on direct-mail techniques, but now incorporating Web technology, CWA alerts members about upcoming legislative action through informational letters or brochures. Sometimes the informational packet includes a letter to be filled out and sent to a specific legislative representative, while in other instances members are urged to call the offices of key legislators to express their opinions on specific issues. The issues targeted by CWA are varied and have grown from the initial antifeminist (specifically anti-ERA) rhetoric to a much more encompassing, albeit consistently conservative, agenda. Organizational literature and website reports today emphasize issues as varied as homosexuality and national sovereignty. CWA's particular emphasis is on traditional family values, but their policy interests are much broader than those that can be simply reduced to preserving or protecting a traditional family ideal. CWA believes that a woman's most important role is as a nurturer or caregiver to her family. At the same time, CWA believes that women have to take a stand to "save" their families from the negative influences of contemporary society. The elements of this stand are diverse and include fighting for (1) more parental control in the socialization of children through public education and federally funded day care; (2) legal restrictions on ABORTION; (3) prohibiting the legal sanctioning of gay and lesbian families; (4) traditional definitions of sex and gender roles; (5) an end to the progress of radical and liberal FEMINISM; (6) the censoring of PORNOGRAPHY; (7) limited government involvement in most areas of private life; and (8) a strong national defense.

The way in which CWA mobilizes its members around these issues speaks to the efficacy of the organization in providing the means for members to become politically active within the context of their life situations. One of CWA's training pamphlets, "How to Lobby from Your Kitchen Table," instructs members in the basic skills of writing letters to legislators and describes the impact one voice can have in an open democratic process. CWA also makes use of its 535 Program (referring to the 435 members in the U.S. House of Representatives and the 100 senators) when it needs to organize a political or prayer effort around a piece of legislation. In this way, CWA relies on an existing structure to affect national politics. The same structure may be implemented at lower levels (in state or local government) when the need arises.

Accounts of CWA's political efficacy are numerous, and candidates who rely on the votes of conservatives are aware and responsive in many cases to the interests of CWA members. As is their intent, their action is most often successful at local or precinct levels and includes decisions that affect schools, libraries, day-care facilities, and health clinics. Although Beverly LaHaye stepped down from the presidency of the organization in the late 1990s, she remains active in CWA's national leadership and continues her radio shows and her writing, and is still considered the ideological leader of CWA.

See also CHRISTIAN COALITION; EAGLE FORUM; FAMILY RESEARCH COUNCIL; FOCUS ON THE FAMILY.

—R. Lorraine Bernotsky

Cone, James (1938–) *theologian*

James Cone, born on August 8, 1938, in Fordyce, Arkansas, is currently Charles A. Briggs Distinguished Professor of Systematic Theology at Union Theological Seminary. He is widely credited with having given birth to a theological movement that emerged from the black experience in America and the black church. LIBERATION THEOLOGY in America surfaces in his work.

One of the ways to gain clarity on a theological position is to establish what it is refuting. Cone is writing against the assumption that one can conceive a universal theology—one form fits all. Even when the theologian contends that he or she is writing in midair, the reality is that there is a context that is informing and deforming the contours of the Christian faith. Everyone has a context; everyone has a location. There is no immaculate viewing of the content of the faith. While theologians have a history of presuming their version of the faith is

appropriate for all, the problem for Cone with white theology is twofold. On the one hand, white theology has loaded into it the interests and values of the dominant order and tends to canonize the injustices of the present. On the other hand, it is written as if the black/oppressed community does not exist. Preservation of the status quo is an inevitable consequence, even when there is a presumption of prophetic behavior.

Cone's contention is that theology is inherently defined by where one begins. He begins in the black experience. His data are slave ships, segregated schools, lynch mobs, suffering, and humiliation, as well as creative expression of resistance, courageous acts of rebellion, and stealthy subversion of injustice. When those experiences and those of the black faith community are the point of departure, what emerges is a recognition that the biblical tradition reads differently than in white churches. God can no longer be rendered as the tool of the state and the instrument of the religious establishment. God, now, is understood as one with the oppressed of the land, working for their liberation. God becomes good news for the poor and bad news for the rich. "Honkies" are on notice that they are the opposition party to what God is doing in human history.

Cone is richly rooted in the religious experience of the black church. He consistently harkens back to his formation in the AFRICAN METHODIST EPISCOPAL (A. M. E.) CHURCH. It was there that he came to understand the presence of the divine spirit as expressed through music, sermon, and prayer. There he learned that there was another Home than the one at hand. And it was there he was introduced to the art of survival in a world where one's dignity was perpetually under assault. There he formed a different sense of his reality than the one forced on him by the white people in Bearden, Arkansas. In later times this meant he would write about the spirituals and how black experiences and the promises of God played on each other. The practice of piety was rich and real for him in the church and continues to be.

But this piety does not feed on itself and simply perpetuates personal resources for coping. While Cone values the private sphere and its spiritual expression, his work falls under the category of PUBLIC THEOLOGY. The Christian faith finds expression in the soul, to be sure, but the political sphere is where its implications come to rest. That there is an "over yonder" (Heaven) is a sure belief and the grounds for "keeping on keeping on." Yet the Hebrew and Christian Scriptures center on events in history and the need for a different world in this one. The Exodus was an economic event; the slave labor on which the economy depended was liberated. The birth of Jesus was a political event; Herod the King was confounded and threatened. James Cone critiques a sheltered piety that leaves the order of society uncontested. He affirms a faith that lives the future in the present and relentlessly undermines oppressive structures.

At the heart of his theology is the contention that the oppressed "get it right" when it comes to the rendering of Scripture into affirmation. They have a privileged access, a lens that reads the story as it was once lived. There is a structural similarity between their existence and that of those on whose behalf God acted in the Bible. Perhaps that clarifies why his first book bore the title *Black Theology and Black Power.*

Further reading: Cone, James. *A Black Theology of Liberation.* Philadelphia: Lippincott, 1970; ———. *The Spirituals and the Blues.* New York: Seabury Press, 1972; ———. *God of the Oppressed.* New York: Seabury Press, 1975; ———. *Martin and Malcolm and America: A Dream or a Nightmare.* Maryknoll, N.Y.: Orbis Books, 1991.

—David O. Woodyard

Congress of Racial Equality (CORE)

Founded in 1942, the Congress of Racial Equality (CORE) was started by students in Chicago who sought to change racial problems using nonviolent methods as taught by Mahatma Gandhi. CORE was one of the first organizations to use nonviolent protest methods such as sit-ins, jail-ins, and picketing. After the Greensboro, North Carolina, student lunch counter protest during 1960, CORE became recognized nationally as a civil rights organization. CORE was an important organization in President Kennedy's Voter Education Project, cosponsored the MARCH ON WASHINGTON in 1963, and in 1964 helped to organize FREEDOM SUMMER. As financial problems beset CORE in the late 1960s, leadership changed and CORE began to embrace the Black Power movement in hopes of cultivating more support in the African-American community.

The founding members of CORE belonged to a Christian pacifist organization at the University of Chicago called the Fellowship of Reconciliation (FOR). They were concerned with racial problems and started the Chicago Committee of Racial Equality (the name of the organization would drop "Chicago" and replace "Committee" with "Congress"). At its inception CORE was largely dominated by white, Midwestern, middle-class college students—the organization was dedicated to interracialism.

In 1942, CORE protested against "segregation in public accommodations" employing the nonviolent tactic of sit-ins. Through the use of nonviolent protest, CORE was successful in integrating northern public buildings throughout the 1940s. To build on their northern successes, in 1947 CORE gained national attention when they decided to test the Supreme Court ruling that stated "segregation in interstate travel was unconstitutional." The "Journey of Reconciliation" resulted in four of the eight riders being arrested in North Carolina, while three others were sent to work on a chain gang. These events placed CORE at the forefront of a growing movement that employed nonviolent protest methods. Although CORE became less active in the early 1950s, the Supreme Court ruling of *Brown v. Board of Education* (1954) spurred new activism. CORE's early successes also convinced members that to have an impact nationwide, there should be a leader of the organization—James Farmer became the first national director in 1953.

The spark for civil rights that *Brown v. Board of Education* set off was further heightened with the Montgomery BUS BOYCOTTS (1956). The philosophy of CORE and its dedication to nonviolent protest became the blueprint for the bus boycotts. As the South became the hotbed for the CIVIL RIGHTS MOVEMENT, CORE began to shift its focus from the North to the racial problems of the South. As the geographical focus changed from North to South, the membership of CORE changed as well. Once dominated by white, middle-class college students, an increasing number of African Americans joined the effort.

As more people began to join the Civil Rights movement and protest using methods pioneered by CORE, CORE became an important component of the movement. CORE partnered with the black churches and ministers to mobilize citizens in the South, though CORE was considered an "outside" organization and therefore met with some skepticism by southern African Americans. However, CORE overcame its "outside" status by cultivating relationships with one significant institution in the African-American community—black churches.

CORE was an integral part in the organization of Freedom Summer in 1964, during which three CORE activists were killed: James Chaney, Andrew Goodman, and Michael Shwerner. Their deaths helped build national attention and sympathy for the CIVIL RIGHTS MOVEMENT.

As the Civil Rights movement began to change with the murder of MARTIN LUTHER KING JR. in 1968, so did CORE. Members were skeptical about the nonviolent methods that were used and also questioned Farmer's leadership abilities. Farmer left the position in 1966 after financial troubles and decreasing membership beset the organization. Floyd McKissick replaced Farmer and represented African Americans who embraced black power. McKissick was unable to solve the financial difficulties, and in 1968 Roy Innis took the position of national director, which he maintains.

Further reading: Congress of Racial Equality. Available on-line. URL: www.core-online.org/history/history.htm/. Accessed 2001; Meier, August, and Elliot Rudwick. *CORE: A Study in the Civil Rights Movement: 1942–1968.* New York: Oxford University Press, 1973; Morris, Aldon D. *The Origins of the Civil Rights Movement.* New York: Free Press, 1984.

—Caroline M. Nordlund

conscientious objection

Conscientious objection refers to exemptions from complying with certain legal demands or duties where compliance would violate an individual's religious or religionlike values and beliefs. While most closely identified with litigation over objections to bearing arms in times of war (as repeatedly addressed by the Supreme Court), the concept also applies in the medical setting where caregivers may be excused from the professional duty to render nonemergency health care when carrying out the procedure would violate the conscience of the caregiver. This provision most commonly applies to ABORTION, sterilization, EUTHANASIA, or practices related to the termination or withdrawal of life support.

At the very heart of First Amendment efforts to protect religious freedom lies the belief that there are limits to the authority of the state. As noted by Justice Charles Hughes, although all citizens owe an exacting duty to the state, "in the forum of conscience, duty to a moral power higher than the state has always been maintained" (UNITED STATES V. MACINTOSH cited with approval UNITED STATES V. SEEGER). In the Macintosh case, Justice Harlan Stone argued: "So deep in its significance and vital, indeed, is it to the integrity of man's moral and spiritual nature that nothing short of the self preservation of the state should warrant its violation."

Nowhere is this conflict more pronounced than when the state is confronted by a conscientious objector to war. This issue first arose at the very founding of the American nation, prompting the Continental Congress in 1775 to pass a resolution respecting the religious pacifist and recommending that in lieu of armed service, the objector should contribute to the war effort through nonmilitary means. And while omitted from the text of the Constitution (though JAMES MADISON proposed including a religious exemption to bearing arms as a part of the BILL OF RIGHTS), a number of states adopted a right of conscientious objection to war in their state constitutions.

As litigated before the Supreme Court, the issue has repeatedly arisen as a matter of statutory interpretation. It has evolved through a series of cases primarily involving conscious objector exemptions to the selective service and draft laws (*Arver v. United States* 1918; *Gillette v. United States* 1971) and immigration and naturalization laws requiring an oath to bear arms in defense of the country (UNITED STATES V. SCHWIMMER; GIROUARD V. UNITED STATES).

Exempting an individual from military service (or any other duty) on its face appears discriminatory; it confers a benefit on one individual because of religious conscience that is not available to others. To avoid this perception, the Supreme Court has focused on three aspects of conscientious objection: its constitutional grounding, the categorization of conscience, and the location of conscience.

First, the Court avoids finding a constitutional grounding that would identify conscience with a group or status (such as a particular religion). While often litigated as a Free Exercise right, conscientious objection has no constitutional grounding. "The conscientious objector is relieved from the obligation . . . in obedience to no constitutional provision, express or implied; but because, and only because, it has accorded with the policy of [the legislature] thus to relieve him." While the state has the power to exact a duty from all citizens regardless of any religious or conscientious objection to its performance, the legislature is allowed to accommodate conscientious or religious objection.

As originally enacted, most conscientious objector statutes required that the objector be a clergy person, theological student, or member of a religion with well-established objections to bearing arms. The exemption was not to apply to "essentially political, sociological, or philosophical views or a merely personal moral code." To avoid discriminating between "religion" and "irreligion," the Supreme Court progressively reinterpreted conscientious objection to include any person whose objection was based on moral or ethical beliefs that were equivalent to traditional religion. (The Court did not extend this protection to "selective" objection to particular wars, as opposed to a general pacifism: *Gillette.*)

Finally, in contrast to the traditional suspicion expressed in REYNOLDS V. UNITED STATES (1879) that relying on individual conscience risks anarchy, in order to avoid limiting conscience to a single religious concept, the Supreme Court acknowledges that conscience attaches according to the sincerely held beliefs of the individual.

See also COX V. NEW HAMPSHIRE; JEHOVAH'S WITNESSES; LOVELL V. GRIFFIN; MENNONITE TRADITION; PACIFISM.

Further reading: Miller, Robert T., and Ronald B. Flowers. *Toward Benevolent Neutrality: Church, State, and the Supreme Court.* 5th ed. Waco, Tex.: Baylor University Press, 1996.

—David E. Guinn

conservatism

Conservatism, once at the periphery of American politics, now occupies a central and strategic position in the seat of political power. The election of RONALD REAGAN in 1980, followed by the congressional realignment of 1994 and the narrow victory of GEORGE W. BUSH in 2000, provides evidence of the continuing power of the conservative portion of the American electorate. Despite these successes, critics charge that conservatism is not well represented in Hollywood, the mass media, or university faculty.

Conservatives have been reluctant to define what they mean by the term, but conservatism is an ideology that defends the political, economic, religious, and social status quo from the forces of abrupt change. Conservatives believe that established customs, laws, and traditions provide continuity and stability to the guidance of society. It is a conservative's responsibility to keep cultural and moral traditions intact.

The resurgence of American conservatism began after World War II, when the acceptance of a large national government was an axiom of politics following the collapse of the national economy. The popular New Deal of President FRANKLIN DELANO ROOSEVELT was in its heyday, and the successful national mobilization during the war effort seemed to confirm the necessity of an expanded central government. Lionel Trilling pronounced the "last rites" of conservatism in 1950 when he said, "LIBERALISM is not only the dominant but even the sole intellectual tradition" in American politics. An entire generation seemed to accept the idea that government should set the economic agenda and care for the welfare and security needs of society.

The glittering optimism of a bountiful liberal future floundered in the sweeping cultural changes that it ushered into American society. Conservatives charge that everything associated with what they call the contemporary cultural malaise emerged during the era of liberal hegemony in the 1960s and 1970s: divorce rates went up, the urban underclass was marginalized, pop therapies mushroomed, school desegregation and busing alienated middle-class voters, the academy floundered, and talk of identity and victim politics emerged. Conservatives also argue that problems arose in the 1970s thanks to bilingualism, which led to the nonassimilation of immigrants; FEMINISM, which liberated men from sexual responsibility; as well as the gay rights and "political correctness" movements. The administration of President JAMES EARL CARTER was offered as a metaphor for a nation enduring a collapse of confidence in its institutions and rising cynicism about its politics. The worsening economic condition, and the national traumas of Watergate and Vietnam, eroded Americans' confidence in a strong national government.

The repudiation of liberal expectations began with the election of Ronald Reagan in 1980. Conservatives saw this election as a giant step in the long swing of ideological change that started with the 1964 presidential campaign of Barry Goldwater. The Reagan administration was, in the words of one observer, more ideological than partisan. When it came to policy, liberal Republicans were as much an anathema to the Reaganites as liberal Democrats. Reagan envisioned a smaller government as the key to a greater America, and early in his presidency he dealt skillfully with Congress to bring about tax cuts and reduced business regulation.

Reagan was not an original thinker who added to the body of conservative thought, but his popularity and optimism allowed the public to see conservatism in a new light. Virtually all conservatives, in the Reagan administration and since, have held to two core beliefs: that flawed human nature is an unchanging mixture of both good and evil, and that an objective moral order exists independent of humanity.

Conservatives trust that the crisis they see in America is primarily moral and spiritual. The West has abandoned its belief in absolute and eternal truths, placing its faith instead in relativism, rationalism, and human perfectibility. Eric Voegelin, Leo Strauss, Richard M. Weaver, and Russell Kirk were foundational scholars who explored Western history for the sources of its decadence. They wanted a return to the "Great Tradition," the moral foundations that made Western civilization unique, and they saw such a rebirth as the only way to escape the madness and deadly relativism of the 20th century. Most of these thinkers turned to Christianity as the necessary foundation for an orderly society.

Conservatives believe that civic revitalization must come from local communities, whose strengths rest on the pillars of family, neighborhood, church, and synagogue. They believe that government has its limitations and that many things in life are more important than politics, among them religion, art, study, family, friends, music, and duty. In the eyes of American conservatives, these intermediary institutions, which stand between citizens and their government, are the womb of culture. Government should leave well enough alone and let these institutions nourish society.

See also RELIGION IN THE 1980 PRESIDENTIAL ELECTION; RELIGION IN THE 1984 PRESIDENTIAL ELECTION; RELIGION IN THE 2000 PRESIDENTIAL ELECTION.

Further reading: Dunn, Charles W., and J. David Woodard. *The Conservative Tradition in America.* Lanham, Md.: Rowman and Littlefield, 1996; Trilling, Lionel. *Liberal Imagination: Essays on Literature and Society.* New York: Viking, 1950.

—J. David Woodard

conservative Christian litigators

Conservative Christian law firms are some of the most active and best-funded interest groups in the nation. Since the 1970s, conservative Christian litigators have maintained a constant presence in both state and federal courts. Throughout the 1980s, they participated primarily in ABORTION rights cases. In response to political changes during the 1990s, however, they successfully shifted the movement's primary concerns in court away from abortion and toward FREE EXERCISE of religion and other First Amendment issues. Their participation in court is an essential component of the Christian conservative movement's overall political strategy. Because they employ sophisticated litigation techniques pioneered decades earlier by liberal interest groups, they have been extraordinarily successful at exerting influence in the legal system.

Conservative Christians became fully engaged in politics during the 1970s, largely in response to the Supreme Court's decision in ROE V. WADE (1974), granting women the right to obtain abortions. Because of trends within the movement, the first instinct of conservative Christian leaders was to focus primarily on lobbying legislatures. But, even during this period, conservative Christians helped solidify their victories in Congress and the states by defending legislation in court. For example, in *Harris v. McRae* (1980), the movement successfully defended the HYDE AMENDMENT in court. This legislation halted federal funding of abortions. In many other cases, the Christian Right supported state efforts to regulate abortion services through consent provisions, parental or spousal notification, doctor limitations, funding provisions, and record-keeping requirements. Although not entirely successful, conservative Christian litigators exerted influence on case outcomes by framing the issues in ways that suited their goal of chipping away at the *Roe* decision. Although abortion rights litigation continued into the 1990s, other trends in conservative Christian litigation emerged. As the abortion issue became less salient in electoral and legislative politics, conservative Christian litigators began to turn their attention to other civil rights issues. These issues include the exercise of religion in public places and schools, abortion protestation, and support for "family values" legislation such as anti-PORNOGRAPHY statutes.

Primarily, conservative Christian law firms employ the "test case strategy" as a means for influencing case outcomes. This strategy requires a firm to sponsor (bear the cost of) litigation from trial court through to its final disposition before an appellate court like the U.S. Supreme Court. However, there are other options for these groups to pursue. These include submitting an amicus curiae, or friend of the court, brief or participating as Counsel on Brief. An amicus curiae brief is submitted to a court by a concerned party not named in the lawsuit to supply the court with reasons for ruling in their favor. An amicus curiae generally demands less group involvement than the test case strategy (though it may cost $10,000 or more). When participating as Counsel on Brief, a firm can contribute to preparation for argument but bears few if any of the costs of litigation. Counsel on Brief participation offers a way for groups to influence the arguments courts hear without having to invest significant resources.

The leading group among 1990s conservative Christian litigators is the AMERICAN CENTER FOR LAW AND JUSTICE (ACLJ). After years of expressing concern over the influence of the AMERICAN CIVIL LIBERTIES UNION in court, the Rev. PAT ROBERTSON began to implement plans for a high-powered Christian litigating firm. This law firm has exerted tremendous influence on the central logic of Christian litigators, seeks long-term influence on court-crafted policy, preferring to employ the test case strategy, and has taken 13 cases to the Supreme Court. It has a massive and stable budget and is the only conservative Christian firm with its own endowment.

But the ACLJ is not the only conservative Christian litigating firm. Various others were founded during the late 1980s and 1990s. These include the Becket Fund for Religious Liberty, Northstar Foundation, AMERICAN FAMILY ASSOCIATION–Center for Law and Policy (AFA-CLP), Liberty Counsel, CHRISTIAN LEGAL SOCIETY, and the Alliance Defense Fund. Many of these groups litigate for the express purpose of exerting long-term influence on the policy decisions of courts. But they also identify other kinds of goals. Some, like the AFA-CLP litigate almost entirely on behalf of grassroots supporters, providing free legal counsel for those who feel their religious rights have been violated. Others, like the Liberty Counsel, see education (of both public officials and their own members) as an important goal. Still others, like the Christian Legal Society, identify building networks among Christian attorneys and providing legal representation to churches and religious charities as their central goal.

The primary vehicle for carrying the conservative Christian goals into the courts has been the free expression argument. Firms like the ACLJ and the Liberty Counsel have had tremendous success in making a free speech defense in cases involving ESTABLISHMENT CLAUSE claims. The central logic of the argument is that the free exercise of religion often involves an expression of faith, and that the Constitution protects religious expression as free speech over concerns of government entanglement with religion. Conservative Christian attorneys have applied this logic in cases dealing with public expressions of faith (*U.S. v. Koklinda* 1989), equal access to public property (*LAMB'S CHAPEL V. CENTER MORICHES SCHOOL DISTRICT* 1992), and abortion protests (*NOW v. Scheidler* 1992).

Despite their particular ideological and moral perspective on society and politics, Conservative Christian litigators use the courts in much the same way that other public interest litigators do—developing a legal logic, using the test case strategy as a means for influencing policy, and respecting the preferences of courts for slow and incremental policy changes. In short, Conservative Christian litigators behave in very much the way we should expect them to behave, given the legal adversarial context of courts and the political context of interest-group politics.

See also HERITAGE FOUNDATION; PEOPLE FOR THE AMERICAN WAY; RUTHERFORD INSTITUTE.

Further reading: Craig, Barbara H., and David M. O'Brien. *Abortion and American Politics.* Chatham, N.J.: Chatham House, 1993; Epstein, Lee, and Joseph Kobylka. *The Supreme Court and Legal Change: Abortion and the Death Penalty.* Chapel Hill: University of North Carolina Press, 1992; Hacker, Hans J. "Defending the Faithful." In *The Interest Group Connection.* Edited by Paul S. Herrnson, Ronald G. Shaiko, and Clyde Wilcox. Chatham, N.J.: Chatham House, 2002.

—Hans J. Hacker

Conservative Judaism

Conservative Judaism was founded in New York City in 1887 with the establishment of the Jewish Theological Seminary (JTS), the movement's rabbinical school. It was the first truly American brand of Judaism and can be properly understood as a response to the virtually outright rejection of Jewish law (Halakah) by the Reform movement, as embodied in the adoption of the Pittsburgh Platform. The daunting task of striking a balance between the secularism of REFORM JUDAISM and the unbending emphasis placed on tradition within ORTHODOX JUDAISM has defined the Conservative mission. Today, the Conservative movement has well over 1 million members in the United States and is the largest of the major Jewish denominations.

In 1902, Rabbi Solomon Schechter moved to New York City from England to head JTS. An eminent and respected scholar, he was a "passionately committed religious Jew." Under Schechter's leadership, JTS blossomed into the preeminent American Jewish educational institution that it is today. Many of the tenets of Conservative Judaism trace back to Schechter's own beliefs. A tribute to his influence, the movement calls its day schools Solomon Schechter schools.

Before inquiring into the foundations of Conservative belief and practice, a caveat: The only thing that is certain when using the label "Conservative" is that an individual associates herself with a synagogue that belongs to the United Synagogue of America, the umbrella organization of the Conservative movement. The movement embraces a wide variety of practices and beliefs, so that while one member or congregation may appear closer to the Orthodox movement, another may lean toward Reform Judaism.

With this established, the foundational tenets of Conservative Judaism are well put by Simon Greenberg, the former vice chancellor of JTS:

> The Conservative movement . . . embrac[es] within itself both poles of the polarities that are ubiquitously inherent in all of human life generally, and in Jewish life in particular; the insistence upon the validity of *Halakha* and the need for taking the needs of modern American Jewish life into consideration; the place of centrality of *Eretz Yisrael* [the land of Israel] in Jewish life and thought, and the indispensable role of the Diaspora [Jews living outside of Israel]; the role of ritual in Jewish religion and the dominant place of the moral and ethical law; the ceaseless striving for unity in Jewish life and the acceptance of the diversity through which it expresses itself.

With respect to religious practices, Conservative Judaism does fall somewhere between Reform and Orthodox Judaism. Notwithstanding the wide spectrum of observance within the movement, members and synagogues have generally taken the middle road, attempting to balance tradition with modernity. For instance, women are permitted and encouraged to participate in virtually every religious undertaking alongside men, including training and ordination as cantors and rabbis. In general, the movement has tended to interpret Jewish law with increasing flexibility, e.g., permitting driving to synagogue on the Sabbath to facilitate attendance. Discussing Conservative religious services, Marshall Sklare has observed that they "must be 'Jewish' enough so that there will be continuity with previous experience, but at the same time they must take the new norms into account." As Conservative Jews enter the 21st century, the movement will continue to grapple with the challenges of balancing modernity and tradition.

Further reading: Nadell, Pamella S. *Conservative Judaism in America: A Biographical Dictionary and Sourcebook.* New York: Greenwood Press, 1988; Sklare, Marshall. *An American Religious Movement: Conservative Judaism.* Lanham, Md.: University Press, 1985; Telushkin, Joseph. *Jewish Literacy: The Most Important Things to Know about the Jewish Religion, Its People, and Its History.* New York: William Morrow, 1991.

—Matthew L. Eanet

consistent ethic of life

In the United States, the expression "consistent ethic of life" is most associated with JOSEPH CARDINAL BERNARDIN, chair of the NATIONAL CONFERENCE OF CATHOLIC BISHOPS' Committee on Pro-Life Activities, from 1983 to 1989. Bernardin introduced the concept to the general public in 1983, during the Fordham University Gannon Lecture, and expounded on the theme in subsequent forums until his death in 1996. The consistent life ethic was endorsed by the U.S. Catholic Bishops in their 1985 Pro-Life Pastoral Plan, and was implicitly adopted by Pope JOHN PAUL II in his 1995 encyclical, *The Gospel of Life.* Also known as the "seamless garment" approach, this idea is embraced by diverse religious and secular groups including Sojourners, EVANGELICALS FOR SOCIAL ACTION, Feminists for Life, and other members of the Seamless Garment Network.

Advocates believe humans are inherently sacred or dignified beings, as well as social creatures who share responsibility for each other. Human life is considered worthy of protection from conception until natural death. Advocates share concern for a spectrum of threats to human life and well-being, including poverty, inadequate HEALTH CARE and education, ABORTION, war and defense spending, the death penalty, EUTHANASIA, domestic violence, and more. Many advocates include threats to supporting ecosystems among their interests. The approach scrutinizes solutions to social problems that employ violence, pit one constituency against another, or focus so narrowly on one threat to life that other threats are ignored.

Two concerns prompted Bernardin's formulation of the consistent life ethic. First was his concern for human well-being. Although many threats to humanity are ancient, new forces in our contemporary context exacerbate their impact. These include powerful technology, an expanding and skewed sense of privacy, and the right to redress grievances, perception of diminishing resources, cultural fixation on efficiency and immediate gratification, loss of vision and values that transcend time and individual choice—particularly as these influence our approach to pain and sacrifice. Plagued by individualism, shortsightedness, and an assumption that we can devise a "quick fix" to any problem, we often ignore our brothers and sisters in need, or try to make problems disappear by simplistic and destructive means.

Second, Bernardin was concerned for the ROMAN CATHOLIC CHURCH's credibility. He thought consistent witness to sanctity of life, in word and deed, would strengthen the church's persuasiveness as a prophetic teacher and maximize its potential in providing services to needy populations.

While Bernardin realized many people were not in the habit of thinking systemically about life issues, he thought any reasonable person could find this approach compelling. He noted that the premise of human sacredness is founded on the biblical theme of humanity created in God's image, but is also supported through the Western political tradition that certain inalienable rights are due to all humans, precisely because they are human. Promoting quality of life (beyond protection against directly taking life) is rooted in the biblical message that the poor, the sick, widows, and orphans are special in God's eyes and that communities have a grave responsibility to care for them. Yet, concern for quality of life is reinforced by that strand of political philosophy that says the state has a proactive purpose in promoting life, liberty, and the pursuit of happiness; it does not exist merely to restrain competing groups from harming each other. Linking concern for direct attacks on human life and threats to quality of life is also a matter of practical realism, for the latter (RACISM, materialism, poverty, inadequate health care) often contribute to the former (war, abortion, euthanasia, death by disease and malnutrition).

Bernardin encountered criticism from the political Right and Left. Some said linking many issues eroded attention to single issues of special importance. Others said Bernardin expected people to find energy to devote to too many causes. In response, Bernardin said the church as a whole must give comprehensive witness to human dignity, and each member must do what is possible, given his or her resources and unique vocation, to contribute to this witness. Most important, "it is very necessary for preserving a systemic vision that individuals and groups who seek to witness to life at one point of the spectrum of life not be seen as insensitive or even opposed to other moral claims on the overall spectrum of life. . . . No one is called to do everything, but each of us can do something."

See also CATHOLIC BISHOPS IN AMERICAN POLITICS; CATHOLIC BISHOPS' 1975 PASTORAL LETTER ON ABORTION; CATHOLIC BISHOPS' 1986 PASTORAL LETTER ON THE ECONOMY; CATHOLIC BISHOPS' 1983 PASTORAL LETTER ON WAR AND PEACE; HUNGER AND HUMANITARIAN AID; PACIFISM; UNITED STATES CATHOLIC CONFERENCE.

Further reading: Feuchtmann, Thomas, ed. *Consistent Ethic of Life.* Kansas City, Mo.: Sheed and Ward, 1988; Langan, John, ed. *A Moral Vision for America.* Washington, D.C.: Georgetown University Press, 1998.

—Florence Caffrey Bourg

Constitution Party (formerly U.S. Taxpayers Party)

In 1992, a collection of like-minded state parties merged to form the U.S. Taxpayers Party. The fundamental goal was to shrink the federal government back to its original size and scope, virtually eliminating federal taxes in the process. Howard Philips, former director of the U.S. Office of Economic Opportunity under RICHARD NIXON, has run as the party's presidential candidate in all three presidential elections since 1992 (receiving 12,623 votes that year). By 1996, the party reached its apex of support at 170,869 votes (less than 0.2 percent), dropping back below 0.1 percent (98,004 votes) in the 2000 election. By 2000, however, the party was on the ballot in 42 states, with write-in status in another six. At their national convention in St. Louis, Missouri, in September 1999, the delegates of the U.S. Taxpayers Party officially changed their name to the Constitution Party. The party's national chairman, Jim Clymer, explained, "Anyone who knows much about us at all knows that we are anything but a one-issue party." Indeed they are not, having a wide-ranging platform predicated on a blend of limited government and conservative Christianity. Since they have no elected officials, their platform is more a statement of what they would accomplish, rather than what they do or have done.

For the party, the Constitution is the embodiment of the principles of life, liberty, and the respect for property, but not the source of them. The Constitution Party interprets the rights enjoyed by Americans as rooted in the higher law of the Creator, who sent his only son, Jesus Christ, to redeem the world. A sense of Christian ethics is to inform all actions of elected leaders and their appointed representatives in the executive and legislative branches.

The distinction between a republic and a democracy is extremely important for members of the Constitution Party. Laws are to be made by elected representatives only. No other body is empowered to create regulations, and the party would eliminate virtually all regulatory agencies, including the Department of Education and the Environmental Protection Agency. Referenda and other methods of creating legislation outside of a legislature are deemed unconstitutional, and constitutional conventions are opposed because they cannot be limited to a single issue and thus hold the potential to erode existing rights.

Party members demand a strict interpretation of the U.S. Constitution. Informed by THOMAS JEFFERSON's principle that the government that governs best governs least, the federal government is to be limited only to powers explicitly listed in the text of the constitution, and even those powers are to be used as little as possible. Accountability of the elected to their constituents is strongest when closest to home, and when the polity deems legislation necessary, it should be created at the state level whenever possible. This includes passing and enforcing criminal laws.

Taxes are a central issue to the group that originally called itself the "U.S. Taxpayers Party." The party's platform calls for the elimination of the Internal Revenue Service and a repeal of the Sixteenth Amendment, allowing for a federal income tax. To the degree that tariffs on imports fail to cover the expenses of federal expenditures, the difference would be raised on what is called a "state-rate" tax, in which each state is assessed in proportion to its share of the total U.S. population. States themselves would determine how their own taxes are assessed, allowing for the greatest level of accountability possible to the taxpayers. The Social Security system would remain in place, although individuals would have the right either to opt out entirely or to place their funds in private investment portfolios. Federal programs redistributing wealth are not only considered unconstitutional but also immoral, running against the biblical injunction against theft. Instead, they would be replaced by individual Christian charities, sustained by the liberated funds citizens would no longer be paying in taxes.

Consistent with individual liberty at home, the nation should protect its liberty abroad by removing itself from all alliances and treaties that compromise the country's independence, such as the United Nations, as well as GATT, NAFTA, the World Bank, and the International Monetary Fund.

The American statesman John C. Calhoun noted that when a group believes they will be part of a permanent minority, "the only resort left [to] them would be a strict construction of the Constitution." The Constitution Party appears to be a living example of this.

Further reading: Calhoun, John C. *A Disquisition on Government and Selections from the Discourse.* C. Gordon Post, ed. Indianapolis: Hackett, 1995; Constitution Party on the Web: URL: http://www.constitutionparty.com/.

—Brian J. Glenn

Contract with the American Family

The Contract with the American Family was a set of 10 social policy suggestions proposed by the CHRISTIAN COALITION in May 1995. Following on the heels of the House Republican–instigated Contract with America, the coalition believed it was time to shift Congress's policy focus from economic and regulatory issues to social ones. The Contract with the American Family focused on the following 10 areas:

1. Restoring Religious Equality: Perhaps the most important of the 10, this proposed constitutional amendment would protect voluntary religious expression in public places. While not intended to reinstate mandatory PRAYER IN PUBLIC SCHOOLs or Bible reading, it sought to ensure the rights of voluntary and community-led prayers at public events.
2. Return Education Control to the Local Level: The intent of this proposal was to return total control and funding of education to local communities and school boards, abolishing the federal Department of Education.
3. Promoting School Choice: Including VOUCHERS, tax credits, and school choice programs, this proposal sought stronger federal support for a wide range of alternative school selection and funding initiatives.
4. Protecting Parental Rights: Seeking to enact a parental rights act, this proposal was also aimed at blocking the United Nations Convention on the Rights of the Child. The proposed legislation would protect parents' right to make most decisions for their children.
5. Family-Friendly Tax Relief: This proposal encouraged significant reforms in the federal income tax structure for families. It included a parental tax credit, elimination of the "marriage penalty," and reform of the Internal Revenue Service's regulations to allow homemakers to contribute equally with their working husbands.
6. Restoring Respect for Human Life: While affirming the coalition's desire to see the end of all ABORTION, this proposal focused primarily on three less comprehensive goals. First, they emphasized outlawing all late-term abor-

tions, especially partial-birth. Second, they called for the repealing of laws requiring states to pay for abortions in the cases of rape and incest. Third, they stressed ending federal funding to organizations, domestic and international, that perform or promote abortion.
7. Encouraging Support of Private Charities: As a first step in transforming the welfare system into a private and faith-based arrangement, this proposal sought to enhance private giving through tax relief and incentives.
8. Restricting PORNOGRAPHY: Intended to make existing laws tougher, this proposal specifically sought to protect children from viewing pornography, both on the Internet and through inadequately scrambled cable signals.
9. Privatizing the Arts: This proposal sought the privatization of the National Endowment for the Arts, National Endowment for the Humanities, and the Corporation for Public Broadcasting. Believing that the federal government should not be the arbiter of "good" or "bad" art, the Christian Coalition proposed the end of public funding for all art.
10. Crime Victim Restitution: As part of a larger program intended to reduce recidivism in America's prisons, this proposal sought legislation that would require convicted criminals to make restitution to their victims. It would also require states that receive federal money for prisons to ensure that all inmates were part of a work or educational program.

The contract, introduced in a press conference attended by several high-profile Republican leaders, was strongly supported by conservatives in the House of Representatives. House Speaker Newt Gingrich (R-Ga.) pledged that the House would vote on the proposals outlined by the contract. Seen by many as payback for the Christian Coalition's strong support of the earlier Contract with America, coalition leader RALPH REED even made mention of the coalition's million-dollar campaign to pass the earlier contract in his remarks introducing the Contract with the American Family.

While enjoying considerable support among NEW EVANGELICALS IN CONGRESS and the electorate, reaction to the Contract with the American Family was strongly mixed. Many leaders of less conservative religious denominations and spokespersons of minority groups roundly criticized the contract for being a contract with the white middle-class Christian American family, not a broad gesture in the interests of all.

These criticisms, combined with waning support in a Congress concerned more with economic- and regulatory-oriented legislation, were a prelude to the failure of the contract. The 104th Congress passed none of the proposed legislation. Although several of the propositions have subsequently been passed, instituting the $500-per-child tax credit and removal of the marriage penalty, none were passed under the aegis of religious conservative pressure.

See also CHRISTIAN RIGHT AND THE REPUBLICAN PARTY; RELIGION IN CONGRESS.

—Kimberly Conger

Coughlin, Father Charles (1891–1979) *Catholic priest*

Born on October 25, 1891, in Hamilton, Ontario, Canada, Coughlin was the first religious figure to take his sermons and ideas to the airwaves. He became outspoken about President FRANKLIN DELANO ROOSEVELT and his New Deal in the 1930s through his weekly radio sermons and his newspaper, *Social Justice*, until his controversial topics forced him off the air and ceased the printing of his journal. Some estimates indicate the sermons drew an audience of nearly 40 million people during Coughlin's height of popularity, in the 1930s.

Coughlin graduated from St. Michael's College in 1911. He desired to become a politician, but he knew his Roman Catholic parents wanted him to become a priest, so he made the decision to combine these two ambitions. He entered St. Basil's Seminary and was ordained on June 29, 1916. He was incardinated into the Detroit diocese on February 26, 1923, after a change in the Basilian Order allowed him to retain his priestly duties, but as a secular clergyman.

Coughlin built "The Shrine of the Little Flower" church in nearby Royal Oak, Michigan, on the request of Bishop Michael Gallagher, but soon realized that local anti-Catholic sentiment and a lack of funds threatened the church. To raise money, he decided to take to the airwaves.

Coughlin's first Sunday radio sermon aired on October 17, 1926, on WJR in Detroit. By early 1927, he had hired clerks to deal with the massive amounts of mail coming in every week. He formed the Radio League of the Little Flower to continue raising funds for the church. It was not until the stock market crash in October 1929 that Coughlin launched nationally. In 1930, he signed a contract to broadcast across 16 stations nationwide. Though he denounced communism on air for the first time in 1930, it was not until October 1931 that his sermons became overtly political, as Coughlin attacked President Herbert Hoover for the growing depression.

In 1932, Coughlin met Franklin Roosevelt and supported his run for the presidency. He soon became displeased with Roosevelt's programs, though, feeling they would not end the Great Depression. Publicly, Coughlin still maintained the phrase he had coined on air, "Roosevelt or Ruin," but he was feeling betrayed by the president's proposals.

On December 11, 1934, Coughlin founded the National Union for Social Justice (NUSJ) to uphold the rights of private ownership and protect against greed. The organization was based on 23 principles of SOCIAL JUSTICE, all supporting the belief that increased government regulation would remedy the effects of the depression. The main reason for the split between Coughlin and Roosevelt, therefore, was Roosevelt's inability to end the depression. However, a disagreement in the wording of the Wagner Act and Coughlin's belief that the United States was supporting communism also stoked the growing tension. Coughlin's alliance with Louisiana senator Huey Long also prompted attacks from the Roosevelt administration on the priest. By November 1935, two months after Long's assassination, Coughlin was using the phrase "Roosevelt and Ruin."

Father Charles Coughlin *(Library of Congress)*

Father Coughlin branched out to print media on March 13, 1936, when he launched the weekly journal *Social Justice*. In June 1936, Coughlin, William Lemke, Francis Townsend, and the Rev. Gerald L. K. Smith formed the Union Party, as a force against Roosevelt's New Deal policies. Lemke became the party's presidential nominee, but the party garnered fewer than 1 million votes in the November election.

After the 1936 election, the Vatican ordered Coughlin to stop leading political movements. Coughlin agreed but believed he could still voice his opinion and soon formed the Christian Front. The organization, dedicated to ending communism, disallowed Jews from membership. After 1938, Coughlin's radio sermons and newspaper articles grew increasingly controversial and marginal—they were exceedingly anti-Semitic, and he demanded U.S. neutrality in the intensifying war overseas.

In 1939, the National Association of Broadcasters limited the amount of radio time allotted for controversial programs. The September 23, 1940, issue of *Social Justice* announced that Father Coughlin was retiring from the airwaves temporarily, but he never returned to the air. On May 4, 1942, after an FBI hearing, *Social Justice* lost its second-class mailing privilege on the grounds of printing seditious material under the Espionage Act. Coughlin soon announced that he was obeying the church and ceasing his political activities, including publication of his newspaper.

Coughlin returned to the Little Flower, where he served as priest until 1966; he died in a Detroit suburb in 1979.

See also MARXISM/COMMUNISM; ROMAN CATHOLIC CHURCH.

Further reading: Bennett, David H. *Demagogues in the Depression: American Radicals, and the Union Party*

1932–1936. New Brunswick, N.J.: Rutgers University Press, 1969; Brinkley, Alan. *Voice of Protest: Huey Long, Father Coughlin, and the Great Depression.* New York: Knopf, 1982; Marcus, Sheldon. *Father Coughlin: The Tumultuous Life of the Priest of the Little Flower.* Boston: Little, Brown, 1973; Tull, Charles J. *Father Coughlin and the New Deal.* Syracuse, N.Y.: Syracuse University Press, 1965.

—Alison L. Davis

Council of Fifty

On March 11, 1844, JOSEPH SMITH, the Mormon prophet, admitted several men to a special council that came to be known as the Council of Fifty. Smith taught that this council constituted the nucleus of the Kingdom of God on Earth. Some scholars argue that the Council of Fifty was the driving agent of Mormon history between 1844 and the late 1800s. However, more recent research has revealed that the impact of the council was less substantial, though still significant.

Smith organized the Council of Fifty to fulfill the biblical prophecy in Daniel 2:44: "And in the days of these kings shall the God of heaven set up a kingdom, which shall never be destroyed . . . it shall break in pieces and consume all these kingdoms, and it shall stand forever." The council, composed of many LATTER-DAY SAINTS (LDS) leaders (but also three individuals who were not LDS), was intended to govern the world during Jesus Christ's millennial reign. But its authority diminished over time until the ecclesiastical hierarchy of the LDS Church subsumed its duties.

While the Council of Fifty never seemed to operate to the extent that Smith envisioned, it still served some important functions. The first significant duty was to organize and promote Joseph Smith's 1844 presidential candidacy. Smith's quixotic campaign was cut short, however, when he was killed in 1844 in Carthage, Illinois.

Smith's other major assignment for the council was to oversee the Saints' exodus from Illinois. As tensions with non-LDS citizens grew, three sites were under consideration: Texas, Oregon, and Utah. A treaty between the Mormons and the government of Texas had been drafted and awaited approval. But in the midst of these negotiations, Smith was killed. Under the leadership of BRIGHAM YOUNG, the council chose the Salt Lake Valley as the growing church's gathering place. Lyman Wight was excommunicated for his attempts to move the Saints to Texas. Young organized the migrating Saints groups to be supervised by captains, a majority of whom were members of the Council of Fifty.

Shortly after the first Mormons reached the Salt Lake Valley in 1847, Young and several others returned eastward to assist the remaining Saints migrating to Utah. He left civil governance to a council of church leaders, many of whom were members of the Council of Fifty. Thus began the theocratic rein of the LDS Church in the Utah territory.

When Young returned to Utah in December 1848, the Council of Fifty took over as the provisional government of the Saints. Minutes from the council's meetings show that it exercised broad legislative power. They defined the boundaries of the territory, oversaw the procurement of public arms, organized a militia, contracted for public works projects, established standards of weights and measures, planned city development, and created laws defining crimes and punishments.

The Council of Fifty pushed statehood for Utah. They drafted a constitution and arranged for elections to be held in March 1849. The ballot listed a slate of officers, which voters could either approve or disapprove. A democratic political convention assembled the list of proposed officers, but a slate drafted by the Council of Fifty (which differed from the slate of the convention) actually appeared on the ballot and prevailed. Some of the offices prescribed in their constitution were not filled by the council's slate, and others who were not mentioned in the constitution were listed. All officials in this government were members of the Council of Fifty, which took power in July 1849 and lasted until September 1850, when the U.S. Congress passed a law organizing the territory of Utah.

Under the reign of the council, there had been no separation of church and state; after the election, the council began to cede its governmental authority to the territorial government. As the council's civil power diminished, the leading bodies of the LDS Church began to take control of the political activities of the church. The council continued to meet regularly until October 1851, after which they met sporadically through the late 19th century. In its later years, the council was more of a discussion forum than a decision-making body. The last meeting of the council was held in 1884.

Though the council formally governed in the Utah territory for only a short time, its legacy is substantial. They planned the physical and legal infrastructure of the eventual state of Utah. Additionally, its members held prominent positions in the government (though over time, the practice shifted to appointing political figures to the council, not the reverse). Today, LDS political activities continue to be guided by the church's first presidency. However, faithful Latter-Day Saints familiar with the millennial prophecies of their faith anticipate the eventual revitalization of the Council of Fifty with the establishment of the political Kingdom of God on Earth.

See also MORMON EXTERMINATION ORDER; POLYGAMY; *REYNOLDS V. UNITED STATES.*

Further reading: Andrus, Hyrum L. *Joseph Smith and World Government.* Salt Lake City: Deseret Book, 1958; Arrington, Leonard J. *Brigham Young: American Moses.* New York: Knopf, 1985; Hansen, Klaus J. *Quest for Empire: The Political Kingdom of God and the Council of Fifty in Mormon History.* East Lansing: Michigan State University Press, 1967; Quinn, D. Michael. "The Council of Fifty and Its Members, 1844–1945." *Brigham Young University Studies* 20 (winter 1980): 163–197.

—Damon M. Cann

covenant theology

Covenant theology, also called federal theology, is a system of interpretation that explains humankind's relationship with God according to a series of covenants. Although the notion of covenant is ancient—the Old Testament records God's covenant with Israel—the development of an overall covenant theology originated with the Protestant Reformation. At the time of the Reformation, covenant (Latin, *foedus,* from which the word *federal* is derived) was understood to denote a compact between two individuals in which they obligated themselves to each other, under an oath, to accomplish some purpose. Reformation figures instrumental in the development of covenant theology include Ulrich Zwingli (1484–1513), John Calvin (1509–64), and Heinrich Bullinger (1505–75). Reformed covenant theology emphasized that, by God's grace, humankind is offered salvation and receives it through faith, entering into an assured covenantal relationship with God. According to Reformed thought, especially that of Bullinger, the covenant was seen as the "divine framework for human life . . . in both religious and civil affairs."

Theologians generally specify three covenants: the Covenant of Works, the Covenant of Grace, and the Covenant of Redemption. Within these covenants is the notion that God initially entered into a covenant of works with Adam, promising eternal life for obedience, and after Adam rebelled God resolved the dilemma by entering into a covenant of grace with Adam and the human race. By faith, humans can be redeemed and saved. One of the first, and perhaps most enduring, statements of covenant theology is the *Westminster Confession of Faith* (1647), the foundational document for present-day Presbyterians, Baptists, and Congregationalists.

The covenant approach to theology, and the attendant notions of obligation, mutuality, and individualism influenced English Puritanism. With the settling of the New World, these covenant ideals were exported to America and achieved a large measure of influence, especially through the writings of William Perkins, Richard Sibbes, William Ames, John Preston, and JOHN WINTHROP. While the covenant doctrine offered PURITANS God's graciousness and eternal assurance, Puritan writers also emphasized covenantal obedience and that the "process of adoption was the result of a bargain between God and man in which human will played a significant role."

In America, Puritan Congregationalists used covenant theology to reject the established episcopacy of the Anglican Church. Based on the assumption that believers can minister and govern themselves through vote and participation, Congregationalists formed churches based on covenants between God and themselves. In the Watertown Covenant (1630), for example, Pilgrims established a congregation through a "Covenant with the Lord our God, and before him with one another . . . [to] Worship God; and . . . give ourselves wholly unto the Lord Jesus."

Covenantal ideals significantly influenced civic and political life in early America. The political principles implemented in colonial America were elaborations of Puritan covenant theology that saw all society—including civic and political institutions—as a derivative of the "basic biblical covenant between God and his people." William Ames (1576–1638) wrote that just as a church is formed by believers joining by covenant, so too "the same believing men may join themselves in covenant to make a city or some civil society." Undermining the logic of hierarchical government and royal absolutism, Puritans often used covenantal language when establishing townships in the New World.

One of the first organizing documents in the New World was the Mayflower Compact (1620), wherein the PILGRIMS, having "undertaken for the glory of God . . . a voyage to plant the first colony in the Northern parts of Virginia," formed themselves into a "Civic Body Politick" through a covenant. Similarly, the town of Providence in Rhode Island (1636) and the Fundamental Orders of Connecticut (1639) were formed by covenants.

Ultimately, covenantal ideals provided a model for community, religious or civil, wherein equal individuals come together and through a mutual and morally binding pact (witnessed by God) establish a new polity and governing institutions. Entering into a covenantal relationship does not sacrifice member individuality, and the covenant can be dissolved by mutual consent. Covenant ideals gained influence during the 17th and 18th centuries through the writing of Thomas Hobbes (1588–1679) and JOHN LOCKE (1632–1704), and the derived notions of consent and popular sovereignty are strongly reflected in the U.S. DECLARATION OF INDEPENDENCE and the Constitution.

See also CALVINISM; CIVIL RELIGION.

Further reading: Baker, J. Wayne. "Faces of Federalism: From Bullinger to Jefferson." Publius 30, no. 4 (2000): 25–41; Elazar, Daniel J. *Covenant and Commonwealth.* New Brunswick, N.J.: Transaction, 1996; ———. *Covenant and Constitutionalism.* New Brunswick, N.J.: Transaction, 1998; Enns, Paul. *Moody Handbook of Theology.* Chicago: Moody Press, 1989; Lutz, Donald S. *Colonial Origins of the American Constitution.* Indianapolis: Liberty Fund, 1998.

—Franklyn C. Niles

Cox v. New Hampshire 312 U.S. 569 (1941)

In *Cox v. New Hampshire*, the JEHOVAH'S WITNESSES challenged the New Hampshire statute requiring a permit from local authorities before staging a parade. Willis Cox, a Witness, along with 68 of his coreligionists and 20 apparent sympathizers, marched through the streets of Manchester, New Hampshire, without having obtained a parade permit from local officials. Apparently the participants had no intention of procuring a permit. To obtain a permit, the Witnesses would have had to appear before a licensing board and pay a fee of not more than $50.

The middle of the 19th century witnessed movements by various religious groups seeking the Second Advent of Christ.

The Jehovah's Witnesses arose out of this Adventist movement and are formally known as the WATCHTOWER BIBLE AND TRACT SOCIETY in the United States. Witnesses were disillusioned with mainstream churches and society, which spawned a period of political activism by many in the Adventist denominations, but particularly by the Witnesses.

One of the features that distinguished the Witnesses from other Adventists was their refusal to submit to civil authority. Cases that came before the U.S. Supreme Court debated the extent to which the Witnesses were required by the civil authority to "render unto Caesar." Throughout their history, but more particularly in the late 1930s and early 1940s, when the federal Bill of Rights was being incorporated to cover the states, the Witnesses challenged a variety of government strictures claiming FREE EXERCISE protections, including government mandates against leafleting and for military service.

As a historical sidenote, one of the named defendants is Walter Chaplinsky. He is famous for being the lead appellant in *Chaplinsky v. New Hampshire* (1942), in which the Supreme Court established the "fighting words" exception to the free speech clause of the First Amendment.

While Jehovah's Witnesses often won striking victories in court, in the *Cox* case they did not. They were convicted in the municipal court of Manchester of violating the state statute by "holding a 'parade or procession' upon a public street without a special license." The challenge to the state was multifaceted. The Witnesses claimed that they were, by enforcement of the law, deprived of their rights of freedom of worship, press, speech, and especially freedom of assembly. They also alleged that the laws were vague and indefinite and therefore unenforceable.

The Supreme Court did not agree with Cox and his coreligionists. Chief Justice Hughes, writing for the Court, concluded that the maintenance of a civil society and protecting civil liberties included the maintenance of public order and regulation of traffic: "One would not be justified in ignoring the familiar red traffic light because he thought it his religious duty to disobey the municipal command or sought by that means to direct public attention to an announcement of his opinions." Moreover, Hughes suggested: "The argument as to freedom of worship is . . . beside the point. No interference with religious worship or the practice of religion in any proper sense is shown, but only the exercise of local control over the use of streets for parades and processions."

This restriction of the freedom of assembly was held to be a traditional exercise of local authority. The problem for local officials, as laid out by the Court, was that any regulation was not to unreasonably interfere with that "right of assembly and the opportunities for the communication of thought and the discussion of public questions immemorially associated with resort to public places." Thus, streets, byways, and public areas are dedicated to the use of the people so long as they do not interfere with other citizens. By this case, the adage that "my right to swing my arm stops at the end of your nose" has been guaranteed to citizens in public areas. Further, *Cox* leaned

toward the state in maintaining the integrity of secular, neutral laws, on sands that would shift away from the state by the 1960s.

See also *CANTWELL V. CONNECTICUT; CONSCIENTIOUS OBJECTION; LOVELL V. GRIFFIN; MARTIN V. STRUTHERS; OHIO, AND MURDOCK V. COMMONWEALTH OF PENNSYLVANIA.*

—StanLey M. Morris

Creech, Jimmy (1945–) *activist, former minister*

Jimmy Creech was born in Goldsboro, North Carolina. He holds a Bachelor of Arts in biblical studies from the University of North Carolina–Chapel Hill and a Master of Divinity from the Duke University Divinity School. Creech served as a pastor in the UNITED METHODIST CHURCH between 1970 and 1999, receiving numerous regional and national awards for his contributions to and ministries for SOCIAL JUSTICE.

Jimmy Creech is best known for his commitment to GAY RIGHTS, in particular for performing same-gender unions in opposition to the Methodist Church's official teachings. When Creech was a minister at First United Methodist Church in Omaha, Nebraska, he was removed from the ministry by his denomination for performing a "recommitment ceremony" for two gay men in Chapel Hill, North Carolina, in 1999. Just a year earlier, Creech was acquitted by the Methodists' Nebraska Annual Conference for a same-gender covenant service he had performed in 1997, and following the acquittal Creech took a voluntary leave of absence to write a book, travel, and speak across the country about the struggle to include and affirm gays and lesbians in the United Methodist Church. Following his participation in the 1999 commitment ceremony, a formal complaint was filed against him, and Creech was found guilty of violating the Order and Discipline of the United Methodist Church and stripped of his ministerial credentials.

From early in his ministry, Creech was recognized for his passionate commitment to social justice. In 1987 he was named head pastor at Fairmont United Methodist Church in Raleigh, North Carolina, where his early sermons revolved around his main interest at the time, human rights abuses in Central America. When the issue of adding sexual orientation to Raleigh's nondiscrimination statute was raised, several clergy, including Creech, were moved by testimonies of gays and lesbians who viewed the church as a source of persecution and bigotry. Shortly afterward, local clergy organized a conference on homosexuality and the church. Out of that conference the Raleigh Religious Network for Gay and Lesbian Equality (RRNGLE), an ecumenical group that sought to counter antigay religious rhetoric with a message of God's love for all people, was born. Creech was offered the position of convener, and he took several public stands in support of gay and lesbian rights, including marching in the Gay and Lesbian Pride Parade and personally endorsing a letter supporting gay and lesbian equality that RRNGLE distributed to all area clergy in 1988. These actions prompted a backlash among his congregation members at Fairmont, and many withheld their contributions in protest of Creech's actions. Facing serious internal dissent and virtually empty coffers, Creech consented to the bishop's request to reassign him.

But all the publicity Creech had received for his involvement with gay and lesbian rights made it difficult for him to find a new church home. In 1990, Creech was offered the position of program associate with the North Carolina Council of Churches, where he focused on issues of criminal justice, HEALTH CARE justice, and improving the lives of migrant farm workers (Hartman 1996: 24). During his tenure, the METROPOLITAN COMMUNITY CHURCHES were admitted into membership with the North Carolina Council of Churches. North Carolina was the first state council in the country to admit the MCC, and the move prompted several evangelical pastors to cut off funding to the council.

In 1996, Creech was assigned head pastor of the 2,000-member First United Methodist Church in Omaha, Nebraska. Here he continued to perform same-gender covenant ceremonies, for which he was brought to trial by a 13-clergy member court for disobeying the bishop's ban on such unions. Although he was acquitted, the bishop declined to reappoint him as pastor at First United Methodist. Creech took a voluntary leave of absence but still continued to perform holy unions and be a vocal advocate for gay and lesbian rights. Since his removal from the ministry, Creech has assumed his place among the laity of the United Methodist Church and continues his call to "resist evil, injustice, and oppression in whatever forms they present themselves."

See also GAY AND LESBIAN MARRIAGE.

Further reading: Concerned Methodists. "Case Studies: An Historical Record of Jimmy Creech." URL: http://www.cmpage.org/jcreech.html. Posted 1998; Creech, Jimmy. "Gratitude and Hope: A Letter from Jimmy Creech." December 2, 1999; Epley, Kris. "Creech Convicted, Defrocked." *Grand Island (Nebr.) Independent,* November 18, 1999; Hartman, Keith. *Congregations in Conflict: The Battle Over Homosexuality.* New Brunswick, N.J.: Rutgers University Press, 1996.

—Krista McQueeney

culture war

The "culture wars" is the controversial metaphor to describe the restructuring of religious and cultural conflict in the United States since the 1960s. The culture wars thesis was first advanced by sociologist James Davison Hunter in a book entitled *The CULTURE WARS* (1991). According to Hunter, "the dominant impulse at the present time is toward the polarization of a religiously informed public culture into relatively distinct moral and ideological camps." Building on the work of Robert Wuthnow, Hunter locates the sources of this new cleavage in changes in American society after World War II, most notably, the expansion of access to higher education, the growth of a new professional class of "knowledge workers," the movement of women in large numbers in the workforce, and innovations in communications technology. Hunter argues that these social changes, along with the divisive politics of the CIVIL RIGHTS MOVEMENT, VIETNAM WAR, and sex and gender transformed American culture and institutions by undermining the long-standing biblical theistic normative assumptions that undergirded public life. The collapse of the Judeo-Christian moral consensus exacerbated historical religious tensions and produced a realignment of American religious pluralism by superimposing a new division atop older ones. The new cleavage cut across denominational boundaries that separated, for example, Baptists from Episcopalians, Protestants from Catholics, and Christians from Jews, and is now producing divisions within as well as between religious traditions.

The new cleavage aligns persons who remain committed to "orthodox" religious beliefs and practices against secularists and persons who have abandoned traditional orthodoxy in favor of modern or liberal religious views. The tension between these two opposed camps, the "orthodox" and the "progressive," is animated by two competing religious/moral worldviews concerning what normative standards ought to govern individual behavior and social arrangements. On the orthodox side are people who locate moral authority in a transcendent source (e.g., God, nature's law, the Bible, Torah, etc.). Its standards are absolute, universally valid, and independent of human construction and preference. On the progressive side are people who locate moral authority in reason, science, and personal experience. Moral progressivists reject transcendent sources of moral authority and anchor it instead in "humanistic ethics" or "this worldly" considerations. Progressivist moral rules are "loose-bounded," relative to circumstances, pluralistic, and dependent on personal preference. The culture war is the struggle between religious and cultural elites, activists and special-interest organizations allied with these rival moral and ideological camps to shape and define public culture.

The conflict between the progressivist and orthodox camps has expanded beyond religion into secular politics. The principal arenas of conflict are the family, education, media, and the arts. The logic of each worldview has led allies of the orthodox and progressive camps to diametrically opposed stances toward contentious issues such as ABORTION, PRAYER IN PUBLIC SCHOOLS, multiculturalism, GAY RIGHTS, federal funding of the arts, and the like. Because of the centrality of values to personal identity, and the intensity in which they are held, compromise is more difficult to reach in the culture wars than on political disagreements over tax cuts, fiscal policy, and government economic activism.

There is some empirical evidence that the culture wars have produced a religious realignment of the American party system among elite activists as well as mass supporters. This restructuring is seen in the movement of seculars and religious liberals into the Democratic Party, the counterpush of religious and moral traditionalists toward the Republican side, and in the increasing polarization of the two parties' platform planks on moral and cultural issues. The escalation of the culture wars is also evident in the polarized attitudes in the general public toward fundamentalist and evangelical Christians and the use of these two religious groups by cultural progressives as negative political referents.

See also CHRISTIAN RIGHT AND THE REPUBLICAN PARTY; EQUAL RIGHTS AMENDMENT; SECULAR HUMANISM; SOUTHERN REPUBLICAN REALIGNMENT.

Further reading: Bolce, Louis, and Gerald De Maio. "The Anti-Christian Fundamentalist Factor in Contemporary Politics." *Public Opinion Quarterly* 63 (1999): 508–542; Green, John C., James L. Guth, Corwin E. Smidt, and Lyman A. Kellstedt, ed. *Religion and the Culture Wars: Dispatches from the Front.* Lanham, Md.: Rowman and Littlefield, 1996; Hunter, James Davison. *The Culture Wars: The Struggle to Define America.* New York: Basic Books, 1991; Layman, Geoffrey C. *The Great Divide (Power, Conflict, and Democracy): American Politics into the Twenty-first Century.* New York: Columbia University Press, 2001; Wuthnow, Robert. *The Restructuring of American Religion: Society and Faith since World War II.* Princeton, N. J.: Princeton University Press, 1988.

—Louis Bolce

Culture Wars: The Struggle to Define America

(1991) By James Davison Hunter. New York: Basic Books

James Davison Hunter's *Culture Wars: The Struggle to Define America* (1991) explores the cultural conflict that marked the cultural and political divisions in the United States during the final decades of the 20th century. Hunter, a sociologist, relied on historical analysis of the cultural divisions marking contemporary American life and politics to support his thesis of a CULTURE WAR that provokes "reverberations not only within public policy but within the lives of ordinary Americans everywhere." Cultural conflict in the United States is the result of "political and social hostility rooted in different systems of moral understanding," each desiring to dominate the others. Hunter contends that these conflicting moral visions do not stem from differing theological or ecclesiastical allegiances, nor are they between the religious and the irreligious. Rather, the fundamental divide is deeper, rooted in polar understandings of moral authority that result in conflicting worldviews.

The polar impulses in the culture war—the "orthodox" and the "progressive"—begin from such widely divergent assumptions that there is little common ground from which to engage in productive debate or compromise. The orthodox are committed to "an external, definable, and transcendent authority . . . sufficient for all time" and find their moral authority from outside of themselves. Progressivism, by contrast, is "defined by the spirit of the modern age, a spirit of rationalism and subjectivism." Progressives tend to view moral authority as residing "in personal experience or scientific rationality," rather than in a transcendent moral authority or historic faith.

Hunter's fundamental argument is that these two polarizing tendencies are a product of a "historically unnatural" religious realignment, with the orthodox wings of PROTESTANTISM, ROMAN CATHOLICISM, and Judaism forming alliances with one another to oppose the more progressive camps within their own faith traditions. *Culture Wars* is essentially an analysis of this realignment of religion in the United States and its impact culturally and politically. Hunter's basic assumption is that this religious realignment has deep political and cultural significance, for "politics is, in large part, an expression of culture. . . . At the heart of culture, is religion. . . . And at the heart of religion are its claims to truth about the world."

One reason the conflict is significant, maintains Hunter, is because of the magnitude of what is at stake. The debate is not simply over trivial or transient issues but the fundamental question of how we will order our lives together; it is, in essence, a "struggle to define the meaning of America."

Another reason the conflict is significant is because it is between political activists and cultural elites and therefore dominates public dialogue and debate. In fact, this is related to a frequent criticism of Hunter's thesis, that the culture war's argument is "overheated rhetoric," and the conflict is made out to be more than it really is. The mass public, as critics have demonstrated, are not divided along the lines Hunter contends. While they are divided along cultural, religious, and political lines, these cleavages are diffused and crosscutting rather than clustering around the polar impulses identified by Hunter. And even if they do occupy polar positions, as Hunter argues, Americans are not attentive to the issues being contended, nor are they engaged in the debate itself. Rather, they try to avoid conflict whenever possible.

Yet Hunter does not contend that the cultural conflict divides all Americans into two opposing camps. He recognizes that the mass public "occupy a vast middle ground between the polarizing impulses" and are thus not active participants in the culture war. The conflict is significant for American culture not because of its breadth, but rather because of its prominence—it is a conflict between cultural elites and political activists defending polar understandings of the meaning of our existence, and it is they who dominate public debate. With the foundation of the conflict so deep, with so much at stake, and with cultural elites occupying vastly different positions, the conflict dominates public discourse, a discourse "more polarized than the public itself." Unable and unwilling to find a common frame of reference from which to have a dialogue or come to some compromise on key issues, a divided elite poses serious challenges to American democracy.

Further reading: Wolfe, Alan. *One Nation, After All.* New York: Viking, 1998.

—Beverly Gaddy

D

Davis v. Beason 133 U.S. 333 (1890)

On February 3, 1890, the U.S. Supreme Court delivered a 9-0 opinion on a controversial POLYGAMY case. The state of Idaho established a law that prevented from voting those "who advocated or practiced plural marriage or belonged to an organization that did."

Samuel B. Davis, a member of the LATTER-DAY SAINTS, and various other Mormons who did not practice polygamy were not allowed to vote because of their religious affiliation and decided to take action. Justice Stephen Field delivered the Court opinion, stating that the FREE EXERCISE CLAUSE is subservient to the criminal laws of the United States. At that time, under *REYNOLDS V. UNITED STATES* (1878), polygamy was considered illegal. Thus, the Court upheld the decision in favor of Beason.

During this time in U.S. history, dissent was widespread against bigamy and polygamy. The Court stated: "While legislation for the establishment of a religion is forbidden, and its free exercise permitted, it does not follow that everything which may be so called can be tolerated. Crime is not the less odious because sanctioned by what any particular sect may designate as 'religion.'" The Court found that the statute in Idaho was in concert with the voting laws in Idaho and those of the United States, and that disallowing polygamists or those belonging to sects that support polygamy was, in fact, legal.

Meanwhile, Congress declared on March 22, 1882, "that no polygamist, bigamist, or any person cohabiting with more than one woman, and no woman cohabiting with any of the persons described as aforesaid in this section, in any territory or other place over which the United States have exclusive jurisdiction, shall be entitled to vote at any election held in any such territory or other place, or be eligible for election or appointment to, or be entitled to hold any office or place of public trust, honor, or emolument in, under, or for any such territory or place, or under the United States." Thus, the Court unanimously decided that the lower court's decision would be upheld and that the Free Exercise Clause was not violated owing to the nature of the criminality of polygamy.

—Kelli R. Williams

Day, Dorothy (1897–1980) *Christian activist*

Dorothy Day was born in Brooklyn, New York, and spent most of her childhood in Chicago. As a journalist and author, social activist and pacifist, and founder of the CATHOLIC WORKER MOVEMENT, Day was largely responsible for inaugurating a radical evangelical Roman Catholic social witness that continues to shape a segment of American Catholicism.

Day's parents were nominal Protestants and she attended church as a child. Despite a constant interest in religion, Day decided while a student at the University of Illinois "that religion was something that I must ruthlessly cut out of my life." Day's rejection of religion was accompanied by increased involvement in radical politics and growing frustration with the reality of poverty. She joined the Socialist Party and began writing columns for the local newspaper. In 1916, after two years in college, Day moved to New York. She became involved in the radical intellectual community centered in Greenwich Village and was employed as a writer with such left-wing publications as the *New York Call* and *The Masses.* During these years, she was involved in various political causes, spent 30 days in jail following a protest in Washington for women's suffrage, and was impregnated and procured an illegal ABORTION.

Over the course of several years, Day was increasingly drawn to the ROMAN CATHOLIC CHURCH. She was baptized a Catholic on December 28, 1927. Though conversion ended her relationship with leftist political movements, her commitment to the poor and her opposition to capitalism did not end. In 1932, while in Washington to cover the communist-organized Unemployed Council's Hunger March for *COMMONWEAL,* she prayed "that some way would open up for me to use what talents I possessed for my fellow workers, for the poor." When Day returned to New York, Peter Maurin, the itinerant son of French peasants, suggested Day produce a newspaper that would advocate radical social action based on Christian principles. The result was *Catholic Worker,* the first issue of which was published and distributed in May 1933. The newspaper, along with Houses of Hospitality to serve the poor, were the mainstays of what would become the Catholic Worker movement. The paper continues to be published (and is still sold for a penny), and the movement now supports over 175 Houses of Hospitality in 36 states and eight foreign countries.

Day's social vision epitomized the EVANGELISM of Christian social action. She believed the church was called into the world to demonstrate a radical and prophetic witness to justice that imitated the life of Christ. Drawing on the Gospel message (especially the Beatitudes), as well as the "personalist" philosophy advanced by European Catholics such as Emmanuel Mounier and Jacques Maritain, Day sought, in the words of Maurin, to create "a new society within the shell of the old." This new Christian society would stand in solidarity with the poor and seek to change society through practicing love in action.

In addition to living with the poor, Day also embraced PACIFISM. She rejected the idea that love could be coerced. Her uncompromising commitment to pacifism created a split in the Catholic Worker movement during World War II. Fifteen Houses of Hospitality closed following the U.S. entry into the war, and subscriptions to the *Catholic Worker* declined precipitously. Following the war, Day refused to participate in civil defense drills that simulated nuclear attack. In Rome in 1963, she joined a 10-day fast involving a group of women who wanted the bishops at VATICAN II to condemn war. She was also instrumental in founding PAX CHRISTI USA, organized near the end of the VIETNAM WAR. Day's pacifism inspired left-wing Catholics in America such as Thomas Merton and Daniel and Philip Berrigan.

Almost immediately after her death in 1980, the issue of Day's canonization was raised. The Vatican has approved the late JOHN CARDINAL O'CONNOR's request to consider Dorothy Day's "cause," leaving open the possibility Day will be named a saint of the Catholic Church.

Further reading: Coles, Robert. *Dorothy Day: A Radical Devotion.* Reading, Mass.: Addison-Wesley, 1987; Day, Dorothy. *From Union Square to Rome.* Silver Spring, Md.: Preservation of the Faith Press, 1938; ———. *The Long Loneliness: An Autobiography.* San Francisco: Harper and Row, 1952; Piehl, Mel. *Breaking Bread: The Catholic Worker and the Origin of Catholic Radicalism in America.* Philadelphia: Temple University Press, 1982.

—Zachary R. Calo

Declaration of Independence

Along with the U.S. Constitution, the Declaration of Independence is one of the founding documents of American political thought. It is generally believed to be a more democratic and universalistic statement than the Constitution, however, which in its original form excluded from full citizenship all women, most nonwhites, and some white males. The Declaration makes no such distinctions, either explicitly or implicitly.

On June 11, 1776, the Continental Congress assigned the task of drafting a resolution of independence to a committee consisting of JOHN ADAMS (1735–1826), BENJAMIN FRANKLIN (1706–90), THOMAS JEFFERSON (1743–1826), Robert R. Livingston (1746–1813), and Roger Sherman (1721–93). The bulk of the work fell to Jefferson, whose rough draft of the Declaration was submitted to the Continental Congress on June 28, 1776. After several days of debate, and a few revisions, the Declaration was unanimously approved (with the New York delegation abstaining) on July 4, 1776. Most notable among the revisions was the deletion of Jefferson's powerful condemnation of slavery, which his colleagues thought too inflammatory and divisive to achieve widespread support. The signatures of 55 delegates, including the well-known clergyman JOHN WITHERSPOON, were subsequently added.

The Declaration invokes the Lockean theory of natural law, and a long list of specific grievances against King George III, as legal and moral justification for the rebellion of the colonies against Great Britain. Although the text of the Declaration mentions the natural rights of life, liberty, and the pursuit of happiness, it makes no explicit reference to freedom of religion or conscience. Similarly, the Declaration fails to identify favoritism toward the Church of England among the complaints against the king, although some VIRGINIA patriots were beginning to make this claim, especially after the king disallowed the Two-Penny Act of 1759, which had reduced the value of the salaries of Virginia's Anglican clergymen.

Although many deists and radical pietists wanted the state out of religion, and Jefferson himself leaned toward DEISM, most of the country was not ready for radical talk about disestablishment or the SEPARATION OF CHURCH AND STATE. When the Declaration was drafted, the vast majority of Americans still believed that the state should have a significant role in promoting religious belief and practice. Many southern Anglicans and New England Congregationalists, for instance, believed that the state could encourage and support Christian worship without violating religious liberty.

The Declaration does make frequent explicit references to God, natural law, nature's God, the creator, and divine providence. Even Jefferson, whose religious beliefs were far from orthodox, and who was inclined to minimize the significance of God and providence in human affairs, did nothing to limit the appearances of nature and nature's God in his political rhetoric. This is not surprising, given that God and natural law were vital features of the language of politics in 18th-century America. Just about everyone accepted that God's will could be known through human reason by studying nature, including humankind's own nature.

The rhetoric of the Declaration of Independence has inspired generations of American revolutionaries, reformers, rebel, and radicals. Frequently invoked, quoted, paraphrased, and outright copied, echoes of the Declaration can be found in the writings of the Anti-Federalists, in Stephen Douglas's popular sovereignty arguments (and in ABRAHAM LINCOLN's criticisms of them), in the polemics of ABOLITIONISTS, in the Seneca Falls Declaration of Sentiments, and so on.

Although Americans celebrate July 4 as Independence Day, the separation of the colonies from the motherland technically occurred on July 2, 1776, as the result of a largely forgotten Resolution of Independence by the Continental Congress, not as the result of the adoption of the Declaration of Independence.

See also RELIGIOUS ESTABLISHMENT IN THE COLONIES.

Further reading: Bailyn, Bernard. *The Ideological Origins of the American Revolution.* Cambridge, Mass.: Harvard University Press, 1967; Becker, Carl. *The Declaration of Independence.* New York: Vintage, 1922; McLoughlin, William G. "The Role of Religion in the Revolution." In Stephen G. Kurtz and James H. Hutson, eds. *Essays on the American Revolution.* New York: Norton, 1973; Peterson, Merrill D., ed. *The Portable Thomas Jefferson.* New York: Penguin, 1975; Rossiter, Clinton. *The Political Thought of the American Revolution.* New York: Harcourt, Brace and World, 1953 [1963].

—Jason A. Scorza

deism

Deism is the view that the existence of God is demonstrated in the natural world, rather than in a supernatural revelation. Deists focus on morals and ethics, rather than doctrine. Deism became widespread in 18th-century Europe, as a result of the Enlightenment; many of those active leaders in the American Revolutionary period were deists.

The most famous deist of the early republic was THOMAS JEFFERSON. He had little patience for squabbles over fine points of religious beliefs that, he felt, violated the voice of reason. He edited his own version of the New Testament, excising the supernatural elements, and leaving the moral teachings. Jefferson's deist views were key in shaping his thoughts on freedom of religion and the separation of church and state. He established the University of Virginia along nonsectarian lines, and drafted the Virginia Statute for Religious Freedom, which was adopted by the Virginia legislature in 1786.

Jefferson's deism was influenced by the writings of the Unitarian minister Joseph Priestley and the pamphleteer Thomas Paine, an Englishman who supported American independence and who eventually immigrated to the United States after the war. Thanks to Priestley, Jefferson began to hold Jesus in a much higher estimation than he had previously, but Jefferson maintained his position that Jesus was wholly human and not divine. Paine wrote *The Age of Reason,* an incendiary book divided into two parts. Part one argued for basic deist ideas: one God, who never became incarnate, who created the world to run on by itself without supernatural interference, who provided his word in the form of nature, and who gave people their proper rewards after death. Part two was a full-fledged attack on the idea of the divine inspiration of the Christian Bible, pointing out contradictions and inconsistencies in the sacred texts. Jefferson corresponded with both Priestley and Paine extensively.

In 1794, Elihu Palmer organized a "Deistical Society" in New York, but deism as a prominent religious movement had declined significantly by the early 19th century. Critics of deism often accused it of sliding very easily into AGNOSTICISM and ATHEISM. They argued that a God who merely created the world and no longer became involved in the world was, for all intents and purposes, no God at all. Prayer to such a God went unanswered; the love of such a God was ineffective. Today, many members of UNITARIAN UNIVERSALIST churches hold beliefs very much in line with deism.

—Eric L. Thomas

Democracy in America

Alexis de Tocqueville (1805–59), a French aristocrat and scholar, came to the United States in 1831 intending to study the American penal system. Instead, he produced *Democracy in America* (1835/1840), a magisterial work on American politics, government, society, and culture, which has intrigued generations of social scientists and inspired efforts by some to revitalize American civil society.

Tocqueville understood freedom in a democracy to depend on the relationship between public and private life, including religious life. For Tocqueville, religion is important for at least two reasons. First, widespread religious faith helps moderate (although not eliminate) the powerful materialistic and egoistic impulses of democratic life. Second, free religious associations and communities help incubate democratic mores and virtues.

According to Tocqueville, human beings cannot easily live without fixed ideas about God and their own place in the cosmos. This is particularly true for individuals living in a democracy, where political authority is weak, civil liberty is extensive, and self-interest runs rampant. Tocqueville accepts that most individuals in a democracy will seek to enrich themselves. However, he hopes that the pursuit of wealth can be chastened by moral considerations. Regardless of whether religion can actually save our souls in the next world, Tocqueville concludes, it contributes to human happiness and dignity in this world by reminding individuals of their "obligations toward mankind."

At the same time, Tocqueville argues, moral and religious associations—even more so than economic or political associations—are great seedbeds of virtue for democratic peoples, teaching individuals how to cooperate with one another to achieve long-term social goals. Tocqueville explains, "Feelings and ideals are renewed, the heart enlarged, and the understanding developed only by the reciprocal action of men one upon another."

Although Tocqueville identifies a crucial role for religion in democratic society, he explicitly rejects a role for government in promoting religion, expressing concern that in the hands of the state, religion could become just another political weapon. Tocqueville views government interference in religious matters, and in particular the co-option of clergy, as part of a broader pattern in which the charitable, educational, and moral associations of a nation are gradually undermined and supplanted by the state, at the expense of freedom.

Tocqueville also explicitly rejects a formal political role for clergymen, fearing that the temptations of power would lead to the decline of religious faith. The complete SEPARATION OF CHURCH AND STATE, he insists, contributes to the influence of religion in a democracy, rather than reducing it. By distancing itself from the bickering, rivalries, and compromises of politics, religion can remain above reproach, spreading its benefits without alienating or offending anyone. According to Tocqueville, "any alliance with any political power whatsoever is bound to be burdensome for religion. It does not need their support in order to live, and in serving them it may die."

Tocqueville, himself a practicing Roman Catholic, suggests that in a democratic society the details and outward forms of worship will tend to lose their attractions, or even grow repugnant to individuals. For the sake of the overall benefits of religion and religiosity, therefore, Tocqueville believes that ceremonies and rituals should not be permitted to proliferate unnecessarily. They should be maintained, instead, only when they directly support and reinforce the central dogmas of faith.

For Tocqueville, the general spirit of religion, rather than particular observances, helps shape the mores of a democratic people. This general spirit, Tocqueville observed, was extremely strong in the United States, to the point that even nonbelievers felt compelled to profess the Christian faith publicly. But while Tocqueville identifies the tyranny of the majority over public opinion as the most serious threat to liberty in a democracy, he does not extend this critique to the influence of religious faith, which in his judgment is most beneficial when it is most pervasive.

See also BOWLING ALONE; HABITS OF THE HEART; POLITICAL PARTICIPATION.

Further reading: Bellah, Robert, et al. *Habits of the Heart: Individualism and Commitment in American Life.* New York: Harper and Row, 1985; Gargan, Edward T. *De Tocqueville.* New York: Hillary House, 1965; Putnam, Robert D. *Bowling Alone: The Collapse and Revival of American Community.* New York: Simon and Schuster, 2000; Tocqueville, Alexis de. *Democracy in America.* Edited by J. P. Mayer; translated by George Lawrence. New York: Harper and Row, 1988.

—Jason A. Scorza

denominationalism

The word *denomination* is derived from the Latin word *denominare*, which means "to name." A denomination is an association of churches, related mission organizations, educational institutions, and formal administrative agencies who share common beliefs and practices, and who cooperate for the achievement of shared goals. In addition, groups of denominations that share a common history and basic beliefs,

and often include similar ethnic groups, such as Baptists, constitute a "denominational family." Denominational families, prevalent among Protestant Christians, are a result of religio-cultural movements such as the Reformation, the FIRST GREAT AWAKENING, and the SECOND GREAT AWAKENING.

Like other social organizations, religious denominations are important socializing contexts that help generate worldviews, reinforce behavioral expectations, and provide believers with a sense of self-identification. In this way, denominations play a foundational role in the transmission of cultural values and traditions in a society, and thus contribute to social and political stability.

Denominationalism, however, is not without its critics. Perhaps most notably, H. Richard Niebuhr argued that "Denominationalism . . . represents the moral failure of Christianity," since denominations are "laden with ethnic, racial, and class-based divisions" and thus violate the spirit of Christian brotherhood. According to Niebuhr, denominations "are not religious groups with religious purposes, but [rather] . . . represent the accommodation of religion to the caste system."

Denominationalism is a relatively recent phenomenon, having its roots in the theological distinction made by John Wycliffe and John Hus and expressed by the Protestant Reformers between the visible and invisible church. In addition, 18th-century REVIVALISM in America, especially associated with John Wesley and GEORGE WHITEFIELD, greatly contributed to the growth of denominationalism in the New World. Yet when compared with European religious organizational development, America's denominational growth is unique. During America's founding era, antagonism among colonists toward organized Anglicanism, constitutional provisions guaranteeing the SEPARATION OF CHURCH AND STATE and increased cultural diversity resulting from immigration meant that no denomination had sufficient power or institutional development to become dominant. Instead, numerous diverse minority religious organizations developed, and thus each religious body was forced to coexist with other religious groups. Within this milieu, religious tolerance flourished, and new religious groups emerged.

While there are numerous methods available to classify the bewildering number of denominations in America, most classification schemes are elaborations of Ernst Troeltsch's church-sect typology. Troeltsch viewed the church as a universal body that supports secular authority and has as its goal worldwide religious conversion. The church is an inclusive organization wherein membership is socially determined. Sects, in contrast, are small, voluntary organizations that require members to remain separate from society, adhere to strict religious values, and practice personal holiness. Some sects "mature" and become denominations (such as the SOUTHERN BAPTIST CONVENTION), while others, such as the QUAKERS, the AMISH, and the MENNONITES, remain separatist groups. In Niebuhr's interpretation, denominations are simply religious, churchlike bodies that accommodate themselves to political and social structures and social values.

Based on Troeltsch's typology, and incorporating the notion of denominational families, scholars assign denominations to one of five religious traditions: Mainline Protestant (such as the EPISCOPAL CHURCH and the UNITED METHODIST CHURCH), White Evangelical Protestant (including the Southern Baptists and the ASSEMBLIES OF GOD), ROMAN CATHOLIC, Black Protestant (for instance, the NATIONAL BAPTIST CONVENTION and the AFRICAN METHODIST EPISCOPAL CHURCH), and Jewish. Mainline Protestant denominations tend to be ECUMENICAL in orientation and liberal in theology, while Evangelical Protestant denominations are often PIETISTIC, separatist, and theological conservative.

Religious denominationalism is such a defining characteristic of America that Andrew Greeley called America the "denominational society." And while significant denominational changes have occurred since Greeley wrote those words—most notably the decline of membership in mainline Protestant denominations—the number of Americans affiliated with churches remains exceedingly high, especially compared with Europe, and is actually increasing. For example, according to David Barrett's *Survey of Churches and Religions,* there were 2,050 denominations in the United States in 1980, but by 2000 there were 4,684 denominations comprising 600,000 congregations, representing over 133 million adult members, and nearly 192 million affiliated people. According to the recent *American Religious Identification Survey,* 52 percent of Americans claim Protestant religious affiliation, 24.5 percent Catholic, 1.3 percent Jewish, 2.4 percent "some other" religious identification, and 14.1 percent claim not to affiliate with any religion.

Despite the continuing existence of congregational life in America, social and religious changes—such as modernism and ecumenism—during the 20th century eroded denominational loyalty, especially among the youngest generations. Some scholars label the current era "post-denominational." Characterized by the dual trends of declining membership in mainline Protestant churches and the emergence of informal networks of Evangelical Protestant churches and organizations that worship in less structured ways (often termed "new paradigm" churches), post-denominational America is increasingly spiritual, but less attached to specific churches or denominations. Perhaps as a testament to these spiritual yearnings, presumably unfulfilled by liberal mainline Protestant churches, membership in "strict churches"—theologically conservative churches such as the Vineyard Church, Assemblies of God, and Southern Baptist Convention—is on the upswing.

Clearly, growth rates of religious bodies reflect their values and goals as well as cultural trends. At the turn of the 21st century, America's religious life is undergoing a transformation. There is great fluidity among church members, with parishioners moving among different denominations in search of more meaningful religious experiences. And while "taken-for-granted" denominational culture still exists—especially in rural, southern, and midwestern regions—the current religious climate in America is rewarding churches and groups that are theologically conservative, spiritually vital, and "open and connected to the larger world," yet not socially divisive (Ammerman 2002: 307).

Further reading: *American Religious Identification Survey.* Available on-line. URL: http://www.gc.cuny.edu/studies/key_findings.htm; Ammerman, Nancy T. "New Life for Denominationalism." *Christian Century* (March 15, 2002); Greeley, Andrew M. *The Denominational Society.* Glenview, Ill.: Scott, Foresman, 1972; Kellstedt, Lyman A., and John C. Green. "Knowing God's Many People: Denominational Preference and Political Behavior." In *Rediscovering the Religious Factor in American Politics.* New York: M. E. Sharpe, 1993; Miller, Donald E. "Postdenominational Christianity in the Twenty-First Century." *Annals of the American Academy of Political and Social Science* (July 1998); Niebuhr, H. Richard. *The Social Sources of Denominationalism.* New York: Meridian Books, 1929; Troeltsch, Ernst. *The Social Teaching of the Christian Churches.* Trans. Olive Wyon. New York: Macmillan, 1912/1976.

—Franklyn C. Niles

Dewey, John (1859–1952) *scholar*

After graduating from the University of Vermont in Burlington, the city where he was born, and receiving a Ph.D. from Johns Hopkins University, John Dewey spent the rest of his life in academia, first at the University of Michigan (1884–94), then at Chicago (1894–1904), and, finally, at Columbia (1905–52). A major figure in the emerging national university and its developing disciplinary organizations, Dewey was president both of the American Psychological Association in 1899 and of the American Philosophical Association in 1904.

His interrelated philosophical, psychological, and educational ideas were developed first within a romantic-evangelical framework, in which God's spirit is progressively revealed through human experience. Through the combined influence of the evolutionary organic idealism of G. W. F. Hegel in Germany and T. H. Green in England, Dewey's project was to shape a philosophy of democratic experience, democratic education, and democratic social, economic, and political reform that would guide America toward the full realization of justice and righteousness.

His early essays, "The Ethics of Democracy" (1888), "Christianity and Democracy" (1892), and "The Relation of Philosophy to Theology" (1893), all attest to this personal sense of calling. In the last essay, he stated his position: "The next religious prophet who will have a permanent and real influence on men's lives will be the man who succeeds in pointing out the religious meaning of democracy, the ultimate religious value to be found in the normal flow of life itself." After his move to Chicago, Dewey broke formal connections with Christian churches and ceased to address theological issues from inside Christian teachings; and yet a kind of

"Protestantism without [creedal] Christianity" continued to pervade his writings, in a way that paralleled the social reform activities and writings of JANE ADDAMS and Graham Taylor, and the teachings of Christian sociology represented by his Chicago colleagues Albion Small and Shailer Mathews.

In Dewey's educational writings, the common school becomes transformed into something like an embracive national church. Excerpts from two essays, "My Pedagogic Creed" (1897) and "Religion and Our Schools" (1908), are testaments to the idealism of his earlier evangelical faith, now incorporated into his philosophy: "education is . . . the process of coming to share in the social consciousness; . . . social consciousness is the only sure method of social reconstruction." "In bringing together those of different nationalities, languages, traditions, and creeds [our schools] are performing an infinitely significant religious work . . . they are promoting the social unity out of which . . . genuine religious unity must grow." "I believe that in this way the teacher always is the prophet of the true God and the usherer in of the true kingdom of God."

Even though Dewey later joined others in the 1920s to condemn the churchgoing evangelical middle classes, he recognized that they constituted the core constituency for American social reform. *A Common Faith* (1934) may be read as an attempt to rescue the religious qualities of moral aspirations and intensely felt experience from the grip of static intellectual propositions and formal religious creeds. This same impulse was conveyed in what were perhaps Dewey's two most influential works, *Democracy and Education,* published continuously from 1915 to 1953, and *Ethics,* a college textbook written with James Tufts, widely used from 1908 to 1942.

See also ADAMS, HENRY CARTER; EVANGELICALISM; SOCIAL GOSPEL.

Further reading: Crunden, Robert M. *Ministers of Reform: The Progressives Achievement in American Civilization 1889–1920.* Urbana: University of Illinois Press, 1984; Damico, Alfonso. *Individuality and Community: The Social and Political Thought of John Dewey.* Gainesville: University Presses of Florida, 1978; Eisenach, Eldon. *The Lost Promise of Progressivism.* Lawrence: University Press of Kansas, 1994.

—Eldon J. Eisenach

divine right of kings

The divine right of kings is the theory or doctrine that monarchs rule by divine ordinance. According to theories of divine right, the authority of monarchs is ordained by God and acquired through heredity, with any resistance to this authority being considered illegitimate. As a legitimation of authority, assertions of the divine right of kings extend back as far as the practice of monarchy itself, with acceptance of the theory flourishing until the 17th century. The political revolutions of the 17th and 18th centuries challenged and eventually discredited belief in the divine authority of monarchs.

Although divine right as a concept can be found in earlier history, as in the use of the title *pontifex maximus* and in the cult of the emperor promoted by Augustus (63 B.C.E.–14 C.E.) in the early Roman Empire, Augustine of Hippo (354–430) provided a theoretical foundation for the belief in the divine right of Christian monarchs. According to Augustine, monarchs were awarded temporal power over the political realm, while the church exercised power in the spiritual realm, and to question either type of authority was in essence to question the will of God. This division remained in place, with the eventual exception of England, where political and spiritual authority came to be seen as converging in the monarch.

The divine right of kings continued to be relatively unchallenged until the 17th century, when, owing in part to the influence of the Protestant Reformation, national monarchs began asserting their authority in both political and ecclesial matters. An emerging group of thinkers influenced by the work of Hugo Grotius (1583–1645) believed that political entities, such as states, were governed by natural laws, and that these laws were both constant and universally applicable. In both France and England, however, support for the divine right of kings continued. In France, the Catholic bishop Jacques-Bénigne Bossuet (1627–1704) asserted that the king's authority was divinely ordained and followed a patriarchal model. Further developing a formal doctrine of the divine right of kings, Bossuet asserted that any legally formed government expressed the will of God; that the authority of such a government was sacred; and that resistance against it was illegitimate. In England, Robert Filmer attempted to establish that the Stuart crown was the heir of a divine right that could be traced back to the biblical Adam. In his treatise *Patriarcha* (1648), Filmer asserted that the state was a family, the king was its father, and Charles I (1600–49) was both Adam's heir and ruler of England.

Responding to *Patriarcha,* the empiricist philosopher JOHN LOCKE (1632–1704) wrote his *First Treatise of Civil Government* (1689) with the expressed intent of refuting Filmer's doctrine of the divine and absolute right of the monarch. Locke asserted that the state was formed through a social contract and guided by natural law, which guaranteed the inalienable rights of human beings, and that revolution, considered illegitimate by adherents of divine right, was not only a right in some circumstances but also an obligation. Locke also contributed to the development of the concept of SEPARATION OF CHURCH AND STATE, arguing that religion is a personal concern decided by faith, and as such is outside the jurisdiction of the civil magistrate. In addition to developments in philosophy and political theory, several political events, including England's Revolution of 1688, the American Revolution, the French Revolution, and the Napoleonic era, effectively discredited the doctrine of divine right.

The Revolutionary War and the new form of government it generated in America were directly influenced by the political theories developed in reaction to doctrines of the divine and absolute rule of monarchs. The separation of church and state, as stated in the First Amendment of the U.S. Constitution, holds that "Congress shall make no law respecting an establishment of religion, or prohibiting the free exercise thereof;" it demonstrates the importance the founders placed on preventing the establishment of a national religion. Their concern was that a national religion or official state church, such as those that had historically restricted or denied citizens their civil liberties as well as their "inalienable rights," would be instituted and subsequently reinstate the political conditions against which they had revolted.

Further reading: Levy, Leonard. *The Establishment Clause.* Chapel Hill: University of North Carolina Press, 1994; Lovell, Colin Rhys. *English Constitutional and Legal History.* New York: Oxford University Press, 1962; Marshall, John. *John Locke: Resistance, Religion, and Responsibility.* New York: Cambridge University Press, 1994; Rives, J. B. *Religion and Authority in Roman Carthage from Augustus to Constantine.* New York: Oxford University Press, 1995.

—Lora L. Stone

Dobson, James (1936–) conservative activist

James Clayton Dobson Jr. was born in Shreveport, Louisiana. He is the founder and president of FOCUS ON THE FAMILY, a nonprofit, conservative Christian organization that seeks to promote and sustain the traditional family and traditional values. Dobson's radio show, news updates, and commentaries, still the heart of Focus on the Family, are broadcast in 12 languages, reaching 550 million radio listeners on more than 4,000 facilities worldwide.

Dobson received a bachelor's degree in psychology in 1958 from Pasadena College (now relocated to San Diego and renamed Point Loma Nazarene University), a Christian liberal arts school, and a Ph.D. in 1967 from the University of Southern California in the field of child development. His experiences in the pediatric and child development fields led to intense frustration with the lack of a comprehensive, rational, biblically based conception of the family for those experiencing the trials of modern life. Started in 1977 in Arcadia, California, and broadcast on only a few dozen stations, Dobson's weekly radio program was designed to address these concerns. Now based in Colorado Springs, Colorado, Focus on the Family has since evolved into a wide array of 74 different ministries designed to assist and provide resources to, among others, families, clergy, doctors, teachers, the elderly, and young people.

Dobson and his organization have been instrumental in generating networks of conservative Christians and propagating the general social attitudes and values necessary for groups, such as the Christian Coalition, to organize their constituencies on behalf of conservative Republican candidates and proposals. By fighting for the same sets of goals, Dobson and his contemporaries, such as PAT ROBERTSON, GARY BAUER, and Phyllis Schlafly, have intentionally, and unintentionally, aided one another by circulating and supporting traditional values and influencing how conservative Christians conceptualize the role of government in their everyday lives. Dobson strongly believes that conservative Christians have an obligation to make their voices heard. He notes, "When the church reaches the point that it has no stomach for the fight against evil, especially in a day when moral foundations are crumbling, then its powerful voice for righteousness is muted and its influence in the culture is ineffective."

Dobson has earned the respect of many on both sides of the debate because of his unfailing commitment to his principles. Despite general support for Republican causes, Dobson does not shy away from criticizing the party when his principles demand action. During the 1996 and 1998 electoral campaigns, for example, he called on Republicans to pursue the moral agenda of the Christian Right or face the consequences at the polls. He warned that if they failed to take up a morally conservative agenda, he would "do everything I can do to take as many people with me [away from the polls] as possible." Keenly recognizing his influence at the grassroots, Republicans made more of an effort to reach out to Dobson and his agenda. Indeed, Focus supporters besiege Congress with phone calls and letters when Dobson weighs in on an issue on his radio program or in mailings to constituents. By providing constituents with key information about policy, Dobson has been able to influence Republican policy makers and shape legislation.

Dobson's prominence in the pro-family movement has resulted in a number of high-level government advisory appointments concerned with the American family. President RONALD REAGAN appointed him to serve on the National Advisory Commission to the Office of Juvenile Justice and Delinquency Prevention, as the cochairman of the Citizens' Advisory Panel for Tax Reform, and as the chair of the United States Army's Family Initiative. Dobson also was frequently invited to the White House to consult with Presidents Reagan and George H. W. Bush and their staffs on issues related to the family. Most recently, in 1994 Senate Majority Leader Robert Dole appointed Dobson to the Commission on Child and Family Welfare, and by Leader Trent Lott to the National Gambling Impact Study Commission in 1996. He also received a special commendation from President JAMES EARL CARTER for his work on a family task force in 1980. Dobson's unfailing dedication to his principles has led many conservative Christians to look to him for moral leadership for the movement; this strong devotion to his beliefs ensures James Dobson will remain a steady and powerful voice in conservative Christian circles.

Further reading: Apostolidis, Paul. *Stations of the Cross: Adomo and Christian Right Radio.* Durham, N.C.: Duke University Press, 2000; Dobson, James C. "The New Cost of Discipleship." *Christianity Today,* September 1999; Focus on the Family website. URL: http://www.fotf.org; Watson, Justin. *The Christian Coalition: Dreams of Restoration. Demands for*

Recognition. New York: St. Martin's Press, 1997; Zettersten, Rolf. *Dr. Dobson: Turning Hearts Toward Home.* Dallas, Tex.: Word Publishing, 1989.

—Brett M. Clifton

Drinan, Robert (1920–) *Jesuit priest*

Father Robert Frederick Drinan is a Jesuit priest and former five-term member of Congress. He was born in Boston and later ordained a ROMAN CATHOLIC CHURCH priest in 1953. He earned a B.A. and M.A. from Boston College and an L.L.B. and L.L.M. from Georgetown University Law Center in 1949 and 1950, respectively. In 1954, he was awarded a Th.D. from the Gregorian University (Rome). He was admitted to the District of Columbia Bar, the Commonwealth of Massachusetts Bar, and the U.S. Supreme Court Bar between 1950 and 1956. From 1956 to 1970, he served as dean of the Law School at Boston College.

Father Drinan represented the Fourth Congressional District of Massachusetts as a Democrat from 1971 to 1981. He served as chairman of the Subcommittee on Criminal Justice of the House Judiciary Committee. His travels included official congressional delegations to Vietnam, Thailand, Hong Kong, China, and Japan. He also served on private delegations to the Netherlands, South Africa, Sudan, ISRAEL, and the Soviet Union, and privately sponsored human rights missions to Chile, the Philippines, El Salvador, Guatemala, Nicaragua, Argentina, France, and Vietnam.

A change in papal leadership in 1978 ended Drinan's congressional service. Pope JOHN PAUL II directed him not to seek reelection to Congress in 1980. Canon law generally prohibited priests from holding public office, although Drinan had the permission of his superior. His fellow members of Congress praised Drinan for his devotion to "the oppressed, the indigent and the underprivileged." Drinan was not pleased with the pope's action because he saw his congressional service as "priestly work." However, an aide reported, "He never once considered defiance." Since 1981, Father Drinan has been a professor of law at Georgetown University Law Center.

In addition to teaching courses in international human rights, constitutional law, civil liberties, legislation, professional responsibility, and the advanced legal ethics seminar at Georgetown, Father Drinan is a nationally known author, lecturer, and public advocate. He has espoused political positions that have caused controversy with conservatives and church hierarchs. Conservatives saw him as a pioneer in the practice of being "personally opposed to ABORTION but pro-choice." In 1996, Drinan publicly supported President WILLIAM JEFFERSON CLINTON's veto of the partial-birth abortion ban because he believed the congressional bill did not outlaw abortions after 20 weeks, but did prohibit the most statistically safe method for performing such abortions. He received strong public criticism from JOHN CARDINAL O'CONNOR of New York and James Cardinal Hickey of Washington, D.C. His Jesuit superior also expressed disagreement. Drinan later retracted his position, saying he had been mistaken and the bill did not ban the method with the best safety record.

On the issue of the death penalty, Drinan criticized his fellow Jesuit, Avery Cardinal Dulles, who agreed with the pope's opposition to the death penalty but classified it as a "prudential conclusion" that does not change church teaching or bind Catholics in conscience to agree with it. Drinan stated that Dulles's position could not be justified and cited the American bishops' opposition to capital punishment. Drinan also joined a coalition of religious leaders in urging passage of the McCain-Feingold Campaign Finance Bill.

Father Drinan has published numerous books and has published in such periodicals as *Christian Century, London Tablet, America,* and the *Boston Globe.* He has also been a frequent contributor to the *Journal of Church and State,* the *National Catholic Reporter,* and *Family Law Quarterly.* He writes regularly for several law reviews and journals of policy and opinion and is the author of 10 books.

Drinan holds national leadership positions in several organizations, including the Lawyers Committee for Human Rights, Common Cause, and the NAACP Legal Defense and Educational Fund. He has been an active leader in the American Bar Association along with numerous other professional organizations. He is past president of Americans for Democratic Action, is honorary president of the World Federalist Association, was founder of the Lawyers Alliance for Nuclear Arms Control and the National Interreligious Task Force on Soviet Jewry, and is a member of numerous other political associations. He also holds 23 honorary degrees from institutions such as Georgetown University, Loyola University (Chicago), and Villanova University.

Further reading: Hennesey, James. *American Catholics.* New York. Oxford University Press, 1981.

—Anthony J. Pogorelc

Dutch Reformed tradition (Christian Reformed Church, Reformed Church in America)

The Christian Reformed Church in North America (CRC) and the Reformed Church in America (RCA) are two small Protestant denominations of approximately equal size (300,000 members each), yet their cultural significance exceeds their size. Not only do the two denominations share a common theology with some of America's earliest settlers, the PURITANS, but their emphasis on integrating faith with reason has helped generate a substantial and influential body of Christian scholarship.

Both the CRC and the RCA have Dutch, Calvinist roots and both adhere to the same confessional tests of orthodoxy—the Belgaic Confession, the Canons of Dordt, and the Heidelberg Catechism. Nonetheless, the two denominations differ significantly in terms of historical development, certain doctrinal issues, and, especially, their relationship to American PROTESTANTISM. The differences are sufficiently notable that the RCA is best classified as a mainline denomination, while the CRC is, at least arguably, best classified as an evangelical denomination. Although the RCA is sometimes viewed as more theologically conservative than most mainline denominations, the RCA was a charter member of both the World and NATIONAL COUNCIL OF CHURCHES. In contrast, the CRC has never joined those mainline organizations. Rather, it has loosely aligned itself with American evangelicalism, as signified by its on-again, off-again membership in the NATIONAL ASSOCIATION OF EVANGELICALS.

The RCA is America's oldest Protestant denomination, tracing its heritage to the settlement of New Amsterdam by Dutch colonists in the 17th century. Before the British took control, the RCA, then known as the Reformed Protestant Dutch Church, was the official church of the colony. During its formative years, the RCA struggled with reconciling its Dutch roots with Anglo-American culture. By the mid-19th century, however, the issue was largely settled in favor of Americanization, and in 1869 the denomination officially changed its name to Reformed Church in America.

During the mid-19th century, the RCA attracted waves of immigrant seceders from the Dutch Reformed Church in the Netherlands, concerned about a perceived erosion of orthodoxy in the Dutch church. In contrast to the established membership of the RCA, which was largely located in New York and the Middle Atlantic states, the new immigrants tended to settle in such Midwestern states as Michigan, Illinois, and Iowa. These newcomers tended to be culturally closer to the "old country" and theologically more orthodox than the established membership of the RCA.

The RCA continues to reflect this cultural and theological bifurcation, with the two wings of the denomination often differing over theological matters. Issues such as whether or not to ordain women to the ministry frequently pit more conservative Midwesterners against less conservative Easterners. Similar political divisions have developed in the RCA, with Midwestern members tending to be more politically conser-

vative than are members from the East. Although the Synod of the RCA has tended to support many of the politically liberal positions of mainline church councils, internal debates on these positions have been contentious, and votes have frequently been very close.

The CRC originated in 1857 when a group of members of the Reformed Protestant Dutch Church (now RCA) seceded from the mother church. A variety of factors prompted the secession, including concerns over the mother church's acceptance of FREEMASONRY and, more generally, its accommodation to American culture. Since the CRC adhered more strongly to its Dutch cultural and theological heritage, Dutch immigrants to the United States in the late 19th century tended to join the CRC rather than the RCA. The same phenomenon occurred after World War II, but this time in Canada, as waves of Dutch immigrants to Canada formed new CRC congregations. Hence, the denomination is now officially called the CRC in North America.

While the CRC fiercely maintains its theological orthodoxy, it has tended to reject FUNDAMENTALISM and biblical literalism. Neither has the denomination felt completely at home with American EVANGELICALISM, seeing the movement as neglecting the "life of the mind." Following the tradition established by former Dutch prime minister Abraham Kuyper, many members of the CRC have emphasized the importance of transforming culture in the name of Christ and of establishing a system of Christian schools to facilitate that activity.

Although the membership of the CRC is located primarily in the American Midwest and in Ontario, the church has become more geographically and theologically diverse in recent years. Thus, debates over such issues as the ordination of women and biblical interpretation have generated considerable controversy. Politically, members of the CRC tend to be conservative, but the denomination's emphasis on the pursuit of social justice has moderated that conservatism.

—James M. Penning

E

Eagle Forum

Phyllis Schlafly, a lawyer and Republican political activist, founded Stop ERA in 1972 with a small group of women volunteers. In 1975, they became the Eagle Forum and described themselves as an organization for believers of all faiths who would work toward specific political goals. While Schlafly was active in conservative politics and published her first of many books in the mid-1960s, she is best known for her work as the leader of the Eagle Forum. Although it does not focus exclusively on issues of morality or traditional family values, as many Christian Right organizations do, the Eagle Forum nonetheless espouses an ideology that is congruent with the Christian Right. What distinguishes it from other Christian Right women's organizations is the emphasis it places on economic and foreign policy issues in addition to its focus on more clearly moral or social issues.

Despite the wide range of issues it takes on today, the Eagle Forum's initial goal, as Stop ERA was to defeat the EQUAL RIGHTS AMENDMENT (ERA) to the Constitution. Proposed in 1972, the ERA called for men and women to be given equal treatment under the law. Schlafly's Stop ERA campaign was launched at a time when victory for the amendment seemed inevitable. The proposal for the amendment passed with overwhelming majorities in the U.S. House (23 opposed) and in the Senate (eight opposed). Once it reached the state legislatures, 30 of the 38 states needed to ratify it did so within 12 months. Responding to the seemingly imminent passage of the amendment, Schlafly organized women all across the United States to take a stand against what she described as the ERA's radical FEMINIST agenda aimed at destroying the traditional roles of women. Arguing that women already had equality under the law and that passage of the ERA would result in coed bathrooms, women being subject to the military draft, and wives losing the right to be supported by their husbands, Schlafly drew support from conservative politicians and religious leaders, as well as from women and men who feared the aftermath of an ERA. By 1982, despite an extension granted by Congress to increase the time allowed for ratification by the state legislatures, only 35 states had ratified the

ERA and five had voted to rescind their earlier ratification. The proposed amendment failed when the deadline for ratification expired in June 1982. In spite of defeating the ERA at the national level, the Eagle Forum still fights ERA-related battles as they emerge in state legislatures and courtrooms throughout the United States.

Her stand against the ERA kept Schlafly and the Eagle Forum in the national spotlight for a decade and enabled her to mobilize thousands of supporters from numerous states. Today the Eagle Forum focuses on a full agenda of issues including education, ABORTION, strategic defense, foreign policy, privacy rights, environmental policy, global issues, and GAY RIGHTS. Eagle Forum's position on these issues reflects a typical conservative ideology and in most cases resembles that of the Christian Right. Organizational literature states that the Eagle Forum opposes all tax increases, supports American sovereignty, supports private enterprise, supports the sanctity of human life, and supports conservative and pro-family policies at every level of government.

Her work as the leader of Stop ERA and her previous work as a Republican activist have provided Schlafly with access to numerous influential political leaders and have kept Eagle Forum at the center of conservative politics in the United States. Schlafly has written continuously since the mid-1960s and to date has published 16 books. Her newsletter, now available on the Eagle Forum website and circulated to more than 80,000 subscribers, has been published continuously since 1967. Schlafly also addresses the public through her weekday Eagle Forum radio show, which is broadcast on hundreds of radio stations around the country.

In recent years, Eagle Forum has expanded its membership to include young people as well. The Teen Eagles, intended for students 12 to 17 years old, provides teen members with a newsletter from the Eagle Forum targeting issues of interest to teens. The newsletters are also meant to serve an educational purpose, teaching teens about politics in the United States, albeit from a clearly conservative perspective.

The influence of Schlafly and Eagle Forum activists on national and state politics is undeniable. The organization has had significant success battling issues in the courtroom through the practice of filing AMICUS CURIAE BRIEFS in the Supreme Court and in circuit course cases. The issues addressed in these cases range from the adoption of English as an official language to privacy rights. In addition, the Eagle Forum has been successful in mobilizing support or opposition around various pieces of legislation at the state and national levels. In recent years, the organization has fought legislative battles over abortion rights, gay and lesbian rights, education, public funding of the arts, and HEALTH CARE provision. However, the impact of the Eagle Forum is not limited to political action around specific issues and legislation. Eagle Forum has its own political action committee and has helped numerous conservative candidates win Republican nominations.

Although it started as a single-issue organization (Stop ERA) aimed at defeating a specific amendment to the Constitution, the Eagle Forum today represents a highly organized group of volunteers who can be effectively mobilized around numerous issues through a network of state-run chapters. While the group is clearly religious in its orientation, specifically espousing Judeo-Christian values, its membership represents a diversity of denominational affiliations within this general ideology. As such, Eagle Forum holds a unique place among conservative religious political organizations in the United States.

See also CHRISTIAN COALITION; CHRISTIAN RIGHT AND THE REPUBLICAN PARTY; CONCERNED WOMEN FOR AMERICA; FAMILY RESEARCH COUNCIL; FOCUS ON THE FAMILY.

—R. Lorraine Bernotsky

Eastern Orthodox Churches

The Eastern Orthodox Churches are a fellowship of self-governing jurisdictions united in worship and doctrine that constitutes, alongside the ROMAN CATHOLIC CHURCH and Protestant churches, one of the three major expressions of Christianity. Worldwide, Orthodox Christians number between 200 and 250 million, with their greatest concentrations being in Russia, Romania, and Greece. In the United States, there are an estimated 4–5 million Orthodox Christians belonging to one of nearly a dozen jurisdictions with ties to "mother churches" in Europe and the Middle East. The three largest American jurisdictions are the Greek Orthodox Archdiocese of America, the Orthodox Church in America (OCA), and the Antiochian Orthodox Christian Archdiocese of North America.

The term *orthodox,* derived from Greek, means both "right-believing" and "right-worshipping." Orthodox Christians understand themselves as both the guardians and the teachers of doctrinal truth and the believers who properly glorify the true God. Among contemporary Orthodox, doctrine and liturgy remain central. The most basic expression of Orthodox doctrine is the Nicene-Constantinopolitan Creed (381). In addition, Orthodoxy affirms the authority of the Seven Ecumenical Councils held between 325 and 787, as well as of later eastern episcopal synods. The Orthodox Church is doctrinally traditional and is generally conservative on contemporary moral issues. Its theological emphasis is on creative continuity with the spirit and teachings of Greek patristic authors. Liturgically, Orthodoxy is known for its rich worship tradition. Byzantine architecture and icons characterize most Orthodox parishes, even in America. The most frequently used eucharistic rite is the Divine Liturgy of St. John Chrysostom, which is celebrated with a wealth of hymns and a profound sense of reverence.

Orthodox Christians believe that their church is "the One, Holy, Catholic, and Apostolic Church" (Nicene Creed) that was born on Pentecost (Acts 2) and that has remained true to the faith of the Apostles. They emphasize that of the five ancient patriarchates (Rome, Constantinople, Jerusalem, Alexandria, and Antioch), all except Rome continue as part of today's Orthodox Church. The division between Eastern Orthodoxy and Western Roman Catholicism is formally dated to 1054; however, historians note that Rome had been growing away from the four eastern patriarchates since at least the seventh century. The reasons for the Great Schism were multiple, including theological, political, and cultural dimensions. The 16th-century Protestant Reformation that further divided Western Christians occurred independently of the East and forged theological categories that highlighted the differences between Roman Catholics and Protestants but that were largely foreign to the Orthodox Church.

The jurisdictional multiplicity that marks its American presence reflects the fact that Orthodoxy arrived in the New World both through missionary efforts and through immigration. Missionary monks from Russia arrived on Alaska's Kodiak island in 1794, and by 1867, the year of Alaska's purchase by the United States, approximately 12,000 native Alaskans had become Orthodox Christians. After 1867, Alaskans were inundated by a devastating campaign of "Americanization." Sheldon Jackson, Alaska's newly appointed commissioner of education, sought to suppress the Orthodox Church and its affirmation of local Alaskan languages and culture, viewing it as subversive to American Protestant values.

At another corner of the continent, the first Greek immigrants arrived in 1762 in Florida. While these immigrants retained their religious identity, it was not until the last quarter of the 19th century that the first Orthodox parishes were established in the continental United States. As the numbers of Orthodox immigrants exploded during the first two decades of the 20th century, so did the number of parishes. Moreover, it seemed natural for the immigrants to organize along ethnic lines and to request clergy who spoke their mother tongue and who would help them preserve their homeland traditions. Thus, rather than uniting in pan-ethnic communities, the Greeks, Carpatho-Russians, Serbians, Arabs, Bulgarians, Romanians, Albanians, and Ukrainians formed separate parishes and established parallel jurisdictions in most major cities, in spite of their doctrinal unity.

During the 1930s and 1940s, America's Orthodox leaders began to acknowledge the problems that jurisdictional multiplicity posed and to work toward unity. Not only were parallel jurisdictions a violation of Orthodox canon law, but the lack of pan-Orthodox unity impeded the church's ability to contribute to American public life. During and after World War II, efforts to gain official and public recognition were intensified. Most jurisdictions joined the WORLD COUNCIL OF CHURCHES (WCC) and the NATIONAL COUNCIL OF CHURCHES (NCC). Greek Archbishop Athenagoras (Spirou) was featured on the cover of *Life* magazine in 1948, Archbishop Michael (Constantinides) participated in the 1957 presidential inauguration, and Archbishop Iakovos (Coucouzes) gained the nation's attention when he marched on Selma, Alabama, alongside MARTIN LUTHER KING JR. While significant progress has been made toward Orthodox unity in America, no resolution has yet been achieved. The Eastern Orthodox Church has become much more visible on America's public scene, however, and it has done so without lobbying groups or the official endorsement of particular policy issues.

See also MAINLINE PROTESTANT WASHINGTON OFFICES.

—Perry T. Hamalis

economic development

Religious organizations' involvement in community economic development (CED) stems from their location in disadvantaged communities and their theological and social mission to aid the poor. From the start of the CED movement in the 1960s, religious institutions have played critical roles. Congregations or involved clergy founded many of the earliest CED groups; today, some of the largest CED corporations have strong ties to neighborhood churches. President GEORGE W. BUSH has drawn attention to the work of religious groups in CED and other social service areas, although their involvement in implementation of government programs is longstanding. As his faith-based initiatives become formal federal programs, and as national advocates of CED offer increased technical assistance to congregations, it is likely that more religious organizations will take on CED work.

Community economic development involves building assets within low-income neighborhoods. The CED model empowers residents by engaging them in the planning and execution of neighborhood improvement. Initially a reaction to top-down urban renewal efforts, later supported by War on Poverty programs, the CED movement grew significantly during the 1980s, trying to fill the gap left by the federal government's retrenchment from social service provision and urban programs under President RONALD REAGAN. A recent survey found that congregations most likely to engage in services such as CED are large, African American, liberal, and located in needy neighborhoods. Commitment and leadership from clergy also play a key role. A common way that congregations become involved in CED is to found a separate organization affiliated with the church, a community development corporation (CDC). About 14 percent of CDCs (about 500) identify themselves as "faith-based organizations."

Faith-based CDCs work to build the commercial, residential, and financial infrastructure within their neighborhoods. There are numerous examples of successful economic development projects and programs. Newark, New Jersey's, New Community Corporation owns and operates a shopping center anchored by a Pathmark grocery store in Newark's Central Ward. This neighborhood had been without a grocery store for 20 years. Focus: Hope in Detroit operates a Machinist Training Institute for youth, and a job-training center in high-tech manufacturing. Concord Baptist Church in Brooklyn, New York, runs a credit union with $3 million in assets and a thousand members. First African Methodist Episcopal Church operates a micro-loan fund for minority entrepreneurs in South Central Los Angeles.

The impetus for religious groups to engage in CED is rooted in theology. Congregations and clergy may draw on lessons from the Ten Commandments and other biblical teachings about helping others, or about actions required to live a moral life, or they may be trying to "rescue lost souls"; they may feel obligated to work for social justice by engaging in socioeconomic reform efforts, in the tradition of MARTIN LUTHER KING JR. Advocates often say that faith-based support for CED brings a moral credibility to the political advocacy needed to sustain government attention to poor people and their neighborhoods.

While religious organizations have long engaged in CED, recent federal initiatives have raised their visibility and provided new resources. In 1997, the federal Department of Housing and Urban Development (HUD) established a Center for Community and Interfaith Partnerships to coordinate and intensify the involvement of faith-based groups in implementation of HUD programs, including housing and economic development. Under President George W. Bush, similar offices have been established in the Departments of Education, Health and Human Services, Justice, and Labor. He wants to expand the CHARITABLE CHOICE program enabling religious groups to provide government-funded social services, which was part of WELFARE REFORM in 1996. Trade associations for religious-based development organizations have formed, including the Christian Community Development Association. The National Congress for Community Economic Development started a Faith-Based Community Economic Development Program. Many foundations, including the Lilly Endowment and the Enterprise Foundation, have supported faith-based groups entering the field of CED.

Religious organizations that become involved in CED face a number of hurdles, including the difficulty of entering a complex field requiring technical expertise, the potential for business values to clash with social values, and the need for predevelopment funds that may take years to recoup. Participation in government programs may require a higher level of documentation and disclosure than religious groups are accustomed to, and rules may include practices with which religious groups disagree. To some critics, this represents unacceptable entanglement of the state in the operations of religious organizations, and they urge religious groups to decline government funds. Other critics fear that government support for faith-based initiatives is part of a shift in responsibility for helping poor neighborhoods from the state to the private sector. They worry that religious and other nonprofit organizations alone cannot address the social problems in urban centers. But many believe that faith-based groups doing CED are making important contributions to poor communities throughout the country.

See also HUNGER AND HUMANITARIAN AID; WHITE HOUSE OFFICE OF FAITH-BASED AND COMMUNITY INITIATIVES.

Further reading: National Congress for Community Economic Development website. URL: http://www.ncced.org; Thomas, June Manning, and Reynard N. Blake Jr. "Faith-based Community Development and African-American Neighborhoods." In W. Dennis Keating, Norman Krumholz, and Philip Star, eds. *Revitalizing Urban Neighborhoods.* Lawrence: University of Kansas Press, 1999; Vidal, Avis. "Faith-Based Organizations in Community Development." Prepared for U.S. Department of Housing and Urban Development, Office of Policy Development and Research, 2001.

—Mara S. Sidney

eco-theology

Eco-theology is a set of theological responses to the environmental crises of the modern world. In America, hints of eco-theology date back to the early 19th century, but it truly became a conscious theology in the 1960s and 1970s. The term generally refers to theologies that claim that the worth of nature has been ignored all too often by traditional theology. Eco-theologians have been inspired by reinterpretations of sacred scriptures, the CIVIL RIGHTS MOVEMENT and the feminist movement, and modern science.

The roots of American eco-theology can be found among the transcendentalists, specifically RALPH WALDO EMERSON and HENRY DAVID THOREAU, who argued for a renewed appreciation of nature in the face of growing industrialization. Emerson had a profound influence on John Muir, the founder of the Sierra Club and the first prominent fighter for the preservation of wilderness. Not only was Muir an activist, but he was also a religious person in the sense that he maintained that the forests and mountains of California were his churches and temples.

Before the 1960s, most of those arguing for explicit connections linking religion and theology with nature and ecology were outside the religious mainstream. In the 1960s, things began to change. With Rachel Carson's publication of *Silent Spring* in 1962, the environmental movement epitomized in the first Earth Day in 1970, and the growing awareness of the harmful effects of pollution, the state of the environment became a major concern for many. Lynn White's 1967 article "The Historical Roots of Our Ecologic Crisis," which blamed the state of the environment on an anthropocentric Christianity, sparked the creation of a Christian eco-theology, which, in many ways, was a response to White's challenge.

The most conservative eco-theology posits that humanity was given the unique responsibility of caring for nature, and that new interpretations of biblical scripture and reformulations of ecologically relevant elements within Christian history are sufficient in fulfilling this responsibility. H. Paul Santmire is one of the best-known proponents of this reclaiming of Christian sources for ecological renewal. Most environmentally aware Evangelical Protestants hold to this kind of eco-theology as well. Besides remaining wholly within Christianity, this form of eco-theology maintains the special uniqueness and responsibility that God has conferred on humans. Other forms of eco-theology claim that such a position is too anthropocentric, and they thus stress humanity's continuity with nature.

A less traditionally conservative eco-theology stems from process theology, a theological stance that issued from the early-20th-century process philosophy of Alfred Whitehead. Drawing on the advances in modern biology, ecology, and physics, process theology provides a more radical reinterpretation of Christian theology and a new framework in which to discuss humanity's impact on nature. Process theology holds that everything is in a continual process, and that God is himself a process that draws other processes to greater and greater levels of enjoyment. Process theologians, such as John Cobb, see process theology as providing the basis for greater sensitivity to the environment.

Other eco-theologies, though originating from a Christian background, are heavily indebted to other religions, as well as modern sciences. Thomas Berry argues that Christian responses to environmental changes must be heavily informed by modern science and non-Christian religions. Berry's central theme is the development of a new story to replace biblical creation stories, a tale describing the evolution of the universe from energy to humanity, a tale demonstrating humanity's continuity and essential equality with nature. The new story intends to show that people are intimate parts of nature and that humans must let this relationship inform their practical actions in the world. For Berry, the advantage of this new cosmic narrative derived from physics and biology is that, even though it may have similarities with the creation stories of many religions, it is not tied to any one religious tradition, and thus can be shared by people of any religion and no religion. A globally shared story, it is argued, will aid in the global response needed for saving the environment.

Other eco-theologians, such as Rosemary Radford Ruether and Sallie McFague, stem from the feminist camp. Just as accurately described as feminist theologians, they see their FEMINISM as having a direct impact on the environment; the claim is that the oppression of women is intimately related to the oppression and domination of nature, and that the liberation of either presupposes the liberation of the other. Likewise, liberation theologians link imperialism and colonialism to both the oppression of the poor and the destruction of ecosystems.

See also FEMINIST THEOLOGY; PANTHEISM; TRANSCENDENTALISM.

Further reading: White, Lynn, Jr. *"The Historical Roots of Our Ecologic Crisis." Science* 155 (1967): 1,203–1,207; Fowler, Robert Booth. *The Greening of Protestant Thought.* Chapel Hill: University of North Carolina Press, 1995.

—Eric L. Thomas

ecumenism

Ecumenism is a theological movement that promotes unity, either among Christian churches and denominations or, in a wider sense, among different religions worldwide. Unity is accomplished through intentional cooperation and dialogue. Ecumenism has been present in Christianity since the end of the Apostolic Age (27–98 C.E.), after which the shared experience of early Christian apostles and disciples no longer provided unity for the growing numbers of converts. There have been several major divisions since the Apostolic Age that have been countered with various ecumenical efforts. In the 20th century, significant formal developments grounded in ecumenism resulted in the creation of several international movements and councils.

Historically, the controversy over the doctrine of the Trinity in the fourth century, the separation of the Semitic churches in the fifth century, the separation of the church of Rome and the church of Constantinople in the 11th century, and the increasing fragmentation of the Western church since the 16th century all mark divisions that called for ecumenical efforts on the part of church leaders. In the 19th century, in response to a surge in religious fervor and the proliferation of Christian MISSIONARY work worldwide, Protestants began crossing denominational lines and forming interdenominational associations. In Britain, several organizations, such as the British and Foreign Bible Society (1804), the Young Men's Christian Association (1844), the Young Women's Christian Association (1854), and the Evangelical Alliance (1846), formed to promote Christian education, service, mission, and prayer. Ecumenical efforts were also evident in the United States, including those by the Episcopalian William Reed Huntington (1838–1918), who proposed the creation of a united American Church, and by the Methodist John Mott (1865–1955), who founded the World Student Christian Federation in 1895.

In the early 20th century, the World Missionary Conference at Edinburgh (1910), the International Missionary Council (1921), the Life and Work Movement (1925), and the Faith and Order Movement (1927) all worked toward international Christian unity and developed organizational networks that eventually contributed to the establishment of the WORLD COUNCIL OF CHURCHES in Amsterdam (1948). The World Council of Churches developed active programs and official positions on faith, mission, EVANGELISM, international relief work, interfaith dialogue, SOCIAL JUSTICE, and the status of historically oppressed groups, such as women and the poor. Resistant to modern ecumenical projects such as the World Council of Churches, the Vatican restricted the ROMAN CATHOLIC CHURCH's participation in ecumenical activities centered outside the Catholic Church until 1960, when Pope JOHN XXIII created the Secretariat for Promoting Christian Unity. Ecumenism was given further support and definition when VATICAN II was called in 1962, with the "Decree on Ecumenism" (*Unitatis Redintegratio*) being issued by Pope Paul VI in 1964, in which the restoration of unity among all Christians is stated as one of the principal concerns of the Second Vatican Council. Since Vatican II, the ecumenical movement in the Catholic Church has been supported through interfaith dialogues, interdenominational reconciliation, and formal statements.

Since the latter years of the 20th century, the trend in both Catholic and Protestant ecumenical efforts has been toward promoting unity among world religions and engaging in interreligious dialogue. The Catholic Church has created the Secretariat for the Promotion of the Unity of Christians, the Secretariat for Non-Christians, and the Secretariat for Unbelievers in the Roman Catholic Church, while the World Council of Churches has established the Sub-Unit for Dialogue with People of Living Faiths and Ideologies. To some extent, this wider ecumenism is a response to the process of globalization taking place in the economic, political, and social realms. Given the growing interdependency among nations, the development of mass communications, and the radically increased frequency with which people from different cultures engage in personal contact, ecumenism can be seen not only as a necessity for peaceful cohabitation but also as a means of addressing international issues such as mass poverty, conservation of global resources, and human rights. Although some resistance to ecumenism continues, a majority of both Protestants and Catholics have moved toward an ecumenical inclusivity and religious pluralism that parallels the global trend toward democracy in the political realm.

Further reading: Gros, Jeffrey. *That All May Be One: Ecumenism.* Chicago: Loyola University Press, 2001; Kessler, Diane, and Michael Kinnamon. *Councils of Churches and the Ecumenical Vision.* Geneva, Switz.: WCC Publications, 2000; Phan, Peter C. *Christianity and the Wider Ecumenism.* New York: Paragon House, 1990; Rusch, William G. *Ecumenism: A Movement toward Church Unity.* Philadelphia: Fortress Press, 1985.

—Lora L. Stone

Eddy, Mary Baker (1821–1910) *religious founder*

Mary Baker Eddy was born in Bow, New Hampshire, in 1821. She founded the movement known generally as CHRISTIAN SCIENCE, and formally as the Church of Christ (Scientist). Poor and of increasingly poor health as she entered middle age, Eddy became interested in Mind Cure techniques advocated by Phineas Parkhurst Quimby. However, she struck out on her own and in her own direction in 1866 when she fell on the ice in Lynn, Massachusetts, and then, according to her testimony, healed herself from a life-threatening back injury. From this time forward, she gradually developed a fully articulated religious system. In 1875, she and a small number of followers formally organized and took on the name Christian Scientists. That same year she published the first edition of *Science Health* that, along with the Bible, became the central scripture of the group. When she died in 1910, Eddy left a large and often contentious group of followers who looked to her as their charismatic leader and revelator of God's truth to the world.

Occasionally, within the context of her teachings, Eddy advocated for the rights of women or addressed a current political topic. For the most part, however, Eddy stayed away from the political issues of the day, and, in the last two decades of her life, she lived as a virtual recluse protected by a band of loyal followers from the physical and mental attacks of enemies. Eddy's central discovery was that the material, social, and, therefore, political worlds were at base misperceptions of reality. She claimed that God, or Mind, was the only true reality, and that through prayer and internal understanding human beings needed to advance to the point where they realized in the depth of their being the falseness of sickness, disease, and, more generally, the material world: "The chief stones in the temple of Christian Science are to be found in the following postulates: that life is God, good, and not evil; that Soul is sinless, not to be found in the body; that Spirit is not, and cannot be, materialized; that Life is not subject to death; that the spiritual real man has no birth, not material life, and no death." In this view, politics has only a provisional and temporary reality and usefulness as a tool for sustaining human life until a more general spiritual realization takes hold of individuals.

Though Eddy advocated and practiced disengagement with the issues and politics of the day, throughout her life as a religious leader, she was frequently and successfully involved in business affairs and legal cases. Most famously, in 1908, she founded the *Christian Science Monitor* to provide accurate and objective coverage of important events. The *Monitor* grew to be a highly respected newspaper that strove to observe and report the political and social events of the day. Eddy also sued and was sued by a number of disgruntled former students, friends, and family members. Probably the best-known case involved a group of relatives, including her son, who, in the last years of her life, attempted to gain control of her large fortune by claiming that she was senile and that her inner circle had undue influence over her. She triumphed in this case, as she had in many others, and in her refusal to back down, she presented to her followers the interesting case of a religious leader who advocated for the ultimate unreality of the legal and political realms, but who would fully and skillfully engage in these realms and on her adversaries' terms to protect her religious discovery and revelation for her present and future followers.

Mary Baker Eddy *(Library of Congress)*

Further reading: Eddy, Mary Baker. *Science and Health with a Key to the Scriptures.* Boston: Writings of Mary Baker Eddy, 2000.

—Susanna Morrill

Edwards, Jonathan (1703–1758) *theologian*

Jonathan Edwards was a Congregational minister and distinguished theologian, born in East Windsor, Connecticut. He rose to prominence as a key figure in the evangelical movement that arose from the FIRST GREAT AWAKENING. As a spokesman for moderate EVANGELICALISM, Edwards left a legacy that was most pronounced in his efforts to defend the authentic aspect of REVIVALISM against its rationalist critics. Edwards wrote a number of influential theological treatises, culminating in *Dissertation Concerning the Nature of True Virtue* (1765), which sought to defend an evangelical CALVINISM against the secularism of 18th-century thought. Rejecting earlier interpretations of this work as a defense of an antiquarian orthodoxy, recent scholarship has convincingly argued that it is better understood as a sophisticated effort to incorporate aspects of philosophical rationalism into a Calvinist framework. In this aspect, Edwards's work can be understood as bridging traditional Protestant doctrine with the philosophical rationalism of 17th- and 18th-century thought.

The son of Reverend Timothy Edwards and Esther Stoddard, daughter of the Reverend Solomon Stoddard of Northampton, Massachusetts, Edwards was born into a family of distinguished religious tradition in New England. Initially educated in his father's East Windsor parsonage, he entered the fledgling Yale College at the age of 12. Studying under Rector Timothy Cutler, Edwards graduated at the top of his class in 1720. After brief pastoral experience in New York City and Bolton, Connecticut, Edwards returned to Yale in 1724 to take up a position as a tutor. Edwards left Yale in 1726 to be co-pastor and presumptive successor to his grandfather Solomon Stoddard in Northampton. His 25-year tenure at Northampton was a formative experience for the young minister, marked by periods of disillusionment and enthusiasm. Disappointed by the moral lethargy he encountered at Northampton, Edwards made efforts to renew the spiritual energy of parishioners. He developed a hard-hitting sermon style that combined a stark vision of human depravity with

Jonathan Edwards *(Library of Congress)*

the exhilarating potential of salvation by simple faith. In *A Faithful Narrative of Surprising Conversions* (1737), Edwards documented how in the winter of 1734–35 his preaching had triggered a spiritual revival in the community. Seeking to revive this religious spirit, Edwards invited a number of itinerant preachers, including GEORGE WHITEFIELD, to Northampton in 1740–41. The revival frenzy unleashed in the course of this second wave of the First Great Awakening saw Edwards become a principal spokesman for evangelicalism. Distancing himself from the "excesses" of some elements of the revivals, Edwards sought in *The Distinguishing Marks of a Work of the Spirit of God* (1741), *Some Thoughts Concerning the Present Revival of Religion* (1742), and the *Treatise Concerning Religious Affections* (1746) to defend evangelicalism publicly against criticisms leveled against it.

Disappointed at the fleeting nature of these revivals of piety, Edwards decided in 1748 to dispose of an ecclesiastical compromise that had been made famous by his grandfather: the Stoddardean "Halfway-Covenant." Edwards considered this system, whereby intellectual assent to Christian doctrine sufficed for membership, far too lax and requested the imposition of a stricter standard. Edwards's position aroused considerable opposition. The parishioners rejected his request, and in 1750 he was dismissed as pastor. Edwards left Northampton the following year to take up a position as a missionary to Native Americans and pastor to the small European settlement at Stockbridge, on the western border of Massachusetts. His six-year stay at this frontier settlement provided Edwards with an opportunity to undertake his most sophisticated theoretical endeavors. These efforts produced his greatest theological treatises, including, *A Careful and Strict Enquiry into the Modern Prevailing Notions of That Freedom of Will* (1754) and *The Great Christian Doctrine of Original Sin Defended* (1758). All these works sought to defend traditional Reformed doctrine against the optimistic theories of human agency presented by the Arminian "liberal" challenge. To this end, he defended the Calvinist interpretation of original sin and demonstrated the rationality of God's determination of human will. Edwards achieved his most sophisticated theological statement, however, in his posthumously published *Dissertation Concerning the Nature of True Virtue* (1765). While Edwards delineated the limitations of natural morality, he also introduced into the Calvinist scheme a rational theology in which humans in the natural world were part of a divinely sanctioned moral order. By accepting that natural man was furnished with a moral competency in this way, Edwards incorporated a fundamental tenet of the agenda of his "liberal" adversaries even while he upheld a traditional soteriology.

Further reading: Cherry, Conrad. *Jonathan Edwards: A Reappraisal.* Garden City, N.Y.: Doubleday, 1966; Fiering, Norman. *Jonathan Edwards's Moral Thought and Its British Context.* Chapel Hill: University of North Carolina Press, 1981; Miller, Perry. *Jonathan Edwards.* Amherst: University of Massachusetts Press, 1949; Ramsey, Paul. *Jonathan Edwards'*

Ethical Writings. New Haven, Conn.: Yale University Press, 1989; Wilson, John F. "Jonathan Edwards as Historian." *Church History* 46 (1977): 5–18.

—Roland Marden

Edwards v. Aguillard 482 U.S. 578 (1987)

On June 19, 1987, the Supreme Court found Louisiana's Balanced Treatment for Creation-Science and Evolution-Science in Public Instruction Act in violation of the ESTABLISHMENT CLAUSE of the First Amendment. The 7-2 majority concluded that the act, which forbade the teaching of evolution unless taught in conjunction with creation science, had no legitimate secular purpose. Rather, the act was intended to structure the curriculum of the state's public schools to further a particular religious doctrine. This decision supported an earlier ruling in EPPERSON V. ARKANSAS (1968), which rejected Arkansas's attempt to ban the teaching of evolution in public schools altogether.

The act, also known as the Creationism Act, was challenged by parents, teachers, and religious leaders in Louisiana, seeking an injunction and declaratory relief. They charged that the act was invalid because it violated the establishment clause. Louisiana officials responded by arguing that the act had a legitimate secular purpose in protecting academic freedom. Neither the District Court nor the Court of Appeals found merit in the latter argument; both sided with the appellants.

The Supreme Court relied on the test laid out in LEMON V. KURTZMAN in coming to its decision. According to *Lemon*, if a statute or action is to pass constitutional muster, it must have a secular legislative purpose, its primary effect must neither inhibit nor advance religion, and it must not foster excessive government entanglement. The Court found that the Creationism Act evinced no clear secular purpose.

Louisiana's stated purpose for its act was to protect academic freedom. Justice WILLIAM BRENNAN, writing for the majority, exhibited skepticism of this intent when he wrote, "While the Court is normally deferential to a State's articulation of a secular purpose, it is required that the statement of such purpose be sincere and not a sham." As he explained, requiring schools to teach creation science alongside evolution did not serve to advance academic freedom. There were no laws on record prohibiting Louisiana's public school teachers from teaching any scientific theory, and the Creationism Act granted teachers no authority that they did not already possess.

Furthermore, the act's clear preference for the teaching of creation science contradicted its stated intent. Evidence of this preference can be found in the act's specification that curriculum guides be developed for creation science but not for evolution, and by the presence of antidiscrimination policies for the benefit of teachers teaching creation science in exclusion of those teaching other scientific theories.

This information, along with the act's legislative history, led the Court to the conclusion that its intended purpose differed significantly from its stated purpose of protecting academic freedom.

As Justice Brennan wrote:

The preeminent purpose of the Louisiana Legislature was clearly to advance the religious viewpoint that a supernatural being created humankind . . . the Creationism Act is designed either to promote the theory of creation science which embodies a particular religious tenet by requiring that creation science be taught whenever evolution is taught or to prohibit the teaching of a scientific theory disfavored by certain religious sects by forbidding the teaching of evolution when creation science is not also taught.

While Arkansas lawmakers attempted to ban the teaching of evolution entirely in *Epperson*, those in *Edwards*, having that avenue closed to them, attempted to discredit the theory by mandating that it be presented accompanied by their preferred account. Their efforts also failed, however, as the Supreme Court found the Creationism Act, having no secular purpose, to be in violation of the establishment clause.

Justices Powell and O'Connor concurred with the majority opinion, while emphasizing that the Court's decision in no way diminished the discretion of public school boards to select their own curriculum. Justices ANTONIN SCALIA and William Rehnquist dissented, objecting to the use of *Lemon*'s purpose test, while at the same time arguing that the Creationism Act did in fact have a secular purpose. They found such a secular purpose in the idea that "creation science is a body of scientific evidence rather than a revealed belief."

—Steven C. Leidinger

Eisenhower, Dwight D. (1890–1969) *U.S. president*

Dwight D. Eisenhower was born in Abilene, Kansas, and served as 34th president of the United States (1953–60). Eisenhower was a career military officer whose service as Supreme Allied Commander in Europe during World War II, which included planning the successful D-Day invasion of German-occupied France, brought him international fame and political success. As president, he was associated with an ANTICOMMUNIST foreign policy, budgetary restraint, national prosperity, and promotion of public religion.

Eisenhower's personal faith was shaped by his background and career. His family included JEHOVAH'S WITNESSES and a small MENNONITE sect known as the River Brethren. For most of his adult life, however, he had no formal church affiliation. During his army years, he attended nondenominational worship services and worked with chaplains of all three major faiths. These experiences helped develop in him both a commitment to the importance of religious faith in society and an acceptance of American religious pluralism. In 1948, for example, he declared that he was an intensively religious man, but added that such faith did not mean he hewed to any particular sect. In a widely reprinted statement, he proclaimed, "I believe in democracy." After becoming president he was baptized into the PRESBYTERIAN CHURCH. Thereafter, he was a regular churchgoer, usually attending the National Presbyterian Church in Washington. Upon retiring from politics, he joined the Gettysburg Presbyterian Church, where he worshiped regularly until his death.

As president, Eisenhower made several efforts to show respect for religion and promote its public expression in national life. He began his first inaugural address with a prayer asking "Almighty God" to "make full and complete our dedication to the service of the people in this throng, and their fellow citizens everywhere." These words reflected Eisenhower's linkage of patriotism and faith, and he prayed, "May cooperation be permitted and be the mutual aim of those who, under the concepts of our Constitution, hold to differing political faiths; so that all may work for the good of our beloved country and Thy glory. Amen."

Eisenhower identified himself with religious faith and public acts of religion. He began holding annual Presidential Prayer Breakfasts in 1953, a tradition that continues at the White House today (as the National Prayer Breakfast). With his encouragement, Congress added the phrase "under God" to the Pledge of Allegiance. Eisenhower also proclaimed national days of prayer, and his public statements often contained a religious dimension. In his 1954 State of the Union Address, he proclaimed that the people of the United States "have always reserved their first allegiance to the kingdom of the spirit." During his reelection campaign in 1956, billboards in California told voters that "Faith in God and Country; that's Eisenhower—how about you?" At a news conference the following year, he returned to one of his favorite themes: the link between democratic liberty and religious faith. He told the assembled reporters: "I believe all forms of free government are based either knowingly or unknowingly on deeply held religious convictions" and that religion teaches the equality of all people under "a common Creator."

Eisenhower's public piety was more general than specifically Protestant, as had been Woodrow Wilson's faith. His expressions of faith were well received by the public but did engender criticism. Eisenhower once remarked that "America makes no sense without a deeply held faith in God—and I don't care what it is." The comment neatly summarized his views: he saw faith as essential to American democracy but respected the country's religious pluralism. However, critics took the statement as proof of the president's intellectual blandness. Those who supported public expressions of religion at times regarded Eisenhower's religiosity as too shallow. They noted that after he had issued one declaration of a day of prayer, the president went out to play golf.

Eisenhower's generic expressions of support for religion seemed like thin gruel to many in his time who wanted more forceful exhibitions of public faith. From the perspective of the 21st century, however, his frequent statements about God and religion are stronger than most American politicians make. In retrospect, his generalized promotion of religion helped ease the transition from a Protestant-specific American

CIVIL RELIGION to one more accepting of the fact of religious pluralism. However subtly, Eisenhower's support for faith in general may have helped make it possible for his successor to be ROMAN CATHOLIC, and for politicians of other faiths to be considered candidates for national public office.

See also JOHN F. KENNEDY.

—Ryan Barilleaux

Ely, Richard T. (1854–1943) *scholar*

Richard T. Ely was born in New York State, attended Dartmouth College and Columbia University, and did graduate work at Halle and Heidelberg, where he received a Ph.D. Along with HENRY CARTER ADAMS, John Bates Clark, Simon Patten, and others, Ely was one of the founders of the economics profession, serving as the first secretary to the American Economics Association (AEA, 1885–92) and then, in 1900, as its president. As professor at Johns Hopkins (1881–92) and the University of Wisconsin (1892–1925) and author of two leading economics textbooks, Ely shaped the teaching of economics and the training of its professorate for almost half a century.

More active in political and social reform than most of his academic peers, Ely, along with his colleague John R. Commons, was the leading light of the "Wisconsin Idea," which linked the university with progressive reform. Through two popular books published in 1912, one by his student Frederic C. Howe, and another by his colleague and disciple Charles McCarthy (with a glowing introduction by THEODORE ROOSEVELT), Ely became enshrined as a leading public figure in American progressivism, writing extensively in popular weeklies and monthlies on issues of the day.

Permeating Ely's economic writings and reform activities was a deep commitment to the ideals of social Christianity. His first textbooks on economics were written as much for lay Christians and divinity students as for undergraduate university courses, and were used equally in sociology and economics departments. For Ely, economics was an ethical as well as an academic discipline, combining historical, sociological, and psychological elements in the study of the spiritual evolution of humans through their material life. Like Adams and other founders of the AEA (almost half of whom were liberal Evangelical Protestant clergymen), he thought economists should provide guidance to the state so that ethical principles would permeate all economic relationships.

Always active in church-related social reform bodies in America and England, he was the leading intellectual spokesman for what was first termed "Christian socialism" and later came to be called "Christian sociology," with its strong support of labor unions and activist legislation seeking justice for industrial laborers. Given his association with labor leaders and his public support for major strikes, Ely was often the object of controversy. A failed attempt to have him fired at Wisconsin early in his tenure resulted in one of the landmark events in the history of academic freedom.

See also LIBERALISM; SOCIAL GOSPEL; SOCIAL JUSTICE.

Further reading: Crunden, Robert M. *Ministers of Reform: The Progressives' Achievement in American Civilization 1889–1920.* Urbana: University of Illinois Press, 1984; Eisenach, Eldon. *The Lost Promise of Progressivism.* Lawrence: University Press of Kansas, 1994; Rader, Benjamin G. *The Academic Mind and Reform: The Influence of Richard T. Ely in American Life.* Lexington: University of Kentucky Press, 1966.

—Eldon J. Eisenach

Emerson, Ralph Waldo (1803–1882) *writer*

Ralph Waldo Emerson, essayist and poet, was the leading voice of TRANSCENDENTALISM. Although he began his career in 1829 as a Unitarian pastor in Boston, Emerson resigned his position in 1832. By this time, he had become increasingly uncomfortable with many Christian teachings and was developing a new philosophy founded on radical individualism and personal religious vision. The writings that first gained Emerson widespread fame were *Nature,* published anonymously in 1836, and his address to the Harvard Divinity School graduating class of 1838, but he is best remembered today for "Self-Reliance" (1841).

Emerson's ideas marked a radical break with most religious teachings and philosophic schools of his day. He rejected both traditional Christian doctrine, such as the historicity of biblical miracles, and the dominant secular teachings concerning human moral knowledge, such as moral rationalism. In their place, Emerson erected a philosophy founded on intuition. Moral rationalists, influenced by JOHN LOCKE's sensationist psychology, turned to empirical experience of the external world as the basis of all knowledge. They believed that through careful study of sensory experiences, human beings could discern immutable laws of the universe that would provide a foundation for moral reasoning. Rejecting this, Emerson taught that the key to true understanding rests within each individual. To Emerson, the human mind is itself divine, part of the singular ultimate reality, the Oversoul. To understand the truth of things, we must perceive this divinity within ourselves, a divinity that exists independently of any historical circumstances or religious institutions. The divine must be perceived directly through intuition, and not indirectly through the mediated influence of church, priest, or dogma.

At the center of Emerson's social and ethical thought was the autonomous individual, and his great ethical imperative was always to protect this individual's autonomy from outside influences. This emphasis comes through forcefully in his famous essay "Self-Reliance." Emerson wrote: "Society is a joint-stock company, in which the members agree, for the better securing of his bread to each shareholder, to surrender the liberty and culture of the eater. The virtue in most request is conformity." "Self-Reliance" was a call for the reassertion of individual autonomy against social demands for conformity. If as individuals we desire to recapture the divine within our hearts, then

Ralph Waldo Emerson *(Library of Congress)*

we must trust in and assert our own insights and principles. Few ever do so, since society's demand for conformity is so powerful. Most civilized human beings turn away from everything that is true within and allow the outside world to define their life and work. They become cowardly, dependent creatures—dependent on society, from which they try to derive meaning, dependent on physical property, in which they find the stability they lack within, and dependent on government, which protects and maintains both society and property.

While this plea for individual autonomy has obvious implications for democratic thought, Emerson was surprisingly conservative on contemporary social issues. Although he eventually became a more ardent supporter of abolitionism, Emerson was pessimistic about most social reform movements, believing that the efforts of the wise usually are better turned inward. In "Self-Reliance," he derided efforts "to put all poor men in good situations" and to see to "the education at college of fools." And Emerson harbored few hopes for enlightened government. He understood the DECLARATION OF INDEPENDENCE's ideals as promising a land that would protect individual autonomy, but Emerson was no egalitarian. He concluded that while some would become truly wise through perception of the "only reality" of which all physical things are mere reflections, many more would live out their lives in pursuit of lower objects, such as wealth and physical health. Since the masses lack trustworthy perception, democracies will be prone to elevating individuals to stations higher than they merit. As a result, democratic government always will be flawed and corrupt. A corrupt or abusive government cannot be reformed unless the people's character is reformed; however, character is reformed not by social movements but by inner truth. A good government is thus the government that makes it possible for wisdom to develop, and once the wise emerge, the state has little purpose. For Emerson, the proper response to social corruption was not renewed dedication to reform society but a renewed commitment to live independently of society.

See also THOREAU, HENRY DAVID.

Further reading: Beitzinger, Alfons. J. *A History of American Political Thought.* New York: Dodd, Mead, 1972; Emerson, Ralph Waldo. *Emerson's Complete Works.* Boston: Houghton Mifflin, 1921; Rusk, Ralph L. *The Life of Ralph Waldo Emerson.* New York: Charles Scribner's Sons, 1949.

—James Paul Old

Employment Division, Department of Human Resources of Oregon v. Smith 494 U.S. 872 (1990)

Employment Division v. Smith (1990) is among the most controversial religious freedom cases decided by the Supreme Court in the latter half of the 20th century. The case concerned two employees of a drug rehabilitation clinic, both members of the Native American Church, who were fired from their jobs for using peyote—a hallucinogenic drug classified as Schedule I by the Federal Controlled Substances Act—for sacramental purposes at a church ceremony. The two filed for unemployment compensation but were denied since they had been terminated for "work-related misconduct." The Oregon Court of Appeals reversed the unemployment board's decision, ruling instead that the denial of benefits to persons discharged because of conduct related to their religion was a denial of the FREE EXERCISE CLAUSE of the First Amendment.

The Supreme Court first agreed to consider the dispute in 1987. Upon review, the Court remanded the case to the Oregon Supreme Court to clarify whether state laws prohibited the use of peyote for religious purposes. The state court held that Oregon drug laws made no exception for sacramental use of peyote, but it reaffirmed its earlier decision that these laws violated the Free Exercise Clause. State officials appealed again to the U.S. Supreme Court, which granted review a second time.

Justice ANTONIN SCALIA announced the Court's decision. The majority opinion held that the state's interest in preventing abuses of its unemployment insurance fund was sufficiently important to justify its denial of benefits to Native Americans. In reaching this conclusion, the Court

argued that "if prohibiting the exercise of religion . . . is . . . merely the incidental effect of a generally applicable and otherwise valid provision, the First Amendment has not been offended." While the Court noted that a legislature could choose to make religious practices exempt from a generally applicable law, it added that the Constitution does not *require* a legislature to do so. Since Oregon's drug laws applied to everyone and did not target the religious rituals of Native Americans directly, the "incidental" burden on their free exercise was constitutional.

Justice Sandra Day O'Connor filed a separate opinion, part of which was joined by Justices WILLIAM BRENNAN, Thurgood Marshall, and Harry Blackmun, in which she argued that the Court should continue to use the compelling interest test. She argued that such an analysis produces the same outcome as that the majority reached in *Smith.* Brennan, Marshall, and Blackmun did not find a compelling governmental interest here and so found the law to be an unconstitutional infringement of the petitioners' free exercise guarantees.

The Court had been most likely to grant religious exemptions under the compelling interest doctrine when the religious practice at stake affected relatively few people. In cases where the claims of a minority religion might lead to greater costs for the state—for example, the AMISH's claim to an exemption from paying social security taxes, which the Court denied in *UNITED STATES V. LEE* (1982)—the Court usually declared the state's interest "compelling" when proscribing religious activity. Nevertheless, First Amendment advocates saw the compelling interest doctrine as a strong protection against state encroachments on religious practices. In contrast, the *Smith* Court seemed to reaffirm the so-called belief-action distinction first introduced in *REYNOLDS V. UNITED STATES,* a case decided in 1879 that upheld a congressional ban on the Mormon practice of POLYGAMY in Utah territories. In *Reynolds,* the Court held that though government could not punish religious *belief,* it could regulate religiously motivated *actions* that threaten "peace and good order."

Smith was widely interpreted as an abandonment of a legal doctrine forged in a series of cases dating to the early 1960s. In *SHERBERT V. VERNER* (1963), the Court applied a "strict scrutiny" test that forbade the government from burdening religious practices unless it has a "compelling interest" and used the least intrusive means in pursuing that interest. Previous cases had also rejected the *Smith* majority's argument that incidental effects were presumptively constitutional. As Chief Justice Warren Burger argued in *WISCONSIN V. YODER* (1972), "a regulation neutral on its face may, in its application, nonetheless offend the constitutional requirement for governmental neutrality if it unduly burdens the free exercise of religion."

According to the Court, its earlier decisions regarding unemployment benefits for those fired for refusal to engage in certain behaviors because of religious objection (*Sherbert; THOMAS V. REVIEW BOARD OF INDIANA EMPLOYMENT SECURITY DIVISION; HOBBIE V. UNEMPLOYMENT APPEALS COMMISSION OF*

FLORIDA) are distinguishable from this case, because the behavior in question in the other cases (not working on Saturday, for example) were not illegal actions. Here, the Court says, the petitioner is seeking exemption, or to be put "beyond the reach of a criminal law that is not specifically directed at their religious practice" because of its effect on their free exercise of religion. However, a law with a valid purpose that incidentally affects religious exercise is not unconstitutional. The Oregon law did not seek to undermine the Native American Church; it was a generally applicable law aimed at drug use. The Court declined to determine whether or not the government had, in this case, a compelling governmental interest—deeming that requirement "benign."

At the time of the *Smith* decision, most observers had come to view the compelling state interest test as settled doctrine, and *Smith* caught them off guard. Within two years, however, organized groups had developed a broad-based coalition that sought a legislative remedy to the *Smith* decision. The result of their pressure was the RELIGIOUS FREEDOM RESTORATION ACT of 1993 (RFRA), congressional legislation (HR 1308) that attempted to forestall *Smith*'s effects by restoring the compelling state interest doctrine, which President WILLIAM JEFFERSON CLINTON signed into law. But the Supreme Court ultimately struck down RFRA in *BOERNE, CITY OF V. FLORES* (1997), arguing that the separation-of-powers doctrine gives the Court the authority to decide what the Free Exercise Clause means. At present, the coalition is pushing a new law (the Religious Liberty Protection Act) that seeks to alleviate the separation-of-power concern by grounding the legislation in Congress's power to regulate interstate commerce.

Further reading: McConnell, Michael. "Free Exercise Revisionism and the *Smith* Decision." *University of Chicago Law Review* 57 (1990): 1109.

—Sara C. Benesh and Kevin R. den Dulk

Engel v. Vitale 370 U.S. 421 (1962)

On June 25, 1962, the Supreme Court handed down its decision in what would become the first in a long string of controversial cases involving PRAYER IN PUBLIC SCHOOLS. In *Engel v. Vitale*, the Court found New York's practice of using its public school system to encourage the recitation of the Regents' prayer to be a violation of the ESTABLISHMENT CLAUSE, as it applied to the state by way of the FOURTEENTH AMENDMENT. The 8-1 majority, led by Justice Hugo Black, let it be known that the nondenominational and voluntary nature of the prayer was wholly irrelevant and the practice amounted to state sponsorship of religion.

Union Free School District No. 9, New Hyde Park, New York, acting in accordance with the dictates of its school board and the recommendation of the State Board of Regents, provided for the recitation of the following prayer at the beginning of each school day: "Almighty God, we acknowledge our dependence upon Thee, and we beg Thy blessings upon us,

our parents, our teachers and our Country." The prayer, formulated by the state's governing educational body, was intended to instill moral and spiritual values in its students.

Shortly after the school district adopted this practice, the parents of 10 students went to court seeking an injunction on the grounds that both the state law authorizing the prayer, and the school board's order to comply, violated the Establishment Clause of the First Amendment to the Constitution. The New York Court of Appeals upheld the decision of a lower court, agreeing that the recitation of the Regents' prayer did not amount to an establishment of religion owing to its nondenominational character and the fact that students were not strictly compelled to participate.

The U.S. Supreme Court's more separationist view of the establishment clause led to a much different conclusion, and ultimately a reversal of the New York Court of Appeals. Relying heavily on an analysis of the nation's religious history, and an assessment of the founders' intent in authoring the religious clauses of the Constitution, the majority firmly established the government's proper role respective to prayer.

As Justice Black wrote:

> We think that the constitutional prohibition against laws respecting an establishment of religion must at least mean that in this country it is no part of the business of government to compose official prayers for any group of the American people to recite as a part of a religious program carried on by government.

Furthermore, the Court found no merit in the Court of Appeals's assessment that the nondenominational nature of the prayer, or the fact that students could abstain from participating in prayer, rendered the practice any more legitimate. Rather, the Court specifically addressed the shortcomings of this argument:

> Neither the fact that the prayer may be denominationally neutral nor the fact that its observance on the part of the students is voluntary can serve to free it from the limitations of the Establishment Clause. . . . when the power, prestige, and financial support of government is placed behind a particular religious belief, the indirect coercive pressure upon religious minorities is plain.

With its decision, the Supreme Court struck a blow to proponents of school prayer, and *Engel* would prove to be groundbreaking in this respect. For the first time in history, the Court had addressed the issue of prayer in public schools, and its message was resoundingly clear: public education and organized prayer are not to mingle. What is more, the Court's firm stand left few avenues by which to circumvent its ruling. Despite this fact, proponents of school prayer continue to search for a way to combine prayer and public schooling. Their efforts, marked by a long trail of case law, have yet to overturn *Engel*.

In writing for the majority, Justice Black recognized the controversial nature of the Court's decision, which generated considerable public uproar. He was careful to point out that the establishment clause was not intended to handicap religion, but to protect its integrity and the religious freedoms of all Americans. In doing so, he acknowledged that New York's establishment of its Regents' prayer, while not an establishment of a particular sect at the expense of all others, was a dangerous, albeit small, step in that direction. He closed the Court's decision with a quote from James Madison's *Memorial and Remonstrance*. "It is proper to take alarm at the first experiment on our liberties." This attitude has set the tone for cases involving school prayer.

See also CONSERVATIVE CHRISTIAN LITIGATORS.

—Steven C. Leidinger

Episcopal Church, USA

Most Episcopalians belong to the Episcopal Church, USA, a mainline Protestant denomination and the U.S. counterpart of the Church of England. In the 1990s, Episcopalians comprised 2 percent of the U.S. population, with a 44 percent membership drop between 1966 and 1996. In 1991, the median household income of Episcopalians was $33,000, behind only Jews, UNITARIAN-UNIVERSALISTS, and agnostics. Most vote Republican; politically, the church in recent decades has been categorized as liberal, which has often put its leadership at odds with its parishioners.

In Colonial America, the Church of England was the established church in several colonies. During the Revolution, its American clergy generally supported the Tories, while many laity supported independence. In 1789, the Episcopal Church in the United States was reconstituted as an independent church. Episcopalians generally gravitated toward the Federalist Party during America's early party alignments.

The church remained conservative during the 19th century, never becoming very active in the slavery controversy, and easily regrouping after the Civil War because of the ambivalent stance maintained by its leaders. Yet by the time of the Great Depression of the early 1930s, it had developed a SOCIAL GOSPEL contingent that advocated sweeping social reforms and has continued to make its presence felt.

To be an Episcopalian has often meant respectability, wealth, or upward mobility. Many elites in American business and politics have been products of Episcopal schools and social networks. While the political interest of many Episcopalians has been protection of wealth, the denomination has included elements committed to public service and political activism.

Episcopalians were visibly active in the CIVIL RIGHTS MOVEMENT in the 1950s and 1960s. High-ranking church leaders, clergy, and laity spoke out, marched, and engaged in CIVIL DISOBEDIENCE. Church leaders passed resolutions condemning segregation and established a civil rights fund. In the late 1960s, the church appropriated money to aid African-American groups seeking "black economic and political power." These policies were controversial within the church, and the church was not always consistent or coordinated in its pursuit of them. At least in part, the church's membership drop has been attributed to its commitment to political and social activism, including some well-publicized incidents of "helping revolution." Sensationalized media stories about church support for radical causes caused tension between local parishes and the national church, and was a factor in the church's internal political struggles. Recent political causes, such as debt relief for poor countries, continue to reflect a liberal "peace and justice" position, while the church has taken a centrist stance on public funding for "faith-based" social services.

The Episcopal Church established a small lobbying office in Washington, D.C., in 1979, located close to other liberal church offices and the Capitol. It represents the church's leadership, not the more conservative laity. However, it maintains an issue alert system to inform interested laity of legislative activities. Too small to engage alone in effective lobbying, it often coordinates with other mainline denominations.

Historically the Episcopal Church has been overrepresented in the White House and Congress relative to its strength in the population. But its numbers in Congress have declined in recent years. Finally, the Episcopal Church has contributed to the development of American CIVIL RELIGION by building the National Cathedral in Washington, D.C., sometimes called the "semi-official church of America," and St. John's Church near the White House, known as "the Church of the Presidents."

See also ABOLITIONIST MOVEMENT; *GATHERING STORM IN THE CHURCHES, THE;* SECTIONAL DIVIDE OF THE CHURCHES OVER SLAVERY; WHITE HOUSE OFFICE OF FAITH-BASED AND COMMUNITY INITIATIVES.

Further reading: Fowler, Robert Booth, Allen D. Hertzke, and Laura R. Olson. *Religion and Politics in America.* 2d ed. Boulder, Colo.: Westview Press, 1999; Hofrenning, Daniel J. B. *In Washington but Not of It.* Philadelphia: Temple University Press, 1995; Konolige, Kit, and Frederica Konolige. *The Power of Their Glory.* New York: Wyden Books, 1978; Reeves, Thomas C. *The Empty Church.* New York: Touchstone, 1998; Reichley, A. James. *Religion in American Public Life.* Washington, D.C.: Brookings Institution, 1985; Shattuck, Gardiner H., Jr. *Episcopalians and Race: Civil War to Civil Rights.* Lexington: University Press of Kentucky, 2000; Episcopal Church, USA on the Web. URL: http://www.episcopalchurch.org.

—Jane Gurganus Rainey

Epperson et al. v. Arkansas 393 U.S. 97 (1968)

A 10th-grade biology teacher's claim that an Arkansas "anti-evolution" statute was unconstitutional was affirmed by the U.S. Supreme Court in a unanimous decision rendered on November 12, 1968. Speaking for the Court, Justice Fortas applied the purpose and effect test set forth in *ABINGTON V. SCHEMPP* (1963), and concluded that the statute violated the First Amendment's ESTABLISHMENT CLAUSE requirement of strict neutrality.

Arkansas voters had adopted a "monkey law" in 1928, making it unlawful for teachers "to teach the theory or doctrine that mankind ascended or descended from a lower order of animals" or for state-supported schools or universities "to adopt or use in any such institution a textbook that teaches" this theory. A similar law had precipitated the celebrated 1927 SCOPES "MONKEY" TRIAL in Tennessee. In 1965, a public school teacher at Central High in Little Rock faced the dilemma of either refusing to use a newly adopted textbook or teaching from a text containing a chapter on Darwinian evolution. Both alternatives raised the prospect of her dismissal.

The teacher, Susan Epperson, sought a declaration voiding the statute and an injunction preventing her dismissal for violating its provisions. Overturning a lower court judgment, the Arkansas Supreme Court concluded the state had acted within its "power to specify the curriculum in its public schools." On appeal, the U.S. Supreme Court acknowledged that states have the authority to prescribe school curriculum but insisted that authority does not supersede constitutional guarantees to freedom of speech and religion.

Although agreeing with the appellant's contention that the statute was unconstitutionally vague, the Court overturned it on the ground that it violated the establishment clause requirement of strict neutrality in matters involving religion, *EVERSON V. BOARD OF EDUCATION* (1947). According to *Everson*, the First Amendment requires the state to practice strict neutrality among religions and between religion and irreligion. The Court found that the Arkansas statute violated this principle because it "selects from the body of knowledge a particular segment which it proscribes for the sole reason that it is deemed to conflict with a particular religious doctrine; that is, with a particular interpretation of the Book of Genesis by a particular religious group." Protecting the majority's religious beliefs from a nonreligious viewpoint did not constitute neutrality.

The Court used the purpose and effect test set forth in *Abington* to nullify the statute. According to this test, if a law had the primary purpose or effect of advancing or restricting religion, it was null and void. In *Epperson*, the Court said, "It is clear that fundamentalist sectarian conviction was and is the law's reason for existence." The effect of the statute advanced religion by excluding from the classroom a theory that might undermine religious teaching. The Court insisted the Constitution "forbids alike the preference of a religious doctrine or the prohibition of theory which is deemed antagonistic to a particular dogma." The law, deemed to fail both prongs of the purpose and effect test, thus violated the establishment clause as applied to the states under the FOURTEENTH AMENDMENT.

Justice Black concurred with the judgment but questioned whether the case presented a justiciable case or controversy. The state had never attempted to enforce the law, nor was there a controversy after the textbook's adoption. Black reluctantly agreed to strike down the law because of vagueness: "a teacher cannot know whether he is forbidden to mention Darwin's theory at all or only free to discuss it as long as he refrains from contending that it is true." Black objected to the majority's "sweeping" invalidation of the statute under the establishment clause for three reasons: it was impossible to ascertain the motives of the voters adopting the measure; it was possible the Court's action violated strict neutrality by advancing irreligion; and "academic freedom" did not necessarily allow teachers to break their contractual obligations.

Justice Harlan concurred with the majority but wanted the Court's rationale restricted to the statute's violation of the establishment clause. He contended that the Court unnecessarily clouded the issue by addressing vagueness and freedom of speech. Conversely, Justice Stewart's concurrence argued that the Court should have based its reasoning solely on the grounds of vagueness and freedom of speech.

Echoes of this case were heard in 1987 when the Court cited *Epperson* as a guiding precedent in invalidating Louisiana's Creationism Act, which forbade the teaching of evolution unless accompanied by instruction in "creation science," *EDWARDS V. AGUILLARD* (1987).

—Leah Boyd, Jonathan Fidani, and David L. Weeks

Equal Access Act (1984)

In the case of *WIDMAR V. VINCENT* (1981), the U.S. Supreme Court ruled that a public university that provided an open forum for student groups could not discriminate against religious speech without violating the FREE SPEECH CLAUSE. In 1984, Congress responded to the decision by passing the Equal Access Act (EAA). The act provides:

> It shall be unlawful for any public secondary school which receives Federal financial assistance and which has a limited open forum to deny equal access or a fair opportunity to, or discriminate against, any students who wish to conduct a meeting within that limited open forum on the basis of the religious, political, philosophical, or other content of the speech at such meetings.

The act provides that secondary public schools allowing noncurriculum-related clubs to meet on their premises during noninstructional time must afford the same privilege to religious groups without discrimination. A noncurriculum group is defined as any group that forms around a subject that is not taught in the school's basic curriculum and for which there are no plans to develop courses for teaching that subject.

Student meetings protected under the EAA include those involving religious practices such as prayer services, holy book readings, and liturgical exercises. The EAA also provides for use by religious groups of school bulletin boards, public address systems, newspapers, and other campus media for the promotion of their organization and its events. All school policies affecting the use of school facilities by noncurriculum groups must be applied equally and without discrimination to those groups, whether they are secular or religious.

EAA becomes applicable at a particular secondary public school once any noncurriculum-related organization is given the right to use that school's facilities. Granting the use of school facilities to even one noncurriculum group creates a "limited public forum" and triggers equal access rights for religious organizations. Certain restrictions apply to student groups in the creation of limited public forums that invoke the applicability of EAA. Those are:

- Meetings must be voluntary and student-initiated;
- School or government employees or agents may not sponsor meetings;
- School or government employees may be present only in a nonparticipatory capacity;
- Meetings do not interfere with the orderly conduct of educational activities;
- Nonschool persons may not direct, control, or regularly attend activities of student groups.

Substantial bipartisan majorities in both houses of Congress passed the act. Committee reports from both the House and the Senate indicate that the act was intended to address "widespread discrimination against religious speech in public schools." As evidence of this discrimination, the reports cite two federal appellate court decisions holding that it would violate the ESTABLISHMENT CLAUSE to allow student religious groups to meet on school grounds during noninstructional time.

The constitutionality of the EAA was challenged in WEST-SIDE COMMUNITY BOARD OF EDUCATION V. MERGENS (1990). In that case, a school board denied a student group permission to form a Christian club that would have the same privileges as other student groups. In an 8-1 decision, the Court ruled that the act did not violate the establishment clause.

One of the tasks faced by the Supreme Court in *Mergens* was to interpret the term "noncurriculum related student group," in order to determine whether a school offered a limited open forum. The *Mergens* majority defined such a group as "any student group that does not directly relate to the body of courses offered by the school." In dissent, Justice John Paul Stevens argued that the appropriate standard was whether a student group had as its purpose "the advocacy of partisan theological, political, or ethical views."

See also *GOOD NEWS CLUB ET AL. V. MILFORD CENTRAL SCHOOL; ROSENBERGER V. UNIVERSITY OF VIRGINIA.*

—Derek H. Davis and Malia Reddick

Equal Rights Amendment (ERA)

In 1923, the Equal Rights Amendment was first proposed in Congress. In spite of regular introductions in Congress, congressional approval for the amendment has been granted only once—in 1972. It read simply, "Equality of rights under law shall not be denied or abridged by the United States or by any State on account of sex," followed by enforcement and enacting clauses. After struggling for 10 years to gain state approval, the ratification deadline passed, with only 35 of the 38 needed states having ratified it.

The ERA initially faced minimal opposition in 1972. Hawaii's legislature ratified the amendment five minutes after Congress passed it. Five more states ratified in the three days following congressional approval. When hearings were held, they usually consisted of a few ERA supporters. Within a year, 30 states had ratified, usually with near-unanimous votes. However, opposition soon mobilized.

In 1972, Phyllis Schlafly, a conservative, Catholic activist and past vice president of the National Federation of Republican Women (NFRW), organized Stop ERA to fight the amendment. Initially, the opposition movement drew support from subscribers to the *Phyllis Schlafly Report* and Schlafly's supporters from the NFRW. With the passing of time, however, evangelical Christians became a potent force in the campaign against the ERA, with the ERA became a rallying issue for the nascent groups of the Religious Right. While Schlafly's individual supporters made important organizational contributions, it was largely Christian conservatives who supplied the grassroots activists. The churches provided stay-home mothers who had time and speaking skills (from their churches), with a commitment to the literal interpretation of the Pauline admonition that women should be subject to their husbands.

Polls throughout the ratification period showed that the public favored the broad concept of equal rights. ERA opponents, therefore, focused their energies on publicizing purported effects of the amendment. Many claims were unfounded—that ERA would require unisex bathrooms; however, there was debate over whether the amendment would allow women to be drafted to fight in combat, legalize homosexual marriage, and the like. Unfounded rumors were enough to whip some into a frenzy. Other opponents simply feared giving the Supreme Court authority to rule on issues they knew they could win in their state legislatures. Schlafly made no effort to correct individuals whose reasons for opposing the ERA were unfounded.

In 1977, Indiana became the last state to ratify. Congress granted an extension of the ratification deadline until 1982, but no states ratified during that period. Except Illinois, the states that did not ratify were southern or had a strong Latter-Day-Saint presence (Arizona, Nevada, and Utah). Illinois required a three-fifths majority to ratify a constitutional amendment, and because Schlafly had presided over the Illinois Federation of Republican Women, she had many supporters there.

The defeat of the ERA was a significant political matter itself, but two tangential consequences of the ERA battle continue to affect politics today. First, full-time homemakers were mobilized as a political force; Schlafly's group, EAGLE FORUM, continues to be active today. Second, the Right's shift from ANTICOMMUNISM to social issues mobilized religious groups. The Protestant/Catholic divide that had for so long characterized American religion gave way to a fundamentalist/nonfundamentalist dichotomy. The ERA, ABORTION, and other controversial social issues of the 1970s forged a political coalition among conservative religious groups in spite of doctrinal conflicts. Conservative Catholics have also been accepted, tenuously, in the Religious Right, and in spite of the outright enmity that has characterized their relationship, Evangelical Protestants and Mormons have joined forces on social issues. The bonds that formed during the 1970s continue to influence the politics of the religious conservative movement today.

See also CHRISTIAN RIGHT AND THE REPUBLICAN PARTY; FEMINISM; FEMINIST THEOLOGY.

Further reading: Brown, Barbara A., Thomas I. Emerson, Gail Falk, and Ann E. Freedman. "The Equal Rights Amendment: A Constitutional Basis for Equal Rights for Women." *Yale Law Journal* 80 (1971): 955–962; Lee, Rex E. *A Lawyer Looks at the Equal Rights Amendment.* Provo, Utah: Brigham Young University Press, 1980; Mansbridge, Jane J. *Why We Lost the ERA.* Chicago: University of Chicago Press, 1986; Shupe, Anson, and John Heinerman. "Mormonism and the New Christian Right: An Emerging Coalition?" *Review of Religious Research* 27, no. 2 (1985): 146–157.

—Damon M. Cann

establishment clause

The establishment clause is the part of the First Amendment reading, "Congress shall make no law respecting an establishment of religion." The common understanding of the clause is that it mandates a separation of church and state, though the degree of that separation is hotly debated.

American culture at the time of the founding embraced the idea that religion, particularly Protestantism, is a vital part of a good society and that public encouragement of faith is proper. In this context, school prayer, enforcement of the Sabbath, prohibition of blasphemy, and other legal support for religious doctrine was accepted. The establishment clause did not seek to change these practices. Rather, its purpose was to prevent the national government from creating or sanctioning a national church and simultaneously to prevent national interference with state churches or state regulation of religious life. In this way, the clause originally served as a federalism provision, keeping the national government out of matters that were reserved to the states.

State establishment waned in the 19th century for political reasons, though public religiosity persevered. Beginning in the 20th century, a cultural shift toward public secularism took place, marked in law by the Supreme Court's decision in *EVERSON V. BOARD OF EDUCATION* (1947). This case marks a dramatic break from the public religiosity that characterized American life from the time of the founding until, roughly, the

sesquicentennial. In it, the Court held that the establishment clause, which had previously applied only to the national government, applies to the states through the Fourteenth Amendment's due process clause (following a body of law known as "incorporation doctrine" that has gradually applied most of the provisions in the Bill of Rights to the states), meaning that the states, as well as the national government, must make no law respecting an establishment of religion. Further, the Court established a standard of government neutrality with respect to religion, invoking THOMAS JEFFERSON's image of a "wall of separation between church and state."

Since the *Everson* decision, the Court has struggled with competing principles in the interpretation of the clause. Liberal members of the Court have tended to support a view described by the metaphor of a "high wall of separation" between church and state, also known as "strict separation," meaning almost no government entanglement with religion. Conservative members of the Court have tended to support an "accommodationist" approach, in which government aid to religion is permitted so long as it is neutral with respect to particular religions.

Among the most noted establishment decisions is *LEMON V. KURTZMAN* (1971), which articulated the jurisprudential framework the Court typically uses to scrutinize establishment cases. Known as the *Lemon* test, this is a three-part test requiring that a law have a secular purpose (following *ABINGTON V. SCHEMPP*); that a law have a primarily secular effect that neither advances nor inhibits religion (following *BOARD OF EDUCATION V. ALLEN*); and that there be no excessive entanglement of government with religion; the boundaries between church and state must be clear (following *WALZ V. TAX COMMISSION OF CITY OF NEW YORK*).

The *Lemon* test is not a strict rule that formulaically determines judicial decisions, and the Court has not always applied it. The value of the test is to highlight the kinds of questions and criteria that judges should apply when ruling on establishment clause questions. But, this flexibility means that it can be used to justify differing, and sometimes opposite, conclusions about any particular case. Critics question the value of such a malleable test, and Justices William Rehnquist, Sandra Day O'Connor, ANTONIN SCALIA, and Clarence Thomas have called for its abandonment (*KIRYAS JOEL V. GRUMENT*).

Today, the interpretation of the establishment clause is the pivot on which several important issues turn, including school prayer, AID TO RELIGIOUS SCHOOLS, and religious holiday displays. Given its malleability, the *Lemon* test has done little to unify the Court's opinions in these cases, which are often sharply divided. Yet, most establishment decisions are intelligible in terms of the test's three criteria.

The Court has consistently ruled that official steps promoting school prayer are unconstitutional. In *ENGEL V. VITALE* (1962), the Court prohibited public schools from requiring prayer, and in *WALLACE V. JAFFREE* (1985), the Court held that a moment of silence, established to promote voluntary prayer, also violates the establishment clause. But, some accommodation of student-initiated religious activity is allowable. In WEST-SIDE COMMUNITY BOARD OF EDUCATION V. MERGENS (1990), the Court indicated that student prayer meetings do not violate the establishment clause if they are organized by students during an activity period when numerous other activities are available.

The provision of public aid for religious schools has led to many difficult cases. Although direct government funding of religious schools has not been upheld, many limited forms of aid have been allowed. The Court has upheld the provision of textbooks to parochial schools (MEEK V. PITTENGER), financial aid to sectarian universities (TILTON V. RICHARDSON and ROEMER V. MARYLAND PUBLIC WORKS BOARD), the provision of public school teachers to parochial schools to provide remedial education (AGOSTINI V. FELTON), overruling AGUILAR V. FELTON, and government funding of a sign-language interpreter for a deaf student at a religious school (ZOBREST V. CATALINA FOOTHILLS SCHOOL DISTRICT). All these decisions were 5-4 except for Meek v. Pittenger (which was 6-3), illustrating how closely the Court has been divided on these questions.

The issue of religious holiday displays is complicated because many symbols, such as Christmas trees, have both secular and religious significance. In LYNCH V. DONNELLY, the Court held that government displays may not endorse religion, because endorsements send a message of favoritism to believers and a message of exclusion to nonbelievers. In ALLEGHENY V. ACLU, the Court held that the display of a nativity scene in a courthouse violates the clause, but the display of a large menorah next to a large Christmas tree does not, because the dual display undermines any message of endorsement of a particular religion.

In addition to the competing principles of accommodation and strict separation, the establishment clause is sometimes in tension with other parts of the First Amendment. One is the FREE EXERCISE CLAUSE; refusal to accommodate religion can impede free exercise, while accommodation to facilitate free exercise may constitute establishment. Similarly, the establishment clause is sometimes in tension with freedom of speech and the press. In ROSENBERGER V. UNIVERSITY OF VIRGINIA, the University of Virginia denied student activity funds for the religious magazine Wide Awake out of concerns that funding the magazine would constitute an unconstitutional establishment of religion. However, the Court held (again, 5-4) that withholding the funds constituted impermissible discrimination against religious viewpoints.

—Matthew DeBell

euthanasia

Euthanasia, which comes from Greek words meaning "good death," is the term given to assisted suicide and direct actions that lead to the death of individuals who are often experiencing physical difficulties. Proponents assert that euthanasia is humane in instances where quality of life is greatly reduced, while opponents see euthanasia as a violation of the sanctity of human life. The best-known individuals promoting euthanasia are Derek Humphry, founder of the Hemlock Society and author of several books promoting euthanasia, and Jack Kevorkian, the Michigan doctor who has assisted with over 100 suicides. The main groups opposing legal euthanasia in the United States have been pro-life organizations, such as the National Right to Life and the ROMAN CATHOLIC CHURCH. While states may permit assisted suicide, the Supreme Court, in an important decision, asserted that there is no constitutional right to assisted suicide. As of 2002, Oregon is the only state that permits assisted suicide.

Although the Euthanasia Society of America was formed in 1938, euthanasia did not become a social and political issue until the last quarter of the 20th century. Attracting national attention, the case of Karen Ann Quinlan in 1976 brought before the public some of the issues related to euthanasia. Because of injury, Quinlan was unable to make medical decisions. Her parents sought to remove her from life-support systems but were not permitted to do so until the New Jersey Supreme Court ruled on their behalf.

In 1980, Derek Humphry, a native of England and long-time journalist, founded the Hemlock Society in Los Angeles. Humphry has personal experience with issues related to euthanasia. His first wife suffered from bone cancer, and in 1975 he helped her commit suicide, which he described in his first book about euthanasia, *Jean's Way* (1979). He has also written *The Right to Die* (1986); *Final Exit: The Practicalities of Self-Deliverance and Assisted Suicide* (1989), which spent 18 weeks on the *New York Times*'s Bestseller List; and *Dying with Dignity: Understanding Euthanasia* (1992). Humphry speaks widely and has made many media appearances defending physician-assisted suicide.

The best-known practitioner of euthanasia in the United States is Jack Kevorkian, a retired pathologist based in Michigan. Kevorkian has been arrested several times and acquitted all but the last time. He is currently in jail for second-degree murder for the death of Thomas Youk, whose assisted suicide was shown on videotape on CBS's *60 Minutes.*

Neither Congress nor any state legislature has passed legislation permitting assisted suicide. With use of the initiative process, assisted-suicide measures have been placed on the ballot in California (1992), Washington (1991), and Oregon (1994). The pro-euthanasia measures were defeated in California and Washington, but the Death with Dignity Act passed in Oregon with 51 percent of the vote. Opponents of the measure, mostly represented by pro-life organizations, spent $1.5 million on that ballot initiative, while supporters spent approximately $600,000. The measure was immediately challenged in court. Eventually, Oregon courts upheld the measure. A measure to repeal the law was on the ballot in 1997, but that effort failed with 60 percent of the vote.

The federal courts have also addressed euthanasia; citizens of Washington and New York have challenged their respective states' laws prohibiting it. In the case involving the Washington law, first known as *Compassion in Dying v. Washington,* the federal district court declared the law unconstitutional. On March 9, 1995, a three-judge panel of the U.S. Court of Appeals for the Ninth Circuit overturned the decision. On March 6, 1996, the same Court of Appeals sitting en banc reversed the previous appeals court decision. In 1994, three doctors and three terminally ill patients challenged the New York State statute prohibiting physician-assisted suicide. The federal district court upheld the law; on April 2, 1996, the U.S. Court of Appeals for the Second Circuit in part reversed the district court ruling. Both of these cases, known as *Washington v. Glucksberg* and *Vacco v. Quill,* were appealed to the Supreme Court, which heard oral arguments in the cases on January 8, 1997. On June 26, 1997, the Court ruled in a unanimous decision with the opinion written by Chief Justice William Rehnquist that laws prohibiting assisted suicide are not unconstitutional.

Further reading: Euthanasia Research and Guidance Organization website. <finalexit.org>; Michael Uhlmann, ed. *Last Rights: Assisted Suicide and Euthanasia Debated.* Grand Rapids, Mich.: Eerdmans, 1998.

—Michael Coulter

evangelicalism

Evangelicalism in contemporary American culture refers to an identifiable, but imprecisely defined, segment of the population composed of doctrinally conservative Protestants. While evangelicals have become an important political and social force in the latter part of the 20th century, there is no clear consensus on the definition of evangelicalism. For some analysts, the most important characteristic of an evangelical is adherence to a "high" view of Scripture—those who regard the Bible as literally true, or as inerrant. Others have considered religious experience to be a defining characteristic of evangelicalism. Either discrete "born-again" events or more gradual spiritual awakenings are regarded by some as essential components of Christian evangelicalism. Still others have regarded evangelicals as a social group with regular interactions and common identities, and have sought to define evangelicalism as membership in particular denominations, or as self-identification with a social movement.

Despite our inability to define evangelicalism with any degree of precision, there does exist a Wittgenstinian "family resemblance" among the various attempts to define and to measure the concept. Evangelicals do perceive the Bible to be important, and accessible to ordinary believers without the interpretation or intervention of religious leaders. Similarly, evangelicals tend to believe that salvation is available only through Jesus Christ, and are correspondingly unwilling to accept the authenticity of non-Christian religions. Beyond these minimal characteristics, evangelicals in the United States are a remarkably diverse lot. Evangelicalism, as a general concept, includes such subsets as FUNDAMENTALISM, PENTECOSTAL, and CHARISMATIC Christianity, and the HOLINESS tradition.

The importance evangelicals attach to individual salvation has traditionally been thought to inhibit evangelical participation in politics. Evangelicals have been regarded as "otherworldly," and often unconcerned with secular public affairs. But Evangelical Protestants have periodically engaged in political activity. It has been suggested that there have been three important periods of evangelical political activity in the 20th century. The first is thought to have occurred in the aftermath of World War I and extended into the 1920s. The political mobilization of evangelicals may have been occasioned by the sudden visibility of large groups of Roman Catholic and Jewish immigrants, and coalesced around the issue of PROHIBITION. A second wave of evangelical political activity occurred in the 1950s, and appears to have been motivated by fears of international and domestic communism. Finally, the late 1970s and early 1980s saw the rise of a variety of conservative Christian movements and organizations, which were responses to a perceived culture of "permissiveness." Issues such as sexual morality, GAY RIGHTS, ABORTION, and PRAYER IN PUBLIC SCHOOLS provided the issue focus for groups such as MORAL MAJORITY, CHRISTIAN COALITION, FAMILY RESEARCH COUNCIL, and the EAGLE FORUM.

Some observers have suggested that the rise and decline of evangelical political engagement is occasioned by the activation of group-related attitudes. Evangelicals can be mobilized by the sudden visibility of politically assertive groups who do not share their values, such as immigrants, gays, or feminists. However, the resulting political activity often results in the exposure of theological differences among groups of evangelicals, which may contribute to the fragmentation of religiously motivated interest groups. The assertion of what has been termed "religious particularism" has inhibited the formation of political coalitions of doctrinally conservative Christians.

For example, in 1988, PAT ROBERTSON ran for the Republican presidential nomination, but he was unable to attract much support beyond a relatively narrow Pentecostal base. Other groups of evangelicals, such as fundamentalists, appear to have shunned Robertson's candidacy as a response to Robertson's highly specific doctrinal appeal.

The most recent wave of evangelical political activity, however, has also occasioned a strong connection between Evangelical Protestants and the Republican Party. Evangelicals of all theological persuasions have tended to identify with the GOP since the RONALD REAGAN administration. Unlike evangelical interest group activity, the effects of particularism do not seem to have limited evangelical strength within the GOP. Consequently, Evangelical Protestants are an increasingly important component of the Republican coalition, and a formidable force in American elections.

See also ANTICOMMUNISM; CHRISTIAN RIGHT AND THE REPUBLICAN PARTY; FUNDAMENTALISM; RELIGION IN THE 1980, 1984, 1988, 1992, 1996, 2000 PRESIDENTIAL ELECTIONS; TELEVANGELISM.

Further reading: Green, John C. "Pat Robertson and the Latest Crusade: Religious Resources and the 1988 Presidential Campaign." *Social Science Quarterly* 74 (1993): 157–168; Jelen, Ted G. *The Political Mobilization of Religious Beliefs.* Westport, Conn.: Praeger, 1991; Leege, David C., and Lyman A. Kellstedt, eds. *Rediscovering the Religious Factor in American Politics.* Armonk, N.Y.: M. E. Sharpe, 1993; Wilcox, Clyde. "Fundamentalists and Politics: An Analysis of the Impact of Differing Operational Definitions," *Journal of Politics* 48 (1986): 1041–51; Wilcox, Clyde. *God's Warriors: The Christian Right in the Twentieth Century.* Baltimore: Johns Hopkins University Press, 1992.

—Ted G. Jelen

Evangelical Lutheran Church in America

The Evangelical Lutheran Church in America was formed in 1988 by the uniting of the 2.85 million-member Lutheran Church in America, the 2.25 million-member American Lutheran Church, and the 100,000-member Association of Evangelical Lutheran Churches. It now has 5,149,668 baptized members (2,457,252 communing) and has shown small declines in most of the years of its existence.

Beginning with 58 different Lutheran church bodies in the mid-19th century, the movement for Lutheran unity has now arrived at two major Lutheran churches, the ELCA and the LUTHERAN CHURCH–MISSOURI SYNOD. This movement has essentially been one of different ethnically based Lutheran groups gradually losing their ethnic identity and thereby finding they had few reasons to maintain themselves as separate organizations. The Lutheran Church in America, for example, was formed in 1962 out of the Swedish Augustana Synod, the Finnish Suomi Synod, the Danish American Evangelical Lutheran Church, the Slovak Zion Synod, and the United Lutheran Church in America (ULCA). The ULCA was by far the largest of the uniting bodies and also the most Americanized. It was based in the East and had a long history of intraorganizational constitutional efficiency. It was also more hierarchically organized and ecumenically interested. The American Lutheran Church (ALC), founded two years earlier in 1960, was made up of German, Norwegian, Danish, and Icelandic groups that up to that time had their own church organizations. The ALC was more congregationalist and PIETIST than the ELCA.

This lingering disparity between the two major uniting churches has resulted in the most serious institutional challenge the ELCA has faced in its brief existence. After long ecumenical conversations with other mainstream Protestant denominations, the ELCA first approved a Formula of Agreement to enter into full communion with three Reformed churches, including the liberal United Church of Christ. While this agreement surprisingly passed without serious contention, the effort to pass a Concordat of Agreement with the EPISCOPAL CHURCH met with strong opposition. After much internal and external negotiation, however, the ELCA and the Episcopal Church came to a Called to Common Mission (CCM) agreement that established full communion. However,

many ELCA pastors and churches—mostly but not all from the old ALC—have resisted the CCM by organizing the WordAlone Network, which is founded on their passionate conviction that by adopting the historic episcopacy as a necessary component of ordination, the ELCA has fundamentally changed its doctrinal base.

Under pressure from the WordAlone Network, the ELCA provided a loophole for ordinations by nonbishops in "special cases." The Episcopalians reluctantly acceded to the ELCA revision, so the WordAlone Network may no longer have the intense rallying point it once had. Nevertheless, the Network has set up parallel organizations and continues its protest of the direction of the ELCA.

Another major rift in the ELCA has not yet issued in organized resistance. The tensions between "orthodox" and "revisionist" factions are serious and may reach a breaking point over sexuality issues, especially the ordination of openly gay clergy and the blessing of gay and lesbian unions. The church has committed itself to making a decision about these issues in 2005.

The rift between orthodox and revisionist camps has been fueled over the years by the fateful decisions made by the Committee for a New Lutheran Church at the origin of the ELCA. Spurred on by black, feminist, and "progressive" representatives of the small Association of Evangelical Lutheran Churches—the offshoot of the Lutheran Church-Missouri Synod—a strict quota system for representation of "neglected" groups was set in place. This approach to church organization was done in the name of "inclusivity" or "diversity," which themes have defined the identity and mission of the ELCA since 1988.

This strategy, however, has insured that the headquarters "culture" of the ELCA is far more "revisionist" than its membership. That culture—supported by urban and university pastors and churches—is pressing for the ordination of homosexuals in committed relationships, the blessing of gay and lesbian unions, "inclusive language," liberal public policy, a permissive stance on ABORTION, gender FEMINISM, PACIFISM in international conflicts, and, above all, "inclusivity and diversity" in all things, including theology. In all this the ELCA resembles the mainstream Protestant churches with whom it has struck up ecumenical relations. It is also suffering the same sorts of conflicts that those churches have experienced. Up until this point, the controversy over the revisionist agenda on sexual issues has not resulted in organized resistance. But such resistance could well emerge in the next years.

As Lutherans have gradually emerged from their ethnic enclaves, they have faced the same temptations to accommodate to culture as older Protestant groups. Lutherans have always maintained that they are different because of their strong confessional heritage. The next decades will clarify whether that claim is accurate, or whether accommodation will lead to continued loss of members and protests—if not schisms—precipitated by that accommodation.

Meanwhile, the small membership decline has not been offset by efforts at "inclusivity," partly because those efforts have not led to the successful evangelization of minority populations. In 1988 there were 48,261 black members (.92 percent) and 22,766 Hispanic (.43 percent); in 2000 those numbers stood at 52,558 (1.03 percent) and 37,540 (.73 percent), respectively. White membership currently stands at 4,988,085 (97.31 percent).

As of 2000, the ELCA has 17,611 clergy (2,358 female and 435 people of color) in 65 synods in nine geographic regions. It has 10,851 congregations, with its heaviest strength in the upper Midwest. It has eight seminaries, 29 colleges and universities, 28 high schools, and 265 elementary schools. Its churchwide budget for 2000 was $83,375,000, which supports the work of its administrative offices, six divisions, two commissions, and six departments. It supports many social service units, a press, and a Board of Pensions. Its church periodical is *The Lutheran* and its main offices are in Chicago.

See also ECUMENISM; GAY AND LESBIAN MARRIAGE.

Further reading: The ELCA website: URL: http://www.elca.org/.

—Robert Benne

Evangelicals for Social Action

Evangelicals for Social Action (ESA) formed in 1973. Previously, many young evangelical leaders had expressed concern over the lack of emphasis on SOCIAL JUSTICE within evangelical circles. Much of this could be attributed to the historical split between "fundamentalists" and "liberals" within the broader Protestant world. Evangelicals became suspicious of the SOCIAL GOSPEL of mainline Protestantism. There was a perception that social justice had been jettisoned as an evangelical goal for society. Many of those who were concerned attended a meeting in Chicago in 1973 to prepare a statement related to the need for evangelicals to become more involved in helping the poor. A statement was drafted and released by meeting participants, "A Declaration of Evangelical Social Concern." The statement admitted that evangelicals had engaged in RACISM and had taken advantage of the poor and would therefore pledge themselves to the administration of social justice throughout society as a direct part of their evangelical faith. As a direct result of this meeting, Evangelicals for Social Action was created to monitor and encourage implementation of the group's ideals of social justice.

The founder and leader of ESA is RONALD J. SIDER. His book *Rich Christians in an Age of Hunger* provides key insights into ESA's views on social justice. Namely, Western Christians are wealthy when compared to many others throughout the world; Christians have a moral imperative not only to help with immediate needs but also to propose and work toward remedies for the underlying causes of poverty and social injustice. Sider's work continues to speak for the organization, and his leadership continues to be pivotal for ESA. ESA's official doctrinal statement is the Lausanne Covenant.

ESA attempts to keep evangelicals from a variety of groups and denominations engaged in the debate about social justice issues. Additionally, ESA has as a primary goal: the direct effecting of the political and governmental system for the betterment of society. Basically, ESA believes that government can and should be used to foster much good in society and should be encouraged by evangelicals to do so. Communication with its members and the broader society is maintained through newsletters, conferences, and *Prism*, its critically acclaimed bimonthly magazine.

ESA has had numerous successes. First, social justice issues are unquestionably being given greater credence owing to the work of ESA. Because dialogue on social justice issues is a goal for the group, ESA is an unqualified success as an organization. However, successes have not just been limited to keeping dialogue alive. ESA played a key role in helping to form the Evangelical Environmental Network (EEN). ESA and EEN played a significant role in 1995 when they successfully defended, along with other groups, the Endangered Species Act. They compared the Endangered Species Act to Noah's Ark. Many stated that without their help, the Endangered Species Act might have been severely weakened. ESA support for CHARITABLE CHOICE has been an important element in its passing Congress and in being signed into law by President WILLIAM JEFFERSON CLINTON in 1996. ESA continues to support this type of relationship between government and ministries because it strengthens the coalition of forces helping the poor. Some of the other issues important to ESA, all of which fall under the heading of social justice, are racial equality, gender equality, WELFARE REFORM, fair taxation, and family breakdown, just to name a few.

ESA has also been quite involved in the foundation of the ECUMENICAL group CALL TO RENEWAL. This is a progressive grouping of evangelicals, ROMAN CATHOLICS, mainline Protestants, and black and Hispanic Christians. The group calls on all ministries to take a holistic approach to social transformation. Resources have been developed and are available for congregations and other groups to use in the development of these programs.

ESA has successfully worked over the years in affecting the public policy debate and actual policies at both national and grassroots levels. Social justice concerns have been kept in front of the broader religious world and society in general. ESA continues to operate under the leadership of Ron Sider out of their offices in Wynnewood, Pennsylvania.

See also CAMPOLO, ANTHONY; WALLIS, JIM.

Further reading: Evangelicals for Social Action Website. URL: http://www.esa-online.org; Sider, Ron. *Just Generosity: A New Vision for Overcoming Poverty in America*. Dartmouth, Mass.: Baker, 1999.

—William Lester and Julie Smith

Everson v. Board of Education 330 U.S. 1 (1947)

On February 10, 1947, the U.S. Supreme Court rejected a taxpayer's claim that reimbursement for the cost of transportation for children attending private religious schools was a violation of the ESTABLISHMENT CLAUSE. Justice Hugo Black, speaking for a 5-4 majority, applied the establishment clause of the Bill of Rights to state governments through the FOURTEENTH AMENDMENT for the first time, but he rejected the claim that New Jersey acted unconstitutionally.

New Jersey state law allowed local school boards to "make rules and contracts for the transportation of children to and from schools." The Ewing Township Board of Education opted to rely on public transportation for children attending both public and nonprofit private schools and offered to reimburse parents for the expense. Arch Everson, a taxpayer, contended that this state-sponsored program forced him and other similarly situated taxpayers to support ROMAN CATHOLIC CHURCH schools in violation of the First Amendment, made applicable to states via the Fourteenth Amendment's due process clause.

In reviewing the background of the establishment clause, Justice Black recounted the struggle for religious freedom in the Colonial era. So salient, in his mind, was the extended political battle in Virginia over tax levies to support the established church that Black ignored the first amendment's legislative history and relied almost entirely on THOMAS JEFFERSON's "Bill for Establishing Religious Freedom" and JAMES MADISON's "Memorial and Remonstrance against Religious Assessments" as definitive explanations of the religion clauses.

Jefferson and Madison's writings convinced Black that:

The 'establishment of religion' clause of the First Amendment means at least this: Neither a state nor the Federal Government can set up a church. Neither can pass laws which aid one religion, aid all religions, or prefer one religion over another. Neither can force nor influence a person to go to or to remain away from church against his will or force him to profess a belief or disbelief in any religion. No person can be punished for entertaining or professing religious beliefs or disbeliefs, for church attendance or non-attendance. No tax in any amount, large or small, can be levied to support any religious activities or institutions, whatever they may be called, or whatever form they may adopt to teach or practice religion. Neither a state nor the Federal Government can, openly or secretly, participate in the affairs of any religious organizations or groups and vice versa. In the words of Jefferson, the clause against establishment of religion by law was intended to erect 'a wall of separation between church and State.'

Black's separatist interpretation of the First Amendment led him to conclude that government entities cannot directly finance any religious activity. The boundary of this conclusion would become the turf over which establishment cases would eventually be fought, butting up against FREE EXERCISE claims. The establishment clause does not preclude using tax dollars to meet a public need when the expenditure incidentally benefits religion. The key element is that the expenditure must be authorized for a public purpose: Precluding all incidental benefits might infringe on the free exercise rights of the American people and create an adversarial relationship between church and state.

In this case, New Jersey found it in the public interest to provide safe transportation for all school children, including those attending religious schools. Comparing the provision of safe transportation to that of police and fire protection, sewage disposal, and public highways, Black insisted the state had to remain neutral in these matters, offering services equally to everyone. Because funds expended for a public purpose do not violate the Fourteenth Amendment's due process clause, Black famously concluded, "The First Amendment has erected a wall between church and state. That wall must be kept high and impregnable. We could not approve the slightest breach. New Jersey has not breached it here."

The four dissenting justices were quick to point out the discrepancy between Black's invocation of separation of church and state and his approval of state aid in educational matters. Justices Jackson and Rutledge wrote dissents accusing Black of immeasurably compromising the SEPARATION OF CHURCH AND STATE by permitting use of the taxing power to benefit religion. Demanding a "complete and permanent separation . . . by comprehensively forbidding every form of public aid or support for religion," Justices Jackson and Rutledge compared Black to Byron's Julia, who, "whispering 'I will ne'er consent,' consented."

The Court's first major statement on the meaning of the establishment clause, this seminal decision sparked a raging debate between those desiring an absolute separation of church and state and those desiring an accommodation. It also precipitated an inconsistent body of case law, seen in the ensuing years when the Court effectively both upheld and struck down transportation subsidies by summary judgments or by refusing to review conflicting lower court judgments. The issue became even more complex when the Court was called on to resolve many other forms of state AID TO RELIGIOUS SCHOOLS.

See also TUITION TAX CREDITS FOR RELIGIOUS SCHOOLS.

—David L. Weeks

F

Falwell, Jerry (1933–) *televangelist*

Jerry Falwell was born on August 11, 1933, in Lynchburg, Virginia, along with a twin brother, Gene. He is a fundamentalist Baptist minister who rose to prominence in the 1980s as a TELEVANGELIST and as founder and leader of the pioneering conservative Christian group, MORAL MAJORITY. During the 1980s, Falwell emerged as the foremost political spokesman within Evangelical PROTESTANTISM, and his well-publicized stands against ABORTION, PORNOGRAPHY, and GAY RIGHTS helped define the political agenda of the Christian Right. His political engagement helped get evangelical voters to the polls and ensure a number of Republican electoral victories.

Falwell was an outstanding student in high school and graduated as class valedictorian. He was also a fullback and captain of his football team. In 1950, he entered Lynchburg College, where he intended to study engineering. Two years later, he was converted and decided to devote his life to Christ. On the advice of his pastor, Falwell transferred to Baptist Bible College (BBC) in Springfield, Missouri. In his senior year at BBC, Falwell became a youth minister, and after graduation in 1956, he returned to Lynchburg to establish his own church—the Thomas Road Baptist Church. One year after establishing the new church, Falwell married pianist Macel Pate.

Falwell quickly became a popular and well-liked pastor. The Thomas Road Church attracted numerous new members. Falwell's rise coincided with the growth of televangelism. The new medium of television offered a means for Falwell to reach far more potential converts. In 1968, he launched the *Old Time Gospel Hour*, which broadcast the Baptist minister's sermons on both radio and television. The show as enormously popular with evangelicals and was soon syndicated around the country, at its height on more than 200 television stations. The success of Falwell's venture into broadcasting allowed him to establish a university in 1971. Falwell initially used his church staff as faculty, but Liberty University later grew into a four-year liberal arts college with an enrollment of 14,000.

The televangelist was deeply troubled by what he perceived to be the moral decay of American society and culture.

To counter this trend, Falwell founded the Moral Majority in 1979. It identified itself as a secular political organization that supported conservative candidates and causes. Falwell traveled extensively to promote the Moral Majority, and within two years, the organization had a mailing list that included

Reverend Jerry Falwell *(Wayne Scarberry/Getty Images)*

7 million people. In 1980, Falwell worked diligently to support the presidential candidacy of RONALD REAGAN. Falwell and the Moral Majority are generally credited with helping to increase the turnout of Evangelical Protestants. The organization also spurred the creation of numerous other conservative Christian groups, such as the CHRISTIAN COALITION and the FAMILY RESEARCH COUNCIL.

Falwell is the author of several best-selling works including *Listen, America!* (1980), *Wisdom for Living* (1984), and *Falwell: An Autobiography* (1997). He was also involved in a precedent-setting Supreme Court case, *Hustler Magazine v. Falwell* (1988), which dealt with First Amendment freedom of speech issues. Falwell brought suit against *Hustler* because of a lurid cartoon and false interview that the magazine published about him. In its decision, the Supreme Court ruled that parody and caricature were forms of free expression.

While sexual scandals ruined the reputations of fellow televangelists JIM BAKKER and JIMMY SWAGGART in 1987, Falwell remained untouched. In fact, Falwell assumed the chair of the Praise the Lord (PTL) network in 1988, at that time the nation's largest evangelical broadcasting network, when Bakker was forced to resign because of his conduct. However, the series of scandals that affected televangelists in the 1980s eroded Falwell's base. In addition, the increasingly political nature of Falwell's activities alienated some followers who did not support his evident repudiation of traditional evangelical political disengagement.

By the late 1980s, Falwell's religious and political empire had begun to deteriorate. The Moral Majority went out of business, and Liberty University became mired in a nine-figure debt. Meanwhile, under Falwell's leadership, the PTL went bankrupt and he was even forced temporarily to cancel his *Old Time Gospel Hour*. Nonetheless, Falwell consolidated his religious base, and using his Thomas Road Church, slowly rebuilt. Falwell demonstrated his continuing political influence when he worked with fellow evangelist PAT ROBERTSON to defeat the candidacy of Arizona senator John McCain and ensure the victory of the more conservative GEORGE W. BUSH in the competition for the 2000 Republican presidential nomination.

See also CHRISTIAN RIGHT AND THE REPUBLICAN PARTY.

Further reading: Frankl, Razelle. *Televangelism: The Marketing of Popular Religion.* Carbondale: Southern Illinois University Press, 1987; Hadden, Jeffrey K. "The Rise and Fall of American Televangelism." *Annals of the American Academy of Political and Social Science* 527 (1993): 113–131; Lloyd, Mark. *Pioneers of Prime Time Religion: Jerry Falwell, Rex Humbard, Oral Roberts.* Dubuque, Iowa: Kendall/Hunt, 1988; Schultze, Quentin J. *Televangelism and American Culture: The Business of Popular Religion.* Grand Rapids, Mich.: Baker, 1991; Smolla, Rodney A. *Jerry Falwell v. Larry Flynt: The First Amendment on Trial.* New York: St. Martin's Press, 1988; Snowball, David. *Continuity and Change in the Rhetoric of the Moral Majority.* New York: Praeger, 1991.

—Thomas Lansford

Family, The

The Family, originally the Children of God and later, the Family of Love, is an international religious organization of Christian MISSIONARIES founded in 1968 by Moses David Berg (1919–94). The Family emerged out of the Jesus Movement in the late 1960s and grew from a few dozen members to a peak membership of 10,000–15,000 full-time members. The movement emphasizes evangelistic activity and claims to have shared its message personally with over 200 million individuals, to have distributed more than 800 million pieces of literature, and to have personally prayed for salvation with over 20 million people. The Family currently claims 12,000 full-time and associate adult-volunteer members in 1,400 communities located in over 100 countries. Throughout its history, the movement has been best known for its radical sexual practices that included the use of sexual relationships in recruitment, "sexual sharing" among members, and, for a time, sexual relationships between adults and minors.

David Brandt Berg (referred to in the movement by a variety of names–Moses David, Mo, Father David, Dad) was a third-generation evangelist. In 1944 Berg married Jane Miller (known in The Family as Mother Eve); the couple had four children, only one of whom remains active in the movement. Berg became a minister in the Christian and Missionary Alliance but ultimately rejected established churches and formed his own religious group. One of Berg's early revelations, Old Church-New Church, involved his taking a new wife, Karen Zerby (known in The Family as Maria), who became his partner for the remainder of his life. By 1970, the group had grown to 200 members; they settled on a property that was formerly the Texas Soul Clinic and began building "a new nation" modeled on the early Christian church. The movement came under increasing attack from families of converts. Berg and Maria then relocated to London, where they could escape negative publicity. From that time forward, Berg remained in seclusion, with his location known only to a small circle of leaders. To communicate his ideas and principles with the leadership and members in the United States, Berg created "Mo Letters," illustrated guides to life in The Family, and later other publications through which he administered the movement and conveyed spiritual messages. By 1971 Berg had urged members to leave the United States, and his followers began establishing movement "colonies" in a number of European countries. The movement then spread rapidly to nations across the globe—Japan, Australia, New Zealand, India, Southeast Asia, and South America.

The 1970s were a turbulent period in the movement. In 1972, Berg elevated his spiritual status by pronouncing himself God's endtime prophet. In 1974, Berg began experimenting with a new approach to witnessing, personally demonstrating God's love by any means necessary, including sexuality, to bring souls to Christ. This tactic, known as "flirty fishing," spread through the movement in succeeding years. Beginning in 1975, Berg initiated several major reorganizations designed to solidify his authority and replace an entrenched, authoritarian leadership. The most important of these was the Re-organization Nationalization Revolution, which replaced much of the movement membership and reorganized the group as The Family of Love (later The Family). The result of these various changes in the movement produced widespread defection, perhaps as much as one-third of the membership.

The 1980s were a period of major transition for the movement. Early in the decade The Family began rejecting a number of its radical sexual practices—first, sexual contacts between minors and adults, and by 1987, flirty fishing. Sexual sharing between consenting adults has been preserved. Berg's health became increasingly more precarious, and he gradually turned over administration of the movement to Maria and Peter Amsterdam, who married shortly after Berg's death in 1994. Finally, there was a rapid rise in the number of children to as much as two-thirds of total movement membership. The result was a major reorientation of activity toward child care and education.

In the aftermath of the decade of radical sexual practices, The Family faced prosecution on child abuse charges in a number of countries (Spain, France, England, Australia, Argentina) at the instigation of apostate members. In none of these cases were charges of sexual abuse substantiated. The most significant of these events was a child custody case in England in 1993. In that case, The Family was ultimately awarded custody of the child at issue, but the judge required an acknowledgment from The Family of past excesses and abuses.

See also EVANGELICALISM; NEW RELIGIOUS MOVEMENTS AND CULTS.

Further reading: Bainbridge, William Sims. *The Endtime Family.* Albany: State University of New York Press, 2002; Chancellor, James. *Life in the Family.* Syracuse, N.Y.: University of Syracuse Press, 2000; Davis, Deborah. *The Children of God.* Grand Rapids, Mich.: Zondervan, 1984; Lewis, James R., and J. Gordon Melton, eds. *Sex, Slander and Salvation.* Stanford, Calif.: Center for Academic Publication, 1994; Melton, J. Gordon. *The Family/The Children of God.* Salt Lake City: Signature Books, 2001; Van Zandt, David. *Living with the Children of God.* Princeton, N.J.: Princeton University Press, 1991.

—David G. Bromley

Family Research Council

Founded in 1981 by a group of conservative Christian, pro-family leaders, and currently led by Florida attorney and pro-life leader Ken Connor, the Family Research Council (FRC) is a conservative, nonprofit, public policy research and education organization that employs a staff of 120 people and enjoys a $15.3 million annual operating budget. Based in a six-story building inscribed with the motto faith, family, and freedom, in Washington, D.C., FRC has as its mission to produce and advocate high-quality policy initiatives that strengthen and sustain the traditional American family and traditional values.

To accomplish this task, it maintains a comprehensive research and statistical database, seeks to inform and educate citizens about contemporary policy, and promotes Judeo-Christian principles by providing information to the news media, business leaders, academics, and policy makers in the legislative, executive, and judicial branches of the federal government. Through the use of radio, television appearances, newsletters, opinion columns, and the Internet, FRC informs, represents, and relies on the commitment of 480,000 constituents who are encouraged to provide grassroots support for FRC policy initiatives and opposition to "anti-family" legislation.

In 1988, FOCUS ON THE FAMILY rescued the financially strapped FRC, led until that time by Jerry Reiger, incorporating it into Focus's own organization and paying off FRC's debts. Concurrently, GARY BAUER, a former official in the presidential administration of RONALD REAGAN, assumed the presidency of FRC and held the position of senior vice president at Focus. Under Bauer's more than 10 years of leadership, FRC established a firm foothold in Washington politics and eventually dissolved its ties to Focus in October 1992.

The heart of FRC are its research and policy proposals, which it hopes will at least initiate public discussion and at best result in the passage of pro-family legislation. Its domestic policy, cultural studies, national security and foreign relations, and legal studies staff analyze internally and externally commissioned polls and write numerous well-researched position papers, which are distributed for public consumption and legislative consideration by FRC's recently enlarged media and government relations staff, the latter being organized under the purview of American Renewal. Many of these proposals have been adopted and advocated by other conservative Christian and conservative groups, such as the CHRISTIAN COALITION and Americans for Tax Reform, respectively. FRC has worked in concert with these groups to promote pro-family legislation and, as part of larger pro-family coalitions, has enjoyed several victories since the Republican Party gained control of both houses of Congress in 1994. The most notable successes include the $500 per child tax credit, drafted by FRC staffers, and the Defense of Marriage Act, in which FRC initiated and led the legislative effort, providing members of Congress with key information, testimony, and publicity about the goal of protecting the traditional definition of marriage. Other FRC-supported initiatives include passage of the Child Custody Protection Act, the Communications Decency Act, the TEN COMMANDMENTS Defense Act, the Religious Liberty Protection Act, the Unborn Victims of Violence Act, and the Pain Relief Promotion Act. Unfortunately for the FRC, President WILLIAM JEFFERSON CLINTON vetoed many of its initiatives, such as a ban on "partial-birth" ABORTION.

FRC produces a variety of 15 periodicals and special publications intended mainly for families and policy makers, but with a keen eye toward those who influence them as well. Sent to almost 300,000 supporters across the nation, *Washington Watch* has long been FRC's primary publication, providing constituents with information regarding current events and

FRC's activities. Another, *Family Policy*, was created in the late 1980s to enable FRC to share policy research on family issues with policy makers in Congress, the media, academia, think tanks, and other policy institutions across the country. The organization also publishes a periodic collection of papers on national defense, a monthly publication on drug policy, three weekly newsletters regarding, respectively, federal legislative action, education, and culture, and has distributed over 500,000 Ten Commandments school book covers. The building of its own radio studio to produce *Washington Watch*, FRC's daily radio commentary with Janet Parshall (now broadcast on over 400 stations) and the development of a national weekly radio public affairs program, coupled with its new emphasis on educational outreach to the pro-family grassroots movement, seems to ensure that the group will continue to grow and remain a Washington mainstay.

See also CHRISTIAN RIGHT AND THE REPUBLICAN PARTY; GAY AND LESBIAN MARRIAGE; RELIGION IN THE CONGRESSIONAL ELECTIONS OF 1994.

Further reading: "A Decade of Progress: Defending Family, Faith, and Freedom." Washington, D.C.: Family Research Council, November, 1998; *Family Research Council Newsletter.* Washington, D.C.: Family Research Council, June 15, 2000; Fowler, Robert Booth, Allen D. Hertzke, and Laura R. Olson. *Religion and Politics in America.* Boulder, Colo.: Westview Press, 1999; "FRC's Strategic Plan for the New Millennium." Washington, D.C.: Family Research Council, January, 2000; Personal Interview with Brett Rudolph, FRC National Field Director, Washington, D.C. March 25, 1999.

—Brett M. Clifton

Louis Farrakhan *(Getty Images)*

Farrakhan, Louis (1933–) *religious leader*
Louis Eugene Walcott was born on May 22, 1933, in Roxbury, Massachusetts, to Mae Clark, a native of St. Christopher (St. Kitts) in the Caribbean. His father was Jamaican and his stepfather was from Barbados. His mother, who participated in Marcus Garvey's Back to Africa movement, instilled both racial pride and a love of music in her son, who began violin lessons at the age of five. By age 13, he had played with the Boston College Orchestra and the Boston Civic Symphony; at 14 he won a violin competition on a popular television show, the *Ted Mack Amateur Hour.*

Louis Walcott attended Winston-Salem Teachers College in North Carolina for two years before returning to Boston to marry his high school sweetheart, Betsy (now Khadidja) in 1953 in ceremonies at St. Cyprian Episcopal Church, where he was a member. They had nine children.

Louis Walcott's musical talents extended to singing. Known as Calypso Gene or "The Charmer," he sang in Boston nightclubs, where in the early 1950s he met MALCOLM X, then a key member of the NATION OF ISLAM (NOI). His second encounter with NOI came during a 1955 engagement called "Calypso Follies" at the Blue Angel in Chicago, when a friend suggested that he attend the group's annual Savior's Day convention. Louis Walcott heard ELIJAH MUHAMMAD speak, and "the truth dawned on him." Soon thereafter, he joined NOI Temple No. 7 in Harlem and took the name Louis X.

At the insistence of NOI, Louis X gave up his career as an entertainer to devote himself full-time to his new calling as a lieutenant in the Fruit of Islam (NOI's paramilitary wing), where he developed his skill at public speaking. As a protégé of Malcolm X, he also became assistant minister (later, minister) and captain of the Fruit of Islam at NOI's Temple No. 11 in Boston.

Although he could no longer perform, Louis Walcott's musical talents were put to use in other ways. He wrote and directed two stage productions centered on NOI beliefs and composed several popular NOI songs, including "White Man's Heaven is Black Man's Hell."

In 1964, Louis X was named to replace Malcolm X as the minister of Temple No. 7, and he successfully weathered the crisis following Malcolm X's assassination by three gunmen at the start of a speech on February 21, 1965, in the Aragon Ballroom in Harlem. Three years later, he became a national representative of Elijah Muhammad, and around this time also changed his name to Louis Farrakhan.

When Elijah Muhammad died in 1975, his son Wallace D. Muhammad (now WARITH DEEN MUHAMMAD) was named successor as head of NOI. At first, Farrakhan accepted the decision. But the son initiated a reformation process designed to bring NOI closer to mainstream Sunni Islam, and dissention between the two men over inheriting the mantle of Elijah Muhammad increased.

Following visits to Africa and the Caribbean, Farrakhan moved to assert his claim. In November 1977, he signaled his intention to reestablish NOI, calling it a "return to the teachings and program with a proven ability to uplift and reform blacks." Farrakhan announced the reconstituted NOI during Savior's Day celebrations in February 1981. His organization remains the largest survivor of the 17 or more splinter groups formed by NOI members after Elijah Muhammad's death.

During the 1980s, Farrakhan was said to be successful in drawing adherents to this reborn NOI, at least in part because of the economic dislocations in the black community caused by policies of the presidency of RONALD REAGAN. His personal charm and media celebrity also brought worldwide attention to NOI.

In 1988, NOI repurchased its former flagship temple in Chicago for $2.3 million and dedicated it as Mosque Maryam, the National Center for Re-training and Re-education of the Black Man and Woman of America and the World. The National Center includes a preschool and K-12 University of Islam.

In 1992, Farrakhan drew a crowd of 60,000 to the Atlanta Dome for NOI Savior's Day celebration, and in 1995, NOI sponsored the successful Million Man March in Washington, D.C. The same year, NOI also purchased farmland in Dawson, Georgia, and opened a restaurant in Chicago.

Farrakhan reregistered to vote in June 1996 and formed a coalition of religious, civic, and political organizations to "represent the voice of the disenfranchised on the political landscape."

By the 21st century, NOI claimed mosques and study groups in more than 80 cities in North America, the United Kingdom, and Ghana. Membership numbers, however, are not released by NOI. Estimates range from fewer than 5,000 to around 20,000; but Farrakhan's media savvy gives NOI a larger place on the American scene than those numbers would indicate.

In 2002, despite occasional well-publicized bouts with illness and rumors of financial problems, Farrakhan continued to lead NOI as a black nationalist religious movement of African Americans, maintaining its tightly knit network of mosques, schools, and newspaper, *The Final Call*, which is the official communications organ of the Nation of Islam.

Further reading: Nation of Islam website URL: http://www.noi.org; Gardell, Mattias. *In the Name of Elijah Muhammad: Louis Farrakhan and the Nation of Islam*. Durham, N.C.: Duke University Press, 1996.

—Susan McKee

Fard, Wali D. (1891?–1934?) *religious founder*

Wali D. Fard was the founder of the Temple of Islam, an American Black Muslim religious movement later known as the NATION OF ISLAM (NOI). Fard's origins are a mystery. Sources disagree on his birth year (some say 1877; others, 1891), birthplace (possibilities include New Zealand, Oregon, the Indian subcontinent, Arabia, Great Britain, the West Indies, and California), ethnic heritage (British, Polynesian, Kuraishi tribe of Arabia, African American), and even his name.

In the summer of 1930, Fard was a door-to-door apparel salesman in the Paradise Valley area of Detroit, then an enclave of African Americans who had moved to the industrial North in the great migration from the South. In a speech in Detroit on July 4, 1930, Fard announced the formation of the Temple of Islam, which later became Temple No. 1 of the Nation of Islam. One of his early followers, ELIJAH MUHAMMAD, founded Temple No. 2 in Chicago in 1932. Fard himself moved to Chicago in 1933. The following year, Fard mysteriously disappeared and was never heard from again.

Fard's public life is inextricably entwined with that of Elijah Poole, an African American who moved to Detroit from Georgia in the late 1920s. After attending a Temple of Islam service in 1931, Poole approached Fard, who admitted he was the earthly incarnation of God, but cautioned Poole not to reveal that information. Fard later renamed Poole Elijah Muhammad and titled him Supreme Minister of Islam. After Fard's disappearance, Elijah Muhammad assumed the leadership of the Nation of Islam.

Elijah Muhammad was no newcomer to black separatist movements. His father had been an organizer for Marcus Garvey's Back to Africa movement, which reached its zenith in the 1920s. Garvey extolled the virtues of blackness, preached pride in African heritage, and called for blacks to worship a black God, as did the Nation of Islam under Fard and Elijah Muhammad. Both also likely were members of a Moorish Science Temple, established in Detroit around 1928 by Noble Drew Ali.

The separatist movements were attempts to uncouple the history of blacks from whites in America by emphasizing their different origins. Garvey encouraged American blacks to rediscover their African roots by returning to their homeland. Titling himself a Prophet of Allah, Ali considered it more important for American blacks to rediscover their Asiatic or Moorish roots while remaining in the country where fate had led them. Fard and Elijah Muhammad drew from this ready reservoir of myth to create the Nation of Islam.

Fard was considered by some to be the reincarnation of Noble Drew Ali. Others knew him as "the Master," "the Prophet," or as "God-in-Person." Traditional Nation of Islam theology includes this belief: "We believe that Allah (God) appeared in the Person of Master W. Fard Muhammad, July 1930; the long-awaited 'Messiah' of the Christians and the 'Mahdi' of the Muslims."

"All Muslims are Allahs," wrote Elijah Muhammad, "but we call the Supreme Allah the Supreme Being. And He has a

Name of His Own. This Name is 'Fard Muhammad.'" The NOI celebrates a unique holiday, Savior's Day, on February 26 to commemorate Fard's birthday.

Despite the use of Muslim references, including the Arabic word for "God," Fard did not espouse the same ISLAM as revealed on the Arabian peninsula in the seventh century. NOI theology holds that a mad black scientist named Yakub created white people 6,000 years ago as a curse and test for the superior black people. Fard claimed to have been sent by Allah to reclaim his people, the tribe of Shabazz, who had been kidnapped and sent to America in chains.

In the racially charged atmosphere of Depression-era Detroit, Fard and his followers soon ran into conflicts with the white political structure. Rumors of ritual killings came to a head when a NOI member arrested by police in 1932 confessed to having killed a man during a "sacrifice." As leader of the "voodoo cult," Fard also was arrested. Two more arrests for "cult activities" convinced him to leave Michigan in 1933. He last appeared on official records when he was arrested in Chicago for disorderly conduct in September 1933. After his disappearance, Elijah Muhammad revealed that Fard was not a prophet, but God himself, and he, Muhammad, was his messenger.

See also MUHAMMAD; WARITH DEEN.

Further reading: Essien-Udom, E. U. *Black Nationalism: A Search for an Identity in America.* Chicago: University of Chicago Press, 1962; Marsh, Clifton E. *From Black Muslims to Muslims: The Transition from Separatism to Islam, 1930–1980.* Metuchen, N.J.: Scarecrow, 1984; Muhammad, Elijah. *Our Savior Has Arrived.* Newport News, Va.: United Brothers Communications Systems, 1992; Nation of Islam website. URL: http://www.noi.org.

—Susan McKee

Farris, Michael (1951–) *activist*

Michael Farris is an ordained Baptist minister, an attorney, and head of the HOMESCHOOL LEGAL DEFENSE ASSOCIATION. He is also the founder of the nation's first college for homeschooled students and the founder and head of the Madison Project political action committee. He served as the former director of the Washington State MORAL MAJORITY, the legal counsel to CONCERNED WOMEN FOR AMERICA, national treasurer for PAT ROBERTSON's 1988 presidential campaign, and as the Republican nominee for lieutenant governor of Virginia. He was also the plaintiff's attorney in the famed 1986 "Scopes II" trial, *Mozert v. Hawkins County Board of Education.* He is a prolific lecturer, author, and tireless advocate of Christian conservative causes, appearing frequently in leading news media. He and his wife, Vicky, are the parents of 10 children, all educated at home.

With his extensive public profile, Farris is a controversial political figure. The trajectory of his activism has catapulted him from social movement organizations to a position of substantial influence in GOP politics. His efforts have inspired both intense loyalties among Christian Right supporters and harsh denunciations from his detractors. Farris elicits such a range of feelings because his issues and activities are at the heart of the CULTURE WAR in the United States. Ultimately, Farris is most successful as a social movement organizer and legal advocate for homeschooling. His one foray into the electoral realm was a disappointment for him. There are good reasons for his successes in social movement and legal activity and his failure to win election.

Farris's initial notable foray into the political realm was as the executive director of the Washington State Moral Majority in the early 1980s. He was then in his twenties and a recent law school graduate. Farris's political activities in the Moral Majority suggest that he was a dedicated activist who took uncompromising stands and, as a result, was very successful at building a state social movement organization. The Washington chapter was the largest state organization in the Moral Majority. Yet Farris made a break with the Moral Majority, and in 1982 he renamed the state organization the Bill of Rights Legal Foundation.

To mobilize a social movement, leaders frequently seek to attract publicity by issuing extreme statements, engaging in public forums, and organizing demonstrations. As a young man in a highly visible role, Farris did the same. He relished the limelight and a good debate. He appeared in forums with ideological opponents, including drug guru Timothy O'Leary, often on college campuses. The events were spirited, and Farris did not flinch from a heated exchange.

Over time, many of Farris's controversial statements and writings were collected by his opponents and later used to characterize him as an extremist. Most famously, Farris made some strong anti–public school statements that fueled an image of him as immoderate in his use of language. Farris accused the public schools of conforming to "the state's program of values indoctrination." He decried "the vindictive godlessness rampant in our modern school systems" and labeled the public school system "a godless monstrosity." He accused the public schools of having "prescribed orthodox views of politics" such as the belief that "racial integration is good," when such views are "matters of opinion."

Consequently, "the public schools are a multi-billion dollar inculcation machine," and "a far more dangerous propaganda machine" than that which existed in the former Soviet Union. In a 1987 speech, Farris declared public schools unconstitutional. "I believe . . . that public schools are per se unconstitutional. You can't run a school system without inculcating values. . . . Since inculcation of values is inherently a religious act, what the public schools are doing is indoctrinating your children in religion, no matter what." When Farris ran for lieutenant governor of Virginia in 1993, his past statements became effective campaign material for his opponents.

Farris, became active in local and state politics. In 1993 he ran for the Republican lieutenant governor nomination and surprised everyone when he defeated a better-known party leader. He did not win the general election, but as in the past

Farris did not let defeat slow him down politically. He turned to forming the Madison Project PAC using the "bundling" technique originated by Emily's List PAC.

Farris may be best known today for his leadership role in the HOMESCHOOLING movement. He founded and is chairman of the Home School Legal Defense Association (HSLDA), a nonprofit advocacy organization that promotes the interests of homeschooling families. That organization in part is a defensive one: providing legal assistance to protect the homeschools of members. It is also a proactive organization that engages in issue advocacy at the state and federal levels. The HSLDA has a division entitled the National Center for Home Education. The center operates a Congressional Action Program to lobby the federal government through a grassroots network of HSLDA members throughout the country.

Education Week has anointed Farris as one of the 100 "Faces of a Century," and homeschooling is now the fastest-growing segment of the education community in the United States. Farris is widely recognized as a major force in moving homeschooling into the mainstream as a respectable educational alternative.

Farris most recently founded Patrick Henry College in Loudon County, Virginia. The purpose of this institution is to provide a college-level alternative for homeschooled students. Patrick Henry College is a unique higher education institution. The uniqueness of the concept and Farris's goals for Patrick Henry College attracted both attention and controversy. Farris promulgated rules that banned alcohol and required students to wear uniforms and go to chapel daily. Students were prohibited from dating on their own and were expected to inform their parents of any "potential romance." They were also expected to get parental approval and to socialize together only when in groups of other students. According to one school pamphlet, students must "show evidence of a personal relationship with Jesus Christ." They must abide by a seven-point statement of faith, including the belief in the literal resurrection of Christ. The application for admission required that prospective students "Please describe your personal relationship with Jesus Christ." The college's policy of nondiscrimination says: "The college shall maintain its constitutional and statutory right to discriminate on the basis of religion in order to accomplish the religious mission of the college."

In two decades of activism, Farris has made an important impact on the social conservative movement in the United States. His name is not as immediately recognizable as those of JERRY FALWELL or Pat Robertson, but like the better-known movement leaders, Farris has become a major player in the politics of the "culture wars."

—Mark J. Rozell

feminism

Feminism—which means most basically the idea that women are fully human and have the same range of capacities as men—has influenced all the world's religions over the past two centuries. It has also given rise to alternative spiritualities shaped by ancient and contemporary pagan traditions, collectively known as the women's spirituality movement. Feminists who have sought to reform traditional religions have focused on women's ordination, biblical interpretation, gender-inclusive language, and incorporating female images of the deity. Many influential feminist theologians who have critiqued and ultimately split from the established religions were originally trained in the biblical traditions of Christianity and Judaism. These theologians, most notably Mary Daly and Carol Christ, concluded that biblical traditions were simply too sexist to be reformed, and responded by articulating woman-centered theologies. Carol Christ has dubbed this as the "reformist/revolutionary" division, and although these labels have proven controversial, the extent to which theologians remain linked with established religions has probably been the chief point of disagreement among feminist theologians of the past 30 years.

The relationship between feminism and religion in the United States dates back to the 19th-century women's movement. First-wave feminism was pioneered by leaders of the ABOLITIONIST MOVEMENT of earlier decades who were inspired to action by likening their own lack of rights to the situation of slaves. Facing hostility from the churches, slavery proponents, and even some abolitionists for taking a public role in the antislavery movement, many of these women began to articulate arguments for women's rights. The Grimké sisters, the first women to regularly address mixed-sex public assemblies, responded to accusations that their behavior was unwomanly and un-Christian by coming out with a series of pamphlets and lectures addressing women's rights in the mid-1830s. The Seneca Falls Convention of 1848, organized in response to World Anti-Slavery Convention delegates' refusal to allow women seats on the convention floor, launched the American women's movement.

Nineteenth-century feminists were by and large Christian evangelicals, and they and their allies concentrated on women's ordination, the expansion of women's roles into public and religious life, and the existence of the divine feminine. In 1853 Antoinette Brown became the first ordained woman minister in the Congregational Church, and a few women were also ordained by the Methodists, the Universalists, and the Presbyterians during the 1800s, although many churches did not even contemplate ordaining women until the 1970s. In 1895 abolitionist ELIZABETH CADY STANTON published *The Woman's Bible*, a collection of biblical interpretations dealing with women that emphasized gender egalitarianism and the feminine elements of the divine. Although religious issues were not central to first-wave feminists, they often invoked biblical justifications, arguing that God created man and woman as equals.

Feminists of the late 1960s and early 1970s echoed many of the claims of their 19th-century foremothers, but they were able to make greater inroads into established religion and popular consciousness. Women made critical strides in ordination during the 1970s, as the first woman ministers were ordained in the Lutheran and EPISCOPAL Churches as well as rabbis in the REFORM and RECONSTRUCTIONIST JEWISH traditions. A large and influential body of literature also began to develop, proposing ways that inclusive language and rituals recognizing women could be incorporated into worship services. As well, experiments such as Womenchurch and the feminist spirituality movement emerged in the 1970s and 1980s, and although they differed in their affiliation with established religion, both attempted to establish and practice explicitly feminist spiritualities.

Today, feminism continues to influence established religion in the United States. Most religions, except Roman Catholicism, ORTHODOX JUDAISM, and some evangelical Protestant churches, do have at least some women clergy, and their numbers are rapidly growing. As of 1996, one in every eight American clergy was female, and women now make up about 30 percent of all graduate students at North American Christian seminaries. Gender-inclusive language, though still controversial, is being employed in more and more worship services across the United States, and women continue to play more visible roles in both established and alternative religions nationwide.

See also FEMINIST THEOLOGY.

Further reading: Christ, Carol. "The New Feminist Theology: A Review of the Literature." *Religious Studies Review,* no. 4 (1977): 203–212; National Council of the Churches of Christ. *An Inclusive Language Lectionary.* Atlanta: John Knox Press, 1983; King, Ursula. *Women and Spirituality: Voices of Protest and Promise.* New York: Macmillan, 1989; Gross, Rita. *Feminism and Religion: An Introduction.* Boston: Beacon Press, 1996; Murphy, Caryle. "A Chorus of Amens as More Women Take over Pulpit." *Washington Post,* July 25, 1998; Ruether, Rosemary Radford. *Religion and Sexism: Images of Woman in the Jewish and Christian Traditions.* New York: Simon and Schuster, 1974.

—Krista McQueeney

feminist theology

At the most basic level, theology means "thinking about God" (from the Greek words *theos,* "God," and *logos,* "word" or "thought"). FEMINISM is defined as a theory and a movement that wants to create a culture in which women have an equal position with men. Feminist theology, then, is a way to think about God from women's perspectives, keeping in mind women's equality to men. Its defining principle is that "whatever diminishes or denies the full humanity of women must be presumed not to reflect the divine." Some topics in feminist theology are the critique of exclusively male images of God, the uncovering of women's stories and women's traditions in the Bible and religious history, female spirituality, and the inclusion of women in religious studies, teaching, and ministry. Feminist theology is intercultural and has taken on several contextual forms. Some of them are Womanist (from the African-American context), *Mujerista* (from the Hispanic context), Asian and Asian-American, Jewish, Lesbian, North-American, and European feminist theologies.

Historically, feminist theology has its roots in the feminist movement of the 20th century, the women's ordination movement, and the ecumenical movement. It is related to LIBERATION THEOLOGY in that it is based on women's struggle for liberation from patriarchal structures in culture and religion. Feminist theology is inspired by the example of women throughout the ages who have taken a stand in male-dominated societies and religions: the mystic Julian of Norwich (1342–1416), who described God and Jesus with feminine imagery; ANNE HUTCHINSON, who led controversial Bible studies for women in the 1630s; ELIZABETH CADY STANTON, who published the Women's Bible in 1895, to name only a few. Before the 1980s, when feminist theology became a subject at colleges and universities, women discussed feminist theology in local churches and synagogues and in international networks that were first created in the Netherlands, Germany, and the United States.

According to one feminist theologian, Rosemary Radford Ruether, feminist theology has three basic tasks: to critique androcentric religious traditions, pointing out the ways they have been limiting for women; to recover women's stories past and present, showing women's abilities throughout history; to reshape religious doctrines and practices, making the tradition more responsive to the needs and experiences of both genders. Feminist theology reconsiders all areas of traditionally male Western theology that often regard women as inferior, responsible for the origin of evil, and more susceptible to sin than males. In systematic theology, the feminist approach attempts to revise doctrines such as Christology and the understanding of the origin of sin so that these doctrines no longer serve as a means of women's oppression. The doctrine of God, for instance, is expanded to include biblically sound gender-neutral, or both male and female images for God. In liturgical studies, feminist theology develops new liturgies in which women's stories are celebrated. Jewish feminists created feminist rituals such as feminist *Seders* and rites of entrance for a daughter into the covenant. Feminist theology inspires church historians to research the often underestimated role of women in the early church and rediscover women's theological traditions in medieval sects and monasticism. Feminist biblical scholars study the present and past realities of historical women, speak of God by also using biblical female metaphors, and study women in the Bible and how their stories have been interpreted over the centuries.

Feminist theologians acknowledge that the Bible was written by and mainly for males and that religious traditions are patriarchal in nature. For some, this reality has become so overwhelming that they have left their religious affiliations behind because they do not believe that traditions and institutions can be reformed. A minority of them attempt to revive an ancient feminist religion.

Feminist theologians are aware that "in reconstructing the past, exegetes and theologians construct the world." Therefore, feminist theology wants to challenge the scholarly pretense of value-neutrality in theological studies. It seeks to transform male-centered theological scholarship into truly human theological scholarship and construction of the world.

Further reading: Brenner, A., and C. Fontaine, eds. *A Feminist Companion to Reading the Bible.* Sheffield, U.K.: Academic Press, 1997; Johnson, Elizabeth A. *She Who Is.* New York: Crossroad, 1993; Radford Ruether, Rosemary. *Sexism and God-Talk. Toward a Feminist Theology.* Boston: Beacon Press, 1983; ———. "The Future of Feminist Theology in the Academy." *Journal of the American Academy of Religion* 53, no. 3 (1985): 703–713; Schuessler Fiorenza, E. "Feminist Theology and New Testament Interpretation." *Journal for the Study of the Old Testament* 22 (1982): 32–46.

— Claudia Bergmann

financial capital of religious organizations

SOCIAL CAPITAL and human capital have received much more attention than financial capital in the discussion of religious-based organizations. However, the fact that religious-based organizations are producers of financial capital that can be used to support social and community services or to leverage additional funding for community-based services should not be overlooked. In communities were businesses have fled and the tax base is limited, congregations are beginning to take greater stock of how they use their financial capital. By financial capital, we mean the property owned by the congregation (e.g., land, buildings, equipment, inventory, and bank balances).

In a study of congregations in seven cities, Cnaan and his colleagues used traditional economic methods to determine the average financial value of a program provided by a congregation per month. To calculate this value, respondents were asked to report for five social service programs the total value of their operations including direct and indirect expenses. The congregational space in which programs are held has financial value, as do the work of clergy, staff, and volunteers who provide the programs and the in-kind support. The average financial value of each item was calculated by totaling the estimated value reported for all programs and dividing the result by the total number of programs, including programs with no reported values. The estimated average monthly value of space was $722.82 for all 1,005 programs (compared with $1,458.70 for the 498 programs for which the estimated values of space were available). To determine the overall financial value of congregational contributions to social services, the value of clergy/staff/volunteer hour, cash support, in-kind support, value of utilities, and value of space was totaled. On average, the monthly value of congregational contributions was estimated at $3,826.68 per program. Given that the average congregation in this sample had four programs,

the total monthly contribution averaged $15,306.72 per congregation, or approximately $184,000 per congregation per year. This contribution is, for the most part, in the form of volunteer hours and other noncash support.

A study reported in Independent Sector's *From Belief to Commitment* provided some indication of the financial capital congregations represent. This study estimated the annual budget of small congregations at $54,000, of medium-size congregations at $108,000, and of large congregations at $432,000. Based on these 1992 estimates and the mean percentage (22.6 percent) congregations allocated for social programs, the estimated financial contribution of congregations for social services are as follows: $12,204 for small congregations, $24,408 for medium-size congregations, and $97,832 for large congregations. One of the largest African-American congregations, Windsor Village United Methodist Church, allocates over $500,000 annually for social services. While these numbers are based on a limited sample and correlated with data from another source, they are useful in assessing the extent of congregational financial support for social programs.

Several cases also demonstrated how congregations invested their financial capital to transform blighted neighborhoods with declining tax bases into mixed-income development communities. After the Los Angeles riots in 1992, First African Methodist Episcopal (FAME) formed a nonprofit that created a Micro Loan Program to supply low-interest loans to minority entrepreneurs, an equity fund, and other economic development programs. Over the past nine years, FAME has approved 76 loans in excess of $2.5 million. FAME has also secured $2.5 million of their projected $10 million planned for investing in emerging businesses. In Chicago, St. Edmunds Episcopal Church aligned with businesses, activists, and government to form a redevelopment corporation that channeled $40 million into the community. The Collective Banking Group of Prince George's County, Maryland, asserted their financial power to forge partnerships with banks that would recognize their investments and special needs. This group of over 127 congregations representing 21 denominations, 300,000 congregants, and $20 million per year in offerings has leveraged their financial capital to change the way banks do business with their congregations. As a result, several banks have revised their financial mechanisms to address the particular needs of congregations, contribute to their scholarship funds, and provide the best rates for financial services. Congregations are not only investing their financial capital in social services and community development, they have also leveraged their resources to change financial practices and to enlist the government and other organizations in contributing to the economic and social welfare of local communities.

With limited data in this area of study, the community investment of congregational financial capital can best be appreciated by comparing it to the financial contribution of for-profit organizations. Most corporations in the United States designate only about 1 percent of their pretax net income as an investment in social and community services, as compared with the 22.6 percent found in the congregations in Cnaan's study. By these measures, congregations can be viewed as organizations that possess assets that can be leveraged and used as financial capital to benefit congregations and communities.

See also COMMUNITY ORGANIZING; ECONOMIC DEVELOPMENT.

Further reading: Cnaan, R. A., S. C. Boddie, F. Handy, G. Yancey, and R. Schneider. *The Invisible Caring Hand: American Congregations and the Provision of Welfare.* New York: New York University Press, 2002; Galaskiewicz, Joseph. "An Urban Grants Economy Revisited: Corporate Charitable Contributions in Twin Cities, 1979–81, 1987–89." *Administrative Science Quarterly* 42 (1997): 445–471; Hodgkinson, V. A., M. S. Weitzman, A. D. Kirsch, S. M. Noga, and H. A. Gorski. *From Belief to Commitment: The Community Service Activities and Finances of Religious Congregations in the United States.* Washington, D.C.: Independent Sector, 1993.

—Ram A. Cnaan and Stephanie Clintonia Boddie

First Great Awakening (1734–1744)

The First Great Awakening (1734–44) was a series of evangelical revivals experienced throughout the American colonies that were part of a transatlantic spiritual uprising that saw contemporaneous "awakenings" in England and Scotland. The itinerant preaching tours of a number of charismatic evangelists in the early 1740s, most notably GEORGE WHITEFIELD, galvanized earlier revivalist sentiments into a unified mass phenomenon. The fervor of REVIVALISM that swept the colonies caused serious disruption to the religious scene, leading to rancorous dispute and denominational schism. The Awakening's distinctive focus on an individual's unmediated relationship with God has been seen by modern scholarship as contributing to an egalitarian or democratic consciousness prior to the Revolutionary War. Other scholars have focused on the disruptive impact of the Awakening and its unintended theological consequences. It is argued that the Awakening inadvertently accelerated the process by which American PROTESTANTISM came to incorporate rationalism within its theological doctrine.

Most historians mark the beginnings of the First Great Awakening with the outbreak of revivals in New England in 1734–35. Originating in Northampton, Massachusetts, under the pastoral leadership of JONATHAN EDWARDS, the revivals moved in a southerly direction, reaching the mid-Atlantic colonies in 1737. Edwards's report of the sudden outbreak of spiritual conversions, *A Faithful Narrative of Surprising Conversions* (1737), played an important role in publicizing these events. The revivals were distinguished by their injunction to believers to eschew religious formalism and submit themselves to the immediate spiritual workings of God. As clergy led gatherings to personal conversion, revivalism evoked a powerful sense of the capacity of individuals to experience regeneration irrespective of social status.

George Whitefield, an Anglican evangelist, transformed the First Great Awakening into a colonywide mass phenomenon. Arriving from England in November 1739, Whitefield undertook an intensive 14-month tour that ignited unprecedented evangelical enthusiasm. Whitefield led believers into a spiritual frenzy at numerous mass gatherings throughout the colonies. Though many clergy welcomed the renewed attention to experiential faith, the flouting of ecclesiastical boundaries and conventions aroused considerable controversy. Prominent clergy charged revivalist preachers with violating traditional parish and congregational boundaries. Many clergy also objected to the denial of conventional standards of piety and claimed that such an emphasis on personal experience encouraged licentiousness and immorality. The heightened revival enthusiasm catalyzed by Whitefield thus

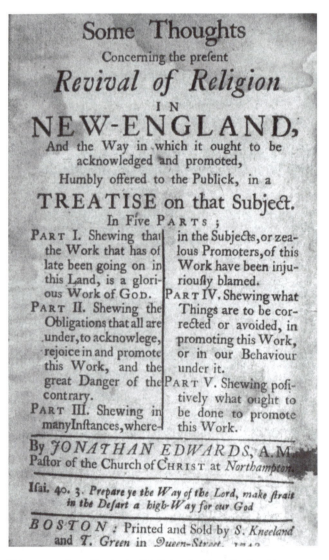

Title page of . . . *Revival of Religion in New England* by Jonathan Edwards *(Billy Graham Center)*

lead to religious "controversies" in which the merits of the nascent evangelical movement were debated.

The wave of enthusiasm continued after Whitefield's return to England, reaching its height in 1742. A number of clergy, most notably Gilbert Tennent, James Davenport, and Andrew Croswell, became prominent preachers of the evangelical gospel whose touring sustained the excitement generated by Whitefield. Skepticism concerning the movement nonetheless began to grow as the revivals became increasingly associated with wild scenes of emotion and extreme denunciations of ecclesiastical authorities. These reservations prompted religious disputes, which led to the adoption of polarized theological positions on the relative importance of reason and spiritual piety. The resultant denominational schism saw the emergence of Congregationalist New Lights alongside the PRESBYTERIAN New Side as supporters of the revival and advocates of spiritual piety, and Congregationalist Old Lights and the Presbyterian Old Side as opponents of the revival and advocates of the use of reason in faith. Ensuing disputes between these two camps saw the emergence of a clear theological delineation between the evangelical and liberal positions. Despite these distinguishing differences, both camps came to incorporate important elements of a philosophical rationalism within their respective theology. The skirmishing between these camps thus obscured an ongoing theological revision that produced a common adoption of theological rationalism. Among liberal clergy, his rationalism was most notably elaborated in the work of Charles Chauncy and Jonathan Mayhew; among evangelical clergy, the later work of Jonathan Edwards and that of his New Divinity followers. In this sense, the First Great Awakening, despite the intent of its protagonists, would prepare the way for a rational vision of natural man that accepted at least a degree of moral agency. Such a theological rationalism would prove amenable to the appropriation of a language of natural law and rights within religious discourse prior to the Revolution.

See also SECOND GREAT AWAKENING.

Further reading: Fiering, Norman. *Jonathan Edwards's Moral Thought and Its British Context*. Chapel Hill: University of North Carolina Press, 1981; Gaustad, Edwin S. *The Great Awakening in New England*. New York: Harper and Row, 1957; Hatch, Nathan O. *The Democratization of American Christianity*. New Haven, Conn.: Yale University Press, 1989; McLoughlin, William G. "'Enthusiasm for Liberty': The Great Awakening as the Key to the Revolution." In *Preachers and Politicians: Two Essays on the Origins of the American Revolution*. Edited by Jack P. Greene and William G. McLoughlin. Worcester, Mass.: American Antiquarian Society, 1977; Stout, Harry S. "Religion, Communications, and the Ideological Origins of the American Revolution." *William and Mary Quarterly* 34 (1977): 519–541; Valeri, Mark R. *Law and Providence in Joseph Bellamy's New England: The Origins of the New Divinity in Revolutionary America*. New York: Oxford University Press, 1994; Wood, Gordon S. "Religion

and the American Revolution." In *New Directions in American Religious History*. Edited by Harry S. Stout. New York: Oxford University Press, 1997.

—Roland Marden

Focus on the Family

Founded by JAMES DOBSON in 1977, Focus on the Family is a nonprofit, international, conservative Christian organization that seeks to sustain and promote the traditional family and traditional values through biblically inspired, commonsense advice. Focus began in Arcadia, California, as a 25-minute weekly radio program, broadcast on only a few dozen stations, but has grown beyond radio into 74 different ministries based in four buildings in Colorado Springs, Colorado. Today, with nearly 1,300 employees and an annual operating budget of more than $100 million, Focus publishes award-winning books, informational newsletters, and 10 monthly magazines. It also produces morally rich and entertaining videotapes and on-air dramas on subjects ranging from marriage and parental advice to the maintenance of religious faith to public policy. Focus also offers counseling and referrals to a network of 1,500 licensed therapists and regularly hosts conferences on a wide variety of subjects. Dobson's radio program, news updates, and commentaries, however, still constitute the heart of the organization and are broadcast in 12 languages, reaching 550 million radio listeners.

After serving nearly two decades in the pediatric and child development fields, Dobson began his radio program as a way to address his frustration with the lack of a comprehensive, rational, biblically based conception of the family for those experiencing the trials of modern life. A quarter of a century later, Focus has a presence in 95 countries, with 17 international affiliates. It even offers a semester-long internship and an academic program for college students through its Institute for Family Studies. More than 2.6 million households receive its flagship publication, *Focus on the Family* magazine; 200,000 people visit the Colorado Springs campus every year; and each week the organization responds to 55,000 letters from people all over the world.

Although not directly organized for political purposes, Dobson and Focus have found several occasions to wade into the political maelstrom. During the 1996 and 1998 election seasons, for example, Dobson insisted that Republican leaders in Congress address moral issues or risk alienating Christian conservatives. National Republican officials recognized the ability of Focus's grassroots supporters to influence party fortunes at the polls and paid more attention to his agenda. When Dobson weighs in on an issue on his radio program or in mailings to constituents, Congress quickly receives phone calls and letters from Focus supporters. By providing constituents with key information about policy, Focus is able to influence Republican policy makers and thereby shape legislation. Recent successes include protecting HOMESCHOOLING rights, strengthening anti-child PORNOGRAPHY laws, and preventing RELIGIOUS DISCRIMINATION.

In addition to Dobson's radio program, Focus disseminates its civic views to its grassroots supporters in several other ways. First, *Family News in Focus,* a daily radio news and commentary program, informs citizens about current events and invites them to take action on pro-family matters. Second, Focus sends out a weekly two-page fax that offers a "Christian perspective on significant current events" and details how to get involved in the "action items" listed. Third, the organization offers a 24-page news magazine, *Focus on the Family Citizen,* which informs its 75,000 readers about the latest developments concerning the issues of the day, such as ABORTION, religious liberty, homosexuality, and sex education. Last, and perhaps most significant, Focus has been instrumental in founding, developing, and nurturing independent, nonprofit, state organizations that coordinate and strengthen pro-family, grassroots activism at the local level. These organizations provide Focus with another venue through which to influence policy and enable the efficient distribution of VOTER GUIDES before elections.

Although the group mostly refrains from taking part in overt political advocacy and partisan politics, it can be linked with many of the other conservative organizations that constitute the Christian Right. From 1989 until 1992, Focus was affiliated with the FAMILY RESEARCH COUNCIL, a conservative think tank based in Washington, D.C. Although the organizations amicably severed their relationship, the ties between their leaders remain strong. Moreover, Focus has been instrumental in generating networks of conservative Christians and propagating the general social attitudes and values necessary for other groups, such as the CHRISTIAN COALITION, to organize their constituencies on behalf of conservative Republican candidates and proposals. By fighting for the same sets of goals, these groups have intentionally, and unintentionally, aided one another by circulating and supporting traditional values, and influencing how conservative Christians conceptualize the role of government in their everyday lives. Dobson's sound leadership ensures that Focus will remain a steady force in conservative Christian circles.

See also CHRISTIAN RIGHT AND THE REPUBLICAN PARTY; RELIGION IN THE 1996 PRESIDENTIAL ELECTION.

Further reading: Apostolidis, Paul. *Stations of the Cross: A dorno and Christian Right Radio.* Durham, N.C.: Duke University Press, 2000; Clifton, Brett M. "Rousing the Faithful to Seek the Promised Land: Analyzing the Christian Right's Penetration of the Republican Party." Ph.D. diss., Brown University, 2002; Dobson, James C. "The New Cost of Discipleship." *Christianity Today,* September 1999; Focus on the Family website URL: http://www.fotf.org, "Meeting Future Needs." *Focus on the Family,* December 1999; Oldfield, Duane M. *The Right and the Righteous: The Christian Right Confronts the Republican Party.* Lanham, Md.: Rowman and Littlefield, 1999; Watson, Justin. *The Christian Coalition: Dreams of Restoration. Demands for Recognition.* New York: St. Martin's Press, 1997.

—Brett M. Clifton

Fourteenth Amendment and the incorporation doctrine

The incorporation doctrine refers to the Supreme Court's interpretation that the due process clause of the Fourteenth Amendment ("nor shall any State deprive any person of life, liberty, or property, without due process of law") extends the protections of selected rights from the Bill of Rights to the states. In the 1940s, the Court interpreted these selective rights to include the right of free exercise in CANTWELL V. CONNECTICUT (1940) and the prohibition against religious establishment in EVERSON V. BOARD OF EDUCATION (1947). Since that time, the vast majority of religious freedom litigation has involved state and local governments.

The original BILL OF RIGHTS (like the Constitution itself) was intended to apply only to the federal government, which was conceived as a government of strictly limited powers. The First Amendment provides that only "*Congress* shall make no laws respecting the establishment of religion or respecting the free exercise thereof," and the Court rejected the idea that the Bill of Rights was equally applicable to the states in its early decision *Barron v. Baltimore* (1833), a decision that has never been overruled. However, the enactment of the Fourteenth Amendment placed this interpretation in question. This amendment, one of the Civil War amendments, was intended to protect the rights of the newly freed slaves. The question became, what were those rights?

A significant historical controversy exists over whether the framers of the Fourteenth Amendment intended it to extend the protections of the Bill of Rights to cover the states. The Court itself complicated the issue with its decision in the *Slaughter House Cases* (1873), decided six years after adoption of the Fourteenth Amendment. Initially, advocates suggested that civil liberties included in the Bill of Rights were "incorporated" within the phrase "the privileges or immunities of citizens of the United States," an obvious point of connection. The Court, however, rejected this interpretation.

Arguably, the Court's decision in the *Slaughter House Case* can be explained as a racist reaction against the first civil rights movement (Black 1997). Nonetheless, this precedent has never been overturned. Consequently, when the Court again attempted to find ways to protect the civil rights of citizens against the actions of the states, it was forced to turn to the due process clause of the Fourteenth Amendment, as in *Gitlow v. New York* (1925). While the due process phrase does offer the advantage that it appears to be a direct quote from the Fifth Amendment (and thereby that the Bill of Rights was "incorporated" within the Fourteenth), the clause itself does nor bear up to this interpretation. The due process of law refers to the *process* of protecting rights—*not* their content. Nonetheless, for historical reasons, incorporation came to rest here.

Despite arguments by such justices as John Harlan Sr., John Harlan Jr., and Hugo Black, the incorporation doctrine has never been held to incorporate all the liberties set forth in the Bill of Rights. Each right had to be recognized individually. Hence, application of the rights guaranteed by the religion clauses to the state level did not occur until the 1940s.

In one sense, the incorporation doctrine has simplified the task of interpreting religious freedom in the United States. The minimum standards of the First Amendment, as interpreted by the Supreme Court, now apply to all levels of government, from the smallest city or township up to the state and federal governments. While the state can provide more exacting protections under its laws and constitution, it cannot abridge the minimums set forth by the Court.

The problem with the incorporation doctrine is that it challenges the interpretive framework of original intent—the idea that the Constitution should be interpreted to mean what its drafters intended. While this method of interpretation is controversial in its own right, the incorporation doctrine presents particular problems; it creates a profound discontinuity between the intent of the framers of the First Amendment and now. The original framers adopted the First Amendment to limit the activities of the *federal* government. It is disingenuous to argue that the framers intended to apply the same limits on the states. Nonetheless, the tactic of citing JAMES MADISON or ALEXANDER HAMILTON as authorities on religious freedom remains popular, even among those scholars who are not committed to original intent.

Further reading: Berger, Raoul. *Government by Judiciary: The Transformation of the Fourteenth Amendment.* Cambridge, Mass.: Harvard University Press, 1977; Black, Charles L., Jr. *A New Birth Of Freedom: Human Rights, Named and Unnamed.* New York: Grossett/Putnam, 1997; Bork, Robert. *The Tempting of America.* New York: Free Press, 1990; Flack, Horace. *The Adoption of the Fourteenth Amendment.* Baltimore: Johns Hopkins University Press, 1908; Hamilton, Alexander, James Madison, and John Jay. *The Federalist Papers.* Clinton Rossiter, ed. New York: New American Library, 1961; Levy, Leonard W. *Original Intent and the Farmers' Constitution.* New York: Macmillan, 1988.

—David E. Guinn

Franklin, Benjamin (1706–1790) *statesman, scientist, writer*

Benjamin Franklin was an extraordinary man. He was a scientist, innovator, printer, statesman, diplomat, philosopher, postmaster general, and writer. His famous kite-flying experiment in a thunderstorm to prove the similarity of lightning and electricity set the stage for later scientific discoveries by Michael Faraday and Thomas Edison. Although this is not an exhaustive account of Franklin's accomplishments, it shows the range of his genius. Franklin was also the only constitutional framer to have signed the Declaration of Independence, the U.S. Constitution, and two treaties with France that ended the Revolutionary War.

Born in Boston on January 17, 1706, Franklin learned the printing trade in his youth from his older brother, James, and at age 22 began his own printing business in Philadelphia. Franklin used the printing press to publish many of his own

Benjamin Franklin. Portrait by Charles Willson Peale *(Library of Congress)*

works. Franklin's famous *Poor Richard's Almanack* (1732), a compilation of witty and wise practical sayings, and his *Autobiography* (1706–57, published posthumously in 1868) are two of his most notable writings.

Perhaps less known are Franklin's writings about religion. For Franklin, religion was another subject of intense interest for his curious mind. Having grown up in a devout New England Congregationalist family, the independent-minded Franklin developed his own ideas about religion that did not square with the Christian orthodoxy of his day. At age 19, he published *A Dissertation on Liberty and Necessity, Pleasure and Pain* (1725), in which he argued against the existence of evil and the immorality of the soul. This essay was followed by the *Articles of Belief and Acts on Religion* (1728), in which Franklin links the goodness of the Supreme Being with human virtue and happiness. According to Franklin, God delights in human virtue because virtue is what makes humans happy. Similar to the DEISTS of early Revolutionary America, Franklin viewed Christianity more in terms of moral teaching than theological doctrine.

Franklin was a deist. American deism held strongly to the ideas of natural religion and social utility. As an offspring of the Enlightenment, deists relied on human reason to discover God and virtue rather than external revelation. "The implied or expressed rejection of the prophecies and miracles of Christianity was the sole factor which distinguished the deists from their orthodox opponents" (Morais 1932: 436). Franklin adhered to the deistic belief that the Supreme Being was "an Eternal Watchman, who had created an immense cosmic machine which whirled on and on in accordance with a set of immutable and regular laws. These edicts were regarded as perfect. To tinker with them by performing miracles would imply the imperfection of the Deity."

Franklin, GEORGE WASHINGTON, and JAMES MADISON, among others, were part of the American FREEMASONRY movement after the Revolutionary War. Although not hostile to Christianity, Freemasonry's principles were similar to deism. "All Masons were to worship God, to love their neighbors, and to avoid excesses. These duties were the substance of 'the universal religion or the religion of nature.'"

Also, Franklin was a member of the Thirteen Club, a group of deists who published the *Liturgy on the Universal Principles of Religion and Morality* (1776), espousing an approach to worship with liturgy that was indisputable and thus universal. The purpose of the *Liturgy* was to create a "form of social worship composed on the most enlarged and general principles, in which all men may join who acknowledge the existence of a supreme Intelligence and the universal obligations of morality, and among such men are included Jews, Christians, and Mohammedans." Prior to that, Franklin assisted Sir Frances Dashwood in the work *Abridgement on the Book of Common Prayer* (1773) by abridging the Psalms and the Catechism. The *Abridgement* was written for the utilitarian reasons of shortening the prayers and removing its unattractive curses on evil.

Franklin resisted the theological dogmatism of orthodox believers; however, he supported organized religion as a necessary influence on society. One scholar has noted: "The paradox in Franklin's religious life is that he completely disbelieved Christianity; yet he was attracted by it as a system of worship, and he enjoyed the company of clergyman of all faiths." Not particularly known for his personal piety because of his self-confessed indulgence in wine and women, Franklin still emphasized the "doing good to others" aspect of Christian belief. One example of this is Franklin's aid to Reverend Samuel Hemphill, who was dismissed from the Presbyterian Church in Philadelphia because of heterodox preaching. The grounds for Hemphill's removal in 1735 represented the type of sectarianism Franklin abhorred. Hemphill was charged as a heretic, "a preacher of morality rather than dogma." Hemphill had equated natural religion and revealed religion, something considered abominable to Presbyterian orthodoxy. Franklin came to Hemphill's defense by publishing attacks on the Presbyterian clergy in his own *Pennsylvania Gazette*. Franklin's argument in this controversy reveals his deistic belief that morality is the end of religion. Identifying the laws of nature with Christianity was completely orthodox to Franklin. Believing that Jesus provided the best system of morality, Franklin was aghast at the Presbyterian insistence that natural religion (morality and virtue apprehended in nature by reason) and revealed religion were opposed to each other. Christensen sums up Franklin's religious ideas as belief in "A benevolent God, a life or morality, a belief in Jesus as a supreme law-giver rather than as the incarnate son of God, and a belief in the inherent goodness of man."

Further reading: Aldridge, Alfred Owen. *Benjamin Franklin and Nature's God.* Durham, N.C.: Duke University Press, 1967; Christensen, Merton A. "Franklin on the Hemphill Trial: Deism Versus Presbyterian Orthodoxy." *William and Mary Quarterly* 10 (1953); Morais, Herbert M. "Deism in Revolutionary American (1763–89)." *International Journal of Ethics* 42 (1932); Williams, David. "More Light on Franklin's Religious Ideas." *American Historical Review* 43 (1938).

—Joanne Tetlow

Frazee v. Illinois Department of Employment Security 489 U.S. 829 (1989)

The Supreme Court's unanimous decision in *Frazee v. Illinois Department of Employment Security* was the final opinion in which the Court applied the compelling state interest standard developed by Justice WILLIAM BRENNAN in *SHERBERT V. VERNER* (1963).

William Frazee, who proclaimed himself a Christian yet was not a member of an established denomination, rejected an offer for temporary retail employment from Kelly Services because the position required that he work on Sunday. Frazee applied for unemployment compensation, stating in his application for benefits that he refused the offer of employment "due to his religious convictions." The Illinois Department of Employment Security rejected his claim and Frazee appealed, asserting that his rights under the FREE EXERCISE CLAUSE of the First Amendment were violated by the denial of unemployment compensation.

On March 29, 1989, Justice Byron White delivered the opinion for a unanimous Court. The Court held that the denial of unemployment benefits in Frazee's case violated his free exercise rights. The opinion distinguished *Frazee* from the previous cases involving unemployment compensation and religious freedom: *Sherbert; THOMAS V. REVIEW BOARD OF INDIANA EMPLOYMENT SECURITY* (1981); and *HOBBIE V. UNEMPLOYMENT APPEALS COMMISSION OF FLORIDA* (1987). In each of the previous cases, the individual seeking benefits had been a member of an established church, and the refusal to work resulted from an established religious belief. The Court rejected the idea that the protection of the Free Exercise Clause extended only to those who belong to organized religious groups. The evaluation of a Free Exercise claim rests on whether the individual has a "sincerely held religious belief."

At the conclusion of the opinion, Justice White reinforced the compelling state interest standard from *Sherbert.* Justice White wrote: "there may exist state interests sufficiently compelling to override a legitimate claim to the free exercise of religion. No such interest has been presented here." In the very next term, the Court found a compelling state interest in *EMPLOYMENT DIVISION, DEPARTMENT OF HUMAN RESOURCES OF OREGON V. SMITH* (1990), and the *Sherbert* standard was limited to unemployment compensation cases.

—Sara A. Grove

Freedom Summer (1964)

Freedom Summer was organized by three main organizations: The CONGRESS OF RACIAL EQUALITY (CORE), National Association for the Advancement of Colored People (NAACP), and the STUDENT NONVIOLENT COORDINATING COMMITTEE (SNCC) during the summer of 1964 in the heart of the CIVIL RIGHTS MOVEMENT. The corps of volunteers sent by these organizations were largely northern, white, college students who could afford to bring $500 for bail in case of arrest. In June 1964, the first wave of students left from the training session at Western College for Women in Oxford, Ohio, for the Mississippi delta to register and organize blacks.

Since 1961, volunteers had been working to register African Americans to vote, and Freedom Summer served as the culmination of these activities. Mississippi became the focal point for voter registration drives because of the extremely low percentage of registered African-American voters there, 6.7 percent—the lowest in the nation. The organizers of Freedom Summer—CORE, NAACP, and SNCC—gained national media attention by recruiting white college students to register voters.

During Freedom Summer, 30 "Freedom Schools" were established in Mississippi. These schools were organized to focus on the racial inequalities in the educational system of Mississippi. The schools that African-American children attended were poorly funded, and teachers often used textbooks and reading materials that were out dated and contained racist remarks. The student volunteers were assigned to teach at schools around Mississippi and aid in teaching about the Civil Rights movement, as well as basic math and reading.

The deaths of three student volunteers—James Chaney, Andrew Goodman, and Michael Schwerner—highlighted the potential dangers that the student volunteers faced as they taught in schools and registered African Americans to vote. They had been arrested for speeding and released from jail. But after their release, they failed to check into Freedom Summer headquarters and were not seen after their jail release. Their bodies were found six weeks later, where it was discovered that Goodman and Schwerner had died from gunshot wounds and Chaney from a beating. These deaths made national headlines, and as a result many citizens outside the South became sympathetic to the Civil Rights movement. The amount of media attention these three murdered white students attracted also angered many African Americans, because these were just three of many murders in the drive for civil rights. Moreover, many African Americans in the South resented whites coming into their communities taking leadership positions in civil rights organizations and the elitist attitude that many African Americans felt from the whites.

Freedom Summer also established the Mississippi Freedom Democratic Party (MFDP), which was organized to challenge the all-white Democratic Party. The MFDP registered over 80,000 citizens to join the party and sent 68 delegates to the 1964 and 1968 national Democratic Party conventions. In doing so, they gained media coverage to spotlight important causes MFDP supported. MFDP demonstrated that African Americans had political power and could be mobilized to use it. The status quo of elite white power was becoming more vulnerable now that African Americans had voting power.

The most important result to grow out of Freedom Summer was the 1965 Voting Rights Act. This piece of legislation ensured that old tactics of intimidation to stop African Americans from voting, such as literacy tests and poll taxes, would no longer be lawful. There was also a new political consciousness and awareness that Freedom Summer helped to establish—African Americans began to feel politically empowered. Freedom Summer also helped change the makeup of the Democratic Party. The birth of MFDP demonstrated that given a fair and equal chance, African Americans could be mobilized. Consequently, more African Americans were represented in the Democratic Party than ever before. The overall success of Freedom Summer can be seen in the increased number of registered African-American voters; by 1969, 66.5 percent of voting-age African Americans were registered to vote.

See also CHURCH BURNINGS; RACISM.

Further reading: Congress of Racial Equality. "Freedom Summer." URL: http://www.core-online.org/History/freedom_ summer [Accessed 5-19-2001]; McAdam, Doug. *Freedom Summer*. New York: Oxford University Press, 1988.

—Caroline M. Nordlund

Free Exercise Clause

The Free Exercise Clause refers specifically to the second religion clause of the First Amendment to the U.S. Constitution: "Congress shall make no law respecting an establishment of religion, *or prohibiting the free exercise thereof.*" The phrase "respecting an establishment of religion" is referred to as the ESTABLISHMENT CLAUSE of the First Amendment.

Several landmark Supreme Court cases have dealt with the Free Exercise Clause and have influenced its interpretation. *CANTWELL V. CONNECTICUT* (1940) "incorporated" the Free Exercise Clause, making it applicable to all 50 states via the due process of law guarantee to all U.S. citizens under the FOURTEENTH AMENDMENT. In the *Cantwell* case, the Court affirmed that the First Amendment "embraces two concepts—the freedom to believe and freedom to act. The first is absolute but, in the nature of things, the second cannot be." This decision reinforced the distinction between the absolute right to religious belief and the more limited right to religious action established by the Court in *REYNOLDS V. UNITED STATES* (1878).

The principal division between Supreme Court justices and their opinions in cases dealing with the free exercise of religion has been over what is often characterized as a "preferred freedoms" versus a "nondiscrimination" interpretation of the clause. Under the preferred freedoms interpretation, presented formally for the first time by Justice Frank Murphy in JONES V. OPELIKA (1942), the First Amendment and its two religion clauses are to be elevated for government protection even above other First Amendment liberties. By contrast, the nondiscrimination interpretation, argued most famously by Justice Felix Frankfurter in MINERSVILLE SCHOOL DISTRICT V. GOBITIS (1940), holds that the right to free exercise is not infringed upon by government laws or actions that are generally applicable to all. In that case, the Court held that the expulsion of public schoolchildren who were JEHOVAH'S WITNESSES because of their refusal to salute the American flag in the classroom was not a violation of their constitutional rights. It was simply the nondiscriminatory application of a law designed to promote national unity. Only three years later in WEST VIRGINIA STATE BOARD OF EDUCATION V. BARNETTE, however, the Court effectively reversed the *Gobitis* decision, stating in an almost identical case that refusal to salute the flag posed no "clear and present danger" to the state.

This division between Supreme Court justices over the preferred freedoms and nondiscrimination interpretations of the Free Exercise Clause has persisted and remains controversial. In EMPLOYMENT DIVISION OF OREGON V. SMITH (1990), Justice ANTONIN SCALIA applied the nondiscrimination test in a case involving members of the Native American Church who were terminated from their jobs for using peyote in a religious ritual in violation of state law and were subsequently denied unemployment benefits. Justice Scalia's decision stated that denial of benefits was not a violation of their constitutional rights because while a state may establish nondiscriminatory exemptions to its laws to accommodate religious practice, it is not constitutionally obligated to do so. Application of the nondiscrimination principle in the *Smith* case provoked considerable legal and political activism by religious groups in attempting to negate its perceived infringement on the free exercise of religion.

See also AMERICAN INDIAN RELIGIOUS FREEDOM ACT; *BOB JONES UNIVERSITY V. UNITED STATES; BOWEN V. ROY; BRAUNFELD V. BROWN; COX V. NEW HAMPSHIRE;* INTERNATIONAL HUMAN RIGHT TO FREEDOM OF RELIGION; *LOVELL V. CITY OF GRIFFIN;* RELIGIOUS FREEDOM RESTORATION ACT; *SHERBERT V. VERNER, THOMAS V. REVIEW BOARD OF INDIANA EMPLOYMENT SECURITY DIVISION; WISCONSIN V. YODER.*

—Derek H. Davis

Freemasonry

Many groups and at least one political party have made the allegation that Freemasonry and the various orders of Freemasons are religious organizations. The secrecy that accompanies the meetings has added to that belief. Instead, as teachers of morality and providers of education, the Lodges of Masonry scattered across the county have in the past been guardians of tradition and transmitters of culture. Thirteen of the 56 signers of the DECLARATION OF INDEPENDENCE were Masons. At least 15 presidents of the United States have been members of various lodges.

Modern Freemasonry arose in England in the early to middle 1700s. It used symbols of the craft guilds of Europe and Great Britain to illustrate its teachings. By the time it reached the American colonies, it was well established as a place for the determination of community affairs, as a fraternal and benevolent society, and as a bond to bring together disparate people in the westward movement after the Revolutionary War.

In spite of these positive traits, the secrecy of Masonic ritual has been seen from the outside as sinister. Because certain rituals speak of shedding of blood to keep the secrets of Masons and Masonry, many churches were opposed to the Masonic orders. As descriptions of their ceremonies leaked out, the lodges were demonized.

Many people, especially some church leaders, were afraid the Masons were controlling much of the economic life of the country. As a result, some political parties arose in the United States that opposed political candidates who were Masons.

One event that sparked this rise in political activity was the disappearance of William Morgan, an anti-Masonic crusader who wrote a book purporting to reveal Masonic secrets. The Masons were accused, without proof, of having murdered him, and in reaction some local organizations arose to oppose Masons running for public office. At the time of Morgan's disappearance, many had come to believe that Freemasonry was a secretive power behind the government, thwarting the will of the people and murdering those who dared cross it. Religious leaders denounced the fraternity as anti-Christian. It did not help the Masonic cause that most of the elected officials brought to trial for Morgan's disappearance were elected officials of surrounding communities.

Various rabble-rousers came forward to denounce the Masons. One such was Thurlow Weed. Weed, who had learned the printer's trade, worked on various upstate New York newspapers and became a leader in the ANTI-MASONIC PARTY. When the Masons forced him out as manager of the Rochester *Telegraph*, he started an anti-Masonic campaign paper in 1830 called the Albany *Evening Journal*, which became a leading organ of the Whig Party. Soon the fear of Masonry manifested itself in the creation of the first major third party in American politics: the specifically named Anti-Masonic Party. Anti-Masonry came to such a fevered pitch that an anti-Masonic Party member, Millard Filmore, was elected vice president and succeeded to the presidency after the death of Zachary Taylor in 1850. By then, anti-Masonic fervor had died down, overshadowed by the rise of the ABOLITIONIST MOVEMENT.

Anti-Masonic feeling has never died in the United States, however. After the Civil War, the National Christian Association declared:

In the United States, occupied by schemes peculiar to young nations, secret orders are not now met or understood as they are in Europe, as working by misrepresentation, intimidation and murder; or even as they were in this country fifty years ago. Then Captain William Morgan said, 'I owe to my country an exposure of its dangers.' He made the exposure and Masons murdered him in 1826.

Various church assaults on Masonic orders have ceased. At the 1992 national gathering of the SOUTHERN BAPTIST CONVENTION, a motion from the floor charged a committee of the convention, the Interfaith Witness Department, to study whether Masonry was a pagan or possibly demonic religion. The study was withdrawn at the 1993 meeting after the charges were found to be false. Criticism of Masonry by churches will undoubtedly continue. The Masonic lodges, in keeping with their tradition, continue to remain silent in the face of the criticism.

Further reading: Freemasonry on the Web: URL: http://freemasonry.org/; National Christian Association. "Consisting Of Forty-three Anti-Secrecy Tracts." Montague, Mass.: Acacia Press. URL: http://www.crocker.com/~acacia/text_amsb.html, 1996 [1883].

—StanLey M. Morris

Free Presbyterians

The issue of slavery during the pre–Civil War years created a schism within the Presbyterian Church. The 1837 division between Old School and New School Presbyterians was the first split within any denomination over the issue of slavery. There were doctrinal and other issues involved in the schism, but slavery was of the utmost significance. The Free Presbyterians arose in the midst of the slavery controversy during this antebellum period. They had one goal: the abolition of slavery (see ABOLITIONIST MOVEMENT). No other principle could compete with that moral conviction, not even denominational unity. To understand the Free Presbyterians, it is necessary to look at the New School Presbyterians arising from the 1837 schism.

The Act of 1818 unanimously declared the Presbyterian Church's antislavery position. Yet despite the fact that the act's language—"slavery was condemned 'as utterly inconsistent with the law of God'"—quelled the concerns of the North, a tolerant attitude toward the South remained. A decade later, abolitionist Presbyterians challenged the church to act on its 1818 proclamation. The issue was filibustered until 1835 by conservative proslavery elements in the denomination. The Philadelphia Presbytery and other moderate Princeton groups opposed to abolitionist activism and concerned about division in the church prevented the issue from coming to the floor of the General Assembly.

Earlier, the Philadelphia Presbytery had worked to spread Presbyterianism in the West and the South. Because of the large presence of Congregationalism in New England, Presbyterians entered into the Plan of Union of 1801 with the Congregationalists to cooperatively spread Calvinist Christianity in the West. But a doctrinal break occurred when the Congregationalists moved away from Calvinism to the Arminian influence of Unitarianism. This set up the Old School–New School schism that would not only reflect the theological divide between CALVINISM and Arminianism, but also represent the proslavery and antislavery partition. The New School Presbyterians, influenced by the New Divinity idea of the Congregationalists, objected to the limits that the Old School doctrine of predestination and election placed on human liberty. More rationalistic and favorable to the goodness of humanity, the New School vehemently opposed slavery as a sin.

Before 1835, the South had not taken a position between the Old and New School difference on slavery, ordering Presbyterians to "Not agitate or discuss this subject in any way whatever. Let there be silence respecting it." Finally, though, in 1835 the issue was unavoidable. The New School evangelist, Charles G. Finney, had started his revivalist movement, and one of his disciples, Theodore Dwight Weld, effectively promoted the thesis that slaveholding was sin. Charles Hodge, the Old School theologian, argued that slaveholding could be consistent with Scripture and that the New Light believers were subordinating the Word of God to their own inner light. Equating New Schoolism with abolitionism and heterodoxy, the Old School hoped to save the South from leaving the church.

When the General Assembly convened in 1837, the South had moved decidedly to the Old School side; however, the tide had turned against the antiabolitionists. In 1836, there had been 35 antislavery Presbyteries compared with 33 antiabolitionist Presbyteries, but now, in 1837, the numbers were disproportionate: 53 antislavery Presbyteries compared with 41 antiabolitionist. The schism was inevitable. During the 1837 General Assembly meeting, the New School severed itself from the denomination. Opposition came from three groups: "the Godly, who were seriously concerned with the purity of the faith, from the conservatives, alarmed by the radicalism and excesses of the New School (of which abolitionism was only a phase), and also from those whose fortunes were directly or indirectly affected by the agitation of the slavery question."

Part of the inspirational vigor of the New School abolitionists was immediatism, which "functioned 'as a kind of surrogate religion.'" The immediatists believed that slaves should be emancipated at once and that the church itself should be purged equally from the scourges of slavery. It was this "devotion to the welfare of mankind" and a "new and higher spiritual life" that motivated the immediatists to embrace abolition as the practical manifestation of Christianity. "For abolitionists, benevolence meant more than mere sympathy for the slave. Action was the infallible test of true benevolence and charity." Since slavery was evil and sinful, there was no reason to delay emancipation. Rather than characterizing slavery euphemistically as an "undefined evil, or calamity, or misfortune," the immediatists specifically charged slavery as a moral evil, a crime that was unacceptable to both church and state.

A decade after the 1837 schism, the Free Presbyterians established themselves as fervent abolitionists who followed the tenets of immediatism. Although opposed to slavery, the Synod of Cincinnati tolerated proslavery sentiments among its members. For the Presbytery of Ripley, Ohio, a complete elimination of slaveholders was necessary, so it called a convention in 1847 to establish an antislavery Presbyterian Church. "The convention met and the Free Presbyterian Church was created by the congregations that withdrew from the Synod of Cincinnati." The Christians of the Free Presbyterian Church "wanted free soil principles to apply in church as well as state." In their minds, God would not abolish slavery until the Church was first purged of this sin.

On April 17, 1850, the Christian Antislavery Convention met in Cincinnati with the Free Presbyterians as a predominant presence. Member churches of the American Home Missionary Society (AHMS) and the American Board of Commissioners of Foreign Missions (ABCFM) were criticized for their connections to slavery. The AHMS had been formed in 1826 to represent all Calvinist churches in the missionary effort to settle the West, whereas Congregationalists established the ABCFM in 1810 as the first American foreign mission society. "The AHMS and the ABCFM became the agents of the New School Presbyterians, Congregationalists, and the smaller evangelical Calvinists at a time when the antislavery movement was greatly agitated." These missionary organizations were not acceptable to Free Presbyterians. At the 1850 convention, the Western Home and Foreign Missionary Association (WHFMA) was formed "to aid antislavery churches that had withdrawn from AHMS." The Board of Home and Foreign Missions of the Free Presbyterian Church, formed in 1848, was merged into the WHFMA. By 1852, many New School Presbyterian churches in the West became a part of the Free Presbyterian Church by association with the WHFMA.

The Free Presbyterians remained part of the New School movement against slavery during the tumultuous years of the Kansas-Nebraska Act of 1854 and the election of 1856, leading to the Civil War in 1861.

See also PRESBYTERIAN CHURCH IN AMERICA; PRESBYTERIAN CHURCH USA; SECTIONAL DIVIDE OF THE CHURCHES OVER SLAVERY.

Further reading: Howard, Victor B. *Conscience and Slavery, The Evangelistic Calvinist Domestic Missions, 1837–1861.* Kent, Ohio: Kent State University Press, 1990; Loveland, Anne C. "Evangelicalism and 'Immediate Emancipation' in American Antislavery Thought." *Journal of Southern History* (1966): 32; Staiger, C. Bruce. "Abolitionism and the Presbyterian Schism of 1837–1838." *Mississippi Valley Historical Review* 36 (1949).

—Joanne Tetlow

fundamentalism

Fundamentalism is an extremely broad term that often used to describe any of a number of doctrinally conservative religious movements. Although precise definitions vary, there appears to exist at least an approximate scholarly consensus on some common elements of fundamentalist movements. First, fundamentalists are thought to emphasize an authoritative view of Scripture. For example, Christian fundamentalists in the United States generally hold that the Bible is literally true in matters of theology, history, and science, and contains no errors of fact. Second, fundamentalist movements are often regarded as antimodern in that their adherents resist certain aspects of contemporary social and economic changes. Finally, fundamentalist movements are explicitly political, in that they seek to use public, authoritative means to accomplish their ends.

Many analysts have attempted to apply the concept of fundamentalism to a wide variety of contemporary religious movements across the globe. Thus, one can read of ROMAN CATHOLIC CHURCH fundamentalist movements such as Opus Dei or the Lefevre movement, or instances of Islamic fundamentalism, such as the Khomeini regime in Iran, or Jama'at-s Islami. The label of fundamentalist as been applied to the Hindu organization RSS in India, and to Jewish movements, such as haredim or Gush Emunim.

Strictly speaking, however, the term *fundamentalist* is most appropriately applied to a movement in U.S. PROTESTANTISM that emerged in the early 20th century. In response to such modernist trends as the rise of science (including the spread of evolutionary theory), the emergence of biblical "Higher Criticism" in American universities, and a generally morally relaxed atmosphere during and after World War I, doctrinally conservative Protestants sought to preserve the core elements of Christian orthodoxy. This trend culminated in the publication of 15 small pamphlets on "the fundamentals" of the Christian faith between 1910 and 1915. These "fundamentals" included such beliefs as the inerrancy of Scripture, the Virgin Birth, the bodily Resurrection of Christ, and Christ's glorious Second Coming.

The emergence and tactics of fundamentalist groups have changed during the 20th century. For much of the movement's history, fundamentalists have sought to achieve a certain separatism from worldly affairs. The "otherwordly" nature of fundamentalism has often inhibited such believers from engaging in overt political activity. But, fundamentalist groups have constituted important political forces in U.S. politics during three distinct periods of American history. In the 1920s, fundamentalist movements became active in response to a sudden increase in Catholic immigration as a result of World War I (providing the impetus for Prohibition) and the popularization of the theory of evolution. In the 1950s, groups such as the CHRISTIAN ANTICOMMUNIST CRUSADE and the JOHN BIRCH SOCIETY arose as a reaction to the threat allegedly posed by international and domestic communism. Finally, the late 1970s and the 1980s saw another increase in fundamentalist political activity, inspired in part by conservative reaction to the Supreme Court's *ROE V. WADE* decision (which legalized ABORTION in most circumstances) and to the emergence of an increasingly visible, assertive GAY RIGHTS movement. Manifestations of this most recent surge in fundamentalist activity include MORAL MAJORITY, the more recent CHRISTIAN COALITION, and PAT ROBERTSON's 1988 campaign for the Republican presidential nomination.

During periods of peak political activity, fundamentalist political movements in the United States have exhibited a strong ecumenical quality. In the 1950s, the largely Baptist Christian Anti-Communist Crusade made common cause with the mostly Catholic John Birch Society. Prominent anticommunist leaders included such Catholic clergy as FATHER CHARLES COUGHLIN in the 1930s and Bishop Fulton Sheen in the 1950s. Similarly, the 1980s witnessed the emergence of a broad coalition of conservative Protestants, ranging from the relatively austere fundamentalism of JERRY FALWELL to the "health and wealth" charismatic Christian message of JIM BAKKER and TAMMY FAYE BAKKER's *PTL Club*.

The history of religiously motivated political movements in the United States, however, suggests that these movements are ultimately fragmented by the effects of religious particularism; that is, since fundamentalists are often very concerned with matters of doctrine, coalitions among doctrinally diverse Christians are often quite unstable. Thus, it has been suggested that the Protestant fundamentalist/Roman Catholic anticommunist coalition of the 1950s could not survive the religious tensions posed by the presidential candidacy of JOHN F. KENNEDY in 1960. Similarly, charismatic Protestant Pat Robertson was unable to mobilize culturally conservative voters beyond his relatively narrow base of PENTECOSTAL Christians. Differences with leaders such as Jerry Falwell over such issues as faith healing and glossolalia (speaking in tongues) limited Robertson's appeal among noncharismatic fundamentalists. It may be, therefore, that strict adherence to doctrinal orthodoxy provides the basis for both the mobilization and the demobilization of fundamentalist political movements.

See also CHRISTIAN RIGHT AND THE REPUBLICAN PARTY; RELIGION IN THE 1988 PRESIDENTIAL ELECTION; SCOPE'S "MONKEY" TRIAL; SOUTHERN REPUBLICAN REALIGNMENT.

Further reading: Jelen, Ted G. *The Political Mobilization of Religious Beliefs.* Westport, Conn.: Praeger, 1991; Marty, Martin E., and R. Scott Appleby. *Fundamentalisms Observed* Chicago: University of Chicago Press, 1991; ———. *Fundamentalisms and the State.* Chicago: University of Chicago Press, 1993; Wilcox, Clyde. *God's Warriors: The Christian Right in Twentieth-Century America.* Baltimore: Johns Hopkins University Press, 1992.

—Ted G. Jelen

G

Gallagher v. Crown Kosher Supermarket 366 U.S. 617 (1961)

One of a set of 1961 U.S. Supreme Court decisions known as the "Sunday Closing Law cases," *Gallagher v. Crown Kosher Supermarket* upheld a Massachusetts law against a challenge that it denied equal protection, constituted an establishment of religion, and prohibited the free exercise of religion. Chief Justice Earl Warren wrote an opinion, joined by three other justices, announcing the judgment of the Court. Two members of the Court concurred with the holding of the Court, although not with the opinion. Three justices dissented from the Court's ruling.

The Massachusetts Sunday Closing Law was similar to those found in many other states through the middle of the 20th century. The statutes here, found in a chapter of state law entitled "Observance of the Lord's Day," generally forbade operating a store or performing any sort of employment on Sunday. Exceptions to the law were provided for charitable and emergency work. Moreover, there were numerous exceptions for the production and sale of a variety of commodities including milk and bread, retail drugs, tobacco, candy, and ice cream. Under the exceptions, Crown Kosher could have operated on Sunday mornings until ten o'clock to sell kosher meats, an option the storeowners declined as economically unfeasible.

Crown Kosher, a corporation under the control of adherents of ORTHODOX JUDAISM, operated in Springfield, Massachusetts, selling kosher meats and other, primarily kosher, foods. Most of the store's customers were also Orthodox Jews; three representatives from among them also challenged the Sunday closing requirements. Joining the store and its customers as a party to the case was Springfield's chief Orthodox rabbi, representing rabbis responsible for verifying that kosher markets were in compliance with Jewish dietary laws.

In its equal protection claim, Crown Kosher argued that the exceptions in the Sunday closing law were so "numerous and arbitrary" that they lacked any reasonable basis. Chief Justice Warren, to the contrary, held that the exceptions provided in the statute could well find justification in a legislative determination. He observed that the legislature had made a reasonable distinction, for example, between the sale of fresh milk and bread and the sale of less perishable groceries. Thus, the equal protection requirement that distinctions have a rational basis had been met.

The establishment of religion claim—that the purpose of the Sunday closing laws was to secure Sunday, the Christian Sabbath, as the Sabbath Day of the state—was also dismissed by the chief justice. He agreed that the laws had originally had a religious goal, but he observed that modifications of the laws over the years indicated that the religious purpose had been lost. The exceptions written into the law and amendments allowing such leisure activities as dancing and most sports demonstrated that the contemporary goal of the Sunday closing law was to promote an atmosphere of rest and recreation, not to aid religion.

Finally, the law was challenged on religious freedom grounds. Crown Kosher was closed from before sundown Friday to after sundown Saturday, when Orthodox Jews are forbidden by their religion to conduct commercial affairs. The store claimed that the Sunday closing laws put it at an economic disadvantage, effectively limiting it to operating four and one-half days a week, whereas other merchants could sell their groceries on six. The Orthodox Jewish customers claimed that the effect of the closing law on them was to deprive them for two days each week of the ability to purchase the kosher food required by their religious dietary laws. The rabbis argued that their work of certifying the quality of the kosher meats was made difficult because meat delivered to the store on Friday could not be sold until Monday. Warren dealt with these claims summarily; the decision in the Sunday closing law case of *BRAUNFELD V. BROWN* meant that these similar claims were also rejected.

See also BLUE LAWS.

—Susan E. Grogan

Gathering Storm in the Churches, The: A Sociologist Looks at the Widening Gap Between Clergy and Laymen (1969) By Jeffrey K. Hadden. New York: Doubleday

Written by sociologist Jeffrey K. Hadden in 1969, *The Gathering Storm in the Churches* remains the landmark assessment of the changing political role of American churches during the 1960s. The work was based on an unprecedented mail survey of almost 10,000 Protestant clergy, primarily from mainline denominations, extensive personal interviews with hundreds of ministers, polls on the religious and political beliefs of laity (and their attitude toward clergy involvement in politics), and several qualitative case studies.

For Hadden, the "gathering storm" was the widening gap between Protestant ministers and their parishioners over theology and politics. He saw a "threefold crisis" of meaning, belief, and authority in Protestant churches, revealed by the contemporary struggle over civil rights. On the one side were many clergy who no longer subscribed to traditional Christian doctrines and, indeed, had often abandoned "otherworldly" religion altogether. For such "New Breed" ministers, the traditional tasks of saving souls and comforting the faithful were replaced by an ecumenical commitment to advance SOCIAL JUSTICE in the present world.

This new public purpose for the church was resisted by committed laity, who often held more traditional religious beliefs and were politically conservative. Not only did clergy and laity differ on doctrine and political perspective, but on the political role of the clergy as well. While New Breed ministers were flooding into social movements against RACISM, the VIETNAM WAR, and other social injustices, most laity regarded these activities with skepticism and, sometimes, downright hostility. Ultimately, then, the "gathering storm" was rooted in divergent clerical and lay understandings about the contemporary meaning of Christian faith.

Given the widespread conflict in local parishes, the most politically active Protestant religious leaders tended to be the clergy most distant from the laity: denominational staff (especially in social mission agencies), campus chaplains, seminary faculty, and those in similar organizational "niches." Hadden showed that organizational location ("structural freedom") was an important predictor of clergy activism: the more insulated the minister, the more active politically. Clearly, political involvement that depended on such freedom was precarious over the long run, given the modest number of such positions.

As a sympathetic observer of New Breed ministers, Hadden hoped they could maintain their political activism. But how might the *gathering storm* be averted? He saw four possible resolutions of the conflict. First, New Breed clergy might withdraw entirely from political involvement or adopt a strategy of nonconfrontational gradualism. A second possible outcome was that traditionalist (Old Breed) clergy and conservative laity might capture denominational institutions, forcing out the New

Breed and their lay sympathizers. Or, more improbably, liberal clergy might seize control of those denominations and eject their opponents. Finally, New Breed ministers might simply leave the church to continue the social struggle from other professional venues. To Hadden, none of these options was at once plausible and desirable. Rather, he admonished New Breed clergy to adopt a fifth option: to discover ways to engage parishioners in the struggle for social justice.

As the first major empirical study of clergy politics, *The Gathering Storm* set the basic framework for later studies. Harold Quinley's *The Prophetic Clergy* (1974) extended Hadden's analysis to a detailed account of the battles in California between liberal clergy and conservative laity over open housing, farm worker unionization, and the Vietnam War. Like Hadden, Quinley lauded the liberal New Breed as the vanguard of clerical activism, regarding conservative ministers as politically irrelevant, but he was more pessimistic about their ability to circumvent or convert conservative laity. And many of the 1960s New Breed pastors had left the church by the late 1970s. Nevertheless, later studies found the New Breed surviving, if not prospering, in the 1990s. Like their 1960s predecessors, the New Breed of the 1990s not only faced skeptical congregations but also confronted invigorated Christian Right ministers, active in conservative causes and enjoying more support from conservative laity.

See also BULLY PULPIT, THE; CIVIL RIGHTS MOVEMENT; WAYWARD SHEPHERDS.

Further reading: Guth, James L., John C. Green, Corwin E. Smidt, Lyman A. Kellstedt, and Margaret M. Poloma. *The Bully Pulpit: The Politics of Protestant Clergy.* Lawrence: University Press of Kansas, 1997; Quinley, Harold E. *The Prophetic Clergy: Social Activism among Protestant Ministers.* New York: Wiley, 1974.

—James L. Guth

gay and lesbian marriage

Gay and lesbian marriage is one of the most controversial issues raised by the GAY RIGHTS movement that began in the 1970s. Although it did not top the movement's agenda in its early years, by the mid-1990s same-gender marriage had become one of the leading issues for both political and religious advocates of gay rights. The legalization of same-gender marriages and their legal alternative, "civil unions," has met with tremendous opposition from both the courts and religious leaders, along with some members of the gay and lesbian community itself, many of whom believe that marriage is a patriarchal institution that should be interrogated rather than sought after. Despite strong popular resistance, the Hawaii Supreme Court raised the possibility of same-gender marriages in 1993 with its landmark decision on *Baehr v. Miike,* in which it ruled that the state's failure to recognize gay

Gay protestors demonstrate outside Chicago's City Hall to call attention to the issue of gay marriage. *(Tim Boyle/Getty Images)*

marriages was a form of gender discrimination. However, the state's voters later rejected proposed legislation to legalize same-gender marriage. Then in July 2000, same-gender civil unions granting the same legal benefits to gays and lesbians as to heterosexual couples were legalized in Vermont, and as of this writing over 1,000 gay and lesbian couples have obtained licenses declaring their unions official under Vermont law.

The 1993 ruling by Hawaii's State Supreme Court in favor of same-gender unions gave rise to a political backlash against gay and lesbian marriage, and since then 35 states have passed legislation barring recognition of same-gender unions. At the federal level, Congress passed the Defense of Marriage Act (DOMA) in 1996, which denied federal recognition of gay and lesbian marriages and allowed states to ignore same-gender unions licensed in other states.

Religious institutions are deeply divided on the issue of gay and lesbian marriage, and several denominations have issued statements prohibiting same-gender unions in recent years. The ROMAN CATHOLIC CHURCH remains unequivocally opposed to same-gender unions, and in 1996 the NATIONAL CONFERENCE OF CATHOLIC BISHOPS released a statement declaring that God created marriage for the purposes of procreation and love solely among heterosexuals. In May 2000, the UNITED METHODIST CHURCH's General Conference voted

overwhelmingly to oppose same-gender commitment ceremonies and to discipline ministers who perform them. In June 2000, the PRESBYTERIAN CHURCH USA reaffirmed its commitment to marriage as restricted to heterosexual couples, prohibiting same-gender unions from being conducted on church property, and in July 2000, the EPISCOPAL CHURCH's House of Bishops rejected a proposal to institute ceremonial rites for same-gender unions.

The debate has raged especially fiercely in ecumenical Protestant circles, and in keeping with the Protestant value of freedom of individual conscience, ministers in several denominations have continued to perform same-gender unions and commitment ceremonies in opposition to their churches' official positions. These acts of conscience have provoked varied reactions by church authorities. In the United Methodist Church, for example, Reverend JIMMY CREECH was removed from his congregation and his ministry in November 1999 for performing a same-gender union ceremony, but in June 2001 General Conference representatives decided not to pursue charges against Reverend Donald Fado, who had presided over a highly publicized holy union between two female church leaders in Sacramento, California. And the General Assembly of the Presbyterian Church USA recently issued a statement that it will not bring charges against ministers who perform same-gender unions so long as they emphasize to the couple that their "union" is not the same as a heterosexual marriage.

Opposition among religious institutions is not uniform, however, as some denominations have taken a quite emphatic and public stand in favor of same-gender unions. The METROPOLITAN COMMUNITY CHURCHES have performed same-gender unions since their establishment in the late 1960s, and founder Reverend Troy Perry has organized several public demonstrations of sorts, holding public "weddings" for gays and lesbians at the 1987 and 1993 National Lesbian, Gay, and Bi Equal Rights and Liberation Marches on Washington, D.C. Other religious bodies, such as the RECONSTRUCTIONIST Rabbinical Association, the UNITARIAN-UNIVERSALIST Association, Open and Affirming congregations in the United Church of Christ, and several meetings of the Religious Society of Friends (QUAKERS) also endorse and perform same-gender unions.

Further reading: Christensen, Jean. "Hawaii Court Stops Gay Marriage." Associated Press, December 10, 1999; Duffy, Shannon. "Pushing the States on Gay Unions." *National Law Journal,* November 27, 2000; Ettelbrick, Paula. "Since When Is Marriage a Path to Liberation?" In *Lesbian and Gay Marriage: Private Commitments, Public Ceremonies.* Edited by Suzanne Sherman. Philadelphia: Temple University Press, 1993; Olsen, Ted. "Presbyterian Court OKs Gay Unions." *Christianity Today,* May 22, 2001.

—Krista McQueeney

gay rights

No aspect of life has elicited greater political involvement on the part of religious groups than sexuality in general, and homosexuality in particular. Religious groups became most active in antigay activities and rhetoric soon after the modern-day gay rights movement in the United States began in June 1969 in New York City, after a police raid on a gay bar, popularly referred to as the Stonewall riot, from the name of the bar. Since then, a number of organizations have been formed to work for gay rights against growing antigay sentiment.

In religious circles, Christian conservatives have tirelessly opposed gay rights, as they have sought to bolster men's and women's traditional roles in the home and the workplace. The FAMILY RESEARCH COUNCIL, a nonprofit organization founded in 1977, produces internationally syndicated daily radio programs, opposes "same-sex marriage," and seeks to maintain the traditional heterosexual understanding of marriage and family. Similar groups, such as FOCUS ON THE FAMILY, a Washington-based nonprofit that promotes Judeo-Christian values, oppose equating homosexuality with civil rights. By the 1990s, such groups' work proved successful when a string of gay rights measures were successfully repealed or amended in state constitutions. For example, in 1992 Colorado became the first state to nullify an existing civil rights protection for homo-

sexuals by amending its constitution. The U.S. Supreme Court would later strike down the provision in 1996.

In terms of politics and public policymaking, groups like Dr. James Dobson's Focus on the Family face opposition from organizations including the Religious Leadership Roundtable, who argue that gay, lesbian, bisexual, and transgender (GLBT) people face pervasive discrimination in the workplace, in housing, in public accommodations, and in other areas. The Religious Leadership Roundtable, a group of some 40 spiritual leaders, seeks to combat the antigay rhetoric of the Religious Right by promoting a more tolerant, faith-based message that affirms GLBT equality on issues such as employment discrimination, adoption, partnership and marriage, and discrimination in the U.S. military. Additionally, organizations such at the Washington-based National Gay and Lesbian Task Force and Lambda Legal Defense Fund work to ensure the civil rights of their members through litigation and legislation. More specifically, AMERICANS UNITED FOR THE SEPARATION OF CHURCH AND STATE, a group that seeks to protect religious liberties, has filed lawsuits on behalf of gay men and lesbians fired on the basis of their sexual orientation.

Members of the GLBT community received support from the American Academy of Pediatrics (AAP) in February 2002 when the group endorsed the adoption of children by gays and lesbians. The AAP cited estimates suggesting that as many as 9 million American children have at least one gay parent when urging its 55,000 members to take an active role in supporting measures that allow homosexual adoption. The TRADITIONAL VALUES COALITION, a Christian lobbying group, dismissed the endorsement as a disservice to medicine.

By the year 2000, the United Church of Christ was the only mainline Protestant denomination to allow GAY AND LESBIAN MARRIAGE. Other Protestant denominations such as the PRESBYTERIAN CHURCH USA, the EPISCOPAL CHURCH, and the UNITED METHODIST CHURCH have considered, but voted not to recognize, unions between two people of the same sex. Under a same-sex union, or marriage, gay and lesbian couples would receive the same benefits, rights, and privileges as any heterosexual couple. As citizens and taxpayers, groups including the National Lesbian and Gay Law Association, established in 1988 as an affiliate of the American Bar Association, argue that gay and lesbian couples should share the same "common benefits" of marriage that the state provides automatically to married couples, such as HEALTH CARE coverage, family leave care, and Social Security benefits. By the mid-1990s, however, many states began explicitly banning same-sex marriages. By 1999, 30 states had done so. Nonetheless, some states, for instance California and Hawaii, do have statewide domestic partnership arrangements, and the Vermont Supreme Court in 2000 passed the most comprehensive legislation giving same-sex couples the same benefits as heterosexual couples.

See also MAINLINE PROTESTANT PRO-GAY GROUPS.

—Veronica Donahue DiConti

Girouard v. United States 328 U.S. 61 (1946)

In *Girouard*, decided on April 22, 1946, Justice William O. Douglas, writing for a sharply divided Supreme Court, held on the basis of statutory construction (with expressly reaching the constitutional issue), that a promise to bear arms in defense of the United States could not legally be made a precondition to the naturalization of a resident alien. In *Girouard*, the Court overruled three earlier statutory construction cases, UNITED STATES V. SCHWIMMER, UNITED STATES V. MACINTOSH, and *United States v. Bland*. Chief Justice Harlan F. Stone and Justices Stanley F. Reed and Felix Frankfurter dissented. Justice Robert H. Jackson, who had joined the Court that term, did not participate in the decision.

James Louis Girouard was a native citizen of Canada. He applied for naturalization to become a U.S. citizen. Girouard stated that he was willing to take the oath of allegiance [8 U.S.C. § 735(b) 8 U.S.C.A. 735(b)], which required him to affirm that he would "support and defend the Constitution and laws of the United States of America against all enemies, foreign and domestic." However, an additional question in the citizenship questionnaire asked, "If necessary are you willing to take up arms in defense of this country?" Girouard wrote, "No, SEVENTH DAY ADVENTIST." Girouard told the examiner that his refusal to bear arms was based solely on his religious commitment. He had claimed exemption from combat duty with the Selective Service Board based on his religious commitments, but was willing to serve in a noncombatant position. The District Court admitted Girouard to citizenship.

The United States appealed to the First Circuit Court of Appeal. With one member of the panel dissenting, the appellate court reversed the decision of the district court, relying on the *Schwimmer, Macintosh,* and *Bland* decisions. Schwimmer then appealed to the Supreme Court.

In his majority opinion for the Court, Justice Douglas first noted that the statute did not by its express language require service in the armed forces or a willingness to bear arms as a precondition to naturalization. He pointed out that there were many other ways to support and defend the country, even in time of great peril or war. He cited physicists developing nuclear bombs, assembly-line workers building war supplies, merchant seamen, construction workers, nurses, engineers, litter bearers, doctors, and chaplains, as others who make "essential contributions." Persons whose religious scruples forbid bearing arms may make equally important contributions in these ways and may love their country as much as those who take up rifle or bayonet to defend America, Justice Douglas stated.

The majority opinion also noted that under Article VI, Clause 3 of the U.S. Constitution, Girouard could not be barred from holding public office because of his religiously based CONSCIENTIOUS OBJECTION to serving in combat. It did not seem reasonable that Congress intended a higher standard for naturalization than for being a member of Congress.

Douglas's majority opinion bluntly conceded that the Court's earlier decisions in *Schwimmer, Macintosh,* and *Bland*

reached the opposite result, and *Bland*, at least, was factually indistinguishable. Relying on Justice Oliver Wendell Holmes's dissent in *Schwimmer* and Chief Justice Charles Evans Hughes's dissent in *Macintosh*, the Court held that the *Schwimmer, Macintosh,* and *Bland* cases were wrongly decided. While not specifically addressing any FREE EXERCISE CLAUSE claim that Girouard might have, Douglas did quote from Holmes's dissent in *Schwimmer*, which was based on the freedom of religion guarantees of the First Amendment. A majority of the Supreme Court has never held that conscientious objector exemptions to Selective Service are constitutionally mandated, but rather are a matter of legislative grace. One assumes that there were not five votes on the Court to base the decision on constitutional grounds, and the constitutional argument for Girouard is never mentioned expressly, but only implicitly in the citation to the *Schwimmer* dissent.

The dissent relied on the legislative history of the then-applicable Naturalization Act of 1940. In *Schwimmer*, the Supreme Court had refused to order the naturalization of a resident alien who proposed to take a modified oath of allegiance stating that the putative naturalized citizen would not bear arms. The *Schwimmer* decision had been decided 10 years earlier when the Naturalization Act was adopted. There had been extensive hearings, and the attorney general as well as the relevant congressional committees had been involved. There was nothing in the legislative history to indicate a desire to overrule *Schwimmer*. Therefore, in the opinion of dissenting justices, the circuit court should have been affirmed.

Girouard v. United States does not create a constitutional right of a resident alien who objects to bearing arms on religious grounds to become a naturalized citizen. Presumably, Congress could amend the naturalization statute to expressly deny naturalization to conscientious objectors without violating *Girouard*. Without such an explicit intention within the statute, however, *Girouard* forbids such requirement being imposed based on principles of statutory construction.

—Stephen R. Prescott

God's Warriors: The Christian Right in Twentieth-Century America (1992) By Clyde Wilcox.
Baltimore: Johns Hopkins University Press

God's Warriors is a careful scholarly account of popular support for the Christian Right, and the book has been well received by its intended audience of social scientists. Wilcox's statistical analysis may confuse readers not versed in quantitative methods, but the substantive conclusions are clear in the text, helping make the book accessible to a general audience as well. The key arguments are as follows: support for the Christian Right is based on conservative religious and political attitudes; the basis of support exhibits significant continuities and differences over time; important divisions exist within the movement; political effects in the 1980s were modest; and there is a potential Christian Right constituency in the black community.

Support Based on Attitudes

Wilcox finds that support for the Christian Right is rational in both the vernacular and social-scientific senses of the word; it is not based on psychopathology, and it represents a choice that is consistent with voters' preferences and beliefs. Wilcox investigates several alternative hypotheses, including claims that political alienation, authoritarian personality, and social status concerns are the foundation for Christian Right support. He finds, however, that support for the Christian Right is best understood in terms of congruence between the religious and political beliefs of supporters and the positions taken by Christian Right leaders. "In this respect, support for the Christian Right is no different in kind than support for the Sierra Club, the National Organization for Women, or any other political group."

Changes Over Time

Wilcox's analysis is focused on three phases of Christian Right activity: the CHRISTIAN ANTI-COMMUNISM CRUSADE in 1964 (though it began in 1952), the MORAL MAJORITY in 1984, and PAT ROBERTSON's presidential campaign in 1988. Although the crusade garnered a relatively broad base of support, including religiously motivated supporters who were moderate on most issues, supporters of the Moral Majority and Pat Robertson were strongly conservative on a host of social, economic, and foreign policy issues, including ABORTION, PORNOGRAPHY, and communism. The broader basis of the crusade's support is probably attributable to its focus on a single issue that was of concern to many Americans. In taking strongly conservative positions on an array of issues, the Moral Majority and 1988 Robertson presidential campaign limited their appeal to a smaller, more conservative bloc of voters than might otherwise have been possible.

Divisions Within the Movement

The success of the movement has been limited by divisions within. The target constituency of the Christian Right—white evangelical Christians—has notable diversity and cleavages within it, particularly between more fundamentalist evangelicals (i.e., SOUTHERN BAPTIST CONVENTION) and PENTECOSTAL AND CHARISMATIC evangelicals (i.e., ASSEMBLIES OF GOD). Although these groups share significant doctrinal overlap and tend to agree about policy (e.g., opposing abortion and pornography and supporting PRAYER IN PUBLIC SCHOOLS) and who their enemies are (e.g., feminists, homosexuals, communists, and liberals), they have important differences in an area that could be termed the epistemology of faith: while fundamentalists find truth in a literal interpretation of the Bible, Pentecostals embrace spirit-filled revelation in a way that many fundamentalists reject. These cleavages are a significant barrier to evangelical political mobilization. Robertson was unable to rally support beyond the Pentecostal and charismatic bloc, while the Moral Majority's strength lay with fundamentalist Baptists. Fundamentalist antipathy toward Pentecostals has limited both the longevity and the effectiveness of the Christian Right's movements.

Political Effects

Popular accounts of the landslide RONALD REAGAN victory in 1980 and the accompanying Republican takeover of the U.S. Senate attributed conservatives' success to the New Christian Right. These accounts probably overstated the movement's political effects, but it does appear to have affected the partisanship and activism of some of its members.

Supporters of the Christian Right were disproportionately likely to vote and to vote for Republicans. However, Wilcox finds no conclusive evidence that the Moral Majority or Robertson was responsible for the shift, as there was a general trend of partisan realignment among evangelicals in the 1980s.

Potential Black Support

Religiosity and social conservatism establish a foundation for a potential Christian Right constituency in the black community. However, as Wilcox notes, it would be "difficult" to mobilize blacks—the single most reliable constituency of the Democratic Party—in support of Republican politics because of partisan attachments and SOCIAL JUSTICE concerns that infuse the agendas of many blacks.

See also ANTICOMMUNISM; CHRISTIAN RIGHT AND THE REPUBLICAN PARTY; RELIGION IN THE 1980, 1984, 1988, 1992, 1996, 2000 PRESIDENTIAL ELECTIONS; SOUTHERN REPUBLICAN REALIGNMENT.

—Matthew DeBell

Goldman v. Weinberger 475 U.S. 503 (1986)

A former Air Force member, Justice William H. Rehnquist wrote the opinion for a slim 5-4 majority in *Goldman v. Weinberger, Secretary of Defense, et al.* The March 25, 1986, decision protected the military's broad discretion in establishing regulations that might conflict with the First Amendment protection of religious FREE EXERCISE. S. Simcha Goldman was an Orthodox Jew, an ordained rabbi, and a commissioned officer serving as clinical psychologist in the Air Force. Goldman's practice of wearing his yarmulke violated Air Force regulations that prohibited personnel from wearing headgear indoors. In the face of a potential court martial, Goldman contested the regulation as an infringement of his right to free exercise. The Court's opinion gave passing recognition to the importance of free exercise. It held, however, that the military represents "a specialized society" with specialized needs. If military officials elect to reduce individual expression to pursue esprit de corps and uniform discipline, courts are unequipped to question their professional judgment of military interests.

Goldman had originally prevailed in the District Court for the District of Columbia, receiving a permanent ban on the regulation as applied to his yarmulke. The Court of Appeals for the D.C. Circuit overturned this ruling, also denying Goldman's request for an en banc rehearing. Of interest is the unlikely combination of three judges who dissented from this denial: Kenneth Starr, Ruth Bader Ginsburg, and ANTONIN SCALIA.

Goldman reflected the late Burger Court's deep uncertainty about how to decide free exercise cases. Scholars are uncertain whether *Goldman* represented a clear break with the line of cases coming out of SHERBERT V. VERNER, or whether the Court's decision merely reflected the case's unique circumstances. *Goldman*'s concurrences and dissents illustrate the complexities of the case and the Court's overall struggle with *Sherbert*'s legacy.

A former Navy man, Justice John Paul Stevens concurred and was joined by Justices Byron White and Lewis Powell—the latter a former Air Force intelligence officer. Stevens emphasized two points. First, that the Court should not underestimate the importance of the military interest in uniformity. Second, he argued that the Air Force regulation, based on a standard of visibility, was the best possible, since it did not require personnel to make evaluations about the character and sincerity of a member's faith. Avoiding such arbitrary evaluations ensured the standard could be applied neutrally to all religions.

Joined by Justice Thurgood Marshall, Justice WILLIAM BRENNAN's dissent clearly addressed Stevens's argument. What cannot be underestimated, said Brennan, is the importance of Goldman's constitutional claim to his rights—rights that follow him even into the military, where majority suppression of minority voices is often most likely. To protect these rights, the Court cannot shirk its responsibility of reviewing potentially offensive military decisions. Any potential discretion must remain within the bounds of reason. The regulations in question, however, fail to establish the particular problem with Goldman's yarmulke—especially in light of other regulations that explicitly recognize the value of individuality and allow room for departure from strict uniformity. The Air Force claimed that it wanted to prevent any divisiveness that could result from Goldman's expression of Orthodox Judaism—yet the code allowed many nonregulation items that offered the same potential for divisiveness. Brennan also chastised Stevens's neutral visibility rule as misguided, extending protection only to those religions that can fit within mainstream standards of dress. Goldman's only hope for protection, Brennan said, lay in congressional action.

In his dissent, Justice Harry Blackmun focused on two "costs." Like Brennan, he agreed that the government failed to show why the "cost" of Goldman's own yarmulke threatened military interests. Relying on the reasoning in UNITED STATES V. LEE, Blackmun also claimed that the government failed to establish that enough members would seek exemptions to dress regulations to make their total "cost" overly prohibitive. Finally, Blackmun chastised Brennan's suggested standard, arguing that a "neat and conservative" rule would also fail to protect minorities.

Picking up on the comments of fellow dissenters, Justice O'Connor sought to preserve the viability of existing standards. Though free exercise precedents were inconsistent, two

themes continually reappear: the need for an overriding governmental interest, and the requirement that such interests be pursued in the least restrictive means—with consideration for the damage of cumulative exemptions. While the military does deserve special discretion, the Court must retain the responsibility of review. Relying on the arguments of Brennan and Blackmun and joined by Marshall, Justice Sandra Day O'Connor claimed that the Air Force regulations failed her hybrid *Sherbert-Lee* test and thus were unconstitutional.

Ultimately, Congress followed Brennan's advice. In September 1987, legislation effectively overturned *Goldman*'s particular holdings but left the status of free exercise jurisprudence unresolved.

—Matthew M. C. Roberts

Good News Club et al. v. Milford Central School
Docket No. 99-2036 (2001)

Good News focuses on whether sectarian (religious) groups have the same right as secular (nonreligious) groups to meet in public schools after the school day ends. Although the case raises clear questions of religious freedom, the Supreme Court's decision hinged on the free speech clause. The specific facts leading up to the controversy are as follows. In accordance with New York law, Milford Central School enacted a policy authorizing district residents to use its building after school for a variety of reasons, including social, civic, and educational functions. Good News Club, a children's Christian organization, submitted a request to hold the club's weekly meetings in the school after school hours. The school denied the request on the ground that the meetings constituted religious worship prohibited by the community use policy. Members of the club filed suit alleging that the prohibition violated their free speech rights under the First and Fourteenth Amendments. The federal district court upheld the school's decision, and argued that because all religious organizations were banned from using the school, there was no constitutional discrimination. The U.S. Court of Appeals for the Second Circuit agreed with this conclusion and ruled that the policy was constitutional *subject* discrimination, not unconstitutional *viewpoint* discrimination. In other words, they argued that it is constitutional to discriminate against a type of speech—in this case, all religious speech—but not to discriminate against specific types of religious speech. Subsequently, the case was appealed to the U.S. Supreme Court.

In a 6-3 decision, the Court reversed the Second Circuit and ruled in favor of Good News Club. The majority opinion, delivered by Justice Thomas, relied on LAMBS CHAPEL V. MORICHES CENTER FREE UNION and ROSENBERGER V. UNIVERSITY OF VIRGINIA and focused on one main argument, that the school was a limited public forum. This means that whoever controls the forum—here, the school—can restrict its use to certain groups or to the discussion of specific topics. The power to restrict speech in a limited public forum, however, is not absolute. As such, restrictions on speech may not discriminate against specific viewpoints and the restrictions must be reasonable. By denying access to the Good News Club on the ground that it was religious in nature, the Court argued that the school discriminated against the club, and therefore violated its right to free speech. The majority went on to conclude that because the school's restriction was viewpoint discriminatory, it did not have to decide whether it was unreasonable.

To counter the club's free speech claim, the school argued that allowing the Good News Club to use its building, even after school hours, would violate the ESTABLISHMENT CLAUSE. The Court rejected this argument and pointed out that the club's meetings would be held only after school hours, were not sponsored by the school, and were open to any student who obtained parental consent to participate. Additionally, the majority argued that the school would not be endorsing the Good News Club's viewpoint by allowing its members to meet in the building, and that the school may actually be perceived as hostile to the group's viewpoint by disallowing it to use the facilities—a phrase now common in Christian conservative circles (see Reed 1994). Thus, the majority argued that disallowing the group to use the school would violate its rights under the establishment clause.

Three justices dissented—Stevens, who dissented alone, and, writing separately, Souter and Ginsberg. Both opinions

differentiated religious speech from secular speech. Stevens attempted a fairly complicated categorization of religious speech: "religious speech that is simply speech about a particular topic from a religious point of view," religious speech that "is aimed principally at proselytizing or inculcating belief in a particular religious faith," and "religious speech that amounts to worship." Similar to Stevens's argument, the argument of Souter and Ginsberg suggested that the school could limit its public forum for religious speech used for religious reasons (to distinguish from *Lambs Chapel*'s religious speech for secular reasons). But their views did not prevail.

Further reading: Reed, Ralph. *Mainstream Values Are No Longer Politically Incorrect: The Emerging Faith Factor in American Politics.* Dallas: Word Publishing, 1993.

—Timothy R. Johnson

Graham, William Franklin (Billy) (1918–   )
evangelist

William (Billy) Franklin Graham Jr. was born on November 7, 1918, near Charlotte, North Carolina. Throughout his long and distinguished career, Billy Graham emerged as America's

Billy Graham (right), with his son Franklin Graham *(Billy Graham Center)*

foremost revivalist and the leader of Protestant evangelicals. Graham also served as religious and spiritual adviser to a succession of presidents from DWIGHT D. EISENHOWER through George H.W. Bush. Globally, Graham was responsible for efforts to spread Christianity throughout the world and was the first Western preacher to conduct open worship services in the communist world, with appearances in countries such as Hungary, the Soviet Union, North Korea, and China.

In 1934, Graham attended a revival meeting where he underwent a religious conversion and decided to devote his life to the ministry. He entered Bob Jones College in South Carolina but found the institution too strict and narrow in focus. Therefore, he transferred to the Florida Bible College in 1937. While at Florida, Graham changed his religious affiliation from Reformed Presbyterian to Southern Baptist and began preaching. Graham then moved on to Wheaton College in 1940, where he met and married Ruth Bell. He also served briefly as a pastor at a local church.

In 1944, Graham's career as an evangelist really began. At the Chicagoland Youth for Christ Rally, Graham led 42 people in a mass conversion. This experience led him to became a field representative for Youth for Christ International. Graham traveled through the United States, Great Britain, and France, working with local churches and Christian organizations to establish youth rallies. In 1949, Graham held an eight-week mass meeting in Los Angeles. The event was a spectacular success and made Graham a nationally known figure. This crusade was followed by similar successful rallies in Boston and Washington. The following year, Graham launched his *Hour of Decision* radio program that further extended his audience.

The 1950s cemented Graham's fame. He became friends with both DWIGHT D. EISENHOWER and RICHARD NIXON. In addition, he held a number of lengthy crusades in the United States, Europe, and Asia. A 16-week crusade in New York attracted 2 million people. In 1957, his appeal led the ABC television network to invite Graham to start a nationwide television program. Graham also launched a magazine, *Christianity Today*. Significantly, Graham's greatest audience was not among FUNDAMENTALISTS, but instead with mainline Protestant denominations. His growing mainstream message led to a break with more conservative fundamentalists but also ensured his lasting attractiveness to the moderate elements in the evangelical movement.

Graham's political power and influence remained significant through the presidencies of Lyndon B. Johnson and Nixon. He enjoyed unprecedented access to the White House and served as spiritual counselor and confidant to both presidents. Nonetheless, he was wary of engaging in partisan politics and avoided participation in or identification with the rise of the Christian Right. During the 1960s, Graham became determined to use his influence to help shape the future of the evangelical movement and maintain its moderate course. To maintain this centrism, Graham formed the Billy Graham Evangelistic Association (BEGA). The BEGA was instrumental in the success of the 1966 World Congress on Evangelism

in Berlin and a similar conference in Lausanne, Switzerland, in 1974. Both meetings were supported financially by BEGA and drew evangelicals from around the world. Other BEGA-sponsored meetings in the 1980s drew more than 10,000 evangelicals from more than 175 nations.

During the 1970s, Graham's proselytizing efforts took an increasingly international focus. By the late 1970s, Graham was acknowledged as the worldwide leader of the evangelical movement. He was granted permission by successive Communist governments to undertake crusades behind the Iron Curtain. Graham was awarded the Presidential Medal of Freedom in 1983, partly because of his efforts. He began to advocate more strongly for world peace and for reconciliation between the United States and both the Soviet Union and China in the 1980s. This conciliatory approach further alienated Graham from conservative religious groups such as the MORAL MAJORITY and later the CHRISTIAN COALITION. This split was further exacerbated by Graham's denunciation of the confrontational tactics of antiABORTION groups such as OPERATION RESCUE.

Graham's visibility and influence declined in the 1990s. Age and Parkinson's disease began to take their toll on his health during this decade, and his influence was further eroded by President WILLIAM JEFFERSON CLINTON's preference for the Reverend JESSE JACKSON as a spiritual adviser. Still, in 1996, Graham was awarded the Congressional Gold Medal, and he remains the spiritual leader of the evangelical movement.

See also ANTICOMMUNISM; EVANGELICALISM; REVIVALISM; TELEVANGELISM.

Further reading: Drummond, Lewis. *The Evangelist.* Nashville: Word, 2000; Graham, Billy. *Just As I Am: The Autobiography of Billy Graham.* Grand Rapids, Mich.: Zondervan, 1999; Martin, William. *A Prophet with Honor: The Billy Graham Story.* New York: Quill, 1991; Pokki, Timo. *America's Preacher and His Message: Billy Graham's View of Conversion and Sanctification.* Lanham, Md.: University Press of America, 1999; Pollock, John. *To All the Nations: The Billy Graham Story.* San Francisco: Harper and Row, 1985; Streiker, Lowell D., and Gerald S. Strober. *Religion and the New Majority: Billy Graham, Middle America, and the Politics of the 70s.* New York: Association Press, 1972.

—Thomas Lansford

Grand Rapids, School District of the City of v. Ball 473 US 373 (1985)

Ball and its companion, *AGUILAR V. FELTON* (1985), were part of the long series of ESTABLISHMENT CLAUSE cases in which the Supreme Court struggled with the constitutionality of state AID TO RELIGIOUS SCHOOLS. The divided decisions striking down assistance programs illustrate not only the intractability of state aid to religious education, but also profound disagreement over the standards for evaluating establishment clause challenges.

Two educational programs supported by the Grand Rapids, Michigan, School District were challenged in *Ball*. The first was a shared-time program, in which public school teachers came into private schools during the regular school day to offer secular enrichment and remedial programs. In the second, the community education program, private school teachers were employed by the state to offer voluntary enrichment programs after school. In finding these program a violation of the establishment clause, Justice WILLIAM BRENNAN, writing for the majority, applied the guidelines enunciated in *LEMON V. KURTZMAN* (1971). The *"Lemon* test" requires that a challenged program have a secular legislative purpose, have a principal or primary effect that neither advances nor inhibits religion, and avoid excessive entanglement between church and state.

Both programs easily passed the first prong of the test; the Court found their educational enrichment purposes "praiseworthy." However, the majority ruled that they failed the second prong of the test, by unconstitutionally advancing religion, for three reasons. First, they risked religious indoctrination by the state. Because the programs were offered in schools "segregated by religion," the Court feared that the religious atmosphere of the schools might influence the tone of the education provided. "Teachers in such an atmosphere may well subtly (or overtly) conform their instruction to the environment in which they teach, while students will perceive the instruction provided in the context of the dominantly religious message of the institution, thus reinforcing the indoctrinating effect." The state might never know this was happening because these classes were "not specifically monitored for religious content."

Second, the programs constituted an unconstitutional symbolic endorsement of religion. Justice Brennan reasoned that the public school presence in a parochial school would provide children with "a powerful symbol of state endorsement and encouragement of the religious beliefs taught in the same class at some other time during the day."

Third, both programs violated the establishment clause by offering impermissible financial subsidies to religious institutions. While not all financial subsidies are unconstitutional, the shared-time program provided programs that the private schools might have provided themselves. The majority feared that approving this program would leave future courts no principled way of limiting the amount of educational program the state might sponsor. "To let the genie out of the bottle in this case would be to permit ever larger segments of the religious school curriculum to be turned over to the public school system, thus violating the cardinal principle that the State may not in effect become the prime supporter of the religious school system."

In summary, the majority concluded: "The symbolic union of church and state inherent in the provision of secular, state-sponsored instruction in the religious school buildings threatens to convey a message of state support for religion to students and to the general public . . . [T]he conclusion is

inescapable that the Community Education and Shared Time programs have the 'primary and principal' effect of advancing religion, and therefore violate the dictates of the Establishment Clause of the First Amendment."

Chief Justice Warren E. Burger and Justice Sandra Day O'Connor concurred with the majority concerning the unconstitutionality of the community education program but dissented to its judgment on the shared-time one. Justices William Rehnquist and Byron White also filed dissents.

The approach embodied in this decision barely survived a decade. In the case of *AGOSTINI V. FELTON* (1997), the majority concluded that changes in establishment clause jurisprudence during the intervening 10 years had undermined the rationale of *Aguilar* and *Ball*. In particular, the Court would no longer assume that a "shared time" program violated the *Lemon* test by impermissibly advancing religion. Thus, *Agostini v. Felton* overturned *Aguilar v. Felton* specifically, and the reasoning on which *Ball* was based.

—Bette Novit Evans

Grove City College v. Bell 465 U.S. 555 (1984)

Grove City College is a small, private, Christian liberal arts college in western PENNSYLVANIA that has long sought to preserve its institutional autonomy. To that end, the college chose not to accept any government assistance—since such dollars always come with strings attached. For example, the college did not participate in the Department of Education's Regular Disbursement System, where grant monies for students were advanced directly to the college itself. Many Grove City students did, however, receive Basic Educational Opportunity Grants (BEOG). The Department of Education claimed that receipt of these funds was enough to force the college to comply with the requirements of Title IX, which prohibited sex discrimination in educational programs receiving federal money. Refusal to comply would allow the department to terminate the distribution of such funds to Grove City students. In the case of *Grove City College et al. v. Bell, Secretary of Education, et al.*, the Supreme Court in effect agreed with the Department of Education. The case was decided on February 28, 1984, and Justice Byron White wrote the opinion for an essentially unanimous Court.

To come to its decision, the Court asked three successive questions. First, did Title IX apply to Grove City, which received no *direct* assistance from the federal government? By recognizing their nondispositive nature, the Court looked for guidance in Title IX's legislative history, in the comments of its legislative supporters, and in Congress's subsequent treatment of the act. When added to the text of the law itself, the Court held that there was no basis on which to believe that Title IX applied only to *direct* financial assistance. In fact, Title IX's nondiscrimination requirements and the BEOG program itself were created by the same piece of legislation. Basic Educational Opportunity Grants were seen as an integral part of federal financial assistance, which was to be covered by Title IX.

The second question that had to be answered was which program at Grove City benefited from the BEOG aid—since such a finding was necessary to determine who had to comply with Title IX. The Court of Appeals had ruled that in the end, such money flowed to the institution as a whole, making the entire school subject to nondiscrimination requirements. Here the Court disagreed, claiming that the lower court's finding rested on faulty logic. Money received by students entered and ultimately benefited only the financial aid department. Thus, it was that department alone that must comply with Title IX. Agreeing with the lower court and with the Department of Education, the Court held that failure to sign an Assurance of Compliance with Title IX could result in the termination of aid to Grove City students.

On its face, the third question was the most important—whether conditioning federal financial aid on Title IX requirements represented a violation of the First Amendment rights of the college and its students. For the Court, the answer to this constitutional question was easily determined on statutory grounds. Since compliance with nondiscrimination requirements only resulted from participation in a voluntary program, no rights were violated. Should Grove City or its students dislike the requirements, they could simply stop participation in the program.

Every justice on the Court signed onto Justice White's decision, making it essentially unanimous. Justices WILLIAM BRENNAN and Thurgood Marshall agreed with the Court's rul-

ing but filed a separate opinion dissenting in part. Their chief contention was with the decision to limit Title IX compliance to the financial aid department. Revisiting the legislative history discussed in the majority opinion, the dissenters held that Congress had clearly intended nondiscrimination laws to apply to the entire institution. Indeed, the *Grove City* decision provoked such a negative response from civil rights groups that in 1988, Congress passed a Civil Rights Restoration Act that essentially reversed *Grove City*.

Though agreeing with the decision, Chief Justice Warren Burger and Justices Lewis Powell and Sandra Day O'Connor wrote a separate concurrence. On purely technical and legal grounds, they said, the case had been correctly decided. But the real issue in the case was actually a trivial one—whether Grove City's receipt of federal funds could be conditioned on a formal acknowledgment of compliance with Title IX. Discrimination had never been the true issue in the case, since Grove City had an exemplary history of nondiscrimination—which had been noted in the record by the original administrative judge. Thus, the college was in full compliance with the *spirit* of Title IX. The enduring legacy of this case, said the three justices, would be the "unedifying example of overzealousness" on the part of the federal government in forcing six long years of prosecution on Grove City—time that could have been spent eradicating actual discrimination.

—Matthew M. C. Roberts

H

Habits of the Heart: Individualism and Commitment in American Life (1985) By Robert Bellah, Richard Madsen, William Sullivan, Ann Swidler, and Steven Tipton. Berkeley: University of California Press

Few sociological texts have had the broad effect on American intellectual, religious, and civic life as has *Habits of the Heart*, co-written by Robert Bellah, Richard Madsen, William Sullivan, Ann Swidler, and Steven Tipton. Though he was careful to give credit to his collaborators, it is clear that the project is associated first and foremost with Bellah. The first edition of the book came out in 1985, a second in 1996. The book is an exercise in normative sociology in the tradition of Daniel Bell, Peter Berger, and Pitirim Sorokin. Like the works of those authors, it is distinct from many other forms of normative sociology because of its "privileging" of both American republican and Christian traditions.

The book had special resonance in the mid-1980s because of the many concerns of intellectuals that the RONALD REAGAN years were the "greed decade." Bellah fueled this suspicion by arguing that Reagan's CONSERVATISM was a sham that disguised policies that gave free reign to economic rationality, which to Bellah was one of the major sources of the INDIVIDUALISM he deplored.

The book's importance has transcended the historical period in which it was written, however, and the political bias that informed it. One of the reasons it has remained influential is because of the interpretative power of its analysis of four ways of viewing and living life in America. The authors' analytic framework of utilitarian individualism, expressive individualism, republican virtue, and biblical virtue remains extremely helpful in understanding American ways of life. His depiction of the latter two draws on the work of Alasdair MacIntyre and Stanley Hauerwas, both of whom helped to bring back the language of tradition, practice, and virtue to our common discourse.

The creative amalgamation of republican and biblical virtue has made up the best part of the American vision. Both traditions—one philosophical, the other religious—are communicated by narratives and born by practices that realize goods internal to them. Both encourage strong connections to others and have persisted over many centuries. These two formative ways of life are being challenged, Bellah argues, by the utilitarian individualism fostered by economic rationality and by the expressive individualism fueled by a decadent romanticism. Each form of individualism subverts true practices, corrodes tradition, and, by weakening persisting connections to others, undercuts any concern for the common good.

These new forms of individualism are increasingly dominant because utilitarian individualism is reinforced by the productive and consumerist demands of expanding capitalism, and expressive individualism is supported by the therapeutic culture made both possible and necessary by capitalist affluence.

Habits of the Heart makes use of many interviews with Americans to illustrate all four ways of life. Both forms of individualism are well depicted by many conversations the field investigators recorded. Even community activists often speak in the language of individualism, so fully has it penetrated our language. Interviews are also used to illustrate the great republican and biblical traditions, though those tend to be fewer.

The number, scope, and location of the interviews have been criticized by other social scientists. They suggest, with some merit, that the interviews are illustrations to bolster a theoretical construct, not sources to build that theoretical construct. However, whether or not the book is adequate empirical sociology is not the main point. The larger points made in the book have been persuasive to many reflective persons. *Habits of the Heart* is social science as public philosophy.

The constructive thrust of Bellah's public philosophy is that the older traditions need to be revived in order to give new life to a vision of the common good and to inspire people to commit themselves to it. It also argues that private life can be redeemed from the corrosive effects of individualism by a return to our older sources of virtue. These are compelling notions that help people find their bearings in something far richer and more enduring than the loneliness and relativism of radical individualism. Unfortunately, Bellah's argument—like

191

MacIntyre's—is often marred by a visceral antipathy to any large-scale economic activity and to the contemporary conservative policies that are supportive of that activity. That tends to make the constructive part of his project attractive mainly to the academic and religious Left.

Nevertheless, the book does for 20th- and 21st-century America what de Tocqueville did for the 19th. It provides a monumental analytic and constructive perspective that has enduring significance.

See also BOWLING ALONE; COMMUNITARIANISM; DEMOCRACY IN AMERICA.

—Robert Benne

Hamilton, Alexander (1757–1804) politician

Alexander Hamilton, the first secretary of the treasury in the administration of GEORGE WASHINGTON, was a strong proponent of a centralized government and financial system at the time the framers drafted the U.S. Constitution of 1787. The only constitutional framer to have been born outside the United States, Hamilton, a native of Nevis, the Virgin Islands, born on January 11, 1757 (although John C. Miller in his biography cites 1755) grew up under the stigma of "illegitimacy." After abandonment by his father and the death of his mother, Hamilton went to work at a sugar refinery in St. Croix. One of the first examples of Hamilton's eloquent prose was his "Hurricane Letter" of 1772, which he wrote at age 15 after observing one of the most devastating hurricanes in the history of the West Indies. Consistent with Presbyterianism, Hamilton saw God's power and wrath in the hurricane, causing him to exclaim: "Where now, oh! Vile worm is all thy boasted fortitude and resolution? What is become of thy arrogance and self-sufficiency?" Hamilton was impressed with the depravity of man and sovereignty of God. In interpreting his "Hurricane Letter" as a realistic rather than gloomy meditation, Hamilton said that it "did not proceed from excessive fear of God's wrath or from a conscience overburdened with crimes of an uncommon cast." Rather, he thought that a logical conclusion of witnessing God's power in the hurricane was to note the weakness and sinfulness of man.

Because of his superior intellectual talents and ambitious temperament, Hamilton was sponsored by his St. Croix employer, Nicholas Cruger, and Scotch-Irish Presbyterian minister, Reverend Hugh Knox, to go to college in America. Hamilton excelled at King's College (now Columbia University) in New York. From there he went on to become a colonel in George Washington's army, a New York State assemblyman, a member of the Continental Congress, a coauthor of *The Federalist Papers,* and a lawyer. With all his political and legal success, writers on Hamilton overlook his religious beliefs.

Although he never joined a church, "there is much persuasive evidence that the young Hamilton who landed in America seeking his fortune in 1773 was conventionally religious, but there is little evidence to show any great depth or intensity of religious feeling." However, Robert Troup, Hamilton's college roommate, observed that "he was a zealous believer in the fundamental doctrines of Christianity; and I confess, that the arguments with which he was accustomed to justify his belief, have tended, in no small degree, to confirm my own faith in revealed religion."

Hamilton's political philosophy was rooted in his view of the natural order established by God. In referring to the oppressive British policy in the colonies, Hamilton stated, "an intelligent, superintending principle . . . the governor of the universe' had erected barriers beyond which governments could not legally go." But from 1777 to 1792, there is scant evidence that Hamilton had an interest in God, religion, or church. Hamilton mentioned God in only two letters during the Revolution. Yet, during this period, Hamilton married Betsy Schuyler, a devout believer and follower of the DUTCH REFORMED TRADITION.

Hamilton, an important leader of the Federalist Party and an enemy of the French Revolution, appealed to God as validation for his opposition to pure democracy and his distaste for THOMAS JEFFERSON. But "actually it is during these years when religious slogans were so often on his lips that Hamilton seems farther from God and from any understanding of his Son, Jesus Christ, than at any time in his whole career." This was to change around 1800, when Hamilton's political career took a severe nosedive, landing him in misery and despair. Many events converged leading to his sudden downfall. Hamilton's beloved Federalist Party was declining and becoming more moderate, appealing to President JOHN ADAMS. Washington died in 1799. Aaron Burr was gaining political power in New York City. Finally, Hamilton resigned as commander in chief after Adams disbanded the army. Adair and Harvey note: "At the end of 1800 Alexander Hamilton, who only a year before had dominated the country like a colossus, was using the tiny shreds of influence left to him trying to block his upstart enemy Burr in order to advance his greatest and oldest enemy Jefferson into that highest office which Hamilton desired so much for himself." In his weakness, Hamilton turned to God. But it was not the God of power and wrath of whom he wrote in the "Hurricane Letter." Rather, it was the God of mercy and compassion. Again, Adair and Harvey: "Nor was this new concern with God merely a matter of outward ritual observance. Hamilton became internally a new and different man." Hamilton's arrogance and need for power was replaced by gentleness, spiritual devotion, and family commitment.

Ironically, the transformed Hamilton was inflicted by a gunshot wound from his political rival Aaron Burr in the famous duel that ended his life on July 12, 1804. Before the duel, Hamilton had confided to a friend that he would not fire the first shot at Burr because of his Christian convictions against taking a life. On his deathbed, after repeated attempts to find a clergyman to administer the sacraments, Hamilton took Holy Communion from an Episcopal bishop.

Another twist of history is that the nonchurched Hamilton was perhaps the most godly and spiritual man of the founding generation. Some of Hamilton's last words were about his faith in Christ, assuring "His firm belief in Christianity, and fervent hope of forgiveness, through the merits and mediations of our Blessed Redeemer."

See also MADISON, JAMES.

Further reading: Adair, Douglass, and Marvin Harvey. "Was Alexander Hamilton a Christian Statesman?" *William and Mary Quarterly* 12 (1955); Miller, John C. *Alexander Hamilton: Portrait in Paradox.* New York: Harper and Row, 1959.

—Joanne Tetlow

Hamilton v. Regents of the University of California 293 U.S. 245 (1934)

In *Hamilton,* on December 3, 1934, the Supreme Court unanimously upheld the constitutionality of a requirement of the Board of Regents of the University of California requiring compulsory military training in the Reserve Officers Training Corps (ROTC) for all male freshmen and sophomore students less than 24 years of age. Justice Pierce Butler wrote the opinion for the Court. Justice Benjamin N. Cardozo concurred specially, finding no constitutional infirmity with required military training, but expressly leaving open the constitutionality of required military service.

Albert W. Hamilton (a minor acting through his father and guardian ad litem, also named Albert Hamilton), whose admission to the University of California had been suspended, appealed from a decision of the Supreme Court of California upholding the constitutionality of the decision of the university to revoke his admission and that of others who refused to participate in ROTC. Hamilton and his co-appellants were all members of the Methodist Episcopal Church and members of its youth organization, the Epworth League. All were minors, and all were the sons of Methodist ministers. The young men and their fathers objected to military service on religious grounds.

A rule of the Board of Regents required all male students less than 24 years of age who were less than juniors academically to participate in ROTC. The content of the courses, prescribed by the War Department, included rifle marksmanship, scouting, patrolling, drill and command, musketry, combat principles, and the proper usage of automatic rifles. Uniforms, weapons, and ammunition were required and were provided free of charge by the War Department.

At the beginning of the fall 1933 term, the appellants petitioned to be exempted from the requirement to participate in ROTC. The Board of Regents refused the petition and suspended the students' admission to the university but granted them leave to apply for readmission at any time that they were willing to participate in the required military service. The appellants filed an action in the California state courts seeking a writ of mandamus, ordering the Regents to readmit them to the university. The state court denied the petition for the writ of mandamus without issuing an opinion.

On petition for rehearing, the court reaffirmed the denial of the writ and issued an opinion noting that the laws of California gave full authority to operate the University of California to the Board of Regents and that these laws expressly included military training as a subject to be taught at the university.

After a lengthy discussion of the basis of jurisdiction, the Supreme Court considered Hamilton and his co-appellants' constitutional claim. The appellants asserted that the FOURTEENTH AMENDMENT, by making the First Amendment applicable to the states, prevented the Board of Regents from expelling students who refused to participate in military training because of religious objections. Without attempting to delineate the precise limits of liberty protection of the Fourteenth Amendment, the Court readily found that freedom of belief, including the right to hold and teach opposition to military training, was a constitutionally protected liberty interest. But, such liberty did not include the right not to be barred from attendance at a state university because of such beliefs.

The Court noted that attendance at a state-supported university was a privilege, not a right. California had not attempted to draft the students or require them to participate in combat. Military training was a part of the course of instruction required of all. Relying on UNITED STATES V. SCHWIMMER, which had upheld the constitutionality of refusing to naturalize a resident alien who was a conscientious objector, the Court rejected the appellants' claims.

Justice Cardozo concurred specially. Cardozo was willing to join the Court's opinion because the young men were required only to take instruction in military science, not to actually participate in military service. Cardozo left open the question of whether required military service of a person who holds religiously based objections to such service would be constitutional. The continued viability of *Hamilton* after the Court's decision in GIROUARD V. UNITED STATES, which overruled *Schwimmer,* is questionable. But *Hamilton* would appear to be distinguishable according to the opinion's distinction between military training and military service.

See also CONSCIENTIOUS OBJECTION.

—Stephen R. Prescott

Hasidic Judaism

Literally, the term *Hasidim* means "pious ones." In the modern period, it refers to those who identify with what has become a very spirited and vibrant Jewish movement founded by Rabbi Israel ben Eliezer (c. 1700–1760), the BA'AL SHEM TOV, or Besht. Originally, it was a mass movement that emphasized mysticism, personal piety, and joy in worship and the performance of other religious rituals. This was in sharp contrast to elite Judaism, with its emphasis on sacred learning.

Viewed as separatist and challenging not only to the elite but also to normative Judaism, the rabbinic establishment staunchly opposed Hasidism, and Rabbi Elijah ben Solomon Zalman (1720–97), the *Goan* (genius) of Vilna (Vilnius), Lithuania, spearheaded a campaign, including a ban of excommunication, against it. The conflict between the Hasidim and their opponents within ORTHODOX JUDAISM did not subside until the 20th century. Today, Hasidism is composed of hundreds of groups, each of which has its own spiritual leader (*rebbe*). Typically, the group's name is derived from the name of the town in eastern Europe where the rebbe lived.

Hasidim suffered tremendous losses in the HOLOCAUST. After World War II, most of the survivors resettled either in the United States or in Israel. Contemporary Hasidim are generally viewed as "ultra-Orthodox." Many Hasidic men dress in black clothing, including black broad-brimmed hats, and have beards and long side locks, either dangling or tied up around the ears. Hasidic women tend to wear wigs, kerchiefs, or hats and full-length, loosely fitting, long-sleeved dresses.

One of the most widely known groups of Hasidim is the Habad movement, who are also known by the name of the town in Belorussia where the leader lived during the 19th century, Lubavitch. This group emphasizes religious outreach to all Jews and utilizes cutting-edge technology in its outreach and public relations activities. In addition, although Habad officially rejects secular ZIONISM, it is a highly nationalistic group.

From 1951 until his death in 1974, Habad's rebbe was Rabbi MENACHEM MENDEL SCHNEERSON, who resided in Brooklyn, New York, which is also the movement's world headquarters. He was ill during his last few years, and some of his followers named him the Messiah. Since his death in 1974, the movement has experienced internal struggles as well as with other Orthodox groups because of its increasing proclamations of Schneerson as the Messiah, a notion that the other movements view as antithetical to Judaism.

Another widely known Hasidic group are the Satmar Hasidim, a sect that was headed by the late Rabbi Yoel Teitlebaum (1888–1979), of Satu-Mare, in present-day Romania, who was a renowned Torah scholar and brilliant anti-Zionist polemicist. The rebbe was rescued during the Holocaust and finally settled in Brooklyn in 1947, where he attracted many followers, and the group experienced significant growth. In 1953, the rebbe was adopted by the ultra-Orthodox, anti-Zionist, Neturei Karta community of Jerusalem, and this contributed to the growing public awareness of Satmar Hasidim. They continue to be, as a rule, adamantly anti-Zionist and anti-nationalist, and they eschew all but purely formal contacts with outsiders.

See also CONSERVATIVE JUDAISM; RECONSTRUCTIONIST JUDAISM; REFORM JUDAISM.

—Chaim I. Waxman

hate crimes

Before the 1980s, the phrase "hate crimes" was nonexistent in government documents, popular magazines, and scholarly journals. It was the introduction of the Hate Crimes Statistics Act (HCSA), by three Democratic representatives, that initiated the use of "hate crimes" in legislation and popular maga-

zines. Enacted in 1990, the act requires the Department of Justice to keep record of, and make public, crimes that are "motivated by racial, religious and ethnic prejudice."

Regardless of the absence of hate crimes before the 1980s, the FBI has investigated biased crimes since the enactment of the Civil Rights Act of 1964. Also, independent organizations such as the AMERICAN JEWISH COMMITTEE (AJC), founded in 1906, and the ANTI-DEFAMATION LEAGUE (ADL), founded in 1913, have recorded instances when hate crimes were committed before the HCSA enactment.

Following the HCSA, amended in 1994 and 1996, the FBI defined hate crime as a "criminal offense against a person or property motivated in whole or in part by the offender's bias against a race, religion, disability, ethnic/national origin, or sexual orientation." Derogatory remarks and racial slurs such as found in white supremacist organizations fall short of being classified as hate crimes because a criminal act is lacking. A hate crime, then, entails a bias motive and criminal conduct.

In 1994, the Hate Crimes Sentencing Enhancement Act, a component of the Violent Crime Control and Law Enforcement Act of 1994, requires that offenses identified as hate crimes fall under stricter penalty; enhancement of penalties varies from state to state. Penalty enhancement is set and limited by two U.S. Supreme Court decisions—*Wisconsin v. Mitchell* (1993) and *R.A.V. v. City of St. Paul* (1992). According to the former ruling, it is constitutionally permissible for states to enhance the penalty of crimes classified as hate crimes.

On October 7, 1989, Todd Mitchell, a 19-year-old black man, of Kenosha, Wisconsin, persuaded a group of black men to assault Gregory Riddick, a white boy; the attack took place after the group and Mitchell watched the movie *Mississippi Burning*. Mitchell was convicted of aggravated assault and given an enhanced penalty because he had "acted out of racial bias in the selection of the victim." The conviction was appealed to the U.S. Supreme Court, which sustained the Wisconsin bias crime statute, which followed ADL model legislation.

In response to a series of arson attacks against African-American churches, President WILLIAM JEFFERSON CLINTON organized the National Church Arson Task Force to investigate attacks against houses of worship committed between January 1, 1995, and October 8, 1998; on July 3, 1996, the Church Arson Prevention Act (18 U.S. Code 247) was enacted with the sole purpose of investigating and eventually prosecuting offender, crimes against churches, synagogues, and mosques. Prejudice and bias motives motivated the perpetrator to attack houses of worship, and consequently resulted in the classification of the offense as a hate crime. Along with African Americans, Hispanics, Jews, Asian Americans, gay men, lesbians, and women are the most common victims of hate crimes.

Although supported by groups such as ADL and AJC, hate crimes legislation has experienced some obstacles. The Supreme Court, in *R.A.V. v. St. Paul* ruled that "fighting words" that provoke others, on the basis of race, color, creed, religion, or gender, to be aroused to violence is protected by the Constitution; to rule otherwise would isolate words and violate the First Amendment.

Because of the vague definition for hate crimes, some argue against the validity of "hate crimes laws" and legislation, maintain that hate crimes appear to be on the rise because there is an increase of agencies that are reporting such crimes, claim there is no evidence to verify that hate crimes are escalating, and claim that the majority of reported hate crimes are low-level offenses punishable by law already. In spite of these dissenting views, lobbying for hate crimes legislation and law, especially by religious groups, will certainly continue as long as bias violence persists.

See also CHURCH BURNINGS.

Further reading: Altschiller, Donald. *Hate Crimes: A Reference Handbook.* Santa Barbara, Calif.: ABC-CLIO, 1999; Jacobs, James B., and Kimberly Potter. *Hate Crimes: Criminal Law & Identity Politics.* Oxford: Oxford University Press, 1998; Lawrence, Frederick M. *Punishing Hate: Bias Crime under American Law.* Cambridge, Mass.: Harvard University Press, 1999.

—Santiago O. Piñon Jr.

health care

Medicine and religion were born twins. All religions employ prayer and rituals to invoke the assistance of the divine in healing. Moreover, illness, suffering, and death, the traditional objects of health care, are also paths to union with or temptations away from the gods. Temples and churches are traditional places of healing, and infirmaries, clinics, and hospitals welcome religious ministry.

In the United States, religious institutions or philanthropists motivated by religion founded many nonprofit and community hospitals in the 19th and early 20th centuries. Although most are no longer explicitly religious in ownership, the ROMAN CATHOLIC CHURCH continues to sponsor about 600 hospitals (about 12 percent of the total), and SEVENTH-DAY ADVENTISTS, Baptists, UNITED METHODISTS, Lutherans, Jews, and other religious traditions have a substantial number of hospitals, nursing homes, and clinics as well. Pastors and theologians reflecting on modern medical moral dilemmas helped to give birth to bioethics, now a mature scholarly field.

When health care moved from religion and folk healing toward science, the role of religious beliefs and institutions became more ambiguous, and the role of government more significant. Medical expertise is now a social possession, largely financed and organized by public or quasi-public institutions. Moreover, the price of medicine is beyond the resources of families or groups of friends and neighbors (and congregations). Through a wide variety of schemes in the modern democratic world, government provides, finances, and regulates health care for its citizens. This means that issues of justice and fairness in access to and payment for health care, and matters of life and death (such as ABORTION, embryonic stem-cell research, and EUTHANASIA) have become inseparably linked with government policy. Yet churches and other religious groups have not lost their interest in health care or in life and death or in justice and fairness. Moreover, the religious beliefs and attitudes of ordinary citizens affect public opinion regarding health care policy.

Thus every significant health care policy draws religious beliefs and religious actors into the political mix. The issue networks that surround Medicare and Medicaid or funding for the National Institutes of Health, for example, have regular participation from organized groups such as the BAPTIST JOINT COMMITTEE, the UNITED STATES CATHOLIC CONFERENCE, the United Methodist Church, and other spokespersons for organized religion. The National Bioethics Advisory Committee invites theologians to contribute to its deliberations. Policies that substantially affect the financial viability of hospitals, home health agencies, and nursing homes (Medicare and Medicaid) or the regulatory environment ("patient's bills of rights") draw lobbyists from trade associations that represent religious health care institutions, the most notable being the Catholic Health Association, a major player in health policy networks.

When issues of health policy directly involve life and death, as so many on the cutting edge of science do (human CLONING/GENETIC ENGINEERING, for example), these same interest groups will be involved, as will others representing more traditional political actors, such as National Right to Life, the CHRISTIAN COALITION, and CATHOLICS FOR FREE CHOICE. It is difficult to think of any significant health care policy issue that does not have substantial input from religious perspectives, organized or unorganized.

These considerations hold a lesson for research and theorizing on the law and practice of American church and state relations. The traditional scenes of contest—PRAYER IN PUBLIC SCHOOLS, AID TO RELIGIOUS SCHOOLS, and religious exercise—are only a small part of the landscape. Religious and government institutions are deeply intertwined in health care and other policy arenas. Researchers have hardly scratched these relationships.

Further reading: Cochran, Clarke E. *Health Care Policy: Where Do We Go from Here?* Luce Monograph Series in Faith and Public Policy. Philadelphia: Crossroads Program, 1997; Cochran, Clarke E. "Sacrament and Solidarity: Catholic Social Thought and Healthcare Policy Reform." *Journal of Church and State* 41 (1999): 475–498; Numbers, Ronald L., and Darrel W. Amundsen. *Caring and Curing: Health and Medicine in the Western Religious Traditions.* Baltimore: Johns Hopkins University Press, 1986; Patel, Kant, and Mark E. Rushefsky. *Health Care Politics and Policy in America.* 2d ed. Armonk, N.Y.: M.E. Sharpe, 1999; Risse, Guenter B. *Mending Bodies, Saving Souls: A History of Hospitals.* New York: Oxford University Press, 1999.

—Clarke E. Cochran

Heaven's Gate

Heaven's Gate was a small, reclusive UFO group located in the western United States through most of its history. The group was led by Marshall "Herff" Applewhite (1931–97) and Bonnie Lu Nettles (1927–85), who died 12 years before the group's collective suicide. The leaders referred to themselves by a variety of names, most recently "Do and Ti" (after the notes on the tone scale). The group lived a highly secluded lifestyle. Its last base was a rented home in Rancho Santa Fe, a fashionable suburb of San Diego, California. In March 1997, all 39 members took their own lives in what they defined as a "transit" to the Next Level, life on another planet. Most of the members died from ingestion of a mixture of alcohol and barbiturates, followed by suffocation with plastic bags placed over their heads.

Applewhite was raised a Presbyterian and taught music at the college level, while Nettles had participated in Theosophical and spiritualist groups and was a registered nurse. They first met in 1972, and both felt their meeting was foreordained. They began traveling together, and the following year Applewhite had a revelatory experience as a result of which he and Nettles concluded that they were the Two Witnesses referred to in Revelations.

Shortly thereafter, Applewhite and Nettles began proselytizing, and by 1976 they counted over 200 followers. However, Heaven's Gate never achieved great size as defections offset conversion; for much of its existence, it consisted of fewer than 100 members. When the group encountered resistance from families of converts, the group almost immediately retreated from public view. For most of its remaining history, Heaven's Gate maintained a highly secluded, migratory, communal lifestyle. The group organized itself as a "classroom" oriented around cultivating the personal attributes required for life at the Next Level and replicating its social forms as closely as possible in an earthly setting.

Applewhite and Nettles taught that members of the Next Level, life forms from another part of the universe, had created conscious life on Earth. Members of the Next Level have returned at various times to "harvest" the result of their endeavor. Jesus was in fact one of these figures, but humans were not yet ready to move to the Next Level. Now two individuals were commissioned to conduct the harvest, Applewhite in the role of Jesus and Nettles as his guide. Humans who followed Applewhite and Nettles would be taken to the Kingdom of Heaven aboard spaceships and would become immortal and androgynous. Preparing humans for the harvest constituted a major challenge, because they are under the influence of Satan, a former member of the Next Level who had turned against God. To be a candidate for transit to the Next Level, it was necessary for humans to break every form of attachment to human life on Earth.

Applewhite and Nettles initially taught that the transit would occur with a corporeal body. But after Nettles's unexpected death in 1985, the group concluded that the human body was a "container" that could be abandoned. This created the possibility of the group voluntarily initiating a transit to the Next Level. Later, Applewhite came to believe that their students were actually members of the Next Level who had been placed on Earth for training that would allow them at some point to move to the Next Level. This belief led the group to begin reconceiving itself as an "Away Team" from the Next Level.

The group's isolation and rejection of conventional society and its identification with the Next Level, defections that reduced dissent and left a core of long-term, aging adherents, Nettle's death and Applewhite's deteriorating health—all combined to move the group toward final closure. The appearance of the Hale Bopp comet in 1995 was interpreted as a sign that the time for departure had arrived. The movement then proceeded to organize its transit and left video messages behind in the hope of deflecting the disparaging interpretations that were sure to follow.

See also NEW RELIGIOUS MOVEMENTS AND CULTS.

Further reading: Balch, Robert W., and David Taylor. "Making Sense of the Heaven's Gate Suicides." In *Cults, Religion, and Violence*. Edited by David G. Bromley and J. Gordon Melton. New York: Cambridge University Press, 2001; Hall, John, Philip Schuyler, and Silvaine Trinh. *Apocalypse Observed*. New York. Routledge, 2000.

—David G. Bromley

Heffron, Michael v. International Society for Krishna Consciousness, Inc. 452 U.S. 640 (1981)

In *Heffron*, on June 22, 1981, the Supreme Court held by a vote of five to four that a rule of the Minnesota Agricultural Society requiring any person or organization that wished to sell, exhibit, or distribute printed or written material during the state fair to do so only from a fixed location was a constitutional time, place, and manner restriction. Justice Byron R. White wrote the majority opinion, joined by Chief Justice Burger and Justices Stewart, Powell, and Rehnquist. Justice WILLIAM J. BRENNAN, joined by Justices Thurgood Marshall and John Paul Stevens dissenting in part, expressed the view that the restriction on sales and solicitations was constitutional, but the ban on the distribution of literature was overly intrusive and thus unconstitutional. Justice Harry R. Blackmun dissented in part, also expressing the view that a ban on the sale of literature or the solicitation of monetary contributions was constitutional, but the ban on the free distribution of literature was unconstitutional, but on different grounds than the other three dissenters.

The Minnesota Agricultural Society (hereinafter Society), a public corporation that operated the Minnesota State Fair, had adopted a rule that required any person or organization that wanted to sell, exhibit, or distribute written or printed material to do so only from a fixed location that had to be rented from the Society. Such locations were rented in a nondiscriminatory fashion on a first-come, first-served basis, without regard to the content of the literature or the religious nature, if any, of the person or organization renting the space. There was no restriction on moving freely about the fair and communicating verbally about one's religious beliefs, only the distribution of literature was prohibited.

The International Society for Krishna Consciousness, Inc. (ISKON), a HINDU sect that worships the god Krishna, believed it had a religious duty to circulate throughout the crowd at the fair distributing literature advocating the Krishna religion. At the time that ISKON members distributed the literature, they also sought donations from the recipients, but did not condition receipt of the literature on the making of a donation. ISKON filed suit in Minnesota state court, asserting that the Society's rule violated its First Amendment FREE EXERCISE rights. The state court ruled against ISKON, but on appeal the Supreme Court of Minnesota reversed. The Society appealed to the U.S. Supreme Court.

The majority held that the Society's rule was a reasonable place and manner restriction on the communicating of the views of the Krishna religion. Undoubtedly, ISKON had a First Amendment right to communicate the tenets of their religion. But, the rights guaranteed by the First Amendment are not absolute but subject to reasonable time, place, and manner restrictions, if nondiscriminatorily applied and based on a significant governmental interest.

It was not disputed that the limitation on the distribution of literature from a fixed location was applied to all who wished to distribute literature at the state fair and was nondiscriminatorily applied. The state of Minnesota had a legitimate significant governmental interest in maintaining the orderly movement of the crowd at the fair, and distributing literature had the potential to significantly impede the movement of the crowd. The rule that did not preclude ISKON from distributing literature, but only limited them to a fixed location, was thus a valid time, place, and manner restriction based on a significant governmental interest.

Justices Brennan, Marshall, and Stevens dissented in part. They believed that the ban on the distribution of free literature was overly intrusive. In the view of the dissenters, the requirement that ISKON remain at a fixed location significantly reduced the number of fairgoers they would have opportunity to reach. Because it dramatically reduced the potential audience, a ban on the mere distribution of literature without an attempt to collect a fee or solicit donations was an overly restrictive time, place, and manner restriction without a sufficient governmental interest. Justice Blackmun agreed with the other dissenters, but on different grounds. Blackmun felt that the mere distribution of free literature no more impeded the flow of the crowd than stopping people and talking with them about the tenets of the Krishna religion, perhaps less so. Thus, the proffered governmental interest in crowd control, while legitimate, did not require a ban on the free distribution of literature.

—Stephen R. Prescott

Heifer International (HI)

Heifer International (HI), formerly known as Heifer Project International, is a nonprofit, sustainable, community develop-

ment organization established in 1944, when they shipped their first cow. Since then, HI has supplied animals and the opportunity to become self-reliant for food and income to families in over 35 states in the United States as well as 48 countries on five continents. They have helped more than 4 million families in initial projects and countless more through "passing on the gift" with programs providing 20 different kinds of food- and income-producing animals.

HI is funded and supported by individuals, congregations, clubs, civic groups, and government, a connection that may grow in the current political climate. A faith-based organization, Heifer Project works in partnership with 12 other faith-based agencies (Covenant Agency) and is also a member of Interaction, a coalition of 160 relief, development, and refugee agencies.

The founder of HI, Dan West, a Midwestern farmer and Church of the Brethren youth worker, ladled out cups of milk to hungry children on both sides of the Spanish Civil War in the 1930s. It struck him that what these families needed was "not a cup, but a cow." He asked his friends back home in the United States to donate heifers, a young cow that has not borne a calf, so hungry families could feed themselves. In return, they could help another family become self-reliant by passing on the gift of one of their animal's female calves. The idea of giving a source of food rather than short-term relief caught on.

HI works in partnership with faith-based groups and civic organizations by providing food- and income-producing animals. The purposes of the projects are to combat hunger, alleviate poverty, and improve the local environment. These are accomplished by providing appropriate livestock, training, and related services to small-scale farmers, though many projects are community-based rather than individual. HI's key concept is that each recipient must pass an offspring of the farm animals they receive to others. This principle, called "passing on the gift," assures that each participant in the program becomes a donor, enhancing dignity and participation in each project. Through this principle, a community becomes more self-reliant for food and income, and the program can be self-sustaining for years to come.

Projects are selected on the basis of 12 "HI Cornerstones for Just and Sustainable Development," including *Passing on the Gift; Accountability* (groups define their own needs, set goals, and plan); *Sharing and Caring* (Sharing what we have and caring for others is central to all faiths, and includes justice for all people and the humane treatment of animals); *Sustainability and Self-reliance* (HI funds projects for a limited time to promote becoming self-supporting); *Gender and Family Focus* (HI encourages men and women to share project decision-making, animal ownership, labor and benefits); *Genuine Need and Justice* (HI project partners give priority to the poorest in the community and do not consider creed or ethnic heritage); *Improving the Environment* (Livestock should not damage the environment and should have a positive effect on soil, wildlife, forestation, and biodiversity); *Full Participation*

(HI works with grassroots groups or organizations representing them); and *Spirituality* (Common values and beliefs about life's purpose and meaning, connecting to the earth, and a shared vision of the future are elements of spirituality that bind all people together). Spirituality provides faith, hope, and a sense of responsibility to work for a better life for all. In all, HI is interested in building social capital and healthy communities by incorporating some of its basic building blocks: faith, economics, and trusting, functional social networks.

Further reading: Heifer International. URL: http://Heifer-project.org/index.shtml. (Accessed April 15, 2001).

—David B. Djupe

Henry, Carl F. H. (1913–   ) *theologian*

Theologian Carl Henry, born in 1913 in New York City to immigrant parents, played a pivotal role in the 20th-century political resurgence of American Evangelical Protestants. Throughout his career, Henry insisted that "social concern is an indispensable ingredient of the evangelistic message." His call for action helped transform evangelicals in just a few decades from an apolitical community into one of the most talked about groups in American politics.

Henry rose to prominence as an in-house critic of FUNDAMENTALISM when he published *The Uneasy Conscience of Modern Fundamentalism* in 1947. Henry argued that fundamentalism's self-imposed separatism troubles the conscience of all right-minded believers. The biblical mandate to be the "salt and light" of the world requires that Christians participate in public life. Only a "rebirth of apostolic passion," he declared, would restore "social vision," "social sensitivity," and "social outreach" among conservative Christians.

This little book became the manifesto of the burgeoning evangelical movement, which progressively distanced itself from fundamentalism. The Reverend BILLY GRAHAM, a key leader in this movement, invited Henry to become the founding editor of *Christianity Today*. Throughout his 12-year editorial tenure, Henry made social involvement a frequent theme in a magazine that reached almost every evangelical leader. Politics, the bane of the fundamentalists, became common fare for evangelicals.

An increasingly receptive audience heard Henry's call to action in many other venues. A popular speaker and preacher, he had opportunities to promote social engagement at events such as the unprecedented 1966 World Congress on Evangelism, where he reminded the 1,200 evangelical leaders present that "the God of the Bible is the God of justice and of justification." His writings are also replete with pleas for engagement. Dozens of articles and many of his nearly 50 books, including his six-volume magnum opus, *God, Revelation and Authority*, address political themes.

Even though Henry was among those theologians defending the Christian faith against the secularizing forces of modernity, he couched his arguments for social activism in mostly positive terms, emphasizing the "biblical mandate" to seek justice—a mandate based on the lordship of Christ, the stewardship of creation, and the servanthood of believers.

By the mid-1970s, Henry's work began to bear fruit. Convinced that political engagement was essential, the next generation of evangelicals returned to the public arena. Although widely acknowledged as the dean of evangelical theologians, Henry did not have a direct role in the practical, political activities of the emerging evangelical political movement. However, both the highly publicized Religious Right and the small, albeit vocal, evangelical left are indebted to Henry.

Henry was a persistent critic of and sympathetic counselor to those evangelicals entering politics. He cautioned against stridency, intolerance, and fanaticism and encouraged moderation, TOLERANCE, and cooperation. Critical of confrontational tactics and single-issue campaigns, Henry urged evangelicals to work through and in obedience to government. He warned Christian activists about exaggerated political expectations, arguing that individual regeneration and broad cultural change were also essential.

Although generally conservative, Henry exhibited moderation on divisive policy issues. He was a foe of ABORTION who was willing to compromise; a critic of the welfare state who insisted that citizens provide for the unfortunate; an enemy of socialism who recognized the dangers of unfettered capitalism. When demanding that public schools not ignore religion, he opposed state-sponsored school prayer; when deploring unlawful forms of protest, he advocated the extension of civil rights; and when defending the military's responsibility to guard against unjust aggression, he questioned the buildup of the military establishment.

In his later years, Henry's political writings turned to fundamental guiding principles. A theologian, not a political philosopher, Henry contended that Christians must look to Scripture, as opposed to natural law, as the source of enduring political principles. The result has been a "biblical politics" that characterizes much of contemporary political discourse among evangelicals.

Among "the revealed moral principles that sustain a healthy society and that indict an unhealthy one," according to Henry, are notions such as social problems result from sin; only spiritual regeneration fully transforms humanity; social justice is demanded of all; human rights have a divine source and sanction; church and state are divinely willed institutions with different purposes; and believers are "citizens of two worlds" with a "sacred duty to . . . extend God's purpose of justice and order."

See also CHRISTIAN RIGHT AND THE REPUBLICAN PARTY.

Further reading: Fowler, Robert Booth. "Carl Henry: Pioneering Moderate." In *A New Engagement: Evangelical Political Thought, 1966–1976*. Grand Rapids, Mich.: Eerdmans, 1982; Henry, Carl F. H. *The Uneasy Conscience of Modern Fundamentalism*. Grand Rapids, Mich.: Eerdmans, 1947; Patterson, Bob. *Carl F. H. Henry*. Waco, Tex.: Word Books, 1983;

Weeks, David L. "Carl F. H. Henry's Moral Arguments for Evangelical Political Activism." *Journal of Church and State* 40 (1998): 83–106.

—David L. Weeks

Heritage Foundation

The Heritage Foundation is a conservative research and policy analysis institute located in Washington, D.C. The foundation has strong ties to the Republican Party and Christian conservative groups. Throughout the 1980s and 1990s, the institute was an important component in the revival of the CHRISTIAN RIGHT AND THE REPUBLICAN PARTY takeover of Congress in 1994. It provided conservative analysis and interpretation of politics and national events, and brought together large corporations and religious groups to promote a conservative agenda. The policy and media success of the Heritage Foundation has led to the establishment of a number of similar think tanks at both the state and the national level.

The Heritage Foundation is a private, nonprofit organization founded in 1973. It was established to serve as a countermeasure to a variety of liberal policy institutes such as the Brookings Institution, which began to exert their political influence during the late 1960s and early 1970s. The Heritage Foundation brought together conservative scholars and writers, as well as politicians who were out of office, to serve as research fellows and provide policy papers for national, state, and local officials and the media. Among the more prominent fellows at the foundation are former Republican cabinet officials such as Edwin Meese, Jack Kemp, and William Bennett. To retain its TAX-EXEMPT STATUS, the foundation may not directly lobby on behalf of legislation. However, conservative politicians use its research output to develop positions or understand policy issues. One of its most influential products was the 1980 report *Mandate for Leadership*. This report was used by the incoming administration of RONALD REAGAN as it developed its policy agenda.

During the 1980s, the Heritage Foundation served as a mechanism to coordinate conservative grassroots groups, wealthy donors, and politicians. It promoted broad free-market and antigovernment policies. The foundation has established a variety of individual institutes that focus on specific issues. For instance, Heritage's Thomas A. Roe Institute focuses on economic policy studies. In addition, the Kathryn and Shelby Cullom Davis Institute concentrates on international studies.

The Heritage Foundation does not claim to be objective in the academic sense, but rather acts to promote specific policies. The foundation opposes ABORTION, affirmative action, and increased government spending. Through its research publications and media briefings, the foundation promotes a return of religious values and teachings to public schools (including PRAYER IN PUBLIC SCHOOLS). It also supports school choice (including VOUCHERS for religious schools) and HOMESCHOOLING. It has also advocated pro-family policies, including the elimination of the marriage tax penalty. The organization has consistently equated the rise in crime and the decline in family life with the rise of the modern welfare state. In its reports and research, it routinely presents the American family as being under siege by groups and forces that run counter to mainstream Christian values. As such, it has championed programs such as President GEORGE W. BUSH's WHITE HOUSE OFFICE OF FAITH-BASED AND COMMUNITY INITIATIVES, which would increase federal funding for religious groups that provide social services. Such programs also mirror the foundation's emphasis on private solutions to societal problems. The foundation further works to promote conservative issues and values around the world. It has particularly strong ties with Asian countries such as South Korea (which has a large Christian population).

One of the major initiatives of the Heritage Foundation has been the State Policy Network, created in 1992. The foundation has supported the establishment of conservative public policy institutions in 35 states and acts as a coordinating body for these organizations. This network links conservative Christian groups throughout the nation and provides policy information for media and local and state politicians. Among the main goals of the network are promotion of school choice initiatives and other socially conservative issues.

The institute was initially founded with a $250,000 grant from beer magnate Joseph Coors. Throughout its history, the foundation has been the beneficiary of generous contributions from corporations and wealthy donors. For instance, during a two-year campaign in the 1990s, it raised $85 million, a sum unmatched by its liberal counterparts. In 2000, the foundation raised almost $28 million.

See also CONSERVATIVE CHRISTIAN LITIGATORS.

Further reading: Bellent, Russ. *The Coors Connection: How Coors Family Philanthropy Undermines Democratic Pluralism.* Boston: South End Press, 1991; Heritage Foundation. *Heritage Foundation: Annual Report 2001.* Washington, D.C.: Heritage Foundation, 2001; Himmelstein, Jerome L. *To the Right: The Transformation of American Conservatism.* Berkeley: University of California Press, 1990; Oldfield, Duane Murray. *The Right and the Righteous: The Christian Right Confronts the Republican Party.* Lanham, Md.: Rowman and Littlefield, 1996; Urofsky, Melvin I., and Martha May, eds. *The New Christian Right: Political and Social Issues.* New York: Garland, 1996.

—Thomas Lansford

Hernandez v. Commissioner of Internal Revenue Service 490 U.S. 677 (1989)

In *Hernandez,* the Supreme Court held on June 5, 1989, that payments to a religious organization for services known as auditing and training were not legitimate deductions under the tax code, and that the code's restrictions on the nature of religious deductions was not an unconstitutional violation of the constitutional guarantee of freedom of religion contained in the First Amendment. The case was decided on a vote of five to two. Justice Marshall wrote the majority opinion, joined by Chief Justice Rehnquist and Justices White, Blackmun, and Stevens. Justice O'Connor filed a dissenting opinion in which Justice ANTONIN SCALIA joined. Justices WILLIAM J. BRENNAN and Kennedy did not participate in the decision.

The CHURCH OF SCIENTOLOGY (hereinafter the Church), provides "auditing" sessions designed to increase members' spiritual awareness and training courses at which participants study the beliefs of the Scientology faith and earn the necessary qualifications to conduct auditing sessions. The Church charges a fixed price to attend the auditing sessions and training classes; the Church believes that this fixed charge is required by what it calls the doctrine of exchange.

Robert L. Hernandez sought to deduct the amounts he paid for auditing and training on his federal income tax as charitable contributions. Under the Income Tax Act, payments made for goods and services are not eligible for the charitable deduction. The commissioner of Internal Revenue disallowed these deductions, and Hernandez sought review by the Tax Court. The Tax Court upheld the commissioner, and the Circuit Court of Appeals affirmed.

The Supreme Court held that Congress had intended to differentiate between gifts and payments for goods or services rendered. If funds are given to a charitable organization as part of a quid pro quo with the donor expecting something in return, it is a purchase, not a donation. Under the plain language of the tax code, such quid pro quo exchanges are not eligible for the tax deduction.

The Court rejected Hernandez's contention that this was an unconstitutional discrimination by imposing harsher tax treatment on religions that impose fixed fees. The code is neutral; it does not discriminate among denominations but forbids all quid pro quo transactions as deductions. Nor does the necessity of determining the value of the goods or services foster an excessive entanglement of state and religion under the test elaborated in *LEMON V. KURTZMAN*.

The two dissenting justices rejected the majority analysis, expressing the opinion that the Church charged a fixed fee to participate in religious services. A disallowance of a deduction for a secular good provided might be acceptable. However, the doctrine of the Church required a fixed charge. Adherents of other faiths could deduct the amounts they donated to their religious body, but Scientologists could not. In the opinion of the two dissenting justices, this was an unconstitutional discrimination among different religious bodies.

Many religious and other charitable organizations offer small gifts or premiums to donors, usually of far less value than the amount of the donation. Since *Hernandez*, donors have been required to reduce the amount of their tax deduction by the value of the goods received. This has affected all charitable organizations from the church that gives a Bible, to the public television station that provides a coffee mug to donors.

—Stephen R. Prescott

Heschel, Abraham Joshua (1907–1972) *rabbi*

By many accounts, Rabbi Abraham Joshua Heschel was one of the 20th century's most profound religious, moral, political, and social leaders. As a theologian and philosopher, he awakened an entire generation to God's presence in the world, challenging contemporary views on religion. As a moral leader, he was committed to activism, to rescuing the Jewish soul and stirring it to action. Standing in defiance of the state to support the moral ideals of justice and nonviolence, he was a powerful advocate in the CIVIL RIGHTS MOVEMENT and anti–Vietnam War movements of the 1960s and 1970s. As an individual, he remained a pious and devoted Jew, unwilling to blindly accept the tenets of Orthodoxy without first challenging their very foundations. He avoided the pitfall of interdenominational squabbling that have divided the Jewish people for the greater part of the 20th century. Seeking to achieve meaningful reconciliation between Jews and Christians, he worked to usher in an era that would be more harmonious than any before.

Born in Poland in 1907, Abraham Joshua Heschel was a true scion of a Hasidic Jewish dynasty, and his family and teachers quickly realized his genius. By age eight, he was already recognized as possessing remarkable intellectual prowess and was ordained as a rabbi while still a teenager. After his rabbinic training. Heschel obtained a doctorate from the University of Berlin and replaced Martin Buber as director of the Central Organization for Jewish Adult Education in Frankfurt, Germany. In 1938, the Nazi German regime arranged for the forced deportation of Heschel and all other Polish Jews living in Germany. Only one week after he and the other Polish Jews were deported, Hitler initiated his program of systematic extermination with *Kristallnacht*, the Night of Broken Glass. Via England, Heschel soon fled from the destruction to begin teaching at the Hebrew Union College in Cincinnati, Ohio. Recounting his escape from Europe just days before his entire village was liquidated, Heschel identified himself as a "brand plucked from the fire of Satan's altar."

In America, Heschel brought a radical new understanding of the religious experience. Focusing not on outward manifestations of religiosity, he advocated radical recentering of the religious perspective, predicated on the "divine-pathos"— that "God is concerned with the affairs of man; that not only does man need God, God is also in need of man." Heschel discussed three paths toward awareness of the Divine Presence: the mystery of revelation, engagement with our present, natural world, and outward manifestations infused by inner intentions, namely, prayer, acts of meta-ethical obedience (*mitvoth*), and prayer. Taken together, all these paths attune the individual to the sublime and the mysterious, which in turn arouse our inner being with awe and "radical amazement."

More than a religious leader, Heschel was a social and political leader as well. He refused to accept human suffering as commonplace or tolerable; many of his positions are summarized in *The Insecurity of Freedom*. His involvement in SOCIAL JUSTICE was a direct outgrowth of his religious commitment. From 1960 to 1972, Heschel's commitment to social activism reached its full potential. He is perhaps most famous for his involvement in the Civil Rights movement and his personal alliance with MARTIN LUTHER KING JR. Known as "Father Abraham" and dressed in the distinctive garb of the old world Jew, Heschel marched in Selma, Alabama, linked arm in arm with Dr. King, Ralph Bunche, and RALPH ABERNATHY. Writing to President JOHN F. KENNEDY, Heschel claimed: "We forfeit the right to worship God so long as we continue to humiliate Negroes."

The VIETNAM WAR also, deeply troubled the aging rabbi. Along with Richard Neuhaus and John Bennet, Heschel founded Clergy and Laymen Concerned about Vietnam, an organization committed to ending the war in Southeast Asia. In 1967, Heschel printed his views on the war in *Vietnam: Crisis of Conscience*. During these last years of his life, Heschel led and participated in protests, lectures, spiritual meetings, and prayer sessions, once commenting: "Oceans divide us, God's presence unites us, and God is present wherever man is afflicted, and all of humanity is embroiled in every agony wherever it may be. Though I am not a native of Vietnam, ignorant of its language and traditions, I am involved in the plight of the Vietnamese."

Heschel was the first major Jewish leader to bring to national attention the suffering of Soviet Jewry. He called for both private and public action to save the spiritual lives of millions of Jews who were being oppressed because of their religious identity.

Heschel was also deeply committed to improving the relationship between Jews and Christians. His greatest concrete impact was his participation in the Second Vatican Council (VATICAN II). As the representative of the AMERICAN JEWISH COMMITTEE, he sought to influence the council to publish an official document rejecting the Catholic mission to the Jews. Although the final declaration fell short of his expectations, Heschel nevertheless felt that it had taken important strides in repairing the damaged relationship. Besides his participation in the council, he also had a profound impact on a number of Christian laypeople and scholars, including W. D. Davies, PAUL TILLICH, and REINHOLD NIEBUHR. Perhaps the most remarkable testament to his influence on Christians is the fact that his religious perspective was quoted in a spiritual address by Pope Paul VI in 1973, the first time a pope ever made public reference to a Jewish religious thinker.

Further reading: Dresner, Samuel, and Edward Kaplan. *Abraham Joshua Heschel: Prophetic Witness*. New Haven, Conn.: Yale University Press, 1998; Heschel, Abraham Joshua. *The Insecurity of Freedom: Essays on Human Existence*. New York: Farrar, Strauss and Giroux, 1966; Heschel, Abraham Joshua, Robert McAfee Brown, and Michael Noval. *Vietnam: Crisis of Conscience*. New York: Association Press, 1967; Kaplan, Edward. *Abraham Joshua Heschel's Poetics of Piety*. Albany: State University of New York Press, 1996; Kasimov, Harold. *Divine-Human Encounter: A Study of Abraham Joshua Heschel*. Washington, D.C.: University Press of America, 1979;

Merkle, John C. *The Genesis of Faith: The Depth Theology of Abraham Joshua Heschel*. New York: Macmillan, 1985.
—Matthew L. Eanet

Hinduism

Hinduism, which originated on the Indian subcontinent, is based on the teachings of sacred scriptures called the Vedas, which date back to the second millennium B.C.E. Today, both Asian immigrants and native-born American converts make up Hindu communities in the United States; one source finds the 1990 American Hindu population at 0.2 percent of the population.

Hinduism first achieved worldwide recognition when Swami Vivekananda spoke at the World's Parliament of Religion in 1893, an event hosted by the World's Fair in Chicago. The parliament was initiated by liberal Protestants who wanted to show the world that Christianity, though the culmination of humanity's religious search, was not inherently exclusive. Vivekananda spoke vigorously on the power of Hinduism. His own teacher was Ramakrishna, a devotee of the Goddess Kali, but Vivekananda's own emphasis was on the more philosophical aspects of Hinduism, coupled with humanitarian service. After the parliament, Vivekananda traveled across the country, initiating the first American-born swamis, and establishing Vedanta societies in New York and California.

Paramahansa Yogananda established the Self-Realization Fellowship in southern California, in 1920. Yogananda's teaching was more devotional than Vivekananda's, including a significant Christian element; one of the claims of Yogananda was that Christ was a practitioner of yoga (a form of spiritual discipline). For Yogananda, the claim of the essential unity of Christianity and Hinduism was part of a larger claim on the essential unity of all religions. The unity of religions would become a regular refrain within American Hinduism.

The next great influx of Hindu teachers occurred in the 1960s. Swami Satchidananda, founder of the Integral Yoga Institute, taught hatha yoga. Maharishi Mahesh Yogi expounded on Transcendental Meditation, and the Beatles rock group helped make Transcendental Meditation a household word. Swami Muktananda introduced Siddha Yoga to the West, eventually establishing one of America's largest ashrams (religious retreat) in New York State.

Many native-born Americans have been exposed to Hindu thought and practice through yoga. Yoga, which is often translated as "union with God," can take many forms, including physical exercises, devotional chanting, and silent meditation. Some native-born Americans deepen their practice of yoga by becoming practitioners of a certain kind of yoga, while maintaining their previous (often Christian or Jewish) religious affiliations. Other Americans devote themselves exclusively to more traditional Hindu communities. Asian-Indian Hindu immigration to the United States has increased since the 1960s.

Further reading: Kosmin, Barry A., and Seymour P. Lachman. *One Nation under God*. New York: Crown, 1993.
—Eric L. Thomas

Hobbie v. Unemployment Appeals Commission of Florida et al. 480 U.S. 136 (1987)

In this case, decided on February 25, 1987, the Supreme Court considered the constitutionality of Florida's refusal to grant unemployment compensation to Paula Hobbie, a SEVENTH DAY ADVENTIST convert who lost her job because she was no longer able to work on Saturday, her Sabbath. Writing for a six-justice majority, Justice WILLIAM BRENNAN argued on the basis of the precedent set in another unemployment compensation case involving a Seventh Day Adventist, *SHERBERT V. VERNER* (1963), in which the Court ruled that compelling a person to choose between his or her religion and eligibility for government benefits burdened the free exercise of religion. Such a burden, the Court then found in *Sherbert,* was subject to "strict scrutiny" and could be imposed only to serve a "compelling state interest."

Brennan insisted there were "no meaningful distinctions" between this and previous cases, including *Sherbert* and *THOMAS V. REVIEW BOARD* (1981). He dismissed the efforts of the Florida Commission to distinguish this case by citing the limited disqualification Hobbie faced and the fact that Hobbie, not her employer, caused the change in her employment situation through her conversion to the Seventh Day Adventist faith. Although the burden Hobbie faced might be less extensive than in previous cases, "[t]he immediate effects of ineligibility and disqualification are identical and the disqualification penalty is substantial." In addition, Brennan saw no reason to treat religious converts differently from others: "The timing of Hobbie's conversion is immaterial to our determination that her free exercise rights have been burdened." Finally, Brennan rejected the Florida commission's contention that accommodating Hobbie's free exercise in this case amounted to the establishment of religion; rather, it merely accorded Sabbatarians the same treatment that Sunday worshipers received.

Writing separately, two justices—Lewis Powell and John Paul Stevens—concurred in the judgment. Justice Powell agreed with the bulk of the majority opinion but took issue with its apparent dismissal of a plurality opinion in which he had joined in *BOWEN V. ROY* (1986). To reach its conclusion, he argued, the Court needed only to distinguish this case from *Bowen,* not reject the latter's line of argument. Justice Stevens also agreed that *Sherbert* and *Thomas* were the controlling precedents, adding only: "granting unemployment benefits is necessary to protect religious observers against unequal treatment."

Chief Justice William Rehnquist's dissent hearkened back to his dissent in *Thomas,* where he argued that "[w]here . . . a State has enacted a general statute, the purpose and effect of which is to advance the State's secular goals, the FREE EXERCISE CLAUSE does not in my view require the State to conform that statute to the dictates of the religious conscience of any group. . . . I believe that although a State could choose to grant exemptions to religious persons from state unemployment regulations, a State is not constitutionally compelled to do so." In addition, he contended in the *Thomas* dissent that the application of the Court's ESTABLISHMENT CLAUSE jurisprudence—in particular, the *Lemon* test—to a hypothetical law that made the accommodations the Court required would lead to the invalidation of the law. His point was not that such a law should in fact be invalidated, but rather that the test was misconceived. He would favor a voluntary state accommodation of religion, but would not constitutionally require it.

Thus in this case the Court sustained a string of decisions in unemployment compensation cases that require the state, on free exercise grounds, to accommodate religious belief. Nevertheless, the plurality argument in *Bowen,* which backed away from requiring strict scrutiny and the assertion of a compelling state interest when a neutral state regulation or practice comes into conflict with an individual's religious practice, returned in *EMPLOYMENT DIVISION V. SMITH* (1990). There, also in the context of an unemployment compensation dispute in which the issue was whether the sacramental ingestion of peyote is a violation of state drug laws and hence an instance of work-related misconduct, the Court limited the scope of the *Sherbert, Thomas,* and *Hobbie* opinions, concluding that free exercise claims do not automatically call for the compelling state interest test. It is unlikely that the position maintained in *Hobbie* will serve as the basis for an expansion of free exercise exemptions from otherwise neutral state laws.

See also BLUE LAWS.

—Joseph M. Knippenberg

Holiness Churches

Pentecostalism, the name that derives from Pentecost, the Greek name for the Jewish Feast of Weeks, which falls on the 50th day after Passover, was the fastest-growing Christian movement of the 20th century, and this growth continues into the 21st century. With over 210 million members worldwide designated as denominational Pentecostals, this group surpassed the EASTERN ORTHODOX CHURCHES as the second-largest denominational family of Christians, exceeded only by the ROMAN CATHOLIC CHURCH. By the latter part of the 20th century, there were an additional 300 million "Charismatic nondenominational" Pentecostals scattered throughout mainline denominations, the Catholic Church, and independent charismatic churches, bringing the total number of Pentecostals and Charismatics worldwide to over a half billion followers. This phenomenal growth pattern requires the Christian world to take notice and to discover the causes of this growth.

The theological roots of Pentecostalism began in the United States around the dawn of the 20th century, first with Charles Parham in Topeka, Kansas, in 1901 and later on Azusa Street with William J. Seymour in Los Angeles in 1906. Yet Pentecostalism is historically grounded in the Holiness movement, primarily the British perfectionistic and charismatic movements. These included the Methodist Holiness movement, inspired by John Wesley (1766–71), the Catholic Apostolic movement of Edward Irving (1831), and the British Keswick "Higher Life" movement (after 1875). A commonality among all three movements was a spiritual experience labeled several things, including "entire sanctification," "perfect love," "Christian perfection," "heart purity," and "baptism in the Holy Spirit." The followers believed that a "second blessing" occurred, a blessing that not only provided evidence in terms of "speaking in tongues," theologically referred to as glossolalia, but also a cleansing or sanctification of the believer in Jesus Christ by the power of the Holy Spirit. Some time during the 1870s in England, probably during the Keswick Conventions, as well as other locations, the second blessing soon became known as an anointing of the Holy Spirit, rather than a spiritual cleansing, which was the Holiness definition.

Pentecostalism is similar in doctrine to other fundamentalist and evangelical Christian denominations, including Baptists and the DUTCH REFORMED TRADITIONS, except with regard to their interpretation and understanding of Scripture regarding the power and presence of the Holy Spirit in a believer's life. Fundamentalists believe that the Holy Spirit baptism did in fact occur at the onset of salvation, but that this experience was limited to the original Apostles and that it gradually ceased to exist toward the end of the first century. Pentecostals adhere to Acts 2: 1–4 and several other places in the New Testament as clear evidence that the baptism of the Holy Spirit is an experience for every BORN-AGAIN Christian believer today. The desire to live a holy life increases after this experience. It is not the experience that brings instant holiness to a believer's life, but it will direct the believer toward Scripture, which, as God's written word, is the basis for living a holy life before God.

The historical roots of the Holiness movement are significant to understanding Pentecostalism. Those who practiced Pentecostal Christianity came almost exclusively from the Holiness movement, including Methodists, former Methodists, and believers from similar denominations. They were all primarily Arminian in their basic theology, which means they believed that human will plays a significant role in eternal salvation. American Methodism experienced a major holiness revival in the mid-to-late 1860s, originating in New York, New Jersey, and Pennsylvania. Camp meetings were the favorite means for Christians to gather together. A camp meeting was usually held in the summer, located outdoors, sometimes lasting weeks at a time, and attracting thousands of persons. Leaders during the late 19th century included Phoebe Palmer, John Inskip, and Alfred Cookman.

Between the mid-to-late 1860s to around 1880, the Holiness movement revived the Christian church worldwide, particularly influenced by the Keswick Conventions and their stress on PENTECOSTAL sanctification. The movement was so strong and influential that many of its adherents believed it would sweep through other denominations. But by the early 1880s, some leaders, such as David Warner, founder of the "Evening Light" Church of God in Anderson, Indiana, stated that they did not believe that the Holiness movement should or could be mainstreamed in traditional Protestant denominations. They were convinced that the

"second blessing" was legitimate, but in their own mind were not convinced that mainline Christianity would accept the Holiness message. So they urged the Holiness adherents to come out of the mainline denominations. Hence was coined the term "comeouters."

The first Pentecostal churches were mostly made up of the down-and-out, the poor and destitute. Specific denominations included the predominantly African-American CHURCH OF GOD IN CHRIST (1897), the Pentecostal Holiness Church (1898), and the Church of God (1906). The Azusa Street movement in Los Angeles, for example, was a merger of white Holiness doctrine with African-American worship styles, which included shouting, dancing, and other forms of verbal and musical expressions. For over three years (1906–9), white and black worshippers came from all over the United States and abroad to experience what is referred to as the "outpouring of the Holy Spirit," which resulted in sanctification, speaking in tongues, prophetic words, tongues and interpretations, and other forms of charisms. Today, these expressions have come to include what the early Methodists and Wesleyans referred to as the second blessing.

By 1906, however, schisms began to take hold, particularly over the practice of speaking in tongues, the result of being baptized in the Holy Spirit. Denominations such as the Nazarenes, SALVATION ARMY, Wesleyans, Church of God (Anderson), and Christian Missionary Alliance broke away from mainline Pentecostalism and the Holiness movement, primarily because of the latter's acceptance and practice of the second blessing. It is now generally accepted among both mainline and Reformed Pentecostals as simply the "baptism in the Holy Spirit."

Several other denominations were offshoots of the early Pentecostal Holiness movements. The International Foursquare Church, founded by AIMEE SEMPLE MCPHERSON in 1927, the charismatic "first lady" of Pentecost from Los Angeles, provided, among other things, a societal forum for the promotion of women into the pulpit ministry. The ASSEMBLIES OF GOD was formed in 1914, and Open Bible Standard was founded in 1935. All three are considered "reformed" Pentecostal denominations, principally because each places less emphasis on the sanctification and holiness issues than does, for example, the International Pentecostal Holiness Church.

Other evidence that spoke of Pentecostalism's influence within Christianity began after World War II, starting with such evangelists as ORAL ROBERTS and William Branham, who preached powerful messages of salvation, holy living, and divine healing. Pentecostalism no longer was relegated to backwoods brush arbors but broke into the living rooms and lives of tens of millions of people worldwide.

A Charismatic renewal began in earnest in the late 1960s and continued through the early 1980s. Individuals from many of the mainline Protestant churches, such as Lutherans, Presbyterians, and Methodists, as well many in the Roman Catholic community, experienced the outpouring of the Holy Spirit with evidence of physical healing, speaking in tongues, and the desire to live holy and pure lives. As Vinson Synan argues in his book *The Holiness-Pentecostal Tradition*, "Pentecostalism has grown beyond a mere passing 'movement' . . . and can now be seen as a major Christian 'tradition' alongside the Roman Catholic, Orthodox, and Reformation Protestant traditions."

—Stephen M. King

Holocaust

The Holocaust (*Shoah*) refers to the most lethal and virulent episode of persecution to have befallen Jews at the hands of Christians or pagans during their long historical existence in Europe. Between January 30, 1933, when the National Socialists (Nazis) came to power in Germany, and May 7, 1945, when Nazi Germany unconditionally surrendered, roughly 6 million European Jews were interned and isolated in ghettos where they were often mistreated and killed, rounded up and shot en masse in territories the Nazi German army occupied, or deported from territories of the Nazi "German Reich" to camps where they were gassed, shot, hanged, tortured, or worked and starved to death, and where cruel medical experiments were often performed on them. After 1945, Jews came to call this 12-year event the Holocaust. The word is derived from a classical Greek word for "burnt offering" or "complete destruction by fire," which in turn translates a Hebrew word for "what is brought up," often translated in English versions of the Jewish writings as "burnt offering" or "whole burnt offering." "Holocaust" in this contemporary usage therefore harks back to Jewish sacrificial practices of antiquity, now depicting Jews as the victims or sacrifices of gentile persecution and systematic murder.

The Holocaust emerged out of a background of long-standing and deep-rooted Christian anti-Semitism, animated by a modern form of European RACISM and a fanatical type of Romantic nationalism. The latter two were combined in Nazi ideology in its doctrine of the role of the state in the historical, racial struggle between the "Aryan" race (of which the Germans were a representative) and "races" that either historically opposed the Aryans, in particular the Jews, or that were to be subject to them, such as the Slavs and other "inferior" races. Under this doctrine, the Nazis were able to establish a policy first of systematic discrimination, then harsh mistreatment, and finally the murder of a large majority of Europe's Jewish population. Traditional Euro-Christian anti-Semitism enabled the Nazis to intern, round up, or deport Jews en masse to be murdered with infrequent (but individually notable) resistance from the non-Jewish population (Denmark, Norway, and Italy were general exceptions) in many cases, and widespread complicity (Poland was a prime example) in other cases.

Figures representing the destruction of European Jewry in the Holocaust are grim: of 3.3 million Polish Jews, 90 percent, or about 3 million, were annihilated. Ninety percent of the 200,000 Jews remaining in Germany after 1939 (there were approximately 500,000 in 1933) died, as did 90 percent of Baltic Jews, more than 75 percent of Greek Jews, 75 percent of Dutch Jews, and 65 percent of Russian Jews. Best estimates are that the 6 million Jews the Nazis murdered represented over two-thirds of the entire European Jewish population. *Holocaust* is sometimes used to refer as well to the approximately 10 million non-Jews, including significant numbers of the German population itself, whom the Nazis murdered, but common usage tends to refer specifically to the Jewish experience.

Allied (especially British and American) complicity in the events of the Holocaust include prewar unwillingness on the part of nearly all free nations to accept Jewish refugees deported from Germany, British unwillingness to allow Jews to settle in Palestine, which the British controlled under a League of Nations mandate, and Allied unwillingness during the war to bomb railway lines and bridges over which trainloads of Jews were being shipped to the extermination camps. German mistreatment of Jews was well known to leaders in the United States, Great Britain, and elsewhere long before 1939, and knowledge of the extermination camps was widely available by 1942. Nazi dedication to the destruction of the Jews superseded the German war effort: German military officers complained that trains, badly needed to ship military personnel and matériel to the fronts, were being diverted for transporting Jewish populations to camps.

Small populations of Jews have remained in Europe since the war, and memorials to the Holocaust exist in many places there. A Holocaust Memorial Museum was opened in Washington, D.C., in April 1993. Human passivity and indifference to suffering and the phenomenon of radical evil remain salient problems raised, but not satisfactorily answered, by the experience of the Holocaust. Theological and religious responses among Christians and Jews alike to the destruction of the Holocaust have ranged from nihilistic and atheistic despair to renewed belief in or hope for a Divine presence and activity in the world.

See also CHRISTIAN IDENTITY.

—Thomas Heilke

Home School Legal Defense Association (HSLDA)

Founded by attorneys MICHAEL FARRIS and Mike Smith in 1983, this membership organization's mission is to support families who desire to teach their children at home. HSLDA's primary means of supporting parents who teach their children at home is legal defense of homeschooling families. Families who pay for a membership are guaranteed legal support if a legal difficulty related to HOMESCHOOLING arises, and one of its attorneys states that each year HSLDA "handles nearly three thousand negative legal contacts on behalf of member-families who faced with public school officials who attempt to exceed the law." HSLDA attorneys have also assisted with significant homeschooling cases involving nonmember families. Through its member families and related organizations,

HSLDA has also sought to encourage a favorable homeschooling environment by being active in legislative developments affecting homeschooling on the state and federal levels.

At first, Farris operated HSLDA out of his home in Washington State; by the end of the first year, it had approximately 200 members. Later the organization moved to the Washington, D.C., area when Farris took a position directing the legal department for CONCERNED WOMEN FOR AMERICA. Chris Klicka joined the organization in 1985 as executive director and the first full-time attorney for the group. Smith began working full-time for the organization in 1986, as did Farris in 1987.

In 1989 HSLDA established the National Center for Home Education to direct advocacy with regard to state and federal legislation. In 1993 this center established the Congressional Action Program, which organizes a network of homeschooling families in congressional districts. In 1993 HSLDA had about 30,000 member families.

With its current headquarters located in Purcellsville, Virginia, about 50 miles east of Washington, D.C., HSLDA has about 50 staff members and 70,000 member families. Farris, who served as president from 1983 to 2000, is the chairman of the board and serves on the legal staff. Smith, formerly vice president, now serves as president.

HSLDA has used its legal staff to support families in many instances, but it considers its victory in *De Jonge v. Michigan* to be one of its most important. This case involved a Michigan family who desired to teach their children at home because of religious convictions. In 1985, Michigan law stated that home instruction had to be provided by a certified teacher. The De Jonges were convicted at trial, and the state appellate court affirmed that decision. With HSLDA lawyers arguing before the Michigan Supreme Court, the court decided in 1993 that religious liberty rights should permit a religious exemption to the requirement of certified teachers.

HSLDA also considers the case of *Texas Education Agency v. Leeper* (1994) to be significant. In this case, homeschools were permitted to operate at private schools. In 1981, the Texas Education Agency (TEA) issued a policy stating that home education could not be considered the same as a private school. HSLDA assisted in a class-action suit against the state's school districts and the TEA. homeschooling advocates won the case at every judicial level, including the Texas Supreme Court, in 1994.

HSLDA also considers its 1993 efforts to defeat an amendment to H.R. 6, the Elementary and Secondary Education Act, to be its most significant effort at influencing federal legislation. Representative George Miller (D-Calif.) offered an amendment requiring states to permit only certified teachers. Farris argues that this amendment would have prohibited noncertified parents from teaching their children at home. HSLDA then coordinated the efforts of homeschooling parents and worked with state homeschooling organizations to communicate opposition to the amendment. HSLDA also worked with members of the Christian Right media to communicate opposition to this amendment. While the amendment passed in committee, it was removed on the floor by a 442 to 1 vote. GARY BAUER, former president of the FAMILY RESEARCH COUNCIL and domestic policy adviser to President RONALD REAGAN, said: "the calls on H.R. 6 . . . surpassed anything I had ever seen on other issues." HSLDA has also been involved with state legislative efforts, providing information to homeschooling advocates and testifying before state legislative committees.

See also CHRISTIAN RIGHT SCHOOL BOARD CANDIDATES; CHRISTIAN RIGHT IN VIRGINIA; TUITION TAX CREDITS FOR RELIGIOUS SCHOOLS; VOUCHERS/SCHOOL CHOICE.

Further reading: Farris, Michael. *The Future of Homeschooling: A New Direction for Home Education.* Washington, D.C.: Regnery, 1997; Home School Legal Defense Association website. URL: www.hslda.org; Klicka, Christopher. *The Right Choice: Home Schooling.* Gresham, Oreg.: Noble, 1995.

—Michael Coulter

homeschooling

Parents who educate their children at home rather than in public or private schools are a growing force in American politics. Current estimates of the number of homeschoolers range from 1.5 million to 1.9 million children, who make up about 2 percent of the primary and secondary school population nationwide. The number of homeschooled children is estimated to be growing at roughly 15 percent annually. Illegal in 30 states as recently as 1980, homeschooling is now commonplace and has been legal in all 50 states since 1993, owing in large measure to the lobbying efforts of parent-educators.

Homeschooling first became popular in the 1960s as a countercultural phenomenon, involving a philosophy of "unschooling," which held that children should tailor their learning individually rather than being restricted by established school curricula. Beginning in the late 1970s, conservative Christian parents began to homeschool their children in response to changes in public school curricula that challenged their religious beliefs. Although parents now homeschool for many reasons, one study of homeschooling parents in three Western states (Washington, Nevada, and Utah) found that the majority are more likely to be strongly committed to their religion than the population at large. Another study of predominantly conservative homeschooling families also found that those parents had more formal education than parents in the general population, and that many homeschooling parents (24 percent) were trained as teachers.

The most prominent Christian political group representing homeschoolers is the HOMESCHOOL LEGAL DEFENSE ASSOCIATION (HSLDA), founded in 1983 by FUNDAMENTALIST Christian attorney MICHAEL FARRIS. HSLDA, which offers its members legal representation in homeschool-related battles, claims a membership of more than 70,000 families.

HSLDA routinely instructs its members on how to be effective lobbyists at the grassroots and national levels of government and enjoys massive political clout. One testament to their ability is a case involving Congress in 1994, when Representative George Miller (D-Calif.) introduced a measure that would have required teachers to be certified in the subject they teach. HSDLA viewed the legislation as potentially threatening to parents who homeschool, so they sent out instructions about opposing the bill to its members and other homeschoolers. The congressional switchboard received so many calls and faxes as a result of the legislative alert that it shut down temporarily. The bill was quickly defeated, 434-1.

In addition to lobbying, HSDLA also routinely champions other "pro-parent" causes that are generally conservative, such as corporal punishment and gun ownership. HSLDA also opposes GAY RIGHTS and the United Nations' Convention on the Rights of the Child. According to one HSDLA staffer, passage of this U.N. convention threatens homeschoolers' ability to physically discipline their children and potentially allows children to claim the right to refuse to be homeschooled.

This lobbying on behalf of other conservative causes by HSDLA has been the source of growing tension between religious and secular homeschoolers, particularly as the movement's popularity grows among parents who homeschool for nonreligious reasons. Secular homeschoolers resent that HSLDA and other exclusive, religious homeschooling groups often represent the "public face" of homeschooling. The distinctive educational and political philosophies of the two groups threaten to fractionalize the homeschool community.

Although the National Education Association asserts that homeschooling cannot provide students with a comprehensive education, public acceptance of homeschooling is growing, particularly as studies indicate that homeschooled children often perform well on standardized tests. Many homeschooled children are college-bound, and more universities are opening their doors to such students. homeschooled children from conservative Christian families also have the option of attending Patrick Henry College, which was founded by Michael Farris in 2000 and has an affiliation with HSLDA. As the only college geared specifically toward homeschooled young adults, its mission is to train students specifically for work in law and government.

See also TEXTBOOK CONTROVERSIES.

Further reading: Cook, Stephanie. "Report Card on homeschooling in the US." *Christian Science Monitor,* March 25, 1999; Cordes, Helen. "Battling for the Heart and Soul of Homeschoolers." *Salon Magazine.* URL: http://www.salon.com.mwt/feature/2000/10/02/homeschooling_battle, 2000; "HSLDA: Who Are We?" URL: http://www.hslda.org/join/tour2.asp. Mayberry, Maralee, J. Gary Knowles, Brian Ray, and Stacey Marlow. *Homeschooling: Parents as Educators.* Thousand Oaks, Calif.: Corwin Press, 1995; McRoberts, Flynn. "The Economics of Karate." *Newsweek,* November 6, 2000; Patrick Henry College, Overview of Institutional Mis-

sion. Available on-line. URL: http://phc.hslda.rg/Overview.asp; Rudner, Lawrence. "The Scholastic Achievement of Home School Students." *Eric Clearinghouse on Assessment and Evaluation* (ED435709), 1999.

—Melissa M. Deckman

homosexual "reeducation" programs

The phrase "homosexual 'reeducation' programs" refers generally to programs that aim to assist individuals who seek freedom from homosexuality. Exodus International, Homosexuals Anonymous, and the National Association for Research and Therapy of Homosexuality (NARTH) are national programs that directly and indirectly support their own local chapters, as well as programs in individual religious traditions. These programs aim generally to help people overcome homosexuality through counseling, support groups, and religious study. Those who believe they have successfully left the "homosexual lifestyle" are often referred to as "ex-gay."

Before 1970, homosexual reeducation programs were largely secular and were based on the techniques of psychotherapy, aversion therapy, castration, electric shock, and medication. The number of programs declined in the 1970s in response to the American Psychiatric Association and the American Psychological Association statements that homosexuality was not a mental illness.

Exodus International, the largest ex-gay organization in the United States, was founded in 1976 as an interdenominational Christian organization that promotes the message of "freedom from homosexuality through the power of Jesus Christ." Exodus ministries believe that freedom from homosexuality is possible as "men and women mature through ongoing submission to the lordship of Christ and His Church." Individual and pastoral counseling, support groups, personal Bible study, and same-sex discipleship groups are important components of this process. Exodus sanctions new ex-gay ministries, supervises and (nonfinancially) supports existing ministries, distributes monthly newsletters, and sustains a phone counseling and referral system to enable individuals to find ministries in their area. Every year an annual conference is held in which over 1,000 ex-gays, pastors, therapists, spouses, parents, and others come together for worship and workshops.

Like Exodus International, Homosexuals Anonymous is a nondenominational Christian organization of men and women who have chosen to help each other to live free from homosexuality. The group is based on the premise that "homosexual activity is not in harmony with the will of God and that the universal creation norm is heterosexuality." The group believes that the "root causes of homosexuality are spiritual, intrapsychic and relational" and that "the grace of God through Christ brings freedom and recovery." Individuals support each other through weekly Homosexuals Anonymous meetings based on 14 steps (modeled after 12-step Alcoholics Anonymous programs). These steps include admitting that you are powerless over your homosexuality, claiming that you are part of God's heterosexual creation, and seeking to mature in relationship with men and women and with God. Two men who had recovered from homosexuality started the group in 1980. Homosexuals Anonymous is organized in local chapters that are part of the worldwide network of chapters that function under the guidance of Homosexuals Anonymous Fellowship Services, based in Reading, Pennsylvania.

Unlike Exodus International and Homosexuals Anonymous, which are based on support for individuals, NARTH is a professional organization dedicated to providing "psychological understanding of the cause, treatment and behavior patterns associated with homosexuality." Charles Socarides, Benjamin Kaufman, and Joseph Nicolosi founded NARTH in 1992. The group's main goal is to "make effective psychological therapy available to all homosexual men and women who seek change." To that end they support scholarly research on the topic, distribute related scientific publications, and maintain a referral service of therapists offering sexual reorientation treatment. Members are professionals who "defend the right to pursue change of sexual orientation."

In addition to these national programs, individual religious traditions have programs devoted to the support and education of ex-gays. Courage in the ROMAN CATHOLIC CHURCH was started in September 1980 and currently has more than 95 chapters worldwide that minister to those with same-sex attractions. The goal of the program is to help those with same-sex attractions to develop a life of inner chastity. Individual chapters are self-supporting and have the approval of their local archdiocese. One by One, an unofficial program in the PRESBYTERIAN CHURCH USA, also ministers to victims of sexual abuse and people who feel their sexual orientation has changed from homosexual to heterosexual. Rather than focusing just on individuals, some UNITED METHODISTS started the Transforming Congregation program in 1988 to provide "information, resources, and training to churches, districts, and annual conferences in understanding and involvement in a ministry of transformation of homosexuals." By "transformation," this group means they provide support in congregations and small groups for ex-gays.

See also GAY AND LESBIAN MARRIAGE; GAY RIGHTS; MAINLINE PROTESTANT PRO-GAY GROUPS.

Further reading: Exodus International website. URL: http://www.exodusnorthamerica.org; Homosexuals Anonymous website. URL: http://members.aol.com/Hawebpage; National Association for Research and Therapy of Homosexuality website. URL: http://www.narth.com.

—Wendy Cadge

Hubbard, L. Ron (1931–1986) *religious founder*
Lafayette Ronald Hubbard was born on March 13, 1911, in Tilden, Nebraska, and died on January 24, 1986. Hubbard was the creator and founder of both Dianetics, a popular self-help therapy, and the CHURCH OF SCIENTOLOGY, which grew out of Dianetics. Hubbard was married three times and fathered seven children. His third marriage was to Mary Sue Whipp in 1952, who gave birth to four children and herself became an important figure in the Church of Scientology. Hubbard led the Church of Scientology from its inception in 1954 until 1966, when he withdrew from formal leadership positions.

L. Ron Hubbard, as he is referred to by Scientologists, was the son of a naval officer, and so he traveled widely during his youth and became an accomplished navigator, sailor, pilot, surveyor, and explorer. During the 1930s, Hubbard supported himself by writing fiction; his greatest success came as a science fiction writer. During World War II, Hubbard served as a naval lieutenant and saw combat in the Pacific. While recovering from an injury, he discovered the basic principles of Dianetics and Scientology, which represent his personal synthesis of philosophy, physics, and psychology.

In 1950, Hubbard published his discoveries as *Dianetics: The Modern Science of Mental Health*. The book immediately became a best-seller and Hubbard a popular lecturer. Dianetics gained popularity because it was much more accessible than psychotherapy, promised more immediate progress, and placed the practitioner rather than a therapist in control of the therapy process. Scientology emerged out of Dianetics when practitioners began reporting experiences from what appeared to be their previous lives emerging during therapy. Hubbard postulated an immortal essence (the thetan) for each individual that existed across lifetimes. These "thetans" gave Dianetics a spiritual dimension that led rapidly to Hubbard's development of Scientology.

The first Church of Scientology was established in Los Angeles in 1954; the following year, Hubbard moved to Washington, D.C., and established the Founding Church of Scientology. Hubbard provided Scientology with both administrative and spiritual leadership until 1966, when he resigned his organizational positions to devote himself to further research and writing. At this juncture, he formed what came to be an elite unit within the Sea Organization (Sea Org), a church unit staffed by advanced members. Sea Org derived its name by virtue of the fact that for nearly a decade it was located on a flotilla of oceangoing ships that cruised international waters. In 1975, Sea Org moved to a land base in Clearwater, Florida. Over the 1970s, Hubbard continued to relinquish control over church organizations, and by 1980 he had withdrawn completely from public view. He retained the title Founder and lived a reclusive life until his death in 1986.

Hubbard never claimed and was not revered as a supernatural figure during his lifetime. Rather, he was understood as an extraordinary man who had discovered principles through which all of humankind could achieve its true, infinite potential. Over his lifetime, Hubbard was a prolific writer by any standard. According to the church, Hubbard's teachings are contained in approximately 500,000 pages of written material and 3,000 recorded lectures, which total some 65 million words. He also produced 100 films and 500 novels and short stories. Since Scientology teaches that individuals possess immortal essences, at the time of Hubbard's death church leaders announced that Hubbard's body had begun to impede his work and that he had moved to another planet to continue his research.

The details of Hubbard's life have been vigorously contested. The church has published an official biography (1996). Various former members and critics have written accounts that challenge important details of Hubbard's life. Among the most significant are a book coauthored by a son of Hubbard's first marriage, Ronald DeWolf, and Russell Miller. Both were released shortly after Hubbard's death in 1986. The most balanced assessment available is contained in Gordon Melton's *The Church of Scientology* (2000).

Further reading: Church of Scientology. *L. Ron Hubbard Images of Lifetime: A Photographic Biography.* Los Angeles: Bridge Publications, 1996; Corydon, Bent, and Ronald DeWolf (L. Ron Hubbard Jr.). *L. Ron Hubbard: Messiah or Madman.* Secaucus, N.J.: Lyle Stuart, 1987; Hubbard, L. Ron. *Dianetics: The Modern Science of Mental Health.* Los Angeles: Church of Scientology of Los Angeles, 1950; Melton, J. Gordon. *The Church of Scientology.* Salt Lake City: Signature Books, 2000; Miller, Russell. *Bare-Faced Messiah: The True Story of L. Ron Hubbard.* New York: Henry Holt, 1987.

—David G. Bromley

Humanae Vitae

Humanae Vitae (Latin, *Of Human Life*) is the title of an encyclical issued in 1968 by Pope Paul VI that reaffirmed the ROMAN CATHOLIC CHURCH's ban on artificial contraception. Papal encyclicals are formal pastoral letters about moral or doctrinal issues circulated to the whole universal church. Most encyclicals are quietly received. This one caused worldwide controversy.

The Catholic Church has traditionally held that, according to natural law, the purpose of human sexuality is procreation, and that any interference with the sexual act for purposes of preventing conception is morally impermissible. This position, traceable to the writings of Clement of Alexandria, Augustine of Hippo, and other patristic writers, was reiterated in the 1930 encyclical *Casti Connubii* (*On Christian Marriage*) by Pope Pius XI. However, developments in modern medicine and public health, as well as changes in the roles of women and the threat of overpopulation, generated new pressures on the Catholic Church to rethink its teaching.

In the early 1960s, Pope JOHN XXIII appointed a special commission to study the question of birth control. After his death in 1963, his successor, Paul VI, removed the issue from debate at the Second Vatican Council (VATICAN II—in session from 1962 to 1965) and insisted that the special commission report directly to him. A majority of the special commission favored liberalization of the church's position, while a conservative minority supported the ban.

Publication of *Humanae Vitae* caused surprise and consternation in the Catholic Church, particularly after it became known that the pope's decision went against the majority report of his own study commission. Paul VI reiterated the traditional teaching condemning artificial contraception. The encyclical calls for responsible parenthood and teaches that "each and every marriage act must remain open to the transmission of life." While acknowledging the unitive purpose of marital love, the pope reemphasized the procreative purpose of human sexuality. Conjugal love should not be separated from the potential for reproduction. While direct interference with the natural purpose of marital sexuality is forbidden, the rhythm method (or natural family planning) is judged acceptable because it does not impede the development of natural processes. Paul VI then discussed possible negative consequences—marital infidelity, sexual promiscuity, loss of respect for women by men, and a general lowering of morality—from the use of artificial contraceptives. The encyclical concludes with practical directives to priests, bishops, doctors, and married couples on how to implement its moral teaching.

Although encyclicals are authoritative for Catholics, they are not infallible pronouncements; Catholics may dissent from such teachings of the church hierarchy when sufficient reasons for so doing exist. Moreover, publication of an encyclical does not imply that the theological issues addressed in the encyclical are closed to further debate. The reception of *Humanae Vitae* in the Catholic world confirms this.

Publication of the encyclical triggered massive public dissent. In the United States, 600 theologians and philosophers signed a statement disagreeing with *Humanae Vitae*. Several national conferences of bishops (Belgian, Canadian, Austrian, English, German) issued statements affirming the individual's right to follow informed personal conscience in the matter of contraception. Lay Catholics increasingly disagreed in practice with the church's teaching. The pope himself was so distressed by the negative reaction to *Humanae Vitae* that he issued no more encyclicals during the remaining 10 years of his pontificate.

Thirty years later, *Humanae Vitae* remains controversial within the worldwide Catholic community, partly because it precipitated a major crisis of church authority. At the same time, its teaching about the importance of not separating human sexual love from reproduction has taken on renewed interest in an age of medical and technological innovations such as in vitro fertilization, surrogate motherhood, stem-cell research, and CLONING.

See also CATHOLIC BISHOPS' 1975 PASTORAL LETTER ON ABORTION, CATHOLIC BISHOPS' 1984 PASTORAL LETTER ON WAR AND PEACE, and CATHOLIC BISHOPS' 1986 PASTORAL LETTER ON THE ECONOMY.

Further reading: Hoyt, Robert G., ed. *The Birth Control Debate.* Kansas City, Mo.: National Catholic Reporter, 1968; Kaiser, Robert Blair. *The Politics of Sex and Religion.* Kansas City: Leaven Press, 1985; Noonan, John T. *Contraception.* Cambridge, Mass.: Harvard University Press, 1965; Callahan, Daniel, ed. *The Catholic Case for Contraception.* New York: Macmillan, 1969; Segers, Mary C. "The Bishops, Birth Control, and Abortion Policy: 1950–1985." In *Church Polity and American Politics: Issues in Contemporary Catholicism.* Edited by Mary C. Segers. New York: Garland, 1990.

—Mary C. Segers

hunger and humanitarian aid

In 1996, the Food and Agriculture Organization of the United Nations requested heads of state and international government leaders to participate in the World Food Summit, held in Rome, Italy. The Summit identified 800 million people worldwide as lacking food to meet basic nutritional needs. Following Amartya Sen, author of *Poverty and Famines: An Essay on Entitlement and Deprivation* (1981) and recipient of the 1998 Nobel Prize in economics, the summit stated that available food has increased but food insecurity continues because people, as well as governments, lack access to food owing to insufficient income. Likewise, natural and man-made disasters were among the contributors to food insecurity.

According to the U.S. Agency for International Development (USAID), an independent federal government agency that assists countries recovering from disaster, trying to escape poverty, and engaging in democratic reforms, and functioning by spending less than half of 1 percent of the federal budget, identifies 200 million people in Africa as experiencing hunger on a daily basis. Also, 68 percent of the world's extreme poor live in Asia and the Near East. In fiscal year 2000, USAID provided 947,900 million metric tons of emergency food aid to 32 countries. In addition, the U.S. Department of Agriculture (USDA) moved nearly 8 million metric tons of farm surpluses to help relieve hunger across the world.

Much of the food that the U.S. government provides is distributed by religious and charitable organizations such as the Church World Services, Catholic Relief Services, Jewish Distribution Committee, Lutheran World Relief, QUAKERS, MENNONITE Central Kitchen, CARE, and others. Although having their own funds from private and public donations, these organizations are unable to "sustain a program in the field during complex emergencies."

Domestically, the U.S. Census Bureau estimates that one in five children, approximately 15 million, live at or below the poverty line. An estimated 31 million people, according to the USDA, are food insecure and rely on emergency food resources to meet their nutritional needs. The Conference of Mayor's 17th Annual Report found that 37 percent of adults requesting food assistance were employed. Contra earlier theories and opinions arguing that poverty is the result of people being unemployed, it is "possible to be fully employed in the formal economy and to live in poverty." Other factors that contribute to hunger in America consist of poverty, lack of affordable housing, household composition, and rising HEALTH CARE costs.

In response to domestic hunger, the U.S. government, through USDA, administers 14 nutrition and food security programs consisting of the Food Stamp Program, Emergency Food Assistance Program, Special Supplemental Nutrition Program for Women, Infants and Children (WIC), National School Lunch Program, School Breakfast Program, Summer Food Service Program for Children, and Child and Adult Care Food. BREAD FOR THE WORLD, the largest grassroots advocacy network in the nation—founded in 1972 and headquartered in Washington, D.C.—claims that nutrition programs and welfare expenditures account for 3 percent of the federal budget. Additionally, the U.S. government is seeking to tap into faith-based communities to assist needy Americans by providing incentives as identified in H.R. 7, Community Solutions Act of 2001. But this act provides hardly any new resources to help people escape poverty. Likewise, it is unlikely that nongovernment organizations will be able to supply the additional resources needed to overcome hunger. With continued federal reductions in the Food Stamp Program via the Personal Responsibility and Work Opportunity Reconciliation Act of 1996, and poor economic conditions, hunger will continue to rise in America.

America's Second Harvest, the largest national hunger relief organization, distributes food to various food banks nationwide; headquartered in Chicago, it estimates that it will be able to make up less than 30 percent of the food shortage resulting from federal cuts. Other organizations that address the problem of hunger in America include Catholic Charities, based in Alexandria, Virginia, Lutheran Social Services based in Baltimore, Maryland, and United Jewish Communities, based in New York City.

See also AID TO POOR NATIONS; HEIFER INTERNATIONAL; WELFARE REFORM; WHITE HOUSE OFFICE OF FAITH-BASED AND COMMUNITY INITIATIVES.

Further reading: Center on Hunger, Poverty and Nutrition Policy. *Analysis of the Capacity of the Second Harvest Network to Cover the Federal Food Stamp Shortfall from 1997 to 2002.* Medford, Mass., 1997; Fainstein, Norman. "A Note on Interpreting American Poverty." In *Urban Poverty and the Underclass.* Edited by Enzo Minzione. Cambridge, Mass.: Blackwell, 1996, 153–159; Natsios, Andrew S. *U.S. Foreign Policy and the Four Horsemen of the Apocalypse.* Westport, Conn.: Praeger, 1997.

—Santiago O. Piñon Jr.

Hunt v. McNair, Governor of South Carolina, et al. 413 U.S. 734 (1973)

A South Carolina taxpayer's claim that a state agency violated the First Amendment's establishment clause by issuing bonds that aid sectarian institutions of higher education was rejected by the U.S. Supreme Court in a 6-3 decision rendered on June 25, 1973. Speaking for the majority, Justice Powell applied the three-prong *Lemon* test and concluded that the state's action passed the purpose, effect, and entanglement prongs.

The South Carolina Educational Facilities Act (Act) empowered the state's Educational Facilities Authority (Authority) to issue revenue bonds for the benefit of public and private higher educational institutions. In 1970, Baptist College of Charleston applied for $1.25 million dollars in revenue bonds to finance capital improvements and the completion of a dining hall. After the Authority gave preliminary approval to the project, a taxpayer filed suit seeking declaratory and injunctive relief, claiming the transaction was unconstitutional.

To resolve the matter, the Supreme Court applied the *Lemon* test. In *LEMON V. KURTZMAN* (1971), the Court had summarized the cumulative criteria used to determine whether statutes withstand ESTABLISHMENT CLAUSE challenges. First, statutes must have a secular legislative purpose; second, their principal or primary effect must neither advance nor inhibit religion; third, statutes must not foster an excessive government entanglement with religion.

In this case, the Court concluded that the Act had the requisite secular purpose, assisting all higher education institutions with financing of construction projects through bond issues. The Act benefited all citizens of South Carolina by helping both public and private institutions provide "sorely needed" facilities to educate the next generation.

When applying the effect test, the Court cited *TILTON V. RICHARDSON* (1971), where they had ruled that federal aid to religiously affiliated institutions is permissible unless an institution is so pervasively sectarian that none of its functions could conceivably be secular in nature. In this instance, although the Baptists controlled the Board of Trustees, there were no religious qualifications for students or faculty members. Nor was there evidence the aid would be used for sectarian purposes, given the Authority's requirements and the College's stated intention—the Authority did not allow construction projects to be used for "sectarian instruction or as a place of religious worship, or in connection with any part of the program of a school or department of divinity," and the college agreed to limit the funded projects to secular purposes. Consequently, the Court concluded that the principal or primary effect of this transaction neither advanced nor inhibited religion.

Nor, according to the majority, did the arrangement entail excessive entanglement. The lease agreement permitted state inspections, but the prospect of state involvement in the financial affairs of the college was minimal, appearing only if the institution defaulted on the bonds.

Thus the Court concluded the South Carolina statute did not violate the establishment clause because it had a secular purpose, its primary effect did not advance or inhibit religion, and the resulting relationship did not entail excessive entanglement.

Justice WILLIAM BRENNAN dissented, joined by Justices William Douglas and Thurgood Marshall, arguing that the scheme would lead to an unconstitutional state policing of the college's affairs. Brennan, who had reservations about the *Lemon* test, applied guidelines from *ABINGTON V. SCHEMPP* (1963). In *Abington*, he had argued "the Constitution enjoins those involvements of religious with secular institutions which (a) serve the essentially religious activities of religious institutions; (b) employ the organs of government for essentially religious purposes; or (c) use essentially religious means to serve governmental ends where secular means would suffice."

Under this test, Brennan concluded the South Carolina statute violated the establishment clause. The state is clearly aiding the college with all its religious activities, even if indirectly. Moreover, because of the required terms of the agreement, the college "surrenders to the State a comprehensive and continuing surveillance of the educational, religious, and fiscal affairs of the College." Such an arrangement, Brennan insisted, violated the establishment clause and inhibited "the College's freedom to engage in religious activities and to offer religious instruction."

—David L. Weeks

Hutchinson, Anne (1591–1643) *religious leader*

Born in Alford, England, the daughter of a PURITAN clergyman, Anne Hutchinson (née Marbury) played a central role in what became known as the "Antinomian controversy" during the early years of the Massachusetts Bay colony. Devoted followers of Puritan minister John Cotton, Hutchinson and her husband, William, journeyed to Massachusetts Bay, as had their oldest son and Cotton himself, in 1634. Governor John Winthrop's *Journal* entry for October 21, 1636, noted with alarm the religious meetings organized by Hutchinson for the women of Boston.

Hutchinson criticized virtually all New England clergy (except for Cotton and her brother-in-law John Wheelwright), insofar as they enjoined their congregants to godly behavior, for preaching a false "covenant of works." Hutchinson effectively held that godly behavior represented no sign of grace and provided no evidence of one's status as a saint. To put it in terms of Puritan theology, Hutchinson held that sanctification—the internal and behavioral transformation of a godly individual—provides no evidence whatsoever of justification. These claims led Massachusetts leaders to view Hutchinson and her followers, literally, as "Antinomians"—individuals whose assertion of inner spirituality entailed a rejection of the basic bonds of law and social morality.

It was not just theology that spurred on disagreements between Massachusetts clergy and magistrates, on the one hand, and Hutchinson and her followers, on the other. Deteriorating relations with the natives formed the background of these disputes as well. Hutchinson's sympathizers refused to serve in expeditions against the Pequots, further conflating theological disputes with disruptive and disloyal civil behavior. Brought before the General Court and questioned about her views, Hutchinson justified herself by claiming an immediate revelation from God. The implication of her claim was clear: a claim to personal divine revelation (to a woman, no less) coupled with a denial that any behavior was required to demonstrate godliness, was being brought to bear against the judgment of the community embodied in its ministers and magistrates. Hutchinson was convicted in 1637 of "traducing

Anne Hutchinson preaching in her house in Boston *(Library of Congress)*

the ministers" and banished in the spring of 1638 after being excommunicated by her church. Moving first to Aquidneck Island (located in what is now Rhode Island) with some sympathizers, Hutchinson later moved to Long Island Sound, where she was killed along with many members of her family in a 1643 Indian attack.

The Hutchinsonian disputes were important in setting the parameters of religious dissent, and orthodox responses to that dissent, in early New England. "The response of the Bay colony to first the Quakers and later the Baptists was shaped by its previous experience in dealing with the criticisms of Anne Hutchinson, ROGER WILLIAMS, and the Presbyterians of old and New England."

Further reading: "The Examination of Mrs. Anne Hutchinson at the Court at Newtown." In Thomas Hutchinson, *The History of the Colony and Province of Massachusetts-bay,* ed. Lawrence Shaw Mayo. Vol. 1. Cambridge, Mass.: Harvard University Press, 1756/1936; Morgan, Edmund. "The Case

Against Anne Hutchinson." *New England Quarterly* 10 (1937): 635–649; Pestana, Carla Gardina. *Quakers and Baptists in Colonial Massachusetts.* New York: Cambridge University Press, 1991; Winthrop, John. *Winthrop's Journal (History of New England, 1630–1649).* Edited by James Kendall Hosmer. New York: Charles Scribner's Sons, 1649/1908.

—Andrew R. Murphy

Hyde amendment

The Hyde amendment has prevented the use of federal funds to reimburse low-income women for the cost of an ABORTION under the Medicaid program since 1976. Before passage of the Hyde amendment, there were an estimated 250,000 to 300,000 federally funded abortions annually.

The original version, sponsored by Representative Henry Hyde (R-Ill.), allowed federal Medicaid funding for abortions only if "the life of the mother would be endangered if the fetus were carried to term." Representative Hyde had introduced the funding restriction as an amendment to a congressional budget bill on the floor of the House, after efforts to bring the abortion issue to debate on a proposed constitutional amendment had failed. Subsequent versions added exceptions for abortion of pregnancies resulting from rape or incest.

Soon after its passage, the Hyde amendment was challenged by a group of low-income women, Planned Parenthood of New York City, several physicians, the Women's Division of the Board of Global Ministries of the UNITED METHODIST CHURCH, and two of its officers. The plaintiffs contended that the Hyde amendment violated constitutional principles of the separation of church and state, specifically, the First Amendment's ESTABLISHMENT CLAUSE and FREE EXERCISE CLAUSE.

The plaintiff's establishment clause argument hinged on the contention that "the magnitude of the organized effort of the clergy and laity of the ROMAN CATHOLIC CHURCH to obtain passage of a right-to-life amendment to the Constitution, and passage of the Hyde amendment in its most restrictive form" constituted an "establishment of religion" in violation of the First Amendment (*McRae v. Califano,* 1980). The Roman Catholic Church had been seeking a constitutional amendment "providing protection for the unborn child to the maximum degree possible" since 1973. By 1975, the NATIONAL CONFERENCE OF CATHOLIC BISHOPS had promulgated a Pastoral Plan for Pro-Life Activities "to bring the civil law into consonance with Catholic teaching." It called for passage of a constitutional amendment, passage of federal and state laws, and adoption of administrative policies that would restrict the practice of abortion as much as possible, narrow the interpretation of *ROE V. WADE,* and support legislation that would provide alternatives to abortion.

The trial court acknowledged that the Catholic Church's effort under the plan was "demonstrably resolute, well organized, and well supported by voluntary workers," and that it "required and obtained very substantial sums of money." The court noted further that the press had given the public "the clear impression that there was a very close identification" between the pro-life movement "and the 'official' view of the Roman Catholic Church." In this context, the court observed, "Roman Catholic clergy and laity are not alone in the pro-life movement, but the evidence requires the conclusion that it is they who have vitalized the movement, given it organization and direction, and used ecclesiastical channels of communication in its support. The union of effort with representatives of other denominations is based on shared religious conviction."

To prevail, however, the plaintiffs had to demonstrate that Congress adopted the Hyde amendment out of religious motivation. In the end, the court denied the establishment clause challenge. The court noted Representative Hyde's observation that "while many Catholic voices are heard in Congress on behalf of innocent pre-natal life the leading Senatorial pro-life spokesmen are mostly non-Catholic. I speak of Senator Jesse Helms of North Carolina, and Senator Dick Schweiker of Pennsylvania."

On appeal, the U.S. Supreme Court affirmed the principle that "it does not follow that a statute violates the Establishment Clause because 'it happens to coincide or harmonize with the tenets of some or all religions.'" The Supreme Court also denied the contention made by some of the plaintiffs that the Hyde amendment violated their free exercise rights. The Court ruled that the indigent pregnant women who brought suit as a class could not maintain a free exercise challenge because none had alleged or proved "that she sought an abor-tion under compulsion of religious beliefs." On the other hand, while the two officers of the Women's Division of the Board of Global Ministries of the United Methodist Church "did provide a detailed description" of their religious opposition to the Hyde amendment, they "failed to allege either that they are or expect to be pregnant or that they are eligible to receive Medicaid." Finally, regarding the Women's Division as an organization, it had conceded that "the permissibility, advisability and/or necessity of abortion according to circumstance is a matter about which there is diversity of view within . . . our membership, and is a determination which must be ultimately and absolutely entrusted to the conscience of the individual before God." Since the members of the Women's Division would thus not have been "coerced" by the Hyde amendment "*as individuals* in the practice of their religion," the organization could not maintain a free exercise challenge.

The litigation over the Hyde amendment, which resulted in a trial court decision that exhaustively reviewed testimony and documents pertaining to the plaintiffs' establishment clause and free exercise challenges over the course of a 112-page published opinion, to which the court appended 101 pages of excerpts from the congressional debates on passage of the Hyde amendment, remains a legal landmark regarding the constitutionality of the influence of religious institutions on the legislative process.

See also CATHOLIC BISHOPS' 1975 PASTORAL LETTER ON ABORTION.

—David T. Ball

I

impeachment of William Jefferson Clinton

Religion permeated the historic impeachment of President WILLIAM JEFFERSON CLINTON in 1998–99. First, the sexual scandal precipitating this action elicited moral judgments from citizens, religious leaders, and political elites, dividing all three along religious lines. Second, prominent figures in the drama had strong religious identities and constituencies, including President Clinton, who publicly drew on his religious allies to avoid removal from office. And, finally, the battle produced an atmosphere especially favorable to religious expression in the 2000 presidential campaign.

On the first count, no scandal was better calculated than this one to evoke the religious divisions in American politics, given the centrality of sexual morality to religious conservatives. The charges against the president, growing out of his relationship with White House intern Monica Lewinsky, elicited religious differences in both elite and public responses. Not surprisingly, Evangelical Protestant clergy were the most outspoken in their condemnation of Clinton and in their calls for his resignation or impeachment, while more liberal religious leaders often called for understanding and forgiveness. Moreover, conservative clergy saw the president's behavior as a legitimate public issue rather than a purely private affair, as many liberal ministers viewed it.

Very similar patterns appeared among the people in the pews: Evangelical Protestants and traditionalist Roman Catholics were more prone to see Clinton's affair as a public issue, with evangelicals especially likely to see it as grounds for removal from office. Other religious groups such as Jews, African-American Protestants, religious liberals from all traditions, and secular citizens were more inclined to think that the matter was entirely a private one and, in any event, did not justify removal.

The leadership of the impeachment drive highlighted the religious component of the battle. Special Prosecutor Kenneth Starr was reared in a strict Church of Christ family (his father was a minister) and continued to move in evangelical religious circles, attending the McLean Bible Church in suburban Virginia, a church home for many prominent conservative politi-

cians. To his admirers, Starr's religious convictions explained his strict ethical sense, personal self-discipline, and devotion to duty. To foes, those same convictions explained Starr's self-righteousness, preoccupation with prurient details of Clinton's affairs, and obsession with bringing the sexual malefactor to trial.

Then, when the action shifted to the House of Representatives, Clinton's most dogged pursuers on the Judiciary Committee were traditionalist Catholics, including Chairman Henry Hyde (R-Ill.), and Evangelical Protestants, such as James Rogan (R-Calif.), Lindsay Graham (R-S.C.), and Asa Hutchinson (R-Ark.). His most prominent defenders were African-American Protestants and Jewish members. Once on the floor, Majority Whip Tom DeLay (R-Tex.), a leader of religious conservatives, spearheaded the impeachment movement. Although the House impeachment votes went almost entirely along party lines, evangelical Republicans were far more likely than members of other religious traditions to vote for all four counts of the indictment.

Clinton himself contributed to the religious tone of the struggle. To ward off impeachment, he appealed to the same religious constituencies from which he drew policy support in his administration, primarily liberal mainline Protestants and religious minorities. Clinton's defenders encouraged friendly liberal clergy, especially in the African-American community, to speak out in favor of forgiveness. To signal his own remorse and repentance, Clinton publicly recruited three religious leaders to serve as spiritual mentors, including J. Philip Wogaman, noted Methodist liberal and pastor of Washington's Foundry United Methodist Church; TONY CAMPOLO, an American Baptist minister and popular evangelistic speaker; and Gordon MacDonald of Grace Chapel in Lexington, Massachusetts. He also remained in touch with William Hybels, pastor of the huge Willow Creek Community Church in suburban Chicago, and with Rev. JESSE JACKSON, who became a frequent White House visitor. Thus, even the president's defense was conducted in religious terms and in religious venues.

Although the Senate quickly acquitted Clinton, the scandal and impeachment controversy affected the subsequent 2000 presidential contest. That campaign saw much discussion of the moral aspects of presidential leadership; candidates in both parties advocated higher standards for presidential behavior and drew on religious language to suggest a priority on virtue. The vice presidential nomination of Senator JOSEPH LIEBERMAN (D-Conn.)—an observant Jew and early moral critic of Clinton—was just one indicator of the role that moral and religious values played in the campaign.

See also RELIGION IN THE 2000 PRESIDENTIAL ELECTION.

Further reading: Guth, James L. "Clinton, Impeachment, and the Culture Wars." In *The Postmodern Presidency: Bill Clinton's Legacy in U.S. Politics.* Edited by Steven E. Schier. Pittsburgh: University of Pittsburgh Press, 2000, 203–222; Rozell, Mark J., and Clyde Wilcox, eds. *The Clinton Scandal and the Future of American Government.* Washington, D.C.: Georgetown University Press, 2000.

—James L. Guth

individualism

Individualism assigns primacy to individual human beings, rather than to groups, cultures, or nations. American individualism may be divided into at least four distinct currents: rights-based individualism, rugged (or entrepreneurial) individualism, religious individualism, and romantic (or expressive) individualism. Each of these varieties of individualism has its own unique aspirations, its own defenders, and its own critics and detractors.

Rights-based individualism finds its most famous expressions in the DECLARATION OF INDEPENDENCE, the U.S. Constitution, and the vast body of American constitutional law. At the heart of the theory of rights-based individualism is a belief in natural rights, including a natural right to conscience. For this reason, religious TOLERATION and the principle of SEPARATION OF CHURCH AND STATE are crucial elements of American rights-based individualism. Many early supporters of the principle of separation of church and state, such as the PURITAN dissenter ROGER WILLIAMS, were primarily concerned with the potential corrupting influence of government on religion. Gradually, however, the emphasis has shifted to protecting public life from religious interference, in the name of individual rights.

The theory of rugged (or entrepreneurial) individualism emerges in its most potent form from mythologies of the frontier and the "self-made man." It is a secular ideology, for the most part, although it is associated closely with the Protestant economic virtues. These virtues, including temperance, order, frugality, industry, moderation, and cleanliness, receive systematic treatment in BENJAMIN FRANKLIN's *Autobiography.* But versions of these virtues enjoy enduring popularity and esteem in the American imagination, associated as they are with the American dream and the American success ethic. During the 19th century, the theory of rugged individualism provided fertile ground for Social Darwinism and laissez-faire conservatism, which drew primarily on the evolutionary individualism of Herbert Spencer. At the same time, Horatio

Alger published more than 100 novels, which formulaically depicted poor boys becoming self-made men through their own labor and virtue. More recently, during the late 20th century, Ayn Rand's popular Objectivist philosophy depicted man as a heroic being, individual happiness as the moral purpose of life, productive achievement as the noblest human activity, selfishness as a virtue, and altruism as a vice.

American egalitarianism, socioeconomic and geographic mobility, and Protestant REVIVALISM all contribute to religious individualism, which focuses on the cosmic battle over the individual soul, rather than on the communal dimensions of religious life. Alexis de Tocqueville identified a strain of religious individualism in American life during the mid-19th century, observing that Americans tend to practice religion for the sake of self-interest. According to Tocqueville, however, the interest Americans place in religion is often of this world, rather than being concerned with salvation. Listening to American preachers, Tocqueville observes, raises the question of "whether the main object of religion is to procure eternal felicity in the next world or prosperity in this." In this respect, at least, religious individualism is related to rugged or entrepreneurial individualism.

Romantic (or expressive) individualism is most urgently articulated by TRANSCENDENTALISTS such as RALPH WALDO EMERSON and HENRY DAVID THOREAU, and is realized also in the romance of the open road, propagated by Walt Whitman, Jack Kerouac, and many others. These authors represent the rebellion of one form of individualism (romantic) against another (rugged). For them, individual achievement had little or nothing to do with material success or acquisition. According to Whitman and Kerouac, the purpose of life is to cultivate and express oneself. For Emerson and Thoreau, it is to think one's own thoughts in spite of the cramped conformity of mainstream society. Twentieth-century social critics such as C. Wright Mills and William H. Whyte also decried social conformity in America. Not unlike Emerson and Thoreau before them, these critics perceived conformist traps in rugged or entrepreneurial individualism. Yet another strain of American political thinking, characterized by communitarians such as Robert Bellah and Robert Putnam, was ambivalent toward both types of individualism, calling attention to feelings of the emptiness of life experienced by many Americans in the absence of "sustaining social commitments."

Further reading: Bellah, Robert, et al. *Habits of the Heart: Individualism and Commitment in American Life.* New York: Harper and Row, 1985; Putnam, Robert D. *Bowling Alone: The Collapse and Revival of American Community.* New York: Simon and Schuster, 2000; Tocqueville, Alexis de. *Democracy in America.* New York: Harper and Row, 1840/1988.

—Jason A. Scorza

Industrial Areas Foundation

The Industrial Areas Foundation (IAF) is a national network of grassroots community organizations, based primarily in religious congregations. The network was founded in 1940 by the late Saul Alinsky, an activist, community organizer, and author. During the 1970s, under the leadership of Alinsky's successor, Ed Chambers, the IAF developed its strategy of organizing congregations. By the 1990s, the IAF could claim a membership of between 700 and 1,000 congregations representing between 1 million and 1.5 million families. Most IAF congregations are Christian, but congregations from other religious traditions are welcome. The IAF also does some organizing around issues related to neighborhood schools. The largest IAF organizations are in Texas, California, and New York.

Although most IAF organizing occurs in congregations, the goal of IAF is secular: to build political power for its constituents, who typically live in impoverished neighborhoods and typically have incomes at or below the poverty level. IAF organizers are quite straightforward about this, and equally straightforward in their claim that self-interest is the primary motivation of their constituents.

The IAF organizes in congregations for several reasons. First, churches and temples are often the only enduring institutions left in poor neighborhoods. Such an enduring institutional base is useful for any community organization that wishes to last longer than a single-issue campaign. Second, church members are likely to have strong social networks. Churches are therefore a rich source of potential community leaders. Third, IAF organizers believe that core values, congruent with those of religious groups, drive their efforts. These include a strong emphasis on SOCIAL JUSTICE, civic involvement, and individual responsibility. IAF's "Iron Rule" states, "Never do for others what they can do for themselves." IAF organizers argue that they are trying to build "relational power," power that flows out of the relationships between individuals and that leads to the ability to accomplish shared goals, also called SOCIAL CAPITAL. Organizers contrast relational power with unilateral power, in which one party dominates others.

Local IAF organizing efforts have often met with considerable success. In San Antonio, Texas, Communities Organized for Public Services (COPS), an IAF affiliate, has been responsible for the distribution of approximately $1 billion in resources to its constituents since 1975. In New York City, IAF affiliates have helped build over 3,000 units of single-family, affordable housing. In some cases, IAF has been able to organize on the state level; Texas IAF organizations worked together to obtain $250 million in state funds to build water and sewage systems for unincorporated rural communities along the Mexican border.

But IAF is not without its critics. They often question the church-based strategy on several grounds. They argue that churches themselves have often been the locus of oppression, particularly of women. They also question whether a church-based neighborhood strategy can address large-scale economic structures that perpetuate oppression. The latter question is of particular importance to IAF. IAF organizers have long seen their goal as the transformation of public life into a more par-

ticipatory, pluralistic form, and IAF will soon have affiliates in approximately 70 congressional districts. Organizers hope to translate this national presence into national power, but it remains to be seen whether IAF's form of church-based, grassroots organizing can be effective on the national level.

See also COMMUNITY ORGANIZING; ECONOMIC DEVELOPMENT; FINANCIAL CAPITAL; SOCIAL CAPITAL.

Further reading: Cortes, E. "Justice at the Gates of the City: A Model for Shared Prosperity." In *Back to Shared Prosperity: The Growing Inequality of Wealth and Income in the United States.* Edited by R. Marshall. Armonk, N.Y.: M. E. Sharpe, 2000; Cortes, E. "Reweaving the Fabric: The Iron Rule and the IAF Strategy for Power and Politics." In *Reducing Poverty in America: Views and Approaches.* Edited by M. R. Darby. Thousand Oaks, Calif.: Sage, 1996; Robinson, B., and M. G. Hanna. "Lessons for Academics from Grassroots Community Organizing: A Case Study—The Industrial Areas Foundation." *Journal of Community Practice* 1, no. 4 (1994): 63–94; Rooney, J. *Organizing the South Bronx.* Albany: State University of New York Press, 1995; Warren, M. R. "Community Building and Political Power: A Community Organizing Approach to Democratic Renewal." *American Behavioral Scientist* 42, no. 1 (1998): 79–92.

—Keith Warren

Interfaith Alliance

The Interfaith Alliance was founded in 1994 by the NATIONAL COUNCIL OF CHURCHES as an educational and lobbying organization and an alternative religious voice of the CHRISTIAN COALITION. Its first president was Dr. Albert M. Pennybacker, a board member of the National Council of Churches. In 2001, its president was an Episcopal bishop, the Right Reverend Jane Holmes Dixon, and its executive director was a Baptist minister, the Reverend Dr. C. Welton Gaddy. Its headquarters are in Washington, D.C. A name frequently appearing in its direct-mail appeals has been former news anchor Walter Cronkite. Board members are a diverse grouping representing mainline Protestant, African-American, UNITARIAN-UNIVERSALIST, Jewish, BUDDHIST, Muslim, and ROMAN CATHOLIC faiths, among others. In 2001, it claimed a membership of 130,000 representing over 50 religious groupings, plus 10,000 "cyber-network" activists, and a network of state and local affiliates.

Its stated objectives and activities fall into three categories. First is promotion of civility and the revitalization of civic life. Examples of civility-promoting activities include calendars listing all the holidays of major religions; guidelines for public prayer, with ideas for appropriately inclusive language, the possible purposes of such a prayer, and choice of persons to deliver the prayer; and a civility pledge for political candidates (however, its election-year report implied that only a small fraction of congressional candidates—"over forty-five"—endorsed the civility pledge).

After the SEPTEMBER 11, 2001, terrorist attacks, the Interfaith Alliance sought to counter anti-Muslim and antiforeign backlash by documenting examples of apparently hate-based incidents, along with examples of cooperation across religious lines, and by offering educational resources on ISLAM, Sikhism, and HINDUISM.

Although some of its literature indicates that maintaining civility is its only agenda, the second category of Interfaith Alliance activism is promotion of the standard array of policy concerns of liberal religious organizations, including religious liberty, public education, civil rights, poverty, and environmental concerns. In the 1990s, campaign finance reform was added to the agenda, followed by opposition to "faith-based" initiatives to expand government funding to religious organizations for social services delivery.

Third, the Interfaith Alliance openly states its intent to counter the "Religious Right," which it describes as promoting intolerance and failing to value diversity. It tracks pertinent legislation and compares its position with that of conservative religious groups. In its first year of operation, it publicly criticized not just the Christian Coalition but also the new Republican majority's legislative program, which it found lacking in Judeo-Christian values.

Its opposition to the Christian Right has drawn vigorous responses from conservative Christian activists. For example, Rev. Louis P. Sheldon of the TRADITIONAL VALUES COALITION called it a "coalition of leftist and New Age religious groups" and a front organization for the Democratic Party. Sheldon also questioned how Gaddy, as a Southern Baptist, could "join hands with spiritualists and witches."

Its efforts to reach the public have included direct-mail appeals, press releases, and an extensive website with an Internet activist network, links to denominational and religion-based sites, plus sites of like-minded secular advocacy groups. The Interfaith Alliance is typical of liberal religious organizations in that it takes positions on a range of issues, many of which are not overtly tied to theology, and it reflects the need for coalitional activity by liberal religious organizations to try to achieve the greater visibility and perceived influence of the Religious Right.

See also AMERICANS UNITED FOR THE SEPARATION OF CHURCH AND STATE; CHRISTIAN RIGHT AND THE REPUBLICAN PARTY; MAINLINE PROTESTANT DENOMINATIONAL WASHINGTON OFFICES; WHITE HOUSE OFFICE OF FAITH-BASED AND COMMUNITY INITIATIVES.

Further reading: Reeves, Thomas C. *The Empty Church: Does Organized Religion Matter Anymore?* New York: Simon and Schuster, 1996; Sheldon, Louis. "Democrat Front Group Stifles Christian Free Speech." Available online. URL: http://www.worthynews.com/. Downloaded December 28, 2001; Interfaith Alliance website. URL: http://www.interfaithalliance.org.

—Jane Gurganus Rainey

international human right of religion

Religious freedom is explicitly recognized as a fundamental human right under international law in Article 18 in each of the Universal Declaration of Human Rights (UDHR) and the International Covenant on Civil and Political Rights (ICCPR). In addition to articulating the right to freedom of conscience and religion, international law explicitly prohibits discrimination on the basis of religion in Article 2 of UDHR, ICCPR, and International Covenant on Economic, Social and Cultural Rights (ICESC).

As a result of the HOLOCAUST of World War II and owing to the advocacy of Eleanor Roosevelt, the United Nations was founded in part on the notion of the fundamental nature of human rights. One of the first actions by the U.N. General Assembly was the adoption of the UDHR (1948). Following 18 years of negotiation, the United Nations issued the ICCPR (1966), which took 10 years to enter into binding force internationally (1976) and took the United States a further decade to ratify.

The full text of ICCPR Article 18 is as follows:

1. Everyone shall have the right to freedom of thought, conscience and religion. This right shall include freedom to have or to adopt a religion or belief of his choice, and freedom, either individually or in community with others and in public or private, to manifest his religion or belief in worship, observance, practice and teaching.
2. No one shall be subject to coercion which would impair his freedom to have or to adopt a religion or belief of his choice.
3. Freedom to manifest one's religion or beliefs may be subject only to such limitations as are prescribed by law and are necessary to protect public safety, order, health, or morals or the fundamental rights and freedoms of others.

Article 18 explicitly recognizes that the right cannot be unlimited and that the state has legitimate roles to play in fostering religion and in balancing religious rights against other interests. The ICCPR language contrasts sharply with the seeming absoluteness of the First Amendment of the U.S. Constitution, which states that Congress "shall make no law respecting the establishment of religion or prohibiting the free exercise thereof."

The biggest contrast between U.S. law and international law is with respect to religious establishment. Under international law, a country can establish an official state religion, e.g., Israel and Saudi Arabia, but it must nonetheless act to insure the FREE EXERCISE of religion by nonadherents. Furthermore, a state can apportion taxes it collects to religion(s), e.g., Switzerland, without violating international law. Although in the United States the ESTABLISHMENT CLAUSE limits the federal government's ability to support religion, it can and does do so through tax exemptions, support for parochial schools (e.g., busing), and the like.

The free exercise aspect of international law includes freedom of conscience, thought, and religion. Unlike a claim made under the U.S. Constitution's religion clauses, actions based on a person's conscience and thoughts need not be grounded in religion to be protected under ICCPR Article 18. One can claim protection under Article 18 merely as a matter of personal morality or ethic under international law, whereas such a claim would not be recognized under the U.S. guarantee of free exercise (see WISCONSIN V. YODER).

Article 18 also protects the practice of religion individually or with others. These practice rights may be limited by the state to protect others and to protect public order, safety, health, and morals. The danger is that a government may interpret this power very broadly and impose significant restrictions, e.g., the Taliban in Afghanistan (1996–2002).

In addition to global human rights treaties, regional human rights treaties in Europe, Africa, and the Americas provide religious rights similar to those in ICCPR. The United States, however, has thus far ignored international standards in developing and in interpreting U.S. law on freedom of religion.

See also CONSCIENTIOUS OBJECTION; RELIGIOUS PERSECUTION.

Further reading: Janis, Mark W., and Carolyn Evans, eds. *Religion and International Law.* Boston, Mass.: Martinus Nijhoff Publishers, 1999; United Nations on the Web: URL: http://www.un.org/. Universal Declaration of Human Rights on the Web: URL: http://www0.un.org/cyberschoolbus/humanrights/resources/universal.asp; Van der Vyver, Johan D., and John Witte Jr., eds. *Religious Human Rights in Global Perspective: Legal Perspectives.* Boston, Mass.: Martinus Nijhoff Publishers, 1996; Witte, John Jr., and Johan D. van der Vyver, eds. *Religious Human Rights in Global Perspective: Religious Perspectives.* Boston, Mass.: Martinus Nijhoff Publishers, 1996.

—Steven D. Jamar

Ireland, Archbishop John (1838–1918) *Roman Catholic archbishop*

John Ireland was the first ROMAN CATHOLIC CHURCH archbishop of St. Paul, Minnesota. He was born in County Kilkenny, Ireland, in 1838 and died in St. Paul, Minnesota, on September 25, 1918. His family immigrated to the United States in 1849 and settled in St. Paul in 1852. Ireland studied for eight years in seminaries in France and was ordained in St. Paul on December 22, 1861. He served as a chaplain during the Civil War and saw action with the Union Army in the Battle of Corinth in 1862. On his return from military service, he served the diocese of St. Paul, becoming coadjutor bishop in 1875 and bishop in 1884. When the St. Paul diocese was raised to an archdiocese in 1888, Ireland became its first archbishop and served until his death in 1918.

Ireland was identified with the Americanist wing of the Catholic Church. *Americanism,* broadly speaking, refers to the adaptation of Catholic practices to the American social and

Archbishop John Ireland *(Library of Congress)*

political context. (*Americanism* also refers to a set of heretical views condemned by Pope Leo XIII in the encyclical *Testem Benevolentiae* [1899]). A dominant aspect of Ireland's Americanism was to allay Protestant suspicion that Catholicism was not compatible with the nation's republican institutions and commitment to political and civil liberties. His best-known statement on the subject, "The Catholic Church and Civil Society," maintained that the church does not endorse any particular form of government and that republicanism was fully embraced by American Catholics.

Ireland's advocacy of Catholic assimilation to America led him to positions that irked more conservative and parochial Catholics, particularly German Catholics, who saw these positions as corrupting the faith. Ireland opposed attempts to form separatist enclaves and was instrumental in refuting the Abbelen (1886) and Lucerne (1890) Memorials, the two major German-American statements calling for greater autonomy of national churches.

Ireland's speeches in France in support of republicanism in 1892 caused suspicion among theological conservatives in Europe who saw American Catholicism tainted with liberalism and rationalism. The perceived heresy of Americanism was condemned in the encyclical *Testem Benevolentiae.* However, the *Americanism* condemned referred to esoteric doctrines that Ireland and other American prelates maintained were never held by Americans. There was a tacit agreement to let this episode pass, and the church adapted pragmatically to the American environment.

As a social reformer, Ireland supported causes such as temperance, the rights of labor, and a colonization program that involved transplanting urban, Catholic slum dwellers to Minnesota. He also opposed racial segregation.

In the late 1880s, the Vatican was contemplating condemning the Knights of Labor. Workers' organizations were perceived as being dominated by nonbelievers and Masons and were associated with socialism. Ireland and James Cardinal Gibbons of Baltimore, in averting condemnation, are credited with saving the Catholic working class in America for the church.

Ireland advocated a cooperative cost-sharing program with public school boards and instituted such a plan in Faribault and Stillwater, Minnesota, in 1891. The plan called for public school boards to rent parish schools and teach a public school curriculum, use state-approved textbooks and examinations, and pay parochial school teachers, including nuns. No religious instruction would occur during the school day. After school the facilities would revert to parish control. This forerunner of later parochial school aid schemes was dismantled because non-Catholics opposed it and conservative Catholics saw a secularizing influence.

Ireland's life was punctuated by other civic and political events. He was a main force in the establishment of the Catholic University of America in 1887. A Republican, he denounced Tammany Hall and the Democratic Party's 1896 election platform. He enjoyed the friendship of Presidents William McKinley, THEODORE ROOSEVELT, and William Howard Taft. He tried unsuccessfully to mediate between the United States and Spain to avert the Spanish-American War. The realization of Ireland's goal of Catholic assimilation became fully realized, though well into the 20th century.

See also CATHOLICS AND THE DEMOCRATIC PARTY; RELIGION IN THE 1896 PRESIDENTIAL ELECTION.

Further reading: Barry, Colman J. *The Catholic Church and German Americans.* Milwaukee: Bruce, 1953; Ireland, John. *The Church and Modern Society: Lectures and Addresses.* 2 vols. St. Paul, Minn.: Pioneer Press Manufacturing Departments, 1905; McAvoy, Thomas T. *The Americanist Heresy in Roman Catholicism 1895–1900.* Notre Dame, Ind.: University of Notre Dame Press, 1963; Morris, Charles R. *American Catholic.* New York: Vintage Books, 1998; O'Connell, Marvin R. *John Ireland and the American Catholic Church.* St. Paul, Minn.: Minnesota Historical Society Press, 1988.

—Gerald DeMaio

Islam

The second-largest world religion (more than 1 billion adherents), Islam is the majority religion in approximately 50 countries and a large minority in many others, including the third-largest religion in the United States. It is the fastest-growing religion in the United States and is expected to surpass Judaism by the year 2010. The Arabic word *islam* means "submission"; in the religious context, it means submission to the will of God, and Muslims are those who submit to God's will. Historical Arabia is the center of Islam, which is where Muslims believe the Quran—the literal word of God—was revealed to Muhammad over the course of 22 years in the first part of the seventh century C.E.

Although great diversity exists within the larger Muslim community, all Muslims are prescribed to follow a core group of principles referred to as the Five Pillars of Islam: the profession of faith, prayer, almsgiving, fasting, and pilgrimage. The profession of faith requires all Muslims to proclaim, "There is no God but God and Muhammad is the Messenger of God," which affirms the absolute monotheistic nature of Islam while also expressing the belief of Muhammad as the messenger of God and the final prophet. Each day, Muslims are called to prayer five times, facing the holy city of Mecca, with a congregational noon Friday prayer. *Zakat* is an alms tax assessed on income and belongings as a means to institutionalize socioeconomic equity. During the holy month of Ramadan, Muslims fast from dawn to dusk; they abstain from food and drink with the exception of those who are traveling or ill. The pilgrimage to Mecca is required of all adult Muslims once in their lifetime if they are financially and physically able to do so; over the last several years, approximately 2 million Muslims made the pilgrimage each year.

The concept of jihad has dual meaning in Islam, sometimes called the greater and smaller jihad. The primary use of jihad is to struggle within oneself to realize the will of God in living a life of virtue and to expand the Muslim community through advocacy, preaching, education, and example. The "smaller jihad" is the struggle for the defense of Islam, or holy war. Although the concept of jihad does not justify aggressive warfare, Muslim extremists have exploited jihad in attempts to rationalize some of their actions. Despite this distinction, the U.S. media have often distorted the concept of jihad to depict Islam as a violent religion.

Islam has two major sects, Sunni and Shia Islam. The question of leadership after Muhammad's death led to a division in the Islamic community. The Sunni believe that Muhammad did not select a successor. As a result, the elders of the community would select a successor to be the political leader of the Islamic community. The Shia believe that Muhammad did assign a successor, the eldest male in his family, his son-in-law and cousin, Ali ibn Talib, and not the first caliph, Abu Bakr. The Sunni compose approximately 85 percent of the Muslim community, and the Shia 15 percent. Although the Shia are the minority, they make up the majority in countries such as Iran, Iraq, and Bahrain. Shia communities exist in the United States, but the overwhelming majority of American Muslims are Sunni.

Although there are no official population figures for religious affiliation in the United States, experts calculate an estimated 6 million American Muslims, with approximately 2,000 mosques to accommodate them. A 2000 Zogby International survey commissioned by the AMERICAN MUSLIM COUNCIL indicated that great ethnic diversity exists in the American Muslim community: 26.2 percent Arab Middle East, 24.7 South Asian, 23.8 African American, 10.3 non-Arab Middle East, 6.4 East Asia, 11.6 other. The slave trade was responsible for the first wave of Muslims to America between the mid-1500s and the mid-1800s. The second wave of Muslims to America immigrated at the end of the 19th century and the beginning of the 20th century, primarily from Lebanon and Syria. The third wave of Muslims to America began in the 1960s and ran through the end of the 20th century, with Muslims coming from all parts of the Islamic world. With new immigration laws following the terrorist attacks of SEPTEMBER 11, 2001, Muslim immigration is expected to change drastically. A number of Islamic organizations founded by the Muslim immigrant community, such as the American Muslim Council and the Council on American-Islamic Relations, seek to increase the POLITICAL PARTICIPATION of the American Muslim population in mainstream political and policy arenas, presenting an Islamic perspective on American issues, and reconciling Muslim values and American interests and ideals.

African-American Muslims, who make up approximately one-quarter of the U.S. Muslim population, are growing at a fast rate for a number of reasons, including a high conversion rate in prisons, African-American political movements with an Islamic element, and the recovery of Islamic identity dating back to the time of slavery. Many African Americans today are converting to Islam as a means of reidentifying with their African heritage. The best-known African-American movement, the NATION OF ISLAM, was founded in Detroit in 1930 by a foreign national named WALLACE D. FARD. Fard's primary follower, Elijah Poole (later ELIJAH MUHAMMAD), carried on the movement in 1934 after Fard's mysterious disappearance. The Nation of Islam lost credibility in the larger Muslim community when the doctrine came to regard Fard as Allah incarnate and Elijah Muhammad as his prophet. MALCOLM X, who converted to Islam while in prison, was an associate of Elijah Muhammad and perhaps the best-known member in the Nation of Islam. After his pilgrimage to Mecca and conversion to normative Islam, Malcolm X was assassinated by members of the Nation of Islam. Elijah Muhammad's son, Wallace Deen Muhammad (later WARITH DEEN MUHAMMAD), became his father's successor in 1975 and changed the Nation of Islam's path toward normative Islam. This change was not embraced by all members of the Nation of Islam; LOUIS FARRAKHAN's leadership has attempted to retain elements of Islam initiated by Warith Deen Muhammad, but also to reintroduce black empowerment and militancy of Fard and Elijah Muhammad in sometimes alarming and provocative rhetoric and discourse. This has led the wider American Muslim community to reject the Nation of Islam as an Islamic movement and their common reference to Farrakhanism.

A number of events, such as the 1979 Iranian Revolution and the Muslim extremist assassination of Egyptian president Anwar as-Sadat in 1981, have shaped American perceptions of Islam. But no event has had such an impact as the terrorist attacks on the Pentagon and New York's World Trade Center on September 11, 2001; they have had a profound and seemingly polarizing impact on American Muslims and on American perceptions of Islam. Many Americans have responded by embracing Islam and learning about it, as made evident by expanded sections in bookstores on Islam and the Middle East, as well as increased book sales on the same subject matters. On the other hand, extreme measures against Muslim individuals, families, mosques, and organizations illustrate American intolerance as well. Between September 11, 2001, and March 2002, over 600 violent incidents against Arabs, Muslims, and those who are perceived as Arab or Muslim have been documented by the Arab-American Anti-Discrimination Committee. As a result, American Muslims have either embraced Islam more publicly to draw strength and guidance, and to educate Americans, or they have chosen to conceal that part of their identity in fear of persecution.

See also RACISM; TOLERANCE.

Further reading: Carla Power, "The New Islam." *Newsweek*, March 16, 1998, p. 34; Esposito, John L. *Islam: The Straight Path.* New York: Oxford University Press, 1991; Gerges, Fawaz A. *America and Political Islam: Clash of Cultures or Clash of Interests?* New York: Cambridge University Press, 1999; Haddad, Yvonne Yazbeck. *The Muslims of America.* New York: Oxford University Press, 1991; Haddad, Yvonne Yazbeck, and John L. Esposito, eds. *Muslims on the Americanization Path?* New York: Oxford University Press, 2000.

—Allen McDuffee

Israel

The modern state of Israel was established in 1948. Most Israelis, however, understand their society to have an ancient history. Religious Israelis in particular believe their country was divinely promised nearly four millennia ago to the patriarch Abraham and his descendants. Under the leadership of Moses, the Israelites left Egypt after four centuries of slavery. This Exodus occurred around the 13th century B.C.E. Around 1000 B.C.E., the first unified Jewish state was established with the creation of the monarchy. Jewish independence was ended by foreign conquests. The land was part of the Babylonian, Persian, and Greek Empires. Under the leadership of the Hasmonean family, a brief period of independence was achieved until the area came under Roman authority. Several revolts against Rome all ended disastrously. Many Jews were exiled from Israel and joined Jewish communities throughout the Mediterranean world that had been established during the previous conquests.

Between the end of the last Jewish revolt in 135 C.E. and the creation of Israel in 1948, generations of Jews retained their attachment to their ancient homeland. After the rise of Christianity, Jews were even forbidden to enter their holy city of Jerusalem. By the seventh century, however, Islam had replaced Christianity as the dominant religion in the area. Small Jewish communities remained precariously in Israel through the Middle Ages and into modern times. Most of these Jews were poor and religious, surviving in great part because of gifts sent by Jewish relatives in Europe and North Africa. By the end of the 19th century, European Jews under Hungarian-born Theodore Herzl (1860–1904) had developed the nationalist movement of ZIONISM, to reestablish a Jewish state. Herzl and his supporters believed that an independent Jewish state was required for Jewish survival in a hostile, non-Jewish world where pogroms were frequent, governments unfriendly, and Jews had no ability to defend themselves.

By 1918, the British had occupied Palestine after expelling the Turks. For the next three decades, Jewish immigration was modest, but it accelerated after the Nazis took power in Germany in 1933 and began systematic persecution of German Jews. Thousands of refugees escaped the German occupation during World War II (1939–45). The HOLOCAUST during the war created a degree of international sympathy for the Jewish plight. When the United Nations partitioned Palestine into Arab and Jewish states, which was acceptable to the Jewish community, the Arabs refused it. Beginning in the 1920s, Palestinian Arabs felt displaced by European Jews. Their resentment was shared by the neighboring Arab states that joined in the first Arab-Israeli War (1948–49) and subsequent wars in 1956, 1967, and 1973. These conflicts established Israel as a permanent presence and first-tier military power in the Middle East.

Israel's population increased from about 600,000 in 1948 to more than 6 million by 2001. It has tremendous demographic diversity and includes immigrants from nearly a hundred countries. In addition, nearly one-fifth of Israelis are of Arab descent. While Israel is the only genuine democracy in the Middle East, its Arab community has been incompletely integrated into the economy and overall society. Arabs and Jews live in separate towns or in separate neighborhoods within towns. They are also separated by religion, language, and culture.

The Arab and Jewish communities are themselves divided. About three-quarters of Israeli Arabs are Sunni Muslims. Christians and Druses make up the remaining fourth. Druses, who make up about 13 percent of the Arab community, are very unlike Muslims and Christians. Druses voluntarily serve in the military and are politically loyal to the Israeli state. Israel's Jewish population includes a large and growing element of Orthodox religionists who desire to apply biblical Scripture to daily life. Examples include their insistence on applying dietary laws, closing businesses on the Sabbath, and banning civil marriage and divorce ceremonies. The more secularized portion of Israel's Jewish population frequently opposes their aims.

Israel's parliamentary system reflects its religious, political, and cultural divisions. The national legislature is a 120-member unicameral chamber, the Knesset. Elections are held at least once every four years. Israel's small area (about the size of New Jersey) and the fact that the country has been surrounded by enemies sworn to its destruction through most of its history has consistently made security concerns a major campaign issue. The three or four religious parties that regularly contest elections collectively draw about 20 percent of the total popular vote, and this proportion has been increasing in recent elections, in great part because of the higher birth rate of religious party supporters.

Although one of the two larger parties (the conservative Likud and the left-of-center Labor Party) normally occupies the top government posts, the Knesset's composition is determined by proportional representation, so no political party has ever been able to secure a numerical majority. Only 1.5 percent of the national vote is required to secure at least one parliamentary seat. Several parties may have only three to five seats. These are not insignificant numbers, since governments majorities may survive by a few seats; some have subsisted on the minimal number of 61. As many as half a dozen parties may participate in the government at any particular time. One or two defections could bring down a government and necessitate new elections before the end of the four-year term. One or more of the religious parties is usually found in any government, whether headed by Likud or Labor.

Interestingly, the greatest Arab-Jewish integration in Israel seems to occur on the political level. Arabs usually form at least one-tenth of the Knesset membership. Some Arab parliamentary members have been strong supporters of Labor governments, and Labor has often depended on them to retain their parliamentary majority.

Israel remains a turbulent country because it is the meeting place and, in many ways, the homeland of the world's three monotheistic faiths. Israel's society is one where religious influence is easily observed. Every day religion directly or indirectly affects both the political and the social lives of its citizens.

Since its establishment, Israel has received a great deal of support from several American Protestant organizations, such as the CHRISTIAN COALITION, which believe the Jewish state must be in place before the second coming of Jesus Christ can occur. American support for Israel is so strong that both the major political parties have consistently referred to Israel as a political and military ally.

See also CONSERVATIVE JUDAISM; HASIDIC JUDAISM; ORTHODOX JUDAISM; RECONSTRUCTIONIST JUDAISM; REFORM JUDAISM.

Further reading: Sprinzak, Ehud, and Larry Diamond, eds. *Israeli Democracy under Stress.* Boulder, Colo.: Lynne Rienner, 1993; Oz, Amos. *In the Land of Israel.* New York: Harcourt Brace Jovanovich, 1983.

—Martin W. Slann

Israeli-Palestinian conflict

The conflict between two nations over the same land was a primary characteristic of the cold war (1945–90) that evolved, mostly in a violent fashion, in the post–cold war era. The conflict preceded the United Nations's 1947 partition plan that divided what was then the British mandate of Palestine into separate Arab and Jewish states. The Jewish community in Palestine (Yishuv) accepted the partition, but theirs was a reluctant acceptance since the Yishuv received only an area the size of Connecticut that to some extent interlaced with the proposed Arab state. The Palestinians utterly rejected the partition plan, arguing that the United Nations had no right to divide sovereign Arab territory. Within Palestine itself, relations between the Arab and Jewish communities had steadily deteriorated during the 1920s and 1930s. The Germans installed a Nazi-dominated government in 1933. Increasing numbers of European Jews, desperate to escape the violent anti-Semitism growing in Germany as well as some of its neighbors, left for Palestine.

When World War II ended in Europe in 1945, some of the Jewish survivors of the HOLOCAUST made their way, often illegally, to Palestine. A three-way civil war broke out between the Yishuv, Palestinian Arabs, and British mandate authorities. By 1947 the British had had enough and announced that on May 15, 1948, their 30-year-old mandate would end and they would evacuate Palestine. The upcoming partition and the British departure intensified hostilities between the Yishuv and Arabs. Both sides committed acts of terror. The Palestinian Arabs received military assistance and diplomatic support from Arab governments and the Soviet Union, while the Yishuv relied on financial help from American Jews and occasional sympathizers in Europe. France, in particular, was most supportive of Israel for the first two decades of the Jewish state's existence because of France's own conflict with Arab communities in North Africa that had been colonized by the French since the early 19th century. The Israeli declaration of statehood occurred the very day the British left. The declaration was followed by an immediate determination by the Arab League members to destroy the Jewish state.

Israel won the first Arab-Israeli war of 1948–49 and settled down for a long siege. The Arabs did not reconcile themselves to Israel's presence. It would take the next three decades and several more wars before Egypt, the largest Arab state, agreed to recognize Israel's existence. Egypt was eventually followed in this regard by Jordan. For most of this period, the Arab-Israeli conflict may successfully be characterized as a secular struggle. Israel was viewed by the Arab Middle East as an agent of Western imperialism. The mainstream resistance group to Israel's existence was the Palestine Liberation Organization (PLO), an umbrella grouping of several secular and leftist movements. The PLO sponsored terrorist acts during the late 1960s that included numerous airplane hijackings. In contrast to what was to follow, most passengers and crewmembers survived these ordeals.

The Six-Day War that occurred in June 1967 altered the course of Middle Eastern geopolitics. Over several days, Israel delivered devastating military defeat to Egypt, Jordan, and Syria. Its army occupied the Sinai Desert, Gaza Strip, West Bank, and the Golan Heights. Israel became the most note-

worthy military power in the region. But Israel also assumed responsibility for the Palestinians who lived in the West Bank and Gaza. In 2002, 35 years after the occupation had begun, the Palestinians, who have one of the highest population growth rates in the world, numbered nearly 3.5 million, more than twice their total in 1967. Israel's current population is a little more than 6 million—20 percent of whom are Arabs with Israeli citizenship.

Between 1979 and 1982, Israel gradually withdrew from the entirety of the Sinai and returned the area to Egyptian sovereignty. The region was demilitarized, and the two countries have lived in peace since Egyptian president Anwar El-Sadat's visit to Israel in 1977. Israel's relationship with the Palestinians, however, was not as simple. The Sinai is practically unpopulated, whereas the West Bank and Gaza Strip are overpopulated. Moreover, economic conditions in both areas rapidly deteriorated due to population pressures, a long drought, and the steadily deteriorating political situation.

Twenty years after the Six-Day War, the first Intifada (uprising) broke out against Israeli occupation. An entire Palestinian generation had grown up under the shadow of the occupation and resented an Arab leadership that was either unwilling or unable to get rid of the Israelis. This new generation began to turn to a quickly evolving alternative that included radical religious organizations unwilling to join a peace process that allows Israel's continued existence. Hamas (an acronym for Islamic Resistance Movement) was in fact created in the very year the 1987 Intifada broke out, and was instrumental in any success the first Intifada experienced.

The Israeli-Palestinian peace process that was initiated during the early months of WILLIAM JEFFERSON CLINTON's presidency, and which was based on the Oslo negotiations that began during the last part of George H. W. Bush's presidency, provided real hope that a two-state solution could be negotiated. By the end of the Clinton administration, though, the hope was dashed, and each side had become completely disenchanted with the other. A second Intifada got under way in September 2000, apparently triggered by the visit of Ariel Sharon, then an aspiring candidate to be Israel's prime minister, to the Al-Aqsa mosque area in Jerusalem's Old City. Known as a hard-line, right-wing Israeli politician, Sharon's appearance especially offended the Palestinians.

Sharon's appearance occurred just as the Clinton administration was making a last effort to work out a deal between Israel, represented by its prime minister, Ehud Barak, and the Palestinian Authority, represented by Yassir Arafat. The talks broke down after Arafat refused the most far-reaching territorial concessions ever offered by an Israeli prime minister. Former prime minister Yitzhak Rabin had been murdered five years earlier for offering less! Barak had essentially promised that Israel would evacuate as much as 96 percent of the West Bank and all of the Gaza Strip, and he even hinted at land swaps to make up for the remaining four percent. Before leaving office, Clinton publicly blamed Arafat for the failure of the negotiations. The administration of GEORGE W.

BUSH went even further and was suggesting by spring 2002 that the Palestinian people might be better served under new political leadership.

The second Intifada entered its third year in September 2002 without an end in sight. Hope is occasionally raised when there is a lull in suicide-bombing attacks on Israelis and their retaliation for such attacks, but then dashed when the cycle inevitably resumes. Morale is suffering on both sides after two years of steadily deteriorating economic conditions. Israelis are frequently afraid to leave their homes to visit shopping malls and restaurants, while the economic infrastructure in West Bank and Gaza, which was not in terrific shape to begin with, has completely collapsed. Once-moderate Israelis increasingly favor building a wall to separate Israel and the West Bank. Extremist Palestinians have been gaining popular support, as has their message that Israel should not exist at all.

Neither side trusts the other and neither side respects the other's political leaders. The impasse will continue until or unless an atmosphere of trust can be somehow re-created.

—Martin W. Slann

J

Jackson, Jesse (1941–) *civil rights activist*

The Reverend Jesse Louis Jackson, president and founder of the RAINBOW COALITION, is an African-American civil rights activist who believes that he has a moral obligation to redeem the soul of the nation. Jackson has been involved in protest, electoral, and diplomatic political efforts throughout his political career, driven by the hope that such actions will decrease racial strife, hatred, and distrust. Jackson is best known for his efforts to increase black ECONOMIC DEVELOPMENT, his Democratic presidential bids in 1984 and 1988, and his unofficial as well as official diplomatic efforts resulting in the release of American and international hostages. Jackson graduated from North Carolina Agricultural & Technical College, is an ordained minister, is married to Jacqueline Lavinia Brown, and is the father of five children. He resides in Chicago.

Jackson's activism in the CIVIL RIGHTS MOVEMENT began in earnest after he married and enrolled at Chicago Theological Seminary (CTS). He accompanied 20 other students and a third of the CTS faculty to Selma, Alabama, to become involved in the demonstrations there. In Selma, Jackson met MARTIN LUTHER KING JR. and talked about the possibility of establishing a Chicago chapter of the SOUTHERN CHRISTIAN LEADERSHIP COUNCIL (SCLC). In the spring of 1966, Jackson became the head of SCLC's Operation Breadbasket. After King's death on April 4, 1968, Jackson would stay with SCLC until December 1971, when he resigned to start Operation PUSH.

As director of Operation Breadbasket, Jackson came up with an ideology that he called "The Kingdom Theory," a premise not that distant from the economic nationalism propagated by the NATION OF ISLAM. Essentially, ministers were to inform blacks that they must control the flow of money that enters and leaves black communities. But unlike the Nation of Islam, Jackson believed that African Americans should be integrated into the American political economy. Starting in the 1970s, Jackson developed what he called "covenants" with corporations.

Establishing Operation PUSH (People United to Save Humanity) in 1971 provided Jackson with the independence needed to operate freely in a northern urban environment. PUSH focused on economic as well as political issues. Jackson entered partisan politics in the summer of 1972, when he and William Singer unseated Mayor Richard Daley's delegate slate at the Democratic convention in Miami. Jackson's involvement in Chicago politics did not result in substantive policy gains from the Daley political machinery; nonetheless, the voter registration and education drives conducted by Operation PUSH were instrumental in 1983, when Harold Washington, Chicago's first black mayor, captured the Democratic primary.

Jackson soon turned his energy to national politics. In the summer of 1983, he set out on a six-state campaign of "political Pentecostalism" through the South. He conducted popular rallies, sometimes as many as 40 a week, in black churches. Jackson became extremely popular with black voters. Yet the nation's black political elite—"the Family", as it was called, consisting of elected officials, civil rights leaders, academicians, and high-ranking Democrats—soon endorsed the idea of a black presidential candidate, but Jackson was not their overwhelming choice. These elites thought a Jackson candidacy could damage fragile coalitions of white and black voters. Nevertheless, Jackson ran for president in 1984. He won 5 percent of the white vote and over 90 percent of the black vote during the Democratic presidential primary season.

Jackson's popularity with black voters was overshadowed by his "Hymietown" remarks made in February 1984. These remarks came three weeks after he successfully negotiated, without permission from the Reagan administration, the release of Lieutenant Robert Goodman Jr., a black pilot whose plane was shot down in Syria. Jackson was engaging in an informal conversation with black journalists at Reagan National Airport in Washington, D.C., about the April primary in New York. He said to reporters, "Let's talk black talk," and in reference to New York's Jewish constituency, Jackson used the terms "Hymie" and "Hymietown." These remarks more or less destroyed the credibility of Jackson's campaign among Jewish and liberal white voters.

Jackson would again try to gain the Democratic presidential nomination, in 1988, relying heavily on his Rainbow

Reverend Jesse Jackson *(Spencer Platt/Getty Images)*

Coalition, formed in 1984 to manage his campaign. This campaign placed less emphasis on black pride and also relied less on black churches for political support. Jackson sought to reach out beyond his black base. Jackson won the majority of votes on "Super Tuesday" in March 1988; southern black voters essentially gave Jackson the victory throughout that region. Jackson came in second in Illinois and first in Michigan, demonstrating his ability to win votes in northern industrial states. Jackson's victory on Super Tuesday gave him the temporary lead in both the popular vote and the number of convention delegates. Some observers believe that if Jackson had won the New York primary, he might have had a legitimate shot at the nomination. However, Mayor Ed Koch of New York City campaigned vigorously against Jackson, telling Jews that they would be crazy to vote for Jackson. Ultimately, Jackson's second-place finishes in New York and Pennsylvania assured Governor Michael Dukakis of Massachusetts the nomination.

This loss did not end Jackson's political ambitions. In 1991, he won the release of hundreds of foreign nationals and

U.S. citizens being held in Kuwait by Iraqi dictator Saddam Hussein. He soon became a fixture on television talk-show circuit. In October 1997 Jackson was appointed a "special Africa envoy" by President WILLIAM JEFFERSON CLINTON. In April 1999, during the KOSOVO CONFLICT, Jackson negotiated the release of three U.S. prisoners of war.

Jackson weathered a serious political crisis in January 2001, when he admitted to having had a child out of wedlock. News of this scandal broke just days before Jackson was scheduled to be part of a massive boycott of President GEORGE W. BUSH's inauguration weekend.

See also MALCOLM X; RACISM; RELIGION IN THE 1984, 1988 PRESIDENTIAL ELECTIONS.

Further reading: Fraddy, Marshall. *Jesse: The Life and Pilgrimage of Jesse Jackson.* New York: Random House, 1996, chapters 8–12.

—Ron Brown

Jakes, Bishop T. D. (1957–) *religious preacher*

Where did Thomas D. Jakes come from, this star rising so swiftly after 1993, when both the Trinity Broadcasting Network (TBN) and Black Entertainment Television (BET) made room for his weekly teaching and sermons? Jakes was born in 1957 in Charleston, West Virginia, the son of Ernest and Odith Jakes, his father the owner of a janitorial service and his mother a teacher. Raised a Baptist, he became a PENTECOSTAL, a member first of the Apostolic Church, and later part of the Higher Ground Always Abounding Assemblies. From the age of 22, Jakes began to pastor storefront churches, and by 1990 he moved to South Charleston, West Virginia, where his church grew from 100 to 300 members.

In 1992, Jakes gave a teaching on "Woman, Thou Art Loosed!" to a Sunday school class in his own church. He expected to be rejected for bringing up the painful subjects of child and spousal abuse. Instead, the women in the class asked for more. In short time, Jakes was traveling to other churches and auditoriums around the country and soon launched his television outreach in 1993. In 1996, he moved to Dallas, Texas, with his family and 50 members of his ministry team to found the Potter's House, a local church that in four years grew to 26,000 members.

In the year 2000, Atlanta's Georgia Dome, over 65,000 women sang and danced the praises of God in the first night of the Woman, Thou Art Loosed! Conference. Jakes set the all-time attendance record for the Dome, over 80,000, the previous year, breaking a mark held by BILLY GRAHAM. It has been said that Jakes defies stereotypes. Women in more than 200 prisons watched Jakes live via satellite hookup, and cameras in three of these prisons allowed the women in Atlanta to see prisoners share in the meeting.

In Atlanta, Jakes sponsored two other events that illustrate the quality and breadth of his ministry. First, he put on a two-day seminar for 9,000 women, mostly African Americans, teaching them entrepreneurial startup skills with the help of successful Christian businesspeople and major corporations. Second, Jakes premiered his second major play, *Behind Closed Doors*, at the Atlanta Civic Center, working with themes from the Sarah and Hagar story in Genesis, addressing the issues of breast cancer, race, sexuality, wealth, relationships, and spirituality in a modern setting. This gospel play has toured in major cities and is sponsored by the T. D. Jakes Enterprises, a for-profit arm of his ministry that also helps to manage his books, plays, and music activities.

Jakes has a substantial television ministry in Europe and in Africa. He travels about a dozen times a year to hold meetings and speaking engagements. In the year 2000 this included trips to London, England, and to Lagos, Nigeria. Meanwhile, Jakes moved aggressively to expand his home base of operations in south Dallas, dedicating a new $35 million church seating over 8,000 people, and starting a major community development initiative valued at $135.2 million called Project 2000.

In elections, Jakes is nonpartisan, which is a somewhat unusual position, since African-American preachers commonly endorse political candidates. However, this political firewall has not stopped Jakes from being a speaker at a Congressional Black Caucus prayer breakfast or from relating to prominent Democrats and Republicans, including President GEORGE W. BUSH.

The *New York Times* published an article listing Jakes as a candidate for the role of national spiritual leader for the new century. As the famous preachers of the 20th century leave center stage, people speculate on their successors. Jakes has the capacity to bear the heavy responsibilities that accompany such a role—if that becomes his destiny.

—Hubert Morken

James Robison (1931–) *theologian, minister*

Robison James, a SOUTHERN BAPTIST CONVENTION minister, college theology professor, and Virginia State representative, was born in Tampa, Florida. He was the moderate theological voice of Southern Baptists during the "fundamentalist takeover" of the 15 million–member national body in the 1980s. A scholar of midcentury Protestant theologian Paul Tillich, James taught at the then-moderate Baptist University of Richmond for three decades, from the 1960s to the 1990s. James was the sparring partner of the Reverend Paige Patterson of the Baptist fundamentalist camp, as well as Richmond professor Robert Alley of the humanist camp. James served four terms in the Virginia House of Delegates, from January 1976 until January 1983, defeating, among others, James Gilmore, who subsequently became governor of Virginia. James focused his legislative agenda on ethics in public education and politics. In 1978 he convened and became president of the Virginia Association for Moral, Civic, and Value Education, a statewide theory and research group, a moderate religious answer to the growing "moral majority" in Virginia.

He was also a member of the Virginia commission recommending one of the first natural death (anti-EUTHANASIA) acts in the United States.

Southern Baptists, a denominational body formed originally from a mid–nineteenth century regional dispute over the viability of missionary agencies and moral viability of slavery, had according to its moderate and liberal adherents been founded on principles of religious freedom that allowed the individual to interpret Scripture according to the leading of the Holy Spirit. Fundamentalist politicos within that movement's national and local organizations argued that this philosophy could not supersede the binding nature of their interpretation of Scripture as the inerrant, inspired Word of God and its accompanying new CALVINIST theology. Fundamentalists believed moderates had turned the Bible into an empty book to be written upon by liberal Baptists, and this called for political resistance to save the denomination. Robison James provided the "moderate" theological voice during these battles, acknowledging the importance of Scripture and the antimodernist concerns of the fundamentalists, while holding to the traditional Baptist doctrine of the competence of the individual to follow Christian Scriptures.

James's attempts at reconciliation within the movement through scriptural interpretation included his much-debated book, *The Unfettered Word*, in which he argued that interpretation of the Scriptures could be a unifying power in the largest Protestant denomination in the United States, the fractured Southern Baptists, but only if both sides understood that the Bible would not be captured by either of their narrow interpretations.

While moderate Baptist theologians were being fired at fundamentalist-controlled Southern Baptist seminaries in Kentucky, North Carolina, and Texas, James and other college theologians were in battles of their own to keep their professorial positions because of the political squeeze between religious conservatives and academic standards of "neutrality" at loosely denominationally affiliated schools such as the University of Richmond, Wake Forest University, and Baylor University.

—Robert Wilson-Black

Jefferson, Thomas (1743–1826) *U.S. president*

Thomas Jefferson was a Virginia-born politician best known for writing the DECLARATION OF INDEPENDENCE and serving as the third U.S. president (1801–9). Jefferson viewed most of organized religion, and particularly state-established religions, as props of the tyrannical pre-Enlightenment regimes he wished to see abolished. For Jefferson, doctrinaire, hierarchical religions were an affront to the right of conscience that, following JOHN LOCKE, he described as an inalienable natural right. In terms of public policy, this abstract right dictated both religious TOLERANCE and the SEPARATION OF CHURCH AND STATE in any legitimate polity. Among Jefferson's proudest accomplishments was his authorship of the Virginia Statute for Religious Freedom. At the same time, Jefferson justified the right of conscience and other rights by asserting that they were God-given, making an omnipotent deity a key support to his preferred version of popular government.

Although he was educated by Anglican clergy, Jefferson's primary religious influence was the Scottish Enlightenment. These thinkers convinced Jefferson that humans possessed an innate moral sense. As a result, he concluded that government-sponsored religious instruction was not necessary to the well-functioning state. In fact, it was a danger, for if religion were closely tied with coercive political power, tyrannical corruption would be facilitated. Perpetually reticent to discuss his religious beliefs, Jefferson thought of God as a largely uknowable creator rather than a comprehensible entity. These were unorthodox views to most Americans, and Jefferson's zeal for freedom of conscience may have been motivated in part by an attempt to forestall inquiries about his own religious convictions.

Though the Second Continental Congress made some modifications of Jefferson's draft of the DECLARATION OF INDEPENDENCE (1776), most of its language is his. Preceding a list of abuses perpetrated by British king George III are religiously tinged phrases that are as widely remembered as any written by an American, Jefferson acknowledged a right of

Thomas Jefferson. Painting by Rembrandt Peale *(Library of Congress)*

revolution by referencing "the Laws of Nature and Nature's God." He followed this assertion with the justification "that all men are created equal; that they are endowed by their Creator with certain inalienable Rights." While God and God-given rights served to legitimate the political actions of the American revolutionaries, Jefferson did not view this support as a contradiction to his preference for separating church and state. Rather than setting down a religious dogma, in Jefferson's mind the Declaration flowed from his few incontrovertible assumptions about God: that He created humans with free will and the reason to use that freedom wisely.

Yet the religious history of the colonies did not reflect that ability to reason. In *Notes on the State of Virginia* (1784), Jefferson pointed out that although his state had eliminated direct support for the Anglican Church during the Revolutionary War, the common law still reflected a discriminatory religiosity. Professing ATHEISM, for example, was a punishable offense, but it should not have been, for "it does me no injury for my neighbor to say there are twenty gods, or no God." Jefferson's hope that such statutes would be eliminated reflected his general preference for minimalist government. Religious requirements stifled reason and freethinking, the only path to greater religious understanding. In an effort to remove these dictates from the common law, Jefferson wrote a Statute for Establishing Religious Freedom in the late 1770s. This bill did not become law until 1786, when JAMES MADISON shepherded it through the Virginia legislature while Jefferson served as U.S. envoy to France.

Jefferson's unorthodox views on religion dogged him throughout his political career. Federalists implied he was an atheist and hostile to Christianity. He refused to respond directly to these attacks, reasoning that religion was a private matter. As president, Jefferson privately refuted the Federalists by asserting that "I am a Christian, in the only sense in which [Jesus] wished any one to be; sincerely attached to his doctrines above all others." He also began to compile the so-called Jefferson Bible, which he worked on into the 1820s. The volume, which Jefferson ultimately titled "The Life and Morals of Jesus of Nazareth," consisted of excerpts from the New Testament that provided moral examples but did not acknowledge Jesus' divinity. The book was intended solely for Jefferson's own use, not for publication. A financial supporter of several churches but a member of none, Jefferson called himself a Unitarian late in life.

See also UNITARIAN-UNIVERSALIST.

Further reading: Boyd, Julian, and Charles T. Cullen, eds. *The Papers of Thomas Jefferson,* Princeton, N.J.: Princeton University Press, 1950-present; Peterson, Merrill D., ed. *Thomas Jefferson: Writings.* New York: Library of America, 1984.

—David J. Siemers

Jehovah's Witnesses

Jehovah's Witnesses are a Christian, international religious community united by a common understanding of the Holy

Bible. Best known for their evangelical work and large conventions, Jehovah's Witnesses receive spiritual direction from a Governing Body located at their world headquarters in Brooklyn, New York. There are approximately 5.8 million Jehovah's Witnesses in some 167 nations. Jehovah's Witnesses are one of the world's fastest-growing religions.

Jehovah's Witnesses believe that Jehovah is the personal name of the Creator. This name appears in the form of the Tetragrammaton 6,828 times in the Hebrew Scriptures (Old Testament) and 237 times in the Greek Scriptures (New Testament). Formerly known as "Bible Students," and "Associated Bible Students," they adopted the name "Jehovah's Witnesses" by general resolution on July 26, 1931, at their summer convention held in Columbus, Ohio.

Central to their faith is a belief in the Kingdom of God, a heavenly government in the hands of Jesus Christ, and 144,000 anointed faithful followers who are selected by Jehovah and who will rule with Jesus as priests and kings over the earth for 1,000 years. At the end of the 1,000-year rule, when all humankind is restored to mental, emotional, and physical perfection on a paradise on Earth, the heavenly government will submit to Jehovah's direct rulership. Their expectations in connection with Jehovah's Kingdom government are closely connected with their responsibility to preach about the Bible's message of good news.

The Governing Body provides spiritual direction and encouragement to congregations primarily by means of *The Watchtower* magazine. The Governing Body does not claim to be infallible, nor is a clergy-laity distinction made within congregations. Teaching and spiritual shepherding are assigned to mature men who meet the spiritual qualifications outlined in the Bible books of Timothy and Titus.

The following are among Jehovah's Witnesses' basic teachings:

- The Bible is inspired by Jehovah God and is the truth.
- Jesus Christ is Jehovah God's son and is not his equal or part of a trinity.
- Jesus Christ was the first of Jehovah's creations and has ruled as King of God's Kingdom since 1914.
- Human death is the result of Adam's sin.
- Hell is not a place of fire or suffering but is humankind's common grave from which the vast majority of the dead will be resurrected to the earth.

For Jehovah's Witnesses, worshipping God properly means avoiding lying, stealing, fornication, adultery, homosexuality, the misuse of blood, idolatry, and other things condemned in the Scriptures. Jehovah's Witnesses eschew tobacco and betel nut, and they avoid any form of substance abuse. Witnesses do not forbid the use of alcoholic beverages, but they warn against the abuse of alcohol. They do not celebrate birthdays or civil or religious holidays. However, they do commemorate Jesus' death once a year by observing the Lord's Supper, a practice also known as the Lord's Evening Meal.

Witnesses receive no monetary compensation for their preaching work or for caring for congregational responsibilities. Volunteers undertake construction work on houses of worship and relief work. Each Witness determines the amount of time and resources he or she will devote to ministry. In addition to public preaching work, congregations of Jehovah's Witnesses worldwide conduct regular weekly meetings for worship. Jehovah's Witnesses encourage strong family life. Witnesses believe that it is their Christian responsibility to be model citizens. For this reason, they show honor and respect toward government authority and obey the laws of the land, as long as the government does not demand that they violate their political neutrality.

Jehovah's Witnesses have had a significant impact on medical communities worldwide. Since the 1940s, Witnesses have taken the position that the use of blood and blood products is contrary to scriptural principle. Since there is no clear scriptural prohibition, the decision to accept donor organs and blood fractions is left to individual Witness as a matter of conscience. Blood salvaging equipment, blood volume expanders, and surgical techniques that have been developed to assist Witnesses have also contributed to the health of many non-Witnesses, since they, too, have been able to obtain qualified medical care without the risk of blood-borne diseases.

See also WATCHTOWER SOCIETY.

—Carolyn R. Wah

Jehovah's Witnesses and religious publishing

The Watch Tower Bible and Tract Society of Pennsylvania publishes *The New World Translation of the Holy Scriptures* in 38 languages. This translation of the Bible was first released in English in six volumes from 1950 to 1960. It was translated and edited by JEHOVAH'S WITNESSES and contains the name *Jehovah* in all 6,828 places where it appears in the Hebrew Scriptures, as well as the 237 places where it appears in the Christian Greek Scriptures.

The Watchtower magazine, formerly titled *Zion's Watchtower and Herald of Christ's Presence*, first appeared in 1879 with a printing of 6,000 copies. The first president of the Watch Tower Society, Charles Taze Russell, wrote most of the sermons, magazines, and books distributed in those early years, including the *Millennial Dawn* series of Bible study books, which was later known as *Studies in the Scriptures*. Russell frequently traveled internationally to debate other prominent clergymen and theologians. He presented the "Photo-Drama of Creation," an eight-hour drama presented in four parts, to some 9 million people in North America, Europe, and Australia during its inaugural year. It depicted the major events of the Bible from the creation to the establishment of the paradise after Armageddon. The "Photo-Drama" combined motion pictures and hand-colored glass slides and synchronized with Bible lectures and music on phonograph records.

In 1924, the Watchtower Society purchased the radio station WBBR, which operated out of New York. At its peak in

1933, 408 stations on six continents were receiving WBBR's Bible message. From 1934 to 1944, the Witnesses used another unique invention to share their message: portable, lightweight phonographs. Witnesses carried these phonographs door-to-door to preach using records of Bible lectures, usually given by Joseph F. Rutherford. The phonograph was designed to allow the operator to hold the machine like a suitcase and start the phonograph with one hand. To support the preaching effort, over 20,000 of these machines were produced. Since 1978 the Governing Body has approved the use of audiocassettes and video to support its worldwide preaching and education work. The entire *New World Translation of the Holy Scriptures* was recorded on audiocassette and is now available to the public in 14 languages.

Today, the Jehovah's Witnesses publish two magazines: *The Watchtower* and *Awake!* *The Watchtower* is a bimonthly magazine published in 140 languages, with an average printing of 23 million copies of each issue. *The Watchtower* carries brief articles on world events and Bible prophecy. Each issue carries at least two articles designated as study articles for use in *The Watchtower* study, a regularly scheduled meeting for worship and study at each congregation of Jehovah's Witnesses. The companion magazine, *Awake!*, originally known as *The Golden Age*, was first published in October 1919. *Awake!* is now published bimonthly and is available in 83 languages.

The Governing Body of Jehovah's Witnesses coordinates the writing, photography, artwork, and graphic layout for these journals, and they are printed at facilities in Brooklyn, New York, and Patterson, New Jersey. During the 1920s the Governing Body decided that volunteer ministers could publish literature more efficiently than commercial concerns. A substantial portion of the effort of preparing and printing these bimonthly journals is borne by an international network of translators at the various branch offices of Jehovah's Witnesses.

See also JEHOVAH'S WITNESSES, POLITICS, AND THE LEGAL SYSTEM; WATCHTOWER SOCIETY.

—Carolyn R. Wah

Jehovah's Witnesses, politics, and the legal system

JEHOVAH'S WITNESSES have historically remained politically neutral and avoided becoming social activists. However, they have appealed to the civil courts for legal protection of their public preaching and their right to assemble for worship. In one of the Witnesses' first encounters with the U.S. legal system, members of the Board of Directors of the WATCHTOWER SOCIETY were arrested and charged with conspiring to violate the Espionage Act of June 15, 1917. The complaint focused on volume 7 of the series *Studies in the Scriptures*, in which comments were made criticizing clergy who had advocated support of World War I. On June 21, 1918, seven of the eight defendants were sentenced to four terms of 20 years each, to be served concurrently. The remaining defendant was sentenced to four concurrent terms of 10 years. In the spring and summer of 1918, Jehovah's Witnesses throughout the United States, Europe, and Canada were arrested, beaten, and abused. Their homes were searched and their Bible literature was seized. On May 5, 1920, the U.S. government dismissed its indictments of the Watchtower directors, and the defendants were discharged from the federal penitentiary in Atlanta, Georgia.

In the late 1930s, Witnesses in the United States again met with organized opposition to their public preaching work. Thousands of court cases nationwide were litigated. This flurry of legal activity culminated in the mid-1940s when the U.S. Supreme Court ruled in a series of victories for the Witnesses (see CANTWELL V. CONNECTICUT), applying Fourteenth Amendment liberty rights to freedom of religion and freedom of speech, protecting the right to preach in a public area; MARTIN V. STRUTHERS/MURDOCK V. PENNSYLVANIA, holding public preaching to be a religious activity protected by the First Amendment; WEST VIRGINIA BOARD OF EDUCATION V. BARNETTE, upholding the right of Witness children to refrain from saluting the national flag.

During World War II, a primary complaint against Witnesses involved divorce actions, when one parent was concerned that his or her children were not taught or encouraged to salute the national flag (see *Salvaggio v. Barnette* 1952), which held that Witness father's refusal to salute the flag and to teach his child to salute the American flag was not a proper reason to deny him custody. In peacetime, child-related complaints have focused on emotional and developmental issues, with allegations that a Witness parent's refusal to celebrate a child's birthday or participate in civil and religious holidays might have a negative impact on the child's development (see *Pater v. Pater*, Ohio 1992), wherein a Witness mother's First Amendment rights were violated when, absent a showing that exposure to the teachings and beliefs of Jehovah's Witnesses presented either present or imminent substantial harm to the child, the trial judge denied her custody of her three-year-old son and ordered her not to expose him to her religious beliefs.

After World War II, litigation continued, but the subject matter changed. The Watchtower Bible and Tract Society held property in several counties of New York. One location in Wallkill, New York, was used as a farm to grow vegetables and raise cattle to feed volunteer ministers living and working at the society's complexes. The Board of Taxation challenged the Watchtower's request for tax exemption for religious use. Success came when the New York Court of Appeals, the state's highest appellate court, ruled in favor of the Witnesses (see *Watchtower Bible and Tract Society of New York, Inc. v. Lewisohn* [1971], holding that the Watchtower Bible and Tract Society of New York, Inc., was organized and conducted exclusively for religious purposes and qualified for exemption under New York real property tax law; *People ex rel. Watchtower Bible and Tract Society, Inc. v. Haring* [1960], holding that Watchtower farm property used to feed its volunteer workers was entitled to exemption under the New York State Real Property Tax Law).

Witnesses' refusal to accept blood or blood products in their health care management has also been the subject of litigation. As a result, appellate courts have considered the issue and ruled in favor of bodily self-determination, holding that the right to refuse any medical treatment that offends the patient's religious beliefs is protected by state and federal constitutions (see *Stamford Hosp. v. Vega,* Conn. 1996), in which the court ruled that a Witness patient's refusal of blood products is protected by common law right of self-determination; *In re Dubreuil* (Florida 1993), in which a Witness patient's refusal of blood was ruled to be protected by state constitutional rights of personal privacy.

In his recent book, *Judging Jehovah's Witnesses: Religious Persecution and the Dawn of the Rights of Revolution,* legal historian Shawn Francis Peters observed: "While protecting their own interests, [Witnesses] prompted courts at all levels . . . to fortify safeguards for this country's most basic democratic liberties, including freedom of religion and freedom of speech."

See also JEHOVAH'S WITNESSES AND RELIGIOUS PUBLISHING.

Further reading: Cote, Pauline, and James T. Richardson. "Disciplined Litigation, Vigilant Litigation, and Deformation: Dramatic Organization Changes in Jehovah's Witnesses." *Journal of the Scientific Study of Religion* 40 (2001): 11–25; Peters, Shawn Francis. *Judging Jehovah's Witnesses: Religious Persecution and the Dawn of the Rights Revolution.* Lawrence: University Press of Kansas, 2000.

—Carolyn R. Wah

Jemison, T. J. (1919–) *activist*

Theodore J. Jemison was born in Selma, Alabama, the son of the Reverend David Vivian Jemison, a prominent pastor of Tabernacle Baptist Church in Selma and then-president of the Alabama Colored Baptist State Convention. Following his own ordination as a Baptist minister, the younger Jemison became pastor of Mount Zion Baptist Church in Baton Rouge, Louisiana, in 1950, a position that he holds to this day. More inclined toward social and political activism than was his father, T. J. Jemison is best known for his role in leading a boycott of the Baton Rouge bus system in the summer of 1953. Jemison, through the bus boycott and other participation in the CIVIL RIGHTS MOVEMENT, gained a measure of national prominence, and was elected president of the NATIONAL BAPTIST CONVENTION (NBC), a position previously held by his father, in 1982. Jemison has used this position to move the NBC, generally regarded as the most conservative of the major national black religious organizations, toward greater social comment and activism.

Jemison's efforts at social change began shortly after he became pastor at Mount Zion. Bristling at the injustice of a Baton Rouge transportation policy that reserved the first 10 rows of seats on city buses for white patrons (often forcing black riders to stand when there were many open seats), Jemison successfully petitioned the city council to soften the restriction considerably. In March 1953, the council revised the bus policy to require only that black patrons start occupying rows from the rear of the bus, while white riders would begin seating from the front. When this change was announced, however, the white bus drivers went on strike, and the City Council capitulated, agreeing to reinstate the old policy. At that point, Jemison led a coalition of black civic leaders in calling for a boycott of the Baton Rouge bus system. An extensive carpool network was organized so that African Americans honoring the boycott would still have transportation to their jobs. After a week of nearly empty buses, the City Council proposed a compromise—the 10 front rows reserved for white patrons would be reduced to two. Jemison, over some objections, accepted this compromise and called off the boycott, even though a vestige of segregation remained. "You cannot change traditions and customs overnight," he argued. "It takes patience, prayer, and downright common sense." The Reverend MARTIN LUTHER KING JR., in his book *Stride Toward Freedom* (1958), credits Jemison's example and personal encouragement with inspiring the more famous Montgomery bus boycott of 1955.

Jemison's social and political activity did not end with the bus boycott. He was present in 1957 at a meeting at Ebenezer Baptist Church in Atlanta that formed the Southern Leadership Conference on Transportation and Nonviolent Integration. This group later grew into the SOUTHERN CHRISTIAN LEADERSHIP CONFERENCE, of which Jemison was a founding member. In more recent years, Jemison has been active in Democratic politics, strongly supporting JESSE JACKSON's two national campaigns and lending his aid to Democratic presidential nominees. Jemison has also sought to involve the National Baptist Convention more thoroughly in national political debates. Under his leadership, the group spoke out against Clarence Thomas's nomination to the U.S. Supreme Court and against U.S. involvement in the PERSIAN GULF WAR. Jemison has also sought changes within the denomination, pushing, for example, for the ordination of women to ministry. Not all his initiatives have been without controversy, however, even within his own denomination. Many black Baptist pastors and women's groups questioned his strong defense in 1992 of boxer Mike Tyson, an athlete with a history of violence against women who was facing rape charges. Yet overall, Jemison remains a respected and influential figure in the civil rights community, both in Baton Rouge and around the United States.

See also ABERNATHY, RALPH; BUS BOYCOTTS.

Further reading: Chestnut, J. L., Jr., and Julia Cass. *Black in Selma: The Uncommon Life of J. L. Chestnut, Jr.* New York: Anchor Books, 1990; King, Martin Luther, Jr. *Stride toward Freedom: The Montgomery Story.* New York: Harper, 1958; Shinkle, Peter. "Civil Rights Saga." *Baton Rouge Advocate,* March 2, 1999, 1; Shipp, E. R. "Baptist President's Support for

Tyson Is Assailed Inside and Outside Church." *New York Times,* March 16, 1992, A10.

—J. Matthew Wilson

Jewish Defense League (JDL)

The Jewish Defense League (JDL) is a militant Jewish organization whose declared aim is to warn and protect Jews against perceived dire threats to their physical security and Jewish identity. Established in 1968, the JDL was for many years synonymous with the name of its founder and national chairman, MEIR KAHANE, an ordained rabbi from Brooklyn, New York. In Kahane's Manichean worldview of gentiles versus Jews, anti-Semitism was all-pervasive, and Jews had to learn to defend themselves by whatever means necessary, including the proactive use of violence. Where most American Jews viewed the United States, and their place in it, as a "new Promised Land," Kahane saw a society hostile to Jews, often comparing his coreligionists' blindness to the dangers with the situation of Jews in Germany as the Nazis took over. The major Jewish organizations, in his view, had failed to adequately protect American Jewry. Even in ISRAEL, Jews faced incessant danger by being surrounded by hostile Arab states. But there at least they had political control and were militarily able and ready to defend themselves. "If I have succeeded in instilling fear in you," Kahane would often end his speeches, "I consider this evening a success."

As its slogan "Never Again!" indicates, the JDL can be seen as a charged reaction to the trauma of the HOLOCAUST and, indeed, more generally to the powerlessness and victimhood that marked the diasporan experience of the Jews for some 2,000 years. As the league declares, the "JDL wants to create a physically strong, fearless and courageous Jew who fights back. We are changing an image, an image born of 2,000 years in the *Galut* [exile], an image that must be buried because it has buried us."

The JDL was heavily influenced by the Revisionist Zionist thinker Vladimir (Ze'ev) Jabotinsky, who, in the early decades of the 20th century, warned of the dangers facing Jews in the diaspora, called for a sovereign Jewish state in the ancient Jewish homeland, and imagined a new kind of Jew—"proud, generous, and fierce." Jabotinsky is reputed to have been a close friend of Kahane's father, and the young Kahane was a member of Jabotinsky's *Betar* youth movement. The JDL presents its philosophy as being grounded in Jewish sources and religious teachings. Its five guiding principles, stated under Hebrew rubrics, are *Ahavat Yisroel*—one Jewish people, indivisible and united; *Hadar*—one of Jabotinsky's key concepts, meaning dignity and pride in being a Jew; *Barzel*, or iron, signifying the need for personal and collective strength, force, and violence; *Mishmaat*—the need for discipline and unity among the Jewish people; and *Bitachon*—"Faith in the greatness and indestructibility of the Jewish people, our religion and our Land of Israel."

Kahane unsettled the American Jewish community not only by the JDL's recourse to violence. He also appealed to Jewish sources to promote the idea of the Jews as the "chosen people" who had exclusive right to the land of Israel, and proclaimed a basic incompatibility between Judaism and Western-style democracy. As Kahane put it, "Judaism is not THOMAS JEFFERSON and the Middle East is not the Midwest."

In 1971, Kahane moved to Israel, where he established the Kach movement. Similar to the JDL in its militancy and appeal to religious sources, it focused on local issues and became notorious for advocating removal of the Arab population from Israel. Running on the Kach platform, Kahane was elected a member of Knesset in 1984, but he was later banned from the electoral process for his extremism.

An Arab extremist assassinated Kahane while he was visiting New York in 1990. Nevertheless, the JDL may be credited with drawing attention to many issues of broad Jewish concern, including, notably, the plight of Soviet Jewry, the whereabouts of Nazi war criminals, and challenges to Jewish continuity. However, it is fair to say that the JDL's reliance on violence and intimidation—including bombings, threatened kidnappings, and sieges of non-Jewish and Jewish institutions—and extreme forms of Jewish nationalism are anathema to the overwhelming majority of Jews whom the movement claims to protect.

See also AGUDAT ISRAEL; ZIONISM.

Further reading: Jewish Defense League website. URL: http://www.jdl.org; Kahane, Meir. *The Story of the Jewish Defense League.* 2d ed. Brooklyn, N.Y.: Institute for Publication of the Writings of Rabbi Meir Kahane, 2000; Katz, Shmuel. *Lone Wolf: A Biography of Vladimir Jabotinsky.* New York: Barricade Books, 1996.

—Geoffrey Brahm Levey

Jewish liberalism

Jewish liberalism refers to the marked tendency of Jews to support left-liberal candidates, political parties, and causes. While not all Jews are liberals, and although Jews, as a group, are not markedly (if at all) liberal on every issue, as a matter of comparison they are generally found to be the most liberal white ethnoreligious group in the United States. LIBERALISM is typically measured in this context by political identification with the Democratic Party; electoral support for Democratic candidates; self-identification as a "liberal" rather than a "conservative"; and support for liberal positions on civil liberties, civil rights, state welfare, and, sometimes, foreign policy issues. A feature of Jewish liberalism has been its registration across all the standard measures of political behavior and attitudes.

The liberal pattern among Jews is often traced to the 1930s realignment in American politics marked by FRANKLIN DELANO ROOSEVELT's New Deal. Some 90 percent of Jews supported Roosevelt in the 1940 and 1944 presidential elections. However, some researchers discern a decided liberal or progressive inclination in Jewish political behavior more or less consistently since the American Revolution. Democratic voting among Jews in more recent times does not match that of the New Deal era, and the Jewish vote has displayed some rightward drift in given elections. Yet as a group, Jews still endorse the Democratic Party at a rate of around 20 percentage points above most other Americans.

The persistence of Jewish liberalism is considered especially puzzling in light of the Jews' rapid upward mobility in the post–World War II period. The rule in American politics is that people become conservative as they become affluent, yet, as Irving Howe observes, the "Jews seem to be the only ethnic community in the United States in which significant numbers of people, though they rise rapidly in socioeconomic condition, do not change their political views." Jewish liberalism is thus an oft-cited example of anomalous group political behavior in the United States. The pronounced degree to which Jews endorse liberal candidates and issues is partly attributable to the Jews' distinctive sociodemographic profile, such as their residential concentration in large cities and their occupational distribution in the liberal professions. Research suggests, however, that conventional factors are unable to explain the full measure of differential Jewish liberalism, especially in regard to civil liberties, state welfare issues, and Democratic Party affiliation.

Explanation of the phenomenon is much debated. The theories, of which there are many, include political interest approaches that ask which parties historically have been most hostile or friendly to Jews, and sociological approaches that stress felt Jewish marginality, status discrepancy, or minority status. Another prominent theory links Jews' distinctive liberalism to Jewish religious values—study and learning, social justice, and nonasceticism; yet religiously observant Jews also tend to be *less* politically liberal and more politically conservative than nonobservant Jews. A more recent theory emphasizes tensions in the relationship between Jews and their own religion and religious authorities. Many commentators have declared or anticipated the demise of differential Jewish liberalism, usually in response to the results of a certain election or survey. This has yet to be borne out.

Further reading: Cohen, Steven M. *The Dimensions of American Jewish Liberalism.* New York: American Jewish Committee, 1989; Forman, Ira N. "The Politics of Minority Consciousness: The Historical Voting Behavior of American Jews." In *Jews in American Politics.* Edited by L. Sandy Maisel and Ira N. Forman. Lanham, Md.: Rowman and Littlefield, 2001; Howe, Irving. "A Time for Compassion and Commitment." In *American Jews and Liberalism.* Edited by Irving Howe et al. New York: Foundation for the Study of Independent Social Ideas, 1986; Levey, Geoffrey Brahm. "Toward a Theory of Disproportionate American Jewish Liberalism." *Studies in Contemporary Jewry* 11 (1995): 64–85; ———. "When Did the Liberalism of American Jews Emerge?" *Jewish Culture and History* 4 (2001): 1–29; Wald, Kenneth D. *Religion and Politics in the United States.* 3d ed. Washington, D.C.: Congressional Quarterly Press, 1997.

—Geoffrey Brahm Levey

Jewish radicalism

Jewish radicalism is not a single movement or episode; rather, it designates the conspicuous involvement of Jews in various Marxist, democratic socialist, labor union, and other leftist radical movements. It is of particular interest because while most Jews in the United States (as elsewhere) have not been radicals (unlike the case with JEWISH LIBERALISM), a disproportionate number of Jews, given their small percentage of the general population, typically has been engaged in radicalism. Moreover, their participation often has been highly influential as theoreticians, polemicists, or organizational leaders. Jewish radicals may be distinguished from "radical Jews" or those who turn to political agitation in behalf of specifically Jewish causes, such as those who associate with the JEWISH DEFENSE LEAGUE.

The history of Jewish radicalism in the United States largely begins with the mass immigration of eastern European Jews from roughly 1880 to 1920. In czarist Russia, two broad categories of Jews became radicalized: a small group of semiassimilated, Russian-speaking, middle-class intellectuals, and a mass of traditionally Jewish, Yiddish-speaking, largely impoverished workers. A similar pattern of Jewish radicalism obtained among the immigrant generations in the United States, especially in the dense immigrant enclaves such as the Lower East Side of New York City. After 1903, immigrant Jewish activists and intellectuals were influential in the Socialist Party of America. Several Jewish figures attained prominence on the Socialist ticket, such as Congressman Meyer London and New York mayoral candidate Morris Hillquit. It has been estimated that up to 15 percent of the Communist Party and the Communist Labor Party memberships was Jewish in the 1920s, and as much as 50 percent in the 1930s.

At the same time, the immigrant Jewish working class helped to spearhead union politics and labor agitation. At its height in 1916, the Jewish Socialist Federation, an autonomous Yiddish-speaking organization within the Socialist Party, had some 8,000 members. By 1914, the United Hebrew Trades, the parent institution of the Jewish labor movement in America, numbered 104 constituent unions, with 250,000 members. Beyond the numbers is Daniel Bell's observation that the eastern European Jews "provided the sinews which sustained the American Socialist Party until 1932." Jewish radicalism declined in the 1940s and 1950s along with the radical parties, becoming prominent again in the 1960s with the rise of student activism, the counterculture, and the New Left.

Many theories have been advanced to explain the extraordinary Jewish involvement in radical movements. Some highlight general radicalizing factors such as working-class conditions and economic hardship. Others stress factors especially affecting, or specific to, Jews. Among these are the heightened sense of social justice that springs from enduring social discrimination (anti-Semitism was especially acute in the 1930s); the loss of Jewish identity through assimilation and the search for a substitute through universal ideologies or fraternal organizations; and a related sense of estrangement from Jewish community and religion coupled with an ambition to be accepted by general society, in some cases bordering on Jewish self-hatred. Another theory is that Jewish radicalism represents the secularization of Jewish religious values, in particular, MESSIANISM and the quest for a just world.

The preponderance of Jews in the New Left has been explained in yet other terms, from expressing the values of their erstwhile radical parents ("red diaper" thesis), to psychosocial dynamics of authority, power, and permissiveness in the Jewish family. In recent years, increasing attention has been paid to the role of Jewish women in early radical movements, a tradition continued by their prominence in the feminist movement since the 1960s (see FEMINISM).

See also MARXISM/COMMUNISM.

Further reading: Bell, Daniel. *Marxian Socialism in the United States.* Princeton, N.J.: Princeton University Press, 1967; Liebman, Arthur. *Jews and the Left.* New York: Wiley, 1979; Rothman, Stanley, and S. Robert Lichter. *Roots of Radicalism: Jews, Christians, and the Left.* 2d ed. New Brunswick, N.J.: Transaction, 1996; Sorin, Gerald. *The Prophetic Minority: American Jewish Immigrant Radicals 1880–1920.* Bloomington: Indiana University Press, 1988.

—Geoffrey Brahm Levey

Jews and the Democratic Party

In the 1930s, Judge Jonah Goldstein quipped that American Jews lived in three *velten* (Yiddish for "worlds"); *die velt* (this world), *yene velt* (the world to come) and *Roosevelt.* The 1932 presidential election that catapulted FRANKLIN D. ROOSEVELT to the White House captured an American Jewish fascination with the Democratic Party that began with THOMAS JEFFERSON and continues to the present day. American Jews remain the most liberal white ethnic group in the United States, offering the Democratic Party upwards of 80 percent of its votes in any given election.

In the 18th century, America's tiny Jewish population, estimated at 15,000, offered almost unanimous political support to Thomas Jefferson and his Democratic Republican Party. (Jefferson's Democratic Republicans would eventually become the Democratic Party.) For Jews concerned about the power of the state, Jefferson's anti-Federalist positions promised greater security. While ALEXANDER HAMILTON and his Federalist cohorts lobbied for a more powerful central government, Jefferson called for a BILL OF RIGHTS that included special protections for religious minorities.

During the 19th century, the immigration of about 100,000 German Jews to the United States changed the fabric of American Jewish political culture. Although many German-Jewish arrivals favored the Democratic Party over the often xenophobic Whigs, the eventual Democratic split on the issue of slavery primed the northern Jewish community to join the ranks of ABRAHAM LINCOLN's Republican Party. Southern

Jews remained faithful to the Democrats throughout the century. When the Civil War ended in 1865, Jews in both regions joined the Republican Party in disproportionate numbers, anticipating a century-long Jewish commitment to equal rights and the rule of law.

When approximately 2 million eastern European Jews immigrated to the United States at the turn of the 20th century, they challenged their German-American brethren's political leanings. While many continued to flock to the Republican Party, especially after President THEODORE ROOSEVELT launched his impressive progressive reform measures, others looked to the Democratic Party when it reinvented itself as the voice of ordinary people during the 1896 general election. Some of the new Jewish arrivals preferred leftist politics and threw their support to Socialist or even Communist candidates.

The American Jewish community's love affair with the Democratic Party began in earnest with the election of Franklin D. Roosevelt in 1932. In subsequent elections, Jews gave the Democratic incumbent an astronomical 90 percent of their vote, securing for him legendary status in the annals of American Jewish political history. Though his refusal to take more decisive action in defense of wartime European Jewry has inspired a reevaluation of his presidency, FDR refused to allow anti-Semitism to guide his administrative and judicial appointments—he opened up the federal government to scores of influential Jews. Jewish social workers helped design many New Deal programs including the landmark Social Security system. During World War II, Jews relied on the Democratic chief executive to guide Allied forces to victory over the Axis powers.

In the postwar period, Jews continued to vote for Democratic candidates, even as liberal ANTICOMMUNISM often blurred distinctions between left and right. Jewish organizations such as the AMERICAN JEWISH COMMITTEE and AMERICAN JEWISH CONGRESS pressed for fair employment practices legislation, while the Jewish rank and file backed the efforts of MARTIN LUTHER KING JR. and the CIVIL RIGHTS MOVEMENT. More than half of all white civil rights workers claimed Jewish ancestry, and Jewish philanthropists filled the coffers of many national civil rights groups.

By the late 1960s, the Jewish community's affection for the Democratic Party endured its greatest test when President Lyndon Johnson pressed for group-based domestic liberal programs and an unpopular VIETNAM WAR. American Jews offered mixed reviews of affirmative action programs but were resolute in their opposition to mandatory hiring quotas. A disproportionate number of Jewish activists participated in antiwar demonstrations. The strident CONSERVATISM of both Barry Goldwater and RICHARD NIXON helped ensure continued Jewish support of Democratic candidates.

Since 1965, the Jewish community has borrowed aspects of group-based LIBERALISM to power an unprecedented ethnic revival. Jewish women emerged as the greatest beneficiaries of affirmative action programs, while American ZIONISTS, neo-Orthodox Jews, and even Jewish New Leftists borrowed a page from the ethnic nationalists' handbook when they articulated public and unapologetic forms of Jewish expression.

See also JEWISH LIBERALISM; JEWISH RADICALISM; LIEBERMAN, JOSEPH; MARXISM/COMMUNISM; RELIGION IN THE 1896 PRESIDENTIAL ELECTION.

Further reading: Cohen, Steven M. *The Dimensions of American Jewish Liberalism.* New York: American Jewish Committee, 1989; Dollinger, Marc. *Quest for Inclusion: Jews and Liberalism in Modern America.* Princeton, N.J.: Princeton University Press, 2000; Fuchs Lawrence. *The Political Behavior of American Jews.* New York: Free Press, 1956; Isaacs, Stephen D. *Jews and American Politics.* Garden City, N.Y.: Doubleday, 1974.

—Marc Dollinger

John XXIII (1881–1963) *pope*

As John XXIII (1958–63), Angelo Roncalli became the history-making pope of the Second Vatican Council (VATICAN II). Surprising many of his advisers, he quickly proposed a worldwide ecumenical council of bishops to address the situation of the church in the modern world. In October 1962, John convened the council, which fundamentally changed the ROMAN CATHOLIC CHURCH's stands on political, social, and cultural questions. John died between the council's first and second sessions and was succeeded by Paul VI.

John XXIII's personality was as important as the council in presenting a new face of the church. Despite his long service in the papal diplomatic corps, his humble rural origins gave him an accessibility and geniality his immediate predecessors lacked. Breaking centuries of precedent, he made pastoral visits to hospitals, old-age homes, and prisons. This pastoral style was imitated and extended by his successors, especially through JOHN PAUL II's (1979–   ) extensive world travels and direct contact with people.

John XXIII's purpose in calling Vatican II was to renew a church that had ossified in the wake of the Reformation and Counter-Reformation. This renewal (*aggiornamento*) was not intended to change fundamental dogma or doctrine, but rather to express them in words and practices more capable of engaging an age radically transformed by world capitalism, ideological movements such as LIBERALISM and MARXISM/COMMUNISM, rapid scientific and technical changes, and religious pluralism. John envisioned a genuine dialogue between church and world, instead of a monologue addressed by the church to an uncomprehending world.

Two important encyclicals (letters on faith and morals addressed to the whole church) marked John XXIII's papacy. The first, *Mater et Magistra* (*Mother and Teacher*), was issued in 1961 to mark the 70th anniversary of Leo XIII's encyclical *RERUM NOVARUM*. John's letter largely summarized familiar themes in Catholic social teaching but broke ground in addressing new aspects of the social question. He praised positive economic, social, and political developments. He recom-

mended unions and worker participation as ways for ordinary workers to share in the economic sphere and praised active state defense of political and economic rights. Yet John raised concerns about the plight of agricultural workers in the new economic system and the need for assistance from the developed world to new nations emerging from colonialism. He expressed deep unease over the profound inequalities within and between nations. John argued that the education of clergy and laity in social responsibility and SOCIAL JUSTICE is an essential part of Catholic doctrine and teaching.

John XXIII's second encyclical, *Pacem in Terris* (*Peace on Earth*), was issued in April 1963, shortly after the Cuban Missile Crisis and just before his death. It was the first papal encyclical addressed to "all men of good will," instead of the church alone, and it urged active cooperation toward peace between Catholics and persons of other (or no) faiths. The reality of nuclear weapons and threats to use them was a strong stimulus to this document, in which John XXIII firmly linked justice and peace. John pleaded for an end to the arms race, a ban on nuclear weapons, and international disarmament agreements. It was not weapons, however, or international disputes alone that threatened peace; rather, profound social and economic injustice produced violence, wars, and civil strife. This encyclical for the first time specified a Catholic account of fundamental human rights (including HEALTH CARE, education, and conscience). In addition, *Pacem in Terris* warmly recommends democracy and qualifies traditional Catholic theory on JUST WAR (without abandoning it) in light of nuclear and conventional weapons capable of unprecedented destruction.

John XXIII's ideas shaped key documents of Vatican II. His writings and his personal style inspired as well a generation of Catholic justice and peace activists in the 1960s and 1970s in the United States and Europe.

See also CATHOLIC BISHOPS' 1983 PASTORAL LETTER ON WAR AND PEACE.

Further reading: Hebblethwaite, Peter. *Pope John XXIII: Shepherd of the Modern World.* Garden City, N.Y.: Doubleday, 1985; Mich, Marvin L. Krier. *Catholic Social Teaching and Movements.* Mystic, Conn.: Twenty-Third Publications, 1988; Pope John XXIII. *Journal of a Soul.* Translated by Dorothy White. New York: McGraw-Hill, 1965; Walsh, Michael, and Brian Davies, eds. *Proclaiming Justice and Peace: Papal Documents from* Rerum Novarum *Through* Centesimus Annus. Revised and expanded. Mystic, Conn.: Twenty-Third Publications, 1991.

—Clarke E. Cochran

John Birch Society (1920–   )

The John Birch Society is a conservative organization that emerged during the 1950s and 1960s as one of the nation's staunchest anticommunist groups. The organization was founded around religious principles and named after an American missionary murdered by Chinese Communists in 1945. The membership and influence of the society reached its peak during the VIETNAM WAR, when it became a symbol of CONSERVATISM in the nation. Since that period, however, the society has declined in stature and membership.

The John Birch Society was established as a result of the work of Robert Welch; however, the organization was named after missionary John Morrison Birch (1918–45). Birch was a Christian missionary who traveled to China in 1920. After World War II broke out, Birch joined the American forces fighting the Japanese in China as an intelligence officer who often undertook missions behind enemy lines. He eventually rose to the rank of captain. The society claims Birch was killed by Chinese Communists on August 25, 1945, 10 days after World War II ended.

Robert H. W. Welch Jr. (1899–1985) was a wealthy Boston candy magnate who, in the aftermath of World War II, became convinced that international communism was the greatest threat to the United States and the American way of life. During the McCarthy era of the early 1950s, Welch supported the efforts to suppress known and suspected communists in the United States. In the 1952 presidential election, Welch supported Robert A. Taft for the Republican nomination. He opposed DWIGHT D. EISENHOWER because he perceived that the former general was too moderate. In 1958, Welch decided to establish a private organization to support anticommunist efforts and expose what he saw as the domestic conspiracy to undermine American values. Welch believed that Birch was the first real casualty of the cold war and named the new society in his honor.

The 1959 rise to power of Communist forces in Cuba seemed to confirm for Welch the weakness and ineffectiveness of the Eisenhower administration. Welch wrote a number of works, including a biography, *The Life of John Birch*. The society's right-wing message resonated with many conservative Christians in the United States. The basic themes of the society centered on the importance of faith, morality, and always anticommunism. The society strove to combat communism and socialism on both the domestic and the international level. Ultimately, its most significant influence was on domestic politics.

The John Birch Society eventually established branches in all 50 states. Membership rose into the hundreds of thousands. The society began to publish a regular series of journals and books that were often based on conspiracy theories and championed the belief that there was a vast coalition of liberals, communists, and moderate Republicans who worked to undermine the Christian values of the nation. The main journal of the society was the *American Opinion* and, later, *The New American*. It also published a monthly bulletin and a variety of books, including the *Blue Book,* which outlines the main beliefs and purpose of the society.

By the early 1960s, the John Birch Society was one of the largest and best organized of the right-wing groups in the United States. The society became very adept at organizing letter-writing campaigns and organizing demonstrations. Through its monthly publications, the organization could disseminate information to its members and coordinate grassroots efforts. The effectiveness of the society also brought it to the attention of the public, and it became one of the nation's most visible right-wing groups. The John Birch Society presented a variety of problems for the Republican Party. The tactics and messages of the society alienated many moderate Americans and reinforced the image of the Republicans as ultraconservative. In the 1964 presidential election, Republican candidate Barry Goldwater was perceived to be an extremist by many Americans (a perception that was used as a campaign tactic by the Democratic Party) because of supporters such as the John Birch Society.

Membership in the society declined throughout the 1980s and 1990s, partially as a result of the death of its founder in 1985 and partially as a result of the end of the cold war. Nonetheless, the organization continues to promote its ultraconservative brand of Christianity and to oppose liberal politicians and policies. One of the society's main goals continues to be the removal of the United States from the United Nations.

See also MARXISM/COMMUNISM.

Further reading: Broyles, J. Allen. *The John Birch Society: Anatomy of a Protest*. Boston: Beacon, 1964; Himmelstein, Jerome L. *To the Right: The Transformation of American Conservatism*. Berkeley: University of California Press, 1990; Perlstein, Rick. *Before the Storm: Barry Goldwater and the Unmaking of the American Consensus*. New York: Hill and Wang, 2001; Schomp, Gerald. *Birchism Was My Business*. New York: Macmillan, 1970.

—Thomas Lansford

John Paul II (1920–) *pope*

Pope John Paul II, born Karol Wojtyla on May 18, 1920, in Wadowice, Poland, was elected Roman Catholic pontiff on October 16, 1978, following the 33-day pontificate of John Paul I (d. September 28, 1978), successor to Paul VI (d. August 6, 1978). He is the first Polish pope, the first non-Italian pope since Hadrian VI (who was Dutch, elected in 1522), and the youngest pope elected since Pius IX (1846). Before his election, Wojtyla was archbishop of Cracow, Poland (since 1964, elevated to cardinal in 1976).

Karol Wojtyla studied for the priesthood in secret during Poland's occupation by Nazi Germany and was ordained a priest on November 1, 1946. Named auxiliary bishop of Cracow in 1958, Wojtyla was a participant in the Second Vatican Council (VATICAN II, 1962–65). His ministry in Poland, as priest, professor, and member of the Polish Catholic hierarchy, coincided with the era of the Soviet-sponsored Polish government. As pope, John Paul II's several visits to his homeland are thought to have contributed to the end of communism in Poland by his public and private support for Poland's Solidarity labor union movement.

John Paul II has been among the most active popes in the history of the ROMAN CATHOLIC CHURCH. Fluent in many languages, he has traveled to more than 120 countries, including three pastoral visits to the United States: in 1979, visiting Boston, New York, Philadelphia, Des Moines, Chicago, and Washington, D.C.; in 1987, Miami, Columbia, New Orleans, San Antonio, Phoenix, Los Angeles, Monterey, San Francisco, Detroit, and Fort Simpson; and in 1995, visiting Newark, New York, and Baltimore. In addition, he made two visits to Alaska, in 1981 (Anchorage) and 1984 (Fairbanks), and was in Denver in 1993 for the international celebration of World Youth Day. The pope has written 13 encyclical letters on theological and social topics, as well as several books for the general public, including the bestseller, *Crossing the Threshold of Hope* (1994).

John Paul II was the victim of a failed assassination attempt, shot by Mehemet Ali Agca on May 13, 1981. Agca's motives have remained a mystery; some have speculated that Agca, a Turk, was associated with the Soviet KGB (secret police) through operatives in Bulgaria. John Paul II publicly forgave his would-be assassin during a visit with Agca in his prison cell in 1983. Agca was granted clemency in June 2000.

John Paul II was one of the most politically active of modern popes. His vested interest in Poland gave him an important role in the political changes in the Soviet Union and Eastern Europe in the 1980s. Full diplomatic relations were established between the United States and the Vatican on January 10, 1984. The pope took a vocal stand against the PERSIAN GULF WAR in 1990 and has been active in diplomacy throughout the Middle East. On June 15, 1994, the Vatican established diplomatic relations with Israel; on October 25, 1994, a working relationship with the Palestine Liberation Organization was established. John Paul II's and President WILLIAM JEFFERSON CLINTON's differing positions on birth control and ABORTION led to open disagreement at the United Nation's World Conference on Population and Development at Cairo in 1994.

John Paul II's relationship with the faithful of the United States is complex. While generally supportive of American civil liberty, the pope is critical of American materialism and what he sees as the moral laxity of the American people, especially concerning the ethical issues of birth control, ABORTION, and divorce. The pope's defense of the liberty of the human person before God, a freedom tempered by a particular vision of truth, often contrasts with the messages of American culture, in which freedom is defined in terms of INDIVIDUALISM. The pope's use of his authority to uphold church teachings is experienced by some American Catholics as authoritarian. Yet despite such differences, the enthusiasm with which the pope was received on his U.S. visits is evidence of his powerful presence.

See also CONSISTENT ETHIC OF LIFE; JOHN XXIII.

Further reading: Gneuhs, Geoffrey. ed. *The Legacy of Pope John Paul II: His Contribution to Catholic Thought.* New York: Crossroad, 2000; Pope John Paul II. *The Pope Speaks to*

Pope John Paul II *(David Brauchli/Getty Images)*

the American Church: John Paul II's Homilies, Speeches, and Letters to the Catholics in the United States.* New York: HarperCollins, 1992; Szulc, Tad. *Pope John Paul II: The Biography.* New York: Simon & Schuster, 1995.

—Susan Gleason Anderson

Jones v. Opelika I 316 U.S. 584 (1942) and *Jones v. Opelika II* 319 U.S. 103 (1943)

The two cases addressed the constitutionality of municipal licensing fees and taxes on the sale of books and pamphlets. In *Jones I,* the Supreme Court consolidated several appeals arising out of Alabama, Arizona, and Arkansas that concerned a group of JEHOVAH'S WITNESSES who were convicted of selling literature without a license. In *Jones I,* the Court determined that the application of nondiscriminatory licensing fees and taxes to the sale and distribution of religious materials did not violate the FREE EXERCISE CLAUSE of the First Amendment. However, the Court ordered reargument of the *Jones* decision in 1943. In its subsequent decision, *Jones II,* the Court vacated its prior decision and reversed the convictions of the Witnesses.

In *Jones I,* the Jehovah's Witnesses argued that their evangelistic activities should be exempt from laws that require licenses to engage in the sale and distribution of religious materials. For the Witnesses, a license requirement limited their First Amendment rights to freely exercise their religion and engage in the prosyletical activities required by their faith. Moreover, licenses and taxes also infringed on the freedom of speech and press. Justice Reed, writing for the majority, disagreed. For Reed, "one man, with views contrary to the rest of his compatriots, is entitled to the privilege of expressing his ideas by speech or broadside to anyone willing to listen or read." Yet, as Reed further notes, "that hearing may be limited . . . to times, places, and methods" necessary to the "preservation of peace and good order." The First Amendment requires an "adjustment of interests" between the speaker/evangelist and the interests of the community. Justice Reed focused on the economic nature of the Witnesses' conduct, and noted that they sold their religious materials to raise funds to propagate their ministries. They used "the ordinary commercial methods of sales of articles to raise propaganda funds," and thus fell under the natural power of the state to regulate that economic activity. As Justice Reed concluded, "we see nothing in the collection of a nondiscriminatory license fee, uncontested in the amount, from those selling books or papers, which abridges the freedoms of worship, speech or press. . . . the First Amendment does not require a subsidy in the form of fiscal exemption."

Justices Murphy, Black, Douglas, and Chief Justice Stone dissented. Justice Murphy wrote the dissenting opinion, arguing that the Witnesses' motivation was not commercial or economic, but evangelical. Their distribution and sale of literature was grounded in their faith. Moreover, the conduct of the Witnesses had no appreciable impact on the finances or services of the cities in question; thus imposition of the tax was difficult to justify on their relatively benign conduct. As Justice Murphy concludes, the "taxes on [the Witnesses'] efforts to preach the 'news of the Kingdom' should be struck down because they burden [the Witnesses'] right to worship the Deity in their own fashion and to spread the Gospel as they understand it."

In its subsequent term, the Court consolidated several appeals involving licensing fees and evangelism by Jehovah's Witnesses into MARTIN V. STRUTHERS/MURDOCK V. PENNSYLVANIA. Since the Court was revisiting this issue, it also ordered a reargument of the *Jones I* case. *Murdock* and the reargued *Jones I* (now *Jones II*) were decided in May 1943. *Jones II* simply states that for the reasons announced in *Murdock*, *Jones v. Opelika* (1942) is vacated, and the convictions of the Jehovah's Witnesses reversed. Justice Douglas wrote the majority opinion in *Murdock*, and stipulated that the license requirements at issue were essentially taxes on conduct protected by the First Amendment. As he noted, "the power to tax the exercise of a privilege is the power to control or suppress its enjoyment. . . . Those who can tax the exercise of this religious practice can make its exercise so costly as to deprive it of the resources necessary for its maintenance. . . . Those who can deprive religious groups of their colporteurs can take from them a part of the vital power of the press which has survived from the Reformation." Thus, the First Amendment free speech, press, and free exercise clauses exempt evangelists,

colporteurs, and the like from state-imposed financial regulations that target their evangelistic activity and conduct.

—John Blakeman

judicial review

Judicial review is the power of the judiciary to invalidate government action on constitutional grounds and renders the U.S. Supreme Court the final arbiter of how the federal Constitution is to be interpreted.

The first Supreme Court acknowledgment of the power of judicial review is found in Chief Justice John Marshall's opinion in *Marbury v. Madison* (1803). Scholars disagree, however, as to the nature of *Marbury*'s significance. Some hold that *Marbury* was innovative, even daring, in proclaiming the power of judicial review. Others consider *Marbury* to be nothing more than the ratification of a foregone conclusion, the long-awaited official recognition of views already generally accepted. Still a third group view *Marbury* as nothing more than judicial review's point of entry into Supreme Court jurisprudence, a starting point for later, drastic expansion. Despite these divergent views, *Marbury* remains the touchstone by reference to which the history of judicial review is analyzed.

Since the Constitution does not expressly provide for or mention judicial review, constitutional historians have also inquired as to whether the framers of the Constitution intended the judiciary to possess this power or whether the judiciary has usurped it.

Scholarly disagreement over the historical origins of *Marbury,* and thus of judicial review, is even more pronounced. One scholar maintains that *Marbury* had no significant historical source other than the political motives of Chief Justice John Marshall. Others locate *Marbury*'s historical roots in the theologically and biblically based legal principles of colonial MASSACHUSETTS; or in the colonial experience of parliamentary despotism; in the colonial experience of subjection to the Privy Council; in the era of the Articles of Confederation; in the early constitutional era; in certain aspects of John Marshall's educational and legal background; in the confluence of several influences, including the nature of early parliaments, ancient ideas of fundamental law, and the change from legislative to popular sovereignty; in the English Common Law; in natural law principles; or in the colonists' struggle for independence.

None of these theories, fully accounts for why the judiciary, in particular, as opposed to the other branches of government, is the ultimate arbiter of constitutionality. Ironically, in a culture whose political theory has long been secular in nature, the origins of the judiciary's role as final constitutional arbiter can best be traced to the theology of John Calvin. Calvin opposed the idea of private citizens resisting civil authorities, for in Calvin's theology the civil authorities had been established by God. On the other hand, according to Calvin, those same civil authorities were duty-bound to protect the citizenry from tyrannical rulers. Calvin's sense of the duty of civil authorities to protect the people from tyrannical monarchs was transposed at the time of the American Revolution into the duty of legislators to protect the people from tyrannical monarchs and, shortly thereafter, into the duty of the judiciary to protect the people from tyrannical legislators (Ball 1998 and forthcoming). This final step in the emergence of judicial review from the theology of John Calvin was taken in November 1782 by Virginia jurist George Wythe, John Marshall's law professor, in *Commonwealth v. Caton* (1782). Just three months later, Marshall became the first to annul an act of a legislature on constitutional grounds in what is known as the *Posey* affair.

See also CALVINISM.

Further reading: Ball, David T. *John Calvin's Contribution to the Emergence of Judicial Review: Source of the Judicial Duty to Disobey Unconstitutional Laws.* Ann Arbor: University of Michigan Press, 1998; ———. *John Calvin and the Emergence of Judicial Review.* Lewiston, N.Y.: Edwin Mellen Press, forthcoming; Crosskey, William W. *Politics and the Constitution in the History of the United States.* Chicago: University of Chicago Press, 1953; Haskins, George L. *Foundations of Power: John Marshall, 1801–15.* In *The Oliver Wendell Holmes Devise History of the Supreme Court in the United States.* Vol. 2. Edited by Paul A. Freund. New York: Macmillan, 1981.

—David T. Ball

just war

The just-war tradition reflects the classical and historical Christian teachings on the use of military force. That tradition is known by the Latin terms *jus ad bellum* (literally, justice toward war) and *jus in bello* (justice in war). The *jus ad bellum* criteria provide guidance about the resort to war. The *jus in bello* criteria place moral restraints on the means used to conduct war.

Jus in bello consists in the criteria of proportionality of means and discrimination (or noncombatant immunity). The criterion of proportionality of means places restrictions on gratuitous and otherwise unnecessary violence. The criterion of discrimination prohibits the direct and intentional targeting of noncombatants. The Christian just-war tradition has been embodied in positive international law and military manuals on the law of war.

Classically, the *jus ad bellum* requires that before war can be waged, there must be legitimate authority, just cause, and right intention. Each of these criteria is related to a fundamental political good: *right authority* is related to the political good of order, *just cause* is related to the political good of justice, and *right intention* is related to the political good of peace. As the tradition developed, other criteria were added to the *jus ad bellum* criteria as prudential considerations to guide statesmen when they contemplated the use of force. Is there

a *reasonable chance for success*? Will the overall good exceed the harm done (*proportionality*)? Have other means to redress a harm been attempted (*last resort*)? Can peace among the combatants really be achieved (*the end of peace*)?

Traditionally, the criteria for *just cause* explicitly included one or more of three possibilities: defense against wrongful attack, retaking something wrongly taken, or the punishment of evil. Since the Peace of Westphalia (1648), just cause has been understood in international law almost exclusively as just defense—although in recent years, a more expansive concept of just cause has been developed in light of attempts to justify humanitarian intervention for particularly egregious human rights abuses. *Right intention* has since the time of Saint Augustine meant, negatively, that war should not be undertaken because of implacable hatred, personal glory, or blood lust. Positively, right intention has insisted that the aim of war is to bring about peace—neither a utopian peace nor the peace of the new heavens and the new earth, but as Augustine called it, a tranquility of order (*tranquillitas ordinis*) in international relations. *Legitimate authority* classically meant that the right to employ force was reserved to persons or communities with no political superior—that is, to sovereign entities.

In light of the war on international terrorism, it is worth recalling that in asking whether war could be waged justly, Thomas Aquinas, who summarized a century of Christian reflection on the subject, began not with just cause, but with legitimate authority, citing as biblical support Romans 13:1–6. By legitimate authority, Aquinas (and classical Christian thought, more generally) was referring to a political authority to which there was no superior. Beginning with Saint Augustine and developing throughout the Middle Ages, Christian thinkers sought to curb violence by declaring illegitimate any use of force by subordinate nobles, private soldiers, criminals, and the church. When confronted with a militaristic Germanic culture in which princes frequently engaged in and gloried in combat for private ends, Christian thinkers repeatedly insisted that warfare was a *public* issue. War could not merely be an extreme tool of private parties but had to be a legal instrument, a part of the coercive power of law itself. Historically and theoretically, securing a public monopoly on the use of force was a necessary (though not sufficient) precondition for a peaceful and civilized society. From this perspective, the freelance terrorism of our time can be regarded as a direct assault on this achievement of civilization.

Thus, for classical Christian just-war theory, it is not merely the potential destructiveness of modern terrorism that raises heightened moral concern. Rather, terrorism by its nature aims to undermine the goods of justice, order, and peace, which are secured by political authority. In attacking these political goods, terrorism thus attacks every human being who benefits from them, and the nation-states in which they reside as citizens.

Diverse theological traditions—Roman Catholic, Anglican, DUTCH REFORMED TRADITION, Lutheran—have adopted the just-war tradition as a central tenet of teaching in Christian moral and political theology. The tradition has faced two competing moral views. The first might be called Machiavellian realism, which rejects the idea that war can be a just and moral enterprise. For the realist, the *resort* to war, when all is said and done, is justified by the requirements of Realpolitik and is merely an extension of day-to-day politics. And for the realist, the *conduct* of war is, in principle, subject to no moral limitation.

The other challenge to the just-war tradition is pacifism, which involves the moral renunciation of violence *tout court* and which views military service as incompatible with Christian discipleship. Between PACIFISM and realism lies the just-war tradition, an understanding of statecraft in which the use of force in the service of justice, order, and peace is both permitted and restrained and in which military service is a legitimate and honorable Christian vocation.

—Keith Pavlischek

K

Kahane, Meir (1932–1990) *radical activist*

As the founder and long-term leader of the JEWISH DEFENSE LEAGUE (JDL), in the 1970s Meir Kahane became a disturbing presence for mainstream Judaism in both the United States and ISRAEL. The JDL came to be associated in the minds of its critics with terrorist activities. As its leader, Kahane, who was ordained a rabbi and completed law school in 1956, advocated the position that Jews will always be victims until they adopt a more aggressive posture toward their tormentors. The Soviet Union was one of the JDL's primary targets because of its refusal to allow Soviet Jews to immigrate. JDL operatives in New York City sometimes pushed Soviet diplomats stationed at the United Nations into busy streets, with the result that a number of them were injured. In other instances, JDL groups harassed Soviet journalists.

Kahane was uninhibited when it came to denouncing those whom he considered to be "establishment Jews." Authentic Jews, he asserted, could live only in Israel. Kahane did not distinguish between Jews and Zionists because he regarded them as inseparable. Jews had been divinely instructed, according to Kahane, to settle the land of Israel. Thus, anyone who opposes Jewish settlement is a sinner; similarly, any Jew who does not move to Israel is a failed Jew who has been successfully assimilated into gentile culture.

Kahane practiced what he preached and moved to Israel in 1971. He immediately entered Israeli politics, but most of the Israeli political mainstream shunned him. Even the religious parties, presumably his natural allies, found him too extreme. Nevertheless, Kahane formed a radical right-wing party, Kach, and managed to get elected to the Israeli parliament (Knesset) in 1984, where he served a single four-year term. He might have been able to win a second term if the Israeli government had not banned Kach for its radical and inflammatory ideology. Kahane's movement called for the removal of non-Jews from Israel, a state, he maintained, that included the West Bank territories that were occupied by the Israeli military during the Six-Day War in 1967.

It is easy to conclude from Kahane's writings and speeches that he was a political and theological radical. However, Kahane seemed to consider himself as a biblical scholar, quoting the Torah to justify and explain the necessity of a Jewish presence in Israel based on the entirety of the ancient Davidic kingdom. In this sense, Kahane thought of Israel as a land divinely promised to the Jewish people, not one to be partitioned between Jews and non-Jews. Much of Kahane's work was polemical, calling for the retention of historic and biblical Israel. He was demonstrably distrustful of Christians, who, Kahane was convinced, relentlessly persecuted and occasionally massacred Jews for the better part of two millennia, and of Muslims, whom he believed to desire another Jewish Holocaust (in the form of the destruction of the state of Israel).

Through most of his adult life and right up to his murder on November 5, 1990, by an Egyptian American, Kahane refused to consider negotiated compromises with Palestinians as either necessary or justified. His views also contained a racist element. Even Israeli Arabs were not safe from his determination that Israel should be purified by ridding it of all non-Jewish blood, an activity he believed had been pursued during biblical times. Most Israelis worried that Kahane's views would achieve nothing more than the further alienation of a fifth of the country's citizenry.

There is ample evidence in Israel of a Kahane legacy. Zoe Artzenu (This Is Our Land) is an organization founded after Kahane's political party was banned; a part of its program is a call for the removal of all Arabs from the West Bank. Around 450 militants live in a fortified quarter of the West Bank city of Hebron, surrounded by 200,000 Palestinians. Some of the militants are fond of writing graffiti calling for Arab expulsion or death in Palestinian neighborhoods. The breakdown of the peace process during the fall of 2000 and resultant daily violence between Israelis and Palestinians suggest that Kahane's political philosophy might be gaining in popularity among Israeli Jews, more than Kahane could have imagined during his lifetime.

See also ZIONISM.

—Martin W. Slann

Kennedy, John Fitzgerald (1917–1963) *U.S.*
president

John F. "Jack" Kennedy was the epitome of an American political tragedy in many respects. Jack Kennedy never actively sought the presidency of the United States, nor fame as a war hero, nor a Pulitzer prize. Yet these are the achievements and accolades for which he is best remembered. At the same time, he became infamous for leading a lifestyle of wealth and privilege, and his moral fortitude was questioned because of allegations of constant womanizing. Ultimately, though, he is enshrined as one of four American presidents to have been assassinated in office.

It was precisely this contrast that seemed to define John F. Kennedy's tenure as president. As the first Roman Catholic president of the United States, Kennedy was constantly under the microscope. Questions of allegiance to the hierarchy of the Catholic Church came to the fore during his campaign for the presidency. Nevertheless, Kennedy's administration was defined by a series of other national and international events that characterized his presidency, rather than his Catholicism.

John Fitzgerald Kennedy was one of nine children born to Joseph and Rose Kennedy. The Kennedys were a family of wealth and power unprecedented among American families. Rising from an Irish immigrant heritage, the Kennedys rose to success in the saloon and liquor business, eventually moving into banking and, later, politics. In an effort to rise above prejudices against Irish Americans and Catholics, the Kennedys moved from Boston to an upper-class suburb of New York City. The Kennedy family power base thus expanded to a major world financial center, where their fortunes kept growing. While failing in his own pursuit of a career in elected office, Kennedy's father sought to pursue a life of politics vicariously through his sons.

Jack Kennedy attended Harvard University, where he was a mediocre student defined more by his social graces and affable personality. Upon graduation from Harvard, Kennedy joined the navy and was assigned to naval intelligence. Long desiring a combat-related post, Kennedy was reassigned to command a PT boat in the South Pacific during World War II, where he held the rank of ensign. His command of PT-109 and subsequent actions related to surviving a sinking at the hands of a Japanese destroyer while bringing his crew to safety painted the picture of Kennedy as a bona fide war hero.

After the war, Kennedy returned to fulfill his father's political ambition. He established residency in Boston and was elected to Congress by a convincing margin in 1946. Like his Harvard experience, Kennedy's performance as a member of Congress was unremarkable. In 1946, he was diagnosed with Addison's disease, which contributed to a series of health problems with which he would struggle for the remainder of his life. Yet despite frail health and Kennedy family indiscretions, John F. Kennedy ran for the U.S. Senate in 1952. Kennedy swept to victory over the formidable Henry Cabot Lodge. While recovering from debilitating back surgery, Senator Kennedy wrote *Profiles in Courage,* which subsequently won acclaim and a Pulitzer prize (despite a cloud of skepticism about whether Kennedy actually did much of the writing).

His credentials and status as a successful politician, wealthy socialite, war hero, and now prize-winning author propelled Kennedy toward a nomination for vice president of the United States at the 1956 Democratic National Convention. He lost his bid in part because of his less-than-stellar record in Congress. Four years later, though, the story was different. With his family's wealth and access to major media outlets, Kennedy swept to victory on the first ballot in the Democratic National Convention in 1960. His religious affiliation had been an issue in his pursuit of the nomination, and his primary opponent, Senator Hubert Humphrey, emphasized that Kennedy had won many of his past victories in predominantly Roman Catholic congressional districts, which Humphrey saw as a potential liability in any general election. Nevertheless, Kennedy's ability to energize the national convention audience with his vision of a New Frontier riveted Democrats and attracted a nationwide following as well.

In one of the closest presidential elections in American history, Kennedy defeated RICHARD M. NIXON by winning six key states in the South, including Texas. This victory was largely the result of popular Texas senator Lyndon Johnson serving as his running mate. Despite vocal criticism of Kennedy's Roman Catholic faith, the issue proved manageable. Evidence suggests that even MARTIN LUTHER KING JR.'s

John Fitzgerald Kennedy *(John F. Kennedy Library)*

family, whose support was pivotal to securing the votes of African Americans, only reluctantly backed Kennedy's presidential bid because of their concerns about his religious beliefs. In fact, it was only because of Kennedy's personal charm and appeal that the Kings were convinced to support Kennedy's candidacy. Kennedy also helped to alleviate concerns over his Roman Catholic faith by addressing a convention of SOUTHERN BAPTIST CONVENTION leaders at the Greater Houston Ministerial Association in 1960. He tackled the issue head-on and asserted his belief in an absolute SEPARATION OF CHURCH AND STATE. With those assurances and Johnson on the ticket, Kennedy prevailed in the key southern states. Yet it is also clear that Kennedy's ability to carry 78 percent of the Roman Catholic vote assured him of victory.

As president, Kennedy lost no time in advancing a global agenda for the United States by implementing a series of key New Frontier programs and appealing to public demands to match the Soviet Union in the so-called space race by proposing that the United States land a human on the moon by the end of the decade. Kennedy promoted the call for the United States to assume the role of "leader of the free world" to fight communism wherever it existed. This fervent ANTICOMMUNIST policy led the United States to support the ill-fated Bay of Pigs invasion of Cuba, an escalation of the war in Vietnam, and the standoff with the Soviet Union over its deployment of nuclear missile sites in Cuba. The Cuban Missile Crisis was the first time that two major nuclear powers came close to war. After tense negotiations, the Soviets agreed to withdraw the missiles if the United States did the same with its missiles in Turkey, which bordered the Soviet Union. Kennedy emerged from the crisis as a decisive president and effective world leader. At the same time, the Kennedy administration pushed for the establishment of the Peace Corps and the Agency for International Development. It also appealed to individual citizens and the U.S. government to reach out to developing nations desperate for financial assistance.

Domestically, President Kennedy had a mixed record. Although his administration is credited with promoting civil rights for African Americans, the record is not entirely positive. At first, Kennedy urged African-American leaders to go slowly, but he was quick to see the tide of protest from both African Americans and whites, which prompted him to send federal marshals to protect "Freedom Rider" protesters, who were testing the integration of interstate travel and to uphold integration orders: throughout the South. Kennedy signed an executive order to expedite the hiring of African Americans in government, and he endorsed the MARCH ON WASHINGTON, which brought 250,000 to Washington, D.C., to push for civil rights on August 28, 1963. Before his assassination in 1963, Kennedy introduced a comprehensive civil rights bill, which led to the passage of the Civil Rights Act of 1964 soon after his death.

Kennedy occasionally turned to his religious fabric for guidance or resolve in advancing certain policies. For example, when he appeared on national television to support the cause of civil rights, he described it as a moral issue. He invoked Scripture to acknowledge that it was imperative for a good society to solve some problems.

John F. Kennedy cultivated a stylish image along with his fashionable wife, Jacqueline Lee Bouvier Kennedy, and their two young children. During his presidency, the White House was showcased as a center for culture and the arts, which added to the image of a wholesome and perhaps idealistic vision of the Kennedy presidency that came to be likened to Camelot. Yet this stood in sharp contrast to the mostly hidden but soon to be aired rumors of sexual liaisons, questionable underworld contacts, and a less than family-oriented or "churchgoing" White House.

John F. Kennedy's appearance on the political scene ended as unexpectedly as it had begun. On November 22, 1963, the president was assassinated while riding in a motorcade in Dallas, Texas. The Kennedy administration may be remembered as a series of firsts. The youngest president and the first Roman Catholic elected to office became the youngest to die in that office. Kennedy's historic call to public service, when he challenged citizens to "ask not what your country can do for you, but what you can do for your country," was indicative of a new era that called for an engaged citizenry, led by a young, active president. It was ironic that the Kennedy presidency ended on a tragic note, leaving behind a lasting memory of a simpler time and a longing for the idealism epitomized by the youthful Kennedy.

See also CATHOLICS AND THE DEMOCRATIC PARTY; RELIGION IN THE 1960 PRESIDENTIAL ELECTION.

—Robert W. Smith

King, Martin Luther, Jr. (1929–1968) *civil rights leader*

Martin Luther King Jr. was born in Atlanta, Georgia, on January 15, 1929, to Martin Luther King Sr., pastor of the Ebenezer Baptist Church, and Alberta King, a school teacher. At 15 he entered Morehouse Colleges through an early-admissions program for gifted high school students, and graduated in 1948 as an ordained minister, with a bachelor's degree at age 19. He attended Crozer Theological Seminary in Pennsylvania, earning a bachelor of divinity degree in June 1951. While at the seminary, he encountered the teachings of Mohandas Gandhi and began combining his theology with a commitment to nonviolent disobedience as a strategy for political change.

King followed the theological doctrine of "personalism," which "gave metaphysical and philosophical grounding for the idea of a personal God, and it gave me a metaphysical basis for the dignity and worth of all human personality." Personalism led King to believe that "there is no graded scale of essential worth; there is no divine right of one race which differs from the divine right of another. . . . The worth of an individual does not lie in the measure of his intellect, his racial origin, or his social position. Human worth lies in relatedness to God." This philosophy dovetailed with a commitment to non-

Martin Luther King Jr. *(National Archives)*

violent direct action that King learned from Gandhi: actively oppose evil; appeal to adversaries through understanding; attack the evil itself, not those perpetrating evil; willingly accept suffering without engaging in retaliation; love, and refuse to hate, opponents; and believe that God is on the side of justice.

King was named the most outstanding student in his class and awarded a fellowship for graduate study at Boston University, where he earned a Ph.D. in 1955. In Boston, King met Coretta Scott, who was studying at the New England Conservatory of Music. They married on June 18, 1953. The following year, King became minister of the Dexter Avenue Baptist Church in Montgomery, Alabama.

In Montgomery, King emerged at age 26 as a national leader in the CIVIL RIGHTS MOVEMENT when he was elected president of the Montgomery Improvement Association (MIA) and helped mobilize the Montgomery BUS BOYCOTT of 1955. The successful boycott led King and associates like RALPH ABERNATHY to form the SOUTHERN CHRISTIAN LEADERSHIP CONFERENCE (SCLC) in 1957 to coordinate local black churches and mobilize the nonviolent direct action of the civil rights movement. In 1959, he resigned as pastor of the

Dexter Avenue Church and moved to Atlanta to devote his time and energy to leading the SCLC.

With the SCLC, King led protest marches, merchant boycotts, lunch counter sit-ins, and voter registration drives across the South in cities such as Albany, Georgia (1961–62); Birmingham, Alabama (1962–63); St. Petersburg, Florida (1964); and Selma, Alabama (1965), and was arrested and jailed numerous times.

One of his most famous moments was his "I Have a Dream" speech, given at the 1963 MARCH ON WASHINGTON for Jobs and Freedom, in which he called for civic equality based on the principle that people should be judged by their character, not the color of their skin. This march, attended by an estimated 250,000 people, helped push Congress to pass the Civil Rights Act of 1964. In 1964, King was named *Time* magazine's Man of the Year, and became the youngest recipient of the Nobel Peace Prize.

In 1965, King led a civil rights march from Selma to Birmingham, Alabama, to promote voting rights. When the marchers reached the Edmund Pettis Bridge, Sheriff James Clark attacked the marchers with tear gas and billy clubs. The nationally televised images of nonviolent protesters beaten by state troopers spurred President Lyndon Johnson to call Congress into a special session, which eventually produced the 1965 Voting Rights Act.

In 1966, King attempted to bring the Civil Rights movement to northern cities when he temporarily moved into a housing project in Chicago and led an open-housing march in Cicero, Illinois, that was met with mob violence. The resistance King met in Chicago signaled that northern segregation was not going to be changed by the same nonviolent tactics that had succeeded in the South. Further, King's difficulty in maintaining nonviolence signaled declining support for his philosophy among disillusioned blacks, some of whom joined black power organizations such as the Black Panther Party that formed in 1966.

Between 1963 and 1968, King faced critics from all sides. Against segregationists who defended the status quo, he argued that the laws upholding segregation were unjust because they distorted human personality, were imposed on one group without being imposed on all groups, and were created through an unfair process that excluded black people by denying their right to vote. Against white moderates who suggested that King was pushing too far, too fast, King argued that "freedom is never voluntarily given by the oppressor; it must be demanded by the oppressed." Moreover, King decried the white moderate who was "more devoted to 'order' than to justice; who prefers a negative peace which is the absence of tension to a positive peace which is the presence of justice" as an obstacle to change. Against blacks dissatisfied with nonviolent protest who advocated armed self-defense, King steadfastly argued that nonviolent disobedience could produce "creative tension" in which negotiation for change could occur—this was done by appealing to the conscience of, not hating, one's opponent. King maintained that blacks' integration into American society as equals could be achieved at the same time that black people maintained self-respect and pride.

By 1968, King had publicly stated his opposition to U.S. involvement in the VIETNAM WAR, advocated a major restructuring of U.S. economic resources funded through a $12 billion Economic Bill of Rights, and began planning a multiracial Poor People's Campaign for economic justice. But then on April 4, 1968, in Memphis, Tennessee, while supporting striking black sanitation workers, King was assassinated.

Four days after King's assassination, Representative John Conyers introduced legislation to create a national holiday in his honor. Fifteen years later, on November 2, 1983, President RONALD REAGAN signed the bill making the third Monday in January a national holiday honoring King's birthday. The first national King holiday was observed on January 20, 1986.

King's goal of an economically just America has not been realized, but his ideal that people be judged not by the color of their skin but by the content of their character has been invoked in various debates, such as about affirmative action, and by various groups, including other racial/ethnic minorities and religiously motivated groups, such as the CHRISTIAN COALITION.

Further reading: Ansbro, John. *Martin Luther King, Jr.: The Making of a Mind.* Maryknoll, N.Y.: Orbis, 1982; King, Martin Luther, Jr. *Why We Can't Wait.* New York: Mentor, 1964; ———. *Where Do We Go from Here: Chaos or Community?* Boston: Beacon Press, 1968; ———. *Stride toward Freedom.* New York: Harper and Row, 1958.

—Gregory W. Streich

Kiryas Joel Village School District, Board of Education of v. Grument 512 U.S. 687 (1994)

Kiryas Joel Village, located in New York, was formed as a religious commune of Satmar Hasidic Jews. HASIDIC is a very strict form of Judaism, enforcing many ultra-Orthodox rules and regulations. The individuals who constructed Kiryas Joel Village in New York intentionally formed its boundaries under the general village incorporation law of the state of New York to exclude anyone who was not of the Satmar Hasidic faith. The village fell within the Monroe-Woodbury Central School District until a special state statute outlined a separate district that followed proper village lines. Although the statute gives a locally elected school board plenary authority over primary and secondary education in the village, the board ran a special education program for handicapped children. Other village children attended private religious schools that did not offer special educational services. Shortly before the new district began operations, respondents and others brought this action, claiming that the statue violated the ESTABLISHMENT CLAUSE of the First Amendment.

The primary issue in this case involved freedom of religion and whether a state may designate a special school district

intended to serve a particular religious community, such as the Satmar Hasidim. Previous establishment clause jurisprudence required that government maintain a neutral stance toward religion, therefore not creating any form of excessive entanglement with a particular group, and it prevented the government from allocating its power to a religious group. All the children in Kiryas Joel Village School District who did not require special education services attended private religious schools. The purpose of the law was to accommodate the requests of village residents that their children not be educated outside the parameters of the Kiryas Joel Village. The trial and appellate courts attacked the legislation, presuming that the statute endorsed a religion, thereby violating the establishment clause. The U.S. Supreme Court agreed with the lower courts that the legislation unconstitutionally endorsed a religion, and held that the establishment clause prevents a state from entrusting its "civic authority" to a group chosen on religious principles.

Many observers view this decision as a possible replacement for the *Lemon* test, set forth in *LEMON V. KURTZMAN,* for reviewing cases involving establishment issues. Justice David Souter wrote the opinion for the Supreme Court, finding that "the law setting up the district amounted to impermissible favoritism toward religion in general and toward one sect in particular, in violation of the First Amendment's prohibition against the establishment of religion." Justice Souter wrote that the state law violated "a principle at the heart of the Establishment Clause, that government should not prefer one religion to another, or religion to irreligion."

—Ryan S. Solomon

Knights of Columbus

The Knights of Columbus is a Roman Catholic fraternal and insurance society founded by Father Michael J. McGivney, a priest from New Haven, Connecticut. Incorporated on March 29, 1882, the founders envisioned an American Catholic insurance and benevolence society with fraternal aspects, including ceremonials designed, in part, to attract Catholic men away from FREEMASONRY. Established at a time when Catholics were a largely immigrant group and American Nativism predominated, the Knights of Columbus sought to reinforce both Catholic and American identity by recognizing the Catholic contribution to American society, symbolized by Christopher Columbus's arrival in the Americas. By the early 20th century, the Knights of Columbus had expanded throughout the United States and into Canada, Mexico, Puerto Rico, and the Philippines. Since 1925, the Knights have sponsored a youth society for boys, the Columbian Squires. The Knights of Columbus publishes a monthly magazine, *Columbia* (formerly *Columbiad* [1893–1920]), and sponsors the Catholic Information Service. The largest Catholic lay association worldwide, today its members number over 1.6 million.

From its earliest days, the Knights of Columbus has been active in political and civic life. The Knights supported the

United States in the Spanish-American War but criticized America's ensuing imperialism. In World War I, the organization was granted permission to provide spiritual and recreational services to the armed forces, with emphasis on the spiritual needs of Catholics. The Knights sponsored and ran recreation "huts" at army training camps and in Europe as a counterpart to the efforts of the YMCA, the SALVATION ARMY, and the Jewish Welfare Committee. After the war, the Knights provided employment services for soldiers and established a Historical Commission intending to counter Nativism by documenting the contributions of ethnic groups to American society. In the 1920s and 1930s, the Knights failed to persuade President FRANKLIN DELANO ROOSEVELT to alter his Good Neighbor Policy in defense of the suppressed Mexican Catholic Church.

In the 1950s, the Knights of Columbus coordinated an ANTICOMMUNIST speaker's bureau and publicity campaign. The Knights of Columbus participated in the successful 1954 legislative campaign to include the words "under God" in the Pledge of Allegiance to the American flag. Although Knights participated in the CIVIL RIGHTS MOVEMENT, the organization was criticized for its own segregationist practices. While segregation was never part of its constitution, integrated councils were few, and in 1964, membership-voting rules were reformed to encourage integration.

Since the 1960s, the Knights of Columbus has focused on social and family issues promoting Catholic Church teachings. Notably, the Knights provided funding and voice for anti-ABORTION activities and anti-PORNOGRAPHY campaigns and pursued issues pertaining to the relation of church and state, supporting PRAYER IN PUBLIC SCHOOLS and tax relief for families that pay private-school tuition.

While remaining an independent, Catholic lay association, the Knights of Columbus has provided financial assistance for a variety of Catholic projects, including loans for the renovation of churches and support for CATHOLIC CHARITIES and other institutions, including the Catholic University of America in Washington, D.C. The Knights of Columbus has shown support for the papacy by contributing to the pope's special charities, funding Vatican radio and television projects, and contributing to the repair of St. Peter's Basilica in Rome. While remaining independent from the UNITED STATES CONFERENCE OF CATHOLIC BISHOPS, the Knights also provided support for American bishops' efforts, especially for pro-life activities and Catholic education.

Through local councils, the Knights of Columbus provides a wide variety of volunteer services, including pro-life activities, support for the Special Olympics and other services for the handicapped, blood drives, and voting campaigns. Local councils may also have ladies auxiliaries associated with them. Knights of the Fourth Degree are recognizable in their service as honor guards and color corps at a variety of church and civic functions.

The history of the Knights of Columbus is an example of the growing self-confidence of American Catholics in civic and political life. While staunchly patriotic, this has not prevented the Knights from criticizing American policy. While American nativist sentiment and activity have frequently targeted the Knights of Columbus (including the recurring appearance of an inflammatory and inauthentic oath of the Knights' Fourth Degree), the Knights responded repeatedly by asserting the legitimacy of American Catholicism.

See also ROMAN CATHOLIC CHURCH.

Further reading: Kauffman, Christopher J. *Faith and Fraternalism, The History of the Knights of Columbus 1882–1982.* New York: Harper and Row, 1982; ———. *Patriotism and Fraternalism in the Knights of Columbus: A History of the Fourth Degree.* New York: Crossroad, 2001.

—Susan Gleason Anderson

Know-Nothing (American) Party

The Know-Nothing Party was formed in 1849 in New York City to oppose the influx of mostly Roman Catholic immigrants, particularly those from Germany and Ireland, who had arrived in large waves throughout the early 19th century. The party's distinctive name stemmed from members' efforts to keep information about the group secret. In response to questions from outsiders, supporters would reply, "I know nothing." Hence, New York newspaper editor Horace Greeley soon dubbed the group the "know-nothing party." The party, formally named the American Party, began as an alliance of secret societies, one of the more prominent being the Order of the Star Spangled Banner, and remained a force on the national political scene for about a decade. Party membership most commonly was restricted to native-born, and primarily rural, Evangelical Protestants.

Important rallying issues for party members included their perceived threats of immigrants competing for jobs and creating additional tax burdens. Party leaders saw immigrants as a menace to American values, institutions, and the nation's social fabric. Primary targets of their fears were Roman Catholic immigrants, particularly those arriving from Ireland. Subsequent party platforms called for the implementation of such measures as allowing only native-born citizens to vote and hold office, requiring 21 years of continuous residence as a prerequisite for citizenship, and using the Protestant King James Version of the Bible in public schools. Yet party statements additionally supported separation of church and state and (reportedly with the perceived influence of the pope in mind) called for all elected officials to pledge allegiance to no foreign power.

Hence, the Know-Nothing Party was known primarily as a protest movement fearing widespread social and economic changes stemming largely from the industrialization of the nation. News of their intense hatred of Roman Catholics and first-generation immigrants quickly spread and attracted sufficient political support for the party to the extent that it contributed to the collapse of the Whig Party and proved crucial in helping the Democrats win the presidency for James Buchanan. However, helping the Democrats certainly was not the goal of the Know-Nothing Party. They tended to view the Democrats as too eager to win the support of the growing wave of Irish Catholic immigrants and thus largely indifferent to the growing problems of native-born Protestants. Likewise, Know-Nothing partisans additionally scorned Whig leaders for their belated efforts to win the support of Irish Catholic immigrants.

The high point of the Know-Nothing Party's political influence came in the mid-1850s. With its political base in New York and neighboring northeastern states, the party in 1854 won many state offices in MASSACHUSETTS, including the governorship and control of the state legislature. The party also attracted significant numbers of anti–Roman Catholic and anti-immigrant voters in New York and MARYLAND, plus such western states as Kentucky and California. The next year Know-Nothing candidates won governorship in five additional states and lost to the Democrats in New York by only four-tenths of a percent.

In 1856, the party's national convention was deeply divided over the slavery issue. Delegates opposing slavery, primarily from Northern states, walked out of the convention after failing to win passage of a declaration banning the extension of slavery in western territories. Proslavery delegates subsequently nominated a former Whig president, Millard Fillmore, as the party's presidential candidate. That fall, Fillmore attracted almost 22 percent of the popular vote while carrying just one state, Maryland.

Several factors contributed to the quick demise of the Know-Nothings by the 1860 elections. Deep divisions over slavery, a failure to win sufficient offices to enact their programs, and a growing reputation (likely nourished by rival political parties) for inciting violence all contributed to the collapse of the party's coalition, as voters abandoned the Know-Nothings primarily to join the up-and-coming Republican Party. Finally, a dramatic upturn in the economy of several European nations in the mid-1850s greatly reduced the influx of Roman Catholic immigrants by the late 1850s, thereby lessening some of the harsh feelings against them.

See also ABOLITIONIST MOVEMENT.

Further reading: Anbinder, Tyler. *Nativism and Slavery: The Northern Know-Nothings and the Politics of the 1850s.* New York: Oxford University Press, 1992; Billington, Ray A. *The Protestant Crusade, 1800–1860: A Study of the Origins of American Nativism.* Chicago: University of Chicago Press, 1964; Overdike, W. Darrell. *The Know-Nothing Party in the South.* Baton Rouge: Louisiana State University Press, 1950.

—Robert E. Dewhirst

Kosovo conflict (1999)

From March through June 1999, NATO bombed Serbia in response to evidence that its president, Slobodan Milosevic, had launched a campaign of ethnic cleansing against the Albanians in the Yugoslav autonomous region of Kosovo. This area of eastern Europe had been filled with ethnic tension as its diverse populations sought to forge new identities and/or reclaim ancient identities in the wake of the demise of the Yugoslav state. The three major ethnoreligious communities in this region are Serbs (predominantly Orthodox Christian) Croats (predominantly Roman Catholic), and Bosnians (Muslims, Orthodox Serbs, and Catholic Croatians). Croatian and Slovenian declarations of independence in 1991, the secession of Croats and Muslims in Bosnia-Herzegovina in 1992, and the Bosnian War (1991–95) foreshadowed the Kosovo conflict.

The 600th anniversary of the Battle of Kosovo (1389) provided Milosevic with an opportunity to promote himself as a Serb nationalist, not merely a Communist leader of the past. Milosevic fanned the flames of Serbian nationalism to justify ethnic cleansing. Meanwhile, the people of Kosovo, who were 90 percent ethnic Albanian, began to demand greater autonomy. Milosevic responded by claiming the centrality of Kosovo to Serbian history, by referring to Kosovo as the "Serbian Jerusalem," and by promoting Serbian migration into the region. Kosovo Albanians declared independence from Serbia and named Ibrahim Rugova as president of the Democratic League of Kosovo. Rugova, who claimed to be a follower of Mohandas Gandhi's philosophy of nonviolent resistance, increasingly lost influence to more militant ethnic Albanians, who formed the Kosovo Liberation Army (KLA). Milosevic reacted to the KLA by increasing the repression of ethnic Albanians. As evidence of ethnic cleansing mounted, NATO, with strong support from U.S. president WILLIAM JEFFERSON CLINTON, launched air strikes against targets in Serbia.

During the Kosovo conflict, Serb forces in Kosovo killed between 7,000 and 10,000 ethnic Albanians. Nearly 1.5 million more ethnic Albanians fled from their homes and became refugees as a result of the systematic intimidation by Serbian military and paramilitary groups. After Milosevic signed a U.N.-approved peace agreement on June 3, 1999, many Serbian officials were charged with war crimes at The Hague, and many more face prosecution. Militant Albanians, meanwhile, have fanned the flames of ethnoreligious hatred by attacking Serbs who remained in Kosovo.

Most religious communities in the United States responded quite predictably to the Kosovo Crisis. Muslim organizations tended to call for bolder actions by the United States and/or NATO to stop ethnic cleansing. Many Jews, who had vowed that there would never be another Holocaust, identified with the ethnic Albanians and called for humanitarian intervention. On the other hand, the historic peace churches (QUAKERS, BRETHREN, MENNONITES) and the EASTERN ORTHODOX Christian community strongly opposed a military solution to this conflict. Orthodox churches in the United States vacillated between condemning the actions of the Serbian government, as the Serbian Orthodox Church itself had done, and blaming the media for presenting a distorted view of this conflict.

Appealing to its theory of JUST WAR, leaders in the ROMAN CATHOLIC CHURCH argued that the crisis in Kosovo demanded a serious response by the international community, but they simultaneously warned that only dialogue, authentic self-government, and protection of human rights for all minority populations would foster a lasting peace in the region. Meanwhile, Protestant communities seemed to reverse their positions from the PERSIAN GULF WAR. The Christian Right initially opposed U.S. and NATO intervention in this conflict, in part because President Clinton supported it. Furthermore, they bridled at the image of the United States defending Muslims against persecution by Christians. Mainline Protestant leaders, on the other hand, were among the first to lobby for U.N. intervention. Once the hostilities commenced, however, the Christian Right demonstrated its patriotism through support for the war effort, while the mainline Protestant leaders proposed a ceasefire and a return to negotiations.

Further reading: Malcolm, Noel. *Kosovo: A Short History.* London: Macmillan, 1998; Mertus, Julie A. *Kosovo: How Myths and Truths Started a War.* Berkeley: University of California Press, 1999; Ramet, Sabrina P. *Balkan Babel: The Disintegration of Yugoslavia from the Death of Tito to the War in Kosovo.* 3d ed. Boulder, Colo.: Westview Press, 1999.

—Andrew D. Walsh

Ku Klux Klan (KKK)

The Ku Klux Klan is a collection of white supremacist groups that actively oppose ethnic and religious minorities. The Klan, or KKK as it is commonly known, has a history of violence in the United States and Canada. The organization utilizes a variety of religious and quasi-religious symbols and literature as part of its ceremonies and as a foundation of its beliefs.

The KKK was originally established in Tennessee in the aftermath of the Civil War. In 1866, six former Confederate soldiers formed a secret society to undermine Reconstruction governments and subjugate newly freed African Americans. The name was based on the Greek word *Kuklos*, or "circle." The Klan was organized into individual local units known as "klaverns." Many of the first members of the KKK were former Confederate soldiers and white landowners. The first leader, or grand wizard, of the KKK was the Confederate general Nathan Bedford Forrest.

The organization specifically targeted for violence and intimidation officials who were part of the Reconstruction governments in Southern states and African Americans. The Klan employed a variety of tactics. For instance, Klan members would burn a cross on the property of those they wished to intimidate as a warning that they should leave or face increased levels of violence. The Klan would often flog or even lynch targeted individuals. To disguise themselves, KKK

Parade of the Ku Klux Klan through counties in Virginia *(Library of Congress)*

members wore white robes and hoods. They usually operated at night and in a clandestine fashion. This led the Klan to become known as the "invisible empire," and members were often referred to as "night riders." By the late 1860s, Klan-led violence had become so widespread that Congress enacted legislation designed to suppress the organization. Among this legislation was the Force bill, which gave the president the authority to use federal troops to suppress the Klan. In 1869, Forrest officially disbanded the KKK, but many individual klaverns continued to operate and undertake actions against African Americans.

From its inception, the Klan has been rooted in religious symbolism. For instance, cross burning is central to both Klan ceremonies and to intimidation tactics. In the lore of the KKK, the burning cross represents the light of Jesus. In addition, the white robes and hoods of the organization are supposed to be symbolic of Christian purity. While the Klan initially victimized African Americans, when the organization was revived in the 20th century, its focus expanded.

In 1915, a former Methodist minister, Colonel William J. Simmons, resurrected the Klan in Atlanta. Simmons envisioned the new Klan as a broad-based conservative organization with appeal beyond the South. The reconstructed KKK took advantage of the growing nativist sentiment in the United States. It marketed itself as a faith-based Protestant organization that worked to protect what it perceived to be the American way of life. It promoted fundamentalist Protestantism. The Klan now opposed not only African Americans, but also immigrants and religious minorities, especially Jews and Roman Catholics. Membership in the Klan grew dramatically during the 1920s and expanded beyond the South. At its height in the 1920s, it was estimated that the KKK had 4 million members. There were chapters in states ranging from Maine to Ohio to Oregon. The organization also had some strength in Midwestern states, especially Indiana. The KKK

began fielding candidates for political office and had some success at the local and state levels. Meanwhile, it also revived its violent tactics, and there were waves of antiminority and anti-Catholic violence. The Klan was especially important in opposing the presidential candidacy of AL SMITH, a Roman Catholic, in the 1928 presidential election.

The onset of the Great Depression, followed by World War II, led to the demise of the new Klan. An Atlanta doctor named Samuel Green attempted to revive the KKK again in 1946. After his death in 1949, however, the organization split into a number of competing factions. The CIVIL RIGHTS MOVEMENT of the 1950s and 1960s led to a new wave of racially motivated violence across the South. Following spectacular acts of violence, including the murder of civil rights workers and the bombing of a Birmingham church, the Federal Bureau of Investigation began a concentrated effort to examine the illegal activities of the KKK. Many klansmen were arrested and local klaverns were broken up. By the 1970s, membership in the KKK had fallen below 5,000.

Membership in the Klan doubled during the 1980s, as various branches sought to widen the appeal of the group by promoting its religious aspects and opening the organization to women and children. Many klaverns also dropped their anti-Catholic stance. But this resurgence was short-lived. By the 1990s, Klan membership had declined to under 6,000.

Further reading: Davidson, Osha Gray. *The Best of Enemies: Race and Redemption in the New South.* New York: Scribner, 1996; Nelson, Jack. *Terror in the Night: The Klan's Campaign Against the Jews.* New York: Simon and Schuster, 1993; Quarles, Chester L. *The Ku Klux Klan and Related American Racialist and Antisemitic Organizations: A History and Analysis.* Jefferson, N.C.: McFarland, 1999; Ruiz, Jim. *The Black Hood of the Ku Klux Klan.* San Francisco: Austin and Winfield, 1998.
—Thomas Lansford

L

Lamb's Chapel v. Center Moriches Union Free School District 508 U.S. 385 (1993)

In *Lamb's Chapel v. Center Moriches Union Free School District*, members of an evangelical church challenged a local school board's denial of the use of school facilities to show a religion-oriented film series on family values and child rearing. The school district allowed after-hours use of its facilities by groups for "social, civic, and recreational purposes," but denied use for religious purposes. Church members filed suit in a U.S. district court, alleging that the school board's actions violated church members' freedom of speech.

The lower courts agreed with the school district that school property was a "limited open forum" and that the school district's decision to deny access to the church was reasonable and viewpoint-neutral. Church members appealed, and the Supreme Court granted certiorari.

In a unanimous decision, the Supreme Court struck down the school district's policy. The Court pointed out that the school board had not refused to allow use of its property for any film or lecture on family values and child rearing, but only those that dealt with the subject from a religious standpoint. As such, the school board "favor[ed] some viewpoints or ideas at the expense of others."

The Court also rejected the school district's argument that permitting use of its property for religious purposes would violate the ESTABLISHMENT CLAUSE. Applying the three-part *Lemon* test, the Court ruled that allowing the church to use school property to show the film series would have a secular purpose, would not have the primary effect of advancing religion, and would not foster an excessive entanglement with religion. In addition, there was little danger that the community would think the school board was endorsing religion.

Although the decision was unanimous, there was substantial disagreement among the justices over the appropriate standard to apply in establishment clause cases. Justice Anthony Kennedy described the use of the *Lemon* test and the endorsement standard as "unsettling and unnecessary." In an opinion joined by Justice Clarence Thomas, Justice ANTONIN SCALIA used more colorful language to characterize the Court's reliance on *Lemon*:

> Like some ghoul in a late-night horror movie that repeatedly sits up in its grave and shuffles abroad, after being repeatedly killed and buried, *Lemon* stalks our Establishment Clause jurisprudence once again, frightening the little children and school attorneys of Center Moriches Union Free School District . . . Over the years, however, no fewer than five of the currently sitting Justices have, in their own opinions, personally driven pencils through the creature's heart (the author of today's opinion repeatedly), and a sixth has joined an opinion doing so.

According to Scalia, allowing the church to use school property would not violate the establishment clause because it would not "signify state or local embrace of a particular religious sect."

The Court has continued to rely on its holding in *Lamb's Chapel*. In the 1995 case ROSENBERGER V. THE RECTOR AND VISITORS OF THE UNIVERSITY OF VIRGINIA, the Court cited *Lamb's Chapel* in striking down the University of Virginia's policy of denying student-activities funds to groups that advocate particular religions. In a 2001 case, GOOD NEWS CLUB V. MILFORD CENTRAL SCHOOLS the Court ruled that a school board's refusal to permit a religious club to use school facilities during noninstructional time violated its right to free speech.

See also LEMON V. KURTZMAN.

—Malia Reddick

Lapin, Rabbi Daniel (1947–) *rabbi*

Daniel Lapin, an ORTHODOX JEWISH rabbi, is the founder of Toward Tradition, an organization dedicated to building close ties between American Jews and Christians, many of whom are active in the Republican Party. Lapin is politically involved in debates about a number of sensitive issues that some scholars have labeled the CULTURE WAR.

The phases of Lapin's life divide into his early years in South Africa, his education, and rabbinical training (1947–75); his period as a rabbi in Venice, California, at the Pacific Jewish Center (1976–91); and his activism in Seattle as head of Toward Tradition (1992–present).

Lapin is the son of an Orthodox rabbi, Abraham Hyam Lapin, and the grandson of Berel Lapin, also a rabbi, who moved from England to South Africa in 1900. Daniel attended engineering school and had a traditional rabbinical training at Gateshead, Great Britain, where he studied with Rabbi Eliyahu Lapin, his great uncle. Subsequently, on three separate occasions called in Hebrew *Semicha,* Lapin received public ordination as an Orthodox rabbi.

In the mid-1970s Lapin moved to the United States and later joined with Michael Medved, the now well-known author, movie critic, and talk-show host, in the seaside community of Venice, to serve the Pacific Jewish Center (PJC) as its rabbi. The PJC was a community, not a synagogue in the traditional sense. Lapin worked tirelessly to help Jews resist the secularizing mainstream of a California culture so focused on individual fulfillment instead of the commands of God and to avoid assimilation. Lapin says that over a 15-year period, he helped about 2,000 Jewish family units to find their Jewish roots.

Theology was the path to politics for Rabbi Lapin. The Bible for him is a prescription for living, useful for all human beings and especially for those who embrace the Creator as revealed in Genesis. He opposes ABORTION and favors low taxes, private education, restrictions on PORNOGRAPHY, WELFARE REFORM, and (in general) the domestic agenda of conservative Christians. Perhaps more controversially, he claims that these policies are supported by the Bible and ought to be supported by all observant Jews and by Christians because they derive ultimately from God's commands. This is not a prescription for theocracy, he says, but a defense of classical American concepts commonly agreed on in the founding era and well into the 20th century.

In his book, *America's Real War* (1999), Lapin presents the truth claims of traditional biblical authority. Jews and Christians in America, argues Lapin, need to rethink their politics and their religion in view of basic teachings long espoused in their respective traditions because of the extreme threat posed by secular beliefs. In short, he argues that liberty, justice, and the rule of law in America rest on revealed religion, on a spiritual consensus sincerely and rationally embraced, rather than on simple pluralism or a toleration of diversity.

Rabbi Lapin formed Toward Tradition in 1991 as a vehicle to help carry his message to a national audience. Toward Tradition sponsors conferences, issues press releases, addresses public issues, and cooperates with conservative Christians and Republicans who share its agenda. Prominent engagements included Lapin's address to the national 1996 Republican Party convention and his high-profile participation in the clergy meeting of President-elect GEORGE W. BUSH. Lapin is also a regular speaker at the annual CHRISTIAN COALITION conferences. Most of his work with Toward Tradition puts Lapin in contact with non-Jews like JAMES DOBSON and PAT ROBERTSON of the Christian Coalition.

Where is Rabbi Lapin making his greatest impact? Certainly book sales of *America's Real War* are an indicator of who is interested in his ideas. By the year 2000, the book had sold over 70,000 copies. Yet most Jews do not know about the book for two reasons. The Jewish press refused to review the book, and Lapin chose Multnomah Press, a Christian press, as his publisher. Rabbi Lapin's presence and the response of others to him are one more indication that the deep fissures in American religion and politics endure because they attach to basic convictions and cultural sensibilities.

—Hubert Morken

Latter-day Saints (LDS), Church of Jesus Christ of (Mormons)

The Church of Jesus Christ of Latter-day Saints was established by JOSEPH SMITH in Fayette, New York, on April 6, 1830. The church also goes by nicknames Latter-day Saints and LDS, but it is best known as the "Mormon church," a label initially given by its enemies. The LDS church claims to be the restoration of the "fullness of the gospel" that was lost owing to the intermingling of earthly philosophies and Scripture. The church claims no parentage from any existing church. It is unarguably Christian in that its theology is exclusively based on salvation through Jesus Christ, as reflected in the church's official name. But church doctrines deviate in important ways from both PROTESTANTISM and ROMAN CATHOLICISM. Latter-day Saints believe that God the Father, Jesus Christ, and the Holy Spirit are separate beings, in modern prophecy and living prophets, in eternal progression in becoming like God, in the ability of families to be reunited after death, in saving ordinances performed for the dead, in the necessity of both works and grace for salvation, and in the necessity of an ordained priesthood. The church believes the Bible to be valid Scripture but supplements it with three additional works: The *Book of Mormon,* the *Doctrine and Covenants,* and the *Pearl of Great Price.* The *Book of Mormon* is the best-known work and contains the writings of prophets who lived on the American continent from 600 B.C.E. to 400 C.E. The church claims to rectify the theological divides within Christianity through these new scriptures and prophecy. Politically, the church and its members tend to be socially conservative, but there is diversity in members' views on economic and foreign policy issues.

The church has had a tumultuous political history. Its doctrinal uniqueness was only one of many sources of friction between Latter-day Saints and "Gentiles" during the 1800s. Block voting made Latter-day Saints threatening to existing political power relations. Church leaders stressed self-sufficiency and economic COMMUNITARIANISM, which threatened non-Mormon economic fortunes and seemed to many to be "un-American." Likewise, their belief in continuing revelation through modern prophets brought charges of "popery" against church leaders.

These and other sources of friction often led to violence, persecution, and exile. Early church leaders were continually harassed by lawsuits, threatened with violence, and often imprisoned. Church members were driven from their homes in Kirtland, Ohio, from several locations in Missouri, and later from Nauvoo, Illinois, before settling in what is now Utah. The church's predominantly northern and British membership was friendly to Native Americans and opposed slavery, which heightened passions in Missouri, a border proslavery state. The governor of Missouri even issued a MORMON EXTERMI-NATION ORDER: "The Mormons must be treated as enemies, and must be exterminated or driven from the state, if necessary, for the public good." After the expulsion of 10,000 church members from Missouri, church leaders appealed to the national government for redress for their financial losses in Missouri, but President Martin Van Buren and the Senate refused to intercede, calling the events purely a state matter.

Joseph Smith believed political power and autonomy might help minimize persecution, so the Mormons built a new city in Nauvoo, Illinois, and Smith worked to institute a city charter that gave political autonomy to the new city. Smith became mayor of Nauvoo and leader of the Nauvoo Legion, the local militia. But anger at Smith's political power and the city council's order to destroy an anti-Mormon printing press led to his imprisonment and murder while in jail in 1844. Again, the Saints felt the need for political protection and isolation from persecutors. Under the leadership of BRIGHAM YOUNG, the Saints left the United States for the Great Basin (Utah), which was at that time part of Mexico; later it was acquired by the United States after the Mexican-American War.

The Saints were the overwhelming political majority in the new territory, and church leaders inevitably assumed political roles. Church leaders established cities, created businesses, provided basic needs to a flood of convert immigrants, and built public works. The church quickly became the center of the Utah economy and political system. The Saints formed the "State of Deseret" and petitioned for statehood but were denied. "Deseret" was designated Utah Territory in 1850, and Young was appointed governor.

In 1853, the church revealed that it allowed some of its members to practice POLYGAMY. This led to decades of intense conflict between the church and the federal government. In 1860 the Republican Party adopted a platform to eradicate the "twin relics of barbarism": slavery and polygamy. In 1862, Republicans in Congress passed the Morrill Anti-Bigamy Act, which outlawed polygamy in U.S. territories. The church confidently fought the prohibition, considering polygamy to be a fundamental religious practice protected by the First Amendment's FREE EXERCISE CLAUSE. But the Supreme Court upheld the Morrill Act's prohibition of polygamy in REYNOLDS V. UNITED STATES (1870).

Throughout the 1870s and 1880s, federal efforts to eliminate polygamy increased. The Edmunds-Tucker Act (1887) mandated an antipolygamy test oath for Mormons wanting to hold public office, serve on juries, or vote. It also abolished the church's Perpetual Emigration Fund, which enabled poor Saints to immigrate to Utah. Women's right to vote, which had been granted by the territorial legislature in 1870, was also revoked. Congress dissolved the church's legal corporation and seized most of its property and financial assets. The law also disbanded the territorial militia and took control of Utah schools. The Utah Commission was appointed to oversee elections in Utah and boasted of preventing more than 15,000 Mormons from voting, despite the fact that the federal government estimated the number of polygamists in the territory to be only 2,500. The state of Idaho effectively disenfranchised all church members regardless of whether they practiced polygamy. The constitutionality of all these actions was upheld by the U.S. Supreme Court in DAVIS V. BEASON (1890) and LATTER-DAY SAINTS, CHURCH OF JESUS CHRIST OF V. UNITED STATES (1890).

Nearly 1,300 church members were imprisoned in the 1880s. Some members and church leaders tried to escape arrest and prosecution by hiding or fleeing to Mexico or Canada. The federal government even threatened to seize LDS temples, the most sacred places of worship to Latter-day Saints, and members' private property. In 1890, the LDS church was on the verge of legal destruction when church president Wilford Woodruff announced that the church would "refrain from conducting any marriage forbidden by the law of the land." The church ended the practice of polygamy, disbanded its political party, the People's Party, and encouraged members to divide evenly among Republicans and Democrats to diminish LDS political dominance. The church also divested itself of many economic interests. After this and other concessions by the church, Utah was admitted to the union as the 45th state on January 4, 1896.

While partisan politics was a necessary part of Mormonism's early battle for survival, the church is now officially politically neutral and does not endorse political candidates or parties. The church makes fewer political pronouncements than most churches. Yet church leaders periodically speak to social and political questions, particularly moral issues. The church officially opposes gambling of all types, including casinos, parimutuel betting, and lotteries. It also opposed the EQUAL RIGHTS AMENDMENT and continues to oppose ABOR-TION, except in the case of harm to the physical and mental health of the mother. The church also opposes gay marriages, nuclear arms escalation, basing the MX missile in Utah, and physician-assisted suicide. In Utah, the church has opposed liquor by the drink. The church has also publicly supported the RELIGIOUS FREEDOM RESTORATION ACT, sexual abstinence education in schools, and other "family friendly" legislation.

The church today still encourages political diversity among its members. Nevertheless, Utah members are also part of a western political culture that encourages political conservatism, and a large majority of Utah Saints vote Republican. Nevertheless, there is variation, particularly on economic and foreign relations issues, in the political views of members worldwide. In fact, fewer than half of the church's 11 million members live in the United States, and only 14 percent live in Utah. Nonwhite members and those outside of Utah have a variety of political orientations that represent their own political cultures.

Further reading: Firmage, Edwin Brown, and Richard Collin Mangrum. *Zion in the Courts.* Urbana: University of Illinois Press, 1988; Rich, Russell R. *Ensign to the Nations: A History of the LDS Church From 1846 to 1972.* Provo, Utah: Brigham Young University, 1972; Fox, Jeffrey C. "Gauging the Impact of Religion and Culture on Public Opinion." Ph.D. diss, University of Oklahoma, 1998; Smith, Joseph, Jr. *History of the Church of Jesus Christ of Latter-Day Saints.* Salt Lake City: Deseret Book, 1978; ———. *The Doctrine and Covenants of the Church of Jesus Christ of Latter-Day Saints.* Salt Lake City: Church of Jesus Christ of Latter-Day Saints, 1989.

—Jeffrey C. Fox

Latter-Day Saints, Church of Jesus Christ of v. United States 136 U.S. 1 (1890)

This case, which was formally titled *The Late Corporation of the Church of Jesus Christ of Latter-Day Saints v. United States,* was argued jointly with *Romney v. United States,* the decisions for both being written by Justice Joseph Bradley. At issue here were two questions: whether Congress had the authority to repeal the church's charter of incorporation and whether the government had the authority to seize the property of the former corporation. In a 6-3 decision, the Supreme Court upheld both the revocation of the charter and the initiation of proceedings for forfeiture of the property.

In early 1851, the Church of Jesus Christ of Latter-day Saints had been granted a charter of incorporation as a religious and charitable organization by the provisional government of the State of Deseret, an act validated by the Utah territorial legislature in October 1851. In 1862 and 1887, however, Congress enacted legislation specifically annulling the charter. The laws were challenged on several grounds, including that the revocation constituted an impairment of the obligation of contracts, an action the church erroneously claimed was forbidden to Congress by the U.S. Constitution. The Court rejected that claim, holding that Congress had "general and plenary" power over the nation's territories, this authority granted in Article I of the Constitution and, as well, a necessary attribute of Congress's power to acquire territory. Moreover, noted Justice Bradley, the very act that established the Utah Territory provided that all laws passed by the territorial government were subject to the disapproval of Congress.

Justice Bradley then turned to the question of whether the property of the dissolved church was subject to seizure and disposition by the U.S. government. In 1862, Congress had enacted legislation limiting the amount of property that could be held by religious and charitable organizations in the territories and providing that property held in violation of the law was subject to forfeiture. Federal legislation passed in 1887 authorized the attorney general to begin proceedings against organizations that held or had acquired property in violation of the act of 1862, and it further provided that proceeds derived from the sale of such property (in the case of the Latter-day Saints, an amount of some $3 million) be used for "common schools" in the territory where the property was located.

Before turning to his view of the government's power to acquire and dispose of charitable assets, Justice Bradley paused to examine the "character" of the charitable corporation—that is, the church—and the "objects . . . it promoted." He observed that the purpose of these large holdings was to support the promotion of church doctrine, including the "distinguishing" practice of POLYGAMY. Arguing that polygamy is contrary to the dictates of Christianity, Bradley rephrased the questions the Court faced as "whether the promotion of such a nefarious system and practice, so repugnant to our laws and to the principles of civilization, is to be allowed to continue by the sanction of the government itself and whether the funds accumulated for that purpose should be restored to the same unlawful uses as heretofore, to the detriment of the true interests of civil society." Answering no to both questions, Justice Bradley argued that the Constitution's guarantee of freedom of religion grants no protection to the act of polygamy any more than it would to religiously motivated assassination or human sacrifice. Since law forbids the practice of polygamy, the promotion of polygamy cannot be a proper use of charitable and religious funds.

Returning to the precise issue in the case, Justice Bradley concluded that, under the ancient "law of charities," where it was impossible for property held by a charitable organization to be used for the original purposes intended by its donor owing to some illegality or failure in the object of the gift, the government had the right and responsibility to direct it to another charitable or public purpose. Thus, the forfeiture proceedings instituted by the government should continue. Moreover, in Romney's companion suit, representing the members of a reconstituted, unincorporated Church of Jesus Christ of Latter-day Saints and seeking their control over the property of the dissolved church, must be dismissed.

In a brief dissent for three justices, Chief Justice Melville W. Fuller argued that while Congress surely had the power to forbid polygamy in the territories, still it had no constitutional authority to contain the spread of the doctrine by seizing the property of individuals or organizations.

See also *REYNOLDS V. UNITED STATES.*

—Susan E. Grogan

Law, Bernard Cardinal (1931–) *Roman Catholic cardinal*

Bernard Francis Law was born in Torreón, Mexico, the son of a U.S. Air Force colonel. He attended high school in the Virgin

Islands, then went to Harvard University. He completed seminary studies at the Pontifical College Josephinum, near Columbus, Ohio.

Law was ordained a priest in the ROMAN CATHOLIC CHURCH for the diocese of Natchez-Jackson, Mississippi, in 1961. He served as an assistant pastor, and in 1963 he became editor of the diocesan newspaper, *Mississippi Register.* During his five years as editor, Law also served as director of the Diocesan Family Life Bureau, assistant director of vocations, and moderator of the Councils of Catholic Men and Women. He was a president of the diocesan priest senate and a consultant to the bishop. He also served as vicar general for the diocese.

Law was the executive director of the Committee for Ecumenical and Inter-religious Affairs of the NATIONAL CONFERENCE OF CATHOLIC BISHOPS (NCCB) from 1968 to 1971. In October 1973, Pope Paul VI appointed him bishop of Springfield–Cape Giradeau, Missouri, a diocese in the foothills of the Ozarks covering all of southern Missouri. During his 11 years as bishop there, Law worked closely with arriving Vietnamese refugees and was actively involved with national and international church concerns. From 1976 to 1981, he served as a consultant to the Secretariat for Promoting Christian Unity in Rome.

Following the death of Humberto Cardinal Medieros, Bishop Law was appointed archbishop of Boston in January 1984. He was created a cardinal in 1985. His titular church in Rome is Santa Susanna. He is active in the Roman Curia, where he holds membership in the Congregations for Oriental Churches, Divine Worship and Sacraments, Institutes of Consecrated Life and Societies of Apostolic Life, Evangelization of Peoples, Catholic Education, and the Pontifical Council for Culture. He has been a papal appointee to synods of bishops and worked on the international catechism.

As a diocesan bishop, Cardinal Law is know as an able administrator and a man of strong views. He shocked a Boston College commencement audience when he said that he wished the school would become more Catholic. He was one of the strongest critics of JOSEPH CARDINAL BERNARDIN'S 1996 Common Ground Initiative. His lack of a reputation as a consensus builder may explain why he has not held a top office in the NCCB (Reese 1992). He has, however, been elected to many NCCB committees. He has served as chair of the NCCB commissions for Ecumenical and Inter-religious Affairs, Migration, Pastoral Research and Practices, and Pro-life Activities. He has also been a member of the Bishop's Ad Hoc Committee for the Church in Latin America and is chair of the UNITED STATES CATHOLIC CONFERENCE'S committee on International Policy. Cardinal Law is a trustee of the Catholic University of America. He is the founder of the Cambridge Center for the Study of Faith and Culture, a Catholic think tank engaged in interdisciplinary research on contemporary faith and culture issues.

Cardinal Law has been a presence on the U.S. political scene. He was the Catholic prelate closest to President George H. W. Bush. The two shared a conservative moral outlook, par-ticularly on the ABORTION issue. The cardinal was a visitor to the Bush's seaside estate at Kennebunkport, Maine, and to the White House. Law played a key behind-the-scenes role in 1989 when diplomatic tensions flared when Panamanian leader Manuel Noriega, pursued by U.S. troops, sought diplomatic haven inside the Vatican's Panamanian embassy. Law quietly counseled the Bush White House about how to deal with the Vatican. Soon after President GEORGE W. BUSH was inaugurated in 2001, Cardinal Law met with him. Law has supported the Republican Party. He defended former U.S. senator John Ashcroft against charges that he was anti-Catholic because of his association with Bob Jones University in South Carolina.

Cardinal Law has been an advocate for a number of issues. He is a strong opponent of abortion and the death penalty. He has criticized capitalism's disregard for workers and promoted affordable housing. He has worked to improve relations between the Catholic Church and the government of Cuban leader Fidel Castro, visiting Cuba and organizing humanitarian missions to the country. In March 1998, Cardinal Law called on President WILLIAM JEFFERSON CLINTON to end the U.S. embargo on Cuba and also asked him to reformulate U.S. foreign policy toward the island nation.

In 2002, Cardinal Law was severely criticized by the press and Boston Catholics for his secretive handling of allegations of sexual abuse of children by priests, and for continuing to assign accused priests to parishes. This crisis in Boston led to the reexamination of sexual misconduct policies in Catholic dioceses throughout the United States. Law resigned as archbishop of Boston in December 2002.

See also O'CONNOR, JOHN CARDINAL.

Further reading: Reese, Thomas J. *A Flock of Shepherds: The National Conference of Catholic Bishops.* Kansas City, Mo.: Sheed and Ward, 1992.

—Anthony J. Pogorelc

Lee v. Weisman 505 U.S. 577 (1992)

Lee v. Weisman involved the practice of including clergy at middle and high school graduations to provide nonsectarian invocations. In this case, the principal of Nathan Bishop Middle School in Providence, Rhode Island, asked a local rabbi to perform the invocation and benediction at a middle school graduation ceremony. Daniel Weisman, whose daughter, Deborah, was one of the graduating students, sought an injunction to prevent the school from continuing to invite clergy to participate in graduation ceremonies. The district court agreed with Weisman that the inclusion of clergy in a public school graduation violated the ESTABLISHMENT CLAUSE of the First Amendment. The decision of the district court was upheld by the First Circuit Court of Appeals. The case was then appealed to the Supreme Court.

In a 5-4 decision, the Court affirmed the decisions of the lower courts. In cases where the Court is confronted with the question of whether or not government is fostering the establishment of one religion over another or religion over nonreligion, the justices have often relied on the test outlined in *LEMON V. KURTZMAN* (1971). The *Lemon* test, as it has come to be known, asks three questions: Does the government have a secular purpose in engaging in the given activity, in this case including religious leaders in public school ceremonies? Is the primary effect of the activity to advance one religion over another? And does the activity result in an excessive entanglement between government and religion?

Justice Anthony Kennedy, writing for the majority, found that the school policy violated the establishment clause, essentially coercing students to participate in religious activity. The fact that the graduation ceremonies were voluntary, and that students could choose not to attend the service if they objected to clergy participation, did not persuade the Court. The justices held that the services were, in essence, mandatory in that the graduation was a one time event, and students would have no other opportunity to participate in any other similar ceremony. Therefore, the burden on the students was too great for the Court to uphold the school policy. The majority was particularly cognizant of the unique circumstances surrounding schoolchildren, noting that students deserve a heightened level of protection from coercion in the schoolhouse.

The dissenters in this case were strident in their response to the majority opinion. Justice ANTONIN SCALIA, joined by Justices Rehnquist, White, and Thomas, refuted the majority position that the inclusion of clergy to deliver a nonsectarian invocation amounted to coercion. Relying on the intent of the framers, Scalia argued: "The Framers were indeed opposed to coercion of religious worship by the National Government; but, as their own sponsorship of nonsectarian prayer in public events demonstrates, they understood that 'speech is not coercive; the listener may do as he likes.'"

The majority opinion did not explicitly rely on the test enunciated in *Lemon,* resting the decision squarely on the Court's previous school prayer decisions and the coercive nature of the ceremony. This is not to suggest that the Court overturned *Lemon*—it did not. In a concurring opinion, Justices Stevens, Blackmun, and O'Connor continued to push for a standard that did not rely on coercion. They argued that the appropriate standard would ignore coercion entirely; all that needed to be shown is that the state favored one religion over another or endorsed religion generally.

These divergent views point out that the question of prayer in school is one that the Court has struggled with throughout the last 40 years and is not likely to resolve soon. Many schools continue to engage in prayer on school property. During the Court's 2000 term, the justices were faced with student prayer at high school football games, a practice they struck down as violating the establishment clause, relying heavily on the Court's coercion argument in *Weisman* as well as the *Lemon* test in *SANTA FE INDEPENDENT SCHOOL DISTRICT V. DOE* (2000). Although it is not clear whether or not the Court will continue to rely on *Lemon* in deciding school prayer

cases, it is likely that questions involving the propriety of PRAYER IN PUBLIC SCHOOLS will continue to confront the justices in the years ahead.

—Scott Comparato

legislative chaplains

A number of government bodies across the nation, from city councils to the U.S. Senate, open their sessions with prayer. Both the U.S. Senate and the House of Representatives, as well as a number of state legislatures, invite officially designated legislative chaplains to lead these devotional exercises.

The tradition of having a prayer at the start of a legislature's business day dates back to the Colonial era. The House and Senate each hired its own paid chaplain during the First Congress, even as members were debating the language of what would ultimately become the ESTABLISHMENT CLAUSE of the First Amendment, which dictates in part that "Congress shall make no law respecting an establishment of religion."

Establishment clause concerns have inspired a number of political and constitutional challenges against both the custom of opening government meetings with prayers and the institutions of paid legislative chaplaincies. The Supreme Court upheld the constitutionality of both traditions in 1983, basing its decision largely on historical practice. In *MARSH V. CHAMBERS*, Chief Justice Warren Burger wrote for the Court:

> In light of the unambiguous and unbroken history of more than 200 years, there can be no doubt that the practice of opening legislative sessions with prayer has become part of the fabric of our society. To invoke Divine guidance on a public body entrusted with making laws is not, in these circumstances, an 'establishment' of religion or a step toward establishment; it is simply a tolerable acknowledgment of beliefs widely held among the people of our country.

The salaries of the House and Senate's full-time chaplains, as well as their travel and office expenses, are paid from the federal treasury. However, state policies on funding legislative chaplaincies may vary. For example, the Nebraska unicameral legislature, which once paid its part-time chaplain with state funds, now relies on volunteer clergy to lead its opening prayers. Before abandoning the position in 2001, Arizona's paid legislative chaplaincy was funded through private donations.

The U.S. Senate's Web page describes the Senate's chaplaincy as a "nonpolitical, nonpartisan, and nonsectarian" position, with responsibilities including spiritual advising and religious instruction for senators and their family members as well as for Senate staffers.

Yet political conflicts have at least periodically plagued legislative chaplaincies. For example, the selection of chaplains for the 35th Congress (1858–59) appears to have become so mired in politics that no chaplains were hired during that period. Instead, various local clergy members provided the morning prayers. Recently, hiring a chaplain for the House of Representatives again proved a political as well as a partisan business. In 2000, Speaker Dennis Hastert named Father Daniel P. Coughlin as House chaplain on his own authority after the established selection process became mired in controversy. The top choice of a bipartisan committee of House members, a Catholic priest named Father Timothy O'Brien, was bypassed by the House Republican leadership in favor of a Protestant candidate. The ensuing controversy prevented the full House from voting on any candidate and led at least one member of Congress to call for the abolition of the full-time position altogether. Instead, Speaker Hastert named Father Coughlin to fill the post on an interim basis until the end of 2000. Father Coughlin's formal appointment to the 107th Congress was one of the first items of business concluded by the full House in January 2001.

Further reading: Davenport, Paul. "Legislature Will Not Replace Gay Chaplain." *Associated Press Newswires.* January 19, 2001; Foerstel, Karen. "Hastert's Selection of Catholic as House Chaplain Fails to End Recriminations about Process." *Congressional Quarterly Weekly.* March 25, 2000; "Ganske Talks Sense on Chaplain Issue." *Omaha World-Herald.* March 7, 2000; Reed, Leslie. "Ernie Chambers." *Omaha World-Herald.* November 28, 2000; Stokes, Anson Phelps. *Church and State in the United States.* Vol. 1. New York: Harper and Brothers, 1950; U.S. Senate. "Learning about the Senate: The Chaplain of the Senate." Available on-line. URL: http://www.senate.gov/learning/learn_leaders_officers_chaplain.html. Accessed Nov. 7, 2001.

—Staci L. Beavers

Lemon v. Kurtzman and *Earley v. DiCenso* 403 U.S. 602 (1971)

Lemon and *Earley* were companion cases decided on June 28, 1971, involving PENNSYLVANIA and Rhode Island plans that provided state compensation to teachers in parochial and other nonpublic schools for teaching secular subjects. An eight-member majority of the U.S. Supreme Court struck down both plans as violating the ESTABLISHMENT CLAUSE of the First Amendment. In writing for the majority, Chief Justice Warren Burger declared that both programs fostered an excessive entanglement between church and state. In so doing, Burger introduced what would become a standard test utilized by the Court to determine establishment clause violations. The tripartite *Lemon* test united two tests from ABINGTON TOWNSHIP V. SCHEMPP (1963) and another from WALZ V. TAX COMMISSION (1970), requiring that laws have a secular legislative purpose, that their primary effect neither advance nor inhibit religion, and that they not foster an excessive entanglement between church and state.

The Rhode Island Salary Supplement Act, enacted in 1969, supplement the salaries of teachers of secular subjects in nonpublic elementary schools, 95 percent of which were church-related, by paying them an amount not in excess of 15 percent of their current annual salary. Nonpublic school teachers were to be certified in the secular courses they taught, were to use the same materials used in public schools, and were to promise, in writing, that they would not inject religious teachings in the classroom. Schools were to submit financial data to the state to determine how much of the expenditure was utilized for secular subjects. The Rhode Island plan was challenged by a group of state taxpayers, arguing that it violated both the establishment and the FREE EXERCISE clauses of the First Amendment. The federal district court ruled that the plan violated the establishment clause because the ongoing surveillance required to insure the secularity of classes led to an excessive entanglement between church and state.

Similarly, the Pennsylvania Nonpublic Elementary and Secondary Education Act, passed in 1968, authorized the state superintendent of public instruction to "purchase" specified "secular education services" for nonpublic schools. Under this program, the state directly reimbursed nonpublic schools for salaries, textbooks, and instructional materials used for secular education. Separate accounting procedures were to be utilized for the state monies, and the curriculum and instructional equipment were to be approved by the state. A group of Pennsylvania taxpayers challenged the program in federal district court as violating the establishment clause, but their complaint was dismissed for failure to state a claim of relief.

While stating that "we can only dimly perceive the lines of demarcation in this extraordinarily sensitive area of constitutional law," Chief Justice Burger, in his majority opinion, ruled both program unconstitutional. In introducing the *Lemon* test, Burger noted that both programs had the legitimate secular purpose of enhancing the quality of secular education in all schools covered by compulsory education laws. However, he stated that the primary effect test need not be determined because both programs violated the excessive entanglement prong. Noting that the sole beneficiaries of the Rhode Island program were teachers at Roman Catholic schools, many of whom were nuns, Burger concluded that "a dedicated religious person, teaching in a school affiliated with his or her faith and operated to inculcate its tenets, will inevitably experience great difficulty in remaining religiously neutral." As a result, Burger asserted that to ensure that religious indoctrination was separate from secular instruction in this setting would require "a comprehensive, discriminating, and continuing state surveillance."

The Pennsylvania statute raised even greater constitutional problems because the state funds were sent directly to the schools. In one of the most controversial aspects of Burger's opinion, he discussed the political divisiveness that resulted when religious groups competed for government funds. According to Burger, "political division along religious lines was one of the principal evils against which the First Amendment was intended to protect."

In a partial dissent, Justice Byron White challenged the idea that secular and religious instruction could not be sepa-

rated. White claimed instead that no evidence had been given that the teachers in the parochial schools of Rhode Island had inserted religion into their secular teaching. Presaging future debates over the *Lemon* test, White found particularly problematic the emphasis on the excessive entanglement query. For White, the test created an "insoluble paradox" for the state and parochial schools in that attempts to insure the secularity of publicly funded programs would inevitably lead to some sort of excessive entanglement between church and state. This concern, plus the perceived inconsistent and unprincipled application of the *Lemon* test, has led to increasing calls, both on and off the Court, to abandon the *Lemon* test in favor of new guidelines for determining establishment clause violations.

See also *EVERSON V. BOARD OF EDUCATION*.

—J. David Holcomb

Levitt v. CPEARL 413 U.S. 472 (1973)

Levitt v. CPEARL decided the question of whether a state statute that provides for reimbursement of parochial schools for the costs of state-mandated testing and record-keeping activities was a violation of the ESTABLISHMENT CLAUSE of the First Amendment. The Court in particular considered whether Chapter 138 of New York State's Laws of 1970 violated the Constitution. These costs included funding for statewide competency tests as well as tests that individual classroom teachers prepared as part of their curriculum, the latter being the far greater component of the two. Both sectarian and nonsectarian private schools were specifically eligible to receive the state reimbursements. While each school was provided a set amount for specific services, the state statue made no provision for audits of school expenditures to ensure that the moneys provided were spent in accordance with state law, and no provision was made for schools to return any excess funds to the state. A group of New York taxpayers and an unincorporated association, Committee for Public Education and Religious Liberty (CPEARL), sought an injunction to prevent Levitt (the state comptroller) and Nyquist (the state education commissioner) from implementing the act. A three-judge United States District Court for the Southern District of New York ruled that the act violated the establishment clause and permanently halted its enforcement, rejecting the state's argument that the services reimbursed were secular. Appeal was made directly to the U.S. Supreme Court.

Chief Justice Warren Burger argued in his majority opinion that the statute is constitutionally infirm because it does not attempt to ensure that the tests the schools were administering (the costs of which are partially covered by the act) were free from religious instruction. As such, the state may inadvertently have been underwriting religious indoctrination, which is "an impermissible aid to religion . . . because the aid that will be devoted to secular functions is not identifiable and separable from aid to sectarian activities." The Court also compared *EVERSON V. BOARD OF EDUCATION* (1947) and *BOARD OF EDUCATION V. ALLEN* (1968) to *Levitt*. In *Levitt*, the

services for which costs were reimbursed were integral to the teaching process because test construction is based on the teacher's own perspective of the subject being tested. Merely because the state mandates certain activities does not allow states to support religious instruction in that the establishment clause would be frustrated if it were "read as permitting a State to pay for whatever it requires a private school to do." Accordingly, the Court held that Chapter 138 of the New York State Laws of 1970 violated the establishment clause because its primary effect was to advance religion; it, therefore, affirmed the district court's ruling.

Justices William O. Douglas, WILLIAM BRENNAN, and Thurgood Marshall concurred in the Court's opinion. Justice Byron White dissented.

—Drew Noble Lanier

liberalism

Liberalism is strongly associated with liberal learning, that is, the arts and sciences worthy of a free person as defined by the course of studies at English universities in the 14th and 15th centuries. This idea of learning was extended to mean freedom from narrow prejudice or tradition. By the early 19th century and ever after, liberalism has referred interchangeably both to religious and to political ideas and practices associated with openness to change and reform. At any given time, liberalism has been identified with particular programs, social movements, institutions, and philosophical-religious premises. Yet over time, in both its religious and its political meanings, liberalism has come to mean not so much a fixed program or body of doctrines as a spirit and a method that attests to the importance of new knowledge and new revelation as important sources for human belief and conduct.

This priority of procedure over substance and progress over fixed states is best seen historically by tracking the changing forms that both religious and political liberalism have taken in America. From the earliest Colonial days until independence from Great Britain, liberalism in America was closely associated with claims of Anglo-Saxon political, constitutional-legal, and moral and religious superiority over continental European royal absolutism, Catholic clericalism, and religious superstition. When resistance to Britain became calls for revolution, however, older and militantly PURITAN ideas from the English Civil War and regicide of the 1640s combined with dreams of "starting the world over again" with pure republican principles instituted in a virgin land by an uncorrupted people. Thomas Paine's *Common Sense* adroitly connected these dots.

Soon after this defining period, liberalism was associated with national republicanism and active national government through the adoption of the U.S. Constitution and the victory of the Federalist Party. Soon thereafter, though, a Jeffersonian and Jacksonian opposition emerged that combined sweeping continental expansion with states' rights (including slavery), strict constitutional construction, and local democracy. Jeffersonian-Jacksonian liberalism was also strongly associated with calls for strict SEPARATION OF CHURCH AND STATE and from governmental interference in the economy (through such things as high tariffs, internal improvements, and the national bank), thus wedding for a time a kind of SECULAR HUMANISM to laissez-faire economics in a rights-based liberal discourse. The weakness of this form of legalistic, small-republic liberalism was soon apparent. Increasingly associated with the defense of backward and isolated subcultures, rent-seeking local economies, the expansion of slavery, heartless Indian removal, and paternalist family structures, anti-Jacksonian movements and parties quickly arose to vindicate national republicanism as the authentic liberal path. This new national republicanism was closely allied culturally with northern evangelical Protestantism and its ties to antislavery, the women's movement, and compulsory common schools on the one hand, and with Nativism, anti-Catholicism, and Prohibition on the other. The New Deal and the liberalism of post–World War II America was an uneasy amalgam of both national and small-republican traditions—of shared national purpose and individual rights. This uneasy amalgam, in a sense, has always been our condition: through all the changes in the philosophical and ideological expressions of liberalism as a social philosophy, our social practices and institutional arrangements have remained studiously committed both to individualism and to reforming purposes.

The religious expressions of liberalism are equally various. In the late Colonial period, religious rationalists were the earliest supporters of resistance to British policies, but religious evangelicals, reborn in the FIRST GREAT AWAKENING of the 1740s, were the better articulators of revolutionary fervor and state constitutional values. Soon thereafter, and until the SECOND GREAT AWAKENING, liberal religion was associated with natural theology, deism, and rationalism. Starting in the early 1800s and lasting through the 1920s, however, liberal Evangelical Protestantism, in association first with the Whig and then the Republican Party, provided the intellectual, moral, and institutional energies for most liberal visions and liberal reforms, especially following decisive military, political, and cultural victories by the Union in the Civil War. Through the new national universities, modernist theology, pragmatist philosophy, and the social sciences, all informed by German historicism, would now lead the way under the progressive wing of the Republican Party. Protestant FUNDAMENTALISM in the 1920s was both a reaction to this development and a cultural expression of withdrawal from national political and cultural life increasingly marked by religious pluralism. From the 1930s to the present, a distinctly Protestant religious liberalism has been steadily eroded by purely secular formulations of economic, social and political advance, and somewhat demoralized by the evangelical energies of fellow Protestants who do not share its claims to national cultural and moral-intellectual leadership. Moreover, given the massive electoral victories of the Democratic Party in the middle of the 20th century, Jews and Catholics rose to a coequal status. A distinctly religious voice of liberalism in political life is now almost wholly subordinated to a legal and constitutionalist faith in religious pluralism itself as a sacred value.

See also CONSERVATISM.

Further reading: Cuddihy, John M. *No Offense: Civil Religion and Protestant Taste.* New York: Seabury Press, 1978; Ferguson, Robert A. *The American Enlightenment, 1750–1820.* Cambridge, Mass.: Harvard University Press, 1996; Greenstone, David. *The Lincoln Persuasion: Remaking American Liberalism.* Princeton, N.J.: Princeton University Press, 1993; Hutchison, William R. *The Modernist Impulse in American Protestantism.* Cambridge, Mass.: Harvard University Press, 1976; Rawls, John. *Political Liberalism.* New York: Columbia University Press, 1993.

—Eldon J. Eisenach

liberation theology

In its written form, liberation theology had its inception with the publication in 1971 of *A Theology of Liberation*, by Gustavo Gutierrez. The setting of his work is Latin America, and his goal is to rethink the themes of the Christian faith from the perspective of those who are marginalized and their struggle for liberation. In many of its forms, liberation theology tends to be traditional in relation to the faith and radical in relation to society. The identification of God with the oppressed rather than the privileged is a new perspective warranted by the biblical faith. Particular expressions of liberation theology form around issues of race, gender, and class. Here we need to suggest more common aspects of liberation theologians.

One of the most important issues for liberation theology is, who does theology and from where? Traditionally, theology is a product of the academy and church bodies. It is thought by liberation theologians as "theology from above." It is formulated in air-conditioned libraries and ecclesiastical bodies. And the text may be a creed or council, usually related somewhat to biblical texts. "Theology from below" is theology from the streets. It does not begin in historical scholarship or forms of speculation. The starting point is the lived experience of the "wretched of the earth," the voiceless, exploited, and victimized. And it focuses on their resistance on behalf of a new humanity. For liberation theologians, theology begins in the cries of the poor and in their struggle for freedom. From that vantage point, the themes of faith and the texts of Scripture are rethought.

Liberation theology is not dismissive of the travails of the soul but focuses on the dehumanization engendered by social, political, and economic structure. Oppression is not self-inflicted; it is programmed into the orders of the world. The poor are not poor because of character flaws. The global economic order is a defining phenomenon that manufactures the rich and the poor. The fundamental reality of the poor is powerlessness. Their oppression is structural, not a personal fault. And they are without recourse.

Reading the Bible "from below" renders a different understanding of the text. It has been common for political figures to drape the American experience in the image of the Exodus event; we are the "New Israel." And God is on the side of the United States in the war against Godless communism. But for liberation theology it is more than an egregious reach to associate the most powerful nation in the world with the Israelites in Egypt. Americans are not slave labor in the world market. The Exodus story was a different one when MARTIN LUTHER KING JR. embraced it for the CIVIL RIGHTS MOVEMENT. There was a "structural similarity" between the Israelites in Egypt and the black community in America. From below, Exodus is a story of resistance to oppression; from above it is a story of conquest. From below it is the subversion of the empire; from above it is the preservation of privilege. From below it is the story of a God who hears the cries of the oppressed; from above it is about a God who sanctions the domination of the status quo. The Bible is a different book when read by those who suffer.

Liberation theology makes engagement with society a necessary condition of legitimacy. It emerges from the setting of engagement, and it demands a return to engagement. Theory and practice form a two-way street and the traffic is curricular; action leads to reconsideration and that translates into new action. It is common for theologians like Gutierrez to say that theology is the second act, what one does "after the sun goes down." One labors on behalf of the victims by day and, by night, reconsiders the claims of faith. The next day is shaped by the outcome of the first one.

Liberation theologians have no difficulty understanding why Herod the King was so threatened by the birth of Jesus.

See also MARXISM/COMMUNISM.

Further reading: Brown, Robert McAfee. *Theology in a New Key: Responding to Liberation Themes.* Philadelphia: Westminster Press, 1978; Cone, James. *A Black Theology of Liberation.* Philadelphia: Lippincott, 1970; Gutierrez, Gustavo. *A Theology of Liberation.* Trans. and ed. by Sister Caridad Inda and John Eagleson; Maryknoll, N.Y.: Orbis Books, 1973. King, Paul G., Kent Maynard, and David O. Woodyard. *Risking Liberation: Middle Class Powerlessness and Social Heroism.* Atlanta: John Knox Press, 1988.

Lieberman, Joseph I. (1942–) *U.S. senator*

Born in 1942 in Stamford, Connecticut, Joseph I. Lieberman has represented the state of Connecticut in the U.S. Senate since 1988. In 2000, he was nominated to be the Democratic Party's candidate for vice president along with Al Gore. This nomination was historic because Lieberman is the first Jew to run for national office on the ticket of a major political party.

Lieberman brought to the Democratic national ticket a wealth of experience in legislative and executive politics. A graduate of Yale College and Yale Law School, Lieberman was elected to the Connecticut State Senate in 1970, where he

Senator Joe Lieberman (right) with former vice president Al Gore *(Alex Wong/Newsmakers)*

served for 10 years, six of them as Senate majority leader. He then served as Connecticut attorney general for six years, during which he reorganized the office as a consumer defender. In 1988, he ran for the U.S. Senate, defeating three-term incumbent Senator Lowell Weicker. He was elected to a second term in 1994 and to a third term in 2000. (Lieberman ran simultaneously for senator and for vice president, as did Lloyd Bentsen in 1988 and Lyndon Johnson in 1960.)

In the Senate, Lieberman built a reputation as a moderate and a centrist. He supported President WILLIAM JEFFERSON CLINTON's efforts to fashion a more centrist "New Democratic" Party, and in 1995 he was named chairman of the Democratic Leadership Council. Although he was a strong supporter of President Clinton (who as a Yale law student had worked in Lieberman's first political campaign in 1970), Lieberman did not hesitate to condemn Clinton's behavior in the Monica Lewinsky affair in 1998. When he did not vote to remove Clinton from office, Lieberman was the first prominent Democrat to denounce Clinton's conduct as not only inappropriate but immoral.

Lieberman's philosophy of Democratic centrism is evident in his positions on major issues. Like Al Gore, and unlike the left wing of the Democratic Party, Lieberman supported the 1991 PERSIAN GULF WAR resolution that authorized President George H. W. Bush to use military force in the Persian Gulf. He favors U.S. support for ISRAEL, but he also voted for military aid to Saudi Arabia. He has consistently supported international trade measures opposed by organized labor, such as the North American Free Trade Agreement (NAFTA), yet he has taken labor's side on other issues of primary importance to unions, such as increases in the minimum wage and prohibitions against employers' hiring permanent replacements for striking workers.

Lieberman has described himself as "pro-business, pro-trade, and pro-economic growth." As a senator Lieberman has supported measures important to Connecticut's large industries of insurance, health care, and military technology.

But his pro-business attitude appears to go beyond local constituency service, instead reflecting a genuine belief that both the Democratic Party and the nation's economy would flourish when government promoted international trade, business entrepreneurship, and technological innovation. As Lieberman put it, "You can't be pro-jobs and anti-business."

At the same time, Lieberman has been a vigorous advocate of campaign finance reform and supported ABORTION rights, environmental protection, gun control, GAY RIGHTS, consumer protection, and civil rights legislation. During the presidency of GEORGE W. BUSH, Lieberman worked with the White House to forge a revised faith-based initiative that protects civil rights and religious freedom. True to his democratic centrism, Lieberman has supported school VOUCHERS on an experimental basis for District of Columbia inner-city schools.

An observant Orthodox Jew, Lieberman is a religious man. He and his family follow kosher dietary rules, and he does not work or ride in cars, trains, or airplanes on the Sabbath. He makes exceptions for vitally important work, however, and Lieberman's five-mile Saturday walks from his Washington home to the Senate chamber to vote on pending legislation are legendary. Lieberman is an adherent of the branch of Judaism known as Modern Orthodox, whose followers are steeped in biblical studies yet, more than the ultra-Orthodox, are inclined to believe in living in the here and now.

In the 2000 presidential election campaign, Lieberman discussed the role of religion in public life. He suggested that, at the very least, religion should not be excluded from political discourse. Religiously motivated views should be given an equal hearing in our public dialogue. Public debate is impoverished if we remove all references to religious belief and God-talk from the public square.

Lieberman's reasoned discussion of the role of religion in public life was one of the more memorable aspects of the 2000 election campaign. By speaking so openly about religion and his own faith commitments, he may have broken the monopoly of religious discussion held by the Religious Right.

The Lieberman candidacy made history, not only because he was the first Jew nominated for national office by a major party, and not only because he was on the losing end of one of the closest presidential elections in the nation's history, but also because his eloquent statements about the role of religion in public life were real contributions to American political discourse.

See also IMPEACHMENT OF WILLIAM JEFFERSON CLINTON; ORTHODOX JUDAISM; RELIGION IN THE 2000 PRESIDENTIAL ELECTION; WHITE HOUSE OFFICE OF FAITH-BASED AND COMMUNITY INITIATIVES.

Further reading: Lieberman, Joseph I. *In Praise of Public Life.* New York: Simon and Schuster, 2000; Segers, Mary C. "A Historic First: The Lieberman Nomination." In *Piety, Politics, and Pluralism: Religion, the Courts, and the 2000 Election.* Edited by Mary C. Segers. Lanham, Md.: Rowman and Littlefield, 2002.

—Mary C. Segers

Lincoln, Abraham (1809–1865) *U.S. president*

Abraham Lincoln was born in February 1809, near Hodgenville, Kentucky, and died on April 14, 1865, after being shot in Ford's Theatre in Washington, D.C., while attending a performance. The nature and extent of the religious beliefs of the 16th president of the United States (1861–65) remain in dispute. Lincoln never joined a church but was known to quote Scripture in his public speeches. Although Lincoln clearly knew both Testaments and frequently quoted the Bible from memory, the nature and depth of his religious convictions has been debated extensively and inconclusively since his assassination.

Lincoln was well known for his religious activities during his presidency. For example, he attended, particularly regularly after the death of his son in 1862, Sunday services in the New York Avenue Presbyterian Church in Washington, D.C. While attending that church, Lincoln reportedly initiated a tradition of standing for prayer, explaining afterward that he thought he should stand for his commander in chief in much the same manner that his soldiers stood when addressing him. He also was said to have occasionally attended midweek prayer services there. In 1863, Lincoln added a religious dimension to the traditional Thanksgiving holiday, an observance that had largely been secular since its inception by President GEORGE WASHINGTON. Finally, many of his presidential

Abraham Lincoln *(Library of Congress)*

speeches, in particular his famous Second Inaugural address, contained important use of religious references, images, and phrases as he sought to rally the nation mired in the depths of the Civil War. Records at that time also reveal that Lincoln allowed White House visitors to pray with him or asked them to pray for him in carrying out his presidential duties.

Before coming to the White House, Lincoln was exposed primarily to a Calvinistic Baptist perspective (see CALVINISM), but during his formative years he also occasionally heard Methodist preachers. All historic references to Lincoln's religious background have been in connection with Protestant denominations and viewpoints. Throughout his life, however, Lincoln continuously declined to join any denomination. Yet he rented a pew in the first Presbyterian Church in Springfield, Illinois, in the years before his election to the presidency. Moreover, several of his biographers seemed to agree that his early and growing opposition to slavery was in part anchored in his religious beliefs. In his pre-presidential years, Lincoln made public religious references in speeches such as his "Young Man's Lyceum Address" in 1838, and he cleverly used quotes and references to the Bible in his famous "House Divided" speech in 1858.

Many scholars have noted that as Lincoln aged, he made more references to religion and God. Some scholars, such as Nicholas Parrillo, have focused on what they saw as a powerful Calvinist theme in Lincoln's views of God and religion. On the other hand, some analysts, such as Mark Noll, concluded that Lincoln's "faith was genuine, but only partially Christian." Another perspective saw Lincoln as somewhat of a DEIST who, until his later years, did not believe in a personal God. Yet another prominent view over the years has been that Lincoln simply made Scripture references and used religious appeals as rhetorical tools to help him attain political goals. In sum, many analysts have maintained that Lincoln was indeed a Christian, many more observers have tended to agree that Lincoln believed in God, while still more maintained that he was at heart a religious man. Yet interviews of Lincoln's contemporaries and close analyses of all his writings and speeches have yet to provide a definitive answer about Lincoln's religious beliefs.

Whatever the case, Lincoln has been revered in almost religious terms. Clinton Rossiter saw Lincoln as "the martyred Christ of democracy's passion play," while Walt Whitman saw him as the "redeemer president."

See also ABOLITIONIST MOVEMENT; CIVIL RELIGION.

Further reading: Donald, David H. *Lincoln.* New York: Simon and Schuster, 1995; Guelzo, Allan. *Abraham Lincoln: Redeemer President,* Grand Rapids, Mich.: Eerdmans, 1999; Lincoln, Abraham. *His Speeches and Writings.* Roy P. Basler, ed. New York: Da Capo, 1990; Morel, Lucas. *Lincoln's Sacred Effort: Defining Religion's Role in American Self-Government,* Lanham, Md.: Lexington Books, 2000; Noll, Mark. "The Struggle for Lincoln's Soul." *Christianity Today* 42, no. 2 (1998): 64; Parrillo, Nicholas. "Lincoln's Calvinist Transformation: Emancipation and War." *Civil War History* 46, no. 3 (2000); Rossiter, Clinton. *The American Presidency.* New York: Harcourt, 1956.

liturgical churches and politics

Though all churches are liturgical in some sense, what is generally meant by "liturgical churches" is the group of churches that maintains the Western or Eastern liturgical rites that have existed from the early church to the present day. All the Orthodox churches are liturgical in that sense, as are the ROMAN CATHOLIC CHURCH and its various rites. Included as liturgical churches are also those that did not reject the classic liturgy of the Roman Catholic Church at the time of the Reformation. The Anglican (EPISCOPAL CHURCH USA) and Lutheran Churches are liturgical churches of this latter kind.

Liturgical churches, because of their respect for catholic tradition, are also hierarchical. They rely on a chain of authority that proceeds downward from the historic episcopacy. Furthermore, they interpret themselves as being organically connected to each other and to the larger body of the holy catholic church. The biblical image of the church as the Body of Christ is a crucial theme in their lives.

These characteristics have political implications. For example, since they view themselves as an interlocking whole, they are not as likely as congregationally based churches to abandon ministries in difficult areas, be they urban or rural. The church lends support—financial and spiritual—to churches that otherwise could not be sustained. Catholics, Lutherans, and Episcopalians are likely to remain in poor neighborhoods or regions long after churches with congregational polities have left. This means that such churches can speak more authentically on behalf of the poor, since they have not abandoned them. The Catholic bishops, for example, can speak persuasively to American society because their churches have maintained a presence and solidarity with the poor. They can play their "prophetic" roles more powerfully because they have not neglected their priestly and pastoral roles.

Another related capacity of the liturgical churches is that they can speak with a fairly unified and authoritative voice. Since they are more cohesive than more Protestant churches, they develop pastoral letters and social statements that attempt to speak for the church to the society. They also can act in a more concerted fashion when they decide to support a particular social policy. Again, the Catholic Church is a good example. Its statements and actions are more effective because they have ecclesiastical weight behind them.

For many adherents of a strong liturgical approach to church life, and for a new theological school—that of radical orthodoxy—the liturgy becomes a vehicle for creating a sacramental reality that counters the fallen and debased world around the church. The liturgy is crucial in constructing an "ecclesial reality" that has potent political meanings. It is sharply differentiated from a world that is idolatrous and violent. By offering another reality to the faithful, it exposes the "world" for what it is, and points to another reality that transcends and contradicts it. It fulfills the dictum of Stanley Hauerwas, that "the church does not have a social ethic, it is a social ethic."

See also CATHOLIC BISHOPS' 1975 PASTORAL LETTER ON ABORTION; CATHOLIC BISHOPS' 1983 PASTORAL LETTER ON WAR AND PEACE; CATHOLIC BISHOPS' 1986 PASTORAL LETTER ON THE ECONOMY; EASTERN ORTHODOX CHURCHES; EVANGELICAL LUTHERAN CHURCH IN AMERICA; LUTHERAN CHURCH–MISSOURI SYNOD; NATIONAL CONFERENCE OF CATHOLIC BISHOPS; WISCONSIN EVANGELICAL LUTHERAN SYNOD.

Further reading: Hauerwas, Stanley. *A Community of Character: Toward a Constructive Christian Social Ethic.* Notre Dame, Ind.: University of Notre Dame Press, 1998; Milbank, John, Catherine Pickstock, and Graham Ward, eds. *Radical Orthodoxy: A New Theology.* New York: Routledge, 1999.

—Robert Benne

Locke, John (1632–1704) *philosopher*

John Locke, a British philosopher of the early Enlightenment, began to write on political philosophy and religious TOLERATION as a result of his career in government. Born in Wrington, Somerset, England, and educated at Christ Church in Oxford University, Locke rejected scholasticism and began to study and experiment in science. His first introduction to politics came in 1667, as he served as physician, secretary, and adviser to Sir Anthony Ashley Cooper, who, in 1672, became the earl of Shaftesbury and, for a year, lord chancellor. In 1669, Locke wrote a draft constitution for Carolina, then a British colony. Then, at Shaftesbury's request, Locke wrote—but did not publish—his first *Treatise of Government* to justify breaking a line of kingly succession.

Shaftesbury, who believed in tolerating religious dissent, nevertheless took a leading role in an attempt to exclude Roman Catholics from the British throne, fearing the repression of Protestants. As a result, both Shaftesbury and Locke fled to Holland as it became clear that James, duke of York and a staunch Roman Catholic, would come to power. After the Glorious Revolution of 1688, in which Protestants William and Mary assumed the throne and agreed to limits to their rule, Locke returned to England and became a commissioner of appeals. In this favorable environment, Locke began to publish his theories on knowledge, religion, and civil government.

Locke's epistemology, as spelled out in his *Essay Concerning Human Understanding* (1690), is famously anti-Cartesian, although it is not antirationalist. Unlike French philosopher René Descartes, Locke did not think that the mind had any innate ideas, describing a child's mind as a tabula rasa (blank slate). Consequently, Locke promoted a form of empiricism, arguing that knowledge was gained by reflecting rationally on sense perceptions, as one built up from simple to more complex ideas. Locke was aware of the arguments of the ancient Skeptics that all sense experiences were unreliable. But while Descartes felt that skepticism required certainty to be founded on reason alone, Locke chose instead to distinguish between two kinds of qualities to an object: primary and secondary. Primary qualities such as heat or color were defined as those unable to be measured and thus dependent on subjective human descriptions. Secondary qualities such as height and weight were measurable, and so, Locke wrote, provided a reliable foundation for knowledge.

On the whole, Locke was more willing to accept uncertainty and probable knowledge than Descartes, which is partially why he promoted religious tolerance in his four *Letters on Toleration* (1689–1706). Locke distinguished between natural and revealed religion, arguing that it was possible to infer the basics of Christianity without scriptural revelation. This idea of a rational religion led some to accuse Locke of deism, for he did not consider revelation to be a form of knowledge. Locke saw the particularities of religious practice and belief as unprovable and thus irresolvable, but he thought that fundamental principles of ethics and theism should be universally recognized. As a result, all citizens who believed in God and were loyal to the state should be tolerated.

While ethical behavior was divinely commanded, Locke argued that submission to tyrannical rulers was not. In his *Two Treatises of Government* (1690), Locke refuted Sir Robert Filmore's *Patriarcha*, which traced a DIVINE RIGHT OF KINGS to rule from their descent from Adam. Following Hobbes, Locke believed that government was justified by a social contract created as people in a state of nature chose to form a society, but Locke disagreed with Hobbes's absolutism. Once a ruler became a tyrant and considered his or her desires above the good of the people, Locke wrote, it was rightful to rebel. Yet, while Locke maintained that people in a state of nature were all equal, he defended unequal wealth. The labor a person invested in unowned land or other resources legitimated ownership, but no one should take more than he or she could tend. Despite this caveat, Locke is often understood to be a strong defender of property rights.

The role of Locke and other Enlightenment rationalists at the outbreak of the American Revolution has been the subject of much debate. It appears that both Patriots and Loyalists employed Lockean notions of natural rights, social contracts, and private property in defending their positions. However, THOMAS JEFFERSON'S DECLARATION OF INDEPENDENCE pays obvious homage to Locke in both language and argument, defending rebellion against tyranny and citing the natural rights of "life, liberty, and the pursuit of happiness," an echo of Locke's "life, liberty, and property." The U.S. Constitution also draws on Locke in the use of checks and balances, the idea of freedom of worship, and the notion of equality of all citizens, although Locke opposed slavery, which the Constitution permitted.

—Caroline R. Sherman

Lovell v. City of Griffin 303 U.S. 444 (1938)

The case of *Lovell v. City of Griffin, Georgia* (1938) was one of the earliest cases challenging the right of local officials to interfere with, restrict, or regulate First Amendment rights. At stake was the ability of the Jehovah's Witnesses to proselytize without restriction and the extent to which the Supreme Court would carve out FREE EXERCISE exemptions.

In the mid-19th century, there was a movement in American Protestantism by various religious groups seeking the Second Advent of Christ, from which the JEHOVAH'S WITNESSES arose. Known as the WATCHTOWER SOCIETY, the sect is one of the three largest Adventist sects in the country, along with CHRISTIAN SCIENCE and the LATTER-DAY SAINTS. Charles Taze Russell became, along with other 19th-century Protestants, disillusioned with the mainstream churches. His books and pamphlets, principally a seven-volume series entitled *Studies in the Scripture,* along with his magazine *Zion's Watch Tower and Herald of Christ's Presence,* formed the basis of much of Jehovah's Witness doctrine.

Russell's writings, strongly influenced by millenarianism, are basic to the Adventist movement. From these publications developed one of the features that distinguished the Witnesses from other Adventist sects, specifically, their refusal to submit to civil authority in a number of ways. As a result, cases affecting the Witnesses came before the U.S. Supreme Court debating the question of the extent to which the Witnesses were permitted by their beliefs and required by law to "render unto Caesar."

Throughout their history, but more particularly in the late 1930s and early 1940s, the Witnesses challenged government strictures at all levels. Some particularly active demands against the legal system in the context of World War II included protesting antileafleting laws.

The city ordinance challenged by the Witnesses in *Lovell* attempted to regulate, as a nuisance, all distribution, by any means, of "literature of any kind." The chief of police was "directed to suppress the same and abate any nuisance as is described [in the ordinance]." In other words, the chief of police had the authority to say what printed material could and could not be read in the city of Griffin, Georgia.

John Milton feared this state of affairs in 1644 when he published his *Aeropagitica, An Appeal for the Liberty of Unlicensed Printing.* Milton's concerns were cited by the Supreme Court as it undertook a review of Alma Lovell's imprisonment of 50 days for failure to pay her $50 fine. According to some scholars, Milton's *Aeropagitica* heavily influenced the founding fathers to include the freedom of speech and press provisions in the Bill of Rights in the Constitution. Chief Justice Hughes summarized the background of the free speech and press provisions when he wrote the opinion of the Court that struck down the city ordinance as being contrary to First Amendment protections.

Hughes found that citizens must be free to practice their religion in the manner as dictated by their conscience. The opinion refers to Thomas Paine and then states unequivocally: "The press in its historic connotation comprehends every sort of publication." The ordinance purported to regulate only distribution, but Hughes suggested, "Liberty of circulating is as essential to that freedom as liberty of publishing; indeed without circulation, the publication would be of little value." Even minority religious groups such as the Jehovah's Witnesses cannot be subject to the whims of government officials.

See also COX V. NEW HAMPSHIRE; MARTIN V. STRUTHERS; MURDOCK V. PENNSYLVANIA.

—StanLey M. Morris

Lukumi Babalu Aye Inc., Church of the v. City of Hialeah 508 U.S. 520 (1993)

Church of the Lukumi Babalu Aye Inc. v. City of Hialeah is a case involving a law specifically tailored to hinder the practice of a certain religion. Members of the Santeria religion—a combination of traditional African religion and Roman Catholicism that began in the 19th century when African slaves were brought to Catholic Cuba—use animal sacrifice in their religious ceremonies to worship the *orishas* (spirits). The Church of Lukumi, practicing this religion, announced plans to open a house of worship in the city of Hialeah, Florida. The Hialeah city council held an emergency public meeting and adopted several ordinances, one of which banned the practice of animal sacrifice. The church and its president filed suit, claiming that these ordinances violated the First Amendment's FREE EXERCISE clause.

The district court ruled for the city, saying it was merely pursuing the secular goal of prohibiting cruelty to animals and guarding public health and safety. The court found four compelling interests in favor of government regulation of this religious conduct: the health risk of animal sacrifice, the risk of emotional injury to children who witness it, protecting animals from cruelty, and restricting the slaughter of animals to places zoned for slaughter. Balancing the government's and the religious participants' interests, the district court found for the city. The United States Court of Appeals for the Eleventh Circuit affirmed in a one-paragraph per curiam decision. The Supreme Court heard the case and, writing for the majority, Justice Kennedy argued that the ordinances were not neutral, were not of general applicability, were not drawn in narrow terms, did not advance compelling government interests, and were therefore void as violations of the free exercise clause of the First Amendment.

In his opinion, Kennedy argued that the first question before the Court is whether the laws in question were neutral and of general applicability. If they were neither neutral nor of general applicability, the next question is whether the government had a compelling interest and had drawn the laws narrowly enough to meet that interest without placing an undue burden on religion. The ordinances under consideration here failed all of these tests.

They are not neutral because, first, they do not pass facial neutrality, even on their face, the laws seem to single out the Santeria religion for regulation. However, since it may be debatable whether these ordinances have facial neutrality, and because facial neutrality is not determinative, Kennedy determined that the object of the ordinances was not neutral either. He argued that the "design of the laws accomplishes . . . a 'religious gerrymander' . . . an impermissible attempt to target petitioners and their religious practices."

The ordinances were also not generally applicable since they had been drawn, according to Kennedy, to assure that only the religious exercise of the Santeria church members fell under their proscriptions. Some of the ordinances were overly broad and others under-inclusive, such that none was neutral or generally applicable. Without exception, they singled out the Santeria religion and its practice while allowing other behaviors that might also qualify as ordinance violations to continue intact.

Because the ordinances failed the neutrality and general applicability tests, Kennedy determined whether the government had a compelling interest driving these regulations and, if so, whether its interest had been met through narrowly drawn regulations that minimized any effect on the exercise of religion. While Kennedy admitted that the government had compelling interests here, he found that the ordinances were not narrowly tailored to protect those interests. To pursue its interest in public health, for example, the council could have made regulations regarding the disposal of organic materials, but it did not. It could have prevented cruelty to animals, another of its interests, by regulating the conditions around the possession of animals, but it did not. In short, "The ordinances had as their object the suppression of religion," which is abhorrent to the First Amendment's free exercise guarantee.

The decision was, in effect, unanimous, but several justices made it clear that they did not exactly agree with the majority's reliance on *EMPLOYMENT DIVISION V. SMITH* (1990). Justices Souter, Blackmun, and O'Connor all wrote separately to note that they would revisit the *Smith* decision—which held that a generally applicable law that incidentally inhibited religious practice was constitutional—and overrule it as a departure from the Court's First Amendment jurisprudence.

—Sara C. Benesh

Lutheran Church–Missouri Synod

Believing they could no longer practice their confessional brand of Lutheranism because of the growing spread of rationalism in Germany, over 600 Lutherans from the former kingdom of Saxony set out for St. Louis, Missouri, in November 1838. Martin Stephan—a charismatic pastor from Dresden and champion of confessionalism—led the journey to America and was officially appointed bishop during the voyage. Arriving first in the port of New Orleans and then traveling up the Mississippi River, the Saxon Lutherans eventually reached St. Louis early in 1839. Although some stayed in St. Louis, most followed Stephan some 100 miles south to settle in Perry County. Shortly after his arrival in Perry County, Stephan was removed as bishop and forever barred from Missouri, mainly because of his authoritarian behavior, embezzlement of community funds, and sexual liaisons with women. After his

removal, Carl Ferdinand Wilhelm Walther emerged as the Saxon Lutherans' new leader. Walther was pastor of Trinity Lutheran Church in St. Louis, which became the mother and model church for all Saxon Lutherans. Additionally, he organized and edited *Der Lutheraner* (*The Lutheran*), a biweekly publication of Trinity strongly emphasizing confessionalism.

Although the Saxon Lutherans in Missouri were religiously rather well equipped, this was not the case for German Lutherans settling in other parts of America. Friedrich Conrad Dietrich Wyneken—a prominent Lutheran missionary serving in Indiana since 1838—was so dismayed by the quality of ministers that he returned to Germany in 1814 to request that more pastors be sent to America. Wilhelm Loehe—a confessional Lutheran pastor at Neuendettelsau in Bavaria—soon answered Wyneken's request, recruiting people and generating funds for the Lutheran mission in America. Loehe's recruits were primarily sent to Ohio, Indiana, and Michigan. A number of these recruits left the Ohio Synod in 1845, largely over the use of the English language. In 1846, the "Loehe men" from Ohio met in St. Louis with the Saxon Lutheran pastors to draft a constitution for a new synod. They met again in July of that year in Fort Wayne, Indiana, and agreed to hold the founding meeting of the new synod the upcoming spring in Chicago, Illinois. On April 25, 1847, the Saxons and the Loehe men of Ohio, along with a number of Loehe recruits who had recently left the Michigan Synod, gathered at First St. Paul's Lutheran Church in Chicago to hold the first convention of the German Evangelical Lutheran Synod of Missouri, Ohio, and other states. In all, 12 pastors and 16 congregations signed the constitution, while 10 other pastors and a Lutheran schoolteacher became advisory members. Carl Ferdinand Wilhelm Walther was elected as first president of the synod. In 1947, 100 years after its first convention, the Lutheran Church-Missouri Synod (LCMS) was adopted as the official, and still current, title of the synod.

From the very beginning, the Missouri Synod identified itself as theologically conservative. No less is true today, as the LCMS remains committed to upholding the authority of the Bible as the actual inspired and inerrant Word of God. This stance toward the Bible would seem to place the LCMS in the Protestant FUNDAMENTALIST camp. Nevertheless, the Missouri Synod historically has distinguished itself from Protestant fundamentalism—for example, remaining neutral in the Fundamentalist-Modernist controversy of the 1920s—and continues to acknowledge this distinction today. Although the LCMS has never been involved in a merger, its unwavering commitment to theological conservatism caused a schism in the mid-1970s. When in 1974 John Tietjen was removed as president of Concordia Seminary in St. Louis for teaching doctrines contrary to those officially endorsed by the synod, many students and the vast majority of the faculty left to establish Seminex, a seminary in exile. Along with 150 congregations, they formed the Association of Evangelical Lutheran Churches (AELC). In 1987, the AELC merged with the Lutheran Church in America (LCA) and the American

Lutheran Church (ALC) to form the EVANGELICAL LUTHERAN CHURCH IN AMERICA (ELCA).

The Missouri Synod's CONSERVATISM extends beyond theology to politics. The LCMS officially supports the death penalty and holds a strong pro-life position on ABORTION. It opposes EUTHANASIA and the ordination of women, and views homosexual relations as sinful, thus rejecting GAY AND LESBIAN MARRIAGES. As of 2000, the LCMS had 2,582,440 members in 6,220 congregations. The Missouri Synod continues its historical presence in parochial schooling: in 2000, there were 1,299 preschools, 1,010 elementary schools, 71 high schools, 10 colleges, and two seminaries.

See also WISCONSIN EVANGELICAL LUTHERAN SYNOD.

Further reading: Lindsell, Harold. *The Battle for the Bible.* Grand Rapids, Mich.: Zondervan, 1976; Todd, Mary. *Authority Vested.* Grand Rapids, Mich.: Eerdmans, 2000.

—Kraig Beyerlein

Lynch v. Donnelly 465 U.S. 668 (1984)

Much as in *MARSH V. CHAMBERS,* this case debated whether an act was in violation of the *ESTABLISHMENT CLAUSE* of the First Amendment. In question was a Christmas display erected annually by the downtown retail merchants association, in conjunction with the city of Pawtucket, Rhode Island. Residents of the city and members of the local AMERICAN CIVIL LIBERTIES UNION brought the action because of the inclusion of a crèche—a scene depicting the birth of Jesus Christ. The plaintiffs charged that the publicly funded display conveyed a sectarian message and was, therefore, unconstitutional. Applying the three-prong test created in *LEMON V. KURTZMAN* (1971), the United States District Court for Rhode Island concurred. It found that the city's sponsorship of a nativity scene had "the real and substantial effect of affiliating the City with the Christian beliefs that the crèche represents." The case was then appealed to the Supreme Court, where the district court's ruling was reversed in a 5-4 decision.

Chief Justice Burger wrote that in considering *Lynch,* the Court was forced to "reconcile the inescapable tension" between maintaining the separation of church and state and recognizing that "total separation of the two is not possible." As he had in *Marsh,* Burger cited historical precedent as the basis for the Court's reasoning: "There is an unbroken history of official acknowledgement by all three branches of government of the role of religion in American life from at least 1789." Citing the First Congress's allocation of funds for LEGISLATIVE CHAPLAINS, Burger concluded that the intention of the framers was not to prohibit the display of religious heritage; rather, he concluded, religious tradition has a proper place in government activity, manifesting itself in examples such as the motto "In God We Trust," and the line "One nation under God" in the pledge of allegiance.

Following its conspicuous absence in *Marsh,* the Burger Court reinstated the established *Lemon* test in *Lynch.* Burger concluded that the town's display passed the three prongs: One, the display did indeed have a secular legislative purpose—"The display is sponsored by the city to celebrate the Holiday and to depict the origins of that Holiday. These are legitimate secular purposes." Two, the crèche did not have the primary effect of advancing or promoting religion—"We are unable to discern a greater aid to religion deriving from the inclusion of the crèche than from those benefits and endorsements previously held not violative of the Establishment clause." Burger insisted that when compared with the public funding of textbooks, the issue of Sunday closing laws (BLUE LAWS) dealt with in *MCGOWAN V. MARYLAND,* or the upholding of legislative chaplains in *Marsh,* that Pawtucket's actions could hardly be considered a promotion of religion.

Last, the Court ruled that the nativity scene did not lead to an excessive entanglement between church and state. The district court found that the display passed on this prong—the city expended little money, and had little contact with church authorities since purchasing the crèche. Burger concurred: "In many respects the display requires far less ongoing, day-to-day interaction between church and state than religious paintings in public galleries."

In a lengthy dissent, Justice WILLIAM BRENNAN remarked that "[n]othing in the history of such practices or the setting in which the city's crèche is presented obscures or diminishes the plain fact that Pawtucket's action amounts to an impermissible governmental endorsement of a particular faith." Although encouraged by the Court's return to the guidelines set up in *Lemon,* Brennan lamented what he considered to be a "less-than vigorous application" of the test and a "careless decision" by the Court. Finding the nativity scene unconstitutional on all three counts, Brennan criticized the direction the Court had taken in validating the crèche on the grounds of "religious heritage." Brennan claimed that compared to the focused discussion of history in prior cases, Chief Justice Burger's reasoning amounted to an unfocused and personal interpretation: "Without that guiding principle and the intellectual discipline it imposes, the Court is at sea, free to select random elements of America's varied history solely to suit the views of the five members of this Court."

ALLEGHENY V. ACLU (1989) would deal with a number of similar questions in a way that resulted in a partial reversal of *Lynch* and *Marsh.*

—Anand E. Sokhey

Lyng v. Northwest Indian Cemetery Protective Association 521 U.S. 507 (1988)

In 1982, the U.S. Forest Service completed an environmental impact statement for the Chimney Rock area of the Six Rivers National Forest. The study found that Native Americans had traditionally used the area for burial grounds and other religious ceremonies. The study suggested that road construction and timber harvesting should proceed but be completed outside the sacred areas. However, the Northwest

Indian Cemetery Protective Association filed suit against Richard E. Lyng, secretary of agriculture, to prohibit the projects near the sacred areas. The Supreme Court ruled, on April 19, 1988, that the First Amendment's FREE EXERCISE CLAUSE does not forbid the U.S. government from completing proposed roads or from gathering lumber in a national forest that historically had been used by American Indians for sacred purposes. Justice Sandra Day O'Connor announced the 5-3 decision, ruling against the Northwest Indian Cemetery Protective Association (with Justice Anthony Kennedy taking no part in the deliberation or the decision of the case).

In a similar case, *BOWEN V. ROY,* Native Americans argued that using Social Security numbers to receive welfare benefits robbed their children of their religious rights. Here, the Court ruled that the use of Social Security numbers was legal because neither would they be penalized compared with other religious groups, nor would they be forced to act or not act in a particular way in accordance with their religious beliefs. The *Lyng* Court argues, in like manner, that the free exercise clause is not violated because the Department of Agriculture not only made adjustments to its plan by moving the proposed construction and harvesting to alternate locations, but also because it followed the guidelines of the American Indian Religious Freedom Act.

The Northwest Indian Cemetery Protective Association argued that the construction of the roads and the harvesting of timber through the Chimney Rock area would not only destroy their sacred land but also disallow them from freely practicing their religion. They claimed that the land in question is vital to the sacredness of their religious practices and that the damage encountered would make it unsuitable for ritual purposes. However, the majority opinion went on to state that the free exercise clause was designed to protect individuals from government interference in their religion but not to allow an individual to instruct federal actions. In both the *Roy* and *Lyng* cases, the free exercise was not prohibited because religious actions or beliefs were not penalized. The *Lyng* Court went on to say: "The First Amendment must apply to all citizens alike, and it can give to none of them a veto over public programs that do not prohibit the free exercise of religion." This logic was certainly applied in this case.

See also NATIVE AMERICAN SACRED GROUNDS.

—Kelli R. Williams

Madison, James (1751–1836) *U.S. president*

James Madison was a primary architect of the federal Constitution (1787–88), drafted the BILL OF RIGHTS (1789), and served as the nation's fourth president (1809–17). Along with his fellow Virginian THOMAS JEFFERSON, Madison was a champion of religious freedom. He concluded early that politics under the Articles of Confederation was too parochial, allowing overbearing majorities in individual states to usurp rights, including the rights of conscience. As such, he helped pass Jefferson's Statute for Establishing Religious Freedom in Virginia and advocated a stronger national government. After securing ratification of the Constitution, he helped formulate the Bill of Rights, which prohibits a nationally established religion and guarantees the free exercise of religion.

Madison's upbringing was Anglican; his father was a vestryman, and a cousin was an Anglican bishop. While he never seriously fell away from his native sect or its members, Madison's own religious practice became conspicuously unzealous. The Scottish-born Presbyterian JOHN WITHERSPOON taught Madison at the College of New Jersey (now Princeton University). Witherspoon made his name fighting doctrinal orthodoxy within the Presbyterian Church and imbued his students with an appreciation for religious as well as political freedom. Other than Madison's unwavering support for the rights of conscience, his own mature religious beliefs are a matter of conjecture. Though he read theological works with interest, "religious topics simply disappear from his surviving writings after 1776."

Madison's first involvement in politics was occasioned by the persecution of Virginia Baptists in 1773. How exactly he defended these dissenters remains obscure. It is clearer that a long-term alliance between them and Madison was initiated, which helped secure Madison's election to the state legislature and challenge the Anglican establishment. Madison was a member of the revolutionary state legislature that drafted the Virginia Declaration of Rights (1776). He suggested that the drafting committee go much further than the "full toleration" proposed by George Mason. Madison suggested that the legislature acknowledge: "All men are equally entitled to the full and free exercise of [religion] according to the dictates of Conscience." If the right of conscience was an inviolable natural right, it was not the province of the state merely to tolerate dissenting sects. Madison coupled this language with a provision for total disestablishment. That provision failed, but a more moderate amendment entitled citizens to free exercise.

In 1784, Virginia nearly enacted a bill that taxed citizens of all religious persuasions to support their respective

James Madison *(Library of Congress)*

265

denominations. Madison postponed the issue until it could be further digested. In the meantime, he wrote a "Memorial and Remonstrance against Religious Assessments." In the anonymous memorial, Madison presented 15 reasons supporting the SEPARATION OF CHURCH AND STATE. The document echoes the themes of Jefferson's Act for Establishing Religious Freedom, but it is also more systematic. On the strength of Madison's and other similar writings, the Virginia citizenry sent an unequivocal message to the legislature to end the religious establishment. In the next session, Madison shepherded Jefferson's act through to passage, ending state-sanctioned religious discrimination.

Seeing a Presbyterian-Baptist coalition provide a counterweight to the Episcopal establishment made a great impression on Madison. A smaller, less diverse state would not have favored disestablishment. Madison came to realize that the heterogeneity of the nation could temper the parochialism of the states. He was a key member of the Philadelphia Convention, which formulated the Constitution, and he articulated its benefits most famously in the essay *Federalist* #10. Madison there noted that tyrannical majority factions, religious and otherwise, were unlikely to form at the national level. Strengthening the national government would safeguard rights, because no one group could dominate. Because Madison believed a strengthened national regime could solve the problem of parochialism mechanically, he did not feel a bill of rights was needed. Nevertheless, after ratification he acknowledged that it would allay fears about the new government and probably do no harm. Madison thus took the initiative in formulating the Bill of Rights during the First Congress. He suggested that freedom of conscience be guaranteed against both national and state encroachment. Congress watered down Madison's suggestion, merely guaranteeing that there would be no nationally established religion and that the national government would not inhibit "free exercise."

Madison considered the fight for religious freedom among his greatest accomplishments. Consistently wary of mixing religion with politics, Madison even doubted his ability as president to call for a national day of prayer. His was a quintessential Enlightenment approach to religion; he believed religion was a largely private enterprise with no place in public life.

See also ESTABLISHMENT CLAUSE; FREE EXERCISE CLAUSE.

Further reading: Banning, Lance. *The Sacred Fire of Liberty.* Ithaca, N.Y.: Cornell University Press, 1995; Hutchinson, William T., ed. *The Papers of James Madison.* Chicago: University of Chicago Press, 1962–present.

—David J. Siemers

mainline Protestant pro-gay groups

Mainline pro-gay groups exist in many of the mainline Protestant denominations. These groups provide support for gays and lesbians within the denomination, and some lobby at national denominational meetings for changes in denominational policy. Pro-gay groups that individuals join include Affirmation (UNITED METHODIST CHURCH), Integrity (EPISCOPAL CHURCH), More Light Presbyterians (PRESBYTERIAN CHURCH USA), American Baptists Concerned (AMERICAN BAPTIST CHURCHES), Lutherans Concerned North America (EVANGELICAL LUTHERAN CHURCH IN AMERICA), and the United Church of Christ (UCC) Coalition for Lesbian, Gay, Bisexual, and Transgender Concerns. With the exception of the UCC, these groups are not formally supported by their denominations.

The first pro-gay group for individuals, the UCC Gay Caucus, was started in 1972 by Bill Johnson in the United Church of Christ to provide support to gay and lesbian members of the denomination. In 1974, Rev. David Baily Sindt founded Presbyterians for Lesbian and Gay Concerns, and Louie Crew started a newsletter, *Integrity*, that by 1976 had evolved into a 1,200-member grassroots group for gay and lesbian Episcopalians by the same name. In the 1970s, these groups focused on supporting gays and lesbians in their denominations, and in the 1980s some groups began to lobby national denominational bodies to change their policies about homosexuality. At present, these groups continue to support gays and lesbians within their denominations, to do outreach to the gay and lesbian community, and to advocate for change within individual denominations.

Pro-gay groups that individual congregations can join, which are commonly called "welcoming" congregation programs, include the United Methodist Reconciling Ministries Network, Evangelical Lutheran Reconciling in Christ Program, United Church of Christ Open and Affirming Congregation Program, More Light Presbyterians, Oasis Congregations, and Welcoming and Affirming Baptist churches. These programs first started in 1978 when Rev. Robert Davidson, a minister at West Park Presbyterian Church in New York City, wrote a statement of conscience that led to a network of Presbyterian congregations that identified themselves as formally welcoming gays and lesbians into their churches. Davidson's central idea was that congregations who disagree with statements or actions their denominations make around homosexuality should say so publicly, and welcome gay men and lesbians into the life of their congregations. Though the mainline churches have never suggested excluding homosexuals from their congregations, proponents of welcoming congregation programs argue that policies that call homosexuality incompatible with Christian teaching do effectively exclude homosexuals. To become a welcoming congregation, individual congregations normally go through a period of study and reflection about homosexuality and then vote about whether or not to join.

Davidson's statement led to the More Light Churches network in the Presbyterian Church USA, which was copied in the 1980s by people within the other mainline denominations. Gay supportive congregation programs generally tried to shift the focus of discussion in the mainline away from morality toward ministry. Morality questions focus on what the Bible says about homosexuality and about whether individuals can be both gay and Christian. Ministry questions emphasize the question, "Can you be a Christian and exclude people from your church?" This shift in emphasis also personalizes questions about homosexuality. The number of welcoming congregations grew throughout the 1980s and 1990s, and by the summer of 2000, there were more than 800 welcoming congregations in 45 states across the country. An ecumenical welcoming congregation movement started in 1990 and has grown through the joint publication of a journal for welcoming congregations called *Open Hands* and through a series of national welcoming congregation meetings and conferences.

Additional mainline pro-gay groups include That All May Freely Serve in the Presbyterian denomination and the Extraordinary Candidate program in the Evangelical Lutheran Church of America. Both these groups were started to promote gay ordination in these denominations. Cornet, the United Methodist Covenant Relationship Network, supports worship services that celebrate some gender covenant relationships in the United Methodist Church. Pro-gay student groups also exist in several of the denominations.

See also GAY AND LESBIAN MARRIAGE; GAY RIGHTS.

Further reading: Cadge, Wendy. "Vital Conflicts: The Mainline Protestant Denominations Debate Homosexuality." In *The Quiet Hand of God: Faith Based Activism and the Public Role of Mainline Protestantism.* Edited by Robert Wuthnow and John H. Evans. Berkeley: University of California Press, 2002.

—Wendy Cadge

mainline Protestants and the Republican Party

Protestants are, and have been, the most numerous and diverse religious group in the United States. American Protestantism encompasses three major traditions: mainline, evangelical, and African American. The mainline Protestant tradition has historically been predominant; but, in recent decades, both evangelicals and Roman Catholics began to outnumber mainline Protestants. By 1996, mainline Protestants were the second-largest Protestant tradition, accounting for about 22 percent of the adult population. By the year 2000, 20 million identified themselves as part of that Protestant tradition. Among them are several types of mainline Protestant parishioners that include the major "liberal denominations," including the UNITED METHODIST CHURCH, EVANGELICAL LUTHERAN CHURCH IN AMERICA, PRESBYTERIAN CHURCH USA, and the EPISCOPAL CHURCH. Politically active, and with a more worldly focus than evangelicals, mainline Protestants stress social reform over individual salvation.

Since its inception in 1860, mainline Protestant parishioners have supported the Republican Party. They were heavily involved in early Republican social movements, including ABOLITION, temperance, and women's rights. Over the course of the 20th century, mainline Protestants would become one of the most stable Republican voting blocs.

Since the 1960s, however, mainline Protestants have become increasingly centrist in their political views as evangelicals became more and more identified with the Christian Right. Mainline clergy had come to view liberal social action, particularly on race issues, as a central part of their ministry, with varied levels of support from their congregations. As a result of this split, a growing political liberalism in the mainline tradition centered on the clergy as the congregants remained conservative.

Because issue attitudes greatly influence party identification, many mainline Protestants still identify themselves as Republicans despite the views of their clergy. Overall the congregants' beliefs emphasize fiscal conservatism. By 1988, 74 percent of mainline Protestants voted for George H. W. Bush for president.

Nevertheless, support for the Republican Party began to decline in the 1992 presidential election. In that year, mainline Protestants gave a plurality (42 percent) of their votes to Bush, 37 percent to Bill Clinton, and 21 percent to Reform Party candidate Ross Perot. While mainline Protestants are second only to evangelicals in labeling themselves as conservatives, in 1992 only 40 percent identified themselves as conservative (Corbett 1999). By the 1994 midterm election, only 38 percent of mainline Protestants identified themselves as Republican, a figure that is significantly down from 47 percent in 1990. By the 1996 presidential election, only 60 percent of mainline Protestants voted for the Republican Party nominee, Bob Dole.

This overall decline in support for the Republican Party indicates that mainline Protestants as a group have been in numerical decline since the 1960s. For example, the 105th Congress demonstrated a 30-year downturn in the number of congressional representatives belonging to mainline churches. Lawmakers who belonged to mainline churches accounted for 280 seats in both the House of Representatives and the Senate three decades ago, compared with 169 in January 1997.

See also CHRISTIAN RIGHT AND THE REPUBLICAN PARTY; RELIGION IN THE 1988, 1992, 1994, 1996, PRESIDENTIAL ELECTIONS.

Further reading: Corbett, Michael, and Julia Mitchell Corbett. *Politics and Religion in the United States.* New York: Garland, 1999; "Fewer Mainline Protestants in Congress." *Christianity Today* 41 (April 7, 1997): 52; Kohut, Andrew, John C. Green, Scott Teeter, and Robert C. Toth. *The Diminishing Divide: Religion's Changing Role in American Politics.* Washington, D.C.: Brookings Institution, 2000.

—Veronica Donahue DiConti

mainline Protestant Washington offices

Since the Prohibition era, mainline PROTESTANTISM has retained an institutional political presence in American politics at the national level. Each major mainline Protestant denomination in the United States supports an advocacy office in Washington, D.C. These offices function as interest groups by representing the political interests of the denominations and coordinating their national advocacy efforts. The oldest and largest of the mainline offices, the UNITED METHODIST CHURCH's General Board of Church and Society, traces its history to the 1920s. Other mainline denominations added Washington offices in the mid-20th century. As a group, these offices have long advocated liberal political agendas. All except the Lutheran office are housed in the United Methodist Building, conveniently located on Capitol Hill beside the Supreme Court.

The Washington offices pursue what is often called a "peace and justice" agenda by advocating for human rights at home and abroad, working to preserve the environment, questioning the U.S. use of military force, and above all fighting for the disadvantaged. The offices lobby members of Congress and executive branch staff, often working in coalition with religious and secular interest groups alike. They also file AMICUS CURIAE BRIEFS in key federal cases. To connect with local congregations, the offices support "action networks" of interested laity and clergy with whom they communicate about policy. These action networks are designed to stimulate grassroots discussion of politics and involvement in lobbying activities.

Mainline Protestant Washington offices continue to operate in an era when religio-political action is increasingly carried out at the local level. At times, they play important roles in policy debates, particularly over international human rights issues, but they rarely exercise a great deal of political power. The offices themselves do not exist at the apex of the denominations' organizational structures, so they must take direction from denominational officials who rank above them while remaining sensitive to grassroots pressures and demands. And because the mainline Protestant denominations are not headquartered in Washington, D.C., the Washington officials are geographically separated from both the top levels of the denominational hierarchy and their grassroots. For the most part, the offices are underfunded and understaffed.

The work of the Washington offices is further complicated by the tremendous diversity inherent within mainline Protestant denominations. The specific policy areas in which the mainline Washington offices work are dictated by decisions made at national denominational meetings, where the voices of both the hierarchy and the grassroots influence the outcomes of contentious debates. Mainline Protestantism can count its openness and diversity among its strengths, but these factors present a challenge for finding (much less articulating) a unified political voice. There is often substantial disagreement within mainline denominations over issues, positions, and strategies.

Moreover, the Washington offices themselves have faced serious challenges from critics within their own denominations about whether they serve a valuable purpose. In 1998, the United Methodist Office came under attack by conservative Methodists who said the office is too liberal and inappropriately partisan. Controversy has also erupted over the Presbyterian Washington Office, which represents the interests of the PRESBYTERIAN CHURCH USA. The results of a major survey of Presbyterians revealed very little knowledge of or support for the office, and the conservative *Presbyterian Layman* accused the office of wasting the denomination's money by pandering to liberals.

The denominational offices nevertheless constitute an important religious presence in Washington, and they ensure that the voices of mainline Protestants are heard among the cacophony of other organized interests. They advocate for the disadvantaged and met with substantial policy success surrounding the "Jubilee 2000" international debt relief plan. They also continue to question what they consider aggressive U.S. foreign policy.

Further reading: Hertzke, Allen D. *Representing God in Washington.* Knoxville: University of Tennessee Press; Marcum, Jack. "Views on the PC(USA) Washington Office. URL: http://www.pcusa.org/rs/dcoffice.htm; Olson, Laura R. "Mainline Protestant Washington Offices and the Political Lives of Clergy." In *The Quiet Hand of God.* Edited by Robert Wuthnow and John H. Evans. Berkeley: University of California Press.

—Laura R. Olson

Malcolm X (El Hajj Malik El-Shabazz) (1925–1965)

religious leader, activist

Malcolm X was born Malcolm Little in Omaha, Nebraska, on May 19, 1925. He dropped the "slave name" Little and adopted the initial X (representing the unknown) when he became a member of the NATION OF ISLAM (NOI). Malcolm was the seventh of his father's nine children, three by a previous marriage, and his mother's fourth child. His grandfather on his mother's side was Scottish, which gave Malcolm light skin, sandy blond hair, and eyes that were an unusual mixture of brown, blue, and green (depending on the lighting). His father, Reverend Earl Little, was a Baptist minister and an organizer for Marcus Garvey's Universal Negro Improvement Association, a black separatist "back-to-Africa" group of the 1920s.

Malcolm X became a devoted Black Muslim in prison, and on his release he went to work for the organization, eventually becoming minister of the Muslim mosque in Harlem. As an impassioned agitator, moralist, and cynic, Malcolm found the integrationism, gradualism, and nonviolence espoused by the established civil rights leadership to be misguided and unacceptable. Until 1964, Malcolm had accepted Black Muslim theology without question. In 1964, however, he made a pilgrimage to Mecca and was so impressed by orthodox Islam's multiracialism that he rejected NOI. On his return, Malcolm became an orthodox Muslim and eventually a rival to NOI leader ELIJAH MUHAMMAD. After leaving NOI, Malcolm formed the Organization of Afro-American Unity (OAAU) and began reaching out to militant grassroots leaders. In October 1964, while on a tour of Africa, he met with representatives of the STUDENT NONVIOLENT COORDINATING COMMITTEE (SNCC) and convinced them to cooperate with his newly established group.

Malcolm's intellectual legacy became a diverse set of ideas that had both conservative and radical implications. His ideas ironically encouraged a generalized pessimism about the future as well as revolutionary enthusiasm. The quest for black racial and economic justice has been influenced heavily by black religious conceptions of justice, charity, equality, and freedom. During the CIVIL RIGHTS MOVEMENT, Malcolm X expressed his conceptions of divine retribution for racial injustice and the religious basis for healthy black self-esteem through black Islam and subsequently orthodox Islamic belief that accorded with black secular ideas about racial self-determination and cultural pride. Malcolm was a champion of the common black person, and his crusade against the vicious stereotypes that for centuries crippled black communities won him a generation of admirers. He had a take-no-prisoners approach to racial crisis, and therefore appealed to young blacks who were disaffected from white society and alienated from older black generations whose contained style of revolt owed more to MARTIN LUTHER KING JR.'s nonviolent philosophy than to Malcolm's advocacy of self-defense. Competing views of Malcolm X embody the paradoxical nature of black nationalist politics over the past three decades.

According to John White, the troubled life of ex-Black Muslim minister Malcolm X illustrates the dilemma faced by the adherents of the Black Power Movement. If any one man articulated the anger, the struggle, and the beliefs of black Americans in the 1960s, that man was Malcolm X. The transformation of Malcolm X points to some very important challenges to the black power ideologies of the day. Malcolm X influenced many of the leaders who sought to guide the grassroots militancy of the black power era. Despite his rhetorical support for black militancy, Malcolm himself did not lead a protest or insurgent movement. His principal contribution to the black nationalist tradition was to link that tradition with the mass movements of his time, primarily the Nation of Islam and, later, the Organization of Afro-American Unity. Malcolm X evolved into one of NOIs most highly regarded leaders. His proselytizing rhetoric and "street education" added to the allure of his legacy. Today Malcolm is often viewed as a hero, martyr, respected black leader, civil rights advocate, firebrand black nationalist, cultural critic, community activist, and simultaneously one of the most chronicled and equally misunderstood personalities of the 20th century.

Further reading: Malcolm X with Alex Haley. *Autobiography of Malcolm X.* New York: Ballantine Books, 1965; White, John. *Black Leadership in America: From Booker T. Washington to Jesse Jackson.* 2d ed. New York: Longman, 1990.

—Boris E. Ricks

March on Washington

The historic March on Washington, a watershed in the history of the CIVIL RIGHTS MOVEMENT in America, occurred on August 28, 1963. The march was officially led by A. Philip Randolph and owed much of its success to the organizational genius of BAYARD RUSTIN. Rustin, a seasoned organizer, put together the logistics of the march right down to the details of plans for inclement weather, various sorts of emergencies, sanitation, drinking water, and the like. Randolph, to whom MARTIN LUTHER KING JR. referred as "the dean of Negro leaders," had once threatened a march on Washington during the FRANKLIN DELANO ROOSEVELT administration. It was scheduled to take place on July 1, 1941. Under such pressure, President Roosevelt, who had refused to support antilynching legislation earlier that year for fear of alienating southern voters, issued Executive Order 8802, stating "there shall be no discrimination in the employment of workers in defense industries and in Government because of race, creed, color, or national origin."

The 1963 March on Washington culminated at the Lincoln Memorial in a mass rally for jobs and the vote for African Americans and a general end to racial discrimination in all forms. These objectives were given concrete legal formulation in president JOHN F. KENNEDY's first major civil rights initiative (introduced in Congress on June 19, 1963) but left to President Lyndon B. Johnson to push through Congress (signed July 2, 1964, in a significantly strengthened form) after President Kennedy was assassinated in Dallas, Texas, on November 22, 1963. Although some historians and theorists believe that the march's impact was negligible in the passage of the Civil Rights Bill of 1964, a strong argument can be made

An aerial view of the March on Washington, 1963 *(National Archives)*

to the contrary. It may just as well have been that the mass-media coverage, publicity, and projection of new possibilities left such an indelible imprint on the national consciousness that this image of hope was what sustained grassroots efforts (many of them church-based) to consistently apply pressure on Congress, even when it appeared that civil rights legislation had bogged down. We have come to recognize that what occurred on the Mall that day was a national epiphany, the effects of which are still being felt, not only in America but around the world.

More than 250,000 people from every state in the union participated, far exceeding the estimates of march organizers. An estimated 40,000 of march participants were church people, many of whom had been organized and energized by the grassroots organizing activity of the Commission on Religion and Race of the NATIONAL COUNCIL OF CHURCHES. This level of direct church participation had additional significance in that it "was a return to the activism of the early twentieth-century SOCIAL GOSPEL and something of a new departure."

The March on Washington was largely organized under the inspiration of the Rev. Dr. Martin Luther King Jr. and has become largely identified with his almost legendary "I have a Dream" speech, delivered on the occasion. Despite the violence in Birmingham, Alabama, earlier that year that preceded this peaceful demonstration and the violence that would follow, the March on Washington sounded a resonant note of hope and possibility typified that day in King's message of racial justice and reconciliation.

The conciliatory tone of the march was threatened at one point by the fiery rhetoric of a speech prepared by STUDENT NONVIOLENT COORDINATING COMMITTEE leader John Lewis, who, under the influence of Randolph, toned it down. Although King's message is the one with which the march has come to be identified, many considered the speech delivered by Lewis the more forceful: "We shall crack the South into a thousand pieces and put them back together in the image of democracy."

Further reading: Fairclough, Adam. *Better Day Coming: Blacks and Equality, 1890–2000.* New York: Penguin Putnam, 2001; Findlay, James F. "Religion and Politics in the Sixties: The Churches and the Civil Rights Act of 1964." *Journal of American History* 77, no. 1 (June 1990): 66–92; Harding, Vincent, Robin D. G. Kelly, and Earl Lewis. "We Changed the World: 1945–1970." In *To Make Our World Anew: A History of African Americans.* Edited by Robin D. G. Kelly and Earl Lewis. New York: Oxford University Press, 2000, 445–552; King, Martin Luther, Jr. *Why We Can't Wait.* New York: New American Library, 1963.

—Matthew V. Johnson Sr.

Marsh v. Chambers 463 U.S. 783 (1983)

A case dealing with the ESTABLISHMENT CLAUSE of the First Amendment, *Marsh* questioned whether prayer had a right-ful place in the business of government. The Nebraska state legislature opened its sessions with prayer, paying a Presbyterian minister, Robert Palmer, on a monthly basis to serve as chaplain. The suit was brought by Ernest Chambers, a member of the legislature and a taxpayer in the state.

The district court that first heard the case ruled that while opening a legislative session with a prayer was not a violation of the establishment clause, paying the chaplain with public money was. The Nebraska legislature then took its case to the Court of Appeals for the Eighth Circuit, which produced a similar ruling. The court of appeals employed the three-prong *Lemon* test, established in *LEMON V. KURTZMAN* (1971) and applied in *COMMITTEE FOR PUBLIC EDUCATION AND RELIGIOUS LIBERTY V. NYQUIST* (1973), and found that the chaplaincy practice failed on all three counts: The act had a religious purpose, its primary effect was to promote religion, and the use of public funds to pay the minister was excessive entanglement between church and state.

Surprisingly, the Supreme Court reversed this decision. For the first time since its inception in 1971, the Court did not use the *Lemon* test. Led by Chief Justice Burger, the Court employed history and the aims of the Founding Fathers as a measure for constitutionality. The opinion of the Burger Court was that "[i]n light of the unambiguous and unbroken history of more than 200 years, there can be no doubt that the practice of opening legislative sessions with prayer has become part of the fabric of our society." Speaking for Justices Blackmun, O'Connor, Powell, Rehnquist, and White, Burger provided an analysis of the intent of the framers of the First Amendment. The conclusion was that the founders would see no real threat to the establishment clause in this case, "that legislative prayer presents no more potential for establishment than the provision of school transportation, beneficial grants for higher education, or tax exemptions for religious organizations." However, the Court justified the decision to allow legislative prayer because of its "unique history" in the United States. Burger claimed the ruling in *Marsh* to be an exception to the establishment clause rather than a revision of it.

Although public prayer had not been a salient issue since the early 1970s, the context for the Court's decision in *Marsh* was President RONALD REAGAN's crusade to "readmit God to America's classrooms." In 1982, Reagan proposed an amendment before Congress: "Nothing in this Constitution shall be constructed to prohibit individual or group prayer in public schools or other public institutions. No person shall be required by the United States or any state to participate in prayer." The Court's ruling actually came while the Senate was considering this proposal, thereby energizing the Reagan administration and lending support to the PRAYER IN PUBLIC SCHOOLS cause.

Justices Marshall and Stevens joined Justice WILLIAM BRENNAN in dissent. The three objected to the Court's reliance on historical precedent over the established *Lemon* framework. Brennan wrote: "For my purposes, however, I must begin by demonstrating what should be obvious: that, if the Court were to judge legislative prayer through the unsentimental eye of our settled doctrine, it would have to strike it down as a clear violation of the Establishment Clause." The dissenters maintained that Burger invoked originalism to avoid the decision *Lemon* would have forced him into. In a bit of reverse logic, Justice Brennan expressed relief that the outcome of *Marsh* was not reached by means of the *Lemon* guidelines: "That it fails to do so is, in a sense, a good thing, for it simply confirms that the Court is carving out an exception to the Establishment Clause rather than reshaping Establishment Clause doctrine to accommodate legislative prayer."

Likewise, Brennan labeled "the Court's focus here on a narrow piece of history . . . in a fundamental sense, a betrayal of the lessons of history." Justice Brennan viewed Chief Justice Burger's interpretation of and reliance on the "intentions" of the framers of the Constitution both flawed and invalid. Rather than debating the legality of legislative prayer in the eyes of the Founding Fathers, Justice Brennan cited their intent to create a living document to be interpreted in the context of its time. The constitutional interpretation of Chief Justice Burger, he maintained, although valid in 1789, was misapplied in 1983.

—Anand E. Sokhey

Martin v. City of Struthers, Ohio 319 U.S. 141 (1943) and *Murdock v. Commonwealth of Pennsylvania* 319 U.S. 105 (1943)

The JEHOVAH'S WITNESSES cases are part and parcel of American law and politics. The Watchtower Bible and Tract Society (see WATCHTOWER SOCIETY) was one of several religious movements arising from the American political experience (others were the SEVENTH-DAY ADVENTISTS and the LATTER-DAY SAINTS). Adherents to the creeds of the Witnesses, along with the other 19th-century Protestants, became disillusioned with mainstream churches as they presented themselves at that time. This was a period of searching for the Second Advent of Christ and a strong element of millenarianism. This was also a period of political activism by many in the various Adventist denominations.

One of the striking features of the Witnesses' beliefs was their practice of distributing leaflets and pamphlets as a religious duty. Often this duty brought them into conflict with civil authority. The Witnesses many times preferred to litigate their rights and stand firm in their refusal to submit to civil authority. Cases previous to this time had established that the freedom of speech and assembly are the birthright of every citizen of the United States, regardless of the political or religious message. The Supreme Court made no reference to the religious speech of this sect.

Martin v. City of Struthers, Ohio and *Murdock v. Commonwealth of Pennsylvania* were part of a series of independently developed suits that were all argued and decided on the same day. Both cases were independent of each other, but the facts of each arose out of a "Watchtower Campaign" through-

out eastern Ohio and western Pennsylvania during which individual Witnesses were to distribute leaflets and tracks promoting their beliefs and to campaign against the ROMAN CATHOLIC CHURCH. This militant PROTESTANTISM is reflected not only in these cases but also in their companion cases *Douglas v. City of Jeannette,* (1943) and JONES V. CITY OF OPELIKA (1943). It is difficult to understand the cases individually because of the way the Supreme Court divided and scattered the majority opinions in each, and wrote dissents that applied to other cases in the same series.

Murdock v. Pennsylvania arose from the "Watchtower Campaign" in the City of Jeannette. An ordinance dating from the late 1800s required a license for "canvassing within said Borough, orders for goods, paintings, pictures or wares of any kind." Robert Murdock, one of the campaign participants, went canvassing door to door, as did the other Watchtower campaigners without purchasing a required license "for one day $1.50, for one week seven dollars ($7.00)." Murdock and the other Witnesses believed they were doing God's will and believed they were subject not to the temporal, but rather to the divine, law. In a companion case, *Douglas v. City of Jeannette,* the mayor of Jeannette had tried bargaining with the Witnesses as to terms and conditions of the city's permission during the "Watchtower Campaign," but to no avail. After the Witnesses were convicted at the local level, with those convictions affirmed in state courts, the case made its way to the Supreme Court.

Justice William O. Douglas wrote the opinion affirming the constitutional right to distribute clearly religious literature on public streets and forums, writing that the government may not interfere with the raising of funds for religious purposes in public forums. It is a measure of how unpopular Jehovah's Witnesses were that the companion cases, which are basically the dissents to *Murdock* and *Martin,* amounted to little more than attacks on the activities of the Witnesses. The decisions in favor of *Murdock* and *Martin* split the Court 5-4. While common in recent times, decisions decided on a close-to-even split vote were rare before the late 1950s.

Justice Black, together with Justice Murphy concurring, decided *Martin v. City of Struthers* on the basis of freedom of speech. As in other cases, there was a conviction in the municipal court of violation of an antileafleting ordinance, which attempted to ban the distribution of all "handbills, circulars or other advertisements" by coming to a residence and "summoning the inmate or inmates of any residence to the door to receive" the items distributed.

The majority opinion pointed out that the distribution of the ideas expressed in these leaflets and tracts selected by the Witnesses might be unconventional but that was exactly what the founders had in mind when drafting the First Amendment. Recognizing that although the pamphleteers could be a nuisance or a cover for criminal activity, "perhaps the most effective way of bringing [new ideas] to the notice of individuals is their distribution at the houses of the people."

From this opinion, we may see that the Supreme Court reasserted the right of Free Speech of even unpopular speakers, and that barriers to their distribution, such as the city ordinance passed by the governing body of Struthers, Ohio, are unconstitutional. The fact that the nation was engaged in World War II at the time these decisions were rendered seems to give the right affirmed by these cases an extra emphasis.

Lest anyone think that the problem is finally resolved, the case of *Watchtower Bible and Tract Society of New York v. Village of Stratton* was decided by the Supreme Court in 2002. The village of Stratton tried to ban solicitors named by the property owner from coming on to private property—largely Jehovah's Witnesses were named. The Court held that protected activities could not be subject even to such advance notice.

See also COX V. NEW HAMPSHIRE; LOVELL V. CITY OF GRIFFIN, GEORGIA.

—StanLey M. Morris

Marxism/communism

Marxism generally refers to the doctrines of Karl Marx (1818–83) and Friedrich Engels (1820–95). Communism generally refers to the doctrines of their intellectual heirs, who include V. I. Lenin (1870–1924), Leon Trotsky (1879–1940), Josef Stalin (1879–1953), Marshal Tito (1892–1980), Ho Chi Minh (1890–1969), Mao Zedong (1893–1976), and Fidel Castro (1926–   ).

Marx formed his ideas of history, politics, and society over an extended period of time that began with his absorption of Left Hegelian doctrine during his student days in Berlin. After moving to London, England, in 1849, he devoted himself to reading political and economic texts in the British Museum and writing long analyses of economic and social history. Marx's most important writings include *The Manifesto of the Communist Party* (with Engels, 1848) *The German Ideology* (1846, with Engels; not published until 1932), and *Capital* (vol. 1, 1867). Marx and Engels developed a doctrine according to which human history is moving toward an ultimate goal in the following way. Humans are laboring beings; they produce the material things that they need to live and to thrive. Humans, however, are alienated from the things they produce, from themselves, from nature, and from each other; the organizational structures and processes that have arisen for producing things more efficiently cause this alienation. An individual's place in the social structures of production (slave or master, peasant or nobleman, factory worker or factory owner) is known as one's social class. Social class determines "consciousness," namely, how one is placed in and sees the world. Expressions of consciousness include all of human culture: the arts, sciences, law, and religion. The core Marxist point is that human consciousness is determined by material conditions. Technological change in history produces change in the material conditions of production, its organization, and what is produced. The social organization of production (classes) and the "superstructure" of laws and ideas (culture)

based on it also change, and this change produces conflict between classes.

The continuing dynamic of historical-material change will come to a crisis point in the socioeconomic system of capitalism. This system comprises two classes of people: a small and shrinking class of wealthy owners of the means of production (the bourgeoisie) and a large, growing class of dispossessed workers who own only their own labor (the proletariat). The proletariat's increasing penury will lead them to revolt. All social structures known heretofore will be erased in this revolution, and a classless world in which people produce all they need without alienation will come into being. Marx believed that this revolution could occur only in societies like Germany or Great Britain that had reached the final, prerevolutionary stage of advanced industrial capitalism.

Followers of Marx gave this doctrine a more voluntary mode: the historical development that leads to revolution can be considerably shortened and the revolution imported into societies in which industrial development had not yet taken place. Lenin introduced a form of this communist doctrine into Russia in 1917, and Mao did likewise in China in 1949. Both societies were largely preindustrial and agrarian. In these and several other cases, the attempts to rapidly transform traditional, agrarian societies into industrialized communist ones led to widespread oppression and millions of deaths.

From early on in the development of communist doctrine, it was fiercely rejected in the United States, where Marxist and communist movements were vigorously suppressed. Marxist and communist doctrines were ostensibly the ideologies that motivated opposition to the United States and its political interests during the cold war (1947–89). The McCarthyite congressional hearings (1950–54) and the VIETNAM WAR (1954–75) mark American "failures" in this conflict, whereas the Korean War (1950–53), the Berlin airlift (1948–49), and the fall of the Berlin Wall (1989) are examples of American "successes."

Marxist-Communist doctrine is attacked by some American Christians on theologically naive economic grounds, but studied philosophical-theological critiques also exist. Alongside the objection to the expense in human lives that has attended communist revolutions, these critiques include analyses of Marxism-communism as a Gnostic heresy concerning the nature of history, as a millenarian heresy, or as based in a philosophically faulty materialism and a suspect philosophical anthropology. Similar critiques of Marxism and communism on not specifically Christian grounds also exist. LIBERATION THEOLOGY, which originated among Latin American Roman Catholic theologians in the 1950s and 1960s, sought to integrate Christian teachings concerning poverty and oppression with categories of analysis developed by Marx and his intellectual progeny. Debate continues whether such doctrinal integration subverts orthodox Christian teaching or enhances it.

—Thomas Heilke

Maryknoll Order

Maryknoll is the common name for a U.S.-based Roman Catholic mission movement that includes societies for priests and brothers, sisters, and laity. The Catholic Foreign Mission Society of America (M.M.) is Maryknoll's mission community of priests and brothers cofounded by James A. Walsh (1867–1936), a priest of Boston, and Thomas F. Price (1860–1919), a priest of Raleigh, North Carolina. It was approved by the American Catholic hierarchy in 1911 and authorized by Pope Pius X. Maryknoll priests do not take religious vows. The organization is modeled on the French Foreign Missionaries of Paris and was the first U.S. group to focus specifically on overseas missions. In 1912, a parallel society for women religious was founded by Mother Mary Joseph (Molly Rogers, 1882–1955), known as the Foreign Mission (later Maryknoll) Sisters of St. Dominic (M.M.), the first such American congregation founded for foreign mission. The Maryknoll Mission Association of the Faithful, established in 1975 and made a coequal missionary group in 1994, is a community of laypeople, priests, and religious who make short-term, renewable commitments to mission abroad under the auspices of Maryknoll. In addition, Maryknoll's affiliate program, Maryknoll Affiliates, founded in 1991, joins those not in foreign mission service to the work of Maryknoll through local chapters.

The first Maryknoll missions went to China in 1918 and spread throughout East Asia. Maryknoll sisters initially provided missionary support for the priests' foreign work at the seminary in Maryknoll, until they were sent to mission first in Los Angeles and Seattle in 1920, then on foreign mission to Hong Kong in 1921. During the Japanese invasion of China in World War II and the subsequent political turmoil, Maryknollers suffered in prison camps and dangerous conditions along with the people they served. When Communists came to power in China, Maryknollers and other missionaries were arrested, and some were tortured and killed, as suspect foreigners. However, Bishop James E. Walsh, M.M. (1891–1981) was permitted to remain in China when missionaries were expelled in the 1950s and was the last American to be expelled from China, in the 1970s. Missions were established in South America in 1942 and in Africa in 1946.

Initially, Maryknollers envisioned their mission work both as a means for converting individuals and cultures to Christianity and as an opportunity to spread particularly American traits, such as democracy, liberty, adaptability, INDIVIDUALISM, and enthusiasm. In the 1950s, many in Maryknoll shared America's ANTICOMMUNIST spirit, providing stories about communism's disregard for religion in the experiences of their missions, particularly in China. However, the Maryknoll vision, largely influenced by the work of Father John Considine, M.M., was more respectful of both individuals and their cultures than most anticommunists.

In Latin America, where Maryknoll has been a major presence since the 1960s (and in contrast with their work in Asia), Maryknoll missioners saw their work as reinvigorating an already Catholic area. While always attentive to the poor, the Maryknoll vision of mission began to include a social analysis that attended to the causes of poverty, and mission came to be understood as authentic development work. Among the tools for this was a new model of church that developed in Latin America, Base Ecclesial Communities. This social analysis, based on a "preferential option for the poor," often put Maryknoll missioners at odds with the local government, the U.S. government, and the Catholic Church. In contrast with Maryknoll's pro-American beginnings, Maryknollers now found themselves speaking against U.S. foreign policy, particularly in Latin America. The murders of Maryknoll sisters Ita Ford and Maura Clarke, in El Salvador, in December 1980 were a catalyst for Maryknoll raising its voice against U.S. policy in Central America during the Reagan administration. The Maryknoll vision of mission is now one of accompaniment and solidarity with the lives of those they serve.

Mission education for U.S. Catholics has always been a priority for the society and is accomplished through a magazine entitled *Maryknoll* (formerly *The Field Afar*, 1907–39). Maryknoll publishing efforts were expanded when, in 1970, Maryknoll founded a publishing house, Orbis Books, which has been a leading vehicle for the spread of liberation theology in the United States.

See also CONSISTENT ETHIC OF LIFE; MARXISM/COMMUNISM; NETWORK.

Further reading: Dries, Angelyn, OSF. *The Missionary Movement in American Catholic History.* Maryknoll, N.Y.: Orbis Books, 1998; Lernoux, Penny. *Hearts on Fire: The Story of the Maryknoll Sisters.* Maryknoll, N.Y.: Orbis Books, 1993; Nevins, Albert J. *The Meaning of Maryknoll.* New York: McMullen Books, 1954.

—Susan Gleason Anderson

Maryland

Maryland experienced great turmoil in religion and politics throughout the 17th century. Founded in 1634 as a proprietary colony by Cecil Calvert, second Lord Baltimore (on foundations laid by his father), Maryland was intended to be both a commercial venture and a refuge for his Roman Catholic coreligionists. Maryland endured several vicissitudes of church and state before emerging as a royal colony with an established Anglican Church at the end of the century.

To say that Maryland was designed in part as a refuge for Roman Catholics from England is not to imply that it was to be a Catholic colony. The Calverts never intended that Maryland should have a Catholic government on the order of Spain or France. Rather, they pursued a policy of religious freedom that, while lacking an elaborate rationale, was nonetheless rooted in genuine conviction, informed by a century of Catholic recusancy in England.

From the beginning, therefore, Protestants and Catholics lived alongside one another in Maryland. The Catholic minority was carefully instructed to give no offense to its Protestant neighbors, especially in the conduct of worship. Yet Baltimore also authorized Jesuit priests to care for the spiritual needs of his Catholic colonists. Militant Jesuit priests soon introduced a discordant note into the colony, sometimes challenging the proprietor himself. Other problems arose from the colony's charter, where Baltimore's almost feudal proprietary privileges were set alongside the instruction that he was to rule "with the Advice, Assent, and Approbation of the Free-Men of the same Province." The result of these and other anomalies was decades of political and religious turmoil, often exacerbated by the existence of quite different political and religious patterns in neighboring VIRGINIA.

Political and religious developments in England also contributed to turmoil in Maryland. The English Civil War and its aftermath certainly encouraged Maryland's Protestant element (many of whom were PURITANS) to question the propriety of a government that gave Catholics the franchise and even allowed them to hold public office.

Maryland's "Act Concerning Religion" of 1649 must be understood against this background. This product of the colony's assembly protected all Christians in the "FREE EXERCISE" of their religion. Religiously provocative terms such as "heretic, Scismatic, Idolator, puritan, Independent, Prespiterian, popish priest, Jesuite, Jusuited papist, Lutheran, CALVINIST, ANABAPTIST, Brownist, Antinomian, Barrowist, Roundhead, [and] Separatist" were banned. Also condemned were the profanation of the Sabbath, swearing, and the misuse of the name of the Blessed Virgin Mary. Ahead of its times in many ways, the act was nonetheless more restrictive than Baltimore's earlier policies. Likely he approved it because it managed to combine concerns of the Protestant majority with continuing TOLERATION of Catholics.

The proprietor temporarily lost his political authority in the 1650s, as Parliament asserted its dominance over the American colonies. Although the proprietor soon regained his powers, rumors of popish plots and concerns about the religious future of England after the restoration of Charles II caused many to question Maryland's religious policies and even its basic form of government. In 1676, the third Lord Baltimore's opponents authored a "Complaint from Heaven with a Huy and crye and a petition out of Virginia and Maryland" that articulated their political and religious grievances. The ensuing conflict came to a climax after William and Mary came to the English throne. In 1689, an antiproprietary party called the Protestant Association seized Maryland's government. When the dust settled, Maryland was a royal colony. Religious freedom was now defined by the recently enacted English Act of Toleration, which continued to disenfranchise Roman Catholics. Thus, Maryland had devolved from a policy of broad religious freedom in the 1630s to the narrower English pattern wherein full religious and political freedom was reserved to Anglicans, with substantial toleration of other Protestants, but only minimal toleration of Catholics. After 1689, Catholics were under severe restrictions in Maryland. Beginning in 1702, the Church of England was legally established in the colony.

The attempt of the Lords Baltimore to establish extensive religious freedom in Maryland foundered on their failure to enunciate a compelling rationale for such freedom, on the continuing reality of popular anti-Catholicism, and on political developments in England and Maryland over which they had no control. While a lively Catholic community, exemplified by the famous Carroll family, continued to exist in Maryland in the 18th century, both Catholic emancipation and larger notions of religious freedom had to await the coming of the American Revolution.

See also CARROLL, JOHN; PENNSYLVANIA; RELIGIOUS ESTABLISHMENT IN THE COLONIES.

Further reading: Curry, Thomas J. *The First Freedoms: Church and State in America to the Passage of the First Amendment.* New York: Oxford University Press, 1986; Hanley, Thomas O'Brien. *Their Rights and Liberties: The Beginnings of Religious and Political Freedom in Maryland.* Chicago: Loyola University Press, 1984.

—Donald L. Huber

Massachusetts

The political experience of Massachusetts in the 17th and 18th centuries reflects a "moralistic COMMUNITARIAN" culture, wherein political activity is centered on concern for the public good, both religious and temporal. The colonies of Plymouth and Massachusetts Bay were originally settled in 1620 and 1630, respectively, by two groups of CALVINISTS. The PILGRIMS who settled Plymouth sought to separate from the Church of England because of its ROMAN CATHOLIC practices and rituals. The PURITANS who settled Massachusetts Bay wanted to purify the Church of England. Central to both groups was the concept of the Covenant (see COVENANT THEOLOGY). A covenant, having its origins in the Old Testament, is a voluntary agreement by individuals who constitute themselves as a people with God as a witness and securer.

Two documents from early Massachusetts history, the MAYFLOWER COMPACT and JOHN WINTHROP's "A Model of Christian Charity," reflect Puritan notions of covenant and community. The Mayflower Compact called on God as a witness as the settlers "covenant and combine . . . together into a civil Body Politick for [their] better Ordering and Preservation" and to further the "Advancement of the Christian Faith." Moral communalism and covenant also suffuse "The Model of Christian Charity," which Winthrop, who served almost continuously as governor or deputy governor of Massachusetts Bay from 1630 to 1649, composed. The theme of mutual dependence is reflected in such lines as "That every man might have need of other, and from hence they might be all knitt more nearly together in the Bond of brotherly affeccion [*sic*]." In Winthrop's memorable words, the Puritan community must "be as a Citty upon a hill, the eies of all people are upon us."

The importance of social cohesion and the maintenance of orthodoxy during the first generations of the Puritan settlement is exemplified by the expulsion of ROGER WILLIAMS and ANNE HUTCHINSON in 1636 and 1637, respectively, for their unorthodox religious views. Winthrop justified these expulsions as necessary for the "safety and welfare" of the commonwealth, which he conceived of as a family that is "not bound to entertain all comers." By the 18th century, Enlightenment philosophy undermined this Puritan orthodoxy.

The General Court in Massachusetts Bay, which chose the governor, deputy governor, and assistants, was an example of colonial self-government. Although originally limited to a few freemen or stockholders, by 1631 all adult church members were considered freemen. The General Court legislated both for the entire colony and, during the first several decades, for localities as well. By the 1650s, more authority had devolved to towns. Towns chose representatives to the lower house of the General Court or House of Representatives. The institution of the town meeting developed wherein residents participated directly to elect town officials and decide local policy. The Halfway Covenant in 1662 extended the franchise by liberalizing qualifications for church members. In 1691, religious qualifications for citizenship were eliminated when the colonies of Plymouth and Massachusetts Bay were combined under a royal charter.

Under the royal charter of 1691, the governor was appointed by the king. But local self-government and town representation to the General Court prevailed until 1774. During the Revolutionary War period, Massachusetts, as did most other states, wrote a constitution. Republican principles of character formation were a core feature of the Massachusetts Constitution of 1780. Provision for religion was explicit. Article III in the Declaration of Rights provided for public support of Protestant teachers of religion as well as TOLERATION of every denomination of Christians. A Religious test for holding public office in the form of believing in "the Christian religion and [having] a firm persuasion of its truth" was stipulated (Chapter VI). These provisions stand in contrast to the federal Constitution of 1787 and its prohibition of religious qualifications for office. Though the constitutional protections of religion in the First Amendment did not apply to the states well into the 20th century, Massachusetts maintained the official establishment of the Congregational Church until 1833—it was the last state to have an established church.

Further reading: Heimert, Alan, and Andrew Delbanco, eds. *The Puritans in America: A Narrative Anthology.* Cambridge, Mass.: Harvard University Press, 1985; Lutz, Donald S. *The Origins of American Constitutionalism.* Baton Rouge: Louisiana State University Press, 1988; Miller, Perry. *The New England Mind: The Seventeenth Century.* New York: Macmillan, 1939; Morgan, Edmund S., ed. *The Founding of Massachusetts: Historians and Sources.* Indianapolis: Bobbs-Merrill, 1964; Swindler, William F. *Sources and Documents of United States Constitutions.* Vol. 5. Dobbs Ferry, N.Y.: Oceana Publications, 1975; Zuckerman, Michael. *Peaceable Kingdoms: New England Towns in the Eighteenth Century.* Westport, Conn.: Greenwood Press, 1983 [1970].

—Gerald DeMaio

Mather, Cotton (1663–1728) *religious leader*

Grandson and namesake of two giants of early American Puritanism (John Cotton and Richard Mather), Cotton Mather—author, preacher, public figure, and member of the Royal Society of London—remains perhaps the best known of all New England PURITANS. Born in Boston, Mather entered Harvard College at age 12, and by the age of 18 he had received an M.A. degree. Fittingly enough, for this heir of the Puritan tradition in America and scion of New England orthodoxy, Cotton's father, INCREASE MATHER (then Harvard president), bestowed the degree on Cotton. Although he considered a career as a physician (and would continue to develop his interests in science and medicine throughout his life), Mather undertook religious studies, was ordained in 1685, and served as his father's colleague at North Church in Boston. While Increase Mather represented the MASSACHUSETTS Bay Colony in England during the late 1680s, seeking the restoration of their colonial charter that King James II had revoked, his son played an important political role at home, supporting, and possibly fomenting, the opposition to and overthrow of royally appointed governor Sir Edmund Andros in 1689.

Cotton Mather combined a rigorous defense of Puritan orthodoxy worthy of his clerical pedigree with an interest in science and medicine unusual for American clergy of his time. His magisterial *Magnalia Christi Americana, or the Ecclesiastical History of New England*—with its stirring opening passage, "I write the wonders of the Christian religion, flying from the depravations of Europe, to the American Strand"—presents a vivid portrait of New England history, bountiful in its promise but also imperiled by the decline of religious fervor in the land, as the working out of God's providence in the world. At the same time, he was an early supporter of inoculation against smallpox during the 1721 epidemic in Boston, braving the community's wrath by inoculating members of his own family. His *Curiosa Americana* (1712–24), which illustrated both his scientific interests and his enthusiasm for the natural wonders of America, earned him membership in the Royal Society, the first American on whom this honor was bestowed.

Unfortunately, for many Americans Mather's name conjures up the spectacle of the Salem witch trials, which shook New England during the spring and summer of 1692 and saw the execution of 20 accused witches. Although Mather did not play a formal role in the trials, his *Memorable Providences Relating to Witchcraft and Possessions* (1689) was widely read during the years leading up to the trials, and the court of oyer and terminer created by Massachusetts governor William Phips included several of Mather's close associates. Mather himself attended the hanging of former Salem minister George Burroughs and, when Burroughs succeeded in reciting the Lord's Prayer (something thought impossible for a true wizard), he urged the crowd to stand by the court's sentence of death despite their misgivings. After the witch hysteria died down in the autumn of 1692, Mather's continued interest in the topic of possession appeared in his *Wonders of the Invisi-*

ble World (1693). After the death of his father, Increase, in 1723, Cotton Mather became pastor of North Church, but he survived his father by just five years.

Further reading: Lovejoy, David S. *The Glorious Revolution in America.* Hanover, N.H.: Wesleyan University Press/University Press of New England, 1972; Middlekauff, Robert. *The Mathers; Three Generations of Puritan Intellectuals, 1596–1728.* New York: Oxford University Press, 1971; Mather, Cotton. *Magnalia Christi Americana, or The Ecclesiastical History of New England.* Edited and abridged by Raymond J. Cunningham. New York: Frederick Ungar, [1702] 1970.

—Andrew R. Murphy

Mather, Increase (1639–1723) *religious leader*

Increase Mather, Colonial American Congregational clergyman, was born in Dorchester, Massachusetts. He was a preacher, author, emissary, and Harvard president. Mather is best remembered for his role in the Salem witchcraft trials, from which he wrote *Cases of Conscience Concerning Evil Spirits.* Some of his most notable publications include his own sermons, *The Great Blessing of Primitive Counseling,* a biography of Richard Mather, and various tracts concerning puritan doctrine.

At age 12, Mather entered Harvard University and received a bachelor's degree five years later. At graduation, Mather attacked Aristotelian logic, which was central to Harvard's curriculum. Although this led to his dismissal, it was indicative of his independent intellect. The next year, 1657, he preached his first sermon.

Mather came from a religiously prominent family. His father, Richard, was investigated while still living in England for dissension, and his father-in-law, John Cotton, fled to America to escape arrest for dissension. In 1657, Mather sailed from Boston to Ireland and England to visit his brother and continue his education. He received a master's degree from Trinity College; he then went to England, where he served as a Puritan minister until 1661. While Mather was in Guernsey, the Commonwealth ended and so did the political and religious freedoms that the PURITANS had enjoyed since the beheading of Charles I in 1649. Charles II was restored to the throne in 1660, and Anglicanism became the official religion of England. In protest, Mather sailed for Boston in 1661 and became minister of North Church. In 1662, he married his stepsister, Maria.

When Charles II delivered an ultimatum in 1683 to the MASSACHUSETTS colonists—retain their charter with England or have it revoked—they chose to separate themselves rather than submit to what they ideologically opposed. Accordingly, the charter was revoked, and this act marked some of the first tensions that would lead to colonial rebellion.

In 1685, Mather became president of Harvard College. In 1688, he was sent as an envoy of Massachusetts's Congregational churches to restore the charter and thank James II for declaring liberty for all faiths. The charter was restored in 1689 but was unpopular because it made the colony and the Congregationalists dependent on England again. Mather's popularity waned after the Salem witchcraft trials because his book, *An Essay for the Recording of Illustrious Providences,* was blamed for the hysteria. He resigned his presidency of Harvard in 1701. In 1714, his wife died, and he married Anne Lake Cotton, widow of his nephew, the following year.

Mather's reliance on biblical principles is exemplary of the Puritan marriage of the Bible to modern society. Puritans viewed themselves as the New Israel and so held fast to biblical laws. They also thought of themselves as a community, and religious fellowship and the leadership of a pastor were very important to them. Mather emphasized the individual and the individual's need to conform for the preservation of society.

Public justice also showed the importance of community through its civic leaders. Mather observed that the "Magistrate . . . *is the Minister of God to thee for good.*" This idea reinforces the theory of the DIVINE RIGHT OF KINGS. Puritans dissented over divine right while in England, believing that the Puritans themselves, as the elect, were philosophically, religiously, and morally able to make correct decisions about governing themselves and practicing their religion. They rejected the ultimatums of the monarch's word and felt ready to interpret the Bible for themselves. In setting up their new colonial societies in America, the Puritans worked for a completely new society as far as mores were concerned. They advocated reliance on biblical ideals and principles rather than on logical humanistic values, which, being earthly and human, were wrong. Increase Mather interpreted colonial events through the doctrine of divinely instituted dispensation, trying to prove that America was the New Israel and that Puritans were the purveyors of God's plan.

See also MATHER, COTTON.

Further reading: Hall, Michael G. *The Last American Puritan: The Life of Increase Mather.* Middletown, Conn.: Wesleyan University Press, 1988; Lowance, Mason I. *Increase Mather.* New York: Twayne, 1974; Mather, Increase. "Sermon Occasioned by the Execution of a Man Found Guilty of Murder," March 11, 1685.

—Whitney L. Bevill

Mayflower Compact

Signed by 41 of the *Mayflower's* male passengers on November 11 (November 21, new style), 1620, the Mayflower Compact was the "first foundation" of the government of Plymouth Colony. The compact embodied in primitive form the critically important principle that government should be based on the consent of the governed, and is thus regarded as a precursor of both the DECLARATION OF INDEPENDENCE and the U.S. Constitution.

The drafting and signing of the Mayflower Compact were occasioned by necessity. The PILGRIMS—a group of English

This painting shows the Pilgrims signing the compact in one of the *Mayflower*'s cabins. *(Library of Congress)*

separatists from the town of Scrooby—set sail from Plymouth, England, with several other passengers for what was then called Northern VIRGINIA, where they were to establish a colony under a patent from the Virginia Company. But endless delays, bad weather, and the impossibility of accurate navigation put them behind schedule and off course, and eventually they found themselves off the coast of Cape Cod, well north of their intended landfall. Worse yet, they had no legal authority to establish a colony in New England, and thus no basis for legitimate government. Some of the *Mayflower's* passengers thus threatened (as the Pilgrims' historian, William Bradford, put it) that they would "use their own liberty" once ashore, "for none had power to command them."

The Pilgrim leadership acted immediately to forestall any challenge to their authority, establishing, in effect, a contractual agreement that would be "as firm as any patent, and in some respects more sure." The signatories to the Mayflower

Compact agreed, "by these presents solemnly and mutually in the presence of God, and one of another" to "covenant and combine our selves together into a civil body politick, for our better ordering and preservation," and "to enact, constitute, and frame such just and equal laws, ordinances, acts, constitutions, and offices, from time to time, as shall be thought most meet and convenient for the general good of the Colony unto which we promise all due submission and obedience."

In form and substance, the Mayflower Compact was inspired by the CALVINIST doctrine of COVENANT THEOLOGY, which held that God had offered his creatures a contract under which He laid down the conditions of salvation and agreed to offer salvation if the terms of the contract were met. Based on the model of the biblical covenant between God and Abraham, such contracts offered a convenient basis for establishing separatist churches, since the separatists rejected the authority both of the pope and of the Church of England.

From this it was but a small conceptual step to the idea that governments and societies should themselves be established by covenant.

The Mayflower Compact was actually in force only from November 1620 to June 1621, when the colonists received a new patent—this time from the Council for New England—which explicitly granted them title to the lands around Plymouth. In 1691, Plymouth Plantation was absorbed into the MASSACHUSETTS Bay Colony and ceased to exist as an independent colony.

For most of the next century, the compact was largely forgotten. During the revolutionary and constitutional eras, however, the document played an important role in the debates over American independence and early American governance. The revolutionaries, for example, used the compact as a living example of the Lockean social contract; loyalists, citing the Pilgrims' description of themselves as "the loyal subjects of our dread Sovereign Lord King James," used it to underscore their devotion to the British Crown. A few years later, Federalist opponents of French-style democracy enlisted the Mayflower Compact in their cause, pointing to the colonists' adherence to traditional principles and their rejection of "anarchic democracy." Still later, Whig politicians seized on the compact as a weapon in their war against Jacksonians, emphasizing that the Pilgrims were "politic, intelligent, and educated" people whose outlook was essentially conservative (see CONSERVATISM). Downplaying the social contract aspects of the document, the Whigs generally avoided the term "compact" altogether, and instead used such phrases as the "Republican Constitution."

The Federalist and Whig interpretations exerted a significant influence on the modern American perception of the Mayflower Compact. The historical reality of the compact—along with its deep religious roots—have been largely forgotten, and the compact now stands largely as a secular symbol of early American constitutionalism.

See also LOCKE, JOHN.

Further reading: Miller, Perry, and Thomas H. Johnson, eds. *The Puritans: A Sourcebook of Their Writings.* Vol 1. New York: Harper and Row, 1963; Sargent, Mark L. "The Conservative Covenant: The Rise of the Mayflower Compact in American Myth." *New England Quarterly* 61 (1988): 233–251.
—William Lasser.

McCollum, Illinois ex rel. v. Board of Education
333 U.S. 203 (1948)

McCollum addressed the constitutionality of noncompulsory religious instruction in public schools. The U.S. Supreme Court ruled 8-1, in a majority opinion written by Justice Hugo Black, that the instruction violated the ESTABLISHMENT CLAUSE. Justice Felix Frankfurter and Robert Jackson wrote concurring opinions, and Justice Stanley Reed dissented. The decision marked the start of the Court's examination of religious practices in public schools and the first clear invocation of the establishment clause to disallow government-sponsored religious practices.

The case, brought by Vashti McCollum on behalf of her son, resulted from a program begun by the school board of Champaign, Illinois, in which clergy provided weekly religion classes in the schools on a volunteer basis. Clergy applied to participate with selection made by school officials. Attendance records were provided to school officials. Students needed parental permission to participate; however, McCollum felt pressure to sign and said her son was ostracized when she refused. McCollum was an ATHEIST but said she thought "humanist" described her better. Raised in a religious environment, she claimed no interest in attacking organized religion.

The Court's starting point in reversing the rulings of the Illinois courts was the 1947 EVERSON V. BOARD OF EDUCATION definition of the establishment clause, to which, as Black noted, both sides in *Everson* agreed. Rejecting the argument that the *Everson* definition should be repudiated, Black reiterated that under the First Amendment, the government could neither aid nor be hostile to religion. Refusal to allow religion classes in a public school did not amount to hostility, but allowing such a practice did equal government aid to religion. The tax-supported public school, the compulsory education law, and the close cooperation between school and clergy in administering the classes all were forms of aid to religion. In Black's closing words, "This is not separation of Church and State."

Justice Frankfurter, concurring, reviewed the religious roots of organized education, the religious nature of education in Colonial America, and the emergence of modern public education. He observed that insistence on secular education in public schools was accepted as early as 1875 and did not spring from hostility to religion. But he also appreciated the frustration of religious groups seeking to provide religious education to their young. With Sunday schools as effective as the "enforced piano lesson," religious leaders sought ways to teach religion during the time children recognized as their "business hours," i.e., the school day. By 1947, "released time" schemes existed in 2,200 communities. There were wide variations in these programs, and only the specific details of Champaign's program were at stake. Frankfurter expressed concerns about pressures to conform and the potential for religious divisiveness generated by the program. He concluded that in church-state relations, "good fences make good neighbors."

Justice Jackson's concurring opinion expressed concerns about the ideas this case might suggest to those wishing to remove every mention of religion from public education. He noted that such topics as art or music could not be taught properly without reference to religion.

Justice Reed's dissent reviewed areas of cooperation between church and state and found the Court ambiguous as to just which part of the Champaign plan made it unconstitutional. He gave his own view of history in support of the program's validity and urged caution in upsetting long-standing practices.

As the first major establishment clause case involving public schools, this case was also tried in the court of public opinion. Vashti McCollum described sensationalized media treatment, hate mail, a circus atmosphere, and subtle pressures against her husband, a University of Illinois professor. Yet she also acknowledged some objective media coverage, much fan mail, and support from religious organizations. Six amici briefs were filed in her support by Jewish, SEVENTH-DAY ADVENTIST, UNITARIAN, and Baptist organizations, the Ethical Culture Society, and the ACLU.

The McCollum victory was significantly narrowed in 1954 when the Court in ZORACH V. CLAUSON upheld a "released time" program in which instruction occurred away from school property.

See also PRAYER IN PUBLIC SCHOOLS.

Further reading: McCollum, Vashti Cromwell. *One Woman's Fight.* Boston: Beacon Press, 1951.

—Jane Gurganus Rainey

McGowan v. Maryland 366 U.S. 420 (1961)

Unlike the majority of decisions on religious questions in the 1960s, *McGowan v. Maryland* supported the religious community by permitting states to enforce their Sunday closing laws, or BLUE LAWS, as long as the laws did not "use the State's coercive power to aid religion." The case had wide-ranging implications because every state except Alaska had some form of Sunday closing law, with 40 states having comprehensive legislation similar to Maryland's.

William McGowan and six other employees of a discount store were indicted for violating Maryland's Sunday blue laws by selling a three-ring loose-leaf binder, a can of floor wax, a stapler and staples, and a toy submarine. McGowan and the others challenged their convictions, asserting that the Maryland statutes violated the equal protection clause of the Fourteenth Amendment because the statutory scheme permitting the sale of certain items while prohibiting others was arbitrary. Furthermore, McGowan questioned whether Maryland's Sunday closing laws violated the ESTABLISHMENT CLAUSE and FREE EXERCISE CLAUSE of the First Amendment.

Chief Justice Earl Warren delivered the opinion of the Court on May 29, 1961, with only Justice William Douglas dissenting. He dispatched the equal protection challenge expeditiously. The majority of the Court deferred to the Maryland General Assembly and its determination of the goods that could be sold on Sunday within the state. Chief Justice Warren set forth the rational basis test and determined that the state had acted reasonably.

The bulk of the majority opinion was devoted to the potential conflict between the blue laws and the First Amendment. Warren examined the history of Sunday closing laws, reviewing contemporary practices in Maryland, as well as practices dating back to 13th-century England. The chief justice noted that although the original purpose of the Sunday closing laws was for observing the Sabbath, nonreligious arguments for the laws began as early as the middle of the 18th century.

> [B]oth the federal and state governments have oriented their activities very largely toward improvement of the health, safety, recreation and general well-being of our citizens. . . . Sunday Closing Laws, like those before us, have become part and parcel of this great governmental concern wholly apart from their original purposes or connotations. The present purpose and effect of most of them is to provide a uniform day of rest for all citizens; the fact that this day is Sunday, a day of particular significance for the dominant Christian sects, does not bar the State from achieving its secular goals.

Chief Justice Warren distinguished *McGowan* from the Court's decision in MCCOLLUM V. BOARD OF EDUCATION (1948), the only decision in which the Court found a violation of the establishment clause. According to Chief Justice Warren, in *McCollum* the state had alternatives to permitting religious instruction in public school buildings during school hours; Warren dismissed McGowan's argument that Maryland had other avenues through which it could provide a "weekly day of rest." Furthermore, in *McCollum*, there was direct cooperation between state officials and members of the clergy, and "tax-supported buildings were used to aid religion." Neither of these factors was present in *McGowan*.

While the majority opinion dealt exclusively with Maryland's blue laws, both Justice Felix Frankfurter's concurrence (joined by Justice John M. Harlan) and Justice Douglas's dissent applied to three additional cases: TWO GUYS FROM HARRISON-ALLENTOWN, INC. V. MCGINLEY; BRAUNFELD V. BROWN; and GALLAGHER V. CROWN KOSHER SUPER MARKET, INC. In *Braunfeld* and *Gallagher*, Orthodox Jewish retailers and customers asserted that compulsory Sunday closing laws forced them "either to give up the Sabbath observance . . . or to forego advantages enjoyed by the non-Sabbatarian majority of the community." Justice Frankfurter rejected this argument because the states had "legitimate secular ends at which their Sunday statutes may aim."

Justice Douglas dissented. While conceding that states could establish a requirement for a "day of rest," he asserted that the Sunday closing laws did not work toward that end. "They [the Sunday closing laws] force minorities to obey the majority's religious feelings of what is due and proper for a Christian community; they provide a coercive spur to the 'weaker brethren,' to those who are indifferent to the claims of a Sabbath through apathy or scruple." Justice Douglas agreed with the Orthodox Jewish adherents in *Braunfeld* and *Gallagher* that the blue laws served to penalize them for observing their religious beliefs.

While Sunday closing laws remain on the books in many states, enforcement is rare. *McGowan* was the last significant decision by the Supreme Court on this subject.

—Sara A. Grove

McPherson, Aimee Semple (1890–1944) *evangelist*

Aimee Elizabeth Kennedy was born in rural Ontario, Canada, on a farm in Salford on October 9, 1890, to James and Mildred "Minnie" Kennedy. When Aimee was 17 years old, she converted to PENTECOSTALISM after attending a revival led by visiting evangelists Robert Semple and Herbert Randall. She began speaking in tongues (glossolalia) several months after the revival. In two decades, she would become one of the best-known evangelists in America, rivaling such evangelists as BILLY SUNDAY in the size of the crowds who gathered to hear her and for her work at the Angelus Temple in Los Angeles, California.

In 1908, she married Robert Semple and moved with him to Chicago to work with William Durham at the Gospel Mission Church. Two years later, Robert and Aimee left for mission work in Hong Kong, but Robert died of malaria several months later. In 1912, Aimee Kennedy Semple married Harold Steward McPherson and gave birth to Rolf Potter McPherson the following year. After a near-death experience in 1913, she believed God had given her a sign to renew her religious work. In 1915, she left for Germany to participate in Pentecostal camp meetings. She soon received invitations to speak at camp meetings and revivals elsewhere in Europe and the United States. Harold joined her as she began leading revivals throughout the southeast United States. Following her separation from Harold in 1918 and divorce in 1921, Aimee's mother, Minnie, joined her and the children as Aimee continued to travel from one revival meeting to the next.

By 1919, Aimee Semple McPherson's reputation as a dynamic speaker had grown, as had the number of people attending her revival meetings. To the many thousands who heard her speak, she became known simply as Sister. By 1920, she was traveling throughout the United States and Canada. In one gathering in Denver, she drew a crowd of over 100,000.

McPherson's ministry did not go without criticisms. Fundamentalists associated with the Moody Bible Institution and the *Moody Monthly* objected to her practice of healing people at her revivals. They argued that the healings were not biblical because they were usually short-lived. At the same time, she came under criticism from Pentecostals who claimed that she was no longer one of them. In 1922, McPherson further angered some Pentecostals when she returned her ministerial credentials to the ASSEMBLIES OF GOD.

In spite of such criticisms, the early 1920s were the height of Aimee Semple McPherson's career as a nationally recognized evangelist. In 1921, she announced plans to construct the Angelus Temple in Los Angeles, California, in her journal the *Bridal Call*, which she began in 1917 to encourage others in the Christian life. Using monies raised from donations, the Temple opened on January 1, 1923. It became part of the Foursquare Gospel Association, which she founded the previous year.

With the success of the temple, McPherson continued to expand her ministries. She began a radio station, KFSG (Kall Four Square Gospel), beside the temple in February 1924. At the time, radio was the cutting-edge technology for reaching the public. In December 1925, she opened the L.I.F.E. Bible College.

On May 18, 1926, McPherson disappeared while taking a swim in the ocean accompanied by her secretary. After the initial speculation that she had drowned, more sensational stories in the press suggested that she had run off with her radio manager. Six weeks after her disappearance, Aimee called her mother from Douglas, New Mexico, claiming she had been held captive in Mexico but managed to escape. Her credibility was questioned by the press and the police after searches were unable to discover the location where she was held captive.

McPherson continued to preach to enormous crowds; however, stories about financial impropriety and rumors about the kidnapping gradually began to diminish her following. A number of churches left the Foursquare Gospel Association after her brief, troubled marriage to David Hutton. In 1936, Aimee's daughter Roberta left the church, despite her presumed status as heir apparent.

See also RELIGION AND THE MASS MEDIA; FIRST and SECOND GREAT AWAKENINGS; ROBERTSON, PAT.

Further reading: Blumhofer, Edith L. *Aimee Semple McPherson: Everybody's Sister.* Grand Rapids, Mich.: Eerdmans, 1993; Epstein, Daniel Mark. *Sister Aimee: The Life of Aimee Semple McPherson.* New York: Harcourt Brace Jovanovich, 1993; Thomas, Lately. *Storming Heaven: The Lives and Turmoils of Minnie Kennedy and Aimee Semple McPherson.* New York: Morrow, 1970.

—Jean L. McSween

Meek v. Pittenger 421 U.S. 395 (1975)

The Commonwealth of PENNSYLVANIA was authorized to provide certain auxiliary services and loans of textbooks, which were acceptable for use in public schools, to all children enrolled in the nonpublic elementary and secondary schools. These nonpublic elementary and secondary schools were required to meet Pennsylvania's compulsory school attendance law, which requires K-12 schools owned or operated by or under the authority of legitimate religious institutions to register with the state Department of Education. The registration proclamation states that schools will teach subjects approved by the school code in the English language; that the governing religious body is a nonprofit organization; and that the school is otherwise in compliance with the provisions of the Pennsylvania School Code.

In 1972, the Pennsylvania General Assembly passed legislation with the primary purpose of guaranteeing that every pupil in the Pennsylvania Commonwealth would share evenhandedly in the benefits of auxiliary services, textbooks, and instructional material, provided free of charge to all children attending public schools. The auxiliary services included counseling, testing, psychological services, speech and hearing therapy, and other related services for educationally disadvantaged students. The instructional materials included magazines, photographs, maps, charts, recordings, and films, and the instructional equipment included overhead projectors, tape recorders, and laboratory supplies.

The appellants in this case brought this lawsuit challenging the constitutionality of three Pennsylvania statutes for supposedly violating the ESTABLISHMENT CLAUSE. The U.S. Supreme Court endorsed the constitutionality of allowing Pennsylvania to purchase textbooks for nonpublic school students, but did not allow for the purchase of instructional equipment because it "sanctioned the loan of equipment which from its nature can be diverted to religious purposes." Justice Potter Stewart held that only those books and materials that can be used in secular classes could be purchased with the money. He held that the loaning of instructional material to private and religious schools is unconstitutional and violates the establishment clause because it directly supports religion. Schools could easily manipulate the usage of these materials to further religious education for the students at the nonpublic schools. The Court also held that Pennsylvania could not supply staff to assist students with special needs in religious schools because this also inappropriately benefited religion.

The issue in this case also involved excessive entanglement because the government would have to become excessively entangled with the religious schools for the state to ensure that these employees taught only secular subjects in the classroom. The establishment clause is still violated whether or not the promotion of religious ideas in the classroom is intentional. As a result, this decision is consistent with past cases involving the "child-benefit theory"; however, only secular textbooks and no other materials can be provided for nonpublic school students to ensure that only a secular education is being supported by the government.

—Ryan S. Solomon

Mennonite tradition

One of the major "peace church" traditions, the Mennonite tradition traces its origin to the radical wing of the 16th-century Protestant Reformation in Switzerland and southern Germany. Radical reformers believed that the mainstream Reformation had not gone far enough in restoring the church to standards derived strictly from the Bible and from early church practice.

They believed staunchly in adult baptism (opponents labeled them ANABAPTISTS—"re-baptizers") and in a dualistic theology in which the church as Kingdom of God is set apart from and largely in opposition to the kingdom of the world. While they accepted that government was given by God as a necessary restraint on evil, they regarded coercive government as outside the perfection of Jesus Christ. They expected from believers radical discipleship—"taking up the cross" and living out Jesus' demanding ethics. Menno Simons (c. 1496–1561), a Dutch Roman Catholic priest, converted to Anabaptism in the 1530s and quickly became an important leader in defend-

ing nonviolence as a defining characteristic of the movement. By the 1540s, nonviolent Anabaptism became so closely associated with him that believers began to be referred to as "Mennists" and later, Mennonites.

At odds with both Protestant and Catholic establishments, Mennonites immediately met with persecution. Thousands were martyred in the first century of the movement. Persecution strengthened the Mennonite self-conception as a nonconformist community and drove many into rural enclaves and into a pattern of repeated migration in search of land and religious freedom.

When WILLIAM PENN, a QUAKER, offered such freedom in colonial PENNSYLVANIA, many Swiss-German Mennonites made their way to America, where eventually their ideas of the voluntary church and the separation of church and state would, ironically, become mainstream. The first permanent settlement was in Germantown, Pennsylvania, in 1683. To this day, the largest concentration of Mennonites is found in eastern Pennsylvania.

In the United States, the dominant stream of Anabaptism has been Swiss-German, and its historical experience of political alienation contributed to the largely apolitical, sectarian stance that characterized most Mennonites up to World War II. The other major stream is of Dutch origin. In the 1500s, many Dutch Mennonites fled eastward, first to Prussia and then to southern Russia, where they enjoyed relatively more freedom to control their own social and political life. When these Mennonites made their way to North America in the 19th and 20th centuries, they settled mainly in Canada, where they have generally led less separatist lifestyles.

U.S. Mennonites are few yet highly schismatic. Typically, divisions have occurred over permissible levels of conformity with "worldly" standards of dress, technology, and the like. Some groups in the Mennonite tradition are identifiable by their plain clothing and lifestyle (e.g., the AMISH and the Hutterites). In all, the United States accounts for about 290,000 of the estimated 1 million Mennonites worldwide. Yet Mennonites have had an impact on U.S. politics. Their claim of a right to CONSCIENTIOUS OBJECTION from wartime service has tested American TOLERANCE of dissent and its understanding of the FREE EXERCISE of religion.

Moreover, in the 20th century, many Mennonites began thinking about relations with government not exclusively in terms of obtaining exemptions (which had sparked charges of free riding), but in terms of justice and peace. In part as a result of participation in relief and reconstruction projects after World War I and alternative service in World War II, their long-standing ethic of service began to take on more expansive and international dimensions. The most important institutional expression of this was the formation of the Mennonite Central Committee (MCC) in 1920, a relief and development organization supported by most Mennonite denominations. Demographic changes also fueled this trend, as many Mennonites moved off the farm and into universities and diverse professions.

The coming-of-age moment vis-à-vis public life was perhaps in 1968, when the MCC established its Washington office, now the primary lobby for Mennonite concerns. Though lay Mennonites are increasingly conservative, the Washington Office works with the mainline religious Left on many issues (support for social welfare spending and international debt relief, opposition to militarism, and capital punishment). Yet it is somewhat to the right of the mainline on some issues (e.g., ABORTION), to the left on others (e.g., military intervention for humanitarian purposes)—a perspective some have labeled "CONSISTENT ETHIC OF LIFE." One of the most distinctive aspects of Mennonites' political influence stems from their international service and relief work (more than 900 workers in some 50 countries), which gives them widely acknowledged on-the-ground credibility on international issues.

See also FREE EXERCISE CLAUSE; SHAKERS.

Further reading: Driedger, Leo, and Donald B. Kraybill. *Mennonite Peacemaking: From Quietism to Activism.* Scottdale, Pa.: Herald Press, 1994; Miller, Keith Graber. *Wise as Serpents, Innocent as Doves: American Mennonites Engage Washington.* Knoxville: University of Tennessee Press, 1996.

—Dennis R. Hoover

Messianism

Derived from the Hebrew for "Anointed One," Messianism is the hope or expectation that a savior, usually divinely appointed, will come to save a chosen group, releasing it from its suffering or oppression. In Hebrew practice, to anoint was to consecrate a particular person or object or set it aside for a special, often divine purpose, but it was also a sign of election to royal office. Both Saul and later David were "anointed" by the prophet Samuel, who legitimized their claim to rule; prophetic anointing of rulers appears later to have become traditional practice. In Christian interpretations of Jewish messianic prophecies, the priestly and kingly functions of the anointed one are combined. Christians hold Jesus of Nazareth to be the Messiah, or Anointed One, whose divinely appointed function it is to save his people. Out of this Christian interpretation, the emergence of later messianic movements and expectations was born.

Messianic figures are often charismatic, but messianism should be distinguished from the phenomenon of charismatic leadership as such, which sociologist Max Weber first identified and categorized. Messianism is a common feature of millenarian movements, and it rarely, if ever, occurs outside a larger millenarian framework, whereas charismatic leadership frequently does. Millenarism, millenarianism, or chiliasm (all from the Greek or Latin for "thousand," deriving from the "thousand-year reign" of the New Testament *Apocalypse of John*) is commonly defined as a belief in a this-worldly, ultimate, total, imminent, and collective salvation. Talmon (1968) identified these five features, and they have since become standard. The messianic figure is the one who will lead the group to salvation.

Messianism implies a personal element that is not a necessary feature of millenarian movements; a personal, identifiable redeemer or agent of salvation is attached to the movement.

Millenarian and messianic salvation is this-worldly: it does not occur "outside" the normal space-time continuum, as, for example, in standard Christian doctrines of salvation through grace in death, or Muslim doctrines of Paradise; or Buddhist ideas of Nirvana. Millenarism posits the salvific transformation of earthly existence. Such salvation is collective, coming to people as a group. Forms of Jewish messianism in which the anointed one comes to save his people are a prototype of this feature. Class and racialist doctrines of historical conflict and ultimate transformational resolution are secularized versions of the same collectivist doctrine; these movements, too, can posit a messiah to lead them. Individual members do *not* achieve salvation, and it is not individually given out. Third, salvation is about to come to pass. Most millenarian movements postulate the coming of the "millennium," the appearance of this-worldly salvation, as not more than 100 years in the future. When messianic expectations are attached to such movements, the messiah is either already present or soon to come. Fourth, salvation will be complete, constituting a radical alteration of life on earth. There will be an end to all evil, and the world will be transformed. This feature in particular distinguishes millenarian from reform movements; it also distinguishes messiahs, who bring this radical and revolutionary transformation about in some way, from social reformers, whose purposes are more politically pragmatic. Finally, millenarian salvation is ultimate; it is understood to be chronologically the final event in history, the millennium being a symbol for the final state of existence in history. Whatever happens after the salvation event is considered to be "outside" of or "beyond" the normal, historical course of things. The human (moral) condition, and often the material conditions on earth, are altered in some fundamental way. Messianic versions of millenarism look for a saving figure to usher in this event.

Messiahs do not always assume the role willingly: the history of messianism includes many figures in whom the poor, dispossessed, or disaffected placed their messianic hopes without the figure in question having any interest in the role. Frederick I (Barbarossa, ca. 1123–90) and his grandson, Frederick II (1194–1250) are well-known examples. More willing historical messianic figures include John of Leyden (d. 1536) and Tanchelm of Antwerp (d. c. 1115). Recent self-appointed messianic figures in the United States include David Koresh, leader of the BRANCH DAVIDIANS, and Jim Jones, leader of the Jonestown People's Temple cult. While messianism has spread to other religions and cultures and developed in secularized versions, it has remained a phenomenon usually heavily marked by Christian influences.

Further reading: Talmon, Yonina. "Millenarism." In *The International Encyclopedia of the Social Sciences.* New York: Macmillan, 1968.

—Thomas Heilke

Metropolitan Community Churches

The Universal Fellowship of Metropolitan Community Churches (UFMCC), an international Christian denomination of churches whose primary outreach is to gay, lesbian, bisexual, and transgender (GLBT) persons, was established in 1968 by PENTECOSTAL minister Troy Perry. Reverend Perry, who was excommunicated from the CHURCH OF GOD when he came out as gay in the mid-1960s, began to hold informal services for gays and lesbians in his apartment in October 1968. Attendance grew rapidly, and Perry formally dedicated the UFMCC's first church in Los Angeles in 1971. The UFMCC now consists of over 300 churches in 16 countries, with its largest congregations in the Bible Belt states of Texas and Florida.

The MCC is an ECUMENICAL church, embracing seekers from a diverse range of religious backgrounds, but its statement of faith is fundamentally Christian. It professes the belief in "one triune God of three persons—God, the parent-creator; Jesus Christ, the only begotten son of God; and the Holy Spirit, God as our Sustainer," and in the Bible as the divinely inspired Word of God. The MCC embraces two sacraments—communion and baptism—and has six ceremonial rites, including ordination, holy union and holy matrimony, and laying on of hands. Its local congregations range in theological orientation from charismatic-Pentecostal to UNITARIAN, and its clergy study at an array of seminaries in the United States and abroad. Candidates for the ministry must take at least two required courses, one on sex and the Bible and another on MCC polity.

A core element of the MCC's mission is to proclaim the "integration of spirituality and sexuality." The MCC has always been dedicated to developing a "new theology of sexuality." To this end, the MCC has representatives on the NATIONAL COUNCIL OF CHURCHES' Faith and Order Commission and convenes its own Faith, Fellowship and Order Commission, devoted to conceiving a theology of sexuality that is Christ-centered, nonsexist, and nonheterosexist. The MCC also seeks to share its message of GLBT affirmation with traditional mainline denominations. It maintains ties with several mainline Christian denominations, including the United Church of Christ and the Disciples of Christ, with whom it recently backed the New Spirit Community Church in Berkeley, California, to unite Christians of various denominations regardless of sexual orientation. Although it has been denied membership to the NATIONAL COUNCIL OF CHURCHES, the MCC belongs to statewide church councils in Colorado, Hawaii, North Carolina, and Oregon and is an official observer at meetings of the WORLD COUNCIL OF CHURCHES.

MCC leaders and local congregations have been vocal advocates for political and social change throughout the denomination's history. Public relations literature proclaims its commitment to confronting "poverty, sexism, RACISM, and homophobia with Christian social action," and church members have fought for SOCIAL JUSTICE on these issues by lobbying government officials, creating support services for the oppressed and afflicted, and employing more confrontational tactics. In the early 1970s, when there were few formal support systems for gays and lesbians, the MCC created one of the first help lines for gay and lesbian callers and provided comfort and shelter to gays in crisis. Since the early 1980s, it has been at the forefront of HIV/AIDS work, ministering to those afflicted with the disease and their families and friends, while also developing networks to provide education, health care, and comfort for HIV-affected people in local communities. MCC leaders and local congregations have also pursued change in traditional political channels, urging government officials to repeal the ban on gays in the military, legalize GAY AND LESBIAN MARRIAGE, respond to human rights violations in Brazil, and enact stricter HATE CRIME laws. The independent Soulforce group, headed by MCC minister Mel White, has engaged since the late 1990s in more contentious tactics, organizing nonviolent demonstrations at several church conventions and courting arrest to protest bans on gay and lesbian ordination and same-gender unions.

The MCC, the first and only worldwide denomination serving GLBT communities, is a long-standing and fast-growing network of Christian-based churches. Its membership numbers 44,000 internationally, and according to the *Los Angeles Times*, its success has been "a major reason that some mainline denominations are grappling with how to deal with homosexuality."

Further reading: Cherry, Kittredge. *Metropolitan Community Churches Today*. West Hollywood, Calif.: UFMCC, 1994; Dart, John. "Homosexuals' Church Alters Mainline Religions' Views." *Los Angeles Times*, June 7, 1991, Pt. A; ———. "Gay and Mainline." *Christian Century*. March 21–28, 2001, 6–8; DeBaugh, R. Adam. *MCC Handouts*. Gaithersberg, Md.: Chi Rho Press, 1995; Hartman, Keith. *Congregations in Conflict: The Battle over Homosexuality*. New Brunswick, N.J.: Rutgers University Press, 1996.

—Krista McQueeney

Million Man March

The Million Man March took place in Washington, D.C., on October 16, 1995. Minister LOUIS FARRAKHAN of the NATION OF ISLAM and Reverend Ben Chavis, the former executive director of the NAACP, planned the march. Farrakhan, who is viewed as the driving force behind the march, hoped to show the public that its image of African-American men is flawed. Farrakhan had stated that October 16 should be viewed as a "Holy Day of Atonement and Reconciliation." This holy day would provide black men the opportunity to atone for their absence from black families, communities, and religious organizations. By atoning and getting closer to God, black men would have the spiritual power, Farrakhan hoped, to commit themselves to their families, religious organizations, and community groups. The march was also called because organizers and supporters wished to voice their opposition to policies being pushed by the Republican-controlled Congress.

The march was marred by controversy. Activist Angela Davis viewed the march as sexist because it barred women. Abraham Foxman of the ANTI-DEFAMATION LEAGUE criticized the planned march because of Farrakhan's previous anti-Semitic remarks. Farrakhan's conflict with the Jewish community began to receive national attention following the "Hymietown" remarks made by the Reverend Jesse Jackson during the 1984 presidential race. Farrakhan made a number of inflammatory statements in defense of Jackson, many of which were viewed as anti-Semitic. President WILLIAM JEFFERSON CLINTON also criticized Farrakhan indirectly in a speech given on October 17, 1995.

Before the march, Farrakhan enjoyed middling support within the black community. The 1992–93 National Black Politics Study revealed that 43 percent of respondents felt Farrakhan was a positive influence in the black community. A *Time* magazine survey revealed that Farrakhan enjoyed a significant boost following the march, which is estimated to have attracted between 400,000 and 2 million men. A survey on October 5–6, 1995, reveals that one-third of all blacks felt that Farrakhan was a positive force in the black community, but only two weeks later, only half of all respondents gave Farrakhan a positive score. Nevertheless, a year later, the march was still viewed positively. A 1996 *Washington Post* survey revealed that 63 percent of blacks believed that the Million Man March had a positive impact on the black community as a whole.

In the end, the Million Man March was an important symbolic political event; it demonstrated that a populist black leader from a black nationalist religious organization could bring together a sizeable number of black men for a public rally. Prior marches such as the March on Washington in 1963 and the planned march in 1943 were neither planned nor organized by black nationalists. Instead, the leadership of these social movements consisted mainly of black and white activists who strongly believed in racial integration.

The Million Man March generated some dialogue among black Christian ministers. The Reverend Frank Madison of Bethel African Methodist Episcopal Church, Baltimore; Jeremiah Wright of Trinity United Church of Christ, Chicago; and Colleen Birchett of Chicago State University coauthored *When Black Men Stand up for God: Reflections on the Million Man March*. These pastors are extremely popular: Reid has a nationwide television ministry, which in 1996 aired on Black Entertainment Television, and both ministers are often asked to preach or lead worship services in black churches across the nation. In contrast, the Reverend Fred Price of Christian Crenshaw Center, Los Angeles, whose television ministry also reaches into black homes across the nation, preached a series of sermons against the Million Man March. Price also produced *Race, Religion and Racism* in 1999, which is critical of both Farrakhan and white churches. Thus, the march may have generated discussions about race in black churches across the nation.

The march did not bring about any lasting political organizing at the grassroots level, despite the fact that after the march, President Clinton established a Commission on Race that allowed citizens to engage in dialogue about race in local communities. Finally, the march demonstrated that black American males continue to see race as an important factor that impacts their life chances.

See also CIVIL RIGHTS MOVEMENT.

Further reading: Madison, Frank, Jeremiah A. Wright Jr., and Collen Birchett. *When Black Men Stand Up for God: Reflections on the Million Man March*. Chicago: African American Images, 1996; McCormick, Joseph P. "The Messages and the Massagers: Opinions from the Million Men Who Marched." *National Political Science Review* 6 (1997): 142–64.
—Ron Brown

Minersville School District v. Gobitis 310 U.S. 586 (1940)

Minersville School District v. Gobitis involved mandatory flag salutation by students under threat of expulsion. Two public school students in Minersville, PENNSYLVANIA, Lillian Gobitas (the surname was actually misspelled in the case files) and her brother William, refused to salute the flag as part of a daily school ritual, an act of defiance that a growing number of JEHOVAH'S WITNESSES were committing at the time. Jehovah's Witnesses are proscribed, by their religion, not to worship any object before God, the flag being considered such an object. As a result of their refusal to salute the flag, the school board adopted a resolution to require students to salute the flag and to punish those who did not. The superintendent then expelled the Gobitas children for insubordination. Their father objected to the expulsion and asked that the children be allowed to attend school but to abstain from participation in the flag ceremony. The district court agreed, finding that the religious convictions of the children were sincere and that the children should be readmitted and excused from the ceremony. The court of appeals affirmed. The Supreme Court took the case and, with Justice Frankfurter writing for the majority, reversed the lower courts and upheld the mandatory flag salute resolution.

To understand the Court's seemingly absurd decision in this case, it is first important to understand the time in which it was made. At the end of World War I, many states enacted such flag-saluting laws as a result of an American Legion campaign to promote Americanism (Irons 1990). In 1940, when the Court heard this case, the United States was on the verge of World War II, and patriotism and loyalty were foremost in peoples' minds. Therefore, it is not so surprising when Frankfurter argued that the formulation of patriotism is a compelling government interest that should not be compromised by a Court decision preferring individual liberties. Frankfurter wrote:

> The ultimate foundation of a free society is the binding tie of cohesive sentiment. . . . The flag is the symbol of our national unity . . . [It is] the symbol of the Nation's power, the emblem of freedom in its truest, best sense . . . it signifies government resting on the consent

of the governed; liberty regulated by law; the protection of the weak against the strong; security against the exercise of arbitrary power; and absolute safety for free institutions against foreign aggression.

He argued further that it was not within the purview of the Court to negate the means by which the legislature advances this compelling government interest. The end, he said is legitimate and the means of instilling patriotism elusive, so the determination by the legislature (through the school boards) that this ceremony would serve to instill patriotism should not be disturbed. The decision was joined by Justices Hughes, Roberts, Black, Reed, Douglas, and Murphy, and Justice McReynolds concurred in the result.

Although he did not vote against the decision in the conference on the merits, Justice Stone, after reading Frankfurter's opinion, circulated a dissent in which he took issue with the Court's decision. He argued that what the Court did here was deny publicly supported educational privileges to two children because of their religious convictions. He argued that the resolution in this case suppresses both freedom of speech and free exercise of religion as the law seeks to "coerce these children to express a sentiment which, as they interpret it, they do not entertain, and which violates their deepest religious convictions." He granted that civil liberties are not absolutes but argued that the legislature's interest here was not compelling enough to "compel public affirmations which violate [students'] religious conscience." The idea of promoting loyalty and national unity via compulsory expression was not acceptable to Stone. The governmental interest here, that of national unity and school discipline, did not outweigh the constitutionally protected guarantees to free speech and religion. Although begged by Frankfurter not to publish the dissent and to join the majority, Stone persisted.

The decision in this case prompted a violent reaction in which Jehovah's Witnesses were harassed and attacked. Eventually the war effort took over the attentions of the country, but the ramifications of the Court's decision did not go unnoticed. In 1942, Justices Douglas, Black, and Murphy signaled their willingness to overturn the decision, and the seating of two new justices, Rutledge and Jackson, gave them a majority. In 1943, they took the case of WEST VIRGINIA V. BARNETTE and overruled *Gobitis*. This time, Justice Frankfurter dissented.

See also COX V. NEW HAMPSHIRE; LOVELL V. CITY OF GRIFFIN; MARTIN V. STRUTHERS; MURDOCK V. PENNSYLVANIA.

Further reading: Irons, Peter. *The Courage of Their Convictions: Sixteen Americans Who Fought Their Way to the Supreme Court.* New York: Penguin Books, 1990.

—Sara C. Benesh

missionaries

Missionaries have influenced government policies, not only because of the stream of information missionaries have pro-vided the public at home, but also because of their very presence in foreign lands. This has been a presence not only of many American individuals and families, but also of a very large investment that accompanied them in the many educational and medical institutions they founded and the numerous relief efforts they carried out in the lands to which they were sent. Thomas A. Bailey's comment regarding policy in the Far East beginning in the 19th century can be applied to much of the world: "One must remember that the American missionaries, and those church members at home supporting their work, were numerous enough and influential enough to make their wants known in Washington."

Government officials, as well as business representatives, have not always welcomed the influence missionaries and their supporters have exerted, both in the lands to which they were sent and among the people in the homeland. Because of their close contact, which included knowledge of native languages and life in isolated areas, missionaries often have been better acquainted with the people of foreign lands than government and business representatives.

Although more exposed to antiforeign expressions in receiving lands, such expressions against missionaries have been much less than is conventionally thought, even when receiving nations were opposed to "foreign interference." One of the reasons is that, typically, missionaries have tried to draw and have been relatively successful in demonstrating a sharp distinction between themselves, on the one hand, and government and business concerns, on the other; namely, missionaries have said and sought to show that they were in receiving lands to serve the needs of the people, which included not only the spreading of the Christian gospel but also numerous service activities. In the end, and sometimes much sooner, governments, American and foreign, have had to take account of the missionary presence. It is also true that some missionaries, particularly the descendants of missionaries, have become directly active in government, as well as in business and in academia, which exert their own influence on public affairs.

John K. Fairbank (1974) has shed much light on the effect of missionaries in China, which is paralleled by similar influences throughout the Far East, the Middle East, South Asia, the South Pacific, Africa, and Latin America. Historians link the spread of Christianity to these areas with the spread of Western power and influence. This has caused criticism of Christian missions from both Americans and people in receiving societies for the association of Christianity with imperialism. Undoubtedly, some of the resistance to Christianity has been because of this perception. At the same time, and contrary to this perception by critics at home and in receiving lands, missionaries have stimulated nationalism and resistance to dominating Western powers, even when this was an unintended consequence of mission work. This effect is seen especially clearly in the South Pacific and in Africa, but it may be seen in almost all the lands to which missionaries have gone. In all the areas where missionaries went, especially in areas where there was not a written language, translation of the Scriptures was especially effective in creating a sense of identity and national pride among receiving peoples.

There is a long tradition of concern for human rights by missionaries dating back to Bartolome Las Casas (1474–1566) in Latin America, missionaries in the South Pacific who supported the freedom of Polynesians, and missionaries in Africa who opposed slavery. Such actions by missionaries have often created trouble for them, but it also has brought about change. In Korea, Christianity became associated with opposition to Japanese domination. Missionaries, especially in the critical 1919–21 period, exerted influence by publicizing Japanese mistreatment of Koreans and the half-hearted efforts at reform by the colonial government. In the period after World War II, when the United States often backed repressive regimes in Latin America, the Roman Catholic Church in the region found itself divided between those supporting these regimes and those who desired change. LIBERATION THEOLOGY and the analysis of the Latin American bishops at Medellín, Colombia, favored the "option for the poor." Although the church later withdrew from an association with liberation theology, American Catholic missionaries continued to identify with the poor and oppressed, which led to some widely publicized cases of martyrdom, such as the 1980 murders of four U.S. nuns in El Salvador in 1980. This, and the murder of Jesuit priests in the same country, did much to influence U.S. public opinion against repressive regimes in the whole region. In most cases, the basis for the influence of missionaries on U.S. government policies is the close connections of the missionaries to the lives of the people in many lands.

Further reading: Bailey, Thomas A. *A Diplomatic History of the American People.* Englewood Cliffs, N.J.: Prentice Hall, 1980; Fairbank, John K., ed. *The Missionary Enterprise in China and America.* Cambridge, Mass.: Harvard University Press, 1974; Noone, Judith M. *The Same Fate as the Poor.* Maryknoll, N.Y.: Maryknoll Sisters, 1984; Sanneh, Lamin. *Translating the Message.* Maryknoll, N.Y.: Orbis Books, 1991.

—Robert L. Montgomery

Mitchell et al. v. Helms et al. 530 U.S. 793 (2000)

In *Mitchell v. Helms*, the Supreme Court upheld a federal program that permits direct government aid to religious schools through loans of equipment and materials. The 6-3 decision was handed down on June 28, 2000. A four-member plurality, led by Justice Clarence Thomas, upheld the program while offering sweeping new guidelines for adjudicating such cases in the future. In a concurring opinion, Justice Sandra Day O'Connor and Stephen Breyer agreed that the program was constitutional but rejected the plurality's new guidelines; Justice David Souter (with Justices John Paul Stevens and Ruth Bader Ginsburg) filed a vigorous dissent. The case is notable for the uncertain precedent it sets for ESTABLISHMENT

CLAUSE jurisprudence on such controversial issues as CHARITABLE CHOICE and private school VOUCHERS.

Chapter 2 of the Education Consolidation and Improvement Act of 1981 provides for the allocation of federal funds for educational materials and equipment to public and private elementary and secondary schools to implement "secular, neutral, and non-ideological" programs. Chapter 2 Aid to schools is based on their enrollment; in Jefferson Parish, Louisiana, about 30 percent of Chapter 2 funds are allocated for private schools, most of which are Roman Catholic. Mary Helms and other public school parents filed suit in 1985, alleging that the application of Chapter 2 in Jefferson Parish violated the First Amendment's establishment clause. The federal district court agreed, issuing a summary injunction in 1990 and a permanent injunction in 1994 against the dispersal of Chapter 2 funds to religious schools. After the presiding judge retired in 1996, however, a new judge appointed to supervise the case reversed the decision a year later, citing new Supreme Court guidance (especially *ZOBREST V. CATALINA FOOTHILLS SCHOOL DISTRICT*) on the issue. In 1999, the Fifth Circuit Court of Appeals overturned this decision, prompting an appeal to the Supreme Court.

The plaintiffs in *Mitchell v. Helms* conceded that Chapter 2, as applied in Jefferson Parish, had a "secular purpose" and that it did not foster "excessive entanglement" between church and state—two important tests of a law's constitutionality that have guided the Court's establishment clause jurisprudence since *LEMON V. KURTZMAN* (1973). The *Mitchell* Court, therefore, focused on the relevant aspects of the "primary effect" prong of the *Lemon* test, which, as modified by *Agostini v. Felton* (1997), states that a law unconstitutionally "advances religion" if it results in government indoctrination of religion or defines the recipient of government aid with reference to religion.

The plurality (led by Justice Thomas, and joined by Chief Justice William Rehnquist and Justices ANTONIN SCALIA and Anthony Kennedy) utilized the legal principle of neutrality to argue that Chapter 2 did not advance religion since it distributed aid to schools without regard to their religious affiliation (or lack thereof), according to neutral, secular criteria. Furthermore, wrote Thomas, religious indoctrination cannot reasonably be attributed to the government if it is the result of "private choices of students and their parents as to which schools to attend."

In a concurring opinion, Justices O'Connor and Breyer voted with Thomas to uphold Chapter 2 (on the grounds that it did not have the primary effect of advancing religion), but rejected their argument that neutrality ought to be the most important factor in deciding such cases. According to O'Connor, the plurality opinion "announces a rule of unprecedented breadth" and is "particularly troubling," since neutrality should be considered "only one of several factors the Court considers" when adjudicating challenges to school aid programs.

Writing in dissent, Justices Souter, Stevens, and Ginsburg argued that the equipment provided by Chapter 2 directly to "pervasively sectarian schools" is easily utilized for religious indoctrination, and thus the program had the unconstitutional effect of advancing religion. Like O'Connor, Souter averred that the plurality "espouses a new conception of neutrality," though he went further in saying that this new conception "breaks fundamentally with Establishment Clause principle and with the methodology painstakingly worked out in support of it."

Mitchell's impact on both establishment clause jurisprudence and public policy depends in large part on whether the plurality's broad conception of neutrality is ever adopted by the majority of the Court. While this ruling appears to have broadened the scope of permissible government aid to religious institutions, it remains unclear how the Court—particularly Justices O'Connor and Breyer—will apply the precedent when it adjudicates challenges to programs like private-school vouchers and Charitable Choice.

—Erik Owens

Moral Majority

The Moral Majority, founded in 1979, was part of the political movement known as the Christian Right. The conservative Protestant community was viewed as a sleeping giant, and the task of the Moral Majority was to arouse it, aided by secular conservatives, to invigorate the Republican Party. Its president was televangelist JERRY FALWELL. Other prominent names among its leadership included Tim Lahaye, Charles Stanley, Greg Dixon, and D. James Kennedy—pastors of some of America's largest churches. It claimed 47 state affiliates; however, few were very active. While it called itself ECUMUNICAL, its leaders were largely independent Baptists and its members mostly fundamentalist. Its major activities included registering voters, supporting conservative candidates, and lobbying Congress.

Its early success has been attributed to the charisma and skills of Falwell, the energy of its first executive director, Robert Billings, fortuitous timing, adroit use of symbols and rhetoric, and clergy backing. Using direct-mail techniques, the Moral Majority claimed great success in reaching budget and membership goals. But the accuracy of its quantitative claims of success has been questioned.

Falwell developed a model for aggressive voter registration in fundamentalist churches, and claimed to have registered several million new voters in 1980 and again in 1984. The media attributed RONALD REAGAN's 1980 presidential victory to this effort. Subsequent analyses, however, have substantially modified this interpretation.

Moral Majority direct-mail appeals, designed to mobilize their recipients, were festooned with flags and written in sensational language with frequent capital letters and red underlining. These achieved widespread name recognition, aided by frequent use of the group's name by its opponents and the national media. The widespread publicity and seeming success of the Moral Majority prompted the creation of groups such as PEOPLE FOR THE AMERICAN WAY with the primary mission of opposing its agenda.

The Moral Majority developed a sweeping agenda, summed up in a call to "return America to moral sanity," though some argue that the elusiveness of this goal contributed to the organization's gradual decline. The Moral Majority also endorsed Reagan's economic, foreign, and national defense goals. Although trying to keep its own moral agenda in the spotlight, it avoided criticism of Reagan's priorities. This prompted other conservatives to criticize the Moral Majority for opting to play an "advisory" rather than a properly "prophetic" role vis-à-vis government.

The organization also engaged in direct lobbying of Congress, but it lacked the political skills needed for successful lobbying and unwittingly convinced members of Congress that it was not the threat that it had once seemed. One particularly embarrassing defeat was Sandra Day O'Connor's Supreme Court nomination, which sailed through the Senate despite Moral Majority opposition. Another, the failure of the omnibus Family Protection Act, revealed how little Moral Majority lobbyists understood about the legislative process.

Falwell sought to build bridges between the Moral Majority, which he described as a political, not a religious, organization, and conservative elements of the Roman Catholic, Mormon, and Jewish communities. However, his fellow clergy were often not supportive of this effort. Many rivalries and theological differences surfaced within the Moral Majority and between the Moral Majority and other parts of the Christian Right. By the mid-1980s, it had expended its political capital with Congress, worn down its followers with financial appeals, and proven itself sufficiently controversial and irritating as to make expansion unlikely.

In 1986, Falwell unveiled a new organization, the Liberty Federation. In 1987, he gave orders to "wind down" the Moral Majority, and in 1989, he announced its demise. Polls showed that the Moral Majority never gained widespread public respect. Yet, Falwell argued that the Moral Majority made a lasting impact by activating the Christian Right, commanding media attention, and paving the way for its successors.

See also CHRISTIAN COALITION; CHRISTIAN RIGHT AND THE REPUBLICAN PARTY; RELIGION IN THE 1980, 1984, 1988 PRESIDENTIAL ELECTIONS.

Further reading: Liebman, Robert C. "Mobilizing the Moral Majority." In *The New Christian Right.* Edited by Robert C. Liebman, and Robert Wuthnow, New York: Aldine, 1983; Martin, William. *With God on Our Side.* New York: Broadway Books, 1996; Moen, Matthew C. *The Christian Right and Congress.* Tuscaloosa: University of Alabama Press, 1989; ———. *The Transformation of the Christian Right.* Tuscaloosa: University of Alabama Press, 1992; Reichley, James A. *Religion in American Politics.* Washington, D.C.: Brookings Institution, 1985; Wilcox, Clyde. *Onward Christian Soldiers?: The Religious Right in American Politics.* Boulder, Colo.: Westview Press, 1996.

—Jane Gurganus Rainey

Moravians

The Moravian Church is a Christian denomination in the reformed tradition, with roots in the Czech Hussite reformation of the 15th and 16th centuries and the German Pietist movement of the 18th century. The first Moravian congregation in North America was founded in Bethlehem, PENNSYLVANIA, on Christmas day in 1741 by Count Nikolaus Ludwig Zinzendorf. Moravians are known for their missionary efforts, which they understand as a duty of the whole church, as opposed to the duty of a missionary society or of individuals.

Christianity in Moravia, an area that is now in the Czech Republic, began in the ninth century when Cyril and Methodius established a Slavic church. The ROMAN CATHOLIC CHURCH later forced the Latin rite on this church, which was considered religious oppression by the Moravians. Jan Hus (1369–1415), one of the leaders of this controversy, preached against the Catholic selling of indulgences for the remission of sins and the denial of communion wine to the laity, and questioned the moral leadership of the papacy. In 1414, the Council of Constance invited Hus to bring forth his stance but arrested and later burned him as a heretic. Hus's followers then formed their own church in 1457; called it the "Society of Brethren" (Jednota Bratrska); and published the Bible in the Czech vernacular, as Luther did for the German people.

In the 16th and 17th centuries, religious persecution extinguished almost all the estimated 400 congregations in Moravia and Bohemia, but in 1722 a few families fled to Saxony, Germany. Count Zinzendorf offered his estate, Herrenhut, to the refugees and also helped them organize their denomination anew. Zinzendorf, heavily influenced by German Pietism, encouraged the Moravians to place a higher stress on the individual religious experience and a personal relationship with Christ and to become a missionary church. The tradition of printing the Daily Texts, a devotional booklet with both an Old and a New Testament text for each day of the year, is still continued, with 1.5 million copies in 50 languages and dialects published annually. The missionary efforts of the Moravians led them to all continents, to St. Thomas—the oldest Moravian mission in the New World—and under the leadership of Bishop Spangenberg to the state of Georgia (1735–40). Their refusal to bear arms during the war between the British and the Spanish caused the Moravians to leave Georgia and settle farther north in Pennsylvania. They established Nazareth, Pennsylvania, and settled in Bethlehem, Pennsylvania, where they lived in a self-supporting community. Moravians also organized churches in New Jersey, North Carolina, Maryland, Canada, and Greenland in their effort to bring Christian mission to the Native Americans of these areas. Fairfield, Ontario, another Moravian settlement, became a stop for the Underground Railroad in the 19th century. Moravian congregations in the Midwest were formed from the 1840s on.

The Moravian Church in America of today, established as an autonomous church body in 1848, is still centered in Bethlehem, Pennsylvania, and reported 50,000 members in the United States in nearly 160 congregations in the year 2000. Worldwide membership is 750,000, with the majority of Moravians living in Africa and the Caribbean. Clergy are educated at Moravian College and its Theological Seminary. Today, 20 percent of Moravian churches are served by female pastors; the first female bishop was elected in 1998. The Moravian Church is a founding member of the World Council of Churches.

Doctrinally, the Moravians accept the historic creeds of the Christian church and adhere to the motto "In essentials unity, in non-essentials liberty, in all things love." Congregations follow a simplified liturgy and the pattern of the traditional church year. Baptism and Holy Communion are considered sacraments. Moravians practice the "love feast," a service stressing fellowship that includes a shared meal for participants to encourage communal oneness. There is no one distinct political or social stance connected with the Moravians. The Moravian website contains a collection of Moravian positions on social issues taken by synods of the Northern Province, uplifting such issues as the civil responsibility to vote and to support all forces of righteousness; the right to CONSCIENTIOUS OBJECTION of military service; opposition to the death penalty; and support of the Jubilee 2000 campaign advocating debt relief for impoverished nations. The Moravians have not adopted a strong anti-ABORTION stance. The church as a whole invites gay and lesbian Christians but requires their pastors to live in a heterogeneous marriage or adopt a celibate lifestyle. The issue of ordination of noncelibate gay and lesbian clergy has not been decided yet.

See also DUTCH REFORMED TRADITION.

Further reading: Durnbaugh, Donald F. "Brethren and Moravians in Colonial America." In *Unitas Fratrum. Zeitschrift fuer Geschichte und Gegenwartsfragen der Bruedergemeinde* 25 (1989). Hamburg: Friedrich Wittig Verlag, 51–68; Fudge, Thomas A. *The Magnificent Ride: The First Reformation in Hussite Bohemia.* Aldershot, Hampshire, U.K.: Ashgate, 1998; Hamilton, J. Taylor, and Kenneth G. Hamilton. *History of the Moravian Church: The Renewed Unitas Fratrum 1722–1957.* Bethlehem, Pa.: Interprovincial Board of Christian Education/Moravian Church in America, 1957; Mulholland, Kenneth B. "Moravians, Puritans, and the Modern Missionary Movement." *Bibliotheca Sacra* 156 (1999): 221–232; Schattschneider, David A. "Pioneers in Mission: Zinzendorf and the Moravians." *International Bulletin of Missionary Research* 8 (1984): 63–67; Weinlick, John R. *The Moravian Church through the Ages.* Moravian Church in America, 1988; Website of the Moravian Church in America at URL: http://www.moravian.org.

—Claudia Bergmann

Mormon extermination order

On October 27, 1838, Missouri governor Lilburn W. Boggs issued an executive order that condoned the killing of LATTER-

DAY SAINTS (LDS) residing in Missouri. It stated: "The Mormons must be treated as enemies and must be exterminated or driven from the state, if necessary for the public good. Their outrages are beyond all description." The execution of this order led to violent conflict and the eventual migration of the Mormons from Missouri to Illinois, where they stayed until their exodus to Utah.

The Mormons had a tumultuous history in Missouri over the seven years preceding the extermination order. In July 1831, a group of about 60 Mormons settled in Independence, Jackson County, Missouri. Two years after the first Saints arrived in Missouri, there were nearly 1,200 Mormons in Jackson County out of a total county population of 3,500. The local settlers began to fear the Mormons for several reasons. With increased numbers came increased political power for the LDS population. The local settlers, who were largely Southerners with roots in slave culture, feared the position of the Mormons, who were largely Northerners, on slavery. The local settlers feared the peculiar religious doctrine of the Mormons. Finally, the Saints traded among themselves and did not contribute to the local economy. When the Saints asked for more time to resolve mounting conflicts, they were attacked by mobs.

During the winter of 1833–34, the Saints were driven from Independence to Clay County, immediately north of Jackson County. Violence in Clay County began almost as soon as the Mormons arrived. Mormon numbers continued to grow, however, as people from LDS settlements in Ohio came to Missouri, and converts filtered in from across the country.

The Missouri state legislature then intervened, creating a new county, called Far West, and designating it as a gathering place for Mormons. By 1838, there were 5,000 Mormons in a main settlement in Far West, with 15,000 total Saints then in Missouri. Mormons made agreements also to settle in neighboring Daviess County, a site in which Joseph Smith began to associate events of Jesus Christ's Second Coming, thus stimulating an influx of Mormons to the area. Some Saints even told settlers that the Lord would destroy the Missourians and give the land to the Mormons. This did not curry favor with local citizens.

Tensions broke into violence on August 6, 1838. William Peniston, a Whig candidate for the state legislature, realized he could not get the Mormon vote, and thus could not win. In an election day rally at Gallatin, Daviess county, Peniston encouraged the locals to prevent Mormons from voting. A Missourian attacked Samuel Brown, a Mormon preacher, and a brawl ensued. Though few Mormons voted, Peniston still lost. In retaliation, Peniston swore out a false affidavit, saying that an army of 500 Mormons had threatened death to many of the old settlers.

Then, on October 25, Captain Samuel Bogart of the Missouri militia took three Mormon prisoners from Caldwell County. The Caldwell County militia encountered Bogart's troops at Crooked River and tried to retake the prisoners. Exaggerated reports of the Gallatin election day incident and the Battle of Crooked River filtered back to Democratic governor Boggs, who already disliked the Mormons (he was from Jackson County). In response, Governor Boggs issued the extermination order, authorizing the use of any means to rid the state of the Mormons.

When the extermination order was issued on October 27, the Mormons were not immediately made aware of it. But, when a large militia began to converge on Far West, it was apparent that armed conflict was approaching.

JOSEPH SMITH and other Mormon leaders went to negotiate with the militia leaders. Instead of negotiating, the militia took the Mormon leaders prisoner and attacked Far West. For over a week, the militia-turned-mob ransacked the town, looting and raping. Soon after, a settlement at Haun's Mill, Daviess County, was taken by surprise attack on October 30. Seventeen were killed in brutal fashion, including a 10-year-old boy and an elderly man. Because of the destruction of shelter and the loss of property and money, many of the Saints became sick or even died from exposure during the winter of 1838–39.

The siege on Far West ended November 6 as prisoners were taken; the Saints were promised they could stay in Missouri through the winter but could not plant crops. The cease-fire did not last long, however, and the Saints were threatened with death if they did not leave by February 1839. With Joseph Smith in jail in Illinois (where he was later killed), BRIGHAM YOUNG organized the evacuation of an impoverished body of Saints to Quincy, Illinois.

In 1976, Missouri Republican governor Christopher S. Bond formally apologized for the treatment of the early Mormons in Missouri and officially rescinded the extermination order as a token of good will toward modern Latter-day Saints.

See also COUNCIL OF FIFTY; *REYNOLDS V. UNITED STATES*.

Further reading: Arrington, Leonard. *Brigham Young: American Moses.* New York: Knopf, 1985; Durham, Reed C. "The Election Day Battle at Gallatin." *Brigham Young University Studies* 13, no. 1 (1972): 36–61; Lyon, T. Edgar. "Independence, Missouri, and the Mormons, 1827–1833." *Brigham Young University Studies* 13, no. 1 (1972): 10–19; Smith, Joseph Jr. *History of the Church of Jesus Christ of Latter-Day Saints.* Vol. 3. Edited by Brigham H. Roberts, Salt Lake City: Deseret Books, 1948.

—Damon M. Cann

Mott, Lucretia (1793–1880) *activist*

Lucretia Coffin Mott, the most prominent American female ABOLITIONIST, pioneer in women's rights, and preeminent QUAKER minister, was born in Nantucket, Massachusetts. By the time of her death in 1880, she had witnessed radical social and political changes regarding the status of slaves, significant gains in the advancement of women, and liberalizing developments within American religion—each of which owed some debt to Lucretia Mott herself.

Lucretia Mott *(Hulton/Archive)*

Mott's early life shaped her outlook definitively. Her childhood was spent on Nantucket among hardy seafaring people. Nantucket women, like Mott's mother, Anna Folger Coffin, were distinguished by their independence, self-reliance, and hard work. With husbands at sea, the women of the island developed an impressive social and economic support network, which formed Lucretia Mott's first exposure to the eminent capabilities of women. Her family's Quaker religion corroborated what she knew from experience. Marked by a distinctive egalitarianism, it affirmed the equality of men and women and established schools that were open to girls as well as boys. Mott attended such a coeducational Friends school, Nine Partners (near Poughkeepsie, New York), which later hired her as an instructor. Here Lucretia met her future husband, James Mott, with whom she would have six children and enjoy a long, amicable marriage and close partnership in social reform. The seeds of that partnership were sown early, during their time at Nine Partners, when James shared Lucretia's outrage at the gross disparity in pay between male and female teachers. This injustice offended Mott's egalitarian sensibility and ignited her ambition to work for women's equality.

In 1817 Mott faced another pivotal moment, the loss of a child. This event prompted an introspective, religious turn, marked by intense prayer and theological study. Soon Mott

began to speak regularly during Quaker meetings, quickly gaining a reputation for exceptional spiritual gifts. Acknowledged as a Quaker minister at the age of 28, she began to travel widely, giving eloquent sermons on the sufficiency of the Inner Light, Christian duty, and progressive topics, including abolition, women's rights, and temperance. Mott's allegiance to the liberal "Hicksite" faction of the Friends and her consistent preaching against social injustices, especially slavery, provoked fierce opposition from orthodox Quakers, some of whom attempted to remove her from the ministry.

Mott's social activism soon transcended church circles, as she became the most prominent female abolitionist, working alongside figures such as William Lloyd Garrison and Wendell Phillips. In 1837 she cofounded the Philadelphia Female Anti-Slavery Society, the first of its kind, and henceforth campaigned vigorously against slavery, at times facing violent opposition. Taking the cause most personally, Mott offered her home as a station along the Underground Railroad.

In 1840, Mott attended the World Anti-Slavery Convention in London, where female delegates were prohibited from speaking. Incensed at this discrimination, Mott and ELIZABETH CADY STANTON, also in attendance, vowed to fight for women's rights. They organized the 1848 Seneca Falls Convention, which called for a range of feminist reforms, including suffrage, and launched the women's movement in the United States. While abolition and the advancement of blacks would remain Mott's central concerns, she continued to work for women's rights, becoming president of the Equal Rights Association in 1866 and serving as a unifying force in the women's movement.

A tireless activist, in her later years Mott promoted liberal religious developments through groups including the Free Religious Association and assumed leadership roles in the peace movement, presiding over the Pennsylvania Peace Society in 1868. Long noted for her rhetorical eloquence, she delivered her last public address before the Society of Friends at the age of 87.

See also ADDAMS, JANE; ANTHONY, SUSAN B.; WILLARD, FRANCES.

—Jeanne M. Heffernan

Mueller v. Allen 463 U.S. 388 (1983)

On June 29, 1983, the Supreme Court handed down its decision in *Mueller v. Allen.* Its ruling upheld a Minnesota law providing tax deductions for educational expenses incurred by parents with school-aged children. In this decision, authored by Justice Rehnquist, the 5-4 majority refuted petitioners' claim that the law in question violated the ESTABLISHMENT CLAUSE of the First Amendment as it applied to the state of Minnesota by way of the Fourteenth Amendment. The neutrality of the law, in providing benefits to all parents of school-aged children regardless of the private-public nature of the school attended, as well as the fact that state funds became available to religious schools only as a result of parents' private choice, distinguished it from a similar tax law found unconstitutional in COMMITTEE FOR PUBLIC EDUCATION AND RELI-GIOUS LIBERTY V. NYQUIST. The elements of neutrality and individual choice, which arose in *Mueller,* would become key distinctions in future cases, such as WITTERS V. WASHINGTON DEPARTMENT FOR SERVICES FOR THE BLIND, involving aid to sectarian institutions.

The Minnesota statute in question allows state taxpayers to deduct from their gross income monies expended on "tuition, textbooks, and transportation" incurred in the education of their primary and secondary school-aged children. The law was challenged by certain Minnesota taxpayers on the grounds that it violated the establishment clause in providing financial assistance to sectarian institutions. Both the district court and the court of appeals upheld the law, citing its neutrality in providing benefits to all Minnesota parents.

The Supreme Court, in affirming the rulings of the lower courts, found its decision guided by the test laid out in LEMON V. KURTZMAN. According to *Lemon,* if a statute is to meet the requirements of the establishment clause, it must have a secular purpose, must have neither the primary effect of advancing nor inhibiting religion, and must not result in excessive government entanglement in religion. On the first count, the Court found that the law did have a secular purpose in assuring the proper education of the state's citizenry, and in assuring the continued benefits that both sectarian and nonsectarian private schools afford state taxpayers. These benefits included, but were not limited to, easing the burden on the state's public schools, and providing public schools with healthy competition.

As for the primary-effect prong of the test—whether the law had the effect of promoting or inhibiting religion—the Court found that it did not do either. In doing so, the Court appealed to the presence of other tax deductions offered by the state, such as those for medical expenses and charitable contributions, and to the state's discretion in equalizing the tax burden of its citizens. Most important, however, was that the deduction for educational expenses was made available to all parents of schoolchildren, whether they attended public, private, or private-sectarian schools. This element more than any other distinguished the law at hand from that in *Nyquist.* In *Nyquist,* tax deductions were available solely to parents financing their children's educations at parochial schools. In that case, sectarian schools were the primary and intended beneficiary of state funds, whereas the neutral availability of funds in *Mueller* made any contributions to sectarian schools the result of parents' private choices. This element of free choice was enough to release the state from any responsibility for the use of funds allocated as a result of its tax-deduction scheme.

The Court also found that the Minnesota law did not result in an excessive government entanglement with religion. The only possible area of concern arose from the state's responsibility in determining which books could and could not qualify for deductions under the law. However, cases such as *Mueller* had already validated states' ability to make a distinction regarding whether a book was or was not secular in nature and content.

Furthermore, the majority found no merit in the four dissenters' argument that the law was not neutral because tuition was not required of students attending public schools. They believed the law to be neutral on its face and were not inclined to base its constitutionality on the "basis of annual statistical reports." Minnesota's law allowing tax deductions for educational expenses, in meeting each condition of *Lemon,* was found constitutionally valid.

—Steven C. Leidinger

Muhammad, Elijah (1897–1975) *religious leader*

Born Elijah Poole in Sandersville, Georgia, to William Poole and Mariah Hall on October 7, 1897, Elijah Muhammad was the leader of the NATION OF ISLAM (NOI) and a black separatist. Muhammad's NOI was a hybrid of political black nationalism and a reinterpreted ISLAM, though most orthodox Muslims rejected it. NOI drew its membership largely from the lower socioeconomic class of African Americans in northern urban areas, having particularly large centers in Chicago, Detroit, and New York. The majority of its members were males between the ages of 17 and 35. Muhammad taught that NOI doctrine included the beliefs that African Americans are the chosen of God, that WALI D. FARD was the prophet of Allah, or literally Allah, that Elijah Muhammad was the seal of the prophets of Allah, that white people are devils, and that a strict moral and social foundation should be encouraged of African Americans. This foundation also included dietary restrictions and a banning of secular entertainment, such as sports and gambling, as well as the prohibition of alcohol, tobacco, and hair-straightening products. In addition to an independent religious and cultural identity, Muhammad believed economic self-sufficiency was vital for NOI. NOI reached its peak in the 1960s, with an estimated membership of between 100,000 and 250,000. Though relatively small, NOI has been a force in American politics largely because of its dynamic leadership (Elijah Muhammad, MALCOLM X, LOUIS FARRAKHAN); its striking indictment of American history, culture, and society; and its call for black self-knowledge, self-reliance, and self-determination.

After moving to Detroit in 1923 with his wife and two children, Poole was influenced by the black nationalist movements of Marcus Garvey (Universal Negro Improvement Association) and Noble Drew Ali (Moorish Science Temple of America) (Evanzz 1999: 51–65). While a member of the Moorish Science Temple of America (MSTA), Poole met Wallace D. Fard, the founder and leader of the Allah Temple of Islam (ATI), in 1931. Fard claimed that he was descended from the Prophet Muhammad and was the Mahdi, or Messiah. He told Poole that white people are devils, that whites are inferior to blacks, and that, according to the myth of Yacub, the Caucasian race is the result of the genetic engineering of a mad scientist long ago. In addition, according to Fard, Islam is the proper religion of African Americans, not Christianity. Fard also encouraged the separation of the races and a return to Africa for black people. Despite his claims only to messiahship, Fard was thought to be God incarnate by Poole. In 1932 Fard made Poole the Supreme Minister of ATI and renamed him Elijah Karriem. In 1933, ATI became the Nation of Islam and Karriem was renamed Elijah Muhammad. In 1934, when Fard disappeared, Muhammad proclaimed himself the Seal of the Prophets of Allah, the Supreme Minister of the Nation of Islam, and claimed Fard was Allah.

While in prison from 1943 to 1946 in Michigan on charges of draft evasion, Muhammad began to convert fellow inmates, a practice that he would continue after his release. In 1957, the Federal Bureau of Investigation, having long investigated black nationalist movements out of fears of their possible ties to communist movements, began to tap Muhammad's phones and to plant surveillance devices around him. These practices would continue until Muhammad's death.

In the 1960s, NOI developed but had internal struggles over the apparent hypocrisy of Elijah Muhammad. Despite his proscribed ideal of a simple and frugal lifestyle, some NOI members believed Muhammad lived in luxury. In addition, it became clear that Muhammad was having affairs with his secretaries and fathering children, though he denied these charges. In the end, Muhammad fathered 13 children with seven women, in addition to his eight children with his wife, Clara (née Clara Belle Evans, married March 7, 1919). Also, rumors of strict disciplinary actions, fallings from the moral code, and financial problems undermined the success of NOI. Ultimately, Muhammad's actions strained his relationships with his wife, his children, especially his son Wallace, and Malcolm X, the prominent spokesman for NOI.

Muhammad battled diabetes and bronchitis toward the end of his life. After his death on February 25, 1975, his son, Wallace Muhammad (later WARITH DEEN MUHAMMAD) seized control of NOI and later renamed it several times.

See also BLACK THEOLOGY; MESSIANISM; RACISM.

Further reading: Clegg, Claude Andrew III. *An Original Man: The Life and Times of Elijah Muhammad.* New York: St. Martin's Press, 1997; Elijah Muhammad File (á105-24822). Federal Bureau of Investigation. 16 Sections (plus index). 2,798 documents; Evanzz, Karl. *The Messenger: The Rise and Fall of Elijah Muhammad.* New York: Pantheon, 1999.

—Kurt Buhring

Muhammad, Warith Deen (1933–) *religious leader*

Warith Deen Muhammad succeeded ELIJAH MUHAMMAD as head of the NATION OF ISLAM (NOI) and founder of the AMERICAN MUSLIM COUNCIL. Born October 30, 1933, Muhammad is the son of Clara and Elijah Muhammad. Wali D. Fard, founder of NOI, foretold the birth of this "favored child" and named him Wallace Delaney Muhammad, predicting he would succeed his father, already tapped to be Fard's successor, as head of NOI.

W. D. Muhammad began working in the NOI hierarchy after completing high school. Although his rise through the ranks was not smooth, the day after Elijah Muhammad died, this son was named his successor and was unanimously approved during Savior's Day celebrations on February 26, 1975. He began a process of Islamization of NOI that resulted in a splintering of the organization. A dissident group loyal to LOUIS FARRAKHAN took over the NOI name and espoused a different theology, while W. D. Muhammad formed the American Muslim Mission, bringing his followers closer to mainstream Sunni ISLAM in both theology and practice.

In 1961, W. D. Muhammad refused the military draft and was sentenced to three years in jail. While there, he began reading mainstream Islamic doctrine and noticed contradictions with NOI theology. The resulting ideological rift with his father caused him to leave NOI in 1963. After the assassination of MALCOLM X in 1965, he returned to the NOI ranks but was suspended by NOI for his "dissident views" in 1969 and again in 1971.

W. D. Muhammad's assumption of the NOI leadership was not without controversy. Another top NOI official, Farrakhan, felt that *he* should have been named Elijah Muhammad's successor. Farrakhan disagreed publicly with W. D. Muhammad in 1977 over NOI's move toward Sunni Islam, and took a minority of NOI members with him into a splinter group. In 1981, Farrakhan announced restoration of the "old" Nation of Islam, and went forward with Elijah Muhammad's NOI teachings. He continues to be the more media-savvy of the two successors, and was responsible for the dramatic MILLION MAN MARCH in 1995.

Continuing his reform movement within NOI, W. D. Muhammad publicly shunned his father's theology and black separatist views. He forged ties with other American Muslim organizations and in 1976 renamed his own the World Community of al-Islam in the West. That year, he changed his title from supreme minister to the more Islamic one of imam and adopted the name Warith Deen Mohammed. Membership was opened to all believers. Two years later, he changed the name of his organization to the American Muslim Mission.

W. D. Muhammad's embrace of mainstream Islam was rewarded with political and economic benefits. In 1975, he met privately with Egyptian president Anwar el-Sadat in Chicago, and in 1976 he received a gift of $16 million from Sheik Sultan ben Mohammad al-Qasmini, head of the Emirate of Sharjah in the United Arab Emirates, to purchase a mosque and build a school. In 1992, he became the first Muslim imam to offer morning prayers before the U.S. Senate, and later he participated in two Interfaith Breakfasts hosted by President WILLIAM JEFFERSON CLINTON. He was invited to meet Pope JOHN PAUL II at the Vatican in 1996.

W. D. Muhammad resigned as spiritual leader of the American Muslim Mission in 1978. In 1985 he dismantled the leadership council he had set up. Although each mosque then became an independent entity with its own name and leadership, most remained affiliated with the successor organization, the Muslim American Society (MAS, also known as the Ministry of W. Deen Muhammad), based in Calumet City, Illinois. (This Muslim American Society is not the same group as the Muslim American Society based in Falls Church, Virginia.)

Integration of MAS, which is still overwhelmingly African American, with mainstream Sunni Islam in the United States is by no means complete, even 25 years after it began. Mosques, schools, businesses, and organizations (including the International League of Muslim Women) affiliated with W. D. Muhammad's MAS retain their distinctiveness through separate conferences and networks. Also, they cooperate in the distribution of the organization's weekly newspaper. Headquartered in Hazel Crest, Illinois, *Muslim Journal* was known as *Muhammad Speaks* when it was the official publication of the Nation of Islam.

Further reading: Ansari, Zafar Ishaq. "W.D. Muhammad: The Making of a 'Black Muslim' Leader (1933–1961)." *American Journal of Islamic Social Sciences* 2 (1985): 245–262; Gardell, Mattias. *In the Name of Elijah Muhammad: Louis Farrakhan and the Nation of Islam.* Durham, N.C.: Duke University Press, 1996; W. Deen Mohammed Ministry website. URL: http://www.wdmonline.com; Muslim American Society website. URL: http://masba.com/index.htm.

—Susan McKee

Murray v. Curlett 374 U.S. 203 (1963)

In the early 1960s, legal challenges to prayer and Bible reading in public schools filled court dockets. While most American government textbooks recognize that ABINGTON TOWNSHIP SCHOOL DISTRICT V. SCHEMPP (1963) ruled the practices of prayer and Bible reading in public schools unconstitutional, few books discuss the second case decided by the opinion *Murray v. Curlett. Murray* deserves recognition because it represents the beginning of the crusade of Madalyn Murray (O'Hair) to eliminate religion from public life.

Murray, an ATHEIST, challenged the long-standing practice in the Baltimore City School District that provided for the "reading without comment, of a chapter in the Holy Bible and/or the use of the Lord's Prayer." Murray, whose son William attended school in Baltimore, asserted that the Bible reading each morning violated her son's freedom of religion under the First and Fourteenth Amendments, as well as the ESTABLISHMENT CLAUSE's principle of the SEPARATION OF CHURCH AND STATE. A divided (4-3) Maryland Court of Appeals affirmed the trial court's decision in favor of the school district.

Less than one year after the Court's decision in ENGEL V. VITALE (1962), *Murray* and *Schempp* attracted national attention. Attorneys general from 18 states joined the case as amici curiae on behalf of continuing the practices of prayer and Bible reading. The AMERICAN JEWISH COMMITTEE, the *Synagogue Council of America,* and the American Ethical Union filed amici briefs urging the end to these practices.

While the cases were argued separately, Justice Tom Clark delivered the opinion for the Court on June 17, 1963, for both *Murray* and *Schempp.* In an 8-1 decision, the Court held that policies of both school districts violated the establishment clause. Justice Clark reviewed the decisions of the Court relating to both the Establishment and FREE EXERCISE CLAUSES. In examining the history of the establishment clause, Justice Clark wrote: "This Court has rejected unequivocally the contention that the Establishment Clause forbids only governmental preference of one religion over another."

Reviewing the facts in the cases, the Court concluded that the prayer and Bible readings were "part of the curricular activities of students who are required by law to attend school. They are held in the school buildings under the supervision and with the participation of teachers employed in those schools." Despite provisions that excused students at the request of their parents, the Court concluded that the school districts' policies required religious exercises and, thus, breached the wall separating church and state.

The brief majority opinion is buttressed by three concurrences by Justices William Douglas, WILLIAM BRENNAN, and Arthur Goldberg joined by Justice John M. Harlan. Justice Douglas's brief concurrence noted that the policies in question violated the establishment clause because the state violated the neutrality principle required by the First Amendment by conducting a religious exercise. Furthermore, the state was using its public school facilities to support religious activities. "Such contributions may not be made by the State even in a minor degree without violating the Establishment Clause." Justice Brennan authored a lengthy concurrence that outlined the framers' intentions with respect to the establishment clause, as well as decisions promoting the separation of church and state in cases involving church property and disputes regarding doctrinal theology within a denomination. Justice Brennan proceeded to refute the school districts' contentions that daily prayer and Bible reading served a secular educational purpose, specifically "by fostering harmony and tolerance among the pupils, enhancing the authority of the teacher, and inspiring better discipline." Though students could be granted an exemption from participation, Justice Brennan noted the stigma associated with nonconformity.

As he did in *Engel v. Vitale,* Justice Potter Stewart dissented, asserting that the factual record in *Murray* and *Schempp* did not support the Court's decision declaring the school districts' policies violations of the establishment clause. To Justice Stewart, the religious exercises in public schools fostered the free exercise of religious beliefs.

While the Supreme Court, through its decision in *Murray* and *Schempp,* declared the practice of prayer and Bible reading unconstitutional, the controversy over the role of religion in public education was far from decided, as was evidenced in the next decades in WALLACE V. JAFFREE (1985), LEE V. WEISMAN (1992), and SANTA FE INDEPENDENT SCHOOL DISTRICT V. DOE (2000).

See also PRAYER IN PUBLIC SCHOOLS.

—Sara A. Grove

N

Naked Public Square, The: Religion and Democracy in America (1984) By Richard John Neuhaus. Grand Rapids, Mich.: W. B. Eerdmans

The Naked Public Square has been regarded widely as a seminal work in contemporary church and state studies written from a neoconservative perspective. Perhaps more influential than Neuhaus's normative claims has been his metaphor of the "naked public square," which continues to be invoked among both supporters and critics nearly 20 years later.

Neuhaus contends that although the claim "America is a secular society" contradicts both the country's history and the current sociological facts regarding religious beliefs among citizens, it is a "myth" being endorsed increasingly by nonbelievers and mainstream believers alike. This "myth of secular America," he argues, not only describes but also buttresses the "naked public square," the state of affairs wherein religion and religiously grounded values are excluded from public discourse and the conduct of public life. Through a reading of the founding documents and the relevant Supreme Court cases, Neuhaus argues that religious freedom was not intended to protect public space from religion but rather to protect the expression and practice of religion from government intervention. It was intended to protect a plurality of religious voices within the democracy, not to sanitize democratic institutions from religious claims. During the 1950s, he argues, an interpretive shift occurred that has led to the equation of religious freedom with secular society.

The immediate context for Neuhaus's book was the rise on America's political landscape of the religious "New Right" (including the MORAL MAJORITY) during the late 1970s and early 1980s. While quite critical of this movement's strategy, Neuhaus is sympathetic with its effort to reclaim a public space for religion and moral arguments. Neuhaus argues that the rising popularity of this movement was made possible by the mainline churches' failure to maintain a Christian and critical public voice, choosing instead to endorse whatever was au courant in the Democratic Party. The New Right, in contrast, has gathered its support in large part because it rejects the "myth of secular America" and has thus been able to tap

the sentiments of a spectrum of the country's believers who feel betrayed by their own denominational leadership.

Neuhaus's constructive argument throughout *The Naked Public Square* is that democracy cannot endure where religion is reduced to being a strictly private matter, or where the public square is naked. Such a moral vacuum will necessarily be filled if not by religion's claims then by an ideology or by an expanding modern state. Neuhaus concludes with a call for the revival of religion's public legitimacy to reclothe the public square with transcendent meaning and ethical foundations. He notes the need for appeals to the law and moral truth to determine and critique local, state, and federal laws. He also stresses the need for renewed ecumenical dialogue and cooperation among America's religious traditions. Only in this way, Neuhaus contends, will the American experiment in democracy and religious freedom be able to endure.

The author, a former Lutheran pastor to the urban poor, converted to Catholicism in 1990 and continues to write on issues of religion and public life as the editor in chief of *First Things*.

See also ECUMENISM; PUBLIC THEOLOGY.

—Perry T. Hamalis

National Association of Evangelicals

The National Association of Evangelicals (NAE) is a voluntary association of evangelical denominations, organizations, churches, and individuals. It exists to demonstrate unity in the body of Christ by "standing for biblical truth, speaking with a representative voice, and serving the evangelical community through united action, cooperative ministry, and strategic planning." NAE was formed by moderate evangelicals attending the National Conference for the United Action Among Evangelicals in St. Louis, Missouri, in April 1942, who were dissatisfied with the theologically liberal position of the Federal Council of Churches (FCC), yet did not want to be aligned with the separatist and dogmatic fundamentalist AMERICAN COUNCIL OF CHRISTIAN CHURCHES (ACCC), founded a year earlier. Theologically conservative, NAE is committed to fostering cooperation among Christians, witnessing to society, ministering to the poor, addressing human concerns, encouraging cross-cultural involvement, and fostering communication.

NAE currently comprises 43,000 congregations representing 50 denominations and over 250 parachurch organizations and educational institutions nationwide. The association maintains numerous commissions, including Chaplains, Christian Higher Education, Hispanic, Social Action, and Women's Ministries. NAE is also affiliated with the Christian Stewardship Association, Evangelical Fellowship of Missions Agencies, and, before 2002, National Religious Broadcasters. NAE produces numerous publications, including *Washington Insight,* a government affairs periodical, and *Dateline,* an evangelical news bulletin.

The development of NAE was driven by the twin convictions that America desperately needed spiritual revival, yet that "a united Christian coalition could effect revival only by leaving its cloister, engaging the world directly, and showing the relevance of the Gospel to modern life." NAE has tried to avoid the separatism, legalism, and hatefulness that defines other fundamentalist organizations such as ACCC. For example, NAE offers membership to affiliates of the mainline liberal FCC, while ACCC excludes FCC members. Although NAE and ACCC agree in large part concerning doctrinal issues, they differ over policy. This has resulted in hostility between NAE and ACCC, and defined the dominant alignment in conservative Protestantism until the 1980s.

Through resolutions adopted at national conferences, the association has spoken out against "social evils" such as communism, RACISM, ABORTION, PORNOGRAPHY, and, recently, divorce. Between 1978 and 1992, NAE efforts resulted in a number of legislative victories, including the passage of bills on drunk driving, church audit procedures, and EQUAL ACCESS to public school facilities for religious groups.

In addition to domestic involvement, through World Relief, its international assistance organization, NAE helps people around the world who suffer from poverty, disease, and hunger. World Relief works cooperatively with the United Nations, the U.S. Agency for International Development, and national governments in some of the countries where it is active. As a testament to its concern for international SOCIAL JUSTICE, in 1984 NAE launched the Peace, Freedom, and Security Studies program to influence public debate.

Since the 1950s, NAE has arguably been the dominant voice of evangelicalism in America. Despite these accomplishments, NAE has struggled to define itself, attract members, sustain financial stability, and secure effective leadership. According to NAE records, during the 1960s and 1970s, turnover of executive leadership was extremely frequent. Transitional leadership took its toll on membership growth, which slowed considerably from 1960 to 1978. Despite the proliferation of evangelicals in America during the latter 20th century, NAE continues to face the challenge of a shrinking constituency in view of an increasingly young, individualistic,

and "organizationally skeptical" evangelical community. Between 1999 and 2000, NAE donations dropped 36 percent. To address these challenges, NAE broadened its appeal in hopes of attracting minorities and women, as well as other previously excluded Christian groups, such as the liberal mainline NATIONAL COUNCIL OF CHURCHES (NCC).

NAE's inclusive stance has come with some cost to the organization. During the 1990s, many conservative Christians withdrew their support, criticizing NAE for being too ECUMENICAL and accepting of theological diversity. In light of these occurrences, some officials in NAE have argued that the group's problems may be as much theological as demographic. In broadening its appeal, NAE lost its distinct theological identity, and thus failed to represent churches since "it hasn't made itself known as to who it is and what it's about." As NAE enters the 21st century, this will continue to be a struggle, given the theological diversity that exists within the evangelical community in America.

Further reading: Cutrer, Corrie. "NAE President Resigns in Wake of Financial Woes." *Christianity Today.* April 6, 2001; Murch, James DeForest. *Cooperation Without Compromise.* Grand Rapids, Mich.: Eerdmans, 1956; "NAE Seeks Rejuvenation." *Christian Century.* March 18, 1998; National Association of Evangelicals. "Ministry." URL: http://www.nae.net/ministry-mission.html, 2002; Stone, Jon R. *On the Boundaries of American Evangelicalism.* New York: St. Martin's Press, 1997.

—Franklyn C. Niles

National Baptist Convention, U.S.A.

The National Baptist Convention, U.S.A. (NBC) was founded in 1897. It was a result of a merger of three regional black Baptist organizations: the Baptist Foreign Mission Convention of the United States, the American National Baptist Convention, and the National Baptist Educational Convention of the USA. In September 1999, the Reverend William Shaw was elected president of the convention. The convention has 33,000 affiliated churches with 8.5 million members, making it by far the largest single black denomination in the United States.

The formation of NBC was a result of heightened race consciousness and a reaction to the discrimination of Southern, white Baptists and the paternalism of Northern, white Baptists. These conditions helped lay the foundation for an independent church movement among black Baptists in the antebellum period, which intensified during the Reconstruction and its aftermath. Rev. E. C. Morris was elected the first president of the new convention. The main role of the convention was to prepare African Americans for full participation in the life of American democracy. Although the beliefs of NBC are identical to the beliefs espoused by mainline Baptist and other Christian denominations, the National Baptists place a great deal of emphasis on activism. The intentions of the group have always been to give black Baptists the opportunities for leadership, education, political empowerment, and spiritual growth that were not afforded them in other societal structures, including mainline white religions.

NBC became a distinctly black denomination but experienced many internal conflicts. The convention was to experience schism three times. The Lott Carey Foreign Missionary withdrew in 1897 to form its own convention (though, in 1905, it and the National Baptist Convention were ostensibly reconciled). In 1915, the National Baptist Convention of America was formed; in 1961, the Progressive National Baptist Convention was organized. Although there have been innumerable attempts to unite the various Baptist branches spawned from the initial split, none have been successful. Given the autonomy of the associations that make up Baptist conventions, local churches are not bound to any one convention and may belong to more than one.

NBC involved itself in domestic interests. Even before the turn of the century, NBC was active in education, supporting nearly 100 elementary and secondary schools and colleges, as well as providing education of African missionaries. In the first decade of the 20th century, NBC spoke out against racial violence and waged campaigns against segregation in public accommodations and discrimination in the armed services, education, and employment. NBC strongly supported the NAACP and was vocal on such matters as the right to vote and to serve on juries. NBC sought to move the modern church from its passive piety toward a universal activism by incorporating the ideas of the SOCIAL GOSPEL movement to justify demands for black civil rights and first-class citizenship.

In 1953, J. H. Jackson became president of NBC. Although the group was somewhat active in the CIVIL RIGHTS MOVEMENT, they maintained a strict focus on religion as a catalyst for freedom. NBC members participated in the Urge Congress Movement of 1957, in which black and white civil rights groups lobbied congressional representatives urging the passage of civil rights legislation. The convention also drafted a recommendation for addressing the problems of RACISM in America. The recommendation "Re-Affirmation of our Faith in the Nation" dealt with many social issues of the day and emphasized the supremacy of equal rights law, the sinful character of discrimination and segregation, the importance of citizen activism, and voluntary integration of the races.

During Jackson's tenure, the convention became substantially more involved in the cause of civil rights, but it never embraced a separatist philosophy. Jackson represented a strong vocal opposition to MARTIN LUTHER KING JR. and his strategy of CIVIL DISOBEDIENCE and nonviolent protest. King left NBC, as one of the leaders of the Progressive National Baptist Convention, a breakaway group established in 1961. Although King was himself in disfavor with Jackson, the mass movement he led was populated disproportionately by pastors and members of local Baptist churches. Because Baptist ministers are essentially free of accountability to a denominational hierarchy, they have often been less vulnerable to civil and economic sup-

pression, a factor of significance in their traditional involvement in political activity and community advocacy.

Further reading: Jackson, J. H. *A Story of Christian Activism: The History of the National Baptist Convention, USA, Inc.* Nashville, Tenn.: Townsend, 1980; Lincoln, C. Eric, and Lawrence H. Mamiya. *The Black Church in the African American Experience.* Durham, N.C.: Duke University Press, 1990; Raboteau, Albert J. In *Encyclopedia of the American Religious Experience.* Edited by Charles H. Lippy and Peter W. Williams. Vol. 1, 635–648. New York: Scribner, 1998.

—TeResa C. Green

National Catholic War Council/Welfare Conference

The National Catholic Welfare Conference (NCWC) was initially organized in 1918 as the National Catholic War Council. NCWC replaced the War Council at the conclusion of World War I. NCWC was designed to coordinate the ROMAN CATHOLIC CHURCH's activities at the national level and provide a forum for collective statements and action by American bishops. Following changes mandated by VATICAN II, NCWC was disbanded in 1966 and replaced by the NATIONAL CONFERENCE OF CATHOLIC BISHOPS (NCCB). Unlike NCWC, NCCB is a canonical body. All bishops must participate in NCCB, and the body is authorized to make policy, subject to Vatican approval, for the church in the United States.

With the entry of the United States into World War I in 1917, the American Catholic hierarchy established the War Council in Washington, D.C., to coordinate church-supported services and relief efforts. James Cardinal Gibbons of Baltimore gave his assurances to President Woodrow Wilson that Catholic resources would be mobilized in support of the war effort. The War Council was organized to accomplish this task and to promote patriotism among American Catholics.

In 1919, after the end of the war, the bishops saw the need for a permanent institution that could respond effectively to national issues confronting the church. Before NCWC, the bishops met and acted collectively only rarely. From 1789 to 1919, there were only 13 official meetings. The push for a permanent institution revealed the growing recognition that American life was increasingly national in focus. The church had to develop structures beyond the confines of individual dioceses to function in this new environment. The selection of Washington, D.C., as the headquarters for the new conference evinced the church's desire to have a voice in national political affairs.

Before the days of NCCB, the National Catholic War Council was replaced by the National Catholic Welfare Council, and Father John Burke, C.S.P., was selected as general secretary. However, a controversy arose among the bishops regarding the authority of the NCW Council. Some bishops, especially Boston's William Cardinal O'Connell, vehemently opposed the new organization. O'Connell was particularly concerned about maintaining control over his diocese and his dominance in the American Church as a result of being the senior cardinal. Rome intervened and recommended that the NCW Council remain, but that membership should be voluntary, the decisions of the meetings not be binding, and the name be changed from Council to Conference to indicate that the body was noncanonical and thus bereft of plenary authority.

NCWC contained seven departments: Education, Press, Social Action, Legal, National Council of Catholic Men, National Council of Catholic Women, and Immigration and Youth. The most important and controversial of these was Social Action. The department was established to promote the social teachings Pope Leo XIII contained in his 1891 encyclical *RERUM NOVARUM*. The department quickly became the center of progressive thought on social and labor questions. Under the leadership of Rev. JOHN A RYAN (1920–45), a professor at Catholic University and the American Church's leading social theorist, and his assistant Rev. Raymond McGowan, the Social Action Department involved the church in debates on labor, industry, race, international affairs, rural life, and communism. In 1919, NCWC released the *Bishops' Program of Social Reconstruction*, the church's first major statement on economics and SOCIAL JUSTICE. Written by Ryan, the document gave the church's support to such ideas as the abolition of child labor, universal vocational training, a legal minimum wage, labor participation in management, insurance against unemployment and sickness, protection of the right to organize, public housing, and progressive taxation. Following Ryan's death, direction of the Social Action department passed to McGowan (1945–54), then to Monsignor George Higgins (1954–67). Until it was closed in 1968, the department remained at the center of progressive Catholic social thought and action.

Further reading: McKeown, Elizabeth. *War and Welfare: American Catholics and World War I.* New York: Garland, 1988; Slawson, Douglas J. *The Foundation and First Decade of the National Catholic Welfare Council.* Washington, D.C.: Catholic University of America Press, 1992; Warner, Michael. *Changing Witness: Catholic Bishops and Public Policy, 1917–1994.* Washington, D.C.: Ethics and Public Policy Center, 1995; Williams, Michael. *American Catholics in the War: National Catholic War Council, 1917–1921.* New York: Macmillan, 1921.

—Zachary R. Calo

National Conference of Catholic Bishops

The National Conference of Catholic Bishops (NCCB) has been called "the most exclusive men's club in America" because it was an organization made up solely of all the Roman Catholic bishops of the United States. Its membership included the 290 active cardinals, archbishops, bishops, and auxiliary bishops from the almost 200 American dioceses and archdioceses. Under a name change, effective in July 2001, the bishops group is now called the United States Conference of Catholic Bishops (USCCB). It is headquartered in Washington, D.C.

The Second Vatican Council (VATICAN II, 1962–65) encouraged bishops to meet together in their own countries to help develop joint programs for the good of the church in those countries. The national conference allows bishops to corporately practice their mission of sanctifying, teaching, and governing by offering a forum for the bishops to exchange ideas, deliberate on shared concerns, and speak as a group.

The organization was created following the council in 1966, but its roots go back more than 150 years to the first meeting of American bishops as a group, in 1810 in Baltimore. Since that meeting of five bishops, the American Church's hierarchy has tried to meet on a national basis to govern the growing Catholic population. At first the meetings were irregular, interrupted by wars and the hardships of travel, but from 1890 on, the bishops have met every year. In 1919, the bishops formalized their gatherings into an organization known as the NATIONAL CATHOLIC WAR COUNCIL, which, in time, became the National Catholic Welfare Conference, to indicate its collaborative and not legislative function. This conference became the precursor to NCCB.

The business of NCCB, and now USCCB, is to allow the bishops to set policy stances on public issues, teach authoritatively on matters of church doctrine, provide guidance for American Catholic worship, and offer reflections on American life from a Catholic perspective. This is done primarily through the semiannual meetings the bishops hold every spring and fall, when they debate and publish resolutions, statements, and pastoral letters of matters of their concern. The bishops are certainly prolific. According to USCCB's website, in the first six months of 2001, the bishops issued comments in seven areas: refugee protection, the Eucharist, Israeli-Palestinian crisis, global climate change, the execution of Timothy McVeigh, Sudan, and Kenya. From 1989 through 1997, the bishops issued more than 185 statements on various political, ecclesiastical, and social topics. Perhaps the most famous statements have been the bishops' letter on nuclear deterrence, published in 1983, their letter on the U.S. economy, which was issued in 1986, and their "Pastoral Plan for Pro-Life Action," released in 1975.

The bishops' organization, an entity grounded in the church's canon law, has been from 1966 assisted in its task by its incorporated twin, the UNITED STATES CATHOLIC CONFERENCE (USCC). USCC was the public policy arm of the bishops. Here the bishops joined with the laity and clergy both to carry out decisions and proposals from NCCB and to recommend actions for the bishops in their general meetings. It provided the bishops with the organizational resources to reach American Catholics and policy makers at the national and parish levels. Both NCCB and USCC shared the same administrative structure and officers, with bishops elected by the NCCB as president, vice president, secretary, and treasurer for both conferences. This dual structure was reviewed by the bishops and eliminated in July 2001. The United States Conference of Catholic Bishops (USCCB) is doing the same functions as the former joint organizations.

See also CATHOLIC BISHOPS' 1986 PASTORAL LETTER ON THE ECONOMY; CATHOLIC BISHOPS' 1983 PASTORAL LETTER ON WAR AND PEACE; CATHOLIC BISHOPS' 1975 PASTORAL LETTER ON ABORTION.

Further reading: Carey, Patrick W., ed. *Pastoral Letters and Statements of the United States Catholic Bishops, Volume VI, 1989–1997.* Washington, D.C.: United States Catholic Conference, 1998; National Conference of Catholic Bishops. *A Manual for Bishops: Rights and Responsibilities of Diocesan Bishops in the Revised Code of Canon Law: Revised Edition.* Washington, D.C.: United States Catholic Conference, 1992; Nolan, Hugh J., ed. *Pastoral Letters of the United States Catholic Bishops, Volume I, 1792–1940.* Washington, D.C.: United States Catholic Conference, 1984; Reese, Thomas J. *A Flock of Shepherds: The National Conference of Catholic Bishops.* Kansas City, Mo.: Sheed and Ward, 1992.

—Paul Fabrizio

National Congregations Study: Political Activities

The National Congregations Study (NCS) is a survey of a nationally representative sample of religious congregations in the United States. Inspired by the insight that organizations attached to a random sample of individuals comprise a random sample of organizations, the 1998 General Social Survey (GSS)—a representative sample of noninstitutionalized English-speaking adults in the United States—included a set of items asking respondents who say they attend religious services more often than "never" to report the name and location of their religious congregation. This hypernetwork procedure generated a nationally representative sample of 1,456 religious congregations. NCS gathered data via a 60-minute interview with one key informant—a minister, priest, rabbi, or other leader—from 1,236 of the nominated congregations, a cooperation rate of 85 percent. The NCS response rate is 80 percent. The probability that a congregation will appear in NCS is proportional to its size. Because congregations are nominated by individuals attached to them, larger congregations are more likely to be in the sample than smaller congregations. Multiple GSS respondents also nominate some congregations. Weighted only to account for the duplicate nominations, univariate statistics from NCS describe the characteristics of congregations in terms of the numbers of religious service attendees who attend congregations with those characteristics. In this case, each attendee is given equal weight. When the data are weighted inversely proportional to congregational size, each congregation is given equal weight, regardless of its size, and univariate statistics describe the characteristics of congregations as establishments.

NCS contains data on seven types of congregational political activity:

1. Whether people at worship services have been told, within the past 12 months, of opportunities for political activity, including petitioning campaigns, lobbying, or demonstrating.

2. Whether VOTER GUIDES have ever been distributed to people through the congregation and the source of such guides.
3. Whether the congregation had a group, meeting, class, or event, within the past 12 months, to organize or participate in a demonstration or march either in support of or opposition to some public issue or policy.
4. Whether the congregation has a similar group to discuss politics.
5. Whether the congregation has a similar group to register people to vote.
6. Whether the congregation has a similar group to organize or participate in efforts to lobby elected officials of any sort.
7. Whether, within the past 12 months, anyone running for office was a speaker at the congregation.

According to NCS, American religious service attendees are most frequently exposed to the three following political activities in their congregations: telling people at worship services about opportunities for political involvement (such as petitioning campaigns, lobbying, or demonstrating); distributing voter guides; and having a group to organize or participate in a demonstration or march in support of or opposition to some public issue or policy. Thirty-seven percent of religious service attendees are in congregations where opportunities for political activity were offered at worship services, while roughly a quarter of congregations—taken as units without respect to size—offered such opportunities. Slightly over one-fourth of religious service attendees are in congregations that distributed voter guides, representing 17 percent of congregations. Of congregations that knew the source of these voter guides, 39 percent named an organization associated with the Christian Right. This means that 7 percent of congregations distributed Christian Right voter guides, and that 10 percent of congregations distributed voter guides produced by Christian Right organizations.

No more than 13 percent of religious service attendees are in congregations where any of the remaining political activities were practiced. When each congregation is given equal weight, there is a four-percentage-point difference in this number; that is, no other political activity measured by NCS is engaged in by more than 9 percent of religious congregations in the United States. With the exception of distributing Christian Right voter guides, there are larger numbers for each type of political activity when the data are reported in terms of religious service attendees in congregations, instead of congregations without respect to size. This indicates that larger congregations are more likely than smaller ones to be politically engaged, regardless of the type of political activity. The reverse is true only for distributing Christian Right voter guides, as larger congregations are less likely than smaller ones distribute such guides to their congregations.

See also POLITICAL PARTICIPATION.

Further reading: Chaves, Mark, Mary Ellen Konieczny, Kraig Beyerlein, and Emily Barman. "The National Congre-

gations Study: Background, Methods, and Selected Results."
Journal for the Scientific Study of Religion 8 (1999): 458–476.
—Kraig Beyerlein (abstracted from Chaves et al., 1999)

National Council of Churches

In 1999, ANDREW YOUNG was inducted as president of the
National Council of Churches of Christ in the United States
(NCC). This induction ceremony was part of a larger celebration marking the 50th anniversary of NCC and took place in its
birthplace of Cleveland, Ohio. Claiming over 50 million members with official representatives from 35 denominations,
NCC styles itself as the primary national expression of the
movement for Christian unity. However, the celebration,
which was dampened by less-than-spectacular attendance and
the cancellation of keynote speaker Archbishop Desmond
Tutu of South Africa owing to health concerns, may be indicative of the recent condition of NCC.

NCC has long been regarded as the grandest of religious
alliances in the United States, but it has faced increasing challenges in more recent years. The beginnings of the council can
be traced back to 1908 and the organization of the Federal
Council of Churches in America. NCC was born of the Federal
Council of Churches' merger with 11 other interdenominational
bodies in 1949, but it would cling to the goals of its parent organizations—social service and interdenominational cooperation.

Like the Federal Council before it, NCC focused on
social service. By combating hunger, poverty, and other disruptive effects of industrialization, the second goal of interdenominational cooperation was to be achieved through social
education and programs of social service. These goals would
not be restricted to the borders of the United States, but
would become worldwide.

To accomplish its goals both domestically and internationally, NCC formed four main divisions: Overseas Ministries, Church World Services, Education and Ministry, and
Church and Society. The activities of these divisions are far-
reaching. Ranging from the filing of AMICUS CURIAE BRIEFS in
the Supreme Court by the Church and Society division, to
the Church World Services' relief efforts following a volcanic
eruption near Amero, Colombia, NCC's scope of activity is
vast. NCC is recognizable worldwide mostly because of the
activities of the Church World Services division, which has
accounted for well over two-thirds of the NCC budget. Such
a broad range of activities, along with other factors, has taken
its toll on the financial well-being of the organization.

The political highpoint of NCC occurred from 10 to 15
years after the organization's birth. President DWIGHT EISEN-
HOWER laid the cornerstone of the new home of NCC in New
York City, across from Riverside Church on land donated by
John D. Rockefeller Jr. NCC then played a significant role in
the CIVIL RIGHTS MOVEMENT, funding, organizing, and leading
the movement. When a delegation organized by NCC joined the
MARCH ON WASHINGTON in 1963, the leader of NCC's Commission on Religion and Race (Robert Spike), observed tellingly:

When the National Council of Churches delegation . . .
moved into the stream of marchers, one of the deepest
longings of my ministry was for a moment fulfilled—the
longing that the Church of Jesus Christ be in the midst
of the human struggle, not on the sidelines. And we
were there—in an act so full of symbolism that no one
could escape it, and with the satisfaction that we were
no longer token representatives. The power of PROTES-
TANTISM was marching with us, and we had a right to be
there at long last, because we were bearing some of the
far reaching burdens of the struggle.

NCC continued to bear some of these burdens, participating in the successful Midwest strategy targeting key swing
senators to pass the 1964 Civil Rights Act. NCC provided organizational resources and volunteers for FREEDOM SUMMER,
sponsored and advocated for the social service providing Delta
(Mississippi) Ministry, and continued their lobbying in Washington. As the militancy of the black freedom movement esca-
lated, however, culminating in James Forman's demand in a
Black Manifesto for NCC to pay $500 million in reparations to
African Americans, white opinion turned against the Civil
Rights movement, weakening support for the activities of NCC.
The fate of NCC's heavy involvement in civil rights struggles
paralleled the backlash that occurred in its member churches.

Conservative critics have pointed to NCC's supposed liberalization over the past 50 years and how it seems to be less
representative of the churches within its organization and
more a product of a small bureaucratic elite. These critics
point to the relatively few stances the council has taken against
communism and Communist states in comparison with the
number of stances the council has taken against U.S. foreign
policy. "The NCC is a hindrance to the cause of Christian
unity," said Methodist James Heidinger II, accusing the council of "extremely liberal theological and political views."

While accusations of liberal theological and political views
are not new to NCC, as the council fought the "communist" label
during much of its first decade of existence, those within the
organization have recognized other obstacles that may weaken it.
The decline of mainline churches in the United States, such as
the Presbyterian and Methodist Churches, are of concern. Former council general secretary Rev. Joan Brown Campbell suggested: "When they catch cold, we get pneumonia."

Current president Elenie K. Huszagh (2002–03) and general secretary Rev. Dr. Robert W. Edgar (2000–04) oversee the
50-member Executive Committee, which serves as the representative decision-making body for the 280 representatives of
member communions.

See also AMERICAN COUNCIL OF CHRISTIAN CHURCHES;
ECUMENISM; NATIONAL ASSOCIATION OF EVANGELICALS;
WORLD COUNCIL OF CHURCHES.

Further reading: Findlay, James F. Jr. *Church People in the
Struggle: The National Council of Churches and the Black
Freedom Movement, 1950–1970.* New York: Oxford University

Press, 1993; Hadden, Jeffrey. *The Gathering Storm in the Churches.* Garden City, N.Y.: Doubleday, 1969.

—Daniel D. Stratton

National Right to Life

On January 22, 1973, the U.S. Supreme Court ruled in the case *ROE V. WADE,* a legal challenge to Texas's strict abortion law, that "a right . . . was broad enough to encompass" a right to ABORTION. In its opinion, delivered by Justice Harry Blackmun, the Court instituted a trimester system under which an abortion could be performed legally.

Outraged at the Court's decision, groups opposed to abortion organized to fight the new liberal privacy standard set by the High Court. By May 14, 1973, the National Right to Life Committee was incorporated, and the following month it held its first convention in Detroit, Michigan, gathering activists from across the nation to form the largest pro-life organization in the United States. By November of that year, its first newsletter went to press. Since its inception, this ideological advocacy group has been disproportionately, but not exclusively, Roman Catholic. Other prominent religious traditions in the group include FUNDAMENTALIST Protestants, conservative mainline Protestants, and ORTHODOX JEWS. To publicize its cause and possibly win elective office, in 1976 pro-life activists formed a political party by the same name as the parent organization, the National Right to Life Party, to publicize the group's antiabortion position.

An effective grassroots organization that pressures congressional members, the National Right to Life in 1999 was ranked by *Fortune* magazine as the eighth most influential public policy group in Washington on its list of 120 powerful lobbies. The fundamental purpose of the National Right to Life, as perhaps the most powerful pro-life organization in the United States, is to engage in actions that, members argue, will restore and respect the legal protection for all human beings from the moment of conception until natural death. To achieve this goal, the Washington-based group, which has affiliates in all 50 states, pursues legislative and political goals that seek the initiation and defense of pro-life legislation and the development, implementation, and participation in the political process to further the pro-life cause on the national, state, and local levels.

Arguing that life begins at conception, the organization seeks bans on abortion, RU486 (the so-called French Abortion Pill), late-term ("partial-birth") abortion, and CLONING/GENETIC ENGINEERING. The group has had some success in its strategy of enacting pro-life laws and pro-life public policies. Its campaign against late-term abortion, a procedure done in the fifth or sixth month of pregnancy and sometimes later, where, members argue, the fetus is destroyed in the process of birth, has been unsuccessful at the federal level. Although a bill to ban the procedure passed Congress twice, President WILLIAM JEFFERSON CLINTON vetoed it on both occasions. Nevertheless, 27 states have passed laws that ban partial-birth abortion.

The organization's most vocal opponent, a grassroots organization based in Washington, is the pro-choice organization National Abortion and Reproductive Rights Action League (NARAL). Politically active, NARAL focuses on the legislative arena and elsewhere, arguing that the fetus removed in abortions should not be considered a person. Even further, it argues that all women must retain the right to control their own bodies, and therefore to choose to have an abortion.

To oppose their pro-choice opponents in the political arena, the National Right to Life organization engages in numerous activities to galvanize members. The group funds pro-life candidates for federal office, usually Republicans, in two particular ways. It uses its political action committee, the National Right to Life Committee, as well as independent expenditures made on behalf of candidates. Other efforts include voter mobilization efforts (on behalf of the Republican Party in recent presidential elections) and distribution of information and funds to state antiabortion PACs. Its perhaps most newsworthy event occurs each year, when the National Right to Life stages one of the largest marches in Washington, held on the anniversary of the Supreme Court's 1973 decision in *Roe v. Wade.*

See also RELIGIOUS COALITION FOR REPRODUCTIVE CHOICE.

Further reading: Wilcox, Clyde, and Mark J. Rozell. *Interest Groups in American Campaigns: The New Face of Electioneering.* Washington, D.C.: Congressional Quarterly, 1999.

—Veronica Donahue DiConti

Nation of Islam

WALI D. FARD, who later mysteriously disappeared, founded the Nation of Islam (NOI) on July 4, 1930. The first members were recent African-American migrants from the South to a Detroit ghetto. NOI soon expanded to Chicago and other northern cities under the direction of Fard's handpicked successor, ELIJAH MUHAMMAD, drawing followers primarily from the black underclass. Although it is nominally Muslim, NOI is an indigenous religious movement with its roots in Christianity. Its methods and leadership derive from black social movements, and its focus is racial and political. High-profile conversions of black Americans in the 1960s, including boxing champion Muhammad Ali and basketball star Kareem Abdul-Jabbar, drew attention to NOI even as its former rising star, MALCOLM X, withdrew his support following a 1964 pilgrimage to Mecca and his discovery of Elijah Muhammad's extramarital escapades. (Malcolm X was assassinated in 1965, probably on NOI instructions.) Verifiable membership statistics are not available; estimates range between 10,000 and 100,000 at NOI's peak in the late 1960s.

In the first decade after W. D. Fard's 1934 disappearance, the Nation of Islam faltered. Its membership slipped from a peak of some 8,000 to about 100. Then Elijah Muhammad was jailed for resisting the draft during World War II and realized that he and his fellow inmates were virtually ignored by black churches. Once released, Elijah Muhammad began a new recruitment. Focusing on the downtrodden—prisoners, prostitutes, young delinquents—NOI experienced unprecedented growth, which continued through the black power movement of the 1960s. This growth brought economic rewards; NOI now owns extensive real estate and operates several businesses.

When Elijah Muhammad died in 1975, his son and successor, WARITH DEEN MUHAMMAD, led NOI away from its separatist doctrines and toward mainstream Sunni ISLAM. However, a significant number of NOI adherents transferred their allegiance to rival NOI official LOUIS FARRAKHAN, who reaffirmed the original theology and practice of NOI. W. D. Muhammad's group became the AMERICAN MUSLIM MISSION, allied with American Sunni Islam, leaving to Farrakhan the NOI name and tradition. Although Farrakhan publicly embraced his former NOI rival, now known as W. Deen Muhammad, during Savior's Day celebrations in 2000, NOI maintains its separate organizational structure, and a different theology and worldview. NOI has a unique cosmology, including the assertion that W. D. Fard was God-in-Person and Elijah Muhammad was his messenger. Savior's Day, celebrated on February 26, celebrates W. D. Fard's birthday.

The death of Elijah Muhammad in 1975 magnified rifts within the Black Muslim movement. Estimates range as high as 17 for the number of resulting NOI splinter groups, but the American Muslim Mission (now the Muslim American Society of W. D. Muhammad) and the reconstituted NOI under Louis Farrakhan are the largest.

In 1988, NOI repurchased its former flagship temple in Chicago and dedicated it as Mosque Maryam, the National Center for Retraining and Reeducation of the Black Man and Woman of America and the World. The National Center includes a preschool and a K–12 University of Islam. In 1995, NOI sponsored the MILLION MAN MARCH in Washington, D.C. In 2002, Farrakhan continued to lead NOI as a black nationalist religious movement of African Americans, maintaining its tightly knit network of mosques, schools, and a newspaper, *The Final Call.*

The theology of the Nation of Islam bears little resemblance to mainstream American Muslim beliefs. Its rituals and sermons draw on Christian themes, and both its early leaders and its core membership are drawn from the black Christian community. NOI is promoted as a more authentic faith for blacks than white Christianity, a religion imposed during slavery.

As developed by Elijah Muhammad, NOI cosmology holds that 25 black scientists created 25,000-year scenarios, which then unfold, and the cycle repeats. Some 66 trillion years ago, blacks were exiled from the moon. Then, 6,600 years ago, Yakub, a black scientist-god, grafted the white race

(a race of devils) from the superior black race. These whites were given 6,000 years to rule over the earth before it became time again for the black race to rule.

NOI has its roots in black separatism and nationalism, social movements born in the post-emancipation struggle of black Americans for equality. Only African Americans could become NOI members, and immigrants from Muslim-majority countries were barred from attending NOI services. Both Elijah Muhammad's and Malcolm X's fathers were organizers for Marcus Garvey's "Back to Africa" campaign. Elijah Muhammad and W. D. Fard also likely were members of Noble Drew Ali's Moorish Science Temple in Detroit in the late 1920s. Government surveillance of NOI began in the 1930s; FBI files on the group are extensive.

Further reading: Essien-Udom, E. U. *Black Nationalism: A Search for an Identity in America.* Chicago: University of Chicago Press, 1962; Gardell, Mattias. *In the Name of Elijah Muhammad: Louis Farrakhan and the Nation of Islam.* Durham, N.C.: Duke University Press, 1996; Nation of Islam website. URL: http://www.noi.org.

—Susan McKee

Native American sacred grounds

Native American sacred grounds are, like SACRED SPACES in other religious traditions, places of communication with divinity through prayer, movement, or visual contact with an image of the divine; they are places of divine presence, often promising healing, success, or salvation, and they provide meaning to the faithful by metaphorically reflecting the underlying order of the world. Native American sacred grounds include sacred hunting and gathering grounds, medicine wheels, ceremonial grounds, secluded sites dedicated to vision quests and purification ceremonies, sacred mountains, rivers or lakes, burial grounds, and the land inhabited by a tribe or Mother Earth in her entirety.

Disputes over Native American sacred space can be categorized into two groups: disputes between Native Americans and developers who want to utilize the sacred land as a resource, and disputes between Native Americans and scientists over sacred burial grounds. These disputes are related to Native American claims to natural resources, legal disputes over Native American religious freedoms, and disputes over the repatriation of Native American cultural and religious artifacts.

Because sacred space is distinctive and set apart, specific rules strictly delimit access to sacred space and behavior within it. This has led to a large number of disputes between Native Americans and groups who do not abide by Native American religious codes, such as developers, industrialists, or tourists. A prominent example of this type of dispute is the 1870s conflict between the Sioux and Cheyenne, under Sitting Bull, and white gold prospectors over the sacred hunting grounds in the Black Hills of South Dakota. This conflict culminated in the Battle of Little Bighorn and the annihilation of

General George Custer's forces in June 1876. More recent cases have involved a wide variety of actors in disputes over a diverse array of sacred places: litigation by the Inupiat against oil companies seeking to drill in their sacred fishing grounds; protests by the Iowa tribe in Oklahoma against the construction of a prison atop a burial ground; a dispute between several tribes and the Forest Service over public access to the Bighorn Medicine Wheel in Wyoming; a dispute over a ski resort near the location of Navajo and Hopi ancestral shrines; a dispute between South California Indian tribes and Cal State Long Beach over the construction of a mini-mall on top of the pilgrimage site of Puvungna; and many more.

It is, perhaps, because of the wide diversity of these cases that no uniform body of law has developed to deal with disputes over Native American sacred space. Beyond the AMERICAN INDIAN RELIGIOUS FREEDOM ACT of 1978, which promises Native Americans free "access to sacred sites required in their religion, including cemeteries," disputes have been dealt with in an ad hoc fashion. The 1988 Supreme Court decision in LYNG V. NORTHWEST INDIAN CEMETERY PROTECTIVE ASSOCIATION, which permitted the U.S. Forest Service to construct a road through the Six Rivers National Forest, a sacred area used by Yurok, Karok, and Tolowa for vision quests and purification ceremonies, is considered a major setback in the Native American struggle to defend sacred grounds.

A clearer legislative record developed through a series of congressional acts in the second category of disputes, those involving the removal of cultural items, human remains, and funerary objects from Native American graves for display and study in museums and universities. At the core of these disputes is the belief held by many Native Americans that the soul is buried with the body and finds a new home in the grave—burial grounds form an alternative community for the deceased. Native Americans argue that exhuming, studying, or irreverently displaying these remains and artifacts, irrespective of their age, amounts to sacrilege, an affront to Native American dignity, and an attack on the well-being of Mother Earth. The possession and use of religious artifacts necessary to ongoing religious ceremonies, guaranteed under the First Amendment, is essential to their own and their ancestors' spiritual fulfillment.

The practice of excavating Native American burial sites for scientific purposes has early roots. Pilgrim scouts reported removing articles from American tombs in 1620, and in 1784 Thomas Jefferson detailed his own excavations of a Monacan burial mound on his property in *Notes on Virginia* (Query XI). Samuel Morton, a pioneer of American physical anthropology, was the first to systematically collect skeletal remains from tombs to further his study of Native American racial "inferiority," and he amassed the largest collection of skulls in the 1840s. By the surgeon general's order of 1868, all army personnel were instructed to collect crania for the Army Medical Museum, a decree resulting in a collection of some 4,000 skulls. According to estimates by the National Congress of American Indians, between 100,000 and 2 million Native American corpses have been dug up from their graves and are held in collections nationwide.

The 1906 Federal Antiquities Act (PL 59-209; 16 USC 431) was the first general act prohibiting the excavation or destruction of antiquities without permit. Similarly, the 1979 Archeological Resources Protection Act (PL 96-95; 16 USC 470aa-470II) made it illegal to excavate or remove from federal or Indian lands any archaeological resources without a permit. Such permits were issued only to educational or scientific institutions if they could demonstrate that their activities increased knowledge about archaeological resources. Although the 1979 act provided Native Americans with a more active role in determining who would receive permits, both acts defined the contents of burial sites as "objects of antiquity" or "archeological resources" and transferred ownership of these "artifacts" to the nation.

Mounting dissatisfaction with the 1979 legislation led to the emergence of the Indian Burial Rights movement in the 1980s. The movement's campaign culminated in two pieces of legislation. The 1989 National Museum of the American Indian Act (20 USC 80q-80q-1 to -15) required the Smithsonian Institution to inventory and return all culturally affiliated human remains and funerary objects. The 1990 Native American Grave Protection and Repatriation Act (NAGPRA) (PL 101-601; 25 USC 3001-13) assigned full ownership and control of Native American cultural items, human remains, and associated funerary object to Native Americans. NAGPRA also provided for the protection, inventory, and repatriation to culturally affiliated tribes of sacred and ceremonial property found in the possession of federal agencies. This legislation represents a fundamental change in public policy toward Native American sacred grounds.

Since NAGPRA, the Bureau of Reclamation has inventoried the remains of some 2,000 individuals, as well as 30,000 funerary objects in museums across the nation. Most states have passed repatriation acts and legislation to protect unmarked graves, and prohibiting disturbance, sale, or public display of human remains from unmarked graves without a permit. NAGPRA has also led to several conferences and collaborative projects between Native American tribes and scientists, and several universities have agreed to voluntarily return their collections of Native American remains.

Further reading: Bowman, Margaret B. "The Reburial of Native American Skeletal Remains: Approaches to the Resolution of a Conflict." *Harvard Environmental Law Review* 13, no. 1 (1989); Boyd, Thomas H. "Disputes Regarding the Possession of Native American Religious and Cultural Objects and Human Remains: A Discussion of the Applicable Law and Proposed Legislation." *Missouri Law Review* 55 (1991); Echo-Hawk, Roger C., and Walter R. Echo-Hawk. *Battlefields and Burial Grounds: The Indian Struggle to Protect Ancestral Graves in the United States.* Minneapolis, Minn.: Lerner, 1994.

—Ron E. Hassner

neo-Paganism

Neo-Paganism, a NEW RELIGIOUS MOVEMENT stemming from early-20th-century Europe, began in America in the 1960s and 1970s. There are an estimated 150,000 to 300,000 neo-Pagans in America. The vast majority are white and live in cities and suburbs. They tend toward middle-class standing, and the majority has at least some college education. Most members are "first-generation" and in their twenties and thirties, although an older generation has begun raising children in the movement.

The main characteristics of neo-Paganism are an emphasis on wholism; animism, PANTHEISM, and polytheism; the veneration of nature; a magical worldview; ritual practice marked by fantasy and play; and a celebration of sexuality. Neo-Pagans purport that all matter is imbued with divinity, and they search for ways to overcome the modern world's alienation from the natural world, the split between the mind and the body, and the denigration of nature and sexuality. Participants celebrate the cycles of the seasons, the solstices and equinoxes, old European agricultural holidays, and the full and new moons. They also practice magic, by which they seek to tap into the order of the universe and effect changes in it. Magic and ritual are used as a "technology of the self" to celebrate life changes and to access the potentialities within the human psyche.

Neo-Paganism is further characterized as a loose network of ideas, festivals, and smaller groups of people, or covens, in which members work magic, study, and celebrate special days together. There is no governing body or hierarchy, and participants tend to be antiauthoritarian. Some groups have three levels of initiation, others have elders; some have one or two people who regularly act as priestess or priest, and others have no hierarchy whatsoever, constantly rotating the role of priestess among members. Neo-Paganism also has no orthodoxy or canon. Images, myths, and ritual practice are derived principally from European mythology, scholarship from the turn of the last century on comparative religion, mythology, and anthropology, occult literature, some non-European tribes such as Native Americans, and the creativity of the members themselves.

Because neo-Paganism is so diverse, only the most prominent submovements can be discussed here. The dominant form of neo-Paganism is Wicca. Wicca is a Middle English term meaning "witch," from Old English *wik*, "to bend or shape," allegedly signifying skill in magic to effect changes in one's life. Wicca came to America in the 1960s from England by way of Raymond Buckland, a practitioner of Garderian Witchcraft. Gerald Gardner had claimed that, in the 1920s, he had been initiated into a coven of practitioners of Europe's "Old Religion," which extended back into the Paleolithic era and had been forced underground because of the witch persecutions of the Spanish Inquisition. Practitioners still call Wicca the "Old Religion," even though its roots more likely lie in 19th- and early-20th-century England, and arise from a combination of several phenomena: secret soci-

eties that practiced initiation and ritual magic; rural "hedge" witchcraft popularized by folklorists and Romantics; the counter-Christian veneration of the Greeks, who were said to have venerated nature and sexuality as symbolized by Gaia and Pan; and the widespread interest in allegedly timeless folk and peasant traditions, born out of an antiurban, antiindustrialization critique.

Gaia and Pan appear in contemporary Wicca as the Goddess of fertility, the moon, and vegetation, and her consort, the Horned God of the hunt and the solar king. While all-women's groups, called Dianic, venerate only the Goddess, mixed-sex groups tend to worship both Goddess and God. The story of their relationship is a symbolic encoding of the cycle of the sun through the year, the phases of the moon, and the changing seasons. Some authors describe Wicca as a feminist religion, since the central goddess figure allegedly empowers and garners respect for women. Yet despite the high value placed on the "feminine," the quest for new images of masculinity, and the open presence of gays and lesbians in Wicca, the religion's myths and symbols remain largely heteronormative.

Norse Paganism, or Ásatrú (meaning *trust* in the ancient Germanic deities), is a much smaller but growing movement. Its adherents are dedicated to reviving an exclusively Germanic, or Northern, tradition. It is, like Wicca, wholistic, nature-oriented, and fairly antiauthoritarian, with groups called kindreds connected through a network. But the participants tend to be more socially conservative than other neo-Pagans and value a warrior's creed. They rely primarily on the Old Norse sagas and Eddas, Tacitus's *Germania,* and scholarship on Germanic religion as their sources of religious inspiration. They also use the theories of psychologist Carl Jung, especially his 1936 essay "Wotan," to argue that, because cultural heritage is genetically inherited, people should avoid multicultural "confusionism" and return to their ethnic roots. Although some Norse Pagans are antiracialist, others are admitted white supremacists, and racialist concerns predominate in their writings.

Wicca and Ásatrú share another aspect in common: the claim to having shamanistic aspects or roots. Shamanism is often seen as the original and, therefore, most genuine form of religion. American shamans have formulated a practice based on ecstasy and trance. They are said to travel out of the body and into other spiritual realms to seek solutions to problems, often related to healing. The focus on healing is a common theme in both neo-Paganism and the New Age Spirituality movement, with which it overlaps.

Contemporary neo-Paganism is still not very well known. Its magical practice, the term "witch," and the worship of a Horned God raise in the minds of non-Pagans the specter of devil worship, a practice explicitly shunned by neo-Pagans. Thus, despite the First Amendment's guarantee of religious freedom, neo-Pagans are often harassed, threatened, and attacked; and they risk losing their jobs, their homes, and their children in custody disputes. For example, after learning that the army allowed neo-Pagans to hold rituals at Fort Hood,

Killeen, Texas, a Christian minister raised a protest, and a congressional representative likened neo-Pagans to SATANISTS and animal sacrificers. Neo-Paganism pushes at the limits of religious TOLERANCE in the United States; moreover, because witchcraft has for centuries been defined as a maleficent practice, neo-Paganism presents an interesting case of how such deeply embedded cultural stereotypes can—or cannot—be transformed.

There is a trend toward forming larger umbrella organizations to help stabilize neo-Paganism and to provide protection from religious discrimination. For example, some Pagans have joined the Unitarian-Universalist Association to benefit from its institutional organization and to gain more public approval through an affiliation with a mainstream group. For some parents, this church honors their Paganism while allowing their children to claim a more socially accepted religion.

Yet neo-Paganism itself, like all religions, is in a process of internal transformation. Neo-Paganism in the early 20th century arose from a critique of modern culture—its abuse of the environment, secularization and the disenchantment of the world, the loss of a sense of self in mass culture, and the uprooting of people owing to industrialization and urbanization. The cultural critique that has formed a part of the pagan worldview has in America been combined with political activism, especially concerning feminist, antiwar, and environmental issues (a good example is Starhawk); but it has also been connected to a complaint against multiculturalism (most prominently in Ásatrú). Neo-Pagans wrestle with changing ideas about race, gender, and sexual orientation; they also struggle between preserving their antiauthoritarian, eclectic, individualistic religion, while also moving toward mainstreaming and routinization. Which aspects of the neo-Pagan worldview will be strengthened or diminished as the religion develops remains to be seen.

See also ECO-THEOLOGY; FEMINISM; FEMINIST THEOLOGY; NEW RELIGIOUS MOVEMENTS AND CULTS.

Further reading: Adler, Margot. *Drawing Down the Moon: Witches, Druids, Goddess-Worshippers and Other Pagans in America Today.* Revised and Expanded. New York: Penguin, 1986; Berger, Helen A. *A Community of Witches: Contemporary Neo-Paganism and Witchcraft in the United States.* Columbia: University of South Carolina Press, 1999; Gwynne, S. C. "'I Saluted a Witch': An Army Base in Texas Becomes the Hotbed for Earth-Goddess Worshippers Called Wiccans." *Time,* 154, no. 1 (1999): 59; Kaplan, Jeffrey. "Reconstruction of the Asatru and Odinist Traditions." In *Magical Religion and Modern Witchcraft.* Edited by James R. Lewis. New York: State University of New York, 1996; Starhawk (Miriam Simos). *The Spiral Dance: A Rebirth of the Ancient Religion of the Great Goddess.* Tenth Anniversary Edition. San Francisco: HarperSanFrancisco, 1989; York, Michael. *The Emerging Network: A Sociology of the New Age and Neo-Pagan Movements.* London: Rowman and Littlefield, 1995.

—Carrie B. Dohe

NETWORK

NETWORK is a national Roman Catholic SOCIAL JUSTICE lobby that educates, lobbies, and organizes to influence the passage of federal laws to promote economic and social justice. NETWORK was founded in 1971 by 47 Catholic sisters who shared a vision of working collectively through government to seek justice for the poor and marginalized. Through the years, NETWORK has grown to more than 11,000 members—individuals as well as hundreds of religious congregations and parishes—working together for federal policies that reflect gospel values of justice and compassion.

Headquartered in Washington, D.C., NETWORK has a staff of 21 and a budget of close to $1 million. It focuses especially on issue analysis, lobbying, and grassroots organizing. In addition, NETWORK has a partner organization, the NETWORK Education Program (NEP), which focuses principally on educational lectures and workshops to a variety of interested organizations. NEP facilitates nonpartisan issues analysis, skills development for responsible citizenship, and faith reflection on political ministry. NEP's vision of a just society is grounded in gospel values, Catholic social teaching, concern for the integrity of creation, and the life experiences of the poor or marginalized. NETWORK is a 501(c)(4) nonprofit organization; NEP is a 501(c)(3) nonprofit. Contributions to the latter—but not to the former—are tax-deductible.

The 47 Catholic sisters who founded NETWORK did so in response to a call for renewal sounded at the Second Vatican Council (VATICAN II). Meeting in Rome from 1962 to 1965, this council of the world's Roman Catholic bishops stated that Catholics worldwide have a duty to protect and promote human dignity and human rights. This call for church renewal led to the development of the idea of political ministry and to the organization of NETWORK. Members advocate for just access to economic resources, a federal budget that meets human needs, and global economic justice.

NETWORK is a little unusual in its organizational ethos. It supports and builds political will to develop a just, participatory, and sustainable world community. It uses Catholic social teaching and the life experience of the poor as lenses for viewing social reality. As a woman-led membership organization, this lobby values participation, mutuality, cooperation, and stewardship. Equality and mutuality are reflected in several of its policies. With respect to donors, NETWORK chooses not to follow the practice of listing higher-level donors in their annual report, in recognition of the value to their work of every person's contribution. Similarly, NETWORK's policy is that all staff members receive the same salary.

A profile of NETWORK members conveys interesting information about this lobby. Approximately 76 percent of the members are women. Some 54 percent range in age from 45 to 65 years. In terms of marital status, 42 percent are vowed religious, 26 percent are married, 18 percent are single, 5 percent are widowed, and 3 percent are divorced. NETWORK members are highly educated; 91 percent of the members have achieved a college degree or higher. They tend to be educators, professionals, administrators, and health care and social service workers. Understandably, perhaps, they tend to give greatest priority to legislative issues that concern HEALTH CARE, human rights, housing, and WELFARE REFORM.

In its lobbying, NETWORK uses publications and reports, educational videos, and direct lobby visits to members of Congress to convey its positions on issues. Advocates address issues such as international debt, homelessness, hunger, women's rights, racial justice, welfare reform, health care, military spending, and campaign finance reform. NET-WORK also relies on e-mail legislative alerts to members, as well as phone calls, letters, and facsimiles. Staff seek to provide clear, concise, accurate information about key legislation to individual members, religious congregations, parishes, campus groups, and peace and justice groups.

NETWORK's commitment to faith-based advocacy has not gone unrecognized on Capitol Hill. Congress members, senators, congressional staffers, and others attend NET-WORK's press conferences where new reports and studies are announced. Congressman Bernie Sanders (I-Vt.) and the late senator Paul Wellstone (D-Minn.) have frequently shown up for NETWORK's analyses of how welfare reform is proceeding. Former congressman Robert Drinan (D-Mass.) was a long-time supporter of NETWORK because of the excellent information it provided his office. Additional recognition came in January 2001, when President WILLIAM JEFFERSON CLINTON awarded the Presidential Citizens Medal, the nation's second-highest civilian honor, to NETWORK cofounder and first executive director Carol Coston, OP.

Further reading: Sylvester, Nancy. "Post-Vatican II Sisters and Political Ministry." In *Between God and Caesar: Priests, Sisters and Political Office in the United States.* Edited by Madonna Kolbenschlag. New York: Paulist Press, 1985; Coston, Carol. "The Legacy of Sister Clare Dunn, CSJ." In *Between God and Caesar: Priests, Sisters and Political Office in the United States.* Edited by Madonna Kolbenschlag. New York: Paulist Press, 1985; NETWORK on the Internet: URL: www.networklobby.org.

—Mary C. Segers

New Age religion

Simultaneously a look to the future and a reach into the primordial past, New Age religious movements claim ancient roots for modern manifestations of spirituality often heavily infused with environmental concerns. These communities differ from new religious movements in that the former have their origins in Western culture and draw on Western religious traditions. The latter generally are sectarian offshoots of Old World Religions, and operate as institutionalized congregations. While their roots are Eastern, their membership is Western. Many American Buddhist communities consist entirely of Caucasian converts; other examples include Hare Krishna and the UNIFICATION CHURCH. While members of new religious movements often are described as restless young adults, observers usually describe members of the various New Age groups as somewhat older, white middle-class adults.

New Age religions may be seen as emerging from the social upheavals of the 1960s and early 1970s—the natural conclusion to the Age of Aquarius. What is termed New Age, however, is not new to North America. The roots of what is now described as New Age may also be seen in the late 19th century. It can be argued that theosophy and other forms of spiritualism are the underpinnings of movements gaining adherents a century later. CHRISTIAN SCIENCE, another 19th-century religion, also combined spirituality with healing.

Although it might appear that the popularity of New Age religions has peaked, their absence from the media is misleading. Because of their marginalized status and relatively small numbers, New Age communities generally operate outside the view of mainstream America. There are many such organizations, ranging in size from literally a handful of adherents to several thousand. There is no national organization, no sanctioning body; most local groups are autonomous. The best sources of information usually are alternative news publications, especially those focusing on the intersections among health, the environment, and spirituality.

In the early 21st century, the list of religious communities usually described as New Age is fluid. It includes everyone from the Ásatrú (allied with the Old Norse pantheon) to those whose spirituality centers on their personal connections with guardian angels. There are the Bear Clan, Society for Ascension, Crystal Connection, SETH readers, Coven of the Goddess, Temple of Natural Science, Psychic Science Church, Self-Realization Fellowship, Edgar Cayce study groups, at least seven major categories within Wicca, and many more. Some prefer to be labeled "pagan," while others include a medley of religious belief and practice, incorporating, for example, Buddhist meditation techniques with prophecy traditions and Native American ritual. Wiccans gained headlines in the late 1990s by demanding freedom to practice their religion in the military and in prisons.

The designation "New Age" is broad enough to include the occult, extraterrestrial contact, and other nonmainstream beliefs (for example, HEAVEN'S GATE). The worldview includes a wider range of supernatural beliefs than Old World religions, and therefore séances, channeling sessions, and past-life regressions can be included.

New Age religions typically include an emphasis on the intersection of spirit, mind, and body, and many practices once confined to "alternative" lifestyles have found their way into mainstream America, from spiritual retreats and labyrinth walks to natural foods and healing imagery. At-home birthing, dream interpretation, yoga classes, and feng shui also have crossed over from New Age to the ordinary. Astrology columns are found in every newspaper. Ayurvedic medicine has joined acupuncture in the acceptable range of medical treatments. Kinesthetic reflexology, Rolfing, and therapeutic massage are becoming routine. The new field of life coaching (also called "motivational coaching") has emerged from the New Age worldview, which emphasizes the possibility of personal transformation.

Some common buzz words in New Age movements include balance (as in balancing one's electromagnetic fields), auras, channeling, potential energy, synchro-destiny, and whole-life living. The material culture includes Tarot cards, crystals, pyramids, images of angels, and Native American dream catchers. New Age practitioners often are vegetarians who prefer organically grown food. They also tend to belong to environmental action and peace groups, believing that the natural environment plays a key role in the development of human consciousness, identity, and health, and that world peace begins with inner peace.

See also NEO-PAGANISM.

Further reading: Adler, Margot. *Drawing Down the Moon.* Boston: Beacon Press, 1979.

—Susan McKee

new evangelicals in Congress

The influence of new evangelicals in Congress can be traced back to the mid-1980s. While there were certainly members of Congress who espoused an evangelical Protestant faith before then (for example, Mark Hatfield, an outspoken evangelical, was elected to the Senate in 1968), it was at this time that a member's identity as an evangelical became more salient. The evangelicals in Congress in the 1980s concentrated on perennial Christian Right issues such as ABORTION and PRAYER IN SCHOOL. They also helped to engineer the final defeat of the EQUAL RIGHTS AMENDMENT in 1983. But at this time, there was much more focus on the activity of religious conservatives in national organizations influencing politics than on the religious identity of the members of Congress themselves. The real story of evangelicals in Congress is a conflation of two things: Christian Right groups that claimed to speak for evangelicals, and the religious beliefs of the individual members. It is hard to talk about one without the other, so tied are their reputations and outcomes.

The real advent of visible influence by evangelical members of Congress occurred with the 1994 election. Spurred by Christian Right organizations' candidate-recruitment efforts, many evangelicals were elected to the House of Representatives. These and other very conservative members became the main focus of the Republican takeover of Congress. These freshman members wielded considerable power and were universally conservative, though not universally evangelical. While the CHRISTIAN COALITION and other Christian Right groups certainly helped many of these new members get elected, there is considerable doubt about the members' continuing allegiance to the coalition's goals. After successfully bringing to the floor votes on elements of the Contract with America in the first 100 days of the session, few were strong proponents of the Christian Coalition's CONTRACT WITH THE AMERICAN FAMILY. Although several prominent members of

the 104th Congress, both freshmen and returning members, were evangelicals, many of these claimed to vote on their own religious beliefs, not those prescribed by Christian Right organizations. Regardless of the reality of members' vote choice decisions, the perception was certainly that the Christian Right had an extraordinary amount of power in Congress and that a great number of their ranks were elected to the House in 1994.

This perception, increased by the general conservativism of those members who did not share the goals of the Christian Right, became a stumbling block to legislative and electoral success for evangelicals in the next several years. By 1996, though 74 members of the House of Representatives were evangelical, obvious progress on issues important to evangelicals and the Christian Right had halted. None of the socially conservative planks in the Contract with the American Family had passed, and President WILLIAM JEFFERSON CLINTON had vetoed the few that made it past both houses of Congress. Senator Bob Dole (R-Kans.) did not meet the Christian Right's hope for a strong conservative presidential candidate, and President Clinton's Democratic coattails were sufficiently long to reduce the number of conservatives and Republicans in the House of Representatives. Many of the conservative and evangelical freshmen of the 104th Congress had moderated their views with their years in office. So great was this moderation that Christian Right leaders, particularly JAMES DOBSON, became highly critical of their performance. Dobson threatened to lead a mass exodus of evangelicals from the Republican Party in 1998.

In the 1998 election, many conservative and evangelical Republicans in the House based their campaigns on the IMPEACHMENT OF BILL CLINTON. The effort seemed to backfire, and for the first time in six decades, the party not in possession of the presidency lost congressional seats in a midterm election. The subsequent disorder of the impeachment proceedings and Clinton's ultimate acquittal by the Senate caused a break within the conservatives in the Republican Party that was difficult to repair. A new speaker was elected, and though Dennis Hastert (R-Ill.) is himself an evangelical, he has never been strongly linked to the Christian Right and is considered a moderate conservative.

The still substantial number of evangelicals in Congress, particularly among House Republicans, seems to have moderated their strategies, if not their views. Years of experience have also increased their ability to get things done in the compromise-requiring environment of Congress.

See also CHRISTIAN RIGHT AND THE REPUBLICAN PARTY; RELIGION IN CONGRESS; RELIGION IN THE 1994 CONGRESSIONAL ELECTIONS; RELIGION IN THE 1996 PRESIDENTIAL ELECTIONS.

Further reading: Benson, Peter L., and Dorothy L. Williams. *Religion on Capitol Hill: Myths and Realities.* San Francisco: Harper and Row, 1982; Guth, James L., and Lyman A. Kellstedt. "Religion and Congress." In *In God We Trust?*

Religion and American Political Life. Edited by Corwin E. Smidt. Grand Rapids, Mich.: Baker, 2001.

—Kimberly Conger

new religious movements and cults

The terms "new religious movement" (NRM) and "cult" have been applied to roughly the same set of contemporary religious groups that began appearing in the United States and western Europe in the late 1960s. Most scholars working in this area use the term "NRM," while oppositional groups (the anticult movement—ACM) and mass media are more likely to employ the term "cult." The controversy centers on whether the focus of theory, research, and public policy should be on these groups as movements protesting against the existing social order or as exploitive organizations that have deleterious effects on their members. The foundational disputes are whether there are distinctive characteristics through which to distinguish cultic and noncultic groups and whether affiliation with these movements is the product of voluntary choice (conversion) or whether the affiliation is the product of group manipulation (brainwashing, thought reform, coercive persuasion).

There is no dispute that there is a long history of nontraditional religious groups in the United States. Since most new groups survive, the overall number has continued to rise. The period beginning in 1965 was one of exceptional growth in nontraditional groups, particularly of groups of Asian origin, as a result of a relaxation in U.S. immigration statutes. Currently, there are over 1,500 religious groups in the United States, and about half of those are nontraditional (which excludes various mainstream groups, sectarian offshoots of these groups, and immigrant churches). The term "new religious movement" identifies an important but difficult to demarcate set of religious entities. Most often the term "NRM" is used to designate groups that appeared in Western societies since the mid-1960s, are nontraditional and nonimmigrant religious groups, began with first-generation converts as their primary membership base, attracted among their converts higher-status young adults, manifest social movement characteristics, may present an anomalous profile with respect to traditional religious organization, and proclaim themselves to be engaged in spiritual activity.

NRMs are extraordinarily diverse. Categorized in terms of their religious traditions, examples of well-known movements include THE FAMILY (Jesus People Movement), UNIFICATION CHURCH (Christian-related), Gurdjieff Foundation (Sufism), Hare Krishna and the Bhagwan movement of Shree Rajneesh (HINDUISM), Soka Gakki (BUDDHISM), *est*, CHURCH OF SCIENTOLOGY, Dianic and Neo-pagan witchcraft groups (New Age/Human Potential Movement), Church of Satan (SATANISM, satanic churches), and the Raelians (UFO groups). Numerous typologies categorize this diverse array of movements. One of the most basic distinguishes between *world-affirming* and *world-rejecting* movements. The former affirm conventional norms and values and offer a means for adherents to realize untapped individual potential, with minimal distancing from conventional society; the latter are antagonistic to conventional society and require that adherents distance themselves from mainstream social life, which is deemed irreparably corrupted and doomed to destruction.

Probably the most common explanation for the emergence of the broad array of NRMs links them directly to the ferment of the 1960s and 1970s, which was punctuated by the VIETNAM WAR, the Watergate scandal, and countercultural rebellion. In this view, the period was characterized by a crisis of meaning, and NRMs were successor movements to the countercultural movements of the 1960s. There is an ongoing debate over the larger significance of contemporary NRMs. For example, it is argued that the emergence of NRMs constitutes disconfirmation of progressive SECULARIZATION, support for a cyclical process of secularization/religious resurgence, or evidence that secularization continues and exotic religions have become just another consumer product.

The key dispute between NRM scholars and oppositional groups (ACM) centers on whether there is an identifiable set of characteristics that distinguish "cults" from other religious groups. The ACM position identifies various types of practices that substantially undermine adherent autonomy, voluntarism, and pursuit of individual needs. For example, in one such formulation, cults exhibit the following characteristics: (1) authoritarian leaders who claim a special mission and/or knowledge, (2) a charismatic, dominant leadership style, (3) leaders' claims to total allegiance, (4) claims to an innovative and exclusive answer to individual and societal problems, (5) an "ends justifies the means" logic that justifies manipulation of outsiders, (6) totalistic ideological and behavioral control over members, and (7) a major transformation of lifestyle (Singer 1995). NRM scholars counter that groups labeled cults closely resemble a number of conventional organizations in which such characteristics are accepted as legitimate—custodial mental hospitals, communes and intentional communities, correctional facilities, convents and monasteries, armed forces training units, and multilevel marketing organizations. With respect to assertions of brainwashing, they point out that most groups have extraordinarily low recruitment success, membership turnover rates are high, it is implausible that diverse groups all discovered and implemented coercive control techniques at precisely the same time, and that groups described as cults are typically fraught with conflict and dissent. This controversy has now spanned three decades and will continue to be the source of intense academic and public policy debate.

See also HEAVEN'S GATE; PEOPLES TEMPLE.

Further reading: Bellah, Robert. "New Religious Consciousness and the Crisis in Modernity." In *The New Religious Consciousness*. Edited by Charles Y. Glock and Robert Bellah. Berkeley: University of California Press, 1976, 333–352; Bromley, David G. "Listing (in Black and White) Some Observations on (Sociological) Thought Reform." *Nova Religio* 1

(1998): 250–266; Bromley, David G. "A Sociological Narrative of Crisis Episodes, Collective Action, Culture Workers, and Countermovements." *Sociology of Religion* 58 (1997): 105–140; Bromley, David G., and James T. Richardson. *The Brainwashing/Deprogramming Controversy*. New York: Edwin Mellen, 1983; Greeley, Andrew. *Unsecular Man*. New York: Schocken, 1972; Melton, J. Gordon. "The Changing Scene of New Religious Movements: Observations from a Generation of Research." *Social Compass* 42 (1995): 265–276; Singer, Margaret, with Janja Lalich. *Cults in Our Midst*. San Francisco: Jossey-Bass, 1995; Stark, Rodney, and William Bainbridge. *The Future of Religion: Secularization, Revival and Cult Formation*. Berkeley: University of California Press, 1986; Wallis, Roy. *Elementary Forms of the New Religious Life*. London: Routledge and Kegan Paul, 1984; Wilson, Bryan. *Religion in Sociological Perspective*. Oxford: Oxford University Press, 1982; Zablocki, Benjamin, and Thomas Robbins. *Misunderstanding Cults*. Toronto: University of Toronto Press, 2001.

—David G. Bromley

New York v. Cathedral Academy 434 U.S. 125
(1977)

In 1972, a three-judge district court declared unconstitutional a New York law authorizing reimbursement to nonpublic schools for expenses incurred for state-mandated record keeping and testing services. The Supreme Court affirmed the lower court decision in LEVITT V. CPEARL, (1973), and on remand the district court entered an injunction explicitly prohibiting reimbursement to sectarian schools for state-mandated services. In response, the New York State Legislature enacted another law recognizing its "moral obligation to provide a remedy" for private schools that incurred expenses prior to *Levitt,* and provided funds to reimburse schools for expenses incurred for the 1971–72 school year, the academic year prior to the *Levitt* decision. Cathedral Academy sued in the New York Court of Claims to recover certain expenses, and the state of New York argued that the law was unconstitutional. The New York Court of Appeals disagreed and declared the state law constitutional. That decision was appealed to the U.S. Supreme Court, and in *New York v. Cathedral Academy,* the Court reversed, declaring the second New York law unconstitutional as well.

The Court was divided 6-3. Justice Stewart wrote the opinion for the Court and was joined by Justices WILLIAM BRENNAN, Marshall, Blackmun, Powell, and Stevens. Chief Justice Burger, with Justice Rehnquist, filed a dissenting statement, and Justice White authored his own dissent.

For the majority, Justice Stewart noted that the state law providing for recovery of expenses, in seeming violation of *Levitt,* "explicitly authorizes what the District Court's injunction had prohibited: reimbursement to sectarian schools for their expenses of performing state-mandated services." Thus, at issue was "the permissible scope of a Federal District

Court's injunction forbidding payments to sectarian schools under an unconstitutional state statute." As Justice Stewart points out, LEMON V. KURTZMAN offers a useful analogy. In the first *Lemon v. Kurtzman* decision, the Court declared unconstitutional two state laws offering reimbursements to private schools, many of which were sectarian. *Lemon II* concerned the lower district court's order implementing the Supreme Court's decision, and on remand the lower court prohibited state payments to sectarian schools for services provided *after* the date of *Lemon I,* but not prior to the Supreme Court's decision. Thus, the district court reached a fair and equitable decision that did not financially penalize sectarian schools for their conduct prior to *Lemon I.* The Supreme Court affirmed the district court's order in *Lemon II.*

In *Cathedral Academy,* though, the district court expressly prohibited state payments to sectarian schools for expenses "*heretofore* or hereafter expended" (italics in original). As Justice Stewart explained, "the state legislature thus took action inconsistent with the court's order" when it determined that private schools relied on the state's promise of payment that was ultimately declared unconstitutional. Accordingly, the New York legislature determined that equity and fairness demand "retroactive reimbursement." To approve the state law, as Justice Stewart points out, would effectively mean that a state legislature could "modify a federal court's injunction" whenever fairness and equity might dictate.

Yet, instead of pursuing the reasoning that considered the state law a threat to federal judicial power, Justice Stewart's opinion shifts back to the First Amendment ESTABLISHMENT CLAUSE. As he pointed out, the original New York law allowing for reimbursement to private schools was unconstitutional in *Levitt* because it would have the primary effect of aiding religion, since sectarian schools were to be reimbursed in lump-sum payments without regard to whether the payments covered only secular services. Since the second New York law at issue in *Cathedral Academy* authorized payments for the identical services found in *Levitt,* it too must be unconstitutional because it has the primary effect of advancing religion. Even if the private schools in question were audited by state agencies to determine which expenses were sectarian, and nonreimbursable, sectarian schools especially would be placed in the position of "trying to disprove any religious content in various classroom materials," and the state "would have to undertake a search for religious meaning in every cLassroom examination offered in support of a claim [for reimbursement]." Thus, the law not only has the primary effect of advancing religion, but it also leads to the excessive entanglement between church and state.

See also AID TO RELIGIOUS SCHOOLS.

—John Blakeman

Niebuhr, Reinhold (1892–1971) *theologian*
Reinhold Niebuhr was the most politically influential American theologian of his generation. A member of a highly gifted

German-American family that included the well-known Christian ethicist, H. Richard Niebuhr (1894–1962), he was involved in many movements of social reform in American society during the middle third of the 20th century. Besides this activist side of his life, his many writings also shaped an ethical vision known as "Christian realism," which has continuing relevance for social ethics, both Christian and secular.

After serving as a parish pastor in Detroit in the early 1930s, he spent the rest of his life at Union Theological Seminary in New York City. From that platform, he was involved in founding the New Republic, Americans for Democratic Action, and Christianity and Crisis. He inspired several generations of students at Union Seminary, many of whom then went into CHRISTIAN SOCIAL ETHICS.

He was perhaps America's last public theologian, if that means a Christian intellectual who can command the attention of major political actors in society, affect the direction of thinking in many fields of thought, and relate Christian perspectives to pressing contemporary social and political issues.

Christian realism as articulated by Niebuhr consists of three basic elements. It is founded on a biblical anthropology that he elaborated in his magnum opus, *The Nature and Destiny of Man* (1943). First, he reclaimed the classical Christian doctrine of sin, which he thought had been lost in the liberal theology and ethics of the SOCIAL GOSPEL. He argued that humans were centers of self-transcending freedom who inevitably abused that freedom by engaging in two basic forms of sin—sensuality and pride. He applied these notions of sin—especially pride—to the collective actions of human groups. Given the inevitability of sinful expressions of pride in collective life, Niebuhr argued that justice is best assured within and among nations and groups by constructing rough balances of power among competing entities. This approach influenced other American students of domestic and international politics such as Hans Morgenthau, George Kennan, and Kenneth Thompson.

Second, Niebuhr attempted to relate the norm of radical love—agape—to both the principles and the achievement of justice in a realistic way. He intended that his social ethics keep the transcendent norm of love revealed in the Christ event in a creative relationship to justice, the worldly balances of power that encouraged freedom and equality. He wanted to avoid both complacency about the achievement of justice and sentimentalism about the ease by which love can deepen and widen the structures of justice. The affluent classes were tempted to complacency while religious intellectuals were tempted to sentimentalism, which attempted to apply love directly to the power conflicts of the world. In keeping love and justice in creative tension, Niebuhr contributed positively to the perennial problem in Christian ethics of relating the radical love ethic of Jesus to the compromises and ambiguities of social and political reality.

Third, Niebuhr's Christian realism entailed a lively engagement of these first two theoretical elements with the issues and problems of his time. His approach enabled him to recognize the ambiguities and paradoxes of every situation without being paralyzed by them. His writings on foreign, race, and industrial relations provide enduring insights for students of social ethics.

Niebuhr's thought continues to be a live option in Christian social ethics by providing a realistic, reformist alternative to the UTOPIAN, dystopian, or sectarian leanings of many forms of contemporary Christian social ethics. While his thought was a dominant strand of Christian ethics up until the mid-1960s, it went into eclipse with the arrival of black, feminist, ecological, and sexual liberation theology and ethics. These schools charged that Niebuhr's Christian realism is not responsive enough to the claims of oppressed peoples. However, his contributions to Christian social ethics have worn well. Much attention is again given to his writings and life, and he has enough followers for them to break into contentious factions. There are "right-wing" and "left-wing" Niebuhrians, both camps claiming continuity with Niebuhrian realism. That fact witnesses to the richness and complexity of Niebuhr's legacy.

See also CONE, JAMES; LIBERATION THEOLOGY.

Further reading: Works by Reinhold Niebuhr: *Christian Realism and Political Problems.* New York: Charles Scribner's Sons, 1953; *An Interpretation of Christian Ethics.* New York: Harper and Brothers, 1935; *The Essential Reinhold Niebuhr.* Edited by Robert McAfee Brown. New Haven, Conn.: Yale University Press, 1986; *The Nature and Destiny of Man.* New York: Charles Scribner's Sons, 1943; *Reinhold Niebuhr on Politics.* Edited by Harry R. Davis and Robert C. Good. New York: Charles Scribner's Sons, 1960. Works about Reinhold Niebuhr: Fox, Richard. *Reinhold Niebuhr: A Biography.* New York: Pantheon, 1985; Kegley, Charles, and Robert Bretall, eds. *Reinhold Niebuhr: His Religious, Social, and Political Thought.* New York: Macmillan, 1956; Lovin, Robin. *Reinhold Niebuhr and Christian Realism.* New York: Cambridge University Press, 1996.

—Robert Benne

Nixon, Richard M. (1913–1994) *U.S. president*

Richard Milhouse Nixon was the 37th president of the United States, serving from January 1969 to August 1974. He grew up in Whittier, California, graduated from law school at Duke University, and, despite his pacifist upbringing, served in the U.S. Navy during World War II. Nixon, a QUAKER, grew up under difficult family circumstances in California. Two of his younger brothers, Harold and Arthur, died of tuberculosis and tubercular meningitis, respectively, during Nixon's teenage years. At the same time, the family struggled to meet day-to-day bills and pay for expensive medical treatments. For the Nixons, particularly the family matriarch, Hannah Milhouse Nixon, hardship, tragedy, and grinding labor were part of God's plan. She evidently had the soul of repression and many times she would say, "I shouldn't say this," putting her finger to her lips. Richard Nixon was a great deal like his mother.

Although Hannah had hoped that her son would be a preacher, he chose at a very early age to become a lawyer.

Still, Nixon's religious upbringing would have a significant impact on his later public life. Nixon's father, Frank Nixon, though he converted to his wife's church, came from a long line of Methodists. But his mother's Quaker religion, linked to generally LIBERAL policy trends (peace in international affairs, charitable concern for the less fortunate, freedom from racial and religious prejudice), also affected him. Yet Nixon's very public and supportive relationship with BILLY GRAHAM seems closer to his father's religious heritage.

A Republican, Nixon was elected to the U.S. House of Representative in 1947 and again in 1949, then served in the Senate from 1951 to 1953. In 1952 he was elected vice president and spent eight years in that office alongside President DWIGHT D. EISENHOWER. His first run for president came in 1960, when Senator JOHN F. KENNEDY (D-Mass.) narrowly defeated him. In 1968, with Spiro T. Agnew as his running mate, Nixon was elected president in one of the greatest American political comeback stories.

As president, Nixon's successes were many, including the opening up of relations with the People's Republic of China and the withdrawal of U.S. troops from Vietnam. But Nixon's remarkable record was forever ruined by a June 1972 break-in at the Democratic Headquarters in Washington, D.C.'s, Watergate complex. Despite this news, Nixon won reelection in November 1972 by a landslide. But a series of investigative reports printed in the *Washington Post* by two reporters, Bob Woodward and Carl Bernstein, alleged that members of Nixon's reelection committee and White House staff had been actively involved in the break-in and, more important, that the administration later covered up this fact. Additionally, there were other break-ins and also allegations of wiretapping conversations with news reporters who revealed information the Nixon White House did not want uncovered.

After an aide, Alexander Butterfield, disclosed to the Senate Select Committee on Presidential Activities the existence of a tape-recording system in the Oval Office, the committee issued a subpoena requesting the recorded conversations. Nixon refused to comply, arguing that the constitutional separation of powers gave the president executive privilege to withhold his private conversations from Congress. In the case of *United States v. Richard M. Nixon*, the Supreme Court ordered Nixon to turn over the tapes. For Senate committee members, the recorded conversations confirmed Nixon's involvement in the payoffs and cover-ups. When impeachment by the House and removal from office by the Senate appeared to be inevitable after the White House released the tape transcripts on August 9, 1974, Nixon became the first U.S. president to resign from office. The new president, Gerald R. Ford, would later pardon Nixon "for all offenses against the United States which he . . . committed or may have committed" during his presidency. In accepting the pardon, Nixon expressed remorse over Watergate and acknowledged errors of judgment, although he did not admit personal guilt.

Despite the excesses and abuses of Watergate, Nixon's reputation as a foreign policy expert and international statesman grew during his postpresidential years, and he authored numerous books. Nixon's career came to an end with his death on April 22, 1994, which prompted an outpouring of praise, but also reminded Americans of his egregious misconduct in office.

Further reading: Barber, James David. *The Presidential Character: Predicting Performance in the White House.* Upper Saddle River, N.J.: Prentice Hall, 1985; Parmet, Herbert S. *Richard Nixon and His America.* Boston: Little, Brown, 1990; White, Theodore. *Breach of Faith: The Fall of Richard Nixon.* New York: Dell, 1975.

—Veronica Donahue DiConti

O'Connor, John Cardinal (1920–2000) *Roman Catholic cardinal*

John Cardinal O'Connor was archbishop of New York from 1984 to 2000 and was created a cardinal in 1985. Cardinal O'Connor was a Roman Catholic priest and bishop who spent most of his adult life as a military chaplain. He rose within the American Catholic hierarchy to head one of the nation's largest sees. For over a decade, he was one of the most prominent Catholic clergymen in the United States. He was known for his doctrinal orthodoxy, outspoken defense of church teaching, charity at home and abroad, and willingness to challenge the powerful.

John O'Connor spent 27 years as a military chaplain. He entered the seminary at age 16, as was common in his era. He was ordained in 1945 and served in teaching and parish work for several years afterward. He eventually completed advanced degrees in ethics, clinical psychology, and political theory. In 1952, he became a navy chaplain, and his military career included service in Korea and Vietnam, and at the Naval Academy in Annapolis, Maryland. He publicly defended the VIETNAM WAR, although later he repudiated that position. He was decorated for his naval service and rose to the post of chief of navy chaplains. He retired in 1979 with the rank of rear admiral, and later headed the church's Military Vicariate for the United States.

Following his naval career, O'Connor rose quickly in the American Catholic hierarchy. He was named bishop of Scranton, Pennsylvania, in 1983, and the following year was elevated to the office of archbishop of New York. As is common for the head of one of America's principal dioceses, he was created a cardinal in 1985. In the tradition of the outspoken men who have led the New York archdiocese, Cardinal O'Connor frequently made news by proclaiming church teaching and authority in the face of challenges from political leaders and popular culture.

O'Connor was a prominent and tireless defender of Catholic orthodoxy. One aspect of this teaching tended to draw most attention from the news media, particularly the cardinal's defense of Catholic orthodoxy on ABORTION and homo-

sexuality. He was an outspoken critic of liberal abortion laws and the politicians who promoted them. This position brought him into highly publicized clashes with leading Catholic office-holders, especially New York governor Mario Cuomo and Representative (and 1984 Democratic vice-presidential candidate)

John Cardinal O'Connor *(Forest Anderson/Liaison Agency)*

311

Geraldine Ferraro. These officials tried to argue that Catholic politicians could personally oppose abortion but support its acceptance in public policy. Cardinal O'Connor roundly and frequently rebutted their claim, and sought to demonstrate publicly that such a view lay outside of Catholic tradition. While Ferraro's defeat in the 1984 election probably had more to do with the popularity of President RONALD REAGAN than her views on abortion, many analysts have argued that the cardinal's opposition did affect Cuomo's political career. A favorite of liberal Catholic Democrats, Cuomo found it difficult to defend his "personally opposed, but . . ." position before a broader audience of blue-collar and less liberal Catholic voters.

The other aspect of Catholic teaching that O'Connor defended and lived was the practice of charity. He drew heavy criticism for his opposition to GAY RIGHTS and participation by gay activists in New York City's annual St. Patrick's Day Parade, but he felt he used his pulpit to teach his congregation against hatred. He vigorously opposed violence against abortion providers, telling his flock that he would prefer that someone thinking about violence against an abortion clinic should take the cardinal's own life instead. He worked to end a newspaper strike in New York City, spoke against rent policies that he believed hurt the poor, and boycotted Major League Baseball when it held games on Good Friday. His archdiocese provided extensive services to people in need, including considerable sums to treat AIDS patients. He traveled to Bosnia in 1989 to offer assistance and support to those afflicted by the civil war there, and offered solace to families of the victims of the crash of Trans World Airlines flight 800 off Long Island in 1996.

In 1999, he was diagnosed with brain cancer and began a rapid decline. But he maintained his spirited demeanor. As he neared death, Congress awarded him a Gold Medal for service to the nation. After his death, he was lauded by testaments to his faith, service, and charity by leaders in the United States and from around the world.

See also BERNARDIN, JOSEPH CARDINAL; JOHN PAUL II; LAW, BERNARD CARDINAL; NATIONAL CONFERENCE OF CATHOLIC BISHOPS; UNITED STATES CATHOLIC CONFERENCE.

Further reading: Djupe, Paul A. "Cardinal O'Connor and His Constituents: Differential Benefits and Public Evaluations." In *Christian Clergy in American Politics.* Edited by Sue E. S. Crawford and Laura R. Olson. Baltimore: Johns Hopkins University Press, 2001.

—Ryan Barilleaux

O'Lone v. Estate of Shabazz 482 U.S. 342 (1987)

O'Lone v. Estate of Shabazz decided the question whether prison regulations that prevent Muslim inmates from attending their faith's required weekly meeting yet allow them to participate in other religious activities violate their FREE EXERCISE rights. Respondents were Muslim inmates at New Jersey's Leesburg State Prison who asserted that prison policies prevented them from attending Jumu'ah, the central weekly congregational service that must be held every Friday afternoon, attendance at which is mandatory. According to a prison regulation, inmates are classified into one of three categories that vary in level of freedom. Those assigned to the midlevel category are required to work outside the prison because of serious overcrowding. Several security concerns prevented these prisoners from returning to the prison during the day, except in emergencies, thereby preventing Muslim inmates from attending the weekly congregation. Several of them brought suit against the prison, alleging violation of their free exercise rights, in the U.S. District Court for New Jersey. The court held that the regulations in question plausibly advanced "the goals of security, order and rehabilitation," and that no less restrictive alternatives were available without compromising the prison's objectives. The U.S. Court of Appeals for the Third Circuit reversed the district court's decision, holding that the challenged regulations could be sustained only if they advanced the goal of security and if no reasonable alternatives exist without compromising that goal. If reasonable alternatives can be found, then the prison's refusal to accommodate the prisoners' desire to attend this central worship event violates the free exercise clause. The U.S. Supreme Court granted certiorari to resolve the question of what standard is to be applied in reviewing prisoners' free exercise suits.

In Chief Justice William Rehnquist's opinion, he asserted that prisoners do not forfeit all their constitutional rights upon incarceration, but many of the privileges and rights enjoyed by those who are not imprisoned are relinquished upon conviction. When prison regulations are challenged, the Court employs a reasonableness test, which is much less stringent than that applied to infringements of others' constitutional rights. As part of that standard, the Court will consider alternative methods by which the claims can be accommodated. The Court expressly stated that the Third Circuit was wrong when it required prison officials to show that no reasonable alternative existed without sacrificing security, because doing so "fails to reflect the respect and deference that the United States Constitution allows for the judgment of prison administrators." In this particular case, the Court argued that the actions of the prison officials were reasonable. First, the regulation in question must be logically connected to legitimate governmental interests. Here, the prohibition of inmates returning to the prison during the day was clearly connected to such interests in that it fostered greater security owing to the easing of tension within the prison and reduced security risks. Second, the Court stated that alternative worship opportunities existed and the regulation did not foreclose every opportunity for them to practice their faith. While the Court recognized the centrality of attending Jumu'ah, the Court was unwilling to compel prison officials to sacrifice their legitimate objectives to assure that every Muslim inmate had that opportunity. Third, the Court stated that the alternative arrangements suggested were simply unworkable, given the exigencies of prison administration. Accordingly, the Court held that the challenged regulations do not contradict the prisoner's free exercise rights and, thereby, reversed the Third Circuit's holding.

Justices WILLIAM BRENNAN, Thurgood Marshall, Harry Blackmun, and John Paul Stevens dissented. They asserted that the prison officials had not shown that the regulations were necessary to further their important objectives and that the regulations were no more restrictive than necessary. Even under the more deferential reasonableness standard adopted by the majority, the prison officials had not meet their burden.

See also ISLAM.

—Drew Noble Lanier

Operation Rescue

Operation Rescue is an antiabortion group known for its use of CIVIL DISOBEDIENCE in opposing ABORTION. The group, founded in 1987 by Evangelical Christian Randall Terry, drew its membership largely from fundamentalist Christian churches.

In the early 1980s, JOHN RYAN formed the first militant antiabortion citizens group, known as the Pro-Life Direct Action League. The group, composed largely of Roman Catholics, employed tactics of demonstrations and occasional violence. With the sympathy of the courts on their side, Ryan's protesters were seldom punished and hence could be arrested often, even on a weekly basis. But the group began to fall apart when its charismatic leader left his wife and infant for another married woman in the league. His followers rejected his decision and expelled him from the movement, causing the Pro-Life Direct Action League to crumble.

From the ashes of the Catholic movement rose Randall Terry and Operation Rescue. Using organizational and motivational skills gleaned from his religious leadership experience, Terry gathered larger numbers than ever before to demonstrate. Operation Rescue's chief strategy was to stand in front of abortion clinics and discourage women from aborting their pregnancies. Some demonstrators would simply talk to women; others tried to block access to clinics. Some individuals even blocked doctors' cars to prevent them from entering clinics. Demonstrators often displayed graphic pictures of aborted fetuses.

Although Operation Rescue is best known for its on-site abortion clinic demonstrations, it has not limited itself to civil disobedience. In 1989, Operation Rescue planned to begin the transition from clinic-centered activism to Capitol Hill with its DC Project, but the plan ended abruptly when Terry was arrested at a clinic demonstration and the interim leader canceled the project.

Terry left the movement in 1995 to become a radio talk-show host, and Flip Benham, a Protestant minister, took the reins. Benham mobilized members on issues beyond, abortion. For example, when Disney extended insurance benefits to the homosexual partners of its employees, Benham orga-

nized 100 members to protest the action. They also protested the sale of books deemed PORNOGRAPHY at national bookstore chains. Protesters destroyed books in many cities across the country. As a result of Operation Rescue's efforts, the Barnes & Noble bookstore chain was indicted on charges of selling obscenity in several states.

Supreme Court rulings and policy decisions have not favored Operation Rescue's cause. A relatively conservative Supreme Court has upheld the basic right to an abortion. The Freedom of Access to Clinic Entrances Act of 1994 criminalizes blocking access to an abortion clinic. Operation Rescue often ignored the legislation. As a result, members of the group have been repeatedly arrested and fined. In 1998, it was estimated that antiabortion group members owed almost $20 million collectively in fines.

Operation Rescue leaders spoke out against the use of violence in their antiabortion crusade. Benham even insisted that protest participators sign a pledge of nonviolence before participating in demonstrations. However, some individuals felt that abortion is so great a sin that violence is an acceptable response. Burning clinics and murdering doctors seemed like the solution. While Operation Rescue denies any participation in violence, public opinion toward the group—both within and without the group—plummets with antiabortion violence. The most dramatic membership drop was in 1993–94, when five doctors and clinic staff members were shot and killed, despite Operation Rescue's insistence that it did not participate.

Mounting legal pressures have virtually forced Operation Rescue out of existence. Although Operation Rescue may not have decreased the abortion rate, pro-life activism was a driving force in making political activists out of Evangelical Protestants. In 2000, Benham organized a new group, Operation Save America, which carries on Operation Rescue's legacy of clinic demonstrations.

Further reading: Hitt, Jack. "Who Will Do Abortions Here?" *New York Times*, January 18, 1998, sec. 6 p. 20; Lewin, Tamar. "NOW Tries to Seize Abortion Foes' Airline Miles." *New York Times.* January 22, 1998, A19; Risen, James, and Judy L. Thomas. *Wrath of Angels: The American Abortion War.* New York: Basic Books, 1998; Rosenfeld, Megan. "Standing by His Conviction: Flip Benham . . ." *Washington Post.* March 18, 1998, D01.

—Damon M. Cann

Orthodox Judaism

The term *orthodox* connotes adherence to the traditional and established faith and ritual, and is today a source of pride to those Jews who identify as Orthodox. Ironically, a Reform Jew who was contemptuous of religiously conservative Jews coined the term *Orthodox Jews* in the late 18th century as a pejorative.

Orthodox Judaism, especially in the United States, is both more and less homogeneous than the other denominations of

American Judaism. It is more homogeneous in that there is a virtual consensus concerning the divine authority of both written (biblical) law and oral (rabbinic) law, which are the components of Torah and *Halakah,* Jewish religious law as interpreted by the recognized rabbinic scholars. In addition, there is virtual consensus on the imperative not only to practice the law but to study it as well.

Orthodox Judaism is less homogeneous than the other denominations of American Judaism in that it comprises a variety of philosophies and movements, including Hasidism (see HASIDIC JUDAISM); Haredism; Sectarianism, or Ultra-Orthodoxy; and Modern Orthodoxy, or Centrist Orthodoxy—each of which also comprises a variety of perspectives. Whereas each of the other American Jewish denominations has a seminary and a rabbinic organization, Orthodoxy has neither a single seminary nor a single rabbinic organization; it comprises many of both. Despite the variation, however, Orthodox Jews do share the broad core of belief and ritual practice, even as they differ on specific issues. Politically, Orthodox Jews tend to be substantially more conservative than their counterparts in other Jewish denominations.

According to the most recent data available—the 1990 National Jewish Population Survey, which is a national survey of America's Jews sponsored by the Council of Jewish Federations—Orthodox Jews make up approximately 6.4 percent of those who define their current religion as Jewish, and approximately 11 percent among those households in which there is a synagogue member. Their influence on American Judaism and the American Jewish community is much greater than their actual numbers, however, because they are much more involved in the religious and communal life of American Jewry, have greater knowledge of and deeper connections with Israeli society and culture, and are more tied with world Jewry than are other American Jews.

As a result of the immigration of significant numbers of Orthodox rabbis and their followers among the refugees of the HOLOCAUST, the Orthodox developed an extensive system of Jewish education that enabled them to nurture a younger generation of knowledgeable Jews who also obtained high levels of professional education and thus experienced important increases in other levels of social mobility. Accordingly, despite their declining numbers, the Orthodox in the United States became much more organizationally sophisticated during the second half of the 20th century and, as a result, more self-confident and publicly assertive. As was the case with religiously conservative Protestantism, Orthodox Judaism became much more active in the public square and embarked on a variety of well-publicized efforts to recruit new adherents. Available data indicate that Orthodoxy has succeeded in stemming the flow of religious defection and may actually be growing.

The Orthodox have always defined theirs as the only authentic version of Judaism. Until recently, however, this was rarely an important issue within the communal life of the American Jewish community because the Orthodox were a relatively small and not very powerful component. As their self-confidence and arenas of activity have increased, though, they have increasingly come into conflict with those representing other varieties of Judaism, especially CONSERVATIVE JUDAISM and REFORM JUDAISM. The Orthodox control the rabbinate in Israel, where religious status has political implications. This has resulted in intense conflict among the various denominations of Judaism, which has exacerbated the already precarious relationship among them in the United States.

See also LIEBERMAN, JOSEPH; RECONSTRUCTIONIST JUDAISM; ZIONISM.

—Chaim I. Waxman

P

pacifism

While the historical sources and theological and conceptual foundations are diverse, pacifism can be defined as the *moral* opposition to all war and to direct participation in war through military service. Generally speaking, pacifists believe that nonviolent alternatives in response to injustice and violence are always morally preferable to the use of force. Some argue that nonviolent alternatives are also more effective, or would be if they were genuinely attempted, while others believe that nonviolent alternatives are morally preferable regardless of their effectiveness.

The classical Christian pacifist position is articulated in Article 6 of the Schleitheim Articles of 1527. Widely regarded as the theological consolidation of ANABAPTISM and an early expression of MENNONITE theology, the statement explicitly rejected the idea that it was permissible for a Christian to "use the sword against evil people for the sake of protecting the good or for the sake of love." This position may also be identified as "dualistic pacifism" because, while it states that the Christian community is bound to the higher law of Christ-like love and therefore Christians should not themselves wield the sword, it nevertheless agreed with the common Christian view that the basic functioning of society requires the restraint of evil through the use of the sword. As the statement explains,

> Concerning the sword we have reached the following agreement: The sword is ordained by God outside the perfection of Christ. It punishes and kills people and protects and defends the good. In the law the sword is established to punish and to kill the wicked, and secular authorities are established to use it.

Because the civil authority's governance "is according to the flesh" and the ordination of the sword is "outside the perfection of Christ," in contrast to the Christian's governance, which "is according to the spirit," these pacifists concluded that "it is not fitting for a Christian to be a magistrate" and that a Christian may not "hold a position of governmental authority if he is chosen for it." The prohibition against Christian military and police service was thus part of the more general pacifist prohibition against Christians holding judicial and political office of any kind.

This dualistic pacifism must be distinguished not only from that of the tradition of JUST WAR but also from various forms of "vocational pacifism," consolidated in medieval Catholicism, which affirms distinct levels of Christian vocation in which laypeople are permitted to engage in just wars, while clergy are not. Contemporary pacifists such as John Howard Yoder, Stanley Hauerwas, Richard B. Hays, and Walter Wink reject efforts to channel the radical call to nonviolence into a vocational higher way of (clerical or monastic) life based on so-called counsels of perfection. They insist that the renunciation of the threat and use of lethal force is binding on all Christians, that it is a positive affirmation of the gospel's ethic of love and the very essence of Christian witness in the world on the part of a suffering community of believers. Thus, Wink insists, "Non-violence is not an option for Christians. It is the essence of the Gospel," and Hays rejects as "untenable and theologically incoherent" any position that would support a "right" of individual CONSCIENTIOUS OBJECTION but generally sanction a Christian's participation in war.

Although the classic Schleitheim form of pacifism is justly subject to the common criticism that it necessitates a sectarian withdrawal from political life and full civic responsibility, it is immune to the criticism that haunts less absolute forms of pacifism. Partial pacifism, or "war pacifism," which permits the state to use lethal force in its internal jurisdiction to uphold civil law, but yet denounces the resort to war as immoral, seems inconsistent. If a Christian may justly serve as a police officer or judge and employ the threat or use of lethal force in defense of the civil community against internal domestic predators, how can it be unjust to serve in the military to defend one's neighbors against external foreign predators?

Pacifists rightly point out that being a pacifist does not mean being "passive" in the face of injustice, but rather involves "active peacemaking" using alternative nonviolent strategies, as exemplified in the tactics of Mohandas Gandhi and MARTIN LUTHER KING JR. The classic nonpacifist response to active peacemaking is that the effectiveness of these strategies is directly related to the degree of benevolence of the aggressor. While relatively effective against southern segregationists and British imperialists, such strategies are entirely ineffective against Communist, Nazi, or other totalitarian regimes or against Islamic-fascist terrorist organizations.

Finally, another form of pacifism is so-called modern war pacifism, or technological pacifism, which is based less on theological or moral grounds than on the claim that modern warfare is inherently indiscriminate and disproportional such that a modern war can never be waged according to just-war criteria. This position is subject to two counterclaims: first, that modern weaponry is far more discriminate and proportionate in its effects, and second, that a war carried out in an indiscriminate or disproportional manner owes more to the will and intent of the combatants than it does to the nature of the weaponry.

Further reading: Hays, Richard B. *The Moral Vision of the New Testament*. San Francisco: HarperCollins, 1996; Wink, Walter. "Is There an Ethic of Violence?" *The Way* 30 (1990): 103–113.

—Keith Pavlischek

pantheism

Pantheism is the claim that everything that exists constitutes a unity, and that this unity is divine. As a form of Western philosophy, pantheism stems from ancient Greek thought and the 17th-century writings of Baruch Spinoza. Pantheism has been deeply inspired by the findings of modern science and by the decline of the power of traditional, organized religion. Many modern pantheists are active in the environmental movement.

Pantheism most directly counters the claim of theism. Theism posits the existence of a divine person, a God separate from and transcending the universe; DEISM, an extreme form of theism, declares that God is totally separate and wholly transcendent. Pantheism does not deny the existence of God, but it does deny the existence of a God ontologically distinct from the universe. What does exist is the universe as a unified, divine whole.

If, for a pantheist, God is simply the universe as a whole, what then separates a pantheist from a materialist, one who claims that the physical universe is all that exists? The difference lies in the attitude of reverence, of religiosity. Pantheism places upon the universe as a whole attitudes that are commonly thought of as religious and reverent. Pantheism thus claims that the word *God* can be used meaningfully as a synonym for this divinity. The belief that the word *God* is meaningful in this context separates pantheism from atheism, naturalism, and materialism.

Pantheism is often distinguished from panentheism, which claims that all is in God, that God both transcends and includes the universe, that the universe is just one small part of the totality that is God. Proponents of panentheism include feminist theologians like Sally McFague, who argue that the universe is God's body, as well as process theologians, such as Charles Hartshorne. Further, pantheism is not merely a claim for the immanence of God, or merely the claim that there is a divine force permeating the whole universe. In religious polemic, the fine philosophical distinctions drawn between pantheism and divine immanence have often been lost. In the 19th century, MARY BAKER EDDY, founder of the Church of Christ, Scientist (adherents of which are popularly known as CHRISTIAN SCIENTISTS), published an essay refuting the accusation by a Protestant minister that her teachings on divine immanence were pantheist. Pantheism makes the stronger claim that the universe as a divine whole is God, and that there is no other God, or really no other anything at all, beyond this holy universe.

In America, the transcendentalist RALPH WALDO EMERSON often wrote in a pantheist tone, as did the poet Walt Whitman in *Leaves of Grass*. Alexis de Tocqueville, author of the insightful DEMOCRACY IN AMERICA, drew a connection between the rise of democracy and the prevalence of pantheism. A supporter of democracy but antagonistic toward pantheism, he argued that pantheism, regrettably, had "secret charms for men living under democracies" because both pantheism and democracy acted as equalizers, one in the ontological, the other in the political sense. Leaving aside the question of the connection between pantheism and political representation, we note that pantheism as a religious philosophy became more acceptable as the scientific worldview became more prevalent. Charles Darwin's theory of natural selection provided a mechanism by which the diversity of life arose, thus providing reason for many to dispense with the need for a God separate from the universe as a whole.

For many active in the environmental movement, pantheism has provided a means for expressing their awe and reverence for Earth and justifying their protection of ecological balance. The pantheism in such groups stems from various sources, such as Native American religion, Taoism, Buddhism, and Deep Ecology (a radically antianthropocentric approach to environmentalism and human life in general). Earth First! is a controversial environmental group known for taking its pantheism and Deep Ecology seriously in its fight against logging and ecological destruction in the American West.

See also ECO-THEOLOGY.

Further reading: Pepper, David. *Modern Environmentalism: An Introduction*. London: Routledge, 1996; de Tocqueville, Alexis. *Democracy in America*. Edited by J. P. Mayer. Translated by George Lawrence. New York: Harper and Row, 1969.

—Eric L. Thomas

Pax Christi

Pax Christi, the international Roman Catholic peace movement, is a nonprofit, nongovernmental organization. It is composed of autonomous national sections: local groups and affiliated organizations spread over 30 countries. In 2000, it claimed 60,000 individual members throughout the world. It has representation status at the U.N. general headquarters, the U.N. Human Rights Commission, UNESCO, and UNICEF.

Pax Christi began in the south of France in 1945 as a crusade of prayer to reconcile the French and German peoples after World War II. It was founded by Marthe Dortel-Claudot, a teacher, and Pierre-Marie Theas, the Catholic bishop of Montauban, who was imprisoned during the war because of his protests against the deportation of Jews from France. A popular desire for peace at the end of World War II contributed to the growth of Pax Christi. Catholic bishops in both France and Germany supported the movement. A German section was also founded.

In time, Pax Christi expanded its focus and became a crusade of prayer for peace among all nations. It organized international centers and paired people from various countries as pen pals to promote international contact and understanding, especially among young people. In 1952, Pope Pius XII granted official status to Pax Christi by designating it as an international Catholic peace movement. In 1963, Pope JOHN XXIII wrote the encyclical letter *Pacem in Terris* (*Peace on Earth*). Pax Christi adopted this document, which condemned the arms race and affirmed human rights and a universal common good, as its charter. The increasing concentration of the Catholic Church on social justice in the VATICAN II era matched well with Pax Christi's agenda. At Vatican II, the bishops supported the right to CONSCIENTIOUS OBJECTION and condemned military deterrence.

Events of the 1950s and 1960s contributed to greater interest in the movement. The movement of Catholic Action within the church encouraged lay movements such as Pax Christi to participate in the mission of the church to bring about social justice. The cold war era increased people's concern about the possibility of nuclear war. Opposition to the VIETNAM WAR led to new interest in conscientious objection. In the United States, the American Pax Association, predecessor to Pax Christi USA, was founded in 1962. Its principal purpose was to inform Catholics about the stance of Catholic social teaching on issues such as conscientious objection and nuclear weapons. In the 1970s, the arms trade became the focus of new campaigns. In the 1980s, new Pax Christi sections were formed in Europe, North America, and the Asia-Pacific region. Pax Christi sent missions to Latin America that published human rights reports. It also promoted disarmament activities around the world. Since 1988, Pax Christi has given the International Peace Award to individuals or groups working at the grass roots level on behalf of peace and justice.

Today Pax Christi's mission consists of spirituality, research, and action. Reconciliation, which unites opposing parties and forges new relationships, is at the heart of its spirituality. It is a Catholic organization; its presidents have been Catholic bishops. The current president is the patriarch of Jerusalem, Michel Sabbah. It also has an ecumenical thrust manifest in its cooperation with other Christian, Jewish, Muslim, and nonreligious nongovernment organizations (NGOs) and movements. Pax Christi promotes research by sponsoring conferences, seminars, fact-finding missions, and personal interviews to provide information for its members, as well as policymaking agencies, governments, NGOs, and the media. It actively sponsors letter-writing campaigns, essay contests for children, vigils, petitions, and events to "foster a culture of nonviolence." It sponsors the International Youth Forum, a program of training, and activities such as summer camps and seminars that support and network young peacemakers (ages 18–30).

Pax Christi International has a long-term commitment to the demobilization of child soldiers; the abolition of nuclear weapons; human rights in Africa and Latin America; dialogue with the EASTERN ORTHODOX CHURCHES; human dignity of refugees and displaced persons in the Balkans; and the cancellation of debt for poor nations. Pax Christi has promoted the comprehensive ban on land mines, and meetings and joint activities between young Serbs and ethnic Albanians in Kosovo. It has brought victims of human rights abuses to the United Nations to give testimony.

Pax Christi USA, with its 54 bishop-members, advocates peacemaking as a priority for the American Catholic Church. In 1998 the bishops authored a pastoral letter condemning nuclear deterrence. Pax Christi USA has worked to end U.S. sanctions against Iraq, to insure that justice for the poor is part of WELFARE REFORM, and to promote hate crimes legislation.

See also CATHOLIC WORKER MOVEMENT; PACIFISM; ROMAN CATHOLIC CHURCH.

—Anthony J. Pogorelc

PAX-TV

PAX TV, the seventh-largest American broadcast network, was founded in August 1998 as a renaming of PAX NET, a network formed in 1997 by Paxson Communications Corporation. Paxson Communications Corporation, founded by Lowell "Bud" Paxson, has primary control of PAX TV and is the major shareholder in the corporation, which is also partly owned by the National Broadcasting Corporation. In September 1999, NBC bought a 32 percent stake in the firm for $415 million, and has an option to take control of the network if the Federal Communications Commission (FCC) allows in subsequent rulings. In addition to PAX TV, Paxson controls other Christian media-related holdings, including the Christian Network and Praise TV, both of which work in collaboration with PAX TV.

PAX TV provides "quality programming with family values, free of excessive violence, free of explicit sex, and free of foul language," according to company documents. PAX TV broadcasts a combination of hour-long dramas such as "Touched by an Angel," infomercials, paid religious programming, and, since the NBC merger, repurposed NBC programming. Paxson, through its other networks and its in-house production companies, also produces original programming for broadcast on PAX TV. While earlier promotion of the network focused on the Christian nature of the programming, current publicity tends to emphasize the "family-friendly" nature of programming on PAX TV, with the other two networks, the Christian Network and Praise TV, carrying most of the overtly Christian programming.

Paxson founded PAX NET after the purchase of what became a network of local UHF television stations, occupying the 700 MHz band of the spectrum. These stations became viable as a national cable-carried network because of "must carry" regulations reinforced by the Telecommunications Act of 1996 and upheld by the Supreme Court in *Turner Broadcasting System, Inc. v. FCC* (1997). "Must carry" forced cable operators to carry local broadcast signals and thus made PAX NET available to cable and satellite customers. This must carry provision also allowed for the centralized management of the network and its ability to sell time to national advertisers.

Paxson Communications Corporation is considered to be heavily indebted, most likely as a result of the rapid expansion of its network and the preparations necessary to move PAX TV to the digital standard for electronic media transmission as mandated in the coming years by the FCC. The investment by NBC can be considered as one means for the network to remain operable, but it can also be seen as potentially diluting the original mission of PAX TV. As part of the agreement with NBC, NBC affiliate sales staff sells time on local PAX affiliates, thus increasing the efficiency of the local PAX TV affiliate stations. Paxson still controls national programming contracts but also allows for the broadcast of repurposed NBC programming such as news and other current programming. NBC has agreed that it will not use programming that does not meet the PAX TV standard for "family friendly," and this has meant that late-night NBC programming and certain situation comedies have not been repurposed to PAX TV. It is unclear how much this new arrangement has limited PAX TV's use of internally produced programming as opposed to infomercials and other paid programming.

Key issues in the future of PAX TV involve its transition to the digital standard and the release of Paxson's current license ownership of segments of the 700 MHz analog spectrum to wireless communication companies. Paxson still carries considerable debt from its investment in digital technology and is seeking assistance from the federal government to further assist its transition. In addition, Paxson is making any early release of its current broadcast licenses contingent on must carry status for multiple digital channels on cable systems, a move resisted by major cable companies and under consideration by the FCC. In these issues, Paxson has capitalized on the network's conservative Christian base through its own lobbying of Congress and the White House, and through encouraging its audience to lobby Congress to order digital must carry provisions on cable operators. The resolution of these issues and the continued relationship between Paxson and NBC will influence the survival of PAX TV, as well as its focus on family-friendly programming.

See also CHRISTIAN BROADCASTING NETWORK (CBN) AND THE 700 CLUB.

Further reading: McConnell, B. "Ch. 60–69 Occupants Band Together to Demand Multiple Carriage." *Broadcasting and Cable*, February 26, 2001; Securities and Exchange Commission 10-K filing of independent audit of Paxson Communications Corporation by Price Waterhouse Coopers, LLP. March 13, 2000.

—Hillary Warren

Penn, William (1644–1718) *religious leader, activist, colony founder*

Religious controversialist, QUAKER activist, and founder of PENNSYLVANIA, William Penn was a passionate advocate of religious liberty in both England and America. Expelled in 1662 from Christ Church College, Oxford, for religious nonconformity, Penn studied at the Protestant Academy in Saumur, France, returned to England to study law at Lincoln's Inn, London, and converted to Quakerism in 1667. His conversion marked the beginning of a lifelong career as preacher, writer, and spokesperson for the Society of Friends (or, as they were commonly known, Quakers), one of the many sects that emerged from the religious and political ferment of the English civil wars.

Penn spent the decade following his conversion writing and traveling throughout Europe and America on behalf of Quaker causes. He was also increasingly interested in the possibility of an American colony serving as a haven for the persecuted—primarily Quakers, but also "sober people of all sorts"—and parlayed debts owed to his father by the Crown into a colonial charter, granted by King Charles II in 1681. He traveled to America to take up residence as governor in 1682. In the design of his colony, Penn sought to ensure as broad a measure of religious liberty as English authorities would allow. Pennsylvania (named not for the founder but for his father) as Penn envisioned it would have no established church (and thus no system of compulsory tithes to support an established ministry), no doctrinal tests for officeholding, and no requirements for the swearing of oaths in legal settings. Practice did not always fully realize Penn's ambitious plans, since royal assent was required for all colonial laws, but all limitations on religious liberty were forced on an unwilling Penn by royal officials.

Business and legal matters, including Penn's activities on behalf of TOLERATION in England and a protracted border dispute with Lord Baltimore over the colony's southern boundary, kept him away from Pennsylvania for most of the rest of his life. Penn's friendship with King James II landed him under house arrest after the king's ouster in the 1688 Glorious Revolution. Financial woes were almost continuous for Penn as well, and he spent time in debtor's prison in 1708. A series of strokes incapacitated him in 1712, and he died six years later.

Penn's early political writings illuminate his Whig understanding of legitimate English politics as grounded in the ancient constitution, the traditional understanding of English politics in which Parliament and monarch shared in the gov-

This painting shows William Penn negotiating a treaty with Native Americans. *(Library of Congress)*

ernment of the realm. His mature works present the core elements of his arguments for liberty of conscience: belief as a purely intellectual phenomenon, which force was unable to effect; the necessity of positive conviction for salvation; the example of Jesus and the primitive church; the division of spheres into civil and spiritual, with the civil magistrate having firm control over the former but not the latter; and pragmatism, prudence, and prosperity, which appealed to more prosaic, but no less important, earthly concerns. These arguments followed all the conventional routes that had been rehearsed for years in English political discourse. None of Penn's justifications for liberty of conscience was original, but by his active participation in drafting Pennsylvania's founding documents, Penn sought to make religious liberty a practical as well as theoretical part of the colony's life. Regardless of his prolonged absences from the colony, Penn always considered Pennsylvania an attempt to instantiate the fundamental principles of political and religious liberty that he articulated in his writings. His activities on behalf of Quakers as well as reli-

gious dissenters of many stripes have secured him a prominent place in the history of religious liberty and in the Anglo-American tradition more generally.

Further reading: Endy, Melvin B., Jr. *William Penn and Early Quakerism.* Princeton, N.J.: Princeton University Press, 1973; Frost, J. William. *A Perfect Freedom: Religious Liberty in Pennsylvania.* New York: Cambridge University Press, 1990; Moore, Rosemary. *The Light in Their Consciences: The Early Quakers in Britain, 1646–1666.* University Park: Pennsylvania State University Press, 2000; Murphy, Andrew R. *Conscience and Community: Revisiting Toleration and Religious Dissent in Early Modern England and America.* University Park: Pennsylvania State University Press, 2001; Penn, William. *The Political Writings of William Penn.* Introduction and Annotations by Andrew R. Murphy. Indianapolis: Liberty Fund. 2001; Soderlund, Jean R., ed. *William Penn and the Founding of Pennsylvania, 1680–1684: A Documentary History.* Philadelphia: University of Pennsylvania Press, 1983.
—Andrew R. Murphy

Pennsylvania

WILLIAM PENN's "Holy Experiment" in Pennsylvania included three essential elements bearing on the relationship between politics and religion: QUAKER rule, Christian morality, and religious liberty. The last of these receives the most attention today because of its profound impact on the American polity, but all three contributed to the unique character of colonial Pennsylvania.

The irony that Quakers, oppressed and persecuted pacifistic sectarians well outside the pale of political establishment in Britain, became a ruling elite in Pennsylvania was not lost on their contemporaries. Nevertheless, Quakers did effectively rule Pennsylvania from the time of Penn's original charter in 1681 until well into the 18th century. They did so not as a dominant majority, but as a politically adroit minority working from within a position of privilege articulated in Penn's original Frame of Government and in subsequent legislation. Historians have generally been kind to the social benefits of Quaker rule, especially during the period before Penn's death in 1718. It is often noted, for example, that Quaker religious ideals led to a greater liberality in both making and enforcing penal laws. At first, only murder and treason were punishable by death, and fines and imprisonment were less harsh than in most other parts of the empire. Attitudes toward Native Americans were also noticeably different from those in other colonies, at least until the French and Indian War.

To say that Pennsylvania was liberal is not to say that it was libertine. Penn believed that liberty of conscience and a high standard of public morality were not incompatible, as had so often been charged by the critics of the Quakers. He was determined to demonstrate this in the day-to-day life of Pennsylvania also for pragmatic reasons. Because Pennsylvania had been chartered at least partly to provide a place of refuge for

Quakers and other religiously radical folk, neither the Proprietor nor his fellow religionists were about to give British authorities any excuse to revoke the colony's charter on moral grounds. Early Pennsylvania was as "PURITAN" as MASSACHUSETTS in many ways, banning all forms of gambling and riotous conduct, card playing, stage plays, and profane speech.

Penn's policy of religious liberty was rooted both in his personal experience and in his deepest convictions. Believing that the Spirit of God cannot be bound by ecclesiastical dogma or human laws, and having himself been imprisoned for his religious beliefs, he believed that God intended a perfect liberty of conscience for humankind. While the dictates of maintaining a viable social order in a British context meant that public officeholders must affirm that Jesus Christ is "Son of God the Savior of the World," as colonial Pennsylvania law required, Penn and his fellow Quakers were nonetheless at the forefront of 17th-century attempts to redefine the relationship between politics and religion. Pennsylvania therefore welcomed and sought out all sorts and conditions of persons, becoming a haven for members of religious fringe groups. Included were many with origins in Germany who were not welcome in other colonies. Critics charged that such openness toward sectarians and heretics would be the downfall of the colony, but in fact it prospered, not least because of the energy and creativity of its religiously diverse citizenry. Colonial Pennsylvania was close to what the United States would later become, both in its theory and its practice of religious liberty, and in the actual religious diversity of its populace. Penn's fundamental vision had staying power; there were no serious instances of RELIGIOUS PERSECUTION in Pennsylvania during its colonial period. Nor were any church taxes ever collected in the colony.

Tensions within the "Holy Experiment" manifested themselves already in Penn's lifetime and became more noticeable over time. Quaker PACIFISM was much resented by the non-Quaker majority, even before the French and Indian War. Advocacy of religious liberty and a Quaker establishment was theoretically inconsistent and practically difficult as the Quaker population declined as a percentage of the whole. Enforcement of a stringent public morality inconsistent with the religious convictions of some of its citizens invited the charge of hypocrisy and open resistance. Nevertheless, colonial Pennsylvania contributed possibly more than any other colony to the ideals of religious liberty that were to become normative in the fledgling United States.

See also MARYLAND; RELIGIOUS ESTABLISHMENT IN THE COLONIES; VIRGINIA.

Further reading: Bronner, Edwin B. *William Penn's "Holy Experiment": The Founding of Pennsylvania, 1681–1701.* New York: Columbia University Press, 1962; Dunn, Richard S., and Mary Maples Dunn, eds. *The World of William Penn.* Philadelphia: University of Pennsylvania Press, 1986; Frost, J. William. *A Perfect Freedom: Religious Liberty in Pennsylvania.* New York: Cambridge University Press, 1990.

—Donald L. Huber

pentecostal and charismatic

Pentecostalism first emerged in the American context on January 1, 1901, when a student, Agnes N. Ozman, at Bethel Bible College in Topeka, Kansas, founded by Charles F. Parham, began to speak in tongues. The experience of speaking in tongues (glossolalia) is described in Acts 2 of the New Testament as Pentecost in which the apostles of Jesus Christ received the spiritual gift in speaking in different languages so that they might convert others. Pentecostals also emphasize the spiritual gift of healing. In the late 1980s, Pentecostals, along with the many charismatics, increased their involvement in politics after the charismatic televangelist PAT ROBERTSON's unsuccessful run for the Republican Party's presidential nomination.

After the first instance of speaking in tongues, the experience rapidly spread throughout Bethel Bible College and beyond. In 1906, William J. Seymour, an African-American student of Parham's, led a racially diverse Pentecostal revival at the Azusa Street Mission in San Francisco. The following year, the predominately African-American denomination CHURCH OF GOD IN CHRIST adopted Pentecostal teachings. This denomination is now the largest black Pentecostal church in the United States. From these origins, Pentecostalism began to develop separately from the Methodist "Holiness" tradition with the founding of the ASSEMBLIES OF GOD in 1914.

Pentecostalism shares much with EVANGELICALISM and FUNDAMENTALISM. As denominations struggled with their understanding of Scripture in light of the scientific discoveries of the late 19th century, Pentecostals sided with the evangelical ardent support for the fundamentals of the faith, such as biblical literalism. Despite these similarities, fundamentalists as well as many evangelicals have often viewed the experience of speaking in tongues with suspicion.

The charismatic movement began in the late 1950s as the Pentecostal experience began to cross over into mainline Protestant denominations and Roman Catholic churches. One of the first instances occurred in April 1960 with the announcement by California Episcopal priest Dennis Bennett that he had been baptized by the Holy Spirit. The ROMAN CATHOLIC CHURCH accepted glossolalia in 1967 as a genuine religious experience after careful study and discussion of the phenomenon. As the Pentecostal experience moved into the mainline denominations, they were influenced by their more liberal and moderate theological views, including a more open view toward the role of women in leadership positions. The movement also brought a change in the socioeconomic status of charismatics and Pentecostals. At its origin, Pentecostals drew members primarily from the lower classes in urban areas. However, charismatic movement marked the expansion of the Pentecostal experience into the middle class and suburban areas.

With an emphasis on spreading their faith over social action, Pentecostals and charismatics kept largely apart from organized involvement in politics. This changed with the run by Pat Robertson for the 1988 Republican presidential nomination. Robertson had a ready store of supporters from his CHRISTIAN BROADCASTING NETWORK, founded in 1960, and his popular *700 Club* show, in which he preached a charismatic message. In one study of Robertson supporters, 69 percent of donors and 59 percent of convention delegates identified their religious tradition as Pentecostal or charismatic—though few fundamentalists could be found as supporters, attesting to the division within the evangelical camp.

Pentecostals and charismatics generally have conservative political leanings. In a 1988 study, Assemblies of God clergy were strongly orthodox in their religious views, held a conservative political ideology, and a Republican Party identification. At that time, 89 percent of the Assemblies clergy identified with the Republican Party. Other studies have suggested that the politics of Pentecostals and charismatics are more complex and vary between traditions. Evangelical Protestants identified more with conservatives and Republicans when they identified themselves as "spirit-filled" (a marker of Pentecostals and charismatics) than when they did not, though for Roman Catholics, the additional identification as "spirit-filled" had the opposite effect, increasing the identification with liberals and Democrats.

See also CHRISTIAN RIGHT AND THE REPUBLICAN PARTY; SOUTHERN REPUBLICAN REALIGNMENT.

Further reading: Blumhofer, Edith Waldvogel. *The Assemblies of God: A Popular History.* Springfield, Mo.: Radiant Books, 1983; Green, John C., James L. Guth, Corwin E. Smidt, and Lyman A. Kellstedt. *Religion and the Culture Wars: Dispatches from the Front.* Lanham, Md.: Rowman and Littlefield, 1996; Guth, James L., John C. Green, Corwin E. Smidt, Lyman A. Kellstedt, and Margaret M. Poloma. *The Bully Pulpit: The Politics of Protestant Clergy.* Lawrence: University Press of Kansas, 1997; McDonnell, Kilian. *Charismatic Renewal and the Churches.* New York: Seabury Press, 1976; Sherrill, John. *They Speak with Other Tongues.* Old Tappan, N.J.: Spire Books, 1964.

—Jean L. McSween

People for the American Way

Formed in October 1980, People for the American Way (PFAW) is a liberal interest group founded by Norman Lear. The group's original motivation was to counter the emerging political activity of the Christian Right, such as that by the MORAL MAJORITY, in the late 1970s. From the group's first president, Anthony T. Podesta, to its current one, Ralph G. Neas, the actions of the Christian Right continue to be the group's most effective rallying cry.

Deemed "Hollywood Money" by its opponents, PFAW saw its high-water mark late in the Reagan administration during the hearings for Supreme Court nominee Robert H. Bork. Running 60-second television advertisements in which Bork was attacked for his supposed extreme right-wing stances,

PFAW drew considerable media attention to the hearings. The advertisements sparked reaction from the White House, which in turn drew even more attention to the hearings. Many in Washington saw this as the turning point in the confirmation process, as the Senate went on to reject Bork's nomination.

PFAW's agenda includes staples of progressive politics today: civil rights, religious freedom, opposition to CENSORSHIP, civic participation, and publicizing the politics of the far right. Following their role in the Bork defeat, PFAW has remained active on judicial nominations, especially during the GEORGE W. BUSH administration. PFAW also brings suit to further its aims of equal rights. For example, PFAW sued Florida secretary of state Katherine Harris among others on behalf of African-American voters challenging practices and policies that they claim disenfranchised thousands during the controversial 2000 presidential election. Supporting GAY RIGHTS through the courts has also been a major initiative of PFAW.

PFAW has gained notoriety for its annual publication of "Attacks on the Freedom to Learn." This publication has been devoted to documenting supposed censorship attempts in public schools across the country. More recently, PFAW has also produced "Hostile Climate," a publication specifically documenting any sort of antigay public policy from legislative initiatives, referenda, court cases, and attempts at censorship deemed discriminatory.

Suffering from lack of a clear vision, other than that of adversary to the Christian Right, PFAW has struggled to maintain a consistent message or direction. PFAW also suffers from an organizational standpoint. While engaging in extensive lobbying and litigation, PFAW has had far less success in attaining its goal of being a grassroots organization. "They [the Christian Right] have an infrastructure in small towns and all over the country in churches, but there is not a similar infrastructure in the progressive movement," says former PFAW employee Jill A. Lesser.

More recently, former president Carole Shields and current president Ralph G. Neas have tried to move the organization more in the direction of a think tank through development of policy alternatives. The group has a total of 75 staff members, including four full-time lobbyists, at its Washington headquarters and at offices in Chicago, Los Angeles, Miami, and New York City.

Further reading: PFAW on the Web. URL: http://www.pfaw.org/.

—Daniel D. Stratton

Peoples Temple

James (Jim) Warren Jones was born on May 13, 1931, in Crete, Indiana, and died on November 18, 1978, in Jonestown, Guyana. His Peoples Temple Christian Church was founded on April 4, 1955. In its early days, the church was noted for its support of racial equality and other liberal causes. The group subsequently moved from Indiana to California and then to

Guyana. Mounting conflict with federal agencies, former members, and opponents ultimately led to a confrontation with an investigative party led by Representative Leo J. Ryan (D-Calif.). After killing several members of the party on November 18, 1978, Jones organized a mass suicide to avoid the inevitable government prosecution that would follow. Group members died as a result of ingesting purple Fla-Vor-Aid, mixed with lethal potassium cyanide and several sedatives and tranquilizers.

The Peoples Temple began with Jones preaching at the Laurel Street Tabernacle in Indianapolis, Indiana, in 1954. In 1955, Jones formed his own church, the Wings of Deliverance, which was later renamed Peoples Temple. Jones's ministry was notable for its interracial composition (20 percent of the congregation was African American), and its campaign for racial equality. The Peoples Temple affiliated with the Christian Church (Disciples of Christ) in 1960; Jones was ordained as a minister despite a lack of theological training. Jones developed heightened charismatic authority by "discerning spirits," faith healing, and predicting the future. Ultimately, Jones proclaimed himself to be the Second Coming of Christ. Peoples Temple theology was Jones's personal blend of Pentecostalism, socialism, and communism. The Holy Bible initially was the church's text, but Jones later rejected the Bible as containing falsehoods and contradictions. A key element in the group's theology was the idea of "Revolutionary Suicide" drawn from Black Panther leader Huey Newton. Members were to give up all previous social ties and commit themselves to a collective struggle against injustice—racial, economic, and social. Jones predicted an apocalypse in which the United States would be engulfed in race and class warfare and genocide.

The Peoples Temple encountered mounting resistance in Indianapolis, and in 1965 Jones and 70 families moved the Temple to Ukiah, California. The group sought a congenial location and one that would be safe in the event of a predicted thermonuclear war. In 1972, the Temple established a second congregation in San Francisco. The group pooled member resources to provide each individual with economic security and membership in a religious "family." In the wake of political controversy surrounding the Temple in San Francisco that was based on Temple leaders' concern about revocation of their tax-exempt status, the group obtained a lease from the Guyanese government for a tract of land for colonization. Guyana was selected because it was socialist but also enjoyed cordial relations with the United States.

The Peoples Temple Agricultural Mission initially grew slowly, with only about 50 residents by 1977. When the Temple was investigated by the Internal Revenue Service in 1977, Jones began to urge members to relocate in Jonestown, Guyana. Creating a viable community in the midst of a jungle was an immense task that consumed all members' time and energy. The group adopted a centralized, communal lifestyle that included public group punishment for personal infractions, collectivization and redistribution of individual wealth, and encouragement of sexual relationships outside of marriage

to limit family solidarity. What Jones called "White Nights," in which members were awakened at night, told to prepare for the ultimate sacrifice, and ordered to imbibe what was presented as a poisonous liquid, were common events to test member loyalty.

The group's move to Guyana did not, however, eliminate the opposition that was building against it from several former members (most notably those making child custody claims), a group of family members opposed to relatives' membership (Concerned Relatives), and U.S. government agencies. Concerned Relatives finally found an advocate in Representative Ryan.

Ryan flew to Jonestown accompanied by members of Concerned Relatives and media representatives. On November 18, 1978, Ryan and 16 Temple members who indicated they would like to leave Jonestown were ambushed as they headed for the airstrip. Ryan and four others were killed. Jones then announced that revolutionary suicide was the only remaining option. The final body count was 914 dead, including 276 children. Jones himself died from a gunshot to the right temple.

See also FAMILY, THE; HEAVEN'S GATE; NEW RELIGIOUS MOVEMENTS.

Further reading: Chidester, David. *Salvation and Suicide.* Bloomington: Indiana University Press, 1988; Hall, John R. *Gone from the Promised Land.* New Brunswick, N.J.: Transaction, 1987; Hall, John, Philip Schuyler, and Silvaine Trinh. *Apocalypse Observed.* New York, Routledge, 2000.

—David G. Bromley

Persian Gulf War

On August 2, 1990, Iraqi president Saddam Hussein (b. 1937) invaded Kuwait and declared it the 19th province of Iraq. Fearing that Saddam Hussein might use military force to take control of the region's oil supplies, President George H.W. Bush organized a multinational coalition to contain Iraq. The U.N. Security Council imposed economic sanctions on Iraq and set a January 15, 1991, deadline for Iraq to withdraw unconditionally from Kuwait. After Saddam Hussein failed to comply with this deadline, the U.S.–led coalition bombed Iraq from January 16 through April 6, 1991. This war effort succeeded in restoring the government of Kuwait and diminishing Iraq's offensive military capability. President Bush won the support of a Democratically controlled Congress to garner support for his policies (and avoid resistance) in the U.N. Security Council, and to create a remarkable coalition of supporters including key Arab nations. This war effort was supported by over 80 percent of the American people, with the loudest criticism coming from Americans who thought the United States should have marched into Baghdad to remove Saddam Hussein from office. Nevertheless, the Persian Gulf War is unique in American history because it marks the first time that the United States began a war despite the explicit reservations of the Roman Catholic and Mainline Protestant Churches.

Catholic criticism of the U.S.-led forces in the Persian Gulf War is best understood as a reflection of this church's renewed commitment to maintaining the presumption against violence in JUST WAR theory. Throughout much of U.S. history, Catholics have been an embattled minority who attempted to demonstrate that they could be good Catholics and good Americans through support for U.S. war efforts. Three events in particular foreshadowed the Catholic Church's critique of U.S. policy in the Persian Gulf War. First, VATICAN II empowered national conferences of bishops to apply Catholic social teachings to local and national policies. Second, the VIETNAM WAR prompted many Americans, including Catholics, to reexamine their assumptions about the ethics of war. Third, the CATHOLIC BISHOPS' 1983 PASTORAL LETTER ON WAR AND PEACE restored the just-war theory's presumption against violence and reclaimed the principled nature of just-war theory. In the context of the Persian Gulf War, the Catholic bishops were particularly critical of President Bush's policy that there be "no negotiations, no compromises, and no face-saving maneuvers." The bishops insisted that negotiations must be attempted as a matter of principle. If the United States had supported genuine negotiations, and those negotiations had failed, the Catholic bishops seemed poised to support the use of force to restore the government of Kuwait.

Leaders of mainline Protestant denominations (such as the UNITED METHODIST CHURCH, the PRESBYTERIAN CHURCH USA, and President Bush's own denomination, the EPISCOPAL CHURCH) along with their umbrella organization, the NATIONAL COUNCIL OF CHURCHES OF CHRIST in the U.S.A., however, provided an endless litany of reasons for opposing U.S. strategy in the war. Their resolutions portrayed the United States as an imperial power that acted to promote its own economic interests, with little concern for justice. They also highlighted similarities between President Bush and Saddam Hussein inasmuch as President Bush's threats, deadlines, and unwillingness to engage in dialogue implied that the strong do as they can and the weak suffer what they must.

Other religious communities responded in more predictable ways to the war. The historic peace churches (QUAKER, Brethren, MENNONITE) opposed a military solution to this conflict. Muslim communities in the United States feared that the war would exacerbate stereotypes about Muslims as violent and anti-Western. Jewish communities in the United States became even more supportive of containing Iraq when Saddam Hussein launched missiles into Israel.

Many Evangelical Protestants, who had mobilized support for Republicans during the Reagan-Bush years, were supportive of President Bush's strategy from the beginning. They were the U.S. community that was the most likely to portray this conflict as a battle between the forces of good and evil. As a result, they were also the community most likely to ask, "Why did the United States not march into Baghdad to remove Saddam Hussein from power?"

Further reading: Geyer, Alan F., and Barbara Green. *Lines in the Sand: Justice and the Gulf War.* Louisville, Ky.: Westminster, 1992; Johnson, James Turner, and George Weigel. *Just War and the Gulf War.* Washington, D.C.: Ethics and Public Policy Center, 1991; National Council of Churches of Christ in the U.S.A. *Pressing for Peace. The Churches Act in the Gulf Crisis.* New York: NCC-USA, 1991; Walsh, Andrew Dean. "Political Realism and Just-War Rhetoric: The Case of the Persian Gulf War." Ph.D. diss. Drew University, Madison, N.J., 1994.

—Andrew D. Walsh

Pfeffer, Leo (1909–1993) *jurist, scholar*

Leo Pfeffer was a leading authority and jurist of American church-state relations. The son of a Jewish rabbi, Pfeffer was born in Hungary and brought to the United States at the age of two by his parents. A graduate of the City College of New York and the New York University School of Law, Pfeffer was admitted to the bar at age 23. In 1945, Pfeffer began a 40-year association with the AMERICAN JEWISH CONGRESS, serving as director, general counsel, and special counsel of its Commission on Law and Social Action. From 1964 to 1979, Pfeffer held a simultaneous appointment as professor of political science and chair of the department at Long Island University. In addition to these positions, Pfeffer served as counsel for the New York Committee for Public Education and Religious Liberty (CPEARL) and the National Coalition for PEARL.

A prolific author, Pfeffer published eight books and more than 70 articles and book chapters. His magnum opus, *Church, State, and Freedom* (1953), is considered a classic study of church-state relations. Pfeffer's legal advocacy included numerous oral arguments before the Supreme Court, as well as the filing of briefs in more than 120 church-state controversies on behalf of a variety of individuals and organizations.

A leading theoretician and advocate of the strict separationist view of church-state relations, Pfeffer frequently argued that freedom of religion and SEPARATION OF CHURCH AND STATE are a unitary principle, that "separation guaranteed freedom and freedom required separation." A self-described "absolutist" with regard to First Amendment rights, Pfeffer routinely advanced the broad interpretation of the ESTABLISHMENT CLAUSE found in Justice Hugo Black's majority opinion in *EVERSON V. BOARD OF EDUCATION* (1947). In numerous cases, Pfeffer challenged religious exercises in public schools, public AID TO RELIGIOUS SCHOOLS, religious tests for public office, and religious symbols on public property. Pfeffer even broke with some of his separationist allies when filing a brief challenging tax exemption for church property in *WALZ V. TAX COMMISSION* (1970). Pfeffer was equally aggressive in defending FREE EXERCISE rights. Regularly utilizing the compelling state interest standard adopted by the Court in *SHERBERT V. VERNER* (1963), Pfeffer's expansive view of free exercise was evident in his briefs defending CONSCIENTIOUS OBJECTORS, the AMISH, members of the UNIFICATION CHURCH, and Sabbatarians. In many of these cases, Pfeffer contended that because a statute was facially neutral or secular did not absolve it from First Amendment scrutiny. According to Pfeffer, history had regularly proven that seemingly secular and neutral laws had been used to destroy new and unconventional religions.

Pfeffer shaped the Supreme Court's establishment clause jurisprudence for nearly 40 years. While the Court's decisions frequently reflected the argumentation found in Pfeffer's briefs, the Court, at times, directly adopted Pfeffer's legal evidence and reasoning. This is true in *MCCOLLUM V. BOARD OF EDUCATION* (1947), where Justice Felix Frankfurter utilized Pfeffer's social scientific data revealing the negative impact of public school–sponsored religious education programs on children of minority faiths. Similarly, the Court adopted Pfeffer's profile of religiously affiliated colleges and universities in several key funding disputes. Particularly significant was Pfeffer's substantial influence in the Supreme Court's "adaptation of the *Lemon* test and its subsequent use in almost all establishment clause litigation" (see *LEMON V. KURTZMAN*).

Pfeffer's advocacy of the separationist position brought him many critics, including leading American Roman Catholics, with whom he fought a decades-long battle over aid to parochial schools. More recently, Robert Cord's critique of the separationist interpretation of the establishment clause and treatise for its nonpreferentialist reading identified Leo Pfeffer as the leading figure of the strict separationist position. Similarly, in an article entitled "The Pfefferian Inversion," Richard John Neuhaus criticized the Pfeffer-inspired Supreme Court's establishment clause decisions that had the effect of creating a *"NAKED PUBLIC SQUARE"* by pushing religion to the margins of American public life.

While Pfeffer's legacy has suffered some setbacks under the current Court, especially with regard to state funding of religious schools and exemptions from secular laws for religious minorities, the Court continues to grapple with the separationist principles established during Pfeffer's 40 years of church-state litigation, scholarship, and advocacy.

See also *COMMITTEE FOR PUBLIC EDUCATION V. NYQUIST; COMMITTEE FOR PUBLIC EDUCATION V. REGAN; LEVITT V. CPEARL.*

Further reading: Cord, Robert. *Separation of Church and State: Historical Fact and Current Fiction.* New York: Lambeth, 1982; Ivers, Gregg. *To Build a Wall: American Jews and the Separation of Church and State.* Charlottesville: University of Virginia Press, 1995; Neuhaus, Richard John. "The Pfefferian Inversion." *National Review* 13 (May 1988): 44; Pfeffer, Leo. "An Autobiographical Sketch." In *Religion and the State: Essays in Honor of Leo Pfeffer.* Edited by James E. Wood Jr. Waco, Texas: Baylor University Press, 1985, 487–533; ———. *Church, State, and Freedom.* Rev. Ed. Boston: Beacon Press, 1967.

—J. David Holcomb

philanthropy

From the founding of the United States, the PURITAN response to social conditions blurred the lines that separate politics, philanthropy, and religion. The Puritans established a culture of philanthropy geared to strengthen communities and build institutions to help the poor raise themselves out of poverty. This tradition introduced a system of nongovernmental agencies.

Mathew Carey (1760–1839), a political economist, organized one of the first immigrant mutual aid organizations, The Hibernian Society for the Relief of Immigrants from Ireland, in 1792. For Carey, helping the poor meant economic empowerment that would benefit the wider society. Voluntary philanthropy on the part of the wealthy was not only morally praiseworthy, but decreased the likelihood of enforced taxation. Carey argued that voluntary organizations were more efficient and effective than government in meeting the needs of the poor. This argument reemerged under the administration of RONALD REAGAN (1981–89) by contemporary neoconservatives and supporters of a smaller central government.

By the end of the 20th century, religious-based organizations were among the nation's top 10 charities with generous public support. Marilyn Dickey and her colleagues reported that, in 1996, the Salvation Army raised more than $1 billion from private sources, far more than any other charity in America. It was ranked first in public donations, followed by the Red Cross ($480 million). Other religious-based organizations in the top 10 charitable organizations were Catholic Charities ($385 million), Second Harvest ($351 million), YMCA of the USA ($340 million), and Habitat for Humanity International ($334 million).

According to a survey conducted in 2000, the Barna Research Corporation found that churches remain the most likely organizations to receive donations from individuals. They also estimated that about six out of every 10 dollars donated went to churches. An earlier study by Hodgkinson and colleagues found that congregations spent $4.4 billion for human services, $4.0 billion on health and hospital, $1.3 billion for arts and culture, $0.7 billion on human justice and community development, $0.5 billion for environmental programs, $0.5 billion for international welfare, and $2.1 billion on other programs to benefit the community. In a study of 251 congregations in seven cities, Cnaan and his colleagues found that the mean percent of church budgets allocated to social programs (22.6 percent) was higher than that of traditional tithing (10 percent), a baseline measure of charitable giving. But tithing is not the only measure of charitable giving. The United Way of America, for example, asks donors to "Give Five" or 5 percent of their income, whereas American corporations, on average, designate only about 1 percent of their pretax net income for charitable purposes. By any of these three measures, congregations can be considered the most charitable in supporting social programs that benefit the community.

In addition to the significant philanthropic contribution by religious-based organizations, people with a religious commitment have been found to contribute to charities of all kinds. The Russ Reid Company, in conjunction with the Barna Research Corporation, found that "the best predictor of people's giving behavior relates to the intensity and nature of their spiritual commitment. Eighty-two percent of the people who give to nonprofit organizations also give to churches or places of worship." Among the regular donors in the study, 60 percent attended a church or another religious service in the past month, 37 percent volunteered at their place of worship in the past month, and 84 percent agreed that religious faith was very important in their lives. This high correlation between giving to charities and involvement in religious organizations indicates that giving to others is central to their religious beliefs. As the government retrenchment of public services begun in the early 1980s continues to expand support for charitable giving, religious organizations will be expected to play a greater role in philanthropy.

Further reading: Carey, M. *Autobiography.* Brooklyn: Research Classics, 1942; Cnaan, R. A., S. C. Boddie, F. Handy, G. Yancey, and R. Schneider. *The Invisible Caring Hand: American Congregations and the Provision of Welfare.* New York: New York University Press, 2002; Dickey, M., S. Gray, H. Hall, and D. Morris. "The Big Bounty for Big Charities." *Chronicle of Philanthropy* (October 30, 1997): 7–8; Galaskiewicz, Joseph. "An Urban Grants Economy Revisited: Corporate Charitable Contributions in Twin Cities, 1979–81, 1987–89." *Administrative Science Quarterly* 42 (1997): 445–471; Hodgkinson, V. A., M. S. Weitzman, A. D. Kirsch, S. M. Noga, and H. A. Gorski. *From Belief to Commitment: The Community Service Activities and Finances of Religious Congregations in the United States.* Washington, D.C.: Independent Sector, 1993; Nagai, A. K., R. Lerner, and S. Rothman. *Giving for Social Change: Foundations, Public Policy, and the American Political Agenda.* Westport, Conn.: Praeger, 1994; Russ Reid Company. "The Heart of the Donor." Pasadena, Calif.: Russ Reid Company, 1995.

—Ram A. Cnaan and Stephanie Clintonia Boddie

Pierce v. Society of Sisters 268 U.S. 510 (1925)

Pierce v. Society of Sisters invalidated an amendment to an Oregon education law requiring children between the ages of eight and 16 to attend public schools. Exemptions were granted to children with disabilities, those who had completed the eighth grade, and those who had to travel an appreciable distance from the public school for which there was no publicly provided transportation. Parents or guardians who refused to comply would be guilty of a misdemeanor, carrying a fine of up to $100 and/or imprisonment of between two and 30 days. The amendment was adopted by state initiative on November 7, 1922, and was to take effect September 1, 1926. Had this law gone into effect, it would have precluded the ability of parents to choose a nonpublic education for their children in this crucial age group.

The socialization function of fostering common American ideals was the rationale behind the amendment. The threat of foreign and un-American ideas was made explicit by the attorneys for Governor Pierce. They maintained that Oregon voters "felt that by mingling together, during a portion of their education," children of various races and sects would share a common culture and be less prone to accept un-American ideas. The governor's attorneys warned that although the vast majority of nonpublic schools were religious, they could be followed by devotees of "certain economic doctrines entirely destructive of the fundamentals of our government," specifically mentioning "bolshevists, syndicalists and communists."

The arguments of the governor's attorneys were echoed in a voter pamphlet supporting the initiative for its goal of socializing foreign-born school children into American ideals:

> The assimilation and education of our foreign born citizens in the principles of our government, the hopes and inspirations of our people, are best secured by and through attendance of all children in public schools . . . Our children must not under any pretext, be it based on money, creed, or social status, be divided into antagonistic groups, there to absorb the narrow views of life as they are taught.

Justice James McReynolds, writing for a unanimous court, in invalidating this amendment to the Oregon law, cited the protection of "liberty" in the Fourteenth Amendment as developed in *Meyer v. Nebraska* (1923). The Court in *Meyer* invalidated a Nebraska statute forbidding the teaching of foreign languages below the eighth grade. In that case, Justice McReynolds articulated a conception of liberty protected under the Fourteenth Amendment that "denotes not merely freedom from bodily restraint but also the right of the individual to contract, to engage in any of the common occupations of life, to acquire useful knowledge, to marry, establish a home and bring up children, to worship God according to the dictates of his own conscience, and generally to enjoy those privileges long recognized at common law as essential to the orderly pursuit of happiness by free men." In *Pierce*, McReynolds wrote that the Oregon act of 1922 interfered with the liberty of parents and guardians to direct the education of their children. In the most memorable lines of the opinion, Justice McReynolds wrote: "The fundamental theory of liberty upon which all governments in this Union repose excludes any general power of the State to standardize its children by forcing them to accept instruction from public teachers only. The child is not the mere creature of the State; those who nurture him and direct his destiny have the right, coupled with the high duty, to recognize and prepare him for additional obligation."

McReynolds also held that as corporations, the Society of Sisters of the Holy Name of Jesus and Mary and the Hill Military Academy, the other school involved in the case, had businesses and property protected by the Fourteenth Amendment against "arbitrary, unreasonable and unlawful interference" by the state.

Pierce is often cited as the case that safeguarded the liberty of parents to choose private education for their children. It is instructive that the First Amendment's FREE EXERCISE CLAUSE and ESTABLISHMENT CLAUSE were not invoked. The Court did not incorporate, or make applicable to the states, the First Amendment religion clauses until the 1940s.

See also AID TO RELIGIOUS SCHOOLS.

Further reading: Jurinski, James John. *Religion in the Schools: A Reference Handbook.* Santa Barbara, Calif.: ABC-CLIO, 1998.

—Gerald DeMaio

pietism

Pietism refers to a general theological tradition within PROTESTANTISM, in which believers are thought to have direct, unmediated relationships with God. Pietists have historically emphasized the importance of individual conversion, "born-again" experiences, or charismatic "gifts of the spirit," although different strands of the tradition emphasize different manifestations of relationships between individual Christians and God. Pietist denominations are often characterized as instances of "low church" forms of Christianity, in which authority is highly decentralized and in which worship is rather informal. Pietism is often contrasted with liturgicalism or ritualism. The latter set of traditions typically emphasize more formal, hierarchical styles of worship. Pietism often entails a commitment to theological egalitarianism, in which status differences between laity and clergy are minimized.

There is a strain within pietism that emphasizes the importance of godly personal behavior and social reform. Pietists generally eschew moral or cultural relativism, and often seek to create social and political environments in which God's will can be realized on earth.

Denominations in the pietistic tradition typically lack regional or national organizations, centralized doctrinal tenets, sacraments, or uniform forms of worship. Pietistic denominations are generally regarded as particularistic, and often eschew cooperation with other religious bodies. Theological differences that might seem minor to observers from outside the tradition often occasion conflict and separation within and between pietistic organizations. While pietistic congregations tend to emphasize local autonomy, their members are often quite concerned with doctrinal orthodoxy within rather narrow, local contexts. Contemporary examples of pietistic denominations in the United States include Baptists, ASSEMBLIES OF GOD, MENNONITES, QUAKERS, and other varieties of PENTECOSTAL Protestantism. Historically, such modern "mainline" denominations such as Presbyterians and Methodists have pietistic roots but have become more liturgical with the passage of time.

Pietism's history is almost as old as the Reformation itself. Some analysts identify the emergence of pietism with the creation of the earliest ANABAPTIST congregation in 1523 in Zurich, Switzerland. Pietism represents an individualist strand within Protestant theology, and thus found fertile soil in the United States. Pietists have been a formidable force in American politics for most of American history.

It is possible to discern at least three major political effects of pietism on American politics. First, it seems likely that participation in pietistic denominations can enhance the political skills of otherwise politically and economically disadvantaged citizens. Although the evidence is mixed, the relatively unstructured, informal, and egalitarian worship and governance structures that characterize such denominations is thought to promote the development of CIVIC SKILLS (such as negotiating, public speaking, and coalition building) that are transferable to more secular arenas. It has been suggested that church participation may be the *only* civic institution that imparts such characteristics to citizens who lack other opportunities for political learning.

Second, pietistic believers have been periodically active in challenging and changing the agenda of American national politics. Movements such as the ABOLITIONIST MOVEMENT, the temperance movement, and the contemporary Christian Right are all the results of the political activity of pietists. Pietism contains a moralistic, reformist strain, which emphasizes the importance of personal behavior and a generally ethical climate. In several periods of U.S. history, pietistic political activism has provided an ethical, transcendent purpose to American politics.

Finally, although pietistic movements have often succeeded in altering the American political agenda, the tradition contains elements that tend to inhibit the development of stable political, governing coalitions. The pietistic emphasis on individual and congregational autonomy has constrained some members of such denominations from attempting to exercise political influence. For many pietists, the "separation of church and state" is an important value for religious, as well as political, reasons. Moreover, the religious particularism to which pietistic denominations are often prone has often prevented the formation of stable political coalitions. Theological rifts between evangelicals and fundamentalists, or between evangelicals and charismatics, have limited the effectiveness of potentially strong political movements and candidacies. Thus, pietism has provided an important dynamic for American politics by serving as the means by which religiously motivated political activity is both initiated and limited.

Further reading: Fowler, Robert Booth, Allen D. Hertzke, and Laura R. Olson. *Religion and Politics in America.* Boulder, Colo.: Westview, 1999; Jelen, Ted G. *The Political Mobilization of Religious Beliefs.* Westport, Conn.: Praeger, 1991; Jelen, Ted G., and Clyde Wilcox. *Public Attitudes Toward Church and State.* Armonk, N.Y.: M E. Sharpe, 1995; Reichley, A. James. *Religion in American Public Life.* Washington, D.C.: Brookings Institution, 1985; Verba, Sidney, Kay Lehman Scholzman, and Henry E. Brady. *Voice and Equality: Civic*

Voluntarism in American Politics. Cambridge, Mass.: Harvard University Press, 1995; Wilcox, Clyde. *God's Warriors: The Christian Right in the Twentieth Century.* Baltimore: Johns Hopkins University Press, 1992.

—Ted G. Jelen

Pilgrims

Although American history is replete with persecuted religious groups journeying to the nation's shores in search of liberty of worship, the term *Pilgrims* is generally reserved for the group of English Separatists who landed at Plymouth, in what would become MASSACHUSETTS, in December 1620. Unlike their neighbors in the Massachusetts Bay Colony, made up of the settlements in and around Boston, the Plymouth Pilgrims were Separatists. Separatists denied that the Anglican Church was a true church and asserted that communion with it was hazardous to one's spiritual health; thus Separatists withdrew into "gathered" congregations as opposed to the geographically defined parishes of the Anglican system. Furthermore, they denied that the civil government ought to have any role in church affairs, claiming that forced worship and governmentally imposed uniformity corrupted true religion. (In this respect, the Separatist position reverses the later view that religious liberty is desirable to protect the *state* from religious strife.)

The Plymouth community had its origins in the English village of Scrooby, Nottinghamshire, around 1606, when a small number of families gathered into an independent congregation and met secretly in the home of William Brewster. Such an act was illegal in England, and several of its members were imprisoned. The company immigrated to the Netherlands in 1609 and, after a brief stay in Amsterdam, settled in Leiden. Worshiping under the leadership of John Robinson, the Pilgrims continued to suffer economic hardship and struggled to maintain their strict religious principles in the midst of a tolerant Dutch culture. The decision to immigrate to America was made around 1618. After a series of difficult negotiations and the loss of their ship *Speedwell*, which had to be left at Plymouth, England, because of unseaworthiness, a portion of the Leiden congregation sailed for America on the *Mayflower* in August 1620. Aiming for the northernmost point of the Virginia settlement (then roughly at the mouth of the Hudson River), the *Mayflower* sighted Cape Cod in November 1620.

On November 11, 1620, 41 male passengers on board the *Mayflower* signed the MAYFLOWER COMPACT, in which they pledged to "covenant and combine our selves together into a civil body politic." Construction of the Plymouth settlement began the following month, but the harsh winter took a heavy toll on the community: by the spring of 1621, only about half of the original 102 settlers remained. That spring saw the planting of the first crops and the beginnings of friendly relations with the Native Americans: The Wampanoags Samoset and Squanto instructed the settlers in planting and cultivating corn and other crops, and the community reached a peace treaty with the chief Wampanoag sachem, Massasoit. The Pilgrims' first harvest, in the autumn of 1621, was the occasion for a three-day celebration attended by settlers as well as nearly 100 Wampanoag. Since 1863, Thanksgiving, styled after the Pilgrims' harvest celebration, has been proclaimed a national holiday in the United States and is celebrated each November.

The Plymouth settlement remained small compared with the dynamic and growing Massachusetts Bay colony that would later spring up in and around Boston, and Plymouth would eventually be incorporated into the Bay colony. But the Pilgrim voyage and landing, difficult winter, and first Thanksgiving celebration remain integral parts of American lore.

Further reading: Bradford, William. *Bradford's History of Plymouth Plantation, 1606–1646.* Edited by William T. Davis. New York: C. Scribner's Sons, 1908 [1650].

—Andrew R. Murphy

Planned Parenthood of Southeastern Pennsylvania, et al. v. Casey, et al. 505 U.S. 833 (1992)

At issue in this case, decided on June 29, 1992, were five provisions of the Pennsylvania Abortion Control Act of 1982—a requirement that a woman give her informed consent to the abortion and be provided with certain information, such as the probable gestational age of the unborn child, the risks of the procedure, and the availability of medical assistance and child support, a requirement in most cases that a minor seeking an abortion must have the informed consent of one parent; a requirement, which can in certain instances be bypassed, that a married woman seeking an abortion sign a written statement that she has informed her husband; a definition of "medical emergency" that permits these requirements to be bypassed; and a requirement that facilities that provide abortions report certain information to the state. A seriously divided Supreme Court, with no single opinion commanding the support of a majority of the justices, upheld four of the five provisions. Only the spousal notification measure failed to pass judicial muster.

There were five separate opinions. Two, authored by Chief Justice William Rehnquist and Justice ANTONIN SCALIA, represented the opinions of four justices (Rehnquist, Scalia, White, and Thomas), who would have overturned *ROE V. WADE* (1973) and upheld all five provisions. A joint opinion, authored by Justices Sandra Day O'Connor, William Kennedy, and David Souter, delivered the judgment of the Court and offered a rationale for it. In his opinion, Justice Harry Blackmun indicated that by making use of a "strict scrutiny" standard, he would have rejected all the provisions, with the exception of that defining a medical emergency. Finally, Justice John Paul Stevens wrote in support of the Court's positions regarding record keeping, medical emergencies, and spousal notification, but in opposition to those who would uphold the parental and informed consent requirements.

In sum, seven Justices supported many, if not all, of the abortion regulations contained in the Pennsylvania statute, but five voted to retain the precedential force of *Roe v. Wade.* The three authors of the joint opinion are the only justices in both of these apparently opposed camps. At issue is whether their joint opinion is coherent or merely, in the words of Rehnquist, "retains the outer shell of *Roe v. Wade....,* but beats a wholesale retreat from the substance of that case." The argument of the joint opinion turns on its understanding of the "essential holding" of *Roe,* which consists of three parts: first, "a recognition of the right of the woman to choose to have an abortion before viability and to obtain it without undue interference from the State"; second, an affirmation of state's authority "to restrict abortion after fetal viability"; and third, the claim that the state has interests in protecting the health of the woman and the life of the fetus "from the outset of the pregnancy." The emphasis laid in the joint opinion on the third point leads to the formulation of the "undue burden" doctrine: "Only where state regulation imposes an undue burden on a woman's ability to make this decision does the power of the State reach into the heart of the liberty protected by the Due Process Clause." State regulations are permissible where they are "calculated to inform the woman's free choice, not hinder it"; they are impermissible where they have "the purpose or effect of presenting a substantial obstacle to a woman seeking an abortion." Thus a requirement that women considering an abortion be provided with information, even if it favors childbirth over abortion, is not an undue burden, while a requirement that a woman notify her husband—given the possibility that he is abusive or opposed to abortion—is an undue burden.

From the point of view of the relationship between religion and politics, what is most interesting is what the various opinions say or do not say about religion. The core of the joint opinion's view of the freedom to be protected embodies a particular view of individual religiosity: "At the heart of liberty is the right to define one's own concept of existence, of meaning, of the universe, and of the mystery of human life. Beliefs about these matters could not define the attributes of personhood were they formed under compulsion of the State." Prior to viability, abortion must ultimately be a matter of choice, because the definition of life is a matter of choice. At the same time, the state can inform the woman that "there are philosophic and social [not religious] arguments of great weight that can be brought to bear in favor of continuing the pregnancy to full term." Only in the context of a minor woman's consultation with her family does this opinion note the relevance of "values and moral or religious principles" to this decision. In sum, the joint opinion implicitly recognizes that there is a religious dimension to the question of abortion, but it uses this dimension to insulate an individual woman's decision from state regulation and control. At the same time, the conception of religion employed in the opinion is itself quite controversial, emphasizing as it does human autonomy and independence.

In his partial concurrence, Stevens called attention to the religious dimension of the joint opinion's treatment of a woman's autonomy: "A woman considering abortion faces a difficult choice having serious and personal consequences of major importance to her own future—perhaps to the salvation of her own immortal soul.... The authority to make such traumatic and yet empowering decisions is an element of basic human dignity.... [A] woman's decision to terminate her pregnancy is nothing less than a matter of conscience." Abortion, then, is a matter of religious freedom. Stevens makes explicit what the joint opinion merely implies—that the First Amendment prohibits any attempt by a state to "promote a theological or sectarian interest" in its regulation of abortion.

By contrast, the four justices who would overrule *Roe* simply rejected this line of reasoning. Acknowledging that "the power of a woman to abort her unborn child . . . is a liberty of great importance to many women," Scalia explicitly eschews reliance on "anything so exalted as my views concerning the 'concept of existence, of meaning, of the universe, and of the mystery of human life.'" Instead, he and his brethren would rely on legal traditions to determine the meaning of liberty and on political processes to determine how such liberty might reasonably be regulated. Thus, Rehnquist argued that "it can scarcely be said that any deeply rooted tradition of relatively unrestricted abortion in our history supported the classification of the right to abortion as 'fundamental' under the Due Process Clause of the FOURTEENTH AMENDMENT." And Scalia insisted that "the Constitution says absolutely nothing about" abortion. The determination of the status of the fetus, in his view, is "a value judgment," but as such, it can be left to the political process and is not protected as a matter of individual autonomy. "Value judgments, after all, should be voted on, not dictated." Of course, in Scalia's view, even actions influenced by religious values can be subject to reasonable state regulation, so long as the regulation is generally applicable and not narrowly intended to interfere with religious practices (see *EMPLOYMENT DIVISION V. SMITH*). The accommodation of practices based on religious values ought to be left to the political process, not to the decisions of judges.

In sum, in this decision four justices were willing to elevate the religious dimension of the abortion issue only insofar as it dignifies an individual's private choice, but not when it might justify any significant limitations on pre-viability abortions. In these circumstances, the choice to abort (or not to abort) is a matter of religious freedom, protected from "undue" state interference. Four other justices would be willing to leave the regulation of abortion entirely to the political process, so long as a rational (not exclusively religious) basis could be advanced for the regulation.

See also FREE EXERCISE CLAUSE; *WEBSTER V. REPRODUCTIVE HEALTH SERVICES.*

—Joseph M. Knippenberg

pledge of allegiance

The pledge of allegiance was originally written in 1892 to commemorate the 400th anniversary of Christopher Columbus's expedition to the Americas. A committee of scholars years later credited the authorship of the pledge to Francis Bellamy, an ex-Baptist Christian Socialist minister who left the church because of the RACISM he encountered there. Published in *Youth's Companion* magazine, the pledge was backed by President Benjamin Harrison, who urged schoolchildren to recite the pledge on Columbus Day (more than 12 million reportedly did). Originally, Bellamy's pledge read:

> I pledge allegiance to my Flag, and to the Republic for which it stands: one Nation indivisible, With Liberty and Justice for all.

The pledge has been changed several times since 1892; in 1923 a meeting of the American Legion and Daughters of the American Revolution added "the Flag of the United States" to replace "my Flag," so that recent waves of immigrants would be clear about the flag to which they were pledging allegiance. A year later, the words "of America" were appended to the new phrase.

The pledge was given official status by the U.S. government in June 1942 as part of legislation to codify the use and display of the flag. Inspired by patriotism, the legislation was enacted soon after the entrance of the United States into World War II; it stated the pledge in near its current form, and addressed the manner in which it was to be invoked.

In 1954, during an escalation of tensions with the Soviet Union, Congress added the words "under God" to the pledge. The House and Senate both passed the resolution without debate and on a voice vote. At the same time, Senator Joseph McCarthy (R-Wisc.) was riding a wave of ANTICOMMUNISM, chairing public hearings and making accusations about communist infiltration of the U.S. government and liberal churches. The addition to the pledge, therefore, was meant to draw attention to the difference between the United States and the godless Soviet Union. Without the reference to God, many argued, the pledge could be employed in any country, even in the Soviet Union. At the signing ceremony for the legislation, President DWIGHT D. EISENHOWER proclaimed: "From this day forward, the millions of our schoolchildren will daily proclaim . . . the dedication of our nation and our people to the Almighty."

The pledge of allegiance and saluting the flag became embroiled in legal controversy first in 1940, when two JEHOVAH'S WITNESSES were expelled from a PENNSYLVANIA school for refusing to pledge allegiance to and salute the flag. In the ensuing court case, *MINERSVILLE V. GOBITIS*, a divided Supreme Court upheld the expulsion arguing that the need for social cohesion in wartime overrode the religious freedoms of a minority group. The decision was overturned just three years later in *WEST VIRGINIA BOARD OF EDUCATION V. BARNETTE*, in which the Court majority declared:

> If there is any fixed star in our constitutional constellation, it is that no official, high or petty, can prescribe what shall be orthodox in politics, nationalism, religion,

or other matters of opinion or force citizens to confess by word or act their faith therein. If there are any circumstances which permit an exception, they do not now occur to us.

Since that time, the Court has almost unfailingly worked to protect children from coercion in schools from local majorities that JAMES MADISON warned of in his Federalist #10 and *Memorial and Remonstrance.* Of course, this line of jurisprudence has also been some of the Court's most unpopular, banning state sponsored PRAYER IN PUBLIC SCHOOLS (*ENGEL V. VITALE*), moments of silence (*WALLACE V. JAFFREE*), prayer at graduation ceremonies (*LEE V. WEISMAN*), and before football games over the loudspeaker (*SANTA FE INDEPENDENT SCHOOL DISTRICT V. DOE*).

In this same spirit, atheist Mike Newdow challenged the mention of God in the pledge of allegiance as administered in the school near Sacramento, California, that his daughter attends. In June 2002, a federal three-judge panel of the ninth circuit court of appeals ruled 2-1 that the inclusion of "under God" in the pledge violates the establishment clause of the Constitution. The author of the majority opinion, Judge Goodwin, wrote:

> In the context of the pledge, the statement that United States is a nation, "under God" is an endorsement of religion. It is a profession of a religious belief, namely, a belief in monotheism . . . [T]he phrase "one nation under God" . . . is normative. To recite the pledge is to swear allegiance to the values for which the flag stands: unity, indivisibility, liberty, justice, and—since 1954— monotheism.

Judge Goodwin struck directly at the implementation of the pledge in public schools: "[T]he school district's practice of teacher-led recitation of the pledge aims to inculcate in students a respect for the ideals set forth in the pledge, and thus amounts to state endorsements of these ideals." Since the ideals include monotheism, according to Goodwin, reciting the pledge means advocating a particular religious belief.

Judge Fernandez, dissenting, articulated a common defense of God's presence in the pledge: "[W]hen all is said and done, the danger that 'under God' . . . will tend to bring about a theocracy or suppress someone's beliefs is so miniscule as to be de minimus. The danger that phrase presents to our First Amendment freedoms is picayune at most." In past rulings, the Supreme Court has hinted at agreement with Judge Fernandez, suggesting that the official motto "In God We Trust" found on currency had lost meaning and the potential to harm due to its repetition. The Court has not specifically addressed this issue, however. Ironically, the *Gobitis* case may serve as a defense for the current pledge—since no student is forced to recite the pledge, coercion is minimized.

The response to this ruling by the elected officials has been one of shock and horror. President GEORGE W. BUSH called it "ridiculous;" Senate Majority Leader Tom Daschle (D-S.D.) labeled it "nuts." A unanimous Senate and a nearly united House of Representatives (401-5) quickly went on record, passing resolutions backing the 1954 pledge. Due to this overwhelmingly hostile response, Judge Goodwin stayed his own decision pending a re-hearing by the full appeals court.

See also *MITCHELL V. HELMS*.

—Paul A. Djupe

political participation

Defining political participation is not an easy task, as the term has been used in a variety of ways. Sidney Verba, Kay Lehman Schlozman, and Henry Brady's definition has become rather influential in the social sciences: "activity that has the intent or effect of influencing government action—either directly by affecting the making or implementation of public policy or indirectly by influencing the selection of people who make those policies." While most agree that this is an adequate definition of political participation, there is much less consensus over how best to conceptualize such participation.

In the last three decades, social scientists have conceptualized political participation in at least three ways. First, certain scholars have focused on overall levels of political participation. This conceptual strategy aggregates such diverse political activities as voting and protesting into one general measure of political involvement. Second, some have dichotomized political activity into conventional and unconventional forms, with the former consisting of items such as attending party meetings, campaigning, contacting political elites, and the latter consisting of items such as protesting, demonstrating, boycotting, and committing violence. Finally, still others have emphasized the different "styles" or "modes" of political participation. These modes include, but are not limited to, contacting public officials, voting, working for political campaigns, acting collectively to solve community problems, protesting, and engaging in political discussions.

Studies examining the connection between religion and overall levels of political participation have largely used church attendance and participation in church activities—being involved in church decision making, groups trying to solve problems, or practicing civic skills (writing letters, participating in meetings where decisions are made, planning or chairing meetings, and giving presentations or speeches)—to measure religion's effect on participation. These measures are undoubtedly related, but their impact on overall political participation is quite different. Past research has found that although church attendance has a null or negative effect on overall levels of political activity, participating in church activities and practicing civic skills in churches have a positive impact on overall rates of political participation. In the case of overall political participation, then, it seems that being involved in church activities beyond attendance is what really matters.

Very little research has directly addressed the impact of religion on conventional political participation relative to participation of a more unconventional sort. When such research has been done, the impact of religion has been assessed primarily in terms of church attendance. For instance, Rory McVeigh and Christian Smith found that weekly church attendees were no more (or less) likely to participate in protest activities as compared with giving time or money to political organizations or candidates than less frequent church attendees. However, they found that individuals who attend church more than once a week were substantially more likely to protest relative to giving time or money to political organizations or candidates, when compared with individuals who attend church less than weekly. Thus, it appears that frequent church attendance is most important for distinguishing the politically conventional from the politically unconventional.

Of all the different political participatory modes, voting has received the most attention in the religion and politics literature. Similar to research on overall political participation and conventional and unconventional forms of political activity, the majority of this research has operationalized religion as church attendance or involvement in church activities. Generally, these studies have reported a positive relationship between these variables, with increased church attendance or involvement leading to increased voter turnout rates. Somewhat surprisingly, however, researchers have not found that practicing civic skills in churches is associated with voting.

When modes of political participation other than voting are considered, the effects of church attendance and involvement are less clear. On the one hand, researchers have found no relationship between church involvement and campaign activism (recruiting, publicly supporting, attending meetings, volunteering, and monetarily contributing to candidates, parties, or election-related groups), or between church attendance and making political contributions, working for political candidates, and time-based political acts, such as contacting public officials or volunteering for local councils of government. Others have even found that church attendance has a negative effect on communal collective action—working with others or forming groups to solve community problems—and discussing politics. On the other hand, participating in church activities has been reported to positively predict communal collective action, and practicing civic skills in churches has been shown to increase the likelihood of performing time-based political acts.

Although less well studied than church attendance or church involvement, the impact of two other religious variables on modes of political participation is briefly worth mentioning. First, discussing elections with friends at church has recently emerged as an important predictor of voter turnout rates. Second, internal religiosity—praying frequently, feeling close to God, and feeling committed to a particular religion—although unrelated to voting, positively predicts involvement in collective community action.

Further reading: Ayala, Louis. "Trained for Democracy: The Differing Effects of Voluntary and Involuntary Organizations on Political Participation." *Political Research Quarterly* 53 (2000): 99–115; Cassel, Carol. "Voluntary Associations, Churches, and Social Participation Theories of Turnout." *Social Science Quarterly* 80 (1999): 504–517; Djupe, Paul A., and J. Tobin Grant. "Religious Institutions and Political Participation in America." *Journal for the Scientific Study of Religion* 40, no. 2 (2001): 303–314; Guth, James L., Lyman A. Kellstedt, Corwin E. Smidt, and John C. Green. "Thunder on the Right? Religious Interest Group Mobilization in the 1996 Election." In *Interest Group Politics*. Edited by Allen J. Cigler and Burdett A. Loomis. Washington, D.C.: CQ Press, 1998; Harris, Fredrick. *Something Within*. New York: Oxford University Press, 1999; Hougland, James, and James Christenson. "Religion and Politics: The Relationship of Religious Participation to Political Efficacy and Involvement." *Sociology and Social Research* 67 (1983): 405–420; Marsh, Alan. *Political Action in Europe and the USA*. London: Macmillan, 1990; McVeigh, Rory, and Christian Smith. "Who Protests in American: An Analysis of Three Political Alternatives—Inaction, Institutionalized Politics, or Protest." *Sociological Forum* 14 (1999): 685–703; Milbrath, Lester W., and M. L. Goel. *Political Participation*. Chicago: Rand McNally, 1977; Peterson, Steven. "Church Participation and Political Participation: The Spillover Effect." *American Politics Quarterly* 20 (1992): 123–139; Verba, Sidney, and Norman H. Nie. *Participation in America*. New York: Harper and Row, 1972; Verba, Sidney, Kay Lehman Schlozman, and Henry E. Brady. *Voice and Equality*. Cambridge, Mass.: Harvard University Press, 1995; Wald, Kenneth D., Lyman A. Kellstedt, and David C. Leege. "Church Involvement and Political Behavior." In *Rediscovering the Religious Factor in American Politics*. Edited by David C. Leege and Lyman A. Kellstedt. Armonk, N.Y.: M. E. Sharpe, 1993.

—Kraig Beyerlein

polygamy

Polygamy refers to the practice of marrying more than one person at a time. More specifically, polygyny refers to a man having multiple wives, and polyandry refers to a woman having multiple husbands. The practice of polygyny in Western culture is most commonly associated with the 19th-century Church of Jesus Christ of LATTER-DAY SAINTS, or Mormons.

The Latter-day Saint Church (LDS) originated in the "Burned-over District" of western New York State where several religious revival movements experimented with different familial structures (see REVIVALISM). Lawrence Foster noted: "Nearly all the new religious groups in the area were involved to some extent with unorthodox marriage ideals and practices. Such movements as the Shakers and the Oneida Perfectionists were only the tip of the iceberg of dissatisfaction with prevailing marriage, family, and sex roles."

In 1843, JOSEPH SMITH, the founder of the Mormon Church, began to teach polygyny to his closest associates on an individual basis. Those who participated in these early polygy-

nous relationships were commanded to keep them secret. Inevitably, rumors of the practice leaked out, which fueled hostilities toward Smith and the church. Strong anti-Mormon sentiments eventually led to the killing of Smith in Illinois and the forced migration of his followers to Utah.

Once they were isolated in the Rocky Mountains, the Latter-day Saints no longer feared reprisal for openly practicing polygyny. Scholars have estimated the percentage of polygynous LDS families at 15 to 25 percent between 1852 and 1890.

As tales of Mormon polygyny filtered out across the country, public opinion turned against the Saints. In 1860, the Republican Party platform proclaimed opposition to the "twin relics of barbarism—Slavery and polygamy." Following public opinion, Congress passed the 1862 Morrill Anti Bigamy Act, which prevented the church from holding more than $50,000 in property and outlawed polygamy. The prevailing sentiment in Utah held that the act was unconstitutional, but to be safe, church property was deeded to individual leaders of the church. Although the law was not initially enforced, it was finally upheld by the Supreme Court in REYNOLDS V. UNITED STATES (1879).

Because the church had deeded its property to individuals, the Morrill Act was largely ineffective in curbing polygamy. Congress struck again with the 1880 Edmunds Act and the 1886 Edmunds-Tucker Act, which outlawed cohabitation, established fines for polygamy, prohibited inheritance in polygamous families, and disincorporated the LDS Church. Between 1884 and 1889, some 1,300 Mormon males had been imprisoned for polygamy, and many others were forced into hiding to avoid prosecution (Merrill 1990: 12). These laws finally forced the church to disband and turn over its property or to give up polygamy. These three statutes were upheld by the Supreme Court in *Church of Jesus Christ of Latter Day Saints v. US* (1890), which ordered the church to wind up its affairs and hand over its properties to the U.S. government.

At this point, Wilford Woodruff, who had become the head of the church in 1887, declared that the church would no longer sanction plural marriages. However, individuals already living in polygamous relationships were not forced to divorce. While the church had made its statement against polygamy, the stigma of the practice did not fade.

For example, in 1898, Brigham H. Roberts, a leader in the LDS Church and a polygamist, was elected to serve in the U.S. House of Representatives. Opponents swiftly mobilized, arguing that electing a polygamist to Congress would alter the institution of marriage in the United States. The House voted to prevent Roberts from taking his seat.

In 1903, the Utah State Legislature elected Republican Reed Smoot to the U.S. Senate. Smoot was a member of the church's Quorum of the Twelve Apostles, but he was not a polygamist. Still, his appointment to the Senate fanned the waning embers of antipolygamist and anti-Mormon sentiments. Smoot was successfully seated, but was challenged in hearings that lasted for three years. Interestingly, Republicans rallied around Smoot. Since the church's early years in

Nauvoo, Illinois, Latter-day Saints had overwhelmingly sided with the Democratic Party. Republicans saw Smoot's election (and influence as a Mormon leader) as a way to steal Utah from the Democrats. As Democrats voiced fears about the political power Smoot could wield through his position in the Mormon Church, Republicans became increasingly convinced that Smoot would have as much power as the Democrats feared. The resolution to expel Smoot failed in a vote largely on party lines.

During the Smoot hearings, the LDS Church issued a second document confirming its stance against polygamous marriage. But some church members were disaffected by the abandonment of polygamy. Splinter groups formed polygamous colonies in southern Utah and northern Arizona. Until the 1950s, the federal government pursued legal action against these groups, including raids on polygamous settlements. These colonies still exist and continue to grow, but bringing legal action against them is difficult, and seldom pursued.

See also COUNCIL OF FIFTY; MORMON EXTERMINATION ORDER; YOUNG, BRIGHAM.

Further reading: Altman, Irwin, and Joseph Ginat. *Polygamous Families in Contemporary Society.* Cambridge, Mass.: Cambridge University Press, 1996; Embry, Jessie L. *Mormon Polygamous Families: Life in the Principle.* Salt Lake City: University of Utah Press, 1987; Foster, Lawrence. *Religion and Sexuality: Three American Communal Experiments of the Nineteenth Century.* New York: Oxford University Press, 1981; Merrill, Milton R. *Reed Smoot: Apostle in Politics.* Logan: Utah State University Press, 1990.

—Damon M. Cann

pornography

Pornography remains so politically controversial a topic that the term itself proves difficult to define. A deliberately neutral definition is provided by Juson and Lillington: "graphic depictions of sex between individuals conveyed through the medium of videos, films, books, or magazines . . . [whose] function is to sexually arouse its viewers."

What is "pornographic" must be understood as distinct from what is legally "obscene." Under the First Amendment, only obscene materials may be subject to government regulation. The Supreme Court spent many agonizing years attempting to draw a firm line between pornography and obscenity to delineate what remained protected by the First Amendment and what might be proscribed. In *Miller v. California* (1973), the Supreme Court finally established the constitutional test for obscenity that remains in effect today. Under *Miller*, "obscenity" is to be determined by:

(a) whether 'the average person, applying contemporary community standards' would find that the work, taken as a whole, appeals to the prurient interest [cites omitted]; (b) whether the work depicts or describes, in a patently offensive way, sexual conduct specifically defined by the applicable state law; and (c) whether the work, taken as a whole, lacks serious literary, artistic, political, or scientific value (24).

Despite pornography's protection under the First Amendment, battles continue to rage across the country over the production and distribution of sexually oriented materials. For example, two high-level federal commissions have studied pornography in American society. Established by ideologically opposed presidential administrations, the committees reached ideologically opposed conclusions and recommendations. President Lyndon Johnson's Presidential Commission on Obscenity and Pornography released its findings in 1970. This commission found pornography to inflict no evident harm on society and recommended that most pornography and obscenity regulations across the country be abolished. The more socially conservative administration of RONALD REAGAN established a second commission to revisit the issue. The Attorney General's Commission on Pornography (also known as the Meese Commission, after Attorney General Edwin Meese) finished its work in 1986. While the members of this commission could not reach agreement on a single definition for the term *pornography*, the commission determined that at least some pornography was detrimental and that greater efforts should be made to regulate and eliminate pornographic materials from American society. Both commissions were subjected to significant criticism.

Beginning in the 1980s, a controversial alliance was formed between some FEMINISTS and the moral CONSERVATIVE community to combat pornography as a mechanism for oppressing women and thus as a form of gender discrimination. Feminist scholars Andrea Dworkin and Catharine MacKinnon drafted antipornography legislation that was debated in cities across the country, promoted in part by moral conservatives. In 1984, Indianapolis passed an antipornography ordinance based on the Dworkin-MacKinnon approach. Because it sought to regulate materials that could not be classified as "obscene," the ordinance was later struck down as an unconstitutional content-based regulation of speech (*American Booksellers Association v. Hudnut* [7th Cir. 1985]). This feminist attack on pornography, with its ensuing feminist–social conservative alliance, remains a divisive issue within the feminist community.

The Internet has become the latest battleground in the war over pornography. In particular, concerns have been raised regarding how developing technology has made sexually oriented materials more easily accessible to children. Congress's first attempt to regulate sexually oriented materials on the Internet was struck down by the Supreme Court in 1997 in *Reno v. AMERICAN CIVIL LIBERTIES UNION* (1997). Known as the Communications Decency Act, this early legislation painted in broad strokes. For example, the law banned transmitting "obscene or indecent" materials over the Internet to anyone under 18 years of age. The Supreme Court declared such a provision to be unconstitutionally vague and too broadly written to survive a First Amendment analysis. Additional court challenges to state and federal Internet pornography policies continue to work their way through the court system.

See also CHRISTIAN COALITION; CONCERNED WOMEN FOR AMERICA; MORAL MAJORITY.

Further reading: Juson, Justine, and Brenda Lillington. "R. v. Butler: Recognizing the Expressive Value and the Harm in Pornography." *Golden Gate University Law Review* 23 (1993): 651–678.

—Staci L. Beavers

prayer in public schools

The United States has a strong tradition of sponsoring religious activities in public school settings. State sponsorship of religion in schools was a customary practice until the 1960s, with readings from the Bible, religious teaching, and recitation of prayer as primary staples of public religious education. In the early 1960s, however, several interest groups that favored halt-ing state-sponsored religious instruction brought several cases to the Supreme Court. Their initial efforts have resulted in a series of cases spanning several decades. In particular, the conflict over prayer implicates the ESTABLISHMENT CLAUSE of the First Amendment to the U.S. Constitution. In general, the Court has viewed the establishment clause as erecting a "wall of separation" between church and state. This metaphor, adopted by the Court in *EVERSON V. BOARD OF EDUCATION* (1947), has become "the fixed star" guiding the Court's understanding of what constitutes impermissible state action regarding religion, including state-sponsored prayer in public schools.

Modern establishment clause jurisprudence began with *Everson*, a case having nothing to do with prayer in schools. But the legal doctrines emerging from it and subsequent cases provided the Court with the logic for determining whether state-sponsored prayer violated the establishment clause. In *Everson*, the Court noted that "state power is no more to be used so as to handicap religions, than it is to favor them." However, the Court noted that the wall between church and state was both "high and impregnable." Further, while the Court determined that government need not show

Football players at Odessa High School in Odessa, Texas, pray in their locker room, September 1, 2000, in an unsanctioned prayer session. On June 19, 2000, the Supreme Court handed down a ruling banning school-sanctioned pregame prayer. *(Joe Raedle/Newsmakers)*

"callous indifference" (ZORACH V. CLAUSON, 1952) to religion, it maintained a generally rigid view of the establishment clause. The Court noted that government may not provide "invaluable aid" (MCCOLLUM V. BOARD OF EDUCATION, 1948) to religion, or aid that is nonsecular in purpose (BOARD OF EDUCATION V. ALLEN, 1968). Finally, in LEMON V. KURTZMAN (1971), the Court formalized the doctrine it had articulated in these and other cases. To pass scrutiny by the Court, any state action regarding religion must have a "secular legislative purpose," a "neutral primary effect" on the advancement or inhibition of religion, and may not promote "excessive entanglement" between government and religion. This set of requirements, commonly known as the *Lemon* test, became the hallmark of Supreme Court religion clause jurisprudence.

The Court first considered prayer in public schools when it heard the case ENGEL V. VITALE (1962). In this case, a set of interest groups preferring a separationist interpretation of the establishment clause challenged the New York State statute requiring public school teachers to lead students in prayer each day. The prayer was written and approved by the New York State Board of Regents, and participation by students was voluntary. In overturning the New York statute, the Supreme Court noted that "it is no part the business of government to compose official prayers for any group of Americans to recite as part of a religious program carried out by the government." In this case, however, the Court failed to articulate a standard for reviewing other acts of government relating to prayer and religious practice.

The Court remedied this issue the following term when it decided ABINGTON TOWNSHIP V. SCHEMPP (1963). This case involved Bible readings and recitation of the Lord's Prayer in public schools. In striking down the use of Bible recitations in public schools, the Court articulated what would later become the first two prongs of the *Lemon* test. Any state action regarding religion must have "a secular legislative purpose and a primary effect that neither advances nor inhibits religion." Justice Stewart, dissenting from the decision, rejected the requirement that government act neutrally toward religion. He stated that any infringement of the establishment clause must involve government coercion. That students might opt out of the religious exercise was an important consideration. The Rehnquist Court has picked up this rebuttal as the basis for revising the standard articulated in *Abington v. Schempp* and formalized in *Lemon v. Kurtzman*.

The Court did not hear another major prayer in schools case until 1985. In WALLACE V. JAFFREE (1985), the Court considered a challenge to a state-mandated "moment of silence" and struck down the state action, ruling that such state-mandated times of meditation during the school day violated the "secular purpose" prong of the *Lemon* test. But out of *Wallace* came the first stirrings of displeasure with what then Justice Rehnquist called its "rigidly separationist" interpretation of the First Amendment's establishment clause. Rehnquist urged the Court to throw off the metaphor of a wall of separation and abandon *Lemon* as the test for determining unconsti-

tutionality. Further, Justices O'Connor and Powell, while concurring with the majority, suggested that moment of silence legislation could be constructed in such a way that it would not violate *Lemon*.

The issue of prayer in schools shifted ground from debate over the *Lemon* test to concerns about state coercion. In LEE V. WEISMAN (1992), the Court struck down state-sponsored religious invocations in high school graduation ceremonies. However, the majority decision did not consider whether religious invocations violated the *Lemon* test. Instead, the Court concluded that "the school district's supervision and control of a high school graduation ceremony places public pressure on attending students." While three concurring justices in this case argued for use of the *Lemon* test, others dissented, not from the use of a "coercion standard," but from the way the majority applied that standard.

In the early 1990s, the Court took up a series of cases involving equal access policies, some of which involved prayer in schools. The first in this line of cases involved a challenge to the EQUAL ACCESS ACT, passed in 1984 by Congress. This act required public schools to allow religious student-led clubs access to school facilities if those schools also allowed secular clubs to use facilities after hours. Although not the central issue in WESTSIDE COMMUNITY BOARD OF EDUCATION V. MERGENS (1990), prayer in schools played a major role in arguments presented to the Court. In particular, lawyers for the Board of Education argued that allowing student-led Bible clubs to use school facilities violated the establishment clause because students might pray or read the Bible aloud. The lawyer for the Bible clubs ignored whether the statute violated the *Lemon* test, and argued that restricting student-led prayer would violate FREE EXERCISE of religion and speech. The Court sided with the student Bible clubs, finding that restriction of student-led Bible clubs had a tendency to remove religion's capacity to defend itself within the educational context of an open exchange of ideas.

The Court continued to take equal access cases through the early 1990s. In each case, the Court appeared willing to risk establishment, or multiple establishments, of religion in schools so long as equal access was granted to religious expressions, including student-led prayer. But the Court did not formally consider the issue of prayer in schools until eight years after *Lee v. Weisman*. In SANTA FE INDEPENDENT SCHOOL DISTRICT V. DOE (2000), the Court considered religious invocations at extracurricular events (in this case, high school football games). Although the state involvement was minimal (the school district claimed no participation in crafting the prayer or selecting who delivered it), the Court found that the policy violated the establishment clause. The Court rested its decision on the role the school district played in authorizing the practice, on the coercive nature of the policy, and on the *Lemon* test's secular purpose requirement.

Further reading: Ivers, Gregg. *Redefining the First Freedom.* New Brunswick, N.J.: Transaction, 1993; Sorauf, Frank

J. *The Wall of Separation.* Princeton, N.J.: Princeton University Press, 1976.

—Hans J. Hacker

Presbyterian Church in America (PCA)

The Presbyterian Church in America (PCA) is a relatively new Protestant denomination, yet it traces its roots to the Protestant Reformation. The denomination has a strong commitment to EVANGELISM, missionary work at home and abroad (see MISSIONARIES), and Christian education. The PCA organized in December 1973, with a determination to be "faithful to the Scriptures, true to the reformed faith, and obedient to the Great Commission." It separated from the Presbyterian Church in the United States (the southern branch of Presbyterianism) in opposition to what it perceived to be theological liberalism denying the deity of Jesus Christ and the inerrancy and authority of Scripture. The PCA holds to a traditional position on the role of women in church offices, and women are not eligible for ordination.

The Presbyterian Church in America has a firm commitment to the doctrinal standards that have been significant in Presbyterianism since 1645, namely, the *Westminster Confession of Faith* and the *Larger and Shorter Catechisms.* These standards express the distinctives of CALVINISM and the Reformed tradition; foremost among them is the unique authority of the Bible. Calvin and those who followed him based all their claims on *sola scriptura:* the Scriptures alone. This included the doctrine of biblical inspiration, which is a special act of the Holy Spirit guiding the writers of the books of Scriptures in their original autographs so that the words would convey the thoughts God wished humans to know. In the 1920s, the Presbyterian Church split over theology. This debate resulted in a loosening of the church's doctrinal standards, the reorganization of Princeton Theological Seminary, the founding of Westminster Theological Seminary, and the eventual birth of the Presbyterian Church in America.

The Bible is held by PCA officers to be an infallible rule of faith and life, and the concept of infallibility has included the idea of inerrancy. The church maintains the historic polity of Presbyterian governance, namely, rule by presbyters, or elders, and the graded assemblies, or courts. The session rules the local church; the presbytery controls regional matters; and the general assembly holds charge at the national level. The PCA offices in Atlanta, Georgia, coordinate four ministries carried out by program committees: Mission to the World, Mission to North America, Reformed University Ministries on college campuses, and Christian Education and Publication. The denomination maintains a conference center in Rosman, North Carolina; Covenant College in Lookout Mountain, Tennessee; and Covenant Theological Seminary in St. Louis.

PCA is one of the faster-growing denominations in the United States, increasing from 250 congregations with 50,000 members at its inception to over 1,400 churches and missions in the United States and Canada. There were about 300,000 communicant and noncommunicant members of the PCA in 2000, as well as more than 520 missionaries in over 60 countries. Because of a unique relationship between Mission to the World and more than 30 missionary organizations, PCA supports another 690 missionaries in 130 countries around the world. In addition, more than 100 PCA-ordained pastors serve as chaplains in the military.

Presbyterian and reformed beliefs have a special relationship to American history and culture. New England and the middle colonies were originally settled by European Calvinists whose beliefs about human depravity and the limits of government influenced debates about the Constitution and are reflected in documents like *Federalist #10,* where JAMES MADISON writes, "the latent causes of faction are thus sown in the nature of man." Eight presidents of the United States have been Presbyterian, and it can be argued that Calvinism influenced a host of others, especially the EPISCOPALIANS and Congregationalists who took office in the early days of the republic.

PCA believes that ministers and church officers should affirm without compromise the traditional beliefs of Christianity. A summary of the importance of this conviction was provided in a 1924 article in the *New York Times.* J. Gresham Machen, who would later help found Westminster Seminary, wrote that the ultimate guarantor of freedom in any society was not courts and legal guarantees: "freedom must be written not merely in the constitution but in the people's heart. And it can be written in the heart . . . only as a result of the redeeming work of Christ." For PCA, the connection between faith and political power lies in the principle that if true faith is abandoned in the church, then civilization will succumb to the bondage of secular thought.

See also DUTCH REFORMED TRADITION; PRESBYTERIAN CHURCH USA.

—J. David Woodard

Presbyterian Church USA

Founded June 10, 1983, by a reuniting of the United Presbyterian Church in the United States of America (UPCUSA) and the Presbyterian Church in the United States (PCUS), Presbyterian Church USA (PCUSA) is the largest mainline Presbyterian denomination, containing 3,485,332 members in 11,216 congregations. The church operates Geneva Press and Westminster John Knox Press, publishes 11 periodicals, including *Presbyterians Today* and *Church and Society,* and sponsors 68 Presbyterian-related colleges and 11 seminaries. Ecumenical in orientation and theologically Reformed in the Calvinist tradition, PCUSA is a confessional and a connectional church, distinguished by the representation of elders in its governance.

The Presbyterian Church USA is a descendant of the Presbyterian General Assembly and the Presbytery that organized in Philadelphia around 1706. During the 17th and 18th centuries, the Presbytery became an influential force in American religion. In the 1830s, Presbyterians split into the Old School and New School assemblies. Old School Presbyterians held firm to the *Westminster Confession of Faith* and were against social reforms such as abolitionism, while New Schoolers opposed the strict Calvinistic doctrine and discipline of the Old School Presbyterians. With the outbreak of the Civil War, New School and Old School Churches divided regionally. At the conclusion of the Civil War, however, Southern factions merged and formed the Presbyterian Church in the United States (PCUS). Similarly, in the North, Old School and New School factions merged, reuniting into the Presbyterian Church in the U.S.A. (PC-USA). PC-USA focused heavily on mission work among blacks in the South and, after reuniting with the Cumberland Presbyterians, became a national party with a membership of 1.4 million by 1910. In 1958, PC-USA merged with the United Presbyterian Church of North America (UPCNA), and formed the United Presbyterian Church in the United States of America (UPCUSA).

During the late 19th and early 20th centuries, theological conservatives withdrew from what they viewed as increasingly "liberal" Presbyterian churches and formed their own conservative denominations. For example, in 1939, under the leadership of J. Gresham Macham, conservative members of UPCUSA established the Orthodox Presbyterian Church; and in 1974, conservatives in the southern PCUS founded the PRESBYTERIAN CHURCH IN AMERICA (PCA). Of particular significance, the departure of conservatives from PCUS allowed the denomination to join with the liberal UPCUSA to form the PCUSA in 1983. Interestingly, this union healed the regional division among Presbyterians lingering since the Civil War.

According to the PCUSA *Book of Order*, the church exists to advance the gospel, worship God, shelter, nurture, and provide fellowship for Christians, preserve truth, promote social righteousness, and exhibit the Kingdom of God to the world. To these ends, PCUSA is committed to evangelism, local and global missionary activities, civic volunteering, and advancing the cause of the poor and the oppressed through direct aid and supporting social relief legislation.

Despite strong theological traditions and commitments, PCUSA has struggled to maintain unity among parishioners. Issues concerning the ordination of women and homosexuals, interpretation of the Trinity, and biblical inerrancy have generated bitter controversy within the church. To address these tensions, the Theological Task Force was created in 2002 with the goal of discovering a basis for "peace, unity, and purity" within the church, and responses to "current issues that divide the church." Despite recent efforts to unify parishioners, PCUSA will no doubt continue to struggle for self-identity and unity. According to *The Yearbook of American and Canadian Churches 2002*, PCUSA continues to experience a sharp decline in membership (2.87 percent between 1997 and 2000).

Among Protestants, PCUSA has been an important member of the Republican Party coalition. However, while fiscally conservative, PCUSA parishioners are more socially liberal than other Protestants, especially concerning ABORTION. Moreover, PCUSA officially advocates elimination of the death penalty, the establishment of effective gun control laws, the protection of homosexual legal rights (although the church opposes homosexual ordination), and support of social welfare spending. Clearly, these policy positions place PCUSA at odds with other political conservatives in America and perhaps is an explanation for why PCUSA parishioners support Republican presidential candidates at rates considerably less than that of other mainline Protestants and evangelicals.

See also DUTCH REFORMED TRADITION; SOCIAL JUSTICE.

Further reading: Balmer, Randall Herbert. *Grant Us Courage: Travels along the Mainline of American Protestantism.* New York: Oxford University Press, 1996; Balmer, Randall, John R. Fitzmier, and Henry W. Bowden. *The Presbyterians.* New York: Praeger, 1994; Kellstedt, Lyman A., and John C. Green. "Knowing God's Many People: Denominational Preference and Political Behavior." In *Rediscovering the Religious Factor in American Politics.* Edited by David C. Leege, Lyman A. Kellstedt, et al. Armonk, N.Y.: M. E. Sharpe, 1993; PCUSA News Service. URL: http://www.pcusa.org/pcnews/oldnews/2002/02087.htm, 2001; Weston, William J. *Presbyterian Pluralism: Competition in a Protestant House.* Knoxville: University of Tennessee Press, 1997.

—Franklyn C. Niles

Prince v. Massachusetts 321 U.S. 158 (1944)

In this landmark case—one in a series brought by members of the JEHOVAH'S WITNESSES in the 1940s—the Supreme Court voted 5-4 to affirm Sarah Prince's convictions for violating Massachusetts's child labor laws.

As the aunt and legal guardian of nine-year-old Betty Simmons, Prince had been convicted of permitting her niece to distribute copies of the Jehovah's Witness publications *Watchtower* and *Consolation* on the streets of Brockton. Prince acknowledged that state law made it a crime for parents or guardians to permit minors under their control "to sell, expose or offer for sale any newspapers, magazines, periodicals or any other articles of merchandise of any description" on the street. But she argued that the law was unconstitutional.

The state's high court disagreed, concluding: "We think that freedom of the press and of religion is subject to incidental regulation to the slight degree involved in the prohibition of the selling of religious literature in streets and public places by boys under twelve and girls under eighteen. . . ."

Before the U.S. Supreme Court, Prince again raised her First Amendment right to freedom of religion and added a "claim of parental right" as secured by the Fourteenth Amendment's due process clause as well.

Writing for the majority, Justice Wiley Blount Rutledge Jr. noted two opposing considerations. On the one hand, he said, the Court had recognized that "the state has a wide range of power for limiting parental freedom and authority in things affecting the child's welfare; and that this includes, to some extent, matters of conscience and religious conviction." On the other hand, the Court had also previously acknowledged "the rights of children to exercise their religion, and of parents to give them religious training and to encourage them in the practice of religious belief."

Moreover, he thought the Court's decision in PIERCE V. SOCIETY OF SISTERS (1925) (upholding parents' authority to send their children to Roman Catholic rather than public schools) and other cases made it clear that there is a "private realm of family life which the state cannot enter."

In the end, however, Rutledge concluded that the scales were tipped in favor of upholding the state law in this case, and he stressed two factors that led him to that conclusion. First, the Massachusetts law protected children from employment, and second, it protected them from "the street." He wrote:

> The state's authority over children's activities is broader than over like actions of adults. This is peculiarly true of public activities and in matters of employment. A democratic society rests, for its continuance, upon the healthy, well-rounded growth of young people into full maturity as citizens, with all that implies. It may secure this against impeding restraints and dangers, within a broad range of selection. Among evils most appropriate for such action are the crippling effects of child employment, more especially in public places, and the possible harms arising from other activities subject to all the diverse influences of the street.

Justice Jackson dissented to say that although he too would like to affirm the state court, he thought a contrary result was required by the Court's recent decision in *Murdock v. Pennsylvania* (1943), which he tartly described as holding that "going upon the streets to accost the public is the same thing for application of public law as withdrawing to a private structure for religious worship."

—Charles F. Williams

Prison Fellowship

Prison Fellowship (PF), a Christian ministry dedicated to serving incarcerated individuals and their families, was founded in 1976. Utilizing thousands of volunteers, it advocates for rehabilitation and restitution as part of its mission of prison reform. The founder and chair of the organization, CHARLES COLSON (1931–), who was a special counsel to President Richard M. Nixon from 1969 to 1973, voluntarily pleaded guilty to obstruction of justice in the Daniel Ellsberg case and served seven months of a one- to three-year prison sentence. Before serving his term, Colson, a former marine, had a BORN-AGAIN EXPERIENCE he described in his aptly named book, *Born Again*.

Colson argues that crime is a moral and spiritual problem requiring moral and spiritual solutions. The organization believes that offenders do not simply need rehabilitation; they require regeneration of a sinful heart. Regarding restitution, Prison Fellowship maintains that crime victims desire more than survival after a trauma; they "crave new life filled with hope and joy." Also, PF attempts to assist prisoners' families, who as PF argues, "need more than a sprinkling of social services to help them get by; they need to be washed clean of shame and despair, and infused with new confidence to move forward."

Prison Fellowship operates groups in hundreds of U.S. prisons, offering Christian worship and revival services as well as Bible studies and educational training—with the permission and often encouragement of prison officials. It also has branches in 88 additional countries, organized by PF International. PF's mission is "To exhort, equip, and assist the Church in its ministry to prisoners, ex-prisoners, victims, and their families, and in its promotion of biblical standards of justice in the criminal justice system." In 1983, Colson established Justice Fellowship, now the nation's largest faith-based criminal justice reform group. Angel Tree, a nationally recognized program provides Christmas presents to more than 500,000 children of inmates annually on behalf of their incarcerated parents. Although based on EVANGELICAL Christian principles, the institution and its founder, Colson, attempt to use ECUMENICAL Christian ties to promote prison reform more broadly among Christians. His 1987 book, *Kingdoms in Conflict,* was a best-selling directive to the Christian community on the proper relationships of church and state, and it positioned Colson as a centrist evangelical voice for balanced Christian political activism. Colson, winner of the Templeton Prize for Progress in Religion in 1993, is the spiritual and practical leader of this movement turned organization.

Further reading: Colson, Charles. *Kingdoms in Conflict.* Grand Rapids, Mich.: Zondervan, 1987; ———. *Born Again.* Old Tappan, N.J.: Chosen Books, 1973.

—Robert Wilson-Black

Prohibition Party

The Prohibition Party, America's oldest "third party," was organized in 1867. Rooted in the early-19th-century temperance movement as well as the midcentury ABOLITIONIST MOVEMENT, the new party advocated an agenda that included the prohibition of the "manufacture, transportation, and sale of alcoholic beverages."

The movement to create a Prohibition Party was fueled by the social dislocations of post–Civil War American society, in which industrialization, government corruption, and population growth generated widespread anomie and concern over the loss of traditional values. The bright hopes of the abolitionists had been dashed by the corruption of the Grant administration. Since neither the Democratic nor the Republican Party of the day seemed willing or able to promote a pro-family, pro-temperance agenda, concerned citizens formed the new party, which drew support from a diverse array of individuals, including former abolitionists, supporters of women's rights, and "dry" Republicans.

The Prohibition Party held its first national convention in Chicago in 1869, when it organized its initial state-level activities, and held its first national nominating convention in 1872. Some supporters of the new Prohibition Party saw parallels to the formation of the Republican Party a decade earlier. The keynoter at the 1872 convention asserted that "Slavery is gone but drunkenness stays."

The Prohibition Party's first forays into presidential politics produced meager results. Between 1872, when the Prohibition Party fielded its first presidential candidate, through the 1880 election, public support for Prohibition candidates was minimal. The party's first three candidates, James Black (1872), Green C. Smith (1876), and Neal Dow (1880), each attracted less than 1 percent of the popular vote nationwide. The party's fortunes improved, however, in 1884, when it nominated Kansan John P. St. John as its standard-bearer. At the time, Kansas was among the most socially and politically turbulent states in the United States, and St. John, a former Republican governor of the state, saw the Prohibition Party as a vehicle to generate reform. In the 1884 election, St. John garnered 150,000 popular votes, 10 times more than any of his Prohibition Party predecessors had received. Moreover, in subsequent elections through 1920, Prohibition Party presidential candidates equaled or exceeded this total, receiving 150,000–250,000 votes nationwide. From 1920 to today, the party has continued to field candidates and contest elections, but it has never regained the prominence it earned in the early 20th century.

From its founding until 1896, the Prohibition Party officially adopted a "broad-gauge" platform that extended far beyond opposition to the sale, manufacture, and distribution of alcohol. Party platforms included such progressive concepts as advocacy of civil service reform, women's rights, and the direct election of U.S. senators. During this period, party leaders made frequent attempts to join forces with the Populist Party but were rebuffed because of the Populists' refusal to advocate the prohibition of alcohol.

The 1896 convention, however, was captured by "narrow-gaugers," who wanted the party to focus exclusively on prohibition. This capture led to the exodus of many "broad-gaugers" from the party, some of whom formed a competing party called the National or Free Silver Prohibition Party. From 1896 until 1920, tension developed between the Prohibition Party and competing pro-temperance forces, including the WOMEN'S CHRISTIAN TEMPERANCE UNION, the Anti-Saloon League, and political activist Carrie Nation, as these forces demonstrated that they could achieve success outside of normal partisan politics.

Following the repeal of Prohibition in 1933, the party broadened its appeal, advocating states rights, the right-to-life, military preparedness, limitation of immigration, local control of education, religious liberty, and school prayer. Nonetheless, its electoral appeal nationwide remained exceedingly limited.

Ironically, the Prohibition Party's failure to flourish can be traced to the nationwide adoption of much of its initial platform, even if such adoption largely occurred in spite of, rather than because of, its best efforts. The ratification of the Seventeenth Amendment in 1913 (direct election of senators), the Eighteenth Amendment in 1919 (prohibition), and the Nineteenth Amendment in 1920 (women's suffrage) weakened the party by prompting supporters to question its reason for being. In recent years, party members have had difficulty distinguishing themselves from more conservative elements of the Republican Party.

Further reading: Clark, Norman H. *Deliver Us from Evil.* New York: Norton, 1976; Prohibition Party on the Web: URL: http://www.prohibitionists.org/; Spitzer, Robert J. "Prohibition Party." In *Political Parties & Elections in the United States.* Edited by L. Sandy Maisel and Charles Bassett. New York: Garland, 1991.

—James M. Penning

Promise Keepers

During the 1990s, Promise Keepers emerged as one of the largest contemporary men's religious organizations in the United States. Founded in 1990 by former University of Colorado football coach Bill McCartney, Promise Keepers has grown exponentially over the past decade. Attendance at stadium events has grown from fewer than 5,000 men in the first year to more than 4 million over the past 10 years. Membership is encouraged through events that take place in football stadiums across the country, although the organization also strongly encourages men to form small groups in their communities and churches after attending stadium events. Despite financial difficulties in April 1998 that resulted in the layoff of its paid national staff, the organization has continued to grow and has expanded into other countries (including Canada, Australia, Germany, New Zealand, South Africa, and the United Kingdom.

The financial problems faced by Promise Keepers, according to organizational literature, were caused primarily by a dramatic shift from a fee-based income structure to a donation-based income stream. To make its events more accessible to men of various financial means, the organization decided to waive the registration fee for stadium events. After a few months, Promise Keepers announced it was again financially stable and planned to continue to be a donation-based organization. It is not insignificant that an organization that reports an operating budget of $1.7 million per month and a conference cost of $1.1 million (each) managed to stabilize so quickly by calling on its members and their churches to send donations. Yet despite plans to remain donation-based, in 2001 Promise Keepers announced that it would again be charging registration fees for stadium events.

Promise Keepers strongly emphasizes racial equality and the need for what it terms "racial reconciliation." White men are

Men form a show of support by placing their arms on each others shoulders during the Promise Keepers 2002 Conference in Miami, Florida. *(Joe Raedle/Getty Images)*

exhorted to seek forgiveness for the sin of RACISM; men of color are encouraged to share testimony concerning the unjust effects of racial discrimination. This position has been praised by some groups committed to SOCIAL JUSTICE, since many Christian Right organizations have been criticized for their lack of concern about racial inequality. On the other hand, some critics, including some black activist organizations, see this apparent egalitarian effort as a threat to the unity and power of the black community and have spoken out against Promise Keepers.

A further area of criticism has come from those who oppose Promise Keepers' male-only membership position. Promise Keepers makes no apology for being an all-male organization. Organization leaders claim that this is an essential element for carrying out their goals, one of which is a reaffirmation of traditional or patriarchal familial relationships. This position has made them the target of political opposition and protest by a number of FEMINIST organizations.

Promise Keepers are committed to an ideology of the traditional family and traditional male gender roles, although this ideology is distinctly nontraditional in its emphasis on racial reconciliation. At the same time, members of Promise Keepers are committed to social action, whether this takes the form

of community work, church work, or developing relationships with other men to advance racial reconciliation. Organizational literature states that a Promise Keeper is committed to (1) honoring Jesus Christ through prayer, worship, and obedience to His Word, in the power of the Holy Spirit; (2) pursuing vital relationships with a small group of men, understanding that he needs brothers to help him keep his promises; (3) practicing spiritual, moral, ethical, and sexual purity; (4) building strong marriages and families through love, protection, and biblical values; (5) supporting the mission of his church by honoring and praying for his pastor and by actively giving his time and resources; (6) reaching beyond any racial and denominational barriers to demonstrate the power of biblical unity; (7) influencing his world and being obedient to the Great Commandment (Mark 12:30–31) and the Great Commission (Matthew 28:19–20).

Among those groups that have been associated with the Christian Right, Promise Keepers seems an anomaly. It strongly denies any link to the CHRISTIAN COALITION or other Christian Right organizations, yet its religious commitments and goals have led many to classify it as part of the Christian Right. A further label it has resisted is that of a "political" organization. Organizational literature states in numerous places that Promise Keepers is apolitical, has no political agenda, and does not engage in lobbying or public policy activities. However, its well-known men-only position and the ideology it encourages men to embrace, which includes a commitment to traditional patriarchal family values as well as social and community action, has led some scholars to conclude that its agenda is political by definition, despite its lack of overt political activity targeted at any legislature.

A final element that would seem to make the organization anomalous is its insistence that it does not want to continue to grow as an organization based on the structure it currently exhibits. Its goal, as it is defined by organizational leaders, is to have enough men in enough churches around the United States carrying out the "ministry to men" originally espoused by McCartney that the formal organization would no longer need to conduct stadium events to recruit and maintain members. Organizational literature does not make clear the impact this would have on Promise Keepers' current international efforts. Despite this goal, Promise Keepers still holds numerous stadium events and has added events in smaller venues, so it is not possible to measure its progress toward the goal of integration at the local level in churches across the United States.

See also PROMISE KEEPERS "STAND IN THE GAP" RALLY.

—R. Lorraine Bernotsky

Promise Keepers "Stand in the Gap" Rally

During the 1990s, PROMISE KEEPERS became one of the largest contemporary men's religious organizations in the United States. One striking feature of Promise Keepers is its insistence that it is not political. Organizational literature states: "Promise keepers is politically neutral and is not politically motivated in any way." This is strenuously emphasized at stadium events, in organizational literature, and perhaps, ironically, at "Stand in the Gap: A Sacred Assembly of Men," held on October 4, 1997. At Stand in the Gap, an estimated 1 million men covering roughly 115 acres gathered at Independence Mall in Washington, D.C. Organization leaders billed the event as a day for "a multitude of Christian men [to] gather, not to demonstrate strength or political power to the country, but to display their spiritual poverty and failings to a holy God." The event was given its name from Ezekiel 22:30, which states, "I [God] looked for a man among them who would build up the wall and stand before me in the gap on behalf of the land so I would not have to destroy it, but I found none." With that in mind, hundreds of thousands of men descended on the Mall.

Randy Phillips, the Promise Keepers' president, explains that he had the idea for Stand in the Gap while driving on a Colorado highway. He envisioned a field filled with men on their knees and crying. He said it was clear to him that this vision was not of a stadium event but of something more than the traditional stadium activities. Organizational literature states that the name of the event was intended to convey the message: "Christian men, who have forsaken their first love and wandered far from God, are poised to answer the call to stand in the gap on behalf of the church." Another difference that distinguished this event from typical Promise Keepers stadium events is that Stand in the Gap was hosted by Native Americans. A Stand in the Gap conference brochure explains that Native Americans were asked to host the event because the leaders of Promise Keepers wanted to show them that they were "sorry for what transpired on their land, and that as brothers in Christ, we want[ed] them to take the lead in this event." The planning was also meant to incorporate men of the Jewish faith, and this was made clear by the blowing of the shofar (ceremonial ram's horn) at the beginning of the event and throughout the day. One further element that made Stand in the Gap different from traditional stadium events was the use of small groups and interactive participation. At many points in the program, attendees were instructed to break into small groups for prayer or discussion, although individual prayer and reflection were encouraged as well. The entire program consisted of singing, listening to speakers, and having either individual or small group prayers and reflections. The speakers were careful not to state any explicitly political messages, and large television monitors posted throughout the mall reiterated the organization's position that Stand in the Gap was not a political event.

Promise Keepers insistence that they are apolitical in general and at the Stand in the Gap event in particular has been the subject of controversy among scholars as well as political activists. Promise Keepers strongly emphasizes racial equality and the need for what they term "racial reconciliation." White men are exhorted to seek forgiveness for the sin of RACISM; men of color are encouraged to share testimony concerning the unjust effects of racial discrimination. Yet it is well known that this "egalitarianism" is not extended to women. Promise Keepers makes no apology for being an all-male organization. Organization leaders claim that this is an essential element for carrying out their goals, one of which is a reaffirmation of traditional, or patriarchal, familial relationships. This position has made them the target of political opposition and protest by a number of feminist organizations.

The original date for Stand in the Gap was scheduled for one year earlier. But owing to the 1996 presidential election and their overarching intent to remain apolitical, Promise Keepers postponed the event until fall 1997. Despite efforts to keep the event apolitical, Stand in the Gap drew both support and opposition from activists, some representing organized groups, others responding as individuals. The National Organization for Women (NOW), headed by President Patricia Ireland, led a group of women in opposing Promise Keepers' apparently patriarchal ideology and warned feminists to prepare for their "invasion of Washington" and the Promise Keepers agenda for women. On the other hand, more traditionally minded women held signs of support for the men who gathered for the event, and some even identified themselves as "happy" wives of Promise Keepers on the signs they held.

Stand in the Gap ended with a call from Promise Keepers founder Bill McCartney for the attendees to gather on the steps of their respective state capitols on January 1, 2000, to provide evidence of the "vibrant men's ministries" that the event's speakers challenged them to create and to further demonstrate their commitment to racial and denominational reconciliation. The Stand in the Gap covenant, for the most part a reiteration of the "Seven Promises of a Promise Keeper," was read aloud by attendees as the final group activity.

This event was unique in the history of the Promise Keepers organization, and organizational leaders have stated that there are no plans to repeat it, despite its overwhelming attendance by members. Promise Keepers continues to hold stadium events across the United States and has expanded these events to include international venues.

—R. Lorraine Bernotsky

Protestant, Catholic, Jew: An Essay in American Religious Sociology (1955) By Will Herberg.
Garden City, N.J.: Doubleday

Will Herberg (1901–77) was a neoconservative, Jewish social philosopher, graduate professor of Judaic studies and social philosophy at Drew University, and religion editor of the *National Review.* He published a fully revised edition of *Protestant, Catholic, Jew* in 1960 (Anchor Books) and again in 1983, the last time with an introduction by Martin E. Marty. The book presents Herberg's sociological interpretation of the paradoxical religious situation of mid–twentieth-century America, which was marked by "pervasive secularism amid mounting religiosity." Many scholars have praised Herberg for his resolution of this paradox: that the once-multitudinous, ethnically separated Protestant, Roman Catholic, and Jewish religious traditions have, under the impact of secularism, become assimilated into a tripartite religious sensibility, based on a shared belief in the "American Way of Life."

Herberg claims that the American Way of Life has become the "operative faith of the American people." It is based on the principles of democracy, including constitutional government, free enterprise, social equality with high economic competition and mobility, an American-style idealism, individualism, optimism, and the belief in progress, as well as the belief that America represents a new world order. Protestantism, Catholicism, and Judaism form the three branches of "American religion" because they share the same "spiritual values" of American democracy. While these three faiths have been Americanized in their promotion of the American Way of Life, they, in their turn, have been secularized. Thus, the idea of the religions of democracy has led to the religion of democracy.

Herberg describes how this situation arose through three generations. The first generation of immigrants still embraced the customs, languages, and religions it brought with it. The churches in the new land were founded not on shared locality but on a common language, culture, and nationality, thus giving rise to the idea of the ethnic group. Although the first generation

often found itself in a lower position economically and socially, America encouraged upward mobility for those immigrants who could assimilate. To move up to more prestigious social and economic positions, members of the second generation often rejected the social and cultural markers that designated them as members of an "ethnic" group, including their elders' religions.

By the time of the third (and contemporaneous) generation, assimilation was fairly complete; yet this generation was eager to regain its heritage, and therefore returned to the old ethnic church. This tie had never been fully severed because American society has always allowed immigrants to maintain their own faith. At this stage, however, the older (European) ethnic distinctions had been subsumed under the categories Protestant, Catholic, and Jew. Herberg elaborates: "Formerly, religion has been but an aspect of the ethnic group's culture and activities; it was merely a part, and to some a dispensable part, of a larger whole; now the religious community was growing increasingly primary, and ethnic interests, loyalties, and memories were being more and more absorbed in and manifested through this new social structure." Thus, ethnic identity has been replaced by religious affiliation in the tripartite division of Protestant-Catholic-Jew.

The resurgence of religiosity to which Herberg bore witness sprang in part from a desire to belong, which in mid-twentieth-century America meant to identify not along ethnic lines, but religious ones, and specifically as Protestant, Catholic, or Jewish. This need to belong, implies Herberg, extended to the sociopolitical front, where the religions of democracy acted as a salve to help heal the angst created by the instability of contemporaneous world politics and the depersonalization of modernity, as well as a defense against the "demonic threat of communist totalitarianism."

Herberg's interpretation of ethnicity is striking, considering that he wrote and revised his book during the civil rights era. Thus he was unable to foresee the ethnic-identity political movements of the 1970s and 1980s. Other scholars note that America no longer has a tripartite religious framework but is increasingly religiously pluralistic. This trend is in large measure due to the influx of new immigrants after passage of the 1965 Immigration Act, something Herberg could not have predicted. Yet his focus on Protestant-Catholic-Jew may also reflect not just pre-1965 America but his own belief that a common tradition is necessary for any functioning society. Using this book as a basis of discussion, scholars across the country—in classes on religious pluralism, civil religion, Jewish studies, Christian studies, and American intellectual history—continue to investigate the parameters of the common "American" religion and the impact of religious pluralism on it.

See also *BOWLING ALONE;* CIVIL RELIGION; DENOMINATIONALISM; *HABITS OF THE HEART;* SECULARIZATION.

—Carrie B. Dohe

Protestantism

Martin Luther's (1483–1546) nailing of his Ninety-five Theses on the door of the Castle Church in Wittenberg, Germany, on

October 31, 1517, marks the beginning of the Protestant Reformation, or Protestantism. Luther's protest was against the ROMAN CATHOLIC CHURCH and the corruption of the papacy, particularly the selling of indulgences, which promised relief from the pains of purgatory. Luther, a monk and theologian, viewed the long-standing Catholic institution of indulgence "as an external and damnable symptom of so much that was inwardly wrong with the Christian teaching of his generation, a teaching which asserted or suggested that God could be placated by external acts, by forms, by payments, by 'good works.'"

The central doctrine of the Protestant Reformation enunciated by Luther, along with John Calvin, Ulrich Zwingli, and other reformers, was "justification by faith alone," something perceived to be antithetical to the Catholic Church's reliance on human works for salvation. In rejecting the authority of the pope, the indulgence, and scholastic theology, Luther asserted an intellectual position of Protestantism that resonates to this day. Luther said, "I am quite sure that the Church will never be reformed unless we get rid of canon law, scholastic theology, philosophy and logic as they are studied today, and put something else in their place."

What Luther and the second-generation reformer, John Calvin, put in its place was Scripture, God's grace, "the priesthood of all believers," and a strong emphasis on faith in Christ's righteousness alone for salvation. According to Luther, his theology was that of St. Augustine (354–430), of the Bible, and of Christ's church. Eschewing tradition, metaphysics, and human convention, Luther proclaimed a theology of the cross—*theologica crucis*. The fundamental disagreement between Catholic "free will" and Protestant "predestination" is clear in the argument between Luther and Erasmus (1466–1536) in Luther's *Bondage of the Will* (1525).

In response to Luther's unwillingness to change his polemical views as expressed in writings such as *The Open Letter to the Christian Nobility of the German Nation* (1520), Pope Leo X issued a papal bull of excommunication, *Exsurge Domine* (1520). The conflict between Luther and the Catholic Church continued under Luther's unrelenting quest for spiritual, theological, moral, and ecclesiastical reform in the church. The term *Protestant* actually came into use later, when Lutheran princes filed a "protest" against the Holy Roman Emperor Charles V in 1529, at the Diet of Speyer. Charles wanted to withdraw the concessions he had made to the Lutherans since the 1521 Diet of Worms. It was time for Charles to enforce the Edict of Worms, which rejected Luther's teachings and banished him from the empire. At the Diet of Worms, Luther denounced the pope and the Catholic Church's teaching and refused to recant. In asserting the Protestant ideas of individual conscience and private interpretation of Scripture, Luther declared to Charles: "Unless I am convinced by the testimony of the Scriptures or by clear reason (for I do not trust either the Pope or in councils alone, since it is well known that they have often erred and contradicted themselves), I am bound by the Scriptures I have quoted and my conscience is captive to the Word of God. I cannot and I will not retract anything, since it is neither safe nor right to go against conscience . . . May God help me. Amen."

Luther redefined the church as the congregation for believers—the invisible *congregatio fidelium*—rejecting the Catholic claim to special religious and political status. As a result, secular rulers were able to assert authority over the Protestant churches, which was not possible with the Catholic church under the all-encompassing authority of the pope. In 1518, Luther sought the protective cover of Elector Frederick III (Frederick the Wise) of Saxony.

Soon thereafter, Protestant ideas spread throughout Germany into the Scandinavian countries, Scotland, and England. Protestantism had profound religious, political, social, cultural, and economic effects in western Europe. The people were ready to move away from the authoritarian, ecclesiastical jurisdiction of the medieval world. The Protestant appeal to the individual conscience sparked a movement that generated reform, if not revolution. From Thomas Cranmer (1489–1556) in England to John Knox (1505?–72) in Scotland to Zwingli (1484–1531) in Switzerland, the Reformation continued. Protestantism advanced rapidly, creating a schism within Western Christendom.

In essence, Protestantism stands for the proposition that man is free by God's grace. The individualism that arose from Protestantism significantly influenced the rise of political liberalism. JOHN LOCKE (1632–1704), the English political philosopher, penned the *Second Treatise of Government* (1690), promoting the Protestant ideals of humanity as inherently free and equally bound by a constitutional order. Thus, the rise of the nation-state in the 16th century may be attributed to Protestant thought.

Out of Luther's deference to the political power ordained by God arose a more radical group of reformers who had no misgivings about political and religious resistance. ANABAPTISTS, who believed that withdrawal from the world was a biblical mandate, made up the main group of radical reformers. The *Schleitheim Confession of Faith* (1527) is the Anabaptist creed that is "wholly antipolitical: they refused to bear arms or to make use of any 'unchristian, devilish weapons of force'; they declared that 'it is not appropriate for a Christian to serve as a magistrate,' and accordingly refused to use the law courts or to 'pass judgment between brother and brother,' and they declined to pay war-taxes, to recognize existing laws of property or to take any part in civic or political affairs." The view of the radical reformers was at odds with Luther and Calvin's "Magisterial" Reformation, which supported an established church under the authority of the magistrate.

Having made a decisive and complete break with Rome, Luther laid the theological foundation for later reform by Calvin (1509–64). Along with Luther, Calvin affirmed the consistency of Protestantism with the Augustinian theology of faith, grace, and predestination. Calvin quite confidently declared: "Augustine is completely on our side." Calvin developed the Protestant ideas of church polity and the theology of the "Reformed" faith (reformed in relation to Lutheranism). Calvin's great opus, *Institutes of the Christian Religion* (1536), systematized Protestant theology and paved the way for the institutionalization of Reformation ideas. "Calvin believed that in organizing the Church at Geneva he must organize it in imitation of the primitive Church, and thereby reassert the independence of the Church and the divine authority of its ministers." As a result, the more radical reformation movements occurred in countries inhabited by Calvinists, not Lutherans, such as France, the Netherlands, and Scotland, rather than Germany, England, and the Scandinavian countries. "The more hostile the State, the more likely that the Protestants would be Calvinist, for Calvinism established an authority of the ministry free from spiritual subjection to the State authorities."

This brand of Protestant Calvinism inspired the Puritan revolts in England, leading to the American founding. The legacy of Luther and Calvin formed the de facto Protestantism of the American polity. The fundamental doctrines of the Reformation had been formalized in various creeds, such as the *Canons of the Synod of Dort* (1618–19), the *Helvetic Consensus* (1675), and the *Westminster Confession of Faith* (1647), making it easier for the PURITANS and their successors to establish Protestantism as the predominant faith in America. Religious liberty and individual belief marked the character of Protestantism. Yet while Reformed Calvinism flourished in New England, Catholics were persecuted in MARYLAND. Eventually, religious liberty came to all forms of religion through disestablishment of state churches and protection against a national church by the First Amendment to the U.S. Constitution.

Since that time, Protestants have held to the belief that "fidelity to the church must be measured by the degree of the church's fidelity to the gospel." The good news of the Protestant gospel is *sola Scriptura, sola fide, sola gratia*—all having one meaning: *sola Christus*. Then and now, the doctrinal pluralism of Protestantism (Lutheran, Anglican, Congregationalist, Baptist, Methodist, Presbyterian) based on the freedom of the Christian has not undermined the cardinal belief in the Word of God, faith, and grace without human works as the salvation of man through the righteousness of Jesus Christ.

See also DENOMINATIONALISM.

Further reading: Brown, Robert McAfee. *The Spirit of Protestantism.* New York: Oxford University Press, 1965; Chadwick, Owen. *The Reformation.* New York: Penguin, 1990; Dillenberger, John, ed. *Martin Luther: Selections From His Writings.* New York: Doubleday, 1962; Pelikan, Jaroslav. *The Christian Tradition, A History of the Development of Doctrine.* Chicago: University of Chicago Press, 1984; Skinner, Quentin. *The Foundations of Modern Political Thought.* New York: Cambridge University Press, 1978.

—Joanne Tetlow

protests and rallies

Once viewed as radical tactics for those shut out of the conventional political process, some forms of protest have grown into common tools of political participation in the United States. Activists and organizations spanning the ideological and religious spectrums have put protest activities to work to promote their causes.

Peaceful rallies and demonstrations served as powerful weapons in the African-American CIVIL RIGHTS MOVEMENT of the 1950s and 1960s. Denied the right to vote throughout much of the South, black citizens staged marches to demand access to the ballot box. College students staged "sit-ins" at local lunch counters that refused service to African Americans. Black churches played a key role in this peaceful drive for equality, with ministers such as MARTIN LUTHER KING JR. providing much of the movement's leadership. The churches proved a powerful force because the local congregation served as "a bulletin board to a people who owned no organs of communication, a credit union to those without banks, and even a kind of people's court." Ultimately, the success of this movement inspired other disenfranchised groups, including Latinos, Native Americans, women, and Evangelical Protestants to adopt some of these tactics in raising their own demands for equal treatment under the law.

Protest politics tends toward the dramatic, and many protest tactics are intended to be much more confrontational than rallies and demonstrations. Political protest in the United States dates back at least to 1773's Boston Tea Party, in which American colonists flaunted their scorn for British taxes. The Civil Rights movement gained momentum in 1955 when blacks in Montgomery, Alabama, again led partly by black clergy, staged a yearlong boycott of the city's segregated buses. Though a peaceful form of protest, the boycott inflicted heavy losses on local businesses. Using the same strategy, farm laborers led by César Chávez organized a successful boycott against the California grape industry in the late 1960s. The success of this boycott helped win the United Farm Workers labor union the right to bargain for better wages and working conditions for its members.

Even when staged as peaceful events, rallies and demonstrations can turn violent. March 7, 1965, became known as "Bloody Sunday" when law enforcement officials terrorized civil rights marchers in Selma, Alabama, with clubs, tear gas, and high-pressure fire hoses. Here, the brutality ultimately worked in favor of civil rights activists, as the horrifying pictures in newspapers and on television screens helped turn public opinion in favor of greater legal equality for blacks.

The pro-life movement has taken to heart the example of the Civil Rights movement and used protest activities to attempt to bring an end to ABORTION, typically praying, marching, and sometimes blocking access to clinics where abortions are performed. Some extremists have also perpetrated violent crimes in the name of the pro-life cause. In 1993, Congress issued a report identifying more than 6,000 clinic blockades staged against family planning clinics, as well as "at least 36 bombings, 81 arsons, 131 death threats, 84 assaults, two kidnappings, 327 clinic invasions, and one murder." Since this report was released, several additional murders have been committed in the name of the pro-life movement.

Protest activities were traditionally viewed as "last resort" tactics for those otherwise shut out of the political process. But protest activities have increased across the United States, even as participation rights have expanded. Today, protest activists are likely to feel alienated from the political system but still believe "that they can do something to affect political decisions."

The Internet plays a growing role in protest activities. Thousands of protesters descended on the meeting of the World Trade Organization in Seattle in 1999; many used e-mail to help plan their activities. Extremist groups have also put the Web to use, raising serious questions about what speech is protected under the First Amendment. For example, some physicians claim that an antiabortion Web page threatens their safety by labeling them "butchers" and then publishing detailed personal information about them, including their home addresses. First Amendment advocates argue that such sites do not constitute direct threats and are thus protected under the Constitution.

See also BUS BOYCOTTS; CATHOLIC BISHOPS' 1975 PASTORAL LETTER ON ABORTION; OPERATION RESCUE; STUDENT NONVIOLENT COORDINATING COMMITTEE.

Further reading: Branch, Taylor. *Parting the Waters: America in the King Years, 1955–1963.* New York: Simon and Schuster, 1988; Janda, Kenneth, Jeffrey M. Berry, and Jerry Goldman. *The Challenge of Democracy: Government in America.* 6th ed. Boston: Houghton Mifflin, 1999; Senate Report No. 103–117 1993.

—Staci L. Beavers

public theology

Public theology is a term used currently both to describe and to prescribe the expression of normative religious claims in public conversations regarding matters of communal life or the common good. Public theology's core thrust is to affirm the propriety and goodness of such claims against the tendency to "privatize" religion and silence its public voice. Examples of issues with which public theology has been concerned include economic justice, civil rights, PACIFISM and JUST WAR, medical and environmental ethics, and the family.

The term *public theology* was first used in 1974 by Martin Marty (1928–   ) to describe the work and contribution of the American theologian and public intellectual REINHOLD NIEBUHR (1892–1971). Since then, it has been used widely to describe earlier public religious expressions, like Abraham Lincoln's Second Inaugural Address (1865) and the early 20th century's SOCIAL GOSPEL movement, as well as to characterize the work of more recent American figures like John Courtney Murray, S.J. (1904–67) and MARTIN LUTHER KING JR. (1929–68).

Historically, *public theology* has referred primarily to the engagement between religious claims and social issues within the American and Western democratic frameworks. Questions of religious freedom, pluralism, and the structures for civil argument have thus been basic. Yet even within a given socio-historical context, public theology has taken on multiple forms. It is not restricted to a particular religious tradition (although most of its American versions have been Christian), nor is it restricted to particular stances within either religious traditions or politics (i.e., conservative or liberal).

The shared contentions that generally unite today's public theologies include the following: (1) religious claims ought *not* to be confined to the private sphere or to the internal sphere of the religious community but, rather, ought to be offered and considered within the broader sphere of public life; (2) religious claims are *not* purely 'personal preferences' or 'private options' but rather are truth claims pertinent to the common decisions of public life; (3) public claims based in a religious stance are *not,* by definition, violations of the ESTABLISHMENT CLAUSE of the Constitution but are politically legitimate; and (4) public institutions are strengthened, not threatened, by the inclusion of religious arguments in public discourse.

Differentiating factors among the various public theologies include their substantive interpretations of the common good and, behind those, of religious truth; their views on the proper and most effective form of public witness and persuasion; and their understandings of their proper relationship to one another. Thus, for example, members of the Christian conservative movement might disagree with some in the mainline Protestant churches on whether the common good emphasizes the development of individual moral character or the provision of equal access to economic, social, and political resources. Such conflicting interpretations are likely to surface, for instance, in debates over welfare reform. Similarly, theologians from the Christian Realism tradition may defend a government action that is protested sharply by religious pacifists. Yet in each of these cases, both sides agree that religious claims ought to be part of the public conversation—both sides represent public theologies.

In regard to the proper form of public theology, some proponents hold that a religious tradition's public voice must use a vocabulary that nonbelievers will likely find more compelling. Thus they express their religiously grounded claims by utilizing rational natural law arguments, human rights language, or less particularistic religious images and narratives. Historically, many ROMAN CATHOLIC, mainline Protestant, EASTERN ORTHODOX, and Jewish thinkers have defended this approach. Other proponents of public theology, especially Evangelical Protestant leaders, have contended that a religious tradition is most true to itself when it speaks publicly with the fullness of the symbols and language of its sacred scriptures, regardless of the reception received by nonbelievers. Within public theology, therefore, the question of *how* to speak religiously in a given context is fundamental.

Finally, public theologies may disagree on the extent to which public arguments should be made in cooperation with other religious traditions that seek the same results. For example, should conservative Jewish and Christian groups work together on pro-life issues? If so, how should positions be articulated? Similarly, the proper role of ecumenical organizations in publicly representing multiple traditions is a point of frequent disagreement.

Given the rise in religious pluralism and the sustained desire among many American citizens for religious claims to be considered in matters pertaining to the common good, public theology's concerns appear to be of increasing interest and relevance.

See also BARTH, KARL; CONE, JAMES; ECUMENISM; TILLICH, PAUL.

Further reading: Hopkins, Dwight N., ed. *Black Faith and Public Talk.* Maryknoll, N.Y.: Orbis, 1999; Marty, Martin E. *The Public Church.* New York: Crossroad, 1981; Neuhaus, Richard J. *The Naked Public Square: Religion and Democracy in America.* Grand Rapids, Mich.: W. B. Eerdmans, 1984; Stackhouse, Max L. *Public Theology and Political Economy.* Grand Rapids, Mich.: W. B. Eerdmans, 1987; Swatos, William H., Jr., and James K. Wellman Jr., eds. *The Power of Religious Publics: Staking Claims in American Society.* Westport, Conn.: Praeger, 1999; Tracy, David. *The Analogical Imagination: Christian Theology and the Culture of Pluralism.* New York: Crossroad, 1981.

—Perry T. Hamalis

Puritans

A Protestant Christian sect doctrinally related to CALVINISM, the Puritans first appeared in England during the late 16th century. During the 17th century, they emerged as opponents of the political absolutism of the Stuart monarchy and as critics of alleged heresies within the Church of England, with which they were still at least nominally affiliated.

Between 1630 and 1640, approximately 20,000 Puritans migrated to New England, having secured a royal charter through the Massachusetts Bay Company. Unlike the PILGRIMS, who landed in Plymouth in 1620, the Puritans who initially settled in Salem and Boston were not primarily concerned with religious liberty. Rather, they were seeking refuge from the decline and corruption of their native England, and envisioning the creation of an organic Christian commonwealth, a New Canaan based on their own version of orthodox Calvinism.

Under the leadership of JOHN WINTHROP (1588–1649), the first governor of the Massachusetts Bay Colony, Puritan settlements flourished in Massachusetts during the middle part of the 17th century. The Puritan way of life also spread to Connecticut and New Hampshire, as well as to Rhode Island, which became a haven for Puritan dissenters exiled from Massachusetts for their nonconformist beliefs. Prominent exiles included ANNE HUTCHINSON (1591–1643), a brilliant defender of Antinomianism who believed in the direct personal ecstatic revelation of grace; and ROGER WILLIAMS (1603?–83), a charismatic clergyman who argued that the Puritan churches of MASSACHUSETTS had been contaminated by government interference and that the state should have no authority in religious matters.

For the New England Puritans, theology was not merely the path to personal salvation; it was also the basis for the prevailing social and political order. The Puritans believed that their community enjoyed a special covenant with God, modeled on the biblical covenant between God and Abraham. Within the Puritan commonwealth, only "the elect" or "saints" (i.e., regenerate individuals who had visibly achieved grace) were admitted into full membership in the church and full citizenship in the state. The unsaved were considered mere "inhabitants," expected to obey the law and attend church, but given only very limited civil rights and no political rights. The status of each individual—saved or unsaved—was determined by examinations by ministers and other "saints."

An idea of limited government was another important feature of Puritan political thought. The Puritan commitment to limited government was due, partially, to their historical dissatisfaction with the Stuart monarchy, but also had strong theological roots. Puritan theologians and clergymen like Thomas Hooker (1586–1647) and James Cotton (1585–1652) reasoned that if humankind's relationship with God was based on a voluntary covenant, then, surely, the relationship between citizens and their magistrates could not be based on arbitrary or unlimited authority.

Even so, the Puritan leaders had no intention of creating a constitutional republic. Their goal, instead, was to establish a Christian state based on religious principles and governed with a firm hand by magistrates chosen for their special practical and moral wisdom. Puritan citizens did not universally share this view, however, and in 1645 Winthrop himself was formally charged with exceeding his legitimate authority as governor. Winthrop marked the occasion of his acquittal with a "Little Speech on Liberty," in which he argued that the authority of the magistrates came directly from God, although the people themselves elected their leaders.

In 1662, political pressure led to reforms expanding membership in the Puritan church and, simultaneously, increasing the number of full citizens in the Massachusetts Bay Colony. And in 1691, the Puritans abandoned their quasi-independence, officially becoming a royal colony. By the middle of the 18th century, the political and theological dominance of orthodox Puritanism had waned significantly. Factional disputes, internal reforms, changing demographics, and the failure of later generations to inherit the religious fervor that had animated the spiritual and social strivings of their forefathers all contributed to this decline.

Nonetheless, Puritanism continued to cast a long shadow over the political, cultural, and intellectual history of the United States, influencing the writings of Nathaniel Hawthorne, RALPH WALDO EMERSON, Josiah Royce, George Santayana, and many others. The intellectual inheritance of Puritanism includes its deep sense of moral purpose, its commitment to limited government based on contract and consent, its passion for righteousness and justice, and its subordination of material to spiritual ends.

Today, the word *puritanical* is often used pejoratively to connote rigid adherence to morality, abstinence, and strict austerity. However, this would not accurately describe the New England Puritans themselves, who, in spite of being intensely devoted to the service of God, were not generally opposed to comfort, convenience, or bodily pleasures. For instance, they did not believe moneymaking to be immoral, as long as it served the welfare and improvement of the community, rather than merely the personal enrichment of the individual. Likewise, neither sex nor drinking was held to be sinful as long as the former served the purpose of procreation, rather than mere gratification, and as long as the latter did not lead to drunkenness.

Further reading: Commager, Henry Steele. *The American Mind: An Interpretation of American Thought and Character since the 1880s.* New Haven, Conn.: Yale University Press, 1961 [1950]; Miller, Perry. *The New England Mind: The Seventeenth Century.* Boston: Beacon Press, 1961 [1939]; Miller, Perry, and Thomas H. Johnson, eds. *The Puritans: A Sourcebook of Their Writings.* Mineola, N.Y.: Dover, 2001.

—Jason A. Scorza

Q

Quakers (Society of Friends)

Today, Quakers represent a very small segment of the American population, but they enjoy a rich legacy of both religious and political influence throughout American history. Founded in England in 1652, Quakers immigrated to America during the Colonial period and brought with them a vibrant theological perspective that promoted social equality, piety, and an inward journey to become closer to God. Quakers were active in Colonial politics, were major participants in the ABOLITIONIST MOVEMENT, and were instrumental in shaping early American culture.

From the group's founding, Quakers have been conscientious advocates for reform. It is reported in the Society's historical archives that George Fox, the father of the Quaker movement, was a reformer who set out at the age of 19 to find the essence of Christianity. Disillusioned with those who professed to be Christians, Fox traveled throughout England for four years before he heard a voice saying, "there is one, even Christ Jesus, who can speak to thy condition."

This message of reform has resonated throughout the group's collective history, as evident in the Society's theological teachings. Fox and his adherents preached that authentic religious experiences cannot be derived from rituals, sacraments, or other "empty forms." He believed strongly that the original message, as articulated by the apostles, had been lost when the church became institutionalized. His quest was to "free" Christianity from the constraints of "steeple houses" and to return it to a more personal, individualized, and direct relationship with God.

The notion of religion as being constituted by this personal, individual, and direct relationship with God sits at the heart of Quaker doctrine and identity. The Society and its practices are organized to reinforce this belief. As articulated in the writings of Fox, it is the duty of each individual Friend to acknowledge the presence of God within and to find his or her way toward a closer relationship with God. For this reason, the group first called itself "The Way." Only later did they referred to themselves as "Friends of Truth" or "Friends of Jesus" (John 15:5). The term *Quaker* was used by their critics,

and its origin dates back to the time when Fox suggested before a British judge that he (the judge) "tremble at the word of the Lord."

From this reformist theology, we get the organization's commitment to social equality and piety. At the heart of these commitments sits a belief that every human being, irrespective of race, class, or gender, has the spirit of God within. Fox and his earliest followers taught that "in every human soul there is implanted a certain element of God's own spirit and divine energy." Sin prevents the individual from cultivating this inner light, and all things that contribute to sinful behavior are to be avoided and removed.

These theological principles inform every aspect of Quaker culture, and they form the foundation for the group's mode of worship, decentralized organizational structure, and strict social norms. Worship services are often held in silence, and individuals rise to speak only when inspired by God to do so. Quaker communities are connected through their worship services, which are held in meeting houses. Quaker meetings occur at the local level, but several local meetings in a region will also unite monthly and quarterly.

Quakers continue to make significant contributions to American society. But historically, they have not always been well received. Although the Society of Friends first emerged in England, they joined the tide of British immigrants seeking religious TOLERANCE and economic prosperity in America. Once in America, however, Quakers faced fierce competition from other religious groups, especially from the PURITAN community living along the New England coastline. The acts of intimidation and violence inflicted on Quakers by Puritans forced a significant portion of the Quaker community to flee New England for safer havens in the upper South and Delaware valley.

Despite the early setbacks, the Society of Friends quickly emerged as arguably one of the most politically influential groups in early Colonial America. In Rhode Island, Quakers held the post of governor for a combined 36 terms. During the 17th and 18th centuries, Quakers dominated the legislatures of New Jersey, PENNSYLVANIA, and North Carolina. Even today, Quakers are active philanthropists and continue to contribute to international efforts to nourish the "inner soul."

Further reading: Weening, Hans. *Quaker Introductory Booklet.* Friends World Committee for Consultation. Available on-line. URL: http://www.quaker.org/fwcc/EMES/booklet.html. Accessed April 26, 2000.

—Alonford James Robinson Jr.

Quayle, J. Danforth (Dan) (1947–) *U.S. vice president*

J. Danforth (Dan) Quayle was the 44th vice president of the United States, serving under President George H. W. Bush (1989–93). He was born on February 4, 1947, in Indianapolis, Indiana. He received a degree in political science in 1969 from DePauw University and a law degree in 1974 from Indiana University while serving in the National Guard. He married Marilyn Tucker, and they have three children.

Vice President Dan Quayle (right) with President George H. W. Bush *(George Bush Presidential Library)*

Quayle began his public service in 1971, when he was an investigator for the Consumer Protection Division of the Indiana Attorney General's Office. Later that year, he became administrative assistant to the governor. He was director of the Inheritance Tax Division of the Indiana Department of Revenue from 1973 to 1974. After graduating from law school, he worked at his family's newspaper as an associate publisher and practiced law along with his wife. Quayle was first elected to the House of Representatives in 1976 and then to the Senate in 1980, becoming the youngest person ever elected to the Senate from Indiana. During his second term in the Senate, he was tapped as running mate for then vice president George H. W. Bush.

Though he had significant duties relating to foreign policy as vice president, Quayle consistently spoke out about family values and defended his evangelical Christian faith. Mainstream America became familiar with him as a conservative Christian crusader and his fight for values after a speech in 1992 at the Commonwealth Club in San Francisco, during which he spoke on the "poverty of values" in American society. Using the television show *Murphy Brown* as an example, he criticized Hollywood's unrealistic depiction of children born out of wedlock. He asserted that in reality, these children and their mothers often face economic hardship and poverty, and a society that portrays a father's role as unimportant only perpetuates irresponsibility. The media ruthlessly attacked his meaning, but he was steadfast in his position. He was later vindicated for his comments in many forums, including an influential 1993 *Atlantic Monthly* article by Barbara Dafoe Whitehead, entitled "Dan Quayle Was Right."

Quayle took some time off after leaving the vice presidency to write his memoir, *Standing Firm.* This gave him an opportunity to reflect and to set the record straight in many respects. He discussed in one part how a news anchor on a morning TV show asked his wife about her religious beliefs. He stated that she did not understand how being a Presbyterian could be seen as unacceptable, and that their faith in God and belief in the Bible are central to their lives. Quayle also affirmed, "God is personal and cannot be mandated by a government" and concluded another chapter by stating that he "remain[s] a true believer—in [his] principles, in [his] country, and in [his] God and Savior."

Returning to the Commonwealth Club in California in 1999, he was even more candid about his perception of the "demoralization" of American society. He focused on progress that had been made as well as areas of our society that still remained off course. He cited the cessation of posting the Ten Commandments in our schools and discussed the issue of PRAYER IN PUBLIC SCHOOLS. He asserted that if the House and Senate open each day with prayer, it defies common sense that our schools cannot do the same. He concluded: "the crusade against religion has [become] . . . a crusade against basic moral principles in our . . . schools." This speech outlined the basic platform for his upcoming presidential bid.

In his unsuccessful 2000 presidential bid, Quayle was naturally aligned with Christian conservatives. While others courted economic conservatives, he courted social conservatives. He made known his opposition to ABORTION during a meeting with the Iowa CHRISTIAN COALITION. In his 1999 book, *Worth Fighting For,* which was written as a prelude to his 2000 presidential bid, Quayle boldly affirmed his opposition to abortion, stating that the only exception should be in saving the life of another person. He went on to state that the federal government should not promote abortion.

His religious convictions are expounded in great detail throughout this book. In particular, Quayle asserts that "America is a God-fearing nation, and we must proceed from that basic premise." Further, "it is time to end the scoffing at religion and especially at Christianity that goes on among the self-anointed elites in the media, the entertainment industry, and academia." He opines in one chapter that people of faith have realized that their faith requires them to act as responsible citizens and become involved in the political process. He later asserts that our most effective weapons to overcome the demoralization of society are none other than church and faith. This statement naturally follows his long record as a strong supporter of local faith-based organizations' efforts to ameliorate poverty and other forms of suffering.

Though Quayle has not been popular with the mainstream media or political liberals, he has not let this deter him from raising awareness of many of society's trenchant social problems. Whether he has a future in American politics will remain to be seen.

See also CHRISTIAN RIGHT AND THE REPUBLICAN PARTY.

Further reading: Quayle, Dan. *Standing Firm.* New York: HarperCollins, 1994; Quayle, Dan. "Values Matter Most." URL: http://www.commonwealthclub.org, May 19, 1999; Quayle, Dan. *Worth Fighting For.* California: Word, 1999; Schneider, Mary Beth. "Newfound Confidence Propels Quayle on Trail." Available on-line. URL: http://www.starnews.com. February 14, 1999.

—Elisabeth Newberry

R

racism

Racism is the theory that posits the inherent superiority of one race over another by taking different skin color and somatic features as the basis for the alleged inferiority or superiority of different racial groups in areas of beauty, intelligence, and morality. When institutionalized, racism is enforced through formal policies, laws, and informal social practices that perpetuate unequal access to social goods and resources and unequal treatment under the law. Institutionalized racism is further embedded in a cultural context of racial attitudes, stereotypes, cultural norms, and even religious beliefs, which legitimize and perpetuate it.

Modern racial categories were introduced by Swedish botanist Carolus Linnaeus and German zoologist J. F. Blumenbach, in the 18th century. In 1758, Linnaeus developed a four-part classification of "races" based on geography: *Americanus* (the Americas), red, choleric, upright, ruled by habit; *Europeus* (Europe), white, sanguine, muscular, ruled by custom; *Asiaticus* (Asia), pale-yellow, melancholy, stiff, ruled by belief; and *Afer* (African), black, phlegmatic, relaxed, ruled by caprice. In 1795, Blumenbach added a fifth category when he grouped races as Caucasian, Ethiopian, American, Mongolian (now eastern Asia), and Malay (Polynesians and Aborigines of Australia). Blumenbach described Americans and Mongolians as one line of "degeneration," and Malays and Ethiopians as the other line of "degeneration," from the Caucasian "ideal." These categories resonated in the American colonies, as Africans were ascribed the qualities of irrationality, sexuality, and the incapacity for self-governance, while whites were ascribed their positive opposites.

These typologies reflected popular notions of European civilization that helped justify colonial expansion and the transatlantic slave trade in the 17th and 18th centuries. Originally, Europeans enslaved Africans on the basis of a Christian versus heathen dichotomy, but this transformed into a white versus black dichotomy as the American colonies instituted racial slavery by the mid-1600s.

The 17th- and 18th-century environmental theories of race gave way to genetic arguments in the United States by the late 19th century and early 20th century, when theories of "craniology" emerged to explain the alleged criminal propensity and lesser intelligence of different racial and ethnic groups. Furthermore, the belief that intelligence was genetically based and measurable led to the development of the intelligence quotient test.

Since the work of anthropologist Franz Boas, many scholars have argued that race is not a fixed biological or genetic entity but a "social construct" that shifts meaning across time and place. For example, some people socially defined as blacks in the United States would be categorized as whites in Brazil. But while race is considered to be a social construct, it does have a very concrete impact on one's life. For example, in statistics ranging from life expectancy, access to education, access to health care, rates of arrest and incarceration, to wages and income, many argue that chronic racial disparities in these areas are evidence of past and ongoing racial discrimination.

Despite recent scientifically accepted proof that humans are 99.988 percent genetically identical, some scholars have argued that race and intelligence are linked to genetics and heredity, and use this to explain racial disparities in educational testing and achievement. These scholars have faced criticism for reviving discredited genetic theories of race, for ignoring the social context that shapes the opportunities available to individuals from different racial groups, and for opposing any government efforts at improving the quality of education for poor and minority students.

In the United States, racism has been supported and opposed by religion and has, at times, wracked the denominations. To support racism, white Southerners invoked the "curse of Ham" to justify the enslavement of Africans as "God's punishment upon Ham's prurient disobedience" and then defend it for bringing Christianity to blacks. The drive in the mid-1950s to start private secular and parochial schools in the South followed closely on the heels of public school desegregation orders. Recently, racism remains evident in the CHRISTIAN IDENTITY movement, which finds expression in such groups as the ARYAN NATIONS. Moreover, some have argued that the NATION OF ISLAM exacerbates racism by advocating black empowerment resting on anti-Semitic and anti-white beliefs.

To oppose racism, both before and after the Civil War, black and white ABOLITIONISTS opposed slavery as a sin, and in the 1950s and 1960s, black ministers like MARTIN LUTHER KING JR. challenged the United States to live up to its professed ideals of equality for all humans as black churches were the local movement centers for the mass movement against legalized segregation. White churches were also involved in the Civil Rights movement, cosponsoring various initiatives such as FREEDOM SUMMER, offering their prophetic voices to their congregations, and Congress, and appearing at the front of PROTESTS AND RALLIES. Recently, religious organizations such as the SOUTHERN BAPTIST CONVENTION have formally apologized for racism, and organizations such as the National Conference for Community and Justice continue to promote interfaith and interracial respect by emphasizing tolerance, conflict resolution, and education.

The major U.S. Protestant denominations split into northern and southern wings over slavery in the 1840s, with the divisions still evident today in various forms. Even after these divisions, race and racism have been the most divisive issues within the denominations. The United Methodist Church, for instance, has suffered continuing anxiety and tension over racial reconciliation efforts. The ROMAN CATHOLIC CHURCH, too, has been divided by race and racism. One could find local priests, primarily in the North, condoning racist attacks against blacks moving into a parish, while many others, especially in the hierarchy, opposed racism and worked hard for civil rights.

Despite the leadership of American religious institutions in the fight against racism and for civil rights, "eleven o'clock on Sunday morning is the most segregated hour of the week in America." Moreover, civil rights activism by the clergy has been attributed as the primary cause of the membership declines felt in most (white) mainline Protestant churches. That is to say, race remains a potent divisive force in America, and the complicated issues surrounding the achievement of racial equality will likely remain so.

See also ABERNATHY, RALPH; APARTHEID IN SOUTH AFRICA; *BOB JONES UNIVERSITY V. UNITED STATES;* BROWN, JOHN; BUS BOYCOTTS; *CHRISTIANS IN RACIAL CRISIS;* CONGRESS OF RACIAL EQUALITY; CONE, JAMES; FARRAKHAN, LOUIS, *GATHERING STORM IN THE CHURCHES;* JEMISON, T. J.; KU KLUX KLAN; NATIONAL COUNCIL OF CHURCHES; SECTION DIVIDE OF THE CHURCHES OVER SLAVERY; SOUTHERN CHRISTIAN LEADERSHIP CONFERENCE; SOUTHERN REPUBLICAN REALIGNMENT; STUDENT NONVIOLENT COORDINATING COMMITTEE.

Further reading: Findlay, James F., Jr. *Church People in the Struggle.* New York: Oxford University Press, 1993; Fredrickson, George. *White Supremacy: A Comparative Study in American and South African History.* New York: Oxford University Press, 1981; Gould, Stephen Jay. *The Mismeasure of Man.* Rev. ed. New York: Norton, 1996; Jordan, Winthrop. *White Over Black: American Attitudes Toward the Negro,*

1550–1812. New York: Norton, 1977 [1968]; McGreevy, John T. *Parish Boundaries.* Chicago: University of Chicago Press, 1996; Winter, Gibson. *The Suburban Captivity of the Churches.* Garden City, N.J.: Doubleday, 1961.

—Gregory W. Streich

raid on Waco

On April 19, 1993, the Federal Bureau of Investigation ended a three-month standoff with the BRANCH DAVIDIANS at their Mt. Carmel compound in Waco, Texas. The standoff began when agents of the Bureau of Alcohol, Tobacco, and Firearms (ATF) attempted to serve and arrest the Davidians' leader, DAVID KORESH (a.k.a. Vernon Howell), in regard to a weapons violation. The initial, violent confrontation between the ATF and the Davidians occurred in February 1993. During the April raid, approximately 80 Davidians, many of them children, perished in a fire. After eight years of allegations, inquiries, investigations, and lawsuits, the Danforth Commission, an independent government investigation panel headed by former U.S. senator John Danforth (R-Mo.) finally concluded that the Davidians, not the FBI, started the fire that engulfed and destroyed the Mt. Carmel complex.

Two major factors appear to have contributed to the deadly confrontation between federal law enforcement and the Davidians. The first are errors by federal law enforcement. On the day of the initial raid in February 1993, ATF agents ignored information that the Davidians had been tipped off regarding the operation. The failure of the initial raid, which resulted in the deaths of four ATF agents and five Davidians, brought the FBI into the standoff. The FBI waited 55 days before entering the compound under orders from Attorney General Janet Reno. During that standoff, they tried to coax the Davidians out of their compound using a variety of means.

With the assistance of Professor James Tabor of the University of North Carolina at Charlotte's Religious Studies Department, the FBI even tried to negotiate with Koresh. Acting on his own initiative and relying on his knowledge of the biblical Book of Revelation, Tabor and a colleague managed to convince Koresh that he was not the fifth seal of the Apocalypse (see BRANCH DAVIDIANS). Instead, they told Koresh he should complete the commentary he was working on, surrender, and turn it over to them to disseminate. This scenario broke down when the FBI decided that Koresh was manipulating Tabor and his colleague. Unfortunately, they were wrong. When the FBI entered the Mt. Carmel complex after the April 19 raid, they found a computer disk containing parts of Koresh's apocalyptic commentary.

The second major factor that contributed to the deadly confrontation at Waco was Koresh's preoccupation with the Book of Revelation and the seven seals of the apocalypse. These notions had played an important role for Koresh and his community since his assumption of leadership in the late 1980s. Koresh believed that he and his community, after the initial violent confrontation with the ATF and during the 55-

day standoff with the FBI, were involved in the traumatic events of the fifth seal of revelation. As outlined in Revelation 6:9–11, these trials include the death of some of the faithful and the violent persecution of others during a short season of tribulation before the final events of the Apocalypse. The opening of this seal was supposed to take place shortly before the Day of Judgment. As a result, the Davidian community was increasingly edgy and tense as they waited to see what the federal agents would do next. This waiting was the real problem, for Koresh also emphasized a portion of revelation that talks about a deceptive Queen of Babylon. As far as Koresh was concerned, the federal government was this queen.

Koresh and his community were victims of their own selective theological foregrounding and the foregrounding of their predecessors. By the time the ATF became concerned about a fringe religious community that had stockpiled weapons, the community in question saw itself as the *only* real Christian community, surrounded and beleaguered by enemies on all sides. The result was that federal law enforcement stumbled into a conflagration that was waiting to happen with a community under strong authoritarian control that saw itself as only a hair's breadth away from spiritual and physical destruction. By the time the ATF raid failed and the FBI attempted to clean up the resulting political mess, an apocalyptic nightmare was well under way. If the federal agents had backed away at the beginning of the siege, a tragedy might have been avoided. Given Koresh's belief that the Apocalypse and its ultimate battle between good and evil were soon to come anyway, it would have only been postponed.

See also MILLENARIANISM.

Further reading: Tabor, James D. "The Waco Tragedy: An Autobiographical Account of One Attempt to Divert Disaster." In *From the Ashes: Making Sense of Waco*. Edited by James R. Lewis. Lanham, Md.: Rowman and Littlefield, 1994; ———. "Religious Discourse and Failed Negotiations: The Dynamics of Biblical Apocalypticism in Waco." In *Armageddon in Waco: Critical Perspectives on the Branch Davidian Conflict.* Edited by Stuart A. Wright. Chicago: University of Chicago Press, 1995.

—Adam L. Silverman

Rainbow Coalition

The Rainbow Coalition, also known as the Rainbow/PUSH Coalition (RPC), based in Chicago, is a progressive movement organized in 1985 primarily by the Reverend JESSE JACKSON to advance a social, economic, and political agenda for African Americans.

The Rainbow/PUSH Coalition has its origins in the SOUTHERN CHRISTIAN LEADERSHIP CONFERENCE (SCLC). During the mid-1960s Jackson worked for the SCLC, a civil rights organization founded by the Reverend Martin Luther King Jr. In 1966, Jackson helped found the Chicago branch of Operation Breadbasket, the economic arm of SCLC. After

his suspension from SCLC, Jackson founded Operation PUSH (People United to Save Humanity), an organization that continued the work of Operation Breadbasket without SCLC's sponsorship.

Three additional forces contributing to the RPC's foundation were Jackson's historic 1984 campaign for the Democratic presidential nomination; the 1982 National Conference of Black Political Scientists, which examined the questions of whether there should even be an African-American presidential candidate and what impact that candidate would have on the body politic; and the historic National Black Political Convention of 1972, which brought together nearly 8,000 politically active African Americans to set forth a "black agenda." From this convention, the National Black Independent Political Party was formed. Though this "black political party" was short-lived because of minimal support and cooperation from African-American elected officials, it may be considered the precursor to the Rainbow Coalition.

A substantive understanding of RPC and its precursors can be garnered by looking at it through three identifiable stages: the expansionist period (1980–84), the transitional period (1984–88), and the institutional period (1988–present). While such a framework could be open to future review and development, it may serve to synthesize major changes in the Rainbow Coalition, including its relationship with the Democratic Party.

The paramount characteristic of the Rainbow Coalition during the expansionist period was the broadening of the organization's embrace to include an array of radical-to-militant national organizations and disenfranchised groups from the National Black United Front to the National Black Political Assembly, from the Black Leadership Family to gays and environmentalists, and from labor unions to farm workers. Because of these coalitions, the Rainbow Coalition saw its membership expand to over 70,000, which brought media attention to the coalition, its member organizations, and its paramount leader, Rev. Jackson, who was running for the Democratic presidential nomination. Owing to its rapid growth and high visibility, the Rainbow Coalition sought to work on two levels to lay out a progressive agenda that focused on issues with strong moral and social overtones, such as civil rights, economic parity, GAY RIGHTS, empowerment, and the inclusion of disadvantaged minorities. It also hoped to crack the American two-party system and give rise to an alternative party for neglected groups. Though the coalition failed to advance the majority of its platform within the Democratic Party, it did manage to convince the Democrats to embrace a few of its issues, such as affirmative action.

The transitional period reflects the retrenchment of the coalition's organizations and a redirection of its goals and objectives. Nearly every organization suspended its work, merged with another organization, or dissolved altogether. The principal reasons for this, which is conventional for social movements, were the lack of a cooperative agenda and a structural mechanism that would allow each of the suborganizations to remain independent of the coalition. Many wanted the coalition to turn its political fervor into a third party, but it was clear that there was no financial structure to sustain such a conversion. In addition, many began to see the primary spokesman, Rev. Jackson, as more of a liability than an asset because of his desire to respond to breaking news events. The coalition failed to evolve into a party, but many supporters continued to advance the general ideas of the organization in local and congressional elections.

As Jackson became more mainstream in his ideology and more accepted by the Democratic Party, so did the focus of the Rainbow coalition. Thus, the current institutional period has seen the coalition incorporate a large number of elected officials, from the late representative George "Mickey" Leland (D-Tex.) to former New Mexico governor Tony Anaya, and significant organizations (including the Machinists Union, the American Federation of Government Employees, and various farmers' groups). These elites and organizations emphasized the need for developing grassroots subunits, which would ultimately feed into the National Rainbow Coalition's Platform. The other major characteristics of this period were an even greater emphasis on ethical and moral values, a broadening of the way in which issues were framed, and a return to "influence politics" techniques, primarily nationwide voter registration drives. These activities, according to Jackson, provided the margin of victory for eight southern Democratic senators, whose election returned the U.S. Senate to the Democratic Party and ultimately led to the defeat in the Senate of President RONALD REAGAN's ultraconservative Supreme Court nominee, Judge Robert Bork.

The Rainbow/PUSH Coalition, a merger of Operation PUSH and the National Rainbow Coalition in 1986, has a long list of accomplishments, which include registering thousands of voters; assisting in the election of hundreds of local, state, and federal officials; mediating labor disputes; challenging broadcast station licenses to ensure equal employment opportunities in the media; lobbying to include more minorities in all areas of the entertainment industry; negotiating economic covenants with major corporations, which provided hundreds of minority-owned franchises and car dealerships and other business opportunities; influencing political policy toward South Africa and Haiti; and helping to increase the number of minority administrators in college and professional sports.

See also CIVIL RIGHTS MOVEMENT; KING, MARTIN LUTHER JR.; RACISM.

Further reading: Collins, Sheila. *The Rainbow Challenge: The Jackson Campaign and the Future of U.S. Politics.* New York: Monthly Review Press, 1981; Collum, Danny. "Rainbow Solidifies." *Sojourners*, July 1986, 11; Sewell, Said. "From Revolution to Evolution: The Rise of the Rainbow Coalition and Its Impact on the Democratic Party." Paper presented at the National Conference of Black Political Scientists, February 23, 1996; National Rainbow PUSH Coalition on the Web: URL: www.rainbowpush.org.

—Jacquelyn A. Anthony and Said Sewell

Reagan, Ronald (1911–) *U.S. president*

Ronald Wilson Reagan was elected president of the United States in 1980 and won a second term in 1984. He rose from the obscurity of small-town life in the American heartland to a spectacular career that took him to film stardom in Hollywood, leadership of the American conservative movement, eight years as governor of California, and the first successful two-term presidency since DWIGHT D. EISENHOWER.

The popular writer John Updike, who was no Reagan sympathizer, may have best summed up the president in his book *Rabbit at Rest:* "Reagan . . . had that dream of distance; the powerful thing about him as President was that you never knew how much he knew, nothing or everything." After decades in the public eye, Ronald Reagan remains an enigma to both admirers and opponents.

Reagan was born in Tampico, Illinois, and worked his way through Eureka College. There he studied economics and sociology, played on the football team, and acted in school plays. Upon graduation, he became a radio sports announcer when he developed an ability to explain events in ways that appealed to a listener's imagination. A screen test in 1937 won him a contract in Hollywood, where he appeared in 53 films during the next two decades.

Reagan served as president of the Screen Actors Guild, where he became embroiled in disputes over the extent of

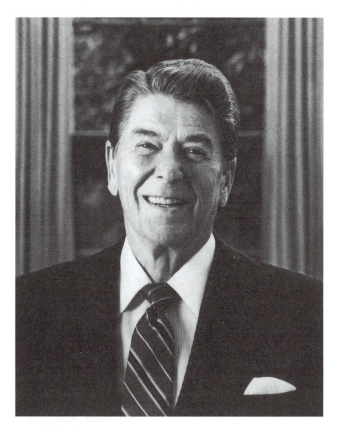

Ronald Reagan *(Ronald Reagan Library)*

the influence of MARXISM/COMMUNISM in the film industry. His political views shifted from LIBERALISM to CONSERVATISM during this period, and he subsequently toured the country touting his ideology as a spokesman for General Electric. In 1966 he ran for governor of California and won by a margin of 1 million votes; he was reelected in 1970.

After leaving the governorship in 1975, Reagan began a daily syndicated radio broadcast consisting of commentary on politics and policy. Without assistance and while maintaining the full travel schedule of a working politician, including a 1976 presidential campaign, he wrote 670 essays in four years. Here he refined the vision and ebullience that would later characterize him as the "Teflon President" and "The Great Communicator."

Reagan was elected in 1980 thanks in part to the votes of millions of Evangelical Protestants, who were beginning to shift their partisan allegiance to the Republican Party following their disappointment with the Carter administration. The emergence of the Christian Right political movement coincided perfectly with Reagan's presidential campaign, and he took great advantage of this fact, appealing successfully with powerful religious rhetoric to newly energized evangelical voters.

When Reagan took office, the nation faced serious foreign and domestic problems. Relations with the Soviet Union had sunk to a new low with the Soviet invasion of Afghanistan in late 1979, and many had been angered by the U.S. boycott of the 1980 Moscow Olympics. In November 1979, Iranians seized over 50 American hostages, and as the nightly newscasts ticked off the days of their captivity, American prestige abroad sank to new lows. At home, Reagan had to deal with stagflation: high inflation and high unemployment. And only 69 days after he took office, a deranged man named John Hinckley shot and nearly assassinated him.

Undeterred, Reagan summarized the goal of his first administration and at the same time rallied his staff to action: "If we get the economy in shape, we're going to be able to do a lot of things. If we don't, we're not going to be able to do anything." By dealing skillfully with Congress, Reagan obtained legislation designed to stimulate economic growth, curb inflation, increase employment, and strengthen the national defense. He embarked on a course of cutting taxes and the size of government and refused to deviate from this plan when the strengthening of defense forces began creating large federal budget deficits.

Reagan's approval ratings soared even as critics discredited him as an ill-informed, half-witted actor dependent on others for his lines. Reagan's grace and wit captured the fancy of the nation as he convinced Americans he had put them on the right track. An apparent renewal of national self-confidence ensued, and by 1984 it helped Reagan win a second term in an electoral landslide.

In foreign policy, Reagan sought to achieve "peace through strength." He increased defense spending by 35 percent and negotiated a treaty with Soviet leader Mikhail Gorbachev to eliminate intermediate-range nuclear weapons. His most spectacular decision was to send American bombers to Libya after evidence showed that Libyan leader Mu'ammar al-Gadhafi had been involved in masterminding an attack on American soldiers in a West Berlin nightclub. Reagan's second term, however, was marred by the Iran-Contra scandal, which came about when the Reagan administration sold American weapons to Iran and illegally used the profits to help anticommunist Nicaraguan rebels.

Despite these setbacks, Reagan left office with a 70 percent approval rating. His admirers saw him as a forceful and confident leader, yet he was criticized for being a disengaged manager who relied on his staff to carry out the responsibilities of the presidential office. Liberal critics labeled him an "empty suit," and some ranked him as a below-average president, but he had a dramatic influence on the history of his time. He moved the entire U.S. political spectrum to the right and imposed harsh fiscal constraints on his successors. He also helped to bring millions of Evangelical Protestants into the Republican fold.

The election of George H. W. Bush in 1988 assured the Reagan legacy. In 1999, Reagan published his autobiography, *An American Life,* and the Ronald Reagan Presidential Library opened in Simi Valley, California, the next year. In 1994, Reagan revealed that he was suffering from Alzheimer's disease and withdrew from the public spotlight. Historian Edmund Morris, Reagan's official biographer, once told the president that after years of studying, observing, and talking to him, he remained an enigma. Reagan replied, "But I'm an open book." "Yes, Mr. President," Morris replied, "but all your pages are blank." Such is the legacy of Ronald Wilson Reagan.

See also CHRISTIAN RIGHT AND THE REPUBLICAN PARTY; RELIGION IN THE 1980, 1984 PRESIDENTIAL ELECTION.

Further reading: Cannon, Joe. *President Reagan: The Role of a Lifetime.* New York: Public Affairs, 2000; Morris, Edmund. *Dutch: A Memoir of Ronald Reagan.* New York: Random House, 1999; Pemberton, William E. *Exit with Honor: The Life and Presidency of Ronald Reagan.* Armonk, N.Y.: M.E. Sharpe, 1998.

—J. David Woodard

Reconstructionist Judaism

The Reconstructionist movement is a branch of Judaism founded in 1922. It is based on an ideology developed by Rabbi Mordecai M. Kaplan (1881–1983), who was reared in ORTHODOX JUDAISM and initially served an Orthodox congregation before affiliating with CONSERVATIVE JUDAISM. As developed by Kaplan, Judaism is not a religion in the Western sense, but a religious civilization. Rooted heavily in Émile Durkheim's sociology of religion, Kaplan viewed religion as a human creation and as the symbolization and reflection of the group's ultimate values. There is debate among Kaplan's admirers, some of whom view him as a towering religious thinker and activist who struggled with traditional religious concepts and precepts, and his antagonists, some of whom view him as a freethinker, a heretic who was weak in character, and a charlatan. The reality was probably somewhere in between.

Although the ideology is essentially atheistic, Reconstructionism did not initially adopt the antipathy to tradition that characterized radical REFORM JUDAISM. On the contrary, Kaplan urged Jews to appreciate Jewish history and culture, including its religious rituals, because the more one practices and internalizes Jewish culture, the greater will be one's sense of Jewish identity. Accordingly, Reconstructionism was always pro-Israel, though it never adhered to a version of ZIONISM that defines immigration to Israel, *aliya*, as a value for all Jews.

Despite its appreciation for Jewish tradition, Reconstructionism has never looked askance at cultural change. On the contrary, an appreciation of change and a willingness to adopt it are necessary to prevent cultural stagnation. Moreover, Jewish culture must be innovative, Reconstructionism avers, if Jewish civilization is to have positive influence on world civilization.

Reconstructionism formally became a denominational movement within American Judaism with the founding of its seminary, Reconstructionist Rabbinical College, in Philadelphia, in 1968. It is the smallest of the Jewish denominations and makes up only a small fraction—approximately 1.5 percent—of American Jewish baby boomers. It is also not clear whether the movement is traditionalist or modernist; this question requires empirical analysis. Theoretically, it could be either. One survey of the Reconstructionist movement found with respect to ritual observances that, "In general, childhood observance was higher in the older (earlier) generation, than in later generations of current married adults." This lends support to the broad perception that the movement was, in the past, more traditional and is now becoming increasingly modernist. Although it has only a small percentage of affiliates, many suggest that the Judaism of most American Jews is, de facto, Reconstructionism.

Further reading: Eisenstein, Ira. *Reconstructing Judaism.* New York: Reconstructionist Press, 1986; Gurock, Jeffrey S., and Jacob J. Schacter, *A Modern Heretic and a Traditional Community: Mordecai M. Kaplan, Orthodoxy, and American Judaism.* New York: Columbia University Press, 1997; Rappeport, Michael. "1966 Demographic Study of the Reconstructionist Movement—Full Report," 1996; Waxman, Chaim I. *Jewish Baby Boomers: A Communal Perspective.* New York: State University of New York Press, 2001.

—Chaim I. Waxman

Reed, Ralph E., Jr. (1961–) *Christian activist*
Ralph Eugene Reed Jr. was born in 1961 and grew up in Miami, Florida, and Toccoa, Georgia. He gained national recognition for his work as the executive director of the CHRISTIAN COALITION. During his tenure, the Christian Coalition was shaped by his vision of a grassroots organization for Christians to become involved in politics. By the time he stepped down as executive

Ralph Reed *(Erik Lesser/Getty Images)*

director in 1997, the coalition claimed a membership of over a million, as well as election victories for Republican candidates for the House of Representatives in 1994.

Reed's interest in politics began at an early age. In 1976, he worked in his first political campaign helping a friend of the family run for Congress. Five years later, he worked on the campaign of Representative Mack Mattingly (R-Ga.), who invited Reed to intern in his office in Washington, D.C. Following his internship and work for the Republican National Committee, Reed became the executive director of the College Republican National Committee, for which he mobilized voters for President RONALD REAGAN's 1984 election bid.

In 1985, Ralph Reed left politics to pursue a Ph.D. in history at Emory University, intending to pursue a career in academia. His dissertation, "Fortresses of Faith: Design and Experience at Southern Evangelical Colleges, 1830–1900," explored the development of evangelical institutions of higher learning and their vision of the institution's role in shaping society. His academic plans were altered in 1989 at an inaugural event for President George H. W. Bush. At the event, Reed spoke to PAT ROBERTSON, the unsuccessful candidate for the 1988 Republican Party nomination and well-known televangelist, about his plans for the future. In the course of the conversation, Robertson discussed the need for a new organization to mobilize Christians into politics and requested that Reed put some of his ideas into a memorandum. Reed suggested a focus on grassroots organizing and the need to teach members about the political process. Later that year, Reed and his wife, Jo Anne, moved to Virginia Beach to begin work creating the Christian Coalition.

Attempting to avoid the missteps of the defunct Moral Majority, Reed emphasized the need for the Christian Coalition to focus more broadly on pro-family issues, not just opposition to abortion and homosexuality. With his leadership, the organization grew rapidly. By the end of 1990, the Christian Coalition claimed 57,000 members and 125 chapters. At its height in 1996, it claimed to have 1.7 million members with over 1,700 chapters in all 50 states.

The explosive growth of the Christian Coalition did not come without challenges. From its inception, the coalition came under scrutiny from the Internal Revenue Service (IRS), which launched an investigation into its tax-exempt status. Eventually in May 2000, the U.S. Court of Appeals supported the IRS's action to strip the Christian Coalition of its tax-exempt status, citing the partisan activity of the organization's VOTER GUIDES. The voter guides displayed a pro-Republican bias in its contrast of candidates on social issues. In addition, Reed came under attack in 1992 for his use of military metaphors to rally Christian Coalition members, particularly the image of opponents ending up in body bags after waging stealth campaigns.

The biggest success for the Christian Coalition came in the 1994 election with the Republican Party's capture of the majority in the U.S. House of Representatives. In 1994, the Christian Coalition distributed over 60 million voter guides. These and other mobilization efforts appeared to work as exit polls showed that evangelical voters made up one-third of the electorate. Following the 1994 election, Reed unveiled the 10-point CONTRACT WITH THE AMERICAN FAMILY as a quid pro quo for the Coalition's strong support, to the tune of $1 million, of the Republican Contract with America. These issues proved too controversial to move in Congress, particularly in light of veto threats by President WILLIAM JEFFERSON CLINTON.

In 1996, the Christian Coalition was less successful than in previous elections. While its membership base continued to expand, they were unable to defeat President Clinton or gain a firmer majority in Congress. At the height of the coalition's success, Reed stepped down as the executive director and started a political consulting firm, Century Strategies. He has recently served as the chair of the Republican Party in Georgia.

See also CHRISTIAN RIGHT AND THE REPUBLICAN PARTY; MORAL MAJORITY; SOUTHERN REPUBLICAN REALIGNMENT.

Further reading: Balz, Dan, and Ronald Brownstein. "God's Fixer." *Washington Post,* January 28, 1996; Glass, Stephen. "After the Fall." *New Republic,* May 26, 1997; Reed, Ralph. *Active Faith: How Christians Are Changing the Soul of American Politics.* New York: Free Press, 1996; Sedgwick, John. "The GOP's Three Amigos." *Newsweek,* January 9, 1995.

—Jean L. McSween

Reform Judaism

Judaism's Reform movement began in 19th-century Europe when Jews sought to take advantage of enlightened government calls for greater civil equality. While Reform Jews rarely achieved parity with their Christian neighbors, they launched an assimilationist religious movement committed to ethical monotheism, universalism, and an embrace of rationality in Jewish practice. Reform Jews held fast to biblical commandments rooted in logic but eschewed ritual as anachronistic.

On American shores, the Reform movement emerged as the most politically liberal of the three main Jewish denominations (including ORTHODOX JUDAISM and CONSERVATIVE JUDAISM). It grew in strength during the mid-19th century, when approximately 100,000 German Jews immigrated to the United States. Under the leadership of Rabbis ISAAC MAYER WISE (1819–1900) and David Einhorn (1809–79), Reform developed into a progressive religious movement challenging many tenets basic to traditional Judaism. Rabbi Wise refused to separate men and women during prayer, while Rabbi Einhorn presaged the Reform movement's entrée into national political issues when he offered his support for the ABOLITIONIST MOVEMENT. Reform Jews rejected ZIONISM and use of the Hebrew language in prayer in a bid to establish the United States as their new promised land.

Reform rabbis codified much of their late-19th-century ideology in the 1885 Pittsburgh Platform. The document established the basic tenets of Reform ideology and theology, offering one of the movement's earliest statements on its larger responsibilities in the world of American politics: "In full accordance with the spirit of the Mosaic legislation, which strives to regulate the relations between rich and poor," the rabbis proclaimed, "we deem it our duty to participate in the great task of modern times, to solve, on the basis of justice and righteousness, the problems presented by the contrasts and evils of the present organization of society."

The interwar period marked dramatic demographic and political changes within the Reform movement. The immigration of almost 2 million eastern European Jews pulled the movement back toward ritual and tradition. The recent arrivals challenged their German-American coreligionists for control of Jewish communal life and demanded a reappraisal of the movement's central tenets. Some Reform leaders came to embrace Zionism in the 1930s, when the rise of Adolf Hitler in Germany brought the movement's non-Zionist position even greater scrutiny. In 1937, the Central Conference of American Rabbis (CCAR) adopted a pro-Zionist position with the publication of the Columbus Platform. Aware, as well, of the growing need for social action in the midst of the Great Depression, the Reform rabbinate called for "application of its teachings to the economic order, to industry and commerce, and to national and international affairs." In response to the many social reform programs of FDR's New Deal, the CCAR emphasized "the duty of charity" and strove "for a social order which will protect men against the material disabilities of old age, sickness, and unemployment."

In the postwar period, the Reform movement, under the leadership of Maurice Eisendrath and Alexander Schindler, placed primary emphasis on social action. Reform Jews participated in the CIVIL RIGHTS MOVEMENT of the 1950s and 1960s, opened a lobbying office in Washington, D.C. (the Religious Action Center of Reform Judaism), applauded the work of Reform Jews such as Kivie Kaplan, who headed the National Association for the Advancement of Colored People (NAACP), and invited MARTIN LUTHER KING JR. to address their annual convention. While some southern Reform rabbis, including Atlanta's Jacob Rothschild, suffered violent retaliation for their public support of racial integration, most southern Reform Jews remained ambivalent about the high-profile civil rights work of their northern counterparts.

The Reform movement's commitment to secular political activism waned in the years after 1964. With the end of the Civil Rights movement and the rise of black power, Jews were marginalized by their one-time allies. When black militants, white leftists, and even many mainstream American churches condemned ISRAEL in the wake of the 1967 Six-Day War, Reform Jews turned inward, focusing their political efforts on the particular needs of the Jewish community. Reform Jews helped lead the movement to save Soviet Jews, committed themselves to a new form of American Zionism that actively encouraged *aliyah* (immigration to Israel), pressed movement leaders to reintroduce ritual, and passed a revised Statement of Principles for Reform Judaism that reflected the movement's new respect for tradition. The Hebrew Union College–Jewish Institute of Religion graduated the first woman rabbi in this period, while the movement as a whole tackled such controversial issues as patrilineal descent, mixed marriages, gay rights, and gender equity.

See also HASIDIC JUDAISM; RECONSTRUCTIONIST JUDAISM.

Further reading: Cohen, Naomi. *Encounter with Emancipation: The German Jews in the United States, 1830–1914.* Philadelphia: Jewish Publication Society, 1984; Meyer, Michael. *Response to Modernity: A History of the Reform Movement in Judaism.* New York: Oxford University Press, 1988; Raphael, Marc Lee. *Profiles in American Judaism: The Reform, Conservative, Orthodox, and Reconstructionist Traditions in Historical Perspective.* San Francisco: Harper and Row, 1984.

—Marc Dollinger

Reform Party

The Reform Party grew out of the presidential ambitions of Texas billionaire H. Ross Perot. On February 20, 1992, Perot declared that he would run for president on the CNN talk show *Larry King Live* if citizens would get him on the ballot in all 50 states. The next day, his office was deluged with phone calls and volunteers. Within a relatively short time, Perot accessed all state ballots. Once on the campaign trail, Perot

spent millions of his own money to broadcast political advertisements in the closing days of the 1992 presidential election, as a way to appeal directly to voters. He avoided the party primary system and, for a short time in early summer 1992, outpolled the Democratic candidate, Arkansas governor WILLIAM JEFFERSON CLINTON, and the sitting Republican vice president, George H. W. Bush.

Perot's campaign advocated fiscal responsibility and a type of vague social LIBERALISM. As an example of Perot's stand on a specific social issue, he favored the status quo on ABORTION laws, not because he thought abortion itself to be a good thing, but because he held it to be none of the government's business if a woman decided to terminate her pregnancy. Perot's main concern was on fiscal matters and the state of the faltering national economy. He was opposed to runaway deficit spending, which President RONALD REAGAN had endorsed, because the government seemed unwilling or unable to address numerous problems arising out of increased budget deficits such as unemployment and higher interest rates.

To a large degree, Perot's fiscal responsibility message succeeded. In 1992, Perot received 19 percent of the popular vote, becoming the most successful third-party presidential candidate since THEODORE ROOSEVELT ran on the Bull Moose ticket in 1912. Perot's success in 1992 and 1996 (in that contest, he drew only 8 percent of the vote) left the Reformists eligible for federal matching funds worth millions of dollars to its nominee. By the 2000 election, Perot was no longer interested in running for president.

Nevertheless, the Reform Party continued to field candidates after 1996. In Minnesota, the Reform Party elected former professional wrestler Jesse Ventura as governor in 1998. But Ventura would soon come under attack when a November 1999 issue of *Playboy* magazine revealed a surprisingly candid interview for a politician. In it, he called organized religion "a sham and a crutch for the weak minded" and blamed it for telling people to "go out and stick their noses in other people's business." That Mr. Ventura would be candid is no surprise: in the spring of the same year, he joined the ranks of Thomas Jefferson in refusing to use his office to promote the National Day of Prayer event.

Ventura's refusal fired the opening round in a battle against what would become his most formidable enemy: organized religion. Branded an antireligious bigot, Ventura faced calls for his resignation from Reform Party chairman Russell Verney, which damaged the Minnesota governor's standing as the uncontested leader of the national Reform Party. In October 2000, Ventura, the party's top elected official, announced that he was leaving the national Reform Party because it "is hopelessly dysfunctional."

Other religious issues have plagued the Reform Party. For example, in October 1999, presidential candidate PATRICK BUCHANAN switched from the Republican Party to the Reform Party, complaining that the GOP had abandoned core principles with its positions on issues such as abortion and GAY

RIGHTS. In August 2000, Buchanan threw his hat in the ring for the Reform Party's presidential nomination. But Buchanan, a former presidential candidate from the Republican far right, remained problematic for Reform Party members. The party stood for moderate conservatism, whereas Buchanan was much more conservative and was labeled a "right-wing" candidate by Perot loyalists. Nevertheless, he won the Reformist nomination. But in the general election, Buchanan failed miserably. He drew only about 1 percent of the popular vote, far short of the 5 percent that would have qualified the Reform Party for further federal campaign funds in 2004.

Further reading: Kohut, Andrew, John C. Green, Scott Teeter, and Robert C. Toth. *The Diminishing Divide: Religion's Changing Role in American Politics.* Washington, D.C.: Brookings Institution, 2000.

—Veronica Donahue DiConti

religion and the mass media

Criticism of (real and imagined) journalistic shortcomings in religion coverage is at least as common as criticism of political news coverage. And when religion stories have a political dimension (or vice versa), the public allows journalists an especially thin margin for error. Yet, notwithstanding the hazards of religion-and-politics news, one of the most important factors explaining the late-20th-century reinvigoration of the religion beat was competition to cover the story of politicized religion.

The special challenge of religion coverage is both an old and a new problem. From the Colonial era through the early years of the 19th century, most newspapers were organs of parties or denominations, not enterprises oriented toward independent news coverage. Newspapers in the modern sense—commercial, mass-circulation dailies—came to the fore only in the 1830s. Technological advances in large-scale printing made possible the "penny press," which in due course supplanted the partisan press. Along with its penchant for yellow journalism, it brought into existence what would eventually be called the religion beat. The journalistic style was typically impressionistic, emphasizing human interest angles, though it did not necessarily shy away from sharp criticism or satire.

In the early 20th century, this tradition of lively religion coverage began to give way to the church page, a journalistic ghetto usually appearing on Saturdays, featuring noncontroversial (even promotional) journalistic content adjacent to church listings. In part, this shift was driven by recognition of the increasing ethnic and religious diversity in the country, and the attendant fear among editors that religion was too divisive a topic. In addition, since religious organizations were now paying for their listings (once published for free as a public service), editors had a new financial disincentive to ruffle religious feathers.

A decline in the volume of religion coverage accompanied this downgrading of the religion beat. And although the post–World War II era saw a temporary surge in religion coverage, the tone was still predominantly consensual, reflecting the cold war culture of Protestant-Catholic-Jewish CIVIL RELIGION.

However, even though some prominent evangelicals like BILLY GRAHAM were held in high esteem (William Randolph Hearst's famous two-word telegram in 1949 instructed the *Los Angeles Examiner* to "Puff Graham"), many evangelicals and most fundamentalists had long felt alienated from the secular media. Of seminal importance in this development was the national coverage of the SCOPES "MONKEY" TRIAL in 1925, which portrayed evangelical opponents of evolutionary theory in a most unflattering light. The journalistic approach, particularly that of H. L. Mencken, recalled the iconoclastic tendencies of the 19th century, and the episode encouraged evangelicals to believe that the journalistic elite were contemptuous of conservative Christians and their politics.

The emerging cultural divide between mainline religion and sectarian EVANGELICALISM had important consequences for the development of broadcast media. While mainline groups gravitated toward the so-called sustaining time system of public service broadcasting allotments, the model for fundamentalists and evangelicals was entrepreneurial. Radio preachers, and later their televangelist heirs, would buy air time or their own stations and aggressively solicit financial support from their audiences.

By the 1970s and 1980s, religious broadcasting's mobilization potential vis-à-vis politics began to be realized. Enraged by recent social trends and Supreme Court decisions (e.g. ROE V. WADE), and emboldened by the growth of their resources, television preachers applied their entrepreneurial skills to the mobilization of the Christian Right. For example, JERRY FALWELL was persuaded to start the MORAL MAJORITY, and PAT ROBERTSON's broadcasting empire provided the backing needed to mount his 1988 run for the Republican presidential nomination, which in turn led to the creation of the Christian Right's flagship interest group, the CHRISTIAN COALITION.

For the secular news media, the rise of conservative religion in politics (and associated conflict over issues like abortion and homosexuality) helped spark a revival of interest in religion coverage. But there were other factor—the rise of Islamic fundamentalism, violence in the Middle East, RELIGIOUS PERSECUTION in a variety of countries, debates over AID TO RELIGIOUS SCHOOLS and social services, to name only a few—that brought the hard news value of religion into sharp relief. After decades of neglect of the religion beat, religion began to be found outside the church page.

Many critics, however, may not have perceived any increase in the quantity of religion news coverage, and in any case were utterly skeptical about any improvement in quality. Conservatives turned up the volume of their complaints about liberal and secular humanist biases in the media, and frequently quoted surveys that suggested journalists at elite news organizations are much less religious than the general public. But criticism came not only from conservatives. In his widely cited 1993 book, *The Culture of Disbelief,* Stephen Carter charged that journalists ignore religion when it spawns politics they like (e.g., the CIVIL RIGHTS MOVEMENT) but highlight and editorially denounce it otherwise. Mark Silk doubted that journalists have an overt secularist agenda but criticized religion coverage for overreliance on stock sentiments and simple morality tales. Ironically, most of these cultural templates are themselves essentially religious, such as the denunciation of false prophets and the lauding of religiously inspired good works.

In response to mounting criticism—and perhaps also because of a realization that religion stories sell well in a news market characterized by declining readers and viewers—the 1990s saw new investments in the religion beat. Dozens of newspapers created faith and values sections, and membership in the Religion Newswriters Association climbed from about 150 in the mid-1980s to about 240 by the end of the 1990s. In 1994, National Public Radio added a religion correspondent, and ABC became the first TV network to hire a full-time religion reporter. A few years later, PBS television added *Religion and Ethics Newsweekly* to its broadcast offerings. New academic centers and foundation initiatives—e.g., the Garrett-Medill Center for Religion and the News Media at Northwestern University, the Leonard E. Greenberg Center for the Study of Religion in Public Life at Trinity College (Hartford, Conn.), and the Pew Program on Religion and the News Media—offered assistance to journalists covering religion-related news.

See also CHRISTIAN BROADCASTING NETWORK (CBN) AND THE *700 CLUB;* GRAHAM, BILLY; PAX-TV.

Further reading: Hadden, Jeffrey K. "Televangelism and Politics." In *Piety and Politics: Evangelicals and Fundamentalists Confront the World.* Edited by Richard John Neuhaus and Michael Cromartie. Lanham, Md.: University Press of America, 1987; Hoover, Stewart M. *Religion in the News: Faith and Journalism in American Public Discourse.* London: Sage, 1998; Olasky, Marvin. *Prodigal Press: The Anti-Christian Bias of the American News Media.* Wheaton, Ill.: Crossway, 1988; Silk, Mark. *Unsecular Media: Making News of Religion in America.* Urbana: University of Illinois Press, 1995.
—Dennis R. Hoover

religion in Congress

Many commentators historically have believed that religion has little impact on the U.S. Congress. While members' religions consistently have been reported, until recently few strayed from the traditional enumerations of Roman Catholic, Jewish, and a few mainline Protestant denominations. This has meant that little is actually known about religion in Congress and how it might affect members' decision-making processes.

Mainline Protestant denominations have provided the significant majority of members of Congress for many years.

While that domination has slipped considerably in the last decade, they still account for the greatest percentage of members' religious affiliation (31 percent) in the 105th Congress. Other religious groups with significant representation in the recent past have been Catholics and evangelicals (25.1 percent and 16.7 percent, respectively). Classical studies of congressional behavior, however, make no mention of religious beliefs as a possible motivating factor in decision making.

By the 1980s, some members of Congress were claiming that religion was a significant factor in their political decision making. This revelation piqued interest in how this commitment might affect voting behavior. A great surge in attention, however, occurred with the advent of the conservative Republican 104th Congress, which was widely perceived as being full of evangelicals.

Existing research suggests that religion has a significant effect on members of Congress. Although this effect is not linked to denominations in particular, it can be linked to families of belief that exhibit similar theological, philosophical, and social characteristics. The earliest work on the role of religion in Congress is a book by two sociologists, Peter Benson and Dorothy Williams. Their *Religion on Capitol Hill: Myths and Realities* compiles information gathered by 82 in-depth interviews with members of Congress about their faith and how it impacts their lives. They found that religion is a significant factor in members' lives and has great impact on their decision making. This was linked not necessarily to denomination, however, but to a broader framework based on their views about God, society, and members' relationship to God and the people around them. Benson and Williams found significant correlation between these types of religious belief and members' political ideology.

More recent studies have found significant relationships between the religious character of a member's district and his or her behavior, and between stated religious denomination and abortion votes and overall ideology. Most compelling, Guth and Kellstedt (2001) show that the type and quantity of religious involvement, regardless of denominational preference, has a significant impact on involved members' social, economic, and foreign policy preferences. Studying the 105th Congress, they find that these religiously involved members tend to be more conservative and Republican. This seems particularly true for Catholics, evangelicals, and to some degree Mormons (see LATTER-DAY SAINTS). Furthermore, they reinforce the finding that the religious character of member constituents has an impact on member decisions, specifically in districts with substantial numbers of evangelical Christians.

Overall, it is clear that religion, whether that of the member herself or the constituents she represents, has a significant impact on voting behavior and decision making in Congress. This seems to be particularly the case for religiously committed members—a finding that is not surprising, given the visibility and power of religiously and politically active Christian conservatives in the past decade. Because EVANGELICALISM practically requires religious involvement and activity on the part of its adherents, it seems logical that these members would be the most guided by their faith—and the most conservative. This suggests, as Fastnow and colleagues point out, that many extant models of congressional behavior are inadequate.

See also CONTRACT WITH THE AMERICAN FAMILY; DRINAN, ROBERT; NEW EVANGELICALS IN CONGRESS.

Further reading: Benson, Peter L., and Dorothy L. Williams. *Religion on Capitol Hill: Myths and Realities.* San Francisco: Harper and Row, 1982; Fastnow, Chris, et al. "Holy Roll Calls: Religious Tradition and Voting Behavior in the U.S. House." *Social Science Quarterly* 80, no. 4 (December 1999): 687–701; Green, John C., and James L. Guth. "Religion, Representatives, and Roll Calls." *Legislative Studies Quarterly* 16, no. 4 (December 1991): 571–584; Guth, James L., and Lyman A. Kellstedt. "Religion and Congress." In *In God We Trust? Religion and American Political Life.* Edited by Corwin E. Smidt. Grand Rapids, Mich.: Baker, 2001.

—Kimberly Conger

religion in the congressional elections of 1994

The elections of 1994 brought about the broadest transfer of power from a majority to a minority party in the 20th century. Backed by broad national support, catalyzed in part by vigorous grassroots efforts by organizations of the Religious Right, the Republican Party gained control of both houses of Congress (for the first time in 40 years) and a majority of governorships, while making substantial gains in state and local legislatures and other elected offices.

Journalists and political scientists often underestimate religion's influence in American elections as a factor in issue selection, voter motivation, and candidates' rhetoric. But in 1994, the so-called Religious Right, represented most prominently by the CHRISTIAN COALITION and FOCUS ON THE FAMILY, was widely credited with providing decisive support for Republican candidates in many close elections across the country. Analysts have estimated that organizations aligned with the Religious Right spent over $25 million (mostly on campaign literature and its distribution) in grassroots efforts to elect Republicans to federal, state, and local offices. By its own account, the Christian Coalition, led by Executive Director RALPH REED and founder PAT ROBERTSON, spent $2 million to support the Republican Party's Contract with America, a 10-point legislative proposal signed in September 1994 by almost every U.S. House Republican incumbent and challenger. (In May 1995, the Coalition announced its own legislative agenda on social issues called the CONTRACT WITH THE AMERICAN FAMILY.) These efforts, undertaken by an energetic base of activists, had a significant impact on the midterm elections, when voter participation tends to drop considerably. National exit polls suggest that white evangelicals (the primary members of the Religious Right) constituted 20 percent of voters in the 1994 elections, and that 75 percent of their votes went to Republican candidates.

The political influence of the Religious Right in the 1994 elections ought not to be overstated, however. Republican electoral victories that year have been attributed to a variety of factors, including widespread disapproval of President WILLIAM JEFFERSON CLINTON, disaffection with the Democratic-controlled Congress, congressional redistricting favorable to the GOP, an infusion of campaign money for GOP challengers, and a strategic decision by Republicans to focus even local elections on national issues. Although white evangelicals clearly contributed to many of these factors and provided important swing votes in close elections, they were but one component of a broad-based conservative movement that swept the Republicans into power. They neither constituted a majority of all voters nor of Republican voters in the 1994 elections.

Though the Christian Coalition suggested that it represented all American Christians (and its well-organized and well-funded advocacy made it the most vocal and visible religious voice in the 1994 campaigns), American Christians evinced a wide range of political views and party affiliations. According to polls from the National Opinion Research Center and the *New York Times,* American Christians in the early 1990s were at least as likely to be Democrats as Republicans; born-again Christians were equally likely to be Democrats as Republicans; and two-thirds of Democrats and Republicans alike claimed that religion is "very important" in their lives. To counter the common linkage in the media between "religious" and "conservative," and to represent religious Americans with liberal political views, in 1994 a group of religious leaders from many faith traditions founded the INTERFAITH ALLIANCE (TIA). Though TIA has not achieved the political prominence of the Christian Coalition (which since 1994 has claimed to have over 1 million members), it remains an active organization today.

See also CHRISTIAN RIGHT AND THE REPUBLICAN PARTY.

Further reading: *Congressional Quarterly's Guide to Congress.* 5th ed. Washington, D.C.: CQ Press, 2000; Green, John C. "The Christian Right and the 1994 Elections: An Overview." In *God at the Grass Roots: The Christian Right in the 1994 Elections.* Edited by Mark J. Rozell and Clyde Wilcox. Lanham, Md.: Rowman and Littlefield, 1995; Pitney, John J., Jr., and William F. Connelly Jr. "'Permanent Minority' No More: House Republicans in 1994." In *Midterm: The Elections of 1994 in Context.* Edited by Philip A. Klinkner. Boulder, Colo.: Westview, 1996; Rice, Jim. "The Armor of the Righteous." *Sojourners* (November 1994): 24; Wald, Kenneth. *Religion and Politics in the United States.* 2d ed. Washington, D.C.: CQ Press, 1992.

—Erik Owens

religion in the 1800 presidential election

The elections of 1800 were the first in which religion played a significant role, reflecting both the rapid growth of evangelicals and the continued development of Federalist and Republican partisan alignments. The Federalists nominated the incumbent president, John Adams, with Charles Pinckney for vice president. The Republicans nominated THOMAS JEFFERSON, Adams's vice president, for president, and Aaron Burr for vice president. However, the electoral college vote resulted in a Jefferson-Burr tie, throwing the final selection to the House of Representatives, which chose Jefferson by a narrow margin.

Religion was used as a scare tactic by Federalists to alarm voters about the dangers of a Republican future. By 1800, popular support for the Federalists had suffered as a result of the Alien and Sedition Acts, and Adams had the image of a haughty aristocrat. Therefore, the Federalists sought to garner support by depicting the election as a choice between "Jefferson and no God" or "God and a Religious President."

Thomas Jefferson described himself variously as a "deist," "theist," "UNITARIAN," or "rational Christian," although he shied away from extensive discussion of his religion, because he believed religion to be a private matter. He was depicted by his enemies as a "howling atheist" and an infidel, accusations that he denied. One source of these accusations was a pamphlet published by the Reverend J. M. Mason entitled "The Voice of Warning to Christians on the Ensuing Election of a President of the United States," prophesying the destruction of religion if Jefferson became president. The Mason pamphlet included an analysis of Jefferson's book, *Notes on the State of Virginia.* Mason criticized Jefferson's treatment of the Flood, his denial that the Jews were the Chosen People, his ambivalence about the status of blacks, and his assertion that ATHEISM was not dangerous for politics. Mason concluded that Jefferson, if not an atheist, was at least an "infidel." For Christians to support him would be treason against God.

Alexander Hamilton urged John Jay, governor of New York, to manipulate the process of choosing New York's electors so as to prevent an atheist from becoming president. New England Puritans were particularly harsh in their attacks on Jefferson. One clergyman warned his audience that they would have to hide their Bibles if Jefferson won the election.

Jefferson's religious views were, in fact, similar to those of Adams, who was critical of this religious mudslinging. Jefferson did not try to publicly clarify his views, but in private correspondence he complained about these religious activists.

Higher-status churches backed the Federalists. In states with established churches, these churches found the Federalists more compatible than the Republicans, while Jefferson won support from populist denominations such as Baptists and Methodists, who found his commitment to religious freedom more persuasive than his personal views on religion. The Republicans were also helped by Aaron Burr's heritage as grandson of the great Puritan leader, JONATHAN EDWARDS. Adams speculated that this fact alone brought the Republicans 100,000 votes.

In office, Jefferson remained circumspect about his religious views. He signed some legislation sought by religious interests but refused to declare federal days of prayer and made only superficial public appeals to a deity.

Further reading: Malone, Dumas. *Jefferson and the Ordeal of Liberty.* Boston: Little, Brown, 1962; Menendez, Albert J. *Religion at the Polls.* Philadelphia: Westminster Press, 1977; Reichley, A. James. *Religion in American Political Life.* Washington, D.C.: Brookings Institution, 1985; West, John G., Jr. *The Politics of Revelation and Reason.* Lawrence: University Press of Kansas, 1996.

—Jane Gurganus Rainey

religion in the 1884 presidential election

By capturing his home state of New York with a slender majority, Governor Grover Cleveland narrowly defeated the Republican presidential nominee, James Blaine, from Maine in an election marked by scandal, blunder, minor parties, and conflicting issues. The final tally was delayed several days because of the narrow vote, as Cleveland defeated Blaine 48.5 to 48.3 percent, with the minor parties earning just over 3 percent of the popular vote. New York provided the deciding votes in the electoral college, as Cleveland earned 219 to Blaine's 182. Cleveland became the first Democratic president in almost 30 years by winning his home state, the South, and some border states, while Blaine secured much of the North and all of the Western states.

At the time, the Republicans were fragmented among three main factions. The Stalwarts represented by President Chester Arthur opposed civil service and other reforms; the "Half-Breeds," represented by the former House speaker and senator Blaine, sought a protective tariff, opposed civil service reform, and wanted more trade with Latin America; while the Reformers rallied behind George Edmunds of Vermont, a proponent of civil service reform and a dissenter regarding the protectionist tariff. The only serious contender to Blaine was Arthur, who failed to unite a New York delegation in his favor. In Chicago, no candidate could defeat Blaine, who won on the fourth ballot. Senator John Logan of Illinois was chosen as his running mate.

The Democratic National Convention, also held in Chicago, saw many challengers, but Governor Cleveland quickly became the favorite. Cleveland, from the largest electoral state, established himself as a reformer in New York by signing a civil service reform law and creating Niagara Falls as a state park, among other reforms. Cleveland did not have the support of some urban Roman Catholics in New York City because of his weakened ties with the Tammany Hall political machine, but he won handily on the second ballot. Cleveland's managers selected the 1876 vice presidential nominee, Senator Thomas Hendricks of Indiana, for the same post for the 1884 campaign.

Cleveland revealed his platform of federal spending reductions, increased civil service reforms, and a one-term limit for the presidency. He also wanted to distinguish himself as the candidate with the better character. The Democratic Party depicted Blaine as a money- and power-hungry politician, which materialized on the editorial pages of national publications. Cleveland came away relatively unscathed when his own extramarital past was uncovered.

Blaine set out on an intense, six-week fall tour and gave more than 400 speeches. He wanted to make tariff protection and a revised stance on civil service reform the focus of his campaign. The Mugwumps, or Reform wing of the Republican Party, refused to acknowledge the new civil service position and decided against supporting him. During his campaign, Blaine also attempted to deflect public persecution over his own marriage scandal and shady dealings with railroad tycoons.

Blaine's electoral strategy also consisted of winning the Irish vote. The Republican candidate avoided any reference to his Blaine Amendment, brought before Congress in 1875, which attempted to eliminate government funding for church-related schools. Irish Catholics turned their support to him mainly as a reward for his harshness toward England while serving in Congress and as secretary of state. In addition, he earned their respect because he was emphatic about his mother being Catholic and his admiration "for her Church."

The deciding factor in Blaine's campaign occurred in the swing state of New York. On October 29, as Blaine finished his whirlwind tour, he attended a rally of supporting ministers at the Fifth Avenue Hotel in New York City. The rally was designed to further humiliate Cleveland and convince voters to deny the man with an illegitimate child. Instead, Presbyterian Dr. Samuel D. Burchard unleashed an infamous and unforgivable alliteration against Blaine's opponents: "We are Republicans and don't propose to leave our party and identify ourselves with the party whose antecedents have been rum, Romanism, and rebellion." Blaine's tardy response to the anti-Catholic comment angered the Irish and made it impossible to maintain their already tenuous support.

Another factor contributing to Cleveland's victory included the Republican slandering of the PROHIBITION PARTY candidate, John St. John, who focused his campaign on upstate New York to steal votes from Blaine.

The 1884 election is typically discussed for its interesting anecdotes, but more important, it demonstrated that voters were interested in choosing among significant programmatic differences between the parties.

Further reading: Prendergast, William B. *The Catholic Voter in American Politics.* Washington, D.C.: Georgetown University Press, 1999; Summers, Mark W. *Rum, Romanism, and Rebellion: The Making of a President, 1884.* Chapel Hill: University of North Carolina Press, 2000.

—John R. LaRaia

religion in the 1888 presidential election

Religion was a minor and uncontroversial issue in the presidential elections of 1888. Republican Benjamin Harrison (1833–1901) won the office over Democrat and incumbent Grover Cleveland (1837–1908). Harrison won 233 electoral votes but lost the popular vote, as Cleveland collected only 168 electoral votes and won the popular vote. This was only the third time in U.S. history that the winner of the popular vote lost the election (1824 and 1876 being the first two instances, 2000 being the fourth). Added to this controversy was the fact that apparently New York and Indiana voters had been paid by Republican Party operatives to cast their lot with Harrison and, in this way, ensure that Harrison won the electoral votes of these two key states.

Grandson to President William Henry Harrison, Benjamin Harrison had previously been a lawyer, Union Army officer, then senator (1881–87) from Indiana. His vice presidential running mate was Levi P. Morton (1824–1920), formerly a U.S. representative from New York, as well as a minister to France in the 1880s. On the other hand, Cleveland had risen through the ranks from local to national politician, starting out as a sheriff, becoming mayor of Buffalo, governor of New York (1883–85), and finally, in 1884, winning the presidency over James G. Blaine (1830–93) of Maine, in a tightly contested election. Cleveland's running mate was Allen G. Thurman (1813–95), formerly a U.S. representative and senator for the state of Ohio.

Though the election ended in some rancor, until the outcome, it was notable for its lack of controversy. Beyond making the expected acceptance speeches, neither candidate actively campaigned, and the only major and real differences between the candidates and their respective party platforms were their positions on tariffs. Harrison sought to maintain the high tariffs already in place to protect American companies from cheaper foreign imports. For this reason, American industry backed Harrison and contributed generously to his campaign. Cleveland argued that tariffs increased the prices of necessities and, therefore, made life difficult for the ordinary worker and citizen. He also saw that high tariffs created dangerously high Treasury surpluses, thereby reducing the free flow of money through the U.S. economy. Cleveland backed the Mills Bill of 1888 as a way to reduce the tariffs and the subsequent surpluses.

Though unsubstantiated rumors circulated that in his early years, Harrison had been a member of the anti–Roman Catholic KNOW-NOTHING PARTY, religious issues surrounding the candidates and voters were ultimately not decisive or important in this election. Rather, the religious issues that arose in 1888 related to larger questions of domestic policy, and were neither emphasized nor controversial during the campaign. On the one hand, both parties sought to show that they had or would stem the flow of Chinese immigrants into the country. This was largely an economic question, but it crossed over into discourse about religion when, during both conventions, speeches were made denouncing the foreign, "pagan," and detrimental influence on the United States from this influx. Also, both parties sought to demonstrate that they were actively attempting to stamp out the Mormon practice of POLYGAMY in Utah. The Republicans explicitly included this goal in their platform; however, this was a largely moot point, since in 1887 the Edmunds-Tucker Act had been passed as the strictest and most successful arsenal of legal weapons against the practice.

—Susanna Morrill

religion in the 1896 presidential election

In the presidential election of 1896, the major issue was metallic. It pitted William McKinley, an Ohio Republican in favor of the gold standard, against WILLIAM JENNINGS BRYAN, a free-silver Democrat from Nebraska. In the end, McKinley bested Bryan 51 to 46 percent, while splinter and minor parties garnered about 3 percent. In the electoral college, McKinley took 23 states and 271 votes to Bryan's 22 states and 176 votes, since McKinley's support centered in population centers with economic power: the industrial Midwest and the Northeast. Bryan carried only one county in New England.

For the Republicans, the nomination was contested but was certainly not a battle. Mark Hanna, an industrialist senator from Ohio, orchestrated support for McKinley and delivered it on the convention floor in St. Louis—McKinley won on the first ballot. While Hanna organized the campaign and drew about $3.5 million from big business, McKinley sat on his front porch and greeted the 750,000 people who came to visit during the campaign with subsidized train fares. In addition to a huge funding advantage, the Republicans also benefited from the timing of a depression, which coincided neatly with Grover Cleveland's Democratic administration. In McKinley, Republicans backed sound money (in the form of the gold standard), while most of those backing the free coinage of silver did not splinter from the party.

The Democratic Party had a tougher row to hoe. Coming out of a depression, they were branded the party of economic failure. They were also the more culturally diverse party and contained the deepest ideological differences. Furthermore, Democrats faced challenges from minor parties, especially the waning People's Party. At their convention in Chicago, the free-silver forces took control of the party, though no one leader was apparently in control. In speeches at the convention, Bryan, only 36 at the time, had the fortune of speaking last and delivered one of the great speeches of American history. He concluded: "We will answer their demand for a gold standard by saying to them: You shall not press down upon the brow of labor this crown of thorns, you shall not crucify mankind upon a cross of gold." Partly on the basis of this speech, he swept to the Democratic presidential nomination.

Bryan crisscrossed the country in one of the great campaign tours, covering, by his own estimate, over 18,000 miles and giving 600 speeches to about 5 million people. It was not enough to overcome the many barriers he faced. His campaign was disorganized and underfunded. Republicans tagged him as a rabble-rouser and a subversive, labels given credence by Bryan's backing from Socialist Eugene Debs and controversial Illinois governor John Peter Altgeld. Bryan's campaign was also hampered by the confusion of "fusion-tickets." He was also nominated by the Populists and carried that label in some states,

while in other states he was a Silver Democrat, among other labels. Moreover, Bryan did not receive the endorsements of major newspapers in urban areas of battleground states.

Most significantly, Bryan needed to create a farmer-labor alliance and make it stick. A combination of economics and ethnicity undermined it, though. Industry allegedly threatened to make purchase orders subject to cancellation if Bryan won. Moreover, Bryan's Protestant pietism did not appeal to urban, ethnic, or Roman Catholic voters, just as the pietistic Protestantism of Republicans candidates did not appeal in earlier elections. At the same time, McKinley and the Republicans were more attractive than they had been in the past; McKinley was not favored by the nativist American Protective Association, and Republicans made overtures to Catholics, one of Hanna's priorities. Support in heavily Catholic areas dropped precipitously from 1892 levels of support for Cleveland.

Rural areas also were not united behind Bryan. Bad weather and poor markets hit hard the South and the Great Plains. Yet some Midwestern farmers, in Illinois and Iowa for instance, were doing relatively better and did not see or need free silver as a savior. Their support for Bryan in November was demonstrably weaker than in states farther south and west.

The 1896 election, in the end, was about power, about sustaining the Jeffersonian and Jacksonian myth of the agrarian or the myth of the "self-made man," both equally powerful but also at odds. The 1896 election resolved that tension in favor of the Republican Party, but the result was to raise, sustain, and eventually resolve some of the basic questions raised in 1896 about monetary policy, the power of special interests, and the democratic process. The election also doomed the Populists, who could not weather their fusion with the Democrats.

Though Bryan did not live up to the assertion of a friend that he would be "greater than any other man since Christ," his campaign performance in 1896 cemented him as one of the great popular politicians of American history.

Further reading: Glad, Paul. *McKinley, Bryan, and the People.* New York: J. B. Lippincott, 1964; Kleppner, Paul. *The Cross of Culture.* New York: Free Press, 1970; Prendergast, William B. *The Catholic Voter in American Politics.* Washington, D.C.: Georgetown University Press, 1999; Schlesinger, Arthur M., Jr., ed. *The Coming to Power: Critical Presidential Elections in American History.* New York: Chelsea House, 1971.

—Paul A. Djupe

religion in the 1928 presidential election

Religion played a significant role in the presidential election of 1928. After Republican president Calvin Coolidge released a statement saying that he did not wish to seek another term, the Republicans nominated Secretary of Commerce Herbert Hoover. Hoover, popular in the party and a distinguished statesman and humanitarian, won the party's nomination on the first ballot at the Republican Convention in Kansas City. However, such a show of unity behind a candidate in the

Democratic Party was not so forthcoming. In 1928, ALFRED E. SMITH (1873–1944), governor of New York, became the first Roman Catholic to run for the presidency on a major party ticket. Nominated after the second ballot at the party's national convention, this was not Smith's first run for the party nomination. He was first suggested as a presidential possibility in 1920. His supporters were more numerous in 1924, when FRANKLIN DELANO ROOSEVELT, who dubbed him the "happy warrior," placed Smith's name into consideration by the party. But his Catholic religion worked against him at the convention, as did his opposition to Prohibition. He was most strongly opposed by William G. McAdoo, and their contest resulted in a deadlock, the nomination going to John W. Davis.

By 1928, Smith secured the Democratic Party's support and became the party nominee. In the general election, Smith appeared to be Hoover's complete opposite. While Hoover was a rural Protestant who never held elective office, Smith was a New York Catholic and longtime member of the Tammany Hall machine, known for its political patronage and corrupting influence on local politics. Both Smith's religion and his New York upbringing made it difficult for him to win a national election. Despite his role as a vigorous reformer as governor of New York, Smith (born on Manhattan's Lower East Side on December 30, 1873, the son of poor parents and the grandson of Irish immigrants who came to America in 1841) was viewed by voters in general and by rural voters in particular as the epitome of the ethnic, urban, machine politician.

Smith's nomination reflected the growing political influence of the ethnic urban North. But Smith was unable to unify the party behind his candidacy, and he became the first Democrat since the Civil War not to carry the South. The loss of the South could also be attributed to his verbal attacks on the KU KLUX KLAN, which undoubtedly alienated him from some southern voters.

Smith did, however, have tremendous strength among immigrant voters, and part of the explanation for Smith's strength in cities was an apparent rise in voting among newly enfranchised Roman Catholic women. For example, heavily Italian precincts in Boston saw female registration rise by 29 percent in 1928, and in Irish precincts the rise in female voting was comparable. A major source of the surge of Democratic votes later in the 1930s was the group of potential Democrats who had been such a large proportion of the electorate in the 1920s. Smith's legacy perhaps is that he supplied an available pool of voters that was mobilized to vote for the first Catholic candidate, but even more so, for the next Democratic candidate, Franklin D. Roosevelt, who would win the presidency in 1932. Attacks made against Smith claimed that if elected, he would make Catholicism the national religion.

In addition to Smith's Catholicism, the other major issue in the campaign was Prohibition. While Smith openly campaigned against Prohibition, Hoover supported its continuation. By election day, the election of 1928 would become another Republican landslide, with Herbert Hoover winning

the presidency with 58.3 percent of the popular vote, compared with Smith's 40.8 percent. Smith carried only eight states, and he lost his own New York. Smith's defeat by Hoover, in large measure, was due to the fantastic and virulent anti-Catholic propaganda that circulated throughout the nation.

After Smith's defeat, it was thought that no Catholic would ever have a chance to win the White House. It would take 32 years and eight more presidential elections to shatter that belief when a Catholic Massachusetts senator, JOHN F. KENNEDY, defeated his Republican opponent, Californian RICHARD M. NIXON, to become the first Roman Catholic president of the United States.

Further reading: Kohut, Andrew, John C. Green, Scott Teeter, and Robert C. Toth. *The Diminishing Divide: Religion's Changing Role in American Politics.* Washington, D.C.: Brookings Institution, 2000; Mayhew, David R. *Placing Parties in American Politics.* Princeton, N.J.: Princeton University Press, 1986; Nie, Norman H., Sidney Verba, and John R. Petrocik. *The Changing American Voter.* Cambridge, Mass.: Harvard University Press, 1979.

—Veronica Donahue DiConti

religion in the 1960 presidential election

JOHN F. KENNEDY's 113,000 popular vote victory in the 1960 election reinstated Democratic Party control over the White House after an eight-year hiatus in the most closely contested presidential race in the 20th century. The Massachusetts senator's narrow win over Vice President Richard Nixon was also reflected in his slender 303 to 219 margin in the electoral college. Yet it was not Kennedy's razor-thin victory but his religion that was the most salient feature of the 1960 election. This election marked the second (and last) time that a presidential candidate's Roman Catholicism emerged as the single strongest factor shaping the vote preferences of the American electorate. The first occasion was in 1928, when the Democrats nominated New York governor AL SMITH, the first Catholic to appear at the top of a major party ticket. In that election, Smith suffered an overwhelming defeat at the polls, losing many traditional Democratic states.

Several reasons have been offered to account for why Kennedy's Catholicism did not handicap him. Kennedy's urbanity, bearing, and wealth were less culturally alienating to native-born non-Catholics than was Smith's Lower East Side, ethnic Irish comportment. The Catholic population, moreover, had undergone remarkable transformation since the 1920s; it was richer, better educated, more assimilated into the mainstream, and represented a significantly larger portion of the electorate, particularly in the eastern and midwestern battleground states. Anti-Catholicism was also much less respectable and out in the open in 1960 than in 1928. Finally, the Republican victories in 1952 and 1956 were deviating elections, attributed largely to the personal appeal of the Republican standard bearer, General DWIGHT D. EISENHOWER. The

Democratic Party was the majority party in 1960, a status it had held since 1932, when FRANKLIN DELANO ROOSEVELT assembled the New Deal coalition, and Kennedy made the appeal to party loyalty a major theme in his speeches on the campaign stump.

Both candidates developed strategies to mute the religious issue. Kennedy met the issue head-on in a televised broadcast during the West Virginia primary, by framing it as a question of TOLERANCE versus intolerance, and again in a September address before a group of ministers in Houston, where he declared his independence from the Catholic hierarchy, opposition to state AID TO RELIGIOUS SCHOOLS, and staunch support for church-state separation. Nixon downplayed the importance of Kennedy's Catholicism and publicly discouraged its exploitation by his supporters.

While issues such as the "missile gap," Kennedy's opposition to the jailing of MARTIN LUTHER KING JR., the economy, and foreign relations were discussed throughout the course of the campaign, Kennedy's Catholicism, more than anything else, had the greatest impact at the polls. The salience of the religious issue was reflected in the strong 30-point shift of Catholics toward Kennedy over what they gave Stevenson in 1956 and in the counter shift of religious Protestants toward Nixon. Although some estimates indicate that Kennedy's religion cost him 1.5 million votes nationwide, the concentration of Catholics in competitive swing states and the bunching of anti-Catholic voters in "safe" southern states had the net effect of enabling Kennedy to pick up 22 electoral votes from states that otherwise would have gone to Nixon.

Another aspect of the 1960 election was its acceleration of the trend toward candidate-centered technologies, political consultants, and campaign organizations, including the use of a variety of mass media, particularly television. The four televised debates, reaching some 70 million out of 107 million voters, disproportionately Catholic, probably represented the high point of this new style of campaign. The first debate quickened Democratic support for Kennedy by rallying wavering Democrats.

Francis Spellman, the archbishop of New York, is flanked by presidential candidates John F. Kennedy (left) and Vice President Richard Nixon. *(Hulton/Archive)*

See also CATHOLICS AND THE DEMOCRATIC PARTY; MAIN-
LINE PROTESTANTS AND THE REPUBLICAN PARTY; SOUTHERN
REPUBLICAN REALIGNMENT.

Further reading: Agranoff, Robert. *The New Style in Elec-
tion Campaigns.* Boston: Holbrook Press, 1972; Campbell,
Angus, Philip E. Converse, Warren E. Miller, and Donald E.
Stokes. *Elections and the Political Order.* New York: Wiley,
1966; Pool, Ithiel de Sola, Robert P. Abelson, and Samuel L.
Popkin. *Candidates, Issues, and Strategies: A Computer Sim-
ulation of the 1960 Election.* Cambridge, Mass.: M.I.T. Press,
1964; Prendergast, William B. *The Catholic Voter in American
Politics: The Passing of the Democratic Monolith.* Washington,
D.C.: Georgetown University Press, 1999; White, Theodore
H. *The Making of the President 1960.* New York: Atheneum,
1962.

—Louis Bolce

religion in the 1976 presidential election

In the 1976 election, there is general scholarly consensus that
the presidential candidacy of JAMES EARL CARTER, a Southern Baptist and self-professed born-again Christian, was the
pivotal religious variable in the election. Jimmy Carter's candidacy marks the ascent of what is now termed the Religious
Right, or Christian Right movement. His candidacy clearly signaled to the Christian community the acceptability, if not the
moral necessity, of integrating religion and politics. Lyman
Kellstedt and colleagues have argued that 1976 represented
the first of several years to be declared "the Year of the Evangelical." Specifically, candidate Carter asked that fellow evangelicals and the conservative Protestant religious community
put aside their distrust in politics and get involved.

The 1976 presidential election was the first election in
which conservative Christian voters were specifically mobilized
as a bloc. Therefore, it also became the first election in which
other politicians recognized that this constituency could be
mobilized for both electoral and policy goals. In the aftermath
of this election, the MORAL MAJORITY was founded in 1978, and
PAT ROBERTSON came into political prominence during the
following decade, including as candidate for president.

Following the 1976 election, scholarly interest started to
recognize the impact of religion on electoral behavior and
issue development. That election represented a watershed in
the growth of scholarly literature in the area of religion and
politics. Since 1980, a born-again question has been included
in the American National Election Study's Presidential Election surveys. There was no such question in 1976. Since then,
there has been considerable research on the political effects of
the born-again phenomenon. It is interesting that the three
major presidential candidates in 1980 (Carter, RONALD REA-
GAN, and independent John Anderson) all claimed to have had
a born-again experience.

The year 1976 was also the first election in which an outsider (Carter) won a major political party's nomination. Carter

was an outsider in two senses. He was a political outsider as a
governor without any national political connection, and he was
a sociocultural outsider as a southern, born-again Baptist who
wore his religion on his sleeve. Carter's unique opportunity was
due in large part to changes in the presidential nomination process brought about in the aftermath of the 1968 Democratic
National Convention debacle in Chicago, and because extensive
media coverage allowed Carter to run as a personality and not as
a party member, thereby ushering in candidate-centered elections. The year 1976 was also the first campaign in which public funds were utilized for a presidential election. Moreover,
Carter stressed values and issues that appealed to religious conservatives, who had long been ignored in political campaigns.

From an ideological perspective, the period from 1965 to
1976 was one of extensive change within evangelical and fundamentalist religious communities. Before the election campaign of 1976, the evangelical and fundamentalist communities
believed that Christianity required the individual to remain
separate from the political and secular world. However, Carter
mobilized these voters because of his own self-professed religious affiliation. Evangelicals were quite supportive of Carter;
fundamentalists, though, criticized him for an interview in
Playboy magazine in which he admitted committing adultery
"in my heart." Nonetheless, many fundamentalists joined
evangelicals in voting for Carter, who was the first avowedly
evangelical candidate in half a century.

This election had two important consequences. First, it
signaled to the political, religious, and secular communities that
there was a voting bloc of evangelicals and fundamentalists to
be tapped. No one had previously considered these individuals as a potential voting bloc because of their long-held preference to remain separated from the secular world. Second,
Carter made a convincing case that Christians had an obligation to participate in politics, thus challenging the notion that
Christians should not mix their religious beliefs with politics.

The period from the 1970s until the middle 1990s is
referred to as the "third wave" of the Christian Right movement
during the 20th century. In the aftermath of Carter's election,
the Moral Majority and CHRISTIAN VOICE were both founded in
1978. These were considered New Christian Right political
organizations, as opposed to strictly religious organizations.

Further reading: Kellstedt, Lyman, John Green, James
Guth, and Corwin Smidt. "Religious Voting Blocks in the 1992
Election: The Year of the Evangelical?" *Sociology of Religion*
55 (1994): 307–326; Leege, David C., and Lyman A. Kellstedt,
eds. *Rediscovering the Religious Factor in American Politics.*
Armonk, N.Y.: M. E. Sharpe, 1993.

—Maurice M. Eisenstein

religion in the 1980 presidential election

The candidates in the 1980 presidential election were the
incumbent president, Democrat JAMES EARL CARTER, Republican and former governor of California RONALD REAGAN, and

RELIGION AND THE VOTE IN THE 1980 PRESIDENTIAL ELECTION

Religious Affiliation	Candidate (Party)			Total
	Carter (D)	Reagan (R)	Anderson (Ind.)	
Mainline Protestant	29.6%	62.8%	7.6%	100%
Evangelical Protestant	34.8	58.2	7.1	100
Roman Catholic	39.5	51.0	9.5	100
Jewish	48.3	37.9	13.8	100
Nontraditional Christian/Orthodox	26.9	65.4	7.7	100
No religion/Atheist/Agnostic	27.9	50.0	22.1	100
Total	33.5	57.1	9.3	100

Source: *American National Election Study, 1992 national adult survey.*
Frequencies: *Mainline: 328; Evangelical: 184; Catholic: 210; Jewish: 29; Nontraditional/Orthodox: 26; No religion: 68; Total: 847.*
Note: *Figures exclude African Americans.*

independent John Anderson. Reagan won by a wide margin, with 50 percent of the popular vote to Carter's 41 percent and Anderson's 6.

The 1980 presidential campaign took place amid several crises, including the Iranian hostage crisis, an energy crisis, and an economic recession. The president's approval ratings were low and people blamed him for the nation's many ills. Thus, the stage was set for an uphill battle against a charismatic actor and former governor (Reagan) and an independent who appealed to estranged Democrats (Anderson). Though the two-party system in the United States makes it difficult for third-party candidates to gain notice, Anderson, a liberal Republican who resigned his congressional seat in Illinois and his party to run for president, received considerable media attention and proved to be a constant thorn in Carter's side.

Studying patterns of vote choice among different religious groups in 1980 provides insights not only into partisan preferences among different faiths, but also into more general political trends taking place in the United States during this uncertain time. The table shows the vote choice among different religious groups as captured by the 1980 National Election Study (NES). When considering the relationship between religious affiliation and vote choice, it is useful to examine nonblack Protestants under two separate categories: mainline (such as Lutheran and Presbyterian) and evangelical (such as Baptist and Church of Christ). Traditionally, white mainline and Evangelical Protestants have tended to diverge in their partisan affiliations and vote choice, in part owing to an historical link between white Southerners and the Democratic Party, though that relationship was in flux toward the end of the 20th century. In this election, Carter's own Southern Baptist and born-again background most likely kept some white evangelical votes that might have otherwise defected to Reagan.

For a variety of historical and continuing social forces, African Americans have tended to be both Protestants and Democrats and overwhelmingly support the Democratic candidate in modern presidential elections. Some 92 percent of

African-American voters supported Carter in 1980 according to the 1980 NES.

Among other religious affiliations, Roman Catholics, nontraditional Protestants (such as CHRISTIAN SCIENTISTS and LATTER-DAY SAINTS, or Mormons), and Eastern Orthodox practitioners voted primarily for Reagan, while Jews voted for Carter more than for Reagan or Anderson. People of non-Judeo-Christian backgrounds (including ISLAM, BUDDHISM, and HINDUISM) and those claiming no religious affiliation preferred Reagan.

This breakdown is largely in accord with the traditional voting patterns of the predominant religious groups in the United States, the main exception being Catholics, who, as a group, have usually considered themselves Democrats and voted accordingly. The defection among Catholics helps to demonstrate that in the end, party loyalty was not strong enough to hand the presidency back to Carter. Anderson's presence gave disaffected Democrats an alternative, as evidenced by his high levels of support among Catholics and Jews. That Carter was unable to secure a majority of the Jewish vote is particularly noteworthy given that Democrats tend to do very well among Jewish voters. Reagan also swayed many Democrats to his side, as evidenced by his high Catholic support (and the new term, "Reagan Democrats").

The Democratic New Deal coalition began to unravel in the 1980 election, leading some to proclaim that the "Roosevelt coalition [had] come to an end." In the past, Democrats had wooed urban immigrants, many of whom were Catholics. The ties that those immigrant groups forged with Democrats had been passed down to subsequent generations. Throughout the 1970s, the Democratic Party came to be identified more and more with nonwhite minorities and social liberals. Since white Catholics were no longer a downtrodden, recent immigrant group, the question of Catholic ties to the Democrats would continue to be raised. Reagan's broad popularity with the American public is clearly demonstrated through an examination of voting patterns among different religious groups, yet it was still too early to tell whether his popularity meant that the Democratic coalition had fallen apart for good.

See also CATHOLICS AND THE DEMOCRATIC PARTY; JEWS AND THE DEMOCRATIC PARTY; MAINLINE PROTESTANTS AND THE REPUBLICAN PARTY; RELIGION IN THE 1984 PRESIDENTIAL ELECTION; RELIGION IN THE 1976 PRESIDENTIAL ELECTION; SOUTHERN REPUBLICAN REALIGNMENT.

Further reading: Erikson, Robert, and Kent Tedin. *American Public Opinion.* 6th ed. New York: Longman, 2000; The National Election Studies, Center for Political Studies, University of Michigan. Electronic resources available at the NES website. URL: www.umich.edu/~nes; McWilliams, Wilson Carey. "The Meaning of the Election." In *The Election of 1980: Reports and Interpretations.* Edited by Gerald Pomper. Chatham, N.J.: Chatham House, 1981; Pomper, Gerald. "The Nominating Contests." In *The Election of 1980: Reports and Interpretations.* Edited by Gerald Pomper. Chatham, N.J.: Chatham House, 1981.

—Deborah Schildkraut

religion in the 1984 presidential election

The candidates in the 1984 presidential election were incumbent Republican RONALD REAGAN and Democrat Walter Mondale, vice president under JAMES EARL CARTER and a former senator. Reagan won in a landslide, with 59 percent of the popular vote (compared with Mondale's 41 percent) and took 49 states. The only state Reagan did not carry was Mondale's Minnesota.

Unlike Jimmy Carter's reelection campaign season in 1980, Reagan's 1984 campaign was free from economic recession and international crises. Perhaps the most memorable quote from the campaign involved Reagan asking the American people, "Are you better off now than you were four years ago?" For many, the answer was yes. And thus, for many, the preferable candidate was Reagan.

The table shows the vote choice among different religious groups as captured by the 1984 National Election Study. In this election, 73 percent of the white evangelical vote went to Reagan. With mainline Protestants normally identifying as Republicans, it is no surprise that Reagan won 70 percent of their votes as well. On the Democratic side, Mondale carried the votes of 91 percent of African Americans.

Looking at the 1984 results by religious affiliation provides insights about how people from different faiths relate to the political world, but it also highlights important trends taking place in the nation at that time. The voting pattern among Roman Catholics is particularly illustrative of this point. Of the Catholics who voted, 50 percent considered themselves Democrats, yet Reagan got 55 percent of their votes. That Reagan won the Catholic vote in two consecutive elections suggests that the 1980s were a time of great change in the electorate. For decades, Catholics had been reliably Democratic, not only in their partisan affiliation but also in their vote choice.

It is possible that Democrats lost the support of Catholics simply owing to Reagan's personal appeal. Yet observers sensed that more important forces were at work. Some argued that religion was ceasing to be a useful predictor of vote choice. Others specifically hailed an end to the New Deal coalition, which had included Jews, union members, Catholics, immigrants, Southerners, and the urban poor. In particular, it was argued that the Democratic leadership had taken its usual Catholic supporters for granted and focused on other disadvantaged groups, such as African Americans and women. The result of this strategy was that the party obtained a new core constituency, a change that facilitated defection among Catholics.

RELIGION AND THE VOTE IN THE 1984 PRESIDENTIAL ELECTION

Religious Affiliation	Candidate (Party)		
	Mondale (D)	Reagan (R)	Total
Mainline Protestant	29.7%	70.3%	100%
Evangelical Protestant	27.0	73.0	100
Roman Catholic	44.7	55.3	100
Jewish	69.4	30.6	100
Nontraditional Christian/Orthodox	41.7	58.3	100
Other	50.0	50.0	100
No religion/Atheist/Agnostic	52.6	47.4	100
Total	36.9	63.2	100

Source: *American National Election Study, 1984 national adult survey.*

Frequencies: *Mainline: 445; Evangelical: 263; Catholic: 365; Jewish: 36; Nontraditional/Orthodox: 24; Other: 12; No religion: 95; Total: 1240.*

Note: *Figures exclude African Americans.*

This new core constituency led others to sever their ties to the Democrats as well, most notably white Southerners. Most white Southerners are evangelical Protestants and were raised as Democrats. Their dramatic shift from one party to another was arguably the most remarkable partisan shift of the 20th century. Jimmy Carter's southern and Christian background helped to delay this defection, but Mondale was not as fortunate. The Republican Party had played the race card, and white Southerners defected in droves.

Among other religious affiliations, Jewish voters and people who claim no religious affiliation were the only groups more likely than not to vote for Mondale. Since these groups make up a very small proportion of the electorate, it is easy to see why Mondale lost.

The 1984 election led many to question whether religion would continue to be a politically relevant distinction in American society. Though Jews and mainline Protestants voted as they more or less always had, shifts in the Catholic and Evangelical Protestant vote certainly raised questions about the relationship between religious affiliation and politics. Many observers proclaimed the end of the Democratic coalition and predicted a Republican "lock" on the presidency.

See also CATHOLICS AND THE DEMOCRATIC PARTY; JEWS AND THE DEMOCRATIC PARTY; MAINLINE PROTESTANTS AND THE REPUBLICAN PARTY; RELIGION IN THE 1980 PRESIDENTIAL ELECTION; RELIGION IN THE 1988 PRESIDENTIAL ELECTION; SOUTHERN REPUBLICAN REALIGNMENT.

Further reading: Abramson, Paul, et al. *Change and Continuity in the 1984 Elections.* Washington, D.C.: Congressional Quarterly, 1986; McWilliams, Wilson Carey. "The Meaning of the Election." In *The Election of 1984: Reports and Interpretations.* Edited by Gerald Pomper. Chatham, N.J.: Chatham House, 1985; The National Election Studies, Center for Political Studies, University of Michigan. Electronic resources available at the NES website. URL: www.umich.edu/~nes.

—Deborah Schildkraut

religion in the 1988 presidential election

The candidates in the 1988 presidential election were Republican George H. W. Bush, the vice president under RONALD REAGAN, and Democrat Michael Dukakis, the governor of Massachusetts. Continuing the Republican hold on the highest office in the land, Bush won with 53 percent of the popular vote compared with Dukakis's 46 percent.

The absence of any pressing national threat in 1988 fostered a political climate that emphasized social issues, and both campaigns relied extensively on symbolic rhetoric. The campaign is remembered for Bush promising "no new taxes" and branding Dukakis a liberal, the campaign's four-letter word. Other potent symbols included Dukakis in an army tank, weekend prison furloughs, and the AMERICAN CIVIL LIBERTIES UNION (ACLU). These objects and concepts were invoked repeatedly and used to communicate and exaggerate the differences between the two candidates.

The table below shows the vote choice among different religious groups as captured by the 1988 National Election Study. As in 1984, more white mainline and Evangelical Protestants voted for the Republican over the Democrat in 1988, with both groups supporting Bush by over 60 percent. Meanwhile, some 92 percent of African-American voters supported Dukakis in 1988 (data not shown).

Challenging those who believed that the traditional link between Roman CATHOLICS AND THE DEMOCRATIC PARTY was lost, Catholics preferred Dukakis to Bush by three percentage points, according to the NES (though polls from the *New York Times* and CNN gave Bush a slight edge among Catholics). Continuing their usual voting patterns, Jewish voters and those with no religious affiliation also gave their support to Dukakis. Nontraditional Protestants (such as CHRISTIAN SCIENTISTS and LATTER-DAY SAINTS) and Eastern Orthodox practitioners overwhelmingly voted for Bush.

Compared with the 1980 and 1984 elections, Democrats made gains in 1988. Though they lost the election, they maintained control of Congress and their traditional New Deal

RELIGION AND THE VOTE IN THE 1988 PRESIDENTIAL ELECTION

Religious Affiliation	Candidate (Party)		
	Dukakis (D)	Bush (R)	Total
Mainline Protestant	36.6%	63.4%	100%
Evangelical Protestant	30.6	69.4	100
Roman Catholic	52.2	47.8	100
Jewish	72.7	27.3	100
Nontraditional Christian/Orthodox	26.3	73.7	100
No religion/Atheist/Agnostic	60.5	39.5	100
Total	42.0	58.0	100

Source: *American National Election Study, 1988 national adult survey.*

Frequencies: *Mainline: 396; Evangelical: 245; Catholic: 299; Jewish: 22; Nontraditional/Orthodox: 19; No religion: 81; Total: 1068.*

Note: *Figures exclude African Americans.*

coalition, whose obituary had been written four years earlier, made a bit of a recovery, with more than half of the Reagan Democrats returning to the fold. This homecoming, however, was not able to supply enough votes to secure the White House. The political landscape had changed sufficiently throughout the 1980s so that a coalition of blacks, Hispanics, Jews, union members, and the urban poor could not capture the presidency. Many of these groups do not vote as regularly as the groups that make up the Republican coalition, and older Americans who experienced Democratic leadership under Franklin Roosevelt were being replaced by a new generation of voters. Furthermore, the loss of white Southerners to the Republicans showed no signs of stopping, and the future of the Catholic vote was far from certain. In short, the theory that Republicans had a lock on the White House was still credible. Among Catholics and evangelicals in particular, a shift in the social issues on the public agenda and the emerging Christian Right enhanced the attractiveness of the Republican Party. Yet observers predicted that fault lines between Christian social conservatives and Wall Street Republicans would worsen and "shake Republican foundations" in the coming years.

Though Dukakis prevented the Democrats from suffering a loss as crushing as the one they experienced in 1984, many observers were still left wondering if religion was ceasing to be a useful predictor of vote choice and where the political preferences of Catholics and white evangelicals truly lay.

See also CATHOLICS AND THE DEMOCRATIC PARTY; CHRISTIAN RIGHT AND THE REPUBLICAN PARTY; JEWS AND THE DEMOCRATIC PARTY; MAINLINE PROTESTANTS AND THE REPUBLICAN PARTY; RELIGION IN THE 1984 PRESIDENTIAL ELECTION; RELIGION IN THE 1992 PRESIDENTIAL ELECTION; SOUTHERN REPUBLICAN REALIGNMENT.

Further reading: McWilliams, Wilson Carey. "The Meaning of the Election." In *The Election of 1988: Reports and Interpretations.* Edited by Gerald Pomper. Chatham, N.J.: Chatham House, 1989; The National Election Studies, Center for Political Studies, University of Michigan. Electronic resources available at the NES website. URL: www.umich. edu/~nes; Pomper, Gerald. "The Presidential Election." In *The Election of 1988: Reports and Interpretations.* Edited by Gerald Pomper. Chatham, N.J.: Chatham House, 1989.

—Deborah Schildkraut

religion in the 1992 presidential election

The candidates in the 1992 presidential election were incumbent Republican George H. W. Bush; Democrat WILLIAM JEFFERSON CLINTON, the governor of Arkansas; and Reform Party candidate H. Ross Perot, a Texas businessman who created his own political party and financed his own campaign. Breaking into the alleged Republican lock on the White House, Clinton won with 43 percent of the vote, compared with Bush's 38 percent. Bush was only the fourth incumbent president of the 20th century to lose a reelection bid. Perot was quite successful for a third-party candidate, capturing a remarkable 19 percent of the popular vote.

The country experienced an economic downturn during the campaign, and Bush was punished in opinion polls for having reneged on his "no new taxes" pledge of 1988. Yet, just a year before the election, basking in the glory of the PERSIAN GULF WAR victory, Bush's job approval ratings were pushing 90 percent, a level of support unseen in the history of polling. As the campaign progressed and as news of the economy replaced news of the war, Bush's approval ratings began to sink. It was one of the most dramatic drops in presidential popularity ratings ever recorded and became a news story in itself. Another important part of the political climate in 1992 was the tension between economic and social conservatives in the Republican Party. A controversial and socially conservative convention speech by PATRICK BUCHANAN, a GOP presidential hopeful, energized that wing of the party and brought the internal tensions to the national stage.

RELIGION AND THE VOTE IN THE 1992 PRESIDENTIAL ELECTION

Religious Affiliation	Candidate (Party)			
	Clinton (D)	Bush (R)	Perot (Ind.)	Total
Mainline Protestant	36.6%	40.0%	23.5%	100%
Evangelical Protestant	30.3	55.1	14.6	100
Roman Catholic	48.2	30.7	21.1	100
Jewish	75.7	8.1	16.2	100
Nontraditional Christian/Orthodox	57.1	28.6	14.3	100
No religion/Atheist/Agnostic	55.8	20.5	23.7	100
Total	42.3	37.6	20.2	100

Source: *American National Election Study, 1992 national adult survey.*

Frequencies: *Mainline: 413; Evangelical: 376; Catholic: 398; Jewish: 37; Nontraditional/Orthodox: 42; No religion: 190; Total: 1469.*

Note: *Figures exclude African Americans.*

The table shows the vote choice among different religious groups as captured by the 1992 National Election Study (NES). As in the past few elections, mainline and Evangelical Protestants gave their support to the Republican candidate, though Perot's presence kept Bush from winning the majority of white mainline votes. Clinton won a plurality of the votes from all other religious affiliations included in the NES. And continuing with their usual voting trends, 92.5 percent of African-American voters supported Clinton in 1992 (data not shown).

Consistent with previous voting patterns, Jews, people from non–Judeo-Christian faiths, and those with no religious affiliation overwhelmingly preferred Clinton to Bush. In a turnaround from previous trends, nontraditional Protestants (such as CHRISTIAN SCIENTISTS) and Eastern Orthodox practitioners also supported Clinton more than Bush or Perot. The table also shows that Perot did best among mainline Protestants, Roman Catholics, and people with no religious affiliation, winning 19 percent of their votes.

That the dependable mainline Protestant vote did not come through for Republicans suggested that new dynamics were at work in the Republican Party. Traditionally, Democrats had been a more fractured party than Republicans. The 1992 election showed the beginnings of cracks in Republican unity. The CHRISTIAN RIGHT and social conservatives, with their emphasis on family values, were a committed and active base. At the same time, fiscal conservatives who might otherwise vote for the GOP were turned off by the party's newfound social conservatism. The ability to satisfy one core party constituency without losing another is no easy feat. It is a balancing act the Democrats faced for years and had become a skill Republicans discovered they needed to master.

Democrats were also helped in that their candidate, like JAMES EARL CARTER, was a Southerner and a Southern Baptist. Moreover, Clinton's "New Democrat" philosophy moved the party back toward the center, helping to win over white urban ethnics, including Catholics, who found the extent of the party's social liberalism in previous elections unappealing. The fractured New Deal coalition, wounded from the previous three electoral losses, managed to hang together.

See also CATHOLICS AND THE DEMOCRATIC PARTY; JEWS AND THE DEMOCRATIC PARTY; RELIGION IN THE 1988 PRESIDENTIAL ELECTION; RELIGION IN THE 2000 PRESIDENTIAL ELECTION; REPUBLICANS AND MAINLINE PROTESTANTS; SOUTHERN REPUBLICAN REALIGNMENT.

Further reading: Burnham, Walter Dean. "The Legacy of George Bush: Travails of an Understudy." In *The Election of 1992: Reports and Interpretations.* Edited by Gerald Pomper. Chatham, N.J.: Chatham House, 1993; McWilliams, Wilson Carey. "The Meaning of the Election." In *The Election of 1992: Reports and Interpretations.* Edited by Gerald Pomper. Chatham, N.J.: Chatham House, 1989; The National Election Studies, Center for Political Studies, University of Michigan. Electronic resources available at the NES website. URL: www.umich.edu/~nes.

—Deborah Schildkraut

religion in the 1996 presidential election

In the 1996 presidential election, President WILLIAM JEFFERSON CLINTON defeated former Senate majority leader Robert Dole 49 to 41 percent (Perot garnered 8 percent) in a campaign without much drama. Clinton lead early and maintained a significant lead until the final days of the election, and swept the electoral college with 379 votes to Dole's 159.

The 1996 election represented a watershed between the midyear 1994 Republican success in attaining control of both Houses of Congress and the 2000 presidential election, where religion was again center stage. Although many observers credited the Christian Right for the GOP electoral success in the 1994 midterm elections, nevertheless, at the 1996 Republican National Convention, Christian Right activists were noticeably absent from the stage because of their perceived negative impact on the 1992 presidential election. In 1992, their extensive views were believed to have cost President George H. W. Bush support from moderate voters. As was the case in 1994, the Christian Right in 1996 had substantial influence in some states and moderate or little influence in others. One of the obvious phenomena of the 1996 election was the Republicans' placement of the Religious Right in the background at their convention and other national forums. Although they were no longer public in national events for the Republicans, they remained a strong force within the party.

According to the University of Michigan's 1996 National Election Study (NES), the religious makeup of the 1996 electorate was as follows: mainline Protestants constituted 22 percent, Evangelical Protestants 33 percent, black Protestant Churches 1 percent, Roman Catholics 26 percent, Jewish 2 percent, Nontraditional or Orthodox 2 percent, Non-Christian/Non-Jewish 1 percent, and no religious identification 13 percent. This distribution had remained constant since the 1990 election.

Although the religious distribution of the electorate remained constant, there were some shifts in voting patterns. Consistent with past elections, white Protestants overwhelmingly and consistently voted Republican, and Jewish voters remained predominantly Democrats. Catholic voters reflected a 9 percent shift in favor of the Democrats. This shift can probably be attributed to a change in the ideological character of the Democratic Party—a shift from class issues to identity issues. As the Democrats shifted their emphasis from their traditional issues of economic and social class improvement to issues of race, gender, and individual identification, they lost the traditional white Catholic voters who had always been conservative on social/moral issues and gained a significant Hispanic, predominantly Catholic, vote. Since the 1992 presidential election, the Hispanic vote grew to 5 percent of the electorate. It is yet to be seen how the Hispanic vote will distribute itself in future elections. Hispanics tend to vote Democratic because of their identity politics; otherwise, they tend to be religiously conservative Catholics.

Compared with the 1994 elections, the 1996 elections were a letdown for the Christian Right. Although they helped the GOP retain control over Congress, there were key defeats at the state level (candidates and ballot propositions).

After 1994, it appeared that the Christian Right had "arrived" on the scene. However, 1996 demonstrated that the Christian Right is not a monolithic national power. Instead, the Christian Right has a niche in national politics, and its real power comes state by state. Obviously, its influence is greater in some states than in others:

> In some states (such as South Carolina and Texas), the Christian Right has become part of a consolidated Republican coalition to the benefit of movement and party alike, while in other states (such as Oregon and Minnesota), the Christian Right has provoked bitter confrontations within the GOP to the detriment of all. Still other states (such as VIRGINIA and California) fall in between, with elements of both consolidation and confrontation. Finally, there are states (including Maine and West Virginia) where the movement is not yet in contention and may never be.

As a social movement, the Christian Right developed its dominant organization the Christian Coalition in 1996. RALPH REED was the executive director of the CHRISTIAN COALITION and the chief strategist for the Christian Right's agenda, which resulted in the formation of Christian Coalition chapters in every state.

One issue that rose in 1996 was the bipartisan legal status of religious organizations. One major problem experienced by the Christian Right was the focus on the Christian Coalition's TAX-EXEMPT STATUS. Essentially, a tax-exempt organization is supposed to be nonpartisan. But because of its strong links to the Republican Party, the coalition's nonpartisan status was challenged by the Internal Revenue Service. Although complaints regarding the tax-exempt status of the Christian Coalition are not purported to have adversely affected the 1996 election, it did have consequences in future years when the coalition lost its tax-exempt status.

There were approximately 200,000 activists nationwide in the Christian Right movement. This was slightly larger than the numbers in 1994. Most activists were part of local chapters, some of well-known organizations such as the Christian Coalition, and others from less-well-known and less-organized groups. Their major activity was providing VOTER GUIDES, many of which were distributed in churches. Those states with higher numbers of evangelicals also reported higher levels of Christian Right activity and mobilization.

The Christian Right's participation in politics is a relatively new phenomenon. Until the election of JAMES EARL CARTER, an openly born-again evangelical Christian (see BORN-AGAIN EXPERIENCE), evangelicals as a group largely stayed out of politics. The perception of the American public was divided on the Christian Right movement—32 percent said they had a positive view of the Christian Right, while 33 percent said they had a negative view. And the Christian Right

was far more popular among white evangelicals (55 percent favorable to 19 percent unfavorable); the secular population was just the opposite (56 percent unfavorable to 14 percent favorable). The Christian Right movement, in totality, consisted of approximately one-fifth to one-sixth of the electorate. But opponents of the Christian Right were better mobilized and more vocal in 1996 than in 1994.

The Christian Right influenced the electoral process in three ways: recruiting candidates, participating in the nominating process, and participating in the general election process. Its weakest participation is in candidate recruitment and its strongest is in voter mobilization.

See also CATHOLICS AND THE DEMOCRATIC PARTY; CHRISTIAN RIGHT AND THE REPUBLICAN PARTY; CHRISTIAN RIGHT IN VIRGINIA; RELIGION IN THE 1992 PRESIDENTIAL ELECTION; RELIGION IN THE CONGRESSIONAL ELECTIONS OF 1994.

Further reading: University of Michigan National Election Studies (NES). Accessed 9-3-01. URL: www.umich.edu/~nes/nesguide/test/tab1b_1c.txt, 2001; Green, John C. "The Christian Right and the 1996 Elections: An Overview." In *God at the Grass Roots, 1996.* Edited by Mark J. Rozell and Clyde Wilcox. Lanham, Md.: Rowman and Littlefield, 1997.

—Maurice M. Eisenstein

religion in the 2000 presidential election

In what proved to be one of the closest elections in American history, the 2000 presidential election was finally decided on December 12, five weeks after Election Day. The Democratic candidate was incumbent vice president Al Gore, a centrist who had served in Congress as a senator from Tennessee. The Republican candidate and eventual winner was GEORGE W. BUSH, son of former president George H. W. Bush and the governor of Texas. The controversy that was to call the election into question was centered on the closeness of the popular vote in the state of Florida. Both candidates needed Florida's 25 electoral votes to obtain the 271 required for victory. Balloting and vote-counting irregularities prolonged the controversy. The vote was finally certified on December 12, after the U.S. Supreme Court halted further recounting procedures.

These problems within the election apparatus in the state of Florida would not have been so significant had the presidential race not been so close. George W. Bush became president of the United States with a 537-vote margin in the state of Florida. The national popular vote, however, favored Al Gore by just under 500,000 voters, making President Bush the first president not to win the popular vote since 1876. The closeness of the presidential election was also echoed in congressional voting returns. The Senate began its session with a 50-50 tie, and the House of Representatives had the fourth-closest division of seats (by percentage) in history. This close election has been attributed to general peace and prosperity of the country, with both candidates pursuing the center of the ideological divide.

RELIGION AND THE VOTE IN THE 2000 PRESIDENTIAL ELECTION

Religious Group	Candidate (Party)		Nonvoters
	Gore (D)	Bush (R)	
Latter-day Saints	12%	88%	29%
White evangelicals	24	76	51
Traditionalists	14	86	37
Centrists	25	75	58
Modernists	54	46	63
White mainline Protestants	39	61	47
Traditionalists	25	75	43
Centrists	40	60	50
Modernists	52	48	46
White Roman Catholics	47	53	47
Traditionalists	25	75	41
Centrists	47	53	47
Modernists	70	30	55
Secular	65	35	52
Hispanic Catholics and Protestants	72	28	70
Jews	77	23	18
Black Protestants	96	4	47
Totals	50.2	49.8	50

Source: Guth et al. 2001: 21

The issues tackled by the candidates primarily concerned social welfare, particularly Social Security, education, and prescription-drug benefits. While Gore focused more specifically on programmatic concerns, Bush seemed to offer a thematic approach to these issues under the rubric of "compassionate conservatism." Both candidates sought the promotion of faith-based social services, citing them as more effective and cost-efficient than their secular, government-run counterparts. Both campaigns proposed federal-funding plans for these types of service providers.

The rhetoric of the 2000 presidential election was saturated with religious references and appeals to faith and family values. This trend was most likely a response to the perceived moral turpitude of President WILLIAM JEFFERSON CLINTON. It allowed candidates to emphasize their "character" over and above their policy plans. This tactic seemed to work better for Bush than for Gore, who was plagued with questions about his political ethics throughout the campaign.

Religion as an issue was present from the start of the primary season. With several religious conservatives including FAMILY RESEARCH COUNCIL founder GARY BAUER and media commentator Alan Keyes, and others sympathetic to that cause such as U.S. senators Lamar Alexander (R-Tenn.) and Orrin Hatch (R-Utah) running for the Republican nomination, the issues of faith and values were strongly emphasized in much of the early primary campaigning. Bush, when asked his favorite political philosopher in a primary campaign debate, replied, "Jesus Christ," and left his opponents scrambling for suitably religious answers.

The issue came to controversy, however, only after the South Carolina primary. By this time, Bush and Senator John McCain (R-Ariz.), war veteran and celebrated "straight-talker," were the leading candidates for the Republican nomination. Bush spoke at Bob Jones University (BJU), a fundamentalist institution in Greenville, South Carolina, known for its anti-Catholic views and a ban on interracial dating. This speech quickly became an issue in the McCain strategy, seeking to link Bush with ultraconservatism and intolerance. Bush later apologized for ignoring BJU's policies in his speech. McCain went further and criticized PAT ROBERTSON and JERRY FALWELL, saying they had an "evil" influence on the Republican Party. Though seeking to delineate between these leaders and evangelical voters, this strategy seemed to damage his standing as a candidate.

Religion became an issue in the Democratic Party as well, though not traditionally predisposed to making religion a centerpiece of campaign rhetoric. Gore needed a way to separate himself from President Clinton morally, if not politically. He found the solution in the choice of his vice presidential running mate JOSEPH LIEBERMAN, an ORTHODOX JEW and senator from Connecticut. Lieberman had been one of the first Democrats to publicly criticize President Clinton during the Monica Lewinsky affair, and one of the main proponents of legislation to reduce violence and sexuality in media during his tenure in the Senate. As the first Jew to appear on either party's presidential ticket, Lieberman's religious commitments raised questions about his willingness and ability to perform his duties on Saturday, the Jewish Sabbath. Citing exceptions to religious law for national security, he effectively resolved these questions. He also drew fire on the campaign trail from the ANTI-DEFAMATION LEAGUE for publicly proclaiming the importance of his faith and the values it engendered. Lieberman, if not enhancing the Democrats' already substantial share of Jewish voters, seemed to lend Gore moral credibility, which may have helped him win other constituencies.

Within the electorate, religion played a significant role in the voting choices of Americans. The table shows the presidential voting percentages broken down by religion. The religious categories are further separated for evangelical and mainline Protestants and Roman Catholics. Taken from the University of Akron/Ethics and Public Policy Center *Survey of Religion and Politics,* the delineations seek to capture the variation in theological, moral, and social beliefs of different members of the same church traditions. "Within each community, 'traditionalists' profess orthodox beliefs, exhibit high levels of public and private religious behavior, and identify with 'sectarian' movements (e.g., for Protestants, 'fundamentalist,' 'PENTECOSTAL,' or 'charismatic'). 'Modernists' hold more heterodox beliefs, exhibit modest levels of religious practice, and identify with church-like movements (ECUMENISM, LIBERALISM). Naturally, 'centrists' fall between the other two camps on all these measures."

Following trends in the past several national elections, Mormons, evangelicals, and mainline Protestants supported the Republican candidate. White Roman Catholics also supported Bush, though their Hispanic coreligionists did not. Again, consistent with past behavior, secular, Jews, and black Protestants overwhelmingly supported the Democratic ticket. What may be the most interesting finding from the survey, however, is the great difference that the type of religious belief makes in the voting choices of adherents. "Traditionalists" and "centrists" were much more likely to vote for George W. Bush than were their "modernist" counterparts. Thus, religious beliefs, over and above simple denominational membership, had a significant impact on voting choice in the 2000 presidential election.

Religion was also a factor at the state level in the 2000 election. Continuing their influence in state-level Republican parties, religious conservatives exhibited strong influence in 18 states, moderate influence in 26 states, and little influence in seven states (Conger and Green 2002). This represents an increase over their influence in the 1994 election. More states show moderate influence and fewer little influence, suggesting that while religious conservatives are making gains in many states, they are not an overwhelming factor in many states.

Religion was important in the 2000 elections, perhaps more visibly so than in any other recent election. Religious rhetoric and policy debates added to the candidates' own professions of faith and beliefs and produced a situation where many voters felt their concerns about political morality were being addressed, while others were alienated by the sometimes overtly religious tenor of the campaign. This appeal to religion by both parties may have contributed to the close voting results in many states.

See also IMPEACHMENT OF WILLIAM JEFFERSON CLINTON; LATTER-DAY SAINTS (LDS), CHURCH OF JESUS CHRIST OF.

Further reading: Ceaser, James W., and Andrew E. Busch. *The Perfect Tie.* Lanham, Md.: Rowman and Littlefield, 2001; Conger, Kimberly H., and John C. Green. "Christian Conservative & State Republican Parties." *Campaigns and Elections.* February 2002; Guth, James L., et al. "America Fifty/Fifty." *First Things.* October: 19–26, 2001; Johnson, Dirk. "The 2000 Campaign: The Voters; Hearing about God but Wondering about Issues." *New York Times.* September 5, 2000: A23.

—Kimberly Conger

religion test oaths for public office

Article 6, clause 3, of the U.S. Constitution states: "The Senators and Representatives before mentioned, and the Members of the several State Legislatures, and all executive and judicial Officers, both to the United States and of the several States, shall be bound by Oath or Affirmation, to support this Constitution; but no religious Test shall ever be required as a Qualification to any Office or public Trust under the United States." With the constitutional prohibition on religious tests for public office, the new Constitution posed a distinct break with the historical trend, found in western Europe and the American colonies and states, of requiring religious tests for all public officeholders.

Religious test oaths were long part of the English political landscape, owing to the established Church of England's preferred status in politics, law, and society. The early American colonists were most familiar with the operation of such oaths in England, especially from the 16th to 18th centuries. As Sir William Blackstone pointedly noted in his *Commentaries on the Laws of England,* religious test oaths were instituted "in order the better to secure the established church against perils from non-conformists of all denominations, infidels, turks, jews, heretics, papists, and sectaries."

Early American colonists, some of whom fled England in part because of religious persecution, were quick to write religious test oaths into their colonial charters. The state constitutions written after 1776 did not necessarily reject religious test oaths either. One example, the Delaware Constitution of 1776, mandated that officeholders must "acknowledge the holy scriptures of the Old and New Testament to be given by divine inspiration," and the Vermont Constitution of 1777 similarly commanded that legislators must "acknowledge the scriptures of the old and new testament to be given by divine inspiration, and own and profess the protestant religion."

At the 1787 Constitutional Convention, the Article VI ban on religious test oaths was the only part of that article that was unanimously approved, and with very little debate. Many early constitutional commentators, such as Joseph Story, viewed the ban on religious test oaths as part of the larger SEPARATION OF CHURCH AND STATE. As Story noted, Article VI is "not introduced merely for the purpose of satisfying the scruples of many respectable persons, who feel an invincible repugnance to any religious test, or affirmation. It had a higher object; to cut off forever every pretence of any alliance between church and state in the national government." Even though the federal Constitution banned religious test oaths for office, such oaths continued to exist in some state constitutions into the 20th century. Whether the state oath requirements were enforced or not is another issue.

The Supreme Court has rarely addressed the Article VI prohibition on religious test oaths. *Torcaso v. Watkins* (1961) is the only Court case in which Article VI is squarely implicated. In the dispute, Torcaso was appointed a notary public by the governor of MARYLAND, but under Maryland's constitution he had to declare his belief in God to serve in his commission. Torcaso refused to take the oath. Maryland state courts upheld the state constitutional requirement, but the U.S. Supreme Court reversed. For the Court, the First Amendment FREE EXERCISE CLAUSE prohibits a state from forcing an individual to profess a belief or disbelief in religion. Importantly, the Court noted that even though Torcaso raised an Article VI argument, it declined to consider it: "because we are reversing the judgment on other grounds, we find it unnecessary to consider appellant's contention that this provision [Article VI] applies to state as well as federal offices." In the Court's reasoning, since the First Amendment further codified protections for individual religious worship and belief (or nonbelief) in the U.S. Constitution, it in a real sense supercedes the Article VI ban on religious test oaths. *Torcaso* prohibits religious test oaths more broadly under the First Amendment free exercise clause, thus linking the Article VI prohibition more squarely to the First Amendment's protections for religious liberty.

Further reading: Blackstone, Sir William. *Commentaries on the Laws of England.* Chicago: University of Chicago Press, 1979; Kurland, Philip B., and Ralph Learner. *The Founder's Constitution.* Chicago: University of Chicago Press, 1987; Madison, James. *Notes of Debates in the Federal Convention of 1787.* New York: Norton, 1987; Story, Joseph. *A Familiar Exposition of the Constitution of the United States.* New York: Harper and Bros. 1883.

—John Blakeman

Religious Coalition for Reproductive Choice

The Religious Coalition for Reproductive Choice (RCRC), formerly known as the Religious Coalition for ABORTION Rights (RCAR), founded in 1973, has been the major conduit for religious involvement in the pro-choice movement. In 2001, it consisted of some 40 Christian, Jewish, and other reli-

gious organizations and included state affiliates in about 20 states. Its national office is in Washington, D.C.

RCAR was formed soon after *ROE V. WADE* in reaction to efforts by pro-life forces to minimize *Roe*'s effects. White liberal clergy had been active in the pre-*Roe* struggle to legalize abortion, RCAR was a product not of these individuals but of denominational leaders and was created as a coalition of religious organizations. It was a project of the UNITED METHODIST CHURCH until 1981, but policy has always been made by a consensus of its member bodies. RCRC has often worked closely with feminist pro-choice organizations; however, its motivations and justifications for pursuing abortion rights differ from those of its secular counterparts.

In its initial stage, it concentrated mainly on lobbying Congress, trying to acquire acceptance and recognition as a source of expertise and to convince Congress by persuading pro-choice clergy and religious organizations that the pro-choice position was not necessarily less religious than the pro-life position. This was less intended to win converts than to reassure supporters in Congress that pro-choice votes that kept abortion a private decision reflected the religious pluralism of American society.

RCRC has also engaged in grassroots activities to educate the public on abortion issues through such tactics as press releases, legislative alerts, and direct mail. RCRC members have also joined in activities with secular pro-choice groups. They have distinguished themselves from secular groups, however, by their emphasis on abortion rights as a First Amendment FREE EXERCISE issue, arguing that different faiths have differing positions on when human life begins and when and whether abortion is moral. Similarly, they have raised the ESTABLISHMENT CLAUSE issue by suggesting that if abortion were to be banned, this would in effect be adopting the ROMAN CATHOLIC CHURCH's position as public policy. They are less likely to talk of a "new morality," abortion on demand, or a woman's right to control her body, preferring to present abortion as sometimes the most moral of a range of difficult choices.

As efforts to curtail the effects of *Roe v. Wade* moved to state legislatures, RCRC stepped up efforts to develop state affiliates, particularly in those states where its presence was deemed crucial. It has also engaged in symbolic politics, trying to find ways to counter the powerful imagery of the pro-life language of its opposition. One such symbolic activity has been the interfaith pro-choice worship services held annually on January 22, the anniversary of *Roe v. Wade*. It has experimented with several slogans over the years such as "Choice—as American as apple pie." A recently adopted slogan is "Pro-faith, pro-family, pro-choice."

In the 1990s, RCRC changed its name from RCAR, reflecting a broadening of its focus from protecting abortion rights to addressing problems of teen pregnancy, sexuality, and other related topics, particularly in multicultural settings.

RCRC has provided a religious pro-choice presence in Washington, D.C., and in state politics, while allowing liberal religious denominations and those for whom abortion has been a divisive issue to maintain a lower level of visible participation and financial support.

Further reading: Hofrening, Daniel J. B. *In Washington but Not of It*. Philadelphia: Temple University Press, 1995; Mills, Samuel A. "Abortion and Religious Freedom: The Religious Coalition for Abortion Rights (RCAR) and the Pro-Choice Movement, 1973–1989." *Journal of Church and State* 33 (1991): 569–594; Rainey, Jane Gurganus. "Religious Involvement in the Pro-Choice Movement." Paper presented at the annual meeting of the American Political Science Association. New Orleans, 1985. RCRC on the Web. URL: http://www.rcrc.org.

—Jane Gurganus Rainey

religious discrimination in higher education

Decades of litigation and federal statutes have opened the doors of colleges and universities to minority students and have also guaranteed student religious groups EQUAL ACCESS to university facilities and resources.

In *Brown v. Board of Education of Topeka* (1954), the Supreme Court declared that racially segregated public schools violated the Constitution's Fourteenth Amendment. In rejecting the "separate but equal" doctrine laid down in *Plessy v. Ferguson* (1896), the Court stated: "in the field of public education the doctrine of 'separate but equal' has no place."

Brown served as the culmination of more than a decade of judicial challenges to *Plessy*. Many of the cases leading up to *Brown* challenged discrimination in higher education. For example, *Missouri ex rel. Gaines v. Canada* (1938) ordered Missouri's state-run law school to admit an African-American student since a comparable law school was not available to him in the state. *Sweatt v. Painter* (1950) declared that the separate institution created for Texas's black law students was significantly inferior to the state's all-white law school with respect to such factors as faculty and school reputation and potential contacts with prominent alumni.

While the cases leading up to *Brown* addressed access to public educational institutions, later federal policies also forced open the doors of many private institutions to racial minorities. For example, Title VI of the Civil Rights Act of 1964 denies federal funding to educational institutions, public or private, that practice race-based discrimination. In *Runyon v. McCrary* (1976), the Supreme Court determined that federal law barred "private, commercially operated, non-sectarian schools" from enforcing race-based admissions policies.

Religious motivations no longer protect schools enforcing race-based policies from government pressure. Bob Jones University began admitting unmarried African Americans as students in 1975, but, in keeping with its fundamentalist biblical teachings, the school prohibited interracial romantic relationships. The school also refused admission to any person who spoke in favor of interracial relationships. In *BOB JONES UNIVERSITY AND GOLDSBORO CHRISTIAN SCHOOL, INC. V. UNITED STATES* (1983), the Supreme Court upheld the Internal Revenue Service's decision to deny tax-exempt status to Bob Jones because of its discriminatory policies, even if the policies were based on the school's religious principles. The Supreme Court denied that reliance on the First Amendment's FREE EXERCISE or ESTABLISHMENT CLAUSE could salvage the school's tax advantages. One consequence of the IRS policy was that Bob Jones donors could no longer claim donations as tax deductions. Thus, even private religious universities practicing racial discrimination now faced significant financial pressures to reverse their policies.

The Supreme Court has put the speech clause to work in defending student religious organizations from discrimination. For example, in attempting to avoid violating the First Amendment's establishment clause, a public university denied a student religious organization access to school facilities for religious activities. *WIDMAR V. VINCENT* (1981) struck down this policy, declaring that when a university had created a "public forum" by making its facilities available to student groups, the First Amendment's protections of the freedoms of speech and association guaranteed student religious groups "equal access" to these facilities. Later, in *ROSENBERGER V. UNIVERSITY OF VIRGINIA* (1995), the Court once again relied on the First Amendment's speech clause to determine that, despite the establishment clause, public universities could not refuse to cover costs for student publications only by student religious groups.

In short, federal government policies have evolved over time to help protect both racial and religious minorities from being singled out for unequal treatment by colleges and universities.

—Staci L. Beavers

religious discrimination in the workplace

Fundamental religious rights and freedoms create special conflicts when religion enters the workplace. When both employees and employers invoke their First Amendment constitutional and international human rights of FREE EXERCISE, the rights may clash and one or the other or both may need to give way. Statutory limits on discrimination on the basis of religion and requirements that employers accommodate religious practices of employees further complicate the picture. With respect to religious organizations, the constitutional prohibition on establishment of religion must be respected. This article sketches the contours of these interrelated themes in U.S. law at the start of the 21st century.

Legal issues concerning religion in the workplace arise in three settings. One setting concerns bona fide religious organizations with religious criteria for employment. For example, a Christian church can require its ministers to believe in Jesus as savior. A second setting involves secular businesses that are barred from discriminating against employees on the basis of religion and that are required to accommodate an employee's religious beliefs and practices, provided the accommodation does not cause the employer undue hardship. The third setting is the most problematic of the three and involves what may be termed a religious secular employer. This sort of employer seeks to infuse the workplace with the employer's religious values, even though the business itself is what would typically be considered secular, e.g., a tool manufacturing plant.

Under Title VII of the Civil Rights Act of 1964, employers are prohibited from discriminating not only on the basis of birthright characteristics such as sex, national origin, color, and race, but also on the basis of religion. In many instances discrimination on the basis of religion is status-based discrimination, with the person being denied employment by a secular employer solely because he or she is Muslim or pagan or a member of a religion different from that of the employer. This sort of garden-variety discrimination can be handled by the law much like other status-based discrimination. In many other instances, religious discrimination raises special concerns. These concerns have been addressed by special provisions in the statute itself, by the regulations promulgated under it, and by court interpretation, and application of law.

For the most part, Title VII exempts religious employees of religious organizations from its provisions; that is, religious organizations are free to discriminate on the basis of religion in employment to a large extent. (*Raybum v. General Conference of Seventh Day Adventists* (4th Cir., 1985). But if the religious organizations is running a commercial enterprise or a nonreligious, not-for-profit charity (e.g., a food bank), employees performing those nonreligious functions may well be protected against religious discrimination by Title VII (*TONY AND SUSAN ALAMO FOUNDATION V. SECRETARY OF LABOR*). Religious organizations are not exempt with respect to all employees with respect to race and sex discrimination (*BOB JONES UNIVERSITY AND GOLDSBORO CHRISTIAN SCHOOL, INC. V. UNITED STATES*).

Religious schools are also generally exempt from the reach of Title VII with respect to religious discrimination, because education is so central to the perpetuation of the faith. However, religious schools may become subject to the strictures against discrimination by accepting public funds (*ROEMER V. MARYLAND PUBLIC WORKS BOARD*).

In contrast to religious organizations that receive a broad exemption, secular businesses have special provisions placing a special burden on them with respect to religious discrimination, which is not present under the other bases such as race. This special burden is to accommodate the religious needs of the employee. Common examples include adjusting work schedules to fit the holy days of an employee (including sabbatarians) (*Dewey v. Reynolds Metals Co.*, 1971), and making exceptions for dress and appearance for certain employees such as permitting an Orthodox Jew to wear a yarmulke or a Muslim woman to wear a scarf when the employer's general rule bans headwear.

Yet, the employer's duty to accommodate is limited. If the accommodation sought or any alternative effective accommodation would cause the employer "undue hardship," the employer need not accommodate the employee (*Trans World Airlines v. Hardison*, 1977). Unfortunately, this term has been applied by

the courts so that the employer needs to make only a very limited showing of hardship; any showing of more than a de minimus effect on the employer's way of doing business is sufficient. Furthermore, the employer has no duty to accommodate an employee unless the employee asks for accommodation.

In the secular workplace, special problems exist relating to workplace speech, including in particular religious speech. For example, may an employee use the duty to honor his or her religious beliefs and practices require an employer to allow her or him to display graphic antiabortion pictures or to wear religious symbols? In most cases, the courts have said no, because the employee has failed to ask to be accommodated and because of the employer's right to avoid disruption and disharmony among employees that such speech could create.

The third setting, the religious secular employer, creates the most difficulties conceptually. Under employment discrimination law, if an employer creates or allows a hostile work environment to exist with respect to any protected class (most typically race and sex), the employer can be liable (*Meritor Savings Bank v. Vinson*, 1986). This creates special problems where religion is concerned, because religious discrimination can be based not only on status (membership in a particular religious group), but also on beliefs and practices. Status cases are easy to treat, like sex or race cases; discrimination against someone merely because he or she is of another faith is simply illegal.

But the circumstance that creates difficulties is where the employer treats the business as an extension of his or her religious actions. For example, some evangelical Christians consider their businesses to be witnesses for their Lord. In fulfilling this conception, they may play religious music, post religious signs, hold religious discussions, and use the Bible as their business manual. A non-Christian, or even a nonevangelical Christian, may find such a religion-infused environment to be offputting or even hostile to the point of feeling unable to continue employment there. The employee may interpret the employer's speech as harassment, which is illegal if based on one of the protected classifications. The employee could then request an accommodation. But what changes, if any, should the employer be required to make?

The law as it has developed favors employees in these settings and has required employers to exempt employees from meetings, to stop "witnessing" on the premises, and has otherwise limited the speech and religious actions of the employer. The courts have generally taken the approach that the business of business is business, not witnessing for the Lord. Thus any speech by the employer that does not conform to the courts' views of what is appropriate for separating the two spheres, sacred and profane, may be targeted by a complaining employee, and an employer's religious speech may be lawfully curtailed.

As commentators have noted, this approach seems to treat as legitimate and favored a compartmentalized approach to religion, which treats as the proper norm Sunday praying followed by Monday morning preying. But for those for whom matters of religion and conscience do not allow this separation, either as employers or as employees, the secular workplace can present special challenges.

Commentators have recommended that courts take a more nuanced approach that balances the interests of the three parties involved (employer, employee, and society) with more care and acceptance than has been evidenced thus far. Both the employer and the employee have free exercise and free speech interests; these interests may at times conflict, and some limits on one or both may be appropriate. Society has an interest in allowing the flowering of ideas, including religious ideas, and in allowing free speech, including religious speech. But society also has other interests in maintaining access to commercial life for all its citizens, promoting social harmony, and effectuating tolerance, acceptance, and equality of diverse members of society. These weighty interests at times conflict, especially in the religious secular employment setting. Experts in the field expect to see significant developments in the law in this area for some time to come.

Further reading: Berg, Thomas C. "Religious Speech in the Workplace: Harassment or Protected Speech?" *Harvard Journal of Law & Public Policy* 22 (1999): 959; Jamar, Steven D. "Accommodating Religion at Work: A Principled Approach to Title VII and Religious Freedom." *New York Law School Law Review* 40 (1996): 719.

—Steven D. Jamar

religious establishment in the colonies

Patterns of religious establishment in the North American colonies ran the gamut from VIRGINIA's attempt at a thoroughly Anglican establishment, to the establishment of dissenting Congregationalism in New England, to a principled lack of any religious establishment at all in Rhode Island, PENNSYLVANIA, New Jersey, and Delaware. The variety of church-state relationships that emerged contributed greatly to the disestablishment of all religious groups under the rational Constitution, a pattern that was eventually followed by all states as well.

Although no American colony ever replicated the situation of the Church of England as it existed in England itself, this ideal did inspire many early leaders of Virginia. Geographical parishes were established, priests were paid by the public authorities, and the formal mechanisms of relating the church in Virginia to the mother church were put into place. Dissenters labored under several disabilities, as they did in England. Unfortunately from the Anglican point of view, bishops were never appointed for Virginia or any other colony. At least partly as a result of this, Anglican clergy were often demoralized and the laity religiously indifferent. This situation was alleviated somewhat, but never reversed, by the activities of the Society for the Propagation of the Gospel, founded in 1701, and by the active interest that Henry Compton, bishop of London, took in Virginia affairs in the early 1700s. Nonetheless, in spite of evident problems in the Virginia establishment, similar patterns extended southward to the Carolinas (1663) and to Georgia (1732). These establishments were considerably weaker, however, which necessitated a practical TOLERATION of dissenters in those colonies that significantly exceeded what was required by the English Act of Toleration of 1689. The evangelical preachers of the FIRST GREAT AWAKENING made significant inroads into all the southern colonies in the three decades before the American Revolution, helping to set the stage for the debates and decisions about religious freedom that would occur in the 1770s and 1780s. These decisions were also shaped by a small but influential group of intellectuals, led by THOMAS JEFFERSON and JAMES MADISON, most of whom had forsaken the doctrines of both the Anglican Church and the evangelicals in favor of a deistic philosophy. This group favored a principled disestablishment of all faiths, which was definitely embodied in the Virginia Statute of Religious Freedom of 1786.

The situation in New England was very different. There, English PURITANS created their own established churches, sometimes denominating themselves as the "purer part" of the Church of England. A large part of the original purpose of the "errand into the wilderness" was to demonstrate the superiority of the Congregational form of Christianity. Because of the very nature of their church polity, however, religious establishment in New England did not result in a religious establishment analogous to the Church of England. In the view of the Congregationalists, only the local church was truly "church." So establishment technically was local, although supported by laws applicable to an entire colony. Most of the familiar features of establishment were present: public funds were used to support the churches, suffrage was linked to church membership, magistrates were endowed with power over religious matters, and dissenting doctrines were suppressed. The New England form of religious establishment began to erode after the 1689 Act of Toleration. The irony that dissenters had established their churches in an English colony was not lost on authorities in the homeland. As the colonies were transformed into royal colonies after the Restoration, the planting of the Church of England was not far behind. Beginning with King's Chapel in Boston in 1686, Anglicanism achieved a significant foothold in New England by the middle of the 18th century. Although an Anglican establishment was impossible under the circumstances, the Church of England nonetheless pressed for whatever prerogatives it could, managing in the process to alienate much of the populace.

Only Rhode Island differed significantly from the New England pattern of religious establishment. From the time that ROGER WILLIAMS fled to Narragansett Bay in 1636, one of the principles of the nascent colony was that of religious freedom. Rhode Island emerged as a haven for QUAKERS, Baptists, Anglicans, Jews, and those of no particular religious persuasion. However, in spite of Williams's eloquent defense of religious liberty, as in his *The Bloudy Tenent of Persecution for the Cause of Conscience Discussed* of 1644, the colony had little direct influence on the political or religious histories of either its closest neighbors or of more distant American colonies.

It was in the middle colonies of Pennsylvania, Delaware, and New Jersey that religious liberty was not only experienced fully but became an ideal held up for all the world to see. Owing to Quaker leadership, specifically that of WILLIAM PENN, these colonies had as a matter of principle no religious establishment. No church taxes were collected, clergy had no special privileges before the law, and there was no RELIGIOUS PERSECUTION. Moral laws were passed that were broadly Christian but did not hinder freedom of conscience. All in all, these colonies were closest to what the United States would later become with respect both to religious liberty and to the relationship between church and state. They were bracketed on the south by Maryland, and on the north by New York, each of which also enjoyed a large degree of religious liberty, in spite of formal Anglican establishments in both colonies in the 18th century. The history of Maryland was in this respect quite complex. Founded on broad principles of religious liberty that extended even to the Roman Catholic confreres of the proprietor. Maryland devolved after the Restoration from its earlier liberal position to one defined by the 1689 Act of Toleration. This involved an Anglican establishment and even the suppression of Roman Catholicism. The Anglican establishment never became very powerful, however, and Roman Catholics managed to maintain a lively communal life. New York's history was complicated both by its origins as a Dutch colony, replete with an established Dutch Reformed Church, and by the later heterogeneity of its population. Anglicanism did not become effectively established in the lower counties of the colony until well into the 18th century, and even then its claims were often disputed by other Christian denominations. Although Trinity parish in lower Manhattan, and King's College, became prominent Anglican institutions, the Anglican establishment in New York did not hinder the growth of a wide variety of religious groups.

The various arrangements regarding religious establishment, and the lively debates that accompanied them, contributed to a growing sense in 18th-century America that the only solution to the problems created by religious establishment was to abolish it altogether. This point of view was embodied in the Virginia Statute of Religious Freedom, in the First Amendment to the Constitution, and was eventually accepted even by those states that continued some form of religious establishment during the early national period.

See also ESTABLISHMENT CLAUSE; FREE EXERCISE CLAUSE; MASSACHUSETTS; SEPARATION OF CHURCH AND STATE.

Further reading: Cobb, Sanford H. *The Rise of Religious Liberty in America: A History.* New York: Macmillan, 1902; Curry, Thomas J. *The First Freedoms: Church and State in America to the Passage of the First Amendment.* New York: Oxford University Press, 1986; Gaustad, Edwin S. *Neither King nor Prelate: Religion and the New Nation, 1776–1826.* Grand Rapids, Mich.: Eerdmans, 1993.

—Donald L. Huber

Religious Freedom (Istook) Amendment

Sponsored and championed by Representative Ernest J. Istook Jr. (R-Okla.) in various forms since his election to Congress in 1992, the proposed Religious Freedom Amendment (RFA) would amend the U.S. Constitution to explicitly permit voluntary PRAYER IN PUBLIC SCHOOLS and other forms of religious expression on public property, including public schools.

The RFA had its broadest support in Congress in 1998, when more than 150 representatives cosponsored the legislation and a number of prominent conservative religious organizations (including the CHRISTIAN COALITION, FAMILY RESEARCH COUNCIL, NATIONAL ASSOCIATION OF EVANGELICALS, and SOUTHERN BAPTIST CONVENTION) strongly lobbied for its passage. That year, the amendment won a simple majority (224–203) in the full House of Representatives but failed to receive the two-thirds' majority needed to pass a constitutional amendment. Neither the House nor the Senate has voted on the RFA before or since 1998.

The proposal amendment, as voted on by the House of Representatives on June 4, 1998, read as follows:

> To secure the people's right to acknowledge God according to the dictates of conscience: Neither the United States nor any State shall establish any official religion, but the people's right to pray and to recognize their religious beliefs, heritage, or traditions on public property, including schools, shall not be infringed. Neither the United States nor any State shall require any person to join in prayer or other religious activity, prescribe school prayers, discriminate against religion, or deny equal access to a benefit on account of religion.

Though Istook and other supporters primarily highlighted the amendment's sanction of school prayer, passage of the RFA would have had broad implications for church-state jurisprudence. For example, the RFA would likely eliminate constitutional challenges to the following practices, among others: public prayer at sporting events, assemblies and graduation ceremonies of public schools; student-led prayer broadcast over the public address systems of public schools; display of religious symbols and texts (including the Ten Commandments) in schools, courthouses, town halls, and public parks; and the formation and meeting of religious groups on government property during working or school hours.

Supporters of the RFA argue that a constitutional amendment is necessary to reverse a series of Supreme Court cases decided since the 1960s that have tightly regulated religious expression in public places. The Court has held, for example, that public prayer constitutes an unconstitutional establishment of religion when spoken in public school classrooms (*ENGEL V. VITALE*) or public school graduation ceremonies (*LEE V. WEISMAN*); that the Ten Commandments cannot be posted in a state courthouse (*STONE V. GRAHAM*); and that in certain circumstances, holiday displays of religious icons on public property are unconstitutional (*ALLEGHENY COUNTY V.*

ACLU). The Court's position on a mandatory moment of silence in public school classrooms is presently unclear. *WALLACE V. JAFFREE* struck down a "mandatory moment of silence" statute in 1985, but in 2001 the Court refused to review *Brown v. Gilmore,* a Fourth Circuit Court of Appeals opinion that upheld a mandatory moment of silence in Virginia public schools.

Critics suggest that the RFA in unnecessary because the First Amendment already constitutionally protects silent public prayers, religious clubs, and noncoercive and nonstate-sponsored group prayers. Opponents of the RFA have further claimed that the amendment could actually restrict religious freedom by forcing all students to endure prayers and religious messages in public schools, allowing teachers to encourage or favor religious expression by students, or limiting parents' rights to determine the religious upbringing of their children.

See also CHRISTIAN RIGHT AND THE REPUBLICAN PARTY; CONTRACT WITH THE AMERICAN FAMILY; NEW EVANGELICALS IN CONGRESS; RELIGIOUS FREEDOM RESTORATION ACT.

—Erik Owens

Religious Freedom Restoration Act (1993)

This federal statute (Public Law 103-144; 107 Stat. 1480), in force between 1993 and 1997, was a congressional attempt to redress a perceived judicial imbalance in the understanding of the constitutional right to the FREE EXERCISE of religion sparked by the Supreme Court's ruling in *EMPLOYMENT DIVISION V. SMITH* (1990). To identify something as a right is to recognize a valid claim to its protection, even in the face of strong conflicting values. Rights are not absolute, however, and sometimes other interests do outweigh rights. Under the U.S. constitutional system, one of the most important duties of the judiciary has been to reconcile conflicts between rights and countervailing public values. The traditional way that courts add extra weight to a rights claim is by placing a heavy burden on the state through the compelling state interest standard.

Ordinarily, the person challenging the constitutionality of a law bears the burden of proof. Failing to overcome this burden leaves the law intact. But the compelling state interest standard reverses this burden of proof, leaving the law's defenders, the state, with the burden of establishing its constitutionality. Such laws are subjected to "strict scrutiny," requiring their defenders to show (1) that the challenged law served not just an important public purpose, but a genuinely *compelling* one; (2) that the law was well tailored to achieve that purpose; and (3) that the purpose could not be achieved by some less burdensome legislative method. Thus, the compelling state interest test requires defenders of a challenged law to persuade a court that its burdens are justified by extremely important state interests that could not be achieved in any less objectionable way.

Beginning with the decision in *SHERBERT V. VERNER* (1963), this approach was considered the dominant method of weighing conflicts between religious free exercise rights and other social interests. In the controversial Supreme Court 5-4 decision in *EMPLOYMENT DIVISION V. SMITH* (1990), the majority rejected this standard, except in a few very specific situations. Almost before the ink had dried on the *Smith* opinion, constitutional scholars and religious advocates assailed its devastating implications for the rights of religious minorities. An unusually broad coalition of religious interest groups formed the Coalition for the Free Exercise of Religion to petition Congress to reverse the effects of the decision. In November 1993, Congress adopted and President WILLIAM JEFFERSON CLINTON signed the Religious Freedom Restoration Act (RFRA), which restored the compelling state interest standard for constitutional review in cases where federally supported programs were involved. The first stated purpose of RFRA is "to restore the compelling interest test as set forth in *Sherbert v. Verner* and *WISCONSIN V. YODER,* and to guarantee its application in all cases where free exercise of religion is substantially burdened."

The key section of the bill states that government may restrict a person's free exercise of religion only if government can show that such a restriction "(1) is essential to further a compelling governmental interest; and (2) is the least restrictive means of furthering that compelling governmental interest."

Under the traditional understanding of the separation of powers, Congress has no authority to reverse a Supreme Court decision by ordinary legislation. But Congress believed it was on safe grounds in adopting the RFRA under its Fourteenth Amendment authority to "enforce by appropriate legislation" constitutional guarantees. Detractors, however, argued that this law was invalid on two grounds—first, that it went beyond enforcing a constitutional amendment by actively changing its interpretation, and that it usurped state authority by extending the requirement to many issues under state jurisdiction.

A constitutional challenge to this law reached the Supreme Court in June 1997 in the case of *CITY OF BOERNE V. FLORES* (1997). In that decision, a divided Court struck down the RFRA, as violating the separation of powers by infringing on the judicial power. The majority ruled that although the Fourteenth Amendment grants Congress the power to enforce a constitutional right, the RFRA went beyond enforcement and altered the meaning of the right, thus infringing on the power of the judiciary and the traditional prerogatives of states. As Justice Kennedy wrote, "Legislation which alters the Free Exercise Clause's meaning cannot be said to be enforcing the clause. Congress does not enforce a constitutional right by changing what the right is."

Since the demise of the RFRA, a number of state legislatures have adopted their own versions of the statute, making many state courts more friendly to religious claims than the federal courts currently are. Thus, when litigants can choose between federal and state venues for hearing religious freedom cases, they may now choose state courts over federal ones.

—Bette Novit Evans

Religious Land Use and Institutionalized Persons Act (RLUIPA) (2000)

RLUIPA is a federal statute protecting against (1) zoning regulations and historical landmark laws that unduly interfere with a religious institution's use or development of its real property and (2) infringement of the FREE EXERCISE rights of persons residing in state or local government correctional, detention, health care, and retirement facilities (42 U.S.C. 2000cc-1[a][1]-[2]). RLUIPA prevents the implementation of land use regulations or institutional policies that impose a "substantial burden" on religious exercise unless the government can show that it has a "compelling" interest at stake.

Congress passed RLUIPA in the wake of the Supreme Court's decision in CITY OF BOERNE V. FLORES that the RELIGIOUS FREEDOM RESTORATION ACT (RFRA), which Congress had enacted in 1993, was unconstitutional, on the basis that Congress did not have the authority to enact RFRA. RFRA had aimed at restoring the free exercise protection previously provided under the First Amendment's free exercise clause, prior to the Supreme Court's decision in EMPLOYMENT DIVISION V. SMITH (1990).

In *Smith*, the Court ruled that, in a "cosmopolitan nation made up of people of almost every conceivable religious preference, . . . we cannot afford the luxury" of thorough constitutional protection for religious liberty under the free exercise clause. After *Smith*, the Court's extremely restrictive interpretation of the free exercise clause required claimants to seek relief, in most situations, from legislative bodies rather than courts.

RFRA had sought to apply the standard that had been applied to free exercise claims prior to *Smith*, the "compelling interest" test, according to which the "[g]overnment may substantially burden a person's exercise of religion only if [the government] demonstrates that application of the burden to the person—(1) is in furtherance of a compelling government interest; and (2) is the least restrictive means of furthering that compelling government interest."

The protection that RLUIPA provides is much more limited in scope than either RFRA or the Court's pre-*Smith* free exercise jurisprudence. As noted, RLUIPA applies only to free exercise infringements on religious land use owing to zoning and landmarking laws or on persons institutionalized in many facilities owned, operated, or managed by a state or local government. Like RFRA, however, RLUIPA requires that any such burden on free exercise must be "in furtherance of a compelling governmental interest" and be "the least restrictive means of furthering that compelling governmental interest."

In the first case decided under RLUIPA, *Haven Shores Community Church v. City of Grand Haven*, the city of Grand Haven, Michigan, agreed in a court-approved consent judgment that its zoning officials had violated RLUIPA by denying a small church the right to use property it had leased in a strip mall. Presumably, RLUIPA will continue to provide significant free exercise protection, but again only in land use disputes and in cases brought by persons in certain government institutions.

Further reading: Becket Fund for Religious Liberty. *Haven Shores Community Church v. City of Grand Haven.* URL: www.becketfund.org, 2001.

—David T. Ball

religious persecution

Religious persecution can come in many forms. Obviously, someone being killed or denied basic human rights because of his or her religious faith constitutes religious persecution.

This cartoon of Pope Pius IX crumbling the U.S. Constitution captured the fears of American Protestants at the height of Irish immigration in the mid-19th century. *(Library of Congress)*

Still, not all punishment, even when religion is involved, can be considered religious persecution. For example, parents/guardians cannot deny a child lifesaving medical care simply because their religion forbids the use of modern medicine, such as CHRISTIAN SCIENTISTS believe. The parent/guardian can be legitimately punished for violating an agreed upon social standard by denying medical care.

This presents shades of gray around the issue of religious persecution, and much of the argument is precisely around where the limits to religious liberty lie. Because of this, one person's or group's definition of religious persecution can run headlong into the society's view of what constitutes the foundational principles for a just society. The temptation to use an expansive definition of religious persecution would trivialize the plain cases of such persecution that have existed in the world and continue to exist to this day. For instance, a kindergartner being told not to pray over her food in an American public school, though certainly religious persecution, is not quite the same thing as a Christian girl in the Sudan being sold into slavery for not being Muslim. One is the obviously mistaken, misguided, and ignorant view of a public school official working outside of the actual law, and the other is a sanctioned and authoritative use of force by a government or society against those who have a different religious tradition. It is a sanctioned and/or authoritative use of force that forms the basis for proceeding with this description of religious persecution.

Examples of religious persecution are legion. They include but are not limited to the ISLAMIC use of jihad; the Crusades; the Inquisition; the Russian pogroms; the HOLOCAUST; Muslim, Hindu, and Sikh strife in Southwest Asia; Catholics versus Protestants in Northern Ireland; Shi'ite Muslims against Sunni Muslims in various countries; and the ongoing conflict between Muslims and Christians in the Sudan. Some of these conflicts and events are historical and some are current, but each represents a real case of religious persecution.

Many of the world's religious conflicts are between different religions. Christian/Muslim/HINDU/BUDDHIST strife exists along with strife involving other religious groups throughout the world. Many of these religions have exclusivist views. The fact that these religions have different belief systems and often-differing goals for society is what makes them unique from one another. It also provides fertile ground for conflict. If some in a religion believe that they have a monopoly on the truth, it is possible for them to rationalize the persecution and defeat of religious opponents because their views are believed to threaten the societal order. This is the psychology present at the root of most religion versus religion conflict.

But the seeds of conflict can still be present within one religious tradition as different sects vie for control. One need only look to conflict between Protestants and Catholics or at tensions between various Muslim sects. Certainly, this exists in other religions as well.

These types of religious persecution reach a boiling point when one group or sect controls the government or other major societal institutions. These governments are then used to inflict and legitimate the persecution of other groups in the name of protecting society. Secular or atheistic governments have also done this to religious groups within their borders. Some of the greatest acts of religious persecution that have ever occurred have taken place in Communist or other authoritarian regimes in the name of protecting society and the state. Millions have lost their lives or faced imprisonment for simply expressing their religious faith. A nonreligious government can be just as detrimental to religious liberty as an opposing religion or sect.

There is some dispute about the formula for ridding a state of religious persecution. Some suggest that TOLERATION of dissenting religious viewpoints seemingly is the key to avoiding the evil that can come from religion. Others, including JAMES MADISON, argue that toleration suggests freedom to worship at the pleasure of the authorities, a state that may change on a whim. Perhaps the formula for avoiding religious conflict is for societies to agree on a set of basic principles that must include rights to freedom of expression in speech and religion.

In the United States, historically, a wide diversity of religious groups have experienced religious persecution, though the top ranks have changed significantly over time. Early on, Jews and Catholics were subject to considerable persecution, including denial of voting rights and coercion by Protestants in public schools and other civic institutions. While Catholic-Protestant tensions undergirded a portion of American politics through the middle of the 20th century, persecution was at its height starting with the mass migrations of European Catholics in the 1840s, with its most public expression the KNOW-NOTHING (AMERICAN) PARTY. Upstart religious sects have also suffered continual religious persecution, especially the LATTER-DAY SAINTS and JEHOVAH'S WITNESSES. The Mormons were driven from their homes in four states, were the target of a MORMON EXTERMINATION ORDER in Missouri, and had their church seized briefly by the government over the practice of POLYGAMY. Jehovah's Witnesses continue to tangle with local governments over their door-to-door EVANGELISM, most recently in *Watchtower Bible Society v. Village of Stratton* (2002).

See also AMERICAN CENTER FOR LAW AND JUSTICE; AMERICAN CIVIL LIBERTIES UNION; ANTICULT MOVEMENT; ANTI-DEFAMATION LEAGUE; CATHOLIC LEAGUE FOR RELIGIOUS AND CIVIL RIGHTS; CHRISTIAN LEGAL SOCIETY; HATE CRIMES; INTERNATIONAL HUMAN RIGHT OF RELIGION; JOHN LOCKE; MARXISM/COMMUNISM; RELIGIOUS DISCRIMINATION IN HIGHER EDUCATION; RELIGIOUS ESTABLISHMENT IN THE COLONIES; TOLERANCE.

Further reading: Haught, James A. 1990. *Holy Horrors: An Illustrated History of Religious Murder and Madness.* New York: Prometheus Books, 1990: Redekop, John H. 1997. "Can Christians Be Tolerant?" *Christian Week.* October 1997.

—William Lester

religious refugees

Religious refugees have figured prominently in U.S. foreign policy considerations and domestic politics. Since 1965, the United States has admitted over 3 million refugees from political and RELIGIOUS PERSECUTION.

From the time that the PURITANS landed, America has been a refuge for people persecuted for their religious faith. In the 19th century, German Catholics and Jews arrived because they felt unwelcome in Germany, and Jews also fled pogroms in Russia. The 20th century ushered in large-scale religious persecution in Nazi Germany and various Communist states. Also, large numbers of religious refugees came from the Middle East, Africa, and Asia. Often, persecutors intertwine religious, political, and ethnic motivations so that they are not easy to distinguish. African religious refugees often flee their countries because they are from a different religion, tribe, or political party than that of the victors who have taken over the government.

The HOLOCAUST and the rise of communism as a self-consciously atheistic political movement created the context for U.S. policy toward admitting religious refugees. In particular the campaign to force the Soviet Union to allow Jews to emigrate became a model for activating domestic politics for support of international religious human rights.

American Jews used their considerable political clout, particularly in heavily Jewish states like New York, to push for freedom of Soviet Jews. Along the way, some American Jewish leaders made common cause with anticommunist secular and Christian conservatives, which initiated a gradual reworking of political allegiances among some Jews. Christian conservative support for freeing Soviet Jews coincided with their attraction to end-times prophecy about the refounding of the state of ISRAEL and their growing interest in politics.

The Soviet Communist Party destroyed practically all of Jewish community, cultural, and religious life. Claiming that Jewish doctors were plotting to poison him, Soviet dictator Josef Stalin, liquidated many leading Russian Jews, especially in the fields of medicine and academia, in the early 1950s. Jews experienced increased discrimination in obtaining education and jobs.

In the early and mid-1960s, American Jews started intense discussions on what could be done to help their counterparts in the Soviet Union. In 1963, several Jewish U.S. senators met with President JOHN F. KENNEDY about assisting Soviet Jews. In the mid- and late 1960s, young Jewish veterans of civil rights marches and anti-VIETNAM WAR protests turned their attention to the oppression of Soviet Jews. Both American and Soviet Jews were emboldened to act by the 1967 Six-Day War, in which Israel decisively defeated the Arab states. By 1971, several organizations to support Soviet Jewry had been formed. That September, the Jewish establishment launched the National Conference on Soviet Jewry and the Greater New York Conference on Soviet Jewry. The AMERICAN JEWISH COMMITTEE provided key personnel and contacts with other religious groups and Soviet Jewry.

In 1975, Senator Henry M. Jackson (D-Wash.) and Representative Charles A. Vanik (D-Ohio) passed through Congress and got President Gerald R. Ford to approve their Jackson-Vanik Amendment to a trade agreement that linked a relaxation of trade restrictions with Soviet permission for its Jewish citizens to emigrate. Scholars debate whether the amendment and other human rights pressure had any effect on the Soviet leadership. Its immediate reaction was to tighten restrictions on Jews. However, the restrictions and ability to emigrate waxed and waned with the ups and downs of the cold war. Most U.S. presidents were ambivalent about having their hands tied by various congressional initiatives linking trade with the Communist bloc to their performance in observing religious human rights.

On May 31, 1977, one of the most prominent Jewish leaders in the Soviet Union, Anatoly (Natan) Shcharansky, was falsely charged with treason as a spy for the CIA. The celebrated case inspired a number of Soviet Jews to become "refuseniks," which meant that they were demanding the right to emigrate in spite of Soviet government opposition. But under the leadership of Soviet president Leonid Brezhnev, the 1970s became known as a time of oppression of Soviet Jews. People who had never thought of themselves as Jews had their identity cards stamped "Jew" and suffered discrimination and state-sponsored anti-Semitic propaganda. Then, Soviet president Mikhail Gorbachev ushered in a reversal of anti-Jewish and antireligious policies upon taking office in 1985. In 1986, Shcharansky was released to go to Israel, and by 1987 glasnost, a policy of openness, brought a new era in Soviet religious policy.

Michael Horowitz, a Jewish activist prominent in Republican circles, brought the lessons he learned in the struggle to free the Soviet Jews to the cause of religious freedom in general and that of persecuted Christians in particular. Horowitz gathered a coalition of evangelical Christians, Jews, and Catholics to deny normal trade relations with Sudan and mainland China as long as they oppressed evangelical Christians and other religionists. Although China eventually received permanent normal trading status with the United States, the coalitions forced the Clinton administration to institute an annual review of religious persecution and to take steps against flagrant offenders. In 1998, the U.S. government established religious freedom as an official policy objective. Clinton appointed an ambassador for international religious freedom and Congress established an independent government-funded U.S. Commission on International Religious Freedom.

See also INTERNATIONAL HUMAN RIGHT OF RELIGION; SANCTUARY MOVEMENT.

Further reading: Orbach, William W. *The American Movement to Aid Soviet Jews.* Amherst: University of Massachusetts Press, 1979.

—Tony Carnes

Religious Roundtable

Ed McAteer, a former Colgate-Palmolive sales manager, began a series of National Affairs Religious Briefings each year in his hometown of Memphis, Tennessee. On his retirement, McAteer founded the Religious Roundtable in 1979 out of his conviction that LIBERALISM, as exemplified by the Supreme Court decisions in *ROE V. WADE* (1973), which legalized ABORTION, and *ENGEL V. VITALE* (1961), which banned PRAYER IN PUBLIC SCHOOLS, was sweeping across the United States with little resistance. McAteer, arguing that America was "imperiled" and that liberalism had stolen the moral high ground, brought together a coalition of CONSERVATIVE business, military, political, and religious leaders to energize conservative constituencies. As president of the Religious Roundtable, McAteer utilizes the organization to bring biblical principles to bear on public policy.

By 1990, the organization boasted more than 100,000 members and chapters in all 50 states that worked to influence the legislative process to adopt "traditional, family-based Christian values." The Roundtable considers itself a public education group and a clearinghouse for information from other groups of the Religious Right. To accomplish this goal, the Religious Roundtable provides its audience with in-depth information about government activities and analyses of issues advancing its positions on political and social issues, such as a pro-life stance on abortion, support for U.S. military strength, and active opposition to PORNOGRAPHY, divorce, and GAY RIGHTS. At the time of its founding, the Roundtable was also a vocal opponent of the EQUAL RIGHTS AMENDMENT.

The Religious Roundtable regularly publishes "The Roundtable Report," a newsletter on proposed and pending legislation concerning the values supported by the Religious Right. A governing board and the Council of 56, named for the same number of signers of the Declaration of Independence, sets policy and direction for the organization. As with most ideological groups, this Religious Right offshoot maintains both a tax-exempt branch and a lobbying arm, Roundtable Issues and Answers. The group is funded by individual memberships. To promote its conservative agenda, the Religious Roundtable holds national affairs briefings, national leadership seminars, rallies, media appearances, and personal appearances, and it also distributes cassette tapes. The Roundtable's National Affairs Briefing in August 1980 was highlighted by an appearance of the Republican presidential candidate, RONALD REAGAN, the only presidential candidate to accept the Roundtable's invitation to the event.

Additionally, the Religious Roundtable holds an annual prayer breakfast to "pray for America." During its National Prayer Breakfast, held in Washington, D.C., each year, the group has used the occasion as an opportunity for Christian Zionists, "in prophetical solidarity with our Jewish brethren, [to] affirm the importance of the state of Israel, and unite against those forces of darkness who wickedly assail them and their beloved state." It also provides a platform from which congressional and other government officials can join with them in proclaiming their unconditional support for "our strategic ally, the only democracy in the Middle East, Israel." In December 2001, McAteer formed a coalition of Jews and

Christians with Herbert Zweibon, chairman of Americans for a Safe Israel, to deplore the killings of Israelis "by [Yasser] Arafat and his cohorts, while simultaneously attempting to kill Judeo-Christian ties to their history and holy places."

Within the religious community, the Religious Roundtable mounted an impassioned attack on the NATIONAL COUNCIL OF CHURCHES (NCC), the national organization of mainline and progressive Protestant churches. McAteer said of the group's efforts to update the Bible to, among other things, include gender-inclusive language, "Powerful forces within the NCC appear to be literally declaring war on our Holy Scriptures," which he calls an "evil scheme to rewrite the Bible."

The Roundtable works as an informational clearinghouse for other groups on the right. Groups that have belonged to the Roundtable's clearinghouse include the CHRISTIAN BROADCASTING NETWORK, the BILLY GRAHAM Evangelistic Association, the (now defunct) MORAL MAJORITY, CHRISTIAN VOICE, the Church League of America, National Religious Broadcasters, Campus Crusade for Christ, Plymouth Rock Foundation, NATIONAL ASSOCIATION OF EVANGELICALS, Gideons, Wycliffe Bible Translators, and Intercessors for America. Moreover, McAteer, along with Howard Phillips, RICHARD VIGUERIE, and Paul Weyrich, helped JERRY FALWELL start the Moral Majority.

—Veronica Donahue DiConti

Rerum Novarum

An encyclical letter of Pope Leo XIII, *Rerum Novarum* was issued on May 15, 1891. Literally translated "Of new things," and more typically referred to as "On the Condition of the Working Classes," *Rerum Novarum* was the first of the ROMAN CATHOLIC CHURCH's great modern social encyclicals. It inaugurated the church's engagement with industrial capitalism and inspired a century of papal teaching, most notably Pius XI's 1931 *Quadragesimo Anno* (*Forty Years After*) and JOHN PAUL II's 1991 *Centesimus Annus* (*The Hundredth Year*).

Prior to *Rerum Novarum*, the Vatican maintained that only a return to a Christian social order could cure the ills of industrial capitalism. Equally opposed both to laissez-faire capitalism and to socialism, yet still wedded to Christendom, the Vatican could offer no relevant solution to the massive suffering that accompanied the rise of industrialism. Though Leo maintained in *Rerum Novarum* that social reform could not happen "without the assistance of Religion and the Church," he conceded that the Catholic Church had to develop a more positive stance on social reform. The church could not simply condemn modernity in toto. Rather, it had to bring the resources of Catholic theology into meaningful dialogue with the pressing social questions of the day.

Rerum Novarum was a conservative document in many respects, but it did mark the entry of the Catholic Church into the field of social reform. *Rerum Novarum* endorsed a middle way between socialism and laissez-faire capitalism. The encyclical reaffirmed the basic right to private property while strongly rebuking socialism as "highly unjust, because it violates the rights of lawful owners, perverts the function of the State, and throws governments into utter confusion." The right of workers to form labor unions was affirmed, although Catholic unions were upheld as the ideal. One of the most important aspects of the encyclical was its affirmation of a worker's right to a living wage. Leo wrote that wage contracts should "not be less than enough to support a worker who is thrifty and upright." Finally, the encyclical declared a role for the state in protecting and assisting workers. Leo believed private associations motivated by Christian charity must be the first means of assistance, but that justice also demanded greater state intervention.

JOHN AUGUSTINE RYAN, the leading American Catholic social theorist of the early 20th century, said of *Rerum Novarum:* "Probably no other pronouncement on the social question has had so many readers or exercised such a wide influence." Yet in spite of the encyclical's seminal importance in the history of Catholic social thought and its eventual influence on American Catholic thought and action, it received only minimal attention in the United States when first published in 1891. Ryan, a seminarian at the time, did not even hear of the encyclical until 1894. Pope Pius XI's *Quadragesimo Anno,* on the other hand, was released at a time of rising Catholic social activity during the Great Depression, and was immediately used by American Catholics to support reform efforts.

Rerum Novarum did have some early influence on American Catholics. German-American Catholics used its message to support a conservative program of social reform based on social education and support for labor. Father Peter Dietz sought to enact the teachings of Leo's encyclical by bringing the church into a closer relationship with organized labor. John Ryan, more than any other American Catholic, brought the message of *Rerum Novarum* to the American Catholic Church. In such books as *A Living Wage* (1906) and *Distributive Justice* (1916), he combined Leo's teachings with American progressive ideology to develop a Catholic program of social reform. Ryan's ideas received the endorsement of American bishops when the National Catholic Welfare Conference issued *The Bishops' Program of Social Reconstruction* in 1919. This document offered the church's support for such policies as the living wage, the right of workers to unionize, and greater state intervention on behalf of the poor. The full flowering of *Rerum Novarum's* teachings in the American church, however, would have to wait until the 1930s.

See also CATHOLIC BISHOPS IN AMERICAN POLITICS; CATHOLIC BISHOPS' 1986 PASTORAL LETTER ON THE ECONOMY.

Further reading: Abell, Aaron I. "The Reception of Leo XIII's Labor Encyclical in America, 1891–1919." *Review of Politics* 7 (1945) 464–495; McShane, Joseph M., S.J. *"Sufficiently Radical": Catholicism, Progressivism, and the Bishops' Program of 1919.* Washington, D.C.: Catholic University of America Press, 1986; Ryan, John A. *Social Doctrine in Action: A Personal History.* New York: Harper, 1941.

—Zachary R. Calo

revivalism

Revivalism is a form of religious worship that developed primarily in Protestant churches but is now practiced throughout Christianity. At a typical revival, a worship leader preaches to a mass audience assembled outside the normal meetings of any one congregation. The style of worship is highly emotional, characterized by singing, dancing, and long, often fiery sermons. Revivalist leaders use their personal charisma and emotional appeals to coax listeners into conversion experiences that will transform their lives. At some revivals, particularly those in the PENTECOSTAL tradition, participants believe that conversion occurs when the Holy Spirit enters into the individual's heart, a moment that is externally manifested by convulsions, fainting, speaking in tongues, or other physical phenomena. In more restrained forms of revivalism, conversion is demonstrated by an "altar call" during which new converts come forward to make public professions of their faith.

Although revivalism is an experiential, rather than doctrinal, form of religion, it has significant theological implications. First, revivalism reintroduced free-will doctrines into American Protestantism. Revivalist practices imply that individuals must consciously choose to accept God's grace, thus inserting an element of free will into the economy of salvation. Revivalist preaching often implies that grace is available to anyone who will accept it, thus placing the matter entirely in the individual's hands. Second, revivalists often are moral perfectionists. They believe that the power of the Holy Spirit is capable of burning sin from the human heart. Many revivalist leaders teach that the moment of conversion is the beginning of a new life, in which sin can be completely conquered. Finally, revivalism has strong millenarian tendencies. Revivalists hope that the "Work of the Spirit" within the individual will lead to a much wider work. Converts will take their newfound faith into the world, perhaps stimulating more conversions and ultimately a religious awakening that will transform an entire region or country. Sometimes expectations for social reform are so intense that revivalists expect to see the emergence of the Kingdom of God.

Revivalism first emerged in America during the FIRST GREAT AWAKENING. By the 1730s, the established clergy of the old Puritan order had become increasingly rationalistic. In response, an aggressively evangelistic breed of pastors emerged who were willing to use the fear of damnation to frighten sinners into conversion. At first, these preachers confined themselves to their own churches, but by 1740 "itinerant preachers" were moving from town to town, preaching to large crowds, often without the permission of local pastors. The most famous of these was GEORGE WHITEFIELD (1714–70), an Anglican minister and associate of John Wesley. Whitefield, known as the Grand Itinerant, preached to crowds of thousands throughout the colonies.

The classic form of revivalism emerged with the SECOND GREAT AWAKENING's huge camp meetings, such as the Logan County (1800) and Cane Ridge (1801) revivals in Kentucky. These revivals lasted several days, requiring the thousands who had come from far away to camp out for the duration. Preachers of several denominations at once exhorted the hearers, and the crowd responded, often with wild enthusiasm. New converts danced, shouted, fainted, screamed, laughed, and even barked. Although established denominations drew back from the emotionalism, the Methodists and Baptists embraced revivalism and experienced dramatic growth.

Revivalism became the dominant form of worship among American Protestants for the first half of the 19th century, particularly in the West and South. In the 1820s, Charles Grandison Finney (1792–1875) led a series of revivals in upstate New York. This area was so frequently exposed to revival passions that it was nicknamed the "Burned-over District." After the Civil War, evangelicals such as DWIGHT MOODY (1827–99) and BILLY SUNDAY (1863–1935) used revivalism to evangelize urban centers. In the 1880s and 1890s, a new wave of revivalism led to the creation of several denominations, including the Church of the Nazarene (1908) and the ASSEMBLIES OF GOD (1914). Revivalism was especially important among African Americans, many of whom had been evangelized in the days of slavery by Methodist and Baptist revivalists.

Although revivalism faded from the "mainstream" by the mid-20th century, it experienced a resurgence after World War II. Rev. BILLY GRAHAM led a famous series of urban revivals in the 1950s. In the 1970s, the charismatic movement brought a form of revivalism to the more staid mainline denominations, such as the EPISCOPAL CHURCH, various LUTHERAN CHURCHES, and even the ROMAN CATHOLIC CHURCH. While many evangelical preachers who might previously have used revivals to reach mass audience now prefer radio and television, mass revival meetings continue. PROMISE KEEPERS, a Christian men's movement, held revival-style meetings in sports stadiums throughout the 1990s. Revivals in Toronto (beginning in 1994) and Pensacola, Florida (beginning in 1995) attracted participants from around the world.

See also ROBERTS, ORAL.

Further reading: Ahlstrom, Sydney E. *A Religious History of the American People.* New Haven, Conn.: Yale University Press, 1972; Beverley, James A. "Toronto's Mixed Blessing." *Christianity Today.* September 11, 1995, 22–27; McLoughlin, William G. *Revivals, Awakenings, and Reform.* Chicago: University of Chicago Press, 1978; Rabey, Steve. "Pensacola Outpouring Keeps Gushing." *Christianity Today.* March 3, 1997, 54–57.

—James Paul Old

Reynolds v. United States 98 U.S. 145 (1878)

George Reynolds (1842–1909) was a member of the Church of Jesus Christ of LATTER-DAY SAINTS (Mormons), an English immigrant, a secretary to Brigham Young, a well-known Mormon author, and, later in life, a member of the church's leadership (Quorum of the Seventy). Reynolds was also the first person convicted of bigamy, or plural marriage, under the Morrill Anti Bigamy Act (Stat. 12:501 [1862]). The Morrill Act outlawed bigamy in U.S. territories and annulled Utah territorial laws allowing it. Conviction carried a penalty of a fine and five years in prison. Prosecutions were generally hard to come by, however, because Mormon temple weddings were not open to public scrutiny, and witnesses were often unwilling to testify against fellow family and church members. Nevertheless, one of Reynolds's wives testified against him, and he was convicted. Reynolds appealed his conviction and challenged the constitutionality of the Morrill Act on the premise that plural marriage was a protected religious practice and that outlawing POLYGAMY violated the FREE EXERCISE CLAUSE of the First Amendment.

Chief Justice Morrison R. Waite wrote the unanimous decision handed down in 1878. The decision upheld Reynolds's conviction and the right of Congress to criminalize polygamy. The Court based its decision on a sharp distinction between religious belief and religious practice. Religious *belief,* the Court argued, could not be regulated in any way. But religious *practice* could be, particularly beliefs deemed "in violation of social duties or subversive of good order." The Court reasoned that polygamy met that criterion because it "has always been odious among the northern and western nations of Europe" and violated British common law. The Court also asked: "Can a man excuse his practices to the contrary because of his religious belief? To permit this would be to make the professed doctrines of religious belief superior to the law of the land, and in effect to permit every citizen to become a law unto himself. Government could exist only in name under such circumstances." The Morrill Act was upheld, and Reynolds was sentenced to two years in prison.

The narrow reading of the free exercise clause in *Reynolds* accelerated the drive to wipe out polygamy, break down Mormon power, and fully assimilate Latter-day Saints into mainstream American culture. Congress passed the Edmunds Act in 1882, which outlawed "unlawful cohabitation"—a crime much easier to prove than bigamy—and provided that those convicted of doing so could not hold public office, serve on juries, or vote. The Edmunds-Tucker Act (1887) went even further and disincorporated the Mormon Church and impounded most of the church's property and financial assets. It also dissolved the Perpetual Emigration Fund, which helped poor Mormon converts from Europe migrate to Utah, revoked women's right to vote, which had been granted by the territorial legislature in 1870, and instituted a "test oath" with a pledge to support the national government and congressional acts against polygamy. Idaho went even further by suspending citizenship rights from Mormons, including those who did not practice polygamy, who were the large majority of Mormons. The constitutionality of the Idaho test oath was upheld by the Supreme Court in DAVIS V. BEASON (1890). The Supreme Court also upheld the disincorporation of the church under the Edmunds-Tucker Act in *Late Corporation of the Church of Jesus Christ of Latter-day Saints v. United States* (1890).

This restrictive reading of the free exercise clause has been criticized and heavily modified in recent years. Critics argue that religion is more than belief, it is also a way of life; the two are not reasonably separated. Also, the free exercise clause specifically protects the *exercise,* or practice, of religion, not just belief. The Court eroded the belief/action distinction in WISCONSIN V. YODER (1972) when it upheld the right of AMISH parents to remove their children from school before the age of 16, as dictated by Wisconsin law. Earlier, in SHERBERT V. VERNER (1963), the Court required that the government show a compelling state interest before restricting the practice. However, some of the restrictiveness of *Reynolds* was resurrected when the Court removed the "compelling government interest" and "least restrictive means" tests in EMPLOYMENT DIVISION V. SMITH (1990).

Further reading: Firmage, Edwin B., and R. Collin Mangrum. *Zion in the Courts: A Legal History of the Church of Jesus Christ of Latter-day Saints.* Urbana: University of Illinois Press, 1988.

—Jeffrey C. Fox

Roberts, Oral (1918–) *evangelist*

Oral Roberts was America's most distinguished 20th-century healing evangelist. He is a religious television pioneer, an educator, and a visionary. He teaches that prayer does not heal, though he laid hands on and prayed for hundreds of thousands of sick people; and that medicine does not heal, though he founded a university, a medical school, and a hospital—because he believes that only God heals. Prayer and medicine are instruments of a creative and loving God and nothing more, in his view.

Speaking to political scientist Aaron Wildavsky about his root conviction, Roberts said that he built his life on the proposition that the God of the Bible, from Genesis to Revelation, is the source of all life and knowledge. In a world broken by sin, poverty, sickness, and hatred, Roberts sees things whole, and perceives his calling to be helping to re-create that wholeness—in short, he said, to bring God's healing power to his generation.

Granville Oral Roberts, the son of Ellis and Claudius Roberts, was born in a log house near Bebee, in Pontotoc County, Oklahoma. His parents were devout Christian PENTECOSTALS. Near death, suffering from tuberculosis, Oral as a teenager confronted his mortality. Touched by God through prayer, it was months before he experienced a full recovery of his strength. He began to preach that same year, making a decision not to enter law and politics, fields that had earlier interested him.

In 1947, Roberts moved to Tulsa, Oklahoma, to be more centrally located and near air travel. In the following years, he held meetings sponsored by local pastors in city auditoriums throughout the nation that took place in a tent he brought along that could seat 12,500 people. His services placed little emphasis on music or entertainment, but rather on preaching, on a one- to two-hour message, designed to build faith in the hearers that God could and would save and heal. Following the sermon and altar call, he prayed for the sick. His services were racially integrated, and African Americans were among his strongest supporters.

In the 1950s, ABC Radio carried his *Healing Waters* program to several hundred stations, and in 1954 he launched into television with the goal of taking the "tent meeting atmosphere" into the homes of America. Soon 130 television stations carried his program to 80 percent of the nation. His support base of partners expanded throughout this period, paying for the costly media exposure and attending his meetings. In later years, Roberts produced prime-time television specials featuring entertainment personalities and maintained a regular Sunday television program.

To secure his legacy, in 1965 Roberts founded Oral Roberts University (ORU). It later expanded to include graduate schools of business, education, theology, nursing, law, medicine, and dentistry. The latter three schools later closed. His son Richard Roberts succeeded him as president of the university when Oral became chancellor.

A lifelong Democrat, Oral Roberts is publicly nonpartisan. He broke from this pattern more as a personal favor when he endorsed PAT ROBERTSON's presidential candidacy in 1988. Roberts identifies with the dispossessed who attended his meetings for decades and with those who fight for them. In the 1970s, ORU granted an honorary doctorate to Rev. JESSE JACKSON. However, as a major employer in Tulsa and a famous person in the region, Roberts is also one of the local elite, sitting on a bank board and holding a membership at the country club.

Roberts is committed to racial reconciliation—one-third of ORU students are racial minorities. He abhors poverty and religious bigotry, maintaining positive ties with the Jewish and Roman Catholic communities. His desire is that the oppressed be set free, that they be educated and prosper in every way, body, soul, spirit, in this life and in the life to come. When civil government, churches, and private associations serve these ends, Roberts is supportive. But when they stray from this agenda, Roberts reminds them that Christ came for the sheep, so that "they might have life, and they might have it more abundantly" (John 10:10).

Further reading: Harnell, David Edwin. *Oral Roberts: An American Life.* Bloomington: Indiana University Press, 1985.

—Hubert Morken

Robertson, Marion C. "Pat" (1930–) *evangelist*

Marion "Pat" Robertson is one of the most important figures in the contemporary Christian Right. Robertson is an ordained minister in the SOUTHERN BAPTIST CONVENTION, and is among the most visible charismatic Christians in the United States (see PENTECOSTAL AND CHARISMATIC).

Robertson's brand of Christianity emphasizes the importance of spiritual gifts (or *charismata*), such as speaking in tongues (glossolalia), prophecy, and faith healing. Robertson has been a central figure in contemporary American politics in a variety of roles.

The basis for much of Robertson's future activities was the founding of the CHRISTIAN BROADCASTING NETWORK (CBN) in 1961 in Portsmouth, Virginia. The network, which broadcast both religious programming and "wholesome" secular programming (including reruns of such popular westerns as *Gunsmoke* and *The Rifleman*) provided Robertson with both a source of income and a platform from which to become a political advocate. The spread of cable television in the 1970s and 1980s, as well as favorable rulings by the Federal Communications Commission regarding religious programming, enabled Robertson to reach a national audience His direct involvement in CBN has been limited in recent years, but Robertson still hosts the *700 Club*. On this program, Robertson provides coverage of contemporary current events from a "Christian" perspective.

In 1988, Robertson ran for the Republican nomination for president. During his campaign, he sought to distance himself from his roles as minister and TELEVANGELIST (a term Robertson did much to popularize). In this capacity, Robertson would occasionally offer secular justifications for conservative positions on social issues. For example, at one point in his campaign, Robertson reiterated his long-standing opposition to the Supreme Court's decision in *ROE V. WADE*, which legalized ABORTION in many instances. As a presidential candidate, Robertson provided an unusual rationale for this position: He suggested that legal abortion threatened the solvency of Social Security by eliminating people who would otherwise be expected to pay into the system as adults. Robertson's quest for the GOP nomination was not successful. Aside from some early successes (typically in caucus states with multicandidate fields), Robertson did not make a credible challenge to the eventual nomination of George H. W. Bush. Some analysts have suggested that Robertson's appeal to religious conservatives was limited by his identification as a charismatic Christian—his emphasis on gifts of the spirit was rejected by other prominent evangelicals, such as JERRY FALWELL. Empirical studies have suggested that Robertson was unable to attract much support beyond a very narrow basis of Pentecostal and charismatic Christians.

After Robertson's presidential campaign folded, he formed an organization called CHRISTIAN COALITION, whose presidency he held until 2000. Christian Coalition was designed as a grass-roots organization to seek electoral success at the state and local levels, as well as providing resources by which churches could engage in political mobilization. Christian Coalition seeks the protection and advancement of Christian values in contemporary American politics, and its communications generally emphasize the various ways in which government policies can limit the religious liberty of doctrinally conservative Christians. The use of the term *Coalition* in the organization's title was intended to emphasize the inclusive nature of the group, and to avoid repeating the religious particularism that characterized Jerry Falwell's MORAL MAJORITY.

Robertson also founded Regent University in Virginia Beach, VIRGINIA, which has an explicitly "evangelical Christian" mission, and the AMERICAN CENTER FOR LAW AND JUSTICE, which Robertson conceived as a Christian alternative to the AMERICAN CIVIL LIBERTIES UNION. Robertson also founded Operation Blessing, an international organization devoted to short-term disaster relief, and CBN Worldreach, an international "evangelizing" (missionary) organization. The latter is devoted to using broadcasting, as well as "personal outreach," to spread the "good news" of the gospel to the developing world. While Robertson himself has become something of an "elder statesman" of American evangelicalism, the organizations he has founded have provided resources for evangelical political activity that transcend his individual activities.

See also RELIGION IN THE 1988 PRESIDENTIAL ELECTION.

Pat Robertson *(Michael Smith/Newsmakers)*

Further reading: Frankl, Razelle. *Televangelism.* Carbondale: Southern Illinois University Press, 1987; Green, John C.

"Pat Robertson and the Latest Crusade: Religious Resources and the 1988 Presidential Campaign." *Social Science Quarterly* 74 (1993): 157–168; Hoover, Stewart M. *Mass Media Region.* Beverly Hills, Calif.: Sage, 1988. Christian Coalition on the Internet: URL: http://www.cc.org. Wills, Garry. *Under God* New York: Simon and Schuster, 1990.

—Ted G. Jelen

Roemer v. Maryland Public Works Board 426 U.S. 736 (1976)

Roemer involved a MARYLAND statute that made annual noncategorical grants to private colleges, including religiously affiliated institutions, provided that the funds were not used for sectarian purposes. Supreme Court Justice Harry Blackmun wrote the majority opinion for the 5-4 decision that upheld the Maryland statute as not violating the constitutionally required SEPARATION OF CHURCH AND STATE.

The Maryland statute provided for qualifying institutions to receive for each student a grant of money equal to 15 percent of the state's per full-time pupil appropriation for a state college student. Students engaged in theological training were to be excluded from the head count, and no money was to be used for sectarian purposes. The Maryland Board of Public Works administered the grant program with the assistance of the Maryland Council for Higher Education. In screening applicants for the grants, the council determined whether or not the institutions primarily awarded theological degrees and whether assurance was given that the funds would not be used for sectarian purposes. In addition, institutions were required to submit annual "Utilization of Funds" reports.

A group of taxpayers in Maryland challenged the statute's constitutionality, claiming that payments of tax funds to church-affiliated institutions violated the ESTABLISHMENT CLAUSE of the First Amendment. Relying on the Court's rulings on aid to religiously affiliated elementary and secondary schools, opponents of the Maryland grant program claimed that the direct funding of religious institutions led to the impermissible advancement of religion. Moreover, they argued that the government oversight necessitated to ensure that government moneys were not used for sectarian purposes led to an excessive entanglement between church and state.

Defenders of the Maryland program argued that the grant system was more like the college building and maintenance grants upheld by the Court in *TILTON V. RICHARDSON* (1971). *Tilton* involved a federal grant program that assisted private colleges, including religiously affiliated ones, in building facilities that were not to be used for sectarian purposes. This requirement, plus the differing atmosphere and level of academic freedom at the college level, led the Court to conclude in *Tilton* that the facilities grant neither advanced religion nor led to an excessive entanglement between church and state.

In writing for the majority, Justice Blackmun upheld the district court's affirmation of the grant program. Applying the three-part *Lemon* test, Blackmun first addressed the contention that the grant program unconstitutionally advanced religion. Blackmun agreed with the district court's finding that the colleges in question were not pervasively sectarian. Other than required theology courses, which were taught in an "atmosphere of intellectual freedom," there were no required religious activities on campus. Moreover, the colleges enjoyed a significant degree of autonomy from their sponsoring church, a religious basis for hiring did not extend beyond the theology department, and the admissions practices led to a student body that was not chosen according to religion. These factors led Blackmun to conclude that the situation in Maryland was similar to that of *Tilton,* and thus there was no "constitutionally significant distinction between them, at least for purposes of the 'pervasive sectarianism' test."

Blackmun similarly ruled that although the schools were required to submit annual reports to the government, the relationship between the church institution and the state did not lead to excessive entanglement. According to Blackmun, the relationship created by this program was no more problematic than the occasional inspection or audit related to state accreditation of the institution. Unlike many religiously affiliated elementary and secondary schools, the universities in question were capable of separating their religious and secular functions and thus diminishing the level of monitoring and investigation required of the government.

The dissent found the direct funding of church-related institutions fundamentally problematic. Justice WILLIAM BRENNAN, joined by Justice Thurgood Marshall, opined that the key question is not whether religion permeates the entire curriculum. "Rather, it is that the secular education is provided within the environment of religion; the institution is dedicated to two goals, secular education *and* religious instruction. When aid flows directly to the institution, both functions benefit." *Roemer,* as a result, reflected the Court's willingness to grant greater latitude in allowing state funding of religiously affiliated institutions of higher education that were not "permeated by religion" than for religiously affiliated elementary and secondary schools. Yet whether this could be done consistent with the excessive entanglement prohibition of the *Lemon* test would continue to be a question raised by both proponents and opponents of public aid to religious institutions.

See also AID TO RELIGIOUS SCHOOLS.

—J. David Holcomb

Roe v. Wade 410 U.S. 113 (1973)

Jane Roe (a pseudonym) claimed that she became pregnant as the result of a rape. She was unable to obtain an ABORTION because her doctor refused to perform the operation. He told her that doing so was illegal under Texas law, except to save the mother's life. Roe obtained counsel and sued on the grounds that the Texas law violated, among other things, her right to privacy and due process. A three-judge district (trial) court provided declaratory, though not injunctive, relief and ruled that the abortion statute was void for vagueness and infringed on Roe's Ninth and Fourteenth Amendment rights. This meant that the court ruled in Roe's favor, but that it would not stop the enforcement of the law, pending subsequent appeals. Roe's attorney appealed directly to the Supreme Court.

In a 7-2 decision, the Supreme Court affirmed the district court's decision. The majority opinion, written by Justice Harry Blackmun, argued that state criminal laws, which allow abortion only as a lifesaving procedure, without regard for the stage of a woman's pregnancy, violate the due process clause of the Fourteenth Amendment. From the Court's view, this clause protects citizens from state actions that impede the right to privacy, which, the justices argued, includes a woman's right to terminate her pregnancy. The majority went on to point out that, while the state cannot override a woman's right to obtain an abortion, it has a legitimate interest in protecting the woman's health as well as the health of the unborn life.

The Court found the right to obtain an abortion fundamental, and in so doing utilized a modified version of the compelling interest test to determine when the state may regulate this procedure. The key modification to the standard was a balance between the interests of a woman's right to obtain an abortion and the state's interest in protecting life. The balance focused on the timing of a woman's right to choose. During the first trimester of pregnancy, the Court ruled that the abortion decision must be left to the woman, relying on the medical advice of her doctor. At the end of the first trimester, and until viability, the state may regulate abortions to protect the mother's health. After viability has been established, the state may regulate, or forbid, abortion except to preserve the life or health of the mother. It may do so to promote the potentiality of human life.

While the decision itself was important, establishing the constitutional right to privacy, *Roe* created a new era in abortion politics, religion's role in politics, and in American politics generally. Specifically, this decision is widely credited with helping to mobilize conservative Roman Catholics, propelling Catholic bishops into politics, eventually awakening Evangelical Protestants to national politics, and providing fertile ground on which to mobilize a new cadre of pro-life and prochoice abortion activists. *Roe* also provided strong evidence that the courts were a viable strategy for shifting public policy, which is evidenced, in part, by the growing number of groups sponsoring and writing friend of the court briefs (amicus curiae) in abortion cases. In short, *Roe* profoundly changed American politics from that point forward.

See also CATHOLIC BISHOPS IN AMERICAN POLITICS; CATHOLIC BISHOPS' 1975 PASTORAL LETTER ON ABORTION; CATHOLICS FOR FREE CHOICE; JOHN CARDINAL O'CONNOR; OPERATION RESCUE; *PLANNED PARENTHOOD OF SOUTHEASTERN PENNSYLVANIA V. CASEY*; RELIGIOUS COALITION FOR REPRODUCTIVE CHOICE; *WEBSTER V. REPRODUCTIVE HEALTH SERVICES*.

Further reading: Craig, Barbara Hinkson, and David M. O'Brien. *Abortion and American Politics.* Chatham, N.J.: Chatham House, 1993; Epstein, Lee, and Joseph Kobylka. *The Supreme Court and Legal Change.* Chapel Hill: University of North Carolina Press, 1992.

—Timothy R. Johnson

Roman Catholic Church

The Roman Catholic Church is the largest Christian body in the world, with close to 1 billion adherents. About half of all Catholics live in Europe or North America, but the church's greatest growth in population is occurring in the developing world. Approximately 60 million Americans claim membership in the church, making it the largest religious group in the United States.

The church claims a lineage back to its founder, Jesus Christ, through an unbroken line of successors to his disciples, called apostles. These successors are the bishops of the church who govern given geographic areas called dioceses. The church has divided the world into almost 2,000 dioceses, each administered by a bishop. There are almost 200 dioceses in the United States. Within these dioceses, Catholics live as part of a community under the leadership of the local bishop. Each diocese is divided into geographical areas called parishes. A priest who ministers to the local community leads the parishes. Catholics are united through their bishop with all other bishops in the world under the leadership of the bishop of Rome, the pope.

The pope, also known as the Vicar of Christ, is the supreme leader of the church. The current pope, JOHN PAUL II (1978–   ), is the 263rd successor to the first pope, St. Peter, one of Jesus' original 12 apostles. The pope is assisted in church governance by bishops who have been promoted by a pope to the rank of cardinal. The cardinals together form the College of Cardinals; from their ranks, they alone elect a new pope. There are 11 American cardinals. Also assisting the pope in his administrative duties is the Roman Curia, a collection of agencies with responsibilities for diplomatic relations with other countries, Catholic doctrine and worship, relations with bishops and priests, evangelization, ecumenical and interfaith dialogue, and other matters.

While Catholics were a part of the American colonies from the earliest days, what is most significant is how few Catholics there were in what would become the United States. By 1785, when the population of the colonies was nearly 4 million, there were only about 25,000 Catholics. For most of American history, their minority status has marked Catholics. Few Catholics served as politicians in the colonies, although MARYLAND did have a significant Catholic presence. Not until Charles Carroll of Maryland began writing in 1773 against the royal government and helped elect a pro-revolutionary government in Maryland did a Catholic leader overcome concerns and prejudice about faith and lead a political party to victory. In three years, Carroll would be one of the signatories of the DECLARATION OF INDEPENDENCE.

From the early days of the country, minority status meant experiencing prejudice. Most Catholic Americans were immigrants from Ireland or Germany, and anti-Catholic feelings were easy to mix up with nativist beliefs. In 1834 in Charlestown, Massachusetts, a convent was burned to the ground, and for the next 20 years, anti-Catholic and anti-immigrant feelings led to violence. There were CHURCH BURNINGS throughout the 1840s and mob violence in New York, Philadelphia, Detroit, St. Louis, and Cincinnati. The KNOW-NOTHING (AMERICAN) PARTY was organized in 1854 with an anti-immigrant, anti-Catholic platform, and the KU KLUX KLAN took up the antipapal banner after the Civil War.

For the American church, the only response was to become more American. Led by its bishops, the church has spent most of American history trying to be accepted by the Protestant majority. This framework for approaching the non-Catholic population has been called "American Catholic Nationalism." The most obvious way that this nationalism was noticed was during wartime. During the Civil War, the archbishop of New York, John Hughes, flew the American flag from his cathedral and encouraged Catholics to fight for the Union side. He even went to Paris to explain to Napoleon III what the North was fighting for. During the Spanish-American War, only one bishop opposed U.S. plans for territorial expansion. Catholic American participation in World War I was enthusiastic, with Baltimore Cardinal James Gibbons taking the lead in promoting enlistment. During that war, more than 1 million Catholics fought for the United States, a number that far exceeded their proportion of the population. Only four CONSCIENTIOUS OBJECTORS (out of 3,989) during that war were Catholic.

During World War II, FRANCIS CARDINAL SPELLMAN of New York, a friend of President FRANKLIN DELANO ROOSEVELT, served as military vicar and made yearly trips to visit U.S. troops. He also carried out diplomatic missions for the president. As a Democrat, Roosevelt needed Catholic votes from large, industrialized cities, so he maintained close ties to Spellman. After the war, Catholicism's strong ANTICOMMUNISM was attractive to foreign policy elites in Washington. With the encouragement of the State Department, Catholic bishops coordinated a letter-writing campaign among Italian Americans to defeat Communists in the 1948 Italian elections. In 1950, the church's help was sought in reaching out to Catholics in the Vietnamese government.

The election of Catholic JOHN F. KENNEDY to the presidency, the work of the church's Second Vatican Council (VATICAN II), and the death of Cardinal Spellman in 1967 effectively ended the era of "American Catholic Nationalism." Through the bishops' own organization, the NATIONAL CONFERENCE OF CATHOLIC BISHOPS, and through the gradual rise in Catholic affluence, the American church began to speak on social and political issues of the day. Although they had made public policy recommendations before, most notably in a 1919 letter "Bishops' Program for Social Reconstruction," whose proposals President Roosevelt partially adopted in his New Deal program, they became active participants in American political debate starting in the early 1970s. When the Supreme Court handed down its ROE V. WADE abortion decision, the bishops even wrote letters to the Catholic faithful providing suggestions on organizing for pro-life activities.

Today, Catholics are fully engaged in public policy debate. U.S. Catholic bishops have described their obligation in the political order as fivefold. First, the church must educate the faithful about its teachings. Second, the church should "analyze issues for their moral and social dimensions." Third, the church must weigh public policy against Christian values. Fourth, the church must participate in debates about public policy. And the fifth obligation flows from the fourth, namely, that the church must speak out forthrightly on public policy issues. Pope John Paul II said that the "Gospel must not be considered a theory, but above all else a basis and motivation for action."

This motivation, the bishops teach, is found in principles that inform Catholic positions on public policy issues. These are an individual dignity that comes from God, protection of human rights, the family as the "basic cell of society," all workers have rights and dignity, poor people's needs must come first, and we are all one human family regardless of race or nationality. When these are applied to specific public policy issues, the results are not surprising. The bishops of the U.S. Catholic Church, for example, oppose ABORTION and EUTHANASIA. They want governments to curb the arms trade and work toward disarmament. They oppose the death penalty and want to end discrimination and RACISM. They teach that economic decisions should be based first on their effect on humans, not profits. Refugees' needs must be met, and immigration policy should allow for family reunification. Violence must be curbed in many ways, including through greater responsibility by the telecommunications industry. These positions have been taken during testimony before Congress, letters written to the Catholic faithful, statements issued to the national media, and parish-level organizing.

The political positions that the Roman Catholic Church takes and the fact that the church even participates in the democratic public policy process at all are, in the end, the result of the church's reflection on its founder and its own history. The church is demonstrating that it wants to be a force to be reckoned with in the modern world, much as it has been in the past.

In 2002, the American Catholic Church faced a highly publicized crisis concerning the molestation of children by priests. High-ranking Catholic officials, most notably BERNARD CARDINAL LAW of Boston, were accused of ignoring and even covering up such molestation. The most common concern was that church leaders had for years moved priests who had sexually abused children to different parishes without explaining the reason for the transfer. High-profile cases of this practice came primarily from the Boston archdiocese (the most attention went to John Geoghan and Paul Shanley, both former Boston priests), but the crisis engulfed other dioceses and archdioceses as well. Further scandal erupted around Milwaukee archbishop Rembert Weakland, who resigned when one of his former students at Marquette University claimed publicly that Weakland had abused him and later bought his silence in a settlement.

Catholic laity grew disillusioned and upset, and the credibility of the church in the United States and abroad was damaged. In reaction to the crisis, church leaders, including Pope JOHN PAUL II, called meetings and attempted to solve what was evidently a longstanding problem. In May 2002, the pope summoned 13 American cardinals to the Vatican, where he encouraged them to find solutions immediately. This meeting was followed in June by a meeting of the UNITED STATES CONFERENCE OF CATHOLIC BISHOPS (USCCB) in Dallas, where attendees voted by a 239-13 margin to allow some past abusers to remain priests. This policy angered survivors of abuse by priests, who called for a zero tolerance policy that would see all abusers permanently defrocked. Nevertheless, the USCCB policy would bar abusers permanently from doing any official church-related work.

See also AID TO RELIGIOUS SCHOOLS; AL SMITH; ASSOCIATION OF CATHOLIC CONSCIENTIOUS OBJECTORS; BERNARDIN, JOSEPH CARDINAL; CATHOLIC ALLIANCE; CATHOLIC CHARITIES; CATHOLIC BISHOPS' 1975 PASTORAL LETTER ON ABORTION; CATHOLIC BISHOPS' 1983 PASTORAL LETTER ON WAR AND PEACE; CATHOLIC BISHOPS' 1986 PASTORAL LETTER ON THE ECONOMY; *CATHOLIC BISHOPS IN AMERICAN POLITICS;* CATHOLICS FOR FREE CHOICE; CATHOLICS AND THE DEMOCRATIC PARTY; CATHOLIC LEGAL SOCIETY; CATHOLIC WORKER MOVEMENT; CONSISTENT ETHIC OF LIFE; DAY, DOROTHY; DRINAN, ROBERT; *HUMANAE VITAE,* IRELAND, JOHN; JOHN XXIII; RYAN, JOHN AUGUSTINE; KNIGHTS OF COLUMBUS; LAW, BERNARD CARDINAL; LIBERATION THEOLOGY; MARYKNOLL ORDER; NATIONAL CATHOLIC WAR/WELFARE CONFERENCE; *NAKED PUBLIC SQUARE;* O'CONNOR, JOHN CARDINAL; PAX CHRISTI; *RERUM NOVARUM;* UNITED STATES CATHOLIC CONFERENCE; VATICAN RECOGNITION.

Further reading: Administrative Board of the United States Catholic Conference. 1995. *Political Responsibility; Proclaiming the Gospel of Life, Protecting the Least among Us, and Pursuing the Common Good.* Washington, D.C.: United States Catholic Conference, 1995; Bunson, Matthew, ed. *2001 Catholic Almanac.* Huntington, Ind.: Our Sunday Visitor, 2000; Ellis, John Tracy. *American Catholicism.* Chicago: University of Chicago Press, 1969; Hanson, Eric O. *The Catholic Church in World Politics.* Princeton, N.J.: Princeton University Press, 1987; Morris, Charles R. *American Catholic: The Saints and Sinners Who Built America's Most Powerful Church.* New York: Random House, 1997; Nolan, Hugh J., ed. "Pastoral Plan for Pro-Life Activities: A Statement Issued by the National Conference of Catholic Bishops. November 20, 1975." In *Pastoral Letters of the United States Catholic Bishops.* Vol. 4, 1975–83. Washington, D.C.: United States Catholic Conference, 1984.

—Paul Fabrizio and Laura R. Olson

Roosevelt, Franklin Delano (1882–1945) *U.S. president*

Franklin Delano Roosevelt (FDR) is perhaps best remembered on two fronts—long-term New Deal presidency, often associated with the growth of large federal government programs, and being the president who led the United States successfully through World War II.

Franklin Roosevelt was born in Hyde Park, New York, of a family that enjoyed high social standing and affluence. The family made its fortune as merchants and sugar refiners in New York City but later amassed fortunes in oil, banking, and other interests. At age 14, Roosevelt enrolled in the Groton School in Massachusetts, where he received rigorous training in social etiquette and was educated in the moral tradition of his EPISCOPAL faith. Although not overtly religious, he served for four years as the warden of St. James Church in Hyde Park. After graduation, he headed to Harvard University, where his academic performance was modest, but he excelled as editor of the *Harvard Crimson* and chair of his class of 1904. Roosevelt next attended Columbia Law School, passing the bar exam but never finishing his LL.B. degree. While at Harvard, he became engaged to Anna Eleanor Roosevelt, a distant cousin and a niece of THEODORE ROOSEVELT. They married in 1905.

It was Republican Theodore Roosevelt who inspired Democrat Franklin Roosevelt to pursue a career in public service. In 1910, FDR ran for the New York State Senate and was easily elected at age 29. Roosevelt embraced the New York Progressive movement, speaking out against political bosses and specifically taking on Tammany Hall politicians in his own party.

Roosevelt's health problems began in 1912. While running for reelection, he contracted typhoid fever. He nonetheless won his reelection and campaigned for anti-Tammany Democrats who supported Woodrow Wilson. This resulted in an appointment as assistant secretary of the navy under Wilson.

Roosevelt earned a reputation as a smart and energetic administrator and attractive Progressive candidate. In 1914, he ran for the U.S. Senate from New York but was easily defeated by the Tammany machine. He soon realized that he would have to reconcile his differences with the Tammany politicians to have a political future in New York. As a rising star in Democratic politics and in Washington, D.C., he was a candidate for vice president in 1920 alongside Governor James Cox of Ohio. When Cox lost by an overwhelming margin to Warren Harding, Roosevelt returned to New York. In 1921 Roosevelt came down with polio, which was to mar his health for the remainder of his life.

Dedicated to pursuing a political career, Roosevelt would not let polio stand in his way. He worked hard at physical therapy to regain strength and the use of his legs and arms. During this time, Roosevelt formed a critical alliance with New York governor AL SMITH. Roosevelt actively supported Smith's reelection bid as governor and managed Smith's presidential campaign in 1924. Smith did not receive the Democratic nomination that year, but he did in 1928. Roosevelt actively supported Smith's candidacy, and at Smith's request, thinking it would help his campaign in New York, Roosevelt ran for governor. Smith lost miserably to Herbert Hoover and even lost New York State. Surprisingly, though, Roosevelt narrowly won election as governor of New York that year.

As governor, Roosevelt quickly established himself as a capable administrator and effective politician. He quickly moved to criticize a number of failures of the Hoover administration, as it proved ineffective in dealing with major economic problems. Roosevelt advocated innovative programs such as unemployment insurance. He easily won reelection and found himself positioned for a run for the 1932 Democratic presidential nomination.

Roosevelt put his campaign theme of "New Deal" programs to work, seeking to turn the tide of the Great Depression that beset the United States and most of the rest of the world. Recognized as a defining moment in forging the modern-day Democratic Party coalition, the 1932 election was seen as a realignment of Roman Catholics, Jews, union workers, white ethnic groups (particularly in the South), African Americans, and the poor. The theme and the coalition worked as Roosevelt defeated Hoover handily in 1932.

Roosevelt moved quickly to establish his administrative appointments and reform measures aimed at jump-starting the economy. He set the tone for what would be his next 12 years in office by calling for a series of emergency economic measures and long-term economic solutions. Roosevelt reached out to citizens through "Fireside Chats" aimed at solidifying public opinion for a number of his reforms.

He moved forward with a series of legislative packages and administrative structures such as the Agricultural Adjustment Administration, the National Recovery Administration, the Public Works Administration, and the Social Security Administration and the creation of entities such as the Tennessee Valley Authority. Roosevelt's programs put millions of people back to work and refinanced farm and home mortgages. The Federal Emergency Relief Administration, created in 1933, ensured quick response and infused billions of dollars into the states. Programs such as the Civilian Conservation Corps were created to cut unemployment among young men.

Roosevelt's bold actions did not come without strong opposition from those concerned about the ever-expanding federal role and the spending of billions of dollars in assistance. Despite the successes of many programs, there were also failures. But undeterred, Roosevelt continued with his New Deal initiatives, sponsoring the Securities and Exchange Act and proposals to restructure federal taxes. He was determined to pursue the agenda supported by his belief in Keynesian economics, where infusion of dollars by government was seen as a proper stimulus for the economy. He attacked opponents as obstructionists, even to the point of proposing increasing the size of the Supreme Court when justices voted against some of his programs. Despite the opposition, he took his unfinished New Deal agenda to the voters in 1936 and was handily reelected.

His creation of the Executive Office of the President in 1939 and support of legislation such as the Fair Labor Standards Act of 1938 continued his domestic efforts to revitalize the economy, improve the efficiency of government, and promote SOCIAL JUSTICE in the workplace and other settings. However, the international scene and World War II would soon overshadow Roosevelt's domestic agenda. The president pursued economic relations with nations including the Soviet Union as a means of improving a depressed economy, but he equally sought to promote a series of "Good Neighbor" policies in the Western Hemisphere. With German and Japanese aggression beginning in Europe and Asia, these policies slowly transformed into mutual defense arrangements. When war broke out in Europe in September 1939, Roosevelt still adhered to a neutrality proclamation while steadily increasing military sales and intelligence-sharing initiatives with other Western nations, especially Great Britain. Reelected to a third term in 1940, Roosevelt now had to apply his skills to the growing international crisis. With the Japanese attack on Pearl Harbor in December 1941, Roosevelt quickly asked Congress to declare war on Japan. Shortly thereafter, Nazi Germany declared war on the United States.

Roosevelt applied his skills in New Deal initiatives to the war effort, creating entities including the War Production Board. As commander in chief, Roosevelt placed military procurement and production in civilian control and strategic issues under the control of the military. His skill as commander equally applied to diplomacy, where he proved to be a skilled compromiser between British prime minister Winston Churchill and Soviet premier Josef Stalin. Roosevelt exerted his influence as a power broker and strategist. As the war was winding down in 1944, he accepted the notion of a United Nations framework for peacekeeping purposes and authorized work on the atomic bomb.

Although his health was deteriorating rapidly, Franklin Roosevelt ran for a fourth term and was easily reelected in 1944. Exhausted from his international travel from the recently completed Yalta Conference; he went on vacation in Warm Springs, Georgia, where he died suddenly on April 12, 1945. Roosevelt can be described succinctly as a politician turned administrator turned warrior. Yet in total, FDR's greatest legacy and enduring contribution to the United States was his uncanny ability to perform well in each of these roles.

—Robert W. Smith

Roosevelt, Theodore (1858–1919) *U.S. president*

Theodore Roosevelt, born in New York City October 27, 1858, and dying January 6, 1919, became the nation's youngest president and its 26th at the age of 43, upon the assassination of President William McKinley in 1901. He was easily elected in 1904 and served until the completion of his term in 1909. He ran on the Bull Moose Progressive ticket in 1912 against his handpicked successor, William H. Taft, causing both himself and Taft to fall to Democrat Woodrow Wilson.

Recent biographies of Roosevelt make scant mention of his religion and religious practices. He was a member of the DUTCH REFORMED CHURCH, which was in keeping with his heritage. Religious practice is not the defining element or lasting impression most observers have of Roosevelt. Yet one might profitably use religious language to describe his style and personal zeal for life and politics. Roosevelt was the leading evangelist for America to the world—and for his own brand of progressive politics to the American populace. He filled the "Bully Pulpit" often, changing the nature and the role of the presidency irrevocably.

Theodore Roosevelt was a believer in the manifest destiny of America, as showcased by his foreign policy endeavors. To demonstrate American power, he sent the Great White Fleet (U.S. navy ships, painted white) around the world. He manufactured a reason to "free" Panama from Colombia, and then he built the Panama Canal. He supported American imperialism wherever it would lead, as shown in his racist justification for the annexation of the Philippines:

> We must treat them with absolute justice, but we must treat them also with firmness and courage. They must be made to realize that justice does not proceed from a sense of weakness on our part, that we are the masters. . . . The insurrection in the Philippines must be stamped out as mercifully as possible, but it must be stamped out. . . . The American flag is to float unchallenged where it floats now.

Domestically, Roosevelt pushed a largely progressive agenda consonant with a SOCIAL JUSTICE perspective, which attacked the corrosive effects of large institutions (interests) on individuals. These large interests, best exemplified in the trusts, wreaked havoc on a populace with no protections from their predations. He therefore enforced existing laws, notably the Sherman Antitrust Act, but also pushed legislation for conservation and the creation of a Department of Commerce and Labor, among other progressive issues. His progressivism deepened as he aged, making his run on the Bull Moose ticket a sincere one.

Nevertheless, Roosevelt was involved with a few religious issues. His agenda and at times his political fortunes brought him into a collision with American Roman Catholics. As president of the New York City Police Board, Roosevelt faced the dilemma that his political future depended on his ability to show results, but the probable results would alienate an important constituency. In particular, New York's BLUE LAWS were not being enforced, generating a lucrative system of bribes for corrupt public officials. Roosevelt decided to enforce the closing laws, despite his own skepticism about the laws themselves and opposition from the working class and many Catholics. At issue, as with many of his campaigns, was the effect of a corrupt system on individual behavior—the law encouraged corruption and undermined faith in the government. The rot had to be driven out by vigorous enforcement,

and Roosevelt did not shy from cracking down on bars selling alcohol on Sundays.

Roosevelt also danced around the concerns of American Catholics as he dealt with the Philippines. If the United States were to annex the country after putting down simmering insurrection of Filipinos against U.S. occupation after the Spanish-American War, how would the extensive lands granted to various orders of the CATHOLIC CHURCH (the so-called Friar's Lands) be handled? Roosevelt agreed to a settlement constructed by Philippines Governor-General William Howard Taft under which the church would be paid $7.2 million for the lands. Moreover, Roosevelt never publicly sided with the nativist wing of the Republican Party of "rum, Romanism, and rebellion" fame; the Catholic voter was much too important to Roosevelt's ambitions (see RELIGION IN THE 1884 PRESIDENTIAL ELECTION). Roosevelt continued the controversial practice (among many Republicans at least) of appointing several Catholics to important positions in his administration.

Further reading: Brands, H.W. *TR: The Last Romantic.* New York: Basic Books, 1997; Genovese, Michael A. *The Power of the American Presidency, 1789–2000.* New York: Oxford University Press, 2001. Morris, Edmund. *Theodore Rex.* New York: Random House, 2001. Prendergast, William B. *The Catholic Voters in American Politics.* Washington, D.C.: Georgetown University Press, 1999.

—Paul A. Djupe

Rosenberger v. University of Virginia Docket No. 94-329 (1995)

The University of Virginia created a Student Activities Fund (SAF) to support student-run organizations. The SAF receives its money from a mandatory fee of $14 for all full-time students, and is designed to support a wide range of extracurricular activities related to the school's educational purpose. University policy authorized student groups, called Contracted Independent Organizations (CIOs), to use SAF funds for many purposes, including paying outside contractors to print their publications. Some CIOs, however, were excluded from SAF funding if the group's activities were primarily religious. This case arose when the university withheld payments to a printer on behalf of Wide Awake Productions because its newspaper, *Wide Awake: A Christian Perspective at the University of Virginia,* was found to promote primarily a particular belief about a deity—a direct violation of SAF policy. The editors of *Wide Awake* filed suit and argued that the refusal to authorize the payment solely because of the paper's religious viewpoint violated the First Amendment right to freedom of speech. The district court granted summary judgment for the university, and the Fourth Circuit Court of Appeals affirmed that decision. In its decision, the Court of Appeals admitted that the university's policy was viewpoint discriminatory but that the discrimination was justified by the necessity of complying with the ESTAB-LISHMENT CLAUSE of the First Amendment.

In a 5-4 decision, the Supreme Court reversed the Court of Appeals. In his majority opinion, Justice Kennedy (writing for Chief Justice Rehnquist, and Justices O'Connor, Scalia, and Thomas), argued that the denial of funds to support *Wide Awake* violated the group's First Amendment right to free speech. Specifically, he relied on *LAMB'S CHAPEL V. CENTER MORICHES UNION FREE SCHOOL DISTRICT*. In so doing, Justice Kennedy argued that, although discrimination against certain speech may be valid if it preserves the limited forum's purposes, it may not be viewpoint discriminatory. Here, the university's actions were of the latter type, not the former. In other words, because the university did not exclude religion as a subject matter but selected it for disfavored treatment, it impermissibly discriminated against *Wide Awake*'s viewpoint.

The university attempted to preempt the Court's use of *Lamb's Chapel* by distinguishing its policy on the ground that it involved the provision of funds rather than access to facilities. The majority found this argument unpersuasive. Citing *WIDMAR V. VINCENT* and *Reagan v. Taxation without Representation of Washington,* it pointed out that the state may regulate the specific content of expression that can be discussed in a limited public forum, but it may not discriminate based on the viewpoint of private persons whose speech it subsidizes. Additionally, the majority found the university's argument, that the scarcity of public money justified the viewpoint discrimination among private speakers, simply wrong.

After finding that the university policy violated *Wide Awake*'s right to free speech, the Court turned its attention to the university's argument that providing it money would violate the establishment clause. Justice Kennedy began by arguing that the SAF funds were distributed in a neutral manner in accordance with *KIRYAS JOEL V. BOARD OF EDUCATION OF GRUMENT;* that is, it found no suggestion that the university created its program to advance religion. More specifically, it found that SAF's purpose was to support various student enterprises, including the publication of newspapers, in recognition of the diversity and creativity of student life. A closer look at the SAF guidelines allowed third-party payments regardless of a group's viewpoint. Thus, *Wide Awake* did not seek subsidies because of its Christian viewpoint but simply to fund its group's communication, like any other CIO.

Finally, the majority argued that SAF did not give money directly to WAP. Rather, in accordance with *ROEMER V. MARYLAND,* and *EVERSON V. BOARD OF EDUCATION,* no public funds flowed directly into *Wide Awake*'s coffers. Thus, the university was not advancing religion by providing *Wide Awake* funds for its newspaper. Overall, then, the Court found that public universities do not violate the establishment clause when they grant access to their facilities on a religion-neutral basis, to a wide spectrum of student groups, even if some of those groups would use the facilities or funds for religious purposes. The Rosenberger decision, therefore, fits within a growing line of narrow establishment clause rulings underpinned by a nondis-crimination or accommodationist view—religious organizations can be supported with public funds if done in a neutral manner—which differs considerably from a preferred freedoms or separationist view, in which the test is stringent for religious organizations to receive funding. This accommodationist view opens considerably the spigot of public funds to religious organizations.

See also CHARITABLE CHOICE; WHITE HOUSE OFFICE OF FAITH-BASED AND COMMUNITY INITIATIVES.

—Timothy R. Johnson

Rustin, Bayard (1912–1987) *activist*

A major strategist for human rights and economic justice, Bayard Rustin was born in West Chester, Pennsylvania, and was educated in the public schools of that city. He attended Wilberforce University, Cheyney State College, and the City College of New York (CCNY). During his leave from Cheyney and his matriculation at CCNY, he was invited to attend the AMERICAN FRIENDS SERVICE COMMITTEE's Peace and Goodwill training. This two-week training program taught Rustin about the need for peace in the world, as well as the tactics for CIVIL DISOBEDIENCE. From this training ground, he joined the Young Communist League in New York as a youth organizer. Like many African-American activists of this time, Rustin understood that the philosophy of democracy was systemically flawed in favor of white male economic elites. Such elites began to question the probability of this government system becoming fair and equitable. As a result of their analysis many of them subscribed to the tenets of communism and became members of the Communist Party. Though the communist movement in America has never been a usual partner for African-Americans advancement, it did play a critical role in advancing and supporting many of their causes, particularly high-profile issues.

Nevertheless, his association with the Young Communist League proved to be a success for Rustin on many levels. First, he challenged the racial segregation of CCNY and the pro-American ideology of many campus organizations, which ultimately led to the takeover of the school's newspaper, student senate, and student union by the league, led by Rustin. During his later disillusionment with the Communist Party over World War II, he joined A. Phillip Randolph's embryonic MARCH ON WASHINGTON movement as director of youth initiatives. The goal of this organization, though never achieved formally, was to challenge escalating discriminatory practices in employment. After Rustin realized that Randolph had capitulated to President FRANKLIN DELANO ROOSEVELT's demand that the demonstration be called off, he began working as a field secretary for youth and general affairs for the Fellowship of Reconciliation (FOR). This position allowed Rustin to travel across the country as an advocate for opening lines of communication regarding race. He understood clearly that if people were willing to have open and earnest dialogue, then they would see that what really separates them is not hatred for the most part, but fear.

Thus, in 1940, he (along with civil rights activist and educator James Farmer) took the ideas of FOR from passive discussion to active engagement by organizing the CONGRESS OF RACIAL EQUALITY (CORE), which had as its fundamental mission the liberation of black people from racial bondage. Rustin adopted the nonviolent philosophy of Mohandas Gandhi, and (long before the CIVIL RIGHTS MOVEMENT) a group of students from the University of Chicago started the first nonviolent sit-in in a Chicago restaurant. Likewise, he led delegations of students on many nonviolent freedom rides, marches, rallies, and demonstrations. In 1942, he assisted in organizing protest rallies against the federal government for arresting and interning over 3,000 Japanese-Americans from California in concentration camps.

In 1946, after serving a three-year sentence for refusing to join the war effort, he launched a major effort, the "Journey of Reconciliation," to enforce the Supreme Court's ruling in *Morgan v. Virginia* that interstate buses were to be integrated. This movement was met with great resistance in the South; however, it was considered by many to be the forerunner of 1960s freedom rides. In explaining why he organized the rides, he said, "The Journey of Reconciliation was organized not only to devise techniques for elimination of Jim Crow in travel, but also as a training ground for similar peaceful projects against discrimination in such major areas as employment and in the armed services." Because of the attention that Rustin's movement attracted from many southern civil rights activists, mainly the Rev. MARTIN LUTHER KING JR., president of the Montgomery Improvement Association, Rustin was asked in February 1956 to assist in organizing the Montgomery bus boycott. King understood that for an initiative of this magnitude to be sustained, they would need someone who was either a strong organizer or a gifted motivator. Rustin was both. In addition, Rustin recognized that King needed an organization that would link him directly to the struggle of blacks and catapult him into the national media. Thus, Rustin, along with Ella Baker and Stanley Levison, drew up the original plan for what became the SOUTHERN CHRISTIAN LEADERSHIP CONFERENCE (SCLC) with King as its founding president.

During this association with SCLC, Rustin, who by many accounts taught the philosophy of Gandhi and nonviolence to the movement, organized several high-profile, nonconfrontational activities (such as the Prayer Pilgrimage for Freedom and the Youth March for Integrated Schools I and II) that dramatized the injustices in the South to Americans. Feeling threatened by the new brand of leadership, many seasoned black activists, primarily in the North, sought to fragment the movement by threatening to expose Rustin as a homosexual and accuse him of having a sexual affair with King. Though the latter, according to D'Emilio (1995) and others, was totally untrue, Rustin resigned from SCLC and was subsequently absent for nearly three years from the 1960s Civil Rights movement. Rustin then seized on this opportunity to expand his audience by advocating for justice elsewhere in the world.

In June 1963, African-American leaders began planning a March on Washington to urge the federal government to reexamine national economic issues, particularly the need for jobs, a higher minimum wage, and fair-hiring practices for African Americans. According to John Lewis, then chair of the STUDENT NONVIOLENT COORDINATING COMMITTEE (SNCC) and organizer of the March on Washington, "There was no one better prepared to lead and give direction, and mobilize—Rustin was that person." Rustin was selected as the deputy director of the march. Historians have failed to note that it was Rustin who suggested to the sponsors, chiefly A. Phillip Randolph, that the march needed to include a call for civil rights. Thus, the March on Washington was renamed the March on Washington for Jobs and Freedom. Rustin had fewer than two months to organize what was expected to be the largest peaceful demonstration in U.S. history. Not succumbing to the pressure, Rustin within days had drafted a mission statement; raised over $15,000 to bring the poor to Washington; designed a plan for security; contracted with bus companies to transport thousands of marchers; arranged for 1,000 beds to be available for those arriving the night before; and enlisted hundreds of volunteers to prepare bag lunches for those who had not brought their own. The words of future representative John Lewis (D-Ga.) underscored the significance of Rustin's work with the march: "Without Bayard Rustin as leader the March on Washington would have been like a bird without wings."

After the march, Rustin continued to advocate for the rights of African Americans, as well as other disadvantaged groups, particularly black South Africans struggling against apartheid, and gays and lesbians desiring equal protection under the law. But because of the stigma of his homosexuality, Rustin's work in the Civil Rights movement has never been acknowledged or given the honor he deserved. At the time of his death, Rustin was cochair of the A. Phillip Randolph Institute, president of its educational fund, and chair of the Social Democrats U.S.A., as well as the recipient of 12 honorary doctoral degrees.

See also GAY RIGHTS.

Further reading: Anderson, Jervis. *Bayard Rustin: Trouble I've Seen.* New York: HarperCollins, 1997; D'Emilio, John. "Homophobia and the Trajectory of Postwar American Radicalism: The Case of Bayard Rustin." *Radical History Review* 62 (1995): 80–103.

—Said Sewell

Rutherford Institute

Founded in 1982 by attorney John Wayne Whitehead, this nonprofit litigation firm draws its name from a 17th-century Scottish philosopher. The Rutherford Institute litigates primarily in First Amendment, religious freedom, and ABORTION protest cases. While formally nonpartisan and religiously non-affiliated, the institute generally takes cases pitting religious conservatives against government policies it considers intrusive. However, the organization has become involved in issues of a nonreligious nature, and has opposed the Bush administration in several high-profile matters. In recent years, it has sponsored cases contesting public school "zero-tolerance" policies against violence, opposed administration antiterrorism initiatives that may infringe on personal liberties, and included religious liberties cases originating in the European Union on its broad agenda. The institute is perhaps best known as the firm that represented Paula Jones, recruiting an attorney to represent her in her sexual harassment suit against President WILLIAM JEFFERSON CLINTON.

The Rutherford Institute describes itself as an "international and educational organization dedicated to preserving human rights and defending civil liberties." Based in Charlottesville, Virginia, the institute employs 50 lawyers and staff. It has a stable base of supporters and collects the majority of its $4.5 million yearly budget from direct-mail solicitation. It has also developed a network of over 1,000 volunteer attorneys, who function as local counsel and coordinate litigation with the institute's lawyers.

The institute identifies eight areas in which it hopes to influence policy. These include conflicts over freedom of expression (such as religious expression and religious employment discrimination), abortion and other protestation, gender discrimination and sexual harassment, student's rights, religion in public places, parental rights, sanctity of life issues, and international human rights. Although its litigation agenda includes primarily religious cases, the institute has defended a variety of clients, including public school students who alleged racial discrimination by administrators and a website owner who may sue President GEORGE W. BUSH for defamation of character. It has also sued the Maryland Department of Transportation over a policy prohibiting the display of the Confederate flag on vehicle license plates.

Recent notable cases in which the institute participated include contesting a school district's distribution of a survey asking questions about students' drug use and sexual attitudes. It has defended OPERATION RESCUE, a group organizing abortion protests, in a Racketeering Influenced and Corrupt Organizations (RICO) law suit, and sued pharmacy chains that disciplined employees who refused to sell the abortion drug RU-486.

Because of the institute's wide-ranging agenda, it often works with groups that are not always allies. It recently joined a broad coalition of religious groups including Jews and Protestants that lobbied for a "compelling public interest" statute protecting religious freedoms in Illinois. In late September 2001, the Rutherford Institute joined the AMERICAN CIVIL LIBERTIES UNION (ACLU) and PEOPLE FOR THE AMERICAN WAY in protesting the Bush administration's antiterrorism legislation. In the mid-1990s, it joined with the ACLU in supporting a religious group's EQUAL ACCESS claim to use of a public facility.

The participation of the institute in Paula Jones's case had tremendous influence over the investigation of Bill Clinton by Independent Counsel Kenneth Starr. An anonymous call to the Rutherford Institute caused attorneys for Jones to depose the president about his relationship with Monica Lewinsky, thereby setting off a broader investigation into the truthfulness of the president's testimony. Furthermore, the institute provided counsel who argued Jones's Supreme Court case. In that case, Jones's attorneys requested that the Court support the lower court decision not to grant Clinton temporary immunity from civil suits involving alleged acts before his term as president in *Clinton v. Jones*. They were ultimately successful in their effort. But, Jones's relationship with the Rutherford Institute and outside counsel soured after she refused their advice to settle her case with Clinton. The institute has taken two other women's rights cases since the Paula Jones lawsuit, and it sees sexual discrimination as a possible area of growth for the organization.

Rutherford Institute president and general counsel John Whitehead is an influential figure within the Conservative Christian Bar (see CONSERVATIVE CHRISTIAN LITIGATORS). He is a University of Arkansas–educated attorney who founded the institute because of his concern about government intrusion on the religious rights of Christians. However, the institute will (and has) sponsored or supported the cases of those who practice other religions. Its involvement on various fronts has won Whitehead the attention of the media. He has made appearances on many popular news programs including *Crossfire* and *Nightline*. For his involvement in religious liberties cases in Hungary, he was presented the Hungarian Medal of Freedom.

See also AMERICAN CENTER FOR LAW AND JUSTICE; CHRISTIAN LEGAL SOCIETY; ESTABLISHMENT CLAUSE; FREE EXERCISE CLAUSE; HERITAGE FOUNDATION; IMPEACHMENT OF WILLIAM JEFFERSON CLINTON.

Further reading: Posner, Richard A. *An Affair of State: The Investigation, Impeachment, and Trial of President Clinton.* Cambridge, Mass.: Harvard University Press, 2000; Rozell, Mark J. and Clyde Wilcox, eds. *The Clinton Scandal and the Future of American Government.* Washington, D.C.: Georgetown University Press, 2000.

—Hans J. Hacker

Ryan, John Augustine (1869–1945) *Roman Catholic priest, scholar, activist*

John Augustine Ryan was born in the rural town of Vermilion, Minnesota, and died in St. Paul. Inspired by Pope Leo XIII's encyclical on labor, RERUM NOVARUM (1891) and the Populist ferment he encountered as a youth, Ryan focused on the application of Christian ethical principles to social and economic questions. A priest, moral theologian, and economic theorist, Ryan became the ROMAN CATHOLIC CHURCH in America's leading champion of progressive social action. His original scholarship left a lasting influence on the shape of Catholic social thought in America.

In 1887, Ryan left the family farm to enter St. Thomas Seminary (later St. Paul Seminary) and was ordained a priest of the Catholic Church on June 4, 1898. He then proceeded to the Catholic University of America in Washington, D.C., to pursue graduate studies. He received a licentiate in moral theology in 1900. Ryan returned to St. Paul Seminary in the fall of 1902 as a professor of moral theology and remained there for 13 years. During this time, he completed his dissertation and in 1906 was awarded a doctorate in sacred theology from Catholic University. Ryan's dissertation became his first book, *A Living Wage: Its Ethical and Economic Aspects* (1906). This work quickly established him as the leading American Catholic social theorist. He began publishing more frequently and widely, and in a 1909 *Catholic World* article, "A Programme of Social Reform by Legislation," he defended such wide-ranging progressive initiatives as the living wage, an eight-hour workday law, and social insurance.

In 1915, Ryan joined the faculty of Catholic University, first as a professor of political science and then theology. The most significant scholarly achievement of his career came with the publication in 1916 of *Distributive Justice*, a comprehensive analysis of economic ethics. Yet no comparable work would follow, as Ryan now embarked on a career more devoted to advocacy and popularization of his social reform ideas than serious scholarship. In 1917, he founded the *Catholic Charities Review,* which served as a major platform for his ideas. In 1919, he wrote the *Bishops' Program of Social Reconstruction,* which advocated minimum-wage legislation, unemployment insurance, public housing, progressive taxation, and greater rights for organized labor. Publication of this document by the NATIONAL CATHOLIC WAR COUNCIL (NCWC, later Welfare Conference) demonstrated the influence of Ryan's ideas in the church. The following year, Ryan became director of the Social Action Department of NCWC, a position he held until his death. Ryan lectured and wrote widely throughout the 1920s on issues such as PROHIBITION, a proposed child labor amendment, and minimum-wage initiatives occupying much of his attention. He also wrote extensively on political theory and the relationship of Catholicism and LIBERALISM. His views were compiled in *The Church and the State* (1922), which generated much attention during the 1928 presidential campaign.

With the onset of the Great Depression after 1929 and the election of FRANKLIN DELANO ROOSEVELT in 1932, Ryan became a vigorous advocate of the New Deal. The appearance of Pope Pius XI's encyclical *Quadragesimo Anno* (1931) bolstered Ryan's support for thoroughgoing social reorganization. Ryan was particularly enthusiastic about the National Recovery Act, which he at times came close to equating with Catholic social theory. Ryan strongly supported Roosevelt during all four presidential elections. His staunch support for Roosevelt angered conservative Catholics and earned him the moniker "Rt. Reverend New Dealer." Ryan was unmoved, and in 1936 he delivered a famous national radio address, "Roosevelt Safeguards America," in which he praised the president and countered the criticisms of CHARLES COUGHLIN.

Ryan's career was devoted to blending Catholic social thought with American progressive liberalism. His writings on social and economic affairs established the framework for a progressive Catholicism and, in a less direct way, helped reconcile Catholics and American political institutions. Ryan's dependence on legislation and the state and his general disinterest in spiritual reform placed him in opposition to emerging reform movements such as the Dom Virgil Michel's liturgical revival and the CATHOLIC WORKER MOVEMENT. But Ryan's methodology proved to be the dominant one in American Catholicism, and it fundamentally shaped Catholic thought about the relationship of church and economics.

Further reading: Broderick, Francis L. *Right Reverend New Dealer: John A. Ryan.* New York: Macmillan, 1963; McShane, Joseph M., S.J. *"Sufficiently Radical:" Catholicism, Progressivism, and the Bishops' Program of 1919.* Washington, D.C.: Catholic University of America Press, 1986; Ryan, John A. *Social Doctrine in Action: A Personal History.* New York: Harper, 1941.

—Zachary R. Calo

S

sacred space

Sacred spaces are religious centers at which the heavenly and earthly meet, a means of access between the human and the divine worlds. Three functions are characteristic of sacred spaces: they are places of communication with divinity through prayer, movement, or visual contact with an image of the divine; they are places of divine presence, often promising healing, success, or salvation; and they provide meaning to the faithful by metaphorically reflecting the underlying order of the world. Sacred places are imbued with forms, actions, and objects that convey religious meaning.

The great religious traditions display an infinite variety of sacred spaces, varying in shape, location, importance, and purpose. Their prevalence has suggested to some students of religion that sacred space is an essential, perhaps the most essential, component in all great religious traditions. Sociologist Émile Durkheim argued that the clear distinction between the sacred and the profane is the basis of all religious practice. Mircea Eliade, the foremost student of sacred space, has recognized that sacred places are historical, spiritual, and cosmological centers, axes connecting heaven and earth, around which the entire cosmic world revolves. Pilgrims who journey to sacred places travel toward the center, seeking in the sacred space a microcosm of the universe and of the specific religion it represents.

The phenomenon of sacred space concretizes religion, giving it an earthbound, material facet. Sacred space may encompass an entire land, a sanctified structure, such as a temple or shrine, or a natural site interpreted as sacred, such as a mountain, river, forest, or lake. The sanctity of some sites is communicated by the gods through a special sign, others because a religiously significant event took place there, or because of the presence of relics.

Where conflict over sacred space erupts, it is often linked to ethnic or sectarian disputes, and has the potential of aggravating existing regional and international issues. Disputes over sacred space erupt either as a result of competition between religious actors or as a result of clashes between secular and religious forces.

When religious traditions split into rival branches, they create competition over a common sacred space. This was the case in Independence, Missouri, for example, where two churches that seceded from the Church of Jesus Christ of Latter-day Saints vied over the site of the future Temple of Christ, to be established on Christ's Second Coming. By staking claim to a sacred site that once united the religious movement, each rival asserts its claim as inheritor of the true faith.

Concretizing of the sacred through attachment to mundane space creates clashes with secular forces who want to use the land for development, exploration, or tourism. This is the most common type of dispute over sacred space in the Americas and Australasia, for example, where Native Americans and Aborigines protest the desecration of their burial, hunting, and ceremonial grounds.

Finally, political actors seek control over sacred space to symbolize their control over the community, or by virtue of the social, economic, and political centrality of that space in the daily life of the community. Rulers have barred access, desecrated or destroyed sites, or funded the construction or restoration of sacred sites as a means for penalizing or rewarding their subjects. Control over shrines is the most crucial when these shrines attract mass pilgrimages. Pilgrimage offers the host regime opportunities for sanctioning rival regimes or demonstrating exceptional generosity and hospitality. To opponents of the host regime, these mass events offer a forum for organized protests and subversive activities, examples of which have erupted in recent years in Saudi Arabia, Iraq, Northern Ireland, and Israel.

The attributes of sacred space complicate the resolution of such conflicts. The clearly defined boundaries of sacred space hamper compromise over the size and location of the disputed space. The more central the space in the religious landscape of the community, the greater the divine power vested in the place, the greater the obligation of the community to defend the sanctity of the space, and the greater the risk that foreign presence or conduct will be interpreted as an offensive act.

Forced arrangements of shared control over sacred space tend to be highly unstable, routinely violent, and exceedingly

A Salvation Army member with guitar on the streets of San Francisco *(Library of Congress)*

short-lived. Rarely, change in the status of a sacred place is possible without the cooperation of religious actors, as witnessed by the great iconoclastic revolutions in the Christian West. Unilateral changes of this sort are possible when political actors are willing to incur the wrath of religious actors or are impervious to the influence of such actors. Political leaders may also be capable of coercing or convincing religious actors to issue rulings that favor changes in the status of sacred space. At the very least, religious actors can supply crucial information about the meaning, importance, and boundaries of a disputed site—information that could help ameliorate conflict over sacred space.

See also *LYNG V. NORTHWEST INDIAN CEMETARY PROTECTIVE ASSOCIATION;* NATIVE AMERICAN SACRED GROUNDS.

Further reading: Chidester, David, and Edward T. Linenthal, eds. *American Sacred Space.* Bloomington: Indiana University Press, 1995; Durkheim, Émile. *The Elementary Forms of the*
Religious Life. Translated by Joseph Ward Swain. London: Allen and Unwin, 1976; Eliade, Mircea, ed. *The Encyclopedia of Religion.* Vol. 12. *Sacred Space.* New York: Macmillan, 1987; Smith, Jonathan Z., *Imagining Religion: From Babylon to Jonestown.* Chicago: University of Chicago Press, 1982.

—Ron E. Hassner

Salvation Army, The

Founded in 1865 by William Booth in London, the Salvation Army is a "Protestant Evangelical church" whose mission is both spreading the Christian faith and assisting people with social needs. Initially, Booth wanted to convert the poor of London without establishing another church; however, because many churches, specifically the Wesleyan church, failed to welcome the new converts, Booth founded the Christian Mission, which was later named, in 1878, Salvation Army.

On October 5, 1879, the Salvation Army conducted its first meeting in the United States under the direction of Eliza Shirley and her parents. Shirley was converted in 1878 while in London, and quickly emerged as a leader. Responding to her father's request to join him in Philadelphia, Shirley asked to be transferred. In America, Eliza Shirley conducted successful open-air campaigns, but she was forced by the police to find a hall. Initially, meetings in the new lot proved to be a failure, but they quickly became successful. Eventually, another lot had to be obtained.

After the successful establishment of the Salvation Army in America, Shirley wrote to Booth requesting that he take command of the work. Booth responded to Shirley's request by sending George Scott Railton. In 1880, the Salvation Army officially arrived in America with Railton and a group of seven women known as the "Hallelujah Seven."

With Booth's publication of *In Darkest England and the Way Out* (1890), the Salvation Army officially shifted its emphasis from religious services to social benevolence as a means of converting people. In America, social service reached a high point when W. Kenneth Wheatley was appointed in 1971 as the national consultant for agency relationships and special services; Wheatley was also responsible for the Salvation Army's being recognized as an "official disaster agency."

In 2000, the Salvation Army served 36 million Americans. With an operating income of $1.8 billion, the plurality (29 percent) coming from contributions, the Salvation Army has developed a variety of social service programs. The adult rehabilitation center is the largest resident substance abuse program in America, treating men and women who suffer from alcohol and chemical dependency. Other services include youth programs and corrections programs, in which ex-convicts reside in halfway houses while participating in a work-release program. Its holiday assistance is the most visible service of the Salvation Army. Donations raised through the red kettle campaign are used to provide Christmas dinners, clothing, and toys to disadvantaged families; assistance to these recipients is continued for months after the Christmas season.

The success and importance of the Salvation Army is evident from the fact that President GEORGE W. BUSH asked John Busby, national commander of the Salvation Army, along with 34 other faith-based and civic leaders, to support the Community Solutions Act of 2001 (H.R. 7), as a means to integrate religious groups and federal funding of social services and community programs. Likewise, the Salvation Army has played a significant role in providing relief efforts to the SEPTEMBER 11, 2001, victims who were directly affected by the terrorist attacks on the World Trade Center in New York.

Organizationally, the Salvation Army follows a military model for the sake of efficiency. The general, based in London, is the international leader and has a term limitation of five years, or until his sixty-eighth birthday. At the general's retirement, senior officers elect a new general. The organization is subdivided into 50 territories, each headed by a territorial commander, and having its own headquarters. For instance, the U.S. National Headquarters is located in Alexandria, Virginia. Territories are composed of Divisions, which, in turn, are encompassed by various Corps—local centers. Leaders of the Salvation Army receive minimal compensation, which may increase according to family size.

Although failing to see an increased membership in its religious services, the Salvation Army is poised to remain a significant and influential provider of all types of social services worldwide to the disadvantaged. These services may be limited if general contributions decline.

See also HUNGER AND HUMANITARIAN AID; WHITE HOUSE OFFICE OF FAITH-BASED AND COMMUNITY INITIATIVES.

Further reading: Clifton, Shaw. *Who Are These Salvationists?* Alexandria, Va.: Salvation Army National Publications, 1999; Hattersley, Roy. *Blood and Fire.* New York: Doubleday, 1999; McKinley, Edward H. *Marching to Glory: The History of the Salvation Army in the United States, 1880–1992.* Grand Rapids, Mich.: Eerdmans, 1995; Taiz, Lillian. *Hallelujah Lads & Lasses: Remaking the Salvation Army in America, 1880–1930.* Chapel Hill: University of North Carolina Press, 2001.

—Santiago O. Piñon Jr.

Sanctuary movement

The Sanctuary movement was a loosely organized network of churches and communities that provided assistance and support to Central American refugees in the 1980s. Southside Presbyterian Church in Tucson, Arizona, and the East Bay Sanctuary Covenant in San Francisco made the first public declarations of sanctuary on March 24, 1982, the second anniversary of the murder of Salvadoran archbishop Oscar Romero by a professional assassin sent by leaders of El Salvador's far right. Sanctuary had no official organizing body. But the Chicago Religious Task Force on Central America provided coordination. Religious communities as far north as Milwaukee, Rochester, New York, and Weston, Vermont, declared public sanctuary.

The communities that offered sanctuary believed themselves to be acting in continuity with the Judeo-Christian tradition. Yet, the offer of sanctuary often publicly defied U.S. immigration law. The confrontation between sanctuary activists and the U.S. government came to public attention in 1985 with the federal indictment of 16 sanctuary activists charged with 71 counts of conspiracy, harboring, concealment, and transporting illegal aliens. The case of *United States of America v. Maria del Socorro Pardo de Aguilar et al.*, heard in the U.S. District Court for the District of Arizona, was widely publicized and controversial. The government's case was based on evidence gathered by an informant who secretly infiltrated the movement. The judge restricted testimony regarding the defendants' motivations, religious freedom, as well as the conditions in Central America. Eight of the 11 brought to trial were found guilty of charges ranging from misdemeanors to conspiracy; three were later acquitted. Most received probation or suspended sentences.

Sanctuary activists sought to provide humanitarian aid to individual refugees and to speak in protest against both U.S. immigration policy and foreign policy in Central America. In the 1970s and 1980s, violence in Central America, primarily in El Salvador and Guatemala, caused an estimated 500,000 to 750,000 people to flee north to the United States. The refugees reported instances of unlawful arrest, summary executions, and torture in their homelands. The refugees and sanctuary activists believed that U.S. support for these governments made Americans partly responsible for the violence. U.S. officials attributed the violence to guerrilla movements and argued that the refugees' motivations were economic, not political. Lacking direct evidence of persecution, refugees were not entitled to asylum in the United States and were then subject to deportation.

The precedents claimed by Sanctuary activists were religious, historical, and civic. Mandates from Hebrew Scripture included parallels in the Israelites' Exodus from Egypt and the legal command of hospitality toward aliens. New Testament justification for sanctuary included Jesus' Great Commandment, the Beatitudes, and the parable of the Good Samaritan. Historical precedent included the medieval practice of church sanctuary for fugitives. In some countries, the sanctuary of churches was granted in civil legal codes; it remained in the Roman Catholic Code of Canon Law until its 1983 revision. In addition, sanctuary activists recalled U.S. immigration history and emphasized parallels with the 19th-century Underground Railroad for fugitive slaves. However, sanctuary activists just as often indicated that they were modeling the hospitality of churches in Central America and Mexico.

The Sanctuary movement shows the complicated relationship between faith and political activity in the United States. For the most part, Sanctuary activists were people of faith who believed they were acting on their faith in support of people in need who came into their midst. The result led them to challenge U.S. immigration and foreign policies. Thus their activities were both religious and political. The tensions between the religious and the political nature of sanctuary activities found expression within the movement and in the government's efforts to oppose it. The numbers of Central Americans who received assistance through their efforts was small. However, the effect of their activity in raising public consciousness about the plight of Central Americans in their homeland and as refugees was significant.

See also CATHOLIC WORKER MOVEMENT.

Further reading: Bau, Ignatius. *This Ground Is Holy: Church Sanctuary and Central American Refugees.* New York: Paulist Press, 1985; Crittenden, Ann. *Sanctuary: A Story of American Conscience and Law in Collision.* New York: Weidenfeld and Nicholson, 1988.

—Susan Gleason Anderson

Santa Fe Independent School District v. Doe
Docket No. 99-62 (2000)

Until 1995, a student council chaplain at Santa Fe High School recited a prayer over the public address system before varsity football home games. Several Mormon and Catholic students took offense at this practice and filed a suit that challenged it as a violation of the ESTABLISHMENT CLAUSE of the First Amendment. While the suit was pending, the school district implemented a new policy meant to account for any possible First Amendment violations. It authorized two student elections. The first was held each year, and was used to determine whether prayers should be delivered at games. If a majority of students voted yes, then a second election was held to choose a single student to deliver prayers for every game that season. The district court ruled that the school could hold prayers if it followed this policy, as long as they were nonsectarian and nonproselytizing. The Fifth Circuit Court of Appeals reversed the district court, holding that, even as modified, the football prayer policy was invalid.

Writing for a 6-3 majority, Supreme Court Justice Stevens wrote an opinion that affirmed the Fifth Circuit's decision and unequivocally ruled that the policy violated the establishment clause. He made several main arguments. First, following the *Lemon* test, he argued that prayers constituted an impermissible government endorsement of religion, and rejected the school district's argument that this principle is inapplicable because the prayers in this case were private student speech, not public speech. According to the Court, the prayers were public—they were delivered on school property, at a school-sponsored event, over the school's public address system, by a speaker representing the student body, under the supervision of school faculty, and pursuant to a school policy that encouraged public prayer.

Second, Stevens relied heavily on *LEE V. WEISMAN.* In *Lee,* the Court concluded that a prayer delivered by a rabbi at a public graduation ceremony coerced those in attendance to participate in a religious practice. The majority found that allowing such a practice establishes state support for a religion in violation of the establishment clause. The Santa Fe School District argued that, unlike in *Lee,* the pregame football prayers did not coerce students to participate in religious observances because attending a game is completely voluntary. Stevens rejected this argument. He countered by pointing out that there are some students who must be in attendance at the football game—including cheerleaders, band members, and the team. Thus, some students may be coerced to participate in the prayers.

Third, the majority argued that the majority rule provision—which allowed the students to decide whether prayers should be used before football games—simply demonstrates that the students' views are not unanimous and that the school is choosing one particular view over another. In sum, the majority argued that the Constitution demands that schools not force on students the difficult choice between whether to attend these games or to risk facing a personally offensive religious ritual.

Finally, the justices in the majority argued that the prayer policy was a direct violation of the *Lemon* test's requirement that all government policies have a secular purpose. Despite the school district's argument, they concluded that the primary purpose of allowing the student-led prayers was religious. Thus, the policy failed a second prong of the *Lemon* test, and therefore violated the establishment clause.

Chief Justice Rehnquist and Justices ANTONIN SCALIA and Thomas dissented. They argued that the majority reached the wrong outcome and did so in a way that was openly hostile to religion in the public sphere. More specifically, the dissenters pointed out that the United States has a tradition of voluntary religious expression at public events, such as the football games at issue in this case. Thus, the prayers should be allowed to continue if the student population votes to do so.

See also *GOOD NEWS CLUB V. MILFORD CENTRAL HIGH SCHOOL.*

—Timothy R. Johnson

Satanism

What is currently termed "Satanism" empirically has three distinct, independent referents. The first consists of conservative Christian constructions of Satan used theologically to define the shape of evil, which is not of interest here. The second consists of countercultural satanic churches, which achieved popularity in the 1970s. The largest and most visible of these are Anton La Vey's Church of Satan and Michael Aquino's Temple of Set. Other satanic churches have been small and short-lived organizations, and most are schismatic offshoots of the Church of Satan. The third is an outbreak of satanic cult fears that swept the United States and Europe during the 1980s. Satanic cults were believed to be organized into an underground network involved in a variety of nefarious activities, but no convincing evidence of this network has ever been uncovered.

The Church of Satan was founded by Anton Szandor La Vey (1930–97), who may best be characterized as an entrepreneurial deviant. He ran away from home at age 16 then worked successively in jobs such as a circus lion tamer, stage hypnotist, nightclub organist, and police department photographer. During the 1960s, La Vey became something of a celebrity. On April 30, 1966, La Vey shaved his head, donned a black robe, and pronounced himself the Black Pope. For La Vey, Satan was conceived not as an anthropomorphic being but as a force of nature, a reservoir of power within each being that permits humans to be their own gods. In the *Satanic Bible* (1969), La Vey advocated indulgence and gratification over abstinence; vital existence, not spiritual pipe dreams; undefiled wisdom, as opposed to hypocritical self-deceit; deserved rather than wasted love; and responsibility only to the responsible. Sex, magic, healing, and destruction are the major rituals. The church prospered during the 1970s when its "grottoes" could be found in major cities across the country, but suffered continuous membership losses with the decline of the 1960s counterculture.

The Temple of Set was founded in 1975 by Michael Aquino, at the time an army lieutenant. Aquino initially joined the Church of Satan but subsequently became disillusioned with La Vey. Set, the Egyptian god of night, is a metaphysical being formerly known under the Hebrew misnomer "Satan," that occasionally violates the laws of the universe. Over a period of millennia, Set has altered the genetic makeup of humans to create a species possessing an enhanced, nonnatural intelligence. The objective of the Temple is to realize that potential through individual empowerment. Setians organize into local chapters called pylons. The total membership of the pylons has never been more than a few hundred.

The other major form of Satanism that swept North America and Europe in the 1980s centered around claims of the existence of a massive network of Satanists involved in a range of nefarious activities. The most horrific allegations involved the abduction of children, child abuse, commercial production of child pornography, sexual abuse and incest, and ritualistic sacrifices of young children. Allegedly at the core of satanic cult belief and practice is the quest for personal power. A central tenet of Satanism is that individuals can enhance their personal power by absorbing the life energy of other individuals. Ritual sacrifice, particularly of children, thus becomes a means of self-empowerment. At the height of the subversion episode, ritual abuse victims were estimated at 50,000 annually.

There are alleged to be five levels of satanic organization: dabblers, self-styled Satanists, organized Satanists, members of public satanic churches, and traditional Satanists. As in the case of other subversion episodes, the five components of satanic subversion are pieced together from apparently unrelated sources. Dabblers are adolescents lured into Satanism through experimentation with satanic material, such as fantasy games and heavy metal rock music. Organized Satanists include a variety of criminals who rationalize their antisocial acts as satanically inspired. Public satanic churches include the Church of Satan and Temple of Set, as well as a myriad of smaller groups. Traditional Satanists are the members of the putative international, underground, hierarchically organized satanic cult network that orchestrates all five levels of satanic activity.

The public evidence of satanic activity was used to buttress claims of satanic ritual abuse and sacrifice by traditional Satanists. This core group purportedly was so tightly organized and effective in its use of terrorism and brainwashing that no direct evidence of its activities could be provided. There was a succession of high-profile ritual sexual abuse cases, most notably the case of the McMartin preschool in Manhattan Beach, California. In virtually all cases of this kind, the only significant evidence of satanic activity involved the testimony of very young children. Convictions were obtained in a number of cases, which supported claims of massive underground satanic activity.

Within a relatively short time, satanic subversion claims were challenged on a variety of grounds. A series of scholarly books discredited the elements of the subversion theory. And a range of government officials and agencies issued investigative reports critical of ritual abuse claims. As a result, the outbreak subsided and a number of criminal convictions in ritual abuse cases were overturned.

See also NEW RELIGIOUS MOVEMENTS AND CULTS.

Further reading: Bromley, David. "Satanism: The New Cult Scare." In *The Satanism Scare.* Edited by James T. Richardson, Joel Best, and David G. Bromley. Hawthorne, N.Y.: Aldine de Gruyter, 1991, 49–72; Bromley, David, and Susan Ainsley. "Satanism and Satanic Churches: The Contemporary Incarnations." In *America's Alternative Religions.* Edited by Timothy Miller. Albany: State University of New York Press, 1995, 401–9; Crime Commission Task Force Studying Ritual Criminal Activity. *Final Report of the Task Force Studying Ritual Crime.* Richmond, Va., 1991; Hicks, Robert. *In Pursuit of Satan: The Police and the Occult.* Buffalo, N.Y.: Prometheus, 1991; Jenkins, Philip. *Intimate Enemies.* Hawthorne, N.Y.: Aldine de Gruyter, 1992; Lanning, Kenneth. "Satanic, Occult, Ritualistic Crime: A Law Enforcement Perspective." *The Police Chief* 56 (1989): 62–83; La Vey, Anton. *The Satanic Bible.* New York: Avon Books, 1970; Nathan, Debbie, and Michael Snedeker. *Satan's Silence.* New York: Basic Books, 1995; Richardson, James, Joel Best, and David Bromley, eds. *The Satanism Scare.* Hawthorne, N.Y.: Aldine de Gruyter, 1991; Victor, Jeffrey. *Satanic Panic.* Chicago: Open Court, 1993.

—David G. Bromley

Scalia, Antonin (1936–) *U.S. Supreme Court justice*

Antonin Scalia was born on March 11, 1936, in Trenton, New Jersey, into a devout Roman Catholic family. Both of his parents were educators, and the family moved to Long Island when he was young. Scalia was an excellent student, graduating first in his class from a military preparatory school. He attended college at Georgetown University, where he graduated summa cum laude in 1957. Scalia then attended Harvard Law School, where he was editor of the *Harvard Law Review,* graduating in 1960. After law school, Scalia practiced in the private sector until 1967, specializing in commercial law until he joined the faculty at the University of Virginia Law School. Scalia taught at Virginia until 1974, when he left to take a position as general counsel of the White House Office of Telecommunications Policy. In 1974, he was appointed assistant attorney general of the Office of Legal Counsel in the Department of Justice. Scalia left the Justice Department to return to teaching at the University of Chicago in 1977. He returned again to public service in 1982, when President Ronald Reagan appointed him to the U.S. Court of Appeals for Washington, D.C. In 1986, Reagan promoted William Rehnquist, then an associate justice on the Supreme Court, to the position of chief justice to replace Warren Burger. Reagan then turned to the 50-year-old Scalia to fill the seat vacated by Rehnquist. Scalia was nominated to the Supreme Court on June 24, 1986, and was confirmed by the

Senate by a vote of 98-0 on September 17, 1986, to become the Court's first Italian-American justice.

Since his confirmation, Scalia has come to be known as one of the most articulate, colorful, and, at times, combative justices on the Court. He adheres to a judicial philosophy that has been described as "originalism" or "textualism. Rather than relying on other modes of judicial decision making that emphasize the current needs of society or balancing the needs of one segment of society against those of another, Scalia relies heavily on the original text of the Constitution or the law in question to reach a decision. This approach emphasizes the meaning of the words at the time that they were written. As might be expected, Scalia also believes in judicial restraint, showing an unwillingness to extend laws beyond their original intended purpose. It is precisely this strict adherence to his stated judicial philosophy that has angered many of his critics. They suggest that the originalism practiced by Scalia leads to rigid interpretations of the Constitution, resulting in inconsistent outcomes. In their opinion, the Constitution is a flexible document, designed in such a way so that it can be applied to modern problems unforeseen by the framers.

Scalia's approach to the Constitution has led to a voting record that occasionally defies traditional interpretations that would classify him as a conservative. He has voted to uphold the right of protesters to burn the American flag and has voted against anti–hate crime laws, arguing that they violate freedom of speech protections contained in the First Amendment. However, he is also a vociferous opponent of the Court's decisions upholding the right to abortion, and has voted to support the rights of states in conflicts with the federal government. Despite such inconsistencies, Scalia is still considered one of the most conservative justices on the Court, voting consistently with fellow conservatives William Rehnquist and Clarence Thomas.

Some suggest that Scalia's strong religious background is an important factor in understanding his decisions. He and his wife are devout Roman Catholics and have nine children. In the case EMPLOYMENT DIVISION V. SMITH (1990), Scalia wrote the majority opinion, which allowed states to place restrictions on the exercise of religious practices if they conflicted with legitimate government goals. This decision has been interpreted as an attempt to limit less well known and less widely accepted religions, instead favoring more common religious faiths with broad levels of public support. It is difficult, if not impossible, to determine the role that Justice Scalia's faith plays in his decision making, but it is an issue that both his supporters and his opponents point to when attempting to discern how he behaves when confronted with cases involving the freedom of religion.

—Scott Comparato

Schneerson, Menachem Mendel (1902–1994)
religious leader

Rabbi Menachem Mendel Schneerson was born April 18, 1902, in Nikolayev in southern Ukraine. He died in New York

City at the age of 92, following a stroke on June 12, 1994. Rabbi Schneerson was the most recent rebbe, or head of the Lubavitch movement of HASIDIC JUDAISM. He held the position of rebbe for 44 years.

Politically, he had three significant influences. First, he rejuvenated the Lubavitcher Hasidic movement in the United States and Israel after its devastation during the HOLOCAUST. Second, the rebbe extended the influence of Judaism and in particular ORTHODOX JUDAISM by sending emissaries to all corners of the world. Finally, in the late 20th century, unlike other Ultra-Orthodox Jewish groups, he was able to integrate modernity's knowledge into Hasidic belief. In direct political action, his word had a significant effect on U.S. politics through the influence of New York State elections, both through voter turnout and monetary contributions, and he had a significant effect on Israeli politics thanks to the support his followers and other Orthodox Jews gave to his political pronouncements.

An example of his importance in U.S. politics occurred shortly after his death in 1994. A bill to bestow on the rebbe the Congressional Gold Medal was introduced in the U.S. House of Representatives by Representatives Charles Schumer, John Lewis, Jerry Lewis, and Newt Gingrich. This bill passed both the House and the Senate by unanimous consent, honoring the rebbe for "outstanding and lasting contributions toward improvements in world education, morality, and acts of charity."

The rebbe's upbringing reflected the many contradictions of his life. As the son of a renowned Kabbalist and Talmudic scholar, Rabbi Levi Yitzchak Schneerson, his early training was in Jewish knowledge, and by the time he reached his bar mitzvah, he was under private tutoring and was considered a Torah prodigy. In 1923, at the age of 19, he met Rabbi Yosef Yitzchok Schneerson, the then Lubavitcher rebbe (the teacher and leader of the worldwide Chabad-Lubavitch movement). Schneerson became part of the rebbe's inner circle, with increased responsibilities for the welfare of the community. For the next four years, he helped the rebbe in the secretive and at times dangerous work of keeping fragments of Jewish life alive in the USSR. In 1927, the rebbe was arrested in Leningrad by Soviet police and sentenced to death, a sentence that was commuted under worldwide pressure. Later that year, Schneerson was allowed to leave the Soviet Union as one of the select family members of the rebbe. The rebbe's second-eldest daughter, Chaya Mushka (1901–88), married Schneerson in Warsaw a year later. At that time, he began pursuing a secular education.

After their marriage, the couple moved to Berlin to continue Schneerson's studies in philosophy, mathematics, and science at the University of Berlin. In 1933, with the rise of Nazism, the family left Berlin for Paris to continue studying at the Sorbonne and a French school of engineering. Secular education was not generally accepted during this time by much of the Orthodox Jewish community. It was viewed as a way of undermining religious faith and generally a waste of

time that could be better utilized in studying the Torah and other holy works. But Schneerson, as he would argue his whole life, saw science and the Jewish religion as complementary, not oppositional.

For the future rebbe, faith and science were collaborative in their efforts to support the aim of Judaism to promote a better, more harmonious, godly world. In addition to understanding the workings of the world, the goal of science enabled the believer to understand and to come in touch with God through his creation. There are some complementary aspects of this belief in the Roman Catholic arguments of St. Thomas Aquinas and the place of natural law. For Hasidic Jews, God is everywhere, including science. Therefore, science becomes one of the many ways by which the divine is to be experienced and revealed.

When the German army marched into Paris in 1940, Schneerson and his wife first fled to Vichy France. Then they sailed via Portugal to New York City, arriving in June 1941. The sixth Lubavitcher rebbe, Joseph Yitzchak Schneerson, died on January 28, 1950. A year later, Menachem Mendel Schneerson became the seventh Lubavitcher rebbe.

During the rebbe's 44 years leading the Lubavitcher movement, it grew from the remnant that was left after the twin devastations of the Holocaust and Communist persecution in the Soviet Union to a community of more than 250,000, concentrated in New York City and Israel. The two unique and most modern institutions that the rebbe instituted were *shaliach* and "mitzvah tanks." *Shaliach,* which means "emissary," were representatives of Lubavitcher Judaism who spread to all corners of the world. This was an attempt to reach all remaining Jewish communities. The rebbe established a cadre of these emissaries who were sent, usually as whole families, to build Chabad-Lubavitch centers to provide humanitarian aid to local Jewish communities. Currently there are over 1,500 such centers in over 40 countries. The "mitzvah tanks" are outreach buses to bring back American Jews to practice the mitzvah, or one of the 613 divine instructions to the Jewish community contained in the Torah. These two activities are believed to have been among the most influential factors spurring a significant growth in Orthodox Judaism in the last part of the 20th century.

—Maurice M. Eisenstein

Schuller, Robert Harold (1926–) *televangelist*

A Protestant minister turned television evangelist, born September 16, 1926, in Alton, Iowa, Robert Schuller is the founder and senior pastor of Crystal Cathedral Ministries and Hour of Power television ministry in Garden Grove, California.

Schuller was the youngest of five children of a hardworking and religious Iowa farmer. Educated in a one-room schoolhouse, Robert committed early to his goal of the ministry. He worked his way through college as a janitor, and received the Bachelor of Arts degree from Hope College and a Master of Divinity Degree from Western Theological

Seminary, both in Holland, Michigan. The Reformed Church in America ordained him in 1950, and he entered the pastorate in 1951 at Hope Church in Chicago.

Schuller moved to Garden Grove, California, in 1955 to found a congregation of the Reformed Church in America. With only $500, he rented the Orange Drive-In Theater and conducted Sunday services from the roof of the snack bar. The congregation's growth over the years dictated the decision to build the internationally acclaimed Crystal Cathedral, from which he now preaches for the Reformed Church of America, to a congregation of over 10,000. In 1970, he began a popular television ministry, preaching in weekly hour shows called the *Hour of Power.*

Schuller has forged friendships with many political leaders. He has had a personal connection with every president for the last two decades. Former president Gerald Ford was a guest on *Hour of Power;* he met former president RONALD REAGAN in the Oval Office. Bob Dole and Elizabeth Dole are Schuller's longtime friends. Schuller also had a close relationship with Senator Hubert Humphrey (D-Minn.). While they did not personally visit each other often, they forged a friendship through correspondence, and Schuller delivered an inspirational message at Humphrey's 1978 funeral. Schuller also has associations with Palestinian leader Yasser Arafat, former Soviet president Mikhail Gorbachev, and Pope JOHN PAUL II.

Schuller has authored more than 30 books, five of which have appeared on the *New York Times* best-seller list. He is also the recipient of numerous accolades, including several honorary doctoral degrees. Schuller and his wife, Arvella, have five children and 17 grandchildren. His only son, Robert Anthony, an ordained minister of the Reformed Church in America, will be his successor at the Crystal Cathedral.

See also DUTCH REFORMED TRADITION; TELEVANGELISM.

Further reading: *Hour of Power* website. URL: http://www.hourofpower.org.

—Jacquelyn A. Anthony

Scopes "Monkey" trial (1925)

The Scopes "Monkey" trial was a major media event of the early-20th-century culture wars between defenders of traditional religion, emphasizing the literal truth of the Bible, and the forces of modernism, relying on rationalism and the scientific method. The trial took place in Dayton, Tennessee, July 10–21, 1925. At issue was the charge that John T. Scopes, a science teacher in the public high school in Dayton violated the statute prohibiting the teaching of the theory of evolution, defined as "any theory that denies the story of the Divine Creation of man as taught in the Bible, and to teach instead that man has descended from a lower order of animals." Scopes used a popular textbook that contained a section on Charles Darwin's *Origin of Species* (1859), the seminal statement on evolution.

The trial is known for its two principal antagonists. WILLIAM JENNINGS BRYAN, three times Democratic presiden-

tial candidate, assisted the prosecution and was a proponent of populism and biblical literalism. Bryan viewed evolution as inextricably bound with materialism, social Darwinism, or the application of the notion of "survival of the fittest" to the social world, eugenics, militarism, and determinism, which he saw as undermining traditional and religiously based American morals and values. He viewed the Tennessee statute as a valid exercise of majority rule by the people of the state speaking through their legislature. Clarence Darrow, assisting the Scopes defense team, was a well-known trial lawyer who had recently saved two teenagers from execution by arguing determinism based on psychological theories. He was associated with labor, and the fledgling AMERICAN CIVIL LIBERTIES UNION (ACLU), and was a leading antagonist of religion.

The state's governor, Austin Peay, did not believe that the law would be actively enforced. The trial came about because the ACLU was looking for a test case to challenge the Tennessee law, and civic leaders in Dayton were looking for a way to gain publicity for their town. Scopes was convinced by the civic leaders to challenge the law. Reporters from major newspapers, including the acerbic antifundamentalist H. L. Mencken, and live radio broadcasts to WGN in Chicago gave the trial a national audience and significance.

The trial opened July 10. The state's prosecutors tried to limit the issue to whether Scopes had violated the law. The defense, with the assistance of the ACLU, had assembled a group of expert witnesses who would testify as to the scientific bases of evolution. Presiding judge John Raulston, feeling the pressure of state leaders, including Governor Peay, refused to allow expert testimony but allowed it to be part of the record for appeals purposes. With experts ruled out, the defense settled on a strategy of calling Bryan as a witness on the Bible. This was the most famous part of the trial, with Darrow questioning Bryan on the literal truth of Jonah and the whale story, the origins of Cain's wife, the age of the earth, and the meaning of six "days" of creation. It was generally accepted that Darrow made Bryan look foolish. The trial ended the next day (July 21). Scopes was found guilty and fined $100 by the judge. Bryan was prepared to continue the battle over evolution but died several days later on July 26. The effects of the controversy were indirect, as evolution and Darwin were deemphasized in textbooks until the late 1950s.

The verdict was appealed to the Tennessee Supreme Court. The court, aware of the political and cultural implications, reversed the judgment on a technicality—the jury, not the judge, should have set the fine. The law was finally repealed in 1967. In *EPPERSON V. ARKANSAS* (1968), the Supreme Court ruled a similar Arkansas statute unconstitutional, citing the First Amendment's ESTABLISHMENT CLAUSE.

The Scopes trial was popularized by the 1955 play *Inherit the Wind,* which was made into a popular movie in 1960. The trial serves as a symbolic event for those who wish to point to the tensions between individual liberty and majoritarian democracy, and between SECULAR HUMANISM and FUNDAMENTALISM.

Further reading: Ginger, Ray. *Six Days or Forever.* Chicago: Quadrangle Books, 1969 [1958]; Larson, Edward J. *Summer for the Gods: The Scopes Trial and America's Continuing Debate over Science and Religion.* New York: Basic Books, 1997.

—Gerald DeMaio

Second Great Awakening

American history has been periodically marked by expansions in the increase in support for traditional religions and places of worship. Such expansions have often been associated with religious awakenings, a phrase originally coined in the late 18th century to describe a new phenomenon occurring at religious revivals held by evangelicals (see EVANGELICALISM). During a revival, churchgoers experienced an unexpected "awakening" of spiritual concern that led to unprecedented numbers of intense and "surprising conversions."

In general, though, the label sought to describe a broad religious phenomenon that transcended sectarian and denominational boundaries. The Second Great Awakening occurred in the United States from approximately 1790 through the 1830s, and was founded on the notion of bringing about significant social reforms. The religious revitalization that the awakening manifested itself in different ways, depending primarily on the local population and church establishment, but it was definitely a Protestant phenomenon.

It was in the transformation of CALVINIST theory, however, that the Second Great Awakening had the most impact on American religious culture. One important result of the new REVIVALISM was a further erosion of older Calvinist beliefs, especially the doctrine of predestination that marked the FIRST GREAT AWAKENING, which occurred during the 1730s and 1740s. The First Great Awakening was a Calvinistic, evangelical religious revival during the U.S. Colonial period that set the stage for the American Revolution by preaching the importance of individual conscience and stressing the rights of the common people. Eighteenth-century Calvinists such as JONATHAN EDWARDS and GEORGE WHITEFIELD stressed the sinful nature of humans and their incapacity to overcome this nature without the direct action of the grace of God.

The Second Great Awakening was ignited by the preaching of James McGready, a Presbyterian, in the area of Logan County, Kentucky. This outbreak of revivalism ignited other revivals at Gasper River, and Barton Stone, who latter founded the Christian Church (Disciples of Christ), led the Cane Ridge Revival (which became the most famous). This meeting was a vast gathering of 10,000 to 25,000 people. These large gatherings represented a break from the isolation of frontier life. During the first half of the 19th century, as the U.S. population grew from 5 million to 30 million and the nation moved westward, revivals became the primary means of Christianizing the growing population. Revivalism represented a crucial source of stability in American society, integrating huge numbers of people under the common umbrella of Protestantism.

Just as the individual soul could be redeemed through the exercise of free will, a national redemption could also follow from collective efforts toward social improvement. For example, religion's influence on politics was quite salient in the ABOLITIONIST MOVEMENT. New England churches, for example, supported by the Bible, fought passionately for abolition while their opponents, largely Southern evangelicals, supported slavery that, they argued, was sanctioned by the Bible. Still, the growing antislavery movement would emerge in the South. From 1808 to 1831, the South became the nation's leader in antislavery societies, and by 1826 it had 45 societies. More notably, the region also led the nation in the number of antislavery newspapers.

A number of other general movements to better society through improved education and strengthened morals also began in New England in the early 1800s. For example, Congregationalists and Presbyterians focused on literacy so that people could read Bibles. Unitarians were also active in the establishment of public education and in working for more humane care of mentally ill, deaf, and blind persons.

A great encourager of such reforms was the evangelist Charles G. Finney. Finney, an abolitionist, encouraged Christians to become involved in addressing social concerns such as prison reform, temperance, and women's rights, to name a few. As a result, the Second Great Awakening resulted in the establishment of numerous societies to aid in the spreading of the gospel. These organizations became known as the Benevolent Empire. The Second Great Awakening, in the end, would have a greater effect on society than any other revival in America.

See also BORN-AGAIN EXPERIENCE.

—Veronica Donahue DiConti

sectional divide of churches over slavery

Many students of history fail to appreciate that the movement to abolish slavery was waged largely in the vestibules of churches. For the Society of Friends (QUAKERS), METHODISTS, Baptists, and Presbyterians, among others, the debate over slavery and its abolition brought conflict and, in a few cases, denominational schism. That was the reality for many of the largest and most geographically dispersed denominations, such as Methodists and Baptists.

During the early years of the ABOLITIONIST MOVEMENT (the 18th century), most denominations tried to avoid dealing with the issue of slavery. Ambivalence became the de facto policy governing how most churches dealt with slavery, including the Methodists, Baptists, Roman Catholics, Lutherans, and Calvinists. For many church leaders at this time, slavery was considered a secular matter and the church had no compelling reason to interfere in the matters of civil society.

Abolitionists within each of these denominations worked tirelessly to convince their peers that slavery was a matter of church concern. They argued that slavery was a sin and the church, as a religious institution, ought to lead the battle to eliminate this sin. However, there was considerable disagreement within the American religious community as to whether slavery was *really* a sin.

That disagreement often fell along sectional lines, with Northern congregations expressing sympathy for the antislavery position and Southern congregations speaking out loudly for their "right" to trade and to own slaves. The disagreement over the church's role in sanctioning slavery would lead to the division of several denominations. The two most commonly discussed in history books, the Methodist and Baptist churches, were also two of the largest denominations during the mid-19th century.

When the Methodist Episcopal Church in America was founded, it issued an unambiguous statement expelling all members who bought and sold slaves "with no other design than to hold them as slaves." However, as the Methodist Church began to spread and its membership continued to grow, the rule was rarely enforced. By the 1820s, the prohibition against owning slaves existed only in theory and was applied sparingly.

Antislavery activists within the Baptist Church found a similar situation. By the 1830s, the Baptist Church had become the largest denominational body in America, and its significant Southern membership made church leaders reluctant to discuss slavery. The Baptist Church was also organized without a centralized governing structure, and this arrangement placed a great deal of autonomy in the hands of local congregations. Therefore, the Baptist Church never issued a sweeping policy on slavery unlike their Methodist counterparts.

A few Baptist churches, mostly in the North, did issue antislavery policies. Among those were the New York Baptist Association and the Friends of Humanity associations of Kentucky. But as the Baptist Church continued to grow and continued to welcome more Southern members, the issue of slavery and slaveholding members moved to the forefront.

By the 1840s, very few institutions, either religious or secular, could continue to avoid the debate over slavery. As the abolitionist movement gained steam in the North, it gradually began to sway public opinion. Most Americans did not endorse immediate and unconditional abolition, but they were willing to entertain some notions of the gradual and systematic emancipation of slaves.

Church leaders in the North found it increasingly difficult to detach themselves from popular opinion, and they began to experience a great deal of pressure to make a definitive statement against owning slaves. These pressures were exacerbated by a growing number of church members, particularly Methodists, who were choosing to secede and form their own associations with unambiguously abolitionist policies at their core. Led by Orange Scott, LaRoy Sunderland, and George Storrs, a group of abolitionist Methodists in the North seceded in 1842 and formed the Wesleyan Methodist Connection.

Although relatively few Methodists followed, it was a clear statement that slavery and its abolition had begun to divide the church. This was not an isolated phenomenon.

Compromise and conciliation governed church policy in the years and decades leading up to the 1840s, but those policies were challenged by both sides. Northern evangelicals of all denominational stripes wanted clear policies prohibiting members from owning slaves. Southern evangelicals, once satisfied with ambiguous policies that rarely were enforced, now wanted church leaders to issue statements that embraced slavery as an institution and recognized the right of church members to own slaves.

This is what happened during the Methodist General Conference of 1844. Church leaders, unwilling to go as far as endorsing the institution of slavery, chose to expel a Southern bishop who had recently inherited slaves. Southern members reacted angrily and would eventually vote to secede, forming the Methodist Episcopal Church, South. One year later the Baptists would experience a similar schism.

By the 1850s two of the largest and most influential denominations in America were divided along sectional and ideological lines over the issue of slavery. At its core, the divisions centered on the role of the church in navigating one of the most controversial political issues in American history.

See also BROWN, JOHN.

—Alonford James Robinson Jr.

secular humanism

Today "secular" implies the opposite of ecclesiastical, a lack of concern with religion, and the doctrine that morality should be based on individual well-being in this life. This is ironic, because the term was first used by St. Augustine to refer to an era within sacred history when prophecy and dramatic interventions by God had ceased, awaiting the onset of the final age. In the early medieval period, "secular" also referred to noncloistered canons and other clerics; thus it came to mean "in the world," leading to the distinction between "regular" and "secular" cathedrals. Annexed to *humanism,* which arose from the revival of classical learning and art in the Renaissance, the idea, if not the term, secular humanism, gained ground from the early 19th century onward as a nontheistic ground of human purpose and flourishing, to distinguish it from the long tradition of Christian humanism in both the ROMAN CATHOLIC CHURCH and Protestantism—taking Augustine's era and making it the whole of the human condition.

"Secularism" as a stand-alone worldview is typically a stridently atheist doctrine (as in, for example, the 19th-century English radical G. J. Holyoake's *Principles of Secularism*). "Humanism," however, has had an enduring relationship to Christianity, through both Aristotelian natural law in the Roman Catholic tradition and the appropriation of Renaissance humanist learning by Catholics and Protestants, Dutch theologian Erasmus standing in the middle of this intersection. The struggle, then, has been between sacred and secular understandings of humanism as the flourishing of human capability and well-being. Auguste Comte (1798–1857) is credited with the simultaneous creation of a thoroughly positivist science of humanity (*Course of Positive Philosophy*) and an empowering "religion of humanity" providing symbolic, ceremonial, and emotive supports for its realization (*System of Positive Polity*). John Stuart Mill, some of his followers, and many UNITARIAN intellectuals in England and America were attracted to both projects, objecting only to the Catholic features of Comte's secular religion and to his highly centralized political formulations. Sociology became the master science, and human moral and intellectual progress the organizing sacred principle, of contemporary secular humanism.

America has long been an attractive market for secular humanist values and ideas. Given its pervasive religiosity, this receptivity might appear strange but results from the fact that America has had a Protestant culture of such creedal variety and organizational diversity that the common civic and political expression of this culture has been a national gospel, a covenantal commitment to moral reform and human progress preparatory to the fulfillment of human history. First came Unitarianism at Harvard University in the 19th century, then came the SOCIAL GOSPEL movement and modernism in mainline Protestant denominations. Finally, the institutionalization of these values that took place in the modern research universities are all expressions of this receptivity. Under the canopy of this shared CIVIL RELIGION, humanist values in America are both sacred and secular, and the line between them among national elites in all areas of American life is a very blurry one.

Among adherents of the Christian Right in America, the line is not blurry at all: secular humanism is an aggressive, nontheistic religion systematically promulgated in the universities, the public schools, the federal courts, and the national news and entertainment media to supplant Judeo-Christianity in American public life and culture. The battleground is the relationship of church and state and religion and public life, especially education. If secular humanism is a religion in competition with theistic and biblically based religion, then it should either be purged from public life as theistic religion is, or stand as an equal competitor on an open field where all religious voices are welcome. While the European history of secular humanism is that of an alternative faith directed explicitly against Christianity, therefore giving some warrant for this view, the larger American picture is more ambiguous. The U.S. Supreme Court has lent some support to this view in cases involving CONSCIENTIOUS OBJECTION to military service by allowing secular humanism to stand alongside theistic religion as a justifiable claim for exemption. Earlier, beginning in 1933, (secular) humanist manifestos were issued by modernist clergy and prominent academic intellectuals. The first one was occasioned by a fear on the part of the signers that neoorthodox Christianity was suddenly (and, to them, inexplicably) gaining ground even among some progressive intellectuals. They were not mistaken in this fear, and this manifesto, like the later ones, was quickly forgotten.

Explicitly secular formulations of humanism have never been dominant features of higher or middlebrow intellectual culture in America. The more important struggle takes place on a different dimension. If secular humanist ideas have been prominent in universities, professions, and public policies, it is because leaders whose commitment to American sacred and patriotic values are assumed to have articulated them from within our publicly shared religious values. This is perhaps even truer today than either in the 1920s, when faith in social science and expertise was treated as revelation itself, and in the 1970s and 1980s, when the adversarial counterculture thought victory could be won through negative argument alone.

See also AGNOSTICISM; ATHEISM; CONSERVATISM; DEISM; LIBERALISM.

Further reading: Bloom, Harold. *The American Religion: The Emergence of a Post-Christian Nation.* New York: Simon and Schuster, 1992; Dewey, John. *A Common Faith.* New Haven, Conn.: Yale University Press, 1960 [1934]; James, William. *The Varieties of Religious Experience.* New York: Library of America, 1990 [1901]; Marsden, George. *The Soul of the American University: From Protestant Establishment to Established Nonbelief.* New York: Oxford University Press, 1994; Neuhaus, Richard John. *The Naked Public Square: Religion and Democracy in America.* Grand Rapids, Mich.: Eerdmans, 1986; Turner, James. *Without God, Without Creed: The Origins of Unbelief in America.* Baltimore: Johns Hopkins University Press, 1986; Wright, T. R. *The Religion of Humanity: The Impact of Comtean Positivism on Victorian Britain.* Cambridge: Cambridge University Press, 1986.

—Eldon J. Eisenach

secularization

Secularization is the process through which religious beliefs and institutions become less influential within civilization. One commonly held theory—often referred to as the "secularization thesis"—predicts that scientific advancement and the diffusion of knowledge throughout human society will hasten the secularization process. This thesis has been suggested in various forms since the Enlightenment, but in recent years it has been particularly influential among sociologists who study religion.

Although the phrase *secularization thesis* is recent, the idea that religion will decline with the passage of time has existed for centuries. In the early 18th century, this expectation became particularly intense. Many leading figures of the Enlightenment expected that long-established religious doctrines and traditions would simply collapse after exposure to rational scrutiny. But religious faith persisted throughout the 19th and 20th centuries, leading to the development of more complex versions of the secularization thesis. One new version was rooted in Freudian psychology. This approach understands religious belief as a symptom of deep psychological neurosis. Psychologists who accept this theory expect that as new treatments for the underlying neurosis are developed, the prevalence of religious belief in society will decline. Another form of the secularization thesis is rooted in Marxist social analysis (see MARXISM/COMMUNISM). Marxists understand religion as a form of false consciousness used by the bourgeoisie to maintain a servile and docile worker class. According to this version, the bourgeoisie use religion to hinder the workers' perceptions of their common interests by focusing attention on false promises in a future world. The theory also predicts that class consciousness will emerge as an inevitable consequence of historical trends and that religious beliefs will fade as this consciousness emerges.

In the second half of the 20th century, a new version of the secularization thesis became influential among sociologists. Peter Berger's work (1967, 1979) was seminal, and he received broad media attention for his prediction that religious beliefs would be overwhelmed by a worldwide explosion of secularism ("Bleak Outlook" 1968). While Berger was more sympathetic to religious faith than either Freudians or Marxists, he predicted that traditional religious faith would not survive the social and psychological forces of the modern world. Berger argued that in modern secular society, any religion's claim to represent complete and exclusive truth is undermined by the presence of competing religions. In a pluralistic society, churches cannot create the social structures—such as social customs and legal mandates—that are necessary to reinforce religious belief. Without such structures to protect it, religion will be challenged by uncertainty. As uncertainty spreads and religious beliefs become more subjective, each religion will experience a crisis of credibility that undermines its claim to authority.

In the 1990s, secularization theory was vigorously challenged by a conception of the dynamic between religion and culture derived largely from economic theory. Noting that secularization theory had failed to predict the impressive vitality of evangelical Christianity within many highly modernized nations, sociologists such as Roger Finke and Rodney Stark (1992) suggested that the pluralistic environment of modern culture is highly conducive, rather than inimical, to religious belief. Conceiving of religion as a sort of commodity offered by sellers (denominations) to buyers (potential converts), Finke and Stark argued that the greater variety of products allows the religious needs of a greater variety of "market segments" to be met. They further argued that the pluralism that Berger expected to create a credibility crisis could actually reinforce religion. The most successful churches are those that create the strongest sense of community. One way to create a strong community is to emphasize differences in belief between members and outsiders. These differences thus function as a form of product differentiation, making the believer more aware of benefits received from membership in a particular religious denomination.

Partly in response to this challenge, more recent secularization theorists have revised the theory by predicting that secularization will occur more narrowly than previously expected. For example, José Casanova argues that the secularization thesis is incorrect in predicting the decline of religious faith, but

correct in recognizing the modern trend toward social "differentiation," understood as the "emancipation of the secular sphere [such as the spheres of the state and the market] from religious institutions and norms." Through the process of "differentiation," the religious sphere becomes only one among several that exist independently of each other. In Casanova's understanding, secularization will not necessarily undermine religious faith, but will transform it. Each church will have to accept that it no longer can be an all-encompassing authority over social life. Only those churches that embrace differentiation will flourish within a differentiated, pluralistic society.

Further reading: "A Bleak Outlook Is Seen." *New York Times.* February 25, 1968, 3, 1968; Berger, Peter. *The Sacred Canopy: Elements of a Sociological Theory of Religion.* Garden City, N.Y.: Doubleday, 1967; ———. *The Heretical Imperative: Contemporary Possibilities of Religious Affirmation.* New York: Doubleday, 1979; Casanova, José. *Public Religions in the Modern World.* Chicago: University of Chicago Press, 1994; Finke, Roger, and Rodney Stark. *The Churching of America: Winners and Losers in Our Religious Economy.* New Brunswick, N.J.: Rutgers University Press, 1992.

—James Paul Old

separation of church and state

The separation of church and state is the concept that religious and political authority ought to be clearly distinct, though both may claim the allegiance of the people. The concept lays at the heart of the U.S. Constitution's treatment of religion in the First Amendment: "Congress shall make no law respecting the establishment of religion, or prohibiting the free exercise thereof." Yet despite the First Amendment, the precise boundaries of church and state have remained unsettled throughout American history. Some have argued that the government cannot support or otherwise accommodate religion in any way, while others have insisted that government must acknowledge the importance of religion and provide religious groups access to the same public resources available to secular groups.

The historical record provides few unambiguous clues as to how the nation's founders would resolve these arguments. There was little disagreement among members of the founding generation that the national government must refrain from establishing any single religion. For many colonists, the privileges of the established Church of England, as well as the attendant persecution of religious minorities, were fresh memories that argued against a similar arrangement in the United States. But beyond this narrow form of church-state separation, the founders' intentions become less clear. On the one hand, a wide range of groups, from Baptists and QUAKERS to deists and secularists, were uncomfortable with most forms of state support of religion, as summed up in THOMAS JEFFERSON's famous declaration that the First Amendment erected "a wall of separation between Church and State." On the other

The first prayer in Congress illustrates the complex relationship of religion and government in the United States. *(Billy Graham Museum)*

hand, the First Congress of the United States, which proposed the First Amendment, did not prohibit state-level establishment. Many states provided direct support to Protestant denominations well into the 19th century.

Even after the states abandoned legal establishments—the last state to do so was MASSACHUSETTS, which removed its financial support of the Congregational Church in 1833—Protestant denominations continued to enjoy the de facto support of state governments. Some states banned blasphemy, recognized Christmas and Easter as official holidays, and enforced the Christian Sabbath. Public schools favored a Protestant style and curriculum, complete with prayers and readings from the Protestant King James Bible. As a result, the dominant Protestantism clashed repeatedly with religious minorities throughout the 19th century. Disputes between Catholics and Protestants were especially acute—even violent—as waves of European immigration swelled the Catholic population and the ROMAN CATHOLIC CHURCH began to make greater demands on the Protestant-dominated political system.

In summary, religion in the 19th century was aligned with the government in many different ways, though direct establishment of any church was strictly avoided. Religion could not

be institutionalized in the form of a state church, but it could be supported as an integral feature of cultural life through public education and other means. It was not until the early 20th century that these traditional church-state alignments began to lose some of their influence. The cultural changes that provided an impetus for altered church-state relations are quite complex; increasing religious pluralism and new theories in science, theology, and law played a role. Far from the 19th-century belief that religion was fundamental component of public order and therefore worthy of state support, intellectuals and other elites began to suggest that religion was often an obstacle to social progress and, in any event, was a private affair that no longer needed special accommodations from the state.

The judicial system reinforced these cultural changes. In the 1940s, the Supreme Court moved decisively to buttress the wall between church and state by nationalizing the religion clauses of the First Amendment and placing greater constraints on how closely government could interact with religion. In *EVERSON V. BOARD OF EDUCATION* (1947), the Supreme Court for the first time applied the ESTABLISHMENT CLAUSE of the Constitution against the states. Writing for the majority, Justice Hugo Black argued that state aid to parochial school children was constitutional only if it went directly to parents, not schools. Barring such "neutral" arrangements, aid to any religious institution would no longer pass constitutional muster. So began a series of decisions that have demanded government neutrality toward religion that had never been experienced in American history.

The efforts to enforce state neutrality can be easily overstated, however. The modern Court has been skeptical of state support of religion, especially in terms of state aid to parochial schools, religious practices in the public schools, and public displays of religious symbols. But state and federal legislatures continue to devise ways to provide public acknowledgment and support of religion and religious institutions. The recent effort to provide educational vouchers so parents can afford to send their children to private religious schools is a case in point. Moreover, the Court's church-state jurisprudence has been widely criticized as confusing and downright contradictory, allowing certain forms of aid in one case and banning similar forms of aid in the next. In light of the totality of its decisions, it is difficult to argue that the Court has declared a wholesale disestablishment of religion, at least if one means by "establishment" any interaction of government with religion.

The debates over the practical meaning of the separation of church and state are reflected in the group politics and mass opinion as well. Though coalitions constantly shift and groups often differ in subtle ways, two main sets of organized groups seek to influence government decisions on the status of church and state: separationists, who seek less church-state interaction, and accommodationists, who seek support of religion in various ways. In terms of mass opinion, social surveys indicate that, in the abstract, American citizens are overwhelmingly committed to the concept of church-state separation, yet most support practical initiatives that would seem more accommodating to religion (for example, a government-funded military chaplaincy or moments for prayer in public schools).

See also FOURTEENTH AMENDMENT AND THE INCORPORATION DOCTRINE; FREE EXERCISE CLAUSE.

Further reading: Levy, Leonard W. *The Establishment Clause.* Chapel Hill: University of North Carolina Press, 1994; Gedicks, Frederick Mark. *The Rhetoric of Church and State.* Chapel Hill: University of North Carolina Press, 1995; Hall, Timothy. *Separating Church and State: Roger Williams and Religious Liberty.* Urbana: University of Illinois Press, 1998; McConnell, Michael. "Accommodation of Religion." In *The Supreme Court Review 1985.* Edited by Philip Kurland. Chicago: University of Chicago Press, 1988; Pfeffer, Leo. *Church, State, and Freedom.* Boston: Beacon Press, 1967.
—Kevin R. den Dulk

September 11, 2001

At 8:45 A.M. on September 11, 2001, a hijacked commercial airliner destined for San Francisco slammed into the North Tower of the World Trade Center in New York City; about 15 minutes later, another cross-country flight ended in the South Tower. The two towers collapsed not long after, killing thousands of police officers, firefighters, and civilians who were unable to escape. A third airplane dove into the Pentagon 40 minutes later, while passengers of a fourth prevented the use of the plane as a weapon by attempting to retake control of the aircraft, during which time the plane crash-landed in a rural Somerset County, Pennsylvania, field. The combined efforts of 19 terrorists with ties to Osama bin Laden and his al Qaeda organization was the worst terrorist attack on American soil, with a death toll of over 3,000 people.

The response by Americans and the rest of the world was swift and proportionate, and infused with religion on many levels. As the leader of America's CIVIL RELIGION, President GEORGE W. BUSH almost immediately invoked religious language, spoke at religious events, and met with religious leaders. His actions reaffirmed Americans' connection to religion and invited religious backing for new U.S. retaliatory missions. In many ways, however, one of the most striking events in American history yielded reactions among Americans that were plain and ordinary; that is, the tragedy highlighted what many Americans do on a regular basis—assist the unfortunate in a wide variety of ways.

Almost immediately came widespread stories of discrimination against people who appeared to be of Middle Eastern descent. Nationally, however, Americans reported increasing trust for those of different ethnic lineage, though trust for Arab Americans lagged behind trust for Hispanics and African Americans. The "rally around the flag" effect thus rippled through society.

In the wake of the tragedy, more Americans than usual turned to church and religious leaders to help make sense of the events. One Gallup poll pegged 47 percent of Americans attending church the weekend after the attacks; that figure returned to its usual level of about 42 percent a few weeks later. Individual religious practices, such as prayer and reading a religious text, were unchanged throughout the period. There was not a great religious revival in America after September 11, as the son of BILLY GRAHAM, evangelist Franklin Graham, had insisted would happen. Instead, pragmatic Americans looked to one another during a brief period of mourning then moved on.

Similarly, there was an outpouring of donations and VOLUNTARISM from Americans in the aftermath of the terrorist attacks. Americans donated millions of dollars to the Red Cross, among other charities; millions donated blood; others donated goods and services; some drove from the Midwest and South to volunteer at "ground zero," the former site of the World Trade Center twin towers. In some respects, the magnitude of the human tragedy overwhelmed PHILANTHROPIC organizations, though the complexity of figuring out who had actually been affected by the tragedy has remained a significant problem for private and governmental relief.

The relief effort was not simply carried out by national organizations, but was coordinated and assisted by local organizations near and far from the tragedy. For instance, one lower Manhattan EPISCOPAL CHURCH, St. Paul's Chapel, proved critical to some of the thousands of relief workers. With local members and volunteers from around the country, the church immediately set up food service and logistical support for the workers. A priest of another nearby Episcopal church explained, "Trinity has never been more relevant to this neighborhood. We didn't have to invent what to do; we just had to be who we are." These stories could be repeated a hundredfold with different names and places. Just like church attendance, however, Americans' involvement in voluntaristic activities returned to their normal levels not long after the attacks. Americans rose to the initial challenge and then settled back into their customary practices.

The terrorist attacks also motivated a scathing public indictment of America's SECULAR culture from televangelists PAT ROBERTSON and JERRY FALWELL, who appeared on the television show the *700 Club*. On the air, Falwell announced:

> The ABORTIONists have got to bear some burden for this because God will not be mocked. And when we destroy 40 million little innocent babies, we make God mad. I really believe that the pagans, and the abortionists, and the FEMINISTs, and the gays and the lesbians who are actively trying to make that an alternative lifestyle, the A.C.L.U., PEOPLE FOR THE AMERICAN WAY, all of them who have tried to secularize America, I point the finger in their face and say, "You helped this happen."

To which Robertson replied: "I totally concur." Robertson later released a statement suggesting God had lifted his protection from the United States because of greed, PORNOGRAPHY, and a lack of prayer. Both were roundly criticized in the national media, disavowed by the White House, and challenged by mainline Protestant churches. In evangelical circles, the controversy seemed to be more about Falwell's errors of selecting the particular sins that incurred God's wrath, not the basic notion that the terrorist attacks were a sign of God's displeasure and a call for repentance.

The U.S. response to the terrorist attacks—an invasion of Afghanistan—also challenged the beliefs of many "peace church" traditions. In many MENNONITE churches, for instance, a deeply ingrained commitment to PACIFISM was questioned by the severity of the September 11 attacks that occasioned some heated meetings. Agonizing over the response, however, was confined to an extremely select group of Americans.

The September 11 terrorist attacks will have a lasting historical significance because of the Bush administration's prosecution of a global war on terrorism, restrictions on civil liberties, increased focus on foreign affairs, and an augmented national defense. The legacy of the attacks for the American public is more limited. Americans will not soon forget the tragedy, but it did not significantly alter their way of life. Robert Putnam suggested even a lost opportunity, "In the aftermath of September's tragedy, a window of opportunity has opened for a sort of civic renewal that occurs only once or twice a century. And yet, though the crisis revealed and replenished the wells of solidarity in American communities, those wells so far remain untapped."

See also RELIGIOUS PERSECUTION; REVIVALISM; TOLERANCE.

Further reading: Putnam, Robert. "Bowling Together." *American Prospect* 13, no. 3 (February 11, 2002).

—Paul A. Djupe

Seventh-day Adventists

Seventh-day Adventism was formally and legally established between the years 1860 and 1863. However, Adventism developed out of an earlier, millennial movement called Millerism. In the early 19th century, preacher William Miller (1782–1849) studied the chronology of the Bible, especially the Book of Daniel, and came to the conclusion that the Second Coming of Jesus Christ would occur between 1843 and 1844. In 1840, he met up with promoter and publisher Joshua V. Himes, who set about organizing lectures and publications so that Miller could spread the word throughout the northeastern United States. Miller was quite successful in convincing his listeners and readers, and by 1844 he had gained tens of thousands of believers. Many of these followers began to detach from the world, some even selling or giving away their possessions as they awaited the advent of Jesus Christ. When the Second Coming failed to materialize, never fully organized, the movement fell into disarray and disagreeing factions.

The most enduring faction formed around a young woman named Ellen Harmon White (1827–1915), who had accepted Millerism in 1840 as only a teenager, and who had then begun to have prophetic visions and dreams related to the imminent end of the world. After the Great Disappointment of 1844, she and a group of Millerite preachers began to reinterpret the events of that year, eventually coming to the conclusion that Jesus Christ had not come to earth, but had, instead, entered the holiest inner sanctum of heaven and was there engaged in a thorough judgment of all of humankind. According to White, Jesus Christ would come to earth only when he had finished this judgment process. The group grew steadily in numbers and organization, and White and her prophetic visions became its central guiding light. White's husband, James White, was also instrumental in formalizing the group and spreading White's message through various publications and periodicals. By 1863, Seventh-day Adventism was fully organized as a church.

Seventh-day Adventists still firmly believe that the Second Coming of Jesus Christ is imminent, but White and subsequent Adventist leaders refused and continue to refuse to speculate on the exact date that it will occur. Instead, these leaders encourage their members to live according to the correct interpretation of biblical laws and restrictions so that they will be separated from the world and prepared for the end of the world, whenever it should happen. For this reason, Adventists are to live in the world, but not to be of the world. As Adventists strove to live apart from mainstream society, they adopted characteristic practices and behaviors to facilitate and mark this separation. For instance, Adventists celebrate their Sabbath on the seventh day of the week, Saturday, and, ideally, they abstain from alcohol, tobacco, stimulants, and meat, as they also shun distracting recreations and clothing. To further advance this separation, Adventists also developed an extensive educational and health system that still exists today in the form of Adventist schools and hospitals.

In line with this thinking, Adventism as an institution and Adventists as individuals have stayed away from the political realm, and there have been few major interactions between this group and the legal or political system of the United States. Still, there has been a gradual shift in the overall political and social leanings of the church and its membership. In the 19th century, Adventism was part of the health reform and dress reform movement and was fairly liberal in its interpretation of the role of women within the home and church. As the church entered the 20th century, it became increasingly identified as a conservative movement that attempted to preserve traditional family and church structure. In the 21st century, many of its positions on political issues have been identified with those of fundamentalist and evangelical Christianity, though, at the same time, Adventism is clearly theologically and institutionally distinct from these forms of Christianity.

There is, nonetheless, an inherent clash between a group that preaches the corruption and imminent end of the world and the government institutions that seek to sustain that same world. This clash can be seen most clearly in the history of Adventism in other countries. By 2000, the church had a membership of 11 million, and 90 percent of those members resided outside the United States, especially in Latin America and Africa. Occasional problems have come with the increasing international success of the group. The former Soviet Union, China, Cuba, and Nicaragua have jailed Adventists for promoting their beliefs and practices. In this sense, the political history of Seventh-day Adventists lies more in present and future challenges to a worldwide church than in its relatively quiet past.

See also JEHOVAH'S WITNESSES.

—Susanna Morrill

Shakers

The Shakers are one of the largest and longest-lived communal religions in American history. Formally known as the United Society of Believers in Christ's Second Coming, the Shakers expressed their religious beliefs through celibacy, communal living, hard work, austere lifestyles, equality between the sexes, and expressive ceremonies filled with singing, dancing, speaking in tongues, and frenzied move-

ments sometimes described as shaking, from which they earned the name "Shaking Quakers," or simply, "Shakers."

The movement was founded in 1758 by a Manchester, England, factory worker named Ann Lee. Lee was a former Quaker who lost all four of her children during their infancy. In 1770 a revelation about Adam and Eve in the Garden of Eden convinced Lee that lust was actually the original sin. Only those who "neither marry nor are given in marriage" could reconcile themselves with God, and thus celibacy was demanded of all followers. Lee brought a small group of followers to America in 1774 and settled near Albany, New York, in a small village named Watervliet.

The early phase of the movement under Lee was largely charismatic (see PENTECOSTAL AND CHARISMATIC), with her followers believing that she had been infused with the Spirit of Christ. After she died in 1784, the movement became formalized and noteworthy in particular for the equality of men and women. By 1800, there were 11 settlements with roughly 1,600 members in Connecticut, Maine, MASSACHUSETTS, New Hampshire, and New York. Later settlements were founded in the South and Midwest. Each settlement was divided into "families" of up to 100 men and women who lived under the same roof but in separate quarters. Each gender had its own leaders, who met together as equals to make decisions for the community.

Shakers are highly entrepreneurial and inventive; they are credited with inventing the washing machine, the metal tip pen, the circular "buzz" saw, the clothespin, and the flat broom, along with a vast quantity of songs and writings. They are probably best known for their high-quality furniture.

Because their membership was not reproducing, the Shakers constantly relied on recruiting new members and were active in proselytizing to find them. The Shakers actively engaged the outside world. Their worship ceremonies were open for all to participate in, and they undertook a wide range of charitable works. Always aware of their need to replenish their ranks, the Shakers were extremely welcoming to those seeking to join, making no distinctions regarding prior faith, gender, or even race. Following the Millerite disappointment of the 1840s, many former Millerites moved to the United Society, and Shakerism reached its peak membership with over 6,000 individuals in its ranks. Membership then began a long, slow decline, so by 1900 there were still 1,000 members, but few converts joined afterward.

The United Society faced numerous legal problems owing to their understanding of property. Following Acts 2:44–45, members held all their goods in common. Shakers believed that property was not owned by humans but rather entrusted to them by God merely to tend. New members were thus asked to donate their worldly possessions irrevocably to the community upon entry, or some time shortly thereafter. This caused problems when a member decided to leave and sought to regain his or her property. Courts in various states almost universally ruled for the community, stating that the covenant formed upon entry was a binding contract.

A second legal complication concerned child custody. After separation, ex-wives with children frequently had difficulty collecting support from spouses who had entered a settlement and had given away all their wealth in the process. This led to suits against settlements for child support. Moreover, another issue arose when families sought to leave the community, taking their children with them. On certain occasions, usually when the families had been members for long periods of time, settlements claimed the right to keep the children as members.

Finally, as pacifists, Shakers found themselves in conflict with certain states during the Revolutionary War for refusing to enter or acknowledge the draft. Later, during the Civil War, President ABRAHAM LINCOLN himself met with leaders from Northern settlements, giving all members of the United Society dispensation. Shakers in the Kentucky settlement instead paid a fine.

Although there is still one active settlement in Maine, Shakerism today is more about a legacy of ideas: gender equality, charity, tolerance, and the development of a First Amendment jurisprudence of FREE EXERCISE regarding religious communities and the state.

See also CONSCIENTIOUS OBJECTION; QUAKERS.

Further reading: Andrews, Edward Deming. *The People Called Shakers.* New York: Oxford University Press, 1953; Brewer, Priscilla J. *Shaker Communities, Shaker Lives.* Hanover, N.H.: University Press of New England, 1986; Campion, Nardi R. *Ann the Word: The Life of Mother Ann Lee, Founder of the Shakers.* Boston: Little, Brown, 1976; Weisbrod, Carol. *The Boundaries of Utopia.* New York: Pantheon, 1980; White, Anna. *Shakerism: Its Meaning and Message.* Columbus, Ohio: Heer, 1904.

—Brian J. Glenn

Sherbert v. Verner 374 US 398 (1963)

The U.S. Supreme Court decision in *Sherbert v. Verner* helped define the contemporary understanding of the FREE EXERCISE CLAUSE. The Court ruled that the First Amendment is violated not only by laws prohibiting the free exercise of religion but also by other kinds of burdens, including the denial of benefits for religious reasons. Moreover, government may not burden religious freedom unless the burden is justified by a compelling state interest. In addition, the concurring and dissenting opinions recognized an unresolved conflict between free exercise and ESTABLISHMENT CLAUSE jurisprudence, which has yet to be resolved.

Adelle Sherbert, a SEVENTH-DAY ADVENTIST, was terminated from her job in a South Carolina textile mill for refusing to work on Saturdays, her Sabbath. Unable to find other employment that did not require Saturday work, she filed a claim for unemployment compensation. Her claim was denied on the grounds that she "had failed without good cause, to accept available suitable work when offered." Sherbert chal-

lenged the denial as a violation of her First Amendment right to free exercise of religion. In upholding her claim, the U.S. Supreme Court significantly expanded constitutional religious protection.

Justice WILLIAM J. BRENNAN JR., writing for the majority, made it clear that the denial of a benefit on religious grounds suffers the same constitutional defect as an actual penalty on the free exercise of religion. Although the state had not literally prohibited the practice of Sherbert's religion, it:

> forces her to choose between following the precepts of her religion and forfeiting benefits, on the one hand, and abandoning one of the precepts of her religion in order to accept work, on the other hand. Governmental imposition of such a choice puts the same kind of burden upon the free exercise of religion as would a fine imposed against appellant for her Saturday worship.

Although no one has a right to unemployment compensation benefits, once a state grants those benefits, they may not be denied for religious reasons. "It is too late in the day to doubt that the liberties of religion and expression may be infringed by the denial of or placing of conditions upon a benefit or privilege."

> [C]onditions upon public benefits cannot be sustained if they so operate, whatever their purpose, as to inhibit or deter the exercise of First Amendment freedoms. . . . Likewise, to condition the availability of benefits upon this appellant's willingness to violate a cardinal principle of her religious faith effectively penalizes the free exercise of her constitutional liberties.

Equally significant, the majority ruled that burdens on religious freedom can be justified only by compelling state interests: "Only the gravest abuses, endangering paramount interests, give occasion for permissible limitation."

This reasoning did not go unchallenged. Both Justice Stewart's concurring opinion and Justice Harlan's dissent recognized some serious potential conflicts between Brennan's free exercise interpretation and the Court's emerging understanding of the ESTABLISHMENT CLAUSE. Recent establishment clause decisions—including *ABINGTON TOWNSHIP V. SCHEMPP* (1963), handed down the same day—had mandated a strict neutrality regarding religion; yet this decision required the state to accommodate religion by favoring religious over nonreligious reasons for missing work. This approach clearly conflicted with religious neutrality under the establishment clause. In Stewart's view, recent establishment clause interpretations had been in error, and the accommodationist spirit of *Sherbert* was the correct approach. But Justice Harlan, dissenting, reached the opposite conclusion. In his view, the establishment clause forbids that kind of preference for religion. While state legislatures are free to grant a religious accommodation if they choose, there is no constitutional right to such accommodation. His interpretation continues to attract support of many constitutional interpreters.

The *Sherbert* decision was followed by a series of unemployment compensation cases, in which the Court insisted that burdens on religious freedom be subjected to the strict scrutiny of the compelling state interest test (see THOMAS V. REVIEW BOARD OF INDIANA, HOBBIE V. UNEMPLOYMENT APPEALS COMMISSION OF FLORIDA, and FRAZEE V. ILLINOIS DEPARTMENT OF SECURITY). This compelling state interest standard remained the dominant approach to balancing religious rights against other interests until the decision in EMPLOYMENT DIVISION V. SMITH (1990), when the majority opinion explicitly limited the *Sherbert* approach to unemployment compensation cases. Congress attempted to reinstate the *Sherbert* standard by passing the RELIGIOUS FREEDOM RESTORATION ACT. Since the Supreme Court overturned that law in BOERNE, CITY OF V. FLORES (1997), the fate of the *Sherbert* standards remains unclear.

See also BLUE LAWS.

—Bette Novit Evans

Sider, Ronald J. (1939–) *activist, evangelist*

As founder and president of EVANGELICALS FOR SOCIAL ACTION, Ron Sider is best known for his commitment to a biblically rooted notion of economic and SOCIAL JUSTICE. Through his work as an author, speaker, professor, and activist, Sider has continually challenged his fellow evangelical Christians to fulfill what he believes is a moral responsibility to provide for the needs of the poor. Throughout his career, Sider has also championed many other issues he feels the Bible clearly commands, such as gender equality, preserving the natural environment, and promoting international peace. The issues to which Sider and Evangelicals for Social Action are devoted cause them to be characterized as liberal, but Sider's views have evolved steadily since the late 1970s, and his policy agenda resists categorization.

For most of his adult life, Sider's religious faith has found a significant portion of its expression through his political and social activism. Shortly after receiving a Ph.D. in history from Yale University in 1969, Sider was involved in a Chicago gathering of evangelical Christians who had come together to discuss the gospel's call to social activism. There they drafted the "Chicago Declaration of Evangelical Social Concern." That 1973 declaration became the seed out of which Evangelicals for Social Action was officially born in 1978. Around this same time, Sider published what remains his best-known work, *Rich Christians in an Age of Hunger* (1977). In this book, Sider draws attention to the existence of institutions that create inequality (like capitalism) and the Christian's responsibility to combat them. Along with the other members of Evangelicals for Social Action, Sider believed that Christians tended to place too much emphasis on individual sin while ignoring structural sin. These structural sins, which are largely economic, needed to be addressed if Christians were to have any hope of approximating the example of Christian community modeled in the New Testament. To this end, Sider proposed ideas that were perceived as radical (and were sometimes quite unwelcome) by fellow evangelicals. Particularly controversial was Sider's suggestion of a graduated tithe (a model, he said, was utilized in his own family, though he was careful not to prescribe this arrangement for everyone) in which the percentage, not just the amount, of a person's financial offering would increase as annual income increased. Sider's point was not to impose specific guidelines, but to encourage his fellow Christians to think about ways to extricate themselves from what was becoming a very materialistic culture.

After the original publication of *Rich Christians in an Age of Hunger,* Sider drew criticism from a range of detractors. Among his most outspoken critics were fellow Christians, some of whom were uncomfortable with Sider's leaning toward MARXISM/COMMUNISM, and economists who questioned his understanding of their field. Sider continued to publish, answering his critics and beginning a dialogue on the issues. The most recent version of *Rich Christians in an Age of Hunger,* a 20th-anniversary edition, reflects the evolution of Sider's ideas. He admitted to having been naive about economic realities and even expressed some approval of market economies and their ability to help alleviate poverty, particularly in Asia. Sider's approach to the problems he cares about most deeply has evolved into a much more pragmatic one over the years. Recently, he has been willing to support traditionally conservative proposals like school VOUCHERS and faith-based programs that address hunger and poverty if they can be shown to achieve the desired results.

In addition to serving as executive director of Evangelicals for Social Action and professor of theology and culture at Eastern Baptist Theological Seminary in Wynnewood, Pa., Sider continues to publish. His long list of influential books includes *Rich Christians in an Age of Hunger* (1977), *Christ and Violence* (1979), *Nuclear Holocaust and Christian Hope* (with Richard K. Taylor, 1982), and *Just Generosity: A New Vision for Overcoming Poverty in America* (1999).

See also CAMPOLO, ANTHONY; EVANGELICALISM.

Further reading: Fowler, Robert Booth, Allen D. Hertzke, and Laura R. Olson. *Religion and Politics in America: Faith, Culture, and Strategic Choices.* Boulder, Colo.: Westview Press, 1999; Sider, Ronald J. *Rich Christians in an Age of Hunger.* Downers Grove, Ill.: InterVarsity Press, 1977.

—Andrea E. Moore

Smith, Alfred Emanuel (1873–1944) *politician*

One of the many marks that Alfred "Al" Smith left on American politics was his legacy as the first Roman Catholic candidate for president of the United States, in 1928. The religious flavor of Smith's defining political moment would in some ways eclipse the many other notable hallmarks of his long record of public life.

Born and raised in New York City, Al Smith captured the spirit of many immigrant groups, especially those living in large urban areas. Growing up in the tenement buildings of Manhattan's Lower East Side was an equally defining time in Smith's life. Smith served as an altar boy at Saint James Roman Catholic Church and attended the local Catholic school. When his father died, he was forced to drop out of school in the eighth grade. He held a number of odd jobs in his late teens and early twenties but found time to participate in a variety of church-sponsored activities such as performing in the St. James Dramatic Society. Smith married Catherine Dunn in 1890 and they raised five children together.

Like many politicians, Smith's political fortunes were determined at an early age and in the local New York City neighborhoods. Tom Foley, a local Democratic precinct leader and member of the infamous Tammany Hall political machine in New York City, befriended him. Smith's alliance with Foley was to serve him well when, because of his loyal service, Smith was hired to the much-sought-after position of process server. In 1903, Smith became the Democratic nominee for a seat in the New York State Assembly. He followed a path of quick succession in New York State politics using his wit, charm, and reputation for honesty. Smith was appointed head of the powerful Assembly Ways and Means Committee and eventually became speaker of the assembly in 1913.

Speaker Smith was a fervent supporter of progressive reforms in New York City and advanced this agenda in his candidacy for governor of New York. In 1911, on the heels of the famous Triangle Waist Company fire that took the lives of 146 women and children, Smith actively pursued his agenda of reform by pushing for legislation that addressed workers' compensation, health, sanitation, and minimum-wage requirements. Many reforms were enacted despite wide opposition from big business. He equally advanced a number of good government reforms and administrative reorganizations for the city of New York, including home rule provisions. His reform agenda was enough to carry him through in a narrow victory as governor but left a large Republican majority in the state legislature.

As governor, Smith continued actively supporting a series of progressive reforms. He also vetoed several antisedition bills, including one bill that would have required the expulsion of members of the Socialist Party from the State Assembly. His second term as governor witnessed an extension of his agenda that included rather distinctive acts such as granting clemency and pardons to unpopular political dissidents. In addition, he took steps to essentially outlaw the KU KLUX KLAN in New York State.

Smith's gubernatorial career would be characterized as the "in-and-out" governor of New York. Largely as a result of his active support of a progressive agenda, Smith lost his reelection bid but returned as governor in 1922, 1924, and 1926. During this period Smith made a national name for himself as a close ally of the progressive reform movement.

Despite his national stature, Smith was unable to secure the Democratic Party nomination for president in 1924. The religious divides that characterized American politics in an implicit and explicit fashion in the early and mid-20th century squelched Smith's chances to secure a nomination. In 1928, Smith again was positioned as the Democratic standard-bearer but faced criticism over his ties to his ROMAN CATHOLIC CHURCH. Political antagonists strongly suggested that Smith's loyalty would be to the Vatican rather than the U.S. Constitution. Smith vehemently affirmed his belief in the SEPARATION OF CHURCH AND STATE, and he secured the nomination at the convention.

Many political scientists have characterized the 1928 campaign for the presidency as one of the most race- and religion-oriented contests in American history. In many respects, the urban-rural divide, the Catholic issue, the prohibitionist debate, and bigotry (as manifested in many nasty campaign activities) dominated the campaign. Smith's campaign is often highlighted as the beginning of a fundamental realignment in party politics (bringing together urban Catholics and other ethnic voters) that occurred with the election of Democrat FRANKLIN DELANO ROOSEVELT in 1932. However, Smith's campaign strategy equally ignored important states and was too focused on areas of narrow support (such as big business). Smith lost all the southern states and even his home state of New York. Herbert Hoover and the Republican Party swept to victory.

Smith then became president of the Empire State Corporation following the realization that a return to power in New York would be eclipsed by Roosevelt's surprising victory in the gubernatorial race of 1928. Smith's anti-Roosevelt inclinations came to the fore as Smith realized that Roosevelt was quickly rising as a national candidate for the presidential nomination. Once Roosevelt was in the White House, Smith frequently attacked him and his programs on the basis of elitism and concerns about large federal government. His opposition continued in 1932 and again in 1936. The onset of World War II healed the rift between Roosevelt and Smith, though, and Smith actively supported the Roosevelt administration's war efforts.

Smith's wife died in 1943 and Smith died a year later from lung disease at the age of 70. Smith's distinction as the consummate Catholic politician followed him into death. After a major funeral at St. Patrick's Cathedral in New York City, Alfred E. Smith became only the second layperson accorded the honor of lying in state in the cathedral.

See also CATHOLICS AND THE DEMOCRATIC PARTY; RELIGION IN THE 1928 PRESIDENTIAL ELECTION.

—Robert W. Smith

Smith, Joseph (1805–1844) *religious founder*

Joseph Smith was born December 23, 1805, in Sharon, Vermont, and was the founder of the Church of Jesus Christ of LATTER-DAY SAINTS (Mormons). At the age of 14, Joseph Smith was searching for religious truth when he claimed to have a heavily visitation from God the Father and Jesus Christ.

He was told that through him, a restoration of Christ's original church would take place. Nine years later, he translated a record written by ancient prophets that was engraved on gold plates. The resulting book, *The Book of Mormon,* was published in 1830, when Smith was 24 years old. He organized the Church of Jesus Christ of Latter-day Saints on April 6, 1830, in Fayette, New York. In his short life, he established the church's theology through the *Book of Mormon,* the *Doctrine and Covenants,* a book of Joseph's revelations, and the *Pearl of Great Price,* which contains Smith's translations of ancient papyri. He also undertook a retranslation of the Bible, but he was killed before its completion.

Smith's life was consumed with sustaining the church in the face of tremendous persecution. Church members were driven out of their homes in five different locations. Smith himself was harassed by dozens of criminal and civil lawsuits, was often imprisoned, was tarred, feathered, and beaten, and was

Joseph Smith *(Library of Congress)*

even sentenced to die by an illegal court martial of the Missouri militia while they laid siege to the Mormon city of Far West, Missouri. His life was spared when Brigadier General of the Missouri State Militia Alexander Doniphan protested and refused to obey the order; he was imprisoned instead.

In Kirtland, Ohio, he helped introduce the United Order, an egalitarian economic system. He also started a bank, but its failure in the recession of 1837 generated so much hostility that he had to flee to Missouri. Church members were twice evicted in Missouri during the 1830s, the last time after the governor of Missouri gave an order to exterminate the Mormons or remove them from the state. State officials were either indifferent or hostile to the Saints, so Smith appealed to President Van Buren and other federal officials for redress for their financial losses. But federal officials deemed it a state matter and refused to intervene. Joseph Smith briefly ran for president in 1844 to publicize the church members' desperate plight after their expulsion from Missouri, but he was murdered soon after his declaration.

Smith believed political clout and autonomy were necessary to protect church members from persecution. In Illinois, he laid out the city of Nauvoo and successfully instituted a charter granting self-governance to the city. The charter allowed the city government to do anything not in conflict with either the state or the national constitutions. An Illinois court martial elected Smith mayor and leader of the city's militia, the Nauvoo Legion. The Mormons' political dominance in Hancock County was resented by non-Mormons. Tensions mounted when the Nauvoo City Council ordered the mayor to destroy the printing press of the *Expositor,* an anti-Mormon newspaper. Smith was arrested and imprisoned in the Carthage, Illinois, jail, where he was shot and killed by a mob on June 27, 1844. He was 38 years old.

Joseph Smith's teachings and revelations contain many statements relevant to politics. Many were meant to reassure a hostile nation that church members were not disloyal or threatening. He taught: "We believe in being subject to kings, presidents, rulers and magistrates, and in obeying, honoring and sustaining the law." He also taught that governments are "instituted of God for the benefit of man." He introduced the LDS belief that the U.S. Constitution was inspired by God: "The Constitution of the United States is a glorious standard; it is founded in the wisdom of God." Nevertheless, he thought it inadequate to protect unpopular minorities: "Although it provides that all men shall enjoy religious freedom, yet it does not provide the manner by which the freedom can be preserved, nor for the punishment of Government officers who refuse to protect the people in their religious rights, or punish those mobs, states, or communities who interfere with the rights of the people on account of their religion . . . those who have the misfortune to be weak or unpopular are left to the merciless rage of popular fury."

See also COUNCIL OF FIFTY; MORMON EXTERMINATION ORDER; POLYGAMY; *REYNOLDS V. UNITED STATES;* YOUNG, BRIGHAM.

Further reading: Smith, Joseph Fielding. *Teachings of the Prophet Joseph Smith.* Salt Lake City: Church of Jesus Christ of Latter-day Saints, 1938; Smith, Joseph, Jr. *History of the Church of Jesus Christ of Latter-Day Saints.* Salt Lake City: Deseret Books, 1978; ———. *The Doctrine and Covenants of the Church of Jesus Christ of Latter-Day Saints.* Salt Lake City: Church of Jesus Christ of Latter-Day Saints, 1989.

—Jeffrey C. Fox

social capital

Social capital completes a triumvirate that also includes physical and human capital. It specifically refers to connections among individuals, or social networks, that foster trust and norms of reciprocity. From its conceptual beginnings, social capital has been intertwined with the study of religion. Voluntary associations are seedbeds for social networks, and as the most common form of association in the United States, religious organizations thus play an integral role in building social capital.

Although social capital has become synonymous with the work of political scientist Robert D. Putnam, he did not coin the term. Rather, in his landmark book, *Making Democracy Work: Civic Traditions in Modern Italy,* Putnam borrowed the term from sociologist James S. Coleman. While other, earlier uses of the term can be cited, the bulk of contemporary social capital research is an intellectual heir to Coleman's work. Coleman initially employed the concept of social networks as a form of capital to explain the academic success of students in Roman Catholic schools. In the 1980s, Coleman was the principal investigator of a major study that found that students in Catholic schools outperformed their peers in public schools. This finding was contrary to the conventional wisdom among education sociologists, and while still controversial, has nonetheless been replicated in a number of subsequent studies. Coleman credited the tight-knit communities in which many Catholic schools are embedded for the academic success of their students. The personal interaction of neighbors at various social functions, most of which were centered around the parish and/or school, provided a means for social norms to be enforced. Among these norms is the need for youth to succeed in school. In other words, parents were not the only ones watching out for the educational welfare of their children; their neighbors were watching out for them too.

Coleman hoped to use social capital as a theoretical bridge between sociology and economics, and thus he developed general applications of the concept. In that spirit, Putnam adapted Coleman's fundamental insights about the way personal interactions give rise to norms to explain the wide variation in the performance of regional governments in Italy. Putnam argued that it was in those Italian regions where social capital had historically been nurtured through voluntary associations that the dilemmas of collective action could best be overcome. Sounding like a contemporary Alexis de Tocqueville but armed with the tools of modern social science, Putnam characterized voluntary associations as providing social lubricant that smooths the operation of public institutions. Given Coleman's work, it is ironic that Putnam characterized the Catholic dominance of southern Italy as inhibiting social capital. While by no means a focus of the book, Putnam does note that as a hierarchical organization, the ROMAN CATHOLIC CHURCH in Italy does not foster the horizontal relationships that are the wellspring of social capital.

Putnam followed *Making Democracy Work* with an article and then a book sharing the title BOWLING ALONE. In both, Putnam turns his attention to the level of social capital in the United States. The phrase "bowling alone" is a metaphor for the state of civic engagement in America. League bowling has declined precipitously, a trend mirrored in many other forms of association. In "Bowling Alone," the article published in 1995, Putnam restricts his attention to Americans' declining rates of involvement in formal associations, including religious organizations. The book, published five years later, exhaustively details myriad forms of association, both formal and informal. With only a few exceptions, involvement in these associations—and thus, social capital—follows the same downward trajectory.

Trends aside, Putnam details how churches, synagogues, and mosques have long been a primary source of social capital in the United States. Religious participation is correlated with numerous other types of collective action. In particular, the capacity for collective action among members of religious organizations often leads to their members' involvement in politics, giving American politics a moral tinge unique among the world's industrialized democracies.

While this brief summary has focused on the intellectual pioneering of Coleman and Putnam, research on the causes and consequences of social capital burgeons across many academic disciplines, including economics, sociology, political science, urban planning, and public health. This wide diffusion means that the term *social capital* is often defined in different ways, even within a single academic field. Perhaps for this reason, critics have charged social capital with being a nebulous, even theoretically vacuous concept. When reading literature employing the concept of social capital, therefore, one should pay close attention to how it is defined and measured.

See also: DEMOCRACY IN AMERICA; POLITICAL PARTICIPATION; VOLUNTARISM.

Further reading: Coleman, James S. *Foundations of Social Theory.* Cambridge, Mass.: Harvard University Press, 1990; Coleman, James S., and Thomas B. Hoffer. *Public and Private High Schools: The Impact of Communities.* New York: Basic Books, 1987; Putnam, Robert D. "Bowling Alone: America's Declining Social Capital." *Journal of Democracy,* 6, no. 1 (1995): 65–78; ———. *Making Democracy Work: Civic Traditions in Modern Italy.* Princeton, N.J.: Princeton University Press, 1993; ———. *Bowling Alone: The Collapse and Revival of American Community.* New York: Simon and Schuster, 2000.

—David E. Campbell

Social Gospel

The Social Gospel was a social reform movement that emerged in American Protestant churches at the end of the 19th century and flourished into the 20th century. It called for a recommitment by Christians to establishing social justice, criticized capitalistic ideals that propelled American industrialization, and called for specific social and economic reforms. Although movement leaders were concerned about increasing economic disparities and dismal living conditions, particularly among the urban poor, they also were optimistic that modern technology and social science could address these problems. The potential for a new era of social justice led some to conclude that the final conquest of evil and the arrival of the Kingdom of God were at hand. Walter Rauschenbusch wrote that human nature contains an "immense latent perfectibility" that could be actualized if modern social forces could be harnessed through science and used for the development of a just and "true social life." The Social Gospel was criticized by EVANGELICALS and other conservatives for its liberal theological roots that deemphasized the doctrine of original sin and sometimes also for its millenarian inclinations.

Concern for social conditions began to emerge within American churches soon after the Civil War. By 1870, a visible group of American clergy was working to promote awareness of social injustices. These early Social Gospel leader were influenced by European Christian Socialists such as Frederick Denison Maurice and Charles Kingsley and by German liberal theologians such as Albrecht Ritschl. The movement was largely confined to urban mainline PROTESTANTISM, since evangelicals were concentrated in rural areas away from the urban poverty that accompanied industrialization. The early Social Gospel leaders included Washington Gladden, Henry George, and Josiah Strong. Gladden was a Congregational minister who ministered to the poor in Springfield, Massachusetts, and Columbus, Ohio, and also published prolifically. Among his better-known works are *Tools and the Man* (1893) and *Social Salvation* (1902). Throughout his long public life, Gladden advocated for the rights of organized labor and for public ownership of utilities. George was a journalist and tax-reform advocate who published fierce attacks on American capitalism, for example, *Progress and Poverty* (1879), and who proclaimed a millenarian vision of a perfected American society. George ran for mayor of New York City in 1886. Upon his death in 1897, 100,000 people were said to have filed past his funeral bier. From 1886 to 1898, Josiah Strong led the Evangelical Alliance, an interdenominational organization dedicated to advancing mission work within the United States and abroad. Strong was a forceful advocate for the urban poor and organized a series of Interdenominational Congresses (1885, 1887, 1889, and 1893) to address their needs. Although in 1898, Strong's radical social views cost him the leadership of the Evangelical Alliance, his model of interdenominational cooperation already had became a lasting feature of the Social Gospel. The Federal Council of Churches (1908) and the Men and Religion Forward Movement (1911) are both examples of interdenominational cooperation inspired in part by the Social Gospel.

Today, Walter Rauschenbusch is most commonly associated with the Social Gospel. A Baptist minister, Rauschenbusch was pastor of a small church near New York City's Hell's Kitchen from 1886 to 1897. Shocked by urban poverty, he joined the Social Gospel and worked on George's 1886 mayoral campaign. Rauschenbusch soon became a leading Baptist critic of the capitalist system and an advocate of socialist economic reforms. After joining the faculty of Rochester Theological Seminary in 1897, Rauschenbusch wrote *Christianity and the Social Crisis* (1907), considered the classic Social Gospel treatise. In it and in later books, including *Christianizing the Social Order* (1912) and *A Theology for the Social Gospel* (1917), Rauschenbusch interpreted the social teachings of the Old and New Testaments, critiqued the American social order, and called for a new commitment within the church to the realization of the Kingdom of God through social and economic reform.

By the 1920s, the Social Gospel was well established within mainline American Protestantism. Social criticism became a common feature of mainline church publications, and the Social Gospel was well entrenched at leading seminaries. Beyond the churches, the Social Gospel combined with Roman Catholics' social criticisms, as first articulated in the Bishop's Program of Social Reconstruction (1919), to play a prominent role in American public debate throughout the early 20th century. In the 1930s, the movement was vindicated to a degree when much of its platform became government policy through President Franklin D. Roosevelt's New Deal.

Further reading: Ahlstrom, Sydney E. "The Social Gospel." In *A Religious History of the American People.* Edited by Sydney E. Ahlstrom. New Haven, Conn.: Yale University Press, 1972; Hudson, Winthrop S., and John Corrigan. *Religion in America.* 6th ed. Upper Saddle River, N.J.: Prentice Hall, 1999; Rauschenbusch, Walter. *Christianity and the Social Crisis.* New York: Macmillan, 1907.

—James Paul Old

social justice

Social justice is grounded in the general principles of justice. In general, the application of justice aims at giving each person what he or she is due, and implies that members of a community or society are concerned for the equality and rights of all. Social justice can involve substantive, retributive, corrective, commutative, and distributive forms of justice, and although *social justice* as a term is fairly recent in origin, the concept of justice as a social virtue can be found in early Near East texts. Since the 19th century, social justice has referred to the achievement of a socioeconomic situation in which all individuals and groups in a society are treated fairly and equally, regardless of race, gender, or any other attribute.

Social justice includes a concern for individual and human rights, equality under the law, fair application of law, distribution of resources, fairness of wages, and fair exchange of goods. Social justice as a concept has a long association with several world religions, extending as far back as the Mesopotamian Kingdom of Samaria (2850–2360 B.C.E.) and the First Intermediate Kingdom of Egypt (2181–2050 B.C.E.), both of which influenced the concept of social justice that would emerge from neighboring Israel. In early Near East texts, social justice is expressed as communal responsibility for fatherless children, widows, and those considered poor or weak. In Hebrew texts, prophets often address social injustice, taking a critical stance toward unethical social and political behavior.

The concept of social justice emerging from the early Near East was retained in subsequent Western religious thought, with an emphasis on the distribution of society's resources according to need. By the late 19th century, religious institutions began responding to the social transformation emerging from the process of industrialization, resulting in the development of social ethics, and an increased emphasis on the SOCIAL GOSPEL and distributive justice. The actual term *social justice* appeared beginning in the early 19th century in several Roman Catholic political texts, most notably those generated by the French movement for social Catholicism, but by the end of the century had come into common use in other religious and political fields. In 1891, Pope Leo XIII explicitly referred to social justice in the encyclical RERUM NOVARUM (*On the Condition of Workers*), after which the concept was given regular consideration by Catholic writers. In a work entitled *Social Justice* (1900), a collection of university lectures delivered by the American political scientist W. W. Willoughby, *social justice* is defined as involving "the proper distribution of goods" and "the harmonizing of the principles of liberty and law, of freedom and coercion."

In the 20th century, *social justice* was further defined in theoretical works, such as those that addressed related issues of legal justice and its application, as well as through collective action. Social justice became an important issue in several U.S. Christian denominations, and was publicly addressed as early as 1898 in the Congregationalist weekly *The Kingdom*. The Central Conference of American Rabbis adopted their Social Justice Program (1920), and the REFORM JEWISH Congregations adopted a Ritual of Social Justice on the Day of Atonement (1922). In 1931, Pope PIUS XI issued the encyclical *Quadragesimo Anno,* clearly establishing social justice as a necessary, permanent concern of the Vatican and faithful Catholics. In the United States, religious communities have frequently generated discussion and action aimed at achieving social justice. The 19th-century ABOLITIONIST MOVEMENT was an early expression of the concern religious communities and believers had for social justice and the need for religious believers to engage in political action. In the 20th century, the concept of social justice became clearly defined, influencing and motivating many of the leaders and participants, often from religious communities, in the American CIVIL RIGHTS MOVEMENT. Similarly, the concern for social justice continues to play an important role in COMMUNITY ORGANIZING, and the critical attention given by citizens to domestic and foreign policy. Social justice continues to be a concept of primary importance that motivates religious believers and citizens to engage in individual and collective action that advocates an economically and politically just society.

Further reading: Dawley, Alan. *Struggles for Justice: Social Responsibility and the Liberal State.* Cambridge, Mass.: Harvard University Press, 2000; Miller, David. *Principles of Social Justice.* Cambridge, Mass.: Harvard University Press, 1999; Tyler, Tom R. *Social Justice in a Diverse Society.* Boulder, Colo.: Westview Press, 1997; Willoughby, W. W. *Social Justice.* New York: Macmillan, 1900.

—Lora L. Stone

Southern Baptist Convention (SBC)

The Southern Baptist Convention (SBC) is the nation's largest Protestant denomination, with almost 16 million members in over 39,000 congregations. Long the unofficially established church of the South, the SBC is now a national body, extended by migration and evangelism into every state. The SBC's membership growth, increasing CONSERVATISM, and growing activism have made it an important political force.

Southern Baptists have always been involved in politics. Emerging from the Reformation's radical wing, colonial Baptists faced widespread persecution from established churches and gladly joined JAMES MADISON and THOMAS JEFFERSON in the fight for SEPARATION OF CHURCH AND STATE. Their beliefs on adult baptism, individual competence to interpret Scripture, congregational autonomy, and a nonprofessional clergy were both shaped by and fostered American democratic culture. In one sense, however, the SBC itself began in a less democratic vein, when Southern Baptists left the national movement in 1845 in a quarrel over slaveholding MISSIONARIES. A religious harbinger of the Civil War, this breach has never been repaired.

After the Civil War, Southern Baptists began a steady expansion. During the 1920s the SBC centralized by creating the Cooperative Program, in which churches merged funds for mission agencies and seminaries. The program's rousing success created a strong denominational identity and encouraged organizational isolation. With few exceptions, Southern Baptists strenuously avoided ECUMENISM, even with other conservative Protestants, for most of the 20th century.

During this expansionist era, Southern Baptist politics was muted, limited by church-state separationism and premillennialist passivity. But political quietism sometimes gave way to sporadic activism on "moral" issues such as PROHIBITION, gambling, and evolution. Whatever the extent of political involvement, Southern Baptist ideology was deeply conservative, usually buttressing the social, racial, and political status quo. By 1970, however, SBC leaders were inching toward the political center and calling for more civic engagement, a move epitomized by the 1976 election of Southern Baptist JAMES EARL CARTER to the presidency.

This shift toward the center was soon challenged. Beginning in 1979, SBC conservatives, or "fundamentalists," campaigned to eject its "moderate" leaders, who had supposedly allowed infiltration of the denomination by theological and political "liberals." After 15 years of massive mobilization and close elections at annual meetings, the victorious conservatives finally purged their foes from SBC agencies and seminaries.

Beyond the religious ramifications, this revolution fundamentally reshaped SBC politics. The conservative leaders were invariably either Christian Right notables or fellow travelers. During annual meetings in the 1980s, political controversies often garnered as much attention as the theological strife. By 1991, however, SBC annual convention resolutions were fully aligned with the Christian Right agenda on abortion, gay rights, PRAYER IN PUBLIC SCHOOLS, education VOUCHERS, parental choice, and other matters.

The conservative insurgents also "defunded" the BAPTIST JOINT COMMITTEE ON PUBLIC AFFAIRS (BJC). long the SBC's voice on religious liberty issues and a staunch defender of church-state separation. To compensate, they broadened the responsibilities of the Christian Life Commission (CLC), once the SBC's "liberal social conscience," but now veering right. During the 1990s, the CLC was rebaptized the Ethics and Public Policy Commission (EPPC) and built a well-staffed Washington office, led by activist Richard Land. The EPPC quickly moved into a vigorous political role, occasionally on the liberal side (on RACISM and hunger), but most often in alliance with the Christian Right on abortion, gay rights, and other moral issues. Land also encouraged closer SBC cooperation with other orthodox groups, such as the NATIONAL ASSOCIATION OF EVANGELICALS.

During the presidential elections of 1992 and 1996, EPPC activities such as the distribution of VOTER GUIDES in Baptist churches clearly favored the Republican tickets over fellow Southern Baptists WILLIAM JEFFERSON CLINTON and Al Gore. Not surprisingly, SBC leaders provided little help for Clinton objectives while he was in office. His early actions reversing abortion limitations put in place by RONALD REAGAN and George H. W. Bush, proposing to allow gays in the military, and nominating social liberals to important posts quickly eliminated any possibility of cooperation. At the 1993 SBC convention, some 20 resolutions critical of Clinton's policies were finally combined in an admonition to Clinton and Gore to "affirm biblical morality in exercising public office." An abortive effort was even made to "withdraw fellowship" from both men, while representatives from Clinton's church in Little Rock, Arkansas, were required to state their personal opposition to homosexuality before being seated. Ed Young, whose Second Baptist Church of Houston was famous for its extensive program of political activity, was reelected SBC president without opposition.

Throughout the second Clinton administration, SBC leaders remained fierce critics of the Clinton administration's social policies. During the Monica Lewinsky scandal, they also condemned his personal behavior and supported IMPEACHMENT OF WILLIAM JEFFERSON CLINTON. By the end of the decade then, SBC leaders were strongly aligned with the Republican Party. Similarly, Southern Baptists in Congress increasingly were found on the GOP side of the aisle, including party leaders such as Representatives Newt Gingrich (R-Ga.), Tom DeLay (R-Tex.), and J.C. Watts (R-Okla.) in the House, and Trent Lott (R-Miss.), the Senate Republican leader.

In the Republican primaries of 2000, several SBC leaders advised the campaign of Texan GEORGE W. BUSH and, in the general election, Southern Baptist officials clearly favored the UNITED METHODIST Bush over fellow Southern Baptist Al Gore, as did the great majority of local clergy. Thus, the SBC has become a bulwark of the religious coalition within the Republican Party.

This greater political activity coincided with new institutional challenges. SBC growth slowed during the 1990s, and was concentrated among minorities, especially Hispanics and African Americans. Contributions stagnated in part because some moderate churches diverted mission funds to alternative agencies such as the Cooperative Baptist Fellowship, while SBC seminaries suffered from leadership and faculty changes. Despite these internal problems, the SBC remains a consistent voice for conservatism in national politics.

See also CHRISTIAN RIGHT AND THE REPUBLICAN PARTY; RELIGION IN THE 1992, 1994, 1996, 2000, PRESIDENTIAL ELECTIONS.

Further reading: Ammerman, Nancy T. *Baptist Battles.* New Brunswick, N.J.: Rutgers University Press, 1990; Guth, James L. "The Mobilization of a Religious Elite: Political Activism among Southern Baptist Clergy in 1996." In *Christian Clergy in American Politics.* Edited by Sue E. S. Crawford and Laura R. Olson. Baltimore: Johns Hopkins University Press, 2001; Smith, Oran P. *The Rise of Baptist Republicanism.* New York: New York University Press, 1997.

—James L. Guth

Southern Christian Leadership Conference

The Southern Christian Leadership Conference (SCLC) originated in 1957 from antisegregation BUS BOYCOTTS in the South led by African-American clergymen. MARTIN LUTHER KING JR., who became the president of the Montgomery Improvement Association (MIA) in 1955, had been so impressive in his leadership of the Montgomery bus boycott that he was easily made the head of SCLC, which was to be a regional civil rights organization that could draw on the network of black churches in direct action efforts. Traditionally, churches had been the center of the southern African-American community, as they were a safe place for uninterrupted discussion, interaction, and political organization. Although it was not a sectarian organization, most of the members of SCLC were Baptist, as were the majority of the organization's leaders.

King's gospel message of liberation combined with his emphasis, derived from Mohandas Gandhi, of nonviolence garnered considerable media attention, but at first little of the focus was directed toward SCLC itself, but rather to King. On the whole, however, King's nonviolent resistance successfully tapped into two seemingly opposing strands of Christian thought: the ethical imperative to help the poor and suffering, and the otherworldly, self-sacrificial motives of past Christian martyrs. The moral impeccability of King's insistence of refusing to try to right a wrong with another wrong was a strong force in the CIVIL RIGHTS MOVEMENT, although King was frequently demonized by many outside the movement as a radical and troublemaker. As the 1960s drew on, King was more frequently challenged from within the Civil Rights movement as well for using a method that was thought to be too passive and ineffective.

SCLC's first campaign was the notably unsuccessful 1958 "Crusade for Citizenship," an attempt to register African-American voters. After reorganization, SCLC took center stage in the national consciousness in 1963 with a very successful campaign against segregation in Birmingham, Alabama, in which many activists were jailed. The televised images of May 2, however, with peaceful young marchers in the "Children's Crusade" being attacked by police dogs and fiercely hosed back with water shocked many and became a decisive moment. The contrast between the violence of the local government and the suffering dignity of the children is believed to have been crucial in swinging public support toward civil rights. On May 10, official desegregation was announced in Birmingham, although violence toward African Americans continued, and the federal government became increasingly aware of the surging demand for civil rights.

Later, in August 1963, SCLC participated in the MARCH ON WASHINGTON, with over 200,000 marchers, in which King's resonant "I Have a Dream" speech used the cadences of a sermon and allusions to religious meaning and obligation to outline SCLC's vision of attaining brotherhood and equality by "meeting physical force with soul force." The next year, SCLC scored a victory in the passage of the Civil Rights Act of 1964.

Voting rights were still at issue in the South, however, and SCLC joined with the CONGRESS OF RACIAL EQUALITY (CORE) and other civil rights organizations in forming a voter registration drive and planning a 1964 march in Alabama, leading from Selma to Montgomery, to urge the repeal of all the mechanisms, including notoriously unjust voter qualification tests, that local officials could use to deny the vote to African Americans. Once again, television provided shocking images of police brutality against peaceful marchers. Although the police managed to prevent the march at first, SCLC went to court to secure their right to march without interference, which they then completed in March 1964. A year later, the Voting Rights Act of 1965 was passed, another major achievement.

From 1965 on, King began to turn to the North—citing the unspoken discrimination within northern cities as even more difficult to counteract than the legal injustices of the South—and to be more concerned with the staggering racial economic disparities in America, initiating Operation Breadbasket and his 1968 Poor People's Campaign.

On April 4, 1968, however, King was assassinated. This event seemingly lent credence to other civil rights groups that proclaimed the need for stronger forms of struggle than simple nonviolent resistance. Reverend RALPH ABERNATHY took over the presidency of SCLC until 1977, when Reverend Joseph Lowery succeeded him, but without King the organization seemed adrift, having lost much of its power and purpose from its early years. In December 1971, the Reverend JESSE JACKSON, who was to become the most prominent African-American politician of the 1980s and 1990s, split away from SCLC after several years of strained relations following King's assassination. Today the organization, which is headquartered in Atlanta and headed by Martin Luther King III, is still active, broadly concerned with improving social welfare, including preventing AIDS, and responding to injustice of many kinds. SCLC maintains commitment to nonviolent action and the conviction that religion adds unity, integrity, and direction to political and social work.

See also BLACK THEOLOGY; CHURCH BURNINGS; CIVIL DISOBEDIENCE; LIBERATION THEOLOGY; PROTESTS AND RALLIES.

—Caroline R. Sherman

southern Republican realignment

The beginning of the end of the one-party, white, Democratic South started during the JOHN F. KENNEDY/Lyndon Johnson administrations, when national Republican and Democratic leaders repositioned dramatically their party's stances on social policy in response to the CIVIL RIGHTS MOVEMENT and the cultural upheavals of the 1960s. The inversion of the two parties' programmatic appeals on civil rights and the increasing polarization among Democratic and Republican activists in the cultural domain altered sharply preexisting cleavages in the southern electorate by simultaneously undermining white support for the national Democratic Party and providing an ideological rationale for their realignment to the Republican Party. This transformation took shape first at the presidential and then congressional and statewide levels before shaking up coalitional alignments in statehouse and local races. It proceeded unevenly across the South over the next 30 years, yet harbingers of fault lines were already visible in two controversies that flared up earlier in the century and spilled into the electoral arena.

The one-party Democratic South emerged soon after the end of Reconstruction and Republican dominance of the region in 1876. Its origins lay in the fear among whites—particularly plantation owners residing in areas where former slaves made up a majority of the population—of African-American political dominance of local government. The rationale for southern white political solidarity was white supremacy, which was achieved by controlling state government and thwarting federal intrusion into local politics by acting cohesively as a veto block both within the national Democratic Party and the U.S. Senate. The disenfranchisement of blacks through the use of literacy tests, poll taxes, and the "white primary" were mechanisms used to secure white control over the electoral process.

The alliance of culturally traditional and racially conservative southern whites with the Democratic Party was strained on several occasions during the first half of the 1900s before it ruptured during the second half of the century. The first split occurred in 1928, when religious and cultural concerns in response to the Democratic presidential nomination of New York governor ALFRED SMITH, who was also a Roman Catholic and an opponent of Prohibition, roused rural Protestant voters in five southern states to bolt the party. The saliency of religion and culture subsided with the defeat of Smith, and as the electorate realigned along class lines in response to the New Deal policies of FRANKLIN DELANO ROOSEVELT, and as blacks shifted allegiance to the Democratic Party, southern whites reverted to traditional voting habits. The second insurrection occurred in the presidential election of 1948, and its political ramifications were more portentous. The Strom Thurmond–led Dixiecrat revolt was a reaction among state's rights conservatives to the postwar liberalism of the national Democratic Party, particularly to its endorsement of the use of federal power to achieve black civil rights.

The political rationale for a one-party, white, Democratic South was destroyed with the passage of the 1964 Civil Rights Act and the Voting Rights Act of 1965, both sponsored by the national Democratic leadership. With the 1964 nomination of Senator Barry Goldwater (R-Ariz.), a state's rights libertarian and vocal opponent of the 1964 Civil Rights Act, and the switch of Dixiecrat Strom Thurman of South Carolina to the GOP, the ideological and political groundwork was established for a brand of Republicanism acceptable to southern whites.

The process toward realignment was hastened along by Richard Nixon's 1968 "Southern Strategy," the "McGovernization" of the Democratic Party, and RONALD REAGAN's strong appeal to religious conservatives during the 1980s. In particular, the surfacing of social issues, including especially ABORTION and women's rights, gave conservative Evangelical Protestants (and conservative Catholics) issues around which to mobilize. By the first Reagan election in 1980, the 40 percent net advantage in party identification favoring the Democrats 20 years earlier had been replaced by near parity for the Republicans. Moreover, during this same time, the proportion of southern gubernatorial, House, and Senate seats held by Republicans rose from near ground zero (0, 6.6, and 0 percent, respectively) to over 40 percent for each office. At no time before 1960 did a Republican presidential candidate win a majority of the two-party white vote in the region. Since then, no Republican presidential candidate has lost a majority of the southern white vote. At present, competitive two-party politics is the norm in the South. Other factors contributing to the nationalization of the southern electorate are migration into the region, industrialization, and television.

See also CHRISTIAN RIGHT AND THE REPUBLICAN PARTY; EQUAL RIGHTS AMENDMENT; MAINLINE PROTESTANTS AND THE REPUBLICAN PARTY.

Further reading: Key, V. O., Jr. *Southern Politics in State and Nation.* Knoxville: University of Tennessee Press, 1977 [1949]; Lamis, Alexander P. *Southern Politics in the 1990s.* Baton Rouge: Louisiana State University Press, 1999; Petrocik, John R. "Realignment: New Party Coalitions and the Nationalization of the South." *Journal of Politics.* 49 (1987): 347–375.

—Louis Bolce

Spellman, Francis Cardinal (1889–1967) *Roman Catholic cardinal*

Francis Cardinal Spellman, the Roman Catholic archbishop of New York from 1939 until his death in 1967, was born in Massachusetts in 1889. He was ordained a priest in 1916 after study at Fordham University and the North American College in Rome. After an assignment in Boston, he returned to Rome, working at the Vatican Secretariat of State. He was appointed a bishop and returned to Boston in 1932, and after seven years was named to head the New York archdiocese. During World War II, he was appointed vicar for the U.S. military. Pope Pius XII named him a cardinal in 1946.

Cardinal Spellman's influence on American politics sprang from a combination of the times, his friendships with the powerful, and the central location of his see in New York City. During the first 60 years of the 20th century, the American Catholic Church was trying to find acceptance in American life as it moved beyond its recent immigrant status. Catholic insecurity and eagerness to belong often led the church to be very conservative politically (Ellis 1969: 190). Spellman reflected this trend, fusing "the themes of Catholicism and Americanism" in his dealing with both laypeople and politicians.

The most significant partnership he formed was during his stay in Rome during the period 1920–30, when he and Eugenio Cardinal Pacelli became friends. Pacelli later became Pope Pius XII and reigned during World War II and the beginning of the cold war. The American cardinal's closeness with the pontiff, and his close relationship with President FRANKLIN DELANO ROOSEVELT, allowed Spellman to become a conduit for information between the two leaders and an emissary for them. Roosevelt relied on Catholic votes for his election and worked with Spellman to maintain close ties to the Vatican.

After the war, the church's anticommunist stance fit in well with the developing cold war mentality in Washington. Spellman spoke frequently against the "communist menace," and his writings appeared in popular magazines. In 1954, Spellman introduced Senator Joseph McCarthy (R-Wisc.) to 6,000 cheering New York police officers, and implicit endorsement of the senator's anticommunist rhetoric. He also regularly visited U.S. troops stationed in Korea.

Spellman influenced politics in other ways. He built churches, schools, and hospitals in New York, raising more than $500 million for his projects. He forbade Catholics to see "immoral" movies. He was a staunch proponent of public aid for parochial schools and once said that Eleanor Roosevelt was guilty of "discrimination unworthy of an American mother" for her opposition to public aid for Catholic schools. He also had "effective control" of bishop appointments, placing 25 of his former assistants as bishops in various dioceses around the country.

His influence waned in the late 1950s after the death of his friend Pius XII and the emergence of the Catholic peace movement. He remained a strong supporter of the VIETNAM WAR even as Pope Paul VI was asking for a negotiated settlement to the conflict. He also opposed most of the reforms of VATICAN II. But his influence was such that upon Spellman's death, President Lyndon Johnson braved crowds yelling "Hey, hey, LBJ. How many kids did you kill today?" (in reference to the rising casualty tolls in the Vietnam War) to sit in the same church as his arch-rival Senator Robert Kennedy, for the funeral. One biographer summed up Spellman's life and work by calling him the "American Pope."

See also CATHOLICS AND THE DEMOCRATIC PARTY; VATICAN RECOGNITION.

Further reading: Chandler, Russell. "Francis Cardinal Spellman." *Christianity Today* 12. December 22, 1967; Cooney, John. *The American Pope: The Life and Times of Francis Cardinal Spellman.* New York: Dell, 1984; Ellis, John Tracy. *American Catholicism.* 2d ed., Revised. Chicago: University of Chicago Press, 1969; Morris, Charles R. *American Catholic: The Saints and Sinners Who Built America's Most Powerful Church.* New York: Random House, 1997; "Roman Catholics: The Master Builder." *Time.* December 8, 1967; *Time.* "Roman Catholics: Requiem for a Cardinal." December 15, 1967.

—Paul Fabrizio

Stanton, Elizabeth Cady (1815–1902) *activist*

Born in 1815 in Johnstown, New York, Elizabeth Cady Stanton was a pivotal figure in the women's suffrage movement in America. Though less famous than her close associate, SUSAN B. ANTHONY, she is credited with giving early FEMINISM a coherent philosophical expression, which she translated into a rhetorically powerful plan of social reform. Upon her death in 1902, Stanton had played leading roles in a variety of causes, including temperance and ABOLITION, though her most significant contributions concerned the legal, social, and political advancement of women.

Academically gifted, Elizabeth Cady Stanton received a rigorous education in such subjects as Greek, mathematics, logic, and natural rights philosophy, graduating with distinction from the Johnstown Academy and the Troy Female Sem-

Elizabeth Cady Stanton *(Library of Congress)*

inary. Upon graduation, Stanton informally studied law and constitutional history in her father's law office, where she first discovered the systemic legal discrimination against women—a situation she resolved to rectify.

After she witnessed the marginalization of women within progressive movements themselves, Stanton's determination to work for women's rights was radicalized. In 1840, while attending the World Anti-Slavery Convention in London with her abolitionist husband, Henry Stanton, she observed the stinging rebuff of women delegates, whereupon she and LUCRETIA MOTT, also in attendance, vowed to take up the cause of women. Stanton and Mott made good on their promise, organizing the landmark Seneca Falls Convention in 1848 that launched the women's rights movement in the United States. Employing her notable rhetorical gifts, Stanton drafted the convention's famous "Declaration of Sentiments," which skillfully mirrored the DECLARATION OF INDEPENDENCE as it called for an end to women's oppression. After much debate and eloquent argument from Stanton, the list of resolutions passed at Seneca Falls included a demand for women's suffrage.

Stanton encountered stubborn male resistance as well to the equal participation of women in the temperance movement. In protest, she joined her new acquaintance, Susan B. Anthony, in founding the Woman's State Temperance Society (1852). Though the organization was short-lived, the friendship forged in it between Anthony and Stanton would become a lifelong, legendary partnership in social activism.

By the mid-1850s, Stanton's comprehensive vision of women's advancement was taking shape, and her agenda included a wide range of issues, from temperance to property rights to divorce reform to suffrage. Working closely with Anthony, Stanton pressed for feminist changes in New York State law. Her efforts were rewarded with the 1860 passage of the Married Woman's Property Act, which gave New York women the novel right to own property, transact business, and share custody of children. Not content to rest with gains in a single state, Stanton and Anthony campaigned widely for similar changes throughout the country, circulating petitions, giving speeches, and hosting women's rights conventions. Complementing Anthony's organizational skills and efficiency, Stanton contributed to the cause an eloquent pen and persuasive oratory, becoming an engaging public spokesperson for women's rights.

Stanton lent her talents to the cause of abolition as well. Perceiving women's oppression and slavery to be kindred evils, she cofounded with Anthony the National Woman's Loyal League, an emancipation and women's suffrage organization. After the Civil War, she and Anthony campaigned vigorously to render the Fourteenth and Fifteenth Amendments gender-inclusive, publicizing their views in the new feminist weekly, *The Revolution,* for which Stanton served as editor and Anthony as publisher.

Stanton's firm insistence that women's advancement should not be subordinated to the cause of freedmen, in addition to her demand for liberalized divorce laws among other feminist reforms, earned her a reputation for radicalism. Stanton's more conservative allies in the women's movement viewed her positions with alarm. A number of them broke from Stanton and Anthony's National Woman Suffrage Association—dedicated to securing a constitutional amendment enfranchising women—to form a more CONSERVATIVE organization. The two groups eventually reunited in 1890, however, with Stanton serving as president of the newly formed National American Woman Suffrage Association. These developments would be chronicled in the multivolume *History of Woman Suffrage,* a collaborative effort among several prominent feminists, including Stanton, Anthony, and Matilda Gage.

In addition to lecturing and lobbying for women's suffrage, Stanton's last two decades were preoccupied with writing on behalf of women's advancement more broadly. Stanton was the principal author of the Declaration of Rights for Women, featured at the 1876 Centennial Exposition in Philadelphia, and in 1878 she composed a federal suffrage amendment that

was introduced in Congress repeatedly until women were granted the vote in 1920. Most radically, she published *The Woman's Bible* (1895), a feminist critique of biblical justifications for the subordination of women and a product of her long-standing dissatisfaction with organized religion, which she considered a source of women's oppression.

Elizabeth Cady Stanton died at the age of 86, leaving the women's movement an unparalleled legacy of political and social activism coupled with radical philosophical and theological reflection.

—Jeanne M. Heffernan

Stead, William Thomas (1849–1912) *social reformer, writer*

William Thomas Stead, a Gladstonian LIBERAL social and moral reformer and editor of the *Pall Mall Gazette* (1883–89), was born in Northumberland, England, the son of a Congregational minister. His political role in America began with his founding of both a British and an American monthly, *Review of Reviews* (1890). The American *Review,* under the editorship of Albert Shaw, a noted municipal reformer and political economist closely associated with THEODORE ROOSEVELT, amply fulfilled Stead's intention to create an organ to disseminate a common cultural and political viewpoint across the English-speaking world, since, in Stead's words introducing the first edition, "The [British] Empire and the [American] Republic comprise within their limits almost all the territory that remains empty for the overflow of the world. Their citizens, with all their faults, are leading the van of civilization." The American *Review* became the authoritative organ for an internationalist perspective in the Progressive movement and provided the intellectual foundations for an actively international foreign policy.

Following extended stays in America, Stead wrote *If Christ Came to Chicago: A Plea for the Union of All Who Love in Service of All Who Suffer* (1894), a best-selling book that spawned many imitators. Following a glowing tribute to JANE ADDAMS and her Hull-House, Stead concluded with a prophecy: having already achieved first rank as the nation's transport, commercial, and financial center, Chicago was soon to be made the capital of the United States, thereby becoming the "imperial city" of the world. Through Christian-inspired reform, every Progressive's domestic and internationalist dreams had come true in a redeemed Chicago. The fruits of righteousness are harvested. To crown its achievements, the city holds a great festival. The high point is the arrival of the emperor of Germany, who has come to pay homage to "the ideal city of the world."

For Stead, this fictional account of Chicago and America was no idle dream. Both the British and the American *Review* closely monitored international trade and comparative industrial growth patterns in Europe and America. From these reports, Stead wrote a highly influential book, *The Americanization of the World* (1902). America will dominate the world, he said, not only because of its comparative economic efficiencies but also because of its success in forging the energies and talents of all the nationalities within its borders "into one dominant American type . . . [creating] one uniform texture of American civilization." Conceding America's dominance and Britain's secondary role, the book concludes with a quotation from British prime minister William Gladstone: "Will it make us, the children of the senior race, living together under [the American's] action, better or worse? How is the majestic figure, who is to become the largest and most powerful on the stage of the world's history, to make use of his power?" Stead went down with the *Titanic* in 1912.

Further reading: Eisenach, Eldon. "Progressive Internationalism." In *Progressivism and the New Democracy*. Edited by Sidney M. Milkis and Jerome M. Mileur. Amherst: University of Massachusetts Press, 1999; Whyte, Frederic. *The Life of W. T. Stead*. New York: Houghton Mifflin, 1925.

—Eldon J. Eisenach

Stenberg v. Carhart 530 U.S. 914 (2000)

In this case, the U.S. Supreme Court overturned a Nebraska statute that generally prohibited so-called partial-birth ABORTION. Justice Stephen Breyer wrote the decision for a closely divided (5-4) Court, basing the ruling on the precedent of *PLANNED PARENTHOOD OF SOUTHEASTERN PENNSYLVANIA V. CASEY* (1992).

The state law at issue here criminalized performing any partial-birth abortion that was not necessary to save the life of the pregnant woman. Violation of the law was a felony, carrying punishments of fines and imprisonment; the statute also provided for the automatic revocation of the practitioner's medical license. Two aspects of the law led to the Court's finding it unconstitutional. First, the law provided no exception to protect the health of the woman. Second, the law's definition of "partial-birth abortion" could be read to include not only the procedure generally associated with this rarely used method of abortion but also a procedure commonly employed in second trimester abortions.

Justice Breyer argued that a health exception was required in a statute that, as here, banned a particular method of abortion. This was so because under *ROE V. WADE* (1973), it was the state's interest in maternal health that justified its regulation of abortions prior to fetal viability. Furthermore, because the proscribed procedure might be medically deemed the most protective of the woman's health in a particular pregnancy, without a health exception the law would endanger rather than promote her health, just the opposite of what the Court's precedents had determined to be allowed the states in regulating the methods of abortion.

The majority opinion in *Stenberg*, as well as the dissenting opinions of Justice Anthony Kennedy and Justice Clarence Thomas, devoted considerable attention to the statute's language in order to determine whether the law's prohibition was limited to the "D and X" method (generally identified as partial-birth abortion) or could be applied to the fairly common "D and E" method. The five justices constituting the Court's majority concluded that the law's reach was broad enough to include the "D and E" procedure. This being the case, the Court held that the law created an "undue burden" on a woman's abortion choice by limiting her ability to choose the "D and E" method.

Chief Justice William Rehnquist dissented, briefly arguing that, under *Casey*, the law should be upheld. Justice ANTONIN SCALIA called for overruling *Casey* and returning the issue of abortion to the people and their elected representatives rather than leaving it in the hands of the courts. Justice Kennedy, one of the three justices who had written the *Casey* opinion, argued that the decision of the Court here did not follow *Casey's* principles. In his view, the Nebraska law neither denied a woman her right to choose to have an abortion nor placed an undue burden on the exercise of that right. Rather, the law reflected the determination by the people of Nebraska that "moral principles having their foundation in the intrinsic value of human life, including life of the unborn" ought to guide the choice among medical procedures. Justice Clarence Thomas, the final dissenter, took the abortion issue back to its beginnings, arguing that *Roe v. Wade* itself had been wrongly decided.

Several organizations filed AMICUS CURIAE BRIEFS in this case. Among those supporting the law were the FAMILY RESEARCH COUNCIL, the UNITED STATES CATHOLIC CONFERENCE, the AMERICAN CENTER FOR LAW AND JUSTICE, AGUDAT ISRAEL of America, and the KNIGHTS OF COLUMBUS. Briefs urging that the law be overturned were filed by, among others, the AMERICAN CIVIL LIBERTIES UNION and the RELIGIOUS COALITION FOR REPRODUCTIVE CHOICE.

—Susan E. Grogan

Stone v. Graham 449 U.S. 39 (1980)

In November 1980, the Supreme Court provided summary judgment in an unsigned *per curiam* decision that a Kentucky statute requiring the posting of the TEN COMMANDMENTS in public schools violated the ESTABLISHMENT CLAUSE of the First Amendment.

The Court applied the test first laid out in *LEMON V. KURTZMAN* nearly a decade earlier, though did not proceed past the first prong that snared this statute—the Court found it lacked a secular, legislative purpose. However, the Kentucky legislature had made an obvious attempt to pass this prong in the statute: "In small print below the last commandment shall appear a notation concerning the purpose of the display, as follows: 'The secular application of the Ten Commandments is clearly seen in its adoption as the fundamental legal code of Western Civilization and the Common Law of the United States.'" The Court had none of this, arguing: "The preeminent purpose for posting the Ten Commandments on schoolroom walls is plainly religious in nature." In *ABINGTON*

TOWNSHIP V. SCHEMPP, the Court faced a similar issue, striking down the mandatory recitation of the Lord's prayer in public schools, "despite the school district's assertion of such secular purposes as 'the promotion of moral values, the contradiction to the materialistic trends of our times, the perpetration of our institutions and the teaching of literature.'" Moreover, posting the Ten Commandments did not serve an education purpose, the Court argued, because it was not integrated into valid, secular curricula; it merely hangs, inviting veneration and reflection.

Justice Stewart dissented on the merits, while Chief Justice Burger and Justice Blackmun dissented on procedure, favoring a full hearing for the case.

Justice Rehnquist, solely, wrote a dissenting opinion in which he supported the claims of the state legislature and the finding of the trial court that the posting of the Ten Commandments had a valid, secular legislative purpose. He argued, "The Establishment Clause does not require that the public sector be insulated from all things which may have a religious significance or origin." According to Rehnquist, many would claim that the Ten Commandments have had a significant influence on Western legal development, therefore, their public display with a disclaimer of their secular significance should be permitted.

—Paul A. Djupe

Student Nonviolent Coordinating Committee

The trajectory of the Student Nonviolent Coordinating Committee (SNCC) in many ways mirrors that of the CIVIL RIGHTS MOVEMENT of the 1960s writ large. SNCC was founded in April 1960 at Shaw University in Raleigh, North Carolina, as a result of the Raleigh Conference, which was put together by Ella Baker of the SOUTHERN CHRISTIAN LEADERSHIP CONFERENCE (SCLC). The mission statement of the organization followed that of SCLC in emphasizing nonviolent resistance as justified by the "Judaic-Christian tradition," and early editions of *The Student Voice,* the SNCC newsletter, urged "kneel-ins" as the best new way of staging civil rights protest. These kneel-ins were considered to be the next step from the sit-ins, which—beginning with the February 1960 Woolworth's sit-in by students protesting segregation in Greensboro, North Carolina—had first drawn attention to the potential for student involvement in the civil rights struggle.

Marion Barry, who later became mayor of Washington, D.C., briefly served as the first chairman of SNCC. In November 1960, Charles ("Chuck") McDew was elected the second chairman and helped to coordinate the Freedom Rides of 1961 with the CONGRESS OF RACIAL EQUALITY (CORE). These desegregated buses were repeatedly attacked, forcing the federal government to send federal marshals to protect them from the KU KLUX KLAN and mob violence.

SNCC sponsored a variety grassroots projects from protesting segregation to food and book drives and voter registration projects. Voter registration became more prominent in 1962, however, drawing publicity and attacks. Under the leadership of John Lewis, who became chairman in June 1963, and Bob Moses, SNCC organized two 1963 Freedom Ballots, mock elections to prove that the disenfranchised would vote if allowed. SNCC then took a leading role in organizing the 1964 Freedom Summer voter registration drive, which successfully registered many but was also the occasion of the murder of three volunteers from CORE, two of whom were white. This made national headlines, drawing support for the Civil Rights movement but also exacerbating racial tensions within SNCC.

As voter registration efforts continued, SNCC began looking for other ways to help empower African Americans and, more generally, the poor and disenfranchised. Gradually, the focus of the organization turned toward poverty amelioration and SOCIAL JUSTICE, more often promoting Marxist interpretations (see MARXISM/COMMUNISM). Early on, SNCC criticized the VIETNAM WAR, arguing that African Americans and the Vietnamese were both suffering at the hands of white Americans. The emphasis on Christian nonviolence was set aside as too submissive and increasingly ineffective, and a movement began within the organization to limit the group to African-American members.

These trends were confirmed with the election of Stokeley Carmichael to the chairmanship in May 1966. Carmichael was prominent in the black power movement and believed that SNCC should be an organization of and for African Americans alone. White volunteers, even founding members, were no longer welcome, and SNCC's new politics caused a rift with other civil rights organizations, including SCLC, with which it had previously worked.

Radicalization continued in 1967 when H. Rapo Brown, now known as Jamil Abdullah Al-Amin, was elected chairman. Rap Brown emphasized the systemic violence that had historically been used against African Americans and encouraged self-defense over passivity, famously saying that violence was "as American as cherry pie." SNCC's support for the Arab side of the Six-Day War (1967) cost the organization heavily in its fund-raising efforts, and SNCC became increasingly allied with the Black Panther Party, both of which were subject to scrutiny and harassment by the Federal Bureau of Investigation's "counterintelligence programs." After the assassination of MARTIN LUTHER KING JR., the "Rap Brown Amendment" was passed prohibiting civil rights activists to travel across state lines to organize. Under a multitude of pressure, SNCC collapsed in 1970.

—Caroline R. Sherman

Sunday, William Ashley (1862–1935) *evangelist*

William Ashley ("Billy") Sunday was a turn-of-the-century firebrand Presbyterian evangelist, whose primary preaching focus was against the sin of "vile drink." He was born on November 19, 1862, in a log cabin just outside Ames, Iowa. Billy never knew his father, who died of pneumonia at an army camp in Patterson, Missouri, one month after Billy's birth. By early childhood, his mother sent him and his brother George to an orphanage. Without a high school education, he struck out on his own at age 15, working a variety of odd jobs before he used his athletic skills to become a professional baseball player. In 1883, he landed a spot on the roster of the Chicago White Stockings and played a total of eight years in the major leagues.

His life changed forever, however, when in 1886, after leaving a Chicago saloon, he stopped to hear a gospel choir perform at Pacific Garden Mission. There he had a BORN-AGAIN EXPERIENCE and was converted to Christianity. His conversion so moved him that he eventually abandoned baseball and became a full-time evangelist from 1896 until his death in 1935. While still in Chicago, he met Helen Amelia Thompson in December 1887 and married her in September 1888. She later became his strong support and mainstay, and was affectionately called "Ma Sunday."

Beginning in 1894, Sunday worked as an advance man with J. Wilbur Chapman, an evangelist, for $40 per week, turning down as much as $2,000 per month to play baseball for the Pittsburgh Pirates. By 1897, he felt ready to launch out on his own evangelistic crusade, and held his first revival meeting at Garner, Iowa. Ma Sunday began to accompany him on his evangelistic treks in 1907, handling his campaign and financial matters. His popularity was at its height just before America's entry into World War I. For example, his 1916 Detroit crusade led thousands to born-again experiences, and thousands more dollars came into the collection plates. In 1917, in one of his more famous 10-week New York campaigns, the total offering exceeded $100,000, whereupon he turned the entire offering over to the Red Cross and other World War I charities. Some 98,000 people were converted to evangelical Christianity.

Not only did the masses respond to his fiery brand of preaching, but he also attracted well-known elites in all areas of life, including business, finance, and politics. He met with both President Woodrow Wilson and Secretary of State WILLIAM JENNINGS BRYAN in 1915. During his 1916 Detroit campaign, dime-store magnate S.S. Kresge moved out of his mansion so Sunday could use it as his crusade headquarters. After one visit with Sunday, Henry Ford was reported to have commented: "if Michigan voted for PROHIBITION, the breweries could be converted to produce denatured alcohol as fuel for his cars." Michigan, in fact, voted for Prohibition.

Sunday's evangelistic fervor was centered on one primary issue: the consumption of alcohol. Once a heavy drinker himself, Sunday knew all too well the myriad of problems associated with alcoholism: broken marriages, destroyed families, wrecked jobs, and personal destruction. His sermons were laced with such lines as "There isn't a man who votes for the saloon who doesn't deserve to have his boy die a drunkard." He attacked drinkers as "dirty, low-down, whiskey-soaked, beer-guzzling, bull-necked, foul-mouthed, hypocrites." Or he would attack the drinking establishment itself by saying, "The normal way to get rid of drunkards is to quit raising drunkards—to put the business that makes drunkards out of business."

In his famous "booze" sermon, which he preached in Boston just before Prohibition took effect, he said, "I am the sworn, eternal and uncompromising enemy of the liquor traffic. I have been, and will go on, fighting that damnable, dirty, rotten business with all the power at my command." He linked drinking with increased criminal conduct by citing statistics such as "82 percent of the crime [in America, presumably] is committed by men under the influence of liquor." He also tried to show that the very presence of bars contributed to the social debauchery of the community. He ranted and raved: "The saloon is the sum of all villainies. It is worse than war or pestilence. It is the crime of crimes. It is the parent of crimes and the mother of sins." In short, Billy Sunday was one of the first evangelists to tie the gospel's spiritual message to helping to eliminate social problems, even arguing that good government should not be identified with the "saloon business."

By the time he died in 1935, he had preached to millions and led several hundred thousand to embrace Christianity. He contributed to passage of the Prohibition Amendment and the sale of war bonds. At his funeral, which was held at Chicago's

William Ashley Sunday *(Library of Congress)*

Moody Bible Church, over 3,000 people filed past his casket. Billy Sunday's legacy will be remembered as helping to transform culture and government policy through his vivid and realistic interpretation of the gospel message.

See also WILLARD, FRANCES; WOMAN'S CHRISTIAN TEMPERANCE UNION.

—Stephen M. King

Swaggart, Jimmy (1935–) *televangelist*

Jimmy Lee Swaggart was born in Ferriday, Louisiana, to sharecropper parents. Swaggart became one of the most influential leaders of American EVANGELICALISM. He helped pioneer TELEVANGELISM, and at his height, Swaggart's programs were broadcast on more than 200 television stations and 650 radio stations. However, a series of sexual scandals led to his removal from the ministry and ultimately contributed to the demise of the televangelist movement.

Swaggart underwent a religious conversion at age nine after both his parents and grandmother became PENTECOSTAL Christians. As a youth, Swaggart's time was divided between studying the Bible with his grandmother and playing music with his cousin, legendary musician Jerry Lee Lewis. Ultimately, Swaggart's faith won out over his interest in music. Nonetheless, the future preacher would later incorporate music into his ministries with great success.

In 1952, Swaggart joined a newly established ministry that his father had launched. He also met and married Frances Anderson. The couple traveled throughout the South, where Swaggart worked as an itinerant preacher. He often preached on street corners, accompanied by an accordion. On occasion, he would also play the piano in churches. In 1958, he officially joined the ministry as a Pentecostal preacher. Throughout his career, Swaggart remained a fundamentalist Pentecostal. He emphasized a literal interpretation of the Bible, and his services resembled traditional southern revivals.

Swaggart first rose to fame because of his musical talents. With the help of his cousin, he recorded a gospel album, *God Took Away My Yesterdays*, in 1962. The album registered strong sales and led Swaggart to develop his own gospel record label to produce both his work and the music of others. Among Swaggart's best-selling albums were *This Is Just What Heaven Means to Me* and *There Is a River*. In addition to his albums, Swaggart gained national attention through a regular radio show, *The Camp Meeting Hour*, which he started in 1969. Eventually, the program aired on more than 650 stations across the country.

In 1968, Swaggart moved to Baton Rouge and established the Jimmy Swaggart Ministries. The new organization provided the base for Swaggart's radio show and record label. Swaggart's popularity in the South was enhanced through a series of highly successful revivals held throughout the region. In Baton Rouge, the Swaggart Ministries developed a congregation of 4,000 people, and Swaggart also launched a small Bible college.

Swaggart was one of the early televangelists who realized the potential of television. In 1973, he established a television studio at the Swaggart Ministries and began a weekly broadcast program, *The Jimmy Swaggart Telecast*, on the PTL network. Eventually, *The Jimmy Swaggart Telecast* reached 2.1 million viewers weekly, becoming the highest-rated religious program on television. It was also broadcast internationally to some 143 nations.

Unlike other religious programming, Swaggart remained true to his evangelical roots. He did not "go Nashville" like other televangelists, such as JIM AND TAMMY FAYE BAKKER, who dressed and behaved like popular entertainers. Instead, Swaggart's program featured many of the highlights of a southern revival meeting, including miracle healing and speaking in tongues. Swaggart also did not engage in political activism to the extent that figures such as JERRY FALWELL and PAT ROBERTSON did with their open support and close ties to the Republican Party.

Swaggart did develop an extravagant lifestyle financed by contributions and donations from his listeners and viewers. He purchased a mansion and land in Baton Rouge worth $2.5 million. He also maintained a private jet and a variety of expensive automobiles. In 1987, when scandals rocked the Bakkers, Swaggart worked to publicize the events, partially as an effort to gain Bakker's followers and partially out of self-righteous indignation. Before the year was out, though, the media had discovered that Swaggart himself had engaged in a variety of affairs with prostitutes. Swaggart was stripped of his credentials and his empire began to unravel. His television viewership dropped to under 400,000, and the program was cancelled in a number of regions. He endeavored to retain his congregation, but was again caught in 1991 with a prostitute. Swaggart continues to preach at the Family Worship Center in Baton Rouge, but his ministries are a shadow of their former glory.

Further reading: Ide, Arthur Frederick. *Heaven's Hustler: The Rise and Fall of Jimmy Swaggart.* New York: Monument, 1988; Frankl, Razelle. *Televangelism: The Marketing of Popular Religion.* Carbondale: Southern Illinois University Press, 1987; Giuliani, Michael J. *Thrice-Born: The Rhetorical Comeback of Jimmy Swaggart.* Macon, Ga.: Mercer University Press, 1999; Schultze, Quentin J. *Televangelism and American Culture: The Business of Popular Religion.* Grand Rapids, Mich.: Baker, 1991; Seaman, Ann Rowe. *Swaggart: The Unauthorized Biography of an American Evangelist.* New York: Continuum, 1999.

—Thomas Lansford

Swaggart Ministries v. Board of Equalization of California 493 U.S. 378 (1990)

Swaggart Ministries v. Board of Equalization concerned whether the religion clauses of the First Amendment prohibit state sales and use tax liability on the sale of religious materials. Appellate Jimmy Swaggart Ministries was audited by the California Board of Equalization, which in turn advised it to register with the state and report and pay state sales tax on all religious merchandise sold at "evangelistic crusades" sponsored by the ministry within California. Swaggart Ministries paid the requested taxes then sued for a refund. The litigation concerns both the FREE EXERCISE and ESTABLISHMENT CLAUSES. First, Swaggart Ministries argued that the sales tax imposed a burden on its religious practices and belief, thus raising the free exercise issue. In addition, the establishment clause was implicated since the application of state sales tax to religious materials caused excessive government entanglement with religion. The Supreme Court unanimously ruled in favor of the state of California. Justice Sandra Day O'Connor wrote the opinion for the Court.

Swaggart Ministries conducted several "crusades" in California between 1974 and 1981. As the Court's opinion notes, Swaggart's presence in California for that period was 52 days total. Items such as Bibles, study manuals, printed sermons, sermon collections, T-shirts, coffee mugs, and other items could be bought at the crusades, as well as through mail order from Swaggart's corporate headquarters in Louisiana. In 1980, after auditing Swaggart, California concluded that there was sufficient nexus between Swaggart Ministries and the state of California to warrant sales tax payment on sales made to California residents. Swaggart was asked to pay $118,294 in tax, interest of $36,021, and a penalty of $11,829. Swaggart did not contest the sales tax imposition on nonreligious items such as T-shirts and coffee mugs, but he did contest the sales tax payment for religious items.

The Court first addressed Swaggart's free exercise argument. Swaggart argued that the free exercise clause prohibited the sales tax imposed on religious items, because it burdened the evangelical distribution of religious materials by a religious organization. The Court responded, though, by noting that California's sales tax "applies neutrally to all retail sales of tan- gible personal property made in California." Moreover, the tax is applied across the board to most corporate entities, and is imposed "even if the seller or purchaser is charitable, religious, nonprofit, or state or local governmental in nature." Finally, as the Court noted, "the sales and use tax is not a tax on the right to disseminate religious information, ideas, or beliefs *per se;* rather, it is a tax on the privilege of making retails sales of tangible personal property." Thus, if the law burdened the free exercise of religion by interfering with the "evangelical distribution" of religious materials, it did so in such a minimal way as not to violate the First Amendment. As Justice O'Connor concluded, "there is no evidence in this case that collection and payment of the tax violates appellant's sincere religious beliefs."

The Court next addressed Swaggart's establishment clause claim. Swaggart Ministries argued that the sales tax imposed on religious materials violated the clause by causing excessive entanglement between government and religion. Collection and payment of the tax by state authorities would impose severe accounting burdens on Swaggart Ministries, and would also impose tax-collection costs that the organization would have to bear. But as the Court responded, "the fact that appellant must bear the cost of collecting and remitting a generally applicable sales and use tax—even if the financial burden of such costs may vary from religion to religion—does not enmesh government in religious affairs." The tax "requires neither the involvement of state employees in, nor on-site continuing inspection of, [Swaggart's] day-to-day operations." The Court also concluded that "from the State's point of view, the critical question is not whether the materials are religious, but whether there is a sale or a use, a question which involves only a secular determination." Thus, the tax law by its nature was secular, and its imposition had no regard for the type of property being sold and taxed.

See also *JONES V. OPELIKA.*

—John Blakeman

T

tax-exempt status of religious organizations

The tax status of religious organizations has posed a complex set of issues for governments at all levels of the U.S. federal system. The ambiguity inherent in deciding whether and how to tax religious organizations is posed squarely by the religion clauses of the First Amendment. Those who oppose exempting religious bodies from taxation have argued that such exemptions are violations of the ESTABLISHMENT CLAUSE, as these regulations place religion in a favored category relative to secular organizations. Conversely, using Justice Marshall's phraseology in *McCulloch v. Maryland* (1819), proponents of religious tax exemptions have suggested that "the power to tax is the power to destroy," and, accordingly, argue that imposing taxes on religious bodies is a violation of the constitutional right to FREE EXERCISE.

Contemporary church-state jurisprudence has generally steered a middle course between these alternatives. In *WALZ V. TAX COMMISSION* (1970), the Supreme Court, by a vote of 8-1, upheld the view that a property tax exemption for religious worship did not violate the establishment clause. Justice Burger, writing for the majority, suggested that since the tax exemption in question was shared by other nonprofit organizations, religion was not advanced in an unconstitutional manner. Burger also argued that imposing taxes on religious bodies would likely result in an "excessive entanglement" in religious affairs by government. However, the majority opinion in *Walz* simply upheld an existing exemption, and did not support the assertion that such exemptions are constitutionally required. While a majority of state constitutions contain provisions mandating tax exemptions for religious and other nonprofit organizations, the current state of First Amendment law suggests that such exemptions are neither required nor prohibited.

With respect to the federal income tax, the status of religious organizations was spelled out in Section 501(c)(3) of the Internal Revenue Code of 1954. This provision of the tax code creates a single classification for religious, literary, social, educational, and charitable organizations, and exempts these from federal taxation under certain conditions. Recognition as a 501(c)(3) entity allows individuals to deduct contributions to the organization from their income taxes, and exempts the organization itself from paying income taxes.

The exemption provided by 501(c)(3) is limited in three ways. First, an amendment to the Internal Revenue Code (passed in 1969) does not exempt from taxation the profits from businesses owned by religious organizations but that are not directly related to their charitable or religious purposes. Second, 501(c)(3) organizations are prohibited from attempting to influence legislation. This standard is considered by some to be rather vague, and it has been applied rather inconsistently. Third, such organizations may lose their exemptions if they "violated public policy." For example, in the case of *BOB JONES UNIVERSITY AND GOLDSBORO CHRISTIAN SCHOOL, INC. V. UNITED STATES* (1983), BJU lost its tax exemption (despite support from the Reagan administration) because the institution was alleged to practice racial discrimination. This discrimination included formal rules forbidding interracial dating among BJU students. The Court ruled that the federal government had a compelling interest in eliminating RACISM, which outweighed the burden imposed on BJU by the loss of its tax exemption.

Congress has authorized exceptions to the tax code for individuals based on religious considerations, and the Supreme Court has generally upheld these exemptions. However, the Court has not typically supported the claims of individuals or organizations for religiously based tax exemptions without specific legislative authorization.

To summarize, it seems clear that, at this writing, there does not exist a First Amendment right for religious organizations to be exempt from taxation, nor do such exemptions constitute a proscribed "establishment" of religion. The granting of such exemptions is often covered by state constitutions, and such exceptions are frequently enacted by legislatures at the state and federal levels. Such acts of legislative discretion have generally been upheld by the courts, provided that they are applied to broad classes of organizations and individuals, and do not single out religious organizations for special consideration.

See also TUITION TAX CREDITS FOR RELIGIOUS SCHOOLS.

Further reading: Kelley, Dean M. *Why Churches Should Not Pay Taxes.* New York: Harper and Row, 1977; Miller, Robert, and Ronald Flowers. *Toward Benevolent Neutrality: Church, State, and the Supreme Court.* Waco, Tex.: Baylor University Press, 1997; Monsma, Stephen V., and J. Christopher Soper. *The Challenge of Pluralism: Church and State in Five Democracies.* Lanham, Md.: Rowman and Littlefield, 1997; Weber, Paul J., and Dennis Gilbert. *Private Churches and Public Money.* Westport, Conn.: Greenwood, 1981.
—Ted G. Jelen

televangelism

From the very beginnings of radio, religious figures realized the potential benefits of broadcasting their sermons and messages. By the 1970s, religious broadcasting on television, or televangelism, had become a significant force in mainstream American Christianity. By the 1980s, the phenomenon had become the foundation for the political power of the Christian Right.

Christianity is a proselytizing religion, and evangelicals sought to utilize the airwaves to spread their message to the widest possible audience (see EVANGELICALISM). The potential impact of broadcasting was realized as early as the 1930s, when Father Charles E. Coughlin, a ROMAN CATHOLIC priest, attracted as many as 45 million listeners each week with his radio program. However, as time went by, evangelical Christians came to dominate the airwaves. In 1944, a group of Christian broadcasters established the National Religious Broadcasters (NRB) in Washington, D.C., to promote their interests. The NRB successfully lobbied to overcome the reluctance of station owners to schedule religious programming. In 1960, the Federal Communications Commission (FCC) ruled that station owners could sell broadcasting time, and it would still count as public service broadcasting. This opened the way for evangelicals to purchase Sunday airtime—and it provided financial incentives for stations to sell time. By the 1960s, evangelical broadcasters had come to dominate Sunday programming.

The growth of televangelism in the 1960s helped spur a resurgence of evangelical Christianity. Figures including Charles E. Fuller, ORAL ROBERTS, and BILLY GRAHAM utilized radio and television to spread their message; the publicity generated by massive prayer meetings and revivals further solidified their base. One distinguishing feature of televangelism was that in practice, it sought to avoid the denominational strife that marked traditional churches. Many televangelists initially avoided the fundamentalist images of southern REVIVALISM and promoted a more moderate image. As a result, they were able to attract a substantial number of viewers from outside their denominations.

Until the 1970s, televangelists had been limited to local stations and markets since the major networks were reluctant to schedule religious broadcasting for fear of alienating specific audiences. In 1977, PAT ROBERTSON dramatically altered the nature of televangelism when his CHRISTIAN BROADCASTING NETWORK (CBN) began leasing its own satellite. This allowed Robertson and CBN to offer programming to cable and satellite systems and effectively go nationwide. Robertson was soon joined by figures such as Robert Schuller, JIM BAKKER, and JIMMY SWAGGART. By the 1990s, televangelists had increased their viewership from approximately 5 million per week in the 1960s to close to 100 million per week in the 1980s. Religious networks such as CBN and Praise the Lord (PTL) offered 24-hour programming and syndication of shows to non-network stations.

Televangelism also provided a platform for forays into national politics. The televangelists utilized their medium to promote conservative candidates and are credited with mobilizing the Christian conservative vote in 1980 and 1984, which helped facilitate President RONALD REAGAN's electoral victories. In 1979, televangelist JERRY FALWELL formed the MORAL MAJORITY and mobilized the evangelical vote to a degree previously unseen in American politics. In 1988, PAT ROBERTSON utilized his base and network to make credible effort to capture the presidential nomination of the Republican Party.

Even as televangelism reached its height in the 1980s, it also faced a variety of hurdles that led to its dramatic decline. First, during the decade there were a series of spectacular and well-publicized scandals that undermined the moral authority of the medium. In 1987, televangelists Jim Bakker and Jimmy Swaggart both were involved in sexual scandals that eroded their audiences and cast aspersions on the medium. Second, the increasing politicization of televangelists turned many viewers away. Overall ratings for religious broadcasting peeked in 1985 and began to decline thereafter. Third, competition among televangelists has further decreased the individual audience of specific stations or broadcasters. This is especially true with regard to small, independent religious stations, whose numbers increased from 25 in 1980 to over 300 by 1990.

Although the political clout of televangelists has diminished during the 1990s, religious broadcasters continue to have a significant impact on the medium of television. Televangelists are engaged in an ongoing effort to reach new markets by offering family-based, though not necessarily Christian, broadcasting.

See also RELIGION IN THE 1980, 1984, 1988 PRESIDENTIAL ELECTION.

Further reading: Alexander, Bobby C. *Televangelism Reconsidered: Ritual in the Search for Human Community.* Atlanta: Scholars Press, 1994; Apostolidis, Paul. *Stations of the Cross: Adorno and Christian Right Radio.* Durham, N.C.: Duke University Press, 2000; Frankl, Razelle. *Televangelism: The Marketing of Popular Religion.* Carbondale: Southern Illinois University Press, 1987; Hadden, Jeffrey K., and Anson Shupe. *Televangelism: Power and Politics on God's Frontier.* New York: Henry Holt, 1988; ———. "The Rise and Fall of American Televangelism." *Annals of the American Academy of Political & Social Science* 527 (1993): 113–131; Martz, Larry, and Ginny Carroll. *Ministry of Greed: The Inside Story of the Televangelists and Their Holy Wars.* New York: Weidenfeld and Nicholson, 1988; Schultze, Quentin J. *Televangelism and American Culture: The Business of Popular Religion.* Grand Rapids, Mich.: Baker, 1991.

—Thomas Lansford

Ten Commandments

The posting of the Ten Commandments in courtrooms and classrooms has been an issue in American politics beginning in the late 20th century, sparked principally by conservative religious groups. The subject of a Supreme Court decision and some legislative pronouncement, it excited public attention and attracted political support in some areas despite judicial hostility.

The Ten Commandments, or the Decalogue, is a code of moral conduct set forth in varying forms in Exodus 20 and Deuteronomy 5 of the Christian and Jewish Scriptures. They represent moral teachings prevalent in the ancient world. Jesus Christ recognized the commandments, though he taught a broader application of their underlying principles (John 13:34). He also apparently valued some commandments higher than others (Mark 10:17–22).

Though there is evidence that publicists and philosophers of the American revolutionary period were acquainted with the Decalogue, it is impossible to confirm it as the basis of American jurisprudence.

During World War II, a Minnesota juvenile court judge, E. J. Ruegemer, and the members of the Fraternal Order of Eagles started a campaign to post copies of the Decalogue in juvenile court rooms. Later, Cecil B. DeMille, then in the process of producing the film *The Ten Commandments,* latched on to the idea with the difference that it was to be inscribed on granite and given away as monuments in public places. Some 2,000 such monuments were donated to American communities.

A parallel movement called for displays in schoolrooms and other public buildings. An example was an enactment of the Kentucky General Assembly, judicial review of which provided a landmark Supreme Court decision. That statute required that the Commandments be displayed on a wall in each elementary and secondary schoolroom. In small print below the last (Tenth) Commandment were to be the words, "[T]he secular application of the Ten Commandments is clearly seen in its adoption as the fundamental legal code of Western Civilization and the Common Law of the United States." Displays were to be financed by voluntary contributions. Noting that such an "avowed" secular purpose is not sufficient to avoid conflict with the First Amendment," a divided Supreme Court invalidated the act (*STONE V. GRAHAM,* 449 US 39, 1980). The effect was to decide that the statue contravened the ESTABLISHMENT CLAUSE of the First Amendment by expressing a religious rather than a secular purpose.

Outbreaks of violent crime in the latter years of the 20th century stimulated a belief in some circles that public displays of the Decalogue would contribute to public morality and order. The Supreme Court ruling notwithstanding, resistance to removal of Decalogue displays flared up. Circuit Judge Roy S. Moore of Etowah County, Alabama (now on the Alabama Supreme Court), posted the Decalogue in his courtroom and was supported by then governor Fob James, who threatened to call out the National Guard to keep the plaque in place.

On May 29, 2001, the U.S. Supreme Court in a 6-3 decision (*City of Elkhart v. Books*) denied to hear the case, letting stand a decision by the Third District Court of Appeals that Elkhart, Indiana's, six-foot-tall granite monument was tantamount to the endorsement of a particular religious belief. Three dissenters (Justices William Rehnquist, ANTONIN SCALIA, and Clarence Thomas) issued a statement denying that the monument expressed preference for a particular religion, but added the historically misleading comment that the monument "reflects the Ten Commandments' role in the development of our legal system."

The Supreme Court ruling would appear to cast doubt on the validity of similar displays elsewhere. Yet it has not killed the movement. On July 26, 1999, North Carolina enacted legislation allowing its display in all public schools. The U.S. House of Representatives on June 17, 2001, passed 248-180 a nonbinding resolution allowing states to display the Decalogue in every school and courtroom.

Surveys show that while most persons favor its display, they are not necessarily conversant with what the Commandments say. According to a recent Gallup poll, 42 percent of Americans questioned could not name as many as five Commandments.

Further reading: Green, S. K. "The Fount of Everything Just and Right; The Ten Commandments as a Source of American Law." *Journal of Law and Religion,* 6 no. 2 (1999–2000); *City of Elkhart v. Books,* 79 F. Supp. 979 (1999); hearing denied by U.S. Supreme Court May 29, 2001.

—Emmet V. Mittlebeeler

textbook controversies

School textbooks often touch upon sensitive issues with religious and moral dimensions, a fact that has resulted in controversies about the content of history, language arts, science, and health textbooks throughout the past century. In the 1920s, Christian fundamentalists opposed the teaching of evolution, as espoused in Charles Darwin's *Origin of Species,* in public schools. Although history best remembers the SCOPES "MONKEY" TRIAL in Dayton, Tennessee, as the most important defeat of the fundamentalist crusade against evolution (at least in the court of public opinion), fundamentalists succeeded in influencing the content of many science textbooks. Published by companies that were afraid of the controversy that might ensue and harm their sales, many science textbooks over the next few decades omitted references to evolution.

The "space race" with the Soviet Union in the 1960s led scientists to press for more updated science textbooks, ensuring that evolution was brought back into most science classrooms. Societal pressures in that decade, however, brought other controversial textbook changes. Conservative Christians across the nation protested against health textbooks that adopted a more liberal approach to sex education. The CIVIL RIGHTS MOVEMENT and the women's movement pressured educators to eliminate racial and gender stereotypes from textbooks, which also aggravated conservative Christian activists in school districts around the country. In the best-known textbook controversy of the 1970s, fundamentalist Christians in Kanawha County, West Virginia, objected to new titles proposed for their language arts curriculum in 1974, many of which stressed multicultural themes. One conservative Christian board member in Kanawha charged that many of the proposed books were morbid and depressing, especially those written by black authors. Moreover, fundamentalist parents believed that these new books promoted moral relativism and situation ethics that challenged their religious beliefs. The controversy led to school boycotts and widespread violence, with the result that many fundamentalist parents removed their children from the public schools. Instead, parents opted to homeschool or send their children to newly developed Christian academies, a trend that increased dramatically over the next two decades in other school districts.

Since the 1980s, conservative Christians have fought against the encroachment of "SECULAR HUMANISM" in textbooks. One prominent Christian Right group, Educational Research Analysts (founded by Mel Gabler and Norma Gabler), review thousands of textbooks for secular humanism and other themes offensive to them. The Gablers insist that secular humanism is a religion "with an anti-biblical, anti-God bent" that "worships the creature instead of the Creator." Christian Right leaders believe that liberal educators have deliberately brought secular humanism into the classroom to undermine the beliefs and values that they hold sacred. In two separate federal lawsuits, fundamentalist parents unsuccessfully sued their school districts over the content of school textbooks. The courts ruled that exposure to textbooks that offended the religious beliefs of some families (*Mozert v. Hawkins County Board of Education* 1987) and the use of textbooks that purportedly advanced "secular humanism" (*Smith v. Mobile County Board of School Commissioners* 1987) did not violate any First Amendment rights.

In more recent years, religious conservatives have complained that textbooks discriminate against them by deleting many references to religion from history and social studies, denying children the opportunity to learn how religion has affected our nation's development. Calls for book censorship or banning by parents for religious reasons are still heard. Between 1990 and 1999, the American Library Association (ALA) recorded more than 5,000 challenges to materials in schools, school libraries, and public libraries for reasons including sexually explicit material, offensive language, and occult themes. The ALA estimates, however, that for each challenge reported, as many as four or five remain unreported.

See also AID TO RELIGIOUS SCHOOLS; CHRISTIAN RIGHT SCHOOL BOARD CANDIDATES; TUITION TAX CREDITS FOR RELIGIOUS SCHOOLS.

Further reading: "Banned Books Week." American Library Association. URL: www.ala.org/bboks/challenge.html, 2000; Gaddy, Barbara B., T. William Hall, and Robert J. Marzano. *School Wars: Resolving Our Conflicts over Religion and Values.* San Francisco: Jossey-Bass, 1996; Gabler, Mel, and Norma Gabler. *What Are They Teaching Our Children?* Wheaton, Ill.: Victor Books, 1985; Martin, William J. *With God on Our Side: The Rise of the Religious Right in America.* New York: Broadway Books, 1996; Sewall, Gilbert T. "Religion and the Textbooks." In *Curriculum, Religion, and Public Education: Conversations for an Enlarging Public Square.* Edited by James T. Sears with James C. Carper. New York: Teachers College Press, 1998; Wills, Garry. *Under God: Religion and American Politics.* New York: Simon and Schuster, 1990; Woods, James E. Jr. "Editorial: Religious Censorship and Public School Textbooks." *Journal of Church and State* 29 (1987), 401–410.
—Melissa M. Deckman

Thomas v. Review Board of Indiana Employment Security Division 450 U.S. 707 (1981)

In this JEHOVAH'S WITNESS case, the Supreme Court ruled 8-1 that the FREE EXERCISE CLAUSE forbade the state of Indiana from denying unemployment compensation to a worker who had quit his job for religious reasons. Justice William Rehnquist was the lone dissenter from Chief Justice Warren Burger's opinion, while Justice Harry Blackmun concurred in part.

Thomas had worked at the Blaw-Knox Foundry & Machinery Co. for about a year when the company closed the roll foundry where he had helped fabricate sheet steel, and transferred him to a department that produced turrets for military tanks. When Thomas realized that his new job was "weapons related," he looked for other positions in the plant. When it turned out that all of the remaining departments at Blaw-Knox produced military weapons as well, he asked for a layoff. When that request was denied, he quit and sought unemployment compensation benefits, which were also denied. The Supreme Court of Indiana reasoned that Thomas had voluntarily quit his job for personal reasons, and upheld the denial.

In coming to the opposite conclusion, Chief Justice Burger dismissed the state court's objection that Thomas could not offer an articulate explanation of either the nature of his beliefs or their religious basis. "Courts," the chief justice wrote, "should not undertake to dissect religious beliefs because the believer admits that he is 'struggling' with his position or because his beliefs are not articulated with the clarity and precision that a more sophisticated person might employ."

Burger also thought the Indiana court erred in finding it significant that Thomas was unable to explain why a fellow Jehovah's Witness who continued to work at Blaw-Knox did not agree with him that producing military armaments was "unscriptural." Said Burger:

[T]he guarantee of free exercise is not limited to beliefs which are shared by all of the members of a religious sect. Particularly in this sensitive area, it is not within the judicial function and judicial competence to inquire whether the petitioner or his fellow worker more correctly perceived the commands of their common faith. Courts are not arbiters of scriptural interpretation. The narrow function of a reviewing court in this context is to determine whether there was an appropriate finding that petitioner terminated his work because of an honest conviction that such work was forbidden by his religion.

This approach, Burger said, was mandated by SHERBERT V. VERNER (1963), the case in which the Court rejected South Carolina's attempt to deny unemployment compensation benefits to a Sabbatarian who refused to work on Saturday.

Thus, the chief justice concluded: "Where the state conditions receipt of an important benefit upon conduct proscribed by a religious faith, or where it denies such a benefit because of conduct mandated by religious belief, thereby putting substantial pressure on an adherent to modify his behavior and to violate his beliefs, a burden upon religion exists. While the compulsion may be indirect, the infringement upon free exercise is nonetheless substantial."

Such a burden on religion could be sustained if the government could show it was the least restrictive means of achieving some compelling state interest. But Burger concluded that in this case, there was "no evidence" to support the two purposes offered by the state: "to avoid the widespread unemployment and the consequent burden on the [unemployment] fund resulting if people were permitted to leave jobs for personal reasons; and to avoid a detailed probing by employers into job applicants' religious beliefs."

Dissenting Justice Rehnquist thought the majority opinion simply added more "mud" to the Court's First Amendment jurisprudence. In Rehnquist's view, the overarching problem with the Court's religion cases was that by interpreting both the free exercise clause and the ESTABLISHMENT CLAUSE too broadly, the Court had placed the two clauses in unnecessary and increasing tension with each other. That ongoing problem was compounded in this case, he said, when the Court not only took yet another overly expansive view of the free exercise clause, but also failed to explain how such a reading could pass the (equally overly expansive) Lemon test for establishment clause violations that the Court announced in LEMON V. KURTZMAN (1971).

—Charles F. Williams

Thoreau, Henry David (1817–1862) writer

Henry David Thoreau was a transcendentalist poet and essayist from Concord, Massachusetts, who was best known for his two-year experiment in frugal living described in Walden (1854) and his theory of CIVIL DISOBEDIENCE. Thoreau took transcendentalist premises to their logical, if extreme, conclusion. In doing so, he articulated an ethic of self-reliance and advocated philosophical anarchism. The religion of established churches was suspect to Thoreau, who reveled in the spiritual morality he found in nature.

Thoreau was born in Concord and lived there most of his life. His father was a pencil maker who provided only a modest living. But Henry did well in school and was ultimately admitted to Harvard College. Thoreau's performance there was undistinguished, mainly because he preferred independent study to the prescribed curriculum. Before graduating in 1837, Thoreau met the leader of the transcendentalist movement, RALPH WALDO EMERSON, who had just written his inspirational classic Nature (1836). Despite an age difference of 14 years, Emerson and Thoreau became fast friends. Like others in his circle, Emerson often admired the rigor with which Thoreau pursued his TRANSCENDENTALISM, but he was sometimes vexed by his ardor as well. In addition to supporting himself by writing, Thoreau was alternately a schoolteacher, surveyor, and pencil maker. None of these activities was lucrative, but that suited his disdain for wealth. Relative poverty was much more inviting. It freed Thoreau from the nuisance of regular employment and allowed him to spend more time in nature. Thoreau died of tuberculosis at 44 years of age.

Most of Thoreau's published writings began as journal entries. His journal is eclectic, jumping from social commentary to natural observation to literary subjects. Although even his finished essays wander, they do contain a consistent critique of American Christianity. In a posthumous tribute, Emerson noted that Thoreau believed "that without religion or devotion of some kind nothing great was ever accomplished: and he thought that the bigoted sectarian had better bear this in mind." The vast majority of American religious practice seemed sadly bigoted to him. "As for the sacred Scriptures," Thoreau wrote in Walden, "who in this town can tell me even their titles? Most men do not know that any nation but the Hebrews have had a scripture." Thoreau believed that with the Bible as the single accepted source of doctrine, innate curiosity about religiosity withered, leading to an inspired, formulaic religious practice. This formulaic practice took place on Sunday within church confines and meant little in the daily lives of most Americans, who were more interested in material things.

Alternatively, Thoreau consulted the scriptures of diverse faiths. While he found them inspirational, he also treated them as epiphenomena, judging them on their ability to convey truths ultimately contained in nature. Nature, on the other hand, was not just a source of spiritual inspiration to Thoreau but a direct moral guide. This aspect of his thinking, foreign during his own time, is arguably even more foreign today. Nev-

WALDEN;

OR,

LIFE IN THE WOODS.

BY HENRY D. THOREAU,

AUTHOR OF "A WEEK ON THE CONCORD AND MERRIMACK RIVERS."

I do not propose to write an ode to dejection, but to brag as lustily as chanticleer in the morning, standing on his roost, if only to wake my neighbors up. — Page 92.

BOSTON:
TICKNOR AND FIELDS.
M DCCC LIV.

Title page of *Walden; or, Life in the Woods,* by Henry David Thoreau *(Library of Congress)*

ertheless, Thoreau insisted that nature's moral laws were plain and consistent. These moral laws were never systematically delineated, befitting Thoreau's transcendentalist premise that individual intuition trumped logical exposition. Even so, we can discern the main precepts of this natural law. Foremost, Thoreau observes a lack of acquisitiveness on the part of flora and fauna. Unlike humans, other creatures live simply, expending only the energy it takes to satisfy their daily needs. They do not engage in a deadening pursuit of wealth. Problematic social institutions like slavery are also absent in nature. Human institutions are prone to compromise, even on matters as gravely immoral as slavery. Nature does not compromise and is thus pure. What is natural to humans is to use their conscience, but institutions routinely lead people to ignore or stifle their own natural moral sense.

Thoreau's critique of organized politics is similar to his critique of religion. Political institutions rely on compromises that stifle the human conscience and are responsible for much evil. In "Civil Disobedience" (1849), he opined that an individual's conscience-driven acts are more legitimate than the pronouncements of the state. Thoreau justified not paying his poll tax because the state countenances slavery. Thoreau willingly faced the state's physical superiority, spending a night in jail (before someone paid his tax), confident in his moral superiority. Thoreau's ideas served as inspiration to Mohandas Gandhi and MARTIN LUTHER KING JR. Their approach to civil disobedience resembled Thoreau's but was explicitly pacifist. Thoreau, on the other hand, did not rule out violence, as evidenced by his praise for John Brown's actions at Harper's Ferry in 1859.

See also ENVIRONMENTALISM; PANTHEISM.

Further reading: Bode, Carl, ed. *The Portable Thoreau.* New York: Penguin, 1975; Emerson, Edward W., ed. *Emerson's Works.* Boston: Houghton Mifflin, 1883.

—David J. Siemers

Tillich, Paul (1886–1965) *theologian*

Paul Tillich was born on August 20, 1886, in Starzedenburg, Germany, and died on October 22, 1965. He had a well-established career in Germany as professor of philosophy at the University of Frankfurt when Hitler became German chancellor. In 1933, Hitler dismissed Tillich and put his life at risk. Legendary theologian Reinhold Niebuhr was in Germany at the time and subsequently arranged for Tillich an appointment at Union Theological Seminary in New York City. Tillich remained there as professor of systematic theology until his retirement in 1955. For the next five years, until 1960, he was a university professor at Harvard University; he had a third American appointment at the University of Chicago Divinity School after that.

One of the distinctive and most enduring contributions of Tillich is in the orbit of theological method. Even for those of a very different theological orientation, his "method of correlation" is both illuminating and adoptable. Tillich argued that it is in the nature of theology and the theologian to move back and forth between poles: the eternal truth of the Christian message and the situation in which it is received. The situation is all the forms in which existence is interpreted and experienced. The issue both socially and culturally becomes the balance between the situation and the eternal message. A tilt in one direction or the other results in either distortion or irrelevance. The five parts of his theological system are constructed on this model. In each instance, the situation cannot finally answer the question it raises and therefore calls out for the Christian message.

Tillich understood his work to be an "answering theology." This explains his phenomenal impact on those who found themselves at the margin of religious traditions as well as those on the verge of an exit. He was profoundly committed to making contact with the culture and where people found themselves in relation to it. When he preached in New York City, for example, the congregation was always heavily populated by the psychoanalytic community. While in the strictest sense, he did not consider himself an "apologetic theologian," he certainly bordered on that phenomenon. What characterized his mode of theology was a determination to make contact with the dynamics of the age and find a way to articulate an aspect of the faith in relation to it. In simplistic terms, one cannot move the answer until one has uncovered the question. His task was consistently one of mediation.

During the American years of Tillich's career, his impact on the political sphere was not substantial, certainly not explicit. This was in part his own reality was shaped by Germany. There, however, his development of "Religious Socialism" was significant and in particular was a response to his experiences in and after World War I. Religious socialism was not a political party but more of a movement. Tillich's concern was for the role of the church in the new republic and a stance against the militarism of nationalism. To Tillich, a just society requires the intervention of something beyond the dynamic of history. Tillich believed that what was at hand could be described as a *kairos* moment. *Kairos,* a Greek word, means that this is a time when something eternal is presenting itself in the temporal realm and enabling significant transformation. The supreme *kairos* event was Jesus the Christ. This led Tillich to a "theonomous" understanding of culture and history. What this implies is that ultimate meaning assumes cultural form and that culture is transparent to spiritual content. The eternal is poised to act and a new creation is pending. Thus, religious socialism is a spiritual power organized against the demonic in the prevailing order. When the eternal breaks into the temporal and is received there, it is an impetus for a new order of justice.

Obviously, what Tillich has done is breach the sacred/secular divide. The political realm is precisely where the divine Spirit is evident and the movement of resistance to the status quo is formed. What saves this from idolatry is what Tillich called "the Protestant principle." The worry is that a particular party will present itself as the embodiment of the divine will. Tillich makes clear that every authentic manifestation of the divine presence points beyond itself rather than to itself. It is one thing to affirm the presence of the eternal in the temporal and another to claim a specific embodiment, say, in a leader or party.

See also BARTH, KARL; LIBERATION THEOLOGY.

Further reading: Works by Paul Tillich: *Dynamics of Faith.* New York: Harper, 1957; *The Courage to Be.* New Haven, Conn.: Yale University Press, 1952; *The Protestant Era.* Chicago: University of Chicago Press, 1948; *Systematic Theology,* Vols. 1, 2, 3. Chicago: University of Chicago Press, 1951–63.

—David O. Woodyard

Tilton et al. v. Richardson, Secretary of Health, Education, and Welfare, et al. 403 U.S. 672 (1971)

In this case, decided together with several other ESTABLISHMENT CLAUSE cases (including *LEMON V. KURTZMAN*) on June 28, 1971, the Supreme Court considered the constitutionality of federal construction aid to religiously affiliated colleges under the provisions of the Higher Education Facilities Act of 1963. At issue in particular were buildings constructed on the campuses of four Roman Catholic colleges in Connecticut. Writing for a plurality of four justices, Chief Justice Warren Burger distinguished the aid provided to colleges and universities from other government attempts to subsidize "sectarian" elementary and secondary education.

The plurality opinion turned on three principal points. The first concerned the nature of the facilities constructed with federal aid—libraries, a language laboratory, a science building, and a music, drama, and arts building. The findings in the district court record indicated that for all intents and purposes, "these buildings are indistinguishable from a typical state university facility." Not only were no religious services conducted in them, but they were totally free from religious adornment. Second, all the institutions at issue were marked by a high degree of academic freedom and secular academic professionalism. While there might well be sectarian colleges and universities whose principal purpose is to propagate the faith and whose policies ensure a pervasively religious atmosphere, none of the four colleges in the current case had been shown to fit this pattern. The courses taught in these buildings and the books housed in the libraries would be arguably essentially indistinguishable from those at state universities. Finally, Burger noted that there are substantial differences between college students and their elementary and secondary counterparts. They are "less impressionable and less susceptible to religious indoctrination . . . The skepticism of the college student is not an inconsiderable barrier to any attempt or tendency to subvert the congressional objectives and limitations." Taken together with the one-time nature of the construction grant, these three considerations made it unlikely, in the plurality's view, that there would have to be substantial ongoing governmental supervision to ensure that funds granted for permissible purposes could be turned to the impermissible end of advancing religion.

Justice Byron White concurred in the judgment, but not in the opinion, offering his views separately about all the federal and state aid cases. "It is enough for me that the States and the Federal Government are financing a separable secular function of overriding importance in order to sustain the legislation here challenged. That religion . . . may substantially benefit does not convert these laws into impermissible establishments of religion." He was not persuaded by the plurality's attempt to distinguish the higher education cases from their elementary and secondary counterparts. So long as one could rely on the professionalism of the instructors at any level—and White believed that one could—there was no reason to be any less confident that secular subjects could be taught in a secular fashion in a parochial elementary or secondary school than in a religiously affiliated college or university.

There were two separate dissents, one by Justice William Douglas (joined by Justices Hugo Black and Thurgood Marshall) and one by Justice WILLIAM BRENNAN (applying to *Lemon* and *Tilton*). Douglas's argument turned on the nature of parochial schools at all levels. They are "unitary institution[s] with subtle blending of sectarian and secular instruction"; indeed, "religious teaching and secular teaching are so enmeshed in parochial schools that only the strictest supervision and surveillance" could assure that government aid did not advance religion. Either it is impossible to separate religious from secular educational functions or it can be accomplished only by engaging in such excessive entanglement as to compromise the religious freedom of the institution. Finally, however, Douglas seemed to argue that any aid under any circumstance would be impermissible simply because government aid frees other funding to be used to advance religion. Government aid amounts at least to the indirect advancement of religion.

Brennan acknowledged in his dissent that the ends pursued by government may be secular, but he argued that it may not use religious institutions to pursue them, at least not in the absence of an argument that nonreligious means of promoting them are insufficient. He further argued that "a sectarian university is the equivalent in the realm of higher education of the Catholic elementary schools in Rhode Island; it is an educational institution in which the propagation and advancement of a particular religion are a primary function of the institution." It is impossible to promote a secular enterprise embedded in a religious institution without at the same time promoting its religious undertakings. In this respect, Brennan agreed with White that the grounds for distinguishing the federal program from the others are unpersuasive. At the same time, he drew different conclusions from this observation. To guarantee that religion is not advanced, government supervision would have to be so pervasive as to amount to "excessive entanglement."

In sum, although the Court found that certain sorts of government aid to religiously affiliated colleges and universities was constitutional, it did so on grounds that did not persuade a majority of the justices. Justice White would go furthest in supporting such aid, while the other eight justices would probably not have supported aid to pervasively religious institutions. The four justices who, with White, made up the majority could countenance such aid only to institutions in which instruction in most subjects was largely indistinguishable from that at nonsectarian institutions. The four dissenters were unwilling to support any aid under any circumstances.

See also AID TO RELIGIOUS SCHOOLS.

—Joseph M. Knippenberg

tolerance

Religion is frequently associated with political intolerance. Most studies of tolerance in the United States that include religion have reported relationships between the two concepts. Some recent research has challenged these findings, demonstrating that utilizing more sophisticated measures for both religion and tolerance erases the linkages between the two, and suggesting that the characterization of believers as intolerant is really an artifact of measurement approach.

Tolerance refers to "the degree to which we accept things of which we disapprove." Political tolerance can thus be defined as the willingness of individuals to "put up with" the public expression of ideas they oppose, measured by how willingly they support various forms of public expression by members of groups they strongly dislike.

Political tolerance is a fundamental value of liberal democracy, essential for the free exchange of diverse or opposing speech, as well as the freedom to act, without fear of censure or reprisal. An ideal of liberal theory is that open debate will enlighten, resulting in the rejection of false or harmful ideas and permitting societal progress. LIBERALISM views tolerance as necessary not only for societal development but also for the maintenance of social diversity, permitting free pursuit of individual goals and maximization of human potential.

Political tolerance studies have generally found that the religiously committed, particularly those holding to traditional Christianity and those identifying with conservative or fundamentalist traditions, are less supportive of the civil liberties of widely disliked groups than are other citizens. The first major work on political tolerance in the United States—Stouffer's *Communism, Conformity, and Civil Liberties* (1955)—was also the first to demonstrate an empirical connection between religion and intolerance, reporting that church attendance was linked to intolerance toward communists, socialists, and atheists. The tolerance measures developed by Stouffer, in which respondents report their willingness to tolerate members of specific widely disliked groups, have become the standard in tolerance surveys. Studies relying on these measures have consistently found linkages between religion and intolerance of atheists, communists, homosexuals, militarists, racists, and other groups. This is particularly true of those reporting strong religious commitment or frequent church attendance, or those adhering to religious beliefs or with religious traditions identified as fundamentalist, Evangelical Protestant, PENTECOSTAL, or conservative Christian. The association intensifies when there is a moral aspect to the target issue or group. The nonreligious, infrequent church attendees, Jews, and liberal Protestants are generally more willing to support the civil liberties of unpopular groups.

Varied explanations have been proposed for the correlation between religion and intolerance. Fervent religious belief is often associated with rigidity of thinking and hostility toward ideas or groups perceived as threats to religion or the moral order. Also, FUNDAMENTALISM is associated with anti-intellectualism and dogmatism, both of which are correlated with intolerance. A belief in biblical literalism or inerrancy may decrease tolerance since the classic defense of liberalism— that a climate of free and open dialogue is essential to permit nobler views ultimately to prevail, allowing progress toward a fuller understanding of truth—holds little value for those who believe truth has been revealed in Scripture. Fundamentalists or conservative believers may object to the focus on individualism in classic defenses of tolerance, believing it encourages pride, undermines authority, or threatens religious community. The fundamentalist emphasis on social separation may discourage pluralism, or view deliberation as confrontational rather than enlightening. Premillennialist beliefs may cause pessimism regarding human progress, undermining the classic defense of liberalism and tolerance.

Others argue that religious commitment should increase tolerance. Some religious traditions are less judgmental, emphasizing justice, mercy, and charity as hallmarks of authentic Christianity. Believers may be principled supporters of free expression and debate of ideas, open to alternative interpretations of orthodox truth, or they may embrace difference for the opportunity of enhanced community. They may welcome alternative ideas or sources of knowledge, or they may encourage engagement in an effort to evangelize. Faith may even enhance toleration by providing believers with the confidence to engage the opposition in order to expose false or harmful ideas by persuasive religious argument.

There have also been challenges to the conclusion that religion itself—rather than the characteristics of believers—causes intolerance. Predispositions that predict intolerance—dogmatism, threat perceptions, anti-intellectualism, and low support for civil liberties—are dispersed among believers and seculars alike. Attitudes and behaviors known to enhance tolerance—support for principles of democracy and high levels of political interest, knowledge, and engagement—are also as prevalent among believers as they are among nonbelievers. Religion's relationship with tolerance may be an indirect one that disappears with the consideration of other factors.

See also ANTICOMMUNISM; RACISM.

Further reading: Busch, Beverly Gaddy. "Faith, Truth, and Tolerance: Religion and Political Tolerance in the United States." Ph.D. diss., University of Nebraska-Lincoln, 1998; Crick, Bernard. "Toleration and Tolerance in Theory and Practice." *Government and Opposition* 6 (1971): 142–171; Mill, John Stuart. *On Liberty.* Edited by Gertrude Himmelfarb. London: Penguin, 1974; Stouffer, Samuel. *Communism, Conformity, and Civil Liberties.* New York: Doubleday, 1955; Sullivan, John L., James Pierson, and George F. Marcus. *Political Tolerance and American Democracy.* Chicago: University of Chicago Press, 1982.

—Beverly Gaddy

toleration in political theory

The notion of toleration is connected with, but not necessarily identical to, religious freedom. To say, for example, that a denomination or sect is "tolerated" may mean only that as a matter of sovereign or legislative grace (not a natural or civil

right), it is permitted merely to assemble and worship. Toleration of this sort is perfectly consistent with the existence of an established church. Thus the English Toleration Act of May 27, 1689, extended freedom of worship to a limited group of dissenters from the established Church of England, but only on the condition that they take an oath of allegiance and seek licenses in order to meet. Not only were other religious traditions, such as the ROMAN CATHOLIC CHURCH, altogether denied this privilege, those who gained it were still denied access to political office.

Influenced by JOHN LOCKE's *A Letter Concerning Toleration* (1689), the American founders adopted a more extensive understanding of toleration that promises (in the words of GEORGE WASHINGTON) that "every one shall sit in safety under his own vine and fig-tree, and there shall be none to make him afraid." The burden of Locke's argument is to distinguish between "Civil Concernments," such as "Life, Liberty, Health, and Indolency of Body; and the Possession of outward things, such as Money, Lands, Houses, Furniture, and the like," and religious concerns, such as salvation. While human beings can legitimately grant to the state the authority to legislate regarding civil matters, "no man can so far abandon the care of his own Salvation, as blindly to leave it to the choice of any other, whether Prince or Subject, to prescribe to him what Faith or Worship he shall embrace." What is most crucial for salvation, according to Locke, is "inward Sincerity": "no Religion, which I believe not to be true, can be either true, or profitable unto me." If salvation is thus necessarily a personal concern, a church must be an essentially voluntary association.

The preamble of VIRGINIA's "Act for Establishing Religious Freedom," drafted by THOMAS JEFFERSON in 1779 and passed in 1786 thanks to the leadership of JAMES MADISON, shows the influence of Locke's argument: "Well aware that Almighty God hath created the mind free; that all attempts to influence it by temporal punishments or burdens, or by civil incapacitations, tend only to beget habits of hypocrisy and meanness, and are a departure from the plan of the Holy Author of our religion, who being Lord both of body and mind, yet chose not to propagate it by coercions on either." The Virginia establishment of religion was a comparatively modest one, in which individuals—with the exception of QUAKERS and MENNONITES—were taxed to support the preacher of their choice. Still, in his "Memorial and Remonstrance," Madison characterized it as different from the Inquisition "only in degree. The one is the first step, the other the last in the career of intolerance."

Thus in America, toleration came to be understood as a matter of right, not of grace. If I am to be free to reach my own conclusions regarding religion, I must extend the same freedom to others. This assertion of right, however, need not rest on the assumption that all religious opinions are equally valid. Thomas Jefferson in Query XVII of his "Notes on Virginia" might well insist on the civil equality of all religions; all are "good enough; all sufficient to preserve peace and order." But that is not the same thing as saying all are true. Thus Madison concedes in the "Memorial and Remonstrance" that it might be possible to abuse freedom of religion, but that "is an offence against God, not against man: To God, therefore, not to men, must an account be rendered." One might well be tolerant of an opinion of which one disapproves. Conversely, moral or theological disapproval in the context of toleration does not always imply either the right or the inclination to persecute.

In sum, there are three possible versions of toleration. The first follows from the believer's recognition that there are errors that are either impossible or imprudent to eradicate. The second follows from the claim that free assent lies at the core of true religion. The third depends on the assertion that all faiths are essentially personal and not subject to anyone else's judgment. The first and second are consistent with belief in religious truth. The third regards toleration as the consequence of relativism.

See also TOLERANCE.

Further reading: Jefferson, Thomas. *The Life and Selected Writings of Thomas Jefferson.* Edited by Adrienne Koch and William Peden. New York: Random House, 1944; Kautz, Steven. *Liberalism and Community.* Ithaca, N.Y.: Cornell University Press, 1995; Locke, John. *A Letter Concerning Toleration.* Edited by James H. Tully. Indianapolis: Hackett, 1983; Madison, James. *The Mind of the Founder: Sources of the Political Thought of James Madison.* Edited by Marvin Meyers. Indianapolis: Bobbs-Merrill, 1973.

—Joseph M. Knippenberg

Tony and Susan Alamo Foundation v. Secretary of Labor 471 U.S. 290 (1985)

This case presented the question of whether regulation of commercial enterprises operated by a religious organization under the Fair Labor Standards Act violates the FREE EXERCISE CLAUSE or ESTABLISHMENT CLAUSE.

The Tony and Susan Alamo Foundation ("the Foundation") was a California nonprofit religious organization that supported its ministries primarily from revenue generated from its operation of a number of commercial businesses, including service stations, retail clothing and grocery outlets, hog farms, roofing and electrical construction companies, a record-keeping company, a motel, and candy companies in four different states.

These businesses were staffed, for the most part, by approximately 300 "associates," who rather than receiving cash salaries received food, clothing, shelter, and medical and other benefits from the Foundation. The secretary of labor filed an action alleging that the Foundation had violated the minimum wage, overtime, and record-keeping provisions of the Fair Labor Standards Act ("the Act") with respect to these 300 associates.

The Supreme Court initially had to resolve whether the Act even applied to the Foundation, given that the Foundation was a religious organization and that the Foundation considered its "associates" to be volunteers rather than employees. Drawing on a review of the statutory language and the Act's legislative history, the Court concluded that the Foundation's businesses were subject to the Act because they were performed for a "common business purpose," competing in the marketplace with private industry. The Foundation had argued that its enterprises differed from "ordinary" commercial businesses because they functioned as ministries to the needs of the associates by providing rehabilitation and food, clothing and shelter, and because they functioned as "churches in disguise," enabling the Foundation to spread its beliefs to the public. The trial court had ruled that the evidence did not support these claims, however, and the Supreme Court declined to review the trial court's ruling. This was exactly the kind of "unfair method of competition" that the Act was designed to prevent, "and the admixture of religious motivations does not alter a business' effect on commerce," the Court concluded.

As to whether the "associates" were to be considered "employees" under the Act, the Court acknowledged that the associates had testified that they did not expect any cash compensation. As one had put it, "the thought is totally vexing to my soul." Nonetheless, applying an "economic reality" test, the Court ruled that because the associates were "entirely dependent upon the Foundation for long periods, in some cases several years," the exchange of in-kind benefits for services rendered them employees under the Act.

Proceeding to the Foundation's contention that application of the Act's minimum wage and record-keeping requirements would violate the free exercise rights of the associates, the Court declared, "It is virtually self-evident that the FREE EXERCISE CLAUSE does not require an exemption from a governmental program unless, at a minimum, inclusion in the program actually burdens the claimant's freedom to exercise religious rights." The associates' objections centered on their assumption that application of the Act would require them to receive a cash wage. The Act, however, defines "wage" to include the kind of in-kind benefits that the associates were already receiving, apparently far in excess of the minimum wage requirement. Application of the Act, therefore, "will work little or no change in their situation," the Court ruled. Even if the Foundation were to begin paying cash wages, nothing prevented the associates from returning the amounts to the Foundation. Since the Act would not "actually burden" the associates' free exercise rights, their free exercise claim failed.

The Foundation also maintained that application of the Act's record-keeping requirements would have the "primary effect" of inhibiting religious activity and would foster "an excessive government entanglement with religion" in violation of the ESTABLISHMENT CLAUSE. Since the Act would be applied only to the Foundation's "commercial activities" undertaken with a "business purpose," and not to its evangelical activities or to the provision of traditional volunteer services to people in need, however, application of the Act's record-keeping requirements "bear[s] no resemblance to the kind of government surveillance the Court has previously held to pose an intolerable risk of government entanglement with religion." The Act's record-keeping requirements are "not significantly more intrusive into religious affairs," the Court concluded, than the kind of secular government regulations such as fire inspections or building and zoning regulations that had already been found not to violate the establishment clause.

The Supreme Court's distinction between the "commercial" and "religious" activities of a religious organization thus foreclosed the possibility of a constitutionally derived blanket exemption for religious organizations from the Fair Labor Standards Act. Just as the "unrelated business income" of religious organization is taxable income under the Internal Revenue Code, the Fair Labor Standards Act's minimum wage and other requirements apply to the employees of commercial enterprises operated by religious organizations.

See also *LEMON V. KURTZMAN*; RELIGIOUS DISCRIMINATION IN THE WORKPLACE.

Further reading: Lupu, Ira C. "Free Exercise Exemption and Religious Institutions: The Case of Employment Discrimination." *Boston University Law Review* 67 (1987): 391–442.

—David T. Ball

Traditional Values Coalition

The Traditional Values Coalition (TVC) is a conservative, grassroots, religious lobby based in Anaheim, California. Founded in 1980 by the Reverend Lou Sheldon, a Presbyterian minister, the nondenominational, nonprofit organization claims a membership of 43,000 churches across the United States. TVC describes itself as a resource to churches and pastors, whose mission is to educate believers on "pro-family" issues, seeking to mobilize them in grassroots lobbying efforts. The organization's mission includes encouraging believers to become politically involved in support of pro-family policies and other issues of interest to the organization.

A prominent leader in the Christian Right, Sheldon and TVC often ally or form coalitions with other conservative groups or Christian Right leaders in support of pro-family policies. Although primarily recognized for its prominent opposition to GAY RIGHTS legislation, PORNOGRAPHY, ABORTION, and public funding of AIDS research, the organization also lobbies in support of other conservative issues. These include education (supporting educational choice, charter schools, and school VOUCHERS), taxes, and religious liberty. Because of its prominent opposition to the gay rights movement and public funding of AIDS research, Sheldon has been a frequent target of protests by homosexual activist groups. President GEORGE W. BUSH's appointment of Sheldon to the advisory committee on funding faith-based organizations in 2001 prompted protests of the faith summit by gay rights organizations.

TVC's primary tactic is to mobilize support from church attendees by sending "citizen action alerts" and other information to member churches, urging congregants to contact their elected officials regarding specific issues. These are usually sent to the pastor of member churches or someone else in the church designated by the pastor to be the TVC representative. Action alerts, also posted on the organization's Website, provide information on a specific issue, such as a bill that has been introduced in Congress. The alert details the effects of the bill or other item in language familiar to those sympathetic to the Christian Right, and concludes with a "take action" message. The take action message typically includes a plea to contact legislative representatives and the president or governor concerning the issue, and includes phone numbers or other contact information. Sometimes preprinted cards, to be completed and signed by the supporter, are included in an attempt to maximize response.

Although TVC focuses much of its resources on its grassroots lobbying efforts, it also engages in direct lobbying in Washington and in state capitals. Sheldon's daughter, Andrea Sheldon Lafferty, directs its Washington-based lobbying activities. Lafferty, who also serves as the organization's executive director, has a reputation among Republican leaders as a trusted and effective lobbyist on issues of concern to the organization.

In addition to its lobbying efforts, TVC is active in electoral politics, both in ballot initiatives and in candidate support at the state and national levels. While its primary electoral activities are voter registration, education, and get-out-the-vote drives, the organization's electoral efforts include supporting candidates for school boards, city councils, and conservative Republican candidates in congressional and presidential races. TVC budgeted $14 million for its efforts in the 2000 elections—five times its 1998 budget. Over 10 million individuals included on the organization's year 2000 mailing list received direct-mail appeals for support of its electoral activities.

Lou Sheldon, chair and founder of TVC, was born in 1934 and raised as a Jew in Washington, D.C. He converted to Christianity at the age of 15, resolving to devote his life to religion. As an undergraduate at Michigan State University, Sheldon was strongly influenced by Russell Kirk, then a philosopher at nearby Hillsdale College. Following seminary training at Princeton, Sheldon pastored several churches before arriving in California in 1965 to pastor Sacramento's First Presbyterian. Sheldon's political activism began in 1973 with an unsuccessful battle to defeat a gay rights measure in California. Although initially focused on California politics, Sheldon organized TVC in 1980 to mobilize churches nationwide to battle "anti-family" policies at the local, state, and national levels. TVC's high-profile role in the passage of Colorado's Amendment 2 in the late 1990s, an initiative prohibiting the granting of special minority status to homosexuals, brought the organization national recognition and prompted harsh criticism from gay-rights and liberal organizations.

TVC has created a separate foundation, the Traditional Values Education and Legal Institute, with a mission of educating conservative church congregations on pro-family issues and providing support to churches for cultural and political struggles.

See also CHRISTIAN RIGHT SCHOOL BOARD CANDIDATES.

—Beverly Gaddy

transcendentalism

Transcendentalism was a New England–based philosophical movement active from the 1830s to about 1860. Transcendentalists, most notably RALPH WALDO EMERSON, HENRY DAVID THOREAU, and Margaret Fuller, lamented the unthinking formalism of most Americans' lives, urging a rebirth of free thinking and spirituality. The movement privileged intuition as a source of knowledge over reason or doctrine, yielding an individualistic, nature-based mysticism rather than a single logically coherent philosophy. Several transcendentalist leaders had been clergy, but their main contribution to American thinking was a radical critique of prevailing American religious, economic, and political practices.

The immediate philosophical inspiration for transcendentalist thought was Immanuel Kant and his English-speaking popularizers, Samuel Taylor Coleridge and Thomas Carlyle. Kant reacted against the Enlightenment assumption that all knowledge stemmed from sensory perception. By contrast, Kant and the New England transcendentalists posited that there was innate knowledge not dependent on physical experience. In fact, this "transcendental" knowledge was more valuable than sensory or logic-based learning, for it was knowledge of the conscience, which revealed one's moral duty to others and the world. This epistemology was more reminiscent of Plato and Eastern religions than modern Christianity. The transcendentalists frequently quoted from Plato's dialogues, the sayings of Confucius, and the Bhagavad Gita.

The religious roots of transcendentalism were not Eastern, however, but Unitarian. Early leaders George Ripley, William Ellery Channing, Orestes Brownson, and Emerson all came to transcendentalism from their position as UNITARIAN clergy. Not convinced of the trinitarian nature of the Godhead or that all biblical Scripture was divinely revealed, they were unorthodox in their religious thinking before the transcendentalist movement even began. During the 1830s, most of them split from the church, finding its position of justifying religious revelation through natural reason untenable. They came to believe that religious truth could be realized only through individual revelation rather than theology. For inspiration, these thinkers increasingly pointed to the beauty and harmony of nature, rather than words from the pulpit.

Emerson's 1836 essay "Nature" provided momentum to the movement. In the essay Emerson observed: "The moral law lies at the center of nature and radiates to the circumference. It is the pith and marrow of every substance." The goal of this worldview was to partake in the inherent morality of the universe. Such thinking pointed to a divine aspect to humanity: "The purpose of Christianity," wrote George Ripley in 1836, "is to elevate the human soul to a resemblance to God, to make it a partaker of the divine nature." Many transcendentalist essays and speeches, including Emerson's "Divinity School Address" (1838) and Theodore Parker's "Discourse of the Transient and Permanent in Christianity" (1841), were explicitly about religion. While their general purpose was to help individuals recapture spiritualism, these ideas were deeply disturbing to many contemporary Christians.

Younger transcendentalists such as Thoreau and Fuller received inspiration from these leaders, ascribing to a kind of natural mysticism without ever formally breaking from a church themselves. "Respectable" Christianity, they found, meant little in people's daily lives. Obsessed with material advancement, most Americans did not follow the example of Jesus, despite calling themselves Christians. Like political institutions, the church was complicit in the most egregious wrongs of the day. The church accepted, indeed thrived on, acquisitiveness and did not vigorously challenge problematic social practices like war and slavery. By contrast, Thoreau and Fuller advocated radical measures. Thoreau renounced material goods and proclaimed that his own conscience trumped the state's laws. Fuller embraced socialism. Though their visions for the world differed widely, both found the church to be an impediment to a more just world.

The individualist premises of transcendentalism limited its effectiveness. While some participated in communes (Bronson Alcott's Fruitlands and Ripley's Brook Farm being the best known), sustained commitment to these enterprises was lacking and none were particularly successful. Further, the transcendentalist critique of American society was sufficiently deep that widespread conversions would have been surprising. Finally, there was great ambivalence within the movement about leading a movement at all, for the spiritually awake would never thirst for leaders.

Despite its failings, transcendentalism has served as an inspiration to many Americans. Nature writers, anti-institutional movements like the New Left, and participatory democrats have all traced their intellectual roots to transcendentalism. The frequency of such attributions points to the uniqueness of a movement that critiqued society from a spiritual perspective, but outside of organized religion. In doing so, its members found America wanting, but the depth of their disappointment could only be produced by the height of their aspirations.

Further reading: Gilman, William H., ed. *Selected Writings of Ralph Waldo Emerson*. New York: Signet Classics, 1965; Hochfield, George, ed. *Selected Writings of the American Transcendentalists*. New York: Signet Classics, 1966.

—David J. Siemers

Truman, Harry S (1884–1972) *U.S. president*

Harry S Truman served as the 33rd president of the United States, from 1945 to 1953. After military service in World War I and failure in business, Truman found his vocation in a political career. He rose from obscurity as a county government official in Missouri to a seat in the U.S. Senate, then became President FRANKLIN DELANO ROOSEVELT's running mate in 1944. When Roosevelt died in April 1945, Truman became president. He won election in his own right in 1948, then retired from politics in 1953. He returned to Missouri, where he lived in his wife's family home until his death.

Truman was a product of the American Midwestern Protestant experience. He was raised in the small town of Independence, Missouri, where he attended Sunday school at the Presbyterian church that his parents attended. As a young man, he joined the Grandview Baptist Church in a nearby town. He married Elizabeth "Bess" Wallace in the Episcopal Church, to which she belonged for the rest of her life, while Harry remained a Baptist. He once described his religious views by saying "I am by religion like everything else. I think there's more in acting than in talking."

While he possessed a strong belief in God, a Calvinist sense of morality, and a conviction that religion was important, Truman was an erratic churchgoer. He told Bess about how one Sunday when he was in Kansas City, "I made a start for church and landed at the Shubert [Theatre]." Just as important to him was his membership in the Masons, which he joined in 1909. He respected religion, counted clergy and other religious leaders among his friends, and frequently used the language of religion in his public statements. While in the White House, he was a member of the First Baptist Church in Washington, but he often remained at home while his wife and daughter attended church. Nevertheless, he saw Christianity as America's religion.

As president, Truman confronted a world wracked by war. One of the first decisions he had to make in office was whether to use the newly developed atomic bomb. He was attending a conference of World War II Allied leaders at Potsdam, Germany, in July 1945 when he took up the responsibility of making the decision. In preparation, he attended church twice on the morning of Sunday, July 22, a Protestant service and a ROMAN CATHOLIC mass. He wrote to his wife that "I guess I should stand in good with the Almighty for the coming week—and my how I'll need it." Two days later he ordered the use of the weapon and soon the war was brought to an end. While he faced intense criticism for using the bomb against Japan, especially from some religious leaders, Truman went to his death defending the decision as a right and moral one.

Following World War II, Truman shaped U.S. foreign policy to respond to the growing power of the Soviet Union. He often described the struggle between communism and democracy in religious terms. In his Inaugural Address in 1949, he called communism a "false philosophy" and proposed a plan to bring relief to nations made vulnerable to communist influence by hunger and poverty. He concluded the speech with a prayerlike statement: "Steadfast in our faith in the Almighty, we will advance toward a world where man's freedom is secure. To that end we will devote our strength, our resources, and our firmness of resolve. With God's help the future of mankind will be assured in a world of justice, harmony, and peace." Later that year, he told a group of Anglican bishops and then a gathering of Lutheran leaders that the United States was living by the Sermon on the Mount. This fact, he maintained, helped to explain the American position of leadership among the moral forces of the world. By contrast, communists embraced ATHEISM and were therefore evil.

As his presidency wore on, Truman increasingly turned to the language of faith to distinguish the two sides in the cold war. While some critics thought he went too far by casting the world's political divisions in such terms, his strategy for the containment of communism shaped U.S. foreign policy for a half century. It was brought to a successful end when the events of 1989–91 led to a breakup of Moscow's European empire and the collapse of the Soviet Union itself.

See also EISENHOWER, DWIGHT D.; MARXISM/COMMUNISM.

Further reading: McCullough, David. *Truman.* New York: Simon and Schuster, 1992.

—Ryan Barilleaux

Harry S Truman *(National Archives)*

Tubman, Harriet (1820/1821–1913) *activist*

Harriet Tubman was born Araminta Ross to Ben and Harriet Ross in 1820 or 1821 in Dorchester County on the Eastern Shore of MARYLAND, near Cambridge, in an area called Bucktown. She died at the age of 93 in Auburn, New York, in 1913. She was one of 10 children and of pure African descent. Harriet felt early the sting of the whip, the pain of the lash, and the traumatic hardship of slavery. Treated harshly as a young child by a series of masters to whom she was hired out by her own, Harriet developed a hatred of slavery and a deep resentment for its degradation. At the age of 13, Harriet had her first involvement in an attempted escape.

An adult male slave had planned an escape. While he and others were at a store, he made for the door. An overseer who had become suspicious and had accompanied them to keep watch saw him. The overseer threw a two-pound weight at the fleeing slave as he set off in pursuit. Instinctively, Tubman moved to block the overseer's path and the weight struck her in the forehead and fractured her skull. She suffered her entire life from this trauma, which left her with a condition similar to narcolepsy with periodic dizzy spells. This physical condition, however, did not compromise her budding resolve to resist the institution and all its ills. It may have been around this time that she heard of slave revolt leader Nat Turner "and pondered his meaning deep within her."

Tubman was physically strengthened by a hard regimen of field work and jobs usually reserved for men. She was put out to the field after she was declared hopelessly recalcitrant and demonstrated no desire to work in the close quarters of the house.

Harriet married John Tubman, a free African American, in 1844 but bore no children. Shortly thereafter she discovered that her mother ("Rit") should have been free at the death of her mistress. Consequently, Rit and her children were kept in slavery by fraud. In 1849, Tubman escaped to Philadelphia alone, and, in 1850, her labors began on behalf of her people. Between 1850 and 1860, she made a total of 19 trips into the South, freeing over 300 slaves including most of her brothers and sisters and her aged parents, leading most to Canada because of the enactment of the Fugitive Slave Law of 1850. The journeys were fraught with immense hardship and peril, having only the occasional stops along the Underground Railroad for temporary respite and supplies. She was so successful that a $40,000 bounty was placed on her head—dead or alive. None of the slaves she liberated was ever recaptured.

After the outbreak of the Civil War, Tubman carried dispatches for the Union Army and served as a spy, scout, and nurse, as well as missionary for liberated and destitute slaves. Her service was invaluable. Nevertheless, for four years of committed service she received a total of 20 days' rations. She supported herself during this period by cooking cakes, pies, and gingerbread late at night and hiring liberated slaves to sell her goods throughout the camp. Destitute after the war, she turned her house into a home for the aged and indigent. At 80 years she was finally granted a $20 monthly pension by Congress.

Harriet Tubman was known throughout her life, particularly among slaves and those she liberated, as Moses. Her life story is a testimony to the interrelated nature of mystical religious experience and struggle in the history of African Americans. Her spirituality provided her with a limitless reservoir of strength that fueled her superhuman endurance and determination. Her life is one of the greatest arguments against patriarchal assumptions of male superiority in the so-called manly virtues.

See also ABOLITIONIST MOVEMENT; BROWN, JOHN; FEMINISM; FEMINIST THEOLOGY.

Further reading: Bradford, Sarah. *Harriet Tubman: The Moses of Her People.* Bedford, Mass.: Applewood Books, 1886; Eusebius, Mary. "A Modern Moses: Harriet Tubman." *Journal of Negro Education* 19, no. 1 (1950): 16–27; Franklin, John Hope. *From Slavery to Freedom: A History of Negro Americans.* New York: Knopf, 1974; Harding, Vincent. *There Is a River: The Black Struggle for Freedom in America.* New York: Vintage, 1983; White, Deborah Gray. "Let My People Go: 1804–1860." In *To Make Our World Anew: A History of African Americans.* Edited by Robin D. G. Kelly and Earl Lewis. New York: Oxford University Press, 2000.

—Matthew V. Johnson Sr.

tuition tax credits for religious schools

A tuition tax credit is intended to make it easier for students to attend a private school by reducing school costs. Proponents of VOUCHERS AND SCHOOL CHOICE—especially religious conservatives—have encouraged the adoption of tuition tax credits by the federal government and state governments since the 1970s. One argument for tax credits is that parents are paying tuition to private schools as well as taxes for public schools. Tax credits have been promoted as a means of helping individuals attend private religious schools without government monies going directly to those schools.

A tax credit is a reduction in tax liability to a tax authority for tuition paid by a taxpayer or for a donation made to an organization that provides scholarships to students attending religious schools. Tax credits can be refundable or nonrefundable; a refundable credit means that even if a person did not owe tax money, he or she would receive money because of the credit.

On the federal level, there have been discussions of tax credits for religious schools since the 1970s, but no policies have been enacted. The 1976 Republican platform called for the consideration of tax credits for students attending nonpublic schools. RONALD REAGAN spoke in favor tax credits throughout his presidency; in 1983, he transmitted the "Educational Opportunity and Equity Act of 1983" to Congress that would have provided for a $300 tax credit for parents who sent their children to private schools. The bill never made it out of committee. This policy initiative continues to be popular with religious conservatives and the ROMAN CATHOLIC CHURCH. The administration of GEORGE W. BUSH has considered tax credits as part of its educational proposals.

Tuition tax credits have been enacted on the state level in support of students attending religious elementary and secondary schools. In 1987, Iowa enacted a nonrefundable tax credit for parents whose children attended nonpublic schools.

The credit refunded $100 in state income tax for the first $1,000 paid for tuition. In 1998, the credit increased to $250, and about 125,000 families claimed the credit.

An education tax credit was made available in Minnesota in 1998. The refundable tax credit does not cover private-school tuition, but it does pay for any education-related expenses at public or private schools. The credit is limited to $1,000 per student and $2,000 per family. The credit is means-tested, so it applies only to those earning less than $37,500 in 2000. Expenses that qualify for the tax credit include tutoring, fees for after-school programs, nonreligious academic books, and software used for educational expenses. Morgan Brown, executive director of the Minnesota-based Partnership for Choice in Education, noted that some private schools have itemized their fees, thus permitting some parents to utilize the credit. Minnesota has also had a tax deduction for private-school tuition since 1955. The tax deduction only reduces the amount of taxable income. The tuition tax deduction was challenged as a violation of the First Amendment's establishment clause. In MUELLER V. ALLEN (1983), the U.S. Supreme Court ruled that the tax deduction had a secular purpose and did not create excessive church-state entanglement.

Illinois enacted the Educational Expenses Tax Credit in 1999; it became effective in 2000. The law permits parents to claim a nonrefundable credit of up to $500 for tuition, books, and lab fees at any public, private nonreligious, or private religious school. The credit covers 25 percent of educational expenses after $250 and up to $2,250. The law was challenged in Illinois state courts, but it was ultimately upheld.

Arizona passed an education tax credit that assists those attending private religious schools. This credit, passed in 1997, permits individuals to take a $500 nonrefundable credit for voluntary cash donations to school tuition organizations (STOs) approved by the state. Over 30 STOs have been established. STOs must distribute nearly all of their revenue in the form of tuition scholarships. There is no state-mandated income test for those receiving scholarships. In 1999, STOs in Arizona awarded 3,800 scholarships with an average amount of $637. Arizona's teachers unions and the AMERICAN CIVIL LIBERTIES UNION challenged the law, arguing that it violated both the U.S. and the Arizona Constitutions' ESTABLISHMENT CLAUSES, but the Arizona Supreme Court upheld the statute.

Further reading: Olsen, Darcy Ann, and Matthew Brouillette. "Reclaiming Our Schools: Increasing Parental Control of Education through the Universal Education Credit." *Policy Analysis.* December 6, 2000.

—Michael Coulter

Two Guys from Harrison-Allentown, Inc. v. McGinley 366 U.S. 582 (1961)

The Supreme Court's decision that state laws prohibiting various activities on Sunday (see BLUE LAWS) do not violate the U.S. Constitution was announced in a series of four cases decided on the same day in 1961. One of these cases was *Two Guys from Harrison-Allentown, Inc. v. McGinley.*

Two Guys (the odd-sounding title of the case comes from the name of a corporation, and does not refer to two individuals) was a Pennsylvania case that covered substantially the same ground as MCGOWAN V. MARYLAND (1961), which the Court chose as the principal vehicle for the expression of its views on Sunday closing laws. The only complicating factor in *Two Guys* was that the language and history of Pennsylvania's blue laws seemed to be more clearly grounded in religious purposes than that of the Maryland statutes at issue in *McGowan.*

Pennsylvania's earliest regulating conduct on Sunday, for example, were explicitly designed to combat "Looseness, Irreligion, and ATHEISM"; a 1779 statute likewise stated that its purpose was "for the due observation of the Lord's day." The modern statutes involved in *Two Guys* were less directly linked to religious purposes, but they did retain at least vestiges of the earlier terminology.

An 8-1 majority, led by Chief Justice Earl Warren, saw little reason to emphasize either the historical origins of the Pennsylvania statutes or their occasional use of old-fashioned terminology. Consequently, he applied essentially the same analysis in *Two Guys* as he had in *McGowan,* holding that "neither the statute's purpose nor its effect is religious," and thus the statutes do not violate the Constitution's ESTABLISHMENT CLAUSE. As in *McGowan,* Warren also dismissed arguments that the seemingly arbitrary nature of the law's inclusions and exclusions violated the equal protection clause.

Justice Felix Frankfurter—at the time the Court's only Jewish justice—filed a separate concurrence (joined by Justice John Marshall Harlan), primarily to set out the long history of laws regulating conduct on Sundays. Because such legislation serves "an extreme complexity of needs" and involves "distinctions so fine," Frankfurter explained, "Courts must accord to the legislature a wide range of power to classify and to delineate."

Justice William O. Douglas dissented, as he did in the other three Sunday legislation cases. "There is an 'establishment' of religion in the constitutional sense if any practice of any religious group has the sanction of law behind it," he concluded. "There is an interference with the 'FREE EXERCISE' of religion if what in conscience one can do or omit doing is required because of the religious scruples of the community."

—William Lasser

U

Unification Church

The Unification Church, or the Holy Spirit Association for the Unification of World Christianity (HSA-UWC), arrived in the United States in 1959. San Francisco was the first city in which the Unificationists, commonly but derogatively known as "Moonies," obtained a significant presence. The church was officially formed in Seoul, South Korea, in 1954, under the direction of Sun-Myung Moon (b. 1920). Originally a Presbyterian, Reverend Moon found himself increasingly at odds with Protestant churches in Seoul and, after moving to North Korea to proselytize, was held in a North Korean prison camp during the Korean War.

The Unification Church flourished in postwar South Korea, despite troubles with the media and government, and in 1963 the group was legalized. Meanwhile, Japan (1958) and the United States became the initial areas of missionary activity. Reverend Moon first came to the United States in 1965 and moved the center of the U.S. movement to the east coast, indicating a turn toward the financial and political heart of the country.

Unificationists believe their movement to be the final stage of Christianity. Moon argues that Eve was seduced by Satan and spread sexual impurity to Adam, necessitating redemption, which occurred in historical stages through the prophets of the Judeo-Christian tradition. However, Moon believes that Jesus failed in his ultimate mission to bring the Kingdom of God to earth because John the Baptist betrayed him.

Reverend Moon cites the example of Jesus, who did not proclaim himself the Messiah, in his own refusal to declare himself the last savior. However, Unification theology offers many clues that Moon is held to be the Messiah and does acknowledge Reverend Moon and his wife as the "True Parents" of humankind. As such, Moon and his wife are believed to offer their followers the opportunity to perfect themselves as "children," then form perfect families with other church members. Unlike many branches of Christianity, the Unification Church does believe that humans are perfectible, and that our current fallen state brings God great sorrow. The movement states as its goal the unification of all religions and ethnicities into one human family and God-centered kingdom.

American Unificationists gained prominence during the 1970s, when popular concern over "cults" led to well-publicized attempts to "deprogram" members of the Unification Church and other NEW RELIGIOUS MOVEMENTS. To this day, some ex-members of the Unification Church charge that the movement uses deceptive practices in recruiting converts, requires excessive personal and financial commitment, and, by engaging in marital matchmaking, facilitates marriage among people who know little of the partner who has been chosen for them.

In academic literature today, the Unification Church is generally considered a "new religious movement," not a cult, and the notion of "brainwashing" has fallen from favor. However, the American popular press has tended to be less accepting, focusing especially on the mass blessing ceremonies for couples, often misconstruing them as mass weddings.

This has no doubt helped shape the political maneuvers of the movement, which has many organizations and businesses that fall within its umbrella but do not proclaim themselves to be explicitly a part of the Unification Church. At times in the 1990s, political leaders such as George H. W. Bush and Jack Kemp have been associated, knowingly or not, with events sponsored by the organization or its affiliates, and connections to or donations from the Unification Church are still generally considered bad publicity if discovered.

Politically, the movement has been best known for its support of RICHARD NIXON during the Watergate scandal and for being anticommunist but attempting to engage with communist countries, including manufacturing projects in North Korea and Vietnam. In addition, in 1982, the same year that the church won tax-exempt status and other guarantees given to established religions, Moon was convicted of tax evasion. This was later declared unjust by a Senate committee chaired by senator Orrin Hatch (R-Utah) and has sometimes been seen as persecution. More recently, the family-values emphasis has led to the sponsoring of chastity-based sex education in schools, a large donation from the Unification-affiliated Women's Federation for World Peace to the Christian Heritage Foundation to help bail out JERRY FALWELL's Liberty University, and the Million Family March in 2000 with LOUIS

FARRAKHAN. Although the Unification Church has attempted to align itself politically with conservative Christians, PAT ROBERTSON announced his reluctance to allow the movement to benefit from GEORGE W. BUSH's proposed faith-based charity plan.

Current academic estimates of Unification membership in America are in the thousands (Finke and Stark 1992: 241), but the wealth of the worldwide movement, which has allowed it to begin a seminary, own the *Washington Times,* purchase the University of Bridgeport, buy United Press International, and make political contributions all within the United States alone, has combined with its notoriety to give it significant visibility. The movement has more recently been known as the "Family Federation for World Peace."

See also ANTICULT MOVEMENT.

Further reading: Finke, Roger, and Rodney Stark. *The Churching of America, 1776–1990.* New Brunswick, N.J.: Rutgers University Press, 1992.

—Caroline R. Sherman

Unitarian Universalists

The Unitarian faith is an antitrinitarian movement that evolved from various movements in Europe and the United States. It converged with Universalism in 1961 to form a Boston-based denomination that now numbers approximately 250,000 in worldwide membership. American Unitarians claim among their forerunners Europeans such as Spaniard Michael Servetus and other freethinking proto-Protestants. American roots are varied but include English transplant Joseph Priestley's preaching in PENNSYLVANIA in the late 18th century, and a controversy that ensued in 1795 when Boston's Anglican King's Chapel congregation voted to remove Trinitarian language from the Book of Common Worship.

Unitarians' role in fighting the disestablishment of religion in MASSACHUSETTS, which manifested itself in a state constitutional amendment in 1834, ensured for Unitarians an important place in early American political life. In an eloquent sermon in December 1820, titled "Religion a Social Principle," William Ellery Channing, the chief antidisestablishmentarian, defended the marriage of church and state, arguing that religion was not only a personal matter between humans and their creator: "Therefore, Society ought, through its great organ and representative, which is government, as well as by other methods, to pay homage to God, and express its obligation." The Dedham Decision of the Massachusetts Supreme Court (1820) confirmed that those members who remained after disagreement with the Parish (the liberals in that case) would hold church property. The departing conservatives had their beliefs and little else. RALPH WALDO EMERSON's departure from Unitarianism toward TRANSCENDENTALISM in the 1830s was another blow to the small but powerful group of Boston elites. In 1825, a group of young ministers created the American Unitarian Association, an organization of Unitarian individuals who aimed to promote Unitarianism, but such efforts did not quickly reach a national audience.

Because of its historical INDIVIDUALISM and relatively small size (even before merger with the even smaller Universalists in 1961), Unitarians as thinkers and activists have had a greater effect on the American political scene than the movement or church per se. President William Howard Taft was moderator of the American Unitarian Association from 1917 to 1918, and noteworthy Unitarians (in thought or membership) in both centuries include President John Quincy Adams, Vice President John C. Calhoun, President Millard Fillmore, theologian Theodore Parker, journalist and education pioneer Horace Greeley, President JAMES MADISON, and statesman Daniel Webster.

Unitarians were at the forefront of the U.S. Sanitary Commission during the Civil War, generating revenue to improve health conditions for Union soldiers and thereby influencing and forecasting an expansion of federal powers. Horace Mann's role in the formation of public schools, as well as the removal of corporal punishment from these schools and what he considered to be the "sectarian influence" of some religious groups on schools in 19th-century America, is also noteworthy. Other Unitarians have included clergyman Henry Whitney Bellows, women's rights activist SUSAN B. ANTHONY, clergyman John Haynes Holmes, literary critic Margaret Fuller, mental health pioneer Dorothea Dix, and Jenkin Lloyd Jones, influential uncle of architect Frank Lloyd Wright and cofounder of the Parliament of the World's Religions in 1892.

Frederick Elliot, while president of the American Unitarian Association at midcentury, bridged the historical gap between a Unitarian movement known more for its Boston Brahmins, who favored the establishment of religion and Christian theological values, and a Unitarian movement known for its opposition to McCarthyism and support of civil rights, humanism, and ethnic and sexual-orientation diversity. Unitarian leaders also influenced the creation of both the Humanist Manifesto (1933) and the Humanist Manifesto II (1973). Two-time Democratic presidential nominee Adlai Stevenson (1900–65) was the most important national political figure of Unitarianism at midcentury, though Rev. James Reeb, killed while participating in the Selma, Alabama, voting rights campaign of 1965, galvanized Unitarian Universalist participation in that movement.

The Unitarian Universalist Association's public political stances today are based on its membership's dogmatic belief in the inherent worth and dignity of every individual and the interconnected web of all existence. A representative example of Unitarian political activism in the later 20th century was a Unitarian family's response to public school Bible reading in 1959. The Schempp family opposed a 1948 law allowing such activities in Pennsylvania, and their family's case was combined with avowed atheist Madalyn Murray O'Hair's court case in Maryland, leading to the case of ABINGTON TOWNSHIP, SCHOOL DISTRICT OF V. SCHEMPP (1963), wherein the U.S. Supreme Court declared that teaching "about" religion was acceptable in schools but the practice "of" religion was not. Fundamentalist activists decried the case as "the removal of God from the schools." Unitarian and Attorney General Elliot L. Richardson's refusal during the Watergate scandal to obey President RICHARD NIXON's order to fire a special prosecutor is a much-lauded example of Unitarian leadership. In 2001, the Unitarian Universalist Association elected the first African-American head of an Anglo-American denomination, further exemplifying their politically progressive stance among religious bodies.

See also LIBERALISM; SECULAR HUMANISM.

—Robert Wilson-Black

United Methodist Church

The United Methodist Church (UMC) was founded on April 23, 1968, when the Evangelical United Brethren Church and the Methodist Church were united. With over 35,000 churches in the United States, the United Methodist Church makes up one of the largest denominations among Protestant churches in the nation (UMC: 2000)—UMC's membership of over 8 million was second only to the Southern Baptist Convention in the Protestant circle in the 1990s. Over the last 30 years, however, UMC has witnessed a decline in membership of almost 40 percent.

Rooted in the traditions of John and Charles Wesley of the Methodist Church, and Philip William Otterbein of the United Brethren in Christ, UMC's history extends back to the early 18th century. Much of the early growth of UMC can be attributed to the work of circuit-riding clergy. These evangelical, revival-led congregations began to surpass the more established churches of the time, including the Congregational, EPISCOPAL, and Presbyterian churches.

The early Methodist Church was not confined to a particular region of the United States, which led to a split in the church over the issue of slavery. After the Civil War, the Southern church began to decline and the Northern church witnessed an increase of 400 percent in membership over the next 50 years. The issue of race and RACISM in the church continued to be a problem into the late 20th century, however. Racial segregation was evident, for instance, in the geographical organization of the church. Of the six regional jurisdictions (like synods or dioceses), the Central jurisdiction was reserved for national conference groups and all African-American congregations. The abolishment of the Central jurisdiction in 1968 led toward a new stance against racism in the church. On May 12, 2000, the church went a step further by adopting an amendment to stop all forms of racism in the church.

The church has always practiced ECUMENISM, often working together with other Protestant groups in an attempt to minister to the entire world. Both the Methodist Church and the Evangelical Brethren Church became members of the NATIONAL COUNCIL OF CHURCHES in 1950 and the Consultation on Church Union in 1960.

The United Methodist Church practices liberal PROTESTANTISM and is most often categorized as a mainline Protestant denomination. Its fairly affluent members, whose median household income is $25,000, casts a majority of its votes for the Republican Party.

The church interprets its social mission in the world through a SOCIAL JUSTICE lens along with a policy of unconditional acceptance. The church does not condone homosexual practices but asks congregations and clergy not to condemn or reject gay members or friends. The family is held in high regard by the United Methodist Church and divorce is frowned upon, but the church is well aware of the social conditions of the world and remains open to new family groups and divorced members. The United Methodist Church is pro-life but does not rule out all ABORTION. It is willing to accept the practice to protect the life of the mother or, in certain instances, where a legal abortion may be necessary for the mother. Throughout history, the church has been an opponent of alcohol and asks its entire membership to abstain.

Despite a decline of its representatives in Congress since 1960, the Methodist Church has maintained a political voice. In 1996, 11 percent of all members of Congress were affiliated with the Methodist Church, third among all religious affiliations behind Roman Catholics and Baptists. The Methodist presence gained further significance in 1916, when the church founded a lobbying office in support of the Prohibition movement. The church urges its members to become active in the political community through their right and responsibility to vote. The United Methodist Church backs a separation of church and state but encourages dialogue and interaction between the two.

See also MAINLINE PROTESTANTS AND THE REPUBLICAN PARTY; MAINLINE PROTESTANT WASHINGTON OFFICES; SECTIONAL DIVIDE OF CHURCHES OVER SLAVERY.

Further reading: Bradley, Martin B., Norman M. Green Jr., Dale E. Jones, Mac Lynn, and Lou McNeil. *Churches and Church Membership in the United States.* Atlanta: Glenmary Research Center, 1992; Fowler, Robert Booth, Allen D. Hertzke, and Laura R. Olson. *Religion and Politics in America.* Boulder, Colo.: Westview Press, 1999; United Methodist Church. *The Book of Discipline of the United Methodist Church.* Nashville: United Methodist Publishing House, 2000; United Methodist Church website. URL: http://www.umc.org.

—Ryan P. Hite

United States Catholic Conference (USCC)

The United States Catholic Conference (USCC) is the public policy arm of the NATIONAL CONFERENCE OF CATHOLIC BISHOPS. The conference is made up of all the Catholic bishops of the United States with the expressed purpose of facilitating collaboration among them as they chart a course for the internal life of the ROMAN CATHOLIC CHURCH from year to year. USCC is made up of many committees with bishops as members and chairmen, but it is inclusive of other clergy and lay membership as well. The USCC committee structure operates to recommend policy for the bishops on social, political, and moral issues.

It has historical roots in the NATIONAL CATHOLIC WAR COUNCIL, which was set up by James Cardinal Gibbons of Baltimore during World War I. This council's mission was to support U.S. soldiers both financially and with direct personnel assistance in order to develop and sustain resources in religious life and recreational needs. The council took a definitive shift in mission in response to Pope Benedict XV's letter, *Communes Litteras* (1919), wherein the pope asked the American bishops to collaborate with him in the work of peace and SOCIAL JUSTICE. In the light of this early work attending to the needs of soldiers and in the development of a vision of what working for peace and social justice means, the United States Catholic Bishops reorganized the council and gave it a more appropriate name, National Catholic Welfare Council. This council focused on policy suggestions for the bishops in the areas of education, immigration, and social action up until 1966, when the National Conference of Catholic Bishops and USCC were established and remain to this day.

A key aspect of the mission of USCC is to inform members of Congress about the nature of Catholic moral values in light of impending legislation. USCC involves itself in the study of contemporary society with an eye toward how cultural and political trends impact the public expression of Catholicism. USCC's publication, entitled *Faithful Citizenship,* is perceived by journalists and pastoral ministers as one of its most significant works. In this document, published every four years to coincide with the U.S. presidential election, the staff of USCC evaluates the political platforms of the major parties fielding a presidential candidate. The evaluation of platforms is based on Catholic social and moral teaching to give Catholic voters guidance regarding candidate selection.

The work of USCC has also drawn criticism over the years as theologians have cautioned the bishops not to get too partisan in their analysis of political and social policy. The warnings have tried to help the bishops see their mission in the public sphere as spiritual, not simply one of influencing public policy debate, as would ordinary lobbyists. Critics have also noted that the USCC staff and consultants should always include competent lay persons. The Second Vatican Council (VATICAN II) underscored that the affairs of the secular world most rightly belong to the laity, not the clergy. The competence of laity who are expert in social and political matters would lend credence to the bishops' statements, which can be perceived as principled platitudes, even by the church's own members.

The U.S. Catholic bishops, through USCC, endeavor to enflesh the relevant moral truths of Catholic doctrine to influence the public order. The dangers of partisanship and policies that are too generalized to effect any real change are significant. Despite these dangers, however, the bishops continue to analyze contemporary political and moral culture so that they can guide their own people and participate as citizens in their own right in forming just laws and moral political policy. The bishops, in their work through the United States Catholic Conference, endeavor to correct what the Second Vatican Council said was one of the "gravest errors of our time . . . the separation of faith from the practices of everyday life."

See also CATHOLIC BISHOPS' 1975 PASTORAL LETTER ON ABORTION; CATHOLIC BISHOPS' 1983 PASTORAL LETTER ON WAR AND PEACE; CATHOLIC BISHOPS' 1986 PASTORAL LETTER ON THE ECONOMY; *CATHOLIC BISHOPS IN AMERICAN POLITICS.*

Further reading: Benestad, J. Brian. *The Pursuit of a Just Order.* Washington, D.C.: Ethics and Public Policy Center, 1982.

—James Keating

United States v. Ballard 322 U.S. 78 (1944)

In this 5-4 decision, the Supreme Court concluded that a court cannot judge the validity of a defendant's religious doctrines or beliefs—but left open the possibility of examining the sincerity of those beliefs.

The case featured Edna and Donald Ballard and the by-then late Guy W. Ballard, who were convicted of 18 counts of using the mails to defraud their victims of money and other property. Their scheme was to solicit funds by falsely representing that they had the religious power to cure any disease, injury, or ailment, and by falsely claiming that they had in fact already cured hundreds of persons afflicted with such diseases and ailments.

Cognizant of the First Amendment implications, the trial court charged the jury that:

> The question of the defendants' good faith is the cardinal question in this case. You are not to be concerned with the religious belief of the defendants, or any of them. The jury will be called upon to pass on the question of whether or not the defendants honestly and in good faith believed the representations which are set forth in the indictment, and honestly and in good faith believed that the benefits which they represented would flow from their belief to those who embraced and followed their teachings, or whether these representations were mere pretenses without honest belief on the part of the defendants or any of them, and, were the representations made for the purpose of procuring money, and were the mails used for this purpose.

The court of appeals subsequently reversed the Ballards' convictions, but the Supreme Court granted the government's petition for certiorari and on April 24, 1944, reversed the court of appeals. In his majority opinion, Justice William O. Douglas reasoned that the trial court had properly withheld from the jury all questions concerning the truth or falsity of the defendants' religious beliefs:

> Heresy trials are foreign to our Constitution. Men may believe what they cannot prove. They may not be put

to the proof of their religious doctrines or beliefs. Religious experiences which are as real as life to some may be incomprehensible to others. Yet the fact that they may be beyond the ken of mortals does not mean that they can be made suspect before the law.

The case has become equally famous for Justice Robert H. Jackson's dissenting opinion, lamenting that the Court had failed to see that if jurors are told they may judge the "sincerity" of a defendant's religious belief, they will inevitably do so by gauging how "believable" they think the defendant's belief is—thus engaging in the very consideration the majority opinion had sought to put out of bounds. "How," Jackson asked, "can the Government prove these persons knew something to be false which it cannot prove to be false? If we try religious sincerity severed from religious verity, we isolate the dispute from the very considerations which in common experience provide its most reliable answer."

Moreover, he noted, "When one comes to trial which turns on any aspect of religious belief or representation, unbelievers among his judges are likely not to understand and are almost certain not to believe him."

Finally, Jackson asked, "When does less than full belief in a professed credo become actionable fraud if one is soliciting gifts or legacies? Such inquiries may discomfort orthodox as well as unconventional religious teachers, for even the most regular of them are sometimes accused of taking their orthodoxy with a grain of salt." "I would," he said, "dismiss the indictment and have done with this business of judicially examining other people's faiths."

—Charles F. Williams

United States v. Lee 455 U.S. 252 (1982)

United States v. Lee decides the question of whether the statutory requirement that imposes Social Security taxes on individuals who hold religious views that oppose the payment of such taxes, and the receipt of such benefits, violates the FREE EXERCISE CLAUSE. Edwin Lee was a farmer, carpenter, and member of the Old Order AMISH faith. He employed several fellow Amish on his farm and in his carpentry shop, but he did not file the required Social Security tax returns of employers, withhold such taxes from the pay of his employees, or remit the employer's share of those taxes. In 1978, the IRS sought $27,000 from Lee for these unpaid amounts. Lee paid those that accrued during the first quarter of 1973, then sought a refund in a suit filed in the U.S. District Court for the Western District of Pennsylvania, asserting that the tax requirement violated his free exercise rights. The district court held that the requirement was unconstitutional since the Amish believe it a religious obligation to provide for the elderly and needy within their community. As such, they oppose the public insurance system imposed on all citizens. In particular, the court found that Congress previously had granted certain religious groups an exemption from the gen-

eral dictates of the Social Security program, providing dispensation to members of faiths that are conscientiously opposed to such programs and that such religious groups provide for their own members' needs. An appeal was taken directly to the U.S. Supreme Court.

In Chief Justice Warren Burger's majority opinion, the Court stated that Congress's policy was relevant only to self-employed individuals. Accordingly, any further exemption from the general Social Security tax requirement must arise from a constitutional guarantee. The Court first addressed the question of whether the dictates of the Social Security system conflict with Lee's free exercise rights. The Court found that the tenets of the Amish faith conflict with the public insurance scheme. However, merely because a conflict exists does not resolve the dispute, because not all religious burdens are unconstitutional. To justify a law that burdens religious practice, the government must show "an overriding governmental interest." The Court stressed the government's vital interest in the program: it is "indispensable to the fiscal vitality of the social security system" because a voluntary system would simply be unworkable. Hence, the government's interest was sufficiently demonstrated. The Court last addressed the question whether the government could accommodate the Amish views without unduly interfering with that high interest. The Court balanced these factors and, noting the nation's religious diversity, argued that granting exemptions to religious organizations would be highly impractical and, thus, some religious views must "yield to the common good." Moreover, the Court found no distinction between the requirements of Social Security and income taxes. Thus, the Court found that the government's interest in the Social Security system was sufficiently great so that a religious adherent could claim no constitutional violation. While Congress exempted the self-employed, the Court was unwilling to expand that exemption, for to do so would impose the employer's faith on his employees. Hence, the Court held that the Social Security system did not violate the appellant's free exercise rights. Accordingly, it reversed the district court's ruling.

Justice John Paul Stevens concurred and wrote that the individual who challenges an otherwise valid, generally applicable statute carries the burden of showing its constitutional infirmity. Stevens, however, was dubious of the Court's claim of the threat that Amish beliefs represent to the soundness of the Social Security system. Yet Stevens agreed that to grant the appellant an exemption would create exemptions to many other tax laws, and thus there is no violation of the appellant's free exercise rights.

—Drew Noble Lanier

United States v. Macintosh 283 U.S. 605 (1931)

In this narrowly decided (5-4) case, the Supreme Court determined that an individual who refused, on religious principles, to swear without qualifications that he would bear arms in defense of the nation could be denied naturalization. Writing for the Court, Justice George Sutherland held that the privilege of naturalization was subject to Congress's complete control and that the requirements of citizenship were not properly subject to modification even—or perhaps especially—when the source of the individual's reservation was his or her loyalty to a higher, religious authority.

Macintosh, a Canadian, had resided in the United States for several years, first as a student and eventually as a faculty member at the Yale Divinity School. In his preliminary application for citizenship, Macintosh noted that he could not promise in advance that he would support any decision to go to war, but only those he believed not to "be against the best interests of humanity in the long run." At a court hearing on his petition for citizenship, Macintosh further explained that his allegiance to God came before allegiance to any nation and that the principles of Christianity required that he withhold his support of a war not morally justifiable.

Justice Sutherland noted that, while CONSCIENTIOUS OBJECTORS could be excused from their duty to bear arms in defense of the nation, this was solely a privilege provided by Congress and was not in any way required by the Constitution. Moreover, an individual may not impose his view of religion's mandates over the will of the government. "We are a Christian nation," Justice Sutherland wrote, "according to one another the equal right of religious freedom, and acknowledging with reverence the duty of obedience to the will of God. But, also we are a Nation with a duty to survive; a Nation . . . whose government must go forward upon the assumption . . . that unqualified allegiance to the Nation and submission and obedience to the laws of the land . . . are not inconsistent with the will of God."

In dissent, Chief Justice Charles Evans Hughes recast the issue in the case, arguing that the congressional policy on naturalization did not condition citizenship on a promise to bear arms. The words in the oath of allegiance are, Hughes noted, comparable to the oath of office Congress has prescribed for all national and state officials, pursuant to Article VI of the Constitution. This constitutional provision for an oath is followed by an important limitation—"but no religious Test shall ever be required as a Qualification for any Office" Hughes reasoned that, since Congress could not be assumed to have placed a religious test in the officials' oath, it surely could not be seen to have placed one in the oath of naturalization. He amplified this conclusion, that the naturalization oath could not be read as requiring the overriding of religious scruples, by tracing the long history in the United States of providing for religious exemptions from military service. For Hughes, even though the law may be imposed on those who object on religious principle, there is no inherent conflict between duty to nation and duty to God. He wrote, "There is abundant room for enforcing the requisite authority of law as it is enacted and requires obedience, and for maintaining the conception of the supremacy of law as essential to orderly government, without demanding that either citizens or applicants for citizenship shall assume by oath an obligation to regard allegiance to God as subordinate to allegiance to civil power."

See also PACIFISM.

—Susan E. Grogan

United States v. Schwimmer 279 U.S. 644 (1929)

United States v. Schwimmer decided the question whether a court may lawfully deny an application for naturalization when an applicant, who was a conscientious objector, refused to affirm that she was willing "to take up arms in defense of this country," as is required under the United States Code for those seeking U.S. citizenship. Schwimmer, a 49-year-old woman of Hungarian descent who had resided in the United States since 1921, sought to become naturalized. She chose to emigrate from her homeland because she found that the United States was "nearest her ideals of a democratic republic." In her petition, she stated that she was "an uncompromising pacifist with no sense of nationalism" but only had "a cosmic sense of belonging to the human family" that is "shared by all those who believe that all human beings are the children of God," which prevented her from taking up arms in defense of the country. The U.S. District Court for the Northern District of Illinois denied her petition because of its failure to meet the statutory requirements. On appeal, the U.S. Court of Appeals for the Seventh Circuit reversed the district court's ruling and appeal was made to the U.S. Supreme Court.

In the majority opinion, Justice Pierce Butler stated that when an applicant fails to satisfy the statutory requirements for naturalization, she has the burden to show possession of the specific qualifications. If, after examining the evidence, any doubt remains about any material fact, then the application should be denied; doubt should be construed in favor of the United States in that the obligation of each citizen in a just government is to defend it against attack. This is particularly relevant to the statutory requirement at issue here, since if a large number of persons refused to take up arms in the country's defense, then the United States would not "long endure."

In the present case, Butler argued, Schwimmer is a contentious objector, which is even more detrimental to the country's safety because her values and views not only prevent her from taking up arms but require her to oppose "the use of military force in defense of the principles of [the U.S.] government." Moreover, Schwimmer lectured frequently, which was of great import to the Court since she could use her oratorical skills to persuade individuals not to support the government's military efforts and, in fact, she was disposed to do so. Because of her conscientious objections, the Court stated that she is not capable of expressing the needed level of attachment and affection for the constitutional principle affirming a citizen's duty to defend the nation by taking up arms, if necessary, which was required for naturalization. The Court, therefore, reversed the court of appeals' ruling and upheld the district court's denial of Schwimmer's petition for naturalization.

Justice Holmes dissented. Holmes asserted that Schwimmer's refusal to swear to take up arms in defense of the nation was irrelevant in that she was a woman and beyond the draft age. Thus, her refusal to swear defense of the country would have no deleterious effect on national security. Rather, Holmes argued that Schwimmer's view that the United States should always remain peaceful is a mere suggested improvement, which should not disqualify her for citizenship through naturalization. And Schwimmer's pacifistic views are protected under the free speech guarantees of the First Amendment. Justice LOUIS BRANDEIS concurred in the opinion, and Justice Sanford dissented briefly.

—Drew Noble Lanier

United States v. Seeger, United States v. Jakobson, and Peter v. United States 380 U.S. 163 (1965)

In *United States v. Seeger* (a consolidation of three separate appeals), the Supreme Court was called on to interpret a section of the Universal Military Training and Service Act, "which exempts from combat training and service those persons who by reason of their religious training and belief are conscientiously opposed to participation in war." Specifically, the plaintiffs in these cases challenged the statutory definition of the phrase "religious training and belief" as "an individual's belief in relation to a Supreme Being involving duties superior to those arising from any human relation, but [not including] essentially political, sociological, or philosophical views or a merely personal code." In a 9-0 decision written by Justice Tom Clark (with Justice William O. Douglas writing a separate concurrence) and handed down on March 8, 1965, the Court ruled that it was the intent of Congress that the "test of belief 'in a relation to a Supreme Being' is whether a given belief that is sincere and meaningful occupies a place in the life of its possessor parallel to that filled by the orthodox belief in God of one who clearly qualifies for the exemption."

Seeger was a consolidated opinion, joining three cases. While popularly identified with the VIETNAM WAR (one of three major decisions; the others being WELSH V. UNITED STATES (1970) and *Gillette v. United States* (1971), the cases actually resulted from litigation arising in the late 1950s.

While presenting some factual differences, the three cases all challenged the limitation of the CONSCIENTIOUS OBJECTION exemption to beliefs grounded "in a relation to a Supreme Being." Each of the defendants in the underlying cases (Seeger, Jakobson, and Peter) carefully distinguished his belief from traditional religious belief in relation to a Supreme Being. Seeger admitted that he was skeptical about the existence of God; his conscientious objection was nonetheless a "religious faith in a purely ethical creed. . . . Without belief in God, except in the remotest sense." Jakobson asserted a sort of existentialist belief: "'Godness' which was 'the Ultimate Cause for the fact of the Being of the Universe'" existed as the necessary cause of existence; it was possible to relate to "Godness through Mankind and the World." Finally, Peter identified his belief as religious, in the sense of being "the consciousness of some power manifest in nature which helps man in the ordering of his life in harmony with its demands . . . the supreme expression of human nature [religion] is man thinking his highest, feeling his deepest, and living his best." However, he identified the source of his belief as his own meditations upon "our democratic American culture, with its values derived from the western religious and philosophical tradition."

The Court approached the case as one of simple statutory construction and resolved it using three points of attack. The first two points cleared the deck to allow the Court to frame the issue in the way it wanted to pursue it. First, the Court interpreted the facts of the case (without presenting strong arguments) to deny the suggestion that the parties were atheists. Indeed, the Court specifically excepted this possible objection to the statute. Second, the Court very narrowly interpreted the statutory exclusion of conscientious objection that was based on "essentially political, sociological, or philosophic views or merely a personal moral code" to refer to objections that are primarily pragmatic (such as war is wrong for political, economic, or philosophic reasons: 173) or those totally lacking in any substantive grounding outside one's own idiosyncratic belief. Since the Court denies any significance to whether one's objections are externally or internally grounded, this interpretation of the "merely personal" appears extraordinarily limited.

Finally, the Court framed the question to be determined as "a narrow one: Does the term 'Supreme Being' as used in [the statute] mean the orthodox God or the broader concept of a power or being, or a faith, 'to which all else is subordinate or upon which all else is ultimately dependent'?" The Court carefully avoided discussing the constitutional grounding or implications of the decision. Instead, it framed its arguments in terms of statutory interpretation and theological exposition (grounding a significant portion of its decision on the work of PAUL TILLICH). Here again, the Court proceeded in three steps. First, it interpreted the goal of the conscientious objection exemption in broad terms as being grounded in a broad concern for conscience rather than religion. Second, it noted that the basis for exemption had grown over the years from a close association with specific, well-known pacifist sects (such as the QUAKERS) to a sincere religious belief by the individual objector. Similarly, the legislature had sought to avoid a Judeo-Christian bias by altering the criteria for objection from one arising out of a relationship to God to one arising out of a relationship to a Supreme Being. Finally, the Court undertook a detailed theological exegesis of the term *Supreme Being* to reach an interpretation essentially in accord with Tillich's interpretation of God as being an individual's "ultimate concern." Interestingly, in carrying out this exegesis, Justice Clark relied on Christian theological resources, while Justice Douglas, in his concurrence, looked to Eastern religions (especially HINDUISM and BUDDHISM).

The Court then concluded that "relation to a Supreme Being" must be interpreted broadly to encompass any belief comparable to religion—a definition courts refuse to apply in other contexts (*Africa v. Pennsylvania* (1981); *Smith v. Board of School Commissioners of Mobile County* (1987)).

—David E. Guinn

utopianism

The term *utopia* entered our language through a book written in Latin, *De Optimo Reipublicae Statu Deque Nova Insula Utopia* (1516), by Sir Thomas More, humanist, lawyer, and defender of the ROMAN CATHOLIC CHURCH. More was lord chancellor of England under Henry VIII, martyred for his opposition to the king's claim of supremacy over the Church of England, and later beatified and canonized. Utopia, compounded from Greek terms meaning "not" and "place," or "nowhere," thus began as a literary fiction and genre, first depicting an imaginary island and later any perfect place or condition, as evidenced by Francis Bacon's *New Atlantis* and James Harrington's *Oceana* in the 17th century and Samuel Butler's *Erewhon* and Edward Bellamy's *Looking Backward* in the 19th. Jeremy Bentham coined the term *utopianism* early in the 19th century, intending to disparage visionary social and political theories opposed to his own as chimerical, extravagant, and impossibly ideal.

That religious and political elements of utopianism are closely related is obvious from both its defenders and its detractors. The fulfillment of Christian eschatological hopes on earth was a prominent feature of utopian community formations by radical Protestant sects in 17th-century Europe, especially during the English Civil War at midcentury by groups such as Levellers, Diggers, and Fifth Monarchists. Radical Protestants soon carried their experiments to America, both as dominant colonizers in the form of the Puritan settlement in MASSACHUSETTS Bay (the "city on the hill") and as marginal sects such as MENNONITES (in Delaware) and German Pietists (in PENNSYLVANIA). America itself came to be seen by many as a utopian or perfectionist experiment, both through the lens of Christian millennialism and the lens of a new land, an unspoiled wilderness awaiting transformation into a garden. THOMAS JEFFERSON and Thomas Paine vie with evangelical revivalists JONATHAN EDWARDS and Charles Finney in these politicoreligious hopes.

This tension between the American nation or the local and self-contained religious commune as the site of utopia is most evident in the proliferation of isolated religious/utopian communities in 19th-century America, some of which still survive (such as the Amana and Hutterite colonies). This tension is mitigated, however, by the fact that some perfectionist communities were viewed as prototypes or vanguards for the whole nation, most notably the perfectionist community at Oneida, New York, founded by John Humphrey Noyes, a Congregationalist minister educated at Andover, Dartmouth, and Yale, who became a convert of Charles Finney, later president of Oberlin College. A second mitigation of this tension between local isolation and national visions of redemption is evidenced in single-issue social and political reform movements taking inspiration, aspiration, and rhetorical construction from religious national redemption crusades. These movements—antislavery, temperance, single tax—were tinged with utopianism in their claims that, if fulfilled, an era of goodness, brotherhood, and justice would then be instituted. These movements, however, stand in uneasy relationship with electoral politics and constitutional government, which inherently require alliances, compromises, and other pragmatic practices to insure success.

Despite these constraints, however, utopian and millennialist movements and rhetoric are still much in evidence in American political life, exemplified in MARTIN LUTHER KING's oration, "I have a dream," and in some aspects of the ideologies of both multiculturalism and ENVIRONMENTALISM. Because American national identity is itself partly constituted by the covenantal ideas of "errand in the wilderness" and "nature's nation," a utopian style will always mark a democratically mobilizing political discourse, even by those like Dr. King who are not utopians at all. And the never-ending debates concerning "realism" versus "idealism" in our foreign policy, marked by popularly supported international crusades and interventions, are perhaps the best proofs that utopianism lives on in the very heart of America.

See also CIVIL RELIGION; COMMUNALISM; TRANSCENDENTALISM.

Further reading: Bercovitch, Sacvan. *The American Jeremiad.* Madison, Wisc.: University of Wisconsin Press, 1978; Claeys, Gregory, and Lyman Toward Sargent, eds. *The Utopian Reader.* New York: New York University Press, 1999; Manuel, Frank E., and Fritzie P. Manuel. *Utopian Thought in the Western World.* Cambridge, Mass.: Harvard University Press, 1979; Schaer, Roland, Gregory Claeys, and Lyman Tower Sargent, eds. *Utopias: The Search for the Ideal Society in the Western World.* New York: Oxford University Press, 2000.

—Eldon J. Eisenach

V

Vatican II (Second Vatican Council)

The Second Vatican Council, popularly known as Vatican II, was the ROMAN CATHOLIC CHURCH's 21st general or ecumenical council since the dawn of Christianity 2,000 years ago. Called by Pope JOHN XXIII, it opened in the Vatican in Rome in October 1962 and included four sessions before its conclusion in December 1965. Over 2,600 bishops and 400 special observers from throughout the world attended the council, making it the first truly worldwide (ecumenical) meeting of bishops designed to discuss and decide issues of vital importance for the life of the church. John XXIII died in 1963, but the council continued under his successor, Paul VI (1963–78).

At the opening of the council, World War II had ended fewer than two decades earlier. The division of the world into First, Second, and Third Worlds was emerging, and near-instantaneous communications was making Catholicism's universal theological claim a psychological and geographical reality. Whereas previous ecumenical councils had been made up almost exclusively of European and Middle Eastern bishops, two-thirds of Vatican II's attendees came from Asia, Africa, and the Americas.

Most of the Second Vatican Council's decrees and decisions affected internal church organization, the responsibilities of priests and bishops, interpretation of Scripture, and relations with Jews, other Christians, and non-Christian religions. Yet Vatican II also made essential contributions to the development of Catholic social theory. The council's principal importance for religion and politics lies in a remarkable change in the Roman Catholic Church's approach to the political, social, and cultural developments of the 19th and 20th centuries. The council embraced a willingness to "read the signs of the times" and manifested a new openness to democracy and to political and social movements concerned with economic development, global warfare and nuclear weapons, and the collapse of colonial structures. The bishops embodied their outlook in two pathbreaking documents: the *Pastoral Constitution on the Church in the Modern World* (usually called by its Latin title, *Gaudium et Spes*) and the *Declaration on Religious Freedom* (*Dignitatis Humanae*).

The first two documents announced a church that was abandoning a centuries-long siege mentality toward LIBERALISM, democracy, industrial capitalism, and cultural ferment. No longer would the church, in aspiration at least, address the world from a perspective outside its struggles, from a position of inviolable, unchangeable superiority. Instead, the church would now see itself and its mission embedded in the "joy and hope" (*gaudium et spes*), the fears and doubts, the disappointments and achievements of modern life. The bishops desired to read these changes in the light of the gospel and human experience, particularly the distinctly modern experiences of scientific and technical advance, rapid communication, two world wars, the cold war, liberal democracy, and national self-determination.

On the church's social and political mission, Vatican II in these and other documents built on the social encyclicals (letters to the universal church dealing with important matters of faith) of previous popes, beginning with Leo XIII's RERUM NOVARUM (*On the Condition of Labor*) in 1891 and continuing through Pius XI's *Quadragesimo Anno* (*On Reconstructing the Social Order*) in 1931; John XXIII himself wrote key encyclicals: *Mater et Magistra* (*Mother and Teacher*) in 1961 and *Pacem in Terris* (*Peace on Earth*) in 1963. Paul VI continued these themes following the council, as has JOHN PAUL II during his long pontificate.

The themes in these documents constitute the legacy of the council and form the basis of Catholic social teaching. The foundational principle is the dignity and freedom of the human person. Inherent dignity belongs to humans as social and communal beings, created equal to one another in the image of God. These considerations brought the bishops to highlight the rights of conscience and the inherent human rights of every person. Moreover, *Gaudium et Spes* described sin in social as well as personal terms and committed Catholics to challenging sinful social structures. These commitments became, in turn, the foundation of a strong defense of human rights against authoritarian and totalitarian regimes and, indeed, of the Latin American movement known as LIBERATION THEOLOGY. In the United States, these principles, as well as a new emphasis on peace and the terrible scourge of nuclear weapons, brought many Catholic clergy and lay persons into the CIVIL RIGHTS, anti-VIETNAM WAR, and nuclear freeze movements. Vatican II, then, was decisive in legitimating the movement of American Catholicism from a culturally marginal and defensive religious institution to full participation in the controversies of American public life.

In recognizing the rights of conscience, the council also moved away from its old commitment to the confessional state and toward recognition of the primacy of religious freedom for all persons and movements, implicitly accepting the fact of religious pluralism. Its energy then could be directed away from guaranteeing its own access to state power and toward assuring the freedom of the church (and all religions) from domination by state power.

Finally, the bishops of the council reinvigorated local church structures, especially national conferences of bishops. The bishops of the United States, organized as the UNITED STATES CATHOLIC CONFERENCE, used this new authority to address a wide variety of political, social, and cultural issues during the last three decades.

It would be difficult to exaggerate the effect of the Second Vatican Council on the internal and external life of the Roman Catholic Church in the last 40 years. The legacy of Vatican II continues to be a topic of heated internal debate. At the same time that it freed the energies of the church to engage in a wide variety of political and social action, it engendered theological and ideological divisions within the church itself that hinder its ability to act with a united front.

Further reading: Abbott, Walter M., S.J., ed. *The Documents of Vatican II.* New York: Herder and Herder, 1966; Coleman, John A., ed. *One Hundred Years of Catholic Social Thought: Celebration and Challenge.* Maryknoll, N.Y.: Orbis Books, 1991; McBrien, Richard P. *Catholicism.* New ed. San Francisco: Harper and Row, 1994; Mich, Marvin L. Krier. *Catholic Social Teaching and Movements.* Mystic, Conn.: Twenty-Third Publications, 1998; O'Malley, John W. *Tradition and Transition: Historical Perspectives on Vatican II.* Wilmington, Del.: Michael Glazier, 1989.

—Clarke E. Cochran

Vatican recognition

The official recognition by the United States of the Vatican is an issue that has appeared in American politics for well over a century and a half. Several times it has been assumed to have been settled, only to rise again. At present, the United States recognizes Vatican City as a sovereign state and carries on full diplomatic relations with it. Occasionally, such relations have been questioned, and it would be rash to suppose that controversy over this subject has been finally laid to rest.

The problem of recognition of Vatican City is rooted in the fact that the pope, the temporal head of the state, is also the head of the ROMAN CATHOLIC CHURCH, which claims mil-lions of adherents within the United States. In official church doctrine, individual Catholics, including American citizens, owe him spiritual allegiance but not political allegiance. The difficulty comes in distinguishing the two in close cases. A constitutional question appears in the traditional separation of church and state enshrined in the First Amendment of the U.S. Constitution. Should the state recognize a particular international entity, which is blended with a church? Is the state by recognizing Vatican City, giving an unconstitutionally preferred position to a denomination that is actually only one of a number of denominations, albeit the most numerous?

Diplomatic relations began at a time when the status of the Vatican was different from what it has grown into by the 21st century. As early as 1797, President John Adams appointed a Roman citizen as American consul in the Papal States, whose head was the pope. In 1848, when the Polk administration extended diplomatic recognition, the pope's temporal domain extended across the Italian peninsula as a result of the restoration by the 1815 Congress of Vienna of lands that had lain within Napoleon's empire. That state had a reputation for tyranny and misadministration, and when Pius IX ascended to the pontificate in 1846, he began to institute liberal reforms.

Polk extended recognition because he was encouraged by Pius's policy of liberalization and after considering the benefits that recognition might bring to American commerce; he was also interested in annexing Mexican territories whose populations were largely Catholic. In a message to Congress on December 18, 1847, he proposed the opening of relations, and both houses voted to finance the dispatch of a chargé d'affaires. Secretary of State Buchanan instructed the new representatives to avoid all appearance of interfering in ecclesiastical matters.

In 1867, Congress failed to fund the mission, and papal-U.S. relations stagnated, though there never was a formal termination. Issues between the United States and the Vatican were handled on a fairly informal basis, like the settlement of the claims of friars to land in the newly acquired Philippine Islands—called by President THEODORE ROOSEVELT in 1902 "a business matter"—and Secretary of State Lansing's rejection of Pope Benedict XV's peace note during World War I.

After the outbreak of World War II, President FRANKLIN D. ROOSEVELT on December 23, 1939, suggested to Pope Pius XII that he would like to send a personal representative, and after the pope expressed his interest, Roosevelt appointed Myron C. Taylor as his personal representative. Taylor and the pope consulted on such matters as the bombing of Rome and the configuration of postwar Europe. Taylor was not a member of the diplomatic corps, and with his resignation in 1950, direct contacts lapsed.

President HARRY S TRUMAN nominated General Mark Clark as U.S. ambassador to the Vatican on October 20, 1951, but about three months later, Clark withdrew his name. President Richard Nixon restored the post of personal representative in 1970, and his successors have continued the practice.

Principal opposition to a full-fledged ambassador has come from Protestant groups that point to constitutional separation of church and state.

The matter was settled, at least for the present, when President RONALD REAGAN recognized the mutuality of interest in opposing communism in Europe, and the value of the Vatican as a source of intelligence from otherwise inaccessible sources, and elevated the position of personal representative to full ambassadorship. A challenge to this move failed on October 20, 1986, when the Supreme Court declined to hear the case.

Further reading: de Bello, Nino. *The Vatican Empire.* New York: Trident Press, 1968; Fogarty, Gerald P. *The Vatican and the American Hierarchy from 1870 to 1965.* Stuttgart, Germany: Anton Hiersemann, 1982; Grahm, Robert A., and Robert C. Hartnett. *Diplomatic Relations with the Vatican.* New York: America Press, 1952.

—Emmet V. Mittlebeeler

Vietnam War

U.S. involvement in the Vietnam War from 1964 to 1975 raised several questions about "JUST WAR" and the limits of CONSCIENTIOUS OBJECTION that had both been present in terms of military service during conflicts. From its inception, the notion of conscientious objection has been inextricably tied to religion in the United States. Throughout American history, whenever the government has deemed it necessary to draft young men for military service, it has made provisions for those who, by reason of conscience, could or would not participate in military conflicts. For example, the Selective Service Act of 1917 provided exemptions from combatant service for clergy and seminary students. Members of the historic peace churches, such as the QUAKERS, AMISH, and MENNONITES, received exemptions as well.

The eventual evolution of what constitutes a sufficient basis for exemption in the United States reflects the increasing religious pluralism of the nation. Over time, this pluralism would be reflected in a dramatically broadening vision of the grounds for exemption, from membership in one of a few denominations to considerations of individual conscience that sometimes stood apart from religion. For example, in 1948, Congress passed a much more comprehensive measure than previous acts for exemptions by reason of conscience. The Universal Military Training and Service Act extended the exemption to "anyone, who, because of religious training and belief . . . is conscientiously opposed to a combatant military service or to both combatant or noncombatant military service." Originally, under the Selective Service Draft Act of 1917, exemptions were allowed for those who were members of a "well-recognized sect or organization" that had strict PACIFISM as part of its official doctrine. The 1948 act, however, increased the scope of exemption by permitting religious training and belief to include "an individual's belief in relation to a Supreme Being."

Despite U.S. involvement in the early 1950s in the Korean War, not until 1965 did the first challenge to the 1948 act materialize, even though the Selective Service System in the early 1960s was largely unchanged from its World War II counterpart. By 1965, as domestic opposition to the Vietnam War increased in the United States, the Supreme Court would rule in two cases upholding the status of draftees as conscientious objectors, and once again the scope of the term would increase. In *UNITED STATES V. SEEGER* (1965) and then in *WELSH V. UNITED STATES* (1970), the Supreme Court ruled that the meaning of the act required "a given belief that is sincere and meaningful and occupies a place in the life of the possessor (in the Seeger case the draftee was AGNOSTIC) parallel to that filled by the orthodox belief in God of one who clearly qualifies for the exemption." Both decisions shifted the focus of conscientious objector status away from religious belief and toward an individual's sincerity.

As war raged on in Southeast Asia, conscientious objector status became a divisive national issue. Religious groups through their Washington offices weighed in on both sides. Both supporters and detractors cited religious rationales for their views, always noting that they were "on God's side." At home, the purpose of the war received considerable scrutiny, especially from the ROMAN CATHOLIC CHURCH and the NATIONAL COUNCIL OF CHURCHES, which is largely a mainline Protestant organization. Numerous clergy, such as Catholic priests Daniel Berrigan and Philip Berrigan, were involved in various forms of antiwar protest such as the burning of draft cards. Additionally, for the first time, political leaders were met with an increasing rebelliousness among young people who questioned what they perceived as a racist, militarist, elitist, and essentially meaningless culture that supported armed conflict. A lack of political efficacy prevailed among American youth as U.S. involvement in Vietnam, which lasted until the fall of Saigon (now Ho Chi Minh City) in April 1975, became an intrinsic part of that culture.

—Veronica Donahue DiConti

Viguerie, Richard (1930–) *conservative activist*

Richard Viguerie, direct-mail entrepreneur and conservative Republican leader from northern Virginia, gave the Religious Right its publications strategy and plan for outreach during its period of dramatic growth in the 1980s. Founder and publisher of *Conservative Digest* and chairman of American Target Advertising, Viguerie developed computerized marketing technologies, using direct mail, that enabled religious conservatives to participate in the political process in ways never before imagined. He is credited with creating the MORAL MAJORITY through mail. It was a defining moment in American political history, the revolutionary pamphlet for a new revolution in the modern age. RONALD REAGAN's 1968 campaign manager, Cliff White, and journalist William Gill asserted that victory for conservative candidates was made possible in every election from 1966 onward in large measure because the

Viguerie Company broadcasted previously unobtainable political information to millions of voting Americans whose political-religious activism was a sleeping giant in 1970s America. Viguerie was a devotee of Marvin Liebman, a conservative political operative who was one of the founders of Young Americans for Freedom, and provided Viguerie with Barry Goldwater's campaign contributors list, from which Viguerie's coveted database was created. "Direct mail," Viguerie noted, "is like having a water moccasin for a watchdog. Silent but deadly."

Often cited as one of the two Christian Right founders in the 1970s (along with Paul Weyrich), during the 1990s Viguerie pushed beyond the mild conservatism of Ronald Reagan and moved toward a hard-right position that was more in line with televangelist and politician PAT ROBERTSON. Viguerie was among the first conservative fund raisers to understand the practical value of the antigay feelings of the right-wing rank and file of American politics. In his 1983 book, *The Establishment vs. the People: Is a New Populist Revolt on the Way?* Viguerie anticipated the "special rights" argument the Religious Right would rely on to overturn bans on antigay discrimination, beginning nearly a decade later: "I feel we should have the right not to hire, work with, rent to, or live next to a homosexual, or an adulterer, or a sexually promiscuous heterosexual, if we so choose."

Viguerie has been credited with forming and inspiring many conservative organizations, allowing conservatives in local and national races to win elections against more moderate or liberal opponents. In 1979, *Time* magazine named him one of 50 future leaders of America, and Viguerie's direct-mail solicitations have helped to raise many millions for New Right causes and candidates.

See also CHRISTIAN RIGHT AND THE REPUBLICAN PARTY; CONSERVATISM.

—Robert Wilson-Black

Virginia

The Church of England figured prominently in the political affairs of Virginia from the beginning, in spite of the fact that religious motives were not prominent in the founding of the colony. It was the continuing reality of an established Anglican Church, and concomitant dissatisfaction with it in the latter half of the 18th century, that resulted in the Virginia Statute of Religious Freedom of 1786.

Colonial conditions dictated significant differences between the Anglican establishment in Virginia and that in Great Britain. Instead of relatively compact parishes centered on a village or an urban neighborhood, Virginia parishes were strung out for many miles along its rivers, making ordinary parish life difficult. Furthermore, both church and state were affected by the absence of a resident bishop. For the church, this meant serious problems with its policies and practices regarding the ordination, appointment, and discipline of clergy. Laity were also affected, since only a bishop could offer the rite of confirmation. Although nominally under the oversight of the bishop of London, the colonial parishes and clergy became quite independent. The appointment of episcopal representatives, beginning with Commissary James Blair in 1689, improved the situation, though only slightly. And the colonial government took over several functions—for example, in family law—that would have been the province of church courts in Britain.

The "Virginia Way" that emerged was also characterized by the emergence of powerful vestries, oligarchical organizations of lay trustees that ruled over local church affairs and served as stepping-stones to higher political office. The House of Burgesses was dominated by vestrymen, a situation that lasted throughout the colonial period. In the person of these men, affairs of church and state were intermingled even more in Virginia than in Britain. Historians have often noted that the Anglican establishment in Virginia served the interests of political and social control more than those of religion. With generally ineffective clergy, habitual shortage of funds (clergy were often paid in tobacco), and laity who were largely without religious passion, the church became the primary local expression of a genteel planter society built by the labor of African-American slaves.

The Virginia Way survived the Civil War, Interregnum, Restoration, and Glorious Revolution in Britain. It could not, however, so easily withstand the rise of Evangelical PROTESTANTISM. While there had long been religious dissent in the colony, especially after the British Act of Toleration of 1689, the primary threat to Anglican hegemony before the 1740s had been from religious indifference rather than religious rivals. A new phase in the religious and political life of the colony was ushered in by evangelical preachers—mostly Presbyterians and Baptists—who had been influenced by the religious fires of the FIRST GREAT AWAKENING. Their message appealed especially to backcountry folk on the fringes of planter society, although they also made converts among the leading families. They were soon at odds with the religious and political establishment, because they favored more democratic models of church polity, were passionate rather than stately in their preaching and worship, and intensely disliked the cozy relationship between the Church of England and the government.

When revolutionary fervor swept Virginia, the question of the relationship of church and state became critical. Some thought already in 1776 that disestablishment of the Church of England was necessary to ensure the "FREE EXERCISE of religion" guaranteed by the new state's Declaration of Rights. THOMAS JEFFERSON advocated a broader understanding of religious liberty at that time, but his proposals were defeated. After independence, JAMES MADISON took up the cause of disestablishment. His *Memorial and Remonstrance* of 1785 is a classic argument for religious freedom, based as it is on the premise that "no man shall be compelled to frequent or support any religious worship," nor be penalized for "his religious opinion and belief." After turning back attempts to lend government support to all Protestant churches, Madison succeeded in getting the

Virginia Statute of Religious Freedom adopted in 1786. This legislation disestablished the Church of England and provided for the equality of all churches before the law. Both the battle for its adoption and its language significantly influenced the First Amendment to the U.S. Constitution.

See also ESTABLISHMENT CLAUSE; MARYLAND; PENNSYLVANIA; RELIGIOUS ESTABLISHMENT IN THE COLONIES; REVIVALISM.

Further reading: Buckley, Thomas F. *Church and State in Revolutionary Virginia, 1776–1787,* Charlottesville: University of Virginia Press, 1977; Curry, Thomas J. *The First Freedoms: Church and State in America to the Passage of the First Amendment.* New York: Oxford University Press, 1986; Peterson, Merrill D., and Robert C. Vaughan, eds. *The Virginia Statute for Religious Freedom: Its Evolution and Consequences in American History.* New York: Cambridge University Press, 1988.

—Donald L. Huber

Voice and Equality: Civic Voluntarism in American Politics (1995) *By Sidney Verba, Kay Lehman Schlozman, and Henry E. Brady. Cambridge, Mass.: Harvard University Press*

Voice and Equality offers a sophisticated model of the factors contributing to individuals' POLITICAL PARTICIPATION. Through the course of the book, political scientists Verba, Schlozman, and Brady (VSB) develop what they call the Civic VOLUNTARISM Model to explain why people get involved in politics. The model has three components: resources, engagement, and recruitment. More colloquially, if we ask why people do not participate in political activity, three possibilities are they can't; they don't want to; and nobody asked. VSB's discussion particularly focuses on the importance of resources, by which they mean money, time, and, notably, skills—running meetings, writing letters, giving speeches, and the like. In the contemporary United States, religious organizations are a major source of training in these CIVIC SKILLS. This is not the only way religious organizations facilitate political activity, as churches, synagogues, and mosques (hereafter, "churches") also contribute significantly to the other two components of the model.

Voice and Equality is a major addition to the literature on political participation, as it moves beyond the blunt characterization of participation as driven by socioeconomic status (SES). The book is the product of a major survey, the Citizen Participation Study, which was conducted in two stages. First, a representative sample of 15,000 Americans was administered a short questionnaire about their demographic background and political activity. From these 15,000 respondents, roughly 2,500 were selected for a second and far more detailed questionnaire. This "stage two" sample deliberately included a disproportionate number of political activists. The result is a thorough look at both what these activists do and why they do

it. The data from the Citizen Participation Study have subsequently been made publicly available through the Inter-university Consortium for Political and Social Research.

While churches figure in all three components of the Civic Voluntarism Model, their contribution to Americans' training in civic skills leaves a particularly deep imprint on the American political landscape. In VSB's account, civic skills are causally prior to engagement and recruitment. They lie latent until an issue arises that motivates an individual's political involvement and/or someone recruits her into action. Once engaged and recruited, an individual's civic skills are the tools by which she expresses "voice."

Many Americans whose low socioeconomic status would otherwise leave them without many civic skills develop them through involvement in their church. VSB conclude that the high rate of religious involvement in the United States serves to counteract the socioeconomic bias among political activists—thus facilitating "equality."

According to VSB, however, churches differ in their capacity to build their members' civic skills. The more horizontal a denomination's organization, the fewer opportunities the laity have to gain experience chairing committees, running meetings, and so forth. Therefore, all else equal, VSB hypothesize that Protestant churches are more likely to build civic skills than Catholic parishes.

Churches or, perhaps more accurately, religious beliefs also serve as a trigger for the second component of VSB's model—political engagement. American history is replete with examples of religiously inspired political movements. For the antiabortion movement of today, the CIVIL RIGHTS MOVEMENT of decades ago, and the ABOLITIONIST MOVEMENT of well over a century ago, religion has motivated Americans to political action.

Religious beliefs not only give Americans a reason to get involved in politics; religious institutions also provide opportunities for them to do so. VSB demonstrate that churches are a common channel of political mobilization in the United States, mirroring the role labor unions play in Europe.

Perhaps the greatest contribution *Voice and Equality* has made to the study of the nexus between religious and political participation is less the specifics of their model and more the attention their work has drawn to churches' role in shaping the contours of Americans' civic engagement. Significantly, previous research on political participation often ignored, or at least deemphasized, churches as civic engines.

Voice and Equality is by no means the final word on churches and political participation. The very generality of VSB's model leaves many gaps to be filled. For example, their discussion of various American denominations' political capacities can be refined. Likewise, they only touch briefly on the role religious leaders play in political mobilization. Nonetheless, VSB's innovative research design, theoretical insights, and empirical rigor make *Voice and Equality* an unrivaled source in the scholarly conversation about the role churches play in America's civic life.

Further reading: Djupe, Paul A., and J. Tobin Grant. "Religious Institutions and Political Participation in America." *Journal for the Scientific Study of Religion* 40, no. 2 (2001): 303–314; Rosenstone, Steven J., and John Mark Hansen. *Mobilization, Participation, and Democracy in America.* New York: Macmillan, 1993.

—David E. Campbell

voluntarism

Voluntarism is the philosophical view that the will, as an autonomous mental faculty involving choice and preference in human action, is preeminent over all other mental faculties. Emerging from 13th-century debates over natural law, voluntarism has figured continuously in philosophical and theological explanations of both human action and the nature of God. According to voluntarism, voluntary action, caused by volition, desire, interest, intent, or deliberation, is due to inner rather than external compulsion.

Although there existed a related tension in Christian doctrine at least as far back as Augustine of Hippo (354–430), the debate concerning the ultimate nature of God became a critical issue in the late 13th century. At the newly established medieval universities, especially the University of Paris, the controversial influence of Aristotelian texts and the emergence and growth of both the Dominican and the Franciscan religious orders contributed to the escalation of the debate. In disputations at the University of Paris, three movements participated in a debate that was concerned in large part with the presence of non-Christian thought in theology and at universities in general: the radical Aristotelians who sat on the faculty of arts; scholars proposing a synthesis of Christian and Aristotelian ethics, best represented in the work of the Dominican friar Thomas Aquinas (1225–74); and those who advocated voluntarism and were adamantly opposed to the influence of Aristotelian thought on Christian doctrine, led by the Franciscan friar Bonaventure (1221–74). The Thomist approach was rationalist, and asserted that natural law issues from God's reason, with choices of the will being determined by the intellect through cognition, while adherents of voluntarism asserted that the will was autonomous and free to choose following principles of attraction. Thomist rationalism prevailed, yet proponents of voluntarism, including the Franciscan friars John Duns Scotus (1266–1308) and William of Occam (1285–1349), continued to assert that divine will, not human or divine reason, freely chooses what is true and moral. This preeminence of the will was extended to human beings, who, according to voluntaristic theories, freely choose to believe in accordance with their desires.

Subsequent voluntaristic theories continued to assert that the will precedes or is superior to reason. In the 19th century, Arthur Schopenhauer (1788–1860) asserted that the entire phenomenal world is an expression of the will, itself a blind, omnipotent force devoid of reason that creates everything and is present in everything as a drive to live and to perpetu-

ate life. Others, such as Blaise Pascal (1623–62), Søren Kierkegaard (1813–55), and William James (1842–1910), argued that religious belief exists independent of rational proof or evidence, and thus is an autonomous act of the will involving desire, passion, and attraction. In the work of James, voluntarism takes a pragmatic turn, in that something is good and has purpose only to the extent that it is the desired or needed.

The ethical, metaphysical, and theological issues associated with voluntarism continue to be of interest. In the United States, a nation that many have asserted was built on voluntary association, religious and secular organizations exist owing in large part to volunteers who are perceived as being compelled to participate, not from external forces or by rational choice, but rather because of each individual will and principle of attraction. Similarly, the ideas of a participatory democracy and of a voluntary church imply individual choice motivated by individual will. With the political example, the United States was founded in part on an ideological commitment to the pursuit of the "inalienable rights" of the individual, which can be seen as essentially voluntaristic rather than rationalistic. In the instance of religious affiliation and participation, theologians and religious leaders continue to assert that the essence of faith and belief is individual conversion by choice or free will, rather than by external compulsion. In both the political and religious spheres, there continues to be a tension in attempts to define what is ultimately good, true, or ethical in terms of both the will of the individual and an external, collective reality. Likewise, the extent to which human action is the result of will or of reason remains a topic of interest in theological, philosophical, political, and social scientific discussions.

Further reading: Kent, Bonnie. *Virtues of the Will: The Transformation of Ethics in the Late Thirteenth Century.* Washington, D.C.: Catholic University of America Press, 1995; Schneewind, J. B. *The Invention of Autonomy: A History of Modern Moral Philosophy.* New York: Cambridge University Press, 1998; Wuthnow, Robert. *Acts of Compassion: Caring for Others and Helping Ourselves.* Princeton, N.J.: Princeton University Press, 1991.

—Lora L. Stone

voter guides

Interest groups and other organizations employ voter guides as a voter mobilization and educational tool. Typically arranged as side-by-side comparisons of candidates across several issues relevant to the race, organizations are often accused of employing guides to influence the vote for or against specific candidates or ballot measures, and not merely for nonpartisan educational purposes. While many organizations—religious and secular, liberal and conservative—distribute voter guides, the religious organization most widely recognized for voter guides, and the most controversial, is the CHRISTIAN COALITION (CC).

CC is a conservative, grassroots organization of the Christian Right, founded by PAT ROBERTSON in 1989, following his failed 1988 bid for the Republican presidential nomination. The organization first distributed voter guides in 1990, distributing 28 million for the 1992 elections, 45 million through 125,000 churches in 1996, and 70 million in the 2000 elections. Covering some local as well as state and national races, the coalition's guides are $5\frac{1}{2}$-by-6-inch cards containing a photo of the candidates, beneath which the candidates' positions on a number of issues of interest to the organization are identified by the words "support" or "oppose." Candidate positions are determined by sending out questionnaires. If no response is received, the coalition surmises positions from voting records or public statements. When that is not possible, "no response" is listed on the guide. Although the content of the guides varies from one race to another, frequently featured issues include ABORTION, GAY RIGHTS, PRAYER IN SCHOOL, taxes, VOUCHERS, and gun control.

The principal method of distribution of the coalition's guides is through churches. As 501(c)(3) nonprofits under Internal Revenue Service (IRS) code, churches may distribute voter guides but may not engage in partisan political activity. Other organizations—community centers, colleges, and religious bookstores—also distribute the guides, which are mailed just prior to the election to churches and organizations requesting them or who had received them in previous elections. Churches often enclose the guide with the church bulletin the Sunday prior to the elections. Some have ushers distribute the guides or place them on car windshields, while others prefer a more low-key approach, leaving them on a table for interested worshippers.

Some candidates and organizations, such as AMERICANS UNITED FOR SEPARATION OF CHURCH AND STATE (AU) and PEOPLE FOR THE AMERICAN WAY (PFAW), have accused the coalition of bias in its guides. Some candidates have objected that the issues highlighted on the guide are phrased to favor their opponents. In the 2000 California presidential primary, for example, the coalition's guides depicted John McCain, a candidate for the GOP presidential nomination, as a liberal agreeing with Al Gore, the Democratic candidate, on six of nine issues, while not agreeing with George W. Bush on a single issue. The coalition denies its guides are biased, however, claiming they present only "nonpartisan voter information."

Both the Internal Revenue Service (IRS) and the Federal Election Commission (FEC) have investigated the coalition's guides for possible violation of federal law. Although the coalition was denied tax-exempt status in 1999 when the IRS decided its guides did constitute partisan activity, it had already restructured as a corporation, which is permitted to engage in partisan activity. A judge dismissed the FEC's suit against the coalition in 1999. The FEC, charged with ensuring compliance with campaign finance law, contended that as the coalition had "coordinated" with certain Republican candidates, and thus the guides amounted to "express advocacy," and should have been reported as "in-kind" contributions.

When dismissing the suit, the judge agreed with the coalition that the guides were independent expenditures, permitted under federal law. While noting that the guides "made clear which candidates the coalition preferred," the judge determined they did not contain "an explicit directive" to vote for the candidates.

Nonetheless, some churches are concerned that distribution of the coalition's guides could threaten their tax-exempt status. Prior to the 1996 elections, the UNITED STATES CATHOLIC CONFERENCE recommended parishes refrain from distributing guides produced by outside organizations, and distribute only guides produced by the Catholic Church. In 2000 AU sent letters to churches across the nation warning pastors that distribution of the guides may violate federal law. The coalition responded by sending out letters reassuring pastors that they would not be in violation of Internal Revenue Code by distributing the guides. While the AU has asked the IRS to investigate some churches who had distributed the coalition's guides, no church has yet lost tax-exempt status as a result, although some have been assessed monetary or other penalties.

—Beverly Gaddy

vouchers/school choice

In response to failing public schools, particularly in urban environments, some reformers advocate allowing parents more choice in the schools their children attend. In many areas, parents can send their children to a variety of public schools within and between school districts, space permitting. Magnet and charter schools are two other forms of school choice. Magnet schools, which have been around for two decades, are public schools that emphasize science and technology, vocational training, the arts, or other specified themes. Charter schools, a newer development, are "nonsectarian public schools of choice that operate with freedom from many of the regulations that apply to traditional public schools." Legal in 36 states, charter schools are issued a "charter" by a controlling legal entity to produce positive academic results in unorthodox ways. The Department of Education estimates that close to 1,800 charter schools operated in 2000.

The most controversial school choice plan, however, involves vouchers. Vouchers are public monies given directly to parents (or, in some cases, tax credits) to assist them in the payment of private school tuition. Proponents argue that vouchers would force failing public schools to improve, as they would have to compete with private schools for students and the government funds that follow. In particular, the inner-city poor see vouchers as a means to provide them with the same option now enjoyed by more affluent families. Voucher opponents, however, question whether the supply of schools will respond to the new demand in ways that proponents expect. Instead, they maintain that vouchers will divert much-needed resources from public schools. Opponents also fear that vouchers will take the most motivated students and parents from failing schools, weakening even further those schools for those left behind.

Voucher opponents also raise constitutional concerns, as using public money to fund religious education may violate the First Amendment. Voucher supporters, however, maintain that because these subsidies do not go directly to private schools but rather to parents (who then must choose between sectarian or nonsectarian schools), vouchers do not violate the ESTABLISHMENT CLAUSE. But critics dismiss this argument in part because they believe no real "choice" exists since the vast majority of private schools (80 percent) are sectarian.

The legal status of the few existing voucher programs is unclear. In Milwaukee, the site of the first voucher program, selected students from poor families receive city funds to pay for tuition at religious or nonreligious private schools. The Wisconsin Supreme Court upheld the constitutionality of the program in a decision that the U.S. Supreme Court declined to review in 1998. However, a federal district court struck down a similar program in Cleveland, finding that the program results in government-sponsored religious instruction. The Sixth Circuit Court of Appeals upheld this decision in December 2000. The legal status of the only statewide voucher program is also unclear. Although Florida's Opportunity Scholarship Program, which since 1999 has allowed students assigned to schools that receive failing grades for two subsequent years to transfer to higher-performing schools (public or private) using state funds, survived one legal challenge (challengers claimed that the program violated the state constitution's provision to provide education through a system of free public schools), it still faces another lawsuit.

Public opinion about vouchers is mixed, although according to the Gallup Organization, fewer than half of Americans support initiatives where government pays for private tuition. In November 2000, voters in California and Michigan soundly rejected separate ballot initiatives that would have provided statewide voucher programs. Despite these political setbacks, President GEORGE W. BUSH has indicated a desire to begin a national voucher program modeled after the program in Florida.

See also AID TO RELIGIOUS SCHOOLS; TUITION TAX CREDITS FOR PRIVATE SCHOOLS.

Further reading: Cook, Peter W., Jr., and Sonail M. Shroff. "Recent Experiences with Urban School Choice Plans." ERIC/CUE Digest (127). New York: ERIC Clearinghouse on Urban Education, 1997; Gilles, Stephen G. "Why Parents Should Choose." In *Learning from School Choice.* Edited by Paul E. Patterson and Bryan C. Hassel. Washington, D.C.: Brookings Institution, 1998; Newport, Frank, and Joseph Carroll. "No Public Consensus Yet on School Voucher Programs." *Gallup News Service.* URL: www.gallup.com/poll/releases/pr010115.asp, 2001; Sawhill, Isabel V., and Shannon L. Smith. "Vouchers for Elementary and Secondary Education." In *Vouchers and Provisions of Public Services.* Edited by C. Eugene Steuerle. Washington, D.C.: Brookings Institution, 2000; U.S. Charter Schools. "Overview of Charter Schools." URL: www.uscharterschools.org/pub/uscs_docs/gi/overview.htm, 2001.

—Melissa M. Deckman

W

Wallace v. Jaffree 472 U.S. 38 (1985)

In the case of *Wallace v. Jaffree,* the U.S. Supreme Court was confronted with the issue of PRAYER IN PUBLIC SCHOOLS. Specifically, the justices were asked to decide on the constitutionality of a 1981 Alabama law that allowed for a moment of silence in public schools "for meditation or voluntary prayer." By a 6-3 vote, the Supreme Court ruled that the "moment of silence" law was unconstitutional, violating the ESTABLISHMENT CLAUSE of the First Amendment. Writing for the majority, Justice John Paul Stevens relied, in part, on the Court's decision in WEST VIRGINIA STATE BOARD OF EDUCATION V. BARNETTE (1943), in which the Court ruled that the First Amendment protects not only the freedom to speak but also the freedom not to speak. In *Wallace,* Stevens extended the reasoning in *Barnette* to protect individuals from being coerced to espouse certain religious beliefs against their wishes. Stevens argued, "Just as the right to speak and the right to refrain from speaking are complementary components of a broader concept of individual freedom of mind, so also the individual's freedom to choose his own creed is the counterpart of his right to refrain from accepting the creed established by the majority." Despite the state's argument, that it did not affirm any particular religious belief or coerce anyone into participation with the moment of silence, the Court ruled that the Alabama law lacked a secular purpose, and was a blatant attempt by the state legislature to return prayer to public schools.

The Court had already entered into the public debate over prayer in school with its previous decisions in ENGEL V. VITALE (1962) and ABINGTON TOWNSHIP V. SCHEMPP (1963). Some form of religious devotion was common in many public schools prior to the 1960s, but those opposed to such practices challenged these practices as violations of the establishment clause of the First Amendment. In *Engel,* at issue was a New York law that required public school teachers to lead children in a prayer written by school officials. The Court struck down the New York law, holding that the establishment clause prevents government officials to have a hand in composing prayers. In *Abington Township,* the Court took a step beyond *Engel,* by enunciating a standard to guide other courts in dealing with school prayer cases. The test created by the Court rested on two questions: What is the primary purpose of the law; and what is the primary effect of the law? This test was later to be modified in the case of LEMON V. KURTZMAN (1971) and would come to be known as the *Lemon* test. In applying this standard to *Wallace,* the Court found that the primary purpose of the law was to return prayer to the schools, thereby failing one of the prongs of the test the Court created in *Abington.*

Wallace is also noteworthy because of the political climate surrounding the decision. Following the Court's decisions in *Engel* and *Abington,* public opinion remained heavily in favor of prayer in school (75 percent according to the 1964 National Election Study), and there was a reluctance among many school districts to abide by the Court's decisions. On several occasions, members of Congress attempted unsuccessfully to overturn the Court by passing a constitutional amendment. But, those in favor of prayer in school were likely buoyed by the appointment of Warren Burger to the position of chief justice, along with the election of RONALD REAGAN as president in 1980, both staunch conservatives and supporters of prayer in school. In 1982, Reagan proposed a constitutional amendment to allow for prayer in school, but the vote in the Senate was not sufficient to pass the amendment on to the states for ratification. Writing for the majority in another case involving prayer, Burger upheld the use of chaplains to open state legislative sessions with a prayer, relying on the intent of the Framers in MARSH V. CHAMBERS (1983).

As one might expect, with a sympathetic president and apparently more conservative Supreme Court, the political climate appeared to favor those supporting prayer in school leading up to *Wallace.* Despite this, the Court used the *Lemon* test to strike the Alabama law. However, the decision in *Wallace* did not clear up the issue of prayer in school. The Court has been unable to agree consistently on the standard to be used in these cases, employing and then abandoning the *Lemon* text from case to case. The uncertainty on the Court has also caused confusion among the public, with cases continuing to be appealed to the Court seeking a definitive answer to the question to this day.

See also GOOD NEWS CLUB V. MILFORD CENTRAL SCHOOL; SANTE FE INDEPENDENT SCHOOL DISTRICT V. JANE DOE.

—Scott Comparato

Wallis, Jim (1948–) evangelist, activist

Born near Detroit, Michigan, on June 4, 1948, Jim Wallis is cofounder of Sojourners Fellowship in Washington, D.C., editor of Sojourners magazine, and the most widely known leader of the "Evangelical left." Wallis is a dissident voice among white Evangelical Protestants. While most are center-right conservatives (and a substantial minority embrace the hard-right conservatism of the CHRISTIAN RIGHT), he argues that biblical values should support a political perspective that is largely populist-progressive.

Raised in a conservative evangelical church, Wallis came of age in the 1960s. As he recalls in his autobiography, Revive Us Again: A Sojourner's Story, during his teenage years he questioned the racial segregation of his church and of EVANGELICALISM generally, seeking counsel and inspiration from black churches and the CIVIL RIGHTS MOVEMENT. As an undergraduate at Michigan State, Wallis immersed himself in student protest against the VIETNAM WAR. Although Wallis then felt disaffected from religion, he also grew frustrated with the secular left, which to him seemed to lack staying power, to be morally relativistic and irresponsible, and to lack robust solidarity with the poor and commitment to nonviolence.

After college, Wallis rediscovered the Bible, especially Jesus' Sermon on the Mount (Matthew 25), and felt "converted" to a gospel message that he had not been taught growing up—radical identification with and service to "the least of these." Suspecting that theological liberalism was a cousin to bankrupt political liberalism, in 1970 Wallis pursued a seminary education at Trinity Evangelical Divinity School near Chicago. There he found a group of like-minded students who believed in "radical discipleship" and the prophetic tradition. This group began in 1971 to publish the Post-American (forerunner to Sojourners), which accused evangelicalism of supporting an idolatrous CIVIL RELIGION of Americanism.

Wallis generated much controversy, yet earned a hearing among the older generation of evangelical leaders who knew something about generational conflict themselves, having long fought the reactionary separatism of their fundamentalist forebears. Along with other "young evangelicals" (as liberal evangelicals were known), Wallis helped draw together a wide spectrum of leaders to endorse an important 1973 statement, the Chicago Declaration of Evangelical Social Concern.

From the Declaration grew EVANGELICALS FOR SOCIAL ACTION, flagship of the moderate wing of the evangelical left. Wallis and his cohorts, however, remained on a more radical path. In 1975, Wallis and 19 others moved from Chicago to an impoverished neighborhood in Washington, D.C., where they renamed the magazine Sojourners and established Sojourners

Neighborhood Center, which offers a variety of social services. These Sojourners had expanded beyond "prophetic" politics to include building intentional Christian community and modeling obedience to the values of Christ's kingdom. For a time they lived communally, but the experiment eventually proved unsustainable.

The closest thing to a political manifesto from Wallis is his 1976 book, Agenda for a Biblical People, an agenda, Wallis insists, that transcends ideologies of the left and right. (He resists the label "evangelical left.") In practice, though, his affinities with leftist politics have been apparent. For Wallis, militarism, RACISM, poverty, and populist reform of government have been top concerns. Still, Wallis confounds some stereotypes. Though sympathetic to LIBERATION THEOLOGY, his COMMUNITARIAN ethos and wariness of government and politics are more MENNONITE than Marxist. Other influences include the black church, the Franciscans, and the CATHOLIC WORKER movement. He is also sympathetic to the "consistent life ethic" that links opposition to ABORTION with support for welfare. Moreover, in 2001, when most of the religious left opposed President GEORGE W. BUSH's CHARITABLE CHOICE initiative for faith-based social services, Wallis gave guarded support.

In 1979, Time magazine chose Wallis as one of the "50 faces for America's Future," and he has been influential well beyond evangelicalism. Wallis often plays the role of catalyst, rallying diverse coalitions (e.g., the Witness for Peace movement, and the religious coalition opposing the PERSIAN GULF WAR). He is a prolific commentator and author of several books, including Faith Works: Lessons from the Life of an Activist Preacher (2000). By the late 1990s, he appeared to be poised to wield a new level of clout through CALL TO RENEWAL, an effort to counter the Christian Right, build bridges between the Christian left and center-right, and find common ground among evangelicals, black Protestants, mainline Protestants, and Roman Catholics.

See also SEAMLESS GARMENT/CONSISTENT LIFE ETHIC; WHITE HOUSE OFFICE OF FAITH-BASED AND COMMUNITY INITIATIVES.

Further reading: Cerillo, Augustus, and Murray W. Dempster. Salt and Light: Evangelical Political Thought in Modern America. Grand Rapids, Mich.: Baker, 1989; Fowler, Robert B. A New Engagement: Evangelical Political Thought, 1966–1976. Grand Rapids, Mich.: Eerdmans, 1982; Hall, Charles F. "The Christian Left." Review of Religious Research. 39, no. 1 (1997): 27–45; Hoover, Dennis R. "The Political Mobilization of the American Evangelical Left." M. Phil. Oxford University, 1992; Skillen, James W. The Scattered Voice: Christians at Odds in the Public Square. Grand Rapids, Mich.: Zondervan, 1990.

—Dennis R. Hoover

Walz v. Tax Commissioner of New York 397 U.S. 664 (1970)

On May 4, 1970, in an 8-1 decision written by Chief Justice Warren Burger with Justice William O. Douglas dissenting, the Supreme Court held that state property tax exemptions for religious organizations that own and use property solely for religious purposes are constitutional. A real property owner in New York had contended that the tax exemption violated the ESTABLISHMENT CLAUSE because it constituted financial support for religion.

The Court attempted to steer a neutral course between establishment on one side and noninterference (FREE EXERCISE) on the other. The Court stated that its general approach is "that we will not tolerate either governmentally established religion or governmental interference with religion. Short of those expressly proscribed governmental acts there is room for play in the joints productive of a benevolent neutrality which will permit religious exercise to exist without sponsorship and without interference."

The Court used two main tests: Was the legislative intent proper, and would the legislation result in excessive entanglement between church and state? The Court found that the legislature was not seeking to establish religion, but rather was seeking to enable its free exercise. In granting a tax exemption to further this aim, it was neither favoring one religion over another nor one charitable organization over another. Thus the legislative intent was not tainted.

To pass muster, not only must the intent be proper, but the effect of the law must not result in excessive entanglement. The Court noted that both taxation and exemption from taxation involve some degree of entanglement. If the state taxes the religious organization, the state could then become more involved in auditing and examining the financial affairs of religion than it would under an exemption. Thus some involvement either through taxation or exemption is unavoidable. Furthermore, by not requiring that the religion support the state, the exemption reduces involvement of the religion in the state, another purpose of the establishment clause noted by the Court.

The Court buttressed its argument by pointing to longstanding historical practice from the earliest days of the Constitution and by the universal grants of such exemptions by states. Just as important, the Court refused to use "a social welfare yardstick as a significant element" to justify its decision because to do so "would introduce an element of governmental evaluation and standards as to the worth of particular social welfare programs, thus producing a kind of continuing day-to-day relationship which the policy of neutrality seeks to minimize."

The *Walz* case is generally considered to be significant for its explicit emphasis on neutrality as a guiding principle and moving away somewhat from the rhetoric of separation. The Court did not eliminate the principle of separation as one of the guides in this area, but it did make clear that neutrality became the more important guide. Further, *Walz* led the way to the soon to be established *Lemon* test by introducing the concept of entanglement.

—Steven D. Jamar

Washington, George (1732–1799) *U.S. president*

Born February 22, 1732, in Westmoreland County, VIRGINIA, George Washington was America's first president (1789–97). Prior to his presidency, Washington served as commander in chief of the Continental forces during the Revolutionary War and as presiding officer of the Constitutional Convention in Philadelphia (May–September 1787). He was unanimously elected president of the United States in 1789 and reelected in 1792. He declined to run for a third term, instead choosing to retire to his beloved estate at Mount Vernon. He died December 14, 1799, the most admired man of his country.

A man of absolute integrity, Washington's personal religious beliefs have long been debated. After his death, several denominations claimed him as a member. He was baptized and married (to Martha Custis, a devoted churchwoman) in the Anglican Church in Virginia, to which he remained a contributing member throughout his entire life. He also financially supported other churches from time to time. Washington seems to have performed his parish duties faithfully, and he attended religious services consistently, though not necessarily weekly.

Washington's public pronouncements and private correspondence testify to a firm belief in divine providence. Unlike some other leading Founding Fathers, Washington did not subscribe to the DEIST belief of an impersonal God unconcerned with human affairs. In his Circular to the States in 1783, Washington referred to Christ as "the Divine Author of our blessed religion." Most of his statements regarding religion, however, take a more abstract, less sectarian tone. "Being no bigot myself to any mode of worship," he wrote in a private letter, "I am disposed to indulge the professors Christianity in the church, that road to Heaven, which to them shall seem the most direct plainest easiest and least liable to exception." Washington was an ecumenical Christian who downplayed theological differences so as to emphasize the political usefulness of religious belief.

Politically, Washington thought religion essential to republican government. "Of all the dispositions and habits which lead to political prosperity," he wrote in his Farewell Address, "Religion and morality are indispensable supports. . . . [L]et us with caution indulge the supposition, that morality can be maintained without religion." Because republican government secures for its citizens an unparalleled degree of freedom and responsibility, Washington believed its flourishing depended on individual citizens' moral character. According to Washington, for most men most of the time, private and public morality depended upon religious belief.

As president and commander in chief, Washington sought to use his power and authority to support and endorse religious belief. During the Revolutionary War, he requested and obtained public funds for military chaplains, which he believed helped to improve discipline, raise morale, check vice, and fortify courage. As president, he issued two official proclamations declaring special days of prayer and thanksgiving. Washington did not think that government should be or was required to be neutral between religion and irreligion. He favored government support of religion because religion supports republican citizenship. Washington was always careful, however, to encourage religion in a general, nonsectarian way. His presidential proclamations recognize "that great and glorious Being who is the beneficent of all the good that was, that is, or that will be," and render thanks to "the Great Ruler of Nations." Washington's language makes clear that he thought government endorsement of religion should be inclusive.

Washington believed republican government could confidently endorse religion because he thought religion and republicanism teach the same basic moral code of conduct. When the two conflicted, as was the case with Quaker pacifists drafted into his army during the Revolutionary War, Washington acted with moderation and restraint. He sought to accommodate Quaker religious beliefs as the war effort permitted. He did not believe, however, that religious citizens who found their precepts in tension with legitimate laws, had a natural right to exemptions from burdensome laws. Like almost all the Founding Fathers, Washington understood government to arise out of a social contract. While the primary aim of the social contract was to protect civil and religious liberty, government could legitimately require its citizens to uphold reasonable civic obligations, including those in tension with an individual's religious precepts. On matters of church and state, then, Washington would disagree with the Supreme Court's "strict-separationist" interpretation of the ESTABLISHMENT CLAUSE. He favored nonsectarian government endorsement of religion. Regarding the FREE EXERCISE of religion, Washington sought to accommodate religious individuals as much as possible, though, he believed religious citizens, like all citizens, had a moral obligation to fulfill their duties of republican citizenship.

Further reading: Boller, Paul, Jr. *George Washington & Religion.* Dallas: Southern Methodist University Press, 1963; Works by George Washington: "A Proclamation," 1 January 1795." In James D. Richardson, *A Compilation of Messages and Papers of the Presidents, George Washington.* Bureau of National Literature, 1911; "Proclamation. A National Thanksgiving, 3 October 1789." In James D. Richardson, *A Compilation of Messages and Papers of the Presidents, George Washington.* Bureau of National Literature, 1911; "Circular to the States, 8 June 1783." In *The Writings of George Washington.* Edited by John Fitzpatrick. Washington, D.C.: Government Printing Office, 1931–44; "To Marquis de Lafayette, 15 August 1787." In *The Writings of George Washington.* Edited by John Fitzpatrick. Washington, D.C.: Government Printing Office, 1931–44; "Farewell Address, 19 September 1797." In *George Washington: A Collection.* Edited by W. B. Allen. Indianapolis: Liberty Classics, 1988.

—Vincent Phillip Muñoz

Watchtower Society

The Governing Body of JEHOVAH'S WITNESSES, located in Brooklyn, New York, utilizes a variety of legal corporations to support its international religious work. The first corporation, Zion's Watch Tower Tract Society, was formed in 1881 and was legally incorporated in the state of Pennsylvania in 1884. In 1896, the name of the corporation was changed to Watch Tower Bible and Tract Society. Since 1955, it has been known as the Watch Tower Bible and Tract Society of PENNSYLVANIA. This corporation represents the international work of Jehovah's Witnesses. Despite its name, it is located in Brooklyn, New York, at the Witnesses' international headquarters. At this location, the writing and editing of Witnesses literature occurs under the direction of the Governing Body. Graphics design and artwork are prepared at the Watchtower Educational Center in Patterson, New York: a complex located 70 miles north of New York City. At a third complex located in Wallkill, New York, *The Watchtower* and *Awake!* magazines, as well as other tracts and brochures, are printed and prepared for worldwide distribution. Bibles and bound books are produced at the factory location near the Brooklyn headquarters. Approximately 5,500 members of the Religious Order of Jehovah's Witnesses live and work at the three complexes.

A second legal corporation, People's Pulpit Association, was formed in 1909 when the headquarters of Jehovah's Witnesses was moved from Allegheny, Pennsylvania, to Brooklyn, New York. In 1939, the People's Pulpit Association was renamed Watchtower Bible and Tract Society, Inc. Since 1956, it has been known as Watchtower Bible and Tract Society of New York, Inc. This corporation is used to administer to the corporate needs of the ministerial functions within the United States.

A third corporation, International Bible Students Association, was incorporated in London in 1914. This corporation was used in connection with early international missionary work and the establishment of branch offices of Jehovah's Witnesses outside the United States.

The chartered purposes of these three corporations focus on supporting the distribution of Bibles and preaching of the gospel of God's Kingdom. Around the world, local national corporations have been formed to hold title to property and to support the preaching of the good news of God's Kingdom in harmony with local laws. Local congregations of Jehovah's Witnesses are often incorporated to hold title to land and buildings of worship known as "Kingdom Halls."

In October 2000, at the Annual Meeting of the Watch Tower Bible and Tract Society of Pennsylvania, the Board of Directors announced the formation of two new corporations to support the religion's organizational needs. The Christian Congregation of Jehovah's Witnesses was formed for the administration of the congregations, assemblies, education, and public religious worship of Jehovah's Witnesses in the United States. It also administers all circuit assembly programs and coordinates the work of regional building committees, which assist congregations that wish to build Kingdom Halls. The Religious Order of Jehovah's Witnesses caters to the needs of all volunteer ministers who have taken a vow of poverty and obedience. In addition to these corporations, there are corporations in other countries used by the 110 branch offices of Jehovah's Witnesses that oversee the corporate needs of the religious community in some 235 countries.

See also JEHOVAH'S WITNESSES, POLITICS, AND THE LEGAL SYSTEM; JEHOVAH'S WITNESSES AND RELIGIOUS PUBLISHING.

—Carolyn R. Wah

Wayward Shepherds: Prejudice and the Protestant Clergy (1971) By Rodney Stark, Bruce D. Foster, Charles Y. Glock, and Harold E. Quinley. New York: Harper and Row.

Wayward Shepherds was part of the influential "Patterns of American Prejudice" series of the late 1960s and early 1970s, funded by the ANTI-DEFAMATION LEAGUE of B'nai B'rith International. The book had a bifurcated agenda, asking two basic questions:

1. What is the extent of anti-Semitism among the Protestant clergy?
2. What is their role in contemporary affairs?

The authors argue that Christianity generates ANTI-SEMITISM. They also implicitly chastise Protestant clergy for their relative silence from the pulpit on important matters of the day.

The authors' understanding of the religious roots of anti-Semitism begins with orthodox faith in Christianity, meaning belief in the divinity of Jesus Christ and Christian universality. The universal applicability of the Christian faith, they argue, leads believers to be particular: Christianity is the one true way. Religious particularists are generally evangelical, driven to share the good news with others. However, when that faith is rejected, by Jews for instance, a religious particularism can bring hostility. Of course, biblical accounts of Jews' hostility toward Jesus heighten these feelings. Religious hostility can then breed both secular and religiously based anti-Semitism. After a detailed analysis of survey data, the authors conclude: "The process leading from Christian doctrines to anti-Semitism applies to the clergy as well as the laity. Indeed, although the clergy are less likely than the laity to be anti-Semitic, a larger proportion of their anti-Semitism is rooted in these religious factors."

In their last chapter, Stark and associates explore the extent to which their sample of Protestant clergy take stands on important issues. They find "the sounds of silence," estimating that only about 6 percent of sermons during the year were devoted mainly to social and political topics. The authors were shocked, noting the events that occurred from spring 1967 to spring 1968: urban riots across the country, the Tet offensive in the VIETNAM WAR, war in the Middle East, President Lyndon Johnson's withdrawing his candidacy for reelection, and Rev. MARTIN LUTHER KING JR. being gunned down in Memphis. Many clergy "touched upon" a political issue from the pulpit, yet fully one-third of sample clergy claimed never to have taken any stand on a political issue from the pulpit.

The authors turn next to an exploration of why certain clergy address political issues while others do not; their primary finding would set the paradigm for understanding clergy behavior for the next 30 years. They find that theological conservatives were less likely to speak out on politics because they were primarily driven by their otherworldliness. Theological conservatives saw preparation of believers for the next life as the church's primary purpose, for this life shall soon pass away. Theologically liberal "New Breed" clergy, who embraced the world, were far more comfortable involving themselves in politics, because they saw it as their mission to make the world consonant with Christ's teachings. But this relationship between orthodoxy and political silence would melt away not long after this book was published. By 1990, James Guth and his colleagues would find few differences in political engagement between modernist and orthodox Protestant clergy.

The Wayward Shepherds ends on a sour note about the potential of American religion to promote social progress: "So long as efforts to arouse the average parish clergyman on such human issues as peace, poverty, prejudice, and justice are no more successful that they have been so far, Sunday will remain the same: the American silent majority sitting righteously in the pews listening to silent sermons."

See also *BULLY PULPIT, THE; CHRISTIANS IN RACIAL CRISIS; GATHERING STORM IN THE CHURCHES, THE.*

Further reading: Guth, James L., John C. Green, Corwin E. Smidt, Lyman A. Kellstedt, and Margaret Poloma. *The Bully Pulpit: The Politics of Protestant Clergy.* Lawrence: University Press of Kansas. 1997.

—Paul A. Djupe

Webster v. Reproductive Health Services 492 U.S. 490 (1989)

In 1986, the Missouri legislature passed a law to regulate ABORTION. The law had four key provisions. First, the law's preamble unequivocally stated that life begins at conception, and that the state has an interest in protecting the life, health, and well-being of unborn children. Second, it specified that physicians, prior to performing an abortion on any woman believed to be 20 or more weeks pregnant, must perform medical examinations and tests to determine the gestational age, weight, and lung maturity of the fetus. Third, the law forbade public employees and facilities from performing abortions deemed unnecessary to save the mother's life. Finally, the law made it unlawful to use public funds, employees, or facilities for counseling a woman to have an abortion not necessary to save her life.

A group of state-employed health professionals, and private nonprofit corporations providing abortion services, brought suit in U.S. District Court challenging the constitutionality of the Missouri abortion statute. They asked the judge for a declaratory judgment, which means that they asked the judge to rule in their favor without a full trial. Additionally, they asked the judge to provide injunctive relief—meaning they asked that the law not take effect until a court decided on its constitutionality. The district court struck down all five provisions and enjoined the state from enforcing the law. The Eight Circuit Court of Appeals affirmed this ruling and found that the provisions in question violated precedent set in ROE V. WADE. On appeal to the U.S. Supreme Court, Missouri argued that the Court should uphold the law, and simultaneously abandon its precedent in *Roe v. Wade*.

In a 5-4 decision, the Supreme Court upheld the Missouri statute, but the majority did not agree to strike the precedent set in *Roe*. The five justices in the majority (Chief Justice William Rehnquist, who delivered the opinion, and Justices Byron White, Anthony Kennedy, Sandra Day O'Connor, and ANTONIN SCALIA) agreed on the constitutionality of three provisions. Initially, they found no constitutional violation in the preamble of the law. They ruled that a state may, if it chooses, express this sort of value judgment because it is just an abstract proposition. Second, they ruled that a state may restrict the use of public employees and facilities for nontherapeutic abortions. Third, they upheld the provision that disallowed the use of public funds for counseling women to have a nontherapeutic abortion. Only three of these justices (Rehnquist, White, and Kennedy) agreed on the fourth provision—that the state has an interest in performing tests to determine the viability of a fetus when the woman is believed to be 20 weeks into her pregnancy.

More important, only Rehnquist, White, and Kennedy agreed to leave *Roe* undisturbed. Of particular note, Justice O'Connor concurred in the Court's judgment, but argued in her separate opinion that the Court should use an undue burden test to replace the trimester scheme in *Roe*. This standard would strike down any law that unduly burdens a woman's right to have an abortion. For O'Connor, the testing provision met this standard, but the other provisions of the law did not. Thus, *Roe* still stood, but was severely limited.

Webster continued the trend begun in *Roe*. The number of groups participating as amicus curiae grew considerably from 1973 to 1989. Particularly striking is the number of denominations that filed amicus curiae briefs, including the LUTHERAN CHURCH, MISSOURI SYNOD, and the UNITED STATES CATHOLIC CONFERENCE. *Webster* was handed down at the peak of the "abortion wars" and represented, perhaps, the high point of organizing by religiously motivated citizens on the issue.

See also CATHOLIC BISHOPS IN AMERICAN POLITICS; CATHOLIC BISHOPS' 1975 PASTORAL LETTER ON ABORTION; CATHOLICS FOR FREE CHOICE; O'CONNOR, JOHN CARDINAL; OPERATION RESCUE; *PLANNED PARENTHOOD OF SOUTHEASTERN PENNSYLVANIA V. CASEY*; religious coalition for reproductive choice.

—Timothy R. Johnson

welfare provision

From the earliest days of the United States to the present time, congregations have been providing for the social and spiritual welfare of their congregants and communities. In her 1969 book, *Perspectives in Public Welfare*, Coll suggested that religious involvement in municipal social service is a legacy from English colonial rule. She noted that in prerevolutionary VIRGINIA, municipal law officials, who were also Anglican church officials, cared for the old, the sick, the deserted, and the illegitimate children of their communities. Congregations in the United States have carried on this tradition by being the hubs for neighborhood services and organizations, including Red Cross blood drives, Boy/Girl Scout programs, senior citizen centers, and shelters for the homeless.

Historically, religious-based organizations of all denominations have served not only as centers of community life and providers of welfare but also as innovators in social welfare programming, including substance abuse programs and outreach to prisoners and their families. However, in the 20th century, the supposed secularization of society and evolution of the welfare state led to the assumption that religious organizations no longer played a critical role in social service delivery. Moreover, it was assumed that social service delivery by congregations was based not on humanitarianism, but rather was done for evangelistic purposes to increase membership.

Despite dramatic growth in public welfare spending beginning with the New Deal of the 1930s, congregations have not forfeited their social responsibilities. Congregations are providing social services ranging from child care to senior services, community development corporations to community organizing, health services to arts and cultural programs. One reason is that social needs have dramatically increased (e.g., homelessness and AIDS) at a time when funding for public welfare has decreased. To fill the gap, the presidential administrations of RONALD REAGAN (1981–89) and George H. W. Bush (1989–93), as well as local and state governments, called for religious organizations to help shoulder the burden of meeting society's needs. In 1996, under the administration of WILLIAM JEFFERSON CLINTON (1993–2001), the CHARITABLE CHOICE provision was enacted as part of the WELFARE REFORM law. This provision allowed religious-based organizations to compete for federal contracts while preserving their religious character. Under President GEORGE W. BUSH (2001–05), a White House OFFICE OF FAITH-BASED AND COMMUNITY INITIATIVES was established to eliminate federal barriers to creating public/private partnerships and prohibiting religious discrimination. At the beginning of the 21st century, religious-based organizations have gained political support and legitimacy as key players in the restructuring of social welfare.

Recent studies have documented that congregations have not forfeited their social responsibilities. In response to the intensifying need for social services, it was reported that congregations increased their involvement in social and community services in the 1980s and 1990s. One national survey of local congregations found that 92 percent of congregations reported one or more programs in human services or welfare services; 90 percent reported one or more programs in health (primarily visitation of the sick); and 62 percent reported involvement in international relief. These congregations also reported programs for public or societal benefits (62 percent), educational activities (53 percent), activities in arts and culture (50 percent), and programs for the environment (40 percent). In a seven-city study, Ram Cnaan and colleagues found that 93 percent of congregations provided at least one social service. These services included: meal/food programs (39 percent), recreation for children (38 percent), parenting skill classes (28 percent), participation in neighborhood associations (24 percent), cooperation with police (22 percent), voter registration (20 percent), services for homeless people (14 percent), and housing (10 percent). Using different methods, Mark Chaves (1999) found that 57 percent of the congregations from a random, national sample provided social services. As compared to the Cnaan study, congregations in Chaves's study were more involved in meal/food programs (31 percent), housing (15 percent), and services to homeless people (7 percent).

Religious denominations also provide a wide range of health and social services. Catholic orders alone maintain some 645 orphanages and at least 500 hospitals in the United States. A third of all day care in the United States is housed in religious buildings. This makes the religious community the largest provider of day care in the country. Congregations offer special advantages in that most have kitchen facilities that are available during the week—many congregations reported food preparation and delivery by religious groups to people that are homebound, especially those with AIDS. Congregations have also been on the forefront in assisting families and communities addressing tremendous economic dislocation, hardships, and homelessness.

Further reading: Chaves, Mark. "Religious Congregations and Welfare Reform: Who Will Take Advantage of 'Charitable Choice'?" *American Sociological Review* 64 (1999): 836–846; Coll, B. D. *Perspectives in Public Welfare.* Washington, D.C.: U.S. Social and Rehabilitative Services, 1969; Cnaan, R. A., S. C. Boddie, F. Handy, G. Yancey, and R. Schneider. *The Invisible Caring Hand: American Congregations and the Provision of Welfare.* New York: New York University Press, forthcoming; Hodgkinson, V. A., and M. S. Weitzman, A. D. Kirsch, S. M. Noga, and H. A. Gorski. *From Belief to Commitment: The Community Service Activities and Finances of Religious Congregations in the United States.* Washington, D.C.: Independent Sector, 1993; Lindner, E. W., M. C. Mattis, and J. R. Rogers. *When Churches Mind the Children: A Study of Day Care in Local Parishes.* Ypsilanti, Mich.: High Scope Press, 1983.

—Ram A. Cnaan and Stephanie Clintonia Boddie

welfare reform

On August 22, 1996, President WILLIAM JEFFERSON CLINTON, who had promised during his 1992 presidential campaign to "end welfare as we know it," signed the Personal Responsibil-
ity and Work Opportunity Reconciliation Act (PRWORA). PRWORA replaced Aid to Families with Dependent Children (AFDC) with Temporary Assistance for Needy Families (TANF). AFDC, established in 1935 under the Social Security Act to provide a safety net for children of single mothers, had increasingly come under scrutiny by fiscal and social conservatives who argued that welfare promotes poverty and immorality. TANF imposes a limit of two consecutive years and five cumulative years for the receipt of aid, provides obligatory work requirements for recipients, requires unmarried minor parents to live with an adult, reduces assistance to mothers who fail to cooperate with paternity establishment, and permits states to cap benefits when a TANF recipient has another child. As a result of this legislation, changing attitudes toward welfare, and a healthy economy, the number of welfare recipients nationwide was cut in half by 1999, with some states reducing their rolls by 90 percent. What is less clear, however, is which recipients are better off, which are working full-time and remain in poverty, and which have foregone adequate childcare or health care as a result of these changes. It is also uncertain whether philanthropic efforts by nonprofit organizations, spurred by CHARITABLE CHOICE legislation, can fill some of the gaps created by PRWORA.

After Republicans won a majority in the House of Representatives for the first time in 40 years (1994), they articulated their motivation for welfare reform in the Contract with America, which states, "Currently, the federal government provides young girls the following deal: Have an illegitimate baby and taxpayers will guarantee you cash, food stamps, and medical care, plus a host of other benefits worth a minimum of $12,000 per year ($3,000 more than a full-time job paying minimum wage). It's time to change the incentive and make responsible parenthood the norm and not the exception." The CHRISTIAN COALITION, the most influential of the organizations associated with the CHRISTIAN RIGHT, responded to the House Republicans' manifesto by issuing the CONTRACT WITH THE AMERICAN FAMILY, which states, "The welfare system has caused the work ethic of the lowest income groups to collapse and family breakup and illegitimacy to soar." The Christian Coalition, along with other organizations identified with the Christian Right, would portray young women as making a rational, but immoral, choice to have children out of wedlock so that they could comfortably live off the labor of others. The efforts of the Christian Right were particularly important in bringing about welfare reform because white southern evangelicals had been important partners in the Democratic New Deal coalition throughout much of the 20th century.

Consistent with the CATHOLIC BISHOPS' 1986 PASTORAL LETTER ON THE ECONOMY and the Catholic Church's traditional support for New Deal programs, the Catholic bishops criticized PRWORA for using children as pawns to control the behavior of their parents, for perpetuating false stereotypes about welfare recipients, and for fostering conditions that might lead more women to opt for ABORTION. While claiming to support some reform of the welfare system, they would respond to PRWORA by proclaiming, "we oppose abandonment of the Federal Government's necessary role in helping families overcome poverty and meet their children's basic needs . . . Genuine welfare reform should rely on incentives more than harsh penalties."

Leadership of the Jewish community, another traditional partner in the New Deal coalition, also criticized PRWORA. The United Synagogue of CONSERVATIVE JUDAISM issued a position paper on welfare reform, which stated that "welfare benefits must be restructured to 'make work pay,' such that no family with at least one full-time worker will be in poverty." The Religious Action Center of REFORM JUDAISM concurred and insisted that welfare reform ought to "ensure guarantee of child care, job training, health care, and nutrition assistance to help move people out of poverty and into long-term self-sufficiency."

Perceiving themselves as champions of peace and justice, but clearly out of step with their own fiscally conservative parishioners, the leadership of the mainline Protestant denominations also criticized PRWORA. The EVANGELICAL LUTHERAN CHURCH IN AMERICA, for example, formed a Task Force on Economic Life that highlighted the growing inequality in the United States. The EPISCOPAL CHURCH urged its members to "work toward a welfare system that lifts people out of poverty, not simply off of welfare rolls." The NATIONAL COUNCIL OF CHURCHES, the umbrella organization for all mainline Protestant denominations, argued, "poverty is not a mark of having sinned but a result of being sinned against."

Shortly before President Clinton signed PRWORA, prominent leaders from the ROMAN CATHOLIC CHURCH, the National Council of Churches, the Congress of National Black Churches, the Union of American Hebrew Congregations, and the Synagogue Council of America issued a joint warning: "Unholy legislation that destroys the safety net must not be signed into law by President Clinton." Though he claimed to prefer legislation with more rewards for those who successfully moved from welfare to work and fewer penalties for those who did not, President Clinton's signature ensured his reelection at a time when nearly three-fourths of all Americans supported these welfare reforms.

See also SOUTHERN REPUBLICAN REALIGNMENT.

Further reading: Carlson-Thies, Stanley W., and James W. Skillen, ed. *Welfare in America: Christian Perspectives on a Policy in Crisis*. Grand Rapids, Mich.: Eerdmans, 1996; Christian Coalition. *Contract with the American Family: A Bold Plan by the Christian Coalition to Strengthen the Family and Restore Common-Sense Values*. Nashville: Moorings, 1995; Gillespie, Ed, and Bob Schellhas, eds. *Contract with America: The Bold Plan by Rep. Newt Gingrich, Rep. Dick Armey and the House Republicans to Change the Nation*. New York: Times Books, 1994; Massaro, Thomas. *Catholic Social Teaching and United States Welfare Reform*. Collegeville, Minn.: Liturgical Press, 1998; Walsh, Andrew D. *Religion, Economics, and Public Policy: Ironies, Tragedies, and Absurdities of the Contemporary Culture Wars*. Westport, Conn.: Praeger, 2000.

—Andrew D. Walsh

Welsh v. United States 398 U.S. 333 (1970)

Welsh v. United States, handed down on June 15, 1970, was the second of the three famous VIETNAM WAR–era CONSCIENTIOUS OBJECTION decisions (along with *SEEGER V. UNITED STATES* and *Gilette v. United States*). In a plurality opinion for a sharply divided court (four in the majority, one concurring, three dissents, and one abstention), Justice Hugo Black delivered the opinion of the Court, reaffirming the holding in *Seeger* that conscientious objector status adhered to all those "whose consciences, spurred by deeply held moral, ethical, or religious beliefs would give them no rest or peace if they allowed themselves to become a part of an instrument of war." Such beliefs qualify as "religious" belief regardless as to how the individual would characterize them.

Following the earlier decision in *Seeger*, Congress responded to the Court's strained reading of the Selective Service Act by removing the reference to acceptable religious objection being defined by its relation to a Supreme Being, while maintaining the exclusion of "essentially political, sociological, or philosophical views or a merely personal moral code." While this change led several district courts in 1969 to rule the new provision unconstitutional on the basis of both the FREE EXERCISE CLAUSE, by requiring military service of a religious objector, and the ESTABLISHMENT CLAUSE, by favoring one type of religious objector over other religious or non-religious objectors, the Supreme Court waited until 1970 to address the issue in *Welsh*. Interestingly, the Court ignored the intervening activity of Congress and persisted in its effort to construe the statute to fit its objectives.

In *Welsh*, the petitioner had sought exemption from military status based on conscience objection "by reason of religious training and belief." However, in filling out the application, Welsh crossed out the words "religious" and later explained that his belief as having been formed "by reading in the fields of history and sociology."

In the plurality opinion, Black ignored the 1967 amendment to the law, and held that Welsh's objections to military service were indistinguishable from those offered by *Seeger*. The only difference was that Welsh refused to identify his beliefs as in any way being religious. The Black plurality did not find this dispositive, asserting that the Selective Service board should nonetheless seek to determine if the objector's beliefs were seriously held. The only individuals not allowed to claim conscientious objector status were "those whose beliefs are not deeply held and those whose objection to war does not rest at all upon moral, ethical, or religious principle but instead rests solely upon considerations of policy, pragmatism, or expediency."

Justice John Harlan, in his concurring opinion, started by acknowledging that he made a mistake in joining the *Seeger* opinion, which, he asserted, was at best a fanciful "Alice in Wonderland" effort at statutory interpretation; he refused to extend that failure by adopting the attempted "lobotomy" in the prevailing opinion of reading out of the statute any distinction between religiously acquired beliefs and nonreligious beliefs. Instead, Harlan argued that the existing statute failed for violating the free exercise and establishment clauses. However, in light of the long-standing tradition of the conscientious objector exemption, Harlan accepted the results of the decision of the Court, not as statutory interpretation but as a judicial "patchwork" offered to avoid overturning the statute as a whole.

Justice Byron White, in a dissent joined by Chief Justice Warren Burger and Justice Potter Stewart, agreed with Harlan that the majority opinion was a statutory distortion masquerading as statutory construction. However, White disagreed with Harlan's assertion that the statute violated the First Amendment. According to White, Congress's intention could be interpreted in two ways. First, Congress could have been making a judgment that drafting religious objectors would be bad military policy because the objectors would make poor soldiers. Instead, they should be exempted like others who are unqualified for service. Since the intent was to create an effective army, excluding those that are unfit does not violate the establishment clause because it lacks the "primary purpose or effect if furthering religion." Second, Congress could have made a constitutional judgment that it was necessary under the free exercise clause to exempt those with religious scruples against bearing arms. The categorization used by Congress was not necessarily a constitutional flaw. "It cannot be ignored that the First Amendment itself contains a religious classification [protecting religious belief and action]. . . . Although socially harmful acts may as a rule be banned despite the Free Exercise Clause even where religiously motivated, there is an area of conduct that cannot be forbidden to religious practitioners but which may be forbidden to others." While the Court may have the final authority over the interpretation of the constitution (*CITY OF BOERNE V. FLORES*), Congress still has a legitimate role in interpreting the demands of the Constitution on it in the performance of its duties. Justice White argued that the Court should defer to the Congress in its judgment on this issue.

—David E. Guinn

Westside Community Board of Education v. Mergens **496 U.S. 226** (1990)

Following the Supreme Court's decision in *WIDMAR V. VINCENT* (1981), which struck down a state university's prohibition of the use of its facilities for religious worship, Congress passed the EQUAL ACCESS ACT. The Equal Access Act of 1984 required all public secondary schools with "limited open forum" policies to give equal access to "any students who wish to conduct a meeting within that limited open forum," regardless of the "religious, political, philosophical, or other content of the speech

at such meetings." Schools offered a limited open forum whenever "non-curriculum related student groups [were allowed] to meet on school premises during non-instructional time." The constitutionality of the Equal Access Act was challenged in *Westside Community Board of Education v. Mergens.*

The Board of Education of the Westside Community Schools system denied a group of students at Westside High School permission to form a Christian club that would have the same privileges and meet on the same terms and conditions as other Westside student groups. The students filed suit in a U.S. district court, alleging that the board's refusal to allow the proposed club to meet at Westside violated the Equal Access Act.

The district court sided with the school board, ruling that the Equal Access Act did not apply. Westside did not have a "limited open forum" since its other student clubs were curriculum-related and tied to the educational function of the school. The court of appeals reversed, holding that Westside maintained a limited open forum to which the Equal Access Act applied and that the act did not violate the ESTABLISHMENT CLAUSE. The school board appealed, and the Supreme Court granted certiorari.

In addressing whether Westside offered a limited open forum under the act, the Court distinguished between curriculum-related and noncurriculum-related groups. Defining the latter as "any student group that does not directly relate to the body of courses offered by the school," the Court found that Westside allowed several such groups to use its facilities. Since Westside maintained a limited open forum, refusing the students' request to form a religious group constituted a denial of access in violation of the Equal Access Act. The Court went on to uphold the constitutionality of the Equal Access Act, although there was disagreement among the justices regarding the appropriate standard to apply.

Justice Sandra Day O'Connor, writing for Chief Justice William Rehnquist and Justices Byron White and Harry Blackmun, applied the three-pronged *Lemon* test developed in *LEMON V. KURTZMAN*. First, the act had a secular purpose since it guaranteed equal access to both secular and religious speech. Second, the act did not have the primary effect of advancing religion because there was no governmental endorsement of religion. The act expressly limited participation by school officials at meetings of student religious groups and required that such meetings be held during "non-instructional time." Finally, because the act prohibited school involvement with religious meetings, there was no risk of excessive entanglement between government and religion.

Justices Anthony Kennedy and ANTONIN SCALIA relied on the act's neutrality in holding that it did not violate the establishment clause. Any benefits to religion were direct rather than indirect, they argued, and students were not required, or even encouraged, to participate in religious activity.

Justice Thurgood Marshall wrote a separate opinion, in which Justice WILLIAM BRENNAN joined, to caution that schools such as Westside should take steps to ensure that toleration of religious speech is not construed as endorsement of such speech.

Only Justice John Paul Stevens dissented from the Court's decision. Stevens would have defined a noncurriculum-related group more narrowly as one that has as its purpose "the advocacy of partisan theological, political, or ethical views." Since none of Westside's student groups fell within this category, the Equal Access Act did not bind Westside. Stevens went on to argue that the Court's interpretation of the act constituted a "sweeping intrusion by the Federal Government into the operation of our public schools." In Stevens's view, the Court should have demonstrated greater respect for the power of local school districts to shape their educational environment.

—Malia Reddick

West Virginia Board of Education v. Barnette 319 U.S. 624 (1943)

At issue in *Barnette* is mandatory flag saluting and the recitation of the Pledge of Allegiance in public schools. As in MIN-ERSVILLE SCHOOL DISTRICT V. GOBITIS (1940), members of JEHOVAH'S WITNESSES filed suit asking for an injunction against the enforcement of this law. A three-judge panel of the federal district court granted relief and the case was brought to the Supreme Court on direct appeal. The Supreme Court, in an opinion by Justice Jackson, newly on the Court, overruled *Gobitis* and decided that mandatory flag salutes are an unconstitutional violation of freedom of speech.

As the patriotism associated with World War II cooled (since the United States was largely winning), the environment of this second flag saluting case was different from the environment three years earlier in *Gobitis*. There were personnel changes on the Court as well, adding to the number of civil libertarians who would champion free speech and freedom of religion guarantees. Finally, there was much criticism of the *Gobitis* decision by legal scholars, prompted in part by the violence against Jehovah's Witnesses that resulted largely because of that decision. There was hope, therefore, that this decision would be different, and it was. However, it reached a decision contradicting *Gobitis* not by reference to religious freedom, but rather by the establishment of a First Amendment right *not* to speak.

In his majority opinion, Jackson discusses this freedom *from* expression by saying:

> . . . the compulsory flag salute and pledge require affirmation of a belief and an attitude of mind . . . It is now a commonplace that censorship or suppression of expression of opinion is tolerated by our Constitution only when the expression presents a clear and present danger of action of a kind the State is empowered to prevent and punish. It would seem that involuntary affirmation could be commanded only on even more immediate and urgent grounds than silence . . . To sustain the compulsory flag salute we are required to say

> that a Bill of Rights which guards the individual's right to speak his own mind, left it open to public authorities to compel him to utter what is not in his mind.

It matters not, then, that there are religious reasons these individuals do not wish to speak, but rather that do not wish to speak period. While the majority agreed that national unity is a governmental interest, they discounted the finding in *Gobitis* that it is compelling enough to override concerns of individual liberty.

Justices Black, Douglas, and Murphy filed concurring opinions to explain their change of heart; all three were in the majority in *Gobitis*. Black and Douglas based their concurrence on freedom of religion and argued: "Neither our domestic tranquility in peace nor our martial effort in war depend on compelling little children to participate in a ceremony which ends in nothing for them but a fear of spiritual condemnation." Murphy, in a separate concurrence, wrote: "There is before us the right of freedom to believe, freedom to worship one's Maker according to the dictates of one's conscience, a right which the Constitution specifically shelters. Reflection has convinced me that as a judge I have no loftier duty or responsibility than to uphold that spiritual freedom to its farthest reaches." He went on to emphasize that the guarantees in the first amendment encompass "both the right to speak freely and the right to refrain from speaking at all."

Not surprisingly, Justice Frankfurter, the author of the *Gobitis* decision, dissented. In it, he argued that even as "One who belongs to the most vilified and persecuted minority in history" (he was Jewish), he "cannot bring [his] mind to believe that the 'liberty' secured by the Due Process Clause gives this Court authority to deny to the State of West Virginia the attainment of that which we all recognize as a legitimate legislative end, namely, the promotion of good citizenship, by employment of the means here chosen." Here, he focused on the proper role of the Court, and saw nullification of flag salute requirements as beyond that realm.

See also CONSCIENTIOUS OBJECTION; COX V. NEW HAMP-SHIRE; LOVELL V. CITY OF GRIFFIN; MARTIN V. STRUTHERS; MUR-DOCK V. PENNSYLVANIA.

Further reading: Epstein, Lee, and Thomas G. Walker. *Constitutional Law for a Changing America: Rights, Liberties, and Justice.* 4th ed. Washington, D.C.: CQ Press, 2001.

—Sara C. Benesh

Whitefield, George (1714–1770) *evangelist*

George Whitefield was an Anglican evangelist, born in Gloucester, England, whose 1739–41 preaching tour of America galvanized the religious revival that later became known as the FIRST GREAT AWAKENING. A charismatic orator, Whitefield's itinerant preaching drew huge crowds and established REVIVALISM as a major phenomenon in the colonies. Previously limited to sporadic outbreaks in New England, Whitefield's efforts transformed the awakening into a unified mass movement that posed a serious challenge to the religious status quo in the colonies. Though Whitefield produced no distinguished theological writings, his singular success at arousing evangelical fervor set him apart as one of the most important figures of the First Great Awakening.

The son of innkeepers, Thomas Whitefield and Elizabeth Edwards, Whitefield entered Oxford University and came under the influence of John and Charles Wesley. They persuaded him, following his graduation, to become a missionary to the colony of Georgia. With the approval of the Georgia trustees and the Anglican hierarchy, Whitefield sailed for Georgia in February 1738. Upon his arrival in May 1738, Whitefield immediately set out to do missionary work. In his efforts to promote piety, his oratory skills drew attention for allegedly winning "the hearts of his Hearers." He soon decided to establish an orphanage in Savannah, and in September 1738 sailed back to England to raise money for that purpose and to take priest's orders.

Back in England, Whitefield developed a reputation as an evangelical orator. His compelling voice and his appeal to a faith based on emotion proved popular among ordinary people. But, he was unpopular with many Anglican clergymen, whom he had criticized for allegedly not proclaiming the truths of the Bible and the Articles of the Anglican Church. Despite his ill repute among some ministers, the young evangelist secured priest's order and collected about 1,000 pounds for his proposed orphanage.

Whitefield returned to America in November 1739. He immediately set out preaching and drew large crowds. After briefly returning to Georgia, Whitefield embarked on his most distinguished preaching effort, an intensive 14-month tour of the mainland colonies. The frenzy that surrounded his itinerant preaching precipitated widespread controversy. Many were attracted to Whitefield's call for a return to a heartfelt, spiritual religion. JONATHAN EDWARDS, Congregational minister from Northampton, Massachusetts, was one of many clergy who welcomed this movement because of its attention to the spiritual basis of faith. Other ministers, most notably Charles Chauncy and JONATHAN MAYHEW, reacted angrily to Whitefield's challenge to religious convention. Itinerancy was charged with violating traditional boundaries of parish and congregation. And, furthermore, the emphasis on personal religious experience was alleged to have introduced a subjective element into religious practice that overturned objective standards of piety and encouraged licentiousness. The ensuing religious "controversies" debated the merits of the evangelical movement that Whitefield had helped galvanize.

Although preoccupied for most of his stay in America with itinerant preaching, Whitefield did build his orphanage in Georgia. Called Bethesda, the orphanage established a reputation for the education of children under the supervision of two followers of Whitefield, Jonathan Barber and James Habersham.

Whitefield's celebrated preaching tour ended in January 1741 with his departure for England. Though he returned to the colonies five more times—in 1744, 1751, 1754, 1763, and 1769—and attracted sizable audiences, he was never able to generate the kind of frenzied excitement that had distinguished his earlier tour. Whitefield married Elizabeth Burnell James in November 1741; their only child died in infancy. Whitefield's devotion to his work apparently left him little time for family life. He had plans to add a Christian academy and a college to Bethesda, but was successful only in achieving the former. Whitefield died in Newburyport, Massachusetts, and in compliance with his request, was buried in Newburyport beneath the First Presbyterian Church.

Whitefield made a lasting impression on the 18th-century religious scene as a direct result of his instigation of the wave of revivalism of the 1740s. By virtue of his charismatic rhetorical style, railing against the religious status quo and powerfully asserting the merit of EVANGELICALISM, Whitefield's preaching became a symbol of the evangelical movement. Supporters used Whitefield as an example of the emotionalism that they alleged was needed to renew religion; opponents used him as an example of the alleged "excesses" of revival enthusiasm. Ultimately, Whitefield and the movement he catalyzed would profoundly reshape American Protestantism by reintroducing sentiment as a criterion of faith. This theological injunction led to ecclesiastical schism within American Protestantism and the subsequent division into "rational" and "evangelical" factions within the Congregational and Presbyterian churches.

Further reading: Belcher, Joseph. *George Whitefield: A Biography with Special Reference to His Labors in America.* New York: American Tract Society, 1857; Belden, Albert David. *George Whitefield, the Awakener.* New York: Macmillan, 1953; Henry, Stuart Clark. *George Whitefield, Wayfaring Witness.* New York: Abingdon Press, 1957.

—Roland Marden

Whitehead, John Wayne (1946–) *activist*

John Whitehead is the president of the RUTHERFORD INSTITUTE, a Charlotte, Virginia–based international legal and educational nonprofit and nonpartisan organization dedicated to preserving human rights and defending civil liberties. He earned a B.A. from the University of Arkansas in 1969 and a J.D. from the University of Arkansas School of Law in 1974. He served as a lieutenant in the U.S. Army from 1969 to 1971. He and his wife, Carol, have five children and live in Virginia.

He converted to Christianity in 1974 after reading Hal Lindsey's *The Late Great Planet Earth.* Believing God called him to preach, he and his wife packed their belongings and headed out to Hal Lindsey's Light and Power House seminary in Los Angeles. He soon discovered that his legal knowledge and trial skills were helpful to many who felt they had experienced civil liberties infractions in institutions such as the public schools. He wrote his first of 15 books, *The Separation Illusion: A Lawyer Examines the First Amendment,* which strongly argued for Christians not to cede battleground in the fight for legal justice, even if that meant going to court.

By 1981, he wrote his second book, *The Second American Revolution,* which was in a sense a redoing of *The Separation Illusion.* He used militaristic language, imagery, and metaphors to spur Christians on toward confrontation with the "forces of evil" that he believed were aligned against Christians and Christianity. By now the MORAL MAJORITY was founded; PAT ROBERTSON was gaining influence in the political and media world; JAMES DOBSON had formed FOCUS ON THE FAMILY in 1977, and later the FAMILY RESEARCH COUNCIL in 1982. Clearly, other prominent evangelical Christian leaders shared Whitehead's view that Christians should be involved in the political process.

The Second American Revolution sold over 100,000 copies and gave Whitehead the financial freedom to pursue his dream of launching a legal organization that would defend individuals' civil liberties, especially those guaranteed in the First Amendment. He did so in 1982. Today, the Rutherford Institute, which was named after Samuel Rutherford, a Scottish Presbyterian minister of the early 17th century who wrote the legal philosophical treatise *Lex Rex,* is an international organization with various offices in the United States and abroad.

Whitehead does not avoid controversy. After swinging 180 degrees ideologically—from a 1960s radical, who even as a member of the military engaged in anti–VIETNAM WAR demonstrations, to a hard right-wing Christian conservative—he founded the Rutherford Institute with the Chalcedon Foundation and funds from the Coors Foundation. Christian reconstructionist R. J. Rushdoony, who was on Rutherford's first board of directors, founded the Chalcedon Foundation. As a theonomist, Rushdoony argued that laws should reflect Old Testament biblical teaching, which meant among other things supporting the death penalty for ABORTION providers and homosexuals. At the time, Whitehead supported much of theonomy's positions. Today he says he does not believe these things.

He has moved much closer to the center of the political and ideological spectrum, even though he is still associated by most on the left as a "card-carrying" Christian right-winger. Today, for example, instead of solely defending Christians, his organization has taken on a number of cases involving people of other faiths, including Jews, Muslims, Native Americans, and Hindus. He has both angered and confused many in the Christian Right with his recent positions on controversial issues. On the one hand, he angers many evangelical Christians by calling them homophobic and hypocritical in their opposition to homosexuals. He notes, "we didn't change our basic beliefs, but we did change how we approached subjects. For example, we're now making clear that gays have rights. They pay taxes. They're American citizens. Are we going to allow discrimination against them in this day and age in America?" Still, he also confused many in turn by paying Paula Jones's legal fees in her suit against President WILLIAM JEFFERSON CLINTON, while praising Clinton for several policy positions, such as promoting Christian teachers in public schools and Christian rights in the workplace.

His latest book, *Grasping the Wind,* is as he says a book about "humanity's search for meaning." That "meaning" is found through pop culture. He strongly believes that Christians, and especially evangelical Christians, should engage in culture, not disengage from it. To do otherwise is to abdicate their responsibility to be "salt and light" to the world. He continues to address the legal issues in the Institute's *Rutherford Institute Litigation Report,* but now he attacks the popular culture venue with *Gadfly.*

John Whitehead invites opinion, debate, and engagement from the Christian community, even when that engagement does not seem "correct" from those whose interpretation of the Scripture is more narrowly defined. His thinking is constantly evolving, and it is this evolution in process that will produce more controversy in the future.

—Stephen M. King

White House Office of Faith-Based and Community Initiatives

The White House Office of Faith-Based and Community Initiatives (White House OFBCI) was established in January 2001 by executive order of president GEORGE W. BUSH. The White House OFBCI was established within the Executive Office of the President to have lead responsibility in the executive branch to establish policies, priorities, and objectives for the federal government's comprehensive effort to enlist, equip, enable, empower, and expand the work of faith-based and other community organizations to the extent permitted by law. President Bush fulfilled a campaign promise to create the White House OFBCI and appointed University of Pennsylvania criminologist and professor of politics, religion, and civil society, John J. DiIulio Jr., to work with five federal agencies (Justice, Housing and Urban Development, Health and Human Services, Labor, and Education) to convert his proposal into legislation.

The purpose of the office is to integrate the social service efforts of religious institutions and other nonprofits with those financed by the federal government (the faith-based initiative reflects a fundamental difference between Democrats and Republicans about the role of the government in meeting social needs). The Executive Office of the President coordinates a national effort to expand opportunities for faith-based and other community organizations to strengthen their capacity to better meet social needs in American communities. One of the principal functions of the White House OFBCI is to develop, lead, and coordinate the administration's policy agenda affecting faith-based and other community programs and initiatives, expand the role of such efforts in communities, and increase their capacity through executive action, legislation, federal, and private funding, in addition to regulatory relief.

The White House OFBCI builds on past innovations, most notably bipartisan CHARITABLE CHOICE legislation. The Personal Responsibility and Work Opportunity Reconciliation Act (PRWORA) of 1996—WELFARE REFORM—contains in Section 104, a provision known as "Charitable Choice." This provision encourages states to "expand the involvement of community and faith-based organizations in the public anti-poverty effort." The Charitable Choice provision of Congress's welfare reform legislation actively encourages states to include faith-based organizations in public/private partnerships. Authored by then-Senator John Ashcroft of Missouri (who is currently U.S. attorney general), the provision requires that when government agencies choose to contract with private sector organizations in building welfare-to-work programs, faith-based organizations must be eligible to compete for those contracts. Although the term "Charitable Choice" is most appropriately linked with welfare reform and with programs that have been specifically cited by federal Charitable Choice expansion acts, the term now seems to be linked with almost any program that turns to faith-based organizations for public-private partnerships.

Hence, it is the belief of the White House that faith-based and other community organizations are indispensable in meeting the needs of poor Americans and distressed neighborhoods. In response to questions regarding the role of federal funding for faith-based programs, Bush stressed that "government cannot be replaced by such organizations, but it can and should welcome them as partners. The paramount goal is compassionate results, and private and charitable community groups, including religious ones, should have the fullest opportunity permitted by law to compete on a level playing field, so long as they achieve valid public purposes, such as curbing crime, conquering addition, strengthening families and neighborhoods, and overcoming poverty." This delivery of social services must be results-oriented and should value the bedrock principles of pluralism, nondiscrimination, evenhandedness, and neutrality.

In his classic work DEMOCRACY IN AMERICA, Alexis de Tocqueville observed that "Religion in America takes no direct part in the government of society, but it must be regarded as the first of their political institutions." That is the case, he went on to explain, because religion nurtures certain civic virtues or "habits of the heart"—a sense of public morality and civility, of restraint and fair dealing—without which democracies cannot endure. As de Tocqueville pithily remarked: "Despotism may govern without faith, but liberty cannot." Four decades earlier, President GEORGE WASHINGTON expressed similar sentiments in his now famous Farewell Address to the nation, declaring, "Of all the dispositions and habits which lead to political prosperity, religion and morality are indispensable supports."

The welfare reform movement that began with the 104th Congress's Contract with America, was extended by President WILLIAM JEFFERSON CLINTON's signature on the Personal Responsibility and Work Opportunity Act of 1996, and culmi-

nated with the Bush administration's establishment of the White House OFBCI, which marked a radical departure from the long-term federal commitment to meet the basic needs of low-income families. Religious organizations have long been important and widely recognized contributors to the support of low-income families and vulnerable populations in the United States (their programs have often outperformed traditional government funded social programs). The role of religious organizations has taken on a new significance and gained much greater visibility with the implementation of federal welfare reform, especially in areas where they serve populations whose support has been significantly curtailed or who are specifically excluded from the government's revised welfare safety net.

The close connection between political prosperity and religious principles has been widely understood and remarked upon throughout American history. Whether we label it a republican ethnic or a CIVIL RELIGION, the belief has been that a civic culture nourished by deep religiomoral impulses, is absolutely necessary to sustain the American experiment in ordered liberty. The White House OFBCI deserves credit for its good intentions and temperate voices. However, what's missing is an advocate for the point of view that strict SEPARATION OF CHURCH AND STATE is the ultimate guarantee of equality and justice for all.

See also AFRICAN AMERICANS AND FAITH-BASED INITIATIVES.

Further reading: Carson-Thies, Stanley W. "Introduction." In *A Guide to Charitable Choice: The Rules of Section 104 of the 1996 Federal Welfare Law Governing State Cooperation with Faith-Based-Social-Service Providers.* Washington, D.C.: Center for Public Justice, 1997.

—Boris E. Ricks

Why Conservative Churches Are Growing: A Study in Sociology of Religion (1972) By Dean M. Kelley. New York: Harper and Row

Dean M. Kelley, a NATIONAL COUNCIL OF CHURCHES (NCC) official and UNITED METHODIST pastor, wrote in 1972 of a significant shift in church membership. Conservative churches were growing because they challenged parishioners with important religious questions, imposed strict membership requirements, and had a clear sense of mission and purpose. Churches lacking these characteristics saw membership level off or decline. Efforts to be inclusive, ecumenical, and tolerant hurt mainline Protestant denominations. Written by a NCC insider, the work was a call for the ecumenical movement to reexamine its approach to the business of religion.

Based on membership levels in the late 1960s for various religious bodies, Kelley demonstrated how conservative branches were cornering the religious marketplace. The "conservative" LUTHERAN CHURCH–MISSOURI SYNOD reported a slight increase in membership despite an aggregate decrease in the three main Lutheran bodies. The "conservative" Christian Reformed Church added members, while the "liberal" Reformed Church in America saw its membership level off (see DUTCH REFORMED TRADITION). As the "liberal" AMERICAN BAPTIST CHURCHES struggled to keep its members, membership in the "conservative" SOUTHERN BAPTIST CONVENTION skyrocketed. Other conservative faiths that demonstrated significant membership gains were the Church of Jesus Christ of LATTER-DAY SAINTS (Mormons), the SEVENTH-DAY ADVENTISTS, the Church of the Nazarene, the SALVATION ARMY, and the JEHOVAH'S WITNESSES.

Unlike some critics, Kelley does not assail the "wheelhorses" of the ecumenical movement for their social activism. He supported church efforts in the social and political realm, as long as churches and pastors remembered that their primary purpose is to provide religious meaning to their parishioners. However, too many ecumenical churches neglected, in his view, the primary issues of "ultimate meaning" while focusing on secondary issues like helping the needy and providing fellowship activities.

Conduct, as well as content, is important to church growth. Growing churches tend to be serious, strict, costly, and binding, as three historical examples illustrate. Designed to "restore" the Christian Church of the New Testament, the ANABAPTISTS were "rebaptizers" who flourished while imposing restrictive barriers, threats, and persecutions. Persecuted often and driven out of several areas, the Mormons finally found a home in Utah through in part their members' strict adherence to a religious code. The Jehovah's Witnesses demand a costly and binding commitment that includes conformity to a proscribed agenda.

To succeed in the 1970s, Kelley said a church needed specific goals, adequate controls, and clear communication. Other "traits of strictness" would help. Absolutism demonstrates a high commitment to a belief system. Conformity ensures dissent is kept to a minimum. And "fanaticism" compels members to share their message with zeal to the world. What should churches interested in growth avoid? Kelley listed six "traits of leniency"—relativism, diversity, dialogue, lukewarmness, individualism, and reserve. As the church at large includes more educated members in the 20th century, Kelley's warnings deserve attention. How does a contemporary church intent on growth disavow individualism, a primary tenant of American political culture? Church leaders of the future will surely need to balance Kelley's admonitions with the realities of the present and future parish.

Kelley's work provided few specific answers to how ecumenical churches could bolster their numbers. Certainly, they could firm up some of their traits of leniency, and put less emphasis on social activism. At the heart of any recovery is what lies at the heart of any religion, connecting meaning to people's lives. A church needs to know for what it stands, connect that to people's lives, and erect sufficient membership barriers to deter the less devout followers. Rigorous instruction is essential. Attitudinal and behavioral tests of membership are needed. Members need to encourage each other. Only then will all churches bolster their membership rolls.

As a NCC executive, Kelley was in an ideal position to observe the growth of conservative churches—and the stagnation of mainline churches—during the contentious 1960s. His work continues to inform today. Parishioners focus on the spiritual food of the congregation. People want churches to make a difference and be different. Social activism is of secondary importance. Church leaders need to balance these basic worship needs with loftier societal goals of justice, peace, and inclusion in an increasingly heterogeneous population.

—Jeffrey Walz

Widmar v. Vincent 453 U.S. 263 (1981)

In *Widmar v. Vincent*, a student religious group at the University of Missouri at Kansas City (UMKC) challenged a university regulation that prohibited the use of university buildings or grounds "for purposes of religious worship or religious teaching." Between 1973 and 1977, the group Cornerstone had used university facilities for its meetings, which involved praying, singing hymns, and discussing religious experiences. In 1977, UMKC denied the group access, reasoning that allowing religious groups such as Cornerstone to use university facilities would violate the ESTABLISHMENT CLAUSE. Cornerstone members filed suit in a U.S. district court, alleging that the policy violated their rights to FREE EXERCISE of religion and freedom of speech.

The district court upheld UMKC's regulation as being required by the establishment clause, but the court of appeals reversed. The university appealed, and the Supreme Court granted certiorari.

Avoiding the potential conflict between the First Amendment's religion clauses, the Supreme Court applied the public forum doctrine. Since UMKC "created a forum generally open for use by student groups," its decision to exclude certain groups based on the content of their speech must be justified by a compelling interest.

UMKC claimed that it had a compelling interest in avoiding a violation of the establishment clause. While the Court agreed that this was a compelling interest, it applied the three-pronged *Lemon* test, developed in *LEMON V. KURTZMAN*, to determine whether UMKC would violate the establishment clause by adopting an "equal access" policy. The lower courts had held, and the Supreme Court agreed, than an equal access policy would have a secular purpose and would avoid entanglement with religion, as required by the *Lemon* test. The more difficult question was whether the primary effect of such a policy would be to advance religion. The Court held that, although religious organizations might receive incidental benefits from an open forum, the advancement of religion would not be the forum's primary effect.

Concluding that the university regulation was a content-based exclusion of religious speech that could not be justified constitutionally, the Court ruled 8-1 in favor of the student group.

Justice John Paul Stevens agreed with the Court's decision but disagreed with the Court's application of the public forum doctrine and compelling interest standard in this situation. In Stevens's view, because public universities have limited resources, greater deference should be given to their decisions regarding the use of university resources for extracurricular activities. Even under a less restrictive standard, however, UMKC had not adequately justified its decision to exclude Cornerstone from university facilities.

Justice Byron White filed the lone dissent, asserting that the case at hand involved religious worship rather than speech. Accordingly, the burden imposed on Cornerstone members' ability to exercise their religious beliefs should be balanced against UMKC's interest in maintaining a definitive SEPARATION OF CHURCH AND STATE. In White's assessment, the university's desire to avoid claims that it was supporting religious worship took precedence over Cornerstone members being forced to meet off campus.

The Court's decision in *Widmar v. Vincent* that an equal access policy did not violate the establishment clause applied only to public colleges and universities. Congress responded to *Widmar* in 1984 by passing the EQUAL ACCESS ACT, which required all public secondary schools with "limited open forum" policies to give equal access to "any students who wish to conduct a meeting within that limited open forum," regardless of the "religious, political, philosophical, or other content of the speech at such meetings." The Court upheld the constitutionality of the Equal Access Act in 1990 in *WESTSIDE COMMUNITY BOARD OF EDUCATION V. MERGENS.*

—Malia Reddick

Wiesel, Elie (1928–) *writer*

A native of Sighet, Romania, and a survivor of the Nazi German death camps, Elie Wiesel has dedicated his life to ensuring that the world does not forget the HOLOCAUST. Wiesel has written some 36 books and has delivered countless lectures, and he served in the 1970s and 1980s as the chairman of the President's Commission on the Holocaust.

Wiesel was 15 when he and his family were deported from Romania to Auschwitz. Neither his mother nor his father survived the Holocaust. His younger sister was also killed. Somehow Wiesel survived (as did two older sisters); he ended up in Paris, where he studied at the Sorbonne and became a journalist. In 1956 he moved to New York City and applied for U.S. citizenship. In the same year, he published his first book, which, in modified and shortened form, was published in French as *La Nuit* in 1958 and in English, as *Night*, in 1960.

Night, wrote Wiesel, is "the foundation" of his work; "all the rest is commentary." In what is probably his most famous literary passage, Wiesel describes his arrival at Auschwitz: "Never shall I forget that night, the first night in camp, which turned my life into one long night, seven times cursed and seven times sealed. Never shall I forget the faces of the children, whose bodies I saw turned into wreaths of smoke beneath a silent blue sky. . . . Never shall I forget those moments which murdered my God and turned my dreams to dust."

Night, and indeed all of Wiesel's life and work, reflects his commitment to remembering and to communicating "visions that other people cannot have or cannot express." Wiesel begins *The Gates of the Forest* (1964) with a HASIDIC story of a rabbi who sought to overcome misfortune. His predecessor had gone to a special place, lit a fire, and said a special prayer. But the rabbi could do none of these things. Instead, he spoke to God: "All I can do is to tell the story, and this must be sufficient."

Wiesel's writings reveal an inability to comprehend or explain the cruelty and brutality of those who carried out the Holocaust. "Why did human beings act like savage wolves?" he asks in his memoirs. "Why were even inmates so sadistic?" Nor can Wiesel explain or forgive the behavior of those who might have saved at least a few lives had they acted more aggressively. "Why were the tracks to Birkenau never bombed?" he asks. "That not a single Allied military aircraft ever tried to destroy the rail lines converging on Auschwitz remains an outrageous enigma to me."

Wiesel is equally unable to understand how God could have allowed the horrors that he witnessed and experienced. As a young student in Romania, he wrote in *Night*, he had been taught: "it is because of our sins that we had been exiled." In the wake of the Holocaust, Wiesel could not accept such an idea. "No, it is not because of our sins," he wrote. "There were no sins, not that many. I refuse to believe that there could have been so many sins to provoke such a punishment." Wiesel concluded, "I will never cease to rebel against those who committed or permitted Auschwitz, including God. The questions I once asked myself about God's silence remain open. If they have an answer, I do not know it."

Beginning in the 1970s, Wiesel's mission to tell the story of the Holocaust and to ask these disturbing questions took him from the world of literature to the world of politics. Appointed in 1979 as chairman of President JAMES EARL CARTER's Commission on the Holocaust, Wiesel devoted himself to spearheading the drive to build the United States Holocaust Museum in Washington, D.C. The museum, in the words of the President's Commission, was designed to underscore "the moral obligation to remember."

In 1986, Elie Wiesel was awarded the Nobel Peace Prize in recognition of his lifelong pursuit of that moral obligation.

Further reading: Wiesel, Elie. *All Rivers Run to the Sea: Memoirs.* New York: Knopf, 1995; ———. *And the Sea Is Never Full: Memoirs.* New York: Knopf, 1999; ———. *The Gates of the Forest.* New York: Holt, Rinehart and Winston, 1996; ———. *Night.* New York, Hill and Wang, 1960.

—William Lasser

Willard, Frances (1839–1898) *activist*

Frances Elizabeth Caroline Willard was born in Churchville, New York. She was the middle child of Josiah and Mary

Willard. The family moved to Oberlin, Ohio, so that Josiah could study for the ministry. Then, owing to his poor health, they moved to a farm near Janesville, Wisconsin. Here, Frances noted in her autobiography, *Glimpses of Fifty Years: 1839–1889*, she "invested not spent" her childhood.

In 1858, the family moved to Evanston, Illinois, so that older brother Oliver could attend Garrett Biblical Institute, and Frances and her sister, Mary, could attend the Northwestern Female College. After graduation, Frances Willard held a series of teaching posts. She became president of the Evanston College for Ladies in 1871 and in 1873, the first dean of women at Northwestern University.

In 1874, Willard resigned her post as dean to become the national corresponding secretary of the recently founded WOMAN'S CHRISTIAN TEMPERANCE UNION (WCTU). WCTU's main goal was to put a stop to the consumption of alcohol. Its crusade against alcohol was also a protest by women about their lack of civil rights in the United States. In most states, women had no control of their property or custody of their children in case of divorce. Women could not vote, and most local political meetings were held in saloons from which they were excluded. As president of WCTU, Willard relied on political organizing, in addition to moral persuasion, to convince people to embrace total abstinence. Willard's personal motto was "do everything." WCTU adopted this as a policy that recognized that all reform was interconnected, and that social problems could not be separated. The use of alcohol and other drugs was a symptom of larger problems in society. By 1882, WCTU was endorsing women's suffrage, and by 1896, most departments of WCTU were dealing with nontemperance issues. However, temperance in terms of substance abuse remained the force that bound WCTU's social reforms together.

From 1891 until her death, Willard served as WCTU's second national president. She embraced the American national political arena, realizing the empowerment that women would experience if able to vote. In addition to temperance, Willard promoted women's rights, suffrage, equal pay for equal work, and an eight-hour workday. Susan B. Anthony introduced Willard to a U.S. Senate committee as a "general with an army of 250,000." Willard was the first woman, and for 50 years, the only woman, to have her statue displayed in the U.S. Capitol building's Statuary Hall. Today, Willard's home in Evanston is a National Historic Landmark. She lived there from the time her father had it built in 1865 until her death in 1898. She bequeathed it to WCTU. It served as the organization's headquarters from 1900 until the 1920s, when a new administrative building was built behind it.

—Beth Ann Waltz

Williams, Roger (1603?–1683) *colony founder*

Roger Williams, born in London to Alice and James Williams, a merchant tailor, was the founder of Rhode Island and a Puritan intellectual who pioneered arguments for the separation of church and state. Little is known of his early years except that he drew the attention of Lord Chief Justice Sir Edward Coke. After a few years of employment, Coke arranged for the young Williams to enter Charterhouse school, where his academic distinction earned him a scholarship to Pembroke College, Cambridge (B.A. 1627). Williams first served as a chaplain to Sir William Masham in Essex County, marrying Mary Barnard on December 15, 1629, with whom he had six children.

Williams's PURITANical views made living in England uncomfortable, and in the summer of 1629, he met with John Cotton and Thomas Hooker to discuss emigrating to America, which he and his wife did in December 1630. The church in Salem, MASSACHUSETTS, offered him a position, but he declined because he felt the congregation had failed adequately to separate themselves from the Church of England. Instead, he lived for several years in Plymouth, where he spent a good deal of time interacting with the Algonquin Indians, learning their language, and performing MISSIONARY work. In 1633, Williams finally accepted the offer from Salem, where he publicly demanded that all churches separate themselves from the authority of the colony. He also argued that the Massachusetts Bay Colony's charter was invalid, since the British government lacked the power to grant title to American lands, that magistrates could not rule on issues of religion but only on civil or moral ones, that the unregenerate could not take an oath of loyalty (which he understood as a religious act), and that Charles I was an ally of the Antichrist. He later apologized for the last comment, but in 1635 he was summoned before the Massachusetts General Court for stating that the government lacked the right to punish violations of the first four commandments (dealing with religious obligations). On October 9, 1635, Williams was banished from the colony for expressing "new and dangerous opinions against the authority of magistrates."

Williams traveled south with a small group of followers, and after purchasing land from the native Americans living on Narragansett Bay, founded Rhode Island. In April 1636, he arrived at the spot he called Providence, giving it that name for the "Sence of Gods mercefull providence unto me in my destresse." He sailed to England in 1642 to plead for a charter, writing *A Key into the Language of America* en route. While in England, he also authored *The Bloudy Tenent of Persecution, for Cause of Conscience* (1644), which was an argument for religious freedom based on Scripture. After securing the charter, Williams returned to Rhode Island and ran a small trading outpost with the Narragansett Indians.

Political difficulties forced Williams to sell his business to finance another voyage to England (1651–54), where he associated with such prominent individuals as Lord Oliver Cromwell and John Milton. This was a prolific time for Williams. He wrote *Experiments of Spiritual Life and Health*, *The Bloudy Tenent Yet More Bloudy*, and *The Hireling Ministry None of Christs*, all in 1652 alone. From 1654 to 1657, Williams served as president of the colony he founded, and in 1663 Charles II officially granted the colony a permanent charter.

Exiled by the Massachusetts Bay Colony for his radical religious views, Roger Williams found asylum among the Narragansett Indians in what became the colony of Rhode Island. *(Library of Congress)*

The concern for religious TOLERANCE that defined so much of Williams's writing was embodied in the practices of Rhode Island. Unlike the other colonies, Rhode Island lacked an established religion, and numerous sects settled and prospered there. Williams himself helped found America's first Baptist church, although he soon left and called himself a "seeker" for the remainder of his life (his views remained largely orthodox Puritan). He defended the right of QUAKERS to practice their faith, although he himself attacked their views as erroneous, and indeed anticipated debating the Quaker George Fox. When that failed to happen, he wrote a scathing polemic entitled, *George Fox Digg'd out of His Burrowes.*

Roger Williams died in Providence some time between January 16 and March 15, 1683. His belief in religious tolerance was deeply rooted in his understanding of Scripture, and has been rightly celebrated as a lasting contribution to the jurisprudence of church-state relations in America.

See also ESTABLISHMENT CLAUSE; FREE EXERCISE CLAUSE; RELIGIOUS ESTABLISHMENT IN THE COLONIES.

Further reading: Clark, L. Raymond. *Roger Williams: God's Apostle of Advocacy.* Lewiston, N.Y.: E. Mellen Press, 1989; Gilpen, W. Clark. *The Millenarian Piety of Roger Williams.* Chicago: University of Chicago Press, 1979; Morgan, Edmund

S. *Roger Williams: The Church and the State.* New York: Harcourt, 1967.

—Brian J. Glenn

Wilmore, Gayraud (1921–) *theologian, scholar*

Gayraud Wilmore is a theologian, pastor, professor, and historian. An ordained Presbyterian, Wilmore helped shape BLACK THEOLOGY and black religious thought. He was a participant of the National Committee of Black Churchmen (NCBC), which issued the landmark statement on black power, published July 31, 1966, in the *New York Times.* Though the NCBC statement, along with JAMES H. CONE's *Black Theology and Black Power* (1969), is referred to as the formal beginning of black theology, Wilmore maintained it was vital to understand black theology as encompassing all black religious thought, from Africa, the period of enslavement, and through to the present and including Christian, non-Christian, and secular sources. Wilmore thought liberation should be understood not only politically, but also perhaps more important, culturally. Using this methodology, he believed black theology would avoid being simply a reactionary movement against white theological thought. Wilmore's category of black religious thought, then, is wider than and includes black theology and black church history. As a result, Wilmore utilized any aspect of African-American culture that emphasized the liberation of blacks from oppression. Wilmore famously asserted that black theology is "developed . . . in the streets, in taverns and pool halls, as well as in churches."

Wilmore was born in Philadelphia, Pennsylvania, on December 20, 1921, to Gayraud S. Wilmore Sr. and Patricia Gardner Wilmore. He was drafted into the U.S. Army in 1940 when he was a sophomore at Lincoln University, Pennsylvania. Wilmore married Lee Wilson in 1944. He earned a B.A. in 1947, graduating with highest honors, and earned a B.D. in 1950, both from Lincoln University. He earned a master of sacred theology the same year from Temple University's School of Religion while serving as pastor of the Second Presbyterian Church of West Chester, Pennsylvania. Wilmore later began doctoral studies in social ethics at Drew Theological Seminary. After being hired as an assistant professor in social ethics at Pittsburgh Theological Seminary (1959–63), he transferred his doctoral studies from Drew to Temple University.

In 1963, Wilmore put his degree and seminary teaching on hold when he was called by the United Presbyterian Church to be the first executive director of the Commission on Religion and Race. The commission was formed after the interfaith Conference on Religion and Race met in 1963, which Wilmore led until 1972. Over the next few decades Wilmore taught at Boston University School of Theology, Colgate Rochester Divinity School, New York Theological Seminary, and the Interdenominational Center in Atlanta, Georgia, until his retirement in 1990.

Wilmore authored or edited a total of 20 books, including *The Secular Relevance of the Church* (1962), *Last Things First* (1982), the two-volume *Black Theology: A Documentary History* (1993), coedited with James H. Cone, and *Black and Presbyterian: the Heritage and the Hope* (1997). His best-known work is *Black Religion and Black Radicalism: An Examination of the Black Experience in Religion* (1972). There, Wilmore argued that black religious thought had become deradicalized and that black radicalism had become dechristianized. Through an examination of the thought and practices of MARTIN LUTHER KING JR., MALCOLM X, and the nascent black theology movement, he asserted that protest, a turn to African philosophy and social history, and freedom from white domination were necessary for liberation. In this way, black religion and black radicalism could be combined.

Wilmore was a founder and past president of the Society for the Study of Black Religion (SSBR), a founding member of the Ecumenical Association of Third World Theologians (EATWOT), and has been active in the Pan African Skills Project and the Black Theology Project of "Theology in the Americas." Also, he is a life member of NAACP and the PRESBYTERIAN CHURCH U.S.A. representative on the Standing Commission of the WORLD COUNCIL OF CHURCHES' Commission on Faith and Order. In addition, he has served as editor of *The Black Church* and the *Journal of the Interdenominational Theological Center,* and contributing editor of *The Christian Century* and *Christianity and Crisis.*

See also LIBERATION THEOLOGY; RACISM.

Further reading: Cone, James H., and Gayraud S. Wilmore. *Black Theology: A Documentary History, Volume One: 1966–1979.* Maryknoll, N.Y.: Orbis Books, 1993, 1979; Hopkins, Dwight N. *Introducing Black Theology of Liberation.* Maryknoll, N.Y.: Orbis Books, 1999; Turner, Eugene G. *Dissent and Empowerment: Essays in Honor of Gayraud Wilmore.* Louisville, Ky.: Witherspoon Press, 1999; Wilmore, Gayraud S. *Black Religion and Black Radicalism: An Examination of the Black Experience in Religion.* 2d ed. Orbis Books, 1983.

—Kurt Buhring

Winthrop, John (1588–1649) *colony governor*

One of the preeminent early American PURITANS, leaders of the Puritan emigration to New England, and architects of the "New England Way" of church government, John Winthrop served as governor of the MASSACHUSETTS Bay Colony for much of the 1630s and 1640s. Born in Suffolk, England, educated at Cambridge University (where his Puritan sympathies were likely nurtured), Winthrop was admitted to Gray's Inn, London, to study law in 1613. How long he remained there is not entirely clear, though his career flourished: in 1617 he assumed the management of Groton Manor from his father and became a justice of the peace in Suffolk. Ten years later, he was named an attorney in the royal Court of Wards and Liveries.

In 1629, Winthrop was elected governor of the Massachusetts Bay Company. The company was similar to a number of other such colonizing endeavors in 17th-century England, with one important exception: its royal charter did not specify where the company should meet. Taking advantage of this loophole, the company made the daring decision to transport itself *and its charter* to America. The next year, Winthrop crossed the Atlantic on the *Arbella.* During this voyage, he delivered his famous address, the "Model of Christian Charity," which drew on the words of Jesus in referring to the New England settlement as "a city on a hill," reminding his shipmates that "the eyes of all people are upon us." The idea of America as a "city on a hill," and an example to the rest of the world, has been part of the rhetoric of American exceptionalism ever since.

Any discussion of Winthrop's life and career also involves a discussion of the term "Puritan." The term is a broad one, referring to a group of English Protestants who sought further reform within the Anglican Church after its Protestantization under Edward VI (1547–53) and Elizabeth I (1558–1603). Puritans emphasized personal piety, an educated ministry, and strict observance of the Sabbath. They opposed the authority of bishops and archbishops over individual congregations. This Puritan approach gave rise to the term "congregationalism," a system of church government that affirms the autonomy of individual congregations in decisions affecting their collective life. At the same time, these congregations remained bound together by a shared theology (in the English case, CALVINISM) and a commitment to the cooperation of civil and ecclesiastical authorities in creating a social climate conducive to godly behavior. During the 1620s and 1630s, many English Puritans became convinced that divine punishment was coming upon the land for its failure to effect thoroughgoing church reform. Puritans considered themselves the *true* Church of England, keepers of Protestant doctrine even as English authorities, both civil and ecclesiastical (King Charles I [reigned 1625–49] and William Laud, Archbishop of Canterbury 1633–45) veered away from the Calvinism that had been the English church's mainstay since its Reformation under Edward and Elizabeth. Such sentiments influenced Winthrop, along with many of his fellow Puritans, to consider emigrating to America.

Despite the remarkable success of the "New England Way"—the adaptation to American circumstances of the basic tenets of congregational Puritanism outlined above—in maintaining a uniform public religious practice and the close relationship between church and state in Massachusetts, religious dissent was always present. Since he served as governor for virtually all of the 1630s and 1640s—and since, when out of office, he was the colony's most influential private citizen—Winthrop was intimately involved in suppressing the first two significant instances of religious dissent. ROGER WILLIAMS preached a Separatist doctrine of formal withdrawal from the Anglican communion, objected to the administration of loyalty oaths, and called the colony's patent "a national sin"—all at a time when the colony's enemies were mounting a concerted attack on the settlement's charter in England. He was ban-

ished from the colony in 1635 and went on to found Rhode Island. ANNE HUTCHINSON, on the other hand, preached a radical grace theology that downplayed the importance of works to salvation; when questioned about these views by the General Court, she asserted an immediate revelation from God. Her followers included many prominent settlers (among them, Governor Henry Vane), and some of them tumultuously disrupted services conducted by ministers they viewed as preaching false doctrine (Morgan 1958). She and a number of her followers were banished in 1638.

The 1640s saw the Massachusetts Bay Colony, and Winthrop as its chief magistrate, articulating its system of church and state and defending it from critics both domestic and English. In 1643, Winthrop was instrumental in founding the New England Confederation, a union for mutual defense, security, and the settlement of border disputes. As the civil wars broke out in England, and the threat of episcopal and royal control over the colony receded, many Puritans expected an era of godly rule in their homeland, one that could look to New England for insight into the operation of a holy commonwealth, to be forthcoming. It soon became clear, though, that events in England were moving, politically if not theologically, in different directions, and that significant elements of English Puritanism favored Protestant TOLERATION. A vigorous

John Winthrop *(Library of Congress)*

assertion of religious uniformity figured heavily in Massachusetts thought and practice as the decade closed, culminating in the Cambridge Platform of 1648. Winthrop died in Massachusetts in 1649.

Further reading: Morgan, Edmund S. *The Puritan Dilemma: The Story of John Winthrop.* Boston: Little, Brown, 1958; Winthrop, John. *The Journal of John Winthrop, 1630–1649.* Edited by Richard Dunn and Laetitia Yaendle. Cambridge, Mass.: Harvard University Press, 1996; *Winthrop Papers.* 5 vols. Boston: Massachusetts Historical Society, 1929–47.

—Andrew R. Murphy

Wisconsin Evangelical Lutheran Synod

Conservative theologically and politically, the Wisconsin Evangelical Lutheran Synod (WELS) was formed in 1892 out of German synods in Wisconsin, Minnesota, and Michigan. The Wisconsin Synod formed first, at Granville, Wisconsin, in 1850. The Michigan and Minnesota Synods followed in 1860. The addition of Nebraska in 1904 created the Joint Synod of Wisconsin, Minnesota, Michigan, and Nebraska. In 1917 the federation merged and became known as the Evangelical Joint Synod of Wisconsin and Other States. The denomination took its WELS name in 1959.

Still concentrated in the Midwest, WELS includes more than 400,000 communicant members and 1,200 pastors in the United States, Canada, Antigua, and St. Lucia. WELS has its own school system, with more than 350 elementary schools and 22 high schools. World mission programs are also in place.

WELS sits on the far right of the theological and political spectrum, distinguishing itself from the mainline EVANGELICAL LUTHERAN CHURCH IN AMERICA (ELCA) and the evangelical LUTHERAN CHURCH–MISSOURI SYNOD (LCMS). Like LCMS, WELS is a confessional church that places a premium on the Lutheran Confessions and strict church doctrine. In *This We Believe*, written in 1967 and revised in 1980 and 1999, the synod presents its statement of belief. It emphasizes the power of God's revelation, the centrality of justification by faith, and other tenets of confessional Lutheranism.

WELS distinguishes itself from its conservative counterpart, LCMS, in several ways. Confessional agreement in scriptural teaching is required for all forms of church fellowship in WELS. This includes not only pulpit and altar fellowship, but also concerts, conferences, and other public events at which worship takes place. WELS opposes membership in the Boy Scouts of America, believing that "the mandatory Scout Oath and Scout Law promote a spirit of self-righteousness." Finally, WELS restricts its leadership and congregational voting prerogatives to its male members. Based in large part on differences in the doctrine and practice of church fellowship, WELS in 1961 declared a break in fellowship with LCMS.

Unlike ELCA, WELS and its members demonstrate little political activism. Much of this political quietism may be traced to the Lutheran two-kingdom theory of church and state. The church preaches the gospel and brings believers in Christ the good news of eternal salvation. Drawing upon Romans 13, it believes that the state is an authority instituted by God to wield the sword, to keep order and peace in a society of sinful humans.

In *Civil Government: God's Other Kingdom*, WELS pastor and professor Daniel M. Deutschlander emphasizes the caution with which WELS and its members approach politics and government. Political activity by the church may harm the pursuit of its mission, proclaiming the gospel. Pastors and church workers are cautioned against running for office, signing a petition, or giving a media interview, for fear that such efforts would detract from the message of the gospel. Individual members, however, are encouraged to fulfill their roles as responsible citizens by obeying laws, voting, and become otherwise active as they see fit. While resisting the evil of some government action is appropriate, parishioners are admonished not to fall into the "evil of revolution."

Consistent with its belief that the church and the government play distinct roles, WELS objects to use of government chaplains for the armed forces, prisons, and some government-run hospitals. Care for the "the souls and minds" of these government employees is the work of the church, not the state. WELS prefers that a parish pastor or a pastor called by the church administer to the needs of these people.

Finally, WELS questions organized lobbying efforts like the Christian Right. The "earthly kingdom of Christ" that such groups desire, according to WELS, will not occur. Moreover, such divisive movements can have a negative impact on the preaching of law and gospel. Since members' true citizenship is in heaven, they should not become too entangled with the affairs of this world.

Further reading: Brug, John F., Edward C. Fredrich II, and Armin W. Schuetze. *WELS and Other Lutherans.* Milwaukee, Wisc.: Northwestern Publishing House, 1995; Deutschlander, Daniel M. *Civil Government: God's Other Kingdom.* Milwaukee, Wisc.: Northwestern Publishing House, 1998.

—Jeffrey Walz

Wisconsin v. Yoder 406 US 205 (1972)

This landmark Supreme Court case pitted the First Amendment right to FREE EXERCISE of religion against a state's duty to provide for the education of its children. Several AMISH parents challenged Wisconsin's compulsory education law. The Amish, a conservative branch of the MENNONITE CHURCH, live in separate communities, practice material simplicity, and adhere to strict biblical teachings. When consolidated schools began replacing the local schools in their rural community, they perceived a threat to the future of their religious based culture. While willing to educate their children through the eighth grade, they reject further secular education as imparting worldly values in conflict with their religious ones. Their refusal to send their children to school after the eighth grade (about age 13) violated Wisconsin's law, requiring attendance through age 16. The Amish argued that secondary schooling would endanger their children's and their own salvation and cause disintegration of their communities. Upholding their claim, the Supreme Court ruled that the Constitution demanded exemptions from state laws for religiously motivated behavior except when there was a compelling state interest to the contrary.

Chief Justice Warren Burger, writing for the Court, adopted the compelling state interest test for balancing state interests against religious freedom claims: "Only those interests of the highest order and those not otherwise served can overbalance legitimate claims to the free exercise of religion."

Justice Burger's opinion illustrates the reasoning required by the compelling state interest standard. Recognizing that First Amendment protection does not extend to nonreligious cultural preferences, the Court first had to consider whether a genuinely religious interest was burdened. Since neither the religious sincerity of the Amish nor their religious objections to high school education were in doubt, the Court easily concluded that compulsory education threatened a "religiously inspired way of life."

Following the logic of the compelling state interest test, the Court then considered Wisconsin's two justifications for compulsory education: promoting democracy and assuring the economic self-sufficiency of its citizens. Both were clearly compelling, but would these goals be sacrificed by granting the Amish an exception?

To answer this question, Burger considered the long-standing Amish religious tradition and the community's exemplary record of productivity and self-sufficiency. This success suggested that traditional Amish vocational education methods were quite successful in preparing its children for productive and independent lives:

> The record strongly indicates that accommodating the religious objections of the Amish by forgoing one, or at most two, additional years of compulsory education will not impair the physical or mental health of the child, or result in an inability to be self-supporting or to discharge the duties and responsibilities of citizenship, or in any other way materially detract from the welfare of society.

The justices concluded that the state could not show a compelling state interest in forcing the Amish to continue conventional education up to age 16, and ruled that the Amish had a constitutional right to be exempt from the law's requirements. Stated in more general terms, the First Amendment requires states to accommodate the religious needs of its citizens by exempting them from ordinary secular legislation that burdens their religious exercise.

Justices Rehnquist and Powell did not participate in this judgment. Justices Potter Stewart and Byron White wrote brief concurring opinions, and Justice Brennan wrote separately, suggesting that the majority might have understated the importance of public education. Most intriguing was the partial dissent written by Justice William O. Douglas, raising the possibility of a conflict between the religious rights of parents and those of the individual child:

> Our opinions are full of talk about the power of parents over the child's education. . . . Recent cases have clearly held that children themselves have constitutionally protectible interests. . . . These children are "persons" within the meaning of the Bill of Rights.

In addition, Justice Douglas chided the majority for appearing to base its decision on the particular achievements of the Amish people. In his view, the record of the Amish is utterly irrelevant; a religion is a religion irrespective of the record of its adherents, and the rights of its members do not depend on the success of its community in avoiding crime or welfare.

The *Yoder* decision is one of the high-water marks of religious accommodation under the free exercise clause. While its approach was not always followed, it was considered the dominant understanding of the free exercise clause until the Court adopted a much more restrictive view in *EMPLOYMENT DIVISION OF OREGON V. SMITH* (1990). Nevertheless, the *Yoder* decision remains one of the defining statements of religious freedom under the Constitution.

—Bette Novit Evans

Wise, Isaac Mayer (1819–1900) *religious leader*

Isaac Mayer Wise was born in Bohemia (in the present-day Czech Republic). He studied in Austria and is purported to have served as a rabbi in Bohemia for several years before arriving in New York in 1846. He became the foremost institution builder of REFORM JUDAISM in America. As was his traditionalist colleague, Isaac Leeser, Wise was dismayed at the chaotic state of Judaism and Jewish congregational life in the United States, and in 1848 he issued a call for an association of Jewish ("Israelitish") congregations in the United States.

Despite his traditional Jewish upbringing and education, Wise became a spearhead of reform. His first position was rabbi of Congregation Beth El in Albany, New York, where he served from 1846 until he was dismissed in 1850, the result of a growing dissatisfaction with Wise as an individual and with the many reforms he instituted. He was then immediately hired as rabbi of Anshe Emeth, also in Albany, a new congregation that was Reform from its very inception. He remained at Anshe Emeth for four years, during which time he traveled around the United States extensively. He edited two weeklies, the *American Israelite*, in English, and *Die Deborah*, in German. He also published a book, *The Origin of Christianity*, for which he was scorned by traditionalists who viewed the book as heretical and threatening. The book did help create a name for Wise, however, in both Jewish and general American public circles, and he emerged as a major spokesman for American Judaism and Jewry. In 1854, at the age of 46, Wise accepted an offer from Congregation Bene Yeshurun in Cincinnati, where he remained until his death in 1900. During those years, he devoted himself to organizing American Judaism, and although he did not quite accomplish that task, he did play the pivotal role in institutionalizing Reform Judaism in America.

Wise had dreamed of organizing all the congregations in the country, but traditionalists refused to associate with him. In 1873, however, representatives of 34 Reform congregations did convene in Cincinnati and officially organized the Union of American Hebrew Congregations. Though its name identifies it as American, not solely Reform, it became and is today the synagogue and temple organization of American Reform Judaism. Similarly, when Wise's dream of establishing a seminary for the training of American rabbis was realized with the founding of Hebrew Union College in Cincinnati in 1875, its name identified it simply as Hebrew, without the Reform designation. Had there been any question at its inception, its Reform identity was sealed at its first ordination. At the banquet in its honor, nonkosher food was served, and the traditionalists present left in anger. Many of them went on to establish the Jewish Theological Society of America, which later became the seminary of CONSERVATIVE JUDAISM. Hebrew Union College today has branches in New York, Los Angeles, and Jerusalem, and is the school of higher learning of American Reform Judaism. And when Wise's dream of establishing a synod of American rabbis was finally realized in 1889, it called itself the Central Conference of American Rabbis, without the specific Reform designation, though it was, and remains, the rabbinical body of American Reform Judaism.

In all probability, the very personality traits that enabled Wise to achieve his institution-building goals also lost him many friends. He was widely perceived as egoistic, contentious, and impulsive. At the same time, the efforts he undertook forced him to refrain from being viewed as too extremist, and both arch reformers and ardent traditionalists scorned him. Among the former, one of his greatest antagonists was David Einhorn, who had come to America in 1855 to become rabbi of Temple Har Sinai in Baltimore. In contrast to Wise, the organizer and institution builder, Einhorn was an unyielding ideologist of radical Reform. He had neither respect nor patience for Wise's relatively less doctrinaire, pragmatic approach. To him, Wise was a liberal reformer and therefore more dangerous than traditionalists. The two remained bitter antagonists throughout their lives, and each competed with the other for the leadership of Reform Judaism in America. While Wise was successful in his role as institution builder, Einhorn and his followers, especially his disciple and son-in-law, Kaufman Kohler, succeeded in having the principles of radical Reform adopted in the Pittsburgh Platform of Reform Rabbis in 1885, four years before the official founding of the Central Conference of American Rabbis.

Wise also produced the first American prayer book, *Minhag America* (*The Custom of America*), which he intended to be the liturgy that would be adopted by all American Jews. Much to his chagrin, both traditionalists and radicals rejected it—the former because it was too reformed and the latter because it was too traditional.

See also ORTHODOX JUDAISM; RECONSTRUCTIONIST JUDAISM.

Further reading: Heller, James G. *Isaac M. Wise: His Life, Work, and Thought.* New York: Union of American Hebrew Congregations, 1965; Knox, Israel. *Rabbi in America.* Boston: Little, Brown, 1957; Temkin, Sefton D. *Creating American Reform Judaism: The Life and Times of Isaac Mayer Wise.* Portland, Ore.: Littman Library of Jewish Civilization, 1998; Waxman, Chaim I. *America's Jews in Transition.* Philadelphia: Temple University Press, 1983.

—Chaim I. Waxman

Witherspoon, John (1723–1794) *minister, educator*

John Witherspoon was a Presbyterian minister and president of the College of New Jersey (now Princeton University), born in Yester, Scotland. He was a distinguished educator and supporter of the patriot cause during the Revolutionary War. Witherspoon was at the forefront of the movement toward independence, serving with distinction in the Continental Congress and signing the DECLARATION OF INDEPENDENCE. His assiduous political efforts led JOHN ADAMS to describe him as "an animated Son of Liberty." His enduring influence, however, was as an educator. Brought to the College of New Jersey from Scotland, Witherspoon became the most highly regarded professor in America. His course in moral philosophy, loosely based on Francis Hutcheson's *A System of Moral Philosophy*, became widely renowned and was imitated throughout the colonies. Often acknowledging their intellectual debt to Witherspoon, a number of his students went on to become distinguished political figures, including JAMES MADISON, Aaron Burr, and Philip Freneau.

The son of James, a minister, and Anne, the daughter of a minister in Edinburgh, John Witherspoon was born into a distinctly clerical family with solid ties to Scottish Presbyterianism. After attending a grammar school near his home, Witherspoon entered the University of Edinburgh and received a master of arts in February 1739. He then continued his studies at Edinburgh for four more years under the Faculty of Divinity. He was licensed to preach in 1743, and in 1745 he was called as minister of the Church of Scotland parish in Beith, Ayrshire.

Witherspoon made his reputation with his involvement in the "controversies" within the Church of Scotland in the 1750s. Writing on behalf of the Popular Party, Witherspoon took up the evangelical cause in a series of polemics that satirized the liberal opposition, the Moderate Party. Published in multiple editions in Edinburgh, Glasgow, London, Philadelphia, and Utrecht, these works brought Witherspoon fame as an eloquent spokesperson for orthodox Presbyterianism. In addition to its polemical flair, Witherspoon's writing was also admired for its consistent emphasis on the importance of learning. His reputation as an "enlightened" evangelical attracted the interest of the New Side trustees at the College of New Jersey when, in 1766, they found themselves in need of a president. As someone from outside the colonies who was orthodox in his doctrine but insistent on the importance of learning, Witherspoon promised to help heal the schism with the Old Sides.

Witherspoon assumed the presidency of the College of New Jersey in 1768. Almost immediately, he began to exert an influence as an educator, politician, and thinker. His fund-raising efforts around the colonies gave financial stability to the college and enhanced its reputation as an institution. Witherspoon undertook systematic reorganization of the college's curriculum that saw the integration of Enlightenment learning throughout the disciplines. His most profound influence on the curriculum was in the teaching of moral philosophy. Following his own injunction that it was the "superior science," Witherspoon made moral philosophy the capstone of the course of study and, for several years, taught the class himself.

Witherspoon's moral philosophy course followed closely the texts he had encountered in Scotland, particularly Francis Hutcheson's *A System of Moral Philosophy*. Witherspoon described a system of natural ethics by which one could achieve a moral order in the natural world. Witherspoon described how, through the use of their natural faculties, humans could recognize the moral design intended for humankind by God in the "nature" around them. Having discovered this "natural law," human beings could fulfill this design through their own conduct and in relations with others. The acts necessary to perform these duties were thus afforded a moral sanction and described as "rights." Following the mainstream of Enlightenment moral philosophy, Witherspoon thus articulated a theoretical language of rights that followed closely the formulation of Samuel von Pufendorf, J. J. Burlamaqui, and JOHN LOCKE.

After some years of observing the growing tensions between Britain and the colonies, Witherspoon put himself at the forefront of the patriot cause. In July 1774, he joined the Somerset County Committee of Correspondence and successfully advocated for a nonimportation agreement among the various committees of New Jersey. He also contributed several political tracts to the patriot cause where he argued the legitimacy of resistance to British policy and in support for independence. In June 1776, New Jersey selected him as a delegate to the Continental Congress in Philadelphia. Soon after his arrival, he joined 55 other delegates in signing the Declaration of Independence. He served in the Continental Congress for most of the period until November 1782, with appointments to more than 100 committees, including negotiations with foreign powers and drafting the Articles of Confederation. After the war, he was elected to the New Jersey legislature in 1783 and 1789, and in 1787 he was a member of the New Jersey convention that approved the Constitution.

Further reading: Collins, Varnum Lansing. *President Witherspoon*. Princeton, N.J.: Princeton University Press, 1925; Noll, Mark A. *Princeton and the Republic, 1768–1822*. Princeton, N.J.: Princeton University Press, 1989; Scott, Jack. *Annotated Edition of Lectures on Moral Philosophy by John Witherspoon*. Newark, Del.: University of Delaware Press, 1982; Sloan, Douglas. *The Scottish Enlightenment and the American College Ideal*. New York: Columbia University Press, 1971.

—Roland Marden

Witters v. Washington Department of Services for the Blind 474 U.S. 481 (1986)

On January 27, 1986, in a unanimous decision authored by Justice Marshall, the Supreme Court reversed a lower court's ruling that a state grant for vocational assistance finding its way into the coffers of a Christian college would constitute a violation of the ESTABLISHMENT CLAUSE. The decision hinged on the fact that the funds in question would be paid directly to the beneficiary, who would then be free to apply them to *any* pursuit of his choosing, secular or otherwise. The fact that the state aid was made neutrally available, combined with the element of free choice, eliminated any possibility that the program in question served to promote religious instruction.

In 1979, petitioner Larry Witters, suffering from a degenerative eye condition, applied to the Washington State Commission for the Blind for vocational aid. He did so pursuant to a Washington statute authorizing the commission to provide such aid, the intent of which was to help visually impaired individuals become more self-reliant. The commission denied Witters assistance on the grounds that he was planning to apply the state funds to his education at Inland Empire School of the Bible, a Christian college, where he was studying to become a minister, missionary, or youth director. In doing so, the commission relied on its policy statement that "[t]he Washington State constitution forbids the use of public funds to assist an individual in the pursuit of a career or degree in theology or related areas."

After exhausting all avenues of appeal afforded him by the administration, Witters turned to the legal system. The State Superior Court upheld the commission's denial on the grounds employed by the commission. The State Supreme Court later upheld this ruling; however, it did so on different grounds. Rather than basing its decision on the Washington Constitution, the State Supreme Court chose to ground its decision in the establishment clause of the U.S. Constitution. Consequently, the Court came to rely on the test outlined in *LEMON V. KURTZMAN*, according to which, a statute or action must have a secular legislative purpose, its primary effect must neither inhibit nor advance religion, and it must not foster excessive government entanglement if it is to pass constitutional muster. The State Supreme Court found that granting aid to an individual for the purpose of pursuing a religious career violated the second prong of the test; it would have the primary effect of advancing religion and would therefore amount to an establishment of religion and a violation of the U.S. Constitution. This reading of *Lemon* reflects a failure to acknowledge the two main factors that distinguish *Witters* from most previous establishment clause case law: the neutral availability of the aid and the element of free choice.

The U.S. Supreme Court also relied on the *Lemon* test in its assessment of *Witters*, although it came to a much different conclusion. While it agreed with the state court as to the first prong of the test, namely, that the statute had a secular rather than religious purpose in providing vocational rehabilitation, it disagreed with its conclusion on the second prong. The Supreme Court found no reason to believe that the program in question had the primary effect of advancing religion. As Justice Marshall stated, "it is well settled that the Establishment Clause is not violated every time money previously in the possession of the State is conveyed to a religious institution." Direct subsidies to religious institutions are always prohibited, but the aid provided under Washington's program was not direct. Rather, neutrally available funds were paid directly to the benefactor, who then chose where to apply them. According to Marshall, "Aid recipients' choices are made among a huge variety of possible careers, of which only a small handful are sectarian. In this case the fact that aid goes to individuals means that the decision to support religious education is made by the individual, not the state." This distinction, first made in *MUELLER V. ALLEN* (1983), is crucial to breaking the chain of government responsibility for the use of the appropriated funds. Although Marshall did not cite *Mueller* as precedent, a number of his colleagues did so in their concurring opinions.

The fact that the total amount of money falling into the hands of religious institutions under the program in question was miniscule was also used by the Court in justifying its decision. At the time the ruling was handed down, Witters was the first and only applicant ever to propose applying vocational rehabilitation funds to a religious undertaking. The Court saw this fact as further evidence that the program did not endorse religion or violate the establishment clause. The Supreme Court reversed the lower court's judgment and remanded the case for further review.

—Steven C. Leidinger

Wolman v. Walter 433 U.S. 229 (1977)

In this case, Ohio taxpayers challenged the constitutionality of a state law that provided aid to private sectarian (religious) schools. They argued that allowing the use of public funds for religious purposes violates the ESTABLISHMENT CLAUSE of the First Amendment. Under the law, funds could be used in six different ways to aid private schools. First, tax monies could be used to purchase secular (nonreligious) textbooks for students attending sectarian schools. Second, the state could provide money for standardized tests and scoring services as long as nonpublic school personnel were not involved in the test drafting or scoring. Third, nonpublic schools could receive aid for speech, hearing, and psychological services. Fourth, the law provided funds for specialized therapeutic, guidance, and remedial services for nonpublic school students, as long as the services were performed in public schools, public centers, or in mobile units located off nonpublic school premises. Fifth, public money could be used for individual instructional materials and equipment that was equivalent to those used in public schools and was not religious in nature. Finally, the law provided money for field trip transportation and special contract transportation if school district buses were unavailable. A three-judge district court held the statute constitutional in all respects.

The Supreme Court reversed in part and affirmed in part, and attempted to stay true to the precedent set down in *LEMON V. KURTZMAN*. Initially, in an opinion delivered by Justice Blackmun, the Court ruled that the state could provide nonpublic school students with books, standardized tests, diagnostic services, and therapeutic and remedial services. He argued that using taxes for these purposes does not violate the establishment clause. The justices found that providing diagnostic services on nonpublic school premises does not create an impermissible risk of fostering ideological views. Similarly, therapeutic, guidance, and remedial services do not have the impermissible effect of advancing religion because they are not provided on private school premises, and public employees administer them. Thus, there is no excessive entanglement with religion—the third prong of the *Lemon* test.

However, the Court ruled that tax money could not be used to provide instructional materials, equipment, or field trips. Doing so would violate the establishment clause. First, loans for instructional material and equipment may directly and substantially advance a child's sectarian education. In these situations, the justices argued it is impossible to separate the secular education function from the sectarian, which means that the state will inevitably support religion by providing money for these purposes. Second, money for field trips goes directly to the nonpublic schools for field trips. As such, it found this to be impermissible direct aid to sectarian education.

Wolman was consistent with some past establishment clause precedents but inconsistent with others. The textbook portion of the decision follows *BOARD OF EDUCATION V. ALLEN*, and *MEEK V. PITTENGER*, both of which found textbook loans to be constitutional. However, Wolman seemingly reversed the *Pittenger* holding, that testing, equipment, and auxiliary services in private schools cannot be funded with taxpayer money. Finally, Wolman seemingly contradicts *EVERSON V. BOARD OF EDUCATION*, which allowed tax monies to reimburse parents for transporting their children to school.

See also AID TO RELIGIOUS SCHOOLS.

—Timothy R. Johnson

Woman's Christian Temperance Union (WCTU)

The National Woman's Christian Temperance Union (WCTU) was founded in Cleveland, Ohio, in November 1874. It grew out of the Woman's Crusade, formed in the winter of 1873–74. Groups of women meeting in Fredonia, New York, and Hillsboro and Washington Court House, Ohio, were inspired by lectures given by Dr. Dio Lewis to make nonviolent protests against the dangers of alcohol. These housewives held "pray-ins" near and in local saloons and demanded that the sale of alcohol be stopped. Within three months they had driven saloons out of 250 communities, and for the first time realized what they could accomplish by standing together. These women held pre-organizational discussions at Chautauqua, New York, in the summer of 1874 that led to the national convention in Cleveland at which WCTU was formed.

Behind WCTU's temperance reform was the notion of "protection of the home." The slogan "For God and Home and Native Land" (later changed to "Every Land") expressed WCTU's priorities. Through education and example, WCTU hoped to obtain pledges of total abstinence from alcohol and later tobacco and other drugs. The white ribbon bow was selected to symbolize purity, and the WCTU watchwords were "Agitate, Educate, Legislate." Local chapters were called "Unions" and were largely autonomous but closely linked to the state unions and national headquarters. Clear channels of authority and communication helped WCTU to become the largest women's organization in the United States.

The crusade against alcohol was also a protest by women about their lack of civil rights in the United States. In most states women had no control of their property or custody of their children in case of divorce. Women could not vote, and most local political meetings were held in saloons from which they were excluded. In 1879, FRANCES WILLARD became president of WCTU and began relying on political organizing, in addition to moral persuasion, to achieve total abstinence. Willard's personal motto was "do everything." WCTU adopted this as a policy that recognized that all reform was interconnected, and that social problems could not be separated. The use of alcohol and other drugs was a symptom of larger problems in society. By 1882, WCTU was endorsing women's suffrage, and by 1896, most departments of WCTU were dealing with nontemperance issues. However, temperance in terms of substance abuse remained the force that bound together WCTU's social reforms.

Today WCTU is the oldest voluntary, nonsectarian women's organization in continuous existence in the world. WCTU is a founding member (1888) of the National Council of Women (Frances Willard was its first president) and the International Council of Women (1893). It is also a charter member (1945) of the United Nation's Non-Governmental Organizations (NGO).

For more than 125 years, WCTU has trained women to think on their feet, speak in public, and run an organization. WCTU was among the first organizations to keep a professional lobbyist in Washington, D.C. WCTU has proposed, sup-

Currier & Ives print (1874) showing a young woman as a warrior for temperance *(Library of Congress)*

ported, and helped establish protection of women and children at home and work, women's right to vote, shelters for abused women and children, the eight-hour work day, equal pay for equal work, kindergartens, the Parent-Teacher Association (PTA), federal aid for education, stiffer penalties for sexual crimes against girls and women, uniform marriage and divorce laws, prison reform, and passive demonstrations for world peace.

Today WCTU is still concerned that the wide availability of alcohol, tobacco, and other drugs combines with diverse social problems to the detriment of society. *The Union Signal* is the official journal of the organization. It is published quarterly as a digest of current research and information on drugs. WCTU's publishing house is Signal Press, which offers educational materials reflecting their stand for total abstinence. Among recent (1999) publications is a history of WCTU written by National president Sarah F. Ward, *The White Ribbon Story* (1999).

—Beth Ann Waltz

World Council of Churches

The World Council of Churches (WCC) was founded in 1948 at Amsterdam, the Netherlands. In 1937, church leaders agreed to establish the World Council of Churches, but World War II deferred its official organization until August 1948. At that time, representatives of 147 churches assembled in Amsterdam to constitute the new organization WCC. Geneva, Switzerland, is home to council headquarters; an office is also located in New York City.

WCC is an international fellowship of Christian churches, built on the foundation of encounter, dialogue, and collaboration, and dedicated to the search for Christian unity. WCC was formed to serve and advance ECUMENISM—the quest for restoring the unity of the church—by encouraging in its members a common commitment to follow the gospel. The prayer of the churches that belong to WCC is for the renewal and faithful response of the people of God in witness and service to the world. Member churches confess the Lord Jesus Christ as God and Savior.

WCC responds compassionately and effectively to suffering people. It brings together theologians, church leaders, and other thoughtful Christians to explore the doctrinal issues on which their traditions agree and disagree. The agenda is a changing one, often reflecting the concerns of its member churches.

The council works on behalf of the "sinned against" in the struggle for SOCIAL JUSTICE. This engagement may take the form of empowering individuals through moral or financial support; it may involve expert analysis and prophetic exposure of social, economic, and political powers that control lives of millions of people. The contribution the council makes is through patient and effective efforts to hold up the relevance of the churches' message of peace and reconciliation in a conflict-ridden world.

WCC is a complex organization. Its highest decision-making body is the Assembly, which meets once every seven years. In the interim of assemblies, the elected 150 members of the Central Committee meet annually to review the work of WCC. The Executive Committee, made up 19 members, acts on behalf of the Central Committee.

The membership of WCC numbers more than 400 million Christians in 342 churches, denominations, and fellowships in 120 countries and territories around the world, at least nominally. WCC member churches are organized bodies of local parishes or congregations. Member churches have at least 25,000 congregants. The member churches that WCC comprises live in remarkably different social conditions and are found in every part of the world. The international composition of the organization suggests that members speak an array of languages, and their distinctive histories produce different styles of worship and forms of organization and governance. This diversity makes WCC an exciting and challenging forum. WCC member churches today include nearly all the world's EASTERN ORTHODOX churches, scores of denominations from such historic traditions of the Protestant Reformation as Anglican, Baptist, Lutheran, Methodist, and DUTCH REFORMED, and a broad representation of united and independent churches. The world's largest Christian body, the ROMAN CATHOLIC CHURCH, is not a member of WCC.

The World Council of Churches is an action-oriented organization that supports knowledge, understanding, and growth of its member churches. The work of WCC is divided among four clusters of teams—the Cluster on Relations, the Cluster on Communication, the Cluster on Issues and Themes, and the Cluster on Finance, Services, and Administration—that implement the programmatic thrust.

One of the council's active teams is the international relations team. This team informs and addresses public issues, and provides a forum for information sharing and joint advocacy on critical situations of human rights violations, conflict, and peacemaking initiatives. The international work is divided in the following areas: peace and conflict resolution, militarism, disarmament and arms control, human rights, global governance and international institutions, and promotion of a unified coherent and informed witness of the churches on international affairs. The implementation of these foci is accomplished through monitoring, analysis and interpretation of political issues; delegation and pastoral visits to governments; ecumenical study teams; confidential group visits to governments; support for human rights action groups; and support for peaceful resolution of conflicts. In principle, WCC relates to individual governments mainly through the member churches and related national councils of churches.

See also NATIONAL COUNCIL OF CHURCHES.

Further reading: Van Elderen, Marlin. *Introducing the World Council of Churches.* Geneva: World Council of Churches Publications, 2001; Vermaat, J. A. A. *The World Council of Churches and Politics.* New York: Freedom House, 1989; World Council of Churches website. URL: http://www.wcc-coe.org.

—Jacquelyn A. Anthony

Y

Young, Andrew Jackson (1932–) *minister, activist, politician*

Born March 12, 1932, in New Orleans, Louisiana, Andrew Young is an ordained minister, statesman, businessman, humanitarian, civil rights activist, human rights activist, published author, and former public servant. For the past 45 years, Young has devoted his life to fulfilling the biblical mandate "For unto whomsoever much is given, of him shall be much required," a command he refers to as "an easy burden."

Young was born into a well-to-do professional family. His father, Andrew J. Young Sr., was a dentist and his mother, Daisy Fuller Young, was a teacher. Born of this union were Andrew and his younger brother, Walter.

Young was taught the importance of religion and education. He earned a B.A. from Howard University in Washington, D.C., in 1951. Young received a bachelor of divinity degree from Hartford Theological Seminary in Hartford, Connecticut, in 1955, and he was later ordained a minister in the United Church of Christ. Since his calling as a minister and pastor, he has successfully blended faith, religion, and politics to conqueror causes that were larger than himself.

Young worked on the staff of the NATIONAL COUNCIL OF CHURCHES (NCC). In 1957, at 25, Young was selected by NCC leadership to work for the Youth Division of Christian Education. There he was introduced to the global church, and learned to appreciate the church as an institution with enormous political influence as well as personal significance. The experience is credited with laying a foundation that prepared Young for the CIVIL RIGHTS MOVEMENT, the U.S. Congress, and the United Nations. His success in these secular environments was due to his experience in ecumenical Christianity. During his three years of service with NCC, Young learned to transcend his southern roots and prejudices and see religion as a global force. This transcendence would cause him trouble later as a member of President JAMES EARL CARTER's administration because he viewed the world from the perspective of Christian mission, putting him into conflict with the cold war analysis advocated by the U.S. government. Young viewed members of liberation movements in Africa, the Middle East, and Latin America as products of a century of missionary education. He saw them as brothers and sisters to be redeemed, not as enemies to be destroyed. Because of these ecumenical perspectives, Young believes he was later able to bring a new perspective to U.S. policy.

A top aide to MARTIN LUTHER KING JR. during the Civil Rights movement, Young was involved in the movement's inception and served as vice president of the SOUTHERN CHRISTIAN LEADERSHIP CONFERENCE (SCLC). The Civil Rights movement "was church" for him and the other young people involved; and the ECUMENISM of the civil rights movement was absolutely essential to its success.

Young was elected to serve three terms (1973–77) in the U.S. House of Representatives, the first African American to hold that position from Georgia since Reconstruction. President Carter appointed him ambassador to the United Nations (1977–79). He served two terms (1982–90) as mayor of Atlanta, Georgia. In 1990, he ran for but failed to win the Democratic nomination for governor of Georgia. In 1994, President WILLIAM JEFFERSON CLINTON appointed Young as chairman of the Southern Africa Enterprise Development Fund, a $100 million, privately managed fund to provide equity to businesses in 11 countries. In 1999, he was elected to a two-year term as president of the National Council of Churches.

Young's lifelong public service has been rewarded in perpetuity by the naming of two academic entities in his honor: Georgia State University's Andrew Young School of Policy Studies, and the Andrew Young Center for International Affairs at Morehouse College, both in Atlanta.

Young has authored two books. *A Way Out of No Way* is a spiritual memoir revealing the ambassador's vision of equality, justice, and peace, which stem from his biblical insight. Young shares stories of the crucial moments that have forged his personal philosophy. In *An Easy Burden,* Young traces the Civil Rights movement's evolution from the philosophy of accommodation and middle-class aspirations of his parents' generation to the nonviolent, direct-action approach of Martin Luther King Jr.

Young cochaired the 1996 Atlanta Committee for the Olympic Games and currently serves as chairman of Atlanta-based GoodWorks International, a specialty consulting group that provides strategic services to corporations and governments operating in the global economy. His awards include the Presidential Medal of Freedom, the French Légion d'Honneur, the Bishop Walker Humanitarian Award, and over 60 honorary degrees from prestigious universities around the world. Young married the former Jean Childs, now deceased, and to this union were born four children, Andrea, Lisa, Paula, and Andrew III. Ambassador Young resides in Atlanta.

—Jacquelyn A. Anthony

Young, Brigham (1801–1877) *religious leader*

Brigham Young was the second president of the Church of Jesus Christ of LATTER-DAY SAINTS (Mormons). He has been called America's greatest colonizer—an "American Moses" (Arrington 1986). Young was born to a Methodist family in Whitingham, Vermont, in 1801. He had no formal education but was skilled in carpentry and construction. In 1830, Samuel Smith, brother of Joseph Smith, left a copy of the *Book of Mormon* with family members. Young was baptized on April 14, 1832, as was his entire family. When he traveled to Kirtland, Ohio, and met Joseph Smith, Young became convinced that Smith was a prophet and vowed to himself to spend his life aiding and defending "Brother Joseph" and the church. In 1835, he was selected as a member of the Quorum of the Twelve Apostles. He was the senior living apostle when he organized the exodus of 10,000 church members out of Missouri after the governor issued a MORMON EXTERMINATION ORDER. In 1839, Mormons crossed the Mississippi River into Illinois, having been forced out of Missouri. He went on yearly missions abroad and was ordained the president of the Quorum of the Twelve Apostles while in England in 1840. He led the church as president of the Quorum of the Twelve for three years after Joseph Smith was shot by a mob in 1844. Young was ordained as the president of the church in 1847.

In the winter of 1846, the Mormons were driven out of their thriving city of Nauvoo, Illinois. Young organized the trek west to the Salt Lake Valley, built infrastructure to provide food and shelter along the trail, and established the Perpetual Emigration Fund to finance the migration of tens of thousands of converts from the eastern United States and Europe. In the Salt Lake Valley, Young essentially directed the construction of a new civilization. He laid out Salt Lake City and other cities, organized irrigation and agriculture, and established a new government for the "State of Deseret," which stretched from Colorado to California. Church members elected him as governor, and when Congress denied Deseret statehood, President Millard Fillmore appointed him as governor of the Utah Territory.

In 1853, the practice of POLYGAMY (actually polygyny) was made public, which led to a great deal of hostility toward the church from the public and the federal government. Young himself was "sealed" to several dozen wives and he was a strong defender of this unique aspect of early church practice. Persistent, false rumors of Mormon rebellion against the United States led President Buchanan to send the army to Utah to "put down" the insurrection and install a new governor. The bloodless "Utah War" was peacefully settled, Young was removed as governor, and military bases were established to watch over the Mormons. Young continually pushed for Utah statehood to win political autonomy and asserted his support for the U.S. Constitution. He reiterated Joseph Smith's belief that the Constitution was inspired by God, and he wished only to see the FREE EXERCISE CLAUSE of the Constitution protect the Saints' unique religious practices. Young also established "United Orders" to make the church economically self-sufficient in the face of growing economic influence by the nonmember population, many of whom were unfriendly to the church. He established Zion's Cooperative Mercantile Institution (ZCMI) to compete against hostile non-Mormon merchants, to slow the growth of their wealth and power, and to distribute the profits among church members.

Young organized colonizing missions that established more than 400 cities in the American West, Canada, and Mex-

Brigham Young *(Library of Congress)*

ico (Arrington 1985). He also founded Utah's higher educational institutions, major banks and businesses, a newspaper, public works, agricultural and commodity production, postal service, telegraph and railroad lines, church and temple construction, mining enterprises, hospitals, printing, hotels, and more. Young's religious, political, economic, and military influence was far-reaching. His opponents saw him as a theocratic despot, while supporters were awed at his accomplishments and leadership. His outspokenness in defense of the church alienated opponents but also earned him the nickname "Lion of the Lord." No LDS leader since that time has had such great influence in the economic, military, and political domains. The division between church and state was instituted in Utah's constitution, and the church divested itself of most of its economic enterprises. Brigham Young died on August 29, 1877, of appendicitis at the age of 76 after presiding over the church for 33 of Mormonism's most tumultuous years.

See also COUNCIL OF FIFTY; *REYNOLDS V. UNITED STATES.*

Further reading: Arrington, Leonard. *Brigham Young. American Moses.* New York: Knopf, 1985.

—Jeffrey C. Fox

Z

Zelman v. Simmons-Harris Docket No.00-1751
(2002)

Zelman was perhaps the crowning achievement of the Rehnquist court's evolving ESTABLISHMENT CLAUSE jurisprudence that has persistently dismantled THOMAS JEFFERSON's wall of separation between church and state to permit religious organizations to receive government funding. In a 5-4 decision, the Supreme Court ruled that a school voucher program established by the state of Ohio for the Cleveland public school district did not violate the establishment clause.

The state of Ohio was given control of the Cleveland public school district in 1995 on order from a federal district court judge who found the district a shambles. Among other programs, Ohio enacted the Pilot Project Scholarship Program, which supplied participating district families need-based tuition assistance to send their children to schools participating in the program; families under 200 percent of the poverty line could receive 90 percent of tuition costs, up to $2,250, while other families could receive 75 percent of tuition costs, up to $1,875. Assistance was also made available for tutoring costs to students attending Cleveland public schools. Public schools in adjoining districts to Cleveland could choose to participate, as could private schools, both secular and sectarian. No public school adjacent to Cleveland chose to participate. Of the 56 private schools participating in 1996, 46 (82 percent) were sectarian, religious schools. Of the 3,700 students enrolled in the program in 1996, 96.6 percent enrolled in religiously affiliated schools.

Chief Justice William Rehnquist wrote for the majority and was joined by Justices ANTONIN SCALIA, Clarence Thomas, Anthony Kennedy, and Sandra Day O'Connor. Based on the string of cases preceding *Zelman* that the majority has constructed, the outcome was assured. For 20 years, the Court employed the *Lemon* test to decide the constitutionality of questions that engaged religious interests and government: the law must have a secular purpose, neither advance nor inhibit religion, and must not entangle church and state. Members of the *Zelman* majority have disputed the authority of *Lemon* since its writing; tellingly, there is not one citation to LEMON *V. KURTZMAN* in the majority opinion (nor to *Everson* as discussed below). Instead, the Court, in *Zelman*, nipped off one prong of the *Lemon* test (the entanglement prong), and argued that the Cleveland voucher program had a secular purpose and did not advance religion.

Rehnquist first argued that the voucher program had a secular purpose: "There is no dispute that the program challenged here was enacted for the valid secular purpose of providing educational assistance to poor children in a demonstrably failing public school system." He then turned to whether the voucher program had a religious or secular effect.

The Court relied most heavily on three recent establishment clause cases that have built a foundation on which the *Zelman* decision rests: MUELLER V. ALLEN, WITTERS V. WASHINGTON DEPARTMENT OF SERVICES FOR THE BLIND, and ZOBREST V. CATALINA FOOTHILLS SCHOOL DISTRICT. In *Mueller*, the Court upheld a Minnesota law that provided parents with school-aged children tax deductions for educational expenses. In *Witters*, the Court upheld a Washington State program that assisted blind citizens vocational assistance—in this case, Witters attending a Christian college to become a minister, missionary, or youth leader. In *Zobrest*, the Court upheld a program to provide a sign language interpreter for a child attending a religious school. In each, the Court majority argued that a state program offering benefits neutrally to all citizens who may, by their private choice, choose to use those benefits toward a religious end does not violate the establishment clause.

Likewise, the Court ruled in *Zelman* that the voucher program did not give money directly to religious institutions because the voucher went to parents, and did not, on its face, set up a program that channeled money to religious institutions. The majority wrote:

> In sum, the Ohio program is entirely neutral with respect to religion. It provides benefits directly to a wide spectrum of individuals, defined only by financial need and residence in a particular school district. It permits such individuals to exercise genuine choice among

options public and private, secular and religious. The program is therefore a program of true private choice. In keeping with an unbroken line of decisions rejecting challenges to similar programs, we hold that the program does not offend the Establishment Clause.

Moreover, the Court differentiated *Zelman* from COM-MITTEE FOR PUBLIC EDUCATION AND RELIGIOUS LIBERTY V. NYQUIST (1973), in which the Court struck down a New York program that gave tax deductions to private schools facing "increasingly grave fiscal problems" and parents of children attending private schools exclusively.

In an attempt to shift the nature of the debate and gain further public legitimacy for vouchers, Justice Thomas wrote a concurrence to argue that *Zelman* is the moral equivalent to *Brown v. Board of Education,* which ordered schools to desegregate in Little Rock, Arkansas.

In dissent, Justice David Souter, joined by Justices John Paul Stevens, Ruth Bader Ginsburg, and Stephen Breyer, argued that "every objective underlying the prohibition of religious establishment is betrayed by this scheme [vouchers]" and that *Zelman* effectively struck down 50 years of establishment clause jurisprudence. In EVERSON V. BOARD OF EDUCATION, the Court wrote: "No tax in any amount, large or small, can be levied to support any religious activities or institutions, whatever they may be called, or whatever form they may adopt to teach or practice religion." In Cleveland, almost all of the tuition voucher funds would have to be spent to attend religious schools, for which the voucher covers nearly the full cost of tuition. Souter notes:

> The sheer quantity of aid, when delivered to a class of religious primary and secondary schools, was suspect on the theory that the greater the aid, the greater its proportion to a religious school's existing expenditures, and the greater the likelihood that public money was supporting religious as well as secular instruction. As we said in *Meek,* "it would simply ignore reality to attempt to separate secular educational functions from the predominantly religious role" as the object of aid that comes in "substantial amounts."

Souter also attacks the majority's use of neutrality and choice directly. The majority claims that educational choice is not limited to religious schools. But the construction of the question is significant—instead of asking if a family participating in the voucher program is constrained in its choice of how to direct the voucher, the majority frames the question about the choices all families have about where to send their children to school, the answer to which is private, public, magnet, or community schools. The majority sidesteps the essential question about the options available to voucher parents; since those options are overwhelmingly sectarian, the voucher program offends the establishment clause.

Justice Breyer dissented separately to emphasize the concerns JAMES MADISON articulated in his *Memorial and Remon-* strance; Breyer wrote, "[T]o emphasize the risk that publicly financed voucher programs pose in terms of religiously based social conflict. I do so because I believe that the Establishment Clause concern for protecting the Nation's social fabric from religious conflict poses an overriding obstacle to the implementation of this well-intentioned school voucher program." Souter exclaims that under *Zelman,* "Public tax money will pay at a systemic level for teaching the covenant with Israel and Mosaic law in Jewish schools, the primacy of the Apostle Peter and the Papacy in Catholic schools, the truth of reformed Christianity in Protestant schools, and the revelation to the Prophet in Muslim schools, to speak only of major religious groupings in the Republic."

Though *Zelman* opens the door for voucher programs to proceed and permits a major shift in public financing of primary and secondary education, few states and localities are moving to adopt such systems and several have been defeated in state-level referenda. According to the National School Boards Association, voucher plans have been defeated in about 26 states. Three localities had vouchers in place at the time of the decision: Cleveland, Florida (47 students in five schools), and Milwaukee (10,800 students in 103 schools). On August 5, 2002, a Florida circuit court struck down the Florida voucher pilot program as violating the state constitution, which prohibits direct or indirect funding to aid religion. However, a flurry of bills instituting voucher programs have been introduced in state legislatures nationwide and *Zelman* legitimizes the attempt.

See also AGOSTINI V. FELTON; BOARD OF EDUCATION V. ALLEN; GRAND RAPIDS SCHOOL DISTRICT V. BALL; MITCHELL V. HELMS; ROSENBERGER V. UNIVERSITY OF VIRGINIA.

—Paul A. Djupe

Zionism

Zionism refers to the Jewish nationalist movement that began in the late 19th century and resulted in the creation of the Jewish state of ISRAEL by the middle of the 20th. The word *Zion* is a traditional reference to both Jerusalem and Israel. Zionism also refers to the attachment Jews demonstrated for Israel during the many centuries of exile from the land.

Political Zionism is more than a century old. It was first expressed in the writings and efforts of Theodore Herzl (1860–1904). Herzl had come from an upper-middle-class, secularized Jewish family in Vienna and covered the trial of Alfred Dreyfus in 1893. Dreyfus was a French Jew and military officer accused of spying for Germany; it was later determined that Dreyfus was innocent of all charges. However, Herzl saw vehement ANTI-SEMITISM firsthand as Paris mobs yelled anti-Jewish insults at Dreyfus.

Herzl determined that only when Jews had a state of their own would they be able to live in peace. Zionism became his life's mission. He was instrumental in founding the Zionist Organization in 1897, when the First Zionist Congress was convened. Zionism became the vehicle by which Jews all over the world would be removed from persecution and oppression. Herzl and his colleagues began the process from which Israel would eventually emerge. During his lifetime, what is today modern Israel was a province of the Ottoman Empire. Herzl attempted with minimal success to negotiate with the Turkish government to purchase farming land and to encourage European Jews to migrate. He died too soon to see the fruition of his efforts.

The Zionist Organization during the 1920s and 1930s gradually split into different ideological camps as the confrontation with indigenous Arabs and the British mandate authority grew. One group early on argued that a Jewish commonwealth could be established in Uganda, then a mostly unpopulated territory. The suggestion was quickly rejected by the overwhelming majority of Zionists. The most serious and durable fissure developed between mainstream Zionism and Revisionism. The former was convinced that only through patient diplomacy could a Jewish state ever come into reality. Moderation toward and understanding of the Palestinian Arab position was key. Left-wing Zionists were the first to consider the possibility of a binational state that would be composed of both Arab and Jewish citizens living jointly under one political jurisdiction and laws that would be equally applied.

Zionism also faced other problems. Some religious Jews considered the Zionists—most of whom were thoroughly secularized—to be the perpetrators of a terrible blasphemy. They were and remain convinced that Israel could be reestablished only with the coming of the Messiah. Other Jews either opposed Israel's restoration or were at best lukewarm to it because they were convinced that Judaism is a religion, not to be confused with a nationality. Israel's existence, they argued, would present non-Israeli Jews with the difficult challenge of dual loyalties, a problem they felt would attract and encourage rather than dispel and eliminate anti-Semitism.

For the Zionist experiment to work, Israel had to become an attractive place for an "ingathering of exiles." However, at no time since the Roman period has Israel contained a majority of the world's Jewish population. It currently houses about two-fifths, a marked increase from the 5 percent Israel began with in 1948. Dedicated Zionists assumed that most Jews would want to return to live in a Jewish state. Most Israeli Jews, though, are descended from immigrants who came to Israel under duress. Israel's population, for example, doubled in a four-year period between 1948 and 1952, mainly because of the influx of Middle Eastern Jews who had been unceremoniously kicked out of Islamic countries whose governments considered them to be Zionist agents. Few of these Jews even knew of the Zionist movement, and accepted migration to Israel as simply necessary.

Zionism may be a victim of its own success. Israel today is a viable Jewish state with a modern economy that includes state-of-the-art technology. It is also a democracy that has enabled its substantial non-Jewish minority to become full political participants. Current expressions of Zionism seem to be controversial ones, even among Israelis. Zionism has

acquired an increasingly religious content as its most intense advocates have established settlements in the West Bank, an area they refer to as Judea and Samaria, historically the heartland of the ancient Israelite kingdom.

See also AGUDAT ISRAEL; JEWISH DEFENSE LEAGUE; KAHANE. MEIR.

Further reading: Avineri, Shlomo. *The Making of Modern Zionism: The Intellectual Origins of the Jewish State.* New York: Basic Books, 1981; Sternhell, Zeev. *The Founding Myths of Israel: Nationalism, Socialism, and the Making of the Jewish State.* Translated by David Maisel. Princeton, N.J.: Princeton University Press.

—Martin W. Slann

Zobrest v. Catalina Foothills School District 113 U.S. 2462 (1993)

On February 24, 1993, in a 5-4 decision, the Supreme Court found that the Catalina School District of Tucson, Arizona, providing a sign-language interpreter to James Zobrest, a deaf student who attended a private religious institution, did not violate the ESTABLISHMENT CLAUSE of the First Amendment. Zobrest claimed that he was guaranteed an interpreter through the Individuals with Disabilities Education Act (IDEA).

Writing for the majority, Justice Rehnquist used the cases of *MUELLER V. ALLEN* and *WITTERS V. WASHINGTON DEPTARTMENT OF SERVICES FOR BLIND* as precedents for the decision:

> We have consistently held that government programs that neutrally provide benefits to a broad class of citizens defined without reference to religion are not readily subject to the Establishment Clause challenge just because sectarian institutions may also receive an attenuated financial benefit.

In both the *Mueller* and *Witters* cases, the Court found that benefits provided by the state could be extended to parents or students attending sectarian institutions without violating the establishment clause. Here, Justice Rehnquist held that a publicly funded interpreter in a private setting was only the result of the individual choice made by the parents. Further, providing this service did not in any way create a financial incentive for an individual to attend a private/religious institution, and no funding was going directly to religious institutions.

The majority distinguished an interpreter from a teacher or other public employee by declaring that an interpreter, as opposed to a teacher, "would neither add to nor subtract from that environment, and hence the provision of such assistance is not barred by the Establishment Clause." In his final argument, Rehnquist wrote: "the Establishment Clause lays down no absolute bar to the placing of a public employee in a sectarian school."

Rehnquist also took great care in separating *Zobrest* from two cases, namely *MEEK V. PITTENGER* and *GRAND RAPIDS V.*

BALL, presented by the respondents as contrary to *Mueller* and *Witters*.

Zobrest differed from *Meek* and *Ball* in that the federal and state IDEA were not providing direct aid to the private institution, as was the circumstance in the *Meek* case. In the case of *Ball*, funding would be provided to schools that would help in the advancement of religion by placing publicly funded teachers into private schools, thus alleviating cost to the institution. The majority in *Zobrest* argued, however, that the interpreter would not act as a teacher, but merely as a translator, therefore not adding to or detracting from the environment; further, since private institutions generally do not offer interpreter services, it would therefore not diminish costs to the institution.

It is here that the dissent struck most forcefully. Writing for the minority, Justice Blackmun intoned, "Until now, the Court never has authorized a public employee to participate directly in religious indoctrination. Yet that is the consequence of today's decision." Blackmun stated that placing an interpreter in a religious school to communicate a religious message was crossing the boundary of what was acceptable under the establishment clause. He found that the decision in this case "involves ongoing, daily, and intimate governmental participation in the teaching and propagation of religious doctrine," a finding that would clearly suggest a violation of the establishment clause.

—Aaron L. Broomall

Zorach v. Clauson 343 U.S. 306 (1952)

Proclaiming that "We are a religious people whose institutions presuppose a Supreme Being," the Supreme Court, on April 28, 1952, upheld a New York City program that allowed public school students to leave school grounds to obtain religious instruction during school hours. The program required the schools to obtain a written request from parents before releasing any student, and provided that students who were not released were to remain in the classroom. The participating churches were also required to provide the schools with a weekly report of any children who had been released from school but had failed to report for religious instruction.

Writing for a 6-3 majority, Justice William O. Douglas rejected the argument that the New York program should be struck down on the same ESTABLISHMENT CLAUSE grounds that the Court had invoked in declaring a similar Illinois school program unconstitutional in MCCOLLUM V. BOARD OF EDUCA-TION, 333 U.S. 203 (1948). The distinction between New York's constitutional "released time" program and the Illinois program struck down by an 8-1 vote in *McCollum*, Justice Douglas concluded, was that whereas the Illinois program permitted religious instructors to use public school classrooms, the New York program did not. "In the *McCollum* case," he wrote, "the classrooms were used for religious instruction and the force of the public school was used to promote that

instruction. Here, as we have said, the public schools do no more than accommodate their schedules to a program of outside religious instruction."

Douglas readily agreed that if the New York teachers used their offices to persuade or force students to take religious instruction, the program would be unconstitutional. But he said the record in this case contained no evidence of such coercion—all indications were that the teachers "did no more than release students" whose parents so requested. The teachers merely cooperated with the religious program to the extent of permitting their students to participate in it, and Douglas saw no constitutional harm in that.

In addition, Douglas appeared to endorse a position flatly rejected in *McCollum*, writing:

> We sponsor an attitude on the part of government that shows no partiality to any one group and that lets each flourish according to the zeal of its adherents and the appeal of its dogma. When the state encourages religious instruction or cooperates with religious authorities by adjusting the schedule of public events to sectarian needs, it follows the best of our traditions. For it then respects the religious nature of our people and accommodates the public service to their spiritual needs. To hold that it may not would be to find in the Constitution a requirement that the government show a callous indifference to religious groups.

Zorach's three dissenters—all of whom had been in the majority in *McCollum*—attacked those assertions head on. Justice Black objected that under the establishment clause "a state can no more aid 'all religions' than it can aid one." Justice Frankfurter thought the plaintiffs ought to have been given an opportunity to prove that the release program was "inherently coercive" of students and parents, and he urged the advocates of release time to stop "seeking to use the public schools as the instrument for securing attendance at denominational classes." Finally, Justice Jackson warned: "The day that this country ceases to be free for irreligion it will cease to be free for religion—except for the sect that can win political power."

All three dissenters thought Douglas's distinction between permitting religious instruction in public classrooms and releasing students to attend religious instruction off premises constitutionally insignificant.

As Justice Black put it: "In the New York program, as in that of Illinois, the school authorities release some of the children on the condition that they attend the religious classes, get reports on whether they attend, and hold the other children in the school building until the religious hour is over. As we attempted to make categorically clear, the *McCollum* decision would have been the same if the religious classes had not been held in the school buildings."

Eleven years later, however, Justice Brennan, concurring in *ABINGTON SCHOOL DISTRICT V. SCHEMPP* (1963), defended

Douglas's distinction between on-premises and off-premises instruction as being "faithful to the function of the Establishment Clause." Brennan said he too thought it determinative that the *McCollum* program "placed the religious instruction in the public school classroom in precisely the position of authority held by the regular teachers of secular subjects, while the *Zorach* program did not."

See also AID TO RELIGIOUS SCHOOLS; PRAYER IN PUBLIC SCHOOLS.

—Charles F. Williams

Bibliography

Adams, James. *The Growing Church Lobby in Washington.* Grand Rapids, Mich.: Eerdmans, 1970.

Ahlstrom, Sydney. *A Religious History of the American People.* New Haven, Conn.: Yale University Press, 1972.

Ammerman, Nancy Tatom. *Bible Believers: Fundamentalists in the Modern World.* New Brunswick, N.J.: Rutgers University Press, 1987.

———. *Congregation and Community.* New Brunswick, N.J.: Rutgers University Press, 1997.

Baer, Hans A., and Merrill Singer. *African-American Religion in the Twentieth Century: Varieties of Protest and Accommodation.* Knoxville: University of Tennessee Press, 1992.

Battin, Margaret P. *Ethics in the Sanctuary: Examining the Practices of Organized Religion.* New Haven, Conn.: Yale University Press, 1990.

Beatty, Kathleen Murphy, and Oliver B. Walter. "A Group Theory of Religion and Politics." *Western Political Quarterly* 42 (1989): 129–146.

Bellah, Robert N., Richard Madsen, William M. Sullivan, Ann Swindler, and Steven M. Tipton. *Habits of the Heart: Individualism and Commitment in American Life.* New York: Harper and Row, 1985.

Benson, Peter L., and Dorothy L. Williams. *Religion on Capitol Hill: Myths and Realities.* New York: Oxford University Press, 1982.

Blumhofer, Edith L., ed. *Religion, Politics, and the American Experience: Reflections on Religion and American Public Life.* Tuscaloosa: University of Alabama Press, 2002.

Bromley, David G., and Anson Shupe. *Strange Gods: The Great American Cult Scare.* Boston: Beacon, 1981.

Bromley, David G., and Anson Shupe, eds. *New Christian Politics.* Macon, Ga.: Mercer University Press, 1984.

Bruce, Steve. *The Rise and Fall of the New Christian Right: Conservative Protestant Politics in America, 1978–1988.* Oxford: Clarendon Press, 1988.

———. *Pray TV: Televangelism in America.* New York: Routledge, 1990.

———. *Religion and Modernization.* New York: Oxford University Press, 1992.

Butler, Jon. *A Wash in a Sea of Faith: Christianizing the American People.* Cambridge, Mass.: Harvard University Press, 1990.

Byrnes, Timothy. *Catholic Bishops in American Politics.* Princeton, N.J.: Princeton University Press, 1991.

Byrnes, Timothy, and Mary C. Segers, eds. *The Catholic Church and the Politics of Abortion: A View from the States.* Boulder, Colo.: Westview Press, 1992.

Chaves, Mark. "Religious Congregations and Welfare Reform: Who Will Take Advantage of 'Charitable Choice'?" *American Sociological Review* 64 (1999): 836–846.

Cnaan, Ram A. *The Newer Deal: Social Work and Religion in Partnership.* New York: Columbia University Press, 1999.

Cone, James. *A Black Theology of Liberation.* Philadelphia: Lippincott, 1970.

Conklin, Paul K. *American Originals: Homemade Varieties of Christianity.* Chapel Hill: University of North Carolina Press, 1997.

Corbett, Julia Mitchell. *Religion in America.* 2d ed. Englewood Cliffs, N.J.: Prentice Hall, 1990.

Cord, Robert L. *Separation of Church and State: Historical Fact and Current Fiction.* Cambridge, Mass.: Lambeth, 1982.

Crawford, Sue E. S., and Laura R. Olson, eds. *Christian Clergy in American Politics.* Baltimore: Johns Hopkins University Press, 2001.

Cromartie, Michael, ed. *No Longer Exiles: The Religious New Right in American Politics.* Washington, D.C.: Ethics and Public Policy Center, 1993.

———, ed. *The Religious New Right in American Politics.* Washington, D.C.: Ethics and Public Policy Center, 1993.

Daly, Mary. *Beyond God the Father: Toward a Philosophy of Women's Liberation.* Boston: Beacon, 1973.

Davidman, Lynn. *Tradition in a Rootless World: Women Turn to Orthodox Judaism.* Berkeley: University of California Press, 1991.

Demerath, N. J., III, and Rhys Williams. *A Bridging of Faiths: Religion and Politics in a Northeastern City.* Princeton, N.J.: Princeton University Press, 1992.

Dionne, E. J., and John J. DiIulio, eds. *What's God Got to Do with the American Experiment?* Washington, D.C.: Brookings Institution, 2000.

Ebersole, Luke. *Church Lobbying in the Nation's Capital.* New York: Macmillan, 1951.

Eck, Diana L. *A New Religious America: How a "Christian Country" Has Become the World's Most Religiously Diverse Nation.* San Francisco: Harper, 2001.

Emerson, Michael O., and Christian Smith. *Divided by Faith: Evangelical Religion and the Problem of Race in America.* New York: Oxford University Press, 2000.

Epstein, Lee. *Conservatives in Court.* Knoxville: University of Tennessee Press, 1985.

Esposito, John L. *Islam: The Straight Path.* New York: Oxford University Press, 1988.

Findlay, James F. *Church People in the Struggle: The National Council of Churches and the Black Freedom Movement, 1950–1970.* New York: Oxford University Press, 1993.

Finke, Roger, and Rodney Stark. *The Churching of America, 1776–1990: Winners and Losers in Our Religious Economy.* New Brunswick, N.J.: Rutgers University Press, 1992.

Fowler, Robert Booth. *Unconventional Partners: Religion and Liberal Culture in the United States.* Grand Rapids, Mich.: Eerdmans, 1989.

Fowler, Robert Booth, Allen D. Hertzke, and Laura R. Olson. *Religion and Politics in America: Faith, Culture, and Strategic Choices.* 2d ed. Boulder, Colo.: Westview Press.

Garrow, David J. *Bearing the Cross: Martin Luther King Jr. and the Southern Leadership Conference.* New York: Morrow, 1986.

Gilbert, Christopher P. *The Impact of Churches on Political Behavior: An Empirical Study.* Westport, Conn.: Greenwood Press, 1993.

Green, John C., James L. Guth, Corwin E. Smidt, and Lyman A. Kellstedt, eds. *Religion and the Culture Wars: Dispatches from the Front.* Lanham, Md.: Rowman and Littlefield, 1996.

Green, John C., Mark J. Rozell, and Clyde Wilcox. *Prayers in the Precincts: The Christian Right in the 1998 Elections.* Washington, D.C.: Georgetown University Press, 2000.

Guth, James L., and John C. Green, eds. *The Bible and the Ballot Box: Religion and Politics in the 1988 Election.* Boulder, Colo.: Westview Press, 1991.

Guth, James L., John C. Green, Corwin E. Smidt, Lyman A. Kellstedt, and Margaret M. Poloma. *The Bully Pulpit: The Politics of Protestant Clergy.* Lawrence: University Press of Kansas, 1997.

Haddad, Yvonne Yazbeck, and Jane Idelman Smith, eds. *Muslim Communities in North America.* Albany: State University of New York Press, 1994.

Hammond, Phillip. *The Protestant Presence in Twentieth-Century America: Religion and Political Culture.* Albany: State University of New York Press, 1992.

Harris, Fredrick C. *Something Within: Religion in African-American Political Activism.* New York: Oxford University Press, 1999.

Heilman, Samuel C., and Steven M. Cohen. *Cosmopolitans and Parochials: Modern Orthodox Jews in America.* Chicago: University of Chicago Press, 1989.

Hertzke, Allen D. *Representing God in Washington: The Role of Religious Lobbies in the American Polity.* Knoxville: University of Tennessee Press, 1988.

———. *Echoes of Discontent: Jesse Jackson, Pat Robertson, and the Resurgence of Populism.* Washington, D.C.: CQ Press, 1993.

Hofrenning, Daniel J. B. *In Washington but Not of It: The Prophetic Politics of Religious Lobbyists.* Philadelphia: Temple University Press, 1995.

Hunter, James Davison. *Culture Wars: The Struggle to Define America.* New York: Basic Books, 1991.

Iannaconne, Laurence R. "Why Strict Churches Are Strong." *American Journal of Sociology* 99 (1994): 1180–1211.

Inglehart, Ronald. *Culture Shift in Advanced Industrial Society.* Princeton, N.J.: Princeton University Press, 1990.

Jelen, Ted G. *The Political Mobilization of Religious Beliefs.* New York: Praeger, 1991.

———. *To Serve God and Mammon: Church-State Relations in American Politics.* Boulder, Colo.: Westview Press, 2000.

Juergensmeyer, Mark. *Terror in the Mind of God: The Global Rise of Religious Violence.* Berkeley: University of California Press, 2000.

Kelley, Dean. *Why Conservative Churches Are Growing: A Study in Sociology of Religion.* San Francisco: Harper, 1972.

Kellstedt, Lyman A. "The Meaning and Measurement of Evangelicalism: Problems and Prospects." In *Religion and Political Behavior in the United States.* Edited by Ted G. Jelen. New York: Praeger, 1989.

Kellstedt, Lyman A., and Mark A. Noll. "Religion, Voting for President, and Party Identification 1948–1984." In *Religion and American Politics.* Edited by Mark A. Noll. New York: Oxford University Press, 1990.

Klatch, Rebecca E. *Women of the New Right.* Philadelphia: Temple University Press, 1987.

Kleppner, Paul. *The Cross of Culture: A Social Analysis of Midwestern Politics, 1850–1900,* 2d ed. New York: Free Press, 1970.

Kohut, Andrew L., John C. Green, Scott Keeter, and Robert C. Toth. *The Diminishing Divide: The Intersection of Culture, Religion, and Politics.* Washington, D.C.: Brookings Institution, 2000.

Kramnick, Isaac, and R. Laurence Moore. *The Godless Constitution: The Case Against Religious Correctness.* New York: Norton, 1996.

Leege, David C., and Lyman A. Kellstedt, eds. *Rediscovering the Religious Factor in American Politics.* Armonk, N.Y.: M. E. Sharpe, 1993.

Liebman, Robert C., and Robert Wuthnow, eds. *The New Christian Right.* New York: Aldine, 1984.

Lienesch, Michael. *Redeeming America: Piety and Politics in the New Christian Right.* Chapel Hill: University of North Carolina Press, 1993.

Lincoln, C. Eric, and Lawrence H. Mamiya. *The Black Church in the African American Experience.* Durham, N.C.: Duke University Press, 1990.

Loades, Ann, ed. *Feminist Theology.* Louisville, Ky.: Westminster, 1990.

Malbin, Michael. *Religion and Politics: The Intentions of the Authors of the First Amendment.* Washington, D.C.: American Enterprise Institute, 1978.

Martin, William. *With God on Our Side: The Rise of the Religious Right in America.* New York: Broadway Books, 1996.

Marty, Martin E. *Righteous Empire: The Protestant Experience in America.* New York: Dial, 1970.

———. *Pilgrims in Their Own Land: 500 Years of Religion in America.* Boston: Little, Brown, 1984.

———, and R. Scott Appleby. *The Glory and the Power: The Fundamentalist Challenge to the Modern World.* Boston: Beacon, 1992.

McLoughlin, William. *Revivals, Awakening, and Reform: An Essay on Religion and Social Change in America, 1607–1977.* Chicago: University of Chicago Press, 1978.

Menendez, Albert. *Religion at the Polls.* Philadelphia: Westminster, 1977.

Miller, Perry. *Errand into the Wilderness.* Cambridge, Mass.: Harvard University Press, 1956.

Miller, Robert T., and Ronald B. Flowers, eds. *Toward Benevolent Neutrality: Church, State, and the Supreme Court.* Waco, Tex.: Baylor University Press, 1987.

Miller, William L. *The First Liberty and the American Republic.* New York: Knopf, 1986.

Moen, Matthew C. *The Christian Right and Congress.* Tuscaloosa: University of Alabama Press, 1989.

———. *The Transformation of the Christian Right.* Tuscaloosa: University of Alabama Press, 1992.

Monsma, Stephen V. *When Sacred and Secular Mix: Religious Nonprofit Organizations and Public Money.* Lanham, Md.: Rowman and Littlefield, 1996.

Monsma, Stephen V., and J. Christopher Soper, eds. *Equal Treatment of Religion in a Pluralistic Society.* Grand Rapids, Mich.: Eerdmans, 1987.

Morgan, Edmund. *The Puritan Dilemma: The Story of John Winthrop.* Boston: Little, Brown, 1958.

Murphy, Andrew R. *Conscience and Community Revisiting Toleration and Religious Dissent in Early Modern England and America.* University Park: Pennsylvania State University Press, 2001.

Neuhaus, Richard John. *The Naked Public Square.* Grand Rapids, Mich.: Eerdmans, 1984.

Noll, Mark A., ed. *One Nation under God? Christian Faith and Political Action in America.* San Francisco: Harper, 1988.

———, ed. *Religion and American Politics.* New York: Oxford University Press, 1990.

Oldfield, Duane M. *The Right and the Righteous: The Christian Right Confronts the Republican Party.* Lanham, Md.: Rowman and Littlefield, 1996.

Olson, Laura R. *Filled with Spirit and Power: Protestant Clergy in Politics.* Albany: State University of New York Press, 2000.

Pfeffer, Leo. *Religion, State and the Burger Court.* Buffalo, N.Y.: Prometheus, 1984.

Quinley, Harold. *The Prophetic Clergy: Social Activism among Protestant Ministers.* New York: Wiley, 1974.

Reichley, A. James. *Religion in American Public Life.* Washington, D.C.: Brookings Institution, 1985.

Richey, Russell, and Donald Jones, eds. *American Civil Religion.* New York: Harper, 1974.

Roof, Wade Clark. *Spiritual Marketplace: Baby Boomers and the Remaking of American Religion.* Princeton, N.J.: Princeton University Press, 1999.

Roof, Wade Clark, and William McKinney. *American Mainline Religion: Its Changing Shape and Future.* New Brunswick, N.J.: Rutgers University Press, 1987.

Roozen, David A., William McKinley, and Jackson W. Carroll. *Varieties of Religious Presence: Mission in Public Life.* New York: Pilgrim, 1984.

Rozell, Mark J., and Clyde Wilcox, eds. *God at the Grassroots: The Christian Right in the 1994 Elections.* Lanham, Md.: Rowman and Littlefield, 1995.

———, eds. *God at the Grass Roots, 1996: The Christian Right in the 1996 Elections.* Lanham, Md.: Rowman and Littlefield, 1997.

Segers, Mary C., and Ted G. Jelen. *A Wall of Separation? Debating the Public Role of Religion.* Lanham, Md.: Rowman and Littlefield, 1996.

Sigelman, Lee. "'If You Prick Us, Do We Not Bleed? If You Tickle Us, Do We Not Laugh?' Jews and Pocketbook Voting." *Journal of Politics* 53 (1991): 976–992.

Smith, Christian. *American Evangelicalism: Embattled and Thriving.* Chicago: University of Chicago Press, 1998.

Sullivan, Lawrence E., ed. *Native American Religions: North America.* New York: Macmillan, 1987.

Tocqueville, Alexis de. *Democracy in America,* ed. Francis Bowen and Phillips Bradley. New York: Knopf, 1840 [1945].

Wald, Kenneth D. *Religion and Politics in the United States.* 3d ed. Washington, D.C.: CQ Press, 1997.

Wald, Kenneth D., Dennis E. Owen, and Samuel S. Hill. "Churches as Political Communities." *American Political Science Review* 82 (1988): 531–548.

———. "Political Cohesion in Churches." *Journal of Politics* 52 (1990): 197–215.

Weber, Paul J. *Equal Separation: Understanding the Religious Clauses of the First Amendment.* Westport, Conn.: Greenwood Press, 1990.

Wilcox, Clyde. *God's Warriors: The Christian Right in Twentieth-Century America.* Baltimore: Johns Hopkins University Press, 1992.

Wilcox, Clyde. *Onward Christian Soldiers: The Religious Right in American Politics.* Boulder, Colo.: Westview Press, 1996.

Witte, John. *Religion and the American Constitutional Experiment: Essential Rights and Liberties.* Boulder, Colo.: Westview Press, 2000.

Wuthnow, Robert. *The Restructuring of American Religion: Society and Faith since World War Two.* Princeton, N.J.: Princeton University Press, 1988.

———. *The Crisis in the Churches.* New York: Oxford University Press, 1996.

———. *After Heaven: Spirituality in America since the 1950s.* Berkeley: University of California Press, 1998.

Wuthnow, Robert, and John H. Evans, eds. *The Quiet Hand of God: Faith Based Activism and the Public Role of Mainline Protestantism.* Berkeley: University of California Press, 2002.

Index

Boldface page numbers indicate main headings. *Italic* page numbers indicate illustrations.